# COUNTRIES
## AND THEIR
# CULTURES

# EDITORIAL BOARD

*Countries and Their Cultures* was prepared under the auspices and with the support of the Human Relations Area Files, Inc. (HRAF) at Yale University. The foremost international research organization in the field of cultural anthropology, HRAF is a not-for-profit consortium of 19 Sponsoring Member institutions and more than 400 active and inactive Associate Member institutions in nearly 40 countries. The mission of HRAF is to provide information that facilitates the cross-cultural study of human behavior, society, and culture. The HRAF Collection of Ethnography, which has been building since 1949, contains nearly one million pages of information, indexed according to more than 700 subject categories, on the cultures of the world. An increasing portion of the Collection of Ethnography, which now covers more than 365 cultures, is accessible via the World Wide Web to member institutions. The HRAF Collection of Archaeology, the first installment of which appeared in 1999, is also accessible on the Web to those member institutions opting to receive it.

# COUNTRIES
## AND THEIR
# CULTURES/

### VOLUME 1

AFGHANISTAN
TO
CZECH REPUBLIC

*Melvin Ember and Carol R. Ember, Editors*

**Macmillan Reference USA**

*an imprint of the Gale Group*

*New York • Detroit • San Francisco • London • Boston • Woodbridge, CT*

*Countries and Their Cultures*

Macmillan Reference USA
1633 Broadway
New York, NY 10019

Macmillan Reference USA
27500 Drake Rd.
Farmington Hills, MI 48331-3535

**Library of Congress Cataloging-in-Publication Data**
Countries and their cultures / Melvin Ember and Carol R. Ember, editors.
    p.cm.
    Includes bibliographical references and index.
    ISBN 0-02-864950-8 (set : hc.)
1. Ethnology-Encyclopedias. I. Ember, Melvin. II. Ember, Carol R.
GN307 .C68 2001
306'.03-dc21

2001030188

Volume 1: 0-02-864947-8
Volume 2: 0-02-864948-6
Volume 3: 0-02-864949-4
Volume 4: 0-02-864946-X

Printed in the United States of America

Printing number
1 2 3 4 5 6 7 8 9 10

Front cover photos (clockwise from top): Aymara man with llamas © Gian Berto Vanni/Corbis; Japanese kindergarten students © Don Stevenson/Mira; Hooded men at Oaxaca Festival © Liba Taylor/Corbis; Kava Ceremony, Fiji © Charles & Josette Lenars/Corbis; Wedding service in a Russian Orthodox church © Dean Conger/Corbis; Egyptian ranger battalion demonstration © Corbis; Boy eating lobster at Friendship Regatta festivities © Dean Conger/Corbis; Akha villagers perform a Chi Ji Tsi ritual © Michael Freeman/Corbis. Background: Desert Rose block print by Arlinka Blair © Jonathan Blair/Corbis.

# CONTENTS

# EDITORIAL AND PRODUCTION STAFF

# PREFACE

When the Soviet Union broke apart, most of the world was stunned. Many thought of the Soviet Union as a very powerful country, and until the breakup most gave very little thought to the many different and geographically separate cultures that comprised the Soviet Union. Anthropologists were not as surprised by the breakup because they knew that the Soviet Union contained a large number of culturally diverse groups of people, such as Russians, Ukrainians, Belarusians, and Kazakhs, among many others. Most of the countries that became independent after the breakup of the Soviet Union—Russia, Ukraine, Belarus, Uzbekistan, etc.—were populated largely by people speaking a particular language and sharing a particular culture. In retrospect, if more people had known that there wasn't much of a shared culture in what we formerly called the Soviet Union, perhaps the breakup would not have been so surprising. This is not to say that the breakup was caused solely by cultural differences. The fact of the matter is that social scientists are still far from understanding what accounts for why a country splits apart, and why the break-up may be violent or peaceful. We do know, however, that if we want to understand what happens to a country, it is important to pay attention to how the different cultures in the country get along and how much of a national culture has developed.

The focus of *Countries and Their Cultures* is on the cultures of the countries around the world, what is and what is not commonly shared culturally by the people who live in a country. As the reader will see, some countries have a distinctive national culture. That is, most of the people in the country share a distinctive set of attitudes, beliefs, values, and practices. Other countries hardly have a shared culture, and maybe not even a dominant one. Many of these culturally diverse countries like Nigeria and Kenya had their political unity imposed upon them by colonialism. There were hundreds of different cultures, many of them not even politi-

cally unified, before the colonial power imposed control over the whole area. The major new commonality was that the various cultures had to deal with a new overarching political authority, the colonial authority. Often, the eventual achievement of independence was not sufficient to create much in the way of a national culture. Only time will tell whether these new political entities will endure and whether national cultures will develop.

In a country with many cultures, the emergence of a common culture can occur gradually and peacefully as people interact over time or when immigrants voluntarily assimilate to a dominant culture. More often than not, cultural dominance emerges in the context of one group having superior power over the others. Africans brought as slaves to what is now the United States did not choose to come, nor did Native Americans choose to have their lands taken away or their children sent away to boarding school to learn the ways of the dominant culture. But even without force, sheer differences in numbers can have profound effects. There is little doubt that where a particular ethnic group vastly outnumbers others in the country, the culture of that ethnic group is likely to become dominant. Examples are the Han of China and the Russians of Russia.

Multiculturalism is quite characteristic of most of today's countries, but countries vary greatly in the degree to which ethnic groups co-exist peacefully and in the degree to which diversity of culture is tolerated and even sometimes celebrated. Germany for a long time (until the 1930s) was tolerant of Jews, but then it changed and exterminated them in the 1940s. Why ethnic conflict emerges at some times and in some places is only beginning to be understood.

Cultural anthropology and the other social sciences can help us understand. Cultural anthropology got started as a discipline when people began to realize, with imperialism and colonialism, that the ways of life of people around the world varied enormously. In the beginning of the twentieth century, there were still many cultures that depended on hunting, gathering, and fishing, with no agriculture or industry. Villages in many places were hardly linked to their neighbors, much less to state-type polities in the outside world. The world's cultural diversity was greater and more fragmented than it is today. Now the world is a multiplicity of nation-states, multicultural (multiethnic) polities that formed as little or larger empires, or as products of colonialism. In an earlier reference work, the 10-volume *Encyclopedia of World Cultures* (produced under the auspices of the Human Relations Area Files [HRAF] and published by G.K. Hall/Macmillan), the focus was on the cultures typically studied by anthropologists. A different language, not shared by neighbors, is often a key defining feature of a group of people who share (or who shared) a culture. Thus, countries and their usual multiplicity of cultures were not the focus of that encyclopedia.

In this reference work, we focus on the cultures of countries. We have asked our authors to describe what is culturally universal in the country they are writing about and what varies by ethnic group, region, and class. Information on widely-shared behavior and values, as well as on cultural variation within the country, is now recognized as important to understanding politics, civil rights, business opportunities, and many other aspects of life in a country. Our focus on culture makes *Countries and Their Cultures* unique. No other single reference work comes close to matching the range of cultural information offered in these volumes.

Another unique feature of *Countries and Their Cultures* is the discussions of "do's" and "don'ts" for a culture, including what to make "small talk" about and what *not* to talk about. For example, visitors to the United States may be familiar with much of American culture, but if they divulge the real state of their health and feelings to the first American who asks "How are you?," they have much to learn about "small talk" in the United States.

A third unique feature of *Countries and Their Cultures* is the discussion of ethnic relations in a country, including material on whether one particular ethnic group became dominant or whether a national culture developed out of a community of disparate cultures. In some cases, particularly in newly developing nations, there is relatively little shared culture, and so there may be little "national" culture.

We are able to provide the information contained in these volumes through the efforts of more than 200 contributors-social scientists (anthropologists largely, but also sociologists, historians, geographers, and political scientists) as well as others who usually have firsthand experience in the countries they write about and know the language or lingua franca of that country. Thus they are able to provide integrated, holistic descriptions of the countries, not just facts. Our aim was to leave the reader with a real sense of what it is like to live in a particular country.

Our list of countries consists largely of politically independent entities. However, we have included some geographically separate entities that are politically part of other countries. Examples are Anguilla and Bermuda, which are dependent territories of the United Kingdom; French Guiana and Guadaloupe, which are French overseas departments; and Hong Kong, which is a special administrative region of China. Our advisors also suggested we add entries for major divisions of the United Kingdom: England, Northern Ireland, Scotland, and Wales.

Articles all follow the same format to provide maximum comparability. Countries with small populations have shorter entries; those with large populations or complex ethnic composition are longer in length to accommodate the complexity.

## USING *COUNTRIES AND THEIR CULTURES*

This reference work is meant to be used by a variety of people for a variety of purposes. It can be used both to gain a general understanding of a country and its culture(s), and to find a specific piece of information by looking it up under the relevant subheading. It can also be used to learn about a particular region of the world and the social, economic, and political forces that have shaped the cultures of the countries in that region. We provide a substantial bibliography at the end of each country entry.

Beyond being a basic reference resource, *Countries and Their Cultures* also serves readers with more focused needs. For researchers interested in comparing countries and their cultures, this work provides information that can guide the selection of particular countries for further study. For those interested in international studies, the bibliographies in each entry can lead one quickly to the relevant social science literature as well as providing a state-of-the-art assessment of knowledge about the world's countries and their cultures. For curriculum developers and teachers seeking to internationalize the curriculum, this work is a basic reference and educational resource as well as a directory to other materials. For government officials, it is a repository of information not likely to be available in any other single publication; in some cases the information provided here is not available at all elsewhere. For students, from high school through graduate school, it provides background and bibliographic information for term papers and class projects. And for travelers, it provides an introduction to the ways of life in any country they may be visiting.

## FORMAT OF THE VOLUMES

The work comprises four volumes, with the country entries ordered alphabetically. A total of 225 countries are described. In addition to the cultural summaries, there are country maps, photographs, and an index.

The descriptive summaries of the countries and their cultures provide the heart of the work. Each summary provides a mix of demographic, historical, social, economic, political, and religious information on the country. The emphasis is cultural; that is, the summaries focus on the ways of life of the people, and the main forces affecting them. The authors have followed a standardized outline, constructed by the editors with the help of the board of advisors, so that each summary provides information on a core list of topics. The authors, however, had some leeway in deciding how much attention was to be given each topic and whether additional information should be included.

## ACKNOWLEDGMENTS

There are many people to thank for their contributions. Elly Dickason at Macmillan Reference played an important role in the initial conception of the project. The Board of Advisors reviewed the list of countries, made valuable suggestions about the outline of the entries, and suggested potential authors. We want to thank Kirsten Jensen for her help in choosing photographs. For managing the project at Macmillan, we are indebted to Monica Hubbard. We are particularly grateful for her good humor and efficiency. Most of all we thank the contributors for describing the countries and their cultures so well.

MELVIN EMBER, PRESIDENT
CAROL R. EMBER, EXECUTIVE DIRECTOR
HUMAN RELATIONS AREA FILES AT YALE UNIVERSITY

# ALPHABETICAL LIST OF ARTICLES

## VOLUME 1

# VOLUME 4

# DIRECTORY OF CONTRIBUTORS

## A

Jon G. Abbink *(Leiden University, Leiden, The Netherlands)*
Chad
Djibouti
Macau

Luc Alofs *(Instituto Pedagogico Arubano, San Nicolas, Aruba)*
Aruba
Netherlands Antilles

Sima Aprahamian *(Concordia University, Montreal, Quebec, Canada)*
Armenia

M. Cameron Arnold *(New York, NY)*
Anguilla
Monaco
San Marino
Slovenia
Wales

## B

Loretta Baldassar *(University of Western Australia, Perth, Australia)*
Australia

Sally E. Baringer *(Mankato, MN)*
The Philippines

Judith C. Barker *(University of California, San Francisco, CA)*
Niue

William O. Beeman *(Brown University, Providence, RI)*
Iran

O. Hugo Benavides *(Fordham University, Bronx, NY)*
Peru
Venezuela

Giovanni Bennardo *(Northern Illinois University, DeKalb, IL)*
Tonga

Alban Bensa *(EHESS Etudes Oceanistes, Paris, France)*
New Caledonia

Jeffrey W. Bentley *(Cochabamba, Bolivia)*
Honduras

Niko Besnier *(Victoria University of Wellington, Wellington, New Zealand)*
Tuvalu

Theodore E. Bestor *(Cornell University, Ithaca, NY)*
Japan

Maria Enedina Bezerra *(University of Florida, Gainesville, FL)*
Brazil

Sophie Blanchy *(Centre d'Etudes et de Recherches sur l'Ocean Indien, Paris, France)*
Comoros
Mayotte

Miguel Bombin *(Laurentian University, Sudbury, Ontario, Canada)*
Uruguay

Joseph Bosco *(Chinese University of Hong Kong, Shatin, Hong Kong)*
Hong Kong

Caroline B. Brettell *(Southern Methodist University, Dallas, TX)*
Portugal

Alexandra Brewis *(University of Georgia, Athens, GA)*
Kiribati

Sherylyn H. Briller *(Wayne State University, Detroit, MI)*
Mongolia

Inga Brinkman *(University of Cologne, Cologne, Germany)*
Angola

Douglas C. Broadfield *(City University of New York, New York, NY)*
Colombia

Benedicte Brøgger *(Work Research Institute, Oslo, Norway)*
Singapore

Reginald F. Byron *(University of Wales, Swansea, United Kingdom)*
United Kingdom

## C

Robert G. Carlson *(Wright State University, Dayton, OH)*
Tanzania

Laurence Marshall Carucci *(University of Montana, Bozeman, MT)*
Marshall Islands

Douglas Catterall *(Cameron University, Lawton, OK)*
England

D. Douglas Caulkins *(Grinnell College, Grinnell, IA)*
Norway

Barbara A. Cellarius *(Max Planck Institute for Social Anthropology, Halle-Saale, Germany)*
Bulgaria

Bambi L. Chapin *(University of California, San Diego, CA)*
Sri Lanka

Dawn Chatty *(University of Oxford, Oxford, United Kingdom)*
Oman

Hanna Chumachenko *(Ohio State University, Columbus, OH)*
Ukraine

Victoria Clement *(Ohio State University, Columbus, OH)*
Türkmenistan

Colleen Ballerino Cohen *(Vassar College, Poughkeepsie, NY)*
British Virgin Islands

Lisa L. Colburn *(University of Rhode Island, Kingston, RI)*
Madgascar

Donald Powell Cole *(American University, Cairo, Egypt)*
Saudi Arabia

David Coplan *(University of Witwatersrand, Witwatersrand, South Africa)*
South Africa

Sandra Crismon *(University of Georgia, Athens, GA)*
Kiribati

Clark E. Cunningham *(University of Illinois at Urbana-Champaign, Urbana, IL)*
Indonesia

Tim Curry *(Maynard, MA)*
Nigeria

## D

William G. Dalton *(University of New Brunswick, Fredericton, New Brunswick, Canada)*
Libya

Frank Darwiche *(Chenôve, France)*
Lebanon

Rosa de Jorio *(University of North Florida, Jacksonville, FL)*
Mali

Jean de Lannoy *(University of Oxford, Oxford, United Kingdom)*
Belgium

Hülya Demirdirek *(University of Oslo, Oslo, Norway)*
Azerbaijan
Moldova

Madjiguene Diajayette *(New York, NY)*
Senegal

Garba Diallo *(International People's College, Elsinore, Denmark)*
Mauritania

Jeanette Dickerson-Putman *(Indiana University, Indianapolis, IN)*
French Polynesia

Julia Dickson-Gomez *(Arizona State University, Tempe, AZ)*
El Salvador

Molly Doane *(Hunter College, City University of New York, New York, NY)*
United States

Bruce H. Dolph *(Manhattan Beach, CA)*
Malawi

S.B. Downey *(Washington, DC)*
Nicaragua
Northern Ireland

Douglass Drozdow-St. Christian *(University of Western Ontario, London, Ontario, Canada)*
Canada

Deborah Durham *(Sweet Briar College, Sweet Briar, VA)*
Botswana

E. Paul Durrenberger *(Pennsylvania State University, University Park, PA)*
Iceland

## E

Marc Edleman *(Hunter College, City University of New York, New York, NY)*
Costa Rica

John Eidson *(University of Leipzig, Germany)*
Germany

Robert Elsie *(Olzheim, Germany)*
Albania

Jeff Erlich *(Newton, MA)*
Uzbekistan

Grant Evans *(University of Hong Kong, Hong Kong)*
Laos

Pablo B. Eyzaguirre *(International Plant Genetic Resources Institute, Rome, Italy)*
São Tomé e Príncipe

## F

Pamela Feldman-Savelsberg *(Carleton College, Northfield, MN)*
Cameroon

Carmen Alicia Ferradas *(State University of New York, Binghamton, NY)*
Argentina

Thomas K. Fitzgerald *(University of North Carolina, Greensboro, NC)*
Monteserrat

Jason M. Fox *(University of Florida, Gainesville, FL*
Brazil

Susan Tax Freeman *(Chicago, IL)*
Spain

Victor A. Friedman *(University of Chicago, Chicago, IL)*
Macedonia

John Moffat Fugui *(University of Hawaii, Manoa, HI)*
Solomon Islands

## G

Eric Gable *(Mary Washington University, Fredericksburg, VA)*
Guinea-Bissau

Elizabeth Van Epps Garlo *(Concord, NH)*
Dominican Republic

Christian Ghasarian *(University of Neuchâtel, Neuchâtel, Switzerland)*
Reunion Island

Mary Katherine Gilliland *(University of Arizona, Tucson, AZ and Pima Community College, Tucson, AZ)*
Croatia

Michael Goldsmith *(University of Waikato, Hamilton, New Zealand)*
Tuvalu

Nancie L. González *(University of Maryland, College Park, MD and Universidad del Valle de Guatemala, Guatemala)*
Guatemala

Stefan Cornelius Goodwin *(Morgan State University, Baltimore, MD)*
Malta

Alison Graham *(Chicago, IL)*
Gabon

Robert H. Griffin *(Houston, TX)*
Austria
Palestine, West Bank, Gaza Strip

## H

Dieter Haller *(Europa University Viadrina, Frankfurt-Oder, Germany)*
Gibraltar

W. Penn Handwerker *(University of Connecticut, Storrs, CT)*
Barbados

Michael S. Harris *(Florida Atlantic University, Boca Raton, FL)*
Bangladesh

Anne Perez Hattori *(University of Guam, Mangilao, Guam)*
Guam

Wendi A. Haugh *(University of Pennsylvania, Philadelphia, PA)*
Namibia

Jeff Haynes *(London Guildhall University, London, United Kingdom)*
Uganda

Jonathan Hearn *(University of Edinburgh, Edinburgh, United Kingdom)*
Scotland

M. Douglas Henry *(Southern Methodist University, Dallas, TX)*
Sierra Leone

Paget Henry *(Brown University)*
Antigua and Barbuda

Robert K. Herbert *(State University of New York, Binghampton, NY)*
Swaziland

Pierre Claver Hien *(Centre National Dela Recherche Scientifique, Ouagadougou, Burkina Faso)*
Burkina Faso

Kevin Hillstrom (*Munith, MI*)
Greenland

Paul Hockings (*University of Illinois, Chicago, IL and Field Museum of Natural History, Chicago, IL*)
India

G. Derrick Hodge (*New York, NY*)
Cuba

Rosemarijn Hoefte (*Royal Institute of Linguistics and Anthropology, Leiden, The Netherlands*)
Suriname

Erling Høg (*University of Copenhagen, Copenhagen, Denmark*)
Denmark

Ellen Rhoads Holmes (*Wichita State University, Wichita, KS*)
American Samoa

Lowell D. Holmes (*Wichita State University, Wichita, KS*)
American Samoa

Nicholas S. Hopkins (*American University, Cairo, Egypt*)
Egypt
Tunisia

Connie Howard (*Indiana, PA*)
Bhutan
Pakistan

Michael C. Howard (*Simon Fraser University, Burnaby, British Columbia, Canada*)
Burma
Thailand

Judith Huntsman (*University of Auckland, New Zealand*)
Tokelau

Eva V. Huseby-Darvas (*University of Michigan, Dearborn, MI*)
Hungary

**J**

Robert Jarvenpa (*State University of New York, Albany, NY*)
Finland

Helle Johannessen (*University of Copenhagen, Copenhagen, Denmark*)
Denmark

Eric M. Johnson (*Washington, DC*)
Kazakhstan

Amanda Jill Johnston (*Monterey, CA*)
Morocco

Laura Jones (*Indiana University, Indianapolis, IN*)
French Polynesia

**K**

Edgar Kaskla (*California State University, Long Beach, CA*)
Estonia

Sulayman Najm Khalaf (*United Arab Emirates University, Al Ain, United Arab Emirates*)
United Arab Emirates

Robert Ķīlis (*Stockholm School of Economics, Riga, Latvia*)
Latvia

Richard Kuba (*University of Frankfurt-Main, Germany*)
Burkina Faso

**L**

Alan LaFlamme (*State University of New York, Fredonia*)
Bahama Islands

Benjamin Nicholas Lawrance (*Stanford University, Stanford, CA*)
Togo

Lamont Lindstrom (*University of Tulsa, Tulsa, OK*)
Vanuatu

Heather Loew (*San Francisco, CA*)
Kuwait

Ruben A. Lombaert (*Overijse, Belgium*)
Belgium

Timothy Longman (*Vassar College, Poughkeepsie, NY*)
Rwanda

Ludomir Lozny (*Hunter College, City University of New York, New York, NY*)
Belarus

**M**

Cluny Macpherson (*University of Auckland, New Zealand*)
Samoa

Paul J. Magnarella (*University of Florida, Gainesville, FL*)
Turkey

Shaun Kingsley Malarney (*International Christian University, Tokyo, Japan*)
Vietnam

Dennis Mares (*University of Missouri, Saint Louis, MO*)
The Netherlands

Maxine L. Margolis (*University of Florida, Gainesville, FL*)
Brazil

Samuel Márquez (*City University of New York, New York, NY*)
Colombia

John Marston (*Colegio de Mexico, Mexico City, Mexico*)
Cambodia

David Matuskey (*Winter Park, FL*)
Republic of Congo
French Guiana
Mauritius

Allen R. Maxwell (*University of Alabama, Tuscalossa, AL*)
Brunei Darussalem

Douglas Midgett (*University of Iowa, Iowa City, IA*)
Saint Lucia

William F.S. Miles (*Northeastern University, Boston, MA*)
Martinique

Gina Misiroglu (*Toluca Lake, CA*)
Côte d'Ivoire

Adam Mohr (*University of Pennsylvania, Philadelphia, PA*)
Ethiopia

Alessandro Monsutti (*Institute d'ethnologie, Neuchâtel, Switzerland*)
Afghanistan

Alexander Moore (*University of Southern California, Los Angeles, CA*)
Panama

Mary H. Moran (*Colgate University, Hamilton, NY*)
Liberia

Ann Muir (*University of Edinburgh, Edinburgh, United Kingdom*)
Zimbabwe

## N

Beverly Nagel (*Carleton College, Northfield, MN*)
Paraguay

Sharon Nagy (*DePaul University, Chicago, IL*)
Qatar

Karen L. Nero (*University of Auckland, New Zealand*)
Palau

Claus Neukirck (*Hamburg, Germany*)
Moldova

Coleen Nicol (*Tufts University, Medford, MA*)
Lithuania

Marie Kamala Norman (*Carnegie-Mellon University, Pittsburgh, PA*)
Nepal

## O

Tania Ogay (*University of Geneva, Geneva, Switzerland*)
Switzerland

Bryan P. Oles (*Takoma Park, MD*)
Federated State of Micronesia

Michael E. O'Neal (*H. Lavity Stoutt Community College, British Virgin Islands*)
British Virgin Islands

Emily Lynn Osborn (*Johns Hopkins University, Baltimore, MD*)
Guinea

## P

Joseph O. Palacio (*University of the West Indies, Belize City, Belize*)
Belize

Brian C.W. Palmer (*Harvard University, Cambridge, Massachusetts*)
Sweden

Wil G. Pansters (*Utrecht University, Utrecht, The Netherlands*)
Mexico

Yiannis Papadakis (*University of Cypress, Nicosia, Cyprus*)
Cyprus

Amy L. Paugh (*New York University, New York, NY*)
Dominica

Jon Pedersen (*Fafo Institute for Applied International Studies, Oslo, Norway*)
Seychelles

Susan W. Peters (*University of Maryland, University College, MD and Schwäbisch Gmünd, Germany*)
Cayman Islands
United States Virgin Islands

Marilyn F. Petersen (*Petaluma, CA*)
Tajikistan

J.E. Peterson (*University of Oxford, Oxford, United Kingdom*)
Oman

Karen Lynn Pierzinski (*North Richland Hills, TX*)
Grenada

Elizabeth C. Pietanza (*Oakland, CA*)
Iraq

Tim Pilbrow (*New York University, New York, NY*)
Bulgaria

Janet Pollak *(William Patterson University, Wayne, NJ)*
Slovakia

Nancy J. Pollock *(Victoria University, Wellington, New Zealand)*
Nauru
Wallis and Futuna

Marion Pratt *(University of Wisconsin, Madison, WI)*
Tanzania

Joan J. Pujadas *(Universitat Rovira i Virgili, Tarragona, Spain)*
Andorra

Trevor W. Purcell *(University of South Florida, Tampa, FL)*
Jamaica

## Q

Diego Quiroga *(Quito, Ecuador)*
Ecuador

## R

Susan J. Rasmussen *(University of Houston, Houston, TX)*
Niger

Douglas Raybeck *(Hamilton College, Clinton, NY)*
Saint Kitts and Nevis

Deborah Reed-Danahay *(University of Texas, Arlington, TX)*
France

Nancy Ries *(Colgate University, Hamilton, NY)*
Russia

Antonius C.G.M. Robben *(Utrecht University, Utrecht, The Netherlands)*
The Netherlands

Mikhail Rodionov *(Peter the Great Museum of Anthropology and Ethnography, Saint Petersburg, Russia)*
Yemen

James M. Rubenstein *(Miami University, Oxford, OH)*
Luxembourg

Josephine Caldwell Ryan *(Southern Methodist University, Dallas, TX)*
Benin

Sonia Ryang *(Johns Hopkins University, Baltimore, MD)*
North Korea

## S

Reem Saad *(American University, Cairo, Egypt)*
Egypt

Frank A. Salamone *(Iona College, New Rochelle, NY)*
Gambia
Italy
Vatican City

Zdenek Salzmann *(Sedona, AZ)*
Czech Republic

William J. Samarin *(University of Toronto, Toronto, Ontario, Canada)*
Central African Republic

Harry Sanabria *(University of Pittsburgh, Pittsburgh, PA)*
Bolivia

Vilma Santiago-Irizarry *(Cornell University, Ithaca, NY)*
Puerto Rico

Rajasundram Sathuendrakumar *(Murdoch University, Murdoch, Western Australia)*
Maldives

Darlene Schmidt *(Madison, WI)*
Jordan

Ellen M. Schnepel *(Research Institute for the Study of Man, New York, NY 10021)*
Guadeloupe

Timothy T. Schwartz *(Hispaniola Anthropological Association, Gainesville, FL)*
Haiti

Brian Schwimmer *(University of Manitoba, Winnipeg, Manitoba, Canada)*
Ghana

Clem Seecharan *(University of North London, London, United Kingdom)*
Guyana

Ann H. Shurgin *(Waller, TX)*
Austria
Somalia

Kalinga Tudor Silva *(University of Peradeniya, Peradeniya, Sri Lanka)*
Sri Lanka

Patricio Silva *(Leiden University, Leiden, The Netherlands)*
Chile

Ian Skoggard *(Human Relations Area Files, Yale University, New Haven, CT)*
Taiwan

Andris Skreija *(University of Nebraska, Omaha, NE)*
Poland

Vieda Skultans *(University of Bristol, Bristol, United Kingdom)*
Latvia

J. Jerome Smith (*University of South Florida, Tampa, FL*)
Northern Mariana Islands

Chunghee Sarah Soh (*San Francisco State University, San Francisco, CA*)
South Korea

Jon Sojkowski (*Beaufort, SC*)
Zambia

Eleanor Stanford (*Narberth, PA*)
Algeria
Bahrain
Bermuda
Bosnia and Hercegovina
Burundi
Cape Verde
China
Cook Islands
Equatorial Guinea
Falkland Islands
Israel
Kenya
Mozambique
Romania
Serbia and Montenegro
Sudan
Syria

Patricia Osborn Stoddard (*Whittier, NC*)
Lesotho

Andrew Sussman (*University of New Mexico, Albuquerque, MN*)
Bermuda

Susan Buck Sutton (*Indiana University, Purdue University at Indianapolis, Indianapolis, IN*)
Greece

## T

George Tarkhan-Mouravi (*ICGRS, Tiblisi, Georgia*)
Georgia

David S. Trigger (*University of Western Australia, Perth, Australia*)
Australia

Kjetil Tronvoll (*University of Oslo, Oslo, Norway*)
Eritrea

Tiffany Tuttle (*Arcata, CA*)
Kyrgyzstan

## W

Anthony R. Walker (*Universiti Brunei Darussalam; formerly, University of the South Pacific, Suva, Fiji*)
Fiji

Dorothea Scott Whitten (*University of Illinois at Urbana-Champaign, Urbana, IL*)
Ecuador

Norman E. Whitten, Jr. (*University of Illinois at Urbana-Champaign, Urbana, IL*)
Ecuador

Thomas Williamson (*University of Pittsburgh, Pittsburgh, PA*)
Malaysia

Peter J. Wilson (*TeWaka, Gisborne, New Zealand*)
New Zealand

Thomas M. Wilson (*Queen's University, Belfast, United Kingdom*)
Ireland

Jonathan Wylie (*Massachusetts Institute of Technology, Cambridge, MA*)
Faroe Islands

## Y

Kevin A. Yelvington (*University of South Florida, Tampa, FL*)
Trinidad and Tobago

## Z

Wallace W. Zane (*Santa Monica College, Santa Monica, CA*)
Saint Vincent and the Grenadines

Jennifer Ziemke (*Temperance, MI*)
Democratic Republic of Congo

Laura Zimmer-Tamakoshi (*Truman State University, Kirksville, MO*)
Papua New Guinea

# AFGHANISTAN

## CULTURE NAME

Afghanistani, Afghan

## ORIENTATION

**Identification.** The word "Afghan" historically has been used to designate the members of an ethnic group also called the Pashtuns, but Afghanistan is multicultural and multiethnic. The state was formed by the political expansion of Pashtun tribes in the middle of the eighteenth century but was not unified until the end of the nineteenth century. Persian-speaking (Tajiks, Hazaras, and Aymaqs) and Turkic-speaking (Uzbeks and Turkmens) populations have been incorporated in the state. Since the Communist coup of 1987 and the ensuing civil war, those groups have sought for greater political recognition, but the existence of the state has not been seriously questioned. The experience of exile shared by millions of refugees may have given rise to a new national feeling.

**Location and Geography.** Afghanistan is a landlocked Asian country of 251,825 square miles (652,225 square kilometers) bordered by Pakistan, Iran, Turkmenistan, Uzbekistan, Tajikistan, and China. The topography is a mix of central highlands and peripheral foothills and plains. The country has an arid continental climate. Summers are dry and hot, while winters are cold with heavy snowfall in the highlands. Precipitation is low, although some areas in the east are affected by the monsoon. Most of the country is covered by steppes, with desert areas and some patches of cultivated land. Pastoral nomadism, subsistence mountain agriculture, and irrigation are practiced. At the end of the eighteenth century, Kabul became the capital. It is located in a wide basin on the road linking India with Central Asia.

**Demography.** There are no reliable census figures, but in 1997, the population was estimated to be 23,738,000. The great majority of people are rural

(80 percent). The population of Kabul peaked at more than one million in the 1980s but dropped after the fall of the Communist regime in 1992. Mazar-e Sharif, Herat, and Kandahar (Qandahar) are the major cities, with populations of about 200,000 each. Important towns include Jalalabad, Kunduz, Baghlan, and Ghazni.

The demographic importance of the Pashtuns has decreased since 1978, because they have formed the majority of the refugee population in Pakistan. It is estimated that Pashtuns represent 38 percent of the population, principally in the southeast, south, and west, with some pockets in the north; they are divided between the Durrani and Ghilzay confederacies and among many tribes along the Pakistani border. The Tajiks (25 percent) live primarily in the northeast, the northwest, and the urban centers. The Hazaras (19 percent) are found in the center, Kabul, and Mazar-e Sharif. The Uzbeks (6 percent) occupy the north. The remaining 12 percent of the population is made up of Aymaks (Sunni Persian-speaking groups in the northwest), Turkmens (along the border with Turkmenistan), Baluchis (in the southwest), and Nuristanis and Pashays (northeast of Kabul).

Except for a few Hindu, Sikh, and Jewish minorities that have left the country, all the inhabitants are Muslims, divided between Sunnis (estimated at 84 percent), and Shiites (15 percent, most of whom are Hazaras); there are Ismaeli pockets in the east of Hazarajat and in Badakhshan. There has been a huge refugee population outside the country since 1978, numbering over six million in 1990—it constituted the largest refugee population in the world. Although many returned after the fall of the Communist regime in April 1992, several million Afghan refugees are still in Pakistan, Iran, and the Arabian peninsula. Some middle-class persons and intellectuals have settled in the West.

**Linguistic Affiliation.** Many inhabitants are bilingual or trilingual, and all the major languages are

*Afghanistan*

spoken in the neighboring countries. The official languages are Persian (officially called Dari) and Pashto; both belong to the Iranian group of the Indo-European linguistic family. The Persian spoken by the Tajiks, Hazaras, and Aymaks is not very different from the Persian of Iran. Pashto, which is divided into two major dialects, is also spoken in large areas of Pakistan. Despite government initiatives to promote Pashto, Persian is the preferred means of expression among educated and urban people. The Iranian group is also represented by Baluchi and some residual languages. The Nuristani languages are intermediate between Iranian and Indian groups, while Pashay is a conservative Indian language. Turkic languages, represented by Uzbek, Turkmen, and

Kirghiz, are spoken widely in the north. Moghol and Arabic enclaves are disappearing.

***Symbolism.*** Afghanistan has never had a strongly unified national culture, and war has led to further fragmentation. The old flag of green, white, and black horizontal strips has been abandoned, and there is no national anthem. The national currency (the Afghani) is printed in two separate locations, with a locally varying exchange rate.

## HISTORY AND ETHNIC RELATIONS

***Emergence of the Nation.*** The territory of modern Afghanistan was the center of several empires, including Greco-Buddhist kingdoms and the Kushans

*An Afghani man sits in the rubble of Kabul, Afghanistan in 1995. Between 1992 and 1995, the Taliban seized control of southern Afghanistan.*

(third century B.C.E. to the second century C.E.) and the Muslim Ghaznavid and Ghurid dynasties (tenth to the twelfth centuries). It was a base of action for many rulers of India, notably the Mughals.

The modern nation emerged during the eighteenth century by Pashtun tribes in reaction to the decline of the Persian and Indian empires. During the nineteenth century, Afghanistan struggled successfully against the colonial powers and served as a buffer state between Russia and British India. The three Anglo-Afghan wars (1839–1842; 1878–1880; 1919) could have forged a national feeling, but the country's history has been dominated by internal conflicts. The first half of the nineteenth century was marked by a feud between two branches of the Durrani Pashtuns, with the Mohammadzay eventually succeeding and ruling until 1978. Abdur Rahman (Abdorrahman Khan, r. 1880–1901) extended his authority over the whole country by overcoming resistance from his fellow tribesmen and defeating the Ghizay Pashtuns, the Hazaras, and the Kafirs (Nuristanis). Although political unity was forged during his reign, his harsh tactics created enmities between Sunnis and Shiites, between Pashtuns and other ethnic groups, and among Pashtuns, as well as between rural and urban people.

King Amanullah (Amanollah Khan, r. 1919–1929) tried to implement various reforms which failed. An attempt to set up a parliamentary government after 1963 resulted in serious social troubles—leading to the seizure of power by the Communists in 1978, many of whom were young, recently urbanized, detribalized people seeking social advancement. Within a few months the country was rebelling, and in 1979 the Soviet Union intervened militarily. A bitter guerrilla war ensued over the next ten years between the Red Army and the Afghan resistance fighters *(mujâhedin)*, during which about 1.5 million Afghans died and millions left the country. The Soviet withdrawal in 1989 and the fall of the Communist regime in 1992 led to an explosion of tensions and dissatisfactions. In response to this situation, the Taliban (religious students from refugee camps in Pakistan), seized the south in the winter of 1994–1995 and restored security. Since that time they have conquered most of the country, but have been unable to incorporate other groups or obtain international recognition.

***National Identity.*** Until 1978, Afghanistan avoided fragmentation through a shared religion and the relative autonomy of local communities even though the government favored Pashtun culture and folklore. Most inhabitants felt they belonged primarily to a local community and secondarily to the supranational Islamic community. National identity was weak, but the state was not considered disruptive. This fragile equilibrium was destroyed after the coup of 1978. The symbols on which the legitimacy of the government was based (political independence, historical continuity, and respect of Islam) vanished.

***Ethnic Relations.*** Before 1978, ethnic relations were competitive and tense. The pro-Soviet government attempted to promote the rights, culture, and languages of non-Pashtun groups. Although this endeavor failed, it led to an erosion of the Pashtun political hegemony. In the 1990s, political claims evolved progressively from an Islamic to an ethnic discourse. Islam-inspired resistance to the Soviets failed to provide a common ground for building peace and uniting people. Since 1992, the civil war has been marked by ethnic claims that have led to polarization between Pashtuns (who dominate the Taliban movement) and the other ethnic groups (who form the bulk of the opposing Northern Alliance).

## URBANISM, ARCHITECTURE, AND THE USE OF SPACE

There are several historical cities, such as Balkh, Ghazni, and Herat, but after twenty years of war, the preservation of historical monuments is not a priority. The Kabul Museum was looted repeatedly, nothing is left of the covered bazaar of Tashqurghan (Tash Kurghan) in the north, and the Buddha statues of Bamyan (Bamian) have been damaged. Most cities and towns are in ruins, and little reconstruction is occurring.

In the south and the center, the most common form of housing is the multi-story fortified farm with high walls built from a mixture of mud and straw. They are scattered in the fields, sometimes forming loose hamlets. In the north and the west, smaller compounds with vaulted houses of mud brick are prevalent. In the eastern highlands, settlements are grouped; stone and timber are common building materials. In both urban and rural settings, bazaars are not residential areas.

Domestic architecture is based on the separation between the public and private parts of the house so that women do not interact with strangers. Furnishings are generally rudimentary. Many families sleep in one room on mattresses that are unfolded for the night, and no places are assigned. In the morning, the room is tidied, with the mattresses and quilts piled in a corner. Rich families may have a separate guest house, but Afghans do not like to sleep alone and generally do not provide guests with separate rooms.

There is a large semi-nomadic and nomadic population. Two types of tents are used: the Middle Eastern black goat's hair tent and the round Central Asian yurt. Temporary shelters range from reed and straw huts to caves.

## FOOD AND ECONOMY

***Food in Daily Life.*** Everyday food consists of flat bread cooked on an iron plate in the fire or on the inner wall of a clay oven. Bread often is dipped in a light meat stock. Yogurt and other dairy products (butter, cream, and dried buttermilk) are an important element of the diet, as are onions, peas and beans, dried fruits, and nuts. Rice is eaten in some areas and in urban settlements. Scrambled eggs prepared with tomatoes and onions is a common meal. Food is cooked with various types of oils, including the fat of a sheep's tail. Tea is drunk all day. Sugar is used in the first cup of the day, and then sweets are eaten and kept in the mouth while sipping tea. Other common beverages are water and buttermilk. Afghans use the right hand to eat from a common bowl on the floor. At home, when there are no guests, men and women share meals. Along the roads and in the bazaars, there are many small restaurants that also function as teahouses and inns.

The common Islamic food prohibitions are respected in Afghanistan. For example, meat is only eaten from animals that are slaughtered according to Islamic law; alcohol, pork, and wild boar are not consumed, although some people secretly raise these animals for consumption at home. The Shiites avoid rabbit and hare.

***Food Customs at Ceremonial Occasions.*** On special occasions, pilau rice is served with meat, carrots, raisin, pistachios, or peas. The preferred meat is mutton, but chicken, beef, and camel also are consumed. Kebabs, fried crepes filled with leeks, ravioli, and noodle soup also are prepared. Vegetables include spinach, zucchini, turnip, eggplant, peas and beans, cucumber, and tomatoes. Fresh fruits are eaten during the day or as a dessert. In formal gatherings, men and women are separated. Dinners start by drinking tea and nibbling on pistachios or chickpeas; food is served late in the evening on dishes that are placed on a cloth on the floor. Eating abundantly demonstrates one's enjoyment.

***Basic Economy.*** The traditional economy combines cultivation and animal husbandry. Irrigated agriculture dominates, but the products of pluvial

*In southern and central Afghanistan, the most common form of housing is a multi-storied fortified farm built of mud and straw.*

agriculture are considered to be of better quality. Wheat is the principal crop, followed by rice, barley, and corn. The main cash crops are almonds and fruits. Cotton was a major export until the civil war. Today, large zones of agricultural land have been converted to poppy cultivation for the heroin trade. Stock breeding is practiced by both nomadic and sedentary peoples. Nomads spend the summer in the highlands and the winter in the lowlands. Many of them, especially in the east, also trade.

Virtually all manufactured goods are imported; they are financed by remittances from refugees and emigrants.

**Land Tenure and Property.** Most grazing land is held communally, but agricultural land is privately owned. Irrigation canals are shared, following a pre-established schedule. The bulk of the population consists of small landholders who supplement their income by sending a family member to work in the city or abroad. Poor farmers who do not own land often become tenants or hire themselves out on a daily base. Often in debt, they are economically and politically dependent on local headmen and landlords.

**Commercial Activities.** Afghanistan produces few commercial goods. The Taliban have opened commercial routes between Pakistan and Turkmenistan, but no official trade can develop until the govern-

ment is recognized by the international community.

**Trade.** Hides, wool, dried and fresh fruits, and pistachios are exported, but narcotics account for the bulk of export receipts. The country imports tax-free goods through Pakistan, including cars, air conditioners, refrigerators, televisions, radios, and stereo equipment. These consumer products are then smuggled to neighboring countries.

**Major Industries.** After more than twenty years of war, there is no industrial activity.

**Division of Labor.** Most of the Afghan workers present in Iran and the Gulf countries are young, unmarried males. In Afghanistan, people work as long as they are fit.

## SOCIAL STRATIFICATION

**Classes and Castes.** Some groups are egalitarian, but others have a hierarchical social organization. There are great differences in wealth and social status. Society also is stratified along religious and ethnic lines. During most of the twentieth century, members of the king's family played a major role in politics as ministers and ambassadors. Most civil servants and technocrats were Persian-speaking ur-

*A group of children read in a mosque school in Arghandab, Afghanistan. Although education is valued in Afghanistan, only 5 percent of Afghani children receive a primary education.*

ban residents. Ismaelis and Shiites (especially the Hazaras) had the lowest status. In the provinces, most administrative posts were held by Pashtuns who had no connection to the population. Local communities were dominated by the richest landlords, assisted by village headmen. The Sayyeds, supposed to be the descendants of the Prophet Muhammad through his daughter Fatima, played an important role as mediators, relying on prestige rather than personal wealth. Family elders were consulted on local matters, and many disputes were settled by local assemblies. Although Communist land reform was rejected by the population, important changes have occurred. Traditional leaders have lost their preeminence to military commanders and young religious militants. Some smugglers have become immensely rich.

***Symbols of Social Stratification.*** Social stratification is expressed primarily through marriage patterns. The general tendency is for lower social groups to give their daughters in marriage to higher social groups. The lavishness of a wedding is an indicator of status and wealth. Following Taliban decree, men must wear a hat or turban and be bearded. Western dress and fashion, which once distinguished urban from rural people, have almost disappeared.

## POLITICAL LIFE

***Government.*** The Taliban control most of the country. Their government is recognized only by Pakistan, the United Arab Emirates, and Saudi Arabia. The Taliban rule without a constitution, relying on the Koran. There is an informal assembly around their leader in Kandahar. Ministries exist in Kabul, and lower-level civil servants have often remained in place, but there is no real administration. At the local level, the military commanders rule groups of villages, a situation the Taliban have tried to end.

***Leadership and Political Officials.*** Afghanistan does not have a unified government. Political parties linked to the resistance, including Sunni and Shiite, and Islamic fundamentalist, have developed during the war, but now they have imperfectly merged in the two remaining factions—the Taliban and the Northern Alliance. Military commanders have the real leadership.

***Social Problems and Control.*** In their drive to ''purify'' society, the Taliban emphasize moral values. No distinction is made between religious and civil laws, and the religious police are omnipotent. Judges apply a tribal-based conception of Islam. Those who commit adultery and consume drugs and alcohol are severely punished. Beatings, amputations, and public executions (beheading, stoning, and shooting) are commonly practiced. Tens of thousands of persons are jailed without trial by the various factions.

*Military Activity.* The Taliban are backed by Pakistan, while the Northern Alliance is supported by Iran and the former Soviet republics in Central Asia. Military activity is intense, particularly in the spring and summer.

## SOCIAL WELFARE AND CHANGE PROGRAMS

No political leader has attempted to develop welfare programs.

## NONGOVERNMENTAL ORGANIZATIONS AND OTHER ASSOCIATIONS

United Nations agencies and the Red Cross are active, but fighting often interrupts their projects. Hundreds of local and foreign nongovernmental organizations have programs for land mine removal, education, health care, road building, irrigation, and agriculture. Their role is often ambiguous, and they have contributed to social stratification because their actions often are limited to major urban centers and areas near the Pakistani border. By providing nearly all welfare programs, they have made it easier for political leaders to ignore social issues.

## GENDER ROLES AND STATUSES

*Division of Labor by Gender.* Male and female roles are strongly differentiated. The public sphere is the domain of men, and the domestic one is the realm of women. Women take care of young children, cook for the household, and clean the house. They may have a small garden and a few chickens. They weave and sew and in some areas make rugs and felt. Among nomads, women make tents and have more freedom of movement. In a peasant family, men look after the sheep and goats, and plow, harvest, thresh, and winnow the crops. Among both rural and urban people, a man must not stay at home during the day. During war, women take over many male duties; men who work abroad must learn to cook, sew, and do laundry.

*The Relative Status of Women and Men.* Between 1919 and 1929, King Amanullah tried to promote female empowerment. Under the Communist government, many women were able to study in universities. This trend was reversed by the Taliban. Women now must be completely covered by a long veil and accompanied by a male relative when they leave the house. Women face overwhelming obstacles if they seek to work or study or obtain access to basic health care. However, the Taliban have improved security in many rural areas, allowing women to carry out their everyday duties.

Women have never participated publicly in decision making processes. They are admonished to be modest and obey the orders of their fathers, brothers, and husbands. Nevertheless, as guardians of family honor, women have more power. Nomadic and peasant women play an important role in the domestic economy and are not secluded in the same way as many urban women. Shiite leaders stress the right of a woman to participate in the political process, engage in independent economic activity, and freely choose a husband.

## MARRIAGE, FAMILY, AND KINSHIP

*Marriage.* Marriage is considered an obligation, and divorce is rare and stigmatized. Polygamy is allowed if all the wives are treated equally. However, it is uncommon and occurs primarily when a man feels obligated to marry the widow of his dead brother. The general pattern is to marry kin, although families try to diversify their social assets through marriage. The incidence of unions between cousins is high.

The first contacts often are made discreetly by women in order to avoid a public refusal. Then the two families negotiate the financial aspects of the union and decide on the trousseau, the brideprice, and the dowery. The next step is the official engagement, during which female relatives of the groom bring gifts to the home of the bride and sweets are consumed. The wedding is a three-day party paid for by the groom's family during which the marriage contract is signed and the couple is brought together. The bride is then brought to her new home in a lavish procession.

*Domestic Unit.* Traditionally, the basic household consists of a man, his wife, his sons with their spouses and children, and his unmarried daughters. When he dies, the sons can decide to stay united or divide the family assets. Authority among brothers is based on ability, economic skill, and personal prestige more than age. Sometimes a brother asks for his share of the family wealth and leaves the domestic group while the father is still alive. Residential unity does not imply shared domestic ex-

*Men gather water from a mosque well. The roles of Afghani men and women differ strongly, both in terms of daily tasks and personal empowerment.*

penses. Domestic units are larger among tribal people than among urban dwellers.

**Inheritance.** In theory all brothers are equal, but to avoid splitting up family property, brothers may decide to own it jointly or to be compensated financially. Contrary to Islamic law, women do not inherit land, real estate, or livestock.

**Kin Groups.** All groups trace descent through the male line. Each tribal group claims a common male ancestor and is divided into subtribes, clans, lineages, and families. Genealogy establishes inheritance, mutual obligations, and a feeling of solidarity. Disputes over women, land, and money may result in blood feuds. The tribal system is particularly developed among the Pashtuns. The main values of their tribal code are hospitality and revenge. Many inhabitants of Afghanistan do not belong to a tribe or have only a loose affiliation. Neighborhood and other social links, often reinforced by marriage, can be stronger than extended kinship.

## SOCIALIZATION

*Infant Care.* Babies are bound tightly in wooden cradles with a drain for urine or carried by the mother in a shawl. They may be breast-fed for more than two years, but weaning is very sudden. Children are cared for by a large group of female relatives. Although surrounded by affection, children learn early that no one will intervene when they cry or are hurt. Adults do not interfere with children's games, which can be tough. Physical punishment is administered, although parents tend to be indulgent with young children. Children move freely from the female part of the house to the public one and learn to live in a group setting.

*Child Rearing and Education.* Respect and obedience to elderly persons are important values, but independence, individual initiative, and self-confidence also are praised. The most important rite of passage for a boy is circumcision, usually at age seven. Boys learn early the duties of hospitality and caring for guests as well as looking after the livestock or a shop, while girls begin helping their mothers as soon as they can stand. Both are taught the values of honor and shame and must learn when to show pride and when to remain modest.

*Higher Education.* Literacy is extremely low, and in 1980, 88 percent of the adult population had no formal schooling. Only 5 percent of children get a primary education, with a huge discrepancy between males and females. People from Afghanistan must travel abroad to further their education. Although education is valued, there is no professional future for educated people other than working for an international agency or a nongovernmental organization.

## ETIQUETTE

Young people address elders not by name but by a title. A husband will not call his wife by her name but will call her "mother of my son." Family surnames are unusual, but nicknames are very common. Kinship terms often are used to express friendship or respect. Hospitality is a strong cultural value. When food is served, the host waits until the guests have started eating. As soon as the dishes are cleared, guests ask permission to leave unless they are spending the night.

When meeting, two men shake hands and then place the right hand on the heart. Direct physical contact is avoided between men and women. If they have not seen each other for a long time, friends and relatives hug, kiss, and speak polite phrases. When someone enters a room, people stand and greet him at length. When they sit down, more greetings are exchanged. It is considered rude to ask a factual question or inquire about anything specific early in the conversation. To express affection, it is customary to complain, sometimes bitterly, about not having received any news.

## RELIGION

*Religious Beliefs.* Despite their different affiliations, Sunnis and Shiites recognize the authority of the Koran and respect the five pillars of Islam. Nevertheless, relationships between members of different religious sects are distant and tense. Sufism is an important expression of religiosity. It represents the mystical trend of Islam and stresses emotion and personal commitment over a codified conception of faith. It is viewed with suspicion by some Islamic scholars. An extreme form of Sufism is represented by wandering beggars. Supernatural creatures such as angels, genies, ghosts, and spirits, are believed to exist. Exorcism and magic protect people from the evil eye. Although condemned by orthodox religious authorities, these practices may be reinforced by the village mullah.

*Religious Practitioners.* There are two kinds of religious practitioners: scholars, whose power is based on knowledge, and saints, whose authority comes from their ability to transmit God's blessing. Among Sunnis, there is no formal clergy, while Shiites have a religious hierarchy. Village mullahs receive a religious education that allows them to teach children and lead the Friday prayers. Many saints and Sufi leaders claim descent from the Prophet. Their followers visit them to ask for advice and blessing. During the war, a new kind of religious leader emerged: the young Islamic militant who challenges the authority of traditional practitioners and proposes a more political conception of religion.

*Rituals and Holy Places.* Throughout the year, people gather at noon on Fridays in the mosque. Most villages have a place to pray, which also is used to accommodate travelers. The tombs of famous religious guides often become shrines visited by local people. They play an important role in the social life of village community and the local identity. Pilgrimages allow women to get out of the home in groups to chat and socialize.

There are two main religious festivals. The Id al-Kabir or Id-e Qorban (the Great Feast or Feast of the Victim) commemorates the sacrifice of Abraham at

*A muslim bows his head in prayer on the snow-capped mountain border of Pakistan, China, and Afghanistan. Both the Sunnis and the Shiites recognize the authority of the Koran and respect the five pillars of Islam.*

the end of the annual period of pilgrimage to Mecca. Most families slay a sheep and distribute some of the meat to the poor. The Id al-Fitr or Id-e Ramazan (the Small Feast or Feast of the Ramazan) marks the end of the fasting month and is a period of cheer during which relatives and friends visit each other. The fasting month of Ramadan is an important religious and social event. During Muharram (the first month of the Islamic lunar calendar), Shiites commemorate the death of the grandson of Muhammad. It is a period of mourning and sorrow. People gather to listen to an account of the martyrdom, weeping and hitting their breasts. The anniversary of the death of Husain is the climax. Processions are organized, and some young men wound themselves with chains or sharp knives. Other important social ceremonies with a religious dimension include births, weddings, funerals, circumcisions of young boys, and charity meals offered by wealthy people.

***Death and the Afterlife.*** The dead are buried rapidly in a shroud. In the countryside, most graves are simple heaps of stones without a name. Wealthier persons may erect a tombstone with a written prayer. For three days, the close relatives of the deceased open their house to receive condolences. Forty days after the death, relatives and close friends meet again, visit the grave, and pray. After one year, a ceremony takes place to mark the end of the mourning period. Many people believe that if a funeral is not carried out properly, the ghost of the dead will return to torment the living.

## MEDICINE AND HEALTH CARE

Since modern medical facilities are limited, people rely on traditional practices that employ herbs and animal products. Every physical ailment is classified as warm or cold, and its cure depends on restoring the body's equilibrium by ingesting foods with the opposite properties. Another way to cure disease is to undertake a pilgrimage to a shrine. Sometimes, pilgrims put a pinch of sand collected from the holy place into their tea or keep a scrap from the banners on a tomb. Certain springs are considered holy, and their water is believed to have a curative effect. Talismans (Koranic verse in a cloth folder) are sewed onto clothing or hats to protect against the evil eye or treat an illness.

## SECULAR CELEBRATIONS

The Jashn, the National Independence Holidays (celebrating complete independence from the British in

1919) used to be an occasion for the government to promote reforms. Parades and sporting events were organized. The New Year on 21 March dates back to the pre-Islamic period. In the old Persian calendar, it was a fertility festival celebrating the spring. It is still a time for celebration when relatives and friends visit each other and bring gifts for the children.

## THE ARTS AND HUMANITIES

The Taliban have banned artistic expression. High culture is kept alive in Pakistan and in the West, refugees have set up cultural circles that organize concerts, exhibitions (paintings, photographs), poetry contests, and courses in calligraphy, painting, music, and poetry. Some also have modest libraries and film archives and promote theater.

## THE STATE OF THE PHYSICAL AND SOCIAL SCIENCES

All scholars have left the country, and no higher education or scientific research is available.

## BIBLIOGRAPHY

Adamec, Ludwig W. *Historical and Political Gazetteer of Afghanistan*, 1985.

Balland, D., L. Dupree, N. H. Dupree, N. H.; et al. ''Afghanistan.'' *Encyclopaedia Iranica*, 1985.

Canfield, Robert L. ''The Ecology of Rural Ethnic Groups and the Spatial Dimensions of Power.'' *American Anthropologist* 75: 1511–1528, 1973.

Centlivres, Pierre. *Un bazar d'Asie Centrale: forme et organisation du bazar de Tâshqurghân (Afghanistan)*, 1970.

———. ''Exil, Relations Interethniques et Identité dans la Crise Afghane.'' *La Revue du Monde Musulman et de la Méditerranée* 59–60: 70–82, 1991.

———Micheline Centlivres-Demont. *Et si on Parlait de l'Afghanistan? Terrains et Textes 1964–1980*, 1988.

———. ''The Afghan Refugee in Pakistan: An Ambiguous Identity.'' *Journal of Refugee Studies* 1 (2): 141–152, 1988.

Digard, Jean-Pierre, ed. *Le Fait Ethnique en Iran et en Afghanistan*, 1988.

Dorronsoro, Glles. *La Révolution Afghane: Des Communistes aux Tâlibân*, 2000.

Dupree, Louis. *Afghanistan*, 1973.

Edwards, David B. ''Marginality and Migration: Cultural Dimensions of the Afghan Refugee Problem.'' *International Migration Review* 2 (2): 313–325, 1986.

———. *Heroes of the Age: Moral Fault Lines on the Afghan Frontier*, 1996.

Ferdinand, Klaus. ''Nomad Expansion and Commerce in Central Afghânistân: A Sketch of Some Modern Trends.'' *Folk* 4: 123–159, 1962.

*Folk*, 24: 4–177, 1982 (special issue on marriage in Afghan society).

Groetzbach, Erwin. *Afghanistan: Eine Geographische Landskunde*, 1990.

Kakar, Hasan K. *Government and Society in Afghanistan: The Reign of Amir 'Abd al Rahman Khan*, 1979.

Maley, William, ed. *Fundamentalism Reborn? Afghanistan and the Taliban*, 1998.

Mousavi, Sayed Askar. *The Hazaras of Afghanistan: An Historical, Cultural, Economic and Political Study*, 1998.

Orywal, Erwin. *Die Ethnischen Gruppen Afghanistan: Fallstudien zu Gruppenidentität und Intergruppenbeziehungen*, 1986.

Poullada, Leon B. *Reform and Rebellion in Afghanistan, 1919–1929: King Amanullah's Failure to Modernize a Tribal Society*, 1973.

Roy, Olivier. *L'Afghanistan: Islam et Modernité Politique*, 1985.

Rubin, Barnett R. *The Fragmentation of Afghanistan: State Formation and Collapse in the International System*, 1995.

Shahrani, M. Nazif and Robert L. Canfield, eds. *Revolution and Rebellions in Afghanistan: Anthropological Perspectives*, 1984.

Szabo, Albert and Thomas J. Barfield, *Afghanistan: An Atlas of Domestic Architecture*, 1991.

Tapper, Nancy. *Bartered Brides: Politics, Gender and Marriage in an Afghan Tribal Society*, 1991.

Tapper, Richard, ed. *The Conflict of Tribe and State in Iran and Afghanistan*, 1983.

UNHCR. ''Afghanistan: The Unending Crisis.'' *Refugees*, vol. 108, 1997.

—ALESSANDRO MONSUTTI

# ALBANIA

## CULTURE NAME

Albanian

## ALTERNATIVE NAMES

The international terms "Albania" and "Albanian" are based on the root *alb-, *arb-, which also is the source of the word *Arberesh*, which is used to describe the Italo-Albanians of southern Italy. That root also appears as *lab- in *Labëria*, referring to the southern Albanian region from Vlorë southward to the Greek border, and *rab- in early Slavic, as in *raban, rabanski* ("Albanian"). Also related to this basic root are the Turkish and Greek words for Albanians and the Albanian language. Albanians now use the designation *shqiptar* ("Albanian") *shqip* ("Albanian language"), and *Shqipëria* ("Albania").

## ORIENTATION

*Identification.* According to the Austrian linguist Gustav Meyer (1850–1900), *shqip* ("Albanian language"), *shqiptar* ("Albanian"), and *Shqipëria* ("Albania") are related to the Albanian verb *shqipoj* ("to speak clearly") and *shqiptoj* ("to pronounce") and can be linked to the Latin *excipio* and *excipere* ("to listen to, take up, hear"). The Albanologist Maximilian Lambertz (1882–1963) preferred a connection with the Albanian *shqipe* or *shqiponjë* ("eagle"), which is the symbol of Albania. The latter explanation may, however, simply be a folk etymology or constitute the reason why Albanians identify themselves with the eagle.

Albanians can be divided into two cultural groups: the northern Albanians, or Ghegs (sometimes spelled Gegs), and the southern Albanians, or Tosks. The geographic border between the two groups, based on dialect, runs roughly along the Shkumbin River, which flows through the central town of Elbasan to the Adriatic Sea. All Albanians north of the Shkumbin, along with the Albanians of Montenegro, Kosovo, and most of Macedonia (FYROM), speak Gheg dialects with their characteristic nasalization. All Albanians south of the Shkumbin, including the Albanians of Greece, southwestern Macedonia, and southern Italy, speak Tosk dialects with their characteristic rhotacism. Although dialect and cultural differences between the Ghegs and Tosks can be substantial, both sides identify strongly with the common national and ethnic culture.

*Location and Geography.* Albanians live in ethnically compact settlements in large areas of the southwest part of the Balkan peninsula, primarily in the Republic of Albania with its centrally located capital city of Tirana and in the self-proclaimed Republic of Kosovo. The Republic of Albania, which houses only about 60 percent of all the Albanians in the Balkans, is a mountainous country along the southern Adriatic coast across from the heel of Italy. Among the minority groups living with the Albanian majority are ethnic Greeks, Slavs, Aromunians (Vlachs), and Rom (Gypsies). Albania is bordered to the north by the Yugoslav republic of Montenegro, which has an approximate 10 percent Albanian minority living in regions along the Albanian-Montenegrin border. The Montenegrin towns of Ulcinj, Tuz, Plava, and Gucinj were traditionally and are still inhabited by Albanians. To the northeast of the Republic of Albania is Kosovo, still a de jure part of the Federal Republic of Yugoslavia. Kosovo, which the Kosovo Albanians have declared to be a free and sovereign republic and which the Serbs insist must remain an integral part of Serbia, has about 90 percent Albanian speakers and 10 percent Serb speakers, with minorities of Turks, Rom, Montenegrins, Croats, and Cherkess. The Albanian enclaves of Presheva (Presevo) and Bujanovc (Bujanovac) are in southern Serbia, not far from Kosovo. To the east of the Republic of Albania is the former Yugoslav Republic of Macedonia, one-third of which, along the Albanian border, has an Albanian majority. The central Macedonian towns of

ALBANIA

0        25        50        75 Miles

0    25    50    75 Kilometers

*Albania*

assimilated Arvanites who populated much of central and southern Greece in the late Middle Ages. The Albanian language, known there in Albanian as *arbërisht* and in Greek as *arvanitika*, is still spoken to some extent in about three hundred twenty villages primarily in Boeotia (especially around Levadhia), southern Euboea, Attica, Corinth, and northern Andros. Southern Italy also has a substantial Albanian minority, known as the Arberesh, who are the descendants of refugees who fled from Albania after the death of Scanderbeg in 1468. Most of the Arberesh live in the mountain villages of Cosenza in Calabria and in the vicinity of Palermo in Sicily. In addition to these traditional settlements, there are large communities of Albanian emigrants in Greece, Italy, Switzerland, and Germany.

***Demography.*** There are an estimated six million Albanians in Europe. The 1991 census for the Republic of Albania gives a total population of 3,255,891. In addition there are about two million Albanians in Kosovo, about five-hundred thousand in the Republic of Macedonia, and about one-hundred thousand in Montenegro. It is estimated that about one-hundred thousand people from the traditional Italo-Albanian communities in southern Italy can still speak Albanian. Figures for Albanian settlements in Greece are unavailable because the Greek government does not acknowledge the existence of an Albanian minority there. All these figures are estimates and fluctuate because of the extremely high birthrates of Albanians and the high level of emigration from Albania and Kosovo. An estimated three-hundred thousand emigrants from Albania now live in Greece, and about two-hundred thousand reside in Italy. In addition, there are about two-hundred thousand Albanians, mostly from Kosovo, living in central Europe (mainly Switzerland and Germany). In the last ten years, Albanians have emigrated to most other countries in Europe, as well as the United States, Canada, and Australia.

***Linguistic Affiliation.*** The Albanian language, *shqip*, is Indo-European, although it is not a member of any of the major branches of the Indo-European family. Despite its Indo-European affiliation and presence in the Balkans since ancient times, it is difficult to pinpoint the exact ancestry of the Albanian language because of the radical transformations that have taken place within it through the centuries. Among these transformations has been a substantial reduction in word length and extreme morphological alterations. Whether the Albanian language stems from Illyrian or Thracian, both, or neither is a matter of contention. The theory of the

Skopje, Kumanovo, and Bitola have sizable (15 to 50 percent) communities of Albanian speakers, whereas the western Macedonian centers of Tetova (Tetovo), Gostivar, and Dibra (Debar), along with the Struga area, all have an Albanian majority. The Albanians in Macedonia represent about 30 percent of the population, although there are no reliable statistics. The Albanian minority in Greece can be divided into two groups: those living in villages and settlements near the Albanian border and the largely

Illyrian origin of the Albanian people is the one most widely accepted in Albania and has been raised to the level of a national and state ideology. There is little evidence to prove or disprove this theory, since little is known about the Illyrian language. Since ancient times, very substantial strata of Latin and of Slavic and Turkish have been added to Albanian, making the older strata more difficult to analyze.

Albanian is a synthetic language that is similar in structure to most other Indo-European languages. Nouns are marked for gender, number, and case as well as for definite and indefinite forms. The vast majority of nouns are masculine or feminine, though there are a few neuter nouns. The nominal system distinguishes five cases: nominative, genitive, dative, accusative, and ablative; the genitive and dative endings are always the same. Attributive genitives are linked to the nouns they qualify by a system of connective particles. Albanian verbs have three persons, two numbers, ten tenses, two voices, and six moods. Unusual among the moods is the admirative, which is used to express astonishment. Among other particular features of Albanian and other Balkan languages are a postpositive definite article and the absence of a verbal infinitive. Although Albanian is not directly related to Greek, Serbo-Croatian, Romanian, or Bulgarian, it has much in common with all those Balkan languages after centuries of close contact.

The regional variants of spoken Albanian differ such that verbal communication between uneducated speakers of different dialects can be difficult. To overcome these problems, a standard literary language, *gjuha letrare*, was agreed on at an orthography congress in Tirana in late November 1972 and has been in use for the last three decades in virtually all publications and in education throughout Albania, Kosovo, and Macedonia. This Standard Albanian is based about 80 percent on Tosk dialect forms, reflecting the structure of political power at that time in communist Albania. The subject remains controversial, with northern intellectuals having reopened in recent years the possibility of reviving a literary standard for the Gheg dialect. The *gjuha letrare* seems to be a widely accepted standard and probably will survive the current turmoil.

Most Albanian speakers in Albania are monolingual, although in view of the strong cultural influence of Italian television, Italian is widely understood along the Adriatic coast. Greek not only is spoken by members of the Greek minority in southern Albania but also is understood by many Albanians near the Greek border. Most Kosovo Albanians speak and understand Serbo-Croatian.

*Prayer room at the Mosque of Etem Bay, in the capital city at Tirana.*

Ironically, because the Belgrade authorities willfully destroyed the Albanian-language educational system in Kosovo in the mid-1980s, an increasing number of young people there, educated in "underground" schools, no longer speak and understand Serbo-Croatian.

**Symbolism.** The national and ethnic symbol of the Albanians is the eagle, which was used in that capacity in the earliest records. The eagle appears in a stone carving dating from 1190, the time of the so-called first Albanian principality, known as Arbanon, and was used as a heraldic symbol by a number of ruling families in Albania in the late Middle Ages, including the Castriotta (Kastrioti), the Muzakaj (Myzeqe), and the Dukagjini. A black double-headed eagle also was placed by the national hero Scanderbeg on his flag and seal. This form of the eagle, deriving from the banner of the Byzantine Empire, has been preserved as an ethnic symbol by the Arberesh of southern Italy. In the late nineteenth century, the double-headed eagle was taken up by the nationalist movement as a symbol of resistance to the Ottoman Empire and was used on the banners of freedom fighters seeking autonomy and independence. The current flag, bearing this black double-headed eagle on a red background, was officially raised on 28 November, 1912 to mark the declaration of Albanian independence in Vlorë and has been used since that time by the Republic of Albania and by Albanians everywhere as the national symbol.

In Albanian oral literature and folklore, the eagle appears as a symbol of freedom and heroism, and Albanians often refer to themselves as the "Sons of the Eagle." The popularity of the eagle among Albanians derives from the similarity between the words *shqipe* (eagle) and the terms for the Albanian language, an Albanian person, and Albania.

Another beloved symbol is the Albanian prince and national hero Scanderbeg (1405–1468). His real name was George Castriotta (Gjergj Kastrioti). Sent by his father as a hostage to the Turkish Sultan Murad II (ruled 1421–1451), he was converted to Islam and, after being educated in Edirne, was given the name Iskander (Alexander) and the rank of bey. In 1443, after the Turkish defeat at Nish by John Corvinus Hunyadi (1385–1456), Scanderbeg abandoned the Ottoman army, returned to Albania, and embraced Christianity. He took over the central Albanian fortress of Kruja and was proclaimed commander in chief of an independent Albanian army. In the following years, Scanderbeg successfully repulsed thirteen Ottoman invasions and was widely admired in the Christian world for his resistance to the Turks, being accorded the title *Athleta Christi* by Pope Calixtus III (ruled 1455–1458). Scanderbeg died on 17 January 1468 at Lezha (Alessio), and Albanian resistance collapsed a decade afterward. In 1478, his fortress at Kruja was taken by the Turks, and Albania experienced four centuries of Ottoman rule. For Albanians, Scanderbeg is the symbol of resistance to foreign domination and a source of inspiration in both oral and written literature. It is common in the homes of Albanian families living abroad to find not only an Albanian flag but also a bust or portrait of Scanderbeg.

## HISTORY AND ETHNIC RELATIONS

***Emergence of the Nation.*** Albanians are a native Balkan people, although their exact origin is unclear. The national ideology insists on an unequivocal ethnic relationship with the ancient Illyrians. As little is known about the Illyrians and there are no historical records referring to the existence of the Albanian people during the first millennium C.E., it is difficult to affirm or deny the relationship. Albanians entered postclassical recorded history in the second half of the eleventh century, and only in this age can one speak with any degree of certainty

about the Albanian people as they are known today. In his *History* written in 1079–1080, the Byzantine historian Michael Attaleiates was the first to refer to the *Albanoi* as having taken part in a revolt against Constantinople in 1043 and to the *Arbanitai* as subjects of the duke of Dyrrachium. Similarly, the historian John Scylitzes refers (ca. 1081) to the Arbanites as forming part of the troops assembled in Durrës by Nicephorus Basilacius. It can be assumed that the Albanians began expanding from their mountain homeland in the eleventh and twelfth centuries, initially taking possession of the northern and central coastline and by the thirteenth century spreading southward toward what are now southern Albania and western Macedonia. In the middle of the fourteenth century, they migrated farther south into Greece, initially into Epirus, Thessaly (1320), Acarnania, and Aetolia. By the middle of the fifteenth century, which marks the end of this process of colonization, the Albanians had settled in over half of Greece in such great numbers that in many regions they constituted the majority of the population. Despite these extensive settlements, the Albanians, largely a herding and nomadic people, do not seem to have created any substantial urban centers. There were no noticeable Albanian communities in the cities of the Albanian coast during the Middle Ages. Durrës was inhabited by the Venetians, Greeks, Jews, and Slavs; Shkodra, by the Venetians and Slavs; and Vlorë, by the Byzantine Greeks. It is estimated that a considerable proportion of Albanians were assimilated by the time of the Turkish invasion; in other words, the Albanians had been largely marginalized in their own country. Only during the Ottoman period did they began to settle in towns and acquire some of the characteristics of a nation rather than those of nomadic tribes.

***National Identity.*** Until the nineteenth century, collective identity in Albania, as elsewhere in the Balkans, was defined primarily by religion, reinforced at the state level by the Ottoman precept of the *millet*: To be of the Islamic faith was to be Turkish, and to be of the Orthodox faith was to be Greek. There was little room in either culture for the rising aspirations of Albanian nationalism during the national awakening (*Rilindja*) in the second half of the nineteenth century. During this period, nationalist leaders began to understand the divisive effects of religion among their people. The nationalist statesman Pashko Vasa (1825–1892) proclaimed in a widely read poem: "Albanians, you are killing your brothers, / Into a hundred factions you are divided, / Some say 'I believe in God,' others 'I in Allah,' /

*A historical cemetery of martyrs overlooking the city of Korcë. Many graves date back to the independence movement of the early twentieth century.*

Some say 'I am Turk,' others 'I am Latin,' / Some 'I am Greek,' others 'I am Slav,' / But you are brothers, all of you, my hapless people! . . . . Awaken, Albania, wake from your slumber, / Let us all, as brothers, swear a common oath / Not to look to church or mosque, / The faith of the Albanian is Albanianism!'' The last line was taken up by Albanians everywhere as the catchword of the nationalist movement that led to independence in 1912.

***Ethnic Relations.*** The Balkan peninsula is inhabited by a multitude of ethnic groups, and relations among them have never been good. Exacerbated nationalism and age-old rivalry for territory and supremacy have always created ethnic tension. This is especially true in regions with mixed settlement patterns, where ethnic groups are not separated by clear-cut political borders. While ethnic relations between Albanians and Greeks along their common border have improved substantially over the last decade, that cannot be said of relations between Albanians and their Slavic neighbors in the former Yugoslavia. In Kosovo, the Albanian majority was reduced to the status of an oppressed colonial people after the Serb conquest of the region at the beginning of the twentieth century. The open conflict that broke out in 1997 was, however, not initially one between Kosovo Albanians and Kosovo Serbs but between Kosovo Albanians and a hostile Serb regime in Belgrade. Relations between Albanians and Macedonians in the western part of the Republic of Macedonia have been tense since the declaration of Macedonian independence and the downgrading of the status of Albanians there to that of a ''national minority.''

## URBANISM, ARCHITECTURE, AND THE USE OF SPACE

The traditional architecture of Albania almost disappeared during the Stalinist dictatorship of 1944–1990. The old towns and bazaars of Tirana and many other urban centers were demolished and replaced by socialist prestige objects or uniform housing blocks. In the late 1960s and early 1970s, virtually all the churches and mosques were razed or transformed beyond recognition. The Catholic cathedral of Shkodra, for instance, was transformed into a sports hall with a volleyball court, and that of Tirana into a movie theater. With the exception of Berat and Gjirokastër, which were declared museum cities, little of the traditional flavor of Albanian towns can now be found. Most of the older public buildings that survived the communist period in Tirana, such as the main government min-

*Agricultural workers travel between Tirana and Kavajë. While Albania has a large rural population, most families in the countryside can barely raise enough crops to feed themselves.*

istries and the university, date from the Italian period (1930s–1940s). The main thoroughfare of Tirana from Scanderbeg Square to the university was constructed by the Italians as a symbol of Italian fascism. The lack of zoning regulations led in the 1990s to chaos in construction and the use of space, destroying the little that survived the communist regime. Old villas have been demolished, and most parks and public gardens disappeared under a myriad of kiosks and cafés.

## FOOD AND ECONOMY

***Food in Daily Life.*** After half a century of Stalinist dictatorship, food culture is virtually nonexistent. For decades, there was little on the market beyond basic staples, and today, dire poverty has left most Albanians with little more to eat than bread, rice, yogurt, and beans. In as much as it has survived at all, Albanian cuisine is meat-oriented. Traditional dishes, which usually are reserved for guests and special occasions such as weddings, are easier to find among Albanians living abroad.

***Food Customs at Ceremonial Occasions.*** Despite their poverty, Albanians are exceptionally generous and hospitable. A person invited to dinner will be given enough to "feed an army," even though the host may go hungry the next day. It is not unusual for an Albanian family to spend a month's salary to feed a visitor. Meals for guests or for ceremonial occasions such as weddings usually involve copious amounts of meat, washed down with Albanian *raki*, an alcoholic beverage. Animals were formerly slaughtered and roasted on a spit for religious holidays such as the Muslim celebration of Great Bayram and the Christian feast days of Saint Basil on 1 January, Saint Athanasius on 18 January, Saint George on 23 April and 6 May, Saint Michael on 29 September, Saint Nicholas on 6 December, and Christmas on 25 December. These customs have largely died out, although some regional dishes have survived. The Orthodox of southeastern Albania still eat *qumështor*, a custard dish made of flour, eggs, and milk, before the beginning of Lent. During the annual spring festival (*Dita e Verës*), in central Albania on 14 March, the women of Elbasan and the surrounding regions bake a sweet cake known as *ballakum Elbasani*. Members of the Islamic Bektashi sect mark the end of the ten-day fasting period of *matem* with a special *ashura* (pudding) made of cracked wheat, sugar, dried fruit, crushed nuts, and cinnamon.

***Basic Economy.*** Until 1990, Albania had a centralized socialist economy dominated by agricultural production on state farms. Food was in short supply, and despite communist propaganda, the country never attained self-sufficiency. While Albania still has a large rural peasantry, traditionally over 60 percent of the total population, most families in the countryside can do little more than feed themselves. Some farming surplus has reached urban markets in recent years, but food imports remain essential.

*Land Tenure and Property.* Albania is a mountainous country with an extremely high birthrate, and there is not enough farmland. Agriculture was reprivatized in the early 1990s after the fall of the communist regime, and many properties were returned to their former owners. Most families, however, received extremely small plots barely large enough to survive on. Property disputes are common and have been a major cause of blood feuding. Although most political parties have strategies for the further privatization of industry and nonagricultural land, many problems remain.

*Commercial Activities, Major Industries, and Trade.* Aside from agricultural output, Albania is a major producer of chrome. There are also significant deposits of copper and nickel and some oil. The country is still reeling from the radical transformation from a socialist to a free market economy, and commercial activity has not attained its potential. Virtually all the major industries went bankrupt and collapsed in the early 1990s when a free market economy was introduced. Some mines, chrome in particular, are still in production, but most have stagnated under pressure from foreign competition. Among the few sectors of the economy that are doing well is the construction industry. Domestic building materials are now widely available on the local market and increasingly on foreign markets. The European Union is the major trading partner, with Italy, Greece, and Germany leading in imports and exports. The national trade deficit has been compensated to some extent by foreign exchange remittances from Albanian emigrants working abroad.

*Workmen at a metallurgical plant in Elbasan, Albania. Much of the Albanian industrial sector collapsed with the introduction of a free market economy in the early 1990s.*

## SOCIAL STRATIFICATION

*Classes and Castes.* Under the communist regime, which called for absolute equality and the rule of a single working class, there were in fact three social castes. The ruling caste was composed of the extended families of politburo members and related communist families and clans. The majority of the population was in the working class. The lowest caste consisted of once prosperous farming families, the precommunist middle class, and opponents of the regime. Many of those families were sent to the countryside into internment or internal exile and were denied access to many professions and to education for their children. This caste system broke down with the fall of the communist regime and has been replaced by a system where status is determined exclusively by wealth.

## POLITICAL LIFE

***Government.*** The Republic of Albania is a parliamentary republic with a democratic constitution that was promulgated in 1998. Political turmoil has continued since the ousting of the authoritarian Berisha regime in 1997, and there is little sign of consensus or cooperation between the ruling and opposition parties. Political tension remains high.

***Leadership and Political Officials.*** The current president, Rexhep Meidani, is a former university professor from the ruling Socialist Party. The government coalition, now under the leadership of Prime Minister Ilir Meta, is dominated by the Socialist Party. Former president Sali Berisha of the Democratic Party continues to lead the opposition.

***Social Problems and Control.*** Public order broke down in 1997 as a result of a lack of political and economic planning. During the spring of 1997, arms depots were plundered throughout the country; as a result, crime became a major problem. Since the 1997 breakdown, there has been a substantial degree of taking the law into one's own hands. However, this is not a new phenomenon but part of Albanian tradition. For centuries, it was not the central government but Albanian customary or traditional law that governed social behavior and almost every facet of life in northern Albania. This customary law is widely respected today. In its definitive form, the *Kanun* of Lekë Dukagjini had chapters covering church; the family; marriage; house, livestock, and property; work; transfer of property; the spoken word; honor; damages; crimes; judicial law; and exemptions and exceptions. It was strictly observed by the tribes of the northern highlands and had priority over all other laws, ecclesiastical or secular. With the help of this ancient code, the highland tribes were able to preserve their identity, autonomy, and way of life under the Ottoman Empire for five centuries. Some aspects of the *Kanun* may appear harsh to a modern observer. Vengeance, for instance, was accepted as the prime instrument for exacting and maintaining justice. This led to blood feuding that decimated the northern tribes in the early years of the twentieth century and that is again a major problem of social life in northern Albania.

## GENDER ROLES AND STATUSES

***The Relative Status of Women and Men.*** Albania is a patriarchal society based on male predominance. Women are accorded subordinate roles. The communist Party of Labor did much to emancipate women during a revolutionary campaign in the late 1960s and early 1970s, but many of the gains of that social revolution have been reversed since the introduction of democracy and a free market economy. Old traditions have revived, and despite legal equality and acceptance in the workforce, women have much less representation in public life than they did under the former regime.

## MARRIAGE, FAMILY, AND KINSHIP

***Marriage.*** Marriages in Albania are socially and legally restricted to heterosexual couples. They often are arranged at an early age in the countryside, traditionally by the parents of the groom with the help of a matchmaker rather than by the couple. Remaining unmarried is looked on as a great misfortune. In some mountain regions, the bride was stolen from her family, that is, spirited away by an armed bridegroom or by his male relatives and companions. This usually symbolic though occasionally real theft of a bride was also a common custom among the Italo-Albanians of Calabria. In other regions, it was customary to purchase a wife. In zones such as Mirditë and the northern mountains, the father, brother, or another male relative of the bride still presents the groom with a bullet wrapped in straw. The new husband is thus free to kill his wife with the approval of her family if she proves to be disobedient.

Albanian weddings are impressive festivities. They are virtually the only popular celebrations observed today and thus are taken very seriously. Whole villages and, in towns, hundreds of people may be invited to take part in a wedding banquet. The celebrations can last several days. Traditionally, weddings take place during the full moon to ensure offspring. Monogamy was always the rule in Albania, but polygamous marriages existed up to the beginning of the twentieth century in some areas, particularly if the first wife was not able to bear a son. Live-in concubines were not uncommon in the mountains up to World War II. Albanian women were as a rule faithful to their husbands. Since a wife was considered the property of her husband, adultery amounted to theft. Thus, cases of adultery were punished severely under traditional law. Premarital and extramarital sex was more prevalent in the northern highlands, the part of the country with the most rigid moral code. Divorce is now a common phenomenon.

*A group of women near Korçë. In Albania's patriarchal society, women are generally placed in subordinate roles.*

## SOCIALIZATION

***Child Rearing and Education.*** Albanians have always lived in a world of extreme hardship and deprivation. Underdevelopment and a high incidence of infant mortality have been compounded by warring and blood feuding that at times decimated the male population. Reproduction, as the key to survival, therefore took on a more elementary significance among Albanians than it did among neighboring peoples. Even today, Albanian birthrates are significantly higher than those anywhere else in Europe. As in other third world cultures, it is believed that the more children, especially male children, one raises, the more security one will have in one's old age. A childless marriage is considered a great misfortune, and a woman living without a husband and children is inconceivable.

Given the extremely patriarchal nature of Albanian society, greater importance is attributed to the birth of sons than to that of daughters. Even today, pregnant women are greeted with the expression *të lindtë një djalë* ("May a son be born"). In Mirditë and the mountains of the north, the birth of a son was marked by rejoicing throughout the tribe and the firing of rifles. It was often the custom in the north of Albania for a woman to be wed officially only after she had given birth to her first son. In Berat, the main beam of a house was painted black at the birth of a girl as a token of the family's disappointment.

Male children generally were better treated, for instance, by being better protected against the "evil eye." As the Kosova scholar Mark Krasniqi (born 1920) points out, boys are given names such as *Ujk* ("Wolf"), *Luan* ("Lion"), and *Hekuran* ("The Iron One"), whereas girls are named *Mjafte*, or *Mjaftime* ("Enough"), *Shkurte* ("The Short One"), *Mbarime* ("The Last One"), and *Sose* ("The Final One").

## RELIGION

***Religious Beliefs.*** Albania is on the border dividing three religions: Roman Catholicism, Greek Orthodoxy, and Islam. According to the last reliable statistics on religion (1942), among a population of 1,128,143, there were 779,417 (69 percent) Muslims, including the Bektashi; 232,320 (21 percent) Orthodox; and 116,259 (10 percent) Catholics. One can estimate today that approximately 70 percent of Albanians in the republic are of Muslim, including Bektashi, background; about 20 percent, mostly in the south, are Orthodox; and about 10 percent, mostly in the north, are Catholic. In 1967, all religious communities were dissolved when a communist government edict banned the public practice of religion. The law was rescinded only in December

1990 during the collapse of the regime. Despite the return of religious freedom, there seems to be more interest in the revival of Christianity and Islam among foreign missionaries and groups than there is among Albanians. Albanians have never had a national religion with which to identify as a people. For the last century and a half, national (ethnic) identity has predominated over religious identity, and this is unlikely to change in the coming years in a small and struggling nation surrounded by hostile neighbors. Organized religion still plays only a marginal role in public life. Religious fervor is extremely rare, and religious extremism is virtually unknown.

## THE ARTS AND HUMANITIES

*Literature.* The foundations of a national literature were laid in the second half of the nineteenth century with the rise of a nationalist movement striving for Albania's independence from a decaying Ottoman Empire. The literature of this so-called *Rilindja* period of national awakening was characterized by romantic nationalism and provides a key to an understanding of the Albanian mentality today.

At the beginning of the twentieth century, the Catholic education facilities set up by the Franciscans and Jesuits in Shkodra under the auspices of the Austro-Hungarian *Kultusprotektorat* paved the way for the creation of an intellectual élite that produced the rudiments of a more sophisticated literature which expressed itself primarily in poetry. The culmination of Albanian literature before World War II appears in the works of the Franciscan priest Gjergj Fishta (1871–1940), once lauded as the national poet. From 1945 to 1990, for primarily political reasons, Fishta was ostracized from the Albanian literary world and the mention of his name was forbidden.

Virtually all prewar Albanian literature was swept away by the political revolution that took place during and after World War II. Most prewar writers and intellectuals who had not left the country by 1944 regretted their decision to stay. The persecution of intellectuals and the break with virtually all cultural traditions created a literary and cultural vacuum that lasted until the 1960s and whose results can still be felt.

With Albania's integration into the Soviet bloc during the 1950s, Soviet literary models were introduced and slavishly imitated. Writers were encouraged to concentrate their creative energies on specific themes, such as the partisan struggle of the "national liberation war" and the building of socialism. Despite the constraints of socialist realism and Stalinist dictatorship, Albanian literature made much progress in the 1970s and 1980s. One of the best examples of creativity and originality in Albanian letters then and now is Ismail Kadare (b. 1936), the only Albanian writer with a broad international reputation. Kadare's talents both as a poet and as a prose writer have lost none of their innovative force over the last three decades. His influence is still felt among the young postcommunist writers of the 1990s, the first generation to be able to express itself freely.

## BIBLIOGRAPHY

Carver, Robert. *The Accursed Mountains: Journeys in Albania*, 1998.

Durham, Edith. *High Albania*, 1909 (reprint 1970, 1985).

Elsie, Robert. *Anthology of Modern Albanian Poetry: An Elusive Eagle Soars*, 1993.

————. *Albanian Folktales and Legends*, 1994.

————. *History of Albanian Literature*, 1995.

————. *Studies in Modern Albanian Literature and Culture*, 1996.

————. *Kosovo: In the Heart of the Powder Keg*, 1997.

Gjeçovi, Shtjefën. *The Code of Lekë Dukagjini*, translated by Leonard Fox, 1989.

Jacques, Edwin E. *The Albanians: An Ethnic History from Prehistoric Times to the Present*, 1995.

Kadare, Ismail. *The General of the Dead Army*, 1986.

————. *Chronicle in Stone*, 1987.

————. *Doruntine*, 1988.

————. *Broken April*, 1990.

————. *The Palace of Dreams*, 1993.

————. *Albanian Spring: The Anatomy of Tyranny*, 1994.

————. *The Concert*, 1994.

————. *The Pyramid*, 1996.

————. *The File on H*, 1997.

————. *The Three-Arched Bridge*, 1997.

Malcolm, Noel. *Kosovo: A Short History*, 1998.

Newmark, Leonard. *Albanian-English Dictionary*, 1998.

Pettifer, James. *Blue Guide Albania*, 2nd ed., 1996.

Pipa, Arshi. *The Politics of Language in Socialist Albania*, 1989.

————. *Albanian Stalinism: Ideo-Political Aspects*, 1990.

————. *Contemporary Albanian Literature*, 1991.

———— and Sami Repishti, eds. *Studies on Kosova*, 1984.

Prifti, Peter. *Socialist Albania since 1944*, 1978.

Skendi, Stavro. *Albania*, 1956.

Vickers, Miranda. *Albania: A Modern History*, 1994.

————. *Between Serbs and Albanians: a History of Kosovo*, 1998.

———— and James Pettifer. *Albania: From Anarchy to a Balkan Identity*, 1996.

Zymberi, Isa. *Colloquial Albanian*, 1991.

—Robert Elsie

# ALGERIA

**CULTURE NAME**

Algerian

**ALTERNATIVE NAMES**

In Arabic, the country is known as Al-Jaza'ir, which is short for Al-Jumhuriyal Al-Jaza'iriyah ad-dimuqratiyah ash-sha'biyah.

**ORIENTATION**

*Identification.* The name Algeria is derived from the name of the country's oldest continuous settlement and modern capital, Algiers, a strategically located port city with access to both Europe and the Middle East. Most of the population of the country is in the north. While the majority of the population who are Arab (or mixed Arab and Berber) identify with the common Algerian culture, the Berber tribes, particularly in the more isolated southern mountainous and desert regions, retain more of the indigenous Berber culture and identity.

*Location and Geography.* Algeria is in northern Africa. It borders Tunisia and Libya to the east; Niger, Mali, and Mauritania to the south; Morocco and Western Sahara to the west; and the Mediterranean Sea to the north. It covers a total of 919,595 square miles (2,381,751 square kilometers), making it the second largest country in Africa (after Sudan), and the eleventh largest in the world. Almost nine-tenths of this area is composed of the six Saharan provinces in the south of the country; however, 90 percent of the population, and most of the cities, are located along the fertile coastal area known as the Tell, or hill. The climate is desert like, although the coast does receive rain in the winter. Only 3 percent of the land is arable, this along the Mediterranean. Inland from the coast is the High Plateau region, with an elevation of 1,300 to 4,300 feet (396 to 1,311 meters). This is mostly rocky and dry, dotted with vegetation on which cattle, sheep,

and goats graze. Beyond the plateau are the Saharan Atlas Mountains, which form the boundary of the Algerian Sahara desert. Despite efforts by the government to contain the desert by planting rows of pine trees, it continues to expand northward. The vast expanse contains not only sand dunes and typical desert life such as snakes, lizards, and foxes, but also oases, which grow date and citrus trees. There are also striking sandstone rock formations, red sand, and even a mountain, Mount Tahat, the highest point in Algeria, that is sometimes snow-topped.

*Demography.* The estimated population as of 2000 is 31,193,917. Ethnically it is fairly homogeneous, about 80 percent Arab and 20 percent Berber. Less than 1 percent are European. The Berbers are divided into four main groups. The largest of these are the Kabyles, who live in the Kabylia Mountains east of Algiers. The Chaouias live in the Aurès Mountains, the M'zabites in the northern Sahara, and the Tuaregs in the desert.

*Linguistic Affiliation.* The original language of Algeria was Berber, which has varied dialects throughout the country. Arabic came to the country early in its history, along with Arab culture and the Muslim religion. When the French came, they attempted to get rid of native culture, and one of the ways they did this was to impose their language on the people. At independence, Arabic was declared the official language. Arabic and Berber are the languages most spoken in day-to-day life. French is being phased out, but it remains an important language in business and some scientific and technical fields, and it is taught as a second language in the schools.

*Symbolism.* The flag is green and white, with a red star and crescent. The star, crescent, and the color green are all symbolic of the Islamic religion.

*Algeria*

## HISTORY AND ETHNIC RELATIONS

***Emergence of the Nation.*** The Berbers were the original inhabitants of the region. The first invaders were the Phoenicians, whose empire covered the area that is today Lebanon. They began establishing ports along the Mediterranean in 1200 B.C.E. They built the cities of Constantine and Annaba in the east of present–day Algeria, but aside from teaching the Berbers how to raise crops, for the most part they kept their distance from them. The Romans began making inroads into North Africa, declaring a new kingdom called Numidia. Roman rule lasted six hundred years.

The Arabs swept across North Africa in the seventh century (during the lifetime of Muhammad, who died in 632), and again in the eleventh century. The Berbers put up resistance, particularly to the edict that both religious and political leaders could only be Arabian. The second Muslim conquest saw a great shift in Berber civilization, as the people were forced to convert in great numbers or to flee to the hills. However, as internal conflicts began to sway the Muslim stronghold in North Africa in the fifteenth century, Europeans capitalized on this, and by 1510 Spain had seized Algiers, Oran, and other important port cities.

The French took control in the nineteenth century. In retaliation for Algerian debts and insolence toward the European nation, they blockaded several Algerian ports, and when this did not succeed, they invaded Algiers on 5 July 1830. Four years later they declared Algeria a colony, beginning a 132-year reign. In 1840 Abd al-Qadir, an Algerian freedom fighter, led the Arabs in an insurgence against their colonizers, which ended in defeat in 1847. At about the same time, the French began immigrating in large numbers to Algeria, in an attempt by the French government to replace Algerian culture with their own. By 1881 there were 300,000 Europeans (half of them French) in an area of 2.5 million Arabs.

In 1871 Muslims staged the biggest revolt since that of Abd al-Qadir thirty-one years earlier. The French responded by tightening control and further restricting the rights of the Algerians.

Throughout the late nineteenth and early twentieth centuries, the French continued to expand their influence and land holdings, and by 1914 they had extended their domain to include large tracts of land that were formerly wilderness or the property of Berber tribes. During World War I and again in World War II, Algerians were drafted to fight with the French. After World War II, Algerian leaders demanded Muslim equality in exchange for this service. Charles de Gaulle, the leader of the French resistance against Germany during the war and the leader of France's provisional government after the war, agreed to grant French citizenship to certain select Muslims, an unsatisfactory response that resulted in rising tensions between Algerians and their colonizers. Anti-French sentiment had been building for some time—the first anticolonial group was formed in 1926, and another, the Algerian People's Party, in 1937—but it was not until 1945 that the independence movement really began to gain momentum. In 1947, de Gaulle refused to relinquish French hold on the colony. The Algerian war for independence broke out in 1954, when the National Liberation Army (ALN)—the military arm of the National Liberation Front (FLN)—staged guerrilla attacks on French military and communication posts and called on all Muslims to join their struggle.

Over the next four years the French sent almost half a million troops to Algeria. Their tactics of bombing villages and torturing prisoners gained worldwide attention and was condemned by the United Nations and U.S. president John F. Kennedy. In 1959 De Gaulle, who was now president of France, issued a promise of independence to the colony, but the next year proceeded to send troops to restore order. In 1961 leaders of the FLN met with the French government, and the following year, Algeria finally won its independence. Ahmed Ben Bella was declared premier. He was head of the government and of the FLN, the country's sole political party. The extent of his power began to make people uncomfortable, and in 1965 a bloodless coup took him out and put Houari Boumedienne, the former defense minister, in his place. Boumedienne continued but modified Ben Bella's socialist policies, concentrating his efforts on reducing unemployment and illiteracy, decentralizing the government, and taking control of the land back from the French colonizers. When he died in 1978 he was succeeded by Colonel Chadli Bendjedid. During the 1980s, Islamic fundamentalism became an increasingly strong movement, and several times led to riots. A new constitution, introduced in 1989, reduced the power of the FLN, and for the first time allowed other political parties. The first part of a general election was held in December 1991, but the process of democratization was cut short when the Islamic Salvation Front (FIS) came close to victory and forced Bendjedid to resign. The FIS never attained control of the government, however, as Bendjedid was replaced by a military takeover of anti-FIS forces. They established a transitional governing body called the Higher Council of States (HCS). Elections were again scheduled in 1992 but the outcome seemed set to favor the outlawed FIS party, and the elections were canceled. This has resulted in ongoing retaliations and counterattacks, in which both sides have ravaged villages and tens of thousands have been killed. In September 1999, Algerians by a large margin passed a referendum proposed by President Abdelaziz Bouteflika to stop the seven-year-long conflict. However, legal injunctions have not yet manifested themselves to end to the violence.

***National Identity.*** The national identity of Algeria is based on a combination of Berber and Arab cultures. The strong influence of Islam in all aspects of Algerian life creates a sense of identity that extends beyond national boundaries to include other Arab nations. Opposition to the French colonizers also has been a uniting force in defining a sense of identity in Algeria.

*Many of the villages located in Algeria's desert region—such as the oasis town of El-Oved in the Sahara (above)—feature high stone border walls for privacy.*

**Ethnic Relations.** There is some distrust between the Arabs and the Berbers, which dates back centuries to the conquest of the area by Arab settlers. Although most Berbers have adopted the Islamic religion, they remain culturally distinct, and even when they are forced to migrate to the cities in search of work, they prefer to live in clans and not integrate themselves into the dominant Arab society. The Kabyles are the most resistant to government incursion. The Chaouias are traditionally the most isolated of all the Berber groups; the only outsiders their villages received were occasional Kabyle traders. This isolation was broken during the war for independence, when the French sent many of the Chaouias to concentration camps.

## URBANISM, ARCHITECTURE, AND THE USE OF SPACE

The population of Algeria is split evenly between urban and rural settings. The center of old cities is the *casbah* (Arabic for fortress), a market of serpentine alleyways and intricate arches where a variety of traditional crafts are sold, from carpets to baskets to pottery. Outside of this relatively unchanged remnant of the old way of life, Algerian cities are a mix of Western influence and Arabic tradition.

The largest city is the capital, Algiers, in the north, on the Mediterranean coast. It is the oldest city in the country, dating back almost three thousand years, to Phoenician times. It served as the colonial capital under both the Turkish and the French. In the casbah, the old Islamic part of the city, many of the buildings are dilapidated, but the narrow streets are lively, with children playing, merchants selling, and people walking and shopping. The casbah is surrounded by newer, European-style buildings. The city contains a mix of modern highrises and traditional Turkish and Islamic architecture. The port at Algiers is the largest in the country and is an industrial center.

Oran, to the west of Algiers, is the second-biggest city. It was built by the Arabs in 903, but was dominated by the Spanish for two centuries, and later by the French. It thus shows more European influence than any other city in Algeria, housing a large number of cathedrals and French colonial architecture.

Other urban centers include Constantine and Annaba. All of Algeria's cities have been hard hit by overpopulation, and its attendant problems of housing shortages and unemployment.

While most of Algeria's desert is uninhabited, it does have some villages, many of them surrounded by stone walls. Reflecting the same values of privacy and insulation, traditional homes also are walled in. The rooms form a circle around a patio or enclosed courtyard. Most architecture, from modern high-rises to tarpaper shacks, uses this same model. Traditional building materials are whitewashed stone or brick, and in older houses, the ceilings and upper parts of the walls are decorated with tiled mosaics.

Nomads of the desert and the high plateau live in tents woven from goat's hair, wool, and grass. In the Kabylia Mountains, villagers build their one-room homes of clay and grass or piled stones, and divide the room into two parts, one for the animals and one for the family.

## FOOD AND ECONOMY

**Food in Daily Life.** The national dish of Algeria is couscous, steamed semolina wheat served with lamb or chicken, cooked vegetables, and gravy. This is so basic to the Algerian diet that its name in Arabic, ta'am, translates as "food." Common flavorings include onions, turnips, raisins, chickpeas, and red peppers, as well as salt, pepper, cumin, and coriander. Alternatively, couscous can be served sweet, flavored with honey, cinnamon, or almonds. Lamb also is popular, and often is prepared over an open fire and served with bread. This dish is called mechoui. Other common foods are chorba, a spicy soup; dolma, a mixture of tomatoes and peppers, and bourek, a specialty of Algiers consisting of mincemeat with onions and fried eggs, rolled and fried in batter. The traditional Berber meal among the poorer people is a cake made of mixed grains and a drink mixed together from crushed goat cheese, dates, and water.

Strong black coffee and sweetened mint tea are popular, as well as apricot or other sweetened fruit juices. Laban also is drunk, a mixture of yogurt and water with mint leaves for flavoring. Algeria grows grapes and produces its own wine, but alcohol is not widely consumed, as it is forbidden by the Islamic religion.

**Food Customs at Ceremonial Occasions.** Religious holidays are often celebrated with special foods. For the birthday of Muhammad, a holiday called Mulud, dried fruits are a common treat. During the month of Ramadan, Muslims refrain from food and drink during the daylight hours. Each evening, the fast is broken with a family meal. Eid al-Fitr, the final breaking of the Ramadan fast, involves consuming large quantities of foods, sweets, and pastries in particular.

**Basic Economy.** Algeria's economy is based primarily on oil and natural gas. The nation has the world's fifth-largest reserves of natural gas and is the second-largest exporter. It also has the fourteenth-largest reserves of oil.

At independence, the economy was primarily based on agriculture, although since then other industries have eclipsed the importance of farming. Currently 22 percent of the population are farmers, but their production accounts for only 6 percent of the country's economy. The agricultural industry is plagued by droughts, encroaching desert, poor irrigation, and lack of machinery as well as by government policies that favor industry over farming. Most food produced is for local consumption; the most common crops include wheat, barley, corn, and rice, as well as fruits and vegetables. However, Algeria is able to produce only 25 percent of its food needs.

Thirty percent of the labor force is employed by the government; 16 percent in construction and public works; 13 percent in industry; and 5 percent in transportation and communications. The country has a serious problem with unemployment, with a rate of 30 percent. This has lead a number of men to migrate to the cities in search of work. There also are a significant number of Algerians who have immigrated to France to find jobs. Many of them return home in the summer to see their families.

**Land Tenure and Property.** When the country was under French rule, the colonizers owned the best farmland, while the Algerians were forced to work the less fertile areas. In the southern plateau and desert regions in particular, many people are nomadic tent-dwellers, who lead their animals from one pasture to another and lay no claim to any land. At independence, the government set up cooperative farms and made some attempt to redistribute land under a socialist model. Under Ben Bella's March Decrees of 1963, which allowed the takeover of property abandoned by French colonists, the government itself became the owner of the best farmland, as well as factories, mines, banks, and the transportation system. However, economic inequality has remained a pressing problem and has lead to riots and violent outbreaks.

**Commercial Activities.** The center of commercial life in Algeria is the souk, large, open-air markets where farmers and craftspeople sell their products. One can buy locally produced meat, fruits, vegetables, and grains—oats, barley, grapes, olives, citrus fruit—as well as woven rugs, jewelry, baskets, metalwork, and other crafts. Souks are held regu-

*Algerian farmers in Ain Terzine. The Algerian agricultural industry is plagued by several factors, including drought and poor irrigation.*

larly in regional centers, as well as in the old districts of major cities. Traditionally things were bought and sold by the barter method, and while this still exists, most trading today is done with cash.

**Major Industries.** The largest industry in Algeria is the production and processing of oil and gas. Services (trade, transport, and communications) also are important. Other industries include agriculture, construction, mining, and manufacturing.

**Trade.** Algeria's main exports are oil and gas, followed by dates, tobacco, leather goods, vegetables, and phosphates. The primary trading partners are Italy, France, Spain, Brazil, the Netherlands, and[f] the United States. Imports include raw materials, food, beverages, and consumer products. However, the government imposes strict regulations on imports in an effort to make the country more self-sufficient.

**Division of Labor.** Most of Algeria's workers are unskilled. However, many of the jobs in the country's industries require specific training, and this fact contributes to the high unemployment rate. The government has made an effort to change this

by starting specialized training programs. Although they have the freedom to pursue whatever career path they choose, many Algerians are constrained by financial hardship and the unpromising job market.

## SOCIAL STRATIFICATION

**Classes and Castes.** The majority of Algerians are poor. Those who are better off are almost always Arabs, and tend to be urban and well educated. The upper classes generally look down not just upon the Berbers, but also upon rural, seminomadic Arabs who speak a different dialect. However, most Algerians are racially a mix of Arab and Berber, and variations in skin tone and hair color are not reflected in social standing.

**Symbols of Social Stratification.** In the cities, most men, and some younger women, now wear European-style clothing. The traditional garb is a white woolen cloak, called a *gandoura*, worn over a long cotton shirt. A cape called a *burnous* is sometimes draped over the shoulders; it is made of linen for the summer and wool for the winter. Sometimes the burnous is plain, or sometimes it is adorned with fancy embroidery, indicating the wealth of the

*Methods dating back to the Roman era are still employed in the production of pottery by women of the Kabylia and Aures mountains. Pottery, jewelry, and woven works are very popular in the open-air markets.*

wearer. The traditional head covering is a red fez wrapped with a white cloth.

Women's clothing is similar, although more complete in its coverage. The *haik* drapes them from head to foot, and is worn over loose pants, which are gathered at the ankle. Tuareg men can be distinguished by the length of indigo cloth they wear wrapped around the head in a turban, extending over their robes, and covering them completely with the exception of their eyes.

## POLITICAL LIFE

***Government.*** Algeria is officially a multiparty republic. It has been controlled since independence by the FLN. In 1988 a new constitution legalized other parties, although certain militant Islamic groups, such as the FIS, have been outlawed. There is one legislative house, the National People's Assembly, composed of 295 elected deputies who serve five-year terms and are allowed to run for consecutive terms. They prepare and vote on all the country's

*The center of Algerian commercial life is the* souk, *or open-air market.*

laws, excluding issues of national defense. There is universal suffrage. The president is elected to an indefinitely renewable five-year term. He appoints a prime minister, who appoints a cabinet.

The country is divided into forty-eight provinces, or *wilayat*, each of which elects its own assembly. The governor, or *wali*, is appointed by the national government, and serves as the primary liaison between local and federal government. The wilayat are further divided into administrative districts or *diaraat*, which are themselves broken up into communes.

**Leadership and Political Officials.** There is a strongly felt divide in Algeria society between the political elite and the majority of the population, who feel largely disenfranchised and powerless. Because the people feel that they are not represented in the government, many resort to violent action as their only form of political expression.

**Social Problems and Control.** There is a large degree of social unrest, which is exacerbated by both political repression and unemployment. The political repression gives way not infrequently to various forms of terrorism, including kidnaping and the murder of civilians. The high unemployment rate

has contributed to an increase in crime, particularly in the cities.

There are forty-eight provincial courts, one for each wilayat, plus an additional two hundred tribunals spread throughout the country. The tribunal is the first level in the justice system. Above this is the provincial court. The highest level for appeals is the supreme court. Also there are three courts that deal with economic crimes against the state. Their verdicts are final and cannot be appealed. The Court of State Security, composed of magistrates and army officers, tries cases involving state security.

**Military Activity.** The president is commander in chief of Algeria's armed forces, which total 121,700, including an army of 105,000, a navy of 6,700, and an air force of 10,000. There also are 150,000 reservists. Military expenditures are $1.3 billion (U.S.), 2.7 percent of the total budget.

## SOCIAL WELFARE AND CHANGE PROGRAMS

The government provides free health care for children under sixteen and adults over sixty. It also offers pensions to the elderly and disabled, and gives allowances for families with children. The welfare system is financed by contributions from employers and employees as well as the state.

Algeria also receives aid from various countries that send specialists to help with the development of education, industry, health care, and the military.

## NONGOVERNMENTAL ORGANIZATIONS AND OTHER ASSOCIATIONS

Algeria is a member of the Arab League, whose goal is to strengthen ties among Arab nations, to coordinate their policies, and to protect their common interests. Algeria also is part of the Organization of Petroleum Exporting Countries (OPEC), which coordinates policies among its member states.

## GENDER ROLES AND STATUSES

**Division of Labor by Gender.** Women work almost exclusively in the home, taking care of all domestic chores. Anything that involves leaving the house is taken care of by men, including shopping. Only 7 percent of women work outside the home, most of these in traditionally female professions such as secretarial work, teaching, or nursing. (However, this 7 percent does not include women who work in agriculture, and in farming communities; it is common for women as well as men to work in the fields.) Women are allowed to run for public office, but such attempts are still extremely rare.

***The Relative Status of Women and Men.*** As in Arabic culture in general, women in Algeria are considered weaker than men, and in need of protection. Men are entrusted with most important decisions. Women live in a very confined circle of house and family; their only contact aside from male family members is with other women. Men, on the other hand, have a much broader sphere, which includes the mosque, the streets, marketplaces, and coffee shops. Independence did not bring much change in this realm. Although the new government adopted socialist principles, gender equality faced great opposition from conservative Islamic groups.

The Berbers have their own concepts and practices regarding gender, which vary widely among the different groups. The role of Kabyle women is most similar to the Arabic tradition; they are unable to inherit property or to remarry without the consent of the husband who divorced them. The Chaouia women, while still socially restricted, are thought to have special magical powers, which gives them a slightly higher status. The M'zabites advocate social equality and literacy for men and women within their villages but do not allow the women to leave these confines. The Tuaregs are an anomaly among Muslim cultures in that the society is dominated more by women than by men. Whereas it is traditional in Islam for women to wear veils, among the Tuaregs it is the men who are veiled. Women control the economy and property, and education is provided equally to boys and girls.

## MARRIAGE, FAMILY, AND KINSHIP

***Marriage.*** Marriages in Algeria are traditionally arranged either by parents of the couple or by a professional matchmaker. Despite its prevalence in Algeria, the influx of Western culture has had little influence in this realm, as the majority of marriages still are arranged. It is considered not just the union of two individuals, but also of two families. Wedding celebrations last for days, including music, special sweets, and ritual baths for the bride. The groom covers the costs of the festivities.

By a law passed in 1984, women gained the right to child custody and to their own dowries. However, the law also considers women permanent minors, needing the consent of their husbands or fathers for most activities, including working outside the home. The decision to divorce rests solely with the husband. It is still legally permissible, although rare, for men to have up to four wives, a code that is laid out in the Qurán (Koran).

***Domestic Unit.*** Traditionally the domestic unit included whole extended families. The husband, his wives, and their children continued to live with the husband's parents. Grandparents also were part of the household, as were widowed or divorced daughters and aunts and their children. This has changed somewhat since independence, with increasing urbanization and the trend toward smaller families. However, it is still common for Algerian women to have between seven and nine children.

***Inheritance.*** Inheritance passes from father to the eldest son. If there are no children, land and belongings are distributed among other relatives.

***Kin Groups.*** In areas of the country with a stronger Arab influence, affiliations are based mostly on blood relations. Loyalty to family is more powerful than any other relationship or responsibility. Traditionally, kin groups have lived in close proximity. Today these ties are somewhat weaker than in the past, due to the influence of urbanization and modernization, but even in the cities, life still centers around the family.

In the Berber tradition, loyalty breaks down along the lines of village groupings, or *sofs*. These groups are political, and part of a democratic process governing life in the village.

## SOCIALIZATION

***Infant Care.*** As in many cultures, infant care is an exclusively female domain. Most women almost never leave the home and thus are never far from their infant children.

***Child Rearing and Education.*** Children are highly valued in Arabic society and are considered a wealth and a blessing to their parents. However, child rearing standards differ significantly for male and female children: Girls are taught to be obedient to all males, while boys learn that the primary function of girls and women is to attend to the males' needs and desires. Girls typically have more duties and chores than boys, who are free to play and spend more time out of doors. Traditionally, only boys were educated, although this has begun to change in recent times.

In 1977, only 42 percent of the population was literate. This increased to 57 percent in 1990, with a male literacy rate of 70 percent and a female rate of

45 percent. The government has concentrated its efforts more on youth than on adult literacy.

Before independence, the Algerian education system was based on the French model. The majority of Algerian children did not attend school. In the years since 1971, the government made education free and mandatory for children between ages six and fifteen, and has made an effort to use the education system to define the nation. Its program stresses the study of the Arabic language as well as technical skills. Ninety percent of children in the cities and 67 percent of rural children now attend primary school. Half of all eligible secondary-age children are enrolled. Girls now comprise 38 percent of students in the secondary schools, a significant increase from preindependence days, when virtually no females attended schools. Despite its lofty goals, however, the system has had difficulty accommodating the increasing population of students, while the number of qualified teachers has diminished. In 1985 a total of 71 percent of secondary teachers were foreign.

**Higher Education.** During French rule, the sole university in the country, in Algiers, was open only to French students. Today there are more than thirty institutes of higher learning, with universities in a number of cities, including Algiers, Oran, Constantine, Annaba, and Tlemcen. This also includes state-funded institutes for technical, agricultural, vocational, and teacher training. A number of Algerians study abroad as well, and the government pays to send them to the United States, Eastern Europe, and Russia.

## ETIQUETTE

Greetings are lengthy and involved, including inquiries into health and family. Social interactions are much more common among members of the same gender than between men and women. Public displays of affection—touching, hand-holding—between men and women are rare, but not between members of the same sex.

Algerians are known for their hospitality and generosity. Visiting is a mainstay of social life, mostly within the circle of extended family. The host serves tea or coffee and sweets.

## RELIGION

**Religious Beliefs.** Ninety-nine percent of Algeria is Sunni Muslim. There also is a tiny Jewish community, whose presence goes back centuries. Christianity has existed in Algeria since the Roman era, but despite efforts (particularly by the French colo-

nizers) to convert, the number of Algerian Christians is very small. Islam forms the basis not only of religious life in Algeria but also is a unifying force (both within the country and with other Arab nations), creating for all believers a common ground that is both cultural and spiritual. There is a range of observance among Algerian Muslims; rural people tend to hold more strictly to the traditional practices.

There also are remnants of the indigenous Berber religion, which has been almost entirely subsumed by Islam. Despite opposition by both the French colonizers and the Algerian government (who viewed this religion as a threat to the unity of the country), there are still some organizations, called brotherhoods, that hold on to their magical practices and ceremonies.

The term Islam means submission to God. It shares certain prophets, traditions, and beliefs with Judaism and Christianity, the main difference being the Muslim belief that Muhammad is the final prophet and the embodiment of God, or Allah. The foundation of Islamic belief is called the Five Pillars. The first, the Shahada, is profession of faith. The second is prayer, or Salat. Muslims pray five times a day; it is not necessary to go to the mosque, but the call to prayer echoes out over each city or town from the minarets of the holy buildings. Friday is the Muslim Sabbath, and the most important prayer of the week is the noon prayer on this day. The third Pillar, Zakat, is the principle of almsgiving. The fourth is fasting, which is observed during the month of Ramadan each year, when Muslims abstain from food and drink during the daylight hours. The fifth Pillar is the Hajj, the pilgrimage to the holy city of Mecca, in present-day Saudi Arabia, which every Muslim must make at some time in his or her life.

**Religious Practitioners.** There are no priests or clergy in Islam. There are, however, men called *mufti*, who interpret the Qurán (the Muslim holy book) for legal purposes, as well as *khatib*, who read the Qurán in the mosques, and *imam*, who lead prayers in the mosques. There are also *muezzins*, who give the call to prayer. The Qurán, rather than any religious leader, is considered the ultimate authority, and holds the answer to any question or dilemma one might have.

In the indigenous Berber religion, the holy men, called *marabouts*, were thought to be endowed by God with special powers.

**Rituals and Holy Places.** The most important observation in the Islamic calendar is Ramadan. This month of fasting is followed by the joyous

*A rug store in Ghardaia. Traditional Algerian crafts, including woven carpets, have been widely praised for their attention to detail.*

feast of Eid al Fitr, during which families visit and exchange gifts. Eid al-Adha commemorates the end of Muhammad's Hajj.

The mosque is the Muslim house of worship. Outside the door there are washing facilities, as cleanliness is a necessary prerequisite to prayer, demonstrating humility before God. One also must remove one's shoes before entering the mosque. According to Islamic tradition, women are not allowed inside. The interior has no altar; it is simply an open carpeted space. Because Muslims are supposed to pray facing Mecca, there is a small niche carved into the wall pointing out in which direction the city lies.

***Death and the Afterlife.*** Death is marked by visiting the family of the deceased. Family members dress in black. Death also is mourned in a larger, more communal way as part of the Islamic New Year's celebration, called Ashura. Muslims mark the passing of the old year by going to cemeteries to commemorate the dead.

## MEDICINE AND HEALTH CARE

Medical care is free and nationalized. The government concentrates its efforts on preventive medicine and vaccinations, building local clinics and health centers rather than large centralized hospitals. After completing their training, all medical workers are obligated to put in several years at a state medical facility. The biggest health problems are tuberculosis, venereal diseases, malaria, trachoma, typhoid fever, and dysentery.

Virtually all health care facilities and providers are concentrated in the more populous north; most people in rural areas have no access to modern medical care. Overpopulation and housing shortages in the cities have created their own health problems, due to poor sanitation and lack of safe drinking water.

## SECULAR CELEBRATIONS

New Year's Day, 1 January; Labor Day, 1 May; Commemoration Day (anniversary of the overthrow of Ahmed Ben Bella), 19 June; Independence Day, 5 July; Anniversary of the outbreak of the revolution, 1 November.

## THE ARTS AND THE HUMANITIES

***Support for the Arts.*** During the French regime, Algerian culture was largely suppressed in an attempt by the colonizers to supplant it with their own. However, since independence, the government has made an effort to strengthen the native Berber, Arabic, and Islamic culture by giving money to open handicraft centers and by encouraging the traditional arts of rug-making, pottery, embroidery, and jewelry-making. The National Institute of Music revives music, dance, and folklore from the ancient Arabic and Moorish traditions. There is a national film company as well, which produces most Algerian movies.

*Literature.* Algeria counts among its literary stars both French writers who lived and wrote in Algeria (e.g., Albert Camus and Emmanuel Robles) as well as native Algerians, some of whom have chosen to write in the colonial language (such as playwright Kateb Yacine), and some of whom write in Arabic or Berber dialects. One advantage of writing in French is that it allows books to be published in France, and then distributed in both France and Algeria. The choice to write in Arabic or Berber, however, is often an act of national pride, and creates a different audience for the work. Many Algerian writers draw on both the influence of European literature and the ancient Arabic tradition of storytelling.

*Graphic Arts.* Traditional crafts include knotted and woven carpets made from wool or goat hair; basket-weaving; pottery, silver jewelry; intricate embroidery; and brassware. Algerian films have recently won accolades, both within the country and abroad. Many of them are dramas and documentaries that deal with issues of colonialism, revolution, and social issues. The director Mahmed Lakhdar Hamina won the Cannes Film Festival award in 1982 for his film *Desert Wind.*

*Performance Arts.* Algerian music and dance follow in the Arabic tradition. These forms of expression were suppressed during the French regime, but are today experiencing a revival. Arabic music is tied to the storytelling tradition and often recounts tales of love, honor, and family. Technically, it is repetitive and subtle. It uses quarter notes and makes small jumps on the scale. Traditional instruments are the *oud*, a stringed instrument similar to the lute; small drums held in the lap; and the *rhita*, or reed flute.

## THE STATE OF THE PHYSICAL AND SOCIAL SCIENCES

There is the University of Science and Technology at Oran, as well as the Houari Boumedienne University of Science and Technology. There are the Ministry of Energy and Petrochemicals and the Ministry of Agriculture and Fishing, both of which sponsor educational institutes.

## BIBLIOGRAPHY

Adamson, Kay. *Algeria: A Study in Competing Ideologies,* 1998.

Ball, David W. *Empires of Sand,* 1999.

Fuller, Graham E. *Algeria: The Next Fundamentalist State?* 1996.

Graffenried, Michael von. *Inside Algeria,* 1998.

*Journal of Algerian Studies,* 1996.

Laremont, Ricardo Rene. *Islam and the Politics of Resistance in Algeria 1783–1992,* 2000.

Malley, Robert. *Call from Algeria: Third Worldism, Revolution, and the Turn to Islam,* 1996.

McDowall, David. *Let's Visit Algeria,* 1985.

*Morocco and Tunisia Handbook with Algeria, Libya, and Mauritania,* 1995.

Rogerson, Barnaby. *A Traveller's History of North Africa,* 1998.

Stone, Martin. *The Agony of Algeria,* 1997.

Targ Brill, Marlene. *Algeria,* 1990.

Willis, Michael. *Islamist Challenge in Algeria: A Political History,* 1997.

### Web Sites

''Algeria.'' U.S. Library of Congress. www.lcweb2.loc.gov

*CIA World Factbook 2000,* www.odci.gov/cia/publications/factbook/geos/ag.

''Destination Algeria.'' Lonely Planet, 2000. www.lonelyplanet.com/dest/afr/alg

—ELEANOR STANFORD

# AMERICAN SAMOA

## CULTURE NAME

American Samoan

## ALTERNATIVE NAMES

An early explorer, Louis de Bougainville called the Samoan islands the Navigator's Islands, and some early government reports may refer to American Samoa as Eastern Samoa.

## ORIENTATION

**Location and Geography.** American Samoa is part of the greater Samoan archipelago in the South Pacific half-way between Hawaii and New Zealand. The four western islands constitute the independent nation of Western Samoa (now "Samoa"). In American Samoa, an unincorporated territory only 76.1 square miles (197 square kilometers) in area, the largest island is Tutuila, the administrative center. Just offshore is Aunu'u, and sixty miles to the east is the Manu'a Group: Ofu, Olosega, and Ta'ū. The most remote parts are two atolls, Swain's Island and Rose Island.

The main islands are of volcanic origin, with low coastal areas, fringe reefs, and sand beaches where most villages are located. The land rises abruptly to highland ridges with mountain summits as high as 3000 feet. In this tropical climate, vegetation is dense, and mountain slopes are heavily wooded.

**Demography.** The population has been projected to be sixty-five thousand in the year 2000, a 69 percent increase since 1960. This population is 89 percent Samoan, 3.7 percent Tongan, and about 2 percent white (mostly Americans). The remaining 5 percent are small subgroups from other Pacific islands, Asians, and groups of mixed heritage. The increase in population since 1960 can be attributed to improved health care and sanitation, a high birthrate, reduced infant mortality, increased life expectancy, and immigration.

**Linguistic Affiliation.** The Samoan language is part of the Austronesian linguistic family. The Samoic subgroup includes Samoan and the languages of Tokelau and Tuvalu.

Samoan is spoken at home, but most residents also speak English. English is taught in schools from the early grades, and the 1990 census reported that fewer than a thousand people age five or older did not speak English.

**Symbolism.** Fa'aSamoa, "the Samoan way," encompasses attitudes, beliefs, and traditions that symbolize a world view, shared throughout the archipelago. It is their explanation of the appropriate way to live.

## HISTORY AND ETHNIC RELATIONS

**Emergence of the Nation.** The ancestors of present-day Samoans moved out of Southeast Asia and settled in islands just west of Samoa as early as 1500 B.C.E. They arrived on a double hulled sailing craft with domesticated plants (taro and yams), pigs, chickens, and dogs, as well as pottery known as *lapita* ware. By the first century A.D., these people began moving into Samoa and Tonga.

Early contact between Europeans and Samoans occurred in 1722, when the Dutch navigator Jacob Roggeveen's ships called at Ta'ū, followed by French explorers in 1768 and in 1787. Charles Wilkes, commander of the United States Exploring Expedition, observed the culture in 1839 and established a permanent relationship with the Samoans. In the 1800s, Pago Pago's well-protected harbor was a popular port for American whaling ships.

In April 1899, a coaling station was built in Pago Pago harbor by the U. S. Navy, and in February 1900, a deed of cession was negotiated with Tutuila chiefs by Naval Commander B.F. Tilley. In

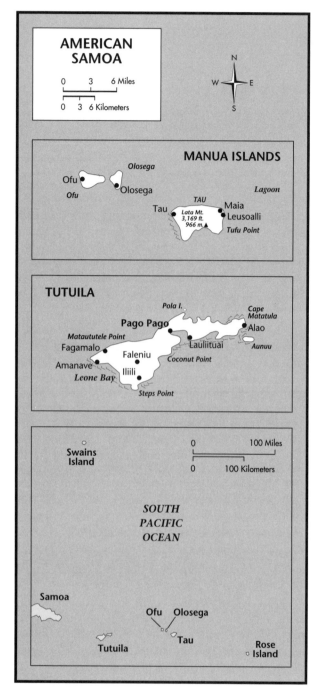

*American Samoa*

1904, the Manu'a group was added when a similar treaty was signed by their king.

**National Identity.** U. S. Navy administration was never oppressive. Samoan customs were preserved if not in conflict with U.S. laws. Hereditary chiefs and talking chiefs were allowed to retain their own forms of assemblage to deal with local political affairs.

Naval officers served as governors until 1951, when the U. S. Department of the Interior assumed responsibility and governors were appointed by the President. Since 1978, governors have been elected by the Samoan people.

Native born American Samoans are U. S. nationals and are free to travel between the two countries and reside in either. Samoans take pride in their status as a U. S. territory and seem uninterested in independence.

**Ethnic Relations.** The American population has never been large, but Americans have held important positions in government agencies and the public school system. Some intermarriage has occurred, and Americans who become long-term residents tend to adapt to the Samoan way of life. Since 1951, there has been an increased flow of Samoan migrants to the United States, where they have established their own churches and often maintain a Samoan lifestyle.

## URBANISM, ARCHITECTURE, AND THE USE OF SPACE

Until the twentieth century, the lifestyle was rural, and this remains the case in outlying islands and most villages outside Pago Pago Bay. Urban development around the bay and near the airport has a small-town quality.

Until the 1950s, traditional houses (*fale*) were oval structures with floors of coral pebbles and round wooden posts supporting a beehive-shaped roof covered with sugarcane thatch. Those very open houses were well adapted to the tropical environment and fostered interaction with passers-by. Privacy was and still is minimal. Most families had a house for sleeping and a small cook house in the back, and some had a guest house for entertaining visitors. Since the 1970s, the American government has promoted the building of concrete "hurricane houses" with corrugated metal roofs to minimize storm damage. These rectangular structures are more enclosed, with doors, windows, and sometimes room partitions. Other houses are built of wood or brick. Furnishings in traditional houses were minimal—mats for sitting and sleeping and little else—but some modern houses are fully furnished, and most have television, and telephones.

Legislative buildings are designed in the traditional oval shape, as are public school buildings, the farmer's market, and parts of the airport terminal building. Some commercial buildings now reflect American architectural designs.

*Fale houses in the village of Fituita. Fale homes were traditionally built with coral pebbles for flooring and sugarcane roof thatch.*

## FOOD AND ECONOMY

***Food in Daily Life.*** Staples of the diet remain taro, breadfruit, bananas, coconuts, papayas, mangoes, some chicken, pork, canned corned beef *(pisupo)* and seafood. Onions, potatoes, lettuce, cabbages, carrots, beans, and tomatoes are also eaten occasionally. Supermarkets carry most foods found in a U.S. market.

In the past, meals were eaten at midmorning and early evening. Food is cooked but may be served cold. Traditionally, most families ate while seated on mats on the floor and many still do. Elders and guests are always served first; children and the women often eat later. With changes in work patterns, three meals daily are now typical.

Most restaurants on Tutuila specialize in American and other foreign foods, but a few offer more traditional Samoan foods.

***Food Customs at Ceremonial Occasions.*** Foods served on ceremonial occasions include daily fare plus whole pigs, potato salad, chop suey, puddings, cakes, and ice cream. *Palusami* (coconut cream bundled in young taro leaves) has become a treat for special occasions. A great quantity of food is served at special events, with guests being expected to eat a portion and take the rest home to share with their households. *Kava*, a nonalcoholic, mildly narcotic drink, is served to chiefs on ceremonial occasions.

***Basic Economy.*** In this traditionally agricultural country, only 989 farms ("plantations") produced for family consumption in 1990 and 137 produced crops for sale. Two-thirds of these farms have less than five acres. U. S. currency is used in American Samoa.

Imports include food, fuel, raw materials for manufacturers, building materials, and mechanical equipment. In 1996, $471 million in goods was imported primarily from the United States, with exports of $313 million.

The government employs 30 percent of the workforce, the tuna canneries employ 33 percent; the remaining 37 percent fill service, professional, and laborer positions. About 56 percent of families live below the poverty level.

***Land Tenure and Property.*** With the exception of small amounts of government and church property, most land is owned by Samoans. Traditionally, communal ownership was by 'aiga and was controlled by the *matai*. This remains true for much land. Some whites married to Samoan women acquired individual ownership of land before the 1930s, when the U. S. Navy outlawed land sales.

*A cruise ship moored at Pago Pago. Visitors to American Samoa help boost the local economy.*

Individual land purchases now are restricted to persons with at least 50 percent Samoan blood.

**Commercial Activities.** Most commerce is based on the sale of imported products. The most common retail trade establishments are places to eat (over 100) and grocery stores (nearly 200), particularly small family-owned general stores.

**Major Industries.** The largest industry is fish processing and canning, with pet food as a by-product. Canned tuna, shipped to the United States, accounts for 94 percent of exports. There is also a garment industry, whose products represent 4 percent of exports.

**Division of Labor.** Age is an important determinant of work roles, with young people engaging in strenuous activities while the elderly play a more sedentary, supervisory and educational role. Children have household responsibilities while leadership roles are given to middle-aged or older persons. In the past some people had specialized skills in building traditional boats and houses, fishing, and medicine.

## SOCIAL STRATIFICATION

**Classes and Castes.** There is no true class system in American Samoa. Chiefs' titles are ranked to some degree based on centuries old traditions. These titles belong to specific families ('aiga), and some are ranked higher and are more respected than others. This is primarily significant ceremonially and determines seating in the *fono* (village council) and the order in which kava is served, but all have an equal opportunity to speak. Any male can aspire to be a matai, since titles are acquired through a democratic process of election by their *aiga*.

## POLITICAL LIFE

**Government.** The governor and lieutenant governor are elected by popular vote for a four-year term. There are two legislative bodies: a Senate of eighteen chiefs *(matai)*, selected by the paramount chiefs of each county, and the House of Representatives, with one member from each of twenty-one legislative districts, chosen by popular vote. American Samoa is represented in the U. S. House of Representatives by a nonvoting delegate. The government is funded in part by local taxes, but the United States provides over 60 percent of funding through grants.

**Leadership and Political Officials.** Village leadership is the function of the village council (fono), made up of the matai of each household. One becomes a matai through service to the family, knowledge of Samoan customs, and personal qualities such as diplomacy, intelligence, and speaking skills. Higher education, experience dealing with non-Samoans, and economic success may also be important. Political campaigns for higher offices may involve American-style rallies and fund-raising events, and candidates for governor tend to identify with the Democratic and Republican parties.

**Social Problems and Control.** A police department handles routine law enforcement, and the legal system is similar to that of the United States. An attorney general is responsible for criminal prosecution, environmental enforcement, consumer protection, immigration, land disputes and disputes over chiefly titles. The High Court has nine judges, including the Chief Justice. The most common crimes are disorderly conduct, assault, burglary, driving under the influence of alcohol, and property damage. Sexual offenses and murder are relatively infrequent.

*A group of Samoan men prepare an earth oven for use. In traditional Samoan culture, men were responsible for daily cooking and preparation of special events.*

***Military Activity.*** American Samoa has no standing military. The United States maintains a Coast Guard Unit on Tutuila, and sends recruiters for various branches of service to Pago Pago. Samoans can enlist in the military, and it is a popular career option. They leave Samoa for training and service.

## SOCIAL WELFARE AND CHANGE PROGRAMS

The Department of Human and Social Services administers federally funded programs that include disability services, foster care, child care subsidies and provider training, drug and alcohol counseling, and vocational rehabilitation. The largest programs provide nutritional education and assistance to the elderly and the WIC (Women, Infants and Children) program for low-income women and children up to age five.

## NONGOVERNMENTAL ORGANIZATIONS AND OTHER ASSOCIATIONS

Villages often have an organization of chiefs' wives. This "women's committee" entertains important visitors and raises money for causes such as equipping village medical clinics and church schools.

Untitled men in villages are organized into a cooperative work group called the *aumaga* that has important ceremonial and labor responsibilities. It is called the "strength of the village," and the leader (usually the son of a high-ranking chief), functions ceremonially as the "village prince," the *manaia*. The *aualuma* is the organization of unmarried women and widows. It engages in communal labor activities, entertains guests, and its members serve as attendants to the "village ceremonial princess," the *taupou*.

## GENDER ROLES AND STATUSES

***Division of Labor by Gender.*** Before the transition to a cash economy, men were responsible for heavy agricultural work, fishing, and house construction. Young men cooked much of the daily food and did the cooking and serving at ceremonial events. Women's activities included sewing, weaving floor and sleeping mats, laundry, child care, and later cooking with modern appliances. Nursing has long been an acceptable role for women. Many of these traditional roles continue today, but new options are important. Men and women now work in tuna canneries, banks, stores, tourist-related businesses, and the school system. Men work in construction, transportation, shipping, and government agencies.

*Imported rice is unloaded in Pago Pago. American Samoa imports many goods, including food, fuel, and building materials.*

***The Relative Status of Women and Men.*** Historically, Samoa has been a male-dominated society. Women exert a great deal of behind-the-scenes power. Professional and authoritative positions are held mostly by men, but women occupy important roles in some government agencies and businesses and in some cases serve as matai.

## Marriage, Family, and Kinship

***Marriage.*** Young people choose their marriage partners, but marriage is primarily an economic alliance between families. In earlier times, high chiefs' sons married high chiefs' daughters, and lower status couples often eloped. One cannot date or marry a blood relative. Nearly everyone marries, usually in the middle to late twenties, and weddings involve elaborate gift exchanges between the two families. Divorce is rare, but remarriage is fairly common among younger people.

***Domestic Unit.*** The household averages seven people and consists of one or more nuclear families and some collateral relatives. It tends to involve three generations and is flexible in composition. The occupants are related through blood, marriage, and adoption. After marriage, couples settle either in the household of the bride or the groom, each of which is headed by a matai. All social and economic activi-ties are under the control of the matai, who is usually a male.

***Kin Groups.*** The largest kin group is the 'aiga, which includes all individuals tracing kinship to a common ancestor. This extended family may have households in different parts of a village or in several villages. The matai of these households exercise various levels of authority within the 'aiga. Matai are members of the village council (fono) which is a regulatory and decision-making body for the community. A matai settles family squabbles and makes decisions about the family's financial contributions to weddings, funerals, and church donations. The entire 'aiga interacts primarily at weddings, funerals, elections and installations of matai, and family emergencies.

## Socialization

***Infant Care.*** Infants receive a great deal of affection and attention and are held and carried during the first year of life. The household usually includes a grandmother, who often serves as primary baby-sitter. Babies are fed when hungry and sleep where and when they doze off.

***Child Rearing and Education.*** Young children are supervised by a grandmother or other women in

*A high school auditorium in Utulei, on the island of Tutuila. American Samoa offers educational programs for preschool children, as well as universal public education through high school.*

the household and often by an older sibling. From an early age, obedience and respect for age and authority are encouraged. There is an educational program for preschool children and universal public school education through high school. There are a few parochial schools.

**Higher Education.** American Samoa Community College on Tutuila offers associate-level degrees. Most students major in liberal arts, teacher education, and business. Some students attend college in the United States. About seven percent of the population age twenty-five and older have a bachelor's or more advanced degree.

## ETIQUETTE

Samoans are meticulous about courtesy, particularly toward the elderly and holders of chiefly titles. One does not stand while others are seated, and if one enters a room where others are sitting on the floor, it is proper to bend slightly and say *"Tulouna"* (''excuse me''). A respect vocabulary is used when speaking to chiefs. Reciprocal courtesy and etiquette are characteristic at ceremonial and political events.

## RELIGION

**Religious Beliefs.** Before the arrival of missionaries in 1830, Tagaloa was recognized as the creator of the islands and their people and matai served as family religious leaders. The first missionaries represented the London Missionary Society, called LMS by Samoans and still used to identify that denomination. Known today as the Congregational Christian Church of American Samoa, it ministers to fifty percent of the population, while the Catholic Church claims twenty percent and Mormon, Methodist, and Pentecostal churches serve the remaining thirty percent. Samoans are faithful churchgoers and generous supporters of village churches and pastors.

**Religious Practitioners.** With the exception of the Catholic Church, which usually includes a few Caucasians among its leaders, most denominations have Samoan religious leaders.

**Rituals and Holy Places.** Church services follow Western rituals, and choral music is an important element. Most villages have at least one church. The dedication of new churches is of supreme importance and involves feasts and choral competitions

*A village council meeting of chiefs. In American Samoa, village leadership is the function of a council made up of the chiefs, or matai, of each household.*

and attracts visitors from nearby islands and the United States.

The second Sunday in October is White Sunday, when church services are conducted by children, who sing, recite Bible verses, and present plays. All wear new white clothing. After church the children are served a meal at home featuring special foods.

***Death and the Afterlife.*** Death is viewed as being "God's will." The traditional belief that dying away from home leads to one's spirit causing trouble for survivors persists. Until the 1980s, funerals were the day after death. Developments of mortuary services allows delayed burial to accommodate overseas relatives. Gifts are given to the family, and burial is done on family land.

## MEDICINE AND HEALTH CARE

American Samoa is a relatively healthy place, but hypertension and obesity are significant health problems in the population. Leading causes of death are heart disease, cancer, and cerebrovascular disease. A hospital on Tutuila provides medical, surgical, obstetric, pediatric, and emergency care. More limited services are available at several small clinics, usually staffed by nurses, in a few outlying villages.

Local air service is used to transport seriously ill people from Manua'a. There is limited reliance on traditional healers (bush medicine), particularly for ailments known before European contact.

## SECULAR CELEBRATIONS

Flag Day is celebrated on 17 April to commemorate the raising of the American flag over American Samoa in 1900, when the islands became a U.S. territory. Activities include traditional group dancing and singing, speeches, cricket games, and races in long canoes, each with about 50 oarsmen.

## THE ARTS AND HUMANITIES

***Support for the Arts.*** The Arts Council and the Government Museum support art instruction for children and adults and subsidize traditional artists to perpetuate traditional arts.

***Literature.*** Oratory is a valued tradition, and a vast body of mythology, legends and poetry survives through use by talking chiefs in village council deliberations and speeches at ceremonial occasions.

***Graphic Arts.*** Samoans value *siapo* (barkcloth tapestries) and finemats as family property to be

*A panoramic view of Pago Pago Bay, a central point for commercial shipping in American Samoa.*

exchanged on ceremonial occasions. Production of siapo and finemats is increasingly rare. At one time being tattooed was a male requirement for *aumage* membership or to qualify for a chief's title. Practice of this art has long been forbidden in American Samoa, but renewed interest in recent years attracts young men to the former Western Samoa for the elaborate knee-to-upper-abdomen tattoos.

***Performance Arts.*** Group singing and dancing are common art forms. Large dance groups of men or women perform movements in unison with hand claps and body slaps. Solo dances are performed by the village ceremonial princess (*taupou*), sometimes flanked by male support dancers.

## BIBLIOGRAPHY

American Samoa government. *American Samoa Statistical Yearbook*, 1996.

Baker, Paul, J. Hanna, and T. Baker. *The Changing Samoans*, 1986.

Bindon, James R. "Dietary and Social Choices in American Samoa." *The World and I*, May: 1986, pp.174–185.

———, Amy Knight, and William Dressler. "Social Context and Psychosocial Influences on Blood Pressure among American Samoans." *American Journal of Physical Anthropology* 103: (May):7–18, 1994.

Cote, James. *Adolescent Storm and Stress: An Evaluation of the Mead–Freeman Controversy*, 1994.

Gray, J. A. C. *Amerika Samoa*, 1960.

Holmes, Lowell D. "The Function of Kava in Modern Samoan Culture." In Efron, D. H., ed., *Ethnopharmacologic Search For Psychoactive Drugs*, 107–118, 1967.

———. "Samoan Oratory." *Journal of American Folklore*, 82:342–355, 1969.

———. *Quest for the Real Samoa: The Mead/Freeman Controversy and Beyond*, 1987

——— and Ellen Rhoads Holmes. *Samoan Village: Then and Now*, 2nd ed., 1992.

Mead, Margaret. *Coming of Age in Samoa*, 1943.

———. *Social Organization of Manu'a*, 2nd ed., 1969.

Oliver, Douglas. *The Pacific Islands*, 3rd ed., 1989.

U.S. Bureau of the Census. *Statistical Abstract of the United States*, 1998.

Whistler, W. Arthur. *Samoan Herbal Medicine*, 1996.

—Lowell D. Holmes
And Ellen Rhoads Holmes

# ANDORRA

## CULTURE NAME
Andorran

## ALTERNATIVE NAMES
Principality of Andorra; Andorranos

## ORIENTATION

**Identification.** The first reference to Andorra appears in the writings of the Greek historian Polybius (c. 200–118 B.C.E), who tells of the military encounter between Andorrans and Carthaginian troops as Hannibal (247–183 B.C.E.) passed through the Pyrenees Mountains en route to Rome. Andorra, historically, was a rural microstate whose population oscillated between four thousand and six thousand inhabitants. In the second half of the twentieth century, as it became a large international commercial center, the nation received larger migratory populations and developed into a multicultural society.

**Location and Geography.** Andorra has a total land surface of 181 square miles (468 square kilometers) making it slightly less than five times the size of the city of Barcelona. It is situated in the Pyrenees Mountains, bordered by Spain and France. The capital of the nation, Andorra la Vella (Old Andorra), lies in the geographic center of the country, where the two tributaries of the Valira River merge.

**Demography.** According to the 1998 census, the population stands at 65,877 of whom only 21.7 percent have Andorran citizenship. The rest of the inhabitants are Spanish (42.9 percent), Portuguese (10.7 percent), French (6.7 percent) or other nationalities (6.5 percent). Moreover, more than 7,589 persons, generally children or youth of immigrant families, have no formal citizenship. According to current legislation, foreigners can acquire citizenship after twenty years of residence in the country. Their children, born in Andorra, acquire citizenship at age eighteen.

**Linguistic Affiliation.** Catalan is the official language of Andorra. It is used throughout public administration, is taught in all schools, and is the language of all road signs. It is also the dominant language in communications media and is the language spoken by the national elites. In commercial signage, Catalan alternates with Spanish and French. Nevertheless, the dominant language of the street is Spanish. The Spanish population represents the largest immigrant community in Andorra and, in addition, the majority of visitors and merchants who come to Andorra are also Spanish. The use of French is limited to populations in the extreme southwest of the country. Portuguese and other languages are limited to private settings.

**Symbolism.** The Sanctuary of the Virgin of Meritxell, patron of the nation, constitutes the most important religious symbol for Andorrans and is also an attractive spot for tourist visits in the summer. Its thirty Romanesque churches and other treasures of medieval art serve as historical referents as well as emblems of identity.

## HISTORY AND ETHNIC RELATIONS

**Emergence of the Nation.** The origins of Andorra can be situated between the Mesolithic and the Neolithic periods. The archaeological site of Balma Margineda dates back eight thousand years, although full territorial occupation was not achieved until 2000 B.C.E. During the Roman era, Andorra had a stable population. Until the epoch of Arab occupation in the eighth century, Iberian populations mixed with peoples arriving from central Europe. At the beginning of the ninth century, the area was repopulated. The first document that refers to Andorra is the Act of Consecration of the Cathedral of Urgel (839 C.E.). In the eighth and ninth centuries, Andorra belonged to the County of Barcelona, which ceded sovereignty over the valleys of Andorra in 988 to the Episcopal see of Urgel (Spain).

*Andorra*

Today, however, both state political powers and Andorran civil society have endeavored to consolidate a national identity that takes as its symbolic referents its medieval past, mythologizing the political peculiarity of the Pareatges. Andorrans also identify themselves as a mountain society and have a special interest in leading sociopolitical and economic movements of the Pyrenean regions. The third pillar of identity is "Catalanness" (*catalanitat*), which it shares with 11 million persons in the northeast of Spain and the southeast of France.

**Ethnic Relations.** As a culture shaped by transhumant (seasonally transient) shepherds in the past and international merchants in the present, Andorrans are open in character and interethnic relations are not conflictive. Moreover, almost all immigrants come from European nations; hence, cultural differences are not strident.

## URBANISM, ARCHITECTURE, AND THE USE OF SPACE

Urbanism in the nation reflects both its rural past and its commercial and urban present. While some municipalities such as Canillo and Ordino demonstrate an urbanism typical of any village of the Pyrenean or Alpine high mountains, the urban center formed by Andorra la Vella and Escaldes-Engordany has the face and structure of any typical Western urban commercial center. Other settlements, such as Sant Julia de Loria and Encamp, show a hybrid rural-urban style.

An urban rule also fixes the invented tradition of the "mountain style." This demands that 30 percent of any facade be constructed of stone masonry. Hence large commercial buildings and the majority of urban public buildings show an amalgam of invented tradition and modernity, combining stone with iron and large surfaces of glass. Nevertheless, the building of the national government is of modern design, constructed in concrete and glass. Meanwhile the seat of the Andorran parliament (the General Council) is a noteworthy sixteenth-century edifice, a kind of palace-fortress constructed totally of stone masonry.

The most notable elements of the Andorran patrimony are its thirty Romanesque churches, almost all of them small, built between the ninth and the thirteenth centuries. Some of them conserve frescoes and wood carvings of great value, such as the Virgin of Canolic (which dates to the twelfth century). There are also remains of old castles and medieval fortifications and magnificent examples of rural homesteads. The small Romanesque sanctu-

At the end of the thirteenth century, after conflicts between the bishop of Urgel and the count of Foix, a Judicial Decision (*Pareatge*) was signed in 1278 that established the regime of coprinces that remains today. Currently, the two coprinces of Andorra are the president of the French Republic and the bishop of Urgel. Medieval rights over Andorra passed from the count of Foix to the king of Navarre in the fifteenth century, and then to the king of France in the sixteenth century; in the nineteenth century, they passed to the president of the republic.

**National Identity.** Historically, Andorra has been a protectorate of France and Spain. This is manifest in several ways: (1) the currencies of the nation are the franc and the peseta; (2) the two systems of public education were, until 1982, the French and the Spanish; and (3) the two languages most commonly spoken are French and Spanish, in addition to Catalan. This dualism has been expressed in multiple ways in recent centuries; Andorran factionalism also always has a pro-Spanish front and a pro-French front.

*A tobacco plantation in Andorra. Tobacco is the only surviving agricultural crop in the country.*

ary of Santa Maria de Meritxell, patroness of Andorra, caught fire in 1972. While it was restored, the famous Barcelona architect Ricard Bofill was commissioned to build a new one. A large building, the new sanctuary uses traditional materials such as stone and black slate despite its modern, functional concepts.

Almost 60 percent of the Andorran population resides in the capital center. Here, the style of life and uses of space are similar to any other European city. Some immigrant communities (such as the Portuguese and Galicians) have taken over certain public spaces (such as cafés and restaurants) as centers for informal reunions, which convert the spaces into semipublic spaces. Yet, there is no pattern of spatial segregation on the basis of ethnicity, even if there exists a clear territorial division of social class: while workers live in small apartments in center city blocks, elites inhabit luxurious mansions on adjoining hills.

## FOOD AND ECONOMY

**Food in Daily Life.** The diet in Andorra is based on consumption of meat, garden vegetables, and some fish. The most common winter dish, in rural and urban zones, is escudella, a soup of veal, chicken,

potatoes, and vegetables. Some immigrant communities have different customs: Portuguese eat more cod and Indians, more vegetarian food. Normally, the midday meal is eaten near the workplace in a restaurant.

**Food Customs at Ceremonial Occasions.** Many Catholic families still avoid eating meat on Fridays. At the feast of the Virgin of Meritxell, Andorran families often eat outdoors after the solemn midday mass: they consume cold cuts, chicken, and rabbit. The Christmas cycle is also an occasion for the organization of family meals.

**Basic Economy.** Until about the middle of the twentieth century, the Andorran economy was based on transhumant shepherding and the breeding of cattle and horses. Andorrans also grew some tobacco, while agriculture was oriented to the production of cereals, potatoes, and garden vegetables. Because of the climate, the rocky relief, and the small size of its territory, the country always ran a deficit in agricultural production. Today, due to the commercial orientation of its economy, agriculture has disappeared. Only tobacco survives, with its production tripling since the early 1970s. Coupled with enormous quantities of imported tobacco, this production feeds a strong tobacco industry serving visitors to the country (as well as smuggling). Almost all that Andorrans consume and sell to millions of visitors comes from importation, principally from Spain and France but also from Japan and other countries of the Far East. Yet another extremely important economic activity for the Andorran economy is the banking sector, because of the nation's condition as a "fiscal paradise."

**Land Tenure and Property.** Most Andorran land is of communal ownership, including the woods and alpine meadows that occupy more than 80 percent of the territory. This situation recurs throughout the Pyrenees, originating in medieval local codes. Private property is found near villages, constituted by homes, rural structures, cultivated fields, and gardens. The exploitation of goods is managed by local administrations (comuns) which, in addition, also exercise many functions typical of city halls. The benefits of the exploitation of these goods revert to citizens in the form of infrastructure, equipment, creation of work, scholarships for students, and social service endeavors. Today, four of the seven municipal units (parroquies) that form the country have one or more winter resorts, from which they also gain great benefits. The only properties of the state are the courses and banks of the rivers, and roads and highways.

***Commercial Activities.*** Andorra has always had fluid commercial relations with France and Spain, including smuggling. During the Spanish Civil War (1936–1939) and the World War II (1939–1945), the volume of exchanges increased, since Andorra was a platform through which to supply belligerent nations. In addition, the economic isolation of Spain during the dictatorship of Francisco Franco, from 1939 to 1975, favored the commercial activity of Andorra, which supplied equipment, machine parts, vehicles, and other consumer goods. The foundation of the new Andorran economy, however, is retail commerce in major consumer goods, oriented toward buyers in nearby regions of Spain and France.

***Major Industries.*** Andorra's industrial development is extremely limited. Apart from tobacco, the most important industry is construction along with its derivative industries, hospitality industries, and semi-artisanal activities such as jewelry.

***Trade.*** Commerce and tourism are based on the importation of all goods and services from third countries. There are sixty import-export companies handling such goods as gasoline, automobiles, beverages, tobacco, machinery, optical and electronic products, food, clothing, and shoes. Electronic goods come from Japan and other Asian sources, while the rest come from Europe.

***Division of Labor.*** Large Andorran firms belong almost exclusively to Andorran citizens, although there are also some enterprises founded by Spaniards and Frenchmen who have acquired citizenship through their years of residence. Foreigners, Spanish and French, dominated professional positions until recently; high enrollments of university students have fostered a process of nationalization in this occupational level. Employment in construction, transport, commerce, and public services (police and sanitation), like work in hotels, tend to employ resident alien workers depending on their ability and level of instruction.

## SOCIAL STRATIFICATION

***Classes and Castes.*** Class differences in Andorra are quite clear and possess marked characteristics, such as residence. Practically all the original Andorran population belongs to the high or medium-high stratum of society as the first group to arrive in the nation. The rest of the Spanish population is basically salaried, although there are executive groups and small entrepreneurs among them. Most Portuguese are found in less-skilled labor positions, especially in hostelry and construction. The French population comprises bureaucrats and small-scale entrepreneurs in hostelry or commerce.

***Symbols of Social Stratification.*** Apart from evocative differences of residence, other indicators of class difference include fashion. The Andorran elite sport well-known international brands, which contrast with the sobriety of the rest of the society. Automobiles are also a highly visible indicator of consumption. Even though the entire society is motorized, only a minority has access to such luxury cars as Rolls-Royce, Mercedes, Audi, and BMW.

## POLITICAL LIFE

***Government.*** Following the 1993 constitution, Andorra is a parliamentary coprincipality, headed by the president of France and the bishop of Urgel. The Andorran parliament (the General Council) includes twenty-eight members, half elected by local constituencies and half by national votes. This system seeks an equilibrium between territory and demography. Elections are held every four years. The winning parliamentary group forms the government.

***Leadership and Political Officials.*** For decades, access to political power in Andorra was linked to two great entrepreneurial families. In the last decade, however, important transformations have emerged from the application of the constitution. There are no real national parties differentiated by ideology and/or in the function of their program of government. Andorran politics are constructed on the basis of influence groups, who defend local and family interests. The elaboration of electoral lists is the result of a complex process of compromise and alliance among client groups. Given the small size of the electorate (some fifteen thousand voters), electoral processes presuppose a face-to-face relation between candidates and electors that is maintained after the election.

***Social Problems and Control.*** The judicial system is constituted at three levels: the Tribunal de Batlles, the Tribunal de Corts, and the Tribunal Superior de Justicia d'Andorra. While all three handle civil and labor affairs, only the first two deal with criminal matters. One might also appeal to a fourth jurisdiction, the Tribunal Constitucional. A corps of judiciary police, distinct from ordinary police, also serves the government. Crime in Andorra is very low. Foreign defendants tend to be extradited to their country of origin. The most frequent crimes are robbery, fraud, and drug trafficking. Labor con-

*Lakes and steep hills dot the landscape of Andorra. The principality has a total land surface of 181 square miles.*

flicts, for unjustified firing, are the most frequent incidents of judicial action.

## SOCIAL WELFARE AND CHANGE PROGRAMS

Since there is no direct taxation in Andorra, the state has limited resources to maintain the level of opulence that characterizes the country. This means its capacity to implement welfare programs is limited. The principal demands of foreign workers, the most fragile and needy social sector, focus on housing and child care in order to secure the position of female workers. Recently, the government attempted a low-interest credit system through Andorran banks to encourage home ownership, but the results were below expectations. The number of child care centers has grown, but still fails to meet demand.

## NONGOVERNMENTAL ORGANIZATIONS AND OTHER ASSOCIATIONS

Andorran organizations are undeveloped, despite the presence of associations in sports, culture, the arts, and business. Unions are not legally accepted, although they exist in clandestine form. All civil associations must be run, legally, by an Andorran citizen. Thus the foreign population has enormous

difficulties in constituting associations. The Spanish Embassy helps the Council of Spanish Residents, an association that looks after the needs and interests of that group. Given Andorra's status as a developed nation, foreign nongovernmental organizations are absent.

## GENDER ROLES AND STATUSES

*The Relative Status of Women and Men.* Andorran society, with its strong rural origins, maintained a marked segregation on the basis of gender roles until the late twentieth century. All public activity was exercised by men, representing the family. Rapid urbanization, changes in lifestyle, and the commercial orientation of the economy have forced a rapid modification in the economic and work roles of women. Today, their public visibility is total, even if their presence in political spheres remains inferior to that of men, despite consistent progress.

## MARRIAGE, FAMILY, AND KINSHIP

*Marriage.* Marriage is not controlled by any limits except class (and not always by that). Marriages between Andorrans and Spaniards or French are normal.

**Domestic Unit.** The family remains the basic social unit, more important than the individual, despite the accelerated evolution of Andorran society. Most enterprises and business are organized through the family, distributing functions according to capacities and the level of study of each member. These family groups, following the institution of the *familia troncal* (stem family), incorporate a married pair and their children.

**Inheritance.** Formerly, the inheritance system passed nearly all the patrimony to one of the sons: the *hereu* (heir). Today, this tendency is maintained only at a symbolic level through the transmission of the family home. In the case of rural holdings, only the inheriting son can marry and reside with his wife and children on the family land; however, current family businesses are different. Any child can remain tied to the family business after marriage, although there remains a tendency towards an heir who will follow the father in the operation of the business.

**Kin Groups.** Networks of kinship are only activated through rituals of sociability for reasons of alliance or political patronage.

## SOCIALIZATION

**Child Rearing and Education.** Andorran children, as in many other European nations, are placed in child care settings before three years of age, and much of the care and instruction of these children thereafter is done by scholastic institutions. Insufficient relationships between parents and children are noticeable at times. The extended work hours of parents, who often do not return home until 8:30 P.M., aggravate this tendency. Cases of youth maladjustment, quite frequent in Andorra and affecting all social sectors, are explained by psychologists as stemming from this relationship deficit.

Until 1982, when an Andorran public school system was created, there were only French and Spanish schools. Each *parroquia* (municipal unit) had a primary school in each system. There were also seven intermediate educational institutions. According to official data, 63 percent of the juvenile population was enrolled in intermediate education in 1999–2000.

**Higher Education.** Roughly 11 percent of the population between eighteen and twenty-four attends university, especially in Spain and France.

*A stone church in a village near Andorra La Vella. Even though Andorra has no formal religion, Roman Catholicism is predominantly practiced.*

## RELIGION

**Religious Beliefs.** Even though Andorra lacks a formal religion, Roman Catholicism is hegemonic. One fundamental element of this presence rests on the role of the bishop of Urgel as coprince and, at the same time, head of the Andorran Church. Apart from the Jehovah's Witnesses, there are no public religious alternatives in Andorra.

**Rituals and Holy Places.** All public ceremonies, including some sessions of the parliament, are accompanied by a Catholic mass. The Andorran festive calendar adapts to the Catholic liturgical calendar, and the nation, like every *parroquia*, has a patron saint and a collection of religious and lay celebrations.

## MEDICINE AND HEALTH CARE

The Andorran medical system is guaranteed through a general hospital, situated in the capital, as well as various clinics and private medical centers. Every population center has a family medical service. Alongside official medicine, traditional curing practices based on herbal knowledge also survive. There are no shamanistic practices of curing (*curanderismo*) in Andorra.

## SECULAR CELEBRATIONS

In addition to the national festival of the Virgin of Meritxell (8 September), each *parroquia* has its own patronal festival. Given the commercial orientation of the nation (which remains open for business especially when neighboring nations have holidays), the only formal holidays are Christmas and New Year's Day.

## THE ARTS AND HUMANITIES

***Support for the Arts.*** Both the state and communal administrations support artistic formation and creativity. Conservatories of music and art schools are scattered around the nation.

***Literature.*** Andorran literary production does not cross the frontiers of the small country, except in the case of writer A. Morell. There are nonetheless groups of historians and folklorists interested in recovering oral traditions and studying and teaching the nation's history.

***Performance Arts.*** In music, the two great figures of classical music, the Claret brothers, who play violoncello and violin, have gained great prestige throughout Europe.

## BIBLIOGRAPHY

Armengol, Lídia. *Approach to the History of Andorra*, 1989.

Baudon de Mony, Charles. "La Vallée d'Andorre et les Êveques d'Urgel au Moyen Age". *Revue des Pyrenees et de la France Meridionale*, 4: 551–571, 1892.

Bladé, Jean François. *The Valley of Andorr*, 1882.

Bricall, Josep M., et al. *Estructura i perspectives de l'economia andorrana*, 1974.

Comas d'Argemir, Dolors, Joan J. Pujadas. *Aladradas y guellas; Trabajo, sociedad, y cultura en el Pirineo Aragonés*, 1985.

———. *Andorra; Un país de frontera*, 1997.

De los Ríos, Fernando. *Vida e instituciones del pueblo de Andorra. Una supervivencia señorial*, 1920.

Deverell, F. H. *All Round Spain by Road and Train, with a Short Account of a Visit to Andorra*, 1884.

Eyre, Mary. *Over the Pyrenees into Spain*, 1865.

Llobet, Salvador. *El medi i la vida a Andorra*, 1986.

Lluelles, M0 Jesús. *La transformació econòmica d'Andorra*, 1991.

López, E.J., Peruga, and C. Tudel. *L'Andorra del segle XIX*, 1998.

Newman, B. *Round about Andorra*, 1928.

Riberaygua, B. *Les Valls d'Andorra:. Recull documental*, 1946.

Riera, Manel. *La llengua catalana a Andorra. Estudi dialectològic dels seus parlars rurals*, 1992.

Sacotte, Jean-Charles. "Les Vallées d'Andorre." *Notes et Etudes Documentaires*, 4087, 2-V-1974.

Sáez, Xavier. "Informe sobre l'economia andorrana, 1995." *Andorra, anuari socio-economic, 1996*, 10–67, 1996.

Sandy, Isabelle. *Andorre: ou les hommes d'airain*, 1923.

Sermet, Jean. *Problemas de la frontera hispano-francesa en los Pirineos*, 1985.

Taillefer, François. *L'Ariège et l'Andorre*, 1985.

Viñas, Ramón. *Nacionalitat i drets polítics al Principat d'Andorra*, 1989.

Violant i Simorra, Ramón. *El Pirineo Español*, 1949.

—JOAN J. PUJADAS,
TRANSLATED BY GARY W. MCDONOGH

# ANGOLA

## CULTURE NAME
Angolan

## ORIENTATION

**Identification.** The word "Angola" derives from the title used by the rulers of the Ndongo state. The title *ngola* was first mentioned in Portuguese writings in the sixteenth century. A Portuguese colony founded on the coast in 1575 also came to be known as Angola. At the end of the nineteenth century, the name was given to a much larger territory that was envisaged to come under Portuguese influence. These plans materialized slowly; not until the beginning of the twentieth century did Portuguese colonialism reach the borders of present-day Angola. In 1975, this area became an independent country under the name República Popular de Angola (People's Republic of Angola). Later the "Popular" was dropped.

Angola may not classify as either a country or a culture. Since 1961, war has destroyed cultural institutions, forced people to flee, and divided the territory between the belligerent. Thus one cannot speak of a single national culture. It is difficult to obtain reliable information because the war precludes research in many areas.

**Location and Geography.** Angola is a country of 482,625 square miles (approximately 1.25 million square kilometers) in western Africa, south of the Equator. There are great variations in climate and geography, including rain forests in the north, drier coastal lands, the fertile central highlands, sandy soils in the east, and desert zones in the Kunene (Cuene) and Kuando Kubango provinces. Apart from large rivers such as the Zaire, Kwanza (Cuanza), Kunene, Kubango (Cubango), Zambezi, and Kuando, there are many smaller rivers, some of which are not perennial. The climate is characterized by a rainy season and a dry season whose timing and intensity differ in the various regions.

Angola borders Namibia to the south, the Atlantic Ocean to the west, Zambia to the east, and the Republic of Congo to the north. The oil-rich enclave of Cabinda lies north of the Zaire river.

**Demography.** Because of the ongoing war, it is difficult to obtain reliable population figures. Also, the numbers fluctuate as people attempt to flee when the fighting is intense and return when the fighting has calmed down. It is estimated that in May 2000, 350,700 Angolans lived outside the country and another 2.5 million to 4 million were displaced within the national borders. About a million residents have died because of the war. Nonetheless the population has increased considerably. In 1973 there were 5.6 million residents; by 1992 that number had risen to 12.7 million. Despite a high annual growth rate, in the beginning of 2000 the population was estimated at 12.6 million. Since a census has not been held since 1970, the figures are difficult to evaluate. Angola has a young population, over 45 percent of which is below fifteen years of age. The population density varies greatly by region. Over the years, the urban population has grown strongly and more than half the people now live in towns. The capital, Luanda, has drawn in many immigrants—a quarter of all residents now live there.

**Linguistic Affiliation.** The official language is Portuguese. Many Angolans are bilingual, speaking Portuguese and one or several African languages. In nearly all cases this is a Bantu language; those speaking a Khoisan language number less than 6,000. Six of the Bantu languages were selected as national languages: Chokwe, Kikongo, Kimbundo, Mbunda, Oxikuanyama, and Umbundu. Many people are able to understand one or more of the national languages, but some forty languages are spoken.

**Symbolism.** The political culture is highly militarized, and in both the National Union for the Total

*Angola*

Liberation of Angola (UNITA) and the Popular Movement for the Liberation of Angola (MPLA) many symbols stem from the military tradition. Parades, uniforms, and flags are prominent during many political meetings. The national flag is red and black with a yellow machete, a star, and a cogwheel segment. UNITA is symbolized by a crowing cockerel.

## HISTORY AND ETHNIC RELATIONS

***Emergence of the Nation.*** Present–day Angola is a construct designed by European politicians at the Conference of Berlin in 1885. Before that time, the area was inhabited by people with different political traditions, ranging from decentralized mobile groups to autocratic kingdoms. The Kongo, Ndongo, and Ovimbundu kingdoms had early contact with the

Portuguese, who in the sixteenth century created colonies on the coast. Wars fought against the immigrant Portuguese, such as that waged by Queen Njinga of the Ndongo kingdom, often have been interpreted in a nationalistic framework. For centuries the communities in this area were affected by the Atlantic slave trade. Portuguese, *mestiço*, (person of mixed descent) and African merchants and middle men sold millions of slaves who were transported to the Americas on Dutch and Portuguese vessels. Although the slave trade was stopped in the 1880s, internal slavery continued into the twentieth century. After the Conference of Berlin, Portuguese colonialism took on a very different character. Through a slow and halting process that met with much local resistance, the Portuguese attempted to expand their control over the interior of the country and enforce a colonial system with taxation and forced labor. After the installation of autocratic rule in Portugal, repression in the colonies became even worse than in the past. The legacy of the colonial divide-and-rule tactics is still felt.

The war for liberation started in 1961 with rebellions in Luanda and the northern region. The anticolonial war ended after Portuguese soldiers, tired of war in the colonial territories, staged a coup in Portugal in 1974. On 11 November 1975, Angola became an independent country. Before that date, fighting had broken out between the three major nationalist parties: the National Front for the Liberation of Angola (FNLA), MPLA, and UNITA. After independence, UNITA received support from South African troops and was later backed by the United States, while the MPLA came to depend largely on Russian and Cuban aid. This division runs through the country's recent history. With Angola's involvement in the war in the Congo and with that war spilling into Namibia and Zambia, the war has taken on international dimensions.

**National Identity.** There is no single national identity. The country is divided along many lines: Ethnic, religious, regional, racial, and other factors interact in the conflict. However, the notion of being Angolan is strong. The Portuguese language sets Angola apart from its neighboring countries and has created long-standing ties not only with Portugal but also with Brazil, Mozambique, and other Portuguese-speaking countries.

**Ethnic Relations.** The civil war is often explained in ethnic terms, with the FNLA considered a Kongo party, the MPLA predominantly Mbundu, and UNITA dependent on Ovimbundu support. The stress on ethnicity is growing in intensity, and eth-

nic differences have become more important. However, many other factors play a role, and ethnicity is only one aspect of identity for Angolan people. Differences between rural and urban populations, regions, religions, and races are some of the criteria on which people classify themselves or are classified by others. The importance of clan as a factor in the construction of identity is disappearing rapidly. Although the small Khoisan-speaking minority is not discriminated against by law, its position is extremely difficult and these people are marginalized in many respects. The closely interlinked political, military and economic elites may be seen as a distinct cultural group. The elites have a number of common characteristics but remain strongly divided and have profoundly different histories. Thus during the colonial era a northern Baptist network came into existence that consisted mainly of Kongo traders with strong ties to French-speaking Zaire. Methodists and Catholics from the central region formed the core of the MPLA and include a relatively high number of *mestiços* and whites, who now make up 2 percent of the population. In the southern elite, Congregationalists from the central plateau are important. This southern elite became prominent in the UNITA leadership.

## URBANISM, ARCHITECTURE, AND THE USE OF SPACE

Angola is relatively urbanized because in the 1980s many people sought refuge in the safer urban areas. The *musseques*, informal settlements around Luanda that are home to nearly a quarter of the population stand in sharp contrast to the modern city center. For people in the countryside, living conditions are very different, although rectangular houses with corrugated iron roofs and zinc are replacing the traditional round wattle-and-daub (straw and mud) houses. Some urban areas are overcrowded, while other regions are almost uninhabited. As it is often dangerous to travel by road or railway, transportation and mobility are a problem. In the 1980s cheap airfares even led to regional trading networks based on transport by air.

## FOOD AND ECONOMY

**Food in Daily Life.** Over half of the population is unemployed, and it is estimated that 70 percent of the people live below the poverty line. Hunger is a threat in many areas. As the usual economic activities are impossible in many regions, local food habits are hardly distinguishable. Coastal people include much seafood in their diet, herders in the

An aerial view of Angola's capital city, Luanda.

southwest rely mostly on dairy products and meat, and farmers eat maize, sorghum, cassava and other agricultural crops. Especially in urban areas but also in the drier rural areas, gathering water and firewood is often time-consuming. Salt is a highly prized product in many areas.

**Food Customs at Ceremonial Occasions.** Many traditional ceremonies and celebrations have disappeared or are held infrequently. If circumstances allow, at a party or ceremony, grilled chicken, soft drinks, and bottled beer are served and consumed in liberal amounts. As these items are costly, most people can only afford local beverages such as maize beer and palm wine.

**Basic Economy.** The farming sector has been neglected by the government. The war has made agriculture impossible in many areas, and transport is often a dangerous undertaking. Although 70 percent of the people engage in agriculture to sustain themselves, over 50 percent of the food supply has to be imported. Farmers plant gardens in which subsistence crops are grown.

**Land Tenure and Property.** Access to land is difficult. There is not a land shortage, but not all arable land is under cultivation. This problem is caused by the fact that war prevents farmers from going to

their fields and often forces people to flee before the harvest. In times of relative calm, land mines render traveling to and working on the land dangerous. Both the MPLA and UNITA have restricted the freedom of movement of the population and imposed rules to curb mobility in specific areas or during certain parts of the day.

**Commercial Activities.** Small retail trade is very important in people's survival strategies. Women are especially important in selling food and firewood, and men predominate in trade in arms, diamonds, and spare parts. Most of the people who work in the transport and building sectors are men. Local commercial activities are largely situated in the extensive *candonga* system, the name for the second economy. The new kwanza, the national currency, is subject to high inflation rates. As the war often makes transport impossible, crafts and repair have become increasingly important again.

**Major Industries.** Angola is a potentially rich country. Petroleum in the Cabinda enclave; diamonds in Lunda; and iron, phosphates, copper, gold, bauxite, and uranium in the other provinces are some of the natural resources. In comparison with other sub-Saharan countries, Angola is industrialized to a considerable degree and has a relatively high income per capita. Oil (90 percent of exports) is

*A group of women selling fish at Luanda Port. In general, Angolan women play a vital role in farming and food trading, while men are herders and wage laborers.*

especially important. Most of these resources are used to finance the military, however, as Angola has a war economy. Only those who have a stake in the war benefit from this system; for most people it means hunger. UNTA (National Union of Angolan Workers), for a long time the only effective labor organization, has been important in the redirection of the economy but rarely manages to represent workers' interests adequately and is strongly connected with the government party. A rival labor organization was established in 1996.

**Trade.** Seventy percent of exports go to the United States, mainly crude oil, diamonds, and other natural resources. Some commercial agricultural products, such as sisal, coffee, and cotton, are sold. The fishing industry also is important. Imports come from Portugal, Brazil, the United States and the European countries and consist mainly of war equipment (50 percent) and food (20 percent). The international drug trade is growing in volume, and UNITA depends largely on the illegal diamond and arms trade.

**Division of Labor.** Most residents take every opportunity to make ends meet, and many historical divisions of labor have been overturned. Thus, women may clear strips of land to prepare the soil for agriculture, while men may collect and sell firewood. Generally, women are important in farming and the local food trade, while cattle herders and wage laborers are usually men.

## SOCIAL STRATIFICATION

**Classes and Castes.** The country is divided along many lines. Before twentieth-century colonialism, the rich trading families formed a local elite that looked down on the *gentio* (''pagans'' or ''crowd''). During the colonial era, an extremely hierarchical society was created in which Portuguese rulers gave some advantages to African *assimilados* (assimilated people) over the great majority of *indigenas* (indigenous people). Although the number of assimilados was never high, they were sharply divided, mainly on regional and religious lines. These divisions are reflected in the founding of political parties and are used for propaganda purposes. Thus, UNITA has tried to denounce the MPLA as 'foreign' because of the continuing importance of whites and *mestiços* in the party. The UNITA leadership is often regarded as populist and opportunistic, and the northern FNLA leadership as capitalist and conservative. However, the various elites have a number of common characteristics, such as regarding wealth and expenditure as the most important indicator of class.

***Symbols of Social Stratification.*** The display of wealth is the most important way to show a superior position in society. This display may take the form of individual material possessions such as cars, yachts, and clothing. It also is manifested in the activities people undertake: Flashy rich youths go to Luanda's expensive discos and nightclubs. Material wealth also may be expressed by acting as a patron, for example, by holding lavish parties for large groups of people and distributing gifts.

## POLITICAL LIFE

***Government.*** Angola is a presidential republic. Until the 1990s, the MPLA monopolized the central state, and, despite the existence of government institutions, presidential powers were extensive. The MPLA leader, Agostinho Neto, was president until his death in September 1979, after which Eduardo dos Santos took over. Since independence, the power center has been rivaled by Jonas Savimbi, the leader of UNITA. The formal government changed in 1992 from a socialist, one-party system to a multiparty, free market system. Many parties have been founded since then, apart from the MPLA and UNITA, but only the revived FNLA continues to have an impact. In April 1997, UNITA joined the government, but it was suspended in August 1998 for failing to observe the peace agreements signed in Lusaka. The parties began fighting again, and the government won considerable terrain from UNITA. UNITA has become internationally isolated, and the whereabouts of Savimbi is unclear, although UNITA continues to buy weapons through the illegal diamond trade. A number of UNITA defectors, including some in leadership functions, have formed a group called UNITA-renovada and are calling for adherence to the Lusaka protocols. The government announced elections for late 2001, but there is no guarantee that they will be held, or will be free and fair.

***Leadership and Political Officials.*** Both in UNITA-held and government areas, political rallies are an important aspect of the political culture. These meetings usually include songs, dances, speeches, and parades. Often they show conflicting tendencies: Although they are used by politicians to bolster their position, many people criticize their leaders during these gatherings. For people from Luanda and the surrounding area, the yearly carnival in Luanda has become a political arena. For a long time, the MPLA government regarded the continuing importance of traditional leaders in local political life with suspicion, while in UNITA the role of chiefs in political life was more widely accepted.

*Street vendors at a market area in Luanda. Small market trade is very important to Angolan survival.*

Many nongovernmental organizations (NGOs) and aid organizations rely on traditional leaders for information and channel aid through them.

***Social Problems and Control.*** Administrative and political life is corrupt, and the bureaucracy often borders on the absurd. "Disappearance" has been the fate of many people suspected of political opposition. The armies have been accused of misbehavior, extrajudicial executions, forced enlistment, and child soldiering. The government has acted against freedom of expression and an independent press, while the Ninjas, a special police force, spread terror among the population. In UNITA areas, reports have confirmed extreme human rights abuses, such as torture, kangaroo courts, and unlawful executions. Civilians regard politics with extreme suspicion, and the continuation of the war is widely regarded as resulting from greed for power among the political leaders. It is remarkable how many people find the courage and creativity to continue living in a context of extreme violence and poverty. Nonetheless, some people do not manage: alcoholism and theft are increasing. Witchcraft is perceived by a great number of people as a problem that is not adequately addressed by politicians, the police, and the judiciary.

***Military Activity.*** Political life is centered on the military. After independence, UNITA held the southeast and continued to hold a sway over the central highlands and Lunda Norte. Despite the ongoing war, there have been intervals of negotiation and peace. Between May 1991 and October 1992 a ceasefire was respected by both parties. After UNITA refused to accept the results of the elections held in September 1992, intense fighting broke out again. It is estimated that in the town Huambo alone, 300,000 people died during this phase of the war. In 1994 the Lusaka Protocol was signed by both parties, and in April 1997 a government of national unity and reconciliation was installed that included representatives of UNITA and MPLA. However fighting began again in 1998. Control over the diamond areas in Lunda Norte became an important war aim. The forces of the MPLA have pushed UNITA out of its former capital, Jamba, in the southeast, but fighting along the Zambian and Namibian borders has remained intense. The same situation exists in the Central Highlands, where UNITA is conducting a guerrilla war. In Cabinda, various factions of the Front for the Liberation of the Enclave of Cabinda (FLEC) have fought for secession for a long time.

## SOCIAL WELFARE AND CHANGE PROGRAMS

There have been attempts to implement long-term social welfare programs. In 2000, the UNDP (UN Development Program) initiated projects focusing on poverty eradication and good governance. Renewed accords with the International Monetary Fund aimed at decreasing the large national debt and reducing the inflation rate. Most of these programs focus on emergency relief. Apart from a host of NGOs, international aid organizations such as the World Food Programme, World Health Organization, UNHCR (UN High Commissioner for Refugees), UNICEF and other UN-related donors are active. With the exacerbating fighting, many people cannot be reached by these organizations, and occasionally the organizations have pulled out all their personnel as the security situation has become problematic. The rural population is hard to reach.

## NONGOVERNMENTAL ORGANIZATIONS AND OTHER ASSOCIATIONS

A wide range of NGOs have been active. Apart from large international emergency relief organizations, such as the Red Cross, Doctors without Borders, and CARE, a host of smaller NGOs have organized campaigns around varying issues, with varying degrees of success.

## GENDER ROLES AND STATUSES

***Division of Labor by Gender.*** The war is primarily a male affair, and few women go off to fight. Many young men have died in the war. As a consequence, a growing number of households are headed by women, and polygamy has not decreased as it has in most other African countries. The fact that the majority of the urban population is male, while women make up the larger part of the rural population, has strengthened these trends. As women are important in agriculture and the regional food trade, they run a higher risk of being hit by land mines than do civilian men. Some 80 percent of land mine victims are women and children. Rape and violence against women continue to rank as important social problems.

***The Relative Status of Women and Men.*** Despite the MPLA's advocacy of gender equality, there are clear discrepancies between the status of women and men. The literacy rate for men is 56 percent, while only 28 percent of women were literate in 1998. Few women are in top positions in political, economic, and military affairs. Often women are paid less than men for the same jobs. The largest women's organization, the Angolan Women's Association (OMA), is strongly tied to the MPLA party. Many smaller women's organizations have been formed, often along professional lines.

## MARRIAGE, FAMILY, AND KINSHIP

***Marriage.*** Marriage and cohabitation take many forms. Some couples are wed in church or by the state, others have their wedding blessed by their parents, and others do not formalize their cohabitation with a ceremony. In most cultures a couple find a home of their own or live with their husband's parents. In some areas there is a high divorce rate that not only is due to the war but also conforms to older patterns of marriage and separation. Many spouses live apart for considerable periods of time; often the economic situation is so desperate that they have to look for means of subsistence on their own. Women often are widowed and as there are more women than men of marriageable age, there is a relatively high number of polygamous households. The age gap between spouses is growing, especially in rural areas.

***Domestic Unit.*** Many households have been disrupted by the war; a considerable number of people have seen relatives die, and communities have been destroyed by the ongoing fighting. People may have relatives in different fighting camps and often live very far from each other, and many Angolans are looking for lost relatives. Especially in rural areas, the extended family remains important: An income may be shared with one or more unemployed relatives; immigrants look for housing, land, and basic assistance from their relatives; and several generations and nuclear families may form a single household. In towns, the importance of the extended family is diminishing.

**Inheritance.** In most Angolan societies, inheritance is patrilineal, with children inheriting from the father. In quite a few communities among the Umbundu, Ngangela, and Ambo, property traditionally was passed to the children of the deceased's wife's brother. This matrilineal system has decreased in importance under the influence of colonialism and the war.

**Kin Groups.** Kinship terminology in many communities is difficult to translate. The children of uncles and aunts may be addressed with the same term used for brothers and sisters. However, there is a sharp distinction between senior and junior "brothers" and "sisters" and uncles and aunts may be differentiated in the maternal and paternal lines. In some cultures a village consists of matrilineal kin and their dependents. As many communities have been torn apart by the war, these structures have often disappeared.

## SOCIALIZATION

**Infant Care.** Young children are most likely to be taken care of by the mother and may be strapped into a cloth on her back while she engages in household chores, agricultural work, or selling at the local market. Other relatives may be equally important in a child's upbringing. Thus, children may stay with their grandparents for considerable periods of time and, especially when they are older, spend a great deal of time with the father or mother's brother's family.

**Child Rearing and Education.** Many children are unable to attend school because of the war, but there has been growth in the literacy rate. In 1970, 12 percent of the population was literate, while the literacy rate currently is approaching 50 percent. The majority of these people are young, reflecting government efforts to develop free educational facilities for all children. There is a lack of educational materials, qualified teachers, and school buildings. In some cultures children are initiated. Sometimes these puberty rites concern only boys, but in groups such as the Nyanyeka, girls are also initiated. In

most communities, the rites have shortened considerably or disappeared. Poverty and the war have caused the number of street children and orphans to grow.

**Higher Education.** There are two universities. The older university, named after the country's first president, is in Luanda, with branches in Huambo and Lubango. As a result of the war, the Huambo branch has been closed down repeatedly, and the university is poorly equipped, badly housed, and overcrowded. A Catholic university opened in 1999 in Luanda.

## ETIQUETTE

In general, dress codes are not strict. In some areas, women are supposed to wear long-hemmed skirts, but this rule is not strictly applied. In many communities, people do not look each other in the eye while speaking. Younger people are expected to address elders politely. The ability to speak well is a highly admired trait, in both men and women. In some communities, men do not eat with women and children.

## RELIGION

**Religious Beliefs.** Especially in the coastal regions, Christianity dates back a long time. A Christian church was established in the Kongo region by the end of the fifteenth century. It is unclear how many residents are Christian; the Roman Catholic Church figures range from 38 percent to 68 percent. Another 15 to 20 percent belong to Protestant denominations, such as Methodist, Baptist, and African churches. For many people there is no contradiction between Christian faith and aspects of African religions. Thus, religious specialists such as diviners and healers hold an important position in society. The government, with its socialist outlook, has been in frequent conflict with religious leaders. Because the Roman Catholic Church has great influence and was associated with Portuguese colonialism, relations with that faith have been especially tense. Since the move toward a more liberal political system, relations with the established churches have eased considerably, although troubling incidents continue to occur. An unknown number of residents do not profess any religion.

**Religious Practitioners.** Traditional healers and diviners have been disregarded by the socialist government. Although the role of these religious practitioners in the community often increased during

*Street children in Luanda. Poverty and war have caused the number of orphaned and homeless Angolan children to grow at a rapid rate.*

the war, the MPLA refused to recognize their function, and at times they were hindered in the execution of their profession. In UNITA areas, the function of healers and diviners has been acknowledged to a far greater extent. There are widespread accusations, however, that UNITA has used healers and diviners to intimidate civilians under their control.

***Rituals and Holy Places.*** Because of the war, many religious practices have been discontinued and cultural institutions are no longer in use. Amid the chaos of the war, many formerly meaningful places and activities have lost their function. Under the influence of the churches, a number of traditional African religious practices have disappeared. In the war context, people attempt to find new ways to address the critical situation. Thus, malign spirits are exorcised in newly established independent churches, children wear amulets to prevent being forced into the army during round-ups, and soldiers strictly follow all the rules given them to make a magic potion against bullets.

***Death and the Afterlife.*** In many Angolan societies, a funeral is an extremely important event; mourning rituals often are regarded as essential for the peace of the deceased's soul. Because of the war,

there is often no opportunity to carry out the appropriate rituals for the dead. Although people have sought alternative forms of mourning, war victims sometimes are left unburied. Apart from the personal trauma this may involve, many people fear that restless spirits will further disrupt social life.

## MEDICINE AND HEALTH CARE

Despite government efforts to extend basic health care services, most people do not have access to medical assistance. Many hospitals face an extreme lack of personnel and do not have the most basic equipment. Only a tiny minority of the population can afford good medical care. For the majority of people, life expectancy is below fifty years. Poverty-related diseases such as cholera, tuberculosis, and measles are a problem in overcrowded urban areas and refugee camps. Many deaths are a direct consequence of malnutrition and undernourishment. The number of people with AIDS is increasing; malaria is common in some areas, especially during the rainy season. One in three children dies before reaching his or her fifth birthday. Angola is one of the few countries where maternal mortality is increasing. A number of health problems are a direct consequence of the war. Over 10 million land mines

*A march to celebrate the 1961 war for liberation, held in a stadium in Luanda, in 1975.*

have resulted in the highest number of amputees in the world, mental illnesses are often related to war trauma, and many children and elderly people have been left without support. With basic health care in disarray, many people seek help from traditional healers. These medical-religious specialists often deal with psychological problems, and many have extensive knowledge of herbal remedies.

## SECULAR CELEBRATIONS

On 11 November 1975 Angola became an independent country. This day is celebrated every year. Apart from Christian holidays, a wide range of occasions are commemorated, such as the founding of the MPLA, the beginning of the armed struggle, and the anniversary of Neto.

## THE ARTS AND HUMANITIES

*Literature.* Angola has an outstanding literary tradition. An important genre has been political poetry, of which the former president Agostinho Neto was a significant representative. The arts, relatively free from censorship, have been an important way to express criticism of the political system. Oral literature is important in many communities, including mermaids in Luandan lore, Ovimbundu trickster tales, and sand graphs and their explication in the east.

The press has been largely controlled by the MPLA and UNITA. Journalists who express alternative views have been curbed in the exercise of their profession: Murder, censorship, and accusations of defamation have been used to suppress an independent press. Radio constitutes an important source of information, but has been dominated by belligerent parties for a long time; although, a Catholic radio station, Rádio Ecclésia, has been established.

*Graphic Arts.* Crafts such as wood carving and pottery are sold in neighboring countries. Luanda has a number of museums, including the Museum of Anthropology.

*Performance Arts.* Angolan music, with its ties to Brazil, has received international attention. The most popular spectator sports are soccer and basketball.

## THE STATE OF THE PHYSICAL AND SOCIAL SCIENCES

Academics face many problems, and the state university is short on staff and teaching materials. As a result of the war, Angola is severely underrepresented in research: Many themes cannot be addressed, many sources have been destroyed, and many areas cannot be reached by researchers. There are well-stocked libraries in Luanda as well as a national archive.

## BIBLIOGRAPHY

Birmingham, David. *Frontline Nationalism in Angola and Mozambique*, 1992.

Bridgland, Fred. *Jonas Savimbi: A Key to Africa*, 1987.

Davidson, Basil. *In the Eye of the Storm: Angola's People*, 1972.

Hare, Paul. *Angola's Last Best Chance for Peace: An Insider's Account of the Peace Process*, 1998.

Hart, Keith, and Joanna Lewis, eds. *Why Angola Matters*, 1995.

Heywood, Linda. *Contested Power in Angola, 1840s to the Present*, 2000.

Kapuscinski, Ryszard. *Another Day of Life*, 1988.

Maier, Karl. *Angola: Promises and Lies*, 1996.

Marcum, John A. *The Angolan Revolution, Vols. I and II*, 1969, 1978.

Miller, Joseph C. *Way of Death: Merchant Capitalism and the Angolan Slave Trade, 1730–1830*, 1988.

Neto, Agostinho. *Sacred Hope*, 1974.

Pepetela. *Yaka*, 1996.

Wheeler, Douglas L., and René Pélissier. *Angola*, 1971.

Wolfers, Michael, and Jane Bergerol. *Angola in the Frontline*, 1983.

### Web Sites

Angola Reference Centre. http://www.angola.org/referenc/index.htm

—INGE BRINKMAN

# ANGUILLA

## CULTURE NAME

Anguillan

## ORIENTATION

**Identification.** Anguilla, a dependent territory of the United Kingdom, is one of the Leeward Islands. According to tradition, Christopher Columbus gave the small, narrow island its name in 1493 because from the distance it resembled an eel, or in Italian, *anguilla*. It is also possible that French navigator Pierre Laudonnière gave the island its name from the French *anguille*.

**Location and Geography.** Anguilla is the most northern of the Leeward Islands in the Lesser Antilles in the eastern Caribbean Sea. Nearby islands include Scrub, Seal, Dog and Sombrero Islands and Prickly Pear Cays. Anguilla is five miles (eight kilometers) north of Saint Martin and sixty miles (ninety-seven kilometers) northeast of Saint Kitts. Anguilla's land area covers thirty-five square miles (ninety-one square kilometers). It is sixteen miles (twenty-six kilometers) long and three-and-one-half miles (six kilometers) wide, with a highest elevation of two-hundred -thirteen feet (sixty-five meters), at Crocus Hill. The largest town, in the center of the island, is The Valley. Relatively flat, Anguilla is a coral and limestone island with a very dry climate. It is covered with sparse vegetation, and there are few areas of fertile soil; most of the land is more adapted to grazing. Anguilla does not have any rivers, but there are several salt ponds, which are used for the commercial production of salt. The climate is sunny and dry year-round, with an average temperature of 80 degrees Fahrenheit (27 degrees Celsius). Anguilla is in an area known for hurricanes, which are most likely to strike from July to October.

**Demography.** Originally inhabited by some of the Carib peoples who came from northern South America, Anguilla was later colonized by the English, in the 1600s. Today the majority of the population is of African descent. The minority Caucasian population is mostly of British descent. The population on average is very young; more than one third are under the age of fifteen. Anguilla has a total permanent population of about nine thousand.

**Linguistic Affiliation.** The official language of Anguilla is English. A Creole language, derived from a mixture of English and African languages, also is spoken by some Anguillans.

**Symbolism.** The flag of Anguilla was changed several times in the twentieth century. The present flag consists of a dark blue field with the Union Jack, the flag of Great Britain, in the upper left corner, and Anguilla's crest to the center-right side. The crest consists of a background that is white on top and light blue below and has three gold dolphins jumping in a circle. For official government purposes outside Anguilla, the British flag is used to represent the island.

## HISTORY AND ETHNIC RELATIONS

**Emergence of the Nation.** Anguilla was first inhabited several thousand years ago and at various times by some of the Carib peoples who arrived from South America. One of these groups, the Arawaks, settled in Anguilla more or less permanently in about 2000 B.C.E. The first Europeans to arrive on the island were the English, who had first colonized Saint Kitts, and then Anguilla in 1650. By this time the Arawaks had vanished, probably wiped out by disease, pirates, and European explorers. However, in 1656 the English in turn were massacred by a group of Caribs, famous for their skill as warriors and farmers. The English eventually returned and attempted to cultivate the land but Anguilla's dry climate prevented its farms from ever becoming profitable.

For the next 150 years, until about 1800, Anguilla, like other Caribbean islands, was caught in

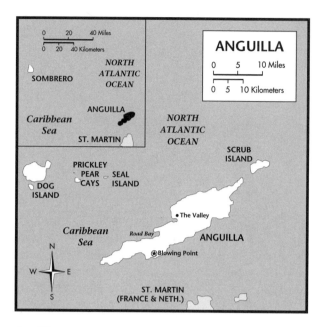

*Anguilla*

the power struggle between the English and the French, both nations seeking to gain control of the area and its highly profitable trade routes and cash crops. Anguilla was attacked by a group of Irish colonists in 1688, many of whom remained to live peacefully with the other islanders. Their surnames are still evident today. The French also attacked Anguilla, first in 1745 and again in 1796, but were unsuccessful both times.

During the 1600s most Anguillans survived by working small plots of land, fishing, and cutting wood for export. Indentured European servants provided most of the labor. However, by the early 1700s, the slave-plantation system was gradually beginning to become the dominant economic system in the eastern Caribbean. The growth of the slave trade was directly tied to the cultivation of sugarcane, which was introduced to the West Indies in the late 1600s from the Mediterranean. It quickly became the most valuable cash crop. Harvesting and processing sugarcane was labor-intensive and required a large workforce. Plantation owners soon discovered that it was more profitable to use slaves, forcibly brought from Africa, rather than indentured servants, to work the sugar plantations. Although Anguilla was never a major sugar producer, its proximity to other West Indian islands caused it to be greatly influenced by the plantation system and the slave trade. As the slave system continued to grow throughout the 1700s, Anguilla's population of people of African descent grew.

In 1824 the government of Great Britain created a new administrative plan for their territories in the Caribbean, which placed Anguilla under the administrative authority of Saint Kitts. After more than a century of independence, Anguillans resented this change and believed that the government of Saint Kitts had little interest in their affairs or in helping them. The conflict between Saint Kitts and Anguilla would not be resolved until the twentieth century. A significant change in Anguilla's social and economic structure occurred when England's Emancipation Act of 1833 officially abolished the slave trade in its Caribbean colonies. By 1838, most of the landowners had returned to Europe; many of them sold their land to former slaves. Anguilla survived for the next century on a subsistence agricultural system, with very little change from the mid-1800s until the 1960s.

Anguillans made frequent requests for direct rule from Great Britain throughout the late nineteenth and early twentieth centuries but continued to remain under the authority of Saint Kitts. In 1967 Anguillans rebelled, disarming and capturing all of Saint Kitts's government officials stationed in Anguilla. Anguillans later even invaded Saint Kitts, and finally, in 1969, the British government intervened, sending in four hundred troops. The British military were openly welcomed by Anguillans and in July 1971 the Anguilla Act was passed, officially placing the island under direct British control. It was not until 19 December 1980 that the island was formally separated from Saint Kitts.

Anguilla's position as first a colony, and then a dependent of another British territory, has prevented it from developing as an independent nation like other larger, Caribbean islands. Since 1980 Anguilla has prospered as a separate dependent territory. With an overall increase in economic prosperity and the end of conflict with Saint Kitts, Anguillans are today optimistic about their future.

**National Identity.** Anguillans are proud of their independence and unique identity as one of the smallest inhabited Caribbean islands. They identify culturally with both Great Britain and the West Indies. Industrious and resourceful, Anguillans are known for working together to help each other through hurricanes, drought, and other problems. Great differences in wealth do not exist; consequently there is a general sense of unity among Anguillans of all backgrounds.

**Ethnic Relations.** Problems of ethnic, racial, and social class conflict have always been minimal in Anguilla. The island's small size and lack of fertile

*A traditional cottage in Lower Valley. To take advantage of the island's temperate climate, Anguillan buildings often feature balconies or terraces.*

soil prevented the plantation system, which had long-lasting negative effects on many Caribbean societies, from developing. Most Anguillans are of mixed West African, Irish, English, or Welsh heritage. The small Caucasian minority is well integrated with the ethnic majority.

## URBANISM, ARCHITECTURE, AND THE USE OF SPACE

Housing conditions are generally good, and urban development greatly improved when badly needed public buildings, roads, and water systems were built in the 1960s. Compared to many other islands, urban planning is generally good. Apart from exclusive resort hotels that cater to a foreign tourist trade, Anguillan buildings are typically simple but rather large concrete constructions. Most construction materials must be shipped in, and the frequent occurrence of hurricanes necessitates particular construction methods. Anguilla's sunny and mild climate easily permits outdoor living year-round. Anguillan buildings often have balconies or terraces and take advantage of Anguilla's brilliant sunlight. Slightly more than half of Anguilla's roads are paved. There are two small ports and one airport.

## FOOD AND ECONOMY

**Food in Daily Life.** With an abundant supply of seafood, fruit, and vegetables, food in daily life is fresh and reflects Anguilla's cultural history. Lobster is common and an important export as well. As the Caribbean has become an increasingly popular tourist destination, the demand for lobster continues to grow. Lobster and crayfish are often prepared with cilantro and plantains. Red snapper, conch, and whelk are also typical to Anguilla. Other dishes include mutton stew with island vegetables, and pumpkin soup. Anguilla also manufactures its own brand of soda, using local ingredients. Salted fish, curried goat, and jerk chicken also are popular.

**Basic Economy.** Tourism is now the mainstay of Anguilla's economy, but other important economic activities include fishing, especially lobster and conch; salt production; raising of livestock; and boat building. There is a small financial services industry that the British and Anguillan governments are trying to expand. Money sent back to the island from Anguillans who have moved abroad also is important to the overall economy. There is no income tax; customs duties, real estate taxes, bank licenses, and the sale of stamps provide revenue for the Anguillan government. Both the eastern

Caribbean dollar and the U.S. dollar are used as currency.

**Land Tenure and Property.** Anguilla's dry climate had always discouraged potential settlers in the past, but with the rise of tourism, land and property values have soared. Strict control of land and inaccessibility to it have helped keep real estate development from growing uncontrollably. Clean beaches and plant and animal life abound. With the end of slavery in the 1830s, land was divided into small plots among the island's residents. A few tourist hotels have been built in recent years, but not the large private resorts found in other parts of the Caribbean.

**Commercial Activities.** Tourism and related activities are now the most widespread commercial concerns. Hotels, restaurants, bars, excursion boating and diving, tourist shops, and transportation services are the most widespread commercial activities. The food business, such as markets and bakeries, also is significant. Anguilla produces and sells collectible stamps and this is a small but lucrative part of the economy.

**Major Industries.** Anguilla is not industrialized. Fishing, particularly lobster, constitutes major exports to other parts of the Caribbean and to the United States. Salt, produced by natural evaporation from salt ponds on the island, occurs in quantities large enough for export. Agricultural production, for Anguillan consumption as well as for other islands, includes corn, pigeon peas, and sweet potatoes. Meat products are from sheep, goats, pigs, and chickens.

**Trade.** Great Britain and its neighboring islands are Anguilla's most frequent and important trading partners. Seafood and salt are still important exports. A large number of consumer goods and materials must be imported. With a stronger economy, Anguillans are able to afford many items that would have been prohibitively expensive twenty years ago.

**Division of Labor.** Anguilla has a low standard of living, and employment is often unsteady. Many younger Anguillans go abroad to find work, either to Great Britain, the United States, or to other, larger Caribbean islands. Since Anguilla's independence from Saint Kitts and the growth of the tourist sector, unemployment rates have dropped dramatically. There is now a shortage of labor, which has led to delays in some of the government-sponsored economic plans as well as price and wage increases.

More work visas are being granted to non-Anguillans, but with the demand for labor high, many Anguillans hold more than one job. The British government provides support for a development and jobs program, and the Caribbean Development Bank also has contributed funds to help provide work and stimulate growth.

## SOCIAL STRATIFICATION

**Classes and Castes.** There is very minimal class distinction among native Anguillans. The small Caucasian minority is not an elite, power-holding group; likewise, the African-descent majority does not discriminate or economically isolate the ethnic minority.

## POLITICAL LIFE

**Government.** As Anguilla is a dependent territory of Great Britain, Anguilla's government is under the authority of the British government at Westminster, London. Anguilla's government consists of the governor, the Executive Council, and the House of Assembly. The governor, who holds executive power, is appointed by the British monarch. The governor is responsible for external affairs, internal financial affairs, defense, and internal security. The Executive Council advises the governor. The House of Assembly has two *ex officio* members, two nominated members, and seven elected members. Other political positions include that of attorney general and secretary to the Executive Council.

**Leadership and Political Officials.** Before Anguilla became a dependent British territory, the chief minister held executive power. For two decades the position of chief minister alternated between two political rivals: Ronald Webster of the People's Progressive Party, and Emile Gumbs of the Anguilla National Alliance. Several coalition governments were formed during this period as Anguillans sought to obtain total independence from Saint Kitts. The chief executive is now the governor. In 1990 the position of deputy governor was created. The three ruling parties are the Anguilla United Party, the Anguilla Democratic Party, and the Anguilla National Alliance.

**Social Problems and Control.** Until recently, Anguilla's most urgent social problem was unemployment. The rapid expansion of the economy and the sudden demand for labor have caused unemployment rates to drop dramatically. However, Anguil-

*A string band plays on Scilly Cay. Tourism is now the most widespread commercial concern in Anguilla.*

lans must now contend with some of the negative effects of the tourism boom: dealing with large numbers of non-Anguillans who sometimes are insensitive to their customs; pollution; rising prices; a strain on the island's resources; and the influence of other cultures on their way of life. Other social concerns include maintaining their cultural traditions without giving up the benefits of increased trade and business with other countries, improving living standards, and keeping the illegal drug trade out of Anguilla.

***Military Activity.*** Great Britain is responsible for Anguilla's defense. The island has a small police force.

## SOCIAL WELFARE AND CHANGE PROGRAMS

As a dependent territory, Great Britain provides economic aid and social programs for Anguilla. Other development and welfare programs are supported by the United Nations and the United States. These programs are for general Caribbean economic development, increasing trade and improving living conditions. They also provide assistance in times of natural disaster.

## GENDER ROLES AND STATUSES

***Division of Labor by Gender.*** More Anguillan women work outside the home than a generation ago, but men still comprise the majority of the workforce. Women own shops or work in the tourist business, in hotels, restaurants, or markets. Women are also employed in agricultural work. However, many women may stop working temporarily when they have young children, returning to work when their children are more independent. Since many businesses and farms are small and family-run, women have a degree of autonomy in work. The recent high demand for labor has also provided jobs for women that previously were nonexistent. Men are more likely than women to be involved in businesses such as fishing, boat construction, and running diving and sailing businesses for tourists.

***The Relative Status of Women and Men.*** General economic and living conditions have improved for all Anguillans. However, more men than women travel abroad to find work, hold political office, and own businesses. The home and family are still considered to be women's main responsibilities, and for the most part women are dependent on male family members or husbands for economic support.

## MARRIAGE, FAMILY, AND KINSHIP

***Marriage.*** The extended family is central to Anguillan and West Indian societies in general. Despite the strong influences of the Methodist and Anglican Churches, historically marriage was not considered obligatory for the creation of a family or a domestic living arrangement. During the eighteenth and nineteenth centuries, apart from the small upper class of English landowners, social conditions and slavery made the creation of long-lasting unions very difficult. Men and women frequently lived together in common law marriages for varying lengths of time. It was not infrequent for women and men to have children with more than one partner. Marriage in the Western sense was more likely to occur among the upper and middle classes. Today marriage is considered a cornerstone of family and social life, and weddings are community events.

***Domestic Unit.*** The basic domestic unit is generally a family headed by a mother and father. Under them are their children, often with one or more older relative, such as a grandparent, living under the same roof. As a result of very minimal class and economic differences, Anguillan family life has generally been more stable from a historical point of

*Shipwright David Hodge, known for building some of the fastest boats in Anguilla, stands by one of the boats he has built by hand.*

view than in some other Caribbean islands, where extremely poor economic and social conditions frequently contributed to the breakdown of the domestic unit. The domestic unit is generally stable until children reach adulthood and leave to start their own families. Daughters generally live at home with their parents until they are married.

**Inheritance.** Today as a British dependent territory, Anguilla's laws governing inheritance are based on Great Britain's. Until recently, inheritance always passed to the oldest son, or to oldest daughter if there were no males heirs. Past inheritance laws also excluded women from holding property.

**Kin Groups.** The extended family, particularly the network of female family members, often extends to include whole communities in Anguilla. The island's population is descended from the small group of people who arrived there two centuries ago, and as a result family groups are the basis for Anguillan society. Kin groups are extensive yet closely-knit, united by their collective past. A kin group can include many related families living near each other, or families in various parts of the island bound by surname. In terms of domestic organization and management, kin groups are matriarchal

in nature, with mother and grandmothers taking responsibility for important family decisions.

## SOCIALIZATION

**Infant Care.** Infants and young children are cared for at home by their mothers or other female relatives. Increased government spending for education has provided funds for early childhood education and care and assistance to working mothers. However, most children remain at home until they begin elementary school at age five.

**Child Rearing and Education.** Anguilla, like many other islands of the West Indies, sought to improve literacy rates and educational standards in the second half of the twentieth century. Between the ages of five and fourteen education is obligatory and free through a public school system. There are several primary schools and a secondary school.

**Higher Education.** For advanced, specialized training or a university degree, Anguillans must either go to another Caribbean country or leave the area. In 1948 the University of the West Indies was established in Jamaica to provide higher education for all English-speaking countries in the region. It has created an intellectual center for the West Indies in general and serves as an important contact with the international academic community.

## ETIQUETTE

Although the daily pace is generally relaxed and unhurried, Anguillans maintain a degree of formality in public life. Politeness and manners are considered important. As Anguilla's popularity as a tourist destination has grown, Anguillans have found themselves faced with confronting the problems that tourism can bring while trying not to lose an important source of income. Nude sunbathing is strictly prohibited, and wearing swimsuits anywhere outside of beach areas is not permitted. Anguillans always address each other by title—Mr., Mrs., etc.—unless they are on very personal terms. People in positions of importance are addressed using their job title with their last names, such as Nurse Smith or Officer Green. In an effort to maintain its low crime rate, Anguilla also enforces a strict antidrug policy, which includes careful search of all items or luggage brought onto the island.

## RELIGION

**Religious Beliefs.** Protestant churches, namely Anglican and Methodist, constitute the largest religious affiliation. Roman Catholicism is the second-largest religious group. Obeah, which is similar to voodoo and based on religious practices of African slaves brought to Anguilla, also is practiced by some.

## MEDICINE AND HEALTH CARE

Health standards are good, and birth and death rates are balanced. Anguilla has a small hospital, and limited health care is available through a government health program. For complicated or long-term medical treatment Anguillans must leave the island.

## SECULAR CELEBRATIONS

Important secular holidays and celebrations include Anguilla Day, 30 May; the Queen's Birthday, 19 June; Caricom Day, 3 July; Constitution Day, 11 August; and Separation Day, 19 December. Carnival is held the first week of August and includes parades, folk music, traditional dances, competitions, and a street fair. Colorful and elaborate costumes are worn in the Carnival parades, and it is a time for Anguillans to celebrate their history.

## THE ARTS AND HUMANITIES

Anguilla has several small art galleries, shops that sell local crafts, and a museum with exhibitions relating to Anguillan history, including prehistoric artifacts found on the island. Although there is no permanent theater on the island, various theatrical performances are held regularly. The Anguilla Arts Festival is held every other year and includes workshops, exhibits, and an art competition.

## BIBLIOGRAPHY

Burton, Richard D.E. *Afro–Creole: Power, Opposition, and Play in the Caribbean*, 1997.

Comitas, Lambros, and David Lowenthal. *Work and Family Life: West Indian Perspectives*, 1973.

Kurlansky, Mark. *A Continent of Island: Searching for Caribbean Destiny*, 1993.

Lewis, Gordon K. *The Growth of the Modern West Indies*, 1968.

Rogozinski, Jan. *A Brief History of the Caribbean: From the Arawak and Carib to the Present*, 2000.

Westlake, Donald. *Under an English Heaven*, 1973.

Williams, Eric. *From Columbus to Castro: A History of the Caribbean, 1492–1969*, 1984.

### Web Sites

''Calabash Skyviews.'' Anguilla history homepage. www.skyviews.com.

—M. CAMERON ARNOLD

# ANTIGUA AND BARBUDA

## CULTURE NAME

Antiguan; Antiguan creole; creole; Barbudan

## ORIENTATION

**Identification.** The culture of Antigua and Barbuda (local creole pronunciation, Antiga and Barbueda) is a classic example of a creole culture. It emerged from the mixing of Amerindian (Carib and Arawak), West African, and European (primarily British) cultural traditions. Specific traces of these parent cultures as well as influences from other Caribbean islands (e.g., reggae from Jamaica) are still very evident in this emergent culture. Before Christopher Columbus arrived in 1493, Antigua and Barbuda had the Carib names of Wadadli and Wa'omoni, respectively.

**Location and Geography.** Antigua and Barbuda are two islands in the Eastern Caribbean chain. Antigua, or Wadadli, has an area of 108 square miles, (280 square kilometers) while Barbuda, or Wa'omoni, is 62 square miles (160 square kilometers) in area, making for a twin island microstate of 170 square miles (440 square kilometers). This state includes the tiny (by Caribbean standards) island of Redonda, which has remained uninhabited. Antigua is an island of both volcanic origin and sedimentary rock (limestone) formation. Its jagged coastline is over 90 miles (145 kilometers) long, producing hundreds of beautiful white sand beaches, bays, and coves. Barbuda is of limestone formation and very flat. The highest point on the island rises to only 128 feet (39 meters). The capital of this state is Saint John's, which is located at the northwestern end of Antigua.

**Demography.** The population census of 1991 estimated the population of Antigua and Barbuda to be 64,252. Approximately 93 percent of this total are Afro-Antiguans and Barbudans, 0.2 percent are Portuguese, 0.6 percent are Middle Eastern, 1.7 percent are whites from Europe and North America,

and 3.4 percent are mixed. The 1997 estimate by the Department of Statistics placed the population at 69,890 and projected a figure of 72,310 for 2000. These increases are the result of significant inflows of migrants from Guyana, Dominica, and the Dominican Republic. Migrants from the latter have given rise to a small Spanish-speaking community on Antigua.

**Linguistic Affiliation.** Given the creole nature of its culture, it is not surprising that the language spoken by the vast majority of Antiguans and Barbudans is a creole, often referred to as Antiguan creole. This makes the culture a bilingual one. The other language is standard English, which is the official language and the language of instruction. This linguistic situation derives from the colonial history of the nation, which was one of 350 years of near continuous British rule. Consequently, Antiguan creole is essentially a hybrid product of West African languages and English. Although linguists have identified African words such as *nyam* (eat) in Antiguan creole, the vocabulary of this language consists largely of English words and distinct creole formations (*gee* = give) or distinct usages of English words. As one moves up the class hierarchy, there is a gradual shift from creole to English as the first language.

**Symbolism.** The cultural symbols that embody the national identity of Antigua and Barbuda emerged out of the anticolonial struggles for political independence, which began in the 1930s. Consequently these symbols tend to be images that celebrate liberation from a number of oppressive conditions and periods in the history of the nation: the ending of slavery in 1834, the rise of the labor movement in the 1930s, the revival of African elements in the national culture during the 1960s, and the still ongoing enhancing of the nation's creole culture vis-á-vis Western and particularly British and American culture. Good examples of these symbols are the national anthem, the flag, and the national

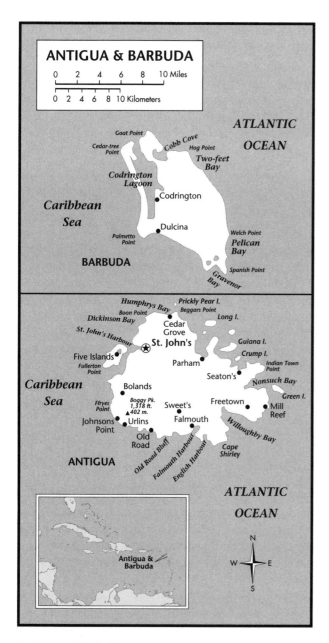

*Antigua and Barbuda*

coats of arm, which display the sun, a pineapple, and the flowers and seas of the state. They can also be seen in more fleeting form in festivals such as carnival.

## HISTORY AND ETHNIC RELATIONS

**Emergence of the Nation.** The emergence of Antigua and Barbuda as an independent nation was the result of the confluence of a number of international currents with the local struggles for decolonization. The turning point in this history of anticolonial struggle was the series of peasant/

worker insurrections that occurred in the Caribbean between 1935 and 1939, with the latter year being the one in which Antiguan and Barbudan workers and peasants revolted. Out of this revolt came the formation of the Antigua Trades Labor Union (ATLU) in 1939. The need for such an organization was recognized by several individuals—a group that included Harold Wilson, Norris Allen, Reginald Stevens, and V. C. Bird. Allen took the lead by calling the meeting at which the union was formed. Stevens was its first president and Berkeley Richards its first general secretary.

As the union got more deeply involved in the struggles of workers against sugar plantation owners, it became increasingly political. It very quickly developed a "political arm," which later became the Antigua Labor Party (ALP). This radicalization increased under the leadership of Bird, the ATLU's second president. Bird vigorously pushed a heady mix of laborism and state capitalism that came to be known locally as milk and water socialism.

Further, through its political arm, the ATLU began successfully contesting the small number of seats in the legislature that were elective. The resulting acquisition of a measure of state power changed the balance of forces in the struggles of workers with plantation owners. Between 1940 and 1951, universal adult suffrage and self-government became high-priority demands of the union. From this point on the labor movement could not be distinguished from the nationalist movement. This politicization led to new rounds of strikes and political confrontations with the planters and the elites of the colonial state. These struggles, reinforced by those in other Caribbean territories, by the struggles in African countries, and by the opposition of the United States and Russia to European colonial policies, finally pushed the British to dismantle their empire. The dismantling was executed via a process of constitutional decolonization that gradually transferred sovereignty to a set of elected leaders such as those of the ALP. Between 1950 and 1981, when Antigua and Barbuda achieved independence from Britain, there were at least five important sets of decolonizing constitutional changes that paved the way to national independence. As the leader of the ALP, Bird was the nation's first prime minister.

**Ethnic Relations.** Behind the late twentieth century reviving and respecifying of the place of Afro-Antiguans and Barbudans in the cultural life of the society, is a history of race/ethnic relations that systematically excluded them. Within the colonial framework established by the British soon after their initial settlement of Antigua in 1623, five distinct and carefully ranked race/ethnic groups emerged. At the top of this hierarchy were the British, who justified their hegemony with arguments of white supremacy and civilizing missions. Among themselves, there were divisions between British Antiguans and noncreolized Britons, with the latter coming out on top. In short, this was a race/ethnic hierarchy that gave maximum recognition to Anglicized persons and cultural practices.

Immediately below the British were the mulattos, a mixed race group that resulted from unions between black Africans and white Europeans. Mulattos were lighter in shade than the masses of black Africans, and on that basis distinguished themselves from the latter. They developed complex ideologies of shade to legitimate their claims to higher status. These ideologies of shade paralleled in many ways British ideologies of white supremacy.

Next in this hierarchy were the Portuguese— twenty-five hundred of whom migrated as workers from Madeira between 1847 and 1852 because of a severe famine. Many established small businesses and joined the ranks of the mulatto middle class. The British never really considered Portuguese as whites and so they were not allowed into their ranks. Among Portuguese Antiguans and Barbudans, status differences move along a continuum of varying degrees of assimilation into the Anglicized practices of the dominant group.

Below the Portuguese were the Middle Easterners, who began migrating to Antigua and Barbuda around the turn of the twentieth century. Starting as itinerant traders, they soon worked their way into the middle strata of the society. Although Middle Easterners came from a variety of areas in the Middle East, as a group they are usually referred to as Syrians.

Fifth and finally were the Afro-Antiguans and Barbudans who were located at the bottom of this hierarchy. Forced to "emigrate" as slaves, Africans started arriving in Antigua and Barbuda in large numbers during the 1670s. Very quickly they came to constitute the majority of the population. As they entered this hierarchy, Africans were profoundly racialized. They ceased being Yoruba, Igbo, or Akan and became Negroes or Blacks. This racialization biologized African identities, dehumanizing and deculturing them in the process. As Negroes, it was the body and particularly its skin color that emerged as the new signifiers of identity. As a result, Afro-Antiguans and Barbudans were reinscribed in a dehumanized and racialized discourse that established their inferiority, and hence the legitimacy of their earlier enslavement and later exploitation as wage laborers.

In the last decade, Spanish-speaking immigrants from the Dominican Republic and Afro-Caribbea immigrants from Guyana and Dominica have been added to this ethnic mosaic. They have entered at the bottom of the hierarchy and it is still too early to predict what their patterns of assimilation and social mobility will be.

## FOOD AND ECONOMY

*Food in Daily Life.* Antigua and Barbuda has long imported most of its food, so it is not surprising that the food eaten by Antiguans and Barbudans consists of creole dishes or specialties that reflect the cuisine of the parent cultures. In recent years, there has been a strong invasion of American fast-food chains, such as Kentucky Fried Chicken. Among the more established creole specialties of Antigua and Barbuda are rice pudding, salt fish and antrobers (eggplant; the national breakfast), bull foot soup, souse, maw, goat water, cockle (clam) water, conch water, and Dukuna. The salted cod used in making the national breakfast is not a local fish. It is an import from the United States and Canada that has been imported since before the revolt of the American colonies.

*Major Industries.* Sugar dominated the economy of Antigua and Barbuda for much of its history. The period of sugar dominance began in the 1660s after the failure of attempts to make money from tobacco. Between 1700 and 1775, Antigua and Barbuda emerged as a classic sugar colony. Because of its exclusive specialization in sugar, the economy was not very diverse. Consequently, it imported a lot, including much of its food from the American colonies and Britain.

After 1775, the economy entered a long period of decline that ended almost two centuries later in 1971. The revolt of the American colonies (1776), the suspension of the British slave trade (1804), the British vote to end slavery (1834), and the British conversion to free trade (1842) all combined to destroy the foundations of the sugar-based economy. The American revolution took away Antigua and Barbuda's cheap food supplies, the changes in British slave policies cut off its labor supplies, while the changes in trade policy took away its guaranteed market. The result was a decline from which sugar never really recovered, along with the need for a new leading sector.

*Antigua's historic windmills are remnants of the island's one-time role as a major sugar producer.*

Concerted efforts at industrialization in the 1940s and 1950s failed. Attracted to Antigua and Barbuda's many beaches, white sands, and sunny climate, wealthy Americans found it a great place to vacation. Out of this demand, tourism emerged as the new leading and rapidly growing sector of the economy. In 1958 tourist arrivals totaled 12,853; by 1970, on the eve of sugar's demise, they had risen to 67,637. In 1998 tourist arrivals reached 204,000. The impact of tourism on the growth of the national economy has been significant. In 1973 the gross domestic product (GDP) of the economy was US $73.3 million. By 1998 the GDP had reached US $423 million. In 1973 the hotel and restaurant sector accounted for 7.9 percent of the nation's GDP. By 1979, the figure had doubled to 14 percent, where it remained into the twenty-first century.

In spite of the growth in tourism and its expansive impact on the construction and transportation sectors, the economy is still not diversified. As in the sugar period, there is an overspecialization that keeps imports high, including food. By the late 1980s, the environmental impact of tourism had become a major political issue, with groups of environmentalists blocking the construction of new hotels.

The newest emerging sector is offshore banking. Because of the secretive and confidential aspects of this industry, it is emerging under clouds of controversy. The government, however, is committed, to its development.

The currency of Antigua and Barbuda is the Eastern Caribbean dollar, which has had a fairly steady exchange rate of approximately 2.70 with the U.S. dollar.

## SOCIAL STRATIFICATION

***Classes and Castes.*** Like many other Caribbean societies, Antigua and Barbuda is a classic case of the superimposition of race on class and vice versa. Consequently, the class structure reflects very much the race/ethnic hierarchy described earlier. Until the rise of the nationalist movement, the dominant class was clearly the British sugar planters. They monopolized the labor of the masses of Afro-Antiguans and Barbudans, who also constituted the subordinate working class. Between these two extremes was a middle class that consisted of the same three groups that occupied the middle layers of the race/ethnic hierarchy—the mulattos, Portuguese, and Syrians. The mulattos dominated the professions (law, medicine, and architecture) and the white-collar positions in banks, businesses, and the

*Antigua's English Harbour. Tourists are increasingly drawn to the region's sunny climate and unique cultural mix.*

though the work has shifted from plantations to hotels.

Important changes have also occurred in the middle levels of the class hierarchy. This layer has ceased to be a predominantly mulatto class and has become one that is predominantly black. This shift was a direct consequence of changes in patterns of black social mobility produced by black control of the decolonized state. Nevertheless, the middle class still retains its mulatto, Portuguese, and Syrian components.

## POLITICAL LIFE

***Government.*** The political institutions of Antigua and Barbuda have gone through three basic stages: a period of colonial plantocratic democracy (1623–1868), a phase of colonial authoritarianism (1868–1939), and a period of liberal democracy (1940–present). Since the enactment of universal suffrage in 1951, elections have been contested every five years without major interruptions. But because of informal pressures and ways of accumulating power, the political system has oscillated between periods of one-party and two-party dominance, with the latter occurring from 1943 to 1967, and the former in two periods: 1968–1980 and 1992 to the present.

## MARRIAGE, FAMILY, AND KINSHIP

***Marriage.*** Families in Antigua and Barbuda are creole formations. Among the white upper class creolization is minimal. Patterns of marriage, family organization, and gender roles are similar to those in the West with minor local adaptations. Much the same is true of the middle classes except for the greater presence of local adaptations. Among the black working class, family life is much more a mixture of the African and European systems. Although the institutions of bridewealth (marriage payments) and lineage groups have been lost, the African view of marriage as a process occurring over many years has been retained. Without the sanction of bridewealth, family for a young couple begins in what have been called visiting relationships, which often become coresidential, and may finally issue in a formal marriage ceremony that is Christian. Like many African families, these creole families are matrifocal, centering on the mother's lineage, with strong traditions of women working outside of the home. There are, as a result, very high rates of labor force participation for Antiguan and Barbudan women.

civil service. Some engaged in small enterprises, but this was primarily a white-collar/professional class. The Portuguese located themselves in the service areas of the retail sector, importing and reselling a wide variety of goods. Consequently, their stores varied from liquor shops, through groceries and gas stations, to stationery stores. Syrians were also in the retail sector importing primarily dry goods such as cloth, clothes, and other household items. Thus unlike the British planters, the latter two groups included small to medium capitalists, who employed small numbers of Afro-Antiguan and Barbudan workers.

In the postcolonial period, there have been significant changes in this class structure even though its basic categories and rank orderings have remained. At the top, hotel owners and offshore bankers have replaced the planters. These are primarily white Americans, with British investors regaining some ground. At the bottom is a working class that is still predominantly Afro-Antiguan and Barbudan. Because of recent changes in immigration policies, however, significant numbers of Afro-Guyanese and Afro-Dominican workers have been added to the ranks of this class. Thus the bottom of the class hierarchy remains primarily black even

*This cannon reflects Antigua's colonial past, which began with British settlement of the island in 1623.*

## RELIGION

***Religious Beliefs.*** The religious life of Antiguans and Barbudans is predominantly Christian. In 1991, 32 percent of the population was Anglican, 12 percent was Moravian, 10 percent was Catholic, and 9 percent Methodist. This Christian orientation, however, is a creolized one that changes as we move up the class hierarchy. For most of their history, the churches of Antigua and Barbuda were colonial institutions—overseas branches of England-based churches, whose pastors were in control. Thus, unlike the African American church, the Afro-Antiguan and Barbudan church does not have a long history of autonomous development. Autonomy came with the independence of the state.

In spite of this Anglicization, religious practices have not escaped creolization. Among Afro-Antiguans and Barbudans, traces of the African religious heritage have survived in the practice of Obeah and in inclinations toward more ecstatic modes of worship. The postcolonial period has witnessed a significant creolizing of church music, which has been influenced by calypso, reggae, and African American gospel music.

## THE ARTS AND HUMANITIES

The more developed art forms of Antigua and Barbuda are mas (street theater), theater, calypso, steel band, architecture, poetry, and fiction. Less well developed are the arts of painting, sculpture, and carving. In the case of the more developed art forms, processes of cultural hybridization have successfully produced distinct creole formations that are expressively linked to the subjectivity and rituals of Antiguans and Barbudans.

***Literature.*** In the area of fiction and poetry, writers include Jamaica Kincaid, Ralf Prince, Elaine Olaoye, and Dorbrene Omard.

***Performance Arts.*** Good examples of distinct creole formations are calypso and steel band. Set to a distinct rhythmic beat, calypsos are songs of social commentary that range from the comic to the tragic. One of the major consequences of decolonization on this art form has been its expansion to include religious themes and situations. Among the calypso kings of Antigua and Barbuda are Short Shirt, Swallow, Obstinate, Onyan, and Smarty Jr.

One of the few musical instruments invented in the twentieth century, steel bands consist of a number of ''pans''—base pans, tenor pans, etc. They are made by pounding the basic notes out of the surface of steel drums used to transport oil. Bands range in size from about ten to one hundred pans. Developed first in Trinidad in the 1930s, the tradition spread quickly to Antigua and Barbuda. Well-known steel bands from Antigua and Barbuda include Brute Force, Hells Gate, Harmonites, Supa Stars, and Halcyon.

## THE STATE OF THE PHYSICAL AND SOCIAL SCIENCES

The sciences are not well developed in Antigua and Barbuda. Natural sciences such as physics and chemistry are particularly weak. This is also true for the larger Caribbean region. The practice of science in the region is located primarily at the University of the West Indies, whose main campuses are in Jamaica, Trinidad, and Barbados. The university's extramural department, however, has a branch in Antigua, where the first year of the bachelor's degree in some of the social sciences can be done, with the remainder being completed at one of the main campuses. The most prominent science journals are in the social sciences, which are led by economics and political science. Among Antigua and Barbuda's outstanding contributions to the pool of regional scientists are Ashly Bryant, Percival Perry, Samuel

Daniel, Ermina Oshoba, Vincent Richards, and Enoch James.

## BIBLIOGRAPHY

Davis, Gregson. *Antigua Black*, 1973.

Gaspar, David Barry. *Bondmen and Rebels*, 1985.

Henry, Paget. *Peripheral Capitalism and Underdevelopment in Antigua*, 1985.

Kincaid, Jamaica. *Annie John*, 1985.

———. *A Small Place*, 1988.

Langhan, Mrs. *Antigua and Antiguans*, 1844.

Olaoye, Elaine. *Passion of the Soul*, 1998.

Oliver, V. *The History of the Island of Antigua*, 1894.

Prince, Ralf. *Jewels of the Sun*, 1979.

Richards, Novelle. *The Struggle and the Conquest*, 1967.

———. *The Twilight Hour*, 1971.

Smith, Keithlyn. *No Essay Pushover*, 1994.

Tongue, Gwen. *Cooking Antigua's Food*, 1973.

—PAGET HENRY

# ARGENTINA

## CULTURE NAME

Argentine, Argentinean

## ALTERNATIVE NAMES

National culture, *ser nacional* (national being), *cultura rioplatense, cultura gauchesca, cultura criolla* (creole culture). In Argentina the word *creole* often has a different connotation than in the rest of Latin America. While in most countries the word is used to refer to the offspring of Europeans born in the Americas, in Argentina it generally connotes a person of mixed origins, European (mainly Spanish) and Native American. Many people use it as a synonym for *gaucho* (Argentine cowboys) and *mestizo*. It is also known as *cultura rioplatense* (River Plate culture). This is a more inclusive concept, as it refers to the culture of Uruguayans and Argentines inhabiting the River Plate Basin region. Official conservative interpretations of the Argentine culture have often emphasized the Spanish and Catholic heritage, rooted in the early contributions made by Queen Isabel of Castille and Ferdinand of Aragon, artifices of the conquest of the Americas in the late fifteenth and early sixteenth century. Latin Americans often identify Argentines as ''*Ches*,'' a colloquial form of address for the second person, similar to the American ''hey, you.'' This is the reason Ernesto Guevara, the Argentine-born commander of the Cuban Revolution, was called ''*el Che*.''

## ORIENTATION

*Identification.* It is generally claimed that by the end of the sixteenth century, Martín del Barco Centenera first used the current name of the country in the poem ''Argentina y Conquista del Desierto.'' The name derives from the Latin word for silver, the metal the Spanish thought they would find in this land. What constitutes Argentina's national culture is a politically loaded debate. Some nationalist and populist sectors see only the *gaucho* tradition as the

defining element of Argentine culture. Only male models enter into these interpretations. The gauchos were horsemen who tended cattle in the central plains region of Argentina. These men were *mestizos*, the product of colonial hybridization who were the offspring of Europeans (mainly Spanish), and indigenous peoples. Ultra-nationalist versions of this culture stress the arabic origins of gaucho culture, claiming that arabic traits were brought by the Spanish who had been profoundly transformed by centuries of Muslim occupation. Nationalist versions also often acknowledge the contributions of indigenous peoples to the national culture. Conservative elite sectors historically traced the origins of the national culture to the Roman Catholic and Spanish tradition. Threatened by the influx of European immigrants at the turn of the century, some landed elite sectors chose to adopt gauchos as a cultural icon. These rural versions of nationality generally clashed with more secular, urban, and modern versions of national identity. Ambivalence dominates the Argentines' self-identity. Depending on the political climate of the times and the dominant ideological orientations, residents of this country oscillate between an identity stressing commonalities with other Latin-American nations; a shared history of four centuries of Spanish rule; and an identity highlighting the uniqueness of this nation, an alleged Europeanized cosmopolitan national culture. Some regional cultural traditions are quite distinct. In the northwest the influence of Pre-Columbian Andean indigenous traditions is very strong while in the northeast (mainly in Corrientes and south of Misiones province) the Guaraní indigenous influence is apparent in speech styles, music, food, local customs, and beliefs.

*Location and Geography.* The Argentine Republic is located at the southernmost part of South America. It extends along 2299 miles (3,700 kilometers) between parallels 22 and 55. It occupies an area of 1.4 million square miles (3.7 million square kilometers). This includes the Antarctica and the South

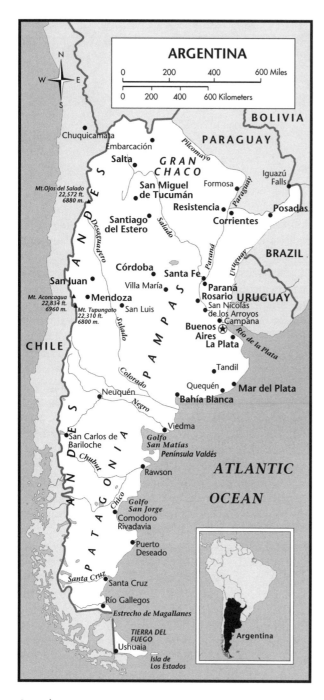

*Argentina*

for ranching. These lands occupy 826,254 square miles (2.14 million square kilometers). There are considerable climatic, soil, and vegetation differences, from subtropical, hot, and humid forests and wetlands in the northeast to arid plains and sierras with dry grasses, scrub, shrubs, and hardwoods in the Chaco, Patagonia, and in the Andes. Uneven regional development characterizes Argentina. Wool, refrigerated meats, and grains are the basis of the thriving economy of the pampas region. Changes in the transportation infrastructure, mainly the construction of railroads, facilitated the integration into the world capitalist economy, from which Buenos Aires and other port cities benefitted greatly. Buenos Aires, the capital, acquired such a dominance that it led many observers to refer to it and its culture as if it were the whole country. The city and the rural areas surrounding it are the source of the most powerful understanding of national identity. The agrarian construct of a national identity is formed by the customs and beliefs of the *gauchos* of the pampas, a group that disappeared with the modernization of the rural economy. The urban constructs of a national culture are centered in the city of Buenos Aires. A dominant version portrays Argentines as sophisticated and highly educated people of European origin. Another urban version highlights aspects of popular culture seen as a product of internal and foreign immigration. Population and wealth are unequally distributed. As of 2000, a third of the national population lived in metropolitan Buenos Aires. Buenos Aires and the neighboring pampas region have a concentration of most of the wealth of the country (roughly 80 percent of Argentina's industrial activity and 70 percent of the agrarian production) and most of the inhabitants (nearly 70 percent of the total population of the country). In the early 1980s President Raúl Alfonsín failed in his efforts to move the capital city to more neutral space to compensate for regional imbalances and to encourage the emergence of other commercial activities.

**Demography.** Argentina's total population is 36.1 million. Estimates for the indigenous population vary. There is no consensus on how an Indian is defined (e.g. place of residence, self-identity), and provincial governments have adopted different definitions.

**Linguistic Affiliation.** The majority of the population speaks Spanish. Argentines say that it is more appropriate to call their language Castilian, because this term expresses more clearly the region in Spain where it originated and from where it was imposed

Atlantic Islands, territories over which Argentina claims national sovereignty. Argentina is the eighth largest country in the world. The country borders Chile to the west, Bolivia to the north, Paraguay to the northeast, and Brazil, Uruguay, and the Atlantic Ocean to the East. The country is organized into twenty-three provinces. Because of its vast length it is comprised of very diverse environments. A large part of the territory is in a temperate zone, mainly plains and the pampas grazelands which are ideal

on other peoples. There are slight regional variations in vocabulary, intonation, and in the pronunciation of certain sounds such as "*y*" and "*ll*." At the time of the Spanish conquest, the land was inhabited by various indigenous groups, but most of the original languages and communities have been irrevocably lost. Two indigenous languages, *Quechua* and *Guaraní*, became lingua franca and were learned by scholars and by nonindigenous settlers in specific regions of Argentina. Quechua was mainly used in northwestern and central provinces, while Guarani was mainly spoken in the northeast. Today, they are spoken by some residents in provinces such as Santiago del Estero and Corrientes. Knowledge of these languages is generally devalued and rarely acknowledged. No serious official efforts exist to preserve indigenous languages. Only a few schools attempt to offer bilingual education for indigenous children. The Argentine school system has never developed special education programs for bilingual children, either during the great migration at the end of the nineteenth century or with the late twentieth century influx of Latin American, eastern European, African, and Asian migrant populations. Besides regional variations of Spanish and indigenous languages, Argentines often employ some *lunfardo* terms and linguistic structure in their colloquial language. Initially used by people such as criminals and prostitutes, Lunfardo became popular through tango music and has been gradually adopted by all class sectors. Lunfardo borrows and transforms words from Spanish, Portuguese, Italian, French, and indigenous languages such as Quechua, reflecting the complex processes of the formation of national cultures in both their popular and cultivated expressions.

**Symbolism**. Argentineans' cultural symbols are mostly the result of hybridization. Football (soccer in the United States) and tango (which encompasses more than just the dance itself) are probably the two strongest symbols of a common national identity. Tango refers to the music, the lyrics, and the dance itself and is a complex urban product that originated in lower-class neighborhoods of Buenos Aires city. The music, its lyrics, and the dance represent the profound transformation of the urban landscape at the beginning of the twentieth century, with the influx of diverse European immigrants. Tango expresses the amalgamation of already existing traditions, themselves a mixture of African, indigenous, and Spanish influences with elements brought by Italians, Spaniards, French, Germans, Polish, and Jews. Argentine nationalists felt threatened by the newcomers because they felt they jeopardized the existing hierarchical system of social relations and refused to see tango as a national cultural product.

Tango was also a moral threat. The sensuality of the dance and the lyrics emphasizing lowlife values and language challenged bourgeois morality and dominant views on appropriate female behavior. It also romanticized a particular male behavior that kept men away from the home. Tango men spent their days in bordellos, sites identified not only with sexual encounters, but also with intense political activity.

The popularization of football is partly explained by social reformers' concerns with appropriate behavior and the proper place of Argentine men and women. British citizens introduced football to the city of Buenos Aires in the early 1860s. The game went unnoticed until Argentine politicians deliberately promoted the sport. From the 1920s to the 1940s military and civilian moral reformers attempted to construct nationhood on the basis of the "true" traditions of Argentina. They encouraged folk music (the music of the motherland) and discouraged tango, which was believed to be the expression of foreigners with dubious morals. As part of this neo-Victorian prudery, Argentina's rulers promoted sports as healthy and hygienic pursuits which would keep men away from the cabarets and bordellos where tango music reigned.

Besides music and sports, food is also a powerful cultural symbol. Argentines sometimes use the expression "she or he is more Argentine than *dulce de leche*." Dulce de leche is a milk-and-sugar spread used in a manner similar to peanut butter in the United States. It appears on toast, pastries, and various confections. Argentine *asado*, a barbecue that is part of the gaucho heritage, is still one of the most important meals in the Argentine diet. Like football, it is a strongly gendered cultural symbol, associated with manliness. Shopping for beef, sausages, and other animal parts that go into a barbecue, as well as the cooking itself, is a male activity. Asados are an important part of Argentine socializing on any occasion.

*Mate* drinking is also seen as a feature of the cultura rioplatense. Mate refers both to the container where a popular infusion is prepared and to the drink itself. The container might be simply made out of a gourd or might be carefully crafted in silver or other metals. It is drunk with a special metal straw with holes in one end to filter leaves. The slightly stimulating infusion is made with leaves

*A fountain in the Plaza del Congreso in Buenos Aires.*

from the *Yerba mate* (*ilex paraguaiensis*) plant which is cultivated in northeast Argentina. Migrants adopted mate consumption and became so adept that some of those returning to their original countries carried this custom with them. Because of this, countries such as Syria and Lebanon now import Yerba mate from Argentina.

Certain men and women stand as undeniable national icons. Historical figures, sportsmen and sportswomen, politicians, and intellectuals contribute to a common identity. Who best represents or plays a role in shaping who Argentines are and had been is a highly contested issue. Several men and women are important in the development of *argentinidad*. However, there would be no agreement on whether they positively or negatively fostered the rise of some kind of national consciousness.

José de San Martín is probably the least controversial of many Argentine icons. Seen as liberator of the Americas in the nineteenth century, he stands as a moral model to be emulated. Some Argentines use him to represent how they would like to think of themselves vis-a-vis other Latin American nations: as messengers of modernity and freedom, without personal or national ambitions of domination. Juan Manuel de Rosas, a landowner from Buenos Aires province, who came to rule Buenos Aires province for almost thirty years and represents the interests

of the provinces before Argentina became unified as a nation, is a good example of the schisms in the process of nation building. Derided by the liberal, modernizing, and urban-oriented sectors of society who regarded him as a tyrant who deliberately kept the masses ignorant, he was an idol for the traditionalists who saw him as and adamant defender of national sovereignty against imperial ambitions. While Rosas was at the center of the disputes around the fate of Argentina in the nineteenth century, Juan Domingo Perón, was the focus of impassioned divisions among Argentines during the last half of the twentieth century. He ruled Argentina from 1946 to 1955 and again in 1973 until his death in 1974. Although some analysts draw parallels between Rosas and Perón, insisting that the two have defended the interests of the people against a foreign colonial order, the two are the products of very different Argentinas. Rosas ruled in an agrarian society of landlords and rural workers; Peron ruled in a predominantly urban society in which internal migrants to cities and the children of immigrants strove for greater participation as well as for recognition as part of the nation. María Eva Duarte de Perón, universally known as Evita, is undoubtedly the most renowned Argentine woman. President Perón's wife played an important role in the political and social recognition of underprivileged groups, mainly workers and women, until her early death in 1952. While political opponents dismissed her by stating that she was a bad actress with questionable morals, the popular sectors were encouraged by carefully crafted governmental propaganda and idolized her, seeing her as a saintly figure. After her death people lit candles next to photographs representing her surrounded by a halo.

Domingo Faustino Sarmiento, a liberal president of Argentina from 1868 to 1874, is probably better known for synthesizing the dilemmas of Argentine identity in his famous literary work, *Facundo*. This text is seen by some critics as the cathedral of Argentine culture. It describes a fragmented country which is torn between civilization and barbarism, with a rural backward interior dominated by authoritarian charismatic populist *caudillos* who refuse to enter into an orderly and rational modern way of life. Sarmiento is held responsible for bringing the country into the modern, literate world; he is the teacher par excellence, the founding father of the Argentine school system, and a role model to be followed—even today attending school every day is equated with "being a Sarmiento."

Sarmiento is either glorified or vilified, but no Argentine is indifferent to him. Although Facundo is meant to attack a rural order and the gaucho way of life, Sarmiento prose ironically continues to mystify the pampas.

While Facundo was intended to highlight the backwardness of the *mestizo* population, *Martín Fierro* by José Hernández exalted the values of gaucho culture. Despite their differences, both literary works became canonical texts for those attempting to define Argentine culture.

Argentines are quite uncertain about who they are. They oscillate between seeing themselves as a highly educated western nation and defining themselves as a Latin-American mestizo nation. This often obsessive search for a national soul became exacerbated when this relatively young nation was dramatically transformed by urbanization and the influx of immigrants. Uncertain about the existence of commonalities, many Argentines tried to find clues about themselves by looking at how other nations saw them. Success of Argentine national or cultural products abroad is translated as approval of the whole national body. Whoever or whatever thrives outside national boundaries rapidly metamorphasizes into even more powerful cultural symbols. It happened with tango after it succeeded in Europe, with soccer and soccer players like Maradona, with tennis players such as Guillermo Vilas and Gabriela Sabattini, with Nobel Prize winners such as Bernardo Houssay, Perez Esquivel, and Saavedra Lamas, with classical dancers such as Julio Bocca, with music composers as different as Alberto Ginastera and Astor Piazzola, with tango singers such as Carlos Gardel, and with folklore singers such as Mercedes Sosa.

Popular card games and table games also express the dilemmas of national culture and the way Argentines sometimes view themselves. One of the most popular card games is *truco* (trick). Supposedly a gaucho game in which country men displayed their ability to deceive their adversary, the game is accompanied by subtle body movements to warn partners about a player's strategy, and by recitation of country-inspired poetry. Country men known as *payadores* used to be valued for their ability to improvise in oral poetry duels showing their wit, sense of humor, and double entendre. Although payadores are a minority today and are unknown to the majority of the national population, many of their playful linguistic games are still present in everyday nicknames, jokes, and many other popular expressions as varied as graffiti and songs created by soccer fans and members of political parties.

For decades, *estancieros* (large landowners) were the richest and most politically powerful citizens. They constituted the ruling elite of the country for generations. For years, young children learned to accept this existing social order by playing games such as *El Estanciero*, a local version of *Monopoly*, in which the players accumulate land, ranches, livestock, and grains. Likewise, the yearly massive attendance to an exhibition in Buenos Aires commonly known as "the rural exhibit," legitimizes the dominant commercial activity of the nation as producer of cattle and grains, ruled by a class of landowners. Although the economy and social structure of Argentina has been dramatically transformed and the landed elites have lost considerable power, it is still commonly suggested that young women marry an estanciero to secure their own and their family's future.

The Argentine flag, the national anthem, and the *escarapela* (a small ribbon or bow worn on patriotic occasions) are the objects of officially prescribed rituals that must be followed by the population at the risk of serious sanctions. These rules had been strongly enforced during authoritarian regimes to the point that people risked imprisonment or even death if they failed to follow them. The population at large feels very strongly about these symbols: they display flags when the country is

A couple dance to the music of street performers in La Boca, a working-class neighborhood in Buenas Aires which was the first stop for many immigrants coming to the New World.

participating in world soccer cup matches or in war times such as when Argentina fought against the British during the Malvinas/Falklands conflict in the 1980s. At a popular level, large drums are always also present at any massive demonstration.

The ruling classes mobilize territory and sovereignty to develop a sense of national identity. The Malvinas/Falklands War clearly illustrates the importance of territory in the construction of national territory. Since early childhood, Argentines are repeatedly exposed to narratives emphasizing the importance of territory to the nation. They are taught that the British attempted to occupy the country on two occasions during the early nineteenth century, but the population resisted bravely by throwing burning oil from the roofs of their homes in Buenos Aires. Since the British occupation of the Malvinas Islands in 1833, statements claiming that the ''islands are Argentine'' and the demand for recovery have always stirred nationalist feelings. Argentine's takeover of the islands was presented as a way of healing wounds inflicted on the national body and as a means to recover dignity.

## HISTORY AND ETHNIC RELATIONS

*Emergence of the Nation.* During the Spanish conquest the territory was occupied by different colonizing attempts. Two of these attempts originated in already established Latin-American colonial centers with one more directly connected to Spain. These early forms of occupation reflected the development of relatively economically and culturally distinct regions, conditioned by the contributions made by indigenous groups and the constraints set by very different environments. Beginning with the early years of the conquest, the majority of the regions maintained strong ties with important Latin American colonial centers, while what came to be known as the Littoral and the Pampas in the east of the territory were in more direct contact with Spain, and consequently, Europe.

By the end of the Spanish Empire, in the late eighteenth century, the Bourbon reforms marked the fate of some regions until today. By creating the Viceroyalty of the Rio de la Plata, and by choosing Buenos Aires as the residence of its authorities, royal authorities acknowledged a process already under way. Buenos Aires was the center of intense smuggling, an activity that flourished as a challenge to the rigid crown regulations on imports. Slaves entered through the Rio de la Plata ports, and hides and tallow were exported from Buenos Aires. Subsequent Bourbon reforms allowed free trade from Buenos Aires. These changes had an extraordinary impact in the configuration of the future national space. The major beneficiary was the city and the neighboring interior. Buenos Aires experienced significant construction and technological improvements. It became the most important commercial and cultural center in South America. Enlightened ideas also came from Europe and influenced the thinking of urban elites, who gradually championed ideas of autonomy and economic liberalism. Most of the interior provinces started an irreversible process of economic decline, intensified after independence because commercial routes and connections were altered. Local craft industries which had developed to supply the demands of the colonial regional markets could no longer compete with the imported goods entering through the port of Buenos Aires.

While independence from Spain was achieved in 1816, Argentina did not become a unified nation until 1880. Confrontations between those who wanted greater regional autonomy (federalists) and those who wanted more centralized forms of government (unitarians) characterized the early post-independence years. Argentine history, mainly written by the victorious liberal elite sectors, refers to these schisms in Argentine society as civilization and barbarism—the modern Europeanized sectors against a traditional rural society characterized as violent, primitive, and vagrant. Some analysts assert that this antimony is misleading because it masks the continuity in the maintenance of power in the hands of landed elites until well into the twentieth century. During the nineteenth century, local identities prevailed, and men were generally recruited by force to participate in armed confrontations. The term *patria*—motherland—was generally used to refer to the native province, rather than to the Argentine nation. The Argentine elites who started to organize the nation after the defeat of what they saw as backwards social forces despised Indians and gauchos and deliberately attempted to whiten and modernize the country by promoting European immigration. The newly arrived immigrants changed both the rural and urban landscape of the *littoral* and pampas regions.

By the 1880s, the majority of the indigenous populations were dominated and pushed to marginal and inhospitable regions. Victory over the Indians of the Pampas and Patagonia was described as the Conquest of the Desert. Vast tracts of land were distributed among the conquerors. The gauchos, who had roamed in open spaces and sometimes escaped into Indian lands to avoid the militia, gradually disappeared from the countryside as a social group. They competed with the immigrants for salaried work in the ranches that were demarcated with barbed wire fences. Many landowners believed that gauchos were ill-suited for agricultural labor and favored the hiring of foreigners. Immigrants arrived by the thousands, to the point that in cities like Buenos Aires foreign-born residents outnumbered the Argentines. Many immigrants joined the industrial labor force. The strategy of encouraging immigration backfired on the ruling classes, who now felt threatened by these newcomers, some of whom introduced such political ideas as socialism and anarchism. These new political ideas, as well as the emergence of forms of popular culture, defied traditional morals and the dominant social and political order, pushing intellectuals and members of the ruling classes to search for what constituted a national soul. They searched for clues in the gaucho culture. This culture which had been doomed to disappearance with the modernization of the country, was reborn as a national myth by the same groups who had contributed to its earlier demise. While the foreign immigrants shook the social order with their labor strikes, and their public behavior became immortalized in popular forms such as

tango music and lyrics, many of their children displayed a more moderate behavior after increasingly becoming part of the mainstream national society and joining the rising middle class.

***National Identity.*** The educational system played an important role in incorporating new social groups into the nation. Despite regional and class differences, state institutions were quite successful in developing nationalist feelings. Although Argentines are overall very nationalistic, there is no agreement on what the basis for the commonality is. Debates over what constitutes a "national being" have been the source of bitter and often violent confrontations. To some, the national culture is a mixture of indigenous, Spanish, and Afro-Argentine traditions, dramatically modified by European immigrants at the beginning of the twentieth century, and experiencing further transformations with globalization in the late twentieth century. For others "true" nationhood is an unmodified essence rooted in the Catholic and Spanish heritage. During the Malvinas/Falklands War the first definition proved to be more powerful. The military government, until then a defender of the more conservative nationalism that emphasized the connection with "Mother Spain" and the Catholic Church and rejected everything that developed in the West after the French Revolution, was compelled to adopt symbols embraced by the population at large to gain their support. The same singers and popular music the armed forces banned because they were not proper manifestations of a "Western and Christian" society, were suddenly summoned when those same armed forces decided to confront a Western nation and justify the war as an anticolonial enterprise. Popular folk music, tango, and national rock were back on the radio and national television to contribute to the national bonding.

***Ethnic Relations.*** With the exception of some areas of the northwest, Argentina was not densely populated at the time of the Spanish conquest. Many indigenous groups disappeared because of harsh forced labor, compulsory resettlement, and diseases introduced by the Spanish conquerors. Those Indians who maintained their autonomy until well into the nineteenth century were brought to near extinction by military campaigns in the 1880s. In the last years of the twentieth century it was estimated that the Indians represent less than 1 percent of the total population (probably around 300,000 people). It is difficult to determine their numbers because those living in urban centers are rarely classified as Indians in official statistics. During colonial times there was an intense slave traffic in the Río de la Plata region. From the late eighteenth century to the mid-nineteenth century, blacks and mulattoes of African and European origin represented between 25 and 30 percent of the total population of Buenos Aires. Their numbers decreased dramatically in the last decades of the nineteenth century: in 1887 only 8,005 Afro-Argentines lived in Buenos Aires out of a total population of 433,375. Epidemics, participation in civil wars, and intermarriage are the most common explanations for the staggering population decline of Afro-Argentines. Less than 4,000 people in Buenos Aires claimed Afro-Argentine identity at the close of the twentieth century. *Mestizo* rural workers and Afro-Argentines resented the presence of European immigrants who competed for scarce housing and sources of labor. By the beginning of the twentieth century, foreign-born immigrants had already taken over many low-paying jobs formerly performed by Argentines. They quickly dominated the urban landscape as they outnumbered Argentine nationals. This contributed to the way Argentines think about their ethnic identity. One of the most dominant defnitions of the country's identity is that the majority of Argentina's population is white with European ancestors. This image is promoted both by outside observers as well as by some local intellectuals. Most of these assertions derive from taking Buenos Aires as representative of the whole nation, but even this city is not as white as it is usually depicted. Industrialization and later economic stagnation both in Argentina and neighboring countries caused migration to the metropolitan area from the interior provinces and from neighboring countries. These new residents are predominantly mestizos. Migrants also include indigenous peoples and a small number of mulattoes and blacks from Uruguay and Brazil. During Perón's government, rural migrants to the city constituted his loyal political base. Middle class and upper middle class opponents of Perón despised these new social sectors and derogatorily called them *cabecitas negras* (black heads). This term, together with *negro/a*, is still used to refer to mestizo and indigenous peoples. While the social conflicts of the 1940s and 1950s were often described in racist terms as cabecitas, and as an "alluvial zoo" invading the urban space, the relationship with those perceived as non-whites by the dominant social groups, has acquired xenophobic overtones. Land and housing occupation, and an increase in crime are attributed to immigrants from neighboring countries. It is difficult to assess the number of Latin American immigrants and internal migrants to cities, and it is

even more difficult to determine how they identify themselves. There are no reliable statistics in the 1990s regarding the ethnic composition of the country. Besides Latin American immigration, immigrants from Eastern Europe, Africa, and Asia were also arriving in Argentina in the late twentieth century. Most of these immigrants are illegal and nobody knows their real numbers.

## URBANISM, ARCHITECTURE, AND THE USE OF SPACE

Although most of the Argentine population is urban (87 percent), Argentina is still quite attached to its past rural glory as a grain and cattle exporter, activities that enabled it to rank among the six wealthiest nations in the world in 1914. The strength of rural imagery is confirmed in the way some Argentines represent themselves to foreigners. Tourists to major cities are offered souvenirs identified with a rural way of life—such as gaucho attire, silver, alpaca knives, and horse stirrups—and are invited to asados in nearby estancias where they can observe gaucho dexterity with horses. Cities founded during colonial times followed a very precise checkers pattern, with a plaza in the center surrounded by government buildings and the church. Since independence, the plaza has represented a place where the people can make claims to the authorities. Plaza de Mayo in Buenos Aires is the most important symbolic space. Major revolutions and popular protests chose this plaza as their epicenter. The *Casa Rosada* (Pink House), facing Plaza de Mayo, is the seat of the executive branch of government. Its color represents the unification of the nation after years of struggle between unitarians (represented by white) and federalists (represented by red). Architecture in major cities reflects the influence of immigrants as well as Argentina's semicolonial relationship to some European nations. Train stations and railroad neighborhoods (neighborhoods near the station that were built and owned until the 1940s—by the British to house railroad employees) follow a definitely British design. Public buildings and museums, many of them formerly the mansions of the landed elites, were generally inspired and/or designed by French architects. Major parks and botanical gardens were also modeled after French designs. Some avenues in Buenos Aires, such as Avenida de Mayo, have a strong Spanish influence in their architecture and resemble streets in Barcelona or Madrid. Some cities in the northwest and in the center of the country, such as Córdoba, Salta, Jujuy, and San Miguel de Tucumán, still have good examples of colonial architecture (adobe walls, central patios, and red-tiled roofs). Although plazas are still favored places for socializing and meeting friends, in some towns and cities the construction of shopping malls is changing the social scene and many people are choosing these sites to spend their leisure time.

## FOOD AND ECONOMY

**Food in Daily Life.** Argentines are very fond of beef and pastas. Most restaurants offer a wide assortment of meat dishes and pastas. Spanish and Italian cuisine inspire everyday cooking, while French-influenced cuisine is reserved for special occasions. It is quite customary to buy fresh pasta for Sunday lunch, which is generally a family event (that often includes the extended family). Breakfast is very light and generally includes coffee or tea and milk, toast, butter, and marmalade. At restaurants and hotels, breakfast also includes small croissants. Lunch is served from 12:30 P.M. to 2:00 P.M. It used to be the biggest meal of the day. This is changing because of tight work schedules that cause some working people to eat increasingly lighter dishes. There is generally an afternoon break for tea or coffee with cookies, sandwiches, pastries, and/or a piece of cake. Dinner is served from 9:00 P.M. to 10:00 P.M. There are no rigid food taboos, but Argentines in general are not very adventurous when it comes to trying unusual foods, flavors, and combinations. The most popular restaurants are steak houses and pizzerias. Because of the strong Italian influence in foods, ice cream stores offering gelatto made on the premises are extremely popular. People meet at any time of the day at cafés for an espresso or a cup of tea. These places are the heart and soul of urban culture in Argentina. People meet there to discuss politics and soccer, to flirt and make new acquaintances, to study, and to socialize with friends and dates.

**Food Customs at Ceremonial Occasions.** Any occasion is a good excuse for having a barbecue. Festive dishes include: *locro* (a stew made with corn, meats, *chorizos*, pumpkins, and sweet potatoes), *empanadas* (generally meat turnovers, but they might also be filled with corn, ham and cheese, or chicken). Spanish *paellas* are also sometimes prepared for special gatherings. As Argentina is a wine-producing country, wine is always served at special gatherings and on holidays. Mate drinks are sometimes offered at some public events.

**Basic Economy.** Since the late nineteenth century, Argentina had been mainly food self-sufficient. With the elimination of trade barriers, some food produ-

cers are finding it very difficult to compete with the price of some imports, causing a crisis in the agricultural sector. The majority of the population is urban and there are very few individuals who produce food for self-consumption. Large agribusinesses are mainly in charge of food production. Argentina's gross domestic product (GDP) is US$338.2 billion and the per capita GDP is US$9,520.

**Land Tenure and Property.** Most land is privately owned. All children have equal rights to inheritance from their parents irrespective of gender or majority. In some isolated areas, the population follows customary law to grant access to land and water. The state owns mineral resources such as oil, and contracts with private business for mineral exploitation.

**Commercial Activities.** Agriculture and livestock continue to be important economic activities, even though only a small number of Argentines live in rural areas. Argentina produces grains (wheat, corn, barley), soybeans, sunflower seeds, lemons, grapes, tobacco, peanuts, tea, apples, and peaches.

**Major Industries.** Argentina specializes in food processing, tobacco products, textiles and garments, shoes and leather goods, paper products, construction materials, domestic appliances, printing, electronics, medical equipment, cars and utility vehicles, furniture, chemicals and petrochemicals, metallurgy, and steel.

**Trade.** Argentine exports in 1997 amounted to approximately US$26 million while imports amounted to approximately US$30 million. Exports include farming and livestock manufactures, 34 percent; industrial manufactures, 31.3 percent; primary products (nonprocessed agrarian and mineral resources), 21.6 percent; and fuel and energy, 12.41 percent. Major exports are cereals, animal feed, motor vehicles (trucks, buses, and tractors), crude petroleum, steel, and manufactured goods. Major imports are motor vehicles (automobiles), organic chemicals, telecommunications equipment, electronics, plastics, and papers.

Brazil is the most important business partner (31 percent exports; 23 percent imports). Other export partners are the United States, 8 percent; Chile, 7 percent; China, 3 percent; and Uruguay, 3 percent. Import partners are the United States, 20 percent; Italy, 6 percent; Germany, 5 percent; and France, 5 percent.

**Division of Labor.** Most jobs are obtained through specific training in technical schools or on the job.

*Avenida 9, the widest street in the world, is a main thoroughfare in Buenos Aires.*

Patron–client relations are mainly political and are sometimes useful to secure a good job. In principal, access to jobs is on the basis of merit and open competition. Traditionally, certain trades were identified with specific ethnic groups. For example, waiters and restaurant owners, grocers and bankers were Spanish; green grocers and contractors were Italian; cleaners and florists were Japanese; deli owners were German; railroad white-collar workers were English; and jewelers were Jewish. These distinctions are no longer meaningful.

## SOCIAL STRATIFICATION

***Classes and Castes.*** Until recently, Argentina had a very large middle class. Upper-class and lower-class sectors can generally trace their origins to more than five generations in the country. Originally the upper class was mainly formed by land-owners of large estates. Urbanization and industrialization processes intensified in the early decades of the twentieth century and greatly affected Argentina's social structure. Merchants and industrialists increasingly joined the ranks of the landed elite. The Argentine middle class was formed mainly by the descendants of immigrants who came to Argentina either at the end of the nineteenth or beginning of

the twentieth century, settled in cities, and worked in the newly created jobs in the industrial, commercial, and public sectors of the economy. In comparison to other Latin American nations, Argentina's income distribution has been fairly equitable throughout most of the twentieth century. Together with Uruguay, it had a very large middle class until quite recently, but that situation changed with the economic crisis of the 1980s and 1990s. Social sciences literature refers to the "new poor," which is made up of former middle class citizens who experienced downward mobility.

***Symbols of Social Stratification.*** Upper classes often wear expensive imported clothes and/or clothes from very exclusive Argentine stores. These distinctions are not fixed; they change with fashion and with the cultural models followed by elite sectors. In the past, British and French culture influenced elite taste. It was not uncommon to hire French or British nannies to educate the children of the upper classes, although this practice faded in the 1970s. North American models are favored by the younger rich generation. Social class also can be easily recognized by speech styles and body language.

*Laundry hanging above a courtyard in La Boca, a working-class neighborhood in Buenos Aires. The economic crises of the 1980s and 1990s caused many middle-class citizens to experience downward mobility.*

## POLITICAL LIFE

***Government.*** Argentina's national constitution was adopted in 1853 and was changed in 1949 by the government of President Juan Domingo Perón. A new constitution was approved in 1994 to allow for a new term in office of former President Carlos Menem. It is a federalist constitution which recognizes three branches of government: the executive, legislative, and judicial. The president and vice-president are elected by direct vote. They hold office for a four-year term and may be reelected for a second term. The legislature has two houses, the house of senators and the house of deputies. The supreme court and lower courts comprise the judicial branch. The power of the provinces is curtailed by the ability of central government to control the distribution of resources from the national to the provincial treasuries.

***Leadership and Political Officials.*** The major political parties are the *justicialista* (formerly *peronista* party) and the radical party. In the presidential elections of 1999, an alliance between the radical party, the *frepaso* (a socialist front party), and other smaller parties won over the justicialista and other newly formed political parties. The two majority

parties have a long tradition of populist politics and they are quite prone to create clientelistic relations.

***Social Problems and Control.*** A police and judicial system is in place to deal with crime. The population is quite skeptical about the power of the police and the judicial system to control crime. There is a great concern about police corruption and police brutality. These issues are hotly debated in the platforms of political parties. The population is ambivalent about the role of the police. Concerned with the increase in violent crimes in the last decades of the twentieth century, many people are demanding a stricter police control and reforms in the penal system which would extend the time of incarceration. However, many people are not willing to grant more powers to the police force because they believe they are part of the problem. Insecurity and violence are closely associated with staggering unemployment, social anomie, and corruption at higher levels of government. There had been some cases of citizens killing criminals in robbery attempts, causing controversy and public debate on the role of common citizens in law enforcement.

***Military Activity.*** Military service was mandatory until the early 1990s. The Argentine military seized power on various occasions. After their defeat in the

*Local boys wait for the schoolbus in Lago Azul. Many middle and upper class parents are influenced by psychoanalytic schools for their children's education.*

Malvinas/Falklands War by the British, the military lost a lot of support. With the return to democracy in 1983, the military budget has significantly been reduced and the armed forces did not escape pressure to privatize which affected other government sectors. Many of the armed forces assets such as factories, buildings, and land holdings had been sold or privatized.

## SOCIAL WELFARE AND CHANGE PROGRAMS

Since the first presidency of Perón, the Ministry of Social Welfare was one of the most powerful governmental institutions. It was mainly used as a political weapon to distribute favors to potential allies. Besides its political goals, the ministry provided very important social services which contributed to the welfare of the population (housing, food programs, training programs, and healthcare). These actions were generally complemented by the social-welfare actions of trade unions. Structural adjustment policies, imposed by the World Bank and the International Monetary Fund (IMF), forced the government to reduce social-welfare services to a minimum. In some parts of the country, nongovernmental organizations (NGOS) are now partially meeting the needs of the most disadvantaged groups.

## NONGOVERNMENTAL ORGANIZATIONS AND OTHER ASSOCIATIONS

The most important organizations involved in solving people's pressing needs are the Catholic Church, other religious denomination organizations, and trade unions. The Catholic Church has taken the most active role in denouncing the effects of globalization on the poor and it is actively involved in social programs to help the population. With the reduction of the labor force and changes in legislation regarding the economic resources unions may control, these organizations are no longer providing the health, housing, and counseling services they used to offer, but they still constitute an important source of help for those who are permanently employed.

## GENDER ROLES AND STATUSES

*Division of Labor by Gender.* Although there are no legal impediments to women performing most roles, their access to some positions of power is limited. Very few women are elected as senators, and there are fewer female than male deputies. The same applies to other governmental positions such as ministers and secretaries of state. There are some professions in which women outnumber men such as architecture.

***The Relative Status of Women and Men.*** Argentine law used to grant men special authority over the children (*patria potestas*). Current legislation states that parents share authority over their children. Children may not leave the country with one parent unless they have the written authorization of the other.

## MARRIAGE, FAMILY, AND KINSHIP

***Marriage.*** Marriage is freely decided by men and women. Only minors (younger than age 18) need parental consent to marry. Argentina is one of the countries with the largest number of consensual unions. The government only recognizes civil marriage. The Catholic Church is very influential in Argentina and has strongly opposed divorce. However, divorce was legalized in the 1980s.

***Domestic Unit.*** The nuclear family is the most common household unit. Small families of one or two children are the norm. Partly for economic reasons and partly because of tradition, sons and daughters often stay with their parents until they are well into their twenties or until they marry. Newlyweds find a new home in which to live, distant from all of their kin. Couples share household responsibilities, although women generally perform more household activities than men.

***Inheritance.*** Land and houses are equally divided between female and male children. Women might inherit their mother's jewelry and some housewares such as china and silverware.

***Kin Groups.*** The extended family gathers regularly. Some members of the extended family might meet on a weekly basis for Sunday lunch. Birthdays, Christmas, and New Year's Eve are also occasions for extended family reunions.

## SOCIALIZATION

***Infant Care.*** Nursing is not concealed as much as it is in the United States. Babies sleep in their own cribs. Child rearing is very similar to the United States.

***Child Rearing and Education.*** Depending on the socioeconomic condition of the parents, children might be raised by nannies and/or baby sitters, maids, or child care providers in day care centers. This may happen even in cases in which the mothers do not work. Working mothers on a low income might rely on relatives and/or neighbors for child care. Large businesses and trade unions offer child care facilities for their female employees often for free. Most public schools have one or two years of kindergarten. Middle class and upper class families are strongly influenced by psychoanalytic schools for the education of their children. It is not uncommon for parents to seek psychological counseling to raise their children and to deal with learning problems at school.

***Higher Education.*** There are 36 state (public) universities and 48 private universities. Public universities are free. Some of them have entrance exams. Higher education degrees are very desirable. Unfortunately, Argentine society cannot employ a great number of its university graduates. Many professionals resort to taking jobs for which they are overqualified.

## ETIQUETTE

Both men and women greet each other by kissing on the cheek. In very formal encounters men and women shake hands. People address each other with the colloquial form *vos* (singular "you," equivalent to *tu* in other Spanish speaking countries). To convey social distance, people employ the more formal *usted* (to talk to superiors or to elders). Social physical distance in everyday encounters is much closer than in the United States. Argentines might touch each other when talking and might feel awkward when North Americans reject physical proximity and contact. Women and men gaze at each other, and it is still quite common that men use *piropos* (flirtateous remarks) when a woman walks by.

## RELIGION

***Religious Beliefs.*** The majority of Argentines are Roman Catholics, even though not all of them actively practice the religion. Jews migrated to Argentina at the end of the nineteenth century from Eastern Europe, Russia, and the Middle East. A significant number also migrated during and after World War II. Estimates of the exact size of the Jewish population vary between 250,000 and 500,000. Pentecostalism and other Protestant denominations are becoming quite popular among the lower class (4.69 percent of the population was Protestant in 1998). New Age and Eastern religions are popular among some middle and upper class urban sectors. People from various classes consult

*A protest in Buenos Aires in 1993. Argentines can be very vocal in their support of political figures and ideas.*

popular healers or "witches," and participate in folk rituals associated with popular forms of religions. For example, some Argentines believe in popular saints thought to have healing powers or to be capable of making miracles, such as Difunta Correa, San La Muerte, and Gaucho Gil.

**Religious Practitioners.** Along with various church specialists, sorcerers and healers are very popular. Some are immigrants from Brazil who carry their Afro-Brazilian beliefs, others combine elements of popular Catholicism with indigenous beliefs, and others are urban men and women who trained themselves in the secrets of the Tarot or I-Ching. Some of these practitioners are becoming so popular that many of them offer their services (mainly palm reading and Tarot) in very popular craft fairs on weekends.

**Death and the Afterlife.** Viewing of the deceased takes place immediately after death, either at a funeral home or at the home of the deceased. No special foods are served and only coffee might be available. In the northeast, there are special ceremonies called *velorio del angelito* for dead children. The ritual includes dancing and singing.

## MEDICINE AND HEALTH CARE

Modern medicine coexists with traditional medical beliefs. While some Argentines make use of a single medical system, others might use both for the same diseases, and still others might go to a doctor for some ailments and to a traditional healer for others. In some regions of Argentina, beliefs in cold and hot principles, which are very common in Latin America, guide the understandings of health. Even in urban centers, women might still cure an upset stomach by *tirar el cuerito* (pulling the skin on the back of the sick person), and they might also employ sulfur and other folk medicine for other sicknesses. Self-medication is quite common and people sometimes recommend medicines to friends for minor ailments. Herbal medicine is used extensively in some regions of the country.

## SECULAR CELEBRATIONS

On 25 May, Argentina commemorates the May Revolution of 1810, when the population of the country decided to appoint its own government after Napoleon invaded Spain.

The Day of the Argentine Flag is 20 June and commemorates the death of the creator of the Argentine flag, Manuel Belgrano.

Independence Day is 9 July. Argentine representatives from various provinces decided to become independent from Spain.

## THE ARTS AND HUMANITIES

*Support for the Arts.* Artists get support from private foundations and national institutions. Very few artists can support themselves. Early in the twentieth century, writers and painters formed groups that led major artistic movements. The two most important ones were the Florida and the Boedo groups. The former was elitist and closely followed European trends, while the latter attracted artists of more humble origins and had a more popular and nationalist orientation. Argentine artists compete for various national prizes offered by foundations and various businesses. Some of the newly privatized energy, telecommunications, and transportation companies sponsor the arts in innovative ways. For example, Subterráneos de Buenos Aires (Buenos Aires Subway) offers dance and theater performances as well as art exhibits to passengers waiting for the train. There are also performances on board.

*Literature.* Argentina is internationally known for some of its writers. Jorge Luis Borges is probably the best known writer. Other acclaimed writers include Roberto Arlt, Ernesto Sabato, Julio Cortazar, Victoria Ocampo, Leopoldo Marechal, Jose Hernández, Domingo Faustino Sarmiento, Manuel Puig, Luisa Valenzuela, Ricardo Piglia, and Adolfo Bioy Casares. Every year, Argentina has an international book fair, with an attendance of more than one million people.

*Graphic Arts.* Institutions of higher education train artists in all types of fine arts. Many Argentine artists have been at the forefront of artistic movements. There are numerous art galleries in the major cities of the country. There are sixty art galleries in Buenos Aires alone. The Centro Cultural Recoleta, the Museo of Bellas Artes, and the Museo de Arte Moderno organize exhibits to promote the work of national artists. Xul Solar, Raquel Forner, Eneas Spilimbergo, Carlos Alonso, Antonio Berni, Carlos Castagnino, Raúl Soldi, Rómulo Macció, Centurión, Benedit, Pérez Celis, Lacámera, and Raúl Russo are renowned painters. Some sculptors such as Fioravanti, Lola Mora, Irurtia, Perlotti, Cossice, LeParc, and Di Stefano have created works for parks and other public spaces.

*Performance Arts.* Argentina has an opera house, the Teatro Colón, where world famous musicians and ballet companies perform. This theater has a classical dance school which produced world-class dancers such as Julio Bocca. Besides the Teatro Colón, other theaters specialize both in classic and modern music and dance and have touring companies. Argentines are very fond of theater. During the military dictatorship in the 1970s, actors organized a theater festival which constituted a very powerful form of social protest. Municipal governments support the arts and generally offer art classes and sponsor artistic events. They promote both classical and popular art expressions. Concerts and dance exhibits take place in parks and large stadiums. Attendance to some of these events is massive.

## THE STATE OF THE PHYSICAL AND SOCIAL SCIENCES

Argentina has many institutions of higher education. The majority of the provinces have national universities as well as various private institutions. The Universidad Nacional de Buenos Aires, Universidad Nacional de Córdoba, Universidad Nacional de La Plata, and Universidad Nacional de Tucumán are some of the largest, oldest, and most prestigious universities in the country.

The major state agency supporting research in the physical and social sciences is the Consejo Nacional de Investigaciones Científicas y Técnicas (CONICET). Other state institutions conduct research in specific fields (for example, nuclear energy at Consejo Nacional de Energía Atómica; agriculture at Instituto Nacional de Tecnología Agropecuaria; geography at Instituto Geográfico Militar; and anthropology at Instituto Nacional de Antropología y Pensamiento Latinoamericano). Both private and public organizations are very actively involved in research. Financing of research is becoming very difficult and many young scientists are leaving the country.

## BIBLIOGRAPHY

Archetti, Eduardo. *Masculinities: Football, Polo and the Tango in Argentina*, 1999.

Bethel, Leslie, ed. *Argentina Since Independence*, 1993.

Burns, Jimmy. *The Land that Lost Its Heroes: Argentina, The Falklands and Alfonsín*, 1987.

Crawley, Edward. *A House Divided: Argentina, 1880-1984*, 1984.

Escolar, Marcelo, Silvina Quintero Palacios, and Carlos Reboratti. ''Geographical Identity and Patriotic Representation in Argentina.'' In David Hooson, ed. *Geography and National Identity*, pp. 346-366, 1994.

Femenia, Nora. *National Identity in Times of Crises: The Scripts of the Falklands-Malvinas War*, 1996.

Foster, David William. *The Redemocratization of Argentine Culture, 1983 and Beyond*, 1989.

———. *Buenos Aires: Perspectives on the City and Cultural Production*, 1998.

———, Melissa Fitch Lockhart, and Darrell B. Lockhart. *Culture and Customs of Argentina*, 1998.

Goodrich, Diana Sorenson. *Facundo and the Construction of Argentine Cultures*, 1993.

Guy, Donna. *Sex and Danger in Buenos Aires: Prostitution, Family, and Nation in Argentina*, 1991.

Keeling, David J. *Contemporary Argentina: A Geographical Perspective*, 1997.

Ludmer, Josefina. *El Género Gauchesco: Un Tratado Sobre la Patria*, 1988.

Masiello, Francine. *Between Civilization and Barbarism: Women, Nation, and Literary Culture in Modern Argentina*, 1992.

Rock, David. *Argentina 1516-1982, from Spanish Colonization to the Falklands War*, 1985.

Rowe, William and Vivian Schelling. *Memory and Modernity: Popular Culture in Latin America*, 1993.

Sarmiento, Domingo F. *Life in the Argentine Republic in the Days of the Tyrants or, Civilization and Barbarism*, 1845, rev. 1961.

Savigliano, Marta. *Tango and the Political Economy of Passion*, 1995.

Shumway, Nicolas. *The Invention of Argentina*, 1991.

Sikkink, Kathryn. *Ideas and Institutions: Developmentalism in Brazil and Argentina*, 1991.

Slatta, Richard. *Gauchos and the Vanishing Frontier*, 1983.

Solberg, Carl. *Immigration and Nationalism: Argentina and Chile, 1890-1914*, 1970.

Waissman, Carlos. *Reversal of Development in Argentina: Postwar Counterrevoultionary Policies and Their Structural Consequences*, 1987.

### Web Sites

Argentine Chamber of Commerce. http://www.amchamar.com.ar

Interaramerican Development Bank (IDB). http://www.database.iadb.org

—CARMEN ALICIA FERRADÁS

# ARMENIA

## CULTURE NAME
Armenian

## ALTERNATIVE NAMES
Hayastan/Hayasdan; Haygagan/Haykakan/Haigagan; Haikakan

## ORIENTATION

**Identification.** The designation "Armenia" applies to different entities: a "historical" Armenia, the Armenian plateau, the 1918–1920 U.S. State Department map of an Armenia, and the current republic of Armenia. The notion "Armenian culture" implies not just the culture of Armenia but that of the Armenian people, the majority of whom live outside the current boundaries of the republic of Armenia.

Armenians call themselves hay and identify their homeland not by the term "Armenia" but as Hayastan or Hayasdan. The origins of these words can be traced to the Hittites, among whose historical documents is a reference to the Hayasa. In the Bible, the area designated as Armenia is referred to as Ararat, which the Assyrians referred to as Urartu. Armenians also identify themselves as the people of Ararat/Urartu and of Nairi, and their habitat as *nairian ashkharh* or *yergir nairian*. Armenians have called themselves *Torkomian* or *Torgomian*. They also call themselves *Haigi serount* or *Haiki seround*, descendants of Haig/Haik.

**Location and Geography.** Armenia has been identified with the mountainous Armenian plateau since pre-Roman times. The plateau is bordered on the east by Iran, on the west by Asia Minor, on the north by the Transcaucasian plains, and on the south by the Mesopotamian plains. The plateau consists of a complex set of mountain ranges, volcanic peaks, valleys, lakes, and rivers. It is also the main water reservoir of the Middle East, as two great rivers—the Euphrates and the Tigris—

originate in its high mountains. The mean altitude of the Armenian plateau is 5,600 feet (1,700 meter) above sea level.

Present-day Armenia—the republic of Armenia—is a small mountainous republic that gained its independence in 1991, after seven decades of Soviet rule. It constitutes one-tenth of the historical Armenian plateau. Surrounding Lake Sevan, it has an area of approximately 11,600 square miles (30,000 square kilometers). Its border countries are Azerbaijan, Azerbaijan-Naxçivan, the Republic of Georgia, Iran, and Turkey. Its climate is highland continental, with hot summers and cold winters. Despite its small size, it was one of the most densely populated republics of the Soviet Union. Half of its inhabitants live in the Ararat plain, which constitutes only 10 percent of its territory and includes the capital city of Yerevan. Yerevan houses one-third of the country's population.

Armenia is a rugged, volcanic country with rich mineral resources. It is highly prone to earthquakes and occasional droughts.

**Demography.** Approximately 3 million people live in the republic of Armenia. Another 3 million Armenians live in various countries of the ex-Soviet Union—mainly in Russia. One and a half million Armenians are dispersed in the Americas. About one million Armenians live in various European countries, and half a million Armenians live in the Middle East and Africa. The ethnic composition of Armenia's population is 93.3 percent Armenian; 1.5 percent Russian; 1.7 percent Kurdish; and 3.5 percent Assyrian, Greek, and other.

**Linguistic Affiliation.** Armenian is the official language. When Armenia was under Russian and Soviet rule, Russian constituted the second official language. The Armenian language is an Indo-European language. Its alphabet was invented by the monk Mesrob in 406 C.E.. There are two major standardized versions of Armenian: Western Arme-

*Armenia*

nian, which was based on a version of nineteenth century Armenian spoken in Istanbul and is used mainly in the Diaspora, and Eastern Armenian, which was based on the Armenian spoken in Yerevan and is used in the ex-Soviet countries and Iran. This latter dialect was subjected to orthographic reforms during the Soviet era. There is also "Grabar" Armenian, the original written language, which is still used in the liturgy of the Armenian national (Apostolic) church.

**Symbolism.** Mount Ararat has had symbolic significance for all Armenians. Today it lies outside the boundaries of Armenia. It may be seen on the horizon from Yerevan, but like a mirage it remains inaccessible to Armenians. Ancient manuscripts depicting the history of Armenia are housed in the national library, Madenataran, and are valued national and historical treasures. Particularly significant symbols of Armenian culture include the statue of Mother

Armenia; Dsidsernagabert, a shrine with an ever-burning fire in memory of the Armenian victims of the 1915 genocide; the ruined ancient monasteries; *khatchkars* engraved stone burial crosses; the ruins of Ani, the last capital of historic Armenia, which fell in 1045; and the emblem of the 1918 first republic of Armenia, its tricolor flag.

## HISTORY AND ETHNIC RELATIONS

***Emergence of The Nation.*** Many prehistoric sites have been unearthed in and around Armenia, showing the existence of civilizations with advanced notions in agriculture, metallurgy, and industrial production, with diverse standardized manufacturing processes and pottery.

The origins of the Armenians have long been subject to debate among historians, linguists, and archaeologists. In the 1980s, linguists drew attention to the existence of many similarities between the Indo-European and Semitic languages. The only way to explain the linguistic similarities between these two linguistic groups would be to geographically move the cradle of the Indo-European linguistic groups farther east, to the Armenian plateau.

The Armenians and their plateau have been subject to various invasions. They witnessed Alexander the Great's expeditions toward the east. They fought the Roman legions and the Sassanid Persians, and in most cases lost. They stopped the Arabian expansion toward the north and provided emperors to the Byzantine throne. Having lost their own kingdom in the eleventh century to the invading Tartars and Seljuks, they managed to create a new kingdom farther south and west, in Cilicia, that flourished until 1375, playing a significant role during the Crusades. Then, they lost their last monarchy to the emerging Ottoman Empire, after the latter's westward expansion was stopped at the gates of Vienna. For more than two centuries, Armenia was devastated by the wars between two empires: the Iranian and the Ottoman. Starting at the end of the eighteenth century, the Russian empire also gained a foothold south of the Caucasus Mountains, defeating the Iranians and the Ottomans in a series of wars. The Armenian plateau thus became subject to the advances of three empires.

At the onset of the twentieth century, historical Armenia was divided between the Russian and the Ottoman (Turkish) Empires. Starting in the 1890s, periodical massacres of Armenians were organized by the Turkish authorities, which culminated in the genocide of 1915–1923. The Young Turk leadership of the Ottoman Empire, which had come to power

*A statue of Russian Communist leader Vladimir Lenin in a square in Yerevan. Armenia was under Soviet rule from 1920 through 1990.*

in 1908, seized the opportunity of World War I to physically remove the Armenian population. They envisioned a new Turkish nation-state (Turan), based on a monoethnic and monoreligious society, extending from Istanbul to Lake Baykal (in Central Asia). The entire Armenian population living under Turkish rule was thus subjected to systematic annihilation and the survivors scattered through the world in the aftermath of what would be known later as the first documented genocide of the twentieth century. Estimates of the Armenian dead vary from six hundred thousand to 2 million. A report of a United Nations human rights subcommission gave the figure of "at least one million."

In late 1917 the Russian empire collapsed and its armies withdrew from the Caucasus front. Eastern or Russian Armenia was left unprotected and by the spring of the next year, the Turkish army was advancing toward the east, trying to reach the oil fields of Baku, on the Caspian Sea. Only a last-ditch effort at the gates of Yerevan saved the Armenians of the east (in Russian Armenia) from the fate of their western compatriots (in Turkey). After the victorious battles of Sardarapat and Bash-Aparan, the Turkish onslaught was contained and reversed, and Armenia declared its independence on 28 May 1918.

Independence, however, was short-lived. After two years, due to the increasing pressure of, on the one hand, advancing Kemalist Turkish forces, and on the other, the Bolsheviks, the small landlocked republic of Armenia was forced to sign treaties that led to the loss of its territories and to its becoming a Soviet republic. Soviet rule lasted seventy years.

Having essentially followed the same path as most other nations under Soviet rule, the Armenians welcomed the dawn of the glasnost era, proclaimed by the last Soviet leader, Mikhail Gorbachev, as a means to correct the decades-old injustices imposed upon them.

Armenians believed in glasnost, and framed their demands in its rhetoric. In February 1988 there were impressive demonstrations in Yerevan and Stepanakert (the capital of Nagorno-Karabakh, an Armenian enclave in Azerbaijan) requesting the reunification of Karabakh with Armenia on the basis of self-determination rights. Following these demonstrations, on 28 May 1988, the seventeenth anniversary of the independence of Armenia was celebrated for the first time since Soviet rule. During the summer of 1988, mass demonstrations continued, followed by general strikes. In November 1988, Armenians were subjected to further massacres in Azerbaijan, leading to massive refugee problems. Emergency measures were established in both republics and Azerbaijan began a blockade of Armenia. The disastrous earthquake in Armenia on 7 December 1988 added to the existing refugee and economic problems. On 12 January 1989, a special commission to administer the Karabakh region, under the direct control of Moscow, was established. On 28 May 1989, the Soviet Armenian government recognized 28 May as the official anniversary of the republic of Armenia. During the summer of 1989, the Armenian National Movement acquired legal status, and held its first congress in November 1989. In January 1990, further Armenian massacres were reported in Baku and Kirovabad. During the spring elections, members of the Karabakh Committee, Soviet dissidents, came to power in parliamentary elections. The republic of Armenia gained its independence on 21 September 1991.

**National Identity.** The Armenian national identity is essentially a cultural one. From the historical depths of its culture and the dispersion of its bearers, it has acquired a richness and diversity rarely achieved within a single national entity, while keeping many fundamental elements that ensure its unity. Its bearers exhibit a strong sense of national identity that sometimes even clashes with the modern concept of the nation-state. It is an identity strongly influenced by the historical experiences of the Armenians. Events such as the adoption of Christianity as a state religion in 301 C.E., the invention of the Armenian alphabet in 406 C.E., and the excessively severe treatment at the hands of foreign powers at various times in its history have had a major impact.

**Ethnic Relations.** The republic of Armenia has thus far escaped the ethnic turmoil characterizing life in the post-Soviet republics. Minority rights are protected by law.

## URBANISM, ARCHITECTURE, AND THE USE OF SPACE

The great majority of Armenians in Armenia and in the Diaspora are urbanites. In the republic of Armenia, 68 percent live in urban areas with a population density of 286 persons per square mile (110.5 per square kilometer).

Contemporary Armenian architecture has followed the basic characteristics of its historical architectural tradition: simplicity, reliance on locally available geological material, and the use of volcanic tufa for facings. During the Soviet era, however, prefabricated panels were used to build apartment

*A woman sells fruit at a roadside stand. Armenia has focused on small-scale agriculture since gaining independence in 1991.*

buildings, many of which collapsed during the 1988 earthquake.

## FOOD AND ECONOMY

**Food in Daily Life.** Staple foods are bread and salt. *Harissa* a traditional meal, consists of wheat grain and lamb cooked over low heat. Armenians everywhere love barbecued meats and vegetables. The pomegranate, with its symbolic association with fertility, is the national fruit. Armenia is also vine and grape country. When speaking of friendship, Armenians say "we have bread and salt among us." In the state protocol, when dignitaries are welcomed, bread and salt are presented.

Breakfasts on nonworking days are sometimes major get-together events. In huge pots *khash* is prepared, cattle legs are boiled and served with spices and garlic and consumed with Armenian brandy.

**Basic Economy.** Since its independence from the Soviet Union, Armenia has been focusing on small-scale agriculture. In 1992, the state-run industries, including agriculture, were immediately privatized as Armenia adopted a Western-style economic system.

*Major Industries.* During Soviet rule, Armenia began to develop and concentrate on computer-based high technology, alongside a manufacturing sphere, the production of brandy, heavy industry, and mining. The 1991 blockade of the country by Azerbaijan led to a fuel shortage that often left its industries at a standstill. Nuclear energy was shut down after the 1988 earthquake as well, but production was resumed after a few years for lack of other reliable sources of energy. The current trend in industrial development is toward small volume/high-value products such as diamond cutting and electronic components, since transportation is still a major problem for the landlocked republic.

*Trade.* Armenia has been subject to an economic blockade since the early 1990s by its neighboring countries, with the exception of Iran and Georgia. Trade relations are newly developing. Armenia exports woven and knit apparel; beverages, including brandy; preserved fruits; art and handicrafts; books; precious stones; metals; and electrical machinery.

## SOCIAL STRATIFICATION

*Classes and Castes.* For several centuries until the end of monarchic historical Armenia in 1045 and Cilicia in 1375, there were aristocratic noble houses with their respective court-related responsibilities. Afterwards, the notion of a generalized middle class emerged. Most Armenians were peasants until the turn of the twentieth century. During the Soviet era, class was de-emphasized. A new elite had emerged, however, based on the nomenclature or system that prevailed during Soviet rule.

## POLITICAL LIFE

*Government.* The republic of Armenia is a democratic constitutional state. A constitution was adopted by national referendum in July 1995. Parliamentary elections were held in July 1995 and May 1999. Presidential elections were held in March 1998.

In 1999, fifteen parties and six political blocs took part in parliamentary elections.

*Leadership and Political Officials.* Robert Kocharian was the second president elected in the republic of Armenia since its independence. There is an elected national assembly (*Azgayin Joghov*), or parliament. The cabinet is formed by a prime minister designated by the president.

*Social Problems and Control.* During Soviet rule, Armenia had followed Soviet criminal and civil law.

Since independence, a new autonomous legal system has been developing. The post independence period has also witnessed a rise in awareness in the media of organized crime and sex service rings.

*Military Activity.* Gradually, an autonomous army and defense system are being developed. Armenia joined the Commonwealth of Independent States (CIS) in March 1992 and signed the CIS Defense Treaty in May 1992.

## SOCIAL WELFARE AND CHANGE PROGRAMS

During the Soviet period, there was a well-established welfare system. Since then, the social welfare system has been affected by the economic crisis. Although the old age security system or pension is still in place, the amount of funding designated as monthly payment is not sufficient to maintain a subsistence living.

## NONGOVERNMENTAL ORGANIZATIONS AND OTHER ASSOCIATIONS

The number of organizations registered as of 31 December 1998 broke down as follows: seventy-six political parties, 1,938 nongovernmental organizations (NGOs), and 905 Media Outlets. The number of NGOs registered with the NGO Training and Resource Center totaled seven hundred.

## GENDER ROLES AND STATUSES

*Division of Labor by Gender.* Armenian culture has historically stressed a division of domains among the sexes. The home/household is a woman's domain. The grandmother/mother-in-law was the manager of the household. Women and men both worked outside the home. In the domestic sphere, women had no choice when it came to the chores. It was their duty and responsibility to maintain the household.

Women and men have equal access to all sectors of the economy. Nevertheless, only five banks, out of the total of 57, are managed by women. In terms of employment, there is a high rate of women's participation in the labor force. Also there is "equal pay for work of equal value." More women, however, are working in lower paid jobs. As a result, the average salary of women constitutes two thirds of men's salaries. The main work areas of women are in the sectors of education and health. The percentage of women working in industry is 40–42 percent. Women constitute 63.9 percent of unemployed workers. Women also account for most of

*An Armenian woman drying grain beside the road in Garni Village, circa 1967. Historically, Armenian women were viewed as having responsibility for domestic chores and maintaining their households.*

the domestic unpaid labor as well as for subsistence farming work.

***The Relative Status of Women and Men.*** During the first republic of Armenia (1918–1920), women enjoyed equal voting and election rights. Four women were elected to the national parliament and one woman, Diana Apgar, became the ambassador to Japan. During the Soviet period, in spite of the legislation that stressed women's equality at all levels, women found it difficult to get into the higher decision-making processes. In 1991, during the first democratic elections in the newly independent republic of Armenia, women candidates won in only nine constituencies out of 240, representing only 3.6 percent of the parliament membership. None of the permanent parliamentary committees include any female members.

## MARRIAGE, FAMILY, AND KINSHIP

***Marriage.*** Armenians are monogamous. In some cases, marriages are arranged. The accepted practice is to avoid marriage with close kin (of up to seven kin-distances). Because of housing shortages in Soviet Armenia, the new couple resided with the groom's family (patrilocality). The preference, however, has been and continues to be for neolocality, that is, the new couple forming a new household.

***Domestic Unit.*** The married couple and their offspring constitute the domestic unit. During Soviet rule, the domestic unit consisted of a multi generational family. Often paternal grandparents, their married offspring, and unmarried aunts and uncles resided together. In pre-Soviet times, each region had its own preference. The most common domestic unit, however, was a patrilocal multi generational family.

***Inheritance.*** Although inheritance laws have undergone changes and reforms over the years, historically, men and women have been treated equally. Diaspora Armenian communities follow the inheritance laws of their respective countries.

***Kin Groups.*** Kin relations are bilateral. Descent, however, is determined by the patrilineal line.

## SOCIALIZATION

***Infant Care.*** Mothers are seen as the main providers of infant care. During Soviet rule, free infant day care was available to all, but Armenians preferred to leave their infants with grandmothers and

*Armenian folk dancers in Yerevan. Armenia has a long tradition of musical art dating back to prehistoric times.*

other close kin. Day-care workers were also mainly women. During the Soviet era, women were guaranteed their employment after a prolonged, paid maternity leave. The practice has continued after independence, pending new reforms, which observers fear may decrease paid maternity leave.

**Child Rearing and Education.** Women are considered to be the bearers and transmitters of culture, customs, and tradition and are seen as responsible for child rearing. Children are highly valued and they occupy the center of attention in households until they reach puberty. At puberty they are disciplined and are expected to take on responsibilities. Education is valued and is given great weight as an agent of socialization. In Armenia throughout the twentieth century, education was free and accessible to all. Because of privatization trends in the post reindependence period, however, there are fears that education may not remain accessible to all.

**Higher Education.** Armenia has stressed free access to education. A national policy directed at the elimination of illiteracy began in the first republic (1918–1920) and continued in Soviet times, resulting in a nearly 100 percent literacy rate. Women enjoy equal rights at all levels of education. A private higher education system was introduced in 1992. Although there is no discrimination on the

basis of sex, some fields have become labeled "female." Of the students in the health-care field, 90 percent are women. In arts and education women constitute 78 percent of the students, in economics the number drops to 44.7 percent, for agriculture, 41 percent, and for industry, transportation, and communications, 40 percent.

## ETIQUETTE

Armenians put great emphasis on hospitality and generosity. There is also an emphasis on respect for guests.

## RELIGION

**Religious Beliefs.** Christianity has been the state religion in Armenia since 301. During Soviet rule, religious expression was not encouraged. The emphasis was on atheism. Armenians had continued to attend church, however, in particular for life-crisis events and rites of passage. The majority of Armenians adhere to the Armenian Apostolic Church. There are also adherents to Catholic, Evangelical, and Protestant denominations.

The church has been a symbol of national culture. It has been seen as the home of Armenians and the bearer of Armenian culture.

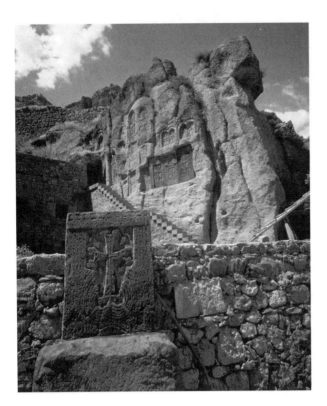

*A temple cut into a Tufa rockface.*

## MEDICINE AND HEALTH CARE

Western medical practices are followed in the health sector. Until recently, medicine and health care were universal and state run. The introduction of a private health sector has been discussed. There are already a number of private clinics operating in the republic of Armenia. In addition, a few clinics operate under the sponsorship of Diaspora voluntary associations, such as the Armenian General Benevolent Union and the Armenian Relief Society.

## SECULAR CELEBRATIONS

New Year's Eve (or Amanor, Nor Dari, or Gaghant/ Kaghand) is a secular holiday. Other secular holidays include: Women's Day 7 April; the commemoration of the 1915 genocide of the Armenians 24 April; the Independence day of the first Armenian republic of 1918, and 28 May; the Independence Day of the current republic of Armenia, 21 September.

## THE ARTS AND HUMANITIES

***Support for the Arts.*** In the republic of Armenia, following the policies put forth during the pre-Soviet and Soviet eras, the state has been supporting the arts and humanities. In recent years, because of economic difficulties, there has been a privatization trend. State support is diminishing. In the Diaspora, the arts and humanities rely on local fund-raising efforts, Armenian organizations, and the initiative of individuals. In the republic of Armenia, artists are engaged full time in their respective arts. In the Diaspora, however, artists are rarely self-supporting and rarely make a living through their art.

***Literature.*** Armenians have a rich history of oral and written literature. Parts of the early oral literature was recorded by M. Khorenatsi, a fourth-century historian. During the nineteenth century, under the influence of a European interest in folklore and oral literature, a new movement started that led to the collection of oral epic poems, songs, myths, and stories.

The written literature has been divided into five main epochs: the fifth century golden age, or *vosgetar* following the adoption of the alphabet; the Middle Ages; the Armenian Renaissance (in the nineteenth century); modern literature of Armenia and Constantinople (Istanbul) at the turn of the twentieth century; and contemporary literature of Armenia and the Diaspora. The fifth century has been recognized internationally as a highly productive epoch. It was also known for its translations of

***Religious Practitioners.*** The Armenian Apostolic Church has two catholicosate sees: the Catholicos of All Armenians at Etchmiadzin, Armenia, and Cilicia, in Antelias, Lebanon. The two sees are organized differently. Each has its own educational system and hierarchy of priests. Among the Armenians there are celibate and married priests. There are also two patriarchates: one in Istanbul and another in Jerusalem. Women are not ordained into priesthood. There is only one women's order: the Kalfayian sisters.

***Death and the Afterlife.*** Most Armenians believe in the Christian vision of death and afterlife. The Apostolic Church, unlike some Christian institutions, does not put emphasis on sin and redemption. Likewise the notion of purgatory is absent. Armenians pay special attention to remembering the dead. After every mass, or *badarak*, there is a memorial service for the dead. The seventh day after death, the fortieth day, and annual remembrance are the accepted way of respecting the dead. Cemeteries are well kept. The communion between the living and the dead is seen in the frequent visits to the graves of loved ones. Food and brandy are served to the dead. The birthdays of dead loved ones are also celebrated.

various works, including the Bible. In fact, the clergy have been the main producers of Armenian literary works. One of the most well-known early works is Gregory Narekatzi's *Lamentations*. During medieval times, a tradition of popular literature and poetry gradually emerged. By the nineteenth century, the vernacular of eastern (Russian and Iranian) Armenia became the literary language of the east, and the vernacular of Istanbul and western (Ottoman Turkish) Armenia became the basis of the literary rebirth for Armenians living in the Ottoman Empire.

Armenian literature has been influenced by European literary styles and movements. It also reflects the tragic history of its people. The 1915 genocide led to the death of the great majority of the Armenian writers of the time. The period immediately after the genocide was marked by a silence. Eventually there emerged a Diaspora literature with centers in Paris, Aleppo, and Beirut. In Soviet Armenia, the literary tradition followed the trends in Russia with a recognizable Armenian voice. Literature received the support of the Soviet state. A writers union was established. At the time of glasnost and perestroika, the emerging leaders belonged to the writers union.

***Graphic Arts.*** Historically, Armenian art has been associated with architecture, bas-reliefs, stone engravings, steles, illuminated manuscripts, and tapestry. Since the Armenian Renaissance during the nineteenth century, interest in drawing, painting, sculpture, textiles, pottery, needlework, and lace has intensified. During the Soviet period, graphic arts were particularly encouraged. A new Armenian style of bright colors emerged in painting. An interest in landscape painting, rustic images, a focus on rural life, and ethnographic genre paintings were noticeable in Soviet Armenia. A national art gallery houses the works of Sarian, M. Avedissian, Hagopian, Soureniantz, and other artists of the Soviet epoch. In the current republic, there are outdoor exhibits of newly emerging painters, and new private initiatives are being made.

***Performance Arts.*** Armenia has a long tradition of musical art, dating back to prehistoric times, and Armenian musicians played a fundamental role in the modernization of oriental music during the nineteenth century. Armenian traditional music differs from its oriental counterparts by its sobriety.

The republic of Armenia has thus far continued the trend set in Soviet years. The opera house, the theaters, and the concert halls are the pride of Armenians and have remained highly accessible to the general public. Armenian folk, classic, and religious music, as well as its composers, such as Komitas and A. Khatchadourian, have been known throughout the world. The folk-dance ensembles have also been participating in various international festivals.

## THE STATE OF PHYSICAL AND SOCIAL SCIENCES

In the republic of Armenia, as in Soviet Armenia, as well as in the Armenian republic of 1918, the state has been the main support system for the physical and social sciences. There is a well-established Academy of Sciences, where the social sciences and humanities have been and are represented. In recent years Armenia has been experiencing a dramatic financial crisis. The state is unable to continue its support of research and development. There have been calls for Diaspora fund-raising support. International foundations have also been approached to provide financing.

## BIBLIOGRAPHY

Alem, Jean-Pierre. *Armenie.* Paris, 3rd ed., 1972.

Aprahamian, S. "Armenian Identity: Memory, Ethnoscapes, Narratives of Belonging in the Context of the Recent Emerging Notions of Globalization and Its Effect on Time and Space." *Feminist Studies in Aotearoa Journal 60,* 1999.

Armenia. *National Report on the Conditions of Women,* 1995.

Bauer-Manndorff, Elisabeth. *Armenia, past and present.* Translated by Frederick A. Leist, 1981.

Berndt, Jerry. *Armenia: Portraits of Survival,* 1994.

Bjorklund, Ulf. "Armenia Remembered and Remade: Evolving Issues in a Diaspora." *Ethnos 58: 3-4,* 335-360, 1993.

Cox, Caroline, and John Eibner. *Ethnic Cleansing in Progress: War in Nagorno Karabakh,* 1993.

Der Manuelian, Lucy, and Murray L. Eiland. *Weavers, Merchants, and Kings: The Inscribed Rugs of Armenia.* Edited by Emily J. Sano, 1984.

Der Nersessian, Sirarpie. *The Armenians,* 1969.

Hamalian, Arpi. *The Armenians: Intermediaries for the European Trading Companies,* 1976.

Hovannisian, Richard G. *Armenia on the Road to Independence,* 1918, 1967.

———. *The Republic of Armenia.* Berkeley: (In six volumes). 1971.

———, ed. *The Armenian genocide in perspective,* 1986.

———, ed. *Remembrance and Denial: The Case of the Armenian Genocide,* 1998.

Kasbarian, Lucine. *Armenia: A Rugged Land, an Enduring People*, 1998.

Kazandjian, Sirvart. *Les origines de la musique Arménienne*, 1984.

Khorenatsi, Moses. *History of the Armenians*. Translated by Robert W. Thomson, 1978.

Lang, David Marshall. *Armenia: Cradle of Civilization*, 1970.

———. *The Armenians, a People in Exile*, 1981.

Libaridian, J. Gerard, ed. *Armenia at the Crossroads: Democracy and Nationhood in the Post-Soviet Era*, 1991.

Lynch, H. F. B. *Armenia, Travels and Studies*, 2 vols., 1901.

Mandelstam, Osip. *Journey to Armenia*, Translated by Clarence Brown, 1980.

Marashlian, Levon. *Politics and Demography: Armenians, Turks and Kurds in the Ottoman Empire*, 1991.

Marsden, Philip. *The Crossing Place: A Journey among the Armenians*, 2nd ed., 1995.

Mouradian, Claire. *De Staline à Gorbatchev: Histoire d'une republique sovietique: l'Arménie*, 1990.

Nersessian, Vrej Nerses, comp. *Armenia*, 1993.

Oshagan, Vahe, special ed. *Armenia*, 1984.

Samuelian, Thomas J., ed. *Classical Armenian Culture: Influences and Creativity*, 1981.

———, and Michael E. Stone, eds. *Medieval Armenian Culture*, 1984.

Somakian, Manoug Joseph. *Empires in Conflict: Armenia and the Great Powers, 1895-1920*, 1995.

Tashjian, Nouvart. *Armenian Lace*, Edited by Jules and Kaethe Kliot, 1982.

Thierry, Jean-Michel. *Armenian Art*. Translated by Celestine Dars, 1989.

Toriguian, Shavarsh. *The Armenian Question and International Law*, 1973.

Utudjian, Edouard. *Armenian Architecture, 4th to 17th century*. Translated by Geoffrey Capner. 1968.

Vassilian, Hamo B., ed. *The Armenians: A Colossal Bibliographic Guide to Books Published in the English Language*, 1993.

Walker, Christopher J. *Armenia, the Survival of a Nation*, rev. ed., 1990.

—SIMA APRAHAMIAN
WITH THE ASSISTANCE OF VIKEN APRAHAMIAN

# ARUBA

## CULTURE NAME
Aruban

## ORIENTATION

**Identification.** Aruba is a multicultural island society, with Caribbean and Latin American features.

**Location and Geography.** Aruba is the most southwestern island of the Caribbean archipelago, located 20 miles (32 kilometers) off the Venezuelan coast. With Curaçao and Bonaire, it forms the Dutch Leeward Islands. Aruba's area is 70 square miles (180 square kilometers). The climate is tropical, with an average temperature of 82 degrees Fahrenheit (28 degrees Celsius). Yearly rainfall usually does not exceed 20 inches (500 mm). Aruba lays outside the Caribbean hurricane belt.

**Demography.** Aruba's population was 93,424 in 1998, as compared to 59,995 in 1987. That growth is attributed mostly to immigration. Not included are an estimated 5,000 illegal aliens. The proportion of foreign-born inhabitants has risen from 18.5 percent in 1981 to 28 percent in 1994. Life expectancy is 71.1 years for men and 77.1 years for women. The population density is 200 legal inhabitants per square mile.

**Linguistic Affiliation.** The traditional language is Papiamento (Talk), a Creole language that is also spoken on Curaçao and Bonaire. The origins of Papiamento are much debated. According to the more popular monogenistic theory Papiamento, like other Creole languages from the Caribbean, originates from one single Afro-Portuguese proto-Creole, which developed as a lingua franca in Western Africa in the days of the slave trade. The polygenetic theory maintains that Papiamento developed on Curaçao with a Spanish base. Aruban Papiamento has a stronger Spanish influence compared to that spoken on Curaçao and Bonaire.

Owing to 360 years of colonial domination, Dutch is the official language in education and public affairs. The oil industry, tourism, and subsequent migration brought English and Spanish to the island and those are the second and third most spoken languages. Most residents are multilingual.

**Symbolism.** Papiamento and the national flag, anthem, and coat of arms are the most important national symbols. They stress the inhabitants love for the island, the close connection to the Caribbean Sea, and the multi-cultural composition of the population. The national anthem is played and sung on many occasions. The Dutch flag functions as a symbol of the unity of Aruba, the Netherlands, and the Netherlands Antilles.

## HISTORY AND ETHNIC RELATIONS

**Emergence of the Nation.** Indian populations inhabited Aruba prior to the European discovery. Between 2000 B.C.E. and approximately 850 B.C.E., the island was populated by preceramic Indians. Around 850 B.C.E., Caquetio Arowaks from western Venezuela migrated to Aruba, introducing pottery and agriculture.

The Spanish discovered Aruba in or around 1499. Because of the absence of precious metals Aruba, Bonaire, and Curaçao were declared *Islas Inutiles* (Useless Islands). In 1515 their inhabitants were deported to Hispaniola to work in the mines. After an unsuccessful colonization effort by Juan de Ampíes (1526–c. 1533), the island was used for cattle breeding and wood cutting. Small numbers of Indians from the mainland migrated to Aruba. Spanish priests from Venezuela attempted to Christianize them.

The Dutch West India Company (WIC) took possession of Aruba in 1636, two years after the Dutch conquest of Curaçao. Indians from the mainland continued to migrate. Colonization of the island was forbidden until 1754. In 1767, the col-

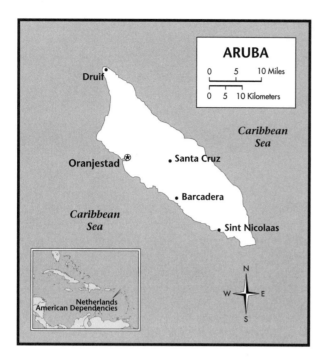

*Aruba*

ony consisted of one hundred twenty households, twelve of which were in the employ of the WIC. Another one hundred were Indian households. After the dissolution of the WIC (1792) and two English interregnums (1801–1803 and 1806–1816), serious colonization started. The elite was mainly active in commercial agriculture and illegal trade with South America. Peasants remained dependant on small scale agriculture, fishing, and labor migration within the region. Slaves never exceeded 21 percent of the population (1849). Slavery was abolished in 1863, when 496 slaves obtained freedom. In the absence of a plantation economy a peasant culture emerged. Colonists, Indians, and blacks intermixed forming the traditional Mestizo-Creole population.

The oil industry arrived in the 1920s and brought rapid modernization and immigration of industrial laborers, merchants, and civil servants from the Caribbean, Europe, the Americas, and China. Aruba became a pluralistic society of over forty nationalities. Afro-Caribbean migrants surpassed the traditional population in economic position and cultural esteem. The position of the traditional elite as commercial entrepreneurs was taken over by Lebanese, Jewish, and Chinese migrants and foreign trade companies.

The Eagle Oil Refining Company (a Royal Dutch/Shell affiliate) ceased its activities in 1953. A major economic setback occurred when the last major international oil company, Lago (owned by EXXON), went out of business in 1985. Tourism, which was first initiated in the 1950s, strongly expanded and became the main economic pillar. The need for labor resulted in a new wave of immigration from the Americas, the Caribbean, the Philippines, and the Netherlands.

Aruba has been part of the Dutch Empire since 1636. Between 1845 and 1954 Aruba, Curaçao, Bonaire, and the windward islands of Saba, Sint Eustatius, and the Dutch part of Sint Maarten formed the colony of Curaçao and dependencies. As a relatively wealthy island, Aruba worked to separate itself from the colony since 1933. Insular nationalism was strengthened by cultural and racial differences with Curaçao. In 1954, the Netherlands Antilles were granted autonomy within the Dutch kingdom. After a rebellion on Curaçao in 1969, the Netherlands pressed for formal independence of the six Antillean Islands. Out of fear of becoming decolonized as a part of the Netherlands Antilles, Aruba opted for separate status. Despite unwillingness on the part of Curaçao and the Netherlands, Aruba became an autonomous part of the Dutch kingdom in 1986. The decision that Aruba would become fully independent in 1996 was revoked; Aruba remains autonomous within the Dutch kingdom.

**National Identity.** Papiamento is the most important marker of Aruban identity. Cultural and historical differences with Curaçao are stressed in the island's national identity. Identification with Dutch culture is weak, while Aruba's unique Indian history and cultural heritage are accentuated. The rural life of the mestizo population during the nineteenth century is an additional source of identity. Mass media, tourism, and massive immigration are agents of rapid change in cultural reality. Some citizens are cultural conservatives because of growing concern about this rapid change.

**Ethnic Relations.** Ethnic tensions focus around the immigrants who came to Aruba since 1988. A division exists between the immigrants from the Netherlands, the United States, and India and the unskilled or semi-skilled laborers from South America, the Caribbean, and the Philippines. The former hold better positions in tourism, trade, and banking, and also work in the government or the educational system. Some eight thousand South American, Caribbean, and Filipino immigrants are employed in lower-level positions in tourism, trade, and the construction sector. Women from Santo Domingo, Colombia, Haiti, and Jamaica work as live-in domestics for upper- and middle class families.

Political participation of non-Dutch immigrants is absent. Participation in trade unions is limited. Ethnic pressure groups do not exist, although internal informal ties are strong. Participation of immigrants in social, cultural, and political life is stagnating. In local newspapers and on radio stations the tensions between lower class Arubians and Latin American migrants are often expressed. The rise in crime is often unjustifiably ascribed to immigrants. The tourism sector and the educational system are the most important areas of social interaction and integration.

## URBANISM, ARCHITECTURE, AND THE USE OF SPACE

Aruba's capital, Oranjestad, is on the southwestern coast. It is the seat of the government and has a growing number of hotels. Cruise ships, shopping malls, and tourists dominate the street scene. A small fort called Fort Zoutman (1798) is Aruba's oldest building and is situated near the harbor of Oranjestad. Interesting monuments in Oranjestad are private homes from the 1920s and 1930s. The National Monument Office promotes the preservation of the 300 registered monuments. Thanks to public and private initiatives, several of these have been restored and relocated. San Nicolas, on the east side of the island, is the second largest town and the industrial center. Its industrial and private buildings date from the 1940s and 1950s. Plans for preservation and restoration are hampered by a lack of funds and political priority. The west and southwest shore form the tourism area. Luxurious hotels are built along the white beaches. Townships are spread over the island. Most important are Noord, Santa Cruz, and Savaneta. In Oranjestad and the townships many unique small colonial peasant houses—so-called "cunucu-houses"—were restored and modernized by their owners. Traditional elements, such as the saddle roof, are frequently incorporated in modern architecture.

Population growth has led to the building of many new residential areas. The lack of town and country planning threatens the balance between urbanization and the preservation of rural and natural landscapes. The hilly northeastern part of the island is the National Park, *Ari Kok*, which is allocated for preservation and eco-tourism.

## FOOD AND ECONOMY

*Food in Daily Life.* In the traditional menu maize dishes (*funchi, pan bati*), goat meat, fish, and *stoba*—stewpots of local vegetables (peas, beans)—dominate. Nowadays, rice, chicken, beef, and fish are eaten most. The number one snack is the *pastechi*, a small pie filled with cheese or beef. International food chains and Chinese, Italian, and other ethnic restaurants have gained popularity. Most food products are imported.

*Food Customs at Ceremonial Occasions.* Food is an important ingredient at most secular celebrations. At children's parties a *piñata* filled with sweets hangs on the ceiling. Blindfolded, the children try to hit the *piñata* with a stick. *Bolo pretu* (black cake) is offered at special occasions.

*Basic Economy.* Having scant natural resources of its own, Aruba has relied on oil refining and tourism as its main sources of income throughout the twentieth century. After the last major refinery close in 1985, government revenues and the standard of living declined 30 percent. Reconstruction of public finances and the expansion of the tourism sector resulted in economic recovery. The number of hotel rooms and time-shares tripled between 1986 and 1999.

Other sectors of the economy boomed after 1988, when unemployment disappeared. The gross domestic product (GDP) doubled between 1987 and 1992. Despite the economic recovery, serious concerns arose because of inflation and strains on the labor market, infrastructure, and the environment. Since about 1995 economic growth has stabilized. The establishment of Coastal Oil in 1988 and the expansion of free zone activities serve to diversify the vulnerable tourist-based economy. Government, hotels and restaurants, construction, transportation, real estate, and business are the nation's major employers.

*Land Tenure and Property.* The government owns approximately two-thirds of the island. Since the decline of agriculture after the arrival of the oil industry, land tenure has been important mostly for the construction of houses. Three types of land tenure occur: regular landed property; hereditary tenure or long lease; and the renting of government grounds. For economic purposes, especially in the oil industry and tourism, government grounds are rented in renewable leases of sixty years.

*Commercial Activities.* Commercial activities are concentrated in tourism and the oil industry. A

*In many townships, small colonial peasant houses have been restored and modernized.*

small number of offshore companies specializing in banking, insurance, and investment are established on the island.

**Major Industries.** Coastal Oil Corporate renovated the remains of the old Lago refinery and started operations in 1988. Wickland Oil Company handles oil transshipment. Small industries, such as breweries and bottling companies, are established in Oranjestad and near the Barcadera free zone area. Production is for local consumption and export.

**Trade.** Like commerce, trade is mainly directed towards tourism and local consumption. The United States is Aruba's largest trade partner. The free zone is becoming increasingly important because of revenues related to port charges and services.

**Division of Labor.** An important division of labor is based on ethnicity. Civil servants are drawn mostly from traditional Arubians and immigrants who arrived between 1924 and 1948, during the oil-boom years. In tourism these groups hold middle- and upper-management positions. Naturalized citizens and permanent residents of Lebanese, Madeirean, Chinese, and Jewish descent focus mainly on trade. Newly arrived Chinese immigrants have opened restaurants and supermarkets all over the island. Recent immigration includes Filipinos, Colombians, and Venezuelans, who hold lower-level positions in tourism and house keeping.

## SOCIAL STRATIFICATION

**Classes and Castes.** Aruba is divided along class, ethnic, and geographical lines, which to a large degree overlap. Although socio-economic inequality is significant, class lines are loosely defined. The upper class consists of traditional elite and Lebanese, Chinese, and Jewish minorities. Economic recovery after 1988 increased upward economic mobility for the middle class, whose spending has increased. Lower class Arubians and recent immigrants from South America and the Philippines form the lower social classes.

**Symbols of Social Stratification.** Social stratification is evident in consumption patterns. Conspicuous consumption is obvious for the upper class. Aruba's middle class has upper class consumptive aspirations. Arubians consider private ownership of houses extremely important. Residential patterns also reveal aspects of social stratification. Oranjestad west and Malmok are the residential areas of the upper class. Oranjestad east and San Nicolas are the poorest districts.

## POLITICAL LIFE

**Government.** Aruba has been an autonomous part of the Dutch kingdom since 1986. The governor of Aruba is the head of the Aruban government and the local representative of the Dutch monarch. The Netherlands' Council of Ministers consists of the Dutch cabinet and two ministers plenipotentiary, one representing Aruba and the other the Netherlands Antilles. The council is in charge of joint foreign policy, defense and justice, and the safeguarding of fundamental rights and freedom.

**Leadership and Political Officials.** Aruba is a parliamentary democracy with a multiparty system. Elections are held every four years. Since achieving the Status Aparte, the government has been dependent on coalitions between one of the two bigger parties and the smaller parties. The biggest parties are the Christian-democratic *Arubaanse Volspartij* (Peoples Party of Aruba) and the social-

democratic *Movimiento Electoral di Pueblo* (Peoples Electoral Movement). Democracy functions with a certain degree of patronage and nationalistic rhetoric. Political parties usually have one powerful leader who carefully selects candidates from different socio-economic, regional, and ethnic backgrounds.

**Social Problems and Control.** Some labor conflicts occur, but these have never led to serious threats to peace in the work place or to economic instability. An increase in petty crime is a concern to many citizens. Serious crimes are rare although armed robbery has increased during the last five years. Alcohol and drug abuse are serious concerns. Drug addicts, *chollers*, are resented. Local social control is provided by the juridical system. Aruba has its own legal powers but shares a Common Court of Justice with the Netherlands Antilles. The Supreme Court is situated in the Netherlands.

**Military Activity.** There has been no military activity on or near the island since 1942, when a German submarine attacked the Lago and Eagle oil refineries. Part of the Dutch Forces Caribbean is in Savaneta where approximately 270 Dutch and Aruban marines are stationed. Their primary task is to protect the island and its territorial waters. The Coast Guard of the Netherlands Antilles and Aruba started operations in 1995 to protect the islands and territorial waters from drug trafficking. In 1999 a division of the Maritime Interdiction Division of the United States Customs Service started surveying international waters for drug trafficking.

## SOCIAL WELFARE AND CHANGE PROGRAMS

Unemployment compensation is available for all persons born in Aruba. Free legal assistance is provided to those who are insolvent and registered. There is an increase in programs concerning child abuse, teenage pregnancy, school drop outs, marital violence, and drug abuse.

## NONGOVERNMENTAL ORGANIZATIONS AND OTHER ASSOCIATIONS

UNOCA (Union di Organisacionnan Arubano—Union of Aruban Cultural Organizations) is a nongovernmental board, which advises the minister of culture on the allocation of subsidies for cultural and scientific projects. CEDE-Aruba (Centro pa Desaroyo Social di Aruba—Center for Social Development of Aruba) is a more autonomous NGO that allocates funds to social and educational projects.

*Men buying shrimp from local vendors at Oranjestad Harbor.*

UNOCA and CEDE-Aruba are funded by the Dutch development aid program. A large number of welfare organizations focus on different topics, varying from the quality of day care centers to the care of the elderly. The government supports many of these with personnel and/or project subsidies.

Service clubs such as Lions, Rotary, and Jaycees have become more influential in recent years. They support welfare institutions with gifts and other forms of aid. Aruba has about ten environmental organizations. Some focus on educational activities, others act as pressure groups.

## GENDER ROLES AND STATUSES

***Division of Labor by Gender.*** The number of women in the labor market has increased enormously. Participation between 20 and 50 years of age varied between 60.3 and 74.4 percent in 1994, as compared to 31.6 and 59.8 percent in 1981. Unemployment for women is higher than for men. Women tend to leave the labor force at an earlier age than men do. Women outnumber men in service and sales positions. The minimum wage for men and women is the same. Discriminatory rules, which hampered female participation in the civil service, have been removed. Nevertheless, men continue to hold the more important positions.

***The Relative Status of Women and Men.*** Gender-oriented groups work for the re-evaluation of the existing position and role of women within the family and society. A feminist movement, which strives for a fundamental reconstruction of gender categories and roles, does not have a strong voice or a large following.

## MARRIAGE, FAMILY, AND KINSHIP

***Marriage.*** Monogamy and legal marriage are the norm, but extramarital and premarital relations are common. Fifty-nine of every one hundred marriages end in divorce. In 1998, 42.2 percent of live births were illegitimate. Intra-ethnic marriages are most common, but far from exclusive. In 1990 and 1991 45.2 percent of Aruban-born men and 24.8 percent of Aruban women married non-Arubans. One cause of this is that by marrying Arubians, foreigners can obtain much-desired Dutch nationality.

***Domestic Unit.*** The conjugal nuclear family is the most common domestic unit, but many other types are also common. The traditional household is matricentric.

***Inheritance.*** Normally all children share in the inheritance.

*A petroglyph on a cave in the inland desert of Aruba.*

**Kin Groups.** Until the beginning of the twentieth century the extended family and the conjugal nuclear-family household were the centers of kinship organization. As a result of patri- or matrilocal settlement, groups of brothers and/or sisters with their spouses lived near to each other on family grounds. Although a shortage of land and urbanization has caused a decrease of patri-and matrilocal settlement and the weakening of the traditional type of kinship organization, the kin group remains the most important locus of social interaction.

## SOCIALIZATION

**Infant Care.** Within the nuclear family the mother predominantly takes care of infants.

**Child Rearing and Education.** Socialization takes place mainly within the family and at school. As a consequence of the growing number of divorces and women's participation in the labor market, the nuclear family is weakening. A growing number of children are attending day care centers before entering the educational system. After-school care is taken up by private enterprise and the government supported project *Tra'i Merdia* (afternoon). Education is based on the Dutch system. At the age of four children attend kindergarten and after age six they attend primary school. After age twelve they enroll in secondary or vocational schools. After secondary education many students leave for Holland for further studies. In 1988 a large-scale renovation project of the educational system at all levels was initiated and was directed at modernizing and Arubanizing the Dutch oriented system.

**Higher Education.** The Aruban Teacher Training College provides higher education. The University of Aruba has departments of law and business administration. Adult education is provided by *Enseñanza pa Empleo* (Education for Employment).

## ETIQUETTE

Etiquette, ceremony, and protocol are enjoying growing popularity for many occasions. Aruban etiquette is basically a variation of the classical European formal tradition, with a Latin American *couleur locale*.

## RELIGION

**Religious Beliefs.** Eighty-six percent of the population is Roman Catholic but church attendance is much lower. Dutch Reformed-Lutheran Protestantism, the religion of the traditional elite, is embraced by less than 3 percent of the population. Twentieth century migration led to the appearance of smaller groups such as Methodists, Anglicans, Evangelists, Jehovah's Witnesses, Jews, Muslims, and Confucianists. The number of and participation in religious sects and movements are increasing.

**Religious Practitioners.** Traditional popular assumptions about the supernatural are called *brua*. Although the term originates from the Spanish word *bruja* (witch), *brua* is not equated with witchcraft. It includes magic, fortune telling, healing, and assumptions about both good and evil. Magic is conducted by a *hacido di brua* (practitioner of brua) and can be applied both beneficently and maliciously. Belief in brua often is not confirmed because of the low social esteem attached to it.

**Rituals and Holy Places.** Aruba has eight Catholic parishes and churches and a growing number of chapels. The chapel of Alto Vista (founded in 1750) is the most famous. The Dutch Reformed-Lutheran community has three churches; other Protestant denominations also have places of worship. The Jewish community (ashkenazim) has a synagogue in Oranjestad. Catholic, Protestant, and Jewish cemeteries are located in Oranjestad. A small cemetery of the free masonry is located next to these. Public cemeteries are located in San Nicolas and Sabana Basora, in the center of the island.

**Death and Afterlife.** Opinions on death and the afterlife are in accord with Christian doctrine. The traditional wake, called *Ocho Dia* (eight days), is the duration of the customary mourning period, in which close kin and friends participate. On the last evening of mourning the altar is taken apart, and chairs are turned upside down. Windows are opened to make sure the spirit of the deceased is able to leave the house. The wake, which has a medieval Spanish origin, is losing popularity.

## MEDICINE AND HEALTH CARE

The Doctor Horacio Oduber Hospital has 305 beds. San Nicolas has a public medical center. The number of private medical centers is increasing. Aruba has three geriatric homes. The introduction of general health insurance has met with many practical and political difficulties. Traditional healing methods (*remedi di tera*) make use of herbs and amulets, and are practiced by a healer (*curado* or *curioso*) who sometimes acts also as practitioner of brua. Modern natural healing methods are growing in popularity.

## SECULAR CELEBRATIONS

Traditional ceremonies typically have a Catholic origin or orientation. On New Year's Eve, best wishes are delivered at homes by small bands singing a serenade called *Dande*. Saint John's Day (24 June) is celebrated with traditional bonfires and the ceremony of *Dera Gai* (the burying of the rooster). Traditionally, a rooster was buried with its head under a calabash above the ground. At present the ceremony is carried out without the rooster. While a small band is playing and singing the traditional song of San Juan, blindfolded dancers from the audience try to hit the calabash with a stick. Of special importance are the celebrations of the 15th, 50th and 75th birthdays. Carnival was introduced on Aruba in the 1930s by Caribbean immigrants, and has become the most popular festival for the entire population.

National festive days are the Day of the National Anthem and the Flag on 18 March and Queen's Day on 30 April. The former stresses Aruba's political autonomy, while the latter celebrates the partnership with the Dutch kingdom. Aruba's former political leader, Francois Gilberto 'Betico' Croes (1938-1986), is commemorated on his birthday, 25 January. Croes is the personification of Aruba's struggle for separation from the Netherlands Antilles. Croes was seriously injured in a car crash a few hours before the proclamation of the Status Aparte on New Year's Eve 1985. He died in November 1986.

International Labor Day is celebrated on 1 May. Many occupational and service organizations groups have their own festive days.

## THE ARTS AND HUMANITIES

**Support for the Arts.** Aruban art life can be divided into two spheres: a commercial one and one directed at tourism and local recreation. Numerous artists are active in both. A lack of funds and clear governmental policy results in a tension between the commercialization of art for the benefit of tourism and the professionalization of local talent for non-commercial purposes. Expositions are mostly held in banks and ateliers. Plans to start a national arts museum are under discussion.

There has been a strong development and a growing popularity of different disciplines and styles since approximately 1986. Aruba's history, tradition, and natural landscape inspire many artists, who interpret in a modern, universal form. In recent years a number of artists have worked from a more individualistic perspective. Training abroad, workshops and interchange with foreign artists residing on Aruba, and participation in expositions abroad keeps the art community from isolation.

*Literature.* Literature focuses on poetry and youth literature. In the 1980s interesting novels, plays, and poetry by Aruban writers were published by the publishing house Charuba. At present little literary work of quality is being published. Most authors publish their own work. Efforts to revive Charuba have not yet been successful.

*Graphic Arts.* The Aruban landscape is a source of inspiration to many professional and leisure painters. Portrait painting is not very widespread. The popularity of both traditional sculpture as well as interdisciplinary three-dimensional graphic arts is rising. Following the economic recovery the number of graphic arts studios has increased since 1988. Most studio artists work as commercial designers. As an art form, graphics is still unrecognized.

*Performance Arts.* Aruba has several theater groups, of which Mascaruba is the oldest and most popular. The *Foundation Arte pro Arte* (FARPA, Art for the Arts) promotes local cultural and artistic projects, especially theatre. The Aruba Dance Foundation organizes international festivals and workshops. Several dance and/or ballet schools focus on youth. A theater, *Cas di Cultura*, is situated in Oranjestad. Aruba hosts biannual international dance and theater festivals. Musicians make a living by playing in the tourist sector and for local audiences. A new generation of Aruban musicians combines traditional Aruban and Caribbean musical styles, with modern influences of hip-hop and reggae. The celebration of Carnival is the high point of the year. The Aruban School of Music offers instrumental music courses. A large number of choirs exist on the island.

## THE STATE OF THE PHYSICAL AND SOCIAL SCIENCES

Archeological research is carried out by the Aruba Archeological Museum under cooperation with the Dutch University of Leiden. The National Historical Archives and the Cultural Institute undertake some historical and cultural research, but scientific research leans heavily on private and foreign initiative. FUNDINI (Fundacion pa Investigacion y Informavcion—Foundation for Information and Investigation) is a foundation for the promotion of social scientific research and information.

## BIBLIOGRAPHY

Alofs, Luc. *Indian Aruba: An Anthropological Perspective,* 2001.

——— and Leontine Merkies. *Ken ta Arubiano?: Sociale integratie en natievorming op Aruba,* 2nd ed., 2001.

DeHaan, T. J. *Antilliaanse Instituties: De Economische Ontwikkelingen van de Nederlandse Antillen en Aruba, 1969–1995,* 1998.

Green, Vera. *Migrants in Aruba* 1974.

Hartog, J. *Arbua, zoals het was, zoals het werd: van de tijd der indianen tot heden,* 1980.

*Labor Force Survey 1994,* 1995.

Lampe, A., ed. *The Future Status of Aruba and the Netherlands Antilles,* 1994.

Oostindie, G. and P. Verton. "ki Sorto di Reino/What Kind of Kingdom? Antillean and Aruban Views and Expectations on the Kingdom of the Netherlands." *West Indian Guide* 72 (1 and 2): 43–75, 1998.

Versteeg, Aad. H. and Stephen Rostain, eds. *The Archaeology of Aruba: The Tanki Flip Site,* 1997.

——— and Arminda C. Ruiz. *Reconstructing the Brasilwood Island: the archaeology and the landscape of Indian Aruba,* 1995.

—LUC ALOFS

# AUSTRALIA

## CULTURE NAME
Australian

## ALTERNATIVE NAMES

"Aussie" is a colloquialism that was used during World War I to refer to Australian-born people of British or Irish ancestry. Initially used to describe a happy-go-lucky character capable of battling through hard times, the term was employed after World War II to distinguish those born domestically from "new" immigrants from western and southern Europe. The term continues to have meaning as a label for Australians representing their country. Among some sectors of society, "Aussie" is regarded as Eurocentric and anachronistic in a nation officially committed to ethnic and racial inclusiveness.

## ORIENTATION

**Identification.** The name "Australia" was formally adopted and popularized in 1817 by the British governor of the colony of New South Wales. The title was suggested in 1814 and derives from the Latin *terra australis incognita* ("the unknown south land") which had been used by mapmakers for centuries before European colonization.

Since its days as a British colony Australia has developed a complex national culture with immigrants from many parts of the world as well as an indigenous Aboriginal and Torres Strait Islander population. The strong sense of societal and historical distinctiveness among the different states and territories has not developed into major subcultural diversity based on geographic regions.

For much of the nation's history, there has been a focus on assimilating different cultural groups into the dominant British Australian traditions; however, in the early 1970s a more pluralist policy of multiculturalism came to prominence. In 1988, bicentennial events were promoted officially as the "celebration of a nation." A commitment was made to the idea that Australia is a collectivity of diverse peoples living in a relatively young society. However, the divisions within the nation continue to find expression in public life, arising from social differences in race, ethnicity, social class, and gender.

**Location and Geography.** Australia is an island continent in the Southern Hemisphere, lying between Antarctica and Asia. It is surrounded by the Indian Ocean to the west; the Timor, Arafura, and Coral Seas to the north; the Pacific Ocean to the east; and the Tasman Sea and Southern Ocean to the south. Much of the continent is low, flat, and dry. The area of the continent is 2.97 million square miles (7.69 million square kilometers).

Although the impact of environmental variation is highly evident in the traditional cultures of indigenous Australians, it has not been as strong a factor in immigrant cultures. The most significant lifestyle differences are affected primarily by variations in climate.

Australia has six states (Western Australia, South Australia, Victoria, Tasmania, New South Wales, and Queensland) and two territories (the Northern Territory and the Australian Capital Territory), whose capital cities are, respectively, Perth, Adelaide, Melbourne, Hobart, Sydney, Brisbane, Darwin, and Canberra. The majority of the population lives in urban areas around the coast.

The capital city, Canberra, is located in the Australian Capital Territory (ACT). The ACT was created in 1909, and the city of Canberra was designed by an American landscape architect in 1912. The Commonwealth Parliament relocated there from Melbourne in 1927. Canberra has a population of over 300,000 and is the largest inland city.

**Demography.** According to the 1986 census, the total population was just over 15.5 million. By 1992 the population had risen to 17.5 million, and

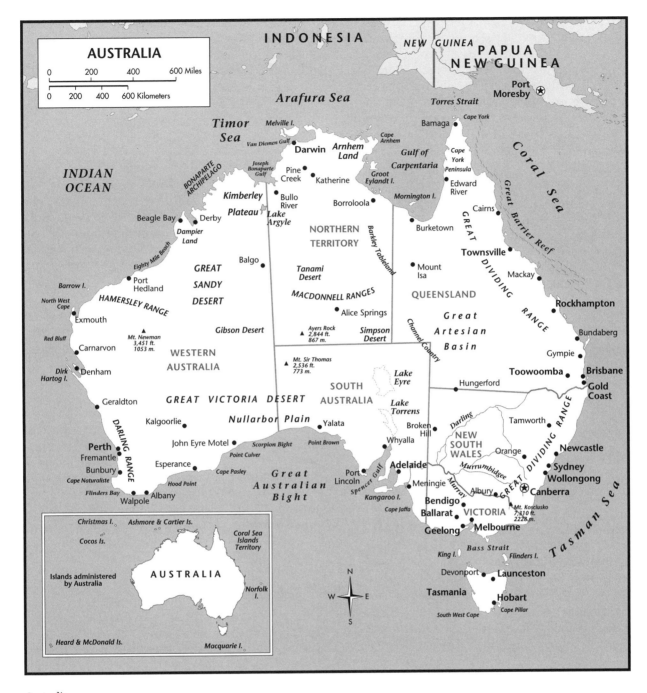

*Australia*

in 1996 it reached 18.3 million. In the year 2000, that number is expected to reach 19 million. In 1997, 4.3 million (23 percent) residents were born overseas. Roughly 2 percent of the population consists of Aboriginal or Torres Strait Islander people, descendants of the original inhabitants of the continent before European colonization. This sector of the population has a higher birthrate than do the others, but also has a higher mortality rate and lower life expectancy. In 1996 the population self-identifying as Aboriginal or Torres Strait Islander was 372,000, probably about the same as in 1788; many of those people have both Aboriginal and non-Aboriginal ancestry.

***Linguistic Affiliation.*** The dominant language since colonization has been English, with little multi-lingualism among the majority population. Nevertheless, both the diverse Aboriginal groups and many immigrants continue to use languages other than English.

Before the European invasion there were around 250 Aboriginal languages, most of which probably had distinct dialects. Perhaps ninety of these languages are still spoken, with around twenty being spoken fluently by indigenous children. The decline in the use of Aboriginal languages is due to the effects of colonization. Among some Aboriginal groups, especially in parts of the north, a number of distinctive creole dialects mix Aboriginal languages with English.

Apart from indigenous languages, some twelve major community languages are spoken at home by at least fifty thousand speakers. These are, in order of the number of speakers, Italian, Greek, Chinese, Serbo-Croatian, Arabic, German, Vietnamese, Spanish, Polish, Macedonian, Filipino languages, and Maltese. Melbourne is the most multilingual city. Migrant groups want their languages to be maintained through government policies such as the Languages Other Than English (LOTE) program in secondary schools.

Australian English probably originated as a combination of British regional dialects used by groups of convicts and others who came to the colonies. Australian English is different from British and American English but does not vary much regionally. Various social factors affect accent and style, including social class, education, gender (women tend to use the cultivated variety more than men do), and age.

**Symbolism.** The flag is dark blue with the British Union Jack in the upper left corner, the seven-pointed white Commonwealth star below the Union Jack, and to the right five white stars representing the Southern Cross constellation. The national animal emblem is the kangaroo, the floral emblem is the golden wattle tree, and the national colors are green and gold. The national coat of arms is a shield supported by a kangaroo and an emu amid branches of wattle. Until 1984 the national anthem was the British "God Save the Queen," but it was changed to "Advance Australia Fair" as part of a movement toward asserting greater separation from the legacy of the colonial power.

These formal symbols have assisted in the establishment of a national consciousness. A highly symbolic national event held annually is Anzac Day which marks the landing and subsequent gallant defeat of Australian troops at Gallipoli during World War I. Throughout the country war memorials and monuments acknowledge the achievements and sacrifices made by Australians in that and other wars.

Flora and fauna native to the continent, such as the kangaroo, koala, emu, and wattle, are symbols of the national ethos, especially in international and national contexts, although this is also the case for unique buildings such as the Sydney Harbour Bridge and the Sydney Opera House. The beach is recognized as a symbol of the national culture.

## HISTORY AND ETHNIC RELATIONS

**Emergence of the Nation.** Australian began as a British penal colony in the eighteenth century, and its national character has formed predominantly through the mechanisms of immigration and race relations. Other factors that have shaped the national culture include the early small female population relative to that of men, which is said to have laid the foundations for a widespread ideology of mateship. The involvement of Australian and New Zealand (Anzac) troops in World War I has been characterized as the symbolic birth of the nation.

A further impetus for the formation of a national culture was the myth of the rural bushman, which developed around early phases of the historical establishment of pastoral and agricultural industries. The "bush" mythology has continued to influence conceptions of the national character despite the fact that the population has always been concentrated in urban coastal centers. The relatively sunny climate has facilitated an image of a sporting, outdoor, beach-loving culture represented by images such as the bronzed Aussie surfer.

**National Identity.** After the invasion in 1788 by British colonists, the indigenous population was dominated by force. Aboriginal societies across the continent experienced violence and disease. After colonization a general history of discrimination and racism was mixed with a range of more benevolent policies. Of lasting effect was the policy of assimilating Aboriginal people into the mainstream culture. The historical stress on assimilation had its most dramatic impact on the children of mixed Aboriginal–European descent who, especially in the first half of the twentieth century, were taken from their Aboriginal parents so that they could be "civilized" and raised in "white" society. These individuals have become known collectively as the "stolen generations" and public acknowledgment of their plight is an important part of the process of reconciliation between Aboriginal peoples and other Australians.

The ideology of assimilation permeated relations not only with the indigenous population but also with immigrants. The early British Protestant

*The Sydney Opera House, one of the most readily-recognizable buildings in Australia.*

colonists were bolstered by the arrival of Irish Catholic settlers who eventually (through their involvement in the development of a Catholic education system and their representation in government) became incorporated into the dominant cultural group. Since that time Australia has been defined as an Anglo-fragment society in which British or Anglo-Celtic culture was and remains dominant. However, immigration over the last two centuries has created a nation that is among the most culturally diverse in the world.

The intergenerational reproduction of minority ethnic identities has produced a national culture that is multicultural, polyethnic, and cosmopolitan. Since the 1970s this diversity has been encouraged through progressive equity legislation that promotes recognition of difference and tolerance of diversity. Nevertheless, multicultural policy has been dominated by a culturalist philosophy in which linguistic and lifestyle (food, dress) diversity has been recognized more readily than have the structural economic difficulties of some immigrant groups. Despite the focus on cultural diversity, the Anglo-Celtic heritage continues to dominate most institutional aspects of society, including the media, the legal system, public education, and the system of health care.

***Ethnic Relations.*** The first migrants were Chinese, attracted by the 1850s and 1860s gold rushes. Fear of miscegenation and xenophobia and the consequent race riots resulted in restrictive legislation against the importation of Pacific and Chinese labor. However, immigration was viewed as important; a well known catch phrase was "populate or perish," reflecting the rationale that population growth would aid both defense and economic development.

The Federation of States in 1901 coincided with the implementation of one of the most influential governmental policies affecting the development of the national culture: The Immigration Restriction Act. This "White Australia Policy" was aimed primarily at combating the perceived "yellow peril" represented by immigrants from neighboring Asian countries. Throughout much of the twentieth century, migrants were selected according to a hierarchy of desirability that was broadened as preferred sources dried up. The British were always at the top of the list, and a number of government subsidies and settlement schemes were implemented to encourage their immigration.

Immigration thus can be defined as a series of waves, with the British dominating until the 1940s, followed by northern Europeans (including displaced persons from World War I), southern Europeans (predominantly in the post–World War II

**115**

period), and eventually, after the White Australia Policy was abandoned in 1972, Asians. Immigration has declined since the 1980s, and it is now difficult to gain entry. The number of migrants has become an issue of debate, particularly in regard to uninvited refugees.

Australia's long history of immigration and the increasing ethnic diversity of its population have spurred debates about the definition of an Australian. Many Aboriginal and Asian citizens still experience a sense of alienation and exclusion from acceptance as "real" Aussies and in difficult economic times often become political and social scapegoats. However, concerted efforts have been made to present these groups in a positive and inclusive light.

New Zealand is the national culture related most closely to Australia. New Zealanders have special entry rights, and there have been large population flows in both directions. Australians and New Zealanders compete energetically in areas such as sport but cooperate closely in international relations.

## URBANISM, ARCHITECTURE, AND THE USE OF SPACE

There has always been a high concentration of urban and suburban dwellers, partly because the harsh physical environment has encouraged people to remain close to the fertile coastal areas. In 1991, 70 percent of Australians lived in thirteen cities that had more than 100,000 people and 39 percent of the population lived in Sydney and Melbourne. Notions of national identity have long been framed around a distinction between the city and the bush, with urban and rural dwellers articulating different economic and social interests.

The cities are characterized by low-density housing and dependence on private cars. In recent decades there has been increased inner-city redevelopment aimed at attracting locals and tourists to central public shopping and recreational areas.

Across cities and towns, significant icons in public spaces include war memorials, sporting grounds, and prominent structures such as the new Parliament House in Canberra. Also of great importance are the "natural" icons such as Uluru, a huge sandstone monolith in Central Australia, and the Great Barrier Reef, which stretches down the east coast of northern Queensland. Major development projects are celebrated as national achievements, especially the Snowy Mountains and Ord River schemes, which were constructed from the 1950s to the 1970s to bring irrigated water to agricultural

areas. The Snowy Mountains project generates hydroelectric power and is regarded as the nation's greatest engineering feat.

Personal home ownership is a common goal, and the nation has one of the highest home ownership rates in the world. In recent decades homes have become larger with more bedrooms and bathrooms, designs have created greater internal spaciousness, and more elaborate fittings and household possessions have been obtained. The quality of private dwellings, however, varies considerably with a household's level of income. Since the 1960s housing has been more diverse in style and size, but the conventional single-story separate house remains predominant.

## FOOD AND ECONOMY

**Food in Daily Life.** Before colonization, Aboriginal peoples were sustained by a diverse range of flora and fauna. The early settlers primarily consumed meat (at first native animals, later beef and mutton), bread, and vegetables, particularly potatoes.

Nearly all regularly eaten foods—except seafood—were introduced after European settlement. However, there have been considerable changes in food preference patterns. In the 1940s meat consumption began to decline, poultry consumption increased dramatically after the 1960s, and there has been a doubling of seafood consumption since the 1930s, in addition to a steady increase in fruit and vegetable consumption since the 1950s.

Since World War II the diet has become highly diversified. Each wave of immigrants has had an impact, including German, Italian, Greek, Lebanese, Jewish, and Southeast Asian foods and cooking styles. Olive and vegetable oils have replaced dripping and lard, and items such as garlic and Asian condiments are used more commonly.

Australian chefs are known worldwide for their "fusion cuisine," a blending of European cooking traditions with Asian flavors and products. Nevertheless, certain foods are recognized as national emblems, including Vegemite (a yeast extract spread), Milo (a powdered base for chocolate milk drinks), Anzac biscuits (oat biscuits sent to soldiers in World War I), and damper (a wheat flour-based loaf traditionally cooked in the ashes of a fire by settlers).

Australians are among the world leaders in fast-food consumption. Burger and chicken chain stores are prominent in the suburbs, having displaced the traditional meat pies and fish and chips. While Australians were long known as tea drinkers, coffee and wine have become increasingly popular.

*A shearer cuts the wool from a sheep in Stawell, Victoria.*

Before World War II Australians drank about twenty times more beer than wine; beer consumption remains high, but wine drinking has increased at a much greater rate, and the country has become a significant exporter of wine.

**Food Customs at Ceremonial Occasions.** No foods are reserved for special occasions, although the religious traditions of some ethnic groups include ceremonial foods. Easter and Christmas are observed by most of the population. Christmas usually is celebrated as it is in Britain, with roast turkey, ham, and roast vegetables followed by a steamed fruit pudding. However, there is an increasing tendency for Christmas to involve a light seafood meal, and barbecues are becoming popular as well. Instead of pudding, many people have ice cream cakes or cold desserts such as pavlova (made from egg whites and sugar). Some people celebrate "Christmas in July," using the coldest month of the year to enjoy the hot dinner of a traditional Christmas.

Special meals are eaten among ethnic groups to celebrate Easter or Passover. Molded chocolate products (Easter eggs) are given to children at this time.

**Basic Economy.** After forty years of settlement, when there was little scope for industrial or commercial enterprises, the pastoral industry became a key force in economic development. In particular, growth in the wool industry was associated with advances in the rest of the economy. Gold surpassed wool as the nation's major export in the 1850s and 1860s, resulting in a rapid expansion of banking and commerce.

From federation until 1930 there was some expansion in manufacturing industries, and with the onset of World War II, the manufacturing sector was developed to respond to the demand for war materials and equipment. Some industries expanded and new ones were developed rapidly to produce munitions, ships, aircraft, machinery, chemicals, and textiles.

After the war exports consisted mainly of primary commodities such as wool, wheat, coal, and metals. High tariffs and other controls were imposed on most imported goods. Although many of those controls were lifted in the 1960s, effective rates of protection remained high. The government continues to be involved in the operation of some public enterprises, including railways, electricity, and post offices and telecommunications. There remains a government interest in the Commonwealth Bank.

A move toward privatization at the state and commonwealth levels of government has been gaining momentum since the early 1980s. Some states, such as Victoria, have embraced this move much more than others have. Australia is highly integrated into the global capitalist economy. Since World War II, much trade has been redirected from Britain and Europe to the Asia-Pacific region, especially Japan. A related trend has been the growth of mineral exports since the mid–1960s.

**Land Tenure and Property.** When the British took control of the continent in 1788, they deemed it *terra nullius* (land that was not owned). According to British law all Australian land was the property of the Crown. In the last two decades of the eighteenth century, land grants were made to emancipated convicts, free settlers, marines, and officers. Land was available to anyone prepared to employ and feed the convicts who were assigned to it as servants. In 1825 sale of land by private tender was introduced.

Land is held as freehold (privately owned through purchase), leasehold (pastoralists and others are given special usage rights for a specified numbers of years), national parks, and Crown Land, which effectively remains under the control of the government. In 1992 a new form of rights in land was legally recognized—"native title"—as a form of continuing Aboriginal and islander connection with the land. To the extent that a system of indigenous customary law can be shown to have continued from the time of European establishment of sovereignty, these groups can make claims to their traditional lands.

**Commercial Activities.** The economy is strong in the service sector in relation to goods-producing industries. Those industries, including agriculture, forestry, fishing, mining, manufacturing, construction, and energy, contributed around 31 percent of gross domestic product (GDP) during the mid-1990s, while the services industries contributed 60 percent. Goods-producing industries provided around a quarter of employment, with the rest provided by service industries.

Service industries include distribution industries (wholesale trade, retail trade, accommodation, cafés and restaurants, and transport and storage) and communication and business services (communications, finance and insurance, and property services). Other service industries are government administration and defense, education, health and community services, and cultural and recreational services.

**Major Industries.** In 1996 and 1997, manufacturing was the most significant sector. Wholesale trade was the only other industry to contribute over 10 percent of GDP, manufacturing accounted for 12 percent of total employment, behind retail at 15 percent. Another major contributor was the property and business services industry. Primary industries in mining and agriculture are of key economic importance. The development of large mines in some remote regions has been associated with the establishment of towns and increased employment.

**Trade.** In order of economic significance, Australia's current major trading partners include the United States, Japan, China, United Kingdom, Republic of Korea, and New Zealand. Australia is one of the world's largest exporters of wool, meat, and wheat and a major supplier of sugar, dairy products, fruits, cotton, and rice.

Major imports include passenger motor vehicles, telecommunications equipment, and crude petroleum oils.

**Division of Labor.** There has been considerable upward socioeconomic mobility, but there is some inequality in the distribution of work. Unemployment has been a problem in recent years, and for some people only part-time or casual employment

is available. Youth unemployment is a major problem in some regions.

Australia is increasingly shifting toward an information economy that relies on a high-skill base. Thus, the workers most at risk of unemployment are laborers, factory workers, and those who learn their skills on the job. Highly skilled managers, medical practitioners, teachers, computer professionals, and electricians have the lowest risk of unemployment.

There has been a widening gap between rich and poor over the past fifteen to twenty years and the household income gap between the poorest and richest neighborhoods has grown considerably. A substantial number of people live below the poverty line.

## SOCIAL STRATIFICATION

**Classes and Castes.** The three main social classes are the working class, the middle class, and the upper class, but the boundaries between these groups are a matter of debate. The wealthiest 5 to 10 percent are usually regarded as upper class, with their wealth derived from ownership and control of property and capital. The growing middle class is defined as individuals with nonmanual occupations.

Nonmanual workers typically earn more than manual workers, although upper-level manual workers such as tradespeople earn more than those in sales and personal service positions. The professions, which include such occupations as accountants, computing specialists, engineers, and medical doctors, have been one of the fastest growing sectors of the economy. Since the 1980s the number of manual workers has been in decline.

Manual workers form the nucleus of the working class; 20 to 40 percent self-identify with this category. Class consciousness includes the acknowledgment of class divisions, but there is also a broad commitment to an ethic of egalitarianism. Australians commonly believe that socioeconomic mobility is possible and exhibit a basic tolerance and acceptance of inequality associated with social class.

**Symbols of Social Stratification.** The upper-class can be signified by expensive clothes, motor vehicles, and homes. In particular, the economic value of housing and other real estate properties varies greatly across different suburbs in all cities.

However, class is not always evident from clothes, cars, and living circumstances. Middle-class people from economically wealthy backgrounds

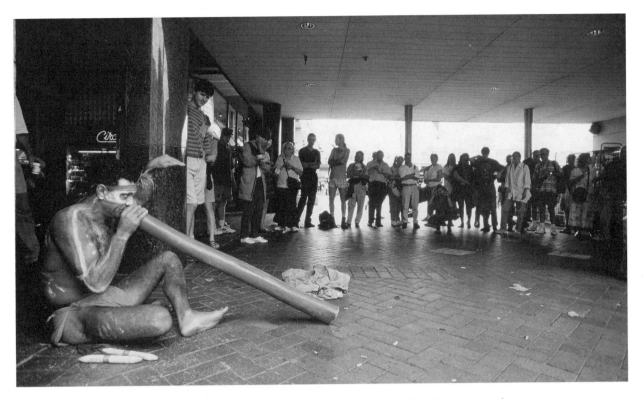

*An Australian aborigine wears traditional face and body paints and plays a didgeridoo for tourists and commuters at Circular Quay.*

may mask their prosperity according to fashion, choice, or participation in particular subcultures. Young people such as students may dress to mimic imagined styles valued for their symbolic rejection of wealth, and some working-class families go into debt to purchase expensive cars and other commodities.

Patterns of speech, consumption patterns associated with entertainment and the arts, and participation in certain sports may be useful indicators of class.

## POLITICAL LIFE

*Government.* Australia is a parliamentary democracy based on the British system of government. Federal, state, and territorial elections are held every three or four years. Voting is compulsory at the federal and state levels but not at the local government level. There are two houses of the federal and state parliaments except in Queensland, the Northern Territory, and the Australian Capital Territory.

Core features of the political party system derive from early twentieth-century arrangements that followed the federation of the states into a commonwealth. There are two major political parties: the Australian Labor Party (ALP) and the Liberal Party. The National Party (formerly the Country Party) allies itself with the conservative Liberal Party. The other large political parties are the Australian Democrats and the Green Party.

Since federation, the constitution has been changed only reluctantly through referenda. In 1999 there was a vote rejecting the proposition that Australia become a republic, ceasing to have an office of governor-general as a representative of the British monarch and thus as the titular head of state. Some argue that the society is already a de facto republic since the constitution has entrenched the primacy of popular sovereignty. The British Union Jack on the flag is for some people an acknowledgment of historical ties with Britain, while for others it is a reason to change the constitution to emphasize the independence of the nation.

*Leadership and Political Officials.* There are three levels of government leadership: the prime minister in the federal government, the state premiers, and the mayors in local government. All officials are elected democratically. At the federal level the governor-general is appointed by the government, as are governors at the state level. Federal and state/territorial governments operate through departments that are organized bureaucratically

*An opal miner working in a field near the South Australian outback town of Coober Pedy. Mining is one of the most important industries in Australia.*

and hierarchically. High-ranking officials are important in the administration of policies and laws.

***Social Problems and Control.*** In the legal system authority is divided between states and territories and the commonwealth. The judicial system is based on the common law of England. The criminal justice system consists of the state and commonwealth agencies and departments responsible for dealing with crime and related issues. The federal criminal justice system deals with offenses against commonwealth laws, and the state systems deal with offenses against state laws. Criminal law is administered mainly through the commonwealth, state, and territorial police forces; the National Crime Authority; and the state and territorial corrective or penal services. Crimes such as stealing are more common than crimes against individuals, such as assault.

***Military Activity.*** The defense forces operate according to three basic priorities: defeating attacks from outside the country, defending the nation's regional interests, and supporting a global security environment that discourages international aggression. Australia has a volunteer army reserve but no national service requirement. There is a navy, an army, and an air force. Twelve percent of regular service positions are held by women.

The nation's strategic stance is broadly defensive, with the expectation that armed force will be used only to defend national interests. The Defence Force has been called on frequently, to assist in international security and humanitarian crises in the Middle East, Namibia, and Cambodia as well as in humanitarian crises in Somalia and Rwanda. The most recent military activity has been peacekeeping in East Timor. The Defence Force also has played a key role in responding to major floods and fires, and its services are called on in search and rescue missions.

## SOCIAL WELFARE AND CHANGE PROGRAMS

The approach to social welfare is based on the notions of "a fair go" for all and egalitarianism. Since the 1970s, legislation has promoted equity and equal access to services for all citizens, often to improve the chances of the disadvantaged. This history of helping "the battler" has been challenged by notions of economic rationalism.

Pertinent social welfare issues include rising unemployment, an aging population, child care, assisting people from diverse cultural backgrounds, assisting people in remote areas, and poverty. Approximately two million people live below the poverty line.

A host of social welfare provisions have been enacted throughout the nation's history. Australia was one of the first countries to give women the vote. It also was the first country to legislate a forty-hour working week (in 1948).

## NONGOVERNMENTAL ORGANIZATIONS AND OTHER ASSOCIATIONS

The government maintains continuing relationships with many large and small Nongovernmental organizations (NGOs) that are active in human rights and community services (Amnesty International, Australian Red Cross, Defense for Children International, and International Women's Development Agency). NGOs provide relevant needs-based community services and welfare and promote changes in government policies and activities. Most not-for-profit NGOs were created by religious orga-

nizations to meet perceived needs or by community members to deal with a specific problem (Salvation Army, Brotherhood of Saint Lawrence, Care Australia). The government encourages the existence of charitable NGOs through tax exemptions and liberal laws of association and incorporation. Often, NGOs are established in response to immediate or emergency social problems. The government will intervene when resources are not being used efficiently and when services are being duplicated.

NGOs, particularly those in the nonprofit sector, are major providers of welfare services and significant contributors in the health, education, sport, recreation, entertainment, and finance industries. The bulk of their revenue comes from government grants, private donations, and service fees.

## GENDER ROLES AND STATUSES

*Division of Labor by Gender.* British ideas and practices involving gender were imported with colonization. Women tend to be associated with the private sphere, unpaid work, and the home, while men tend to be associated with the public sphere, paid work, and the larger society. This division was particularly pronounced in the early years of settlement, when free settler women were seen as homemakers who brought civility to the male population. Migrant women have been valued for their ability to create settled families and generally have entered the country as dependents.

Traditionally, occupation has been sex-segregated, with women predominating as domestics and in the "caring professions," such as teaching and nursing. However, sex discrimination and affirmative action policy since the late 1970s has been directed toward promoting gender equality in all spheres. As a consequence, there have been increases in women's participation in secondary and higher education as well as in the general workforce and an increase in the availability of child care.

*The Relative Status of Women and Men.* Many areas of social, economic, political, and religious life remain gendered, generally to the disadvantage of women. Women are underrepresented in scientific occupations, managerial positions, and the professions and overrepresented in administrative and clerical positions. Women earn on average less than men do and spend more time than men doing unpaid domestic work.

Women's right to vote in federal elections was included in the constitution of 1901. Nevertheless, the progress of women in entering public office was

*A traditional pearling lugger is loaded with supplies at Streeter's Jetty.*

slow. In 1995 women's representation in local, state and federal government was around 20 percent. Although women are more likely to spend time on religious activities than men, the majority of religious ministers are male.

## MARRIAGE, FAMILY, AND KINSHIP

**Marriage.** Most heterosexual couples marry for love and to confirm a long-term emotional, financial, and sexual commitment. Arranged marriages occur in some ethnic groups, but are not considered desirable by most people. Marriage is not essential for a cohabiting relationship or child rearing, but nearly 60 percent of people over fifteen years of age are married. The law grants members of de facto relationships legal rights and responsibilities equivalent to those of formally married couples. Homosexual couples are not recognized by law as married regardless of a long-term relationship. Marriage occurs with a civil or religious ceremony conducted by a registered official and can take place in any public or private location. The ceremony usually is followed by a celebration with food, drink, and music. Guests provide gifts of household goods or money, and the parents of the couple often make substantial contributions to the cost of the wedding. No other official exchange of property occurs.

Divorce has been readily available since 1975 and involves little stigma. It requires a one-year separation period and occurs in approximately 40 percent of first marriages. Upon divorce, the husband and wife agree to divide their mutual property and child-rearing responsibilities; law courts and mediators sometimes to assist with this process. Remarriage is common and accepted. A significant trend in family formation is a dramatic increase in the proportion of marriages preceded by a period of cohabitation.

**Domestic Unit.** The nuclear family is widely considered the norm; the most common household unit in the 1996 census was the couple, followed closely by the couple with dependent children, then the one-parent family with dependent children, the couple with nondependent children, and other family groups.

A pervasive myth is that the extended family does not exist and that society is composed of nuclear families cut off from extended kin. While most people live in couple-only or nuclear family households, the extended family is an important source of support for most people. Blended families and stepfamilies with children from former marriages are becoming more common.

**Inheritance.** Citizens have "testamentary freedom" or the right to declare how they wish their property to be distributed after death. With this freedom, individuals can legally enforce their cultural practices. They also can choose to remove relatives from the will and pass their property to a charitable organization or an unrelated person. If an individual dies without a valid will, the property is distributed to the spouse, then the children of the deceased, and then the parents and other kin. If there are no relatives, the property goes to the Crown.

**Kin Groups.** Broad kin groups are not a significant feature of the national culture, but extended families exist across households and are the basis for emotional, financial, and social support. Many minority ethnic groups recognize kin networks of considerable breadth. Aboriginal cultures encompass principles of traditional kinship in which large networks of relatives form the significant communities of everyday life.

## SOCIALIZATION

**Infant Care.** Child rearing varies considerably with the country of origin, class background, the education and occupation of the parents, and the religious group to which a family belongs. While most practices are aimed at developing a responsible and independent child, Aboriginal and many migrant families tend to indulge young children more than do most Anglo-Celtic parents. Some ethnic groups supervise their young more strictly than the dominant Anglo-Celtic population, encouraging them to mix only with family and friends, be dependent on the family, and leave decision making to the parents.

**Child Rearing and Education.** Mothers are the preferred primary caretakers, although fathers are taking increasing responsibility for child care. In the past mothers were not as isolated in their child care responsibilities, receiving help from older children, extended kin, and neighbors. The reduction in family and household size in recent years has meant that the burden of care falls largely on mothers. There is significant variation in ideas about good parenting, reflecting the diverse cultural values and traditions of parents' ethnic background. Practices justified by recent scientific research usually are considered the best. In the past the values most prized in children were obedience and deference, but today good parenting is commonly associated with having assertive and independent children. There are no formal initiation ceremonies for the "national culture," although the twenty-first birthday often is celebrated as a rite of passage into adulthood.

Access to high-quality education is considered the right of all citizens, and the government provides compulsory primary and secondary schooling for children between ages six and fifteen. Most schools are fully funded by the government. The remainder are nongovernment schools that receive nearly half their funding from fees and private sources such as religious associations. Attendance at nongovernment schools has been increasing since the 1970s because it is felt that independent schooling provides better educational and employment opportunities. Preschool centers are available for children younger than age six. Nongovernment schools are mainly Catholic. Education is aimed at providing children with social and workplace skills. Educational methods vary depending on particular requirements; for example, education for children in remote rural locations relies heavily on advanced communication technologies. Guidelines have been established in all states for dealing with children with special educational needs, such as those with disabilities and those who are intellectually gifted. Some schools with a high percentage of Aboriginal and/or migrant pupils have special language policies that include instruction in languages other than English.

**Higher Education.** Higher education is considered to offer the best employment opportunities. Consequently, tertiary education has become more widely available and is undertaken by an increasingly larger proportion of the population. It is available in two forms: universities and institutions of technical and further education (TAFE). In 1992, 37 percent of women and 47 percent of men received post-school qualifications, and 12.3 percent of the labor force held university degrees in 1993. Universities also attract substantial numbers of overseas students. The government is responsible for funding most universities and institutions, with increasing contributions being made by students in the form of fees and postgraduation tax payments.

## ETIQUETTE

A predominant image among Australians is that they are very casual, easygoing, and familiar. First names are used commonly as terms of address. An ideology of egalitarianism pervades, with men, women, and children treated similarly. Attempts at appearing superior to others in terms of dress, manners, knowledge, and the work ethic are discouraged. A handshake is the most common way to greet a new acquaintance, and a hug, a kiss on the cheek, or a verbal greeting the most common way to greet a friend. The colloquialism, ''g'day'' (good day), is considered the quintessential greeting.

There is an easy friendliness in public places. Personal privacy is respected and staring is discouraged, although eye contact is not avoided. Eye contact during conversation is considered polite among the general population; averting the eyes during conversation is considered a sign of respect among Aboriginal people. When a line is forming, new arrivals must go to the end. In museums and exhibitions voices are hushed. In performance contexts the audience is expected to be silent and attentive. Service attendants consider themselves equal to their guests, and usually are not subservient. Australians also resist being ''served.'' Food may be eaten in the street, but meals usually are eaten at a table, with each person having his or her own plate and eating utensils. Bodily functions are considered inevitable but are not discussed or performed in public.

## RELIGION

**Religious Beliefs**. The constitution guarantees religious freedom, and while there is no official national religion, Australia generally is described as a Christian country. British colonists brought the Anglican belief system in 1788, and three-quarters of the population continues to identify with some form of Christianity, predominantly the Catholic and Anglican faiths. Until recently almost all businesses closed for Christian religious holidays.

Extensive immigration has made Australia one of the most religiously diverse societies in the world. Almost all faiths are represented, with significant numbers of Muslims, Buddhists, Jews, and Hindus. Many indigenous Australians have embraced Christianity, often as a result of their contact with missionaries and missions.

Religious alternatives such as spiritualism and Theosophy have had a small but steady presence since the 1850s. A growing set of beliefs is represented by the so-called New Age movement, which arrived in the 1960s and evolved into the widespread alternative health and spirituality movement of the 1990s. This has opened the way for an interest in paganism and other aspects of the occult among a minority of citizens.

**Religious Practitioners**. There has been an increase in lay religious practitioners in the Christian churches in recent times as a result of decrease in the number of people entering the clergy. Most religious institutions are hierarchical in structure. Religious specialists participate in pastoral care, parish administration, and fund-raising for missions. Many also maintain a host of institutions that deal with education, aged care, family services, immigration, health, youth, and prisoner rehabilitation.

**Rituals and Holy Places**. Every religious denomination has its own places of worship, and most expect their followers to attend religious services regularly. There has been a decline in regular church attendance among the younger generation of Christians, who tend to be critical of church policy and practice. Places of worship are considered sacred and include locations that hold spiritual significance for believers. Among certain ethnic groups shrines are established in places where saints are said to have appeared. There are many Aboriginal sacred sites, which are generally places in the landscape.

**Death and the Afterlife**. The law requires that deceased people be dealt with according to health regulations. A vigil over the body in the family home is practiced in some religious and cultural traditions. Funeral parlors prepare the body of the deceased for cremation or burial in a cemetery. Funerals are attended by family members and friends and often include a religious ceremony.

## MEDICINE AND HEALTH CARE

Most medical health care is subsidized or paid for by the government, for which a small levy is paid by all citizens. Public hospitals often provide free services. People can select a private general practitioner, usually in their neighborhood. The general practitioner provides referrals to specialist doctors where necessary, and payment is usually on a fee-for-service basis. Health professionals may work privately or in a hospital setting. In recent years there has been an attempt to increase the level of private health insurance coverage among citizens.

Prevention of illness is a high priority of the government, with several programs such as vaccination, public health warnings about smoking and AIDS, public education campaigns on nutrition and exercise, and public awareness campaigns regarding heavy drinking and illicit drugs. Individuals are held to be responsible for their own health problems, and most investment goes to individually oriented, high-technology curative medicine. In the 1970s community health centers were established to focus on groups with special needs, such as women, migrants, and Aboriginal people. These centers provide more holistic care by addressing personal and social problems as well as health conditions.

Increasing numbers of people combine Western medicine with traditional and New Age practices. This may include Chinese herbalists, iridology, and homeopathic medicine. These alternative forms of medical treatment generally are not subsidized by the government.

The Royal Flying Doctor Service provides emergency medical assistance to those in remote areas. It was founded in 1928 and is funded by government and public donations. The service also provides emergency assistance during floods and fires.

## SECULAR CELEBRATIONS

Probably the most significant national secular celebration is Anzac Day on 25 April. This is a public holiday that commemorates the Australia and New Zealand Army Corps landing at Gallipoli in Turkey in 1915. However, the event now encompasses participants in all wars in which Australia has been involved. Dawn services are held at war memorials and there are well-attended street parades. On Remembrance Day (11 November), which is not a public holiday, a two-minute silence is observed in remembrance of Australians who fought and died in wars.

Australia Day is celebrated on 26 January to commemorate British settlement, and many capital cities host a fireworks event. Boxing Day occurs on 26 December. The Boxing Day cricket test match is an annual event watched on television by many residents. The day also is treated as an opportunity to extend Christmas socializing, with many barbecues taking place in public parks or at private homes.

Labour Day is a public holiday to commemorate improved working conditions and the implementation of the eight-hour workday. It is celebrated at different times of the year in different states. A significant celebration occurs on Melbourne Cup Day, an annual horse-racing event in Melbourne. Many people attending the race dress formally, and employees in workplaces gather to watch the event on television.

New Year's Day and New Year's Eve are celebrated. Royal Easter Shows and Royal Show Days with annual agricultural shows are held in capital cities with exhibits, competitions, and sideshows highlighting the rural tradition. On Grand Final Days, the annual finals to the national Australian Rules and Rugby League football competitions, large crowds gather to watch the game and friends congregate to watch it on television in homes and public bars. Most states have public holidays to commemorate the founding of the first local colony, and there are annual arts festivals that attract local, national, and international artists as well as multicultural festivals. Some states have wine festivals.

## THE ARTS AND HUMANITIES

*Support for the Arts.* Most people who participate in the arts depend on other professions for their primary income. Full-time arts practitioners are usually highly dependent on government funding. The sale of work in graphic arts, multimedia, and literature earns a substantial income for many practitioners, while the performance arts, in particular dance, do not tend to generate enough income to cover their costs. The Australia Council funds artistic activity, provides incomes to arts workers and projects, and is the primary source of income for dance and theater. The film and television industries receive substantial government support and tax incentives. There is government funding for schools of the performing arts. Approximately 10 percent of large businesses provide some form of support or funding to the arts or cultural events.

*Literature.* Since the 1890s a national literature has been developing with a distinctly Australian voice. This tradition, which is focused largely on the bush as a mythic place in the Australian imagination, has been challenged recently by a new suburban focus for literature. Increasingly, Aboriginal and other authors from diverse cultural backgrounds are having work published and appreciated. Australian authors have won many international awards, and Australians are claimed to be one of the leading nations in per capita spending on books and magazines.

*Graphic Arts.* Painting was dominated by the European tradition for many years, with landscapes painted to resemble their European counterparts until at least 1850. The Heidelberg school was influential in the late nineteenth century. Social-realist images of immigrants and the working class were favored as more "Australian" by 1950. Since 1945, images of the isolated outback have been popularized by artists such as Russell Drysdale and Sydney Nolan. Aboriginal artists were acknowledged in 1989 with a comprehensive display of their art in the Australian National Gallery. Their work is becoming increasingly successful internationally.

***Performance Arts.*** Each state capital has at least one major performing arts venue. Playwrights have been successful in presenting Australian society to theatergoers. Indigenous performance has been supported by a number of theater and dance companies since the early 1980s. Women's theater achieved a high level of attention during the 1980s. The styles of music, dance, drama, and oratory vary significantly, reflecting the multicultural mix of the society. Annual festivals of arts in the states showcase local and international work and are well attended, in particular by the well educated and the wealthy.

Music styles range from classical and symphonic to rock, pop, and alternative styles. Music is the most popular performance art, attracting large audiences. Pop music is more successful than symphony and chamber music. Many Australian pop musicians have had international success. Comedy and cabaret also attract large audiences and appear to have a large talent pool. Ballet is popular, with over twenty-five hundred schools in the early 1990s. The Australian Ballet, founded in 1962, enjoys a good international reputation.

## THE STATE OF THE PHYSICAL AND SOCIAL SCIENCES

The sciences are well served in a number of leading fields, including astronomy, chemistry, medicine, and engineering. Funding is provided by a combination of government and industry. Most universities provide scientific programs. The social sciences are not as well funded mainly because they tend not to produce marketable outcomes. Nevertheless, there is a strong representation in disciplines such as psychology, history, economics, sociology, and anthropology in universities. Social scientists work both in their own country and overseas. There is a tradition of social scientists from certain disciplinary backgrounds working in government and social welfare organizations.

## BIBLIOGRAPHY

Bambrick, S., ed. *The Cambridge Encyclopedia of Australia*, 1994.

Bessant, J., and R. Watts, *Sociology Australia*, 1999.

Bosworth, M. *Australian Lives: A History of Clothing, Food and Domestic Technology*, 1988.

Carroll, J., ed. *Intruders in the Bush: The Australian Quest for Identity*, 2nd ed., 1992.

Castles, S., B. Cope, M. Kalantzis, and M. Morrissey. *Mistaken Identity: Multiculturalism and the Demise of Nationalism in Australia*, 1992.

Clyne, M. "Monolingualism, Multilingualism and the Australian Nation." In *Australian National Identity*, C.A. Price, ed., 1991.

Commonwealth of Australia. *Defending Australia: Defense White Paper*, 1994.

Davison, G., J. Hirst, and S. Macintyre, eds. *The Oxford Companion to Australian History*, 1998.

Forster, C. *Australian Cities: Continuity and Change*, 1995.

Haralambos, M., R. van Krieken, P. Smith, and M. Holborn, *Sociology: Themes and Perspectives*, 1996.

Jose, A.W. *History of Australasia*, 1917.

Jupp, J., ed. *The Australian People: An Encyclopedia of the Nation, Its People and Their Origins*, 1988.

Makin, T. "The Economy" In *Institutions in Australian Society*, J. Henningham, ed., 1995.

Molony, J. *The Penguin Bicentennial History of Australia: The Story of 200 Years*, 1987.

Parrinder, G. *Worship in the World's Religions*, 1976.

Turnbull, C. *A Concise History of Australia*, 1983.

Van Sommers, T. *Religions in Australia*, 1966.

### Web Sites

ABS 1999 Australian Bureau of Statistics Web page. Australia Now—A Statistical Profile. http://www.statistics.gov.au/websitedbs.

—LORETTA BALDASSAR
AND DAVID S. TRIGGER

# AUSTRIA

## CULTURE NAME
Austrian

## ALTERNATIVE NAMES
Republic of Austria; Republik Osterreich

## ORIENTATION

**Identification.** The origins of present-day Austria can be traced back to prehistoric times. The Danube River valley was populated as long ago as the Paleolithic Age (50,000 B.C.E.–8000 B.C.E.). Austria was inhabited by Celtic peoples from prehistory until it fell under Roman control in the first century B.C.E. By the late second century C.E., peoples such as the Slavs, Germans, Huns, and Bohemians began to raid Austria. Christianity, which became the official religion of the Roman Empire, had become established in the region by the end of the fourth century.

Austrians call their country Osterreich (eastern empire). The name dates to about C.E. 800, when Charlemagne, emperor of the Germanic Franks, took control of the region, naming it Eastern March because it was meant to stem invasions by marauders from the east. (A *march* is a protective zone set up to defend a border area.) In the tenth century, German king Otto I named it Ostarichi (eastern kingdom), from which the modern German name, Osterreich, derives. The Latin name, Austria, had appeared by the twelfth century.

Nine provinces comprise Austria. Because the country is landlocked and bordered by eight other countries with their own distinctive cultures, the people of each province tend to be different. Surrounded by so many other cultures, Austria has often been subjected to cultural ''invasions,'' which are a source of the differences among the provinces. Another source of the diversity is the Alps, which cover 62 percent of the country. The distinctions also occurred because different groups settled in Austria. In addition to the Celts, Romans, Asians, Hungarians, and Germanic groups, many groups from central Europe arrived during the Middle Ages (500–1500).

With the advent of Communism in Eastern Europe, many people fled to Austria from the former Czechoslovakia and Hungary. Despite pronounced provincial differences, however, the people of Austria are proud of their country and their independent identity as Austrians.

**Location and Geography.** Located in south-central Europe, Austria is a landlocked, mountainous country, with an area of approximately 32,375 square miles (83,850 square kilometers). It shares borders with Germany, the Czech Republic, Slovakia, Hungary, Slovenia, Italy, Switzerland, and Liechtenstein. Its western portion is a narrow strip that extends between Germany and Italy. The Danube River, Austria's only navigable waterway, flows from southeastern Germany across northern Austria. Areas of major settlement are in the Danube valley and in the lowlands or hills north, east, and south of the Alps.

Austria is divided into nine provinces, Vorarlberg, Tirol, Salzburg, Upper Austria, Carinthia, Styria, Burgenland, Lower Austria, and Vienna, the capital city and a major river port on the Danube.

The Alps are the distinguishing physical feature of Austria, dominating the western, southern, and central regions of the country, with the highest point at Grossglockner, 12,457 feet (3,797 meters). Although the Alps usually did not demarcate the provinces' political boundaries, they were often impassable. Many inhabitants of Alpine valleys were thus isolated and developed their own distinct dialects, dress, folklore, and architecture, and could easily determine the origins of outsiders. Modern mass media and mobility have diminished many of these distinctions.

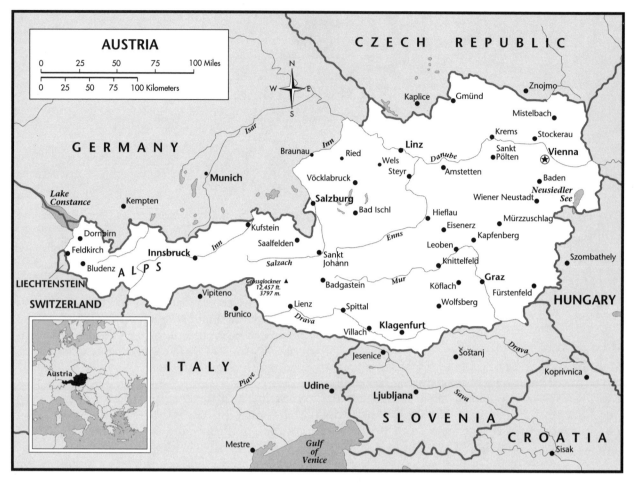

*Austria*

**Demography.** The 1998 population count was 8,078,449 (2000 estimate, 8,131,111), about 95 percent of whom were ethnic Austrian. Other numerically significant ethnic groups include Slovenes, Croats, and Czechs. Austria has one of the world's lowest birthrates, and much of the population is under age twenty-five or over sixty-five. About 65 percent of the population is urban, the largest city by far being Vienna (1.64 million).

**Linguistic Affiliation.** Austria is the only country other than Germany where the official language is German, and approximately 98 percent of the population speaks High German or a dialect of it. Austrian German sounds "softer" from that of Germany, and German speakers can easily discern the difference. There are also regional dialects of German, such as Weinerisch, spoken in Vienna. Austria's Slavic minority, located mostly in the south and the east, speak Slovenian and Croatian as their first language. English is taught in all schools as a second language.

**Symbolism.** The black eagle on the Austrian coat of arms is the national emblem. The civic crown on its head represents Austria's middle classes; a sickle in its left talon represents its farmers; a hammer in the right, its artisans; and broken silver chains hanging from each talon represent freedom from Nazi German control. The red and white bars of Austria's national flag adorn its breast. These represent the blood-stained tunic worn by Duke Leopold V of Babenberg after the Battle of Ptolemais in 1191. Austria's national anthem is "Land of the Mountains, Land on the River."

The edelweiss, *Leontopodium alpinum*, one of the most famous Alpine plants, is also widely associated with Austria. Celebrated in *The Sound of Music*, the edelweiss has white star-shaped flowers and grows on rocks and in crevices.

## HISTORY AND ETHNIC RELATIONS

**Emergence of the Nation.** Austria's geographical location at the crossroads of Europe determined its historical multiethnic makeup. In the late ninth century, Slavs and Magyars (Hungarians) advanced westward along the Danube River valley and over-ran the area. They were defeated by the German king Otto I at the Battle of the Lech in 955. Otto established a strong *march* (protective zone) along Germany's eastern border to keep tribes to the east at bay. Many German colonists settled in the region.

Austria emerged as a distinct political entity in 976 when Otto II gave the area to the Bavarian nobleman Leopold of Babenberg, largely to keep the Magyars at bay. Austria flourished culturally and economically under the three-hundred-year reign of the Babenberg dynasty, who built great for-tresses and beautiful monasteries. The Danube be-came an important trade route, and Vienna was made the capital. Roman Catholicism and German ethnicity took hold in the area.

When the last duke of Babenberg died without an heir in 1246, the Holy Roman emperor Rudolf of Habsburg wrested control in 1278, marking the beginning of the 640-year Habsburg dynasty, one of the most powerful and dynamic in European history. The Habsburgs were extremely successful in expanding their empire through politically moti-vated marriages. The empire became so extensive that at various times it included Austria and sur-rounding countries, northern Italy, Spain and its American territories, and parts of Germany.

By the seventeenth century, Austria was the foremost German state and a major European power. The dominant theme of Austrian history during this period was war, especially under threats from the Ottoman Empire during the sixteenth and seventeenth centuries. The Ottomans launched two great sieges of Vienna (1529 and 1683), but both failed and the Turks were repelled to southeastern Europe.

With the death of Charles VI in 1740, his daughter Maria Theresa (r. 1740-1780) became ruler, although she had to fight off rivals to the throne. Reigning over a golden age in Austria's his-tory, Maria Theresa ruled for forty years. Although she lost Silesia to the Prussians, she—and later her son, Joseph II (r. 1765-1790), who ruled with her jointly beginning in 1765—presided over Austria's transformation into a modern state. She established centralized control of the state, set up a civil service, introduced public education, expanded industry, and reformed the military and the legal system. The cultural life of Austria also thrived during this period.

The turmoil accompanying the French Revolu-tion and Napoleon Bonaparte's rise to power spelled

*Customers explore the shops in the open-air Christmas Market at Hauptplatz in Graz.*

the end of the Holy Roman Empire and also a weak-ening of Austria. The French revolutionary govern-ment, in an effort to expand French territory, de-clared war on Austria in 1792 and began to capture Habsburg territory. Austrian emperor Franz II allied with Britain, Prussia, and Russia to fight the French. The conflict continued until the Congress of Vienna in 1814-1815, convened to plan a permanent settle-ment of European territorial boundaries.

The congress created the German Confedera-tion, a union of thirty-nine small German states with Austria in permanent control of the presi-dency. Austria also regained much of the territory it had lost to Napoleon.

The provisions of the Congress of Vienna con-firmed Austria as the dominant European power. Even after Emperor Franz Joseph I (r. 1848-1916) suffered defeat by the Prussians in 1866, losing some lands, what became known as Austria–Hungary remained a great power. On 12 November 1918, at the end of World War I and after the dissolution of the Habsburg Empire after the assas-sination of its heir, Archduke Franz Ferdinand, a new German Austrian state—known as the First Republic—was established. It was only about one-fourth the size of the Austro-Hungarian Empire.

In March 1938, Nazi German troops occupied Austria, renaming it Ostmark and annexing it as part of Germany. This annexation was known as the Anschluss. Adolf Hitler enlisted Austrian soldiers in the German army until the end of World War II in 1945. After the war, Allied forces occupied Austria, which was divided into four zones. Nullifying the Anschluss, on 27 April 1945 they reestablished an independent Republic of Austria under its 1920 constitution as amended in 1929. Not until the State Treaty of October 1955, however, did the four Allied powers—the United States, Great Britain, France, and the Soviet Union—end their occupation of Austria. Austria's status as a neutral nation was incorporated into the constitution by the Federal Constitutional Law on Neutrality of 26 October 1955.

**National Identity.** Although Austria during the Habsburg Empire was made up of many ethnic groups, the strongest group remained the Germans, and they considered themselves German by culture even though they were loyal to their provinces. During the late 1800s, Austrians began to support the nationalist ideal. Germans in Austria–Hungary divided into three political groups, called *Lager* (camps)—the German Liberals, the Social Democratic Workers' Party, and the Christian Social Party. After World War I, during Austria's First Republic, these camps grew stronger and more divisive, to the point of armed conflict by the 1930s. After the assassination of Christian Social leader Engelbert Dollfuss by Austrian Nazis, the Christian Social Party continued its regime under the leadership of Kurt von Schuschnigg.

Following the Anschluss and then Allied occupation after World War II, Austrian political party leaders discussed ways to rebuild their country and overlook their political differences. After the Nazi war atrocities, Austria no longer wanted to be a part of Germany, and the rise of Communism in Eastern Europe made parliamentary democracy more attractive than ever. However, by 1956 only one-half of Austrians saw themselves as a nation, whereas 46 percent still identified with their German culture. By the late 1980s, nearly 80 percent of Austrians embraced their identity as a distinct nation.

**Ethnic Relations.** Although the Austrian population is strongly homogeneous, there are sizable Croatian (in Burgenland), Slovene (in Carinthia), Hungarian, Czech, and Slovak minorities, and the preservation of their language and culture is guaranteed by Austria's constitutional law. During the late twentieth century, however, the number of

Austrians declaring membership in their ethnic groups dropped by large percentages.

Since 1945, Austria has accepted immigrants, refugees, and transmigrants seeking political asylum from Eastern Europe and the Soviet Union, as well as from South America, Iran, Uganda, and Afghanistan. Gypsies and Jews, who have lived in Austria for centuries, are also considered minority groups. Gypsies maintain much of their life of freedom, and as a result have not become a part of the larger society. Some anti-Semitism still exists in Austria, but attitudes changed somewhat during the 1980s and 1990s.

After World War II, workers arrived from southern Europe, North Africa, and the Balkans to help rebuild northern Europe. Many are still considered "guest workers," although they and their families have made permanent homes in Austria. In 2000, immigrants made up 9 percent of Austria's population. Austria's political conservatives unjustly blame immigrants for taking jobs from native Austrians and for rising crime. Many foreign workers hold low-paying jobs and therefore live in poorer neighborhoods in urban areas, especially in Vienna.

Because of widespread public concern about immigrants, the government tightened immigration controls and strengthened its border patrol in the late 1990s.

## URBANISM, ARCHITECTURE, AND THE USE OF SPACE

Approximately one-third of the Austrians live in the five largest cities—Vienna, Graz, Linz, Salzburg, and Innsbruck—with the remainder inhabiting small towns and the countryside.

Most urban dwellers live in four- or five-story apartment buildings, high-rise buildings, or single-family homes. Many rural areas are dominated by farmhouses that have been in the family for hundreds of years. Usually made of stone and wood, the farmhouses are often equipped with a bell tower to announce mealtimes to those working in the fields. Because of the Alps, Austrian farms are small and isolated, making production relatively expensive.

Western provinces have wooden chalets with steep, pointed roofs, like those in Switzerland, whereas the eastern Danubian houses exhibit more of a Slavic influence, with simple design and stucco plastering.

Urban architecture reflects the broad architectural styles and related cultural movements that

*A fisherman in Attersee. While Austria is highly industrialized, traditional methods and customs are held in high esteem.*

have appeared throughout Europe's history, including the Romanesque and Gothic styles, most notable in churches and monasteries, of the Middle Ages. Other important historical styles include Renaissance, rococo, historicism, and modern.

The church, the state, and the nobility celebrated the ascendancy of the Habsburgs with extravagance, exemplified in large-scale building. The Italian-inspired architecture of the baroque period reflects a combination of religious piety and worldly opulence. Austrian architects created a distinctive national style, Austrian baroque, that featured irregular or undulating outlines, dynamic use of bold and delicate colors, and rich ornamentation.

Vienna achieved its modern-day look in the second half of the nineteenth century with the rise of a prosperous middle class. The medieval wall surrounding the city was razed, freeing up a large tract of land that resulted in the laying out of the Ringstrasse, a great boulevard enclosing the city on three sides (the Danube bordered the fourth). Reviving old architectural styles (historicism), architects and city planners erected buildings with a great diversity of retrograde styles, including Gothic, High Renaissance, and Greek.

Architects in the early 1900s opted for the functionality of modernism, especially in public buildings and transportation systems. Vienna has been in the forefront in providing and maintaining public housing. After the 1960s, architects rejected functionality for illusion and sensualism, focusing on architecture as structures in which individuals "participate".

"Plague columns" are a distinctive type of Austrian monument, erected in town squares throughout the nation in thanks to the Trinity or the Virgin Mary for deliverance from deadly plagues.

## FOOD AND ECONOMY

*Food in Daily Life.* Austrian cooking is one of the most varied in Europe and includes German, Hungarian, Czech, and northern Italian influences.

A typical Austrian's day begins with a light breakfast of coffee or milk with bread and butter or jam. Sausage served with mustard on a hard roll is a typical midmorning snack. Lunch is usually the main meal of the day and consists of soup and a main course of meat—sausage, the widely popular *Wiener schnitzel* (breaded veal), chicken, beef, pork or fish. Fresh vegetables, dumplings, noodles, or potatoes often accompany the main course. A salad may conclude the meal.

Austrian city dwellers often take a midafternoon coffee break at a national institution, the coffeehouse. Part of the Austrian way of life, the coffeehouse serves as a meeting place and a source for breakfast or a snack or light lunch. Most coffeehouses, which usually also serve alcohol, have their own distinctive atmosphere. The evening meal usually consists of light fare, perhaps cold meats, cheese, or smoked fish with bread and wine or beer.

**Basic Economy.** Before World War II, Austrian farmers produced 72 percent of the nation's food requirements. With wider use of commercial fertilizers, mechanization, and scientific methods, they steadily increased that percentage to 90 by the mid-1990s, even though less than 20 percent of the land is suitable for farming. Major crops are wheat and other grains, sugar beets, and potatoes. Austria also grows a variety of other vegetables and fruits, as well as grapes for making wine. Most farmers breed pigs, sheep, and dairy cattle, from which they obtain meat, wool, milk, cheese, and butter.

With increased mechanization, the number of people employed in agriculture decreased, and by the mid-1990s about 7 percent of the population held agricultural jobs. Most farms are small and are owned and operated by families. Many farm families supplement their income by renting out rooms or serving as tour guides or ski instructors.

Austria produces some petroleum and natural gas to meet its own needs, and it also mines coal, iron ore, copper, lead, zinc, antimony, and graphite, used in industry. Its rivers are harnessed to produce hydroelectric energy that provides a substantial portion of the nation's energy needs, with a surplus to export to neighboring countries. Abundant forests provide materials for lumber, paper products, and fuel. Conservation has helped protect farmland from landslides and erosion.

Austria's basic unit of currency is the schilling. Banking and finance are also an important part of the economy.

**Land Tenure and Property.** Austria's urban property market is weak, with many people renting rather than buying housing. Most farms are less than fifty acres (twenty hectares); nearly half are about twelve acres (five hectares) or less. About 70 percent of Austria's forest lands are privately held, with the remainder owned by the federal and provincial governments and by the Roman Catholic Church. Inherited wealth is more highly respected than earned wealth.

**Commercial Activities.** Austria is highly industrialized, but expert craftsmanship is also valued and can be found in products such as leather goods, pottery, jewelry, woodcarvings, and blown glass.

*Costumed Austrians at a festival in Imst.*

Tourism contributes a substantial portion to the economy, especially ski resorts in the Alps and cultural attractions in Vienna and Salzburg. Agricultural products such as wheat, corn, wine, dairy products, and meat are also produced for sale.

**Major Industries.** Manufacturing is the strongest sector of the Austrian economy, accounting for one-third of the workforce and about 40 percent of the gross domestic product. Iron ore is Austria's most important mineral resource, and metal and metal products, especially iron and steel, lead the manufacturing sector. Major products include motor vehicles, locomotives, heavy machinery and equipment, customized electronics, and tools. Other principal manufactured goods include chemicals, petroleum, graphite, wood and paper products, textiles, tobacco products, beverages, and processed foods.

**Trade.** Germany is Austria's principal trading partner, with Austria importing crude oil, machinery and equipment, chemical and manufacturing products, pharmaceuticals, and some foods. Austria's major exports are machinery and equipment, electronics, paper products, clothing and textiles, metals, and transportation equipment. Austria joined the European Union (EU) in 1995. It also conducts wide-ranging foreign trade with Italy,

Switzerland, and other EU countries, as well as the United States, Japan, and other Asian countries.

***Division of Labor.*** Craftsmen serve as apprentices for several years before becoming journeymen and, finally, master craftsmen. Farming is done mainly by families who own the land. Immigrants from a number of nations are employed as unskilled labor and service industry workers. Professional, white collar, factory, and government jobs are held mainly by native Austrians.

## SOCIAL STRATIFICATION

***Classes and Castes.*** Austrian society was traditionally highly stratified, with well-defined social distinctions. In the early 1800s, the three major social classes were aristocrats, "citizens," and peasant-farmers or peasant-serfs. At the beginning of the twentieth century, a small aristocracy remained, along with a small middle class of entrepreneurs, a larger working class, and a large class of peasant-farmers (about 55 percent of the population). During the period between World War I and World War II, these classes developed separate political affiliations as well, dividing the people into camps based on beliefs in either social democracy, conservative Christian politics, or liberalism. These camps dissolved after World War II, and a growing middle class effected change in the social structure.

Prosperity, mobility, and more government benefits in the late twentieth century resulted in a higher standard of living for nearly all Austrians. There are more middle-class citizens than any other group, and education is considered the means to upward mobility. Equality is promoted throughout Austria, although foreign workers, immigrants, and Gypsies are still generally less accepted by the middle class.

***Symbols of Social Stratification.*** An older Austrian family lineage and inherited wealth are still symbols of respect in Austrian culture. Austrians whose families have lived in the country for several generations gain more acceptance than those who are recent immigrants. Symbols of wealth today may be a second home and more material possessions, rather than land, as in earlier centuries.

## POLITICAL LIFE

***Government.*** Austria is a federal republic based on parliamentary democracy. Its constitution was adopted in 1920 and has been amended several times. The federal government has a legislative, an

*Many Austrian cities feature a pleasing blend of "Old World" charm and modern convenience.*

executive, and a judicial branch. The bicameral legislature is known as the Bundesversammlung (Federal Assembly). It is composed of the lower house of parliament, the Nationalrat (National Council), made up of representatives from the political parties, and the upper house, the Bundesrat (Federal Council), representing the nine provinces.

Each of the nine provinces has a provincial government that provides for enforcement of federal laws and policies, and sets laws regarding municipal affairs, education of young children, tourism, and other local matters.

***Leadership and Political Officials.*** Austria has a federal president, elected by the people, who serves as head of state. The president has the power to appoint the chancellor and members of the cabinet and other government posts, to dismiss members, and even, on rare occasions, to dissolve the Nationalrat. However, governmental power rests chiefly with the chancellor (prime minister) and the cabinet, who write most laws. They in turn are responsible to the Nationalrat, which must approve all their actions. Members of the parliament are elected by the people.

From 1945 until 1986, two major political parties, the Social Democratic Party of Austria (SPO) and the Austrian People's Party (OVP) worked together in democratic governance of Austria. As traditional political alliances broke down in the late twentieth century, however, more "floating" voters made it possible for smaller political party candidates to gain a higher percentage of the vote. These parties included the controversial Freedom Party of Austria (FPO), a right-wing party headed by charismatic young leader Jorg Haider. Other, less powerful, small parties are the Liberal Forum and the environmentalist party, the Greens.

In February 2000, the OVP and the Freedom Party formed a coalition, causing the European Union to impose sanctions against Austria because of Haider's alleged racism and Nazi sympathies. Austrians demonstrated to protest the EU's interference in its national politics. Haider stepped down from the party, and the EU lifted its sanctions in September.

**Social Problems and Control.** Austria has traditionally been a peaceful nation with a low crime rate. Police and the law are respected, but since the 1980s some security personnel have been accused of improper conduct and excessive use of force. A variety of political beliefs are tolerated in Austria, and Vienna has long been a center of peace talks between foreign nations and a meeting place for international organizations such as the Organization of the Petroleum Exporting Countries (OPEC). As a result, violence and terrorist attacks have occasionally broken out against visiting members of nations in conflict, although involvement of the Austrian army and tough sentencing of terrorists by Austrian courts have curbed such incidents.

Austrian police divisions are the Federal Police, whose jurisdiction includes Vienna and other urban areas, and the Gendarmerie, responsible for rural and all other areas of Austria. The State Police is a national secret service division.

The criminal court system hears cases of crimes and misdemeanors. Jail and prison sentences tend not to be lengthy, and an effort is made to rehabilitate those incarcerated. Certain acts, such as vagrancy and prostitution, have been decriminalized at the federal level but may still be prohibited by local governments.

**Military Activity.** On 26 October 1955, Austria, by constitutional law, declared its permanent neutrality. It is prohibited from entering into military alliances, and foreign countries are prohibited from establishing military bases on Austrian soil. However, Austria's military does participate in some United Nations peacekeeping missions in other countries.

Although it remains a neutral country, Austria is prepared to defend itself from attack with the Bundesheer (Federal Army), which has an air force but no navy. Military service is on a conscript and volunteer basis. Austrian women have never served in the military. Main objectives until the 1990s were to deter outside forces from crossing Austria in military campaigns against surrounding nations by defending Austria's "key zones" (major routes of military advance) and "area security zones" (remaining Austrian territory). The Austrian security policy was restructured from 1993 to 1995, under the New Army Structure, which focuses on resolving border crises that might occur during instability in neighboring nations, resulting in an influx of refugees.

Austria accepted observer status in the Western European Union in 1995 and participates in the North Atlantic Treaty Organization's (NATO) Partnership for Peace. It is a long-standing member of the United Nations, the Council of Europe, and the Organization for Security and Cooperation in Europe (OCSE).

## SOCIAL WELFARE AND CHANGE PROGRAMS

Austria has one of the world's most highly developed and inclusive social welfare programs, funded by direct and indirect taxes. Benefits include unemployment pay and disability, retirement, and survivor pensions. Health insurance is required by the state and covers 99 percent of Austrians. Workers pay into these plans, but the poor and disadvantaged receive equal benefits. Parents receive many benefits, such as monthly support payments for maternity and paternity leave and child maintenance payments for children, from birth through completion of higher education. Unwed mothers and large low-income families receive additional benefits.

## NONGOVERNMENTAL ORGANIZATIONS AND OTHER ASSOCIATIONS

Austria owes much of its success to its Social Partnership, which brings together farmers, employers and employees, and trade unions. Trade unions and professional groups help gain rights for Austrian workers as well as helping to regulate economic and social matters. Unions use collective bargaining to help set wages and salaries and worker benefits. Professional groups serve to regulate quality of services, pricing, and competition within the professions. Agricultural groups work to improve farming methods and promote production. The major nongovernmental economic organizations are the Austrian Trade Union Federation; the Federation of Austrian Industrialists; the Federal Chamber of Trade and Commerce (or Federal Economic Chamber); the Conference of Presidents of the Chamber of Agriculture; the Regulation of the Professions; and the various chambers of labor, which are public corporations, whereas trade unions are private, volunteer organizations. Membership in a chamber of labor is compulsory for all workers. These organizations work together and with government through a representative council called the Parity Commission, which sets general principles for solving economic problems. Since the late 1980s, the Social Partnership has been criticized for lack of concern over the environment and for social groups that are not represented, such as pensioners, students, and many women.

Catholic Action is the main lay organization of the Roman Catholic Church. Austria's many sports organizations are affiliated with the Austrian Federal Sports Organization.

## GENDER ROLES AND STATUSES

**Division of Labor by Gender.** In spite of efforts to equalize the workforce, a majority of Austrians still consider it women's work to do household chores, cook, and care for children. A growing number of men in younger families help with child care, cooking, and shopping, however. Austrian women hold jobs outside the home less frequently than do women in most other European countries. Except for those with college degrees, women are underrepresented in business and the professions and generally hold jobs that require less education and fewer skills. Women make up only about 40 percent of government workers.

**The Relative Status of Women and Men.** Since the mid-1970s, the Austrian legislature has passed a number of measures aimed at equalizing the treatment of men and women in the workforce. However, most women are still paid less than men for doing the same type of job. The Women's Omnibus Law, passed in 1993, provides for compensation for women who have been discriminated against in the workplace because of their gender or who have faced sexual harassment. The Equal Treatment Law of 1979 has continued to fight discrimination against women.

Austrian men, especially among older and rural families, are still considered the head of the family.

Men have compulsory military service and work in industry, farming, trades, and professions. Austrian men face stresses from uncertain areas, however, as evidenced by their uncommonly high suicide rate.

## MARRIAGE, FAMILY, AND KINSHIP

**Marriage.** Austria saw a boom in marriages from 1945 through the 1960s, a golden age for the economy. Today, however, fewer young people marry, more couples divorce, and more live together and raise children without marrying. More women are opting for having a child but not marrying. Couples marry later in life, and many educated women choose their profession over a family. No-fault divorce was legalized in the 1980s, and divorce has increased, especially in urban areas.

Most weddings are still held in a Roman Catholic Church, although religion plays a lesser part in the lives of urban residents in the late twentieth century.

**Domestic Unit.** The domestic unit varies in Austria. Added to the basic unit of husband, wife, and children are households with a single parent and child, homes of divorced or widowed women and men, single professionals, and households where a man and woman live and raise children outside of marriage. Households in rural areas are still usually conventional, with married couples and several children and possibly grandparents and other relatives living under the same roof.

**Inheritance.** Inheritance of farms varies according to region, with the most common practice being the passing of the property to one son. Remaining siblings then receive cash for their share of the property. In other areas, one heir receives the house and a large share of land, with the rest divided among other family members.

## SOCIALIZATION

**Infant Care.** Infants are well cared for by Austrian parents, with both mother and father allowed paid time off from work when a child is born. Families in urban areas tend to be small, and each child receives plenty of attention. In larger farming families, siblings and other relatives may be available to help care for infants. Most infants receive a traditional baptism in the Roman Catholic Church.

**Child Rearing and Education.** Austrians, whether married or not, receive a special govern-

*A house in the small town of Kaprun. Many rural areas of Austria are dominated by farmhouses that have been in families for years.*

ment payment each month to help provide for children. This continues until the child completes college or vocational training. Parents of handicapped children receive double payments, and thousands of children receive free school lunches. Children's holiday programs are organized by the government, and disabled children receive special training. Austrian children are raised to reflect the Austrian community spirit of peace and compromise as a means of resolving conflict. They are taught to respect others and to appreciate the arts, their beautiful environment, and their heritage.

Austria's education system is one of the world's best, and Austria has a literacy rate of 99 percent. All children have an equal right to free education, with free transportation to and from school and free textbooks provided. Schooling is coeducational and is compulsory through the ninth grade. Between ages six and ten, all children attend a primary school. After age ten, children are separated through a "two-track" system in which some students attend a general secondary school for four more years, and the remainder attend an upper-level secondary school until age eighteen. The decision about which secondary school to attend was once made by children and their parents immediately after primary school, but education reforms since the 1980s have made this decision more flexible, resulting in a larger percentage of children choosing the upper-level schools. Debate over the two-track system continued in the 1990s.

After secondary school, students have the option of attending a university or a vocational school to pursue a specific career. In addition to public schools, the Roman Catholic Church also operates primary and secondary schools that make up about 10 percent of Austria's schools.

*Higher Education*. Students who graduate from upper-level secondary schools may apply to a university. Austria has twelve universities and six fine arts colleges. The University of Vienna, founded in 1365, is the oldest in German-speaking Europe. A university education is free for Austrians, although foreign students pay tuition. Once available only to wealthy males, university training is now available to all Austrian students who pass an entrance exam. As a result, since the 1960s annual enrollment at universities has increased from about 19,000 to 200,000. Women account for about half of the university students, although nearly all professors are male.

## ETIQUETTE

Most Austrians greet one another formally, by shaking hands and saying, "Gruss Gott" (greet God) or "Gruss dich" (greet you). Upon leaving, they shake again and say "Auf Wiedersehen" (good-bye). Older Viennese men may kiss the hand of a lady on introduction, or say "Kuss die Han" (I kiss your hand) and click their heels together. Women enjoy having doors opened for them. When dining, everyone at the table joins in a toast, saying "Prost," and "Guten Appetit" is exchanged before beginning to eat. The formal titles *Frau* (for a woman) and *Herr* (for a man) are universally used.

## RELIGION

*Religious Beliefs*. Freedom of religion and worship is guaranteed in Austria. About three-fourths of Austrians are Roman Catholic. Many Austrians practice "baptismal certificate Catholicism," in which they are Catholic by baptism and religious

formality but do not hold Catholic beliefs on central issues. Another major religion in Austria is Protestantism, and many foreign workers are Muslim or Serbian Orthodox. There is also a small community of Jews, mostly post World War II immigrants and their families, although the Jews have a long history in Vienna, beginning in the tenth century.

*Religious Practitioners*. Catholic priests, Islamic teachers and mosque officials, Protestant ministers, and Jewish rabbis make up the majority of religious practitioners.

*Rituals and Holy Places*. Cathedrals and churches are found throughout Austria. One of the most magnificent cathedrals in Austria is Saint Stephen's, or Stephansdom, in Vienna, built during the fifteenth century. The Augustinian abbey and the statue of Saint Florian in the town of Saint Florian are also important religious sites.

Cathedrals contain carvings depicting the life of Christ, at which worshipers stop to pray. A number of monasteries of the Cistercian order of monks, founded in the twelfth century, still function. A popular pilgrimage and tourist destiny is Melk, a Benedictine monastery on the Danube River. In the countryside, crucifixes are erected at crossroads, and numerous wayside shrines offer a place to rest and pray.

*Death and the Afterlife*. Austrians rely on the churches for funerals, and most hold to the beliefs of their religious faith about the afterlife. Austria has one of the highest suicide rates in Europe, especially among men. Vienna is the site of the large Zentalfriedhof (Central Cemetery), which contains the memorial tombs of such famous composers as Beethoven, Brahms, and Schubert, as well as a memorial to Mozart. Wealthy Austrians are buried in elaborate mausoleums, but nearly all graves are well tended, with flowers neatly arranged.

## MEDICINE AND HEALTH CARE

Austria's health care system is well developed, with 99 percent of its people protected by health insurance plans. These are funded by workers, employers, and the federal, provincial, and local governments. Everyone covered by health insurance is entitled to free outpatient and inpatient treatment. Physicians contract with health insurance agencies but are free to maintain private practices, and patients are free to go to the doctor of their choice.

Cardiovascular diseases, cancer, cirrhosis of the liver, and accidents are the major causes of death.

Life expectancy for newborn males in 1998 was 74.3 years, and for females 80.7 years.

## SECULAR CELEBRATIONS

Major celebrations include Fasching, a Carnival celebration held the week before Lent begins, and the Almahtrieh, a September celebration of the return of herders from Alpine pastures, in which cows decorated with ribbons and bells are led into town in a procession. Austrians also celebrate National Day on 26 October; Independence Day, 12 November; Nikolo (Saint Nicholas) Day, 6 December; New Year's Day, 1 January.

## THE ARTS AND HUMANITIES

**Support for the Arts.** The arts are highly respected in Austria, and Vienna was known during the eighteenth and nineteenth centuries as a world center of culture, especially in music. It was home to some of the greatest classical composers, including Haydn, Mozart, Beethoven, Schubert, and Brahms. During that time, the Habsburg family and the Roman Catholic Church were chief supporters of the arts. Austria is sometimes known as "the Land of Music." Annual festivals throughout the country feature Austrian orchestras, choirs, and other groups. The best known is the Salzburg Summer Festival, founded in 1920. Austria is famous for its Vienna Philharmonic Orchestra and Vienna Boys' Choir.

The Vienna State Opera is a state institution that supports Austria's premier cultural home, the Vienna Opera House, one of the most opulent in the world. It accommodates Austrians on a budget by providing standing room on graded aisles with rails to support viewers during a long opera.

Austrian children have compulsory music and art classes in primary and secondary schools, and private music schools and conservatories abound. Provincial theaters and orchestras bring the arts to rural and town dwellers. The arts are responsible for stimulating a large portion of the tourist trade in Austria as well and so are considered excellent investments for private supporters.

**Literature.** Because it is written in German, Austrian literature is often considered a part of German literature, and the first significant literature in German appeared in Austria in the form of epic poems and songs around 1200. Seventeenth-century minister Abraham a Sancta Clara wrote prose about the social classes that left a permanent mark on Austrian literature. Adalbert Stifter was the best-known fiction writer of the nineteenth century, and

Rainer Maria Rilke was a gifted philosophical poet of the twentieth century. Several Austrian writers wrote plays and operas in addition to verse and fiction. Among them were Hugo von Hofmannsthal, who, with innovative dramatist Max Reinhardt, annually produced the mystery play *Everyman* at the Salzburg Festival. The works of early-twentieth-century novelists Franz Werfel and Franz Kafka are world famous. Well-known interwar novelists are Heimito von Doderer and Robert Musil. Thomas Bernhard and Peter Handke achieved fame in the late twentieth century.

Coffeehouses, especially in Vienna, have long been known as a gathering place for writers and poets. Today, many coffeehouses feature literary readings as part of the culture that makes them so popular.

**Graphic Arts.** As capital of the illustrious Habsburg Empire, Vienna was a center for the fine arts as well as for music and the theater. Realist painter Ferdinand G. Waldmuller and painter Hans Makart were the most famous of the nineteenth century. Gustav Klimt painted in the unconventionally sensuous "secession" style, founded in 1897. Oskar Kokoschka painted the realities of World War I. In the twentieth century, artists such as Herbert Boeckl painted ornamentation on residential blocs and cathedrals. Anton Kolig and Josef Mikl were abstract painters, and Ernest Fuchs and Anton Lehmden were known for "fantastic realism."

The Albertina museum in the Hofburg quarter of Vienna houses a world-famous collection of graphic arts, featuring prints, drawings, and watercolors by artists such as Michelangelo, da Vinci, Rubens, Cezanne, Manet, Modigliani, and Schiele.

**Performance Arts.** Religious drama flourished, especially in Tirol, during the Middle Ages. During the Counter-Reformation, Jesuit priests wrote countless religious dramas and staged plays at Jesuit schools. Vienna became the center for German-speaking drama during the 18th century. Vienna's Burgtheater was the most eminent during the nineteenth century, when playwright Franz Grillparzer's plays were first performed there. Social dramas, folk farces, and satires also premiered during the nineteenth century. Around 1900, the Vienna School of dramatists, led by Austrian playwright Arthur Schnitzler, created a new style of playwriting in Europe, featuring psychological drama. The Salzburg Festival showcases drama as well as music.

## THE STATE OF THE PHYSICAL AND SOCIAL SCIENCES

The sciences are well developed in Austria, and every effort is made to stay in the forefront of research and development, especially with Austria's entry into the European Union in 1995. Research is divided into science-oriented and business-oriented research. Science research is carried out mainly by the universities, whereas business research falls under independent companies and private and state-funded research institutes.

Among Austrians winning the Nobel Prize in the sciences are Julius Wagner-Jauregg (1927, therapy of paralysis); Erwin Schrodinger (1933, physics); Wolfgang Pauli (1945, "Pauli Principle" in quantum theory); and Konrad Lorenz and Karl von Frisch (1973, behavioral science). Famous psychologist Sigmund Freud (1856–1939) did most of his work in Vienna.

Austria participates in the European Space Agency, The European Council for Nuclear Research, the European Molecular Biology Laboratory, the Organization for Economic Cooperation and Development (OECD), and the United Nations Educational, Scientific, and Cultural Organization (UNESCO). Although Austria has pledged not to acquire nuclear weapons and its voters declined the adoption of nuclear energy, Austria is the headquarters for the International Atomic Energy Agency as a center for research and negotiations.

## BIBLIOGRAPHY

*Austria in Pictures.* Rev. ed., 1991.

Berenger, Jean. *A History of the Habsburg Empire: 1273 1700*, translated by C. A. Simpson, 1994.

Brook-Shepherd, Gordon. *The Austrians: A Thousand-Year Odyssey*, 1997.

Honan, Mark. *Austria*, 1999.

Jelavich, Barbara. *Modern Austria: Empire and Republic, 1815 1986*, 1987.

Ladika, Susan. "Europe's Unsettling Immigrants." *The World & I*, 1 May 2000, p. 70.

Robertson, Ian. *Blue Guide: Austria*, 1992.

Sheehan, Sean. *Austria*, 1995.

Solsten, Eric, and David E. McClave, eds. *Austria: A Country Study*, 1994.

Sully, Melanie A. *A Contemporary History of Austria*, 1990.

Sweeny, J., and J. Weidenholzer. *Austria: A Study in Contemporary Achievement*, 1988.

### Web Sites

"Republic of Austria." www.austria.gv.at/e/oesterreich

U.S. Department of State. Background Notes: Austria. July 2000. www.state.gov/www/background_notes/austria

—ROBERT H. GRIFFIN
AND ANN H. SHURGIN

# AZERBAIJAN

**CULTURE NAME**

Azerbaijani, Azeri

**ALTERNATIVE NAMES**

Azerbaijani Turkish, Azeri Turkish. The country name also is written Azerbaidzhan, Azerbaydzhan, Adharbadjan, and Azarbaydjan in older sources as a transliteration from Russian. Under the Russian Empire, Azerbaijanis were known collectively as Tatars and/or Muslims, together with the rest of the Turkic population in that area.

**ORIENTATION**

*Identification.* Two theories are cited for the etymology of the name "Azerbaijan": First, "land of fire" (*azer*, meaning "fire," refers to the natural burning of surface oil deposits or to the oil-fueled fires in temples of the Zoroastrian religion); second, *Atropaten* is an ancient name of the region (Atropat was a governor of Alexander the Great in the fourth century B.C.). The place name has been used to denote the inhabitants since the late 1930s, during the Soviet period. The northern part of historical Azerbaijan was part of the former Soviet Union until 1991, while the southern part is in Iran. The two Azerbaijans developed under the influence of different political systems, cultures, and languages, but relations are being reestablished.

*Location and Geography.* The Azerbaijan Republic covers an area of 33,891 square miles (86,600 square kilometers). It includes the disputed Nagorno-Karabakh region, which is inhabited mostly by Armenians, and the noncontiguous Nakhchivan Autonomous Republic, which is separated from Azerbaijan by Armenian territory. Nakhchivan borders on Iran and Turkey to the south and southwest. Azerbaijan is on the western shore of the Caspian Sea. To the north it borders the Russian Federation, in the northwest Georgia, in the

west Armenia, and in the south Iran. Half the country is covered by mountains. Eight large rivers flow down from the Caucasus ranges into the Kura-Araz lowland. The climate is dry and semiarid in the steppes in the middle and eastern parts, subtropical in the southeast, cold in the high mountains in the north, and temperate on the Caspian coast. The capital, Baku, is on the Apsheron peninsula on the Caspian and has the largest port.

*Demography.* The population of the Azerbaijan Republic has been estimated to be 7,855,576 (July 1998). According to the 1989 census, Azeris accounted for 82.7 percent of the population, but that number has increased to roughly 90 percent as a result of a high birthrate and the emigration of non-Azeris. The Azerbaijani population of Nagorno-Karabakh and a large number of Azeris (an estimated 200,000) who had been living in Armenia were driven to Azerbaijan in the late 1980s and early 1990s. There are about one million refugees and displaced persons altogether. It is believed that around thirteen million Azeris live in Iran. In 1989, Russians and Armenians each made up 5.6 percent of the population. However, because of anti-Armenian pogroms in Baku in 1990 and Sumgait in 1988, most Armenians left, and their population (2.3 percent) is now concentrated in Nagorno-Karabakh. Russians, who currently make up of 2.5 percent of the population, began to leave for Russia after the dissolution of the Soviet Union. The number of Jews decreased as they left for Russia, Israel, and the United States in the late 1980s and early 1990s. Numerous ethnic groups (up to ninety) of the former Soviet Union are represented in small numbers (Ukrainians, Kurds, Belorussians, Tatars). Other groups with a long history of settlement in Azerbaijan include the Persian-speaking Talysh and the Georgian-speaking Udins. Peoples of Daghestan such as the Lezghis and Avars make up 3.2 percent of the population, with most of them living in the north. Fifty-three percent of the population is urban.

***Linguistic Affiliation.*** Azeri (also referred to as Azeri Turkish) or Azerbaijani is a Turkic language in the Altaic family; it belongs to the southwestern Oguz group, together with Anatolian Turkish, Turkmen, and Gagauz. Speakers of these languages can understand each other to varying degrees, depending on the complexity of the sentences and the number of loan words from other languages. Russian loan words have entered Azeri since the nineteenth century, especially technical terms. Several Azeri dialects (e.g., Baku, Shusha, Lenkaran) are entirely mutually comprehensible. Until 1926, Azeri was written in Arabic script, which then was replaced by the Latin alphabet and in 1939 by Cyrillic. With the dissolution of the Soviet Union, Azerbaijan and other Turkic-speaking former Soviet republics reintroduced the Latin alphabet. However, the main body of modern Azeri literature and educational material is still in Cyrillic, and the transition to the Latin alphabet is a time-consuming and expensive process. The generations that learned Russian and read Azeri in Cyrillic still feel more comfortable with Cyrillic. During the Soviet period, linguistic Russification was intensive: although people referred to Azeri as their native tongue, the language many people in the cities mastered was Russian. There were both Azeri and Russian schools, and pupils were supposed to learn both languages. Those who went to Russian schools were able to use Azeri in daily encounters but had difficulty expressing themselves in other areas. Russian functioned as the lingua franca of different ethnic groups, and with the exception of rural populations such as the Talysh, others spoke very little Azeri. Roughly thirteen languages are spoken in Azerbaijan, some of which are not written and are used only in everyday family communication. Azeri is the official language and is used in all spheres of public life.

***Symbolism.*** Azerbaijan had a twenty-three-month history of statehood (1918–1920) before the institution of Soviet rule. The new nation-state's symbols after the dissolution of the Soviet Union were heavily influenced by that period. The flag of the earlier republic was adopted as the flag of the new republic. The flag has wide horizontal stripes in blue, red, and green. There is a white crescent and an eight-pointed star in the middle of the red stripe. The national anthem forcefully portrays the country as a land of heroes ready to defend their country with their blood. The sentiments associated with music in Azerbaijan are very strong. Azeris regard themselves as a highly musical nation, and this is reflected in both folk and Western musical traditions.

*Azerbaijan*

To show pride in country, Azeris first refer to its natural resources. Oil is at the top of the list, and the nine climatic zones with the vegetables and fruits that grew in them also are mentioned. The rich carpet-weaving tradition is a source of pride which is used to highlight the artistic sensibilities of carpet weavers (most of the time women) and their ability to combine various forms and symbols with natural colors. Hospitality is valued as a national characteristic, as it is in other Caucasus nations. Guests are offered food and shelter at the expense of the host's needs, and this is presented as a typical Azeri characteristic. The use of house metaphors was widespread at the beginning of the Nagorno-Karabakh conflict: Armenians were regarded as guests who wanted to take possession of one of the rooms in the host's house. Ideas of territorial integrity and the ownership of territory are very strong. Soil—which in Azeri can refer to soil, territory, and country—is an important symbol. Martyrdom, which has a high value in the Shia Muslim tradition, has come to be associated with martyrdom for the Azeri soil and nation. The tragedy of the events of January 1990, when Russian troops killed nearly two hundred civilians, and grief for those who died in the Nagorno-Karabakh conflict, have reinforced the ritual activity attached to martyrdom.

Azeri women and their characteristics are among the first ethnic markers (attributed characteristics) that differentiate Azeris as a nation. Their moral values, domestic abilities, and role as mothers are pointed out in many contexts, especially in contrast to Russians.

The recent history of conflict and war, and thus the suffering evoked by those events in the form of deaths, the misery of displaced persons, and orphaned children, has reinforced the idea of the Azeri nation as a collective entity.

## HISTORY AND ETHNIC RELATIONS

**Emergence of the Nation.** Azerbaijan was inhabited and invaded by different peoples throughout its history and at different times came under Christian, pre-Islamic, Islamic, Persian, Turkish, and Russian influence. In official presentations, the Christian kingdom of Caucasian Albania (which is not related to Albania in the Balkans) and the state of Atropatena are regarded as the beginnings of the formation of Azerbaijani nationality. As a result of Arab invasions, the eighth and ninth centuries are seen as marking the start of Islamization. The invasions of the Seljuk Turkish dynasty introduced the Turkish language and customs. From the thirteenth century onward, it is possible to find examples of literature and architecture that today are considered important parts of the national heritage. The local dynasty of Shirvan shahs (sixth to sixteenth centuries) left a concretely visible mark in Azeri history in the form of their palace in Baku. Until the eighteenth century, Azerbaijan was controlled by neighboring powers and was invaded repeatedly. In the nineteenth century, Iran, the Ottoman Empire, and Russia took an interest in Azerbaijan. Russia invaded Azerbaijan, and with the 1828 treaty borders (almost identical to the current borders), the country was divided between Iran and Russia. The rich oil fields in Baku that were opened in the mid-nineteenth century attracted Russians, Armenians, and a few westerners, such as the Nobel brothers. The vast majority of the oil companies were in Armenian hands, and many Azeri rural inhabitants who came to the city as workers joined the socialist movement. Despite international solidarity between the workers during strikes (1903–1914), tension

existed between Armenian and Azeri laborers, with the Azeris being less skilled and thus worse paid. This discontent exploded in bloody ethnic conflicts in the period 1905–1918. The fall of the Russian monarchy and the revolutionary atmosphere fed the development of national movements. On 28 May 1918, the Independent Azerbaijan Republic was established. The Red Army subsequently invaded Baku, and in 1922 Azerbaijan became part of the Union of Soviet Socialist Republics. In November 1991, Azerbaijan regained its independence; it adopted its first constitution in November 1995.

**National Identity.** In the early twentieth century, secular Azeri intellectuals tried to create a national community through political action, education, and their writings. Ideas of populism, Turkism, and democracy were prevalent in that period. As a reaction to the colonial regime and exploitation that was expressed in ethnic terms, the formation of Azeri national identity had elements of both Islamic and non-Islamic traditions as well as European ideas such as liberalism and nationalism. The idea of an Azeri nation also was cultivated during the Soviet period. The written cultural inheritance and the various historical figures in the arts and politics reinforced claims to independent nationhood at the end of the Soviet regime. During the decline of the Soviet Union, nationalist sentiment against Soviet rule was coupled with the anti-Armenian feelings that became the main driving force of the popular movements of national reconstruction.

**Ethnic Relations.** Since the late 1980s, Azerbaijan has been in turmoil, suffering interrelated ethnic conflict and political instability. Nagorno-Karabakh Armenians had raised the issue of independence from Azerbaijan a number of times since 1964, and those claims became more forceful in the late 1980s. Armenia supported the Nagorno-Karabakh cause and expelled about 200,000 Azeris from Armenia in that period. Around that time, pogroms took place against Armenians in Sumgait (1988) and Baku (1990), and more than 200,000 Armenians subsequently left the country. The Nagorno-Karabakh conflict turned into a protracted war, and atrocities were committed by both sides until an enduring cease-fire was agreed to in 1994. The massacre of the village of Khojaly in 1992 by Armenians is engraved in Azeri memory as one of the worst aggressive acts against Azeri civilians. Azeris who lived in Nagorno-Karabakh territory were driven out during the war. They are now among the refugees and displaced persons in Azerbaijan and make the conflict with Armenia visible. The Lezgis and

*Carpets for sale in front of a building in Baku. Traditional carpet weaving is a large component of Azerbaijani commerce.*

Talysh also made demands for autonomy, but despite some unrest, this did not result in extensive conflicts. Azeris in Iran have been subject to strictly enforced assimilation policies. Although the opening of the borders has nurtured economic and cultural relationships between the two Azerbaijans, Iranian Azeris do not have much cultural autonomy.

## URBANISM, ARCHITECTURE, AND THE USE OF SPACE

There are various dwellings in different regions. Traditionally, people in towns lived in quarters (*mahallas*) that developed along ethnic lines. Modern Azerbaijan adopted the Soviet style of architecture; however, Baku retains a Maiden Tower and an old town criscrossed with narrow streets as well as examples of a mixture of European styles in buildings that date back to the beginning of the twentieth century. These edifices usually were built with funds from the oil industry.

Soviet-era governmental buildings are large and solid with no ornamentation. Residential complexes built in that period usually are referred to as ''matchbox architecture'' because of their plain and anonymous character. Public space in bazaars and

shops is crowded, and people stand close to each other in lines.

## FOOD AND ECONOMY

***Food in Daily Life.*** There are regional differences in the selection and preparation of food resulting from the availability of agricultural products and membership in different ethnic groups. A mixture of meat and vegetables and various types of white bread constitute the main foods. In rural areas, there is a tradition of baking flat white bread (*churek, lavash, tandyr*). *Kufte bozbash* (meat and potatoes in a thin sauce) is a popular dish. Filled pepper and grape leaves and soups also are part of daily meals. Different types of green herbs, including coriander, parsley, dill, and spring onions, are served during meals both as a garnish and as salad. Pork is not popular because of Islamic dietary rules, but it was consumed in sausages during the Soviet period. The soup *borsch* and other Russian dishes are also part of the cuisine. Restaurants offer many varieties of kebabs and, in Baku, an increasingly international cuisine. Some restaurants in the historic buildings of Baku have small rooms for family and private groups.

***Food Customs at Ceremonial Occasions.*** *Pulov* (steamed rice) garnished with apricots and raisins is

*A dried fruit market in Baku.*

a major dish at ritual celebrations. It is eaten along-side meat, fried chestnuts, and onions. During the *Novruz* holiday, wheat is fried with raisins and nuts (*gavurga*). Every household is supposed to have seven types of nuts on a tray. Sweets such as *paklava* (a diamond-shaped thinly layered pastry filled with nuts and sugar) and *shakarbura* (a pie of thin dough filled with nuts and sugar) are an indispensable part of celebrations. At weddings, *pulov* and various kebabs are accompanied by alcohol and sweet nonalcoholic drinks (*shyra*). At funerals, the main course is usually *pulov* and meat, served with *shyra* and followed by tea.

**Basic Economy.** Azerbaijan has a rich agricultural and industrial potential as well as extensive oil reserves. However, the economy is heavily dependent on foreign trade. The late 1980s and 1990s saw intensive trade with Russia and other countries in the Commonwealth of Independent States. Turkey and Iran have begun to be important trade partners. About one-third of the population is employed in agriculture (producing half the population's food requirements); however, with 70 percent of agricultural land dependent on poorly developed irrigation systems and as a result of delays in the privatization process, agriculture is still inefficient and is not a major contributor to the economy. People in rural areas grew fruits and vegetables in small pri-

vate gardens for subsistence and sale during the Soviet period. The major agricultural crops are cotton, tobacco, grapes, sunflowers, tea, pomegranates, and citrus fruits; vegetables, olives, wheat, barley, and rice also are produced. Cattle, goats, and sheep are the major sources of meat and dairy products. Fish, especially sturgeon and black caviar, are produced in the Black Sea region, but severe pollution has weakened this sector.

**Land Tenure and Property.** In the Soviet period, there was no private land as a result of the presence of state-owned collective farms. As part of the general transition to a market economy, privatization laws for land have been introduced. Houses and apartments also are passing into private ownership.

**Commercial Activities.** There is a strong carpet-weaving tradition in addition to the traditional manufacturing of jewelry, copper products, and silk. Other major goods for sale include electric motors, cabling, household air conditioners, and refrigerators.

**Major Industries.** Petroleum and natural gas, petrochemicals (e.g., rubber and tires), chemicals (e.g., sulfuric acid, and caustic soda), oil refining, ferrous and nonferrous metallurgy, building materials, and electrotechnical equipment are the heavy industries that make the greatest contribution to the gross national product. Light industry is dominated by the production of synthetic and natural textiles, food processing (butter, cheese, canning, wine making), silk production, leather, furniture, and wool cleaning.

**Trade.** Other countries in the Commonwealth of Independent States, Western European countries, Turkey, and Iran are both export and import partners. Oil, gas, chemicals, oil field equipment, textiles, and cotton are the major exports, while machinery, consumer goods, foodstuffs, and textiles are the major imports.

## SOCIAL STRATIFICATION

**Classes and Castes.** The urban merchant class and industrial bourgeoisie of the pre-Soviet era lost their wealth under the Soviet Union. The working class in the cities usually retained rural connections. The most significant social stratification criterion is an urban versus rural background, although the educational opportunities and principles of equality introduced in the Soviet period altered this pattern to some extent. Russians, Jews, and Armenians were mostly urban white-collar workers. For Azerbai-

*Workers on an offshore drill in the Caspian Sea dismantle a drilling pipe.*

janis, education and family background were vital to social status throughout the pre- and post–Soviet period. Higher positions in government structures provided political power that was accompanied by economic power during the Soviet era. After the dissolution of the Soviet Union, wealth became a more important criterion for respect and power. Refugees and displaced persons with a rural background now can be considered the emergent underclass.

***Symbols of Social Stratification.*** As in the socialist era, Western dress and urban manners usually have a higher status than does the rural style. During the Soviet period, those who spoke Russian with an Azeri accent were looked down on, since this usually implied being from a rural area or having gone to an Azeri school. By contrast, today the ability to speak "literary" Azeri carries a high value, since it points to a learned family that has not lost its Azeri identity.

## POLITICAL LIFE

***Government.*** According to the constitution, Azerbaijan is a democratic, secular unitary republic. Legislative power is implemented by the parliament, *Milli Mejlis* (National Assembly; 125 deputies are directly elected under a majority and proportional electoral system for a term of five years, most recently 1995–2000). Executive power is vested in a president who is elected by direct popular vote for five years. The current president Heydar Aliyev's term will end in October 2003. The Cabinet of Ministers is headed by the prime minister. Administratively, the republic is divided into sixty-five regions, and there are eleven cities.

***Leadership and Political Officials.*** Since the late 1980s, the attainment of leadership positions has been strongly influenced by social upheaval and opposition to the existing system and its leaders. However, the network based on kin and regional background plays an important role in establishing political alliances. The system of creating mutual benefits through solidarity with persons with common interests persists.

Generally, political leaders assume and/or are attributed roles described in family terms, such as the son, brother, father, or mother of the nation. Young males have been a source of support both for the opposition and for the holders of powers. The ideals of manhood through bravery and solidarity were effective in securing popular support for different leaders in the 1980s. Personal charisma plays an important role, and politics is pursued at a personal level. There are about forty officially regis-

forms and an authoritarian government, and the Social Democratic Party favors the cultural autonomy of national and cultural minorities and democratization. All these parties are opposed to President Heydar Aliyev's New Azerbaijan Party because of the undemocratic measures taken against their members and in the country at large. The other major parties are the Azerbaijan Liberal Party, Azerbaijan Democratic Party, and Azerbaijan Democratic Independence Party.

***Social Problems and Control.*** According to the constitution, the judiciary exercises power with complete independence. Citizens' rights are guaranteed by the constitution. However, as a result of the uncertainties of the current transitional period, the legacy of the Soviet judicial system, and the authoritative measures taken by power holders, the implementation of legal rules is in practice a source of tension. This means that state organs can break the law by committing actions such as election fraud, censorship, and the detention of protesters. Given the prevalence of white-collar crime affecting investments, savings funds, and financial institutions, the large number of refugees and displaced persons with limited resources has resulted in various illegal business dealings. For example, recent years have seen considerable drug trafficking to Russia and the smuggling of various goods and materials. Despite improvements, people have little faith that they will receive a fair trial or honest treatment unless they belong to the right circles. The ideas of shame and honor are used in evaluating and hence controlling people's actions. Family and community opinion impose limitations on actions, but this also leads to clandestine dealings.

***Military Activity.*** Azerbaijan has an army, navy, and air force. Defense expenditures for the Nagorno-Karabakh conflict placed a sizable burden on the national budget. The official figures for defense spending were around $132 million in 1994.

*Two young shepherds. Cattle, goats, and sheep are major agricultural products.*

tered parties. The largest movement toward the end of the Soviet era was the Azerbaijani Popular Front (APF), which was established by intellectuals from the Academy of Sciences in Baku; members of the APF established several other parties later. The chairman of the APF became president in 1992 but was overthrown in 1993. Currently, the APF has both nationalist and democratic wings. The *Musavat* (Equality) Party has the backing of some intellectuals and supports democratic reforms, the National Independence Party supports market re-

## SOCIAL WELFARE AND CHANGE PROGRAMS

There are laws providing for social security for the disabled, pensions, a guaranteed minimum wage, compensation for low-income families with children, grants for students, and benefits for war veterans and disabled persons (e.g. reduced fares on public transport etc.). However, the level of social benefits is very low. National and international nongovernmental organizations (NGOs) are involved in aid work for displaced persons, especially children.

## NONGOVERNMENTAL ORGANIZATIONS AND OTHER ASSOCIATIONS

Most NGOs concentrate on charity, mainly for displaced persons and refugees and focus on human rights, minority issues, and women's problems (e.g., the Human Rights Center of Azerbaijan and the Association for the Defense of Rights of Azerbaijan Women). Depending on their specialties, these organizations collect information and try to collaborate with international organizations to support people financially, politically, and socially.

## GENDER ROLES AND STATUSES

**Division of Labor by Gender.** Many women were employed outside the home as a result of Soviet policies, but they have traditionally played a secondary role in supporting the family economically. Men are considered the main breadwinners. There are no restrictions on women's participation in public life, and women are active in politics in the opposition and ruling parties. However, their number is limited. Rural women's participation in public life is less common.

**The Relative Status of Women and Men.** With few exceptions, socially and politically powerful women at the top levels have male supporters who help them maintain their positions. Although professional achievement is encouraged, women are most respected for their role as mothers. Women in rural areas usually control the organization of domestic and ritual life. There is a higher degree of segregation between female and male activities and between the social spaces where they gather.

## MARRIAGE, FAMILY, AND KINSHIP

**Marriage.** Even in rural areas, marriages increasingly are arranged in accordance with the partners' wishes. In some cases, girls in rural areas may not have the right to oppose a candidate chosen by their parents; it is also not unusual for parents to disapprove of the chosen partner. Marriages between Azeri girls and non-Muslim non-Azeris (Russians, Armenians) in the Soviet period were very rare, but Western non-Muslims apparently now have a different status. Men, by contrast, could marry Russians and Armenians more easily. Both men and women marry to have children and bring up a family, but economic security is another important concern for women. In addition to the civil marriage ceremony, some couples now go to a mosque to get married according to Islamic law.

**Domestic Unit.** The basic household unit is either a nuclear family or a combination of two generations in one household (patrilocal tendency). In urban areas, mainly as a result of economic difficulties, newlyweds live with the man's parents or, if necessary, the woman's parents. The head of the household is usually the oldest man in the family, although old women are influential in decision making. In rural areas, it is possible for an extended family to live in one compound or house shared by the sons' families and their parents. Women engage in food preparation, child rearing, carpet weaving, and other tasks within the compound, while men take care of the animals and do the physically demanding tasks.

**Inheritance.** Inheritance is regulated by law; children inherit equally from their parents, although males may inherit the family house if they live with their parents. They then may make arrangements to give some compensation to their sisters.

**Kin Groups.** Relatives may live nearby in rural areas, but they usually are dispersed in cities. On special occasions such as weddings and funerals, close and distant relatives gather to help with the preparations. It is common for relatives in rural areas to support those in urban areas with agricultural and dairy products, while people in the cities support their rural relatives with goods from the city and by giving them accommodation when they are in city as well as helping them in matters involving the bureaucracy, health care, and children's education.

## SOCIALIZATION

**Infant Care.** Infant care differs according to location. In rural areas, infants are placed in cradles or beds. They may be carried by the mother or other female family members. In cities, they usually are placed in small beds and are watched by the mother. Parents interact with babies while attending to their daily chores and prefer to keep babies calm and quiet.

**Child Rearing and Education.** The criteria for judging a child's behavior are gender-dependent. Although children of all ages are expected to be obedient to their parents and older people in general, boys' misbehavior is more likely to be tolerated. Girls are encouraged to help their mothers, stay calm, and have good manners. It is not unusual for genetic makeup and thus a resemblance to the behavior patterns and talents of their parents and close family members to be used to explain children's negative and positive qualities.

*An aerial view of Baku, the capital of Azerbaijan.*

**Higher Education.** Higher education has been important for Azeris both in the Soviet and post-Soviet periods. Having higher education makes both boys and girls more attractive as prospective marriage partners. Parents go to great lengths to pay fees for higher education or other informally determined costs associated with admission to schools.

## ETIQUETTE

Issues relating to sex and the body usually are not talked about openly in public. Depending on the age of the speaker, some men may refrain from using words such as ''pregnant''; if they must use them, they apologize. It is not considered proper for adults to openly mention going to the bathroom; in private homes, people of the same age and gender or children can be asked for directions to the toilet. Women seldom smoke in public or at parties or other gatherings, and an Azeri woman smoking on the street would be looked down on. To show respect for the elderly, it is important not to smoke in front of older people of both genders. Young men and women are circumspect in the way they behave in front of older people. Bodily contact between the same sexes is usual as a part of interaction while talking or in the form of walking arm in arm. Men usually greet each other by shaking hands and also

by hugging if they have not seen each other for a while. Depending on the occasion and the degree of closeness, men and women may greet one another by shaking hands or only with words and a nod of the head. In urban settings, it is not unusual for a man to kiss a woman's hand as a sign of reverence. The awareness of space is greater between the sexes; men and women prefer not to stand close to each other in lines or crowded places. However, all these trends depend on age, education, and family background. Activities such as drinking more than a symbolic amount, smoking, and being in male company are associated more with Russian women than with Azeris. Azeri women would be criticized more harshly, since it is accepted that Russians have different values.

## RELIGION

**Religious Beliefs.** Among the total population, 93.4 percent is Muslim (70 percent Shia and 30 percent Sunni). Christians (Russian Orthodox and Armenian Apostolics) make up the second largest group. Other groups exist in small numbers, such as Molokans, Baha'is, and Krishnas. Until recently, Islam was predominantly a cultural system with little organized activity. Funerals were the most persistent religious ritual during the socialist era.

**Religious Practitioners.** In 1980, the sheikhul-Islam (head of the Muslim board) was appointed. Mullahs were not very active during the Soviet period, since the role of religion and mosques was limited. Even today, mosques are most important for the performance of funeral services. Some female practitioners read passages from the Koran in women's company on those occasions.

**Rituals and Holy Places.** Ramadan, Ramadan Bayram, and Gurban Bayram (the Feast of Sacrifice) are not widely observed, especially in urban areas. *Muharram* is the period when there are restrictions on celebrations. *Ashure* is the day when the killing of the first Shia imam, Huseyin, who is regarded as a martyr, is commemorated by men and boys beating their backs with chains while the people watching them, including women, beat their chests with their fists. This ritual was not introduced until the early 1990s, and it attracts an increasing number of people. People go to the mosque to pray and light candles and also visit the tombs of *pir* (holy men) to make a wish.

**Death and the Afterlife.** Although people increasingly follow Islamic tradition, owing to the lack of organized religious education, people's beliefs about the afterlife are not clearly defined. The idea of paradise and hell is prominent, and martyrs are believed to go to heaven. After a death, the first and subsequent four Thursdays as well as the third, seventh, and fortieth days and the one year anniversary are commemorated. When there is too little space, a tent is put up in front of people's homes for the guests. Men and women usually sit in separate rooms, food and tea are served, and the Koran is read.

## MEDICINE AND HEALTH CARE

Western medicine is very widely used, along with herbal remedies, and people visit psychics (*ekstrasenses*) and healers. The sick may be taken to visit *pir* to help them recover.

## SECULAR CELEBRATIONS

The new year's holiday is celebrated on 1 January, 20 January commemorates the victims killed by Soviet troops in Baku in 1990, 8 March is International Women's Day, and 21–22 March is *Novruz* (the new year), an old Persian holiday celebrated on the day of the vernal equinox. *Novruz* is the most distinctive Azeri holiday, accompanied by extensive cleaning and cooking in homes. Most households grow *semeni* (green wheat seedlings), and children jump over

small bonfires; celebrations also are held in public spaces. Other holidays are 9 May, Victory Day (inherited from the Soviet period); 28 May, Day of the Republic; 9 October, Armed Forces Day; 18 October, State Sovereignty Day; 12 November, Constitution Day; 17 November, Day of Renaissance; and 31 December, Day of Solidarity of World Azeris.

## THE ARTS AND HUMANITIES

**Support for the Arts.** State funds during the socialist era provided workshops for painters and other artists. Such funds are now limited, but national and international sponsors encourage artistic activity.

**Literature.** The book of Dede Korkut and the Zoroastrian Avesta (which date back to earlier centuries but were written down in the fifteenth century) as well as the Köroglu *dastan* are among the oldest examples of oral literature (dastans are recitations of historical events in a highly ornamented language). Works by poets such as Shirvani, Gancavi, Nasimi, Shah Ismail Savafi, and Fuzuli produced between the twelfth and sixteenth centuries are the most important Persian- and Turkish-language writings. The philosopher and playwriter Mirza Fath Ali Akhunzade (Akhundov), the historical novelist Husein Javid, and the satirist M. A. Sabir all produced works in Azeri in the nineteenth century. Major figures in the twentieth century included Elchin, Yusif Samedoglu, and Anar, and some novelists also wrote in Russian.

**Graphic Arts.** The tradition of painted miniatures was important in the nineteenth century, while the twentieth century was marked by examples of Soviet social realism and Azeri folklore. Among the widely recognized painters, Sattar Bakhulzade worked mainly with landscapes in a manner reminiscent of "Van Gogh in blue." Tahir Salakhov painted in Western and Soviet styles, and Togrul Narimanbekov made use of figures from traditional Azeri folk tales depicted in very rich colors. Rasim Babayev cultivated his own style of "primitivism" with hidden allegories on the Soviet regime (bright saturated colors, an absence of perspective, and numerous nonhuman characters inspired by folktales and legends).

**Performance Arts.** The local and Western musical tradition is very rich, and there has been a jazz revival in Baku in recent years. Pop music is also popular, having developed under Russian, Western, and Azeri influences. The Soviet system helped popularize a systematic musical education, and people

*An Azerbaijani folk dancer performs a traditional dance.*

from all sectors of society participate in and perform music of different styles. While composers and performers of and listeners to classical music and jazz are more common in urban places, *ashugs* (who play *saz* and sing) and performers of *mugam* (a traditional vocal and instrumental style) can be found all over the country. It is not unusual to find children who play piano in their village homes. Traditional string, wind, and percussion instruments (*tar, balaban, tutak, saz, kamancha, nagara*) are widely used. Uzeyir Hacibeyov, who is claimed to have written the first opera (*Leyli and Madjnun*) in the Islamic East in the early twentieth century, Kara Karayev, and Fikret Amirov are among the best-known classical composers. Both now and in the past, elements from Azeri music have been incorporated into classical and jazz pieces (e.g., the pianist and composer Firangiz Alizade, who recently played with the Kronos Quartet). Beside Western ballet, traditional dances accompanied by accordion, *tar*, and percussion are popular.

## THE STATE OF THE PHYSICAL AND SOCIAL SCIENCES

Universities and institutions of higher education from the Soviet era have been joined by new private universities. The Academy of Sciences has tradition-

ally been the site of basic research in many fields. Social sciences were developed within the Soviet framework, although the directions of study are changing slowly with international involvement. Financial difficulties mean that all research is subject to constraints, but oil-related subjects are given a high priority. State funds are limited, and international funds are obtained by institutions and individual scientists.

## BIBLIOGRAPHY

Altstadt, Audrey L. *The Azerbaijani Turks: Power and Identity under Russian Rule*, 1992.

Atabaki, Touraj. *Azerbaijan: Ethnicity and Autonomy in Iran after the Second World War*, 1993.

Azerbaijan: A Country Study, U.S. Library of Congress: http://lcweb2.loc.gov/frd/cs/aztoc.html.

Cornell, Svante. ''Undeclared War: The Nagorno-Karabakh Conflict Reconsidered.'' *Journal of South Asian and Middle Eastern Studies* 20 (4):1–23, 1997. http://scf.usc.edu/~baguirov/azeri/svante_cornell.html

Croissant, Cynthia. *Azerbaijan, Oil and Geopolitics*, 1998.

Croissant, Michael P. *The Armenia-Azerbaijan Conflict*, 1998.

Demirdirek, Hülya. ''Dimensions of Identification: Intellectuals in Baku, 1990–1992.'' Candidata Rerum Politicarum dissertation, University of Oslo, 1993.

Dragadze, Tamara. ''The Armenian-Azerbaijani Conflict: Structure and Sentiment.'' *Third World Quarterly* 11 (1):55–71, 1989.

———. ''Azerbaijanis.'' In *The Nationalist Question in the Soviet Union*, edited by Graham Smith, 1990.

———. ''Islam in Azerbaijan: The Position of Women.'' In *Muslim Women's Choices*, edited by Camilla Fawzi El-Sohl and Judy Marbro, 1994.

Fawcett, Louise L'Estrange. *Iran and the Cold War: The Azerbaijan Crisis of 1946*, 1992.

Goltz, Thomas. *Azerbaijan Diary: A Rogue Reporter's Adventures in an Oil-Rich, War-Torn Post-Soviet Republic*, 1998.

Hunter, Shireen. ''Azerbaijan: Search for Identity and New Partners.'' In *Nation and Politics in the Soviet Successor States*, edited by Ian Bremmer and Ray Taras, 1993.

Kechichian, J. A., and T. W. Karasik. ''The Crisis in Azerbaijan: How Clans Influence the Politics of an Emerging Republic.'' *Middle East Policy* 4 (1B2): 57B71, 1995.

Kelly, Robert C., et al., eds. *Country Review, Azerbaijan 1998/1999*, 1998.

Nadein-Raevski, V. "The Azerbaijani-Armenian Conflict: Possible Paths towards Resolution." In *Ethnicity and Conflict in a Post-Communist World: The Soviet Union, Eastern Europe and China*, edited by Kumar Rupesinghe et al., 1992.

Robins, P. "Between Sentiment and Self-Interest: Turkey's Policy toward Azerbaijan and the Central Asian States." *Middle East Journal* 47 (4): 593–610, 1993.

Safizadeh, Fereydoun. "On Dilemmas of Identity in the Post-Soviet Republic of Azerbaijan." *Caucasian Regional Studies* 3 (1), 1998. http://poli.vub.ac.be/publi/crs/eng/0301–04.htm.

———. "Majority-Minority Relations in the Soviet Republics." In *Soviet Nationalities Problems*, edited by Ian A. Bremmer and Norman M. Naimark, 1990.

Saroyan, Mark. "The 'Karabakh Syndrome' and Azerbaijani Politics." *Problems of Communism*, September-October, 1990, pp. 14–29.

Smith, M.G. "Cinema for the 'Soviet East': National Fact and Revolutionary Fiction in Early Azerbaijani Film." *Slavic Review* 56 (4): 645–678, 1997.

Suny, Ronald G. *The Baku Commune, 1917–1918: Class and Nationality in the Russian Revolution*, 1972.

———. *Transcaucasia: Nationalism and Social Change: Essays in the History of Armenia, Azerbaijan and Georgia*, 1983.

———. "What Happened in Soviet Armenia." *Middle East Report* July-August, 1988, pp. 37–40.

———."'The Revenge' of the Past: Socialism and Ethnic Conflict in Transcaucasia." *New Left Review* 184: 5–34, 1990.

———. "Incomplete Revolution: National Movements and the Collapse of the Soviet Empire." *New Left Review* 189: 111–140, 1991.

———. "State, Civil Society and Ethnic Cultural Consolidation in the USSR—Roots of the National Question." In *From Union to Commonwealth: Nationalism and Separatism in the Soviet Republics*, edited by Gail W. Lapidus et al., 1992.

———, ed. *Transcaucasia, Nationalism, and Social Change: Essays in the History of Armenia, Azerbaijan and Georgia*, 1996 (1984).

Swietochowski, Tadeusz. *Russian Azerbaijan, 1905B1920: The Shaping of National Identity in a Muslim Community*, 1985.

———. "The Politics of a Literary Language and the Rise of National Identity in Russian Azerbaijan before 1920." *Ethnic and Racial Studies* 14 (1): 55–63, 1991.

———. *Russia and Azerbaijan: A Borderland in Transition*, 1995.

———, ed. *Historical Dictionary of Azerbaijan*, 1999.

Tohidi, N. "Soviet in Public, Azeri in Private—Gender, Islam, and Nationality in Soviet and Post-Soviet Azerbaijan." *Women's Studies International Forum* 19 (1–2): 111–123, 1996.

Van Der Leeuw, Charles. *Azerbaijan: A Quest for Identity*, 1999.

Vatanabadi, S. "Past, Present, Future, and Postcolonial Discourse in Modern Azerbaijani Literature." *World Literature Today* 70 (3): 493–497, 1996.

Yamskov, Anatoly. "Inter-Ethnic Conflict in the Trans-Caucasus: A Case Study of Nagorno-Karabakh." In *Ethnicity and Conflict in a Post-Communist World: The Soviet Union, Eastern Europe and China*, edited by Kumar Rupesinghe et al., 1992.

### Web Sites

Azerbaijan Republic website: http://www.president.az/azerbaijan/azerbaijan.htm.

—HÜLYA DEMIRDIREK

# BAHAMA ISLANDS

## CULTURE NAME
Bahamian

## ORIENTATION

**Identification.** The name Bahamas derives from the Spanish *baja* ("shallow") and *mar* ("sea"). Within the country, a distinction is made between the capital of Nassau on New Providence Island and the out islands of the archipelago. Bahamians recognize their distinctive national culture but emphasize minor differences in speech and customs among the islands. Foreign-born residents from the United Kingdom, the United States, Haiti, Canada, and other countries are referred to by their original nationalities regardless of citizenship or assimilation.

**Location and Geography.** The Bahamas lie in the Atlantic off the eastern coast of Florida and extend for over seven-hundred miles, roughly parallel to Cuba. The archipelago consists of approximately seven hundred islands and cays, plus nearly 2,400 reefs and rock formations. The land area is 5,382 square miles (13,940 square kilometers). There are fourteen island groupings. The climate is subtropical, with a hurricane season from June through November. Flooding is a problem because the islands are low outcrops of limestone, with most settlements barely above sea level. Farming has been practiced since pre–Columbian times, but the soil is thin, sandy, and not fertile. Few of the islands have ground water. The islands are ringed by sandy beaches and surrounded by shallow seas.

**Demography.** Population estimates range from 275,000 to 325,000, with tens of thousands of illegal economic refugees from Haiti who account for 20 to 25 percent of the population. About 85 percent of Bahamians are of African ancestry, and most of the remainder are of European descent. People of Asian ancestry constitute a very small segment of the population. Some racial mixing has occurred. Approximately 60 percent of the population is urban, a proportion that is growing rapidly as young adults migrate from out-island settlements to the urban areas of Nassau and Freeport.

**Linguistic Affiliation.** English is the primary and official language. Regional and class–related dialects vary from "Standard English" among the urban elite to "Bahamian English" among the poorer people. There are finely nuanced differences in vocabulary and pronunciation from island to island. "French Creole" is spoken by immigrants from Haiti. Those immigrants often are able to converse in heavily accented English, but few have been formally educated in the language.

**Symbolism.** Residents sometimes use the term "family islands" to symbolize the desired unity of the scattered population and the image of small, cohesive out-island communities. One of the most familiar symbols is the national flag, which was introduced in 1973. The left side consists of a black triangle with a horizontal yellow stripe flanked by two bright blue stripes. Yellow symbolizes the sunny climate, and blue symbolizes the sea. Many people assert that black symbolizes the African heritage of the people. "Junkanoo" is a Mardi Gras-like celebration that is held on several secular holidays. Both the term and form of the celebration probably come from West Africa. The celebrations combine music, costume, dance, revelry, pride in the African cultural heritage, recognition of slave resistance to authority, and the unity of the people. Junkanoo "gangs" compete for prestige and cash prizes. Tourism officials have transformed these ceremonies into events that draw thousands of visitors. Organizers, scholars, and participants refer to Junkanoo as a social institution that binds the people to each other and to their past.

## HISTORY AND ETHNIC RELATIONS
**Emergence of the Nation.** The first residents were the Lukku-Cairis, or Lucayans, a subdivision of the

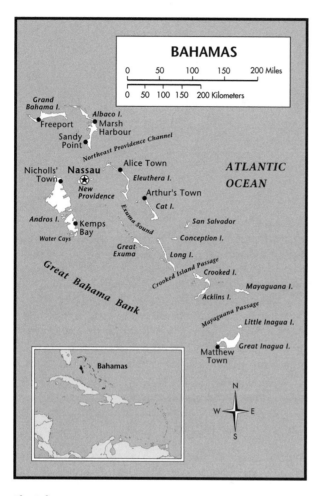

## BAHAMAS

| 0 | 50 | 100 | 150 | 200 Miles |

| 0 | 50 100 150 | 200 Kilometers |

*The Bahamas*

dance, religious concepts, folktales, family patterns, and linguistic influences. New beliefs and behaviors emerged within the Bahamian context as well. Plantations, slave revolts, colonial governance, the insular existence, the sea, hurricanes, and many other elements contributed to the cultural synthesis. The islands remained a British colony until independence was peacefully attained in 1973.

**Ethnic Relations.** Many Bahamians perceive Haitians in terms of negative stereotypes and consider them scapegoats. Haitians often are portrayed as violent, uncivilized, and inclined toward criminality. Because of their poverty, they often do work Bahamians see as undesirable, and thus they are blamed for taking away jobs. Because they speak French Creole and practice voodoo, they are deemed secretive and dangerous. They also are seen as clannish and as a criminal menace. It often is stated that AIDS arrived with the refugees. Americans, whether in the Bahamas as tourists or on business, are seen in a more ambivalent way. Their money is desired, but their influence is not appreciated. Tourism-sector jobs are essential but are perceived as colonialism in modern dress. American investors and businesspeople are portrayed as arrogant, brash, and overly concerned with dominating Bahamians.

## URBANISM, ARCHITECTURE AND THE USE OF SPACE

The population is over 60 percent urban, with over half the people living in the capital city, Nassau. The only other city is the tourism-oriented Freeport. The rest of the population is scattered among dozens of smaller settlements ranging from small villages to regionally important towns. Nassau has neighborhoods that range from exclusive enclaves for the extremely wealthy to slums inhabited by the chronically unemployed and underemployed. Construction materials are roughly evenly divided between limestone and wood. Because of hurricanes, tall buildings are rarely constructed. Where feasible, buildings have porches and many windows. Old colonial structures, from forts to public buildings to houses, are revered. Termites and heavy winds have destroyed many structures, and cement block buildings have become commonplace. Public places such as narrow streets, beaches, and parks encourage human interaction.

## FOOD AND ECONOMY

**Food in Daily Life.** Typical meals for urban residents consist of fruits and vegetables, meat or fish,

Taino Arawak Indians. Christopher Columbus made his first hemispheric landfall in the Bahamas and claimed them for Spain. Many Lucayans were taken to Hispaniola and Cuba as slaves, and the rest died of newly imported diseases. The Spanish never settled the Bahamas, and the region became a haven for pirates. The British claimed the islands in 1629 and started a community on Eleuthera in 1648. The British residents were augmented by loyalists fleeing North America during and after the American Revolution and an influx of enslaved Africans. Blacks have outnumbered whites since the eighteenth century. When the cotton plantations failed, many slaves were freed and given land to farm. During the 1830s emancipation was legally mandated.

**National Identity.** National culture was forged through the interactions of British and African traditions. Britons contributed the English language, Protestantism, a market economy, and European technology. Various West African peoples contributed musical instruments and styles, forms of

bread, and rice. Out islanders tend to eat more fresh fruit, vegetables, and fish. The two national dishes are conch, an easily collected sea snail, rice, and peas. Poor people eat these foods because they are inexpensive and readily available; the more affluent enjoy them as "heritage foods."

**Food Customs at Ceremonial Occasions.** Holiday meals tend to center on local fish or conch, rice and peas, baked goods, and fresh fruit. Bahamian rum, local and imported beer, soft drinks, tea, and coffee are regularly consumed.

**Basic Economy.** Most consumer goods are imported. Farming is unimportant except for a small amount of subsistence gardening in out-island settlements. Tourism accounts for about half the gross domestic product and nearly half of all jobs. The annual per capita income is approximately $10,000, there is little taxation, inflation ranges between 5 and 10 percent, and the unemployment rate is 15 to 20 percent. The national currency is known as the Bahamian dollar

**Commercial Activities.** Commercial farming of cotton, pineapples, and sisal has had little success. Commercial fishing is moderately important, with most of the catch frozen and exported. Sponge fishing is nearly defunct. Cottage industries that produce straw, shells, and wooden items cater to local residents and tourists. Hotels, casinos, restaurants, and sport fishing businesses are common.

**Major Industries.** Manufacturing is unimportant except for a few oil refineries and small factories. Offshore banking and finance are important because favorable tax and corporate laws have been established and widely promoted.

**Trade.** Most consumer goods are imported. Goods such as pharmaceuticals, rum, crawfish and cement are exported. The major trading partners are the United States, the United Kingdom, and Canada.

**Division of Labor.** The government is the largest employer. Out-island children work with their parents or grandparents when they are not in school or at play. In towns and cities, children from poorer families may work as street vendors or do odd jobs. Some occupations are unionized, and unions are an important force. Skilled trades such as fishing, carpentry, and masonry work tend to be family specializations. Small businesses pass from generation to generation within families.

## SOCIAL STRATIFICATION

**Classes and Castes.** The upper class consists of wealthy business owners, corporate managers, professionals, high-ranking government officials, and some foreign citizens. Historically, this class was composed of Britons, white Bahamians, light-skinned Bahamians of mixed race, and a few Americans and Canadians. Most were self-consciously British in speech and behavior. The upper class today includes many more residents of African ancestry. Emulation of the old colonial elite is less common. The middle class consists of small business owners, some professionals, civil servants, and lower-level corporate managers. Most members of this class are of African ancestry, but some are of European and Asian ancestry. Degrees from Bahamian and American colleges are increasingly common. The lower class is the nation's largest and includes roughly equal numbers of urban and out island residents. Almost all the members of this class are of African ancestry. Lower-class Bahamians include fishermen, farmers, laborers, skilled tradespeople, and others who do low-status physical work. Some have high school diplomas, but many have lower levels of educational attainment and are perceived as poor but respectable. The lowest stratum is an underclass that consists of the chronically unemployed and Haitian refugees. Most members of the underclass live in the least desirable and "respectable" sections of the Nassau metropolitan area. They are found in smaller numbers in some out-island communities. Few have a high school diploma.

**Symbols of Social Stratification.** The distinction between old money and new money is not critically important. University degrees, especially from private institutions in Britain and the United States, are common. Most upper-class residents are in the exclusive neighborhoods of Nassau, although some have additional homes in the out islands or abroad. Middle-class people live in "respectable" Nassau neighborhoods or out-island settlements. Many regularly fly to Florida for shopping and entertainment.

## POLITICAL LIFE

**Government.** The Commonwealth is a constitutional, parliamentary democracy with universal suffrage for citizens age eighteen and older. The British monarch is recognized as the head of state and is represented by the governor-general, but executive power is vested in the prime minister. Primary legislative authority resides with an elected

*Produce stalls at a market in Nassau. Fruits and vegetables are a staple of typical Bahamian meals.*

House of Assembly and an appointed Senate. The judicial system includes magistrates' courts, the Supreme Court, and the Court of Appeals. Local government is an extension of the federal government with administration in the hands of appointed district commissioners.

***Leadership and Political Officials.*** There are two major political parties: the Free National Movement (FNM) and the Progressive Liberal Party (PLP). Ideologically, both parties are centrist, with the PLP somewhat to the left of the FNM on most social issues. The personalities of politicians and their relationships with constituents are more important than political philosophy. Most people elected to the House of Assembly since independence have been middle-aged men of African ancestry with university degrees and successful careers in law and/or business. House members need not reside in their districts but normally visit frequently. Political officials are expected to be accessible to their constituents through office visits and the mail.

***Social Control and Problems.*** Bahamian law is based on English common law and statute law. The law is enforced via the paramilitary Royal Bahamas Police Force and federally appointed constables. Legal prosecution is carried out by the attorney general's office. Informal social control occurs through peer pressure, gossip, and fear of harmful magic known as *obeah*. The archipelago is the final staging area for thousands of annual shipments of illegal drugs from South America and the Caribbean to North America. Although illegal and viewed as a social problem by many people, the drug trade is tolerated because it provides income. Money laundering and related international crimes are widely viewed as beneficial and are not criminalized. Crimes such as assault, robbery, and homicide are dealt with routinely. Vigilante groups exist but are not an important aspect of social control.

***Military Activity.*** No military exists and Bahamians rely on the protection of the United Kingdom.

## SOCIAL WELFARE AND CHANGE PROGRAMS

The government has a program of moderate social welfare and change initiatives. The 1990s witnessed education reforms stressing vocational and technical training to combat unemployment and reliance on foreign workers. The low level of taxation and the cultural value attached to independence preclude more elaborate programs.

## NONGOVERNMENTAL ORGANIZATIONS AND OTHER ASSOCIATIONS

Nongovernmental organizations such as churches and labor unions have modest programs of local reform ranging from refugee relief to antidrug initiatives. Regional ad hoc committees lobby for government projects and environmental protection.

## GENDER ROLES AND STATUSES

**Division of Labor by Gender.** Legally, women have equal status under the law, but men tend to dominate the higher-income and higher status positions in the public and private sectors. Men dominate fishing and other maritime endeavors, the building trades, and the transportation industry.

**The Relative Status of Women and Men.** Urban women have many career opportunities and are not discriminated against in obvious ways. Women dominate fields such as nursing, elementary school teaching, and office work. Out-island women tend to be farmers, shopkeepers, craft specialists, and domestics when they are employed. Many self-identify as "housekeepers."

## MARRIAGE, FAMILY, AND KINSHIP

**Marriage.** Marriages are monogamous. In many out-island settlements, the options are marriage and extraresidential unions. In larger towns and cities, consensual unions exist. People are free to select their spouses. Church weddings follow brief engagements. In principle, one should not marry a blood relative, but in small communities marriages between kin more distantly related than first cousins are common. In white-dominated out-island settlements, interracial marriages are stigmatized. Both partners are expected to contribute financially to a marriage. Divorces are available, although many couples simply drift apart and never legally terminate the union. There is no stigma attached to remarriage. A sexual double standard exists in which women are supposed to be chaste until marriage and faithful during marriage whereas men are expected to have premarital and extramarital affairs. Men are widely seen as inherently promiscuous.

**Domestic Unit.** The ideal is the nuclear family household. In cases of extramarital unions, consensual unions, divorce, death, and abandonment, matrifocal households are common. In poorer out-island settlements, parents may move to urban areas to work, leaving their children in the care of

*A float in a Junkanoo parade, Nassau. Parades are common for most secular holidays.*

grandparents. In nuclear family households, authority tends to be evenly divided between the husband and the wife.

**Inheritance.** Sons and daughters inherit from both parents. Inherited property includes land, houses, boats, and household goods. Wills may favor one heir over another, but this is uncommon, especially in the out islands.

**Kin Groups.** No formal kin groups larger than the family exist. Adult siblings tend to look after each other's interests and frequently operate shops or fishing vessels together.

## SOCIALIZATION

**Infant Care.** Infants are cared for by their mothers. Both bottle feeding and breast-feeding are accepted. Infants sleep in the parents' bedroom except among the more affluent, where a separate room is available. Infants are carried in the arms, and baby carriages are used. Caregivers try to calm crying or otherwise agitated infants.

**Child Rearing and Education.** Children are socialized in traditional adult roles. Girls care for younger siblings, play with dolls, and help with

*A town on Man of War Cay. Most buildings and houses are small in height due to hurricane safety measures.*

shopping and household chores. Boys may work with their fathers but are often free to play. Boys are taught to be fun-loving and independent, while girls are expected to be responsible and to remain under close family scrutiny. Corporal punishment and threats are common. The literacy rate is about 90 percent, and public education is available through local elementary schools and regional secondary schools. Private schools in Nassau are available to wealthier families. In public schools, rote learning is common.

***Higher Education.*** Since independence, higher education has been stressed. The College of the Bahamas in Nassau and numerous technical schools provide higher education, although foreign universities are popular among the more affluent.

## RELIGION

***Religious Beliefs.*** Most residents are churchgoing Christians. About 80 percent are Protestant, and 20 percent are Roman Catholic. The largest Protestant denominations are Baptist and Anglican. Obeah is an African system of belief in spirits that often is superimposed on Christianity.

***Religious Practitioners.*** Large congregations are led by ordained ministers and priests, while small congregations are led by unordained preachers. Obeah men are part-time specialists whose activities include placing and removing curses, communicating with spirits, and giving spiritual advice.

***Rituals and Holy Places.*** Most rituals are Christian services and are held in churches. Immersion baptisms and revival meetings are held outdoors. Some Christian services include glossolalia, spirit possession, and faith healing. Obeah rituals tend to be small and private.

***Death and the Afterlife.*** The dead are placed in simple pine coffins, and wakes are held at home. The wealthy buy more expensive coffins and use funeral parlors. Funerals are held in churches, and burials are in churchyards or public cemeteries. It is believed that souls go to heaven or hell, but some believe that ghosts wander before reaching their ultimate destination.

## MEDICINE AND HEALTH CARE

There is one large hospital in Nassau, and over a hundred government clinics are scattered elsewhere. An air ambulance service transports out islanders to the hospital in emergencies. There are about twelve-hundred people per physician, but nurses and paramedics often serve as primary care professionals, especially in remote settlements. "Bush medicine" (herbal treatments) is still found, but its popularity is declining.

## SECULAR CELEBRATIONS

Ten public holidays are recognized: New Year's Day, Good Friday, Easter, Whit Monday (seven weeks after Easter), Labor Day (first Friday in June), Independence Day (10 July), Emancipation Day (first Monday in August), Discovery Day (12 October), Christmas Day, and Boxing Day (26 December). Secular holidays tend to be celebrated with parades, speeches, and concerts.

## THE ARTS AND HUMANITIES

**Support for the Arts.** Artists tend to be self-supporting, although government grants occasionally are given for works of special public significance.

**Literature.** Oral literature, the telling of "old stories," is a revered art form. Written works include historical novels and poetry.

**Graphic Arts.** Graphic arts, especially painting, tend toward landscapes and seascapes and historical events. There are many private gallaries in Nassau.

**Performance Arts.** Plays are performed for tourists and residents at amateur and professional theaters in Nassau and Freeport. Concerts range from youth-oriented popular music (reggae, rock, rap) to more adult-oriented forms (blues, jazz, gospel) to classical music. The largest events are held in Nassau and Freeport, but smaller concerts are held in most out-island communities.

## THE STATE OF THE PHYSICAL AND SOCIAL SCIENCES

Faculty members from the College of the Bahamas conduct a limited amount of scientific research. More is conducted by foreign researchers, especially marine biologists. Social science research tends to be in applied fields such as economic development, finance, social work, and public health. Medicine and engineering are not well developed.

## BIBLIOGRAPHY

Collinwood, Dean W. *The Bahamas Between Worlds*, 1989.

————, and Steve Dodge, eds. *Modern Bahamian Society*, 1989.

Craton, Michael. *A History of the Bahamas.* 3rd ed., 1986.

————, and Gail Saunders. *Islanders in the Stream: A History of the Bahamian People*, vol. 1, 1992.

Crowley, Daniel. *I Could Talk Old Story Good: Creativity in Bahamian Folklore*, 1966.

Dupuch, S. P., editorial director. *Bahamas Handbook and Businessman's Annual*, 1998.

Holm, John A. and Alison Watt Shilling. *Dictionary of Bahamian English*, 1982.

Hughes, C. A. *Race and Politics in the Bahamas*, 1981.

Johnson, Doris. *The Quiet Revolution in the Bahamas*, 1971.

LaFlamme, Alan G. *Green Turtle Cay: An Island in the Bahamas*, 1985.

Otterbein, Keith F. *The Andros Islanders*, 1966.

—ALAN LAFLAMME

# BAHRAIN

## CULTURE NAME

Bahrani

## ORIENTATION

**Identification.** In ancient times, Bahrain was part of an empire known as Dilmun. It was later called Tyros by the Greeks. The name "Bahrain" is derived from the Arabic word *Bahr*, meaning "sea."

**Location and Geography.** Bahrain is an archipelago made up of Bahrain Island and thirty smaller islands. It is located in the Persian Gulf near the Arabian Peninsula, 120 miles southwest of Iran, 14 miles to the east of Saudi Arabia, and 17 miles to the west of the Qatar Peninsula. The main island, which accounts for seven-eighths of the country's area, is thirty miles from north to south and ten miles from east to west. The total area of the country is 240 square miles (620 square kilometers).

The highest point is Ad-Dukhan Hill in the center of Bahrain Island. This area is surrounded by sandy plains and salt marshes. Along the north and northwest coast, there are some springs and aquifers that are used for irrigation. Only 1 percent of the land is arable.

The climate is humid for much of the year, but the country suffers from a scarcity of rainfall which averages three inches a year, falling almost entirely in the winter. Despite the dry climate, the country is home to about two hundred species of desert plants as well as gazelles, hares, desert rats, and mongoose.

**Demography.** According to the *CIA World Factbook*, the estimated population in 2000 was 634,137. The majority of these people are Arabs. There are many temporary immigrant workers, and one-third of the population is foreign-born. Nineteen percent of the population is Asian, 10 percent is non-Bahraini Arab, and 8 percent is Irani. There are significantly more men than women. The population is growing rapidly with a high birthrate and a low death rate. One-third of the people are less than fifteen years old.

**Linguistic Affiliation.** Arabic is the official language and the language of daily life. English is understood in many places and Farsi and Urdu also are spoken by the large numbers of Indian and Persian residents.

**Symbolism.** The national flag is red with a white serrated band of eight points along the left side.

## HISTORY AND ETHNIC RELATIONS

**Emergence of the Nation.** Archaeological evidence dating back to the third millennium B.C.E. indicates that the main island probably was settled by Sumerians. Around 2000 B.C.E. it was known as Dilmun and served as a trading post on the route between Sumeri and the Indus Valley. In the fourth century C.E. Bahrain was annexed into the Sasanian Empire. In the seventh century, Muslims conquered the area and ruled until the sixteenth century. In 1521, Portugal took control, using Bahrain as a pearling post and military garrison. This situation lasted until 1602, when the Persians wrested the country from the Portuguese. The ruler Ahmad ibn Al Khalifah took control from the Persians in 1783; his descendants lead the country to this day.

In the 1830s, the British signed several treaties with Bahrain, offering protection from the Turks in exchange for access to the Persian Gulf. In 1869, Britain put its own emir in place. In 1935, it placed its main Middle Eastern naval base in Bahrain, and in 1946, it stationed the senior British officer in the region there.

Anti-British sentiment rose in the 1950s, but Britain did not decide to pull out until 1971. Bahrain officially declared its independence on 14 August of that year.

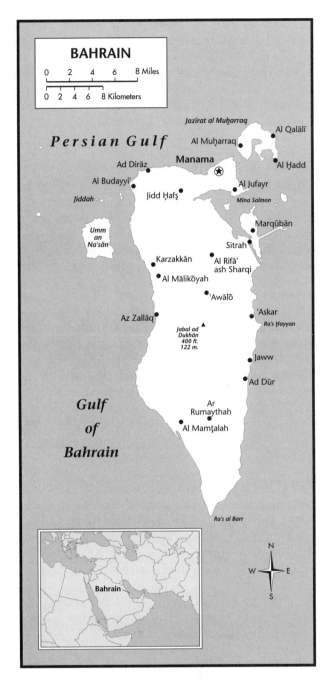

**BAHRAIN**

0 2 4 6 8 Miles

0 2 4 6 8 Kilometers

*Persian Gulf*

*Jazīrat al Muḥarraq*

Al Muḥarraq

Al Qalālī

**Manama**

Ad Dirāz

Al Ḥadd

Al Budayyiʻ

*Al Jufayr*

*Jiddah*

Jidd Ḥafş

*Mina Salmon*

*Umm an Naʻsān*

Marqūbān

Sitrah

Karzakkān

Al Rifāʻ ash Sharqi

Al Mālikōyah

ʻAwālō

*Az Zallāq*

ʻAskar

*Raʻs Ḥayyan*

Jabal ad Dukhān 400 ft. 122 m. ▲

Jaww

Ad Dūr

*Gulf of Bahrain*

Ar Rumaythah

Al Mamṭalah

*Raʻs al Barr*

N W E S

Bahrain

*Bahrain*

Although oil was discovered in 1902, drilling did not begin in earnest until the 1930s. The 1970s and 1980s saw a dramatic rise in the price of oil, which benefitted the economy significantly. In the late 1980s, when other countries in the area experienced economic difficulties, Bahrain maintained its prosperity thanks to earlier economic diversification.

In the 1990s, the country suffered from internal and external problems that began with a push for democratic reforms. When the emir turned this request down, widespread rioting broke out. The country's shaky relations with Iraq led it to cooperate with United Nations' efforts to monitor that nearby country. The United States military buildup in the area also created a tense relationship between Bahrainis and American troops.

***National Identity.*** Bahrainis self-identify as part of the Arab world. There are tensions between the Sunni and Shi'ite Muslims, and religious affiliation is of primary importance in defining one's identity.

***Ethnic Relations.*** Expatriates constitute 20 percent of the population. They come mainly from other Arab nations but also from India, Pakistan, Southeast Asia, Europe, and America. While relations are not unfriendly, foreigners generally are not integrated into Bahraini society. The vast majority are temporary workers and thus constitute a transient population.

## URBANISM, ARCHITECTURE, AND THE USE OF SPACE

Four-fifths of the population lives in cities, the majority in Manama which is the capital and the largest urban center. That city stands on a seabed, parts of which were recently reclaimed from the water. Manama has modern buildings and wide, tree-lined roads as well as an older section with a traditional *souk*, or marketplace.

Muharraq is the oldest town, and used to be the capital. The city has been modernized, but in the old sections one can still see traditional architecture. The houses have tall gates and shuttered windows and are designed around a central enclosed garden or courtyard. Some have wind towers, an old-fashioned form of air-conditioning. These towers are open on four sides at the top to direct passing breezes into the house.

Most rural villages have electricity and running water and are connected to the towns by paved roads. Traditional houses, called *barastis*, were made from palm branches, but today most villagers build homes from modern materials.

## FOOD AND ECONOMY

***Food in Daily Life.*** The best-known dish, *machbous*, consists of fish or meat served with rice. A dessert called *muhammar* is made of brown rice and sugar or dates. *Halwa* is another traditional sweet, a green, sticky dessert filled with spices and nuts. Snacks known as *sambousas* are also popular;

**161**

these are pastries filled with meat and cheese or sugar and nuts.

**Food Customs at Ceremonial Occasions.** Muslim holidays are often the occasion for large family meals. The breaking of the fast month of Ramadan is celebrated with feasts of traditional food, and a variety of special sweets and pastries.

**Basic Economy.** Only 1 percent of the land is arable, and so the country is unable to produce enough food for its population and relies almost entirely on imports. The primary employers are industry, commerce, and services (79 percent of workers are in these fields) and government (20 percent); the remaining 1 percent of the people are farmers. A large number of jobs are held by foreigners, and employment is an ongoing problem, particularly among young people. Three-fifths of the workforce is foreign-born.

The economy is based largely on petroleum production and processing, which account for 60 percent of exports and 30 percent of the gross domestic product (GDP). Bahrain also has well-developed communications and transportation, which has allowed it to become a center for banking and finance, and is the headquarters for a number of multinational firms that do business in the Persian Gulf area.

**Commercial Activities.** The country produces fruits and vegetables, poultry, dairy products, shrimp, and fish that are sold in the souks, along with locally produced handicrafts. Tourism is a growing business, accounting for 9 percent of the GDP. A good deal of international banking is conducted in Bahrain.

**Major Industries.** The main industry is petroleum production, processing, and refining. Others industries are aluminum smelting, offshore banking, ship repairing, and tourism. The country also produces cement blocks, plastics, asphalt, paper products, and soft drinks.

**Trade.** Imports and exports are roughly equal in value. Petroleum accounts for 60 percent of exports, and aluminum for 7 percent. These are exports sent mainly to India, Japan, Saudi Arabia, South Korea, and the United Arab Emirates. Forty-one percent of imports consist of crude oil, which the country processes. Imports, which also include machinery, transportation equipment, and food, come from Saudi Arabia, the United States, the United Kingdom, Japan, and Germany.

**Division of Labor.** Seventy-nine percent of the workforce is in industry, commerce, and services; 20 percent is in the government; and 1 percent in agriculture. Many jobs are held by foreign temporary workers, who account for over 60 percent of the labor force. Expatriates work in every field from manual labor to investment banking.

## SOCIAL STRATIFICATION

**Classes and Castes.** Because Bahrain is one of the wealthiest Gulf states, there are a number of well-to-do people, who are almost all well educated and live in Manama or Muharraq. However, many jobs are staffed by foreigners, and there is an unemployment rate of 15 percent among Bahrainis.

**Symbols of Social Stratification.** Most men wear a traditional long robe called a *thobe*. Wealthier people tend to wear thobes tailored in a more Western style, with side and breast pockets and collars and French cuffs. Men also wrap their heads with a scarf called a *gutra*. Women cover their clothes with the traditional black cloak, which goes over the head, and wear a veil of thin black gauze over the face. Some younger women in the cities leave their faces or even their heads, uncovered, but this is rare.

## POLITICAL LIFE

**Government.** Bahrain is a traditional monarchy in which the king is the chief of state. He appoints a prime minister, who serves as the head of government, and a cabinet. The cabinet has legislative powers with the assistance of an advisory (or *Shura*) council, which was established in 1992, whose members are appointed by the monarch. There is no suffrage, as the monarchy is hereditary, passed down to the oldest son.

**Leadership and Political Officials.** Political parties are prohibited, but there are several small underground leftist and Islamic fundamentalist groups. The main opposition consists of Shi'a Muslim groups that have been active since 1994, protesting unemployment and the dissolution in 1975 of the National Assembly, an elected legislative body.

**Social Problems and Control.** The legal system is based on a combination of Islamic law and English common law. Most potential laws are discussed by the Shura council before being put into in effect.

**Military Activity.** The military consists of a ground force, navy, air force, coast guard, and po-

*Men partake in the traditional past-time of coffee-drinking in the Gulf Hotel in Manama. The scarf that covers a man's head is called a* gutra.

lice force. Males are eligible for service at age fifteen. The country spends roughly 5.2 percent of its GDP on the military.

## SOCIAL WELFARE AND CHANGE PROGRAMS

Bahrain is a welfare state. Medical care is free and comprehensive for both nationals and expatriates. There are programs that provide for the elderly and the disabled. There is an institute for the blind and one for the physically handicapped.

## NONGOVERNMENTAL ORGANIZATIONS AND OTHER ASSOCIATIONS

Groups such as the World Health Organization (WHO) and UNESCO send workers to Bahrain. The country is also a member of the World Trade Organization and the United Nations.

## GENDER ROLES AND STATUSES

*Division of Labor by Gender.* Women are responsible for all domestic work, and few are employed outside the home (only 15 percent of the workforce is female). This is beginning to change as more girls gain access to an education, and foreign influence

has modified traditional views of women's roles. There are no women represented in the government.

*Relative Status of Women and Men.* In the Islamic tradition, women have a lower status than men and are considered weaker and in need of protection. Bahrain has been more progressive than other Arab nations in its treatment of women. The first school for girls was opened in 1928, nine years after the first boys' school.

## MARRIAGE, FAMILY, AND KINSHIP

*Marriage.* While arranged marriage is still common, the bride and groom often have a chance to meet before they marry. While it was traditional for girls to be married at twelve or thirteen years of age, they now tend to wait until they have finished their education and have a job. Upon marriage, a sum of money is paid to the bride by the groom's family. Sometimes she keeps it for herself, but usually the couple uses it to set up a home. Weddings are huge, often with five or six hundred guests. A wedding involves large meals, a religious ceremony, and a henna party in which the bride's attendants decorate her with elaborate patterns. Sometimes celebrations are mixed, but usually they are divided along gender lines.

*A pearl merchant in his shop in Manama. Bahr is an Arabic word meaning "sea."*

**Domestic Unit.** Traditionally, extended families lived together under one roof: parents, children, grandparents, and other relatives. A groom would bring his bride to live with his family. Today it is becoming more common for young couples to live apart from their parents.

## SOCIALIZATION

***Child Rearing and Education.*** Boys and girls are raised separately and according to different stan-

dards. From an early age girls have much more responsibility than their brothers, who have more freedom to play and amuse themselves. Education is free. Primary school lasts for six years, intermediate school for three years, and secondary school for another three years. The literacy rate is 85 percent: 89 percent among males and 79 percent among females.

***Higher Education.*** There are two universities in the country: the University of Bahrain with nine thousand students and the Arabian Gulf University at Manama with seven hundred. The College of Health Sciences trains nurses and hospital technicians. Many families that can afford to do so send their children abroad for higher education.

## ETIQUETTE

Greetings are generally lengthy and involve asking about each other's health and family, although a man does not ask about another man's wife. Everyone stands when someone enters the room, and that person then makes the rounds, shaking hands. After shaking, one touches the hand to the heart in a gesture of affection. Women and men can shake hands, but only if it is initiated by the woman. It is traditional upon visiting someone to be served coffee or tea. This custom includes visits to shops or offices. Failure to make such an offer or to accept it is considered rude.

## RELIGION

***Religious Beliefs.*** Seventy percent of the population is Shi'a Muslim, 15 percent is Sunni Muslim, and the remaining 15 percent is Christian or Jewish or follows indigenous practices. Muslims believe in the equality of all people before Allah. There are several differences between the Sunni and Shi'a sects of Islam. While most Muslims in the world are Sunni, in Bahrain, the majority are Shi'ite. The two groups split in 661, when the Sunnis refused to acknowledge Ali, whom the Shi'ites recognized as their leader.

***Religious Practitioners.*** There are no priests or clergy in Islam. There are men who study the *Quran* (the Muslim holy book) and lead prayers and readings from the text. The Quran, rather than religious leader, is considered the ultimate authority and holds the answer to any question or dilemma one might have. *Muezzins* give the call to prayer and are scholars of the Quran who spend their lives studying and interpreting the text. Sunnis elect their reli-

*A man standing in the doorway of his house in a Bahrain village. Electricity and running water are common in most rural Bahrainian villages.*

gious leaders, whereas in the Shi'a tradition these positions are hereditary.

**Rituals and Holy Places**. The most important observation in the Islamic calendar is Ramadan. This month of fasting is followed by the joyous feast of *Eid al Fitr*, during which families visit and exchange gifts. *Eid al-Adha* commemorates the end of Muhammed's Hajj. The mosque is the Muslim house of worship. Outside the door there are washing facilities, as cleanliness is a prerequisite to prayer, demonstrating humility before God. One must remove one's shoes before entering the mosque. According to Islamic tradition, women are not allowed inside. The interior has no altar; it is simply an open carpeted space. Because Muslims are supposed to pray facing Mecca, there is a small niche carved into the wall pointing out the direction in which that city lies.

**Death and the Afterlife**. Death is not acknowledged with great ceremony. People are buried under simple gravestones that face Mecca. When an important person dies, the house often is closed for a period of time.

## MEDICINE AND HEALTH CARE

The state of health care has improved significantly since independence. The nation has virtually eliminated tropical diseases and raised the life expectancy to seventy-one years for men and seventy-six years for women. There is a large modern hospital in the capital and many local health centers that focus on preventive care. There are facilities to train doctors and nurses, but many medical personnel are foreigners. Particularly in rural areas, some people still rely on traditional herbal cures made from palm tree flowers, pollen, and buds.

## SECULAR CELEBRATIONS

National Day is celebrated on 16 December.

## THE ARTS AND HUMANITIES

**Support for the Arts.** Manama has several galleries that show the works of both nationals and expatriates. Government programs preserve traditional arts and crafts and encourage poor women to take up these art forms to supplement their family income. The Bahrain Museum and the National Heritage Center showcase traditional works.

**Literature.** Bahrain has a strong literary tradition. Most of the work produced is in the classical Arabic style. Well-known contemporary poets that write in this style include Qasim Haddad, Ibrahim al-'Urayyid, and Ahmad Muhammed Al Khalifah. Many younger poets are more influenced by Western literature and write free verse, often with personal and political content.

**Graphic Arts.** The village of Sanabis is known for elaborate embroidery, often with gold thread, which the women sew onto their traditional dresses and cloaks. Fabric weaving also is practiced, as is the weaving of mats from sea grasses. Another popular craft is the production of *dhows*, boats made of wood, according to a traditional design that does not use metal nails. Old-fashioned dhows have sails, and more modern ones use diesel engines.

**Performance Arts.** The music of Bahrain follows the traditional Arabic mode. It is elaborate and repetitive. It is played on the *oud* (an ancestor of the lute) and the *rebaba* (a one-stringed instrument). Bahrain also has a folk dance tradition. The *ardha* is a men's sword dance, which is accompanied by drumming and by a poet, who sings the lyrics.

## THE STATE OF THE PHYSICAL AND SOCIAL SCIENCES

Most scientific research focuses on the oil economy. Bahrain has developed advanced technology for petrochemical plants and oil refineries. While developed primarily for domestic use, Bahrain has also sold some of this technology to other countries.

## BIBLIOGRAPHY

Al Kalifa, Hammad bin Isa. *First Light: Modern Bahrain and Its Heritage*, 1994.

Al Muraikhi, Khalil M. *Glimpses of Bahrain from Its Past*, 1991.

Amnesty International. ''Bahrain: Women and Children Subject to Increasing Abuse,'' July 1996.

''Bahrain,'' *Aquastat*, March 1997.

Bu Shahri, Ali Akbar. *Dilmun Culture*, 1992.

Byman, Daniel L. and Jerrold D. Green. ''The Enigma of Political Stability in the Persian Gulf Monarchies.'' *Middle East Review of International Affairs*, September 1999.

Crawford, Harriet. *Dilmun and its Gulf Neighbors*, 1998.

Darwish, Adel. ''Rebellion in Bahrain.'' *Middle East Review of International Affairs*, March 1999.

Hassall, S. and P. Hassall. *Let's Visit Bahrain*, 1985.

Littleton, Judith. *Skeletons and Social Composition: Bahrain 300 BC–AD 250*, 1998.

Robison, Gordon, and Paul Greenway. *Bahrain, Kuwait, and Qatar*, 2000.

U.S. Department of State, Bureau of Democracy, Human Rights, and Labor. ''Bahrain Country Report on Human Rights Practices for 1997,'' 30 January 1998.

### Web Sites

*Destination Bahrain*, 2000, www.lonelyplanet.com/dest/mea/bah

U.S. Department of State, Central Intelligence Agency. *World Factbook: Bahrain*, 2000, www.odci.gov/cia/publications/factbook/geos/ba

—ELEANOR STANFORD

# BANGLADESH

**CULTURE NAME**

Bangladeshi

**ALTERNATIVE NAMES**

Bengali

## ORIENTATION

**Identification.** "Bangladesh" is a combination of the Bengali words, *Bangla* and *Desh*, meaning the country or land where the Bangla language is spoken. The country formerly was known as East Pakistan.

**Location and Geography.** Bangladesh straddles the Bay of Bengal in south Asia. To the west and north it is bounded by India; to the southeast, it borders Myanmar. The topography is predominantly a low-lying floodplain. About half the total area is actively deltaic and is prone to flooding in the monsoon season from May through September. The Ganges/Padma River flows into the country from the northwest, while the Brahmaputra/ Jamuna enters from the north. The capital city, Dhaka, is near the point where those river systems meet. The land is suitable for rice cultivation.

In the north and the southeast the land is more hilly and dry, and tea is grown. The Chittagong Hill Tracts have extensive hardwood forests. The vast river delta area is home to the dominant plains culture. The hilly areas of the northeast and southeast are occupied by much smaller tribal groups, many of which have strongly resisted domination by the national government and the population pressure from Bangladeshis who move into and attempt to settle in their traditional areas. In 1998 an accord was reached between the armed tribal group Shanti Bahini and the government.

**Demography.** Bangladesh is the most densely populated nonisland nation in the world. With approxi-

mately 125 million inhabitants living in an area of 55,813 square miles, there are about 2,240 persons per square mile. The majority of the population (98 percent) is Bengali, with 2 percent belonging to tribal or other non-Bengali groups. Approximately 83 percent of the population is Muslim, 16 percent is Hindu, and 1 percent is Buddhist, Christian, or other. Annual population growth rate is at about 2 percent.

Infant mortality is approximately seventy-five per one thousand live births. Life expectancy for both men and women is fifty-eight years, yet the sex ratios for cohorts above sixty years of age are skewed toward males. Girls between one and four years of age are almost twice as likely as boys to die.

In the early 1980s the annual rate of population increase was above 2.5 percent, but in the late 1990s it decreased to 1.9 percent. The success of population control may be due to the demographic transition (decreasing birth and death rates), decreasing farm sizes, increasing urbanization, and national campaigns to control fertility (funded largely by other nations).

**Linguistic Affiliation.** The primary language is Bangla, called Bengali by most nonnatives, an Indo-European language spoken not just by Bangladeshis, but also by people who are culturally Bengali. This includes about 300 million people from Bangladesh, West Bengal, and Bihar, as well as Bengali speakers in other Indian states. The language dates from well before the birth of Christ. Bangla varies by region, and people may not understand the language of a person from another district. However, differences in dialect consist primarily of slight differences in accent or pronunciation and minor grammatical usages.

Language differences mirror social and religious divisions. Bangla is divided into two fairly distinct forms: *sadhu basha*, learned or formal language, and *cholit basha*, common language. Sadhu basha is the language of the literate tradition, formal essays

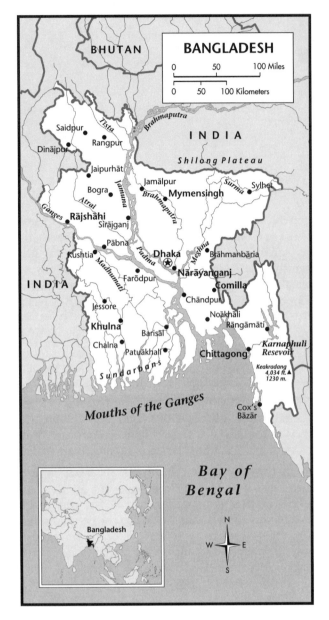

*Bangladesh*

and poetry, and the well educated. Cholit basha is the spoken vernacular, the language of the great majority of Bengalis. Cholit basha is the medium by which the great majority of people communicate in a country in which 50 percent of men and 26 percent of women are literate. There are also small usage variations between Muslims and Hindus, along with minor vocabulary differences.

**Symbolism.** The most important symbol of national identity is the Bangla language. The flag is a dark green rectangle with a red circle just left of center. Green symbolizes the trees and fields of the countryside; red represents the rising sun and the

blood spilled in the 1971 war for liberation. The national anthem was taken from a poem by Nobel laureate Rabindranath Tagore and links a love of the natural realm and land with the national identity.

Since independence in 1971, the national identity has evolved. Islamic religious identity has become an increasingly important element in the national dialogue. Many Islamic holy days are nationally celebrated, and Islam pervades public space and the media.

## HISTORY AND ETHNIC RELATIONS

***Emergence of the Nation.*** The creation of the independent nation represents the triumph of ethnic and cultural politics. The region that is now Bangladesh has been part of a number of important political entities, including Indian empires, Buddhist kingdoms, the Moghul empire, the British empire and the Pakistani nation.

Until 1947 Bangladesh was known as East Bengal province and had been part of Great Britain's India holding since the 1700s. In 1947, Britain, in conjunction with India's leading indigenous political organizations, partitioned the Indian colony into India and Pakistan. The province of East Bengal was made part of Pakistan and was referred to as East Pakistan. West Pakistan was carved from the northwest provinces of the British Indian empire. This division of territory represented an attempt to create a Muslim nation on Hindu India's peripheries. However, the west and east wings of Pakistan were separated by more than 1,000 miles of India, creating cultural discontinuity between the two wings. The ethnic groups of Pakistan and the Indian Muslims who left India after partition were greatly different in language and way of life from the former East Bengalis: West Pakistan was more oriented toward the Middle East and Arab Islamic influence than was East Pakistan, which contained Hindu, Buddhist, Islamic, and British cultural influences.

From the beginning of Pakistan's creation, the Bengali population in the east was more numerous than the Pakistani population in the western wing, yet West Pakistan became the seat of government and controlled nearly all national resources. West Pakistanis generally viewed Bengalis as inferior, weak, and less Islamic. From 1947 to 1970, West Pakistan reluctantly gave in to Bengali calls for power within the government, armed forces, and civil service, but increasing social unrest in the east led to a perception among government officials that the people of Bengal were unruly and untrustworthy "Hinduized" citizens. Successive Pakistani regimes, increasingly concerned with consolidating their power over the entire country, often criticized the Hindu minority in Bengal. This was evident in Prime Minister Nazimuddin's attempt in 1952 to make Urdu, the predominant language of West Pakistan, the state language. The effect in the east was to energize opposition movements, radicalize students at Dhaka University, and give new meaning to a Bengali identity that stressed the cultural unity of the east instead of a pan-Islamic brotherhood.

Through the 1960s, the Bengali public welcomed a message that stressed the uniqueness of Bengali culture, and this formed the basis for calls for self-determination or autonomy. In the late 1960s, the Pakistani government attempted to forestall scheduled elections. The elections were held on 7 December 1970, and Pakistanis voted directly for members of the National Assembly.

The Awami League, led by Sheikh Mujibur Rahman, was largely a Bengali party which called for autonomy for the east. Sheikh Mujib wanted to reconfigure Pakistan as a confederation of two equal partners. His party won one of 162 seats in the East Pakistan provincial assembly and 160 of the three hundred seats in the National Assembly. The Awami League would control national politics and have the ability to name the prime minister. President Yahya, however, postponed the convening of the National Assembly to prevent a Bengali power grab. In response, Sheikh Mujib and the Awami League led civil disobedience in East Pakistan. West Pakistan began to move more troops into the east, and on 25 March 1971, the Pakistani army carried out a systematic execution of several hundred people, arrested Mujib, and transported him to the west. On 26 March the Awami League declared East Pakistan an independent nation, and by April the Bengalis were in open conflict with the Pakistani military.

In a 10-month war of liberation, Bangladeshi units called *Mukhti Bahini* (freedom fighters), largely trained and armed by Indian forces, battled Pakistani troops throughout the country in guerrilla skirmishes. The Pakistanis systematically sought out political opponents and executed Hindu men on sight. Close to 10 million people fled Bangladesh for West Bengal, in India. In early December 1971, the Indian army entered Bangladesh, engaged Pakistani military forces with the help of the Mukhti Bahini, and in a ten-day period subdued the Pakistani forces. On 16 December the Pakistani military surrendered. In January 1972, Mujib was released from confinement and became the prime minister of Bangladesh.

Bangladesh was founded as a "democratic, secular, socialist state," but the new state represented the triumph of a Bangladeshi Muslim culture and language. The administration degenerated into corruption, and Mujib attempted to create a one-party state. On 15 August 1975 he was assassinated, along with much of his family, by army officers. Since that time, Bangladesh has been both less socialistic and less secular.

General Ziaur Rahman became martial law administrator in December 1976 and president in 1977. On 30 May 1981, Zia was assassinated by army officers. His rule had been violent and repressive, but he had improved national economy. After a short-lived civilian government, a bloodless coup placed Army chief of staff General Mohammed Ershad in office as martial law administrator; he later became president. Civilian opposition increased, and the Awami League, the Bangladesh National Party (BNP), and the religious fundamentalist party Jamaat-i-Islami united in a seven-year series of crippling strikes. In December 1990, Ershad was forced to resign.

A caretaker government held national elections early in 1991. The BNP, headed by Khaleda Zia, widow of former President Zia, formed a government in an alliance with the Jamaat-i-Islami. Political factionalism intensified over the next five years, and on 23 June 1996, the Awami League took control of Parliament. At its head was Sheikh Hasina Wazed, the daughter of Sheikh Mujib.

**National Identity.** Bangladeshi national identity is rooted in a Bengali culture that transcends international borders and includes the area of Bangladesh itself and West Bengal, India. Symbolically, Bangladeshi identity is centered on the 1971 struggle for independence from Pakistan. During that struggle, the key elements of Bangladeshi identity coalesced around the importance of the Bengali mother tongue and the distinctiveness of a culture or way of life connected to the floodplains of the region. Since that time, national identity has become increasingly linked to Islamic symbols as opposed to the Hindu Bengali, a fact that serves to reinforce the difference between Hindu West Bengal and Islamic Bangladesh. Being Bangladeshi in some sense means feeling connected to the natural land–water systems of the Ganges, Brahmaputra, and other rivers that drain into the Bay of Bengal. There is an envisioning of nature and the annual cycle as intensely beautiful, as deep green paddy turns

*A man eating a meal on his houseboat in Sunderbans National Park. Fish and rice are a common part of the diet.*

golden, dark clouds heavy with monsoon rains gradually clear, and flooded fields dry. Even urban families retain a sense of connectedness to this rural system. The great poets of the region, Rabindranath Tagore and Kazi Nurul Islam have enshrined the Bengali sense of the beauty and power of the region's nature.

**Ethnic Relations.** The most significant social divide is between Muslims and Hindus. In 1947 millions of Hindus moved west into West Bengal, while millions of Muslims moved east into the newly created East Pakistan. Violence occurred as the columns of people moved past each other. Today, in most sections of the country, Hindus and Muslims live peacefully in adjacent areas and are connected by their economic roles and structures. Both groups view themselves as members of the same culture.

From 1976 to 1998 there was sustained cultural conflict over the control of the southeastern Chittagong Hill Tracts. That area is home to a number of tribal groups that resisted the movement of Bangladeshi Muslims into their territory. In 1998, a peace accord granted those groups a degree of autonomy and self-governance. These tribal groups still do not identify themselves with the national culture.

## URBANISM, ARCHITECTURE, AND THE USE OF SPACE

Bangladesh is still primarily a rural culture, and the *gram* or village is an important spatial and cultural concept even for residents of the major cities. Most people identify with a natal or ancestral village in the countryside.

Houses in villages are commonly rectangular, and are dried mud, bamboo, or red brick structures with thatch roofs. Many are built on top of earthen or wooden platforms to keep them above the flood line. Houses have little interior decoration, and wall space is reserved for storage. Furniture is minimal, often consisting only of low stools. People sleep on thin bamboo mats. Houses have verandas in the front, and much of daily life takes place under their eaves rather than indoors. A separate smaller mud or bamboo structure serves as a kitchen (*rana ghor*), but during the dry season many women construct hearths and cook in the household courtyard. Rural houses are simple and functional, but are not generally considered aesthetic showcases.

The village household is a patrilineal extended compound linked to a pond used for daily household needs, a nearby river that provides fish, trees that provide fruit (mango and jackfruit especially), and rice fields. The village and the household not only embody important natural motifs but serve as the locus of ancestral family identity. Urban dwellers try to make at least one trip per year to "their village."

Architectural styles in the cities show numerous historical influences, including Moghul and Islamic motifs with curved arches, windows, and minarets, and square British colonial wood and concrete construction. The National Parliament building (Shongshad Bhabon) in Dhaka, designed by the American architect Louis Kahn, reflects a synthesis of western modernity and curved Islamic-influenced spaces. The National Monument in Savar, a wide-based spire that becomes narrower as it rises, is the symbol of the country's liberation.

Because of the population density, space is at a premium. People of the same sex interact closely, and touching is common. On public transportation strangers often are pressed together for long periods. In public spaces, women are constrained in their movements and they rarely enter the public sphere unaccompanied. Men are much more free in their movement. The rules regarding the gender differential in the use of public space are less closely adhered to in urban areas than in rural areas.

## FOOD AND ECONOMY

*Food in Daily Life.* Rice and fish are the foundation of the diet; a day without a meal with rice is nearly inconceivable. Fish, meats, poultry, and vegetables are cooked in spicy curry (*torkari*) sauces that incorporate cumin, coriander, cloves, cinnamon, garlic, and other spices. Muslims do not consume pork and Hindus do not consume beef. Increasingly common is the preparation of *ruti*, a whole wheat circular flatbread, in the morning, which is eaten with curries from the night before. Also important to the diet is *dal*, a thin soup based on ground lentils, chickpeas, or other legumes that is poured over rice. A sweet homemade yogurt commonly finishes a meal. A typical meal consists of a large bowl of rice to which is added small portions of fish and vegetable curries. Breakfast is the meal that varies the most, being rice- or bread-based. A favorite breakfast dish is *panthabhat*, leftover cold rice in water or milk mixed with *gur* (date palm sugar). Food is eaten with the right hand by mixing the curry into the rice and then gathering portions with the fingertips. In city restaurants that cater to foreigners, people may use silverware.

Three meals are consumed daily. Water is the most common beverage. Before the meal, the right hand is washed with water above the eating bowl.

With the clean knuckles of the right hand the interior of the bowl is rubbed, the water is discarded, and the bowl is filled with food. After the meal, one washes the right hand again, holding it over the emptied bowl.

Snacks include fruits such as banana, mango, and jackfruit, as well as puffed rice and small fried food items. For many men, especially in urbanized regions and bazaars, no day is complete without a cup of sweet tea with milk at a small tea stall, sometimes accompanied by confections.

*Food Customs at Ceremonial Occasions.* At weddings and on important holidays, food plays an important role. At holiday or formal functions, guests are encouraged to eat to their capacity. At weddings, a common food is *biryani*, a rice dish with lamb or beef and a blend of spices, particularly saffron. On special occasions, the rice used is one of the finer, thinner-grained types. If biryani is not eaten, a complete multicourse meal is served: foods are brought out sequentially and added to one's rice bowl after the previous course is finished. A complete dinner may include chicken, fish, vegetable, goat, or beef curries and dal. The final bit of rice is finished with yogurt (*doi*).

On other important occasions, such as the Eid holidays, a goat or cow is slaughtered on the premises and curries are prepared from the fresh meat. Some of the meat is given to relatives and to the poor.

*Basic Economy.* With a per capita gross national product (GNP) of $350 and an overall GNP of $44 billion, Bangladesh is one of the poorest countries in the world. The only significant natural resource is natural gas.

Approximately 75 percent of the workforce is involved in agriculture, and 15 percent and 10 percent are employed in the service and industrial sectors, respectively. Bangladesh has been characterized as a nation of small, subsistence-based farmers, and nearly all people in rural areas are involved in the production or processing of agricultural goods. The majority of the rural population engages in agricultural production, primarily of rice, jute, pulses, wheat, and some vegetables. Virtually all agricultural output is consumed within the country, and grain must be imported. The large population places heavy demands on the food-producing sectors of the economy. The majority of the labor involved in food production is human- and animal-based. Relatively little agricultural export takes place.

*A Bangladeshi man hanging fish to dry in the sun in Sunderbans. Bangladesh topography is predominantly a low-lying floodplain.*

In the countryside, typically about ten villages are linked in a market system that centers on a bazaar occurring at least once per week. On bazaar days, villagers bring in agricultural produce or crafts such as water pots to sell to town and city agents. Farmers then visit kiosks to purchase spices, kerosene, soap, vegetables or fish, and salt.

**Land Tenure and Property.** With a population density of more than two thousand per square mile, land tenure and property rights are critical aspects of survival. The average farm owner has less than three acres of land divided into a number of small plots scattered in different directions from the household. Property is sold only in cases of family emergency, since agricultural land is the primary means of survival. Ordinarily, among Muslims land is inherited equally by a household head's sons, despite Islamic laws that specify shares for daughters and wives. Among Hindu farmers inheritance practices are similar. When agricultural land is partitioned, each plot is divided among a man's sons, ensuring that each one has a geographically dispersed holding. The only sections of rural areas that are not privately owned are rivers and paths.

**Commercial Activities.** In rural areas Hindus perform much of the traditional craft production of items for everyday life; caste groups include weavers, potters, iron and gold smiths, and carpenters. Some of these groups have been greatly reduced in number, particularly weavers, who have been replaced by ready-made clothing produced primarily in Dhaka.

Agriculture accounts for 25 percent of GDP. The major crops are rice, jute, wheat, tea, sugarcane, and vegetables.

**Major Industries.** In recent years industrial growth has occurred primarily in the garment and textile industries. Jute processing and jute product fabrication remain major industries. Overall, industry accounted for about 28 percent of gross domestic product (GDP) in 1998.

**Trade.** Exports totaled $4.4 billion in 1996, with the United States consuming one-third of those exports. Primary export markets are for jute (used in carpet backing, burlap, and rope), fish, garments, and textiles. Imports totaled $7.1 billion and largely consisted of capital goods, grains, petroleum, and chemicals. The country relies on an annual inflow of at least $1 billion from international sources, not including the humanitarian aid that is part of the national economic system. Agriculture accounted for about 25 percent of the GDP in 1998.

*Transporting straw on the Ganges River Delta. The majority of Bangladeshi, about 75 percent, are agricultural workers.*

**Division of Labor.** The division of labor is based on age and education. Young children are economically productive in rural areas, hauling water, watching animals, and helping with postharvest processing. The primary agricultural tasks, however, are performed by men. Education allows an individual to seek employment outside the agricultural sector, although the opportunities for educated young men in rural areas are extremely limited. A service or industry job often goes to the individual who can offer the highest bribe to company officials.

## SOCIAL STRATIFICATION

**Classes and Castes.** The Muslim class system is similar to a caste structure. The *ashraf* is a small upperclass of old-money descendants of early Muslim officials and merchants whose roots are in Afghanistan, Turkey, and Iran. Some ashraf families trace their lineage to the Prophet Mohammed. The rest of the population is conceived of as the indigenous majority *atraf*. This distinction mirrors the Hindu separation between the Brahman and those in lower castes. While both Muslim and Hindu categories are recognized by educated people, the vast majority of citizens envision class in a more localized, rural context.

In rural areas, class is linked to the amount of land owned, occupation, and education. A landowner with more than five acres is at the top of the socioeconomic scale, and small subsistence farmers are in the middle. At the bottom of the scale are the landless rural households that account for about 30 percent of the rural population. Landowning status reflects socioeconomic class position in rural areas, although occupation and education also play a role. The most highly educated people hold positions requiring literacy and mathematical skills, such as in banks and government offices, and are generally accorded a higher status than are farmers. Small businessmen may earn as much as those who have jobs requiring an education but have a lower social status.

Hindu castes also play a role in the rural economy. Hindu groups are involved in the hereditary occupations that fill the economic niches that support a farming-based economy. Small numbers of higher caste groups have remained in the country, and some of those people are large landowners, businessmen, and service providers.

In urban areas the great majority of people are laborers. There is a middle class of small businessmen and midlevel office workers, and above this is an emerging entrepreneurial group and upper-level service workers.

***Symbols of Social Stratification.*** One of the most obvious symbols of class status is dress. The traditional garment for men is the *lungi*, a cloth tube skirt that hangs to the ankles; for women, the *sari* is the norm. The lungi is worn by most men, except those who consider themselves to have high socioeconomic status, among whom pants and shirt are worn. Also indicative of high standing are loose white cotton pajama pants and a long white shirt. White dress among men symbolizes an occupation that does not require physical labor. A man with high standing will not be seen physically carrying anything; that task is left to an assistant or laborer. *Saris* also serve as class markers, with elaborate and finely worked cloth symbolizing high status. Poverty is marked by the cheap, rough green or indigo cotton cloth saris of poor women. Gold jewelry indicates a high social standing among women.

A concrete-faced house and a ceramic tile roof provide evidence of wealth. An automobile is well beyond the means of most people, and a motorcycle is a sign of status. Color televisions, telephones, and electricity are other symbols associated with wealth.

## POLITICAL LIFE

***Government.*** The People's Republic of Bangladesh is a parliamentary democracy that includes a president, a prime minister, and a unicameral parliament (*Jayitya Shongshod*). Three hundred members of parliament are elected to the 330-seat legislature in local elections held every five years. Thirty seats are reserved for women members of parliament. The prime minister, who is appointed by the president, must have the support of a majority of parliament members. The president is elected by the parliament every five years to that largely ceremonial post. The country is divided into four divisions, twenty districts, subdistricts, union *parishads*, and villages. In local politics, the most important political level is the union in rural areas; in urban regions, it is the municipality (*pourashava*). Members are elected locally, and campaigning is extremely competitive.

***Leadership and Political Officials.*** There are more than 50 political parties. Party adherence extends from the national level down to the village, where factions with links to the national parties vie for local control and help solve local disputes. Leaders at the local level are socioeconomically well-off individuals who gain respect within the party

structure, are charismatic, and have strong kinship ties. Local leaders draw and maintain supporters, particularly at election time, by offering tangible, relatively small rewards.

The dominant political parties are the Awami League (AL), the BNP, the Jatiya Party (JP), and the Jamaat-i-Islami (JI). The Awami League is a secular-oriented, formerly socialist-leaning party. It is not stringently anti-India, is fairly liberal with regard to ethnic and religious groups, and supports a free-market economy. The BNP, headed by former Prime Minister Khaleda Zia, is less secular, more explicitly Islamic in orientation, and more anti-India. The JP is close to the BNP in overall orientation, but pushed through a bill in Parliament that made Islam the state religion in 1988. The JI emphasizes Islam, Koranic law, and connections to the Arab Middle East.

***Social Problems and Control.*** Legal procedures are based on the English common-law system, and supreme court justices and lower-level judges are appointed by the president. District courts at the district capitals are the closest formal venues for legal proceedings arising from local disputes. There are police forces only in the cities and towns. When there is a severe conflict or crime in rural areas, it may take days for the police to arrive.

In rural areas, a great deal of social control takes place informally. When a criminal is caught, justice may be apportioned locally. In the case of minor theft, a thief may be beaten by a crowd. In serious disputes between families, heads of the involved kinship groups or local political leaders negotiate and the offending party is required to make restitution in money and/or land. Police may be paid to ensure that they do not investigate. Nonviolent disputes over property or rights may be decided through village councils (*panchayat*) headed by the most respected heads of the strongest kinship groups. When mediation or negotiation fails, the police may be called in and formal legal proceedings may begin. People do not conceive of the informal procedures as taking the law into their own hands.

***Military Activity.*** The military has played an active role in the development of the political structure and climate of the country since its inception and has been a source of structure during crises. It has been involved in two coups since 1971. The only real conflict the army has encountered was sporadic fighting with the *Shakti Bahini* in the Chittagong Hill Tracts from the mid-1970s until 1998, after which an accord between the government and those tribal groups was produced.

*Road workers undertake construction work in Decca. Laborers make up the vast majority of workers in urban areas.*

## Social Welfare and Change Programs

Bangladesh is awash in social change programs sponsored by international organizations such as the United Nations, the World Bank, Care, USAID, and other nations' development agencies. Those organizations support project areas such as population control, agricultural and economic development, urban poverty, environmental conservation, and women's economic development.

## Nongovernmental Organizations and Other Associations

The Grameen Bank created the popular microcredit practice, which has given the poor, especially poor women, access to credit. This model is based on creating small circles of people who know and can influence each other to pay back loans. When one member has repaid a loan, another member of the group becomes eligible to receive credit. Other nongovernmental organizations include the Bangladesh Rural Advancement Committee, Probashi, and Aat Din.

## Gender Roles and Statuses

***Division of Labor by Gender.*** Women traditionally are in charge of household affairs and are not encouraged to move outside the immediate neighborhood unaccompanied. Thus, most women's economic and social lives revolve around the home, children, and family. Islamic practice reserves prayer inside the mosque for males only; women practice religion within the home. Bangladesh has had two female prime ministers since 1991, both elected with widespread popular support, but women are not generally publicly active in politics.

Men are expected to be the heads of their households and to work outside the home. Men often do the majority of the shopping, since that requires interaction in crowded markets. Men spend a lot of time socializing with other men outside the home.

***The Relative Status of Women and Men.*** The society is patriarchal in nearly every area of life, although some women have achieved significant positions of political power at the national level. For ordinary women, movement is confined, education is stressed less than it is for men, and authority is reserved for a woman's father, older brother, and husband.

## Marriage, Family, and Kinship

***Marriage.*** Marriage is almost always an arranged affair and takes place when the parents, particularly the father, decide that a child should be married. Men marry typically around age twenty-five or older, and women marry between ages fifteen and twenty; thus the husband is usually at least ten years older than the wife. Muslims allow polygynous marriage, but its occurrence is rare and is dependent on a man's ability to support multiple households.

A parent who decides that a child is ready to marry may contact agencies, go-betweens, relatives, and friends to find an appropriate mate. Of immediate concern are the status and characteristics of the potential in-law's family. Generally an equal match is sought in terms of family economic status, educational background, and piousness. A father may allow his child to choose among five or six potential mates, providing the child with the relevant data on each candidate. It is customary for the child to rule out clearly unacceptable candidates, leaving a slate of candidates from which the father can choose. An arrangement between two families may be sealed with an agreement on a dowry and the types of gifts to be made to the groom. Among

175

*The Sitara (star) mosque in Dacca. Religion plays a fundamental role in society, and almost every village has a mosque.*

the educated the dowry practice is no longer prevalent.

Divorce is a source of social stigma. A Muslim man may initiate a divorce by stating "I divorce you" three times, but very strong family pressure ordinarily ensures that divorces do not occur. A divorce can be most difficult for the woman, who must return to her parent's household.

**Domestic Unit.** The most common unit is the patrilineally-related extended family living in a household called a *barhi*. A barhi is composed of a husband and wife, their unmarried children, and their adult sons with their wives and children. Grandparents also may be present, as well as patrilineally-related brothers, cousins, nieces, and nephews. The oldest man is the authority figure, although the oldest woman may exert considerable authority within the household. A barhi in rural areas is composed of three or four houses which face each other to form a square courtyard in which common tasks are done. Food supplies often are shared, and young couples must contribute their earnings to the household head. Cooking, however, often is done within the constituent nuclear family units.

**Inheritance.** Islamic inheritance rules specify that a daughter should receive one-half the share of a son. However, this practice is rarely followed, and upon a household head's death, property is divided equally among his sons. Daughters may receive produce and gifts from their brothers when they visit as "compensation" for their lack of an inheritance. A widow may receive a share of her husband's property, but this is rare. Sons, however, are custom-bound to care for their mothers, who retain significant power over the rest of the household.

**Kin Groups.** The patrilineal descent principle is important, and the lineage is very often localized within a geographic neighborhood in which it constitutes a majority. Lineage members can be called on in times of financial crisis, particularly when support is needed to settle local disputes. Lineages do not meet regularly or control group resources.

## SOCIALIZATION

**Infant Care.** Most women give birth in their natal households, to which they return when childbirth is near. A husband is sent a message when the child is born. Five or seven days after the birth the husband and his close male relatives visit the newborn, and a feast and ritual haircutting take place. The newborn is given an amulet that is tied around the waist, its eye sockets may be blackened with soot or makeup, and a small soot mark is applied to the infant's forehead and the sole of the foot for protection against spirits. Newborns and infants are seldom left unattended. Most infants are in constant contact with their mothers, other women, or the daughters in the household. Since almost all women breastfeed, infant and mother sleep within close reach. Infants' needs are attended to constantly; a crying baby is given attention immediately.

**Child Rearing and Education.** Children are raised within the extended family and learn early that individual desires are secondary to the needs of the family group. Following orders is expected on the basis of age; an adult or older child's commands must be obeyed as a sign of respect. Child care falls primarily to household women and their daughters. Boys have more latitude for movement outside the household.

Between ages five and ten, boys undergo a circumcision (*musulmani*), usually during the cool months. There is no comparable ritual for girls, and the menarche is not publicly marked.

Most children begin school at age five or six, and attendance tends to drop off as children become more productive within the household (female) and agricultural economy (male). About 75 percent of children attend primary school. The higher a family's socioeconomic status, the more likely it is for both boys and girls to finish their primary educations. Relatively few families can afford to send their children to college (about 17 percent), and even fewer children attend a university. Those who enter a university usually come from relatively well-off families. While school attendance drops off overall as the grades increase, females stop attending school earlier than do males.

**Higher Education.** Great value is placed on higher education, and those who have university degrees and professional qualifications are accorded high status. In rural areas the opportunities for individuals with such experience are limited; thus, most educated people are concentrated in urban areas.

Bangladesh has a number of excellent universities in its largest urban areas that offer both undergraduate through post-graduate degrees. The most prominent universities, most of which are state supported, include: Dhaka University, Rajshahi University, Chittagong University, Jahngirnagar University, Bangladesh University of Engineering and Technology, and Bangladesh Agricultural University. Competition for university admission is intense (especially at Dhaka University) and admission is dependent on scores received on high school examinations held annually, as in the British sys-

*A young girl makes matchboxes in the slums of Khulna. There is a marked split between rich and poor in most of the country.*

tem of education. University life in Bangladesh can be difficult. A four-year degree may actually require five to eight years to complete due to frequent university closings. The student bodies and faculties of universities are heavily politicized along national political party lines. Protests, strikes, and sporadic political party-based violence are common, as student groups play out national political agendas on their campuses and vie for members. Virtually every university student finds it easier to survive the system by becoming a member of the student wing of a political party.

While the universities are the scenes of political struggle, they are also centers of intellectual and cultural creativity. Students may obtain excellent training in all fields, including the arts, law, medicine, and engineering. Universities are also somewhat like islands where some of the ordinary rules of social interaction are relaxed. For example, male–female interaction on campuses is more open and less monitored than in society as a whole. Dance and theater presentations are common, as are academic debates.

## ETIQUETTE

Personal interaction is initiated with the greeting *Assalam Waleykum* ("peace be with you"), to which the required response is, *Waleykum Assalam* ("and with you"). Among Hindus, the correct greeting is *Nomoshkar*, as the hands are brought together under the chin. Men may shake hands if they are of equal status but do not grasp hands firmly. Respect is expressed after a handshake by placing the right hand over the heart. Men and women do not shake hands with each other. In same-sex conversation, touching is common and individuals may stand or sit very close. The closer individuals are in terms of status, the closer their spatial interaction is. Leave-taking is sealed with the phrase *Khoda Hafez*.

Differences in age and status are marked through language conventions. Individuals with higher status are not addressed by personal name; instead, a title or kinship term is used.

Visitors are always asked to sit, and if no chairs are available, a low stool or a bamboo mat is provided. It is considered improper for a visitor to sit on the floor or ground. It is incumbent on the host to offer guests something to eat.

In crowded public places that provide services, such as train stations, the post office, or bazaars, queuing is not practiced and receiving service is dependent on pushing and maintaining one's place within the throng. Open staring is not considered impolite.

## RELIGION

*Religious Beliefs.* The symbols and sounds of Islam, such as the call to prayer, punctuate daily life. Bangladeshis conceptualize themselves and others fundamentally through their religious heritage. For example, the nationality of foreigners is considered secondary to their religious identity.

Islam is a part of everyday life in all parts of the country, and nearly every village has at least a small mosque and an imam (cleric). Prayer is supposed to be performed five times daily, but only the committed uphold that standard. Friday afternoon prayer is often the only time that mosques become crowded.

Throughout the country there is a belief in spirits that inhabit natural spaces such as trees, hollows, and riverbanks. These beliefs are derided by Islamic religious authorities.

Hinduism encompasses an array of deities, including Krishna, Ram, Durga, Kali, and Ganesh. Bangladeshi Hindus pay particular attention to the female goddess Durga, and rituals devoted to her are among the most widely celebrated.

*Religious Practitioners.* The imam is associated with a mosque and is an important person in both rural and urban society, leading a group of followers. The imam's power is based on his knowledge of the Koran and memorization of phrases in Arabic. Relatively few imams understand Arabic in the spoken or written form. An imam's power is based on his ability to persuade groups of men to act in conjunction with Islamic rules. In many villages the imam is believed to have access to the supernatural, with the ability to write charms that protect individuals from evil spirits, imbue liquids with holy healing properties, or ward off or reverse of bad luck.

Brahman priests perform rituals for the Hindu community during the major festivals when offerings are made but also in daily acts of worship. They are respected, but Hinduism does not have the codified hierarchical structure of Islam. Thus, a Brahman priest may not have a position of leadership outside his religious duties.

*Rituals and Holy Places.* The primary Islamic holidays in Bangladesh include: *Eid-ul-Azha* (the tenth day of the Muslim month *Zilhaj*), in which a goat or cow is sacrificed in honor of Allah; *Shob-i-Barat* (the fourteenth or fifteenth day of *Shaban*), when Allah records an individual's future for the rest of the year; *Ramadan* (the month *Ramzan*), a month-long period of fasting between dawn and dusk; *Eid-ul-Fitr* (the first day of the month *Shawal*, following the end of *Ramzan*), characterized by alms giving to the poor; and *Shob-i-Meraz* (the twenty-seventh day of *Rajab*), which commemorates the night when Mohammed ascended to heaven. Islamic holidays are publicly celebrated in afternoon prayers at mosques and outdoor open areas, where many men assemble and move through their prayers in unison.

Among the most important Hindu celebrations are *Saraswati Puja* (February), dedicated to the deity Saraswati, who takes the form of a swan. She is the patron of learning, and propitiating her is important for students. *Durga Puja* (October) pays homage to the female warrior goddess Durga, who has ten arms, carries a sword, and rides a lion. After a nine-day festival, images of Durga and her associates are placed in a procession and set into a river. *Kali Puja* (November) is also called the Festival of Lights and honors Kali, a female deity who has the power to give and take away life. Candles are lit in and around homes.

*A young Bengali woman performs a traditional Manipuri dance. Almost all traditional dancers are women.*

Other Hindu and Islamic rituals are celebrated in villages and neighborhoods and are dependent on important family or local traditions. Celebrations take place at many local shrines and temples.

**Death and the Afterlife.** Muslims believe that after death the soul is judged and moves to heaven or hell. Funerals require that the body be washed, the nostrils and ears be plugged with cotton or cloth, and the body be wrapped in a white shroud. The body is buried or entombed in a brick or concrete structure. In Hinduism, reincarnation is expected and one's actions throughout life determine one's future lives. As the family mourns and close relatives shave their heads, the body is transported to the funeral *ghat* (bank along a river), where prayers are recited. The body is to be placed on a pyre and cremated, and the ashes are thrown into the river.

## MEDICINE AND HEALTH CARE

The pluralistic health care system includes healers such as physicians, nonprofessionally trained doctors, Aryuvedic practitioners, homeopaths, fakirs, and naturopaths. In rural areas, for non-life-threatening acute conditions, the type of healer consulted depends largely on local reputation. In many places, the patient consults a homeopath or a nonprofessional doctor who is familiar with local remedies as well as modern medical practices. Professional physicians are consulted by the educated and by those who have not received relief from other sources. Commonly, people pursue alternative treatments simultaneously, visiting a fakir for an amulet, an imam for blessed oil, and a physician for medicine.

A nationally run system of public hospitals provides free service. However, prescriptions and some medical supplies are the responsibility of patients and their families.

Aryuvedic beliefs based on humoral theories are common among both Hindus and Muslims. These beliefs are commonly expressed through the categorization of the inherent hot or cold properties of foods. An imbalance in hot or cold food intake is believed to lead to sickness. Health is restored when this imbalance is counteracted through dietary means.

## SECULAR CELEBRATIONS

*Ekushee* (21 February), also called *Shaheed Dibash*, is the National Day of Martyrs commemorating those who died defending the Bangla language in 1952. Political speeches are held, and a memorial service takes place at the *Shaheed Minar* (Martyr's Monument) in Dhaka. *Shadheenata Dibash*, or Independence Day (26 March), marks the day when Bangladesh declared itself separate from Pakistan. The event is marked with military parades and political speeches. *Poila Boishakh*, the Bengali New Year, is celebrated on the first day of the month of *Boishakh* (generally in April). Poetry readings and musical events take place. May Day (1 May) celebrates labor and workers with speeches and cultural events. *Bijoy Dibosh*, or Victory Day (16 December), commemorates the day in 1971 when Pakistani forces surrendered to a joint Bangladeshi–Indian force. Cultural and political events are held.

## THE ARTS AND HUMANITIES

**Support for the Arts.** Artists are largely self-supporting. The Bangla Academy in Dhaka provides support for some artists, particularly writers and poets. Many artists sell aesthetic works that have utilitarian functions.

**Literature.** Most people, regardless of their degree of literacy, can recite more than one poem with dramatic inflection. Best known are the works of the two poet–heroes of the region: Rabindranath Tagore and Kazi Nurul Islam. Tagore was awarded the Nobel Prize for Literature in 1913. Although from West Bengal, he is respected as a Bengali who championed the preservation of Bangla language and culture. His poem "Golden Bengal" was adopted as the national anthem.

The most famous contemporary writer is Taslima Nasreen, whose novellas and essays question the Islamic justification for the customary treatment of women. Conservative religious authorities have tried to have her arrested and have called for her death for blasphemy. She lives in exile.

**Graphic Arts.** Most graphic arts fall within the domain of traditional production by Hindu caste groups. The most pervasive art form throughout the country is pottery, including water jugs and bowls of red clay, often with a red slip and incising. Some Hindu sculptors produce brightly painted works depicting Durga and other deities. Drawing and painting are most visible on the backs of rickshaws and the wooden sides of trucks.

**Performance Arts.** Bengali music encompasses a number of traditions and mirrors some of the country's poetry. The most common instruments are the harmonium, the tabla, and the sitar. Generally, classical musicians are adept at the rhythms and melodic properties associated with Hindu and Urdu devotional music. More popular today are the secular male–female duets that accompany Bengali and Hindi films. These songs are rooted in the classical tradition but have a freer contemporary melodic structure. Traditional dance is characterized by a rural thematic element with particular hand, foot, and head movements. Dance is virtually a female-only enterprise. Plays are traditionally an important part of village life, and traveling shows stop throughout the countryside. Television dramas portray family relationships, love, and economic advantage and disadvantage. Plays in the cities, particularly in Dhaka, are attended by the educated young.

## THE STATE OF THE PHYSICAL AND SOCIAL SCIENCES

Dhaka University offers courses in most academic disciplines. Sciences such as physics and chemistry have very good programs, although there is a lack of up-to-date laboratories and equipment. In the social sciences, the field of economics is particularly strong, along with anthropology, sociology, and political science. Many top students in the physical and social sciences study abroad, especially in the United States and Europe. The top engineering program is at the Bangladesh University of Engineering and Technology. Electrical, ocean/naval, civil, and mechanical engineering have very good programs. Education in computer engineering is improving rapidly.

## BIBLIOGRAPHY

Ahmed, Nafis. *A New Economic Geography of Bangladesh,* 1976.

Ali, A. M. M. Shawkat. *Politics and Land System in Bangladesh,* 1986.

Alim, A. *Bangladesh Rice,* 1982.

Baxter, Craig. *New Nation in an Old Setting,* 1984.

———— *Bangladesh: From a Nation to a State,* 1997.

Bessaignet, Pierre. *Tribesmen of the Chittagong Hill Tracts,* 1958.

Blanchet, Therese. *Women, Pollution, and Marginality,* 1984.

Bornstein, David. *The Price of a Dream: The Story of the Grameen Bank and the Idea That is Helping the Poor to Change Their Lives,* 1997.

Chowdhury, Subrata Roy. *The Genesis of Bangladesh: A Study in International Legal Norms and Permissive Conscience,* 1972.

Glassie, Henry. *Art and Life in Bangladesh,* 1997.

Hartman, James, and Betsy Boyce. *Needless Hunger,* 1979.

Huq, Syed Mujibul, translator. *Selected Poems of Kazi Nurul Islam,* 1983.

Islam, Aminul A. K. M. *Bangladesh Village: Political Conflict and Cohesion,* 1982.

Majumdar, R. C. *History of Bengal,* 1943.

Nicholas, Marta, and Philip Oldenburg. *Bangladesh: Birth of a Nation,* 1972.

Novak, James J. *Bangladesh: Reflections on the Water,* 1993.

O'Donnell, Charles Peter. *Bangladesh: Biography of a Muslim Nation,* 1984.

Ray, Rajat Kanta. *Mind, Body and Society: Life and Mentality in Colonial Bengal,* 1995.

Sisson, Richard, and Leo Rose. *War and Secession: Pakistan, India, and the Creation of Bangladesh,* 1991.

United States Department of State. *Bangladesh Background Notes,* 1998.

Wennergren, E. Boyd, Charles H. Antholt, and Morris D. Whitaker. *Agricultural Development in Bangladesh,* 1984.

Wood, Geoffrey. *Whose Ideas, Whose Interests?,* 1991.

### Web Sites

Virtual Bangladesh. http://www.virtualbangladesh.com

—MICHAEL S. HARRIS,
WITH THE ASSISTANCE OF ELIZABETH LLOYD

# BARBADOS

## CULTURE NAME
Barbadian

## ALTERNATIVE NAME
Bajan

## ORIENTATION

**Identification.** Barbadians are people born on Barbados and people born elsewhere who have at least one Barbadian parent and maintain cultural ties to the nation. There are emigrant Barbadians communities in Canada, the United Kingdom, the United States, and Guyana that maintain active ties with their families and friends on the island. Barbadians recognize regional identities that correspond to parish districts and distinctive regional accents.

**Location and Geography.** Barbados is a coral limestone outcropping of the South American continental shelf that lies in the western Atlantic Ocean, one hundred miles (160 kilometers) east of the island of Saint Lucia and two hundred miles (320 kilometers) north of Trinidad and the northern coast of South America. Barbados has low, rolling hills, and microclimate variations from rain forest to semidesert.

**Demography.** More than 260,000 people live on this island of 166 square miles (430 square kilometers), with a population density of 1,548 people per square mile (597.7 per square kilometer) in 1996. Large populations have characterized the nation almost since its inception. As early as 1680, the island was home to seventy thousand people.

Until 1960, high birth and death rates generated a large number of young people. Barbadians emigrated in large numbers to the United Kingdom and in smaller numbers to the United States and Canada. Death rates and birth rates fell rapidly after 1960. Aided by continuing emigration among the young and immigration among the elderly, the population aged rapidly. By the year 2050, the proportion of the population age sixty-five and over will range between 25 and 33 percent of the total population.

**Linguistic Affiliation.** Barbadians speak a dialect of English with tonal qualities that reflect the West African heritage of the vast majority of its population. Barbadians also speak an English-West African pidgin called Bajan. The number of native Bajan speakers has declined in recent decades. Both languages have dialect differences that correspond with parish districts.

**Symbolism.** The flying fish serves as a national symbol.

## HISTORY AND ETHNIC RELATIONS

**Emergence of the Nation.** Barbados was colonized by the English early in the seventeenth century. The English found the island uninhabited when they landed in 1625, although archaeological findings have documented prior habitation by Carib and Arawak Native Americans. By 1650, Barbados was transformed by the plantation system and slavery into the first major monocropping sugar producer in the emerging British Empire, and its fortunes were tied to sugar and to England for the next three hundred and ten years. In 1651, Barbados won a measure of independence, and established what was to become the oldest continuing parliamentary democracy in the world outside England. This autonomy encouraged planters to remain on the island rather than returning to Europe when they made their fortunes.

**National Identity.** When West Indian sugar plantations disappeared elsewhere in the 1800s, Barbadian plantations remained productive. In the early twentieth century, the creation of a merchant-planter oligopoly ended the improvement in

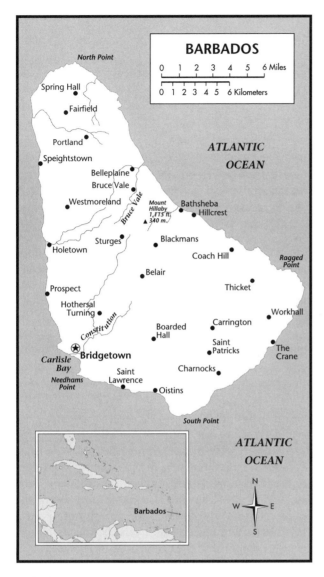

## BARBADOS

0  1  2  3  4  5  6 Miles

0  1  2  3  4  5  6 Kilometers

North Point

Spring Hall

Fairfield

Portland

Speightstown

*ATLANTIC*
*OCEAN*

Belleplaine

Bruce Vale

Westmoreland

Mount
Hillaby
1,115 ft.
▲ 340 m.

Bathsheba

Hillcrest

Sturges

Blackmans

Holetown

Coach Hill

*Ragged*
*Point*

Belair

Prospect

Thicket

Hothersal
Turning

Workhall

Boarded
Hall

Carrington

Saint
Patricks

The
Crane

✪ Bridgetown

Charnocks

*Carlisle*
*Bay*

Saint
Lawrence

*Needhams*
*Point*

Oistins

*South Point*

*ATLANTIC*
*OCEAN*

N
W       E
S

Barbados

*Barbados*

living standards that occurred in the nineteenth century. The Great Depression of the 1930s led to massive labor disturbances. Subsequent investigations of living conditions established the grounds for fundamental political change. The vote, which until the late nineteenth century had been restricted to propertied white males, was made universal in 1943. By the 1950s, the descendants of former African slaves controlled the assembly and set in motion actions that transformed the island in fundamental ways. The island opted for full independence in 1966 but remains a member of the British Commonwealth.

Barbadian culture emerged out of the plantation slavery economy as a distinctive synthesis of English and West African cultural traditions. Regional, race, and class cultural variants exist, but all residents identify with the national culture.

**Ethnic Relations.** About 80% of all Barbadians are the descendants of former African slaves. Barbados also has a high proportion of citizens with a largely European ancestry. Barbados is generally free from ethnic tension.

## URBANISM, ARCHITECTURE, AND THE USE OF SPACE

About 80 percent of the population lives in or around the capital, Bridgetown. The remaining 20 percent live in rural areas in settlements that vary from dispersed homes and occasional plantations to small nucleated villages.

## FOOD AND ECONOMY

**Food in Daily Life.** Coocoo (a creamy blend of cornmeal and okra) and flying fish is the national dish. Breaded and fried flying fish is a popular snack or meal. Bajan meals emphasize fish, chicken, pork, and other foods common in West Africa, such as rice, okra, and Scotch bonnet peppers. Popular fruits include papaya, mangos, guava, bananas, oranges, and pineapples. Meal components such as cornmeal, salt fish, and salt beef were supplied to the original plantation labor forces. A common meal served in rural areas called privilege blends rice, okra, hot pepper, pig tail or salt beef, garlic, salt fish, and onions. Mount Gay distillery has been producing rum since 1703. Mauby, brewed from bark, sugar, and spices, is a popular drink.

**Food Customs at Ceremonial Occasions.** Special occasions often call for pudding and souse, the first a spicy mashed sweet potato encased in pigs belly, and boiled pig's head served with a ''pickle'' of onions, hot and sweet peppers, cucumbers, and lime. Jug, or jug jug, a dish consisting of pigeon, peas, stew and salt beef, onions, Guinea corn flour, and spices, is served with Christmas dishes such as boiled ham and roasted pork.

**Basic Economy.** The economy is fueled by the skills of a diverse population that is one of the world's most educated, with a literacy rate close to 100 percent. The currency is the Barbados dollar, which is linked to the United States dollar. Excellent public and private bus and taxi services take advantage of nearly 1,205 miles (1,650 kilometers) of roads and make it possible to move relatively cheaply around the island. The year 1960 brought a structural change in the economy marked by a decline in sugar production and the growth of industrial manufacturing and tourism. Barbados served as a tourist destination as early as the 1600s. Small numbers of tourists come from South America and other islands in the Caribbean. A significant stream comes from northwestern Europe, primarily the United Kingdom. Most tourists, however, come from the United States and Canada. In an island long known in the Caribbean as "Little England," many Barbadians now claim that its increasingly important ties to the United States have transformed the nation into "Little America."

***Land Tenure and Property.*** Land tenure and property concepts follow precedents set in England.

***Commercial Activities.*** Manufactured goods include garments, furniture, ceramics, pharmaceuticals, phonograph records and tapes, processed wood, and paints.

***Major Industries.*** Light manufacturing firms produce structural components for construction, industrial gases, paper products, electronics components, and solar energy units. Barbados also refines petroleum products.

***Trade.*** Although production declined precipitously in the last half of the twentieth century, sugar remains the major export product. Most manufactured goods are used domestically, but a small quantity is traded to other nations in the Caribbean and Latin America. Barbados carries on a small trade with North America, principally in electronic components, garments, medical supplies, and rum.

## SOCIAL STRATIFICATION

***Classes and Castes.*** Before 1960, Barbadian society consisted of a small merchant-planter elite largely of European ancestry; a slightly larger class of accountants, lawyers, medical personnel, journalists, and teachers of diverse ancestry; and a huge lower class of field laborers and domestic servants primarily of African ancestry. The elite remains about the same size but has grown much more diverse in heritage. The lower class has all but disappeared. In its place, there is now a huge middle class that encompasses everything from skilled blue-collar workers employed in manufacturing firms and hotels to a wide range of white-collar, professional, and managerial occupational groups employed directly or indirectly in the manufacturing and tourist sectors.

## POLITICAL LIFE

***Government.*** Barbados is an independent parliamentary democracy within the British Commonwealth. For administrative purposes, the island is divided into the city of Bridgetown and eleven parishes. The queen of England is recognized as the head of state, and the highest court of appeals is the Supreme Court of the United Kingdom. The queen appoints a governor-general to represent her on the island.

All local governments, including those on the district and municipal levels, were abolished on 1 September 1969; their functions were subsumed by the national government.

***Leadership and Political Officials.*** The Barbados Labour Party and the Democratic Labour Party compete for seats in the House of Assembly; members of the Senate are appointed by the governor-general. The leader of the majority party in the assembly serves as the prime minister. A Cabinet appointed from among the majority party members of the assembly helps the prime minister carry out the executive functions of government.

The Barbados legal system is founded in British common law. The Supreme Court of Judicature sits as a high court and court of appeal; vested by the constitution with unlimited jurisdiction, it consists of a chief justice and three puisne judges, appointed by the governor-general on the recommendation of the prime minister after consultation with the leader of the opposition party. Magistrate courts have both civil and criminal jurisdiction. Final appeals are brought to the Committee of Her Majesty's Privy Council in the United Kingdom.

Some observers have seen a connection between the growth of tourism on Barbados and the rise of such problems as crime, drug use, and prostitution. A more traditional indigenous problem is family violence, which has decreased dramatically within the span of a single generation as women have become empowered by increased educational and employment opportunities, and their economic dependence on men has decreased.

***Military Activity.*** Barbados maintains a small coast guard and the Barbados Defense Force.

## SOCIAL WELFARE AND CHANGE PROGRAMS

A national social security system began operations in 1937, providing old age and survivors' pensions, sickness, disability, and maternity benefits, and (under a January 1971 extension) employment injury benefits. People between the ages of sixteen and

*An arch extends over a road in the capital city of Bridgetown. The majority of the population, about 80 percent, live in or near the city.*

sixty-five are covered. Unemployment insurance was introduced in 1982 and is funded by equal contributions from employers and employees. Sickness and maternity benefits are provided for employed persons, and all government hospitals and clinics maintain public wards for medical treatments, with costs scaled to income.

## NONGOVERNMENTAL ORGANIZATIONS AND OTHER ASSOCIATIONS

Branches of international organizations include the Lions Club, Rotary Club, 4-H Clubs, Boy Scouts, Girl Scouts, YMCA, and YWCA.

## GENDER ROLES AND STATUSES

***Division of Labor by Gender.*** Prior to an increase in educational and job opportunities for women in the 1960s, women depended primarily on their children for economic support. Child support paid by the father, or money earned by the children through chores and small jobs often constituted the family's sole source of income. However, women have since entered many job markets once dominated by men; for example, women held ten of forty-nine seats in Parliament in 1999.

***The Relative Status of Women and Men.*** Although women are well-represented in all aspects of national life, women's rights advocates cite domestic violence as a serious problem. A domestic violence law passed in 1992 requires an immediate police response to reports of violence against women and children.

## MARRIAGE, FAMILY, AND KINSHIP

***Marriage.*** Historically, sexual activity usually began early as women traded sex for economic support and children ("visiting" or "keeper" relationships). Visiting unions gave way to common-law marriages that for older couples might be legitimated by a church ceremony. Childbearing was an investment activity for women. In a woman's youth, children legitimated her claims for income from men, although establishing those claims required subservience. As a woman entered middle age, her daughters took over nearly all household chores and her sons provided financial resources that could make her independent of spousal support and reduced or eliminated her subservience to an autocratic male. In old age, financial and domestic support from children meant the difference between abject poverty and a moderate or even comfortable

*Children walk past a mural in Boscobel, St. Peter Parish. Murals are a common art form for the many artists in Barbados.*

lifestyle. Because men could expect support from their children only if they had maintained a relationship with the children's mother, women dependent on men in their youth found that their men were dependent on them by late middle age.

Since 1960, kin relations have undergone a revolution. Barbadian women have experienced a conjunction of good job opportunities and increased educational levels. The West Indian marriage pattern of visiting, common-law marriage, and legal unions remains, but many women now receive far more domestic help, emotional support, and affectionate behavior. Women now have fewer children and enjoy markedly better relationships with their partners.

**Domestic Unit.** Households range in size from a single man or woman to mixed-gender groups that include as many as fifteen people. Barbadians idealize a household that consists of a married couple and their children, and that pattern characterizes about 45 percent of all households. Around 35 percent of households are organized around a mother and her children. Those households sometimes encompass three generations of women and may include brothers, uncles, sons, and the sexual partners of members of the core family unit. Biological fathers and mothers are distinguished from other

adults who may serve various caregiving and economic support functions for children.

**Inheritance.** Barbadians trace descent and inheritance through both the father and the mother.

**Kin Groups.** Barbadians recognize no organized, corporate groups of kin.

## SOCIALIZATION

**Child Rearing and Education.** Private and public primary and secondary schools offer educational programs modeled on those in the United Kingdom. Child-rearing traditions emphasize gender-based family responsibilities. Traditionally, women took responsibility for the home and taught homemaking skills to their daughters. Men were expected to provide income for the family and work outside the home. Both boys and girls began to work around the home at a very young age, doing chores such as carrying water by age five. Mothers often spoiled their boys. Boys' work was never as continuous as that of their sisters giving boys much more leisure time than girls had. Boys played more often during the day and stayed out later at night. Sons grew into men who were expected to protect their mothers physically, as well as provide for their material needs.

These patterns persist, but increasing affluence has led parents to expect less of their children. Girls now can become lawyers, businesswomen, and university professors. Working women expect their men to help with the children. Women, more than men, help care for elderly parents.

***Higher Education.*** Barbados supports one of the three campuses of the University of the West Indies (UWI). The local campus (Cave Hill) offers degrees in the physical, biological, and social sciences; the humanities; and law and medicine. Barbados Community College follows the practices of the California state community college system, and offers courses in technical fields and the liberal arts. Advanced education is also available through a teacher training college, a polytechnical college, the Extra Mural Centre of the UWI, and a hotel school. The government pays tuition for all citizens who attend the UWI.

## ETIQUETTE

Barbadians are known for their politeness and civility, a legacy both of British influence and of the island's high population density—living in close proximity to others imposes pressure to avoid censure and unpleasant confrontations. Describing his homeland, well-known Barbadian author John Wickham wrote, "The inability of people to remove themselves from one another has led to concern for public order, a compassion for others, and a compelling sense of a neighbor's rights and integrity."

## RELIGION

***Religious Beliefs.*** More than 80 percent of the population is Christian, and more than half belong to the Church of England. A small East Indian community includes some people who practice Hinduism, and Islam is adhered to by a small number of people of diverse backgrounds. A growing number of people practice Rastafarianism. A small Jewish community with Sephardic roots attends services in a synagogue originally built in 1640 C.E.

The Apostolic Spiritual Baptists (popularly known as "Tie–heads") occupy a special place in Barbados' religious spectrum as the island's only indigenous religion. Fashioned after other West Indian revivalist religions, the sect, founded in 1957 by Bishop Branville Williams, combines Christian observance with the foot stomping, hand clapping, and dancing characteristic of African religious practices. Tie–heads, so-called because of the cloth turbans worn by both men and women, sport colorful gowns in colors symbolic of particular qualities.

***Rituals and Holy Places.*** The school day usually begins with a prayer and small revivalist churches abound on the island. Converts to the Tie–Head faith are baptized and then sequestered for seven to ten days in the "Mourning Ground," a special area of the church.

***Religious Practitioners.*** Priests exert some influence over public policy and cultural life (one reason for the absence of casinos on the island), and a substantial amount of radio air time is devoted to religious programming.

## MEDICINE AND HEALTH CARE

Barbadians rely on two bodies of knowledge to prevent and treat illness: a biomedical system organized on a Western model and an indigenous medical system that involves "bush" teas and home remedies.

When economic development began in the 1950s, the health care needs arose from high rates of acute infectious disease, and the government built an outstanding health care delivery system directed at those problems. The medical school at the UWI is located at a six hundred bed acute care facility, Queen Elizabeth Hospital. Separate geriatric and psychiatric hospitals provide specialized care. Public clinics in nearly every parish and private clinics concentrated in heavily populated parishes, serve primary health care needs.

Barbadians currently face two very different sets of health issues. The growing elderly population suffers from arthritis, hypertension, adult-onset diabetes, cancer, and heart disease. Significant proportions of disabled persons have unmet needs for help in seeing, eating, and walking. Youth face behavioral health problems, including AIDS, substance abuse, domestic and street violence, and mood disorders.

## SECULAR CELEBRATIONS

In addition to the major holidays of the Christian calendar, Barbadian holidays include New Year's Day (1 January), May Day (1 May), CARICOM Day (first Monday in August), Independence Day (30 November), and United Nations Day (first Monday in October). This island's major celebration is the Crop Over festival, which takes place in July and early August. The Barbadian equivalent of Thanksgiving in the United States, it is derived from the

*A farm worker harvesting tea. The plantation economy was a large factor in shaping Barbadian culture.*

traditional festival that marked the sugarcane harvest. Events include the ritual presentation of the Last Canes and the judging of costumed groups (called ''bands'') on Kadooment Day (1 August), the climax of the festival. The festivities include calypso music and abundant food.

## THE ARTS AND HUMANITIES

**Support for the Arts.** The arts on Barbados have been supported since the mid-1950s by the Barbados National Arts Council, and tourism has provided many local artists, especially musicians, with patrons. The Barbados Investment and Development Corporation (BIDC) supports the preservation of the island's handcrafts by running numerous shops where local craftspeople sell their wares, as well as offering workshops for beginners and experts alike.

**Literature.** Although Barbados has a long oral storytelling tradition, written literature by Barbadians received its first real debut in the 1940s and 1950s in a Barbadian literary magazine called *Bim*, which was the first showcase of works by a number of Caribbean writers destined for future fame, including Derek Wolcott, the 1992 Nobel laureate in literature, who was born in Saint Lucia but has spent a large portion of his time in Trinidad.

Well-known Barbadian writers include essayist John Wickham, novelist George Lamming (best known for *In the Castle of My Skin*, and poet Edward Kamau Braithwaite, winner of the 1994 Neustadt International Prize for Literature and a professor of Comparative Literature at New York University.

**Graphic Arts.** Barbados has a flourishing community of artists producing paintings, murals, sculptures, and crafts, many of which reflect strong African influences. Barbadian crafts include pottery, mahogany items, and jewelry.

**Performance Arts.** In addition to the popular calypso, reggae, and steel band music that reflects the influence of neighboring Trinidad and Jamaica, Barbados has its own indigenous musical tradition, the *tuk* band, which provides the backbeat for all major celebrations on the island. Composed of pennywhistles, snare drums, and bass drums, it is reminiscent of a British military band, but with a distinctly African flair.

## THE STATE OF THE PHYSICAL AND SOCIAL SCIENCES

State-of-the-art medical research is carried out primarily at the UWI's school of medicine. Social and behavioral research is carried out by UWI faculty and research affiliates of the Institute for Social and Economic Research.

## BIBLIOGRAPHY

Barrow, Errol W., and Kendal A. Lee. *Privilege: Cooking in the Caribbean*, 1988.

Best, Curwen. *Barbadian Popular Music and the Politics of Caribbean Culture*, 1999.

Dann, Graham. *The Quality of Life in Barbados*, 1984.

Hoyos, F. A. *Barbados: A History from the Amerindians to Independence*, 1978.

Schomburg, Robert H. *The History of Barbados: Comprising a Geographical and Statistical Description of the Island; A Sketch of the Historical Events since the Settlement*, 1998.

—W. PENN HANDWERKER

BARBUDA SEE ANTIGUA AND BARBUDA

# BELARUS

## CULTURE NAME

Belarusian

## ALTERNATIVE NAMES

Republic of Belarus, Respublika Belarus; before 1991, the country was known as the Belorussian (also spelled Byelorussian) Soviet Socialist Republic. Sometimes called White Russia or alternatively White Ruthenia, especially in relation to the pre-1918 history of the region. Culture name also known as Belarussian.

## ORIENTATION

**Identification.** The name Belarus probably derives from the Middle Ages geographic designation of the area as "White Russia." Historians and linguists argue about its etymology, but it was possibly used as a folk name referring to northern territories. Some historic sources also mention Red and Black Rus in addition to White Rus. Such labeling probably predates the times when the Kievan Kingdom came into existence. Historic sources mention Belarus during the fourteenth and fifteenth centuries as a geographic name; it later gained specific political meaning, including nation-state identification.

Although Belarusians are the dominant ethnic group in the country, the culture includes people of various ethnicities such as Lithuanians, Poles, Ukrainians, Russians, Jews, and Tartars. The richness and blend of the culture reflects the complexity of ethnic interactions that have been taking place in this region for hundreds of years.

**Location and Geography.** Belarus is bounded by Poland and Lithuania on the west, Latvia in the northwest, Russia in the northeast and east, and Ukraine in the south. Belarus is a large plain about the size of Kansas, with a total area of 80,200 square miles (207,600 square kilometers).

The country is in the western portion of the East European Plains within the basins of the Dnepr, West Dvina, and Neman Rivers. The basins are connected, forming a system of natural waterways that link the Baltic and Black Seas. Much of the country is lowland with gently rolling hills; forests cover one-third of the land and their peat marshes are a valuable natural resource.

Modern Belarus is fairly evenly populated, with the exceptions of the marshes along the southern boundary with Ukraine. The capital, Minsk, is the largest and one of the oldest cities in the region and is centrally located.

Belarus has a moderate continental climate that is influenced by the Baltic Sea and the Atlantic Ocean. The summers are cool with some warm days, and winters are cold, while the average annual precipitation ranges 21.5 inches (546 mm) to 27.3 inches (693 mm). Average temperature ranges are from 63.5 degrees Fahrenheit (17.5 degrees Celsius) in July to 20 degrees Fahrenheit ($-7$ degrees Celsius) in January.

**Demography.** The population of Belarus was estimated to be 10,366,719 in 2000. The major ethnic groups in 2000 were Belarusians (77.9 percent), Russians (13.2 percent), Poles (4.16 percent), Ukrainians (2.9 percent), Jews (1.1 percent), Tartars, and Lithuanians (less than 1 percent). The demographic distribution remained consistent for centuries, but changed profoundly during the course of the twentieth century, especially due to the murder of Jews and Poles during the Holocaust and the influx of ethnic Russians.

The population density was estimated at 127 inhabitants per square mile in 2000. Women make up 53 percent of the population, and men the remaining 47 percent. Approximately 69 percent of the population is urban. The biggest city is Minsk, with around 1.7 million residents.

*Belarus*

### Linguistic Affiliation.
The official language is Belarusian, but Russian is also widely spoken. Furthermore, each ethnic minority—Polish, Ukrainian, and Lithuanian—also speaks its own language. Most Belarusians speak two or three languages, usually including Belarusian and Russian. About 98 percent of adult Belarusians are literate.

The Belarusian language belongs to the family of Slavic languages and is very close to Russian and Ukrainian. All the three languages use the Cyrillic alphabet, with minor modifications in Ukrainian and Belarusian. Until the early twentieth century, the Belarusian language stood out as a symbol of ethnic distinction. In the communist era, Russian became dominant. Since the fall of the Soviet Union, however, Belarusian is again being spoken and taught in schools as the national language.

"Lacinka" is the name of the Latin-script in Belarusian writing. It originated in the mid-sixteenth century as an aftermath of influence from Poland. Reformation, Counter-Reformation, and the expansion of the Western style of education were among the major factors leading to the considerable changes in the archaic Belarusian written language.

### Symbolism.
The state symbols of Belarus changed repeatedly throughout the twentieth century. In 1918 the Belarusian People's Republic took "The Pursuit" emblem (a horseman in motion, carrying a sword and shield) and the white–red–white flag as the state symbols. In 1919 the Belarusian Soviet Socialist Republic approved another state emblem: a hammer and sickle in the rays of the rising sun, surrounded by a garland of wheat. In 1956 the new Belarusian Soviet Socialist Republic (BSSR) approved a flag. It consisted of an upper red stripe and a lower green one. Additionally, there was a white Belarusian folk ornament on the red field. In 1991 the Republic of Belarus acquired the status of an independent sovereign state and "The Pursuit" emblem again became the state symbol and the white–red–white striped flag again became the state flag.

After the referendum in 1995, the state emblem of the Republic of Belarus was changed to an image of the republic's geographic outline in golden sunrays over the globe, with a five-pointed red star above. The image is framed by a garland of wheat, clover, and flax flowers. The golden inscription below reads "Republic of Belarus." The Belarusian national flag, which was accepted in 1995, looks like the 1956 design: two horizontal stripes (red and green) and a vertical element of white folk-design lace presented against the red background. The new state anthem has lyrics and music that reflect the everlasting aspiration of the Belarusian people for freedom and independence, and proclaims their commitment to ideals of humanism, goodness, and justice.

## HISTORY AND ETHNIC RELATIONS

### Emergence of the Nation.
Around the end of the ninth and the beginning of the tenth centuries, the Kievan Rus kingdom formed. Its two administrative provinces, the Polock and the Turov Principalities, covered the area of today's Belarus. For several centuries the Belarusian territories were strongly influenced by the Byzantine culture, including Orthodox Christianity, stone architecture, and literature. After the destruction of the Kievan Rus in the mid-thirteenth century by the Mongols the two Belarusian principalities were incorporated into the Great Lithuanian Duchy. A century later the Duchy formed a union with the Polish Kingdom. This new administrative and political situation brought a strong Western European influence to the region,

including the Roman Catholic religion. A large Jewish population also settled in Belarus in the fourteenth century.

The Polish-Lithuanian Union created a strong political, economic, and military power in Eastern Europe. In 1569 the Great Lithuanian Duchy and the Polish Kingdom fused into a multiethnic federal state, one of the wealthiest and mightiest in Europe of the time, called the Commonwealth (*Rzeczpospolita*). The state enjoyed a powerful position in Europe for two centuries.

Following the partitions of the Commonwealth in 1772, 1793, and 1795 by Russia, Prussia, and Austria, respectively, the Belarusian territories became a part of the Russian empire. Great poverty under Russian rule, particularly among Jews, led to mass emigration to the United States in the nineteenth century. The second half of the nineteenth century witnessed the rapid development of capitalism in Belarus.

Beginning in the late 1880s, Marxist ideas proliferated in Belarus, and the 1905–1907 revolution produced the Belarusian national liberation movement. The nationalist newspaper *Nasha Niva* ("Our Land") was first published around this time. The most significant event in this national awakening process took place in April 1917, when the Congress of the Belarusian National Organizations took place. Its delegates claimed autonomy for Belarus. However, after the October Socialist Revolution in Petrograd succeeded, the Bolsheviks seized power in Belarus. In December 1917, they dissolved the all-Belarusian Congress in Minsk. Regardless of Soviet occupation, the all-Belarusian Congress and the representatives of the political parties declared the Belarusian People's Republic the first independent Belarusian state on 25 March 1918. Ten months later, the Bolsheviks proclaimed the Belarusian Soviet Socialist Republic (BSSR). The new nation-state was formally incorporated into the Soviet Union (USSR), and remained part of that union until 1991.

On 27 July 1991, the Supreme Soviet of the BSSR adopted the Declaration on State Sovereignty. In August 1991, the Supreme Soviet of the BSSR suspended the Communist Party of Belarus and renamed the country the Republic of Belarus. In December 1991, the USSR dissolved and Belarus became a cofounder of the Commonwealth of Independent States (CIS).

In March 1994, Belarus adopted a new constitution, creating a presidency and reconstructing the 260-seat Parliament. On 10 July 1994, Alyaksandr Lukashenka was elected as the first President of Belarus. In 1997, the Treaty on the Union of Belarus and Russia was signed.

***National Identity.*** National identity is symbolically linked to two significant moments in the Belarusian history. The national holiday is officially celebrated on 3 July, commemorating the day Soviet troops entered Minsk in 1944, liberating the city from Nazi forces. For some Bellarussians, 25 March is celebrated as an unofficial Independence Day. The date commemorates the short time period when Belarus broke free from the Bolshevik Russia in March 1918, only to be reoccupied in December 1918.

***Ethnic Relations.*** Throughout the centuries, Belarusian lands were home to an ethnically and religiously diverse society. Muslims, Jews, Orthodox Christians, Roman and Greek Catholic Christians, and Protestants lived together without any major confrontations; Belarusians, Poles, Russians, Jews, Lithuanians, Ukrainians, and Roma (Gypsies) also lived in peace in Belarus. Although the twentieth century brought many challenges to this peaceful coexistence, Belarus is in many senses a culture of tolerance. The current population is primarily Belarusian but also includes Russians, Poles, Ukrainians, and Jews. All ethnic groups enjoy equal status, and there is no evidence of hate or ethnically-biased crimes.

## URBANISM, ARCHITECTURE, AND THE USE OF SPACE

Belarus is predominantly rural with several large cities. Urban centers such as Minsk have been important in the development of Eastern European architecture since the eleventh century. Important religious monuments include the Saint Sophia Cathedral in Polotsk (begun in 1044), and churches such as Saint Euphrocine-Saviour Church in Polotsk, the Annunciation Church in Vitebsk, the Saint Boris and Gleb Church in Grodno (all built in the twelfth century). Many military fortifications and facilities were built between the thirteenth and the seventeenth centuries, in both Gothic and Renaissance styles. Many castles dating from the Middle Ages and Renaissance still stand, and in some cases the original wooden architecture has survived. Baroque churches were built in the sixteenth through the eighteenth centuries, and at the end of the eighteenth century classicism began to dominate local architecture. Russian architects participated in town planning in the late nineteenth–early twentieth centuries, and towns were intensively

*The Graveyard of Villages memorializes the 185 Belorussian towns destroyed by Nazi forces during World War II. The monument stands on the site of one of the towns, Khatyn, which burned to the ground in 1943.*

built up. The architecture of twentieth century was characterized by both modernism and constructivism (such as the National Library of Belarus, built 1930–32).

Belarus is a farming country. Twenty-nine percent of the farm land is devoted to arable land; 15 percent to permanent pastures; 1 percent to permanent crops; 34 percent to forests and woodland; and 21 percent to other uses.

## FOOD AND ECONOMY

**Food in Daily Life.** Belarusian eating habits are not very different from those of people in other Eastern European cultures. They usually have three main daily meals, and staples include red meat and potatoes. Belarusians are also very fond of spending their free time in the woods searching for the many types of mushrooms that are used in soups and other dishes.

Favorite Belarusian dishes include *borscht*, a soup made with beets that is served hot with sour cream; filet à la Minsk and Minsk cutlet; potato dishes with mushrooms; and pickled berries. *Mochanka* is a thick soup mixed with lard accompanied

by hot pancakes. There is also a large selection of international and Russian specialities available. A favorite drink is black tea, and coffee is generally available with meals and in cafés, although standards vary. Soft drinks, fruit juices, and mineral waters are widely available.

Ethnographic studies confirm that most Belarusians in the beginning of the twentieth century subsisted on a rather poor diet. No significant change can be noticed since the inception of the Soviet rules after the Bolshevik Revolution and the picture of a family eating from a common bowl has been changing slowly. After World War II, due to industrialization and economic changes, the eating habits have changed, but not profoundly.

**Food Customs at Ceremonial Occasions.** Food customs often involve women and point out their role in society. For instance, setting a food table was customarily a woman's job. Men would not engage in such activity. An interesting food custom is related to matchmaking, which was always associated with drinking vodka and having food. First the matchmaker would visit a house of a potential bride and offer drinks and food. If the suitor was accepted, he would appear with the matchmaker at the woman's house with vodka and the woman's parents would provide food. Interestingly, the ceremony could be repeated several times until the couple would be officially engaged. If the engagement were broken, whoever broke the engagement would have to repay the other side for all expenses.

After a funeral, the mourners gather together for a meal.

**Basic Economy.** The official currency is the *rouble* (R) (also known as the *zaichik*) divided into 100 *kopecks*. Belarus is an industrial state with developed and diversified agriculture. The main industries include electric power, timber, metallurgy, chemicals and petrochemicals, pulp and paper, building materials, medical, printing, machine-building, microbiology, textiles, and food industries.

The agricultural products are dairy and beef products, pork, poultry, potatoes, and flax. Agricultural production is highly industrialized and is based on the use of modern technology such as tractors, machine tools, trucks, equipment for animal husbandry and livestock feeding, and chemical fertilizers. Agricultural lands make up more than 46 percent of Belarus's territory, and agriculture accounts for about 20 percent of the national income. State-run farms are main producers of agrarian goods. Privately-owned farms are in the state of development.

*A teacher instructs students during a physical education class at their school in Minsk. The state controls child rearing and education.*

The nuclear accident at the Chernobyl (Ukraine) power plant in 1986 had a devastating effect on Belarusian agricultural industry. As a result of the radiation, agriculture in a large part of the country was destroyed, and many villages were abandoned.

Since gaining its independence from the Soviet Union in 1991, Belarus has moved relatively slowly on privatization and other market reforms, emphasizing instead close economic relations with Russia. About 80 percent of all industry remains in state hands, and foreign investment has been hindered by a political climate not always friendly towards business. Economic output, which had been declining for several years, revived somewhat in the late 1990s. Privatization of enterprises controlled by the central government virtually ceased in 1996, and the Belarusian economy was in crisis. The volume of production in all branches of industries has decreased. The Russian financial crisis that began in autumn 1998 severely affected Belarus's Soviet-style planned economy. Belarus is almost completely dependent on Russia, which buys 70 percent of its exports. Belarus has seen little structural reform since 1995, when President Lukashenka launched the country on the path of "market socialism." Belarus's trade deficit has grown steadily since then, from 8 percent of total trade turnover in

1995 to 14 percent in the first quarter of 1997, despite the government's efforts to promote exports and limit imports. Lukashenka also re-imposed administrative control over prices and the national currency's exchange rate, and expanded the state's right to intervene arbitrarily in the management of private enterprise. Given Belarus's limited fiscal reserve, continued growth in the trade deficit will increase vulnerability to economic crisis.

***Land Tenure and Property.*** Prior to the partition of the Commonwealth by the end of the eighteenth century, all land belonged to the local gentry and petty noblemen (predominantly Polish or Polonized Belarusians). Before 1861, when peasants were freed, only small parcels of land were in the hands of Belarusian farmers. Peasants had to work three days a week or one hundred fifty six days a year for the noblemen. Some landlords preferred cash to labor. The landlords also hired peasants (those who did not own land) as paid labor. In the beginning of the twentieth century small stretches of land were owned by the state (about 5 percent), some land was communal (about 34 percent), and the majority was in private hands (60 percent). By 1917 the state, church, and gentry owned 9.3 percent while the individual farmers held 90.7 percent of all arable land. Farms were grouped in small hamlets rather than villages (two to ten households). With each generation the family lots got smaller. Some farmers rented additional land from the noblemen or wealthy farmers. After the Bolshevik Revolution of the 1917, all land belonged to the state and large state-owned collective farms. This situation persisted at the beginning of the twenty-first century.

**Major Industries.** The vast Belarusian forests support a large lumber industry, contributing about one-third of the gross national product (GNP). Among the most developed branches of industry are automobile and tractor building, agricultural machinery, production of machine tools and bearings, electronics, oil extraction and processing, production of synthetic fibers and mineral fertilizers, pharmaceuticals, production of construction materials, textiles, and food industries. Much of the national industry is focused on ready-made products for export.

**Trade.** The country's main trading partners are the other CIS states. Among the primary products traded are buckwheat, chalk, chloride, clay, limestone, peat, potassium, quartz sand, rye, sodium chloride, sugar beets, timber, tobacco, wheat, farm machinery, fertilizers, glass, machine tools, synthetic fibers, and textiles. In 1999 Belarus exported $6 billion (U.S.) worth of goods. Among the most significant export partners are Russia (66 percent of export), Ukraine, Poland, Germany, and Lithuania.

Belarus imports such commodities as oil, natural gas, coal, ferrous metal, lumber, chemicals chemical semi-products, cement, cotton, silk, cars, buses, household appliances, paper, grain, sugar, fish. In 1999 Belarus spent approximately $6.4 billion (U.S.) on goods imported primarily from Russia (54 percent), Ukraine, Germany, Poland, and Lithuania.

## POLITICAL LIFE

**Government.** The Republic of Belarus is united democratic, legal state. It is divided into six administrative regions: five provinces (voblastsi, singular - voblasts'; the administrative center name follows in parentheses): Brestskaya (Brest), Homyel'skaya (Homyel'), Hrodzyenskaya (Hrodna), Mahilyowskaya (Mahilyow), and Vitsyebskaya (Vitsyebsk), and one municipality (horad), Minsk. The basic law is the Constitution of 1994 (with variations and additions), amended by a referendum in 1996. The chief of state, the President, is elected by the population for a five year term. The legislative body, the National Assembly, is composed of the House of Representatives (one-hundred-ten deputies, elected by the population) and Council of Republic (sixty-four members, fifty six elected by domestic councils of deputies, eight appointed by the president). Members of the National Assembly serve four-year terms. A Ministerial Council, headed by the prime minister, is appointed by the President with the consent of the House of Representatives. Local government is managed by local Councils with executive and administrative power. The supreme judicial organ is the Supreme Court, which interprets the constitution.

**Leadership and Political Officials.** Critics and opposition members denounce the increasingly oppressive political atmosphere and human rights violations in Belarus under the Soviet-style authoritarianism of President Alyaksandr Lukashenko. In 1999, the year President Lukashenko was to step down, he held what was internationally considered to be a rigged national referendum. The referendum changed the constitution and allowed Lukashenk to cancel the elections and remain president.

**Military Activity.** Belarus has a sizable army, with approximately 98,400 active duty personnel. Military branches include the army (51 percent of personnel) and the air force (27 percent). The remaining 22 percent is divided among the air defense force, interior ministry troops, and border guards. As a landlocked country, Belarus does not have a navy. Military service is mandatory for males over eighteen years of age. Belarusian military expenditure amounts to approximately $156 million (U.S., in 1998), which is 1.2 percent of the gross domestic product and 1.8 percent of the GNP.

## NONGOVERNMENTAL ORGANIZATIONS AND OTHER ASSOCIATIONS

There are several nongovernmental organizations (NGOs) in Belarus. One of them is The Belarus Project, which supports judges, lawyers, human rights advocates, and journalists in making their case before international audiences and intergovernmental bodies regarding President Lukashenka's violations of human rights and the rule of law in Belarus. Much effort goes toward bringing Belarusian civic leaders to the U.S. State Department and to the United Nations to tell their own stories of the situation in Belarus. This also gives them the opportunity to meet with their international colleagues and with human rights organizations and other NGOs that may be helpful to their cause at home.

*Commuters climb on and off a city bus in Minsk, the largest city, with a population of almost two million.*

## GENDER ROLES AND STATUSES

***Division of Labor by Gender.*** Modern Belarus is a part of the industrialized world. But certain cultural traits, which are observable today, might be traced back to the past. During the last fifty years some changes can be noticed in terms of traditional labor patterns. Today men and women do the same jobs and they might even be compensated equal wages. But ethnographic sources confirm a strong division of labor by gender existing in the beginning of the twentieth century and some of those patterns can still be recognized today. They relate to eating and childrearing patterns. One of them is the obligation of setting the dinner table, which is exclusively a woman's job. It is usually a mother or wife who is responsible for the arrangements. A man would not interfere with this obligation; it may even be considered degrading for a man to perform this task. Also, children under fourteen years old traditionally were under mothers' care and fathers would not interfere.

***The Relative Status of Women and Men.*** Gender roles in Belarus remain very traditional. Men are considered the more powerful gender and as breadwinners, while women are required to take care of the children and household. This traditional structure is slowly changing, and women are be-

ginning to gain more recognition and power. The gay movement is also slowly entering the region, although with some opposition.

Men occupy all top positions in various spheres of the economy and politics. After some gains, a considerable decline in the professional and social status of women has been observed recently. Belarusian women are the least protected social group on the job market, and their unemployment rate is around 65 percent. Part of the gender inequality problem is that Belarusian women do not identify their rights and interests as specifically women's issues. Many Belarusians do not see social injustice in the low status of women, and so do not protest the situation.

The first appearance of feminist initiatives came in 1991, when the Belarusian Committee of Soviet Women was transformed into the Union of Women in Belarus. Other independent women's organizations followed, such as the League of Women in Belarus, the Committee of Soldiers' Mothers, and the Women's Christian-Democratic Movement. From 1993 to 1996, the Ministry of Justice of Belarus registered other organizations that, in addition to the protection of women's rights, were designed to achieve other goals like promotion of the development of culture, the revival of national traditions, and environmental protection. These groups have appeared within the structures of trade unions in order to resolve problems of both working and unemployed women.

In the late 1990s, a number of women's organizations were formed that were tightly linked with certain political structures. For example, the Belarusian feminist movement "For the Renaissance of the Fatherland" united women of social-democratic orientation, while the "League of Women-Electors" were mainly members of the United Civil Party; a women's organization was set up within the Liberal-Democratic Party, called Women's Liberal Association. In 2000, there were more than twenty women's organizations registered by the Ministry of Justice in Belarus.

## MARRIAGE, FAMILY, AND KINSHIP

**Marriage.** Traditionally, marriage was a matter of mutual consent between the young, but the custom also required the consent of the families involved. Daughters enjoyed considerable freedom and had many opportunities to meet young men. Several times a year there were public gatherings in a larger village or town. The young couple had to live with the husband's family and often marriage was a compromise. Both the bride and the groom were expected to contribute something to the marriage and the farm, and most often it was just labor. The most sought qualities of a woman were for her to be a good field worker and housekeeper. Personal beauty and wealth were of secondary importance. Belarusians required high moral qualities from their spouses and virginity of the bride, and occasionally also the groom, was a prerequisite for marriage. The wedding was celebrated in both houses and expenses were shared. Divorce was also by mutual consent.

**Domestic Unit.** Until modern times households based on extended kinship relations (*zadruga* – joint families) were popular. The traditional zadruga household includes the father and all his sons living on one piece of land. Each married son would have his own hut, but the land, animals, and equipment was owned by the entire family. The family also worked and ate together. Private ownership was limited to personal belonging. Such extended family may have included as many as fifty members united under the authority of one senior. Interestingly, the family's head was not always the natural father or grandfather and the extended family often included distant relatives or even strangers who may have been adopted as family members. Labor invested in the farm rather than blood relations regulated the kin membership. A stranger could have become a family member temporarily or for a lifetime and in some situation could have acquired a status of the head of the extended household.

Usually, the father would assume the position of the family's head and after his death any of his sons (usually the oldest), or his brother, or even a stranger, could take up his position in the family. There was no official title of the position, although several folk terms exist. The kinship also regulated profit sharing. If an adult member had been separated from the kin and had not contributed labor, he would not participate in profit sharing. A son who was absent and did not contribute to the welfare of the kin would not get the same share as other family members including those who were not blood related. Some remains of this kin structure persisted until the Soviet times.

The senior of the kin always directed the work of the men, while his wife took care of the women's activities. The father held the legal title to the property, but he was limited in the possibilities to sell or trade the family assets for as long as there were legal heirs. The custom was designed to protect the children and their rights to own property. When the property was sold, minors, after reaching the legal age, could have claimed the sold property as theirs. There are records that on several occasions courts ruled in their favor.

**Inheritence.** With certain exceptions for unmarried daughters, men and women were equal to family property. Whatever they brought in to the marriage remained theirs forever. Only the common investments were considered as family holdings. After the death of the spouse, the property went back to their legal heirs or was returned to the home of their origin. All money that a woman made from selling her garden products was her property and the family had no right over such assets. Also, a daughter's earnings outside a farm, although handed over to the family, were her private property. The wife was not responsible for her husband's debts, but the husband was for his wife's. Belarusian married women enjoyed relative equality in decision-making and economic share. But daughters had no share in the family estates, and brothers were under the obligation to marry off their sisters. When there were only daughters in the family, they inherited the whole estate, and the husband of the eldest one was under obligation to take care of the younger until they married.

## SOCIALIZATION

***Child Rearing and Education.*** Child rearing and education are controlled by the state. Mothers can take paid maternity leaves and paid sick-days when their children are ill. Schooling is free and primary and secondary schooling is mandatory. The state runs affordable kindergartens. More than 10 percent of the population continue their education in several universities around the country. Literacy level is very high; 98 percent of the population age fifteen and over can read and write.

***Higher Education.*** There were fifty-five higher educational institutions in Belarus at the end of the twentieth century, including thirteen private schools. The largest state institutions are the Belarusian University; the University of Informatics and Radio-electronics; the Economic, Technological, Agricultural Technological, and Pedagogical Universities; the Polytechnic Academy; the Academy of Arts; the Academy of Music; the Academy of Physical Training and Sports; the Academy of Agriculture; the Brest, Gomel, Grodno, Vitebsk, Mogilev, and Minsk Linguistic Universities; the Vitebsk Technological University; and medical institutes in Gomel, Grodno, Vitebsk, and Minsk. There were 292 scientific establishments in Belarus, employing 26,000 scientists. The main scientific center is the National Academy of Sciences.

## ETIQUETTE

"Sardechna zaprashayem!" is the traditional expression used when welcoming guests, who are usually presented with bread and salt. Shaking hands is the common form of greeting. Hospitality is part of the Belarusian tradition; people are welcoming and friendly; and gifts are given to friends and business associates.

## RELIGION

***Religious Beliefs.*** Christianity is the dominant faith. Byzantine Christianity was introduced to Belarus with the rise of the Kievan kingdom in the tenth century. With the incorporation of the Belarusian territories into the Great Lithuanian Duchy and later into the Polish-dominated Commonwealth, Roman Catholicism and Protestantism flourished in Belarus. At the end of the sixteenth century, the struggle between the Russian Orthodox and Roman Catholic churches produced the Orthodox Uniate Church, governed by the Vatican. The Orthodox Church dominated following the Russian defeat of uprisings in 1863 and 1864.

*An imposing sculpture decorates the front of an apartment house in Minsk. Historical and domestic subjects were a common theme of early twentieth-century Belarusian art.*

In 2000, Russian Orthodoxy claimed the most Belarusian believers (80 percent), followed by Roman Catholicism. The Christian community in Belarus is currently very diverse and includes several communities of Seventh-Day Adventists, Jehovah's Witnesses, Evangelists, Calvinists, and Lutherans, as well as Roman Catholics Orthodox practitioners, and Uniates. The most prevalent Protestant groups are Evangelic Christians and Christians of Evangelic Faith.

There are now about 44,000 Muslims, including people from the former Soviet republics and about 1,500 Arab students, in Belarus. The country has four mosques (in Ivye, Novogrudok [Navahradak], Slonim, and Smilovichi) and a fifth one at Vidzy in the Braslav district of the Vitebsk region will soon be designated.

Most of the Jews fled the region before World War II, were exterminated during that war, or emigrated after it ended. At the end of the eighteenth century, about 7 percent of Belarus's population was Jewish. At the beginning of the twentieth century, there were 704 synagogues; in 1995, only fifteen of them remained.

The number of Jews in Belarus can be estimated from the current number of members of the Union of Religious Jewish Congregations of the Republic of Belarus. This organization had at least 20,000 members in 2000 and has twelve regional offices. It effectively represents virtually the entire observant community and the Jewish community at large. It supplies humanitarian and medical aid and is affiliated with World Jewish Relief in the United Kingdom and B'nai B'rith in the States. The Main Synagogue of Minsk has daily morning and evening services.

Since the inception of Christianity into the region, the practitioners of Eastern Orthodoxy always outnumbered the followers of other religions. Regardless the times of religious freedom, there were also times of religious intolerance and persecutions. Religious rivalry between Catholicism and Orthodox Christianity amplified after 1839, when the Unite Church was abolished. All major political powers inflicted their policies against certain religions but the Poles and Soviets imposed the most drastic measures. Religious practices were seriously limited during the Soviet area or even outlawed. For instance, Jewish religion and culture, which has strong roots in Belarus, were discriminated under the Soviet rule. Most synagogues have been closed and the teaching of Hebrew and Judaism forbidden. Nevertheless, many Jews practiced their religious activities in secret. Since the Soviet era, the Eastern Orthodox Church in Belarus was a structural part of the Russian Orthodox Church. In February of 1992 the Belarusian Exarchate of the Moscow Patriarchate was created, but Moscow still heavily influences the Belarusian Church. Since 1989 the Vatican has been sending Catholic priests from Poland to work in Belarus.

**Rituals and Holy Places.** Among the most important religious holidays are Easter, Christmas, and days of remembrance. Russian Orthodox Easter is celebrated sometime between late March and early May, and the difference between Orthodox Easter and Catholic Easter may be up to six weeks. Roman Catholic Easter varies according to a lunar calendar. Russian Orthodox Christmas is celebrated on 5 January, and Roman Catholics celebrate on 25 December. Russian Orthodox practitioners observe *Radaunitsa*, a remembrance day, on 28 April, and Roman Catholics celebrate All Souls Day (*Dsiady*) on 2 November.

There are several places in Belarus that are related to various saints of the Eastern Orthodox Church, including Polock, Sluck, Brest, and Turov.

The holiest place of the Russian Orthodox Church is the Garbarka Hill, in eastern Poland.

## MEDICINE AND HEALTH CARE

Hospital treatment and some other medical and dental treatment is normally provided without fee. Belarus has several large, diverse healthcare facilities, both hospitals and outpatient institutions. Specialized medicine is expanding and improving in the country, although students learn medicine in four medical institutes (in Minsk, Vitebsk, Grodno, Gomel), while eighteen medical schools prepare other medical personnel extensive epidemics of diphtheria have been reported in recent years.

Life expectancy at birth is 62 years for men and 74 years for women, with a population average of 68 years.

## SECULAR CELEBRATIONS

Secular celebrations include the following national holidays: 1 January is New Year's Day; 8 March is International Women's Day, honoring the contribution of women to society; 1 May is Labor Day, celebrating the significance and the contribution of the working class and including a parade of citizens; Victory Day, celebrated 9 May, commemorates the victory over Nazi Germany in 1945. Independence Day is celebrated on 3 July and signifies the liberation of Minsk from the Nazi troops during WWII. The October Revolution Holiday, commemorating victory of the 1917 Bolshevik Revolution in Russia, is celebrated on 7 November.

## THE ARTS AND HUMANITIES

*Literature.* The origins of Belarusian literature may be traced to the times of The Kievan Rus. Its formative period was during the fourteenth and fifteenth centuries, and culminated in the sixteenth century when Francisk Skaryna, a publisher, humanist, scientist, and writer, published the first book—the Bible—in Belarusian.

Modern Belarusian literature originated in the nineteenth century, with a sense of national identity. V. Dunin-Marcinkevich, a poet and playwright, was the most dominant figure of the times. He developed literary forms new to Belarus (such as the idyll, ballad, and comedy), and significantly influenced the formation of the literature, dramatic art, and spiritual culture of Belarusians.

Belarusian literature flourished in the twentieth century; key figures were Yakub Kolas and Yanka

*Swimmers and boaters congregate at a bathhouse on the shore of a lake, Minsk. The Baltic Sea and Atlantic Ocean influence the moderate climate.*

Kupala, both poets, novelists, playwrights, critics, publicists, public figures, and founders of the modern Belarusian literature and language.

**Graphic Arts.** Painting first developed in Belarus in the eleventh and twelfth centuries, under influence of Byzantine art. Few works of that period remain, but fresco paintings like those in the Polotsk Sofia Cathedral have been preserved. In the sixteenth century, a fresco painting school was formed in Belarus. Works from the sixteenth through nineteenth centuries were stylistically connected with the painting of Poland and Western Europe; portraiture was popular.

"The Vitebsk School" played a major role in developing the Belarusian national art in the early twentieth century. The best internationally known member of the School was Marc Chagall, who was born near Vitebsk. He emigrated in 1922 and subsequently lived in France, Mexico, and the United States. Often his works depict scenes of his native Vitebsk, and Jewish life in a Belarusian town.

After the October Revolution of 1917, Socialist Realism became popular, with emphasis on historical and domestic subjects. Beginning in the 1940s, artists focused on battle scenes, particularly of the Great Patriotic War. In the 1980s and 1990s, Belarusian painting followed western trends and addressed intellectual and philosophical topics, relying on symbolic meanings and metaphors.

Since the 1980s, decorative and applied arts have been revived. Ceramics, glass, batik, and especially tapestry are popular. Folk art, like weaving from straw, is gaining prominence as well.

**Performance Arts.** Belarusian music shows strong folk and religious influences. During the nineteenth century the collection, publication, and study of Belarusian ethnic songs was begun. Folk influences still inspire many Belarusian composers, and there are many folk music festivals and competitions held annually. Many amateur ensembles of national song and dance, folklore groups, and ensembles of the folklore-scenic form take part in those cultural events.

Belarus has the National Academic Opera and Ballet Theater, as well as the State Musical Comedy Theater and State Symphonic Concert Orchestra. Belarusian opera and ballet are well known and admired internationally. Performing arts centers are found in big cities like Minsk, which has a thriving cultural scene with opera, ballet, theaters, puppet theater, and a circus. Brest also has a renowned puppet theater. Rock music in the Belarusian language first developed in the 1990s.

The Belarusian theater originated from folk traditions from various religious and secular holidays, and from family and domestic rites. One of the longest lasting traditions is puppet theater; it has played a major role in shaping national theatrical traditions. During the eighteenth century, several aristocratic families sponsored their own theaters, and in the twentieth century many new theaters emerged. Today the most famous are the State Theater of Musical Comedy, the Gorkiy State Theater, and the Theater-studio of the Film Actor in Minsk.

Belarusian cinematography tends to focus on heroic and romantic genres, as well as the psychology of characters. Belarusian directors are particularly known for their animated films. There is also an all female film studio in Belarus, Tatyana.

## THE STATE OF THE PHYSICAL AND SOCIAL SCIENCES

All scientific activity is state-funded and organized through academic institutions, universities, or the institutes of the National Academy of Sciences. Belarus has a well-developed scientific community: the National Academy of Sciences, the Belarusian State University, and scientific and research institutes conduct investigations in the fields of quantum electronics, solid-state physics, genetics, chemistry, powder metallurgy, and other research fields.

Traditionally, academic emphasis has been on historical disciplines like archaeology, ethnology, ethnography, history, and art history, but the social sciences like sociology, psychology, and political science are gaining popularity.

## BIBLIOGRAPHY

*Belarus (Now and Then)*, 1993.

Dawisha, Karen. *Democratic Changes and Authoritarian Reactions in Russia, Ukraine, Belarus and Moldova*, 1997.

*Ethnography of Belarus*, 1989.

Garnett, Sherman W., ed. *Belarus at the Crossroad*, 2000.

Kelly, Robert C., ed. *Belarus, Country Review 1999/2000*, 2000.

Levy, Patricia. *Belarus*, 1998.

Marples, David. *Belarus: From Soviet Rule to the Nuclear Catastrophe*, 1996.

———. *Belarus: Denationalized Nation*, 1999.

Novik, Uladzimir. *Belarus: A new country in Eastern Europe*, 1994.

Vakar, Nicholas P. *Belorussia. The Making of a Nation*, 1956.

Zaprudnik, Jan. *Belarus: At a Crossroads in History*, 1993.

———. *Historical Dictionary of Belarus*, 1998.

—LUDOMIR LOZNY

# BELGIUM

## CULTURE NAME

Belgian

## ORIENTATION

**Identification.** *Gallia Belgica* was the Romans' name for the northern part of Gaul, the northern limit of their empire. In early modern times, the name was used as an erudite synonym for the Low Countries. After the 1830 revolution and the establishment of an independent kingdom, Belgium became the official name of the country.

**Location and Geography.** The country is located at the western end of the northern European plain, covering an area of 11,780 square miles (30,510 square kilometers); the neighboring states are France, Luxembourg, Germany, and the Netherlands. The two main rivers are the Schelde and the Meuse, both of which begin in France and flow toward the Netherlands. The land rises progressively toward the south. Flanders (northern part of the country) is less hilly than Wallonia (southern part). The German-speaking population lives at the borders with Germany and Luxembourg. Discoveries of coal in the hills of northern Wallonia led to the early industrialization of the area.

**Demography.** Belgium is one of the most urbanized and densely inhabited countries in the world with about 97 percent of the 10 million inhabitants living in cities in 2000. Brussels, the capital, has approximately 1 million residents, and the second city, Antwerp, has half a million. The central and northern parts of the country are covered by a dense network of medium-size and small cities, and people may live in one city and work in another. Around 55 percent of the population lives in Flanders, 35 percent in Wallonia, and 10 percent in Brussels.

The nation's cultural diversity has been enriched by international and local immigration. The high numbers of Flemish names in the south and Walloon names in the north indicate long time internal mobility. In the last hundred years the most important immigrant groups were Jews who form a sizable community in Antwerp; Poles, who came in the early 1930s and after the fall of communism; Italians (in the 1930s and 1950s); and North Africans and Turks, who arrived in the 1960s. There are many recent immigrants from other countries in the European Union as well as many expatriates working in or around European Union institutions and NATO headquarters. The percentage of noncitizens in the population is high at 15 percent nationally and 28 percent in Brussels.

**Linguistic Affiliation.** The main languages are Dutch and French; they are also the joint official languages. Although German is also recognized as the third national language, it is not used frequently in the national administration. French was introduced as the language of the political elite by feudal lords of French origin, particularly the dukes of Burgundy, who choose Brussels as their main city of residence. In the eighteenth century, French was widely adopted by the bourgeoisie, and in 1830, it was adopted as the official language. Through education and social promotion, French replaced the local dialects in Wallonia and Brussels, but it was not as widely adopted in Flanders.

In Wallonia, a series of Romance dialects rather than a single language were widely spoken but never had official status. Brussels was originally a Flemish city, but the influence of French has always been strongest here, and only a tenth of the population speak Dutch.

The language spoken in Flanders is Dutch, which is commonly called Flemish. The *Taalunie*, an official institution, guarantees the international unity of the Dutch language. There is a great diversity of Flemish dialects which differ in vocabulary and pronunciation. French is still spoken in Flanders by some people in the upper and upper middle

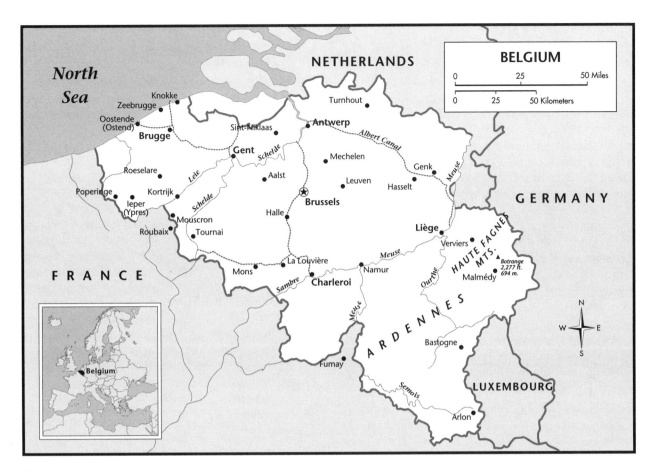

*Belgium*

classes as well as along the linguistic border and around Brussels. The presence of important Francophone minorities in some parts of Flanders has been the source of political conflicts and led in the 1980s to the resignation of several central governments.

**Symbolism.** Political symbolism differs with the region and the sociopolitical environment. The strongest national symbols are the Monarchy and the national soccer team. The national anthem, the *Brabançonne*, is not taught in schools and not widely known. The original song, written during the revolution of 1830, exalted the revolt against the "arbitrary" power of the Dutch king. It was later changed to a milder version that placed obedience to king and law on the same footing as liberty. Symbols are more numerous and more powerful in the Flemish political culture than in the other parts of the country or the nation as a whole.

Much of the mythology in Flanders involves the Lion of Flanders. The lion has been the symbol of the counts of Flanders since the Crusades, and became the symbol of Flemish emancipation since independence.

The oldest elements of Flemish symbolism were developed as Belgian "myths" before the emergence of the Flemish movement. A successful fourteenth-century revolt of cities in the former county of Flanders against a count from the French royal family became an expression of early Flemish/Belgian nationalism. The Flemish national day celebrates the victory of the Flemish militias over the royal French army at the Battle of the Golden Spurs, named after the trophies collected from slain French knights. The Flemish national anthem (the *Vlaamse leeuw*) was composed in 1847. It was adopted as the Flemish movement's anthem in 1900 and became the official anthem of the Flemish community in 1973. Other strong Flemish symbols are the National Song Feast (ANZ) held annually in Antwerp since the early 1930s, in which Flemish songs are mixed with modern expressions of culture.

On the last Sunday of August, the Flemish movement gathers in a pilgrimage at World War I battlefields. Because of the Christian roots of the Flemish movement, the main slogan associated with this has a strong religious connotation. The Walloon movement borrowed the rooster from

France as a cultural symbol. The Francophone community celebrates its national day on 21 September, but it is not emphasized heavily, and an anthem was not adopted until 1999.

In the Middle Ages, Brussels adopted Saint Michael killing the dragon as its patron saint and coat of arms. However, when Brussels became a separate region, its leaders felt they had to find symbols to support the separate identity of the region. They chose the iris and set the regional celebration day in the period in which that flower blossoms.

## HISTORY AND ETHNIC RELATIONS

**Emergence of the Nation.** Although the name of the modern state refers to the original Celtic inhabitants after the Roman conquest in 44 B.C.E., the population was Romanized and adopted the Latin language. Latin gave rise to a series of dialects including, in the southern part of the country, the Walloon dialects. The name "Walloon" derives from a Germanic word meaning "foreign," and refers to the Roman Empire.

Flemish culture came to northern Belgium as a consequence of the Germanic invasions of the fourth century. In the central and southern regions, the Germanic invaders formed small kingdoms and adopted their subjects' culture.

Until the eighth century, conquests and divisions modified the borders of these kingdoms. The last division took place at the treaty of Verdun (843) between the grandsons of Charlemagne, who divided the Holy Roman Empire into three parts, of which the central part, Lotharingia, encompassed the territories between the Netherlands and Italy, including present-day Belgium. However, Lotharingia was absorbed into the German Empire, and the idea of a state between France and the German Empire did not resurface until the fourteenth century. The Burgundian princes inherited, conquered, bought, or received in dowry most of the fiefs constituting the Netherlands, Belgium, and northern and eastern France. They established their court in Brussels and brought the French language to their states. The possessions of the dukes of Burgundy were inherited by the Habsburg dynasty in 1477.

In the middle of the sixteenth century, a religious civil war led to the division of the Low Countries into two parts. The north became the Netherlands, a Dutch-speaking, Protestant state. The south remained Catholic and was associated with the Habsburg dynasty until the French conquest in 1794. Under the Habsburg rulers, the use of Flemish progressively declined, but the position of French was reinforced during the French administration (1794–1814).

After the defeat of Napoleon, the Congress of Vienna established the kingdom of the Netherlands, including present-day Belgium. However, the policy of King Willem I van Oranje Nassau (1772–1843) of favoring the Dutch language and the Protestant religion, led to the revolution of 1830, after which Belgium became independent.

**National Identity.** The Belgian state stipulated freedom of language in its constitution. However, partially as a reaction against the pro-Dutch policy of Willem I, French became the de facto state language. The new government made it the language of administration and education, hoping that it would replace Flemish, Walloon, and German dialects. A Flemish revival initiated by members of the lower clergy and some intellectuals (the so-called Flemish movement) led, over the next two centuries in Flanders, to the progressive replacement of French by Flemish as the language of education, justice, and administration.

In the nineteenth century, the Flemish cultural heritage was an important basis for the definition of a Belgian identity, emphasizing the religious difference with the Netherlands and the wars with France. Thus, the growth of the Flemish movement weakened the feeling of national identity not only in Flanders but in the entire country, leading to the growth of a distinct Brussels identity.

**Ethnic Relations.** The rehabilitation of the Flemish language met with strong resistance from the Francophone establishment and political parties. The "linguistic question" has been the source of political tension for more than a century. In reaction to the Flemish movement, a Walloon movement emerged, mostly linked to the Francophone socialist party. Although the Flemish are the majority population, the Flemish political parties have promoted reforms to protect their language against perceived Francophone domination.

Another Flemish grievance came from the emigration of Francophone inhabitants of Brussels to the surrounding Flemish villages, after which inflation in real estate prices made it impossible for the original Flemish population to stay. The main problem from the Flemish point of view is that the Francophone "migrants" do not learn Dutch but continue to live and work in French-speaking environments and send their children to French schools in Brussels. The Flemish "law of the land" holds that newcomers have to learn the official language

*The three-day carnival at Binche, near Mons, is held just before Lent. During the Gilles carnival men dressed in high, plumed hats and bright costumes lead participants. The majority of Belgians are Catholic.*

of the region. The Francophone population appeals to an individual's rights to speak the language of one's choice, and resents administrative measures favoring the Dutch language in communes situated in Flanders where Francophones constitute 80 percent of the population. More generally, French speakers resent the suppression of French in public administration, public and private education, church services, and business relations. They stress the rights granted to the Flemish minority in Brussels and the petty humiliations faced by the Francophones in the Flemish suburbs. The Flemish feel that their rights in Brussels are justified because that city is the capital of the Flemish region as well as the Belgian state. Most conflicts along the ethnocultural cleavage are fought at the level of politicians, whereas the relations between the population groups remain peaceful.

The main threat to peaceful ethnic relations comes from the extreme-rightist parties, particularly the Vlaams Blok, which thrives on resentment against immigrant communities and the national state. The Vlaams Blok has also recruited some of the most radical elements of the Flemish movement. The rise of the extremist party was historically made possible by the ambiguous attitude of many mainstream Flemish politicians and journalists toward the wartime collaboration of a fraction of the Flemish movement with Nazi Germany. Collaboration in Wallonia was equivalent but was not linked to anything similar to the Flemish movement.

The extreme right in Wallonia has always been fragmented into very small parties, with little political influence. However, one of the main points of the Vlaams Blok, the resentment of the influence of the other language community, is also a major point in the program of the FDF party.

## URBANISM, ARCHITECTURE, AND THE USE OF SPACE

Belgium is essentially a country of medium-size and small cities, many with long histories. In the central parts of these cities, rows of terraced houses are built among a network of ancient churches and marketplaces. Opulent buildings often feature a Belfry in the central marketplace, or, as in Brussels, a city hall and corporation houses.

In nineteenth century, many working-class cities were built in mining and industrial areas. In some cities, new middle-class suburbs were linked to urban centers by large avenues. The stylistic height of this expansion is illustrated by the Art Nouveau houses built by Victor Horta. In the first half of the twentieth century, garden cities were built to provide humane lodgings for the working classes. Today, as the population continues to leave the central cities, one-family houses are organized in small suburban villages.

There is some contrast between the north and south in the use of traditional, rural spaces. While the north has many isolated farms between villages, the southern farms tend to be grouped in villages on both sides of a road.

## FOOD AND ECONOMY

**Food in Daily Life.** Bread and potatoes are the traditional staple foods. Most meals include, pork, chicken, or beef, and Seafood is popular in the northern part of the country. The national drink is beer, but wine is imported in large quantities. In northern cities, popular dishes include mussels with fries and *waterzooi* a broth of vegetables and meat or fish. Throughout the country, French fries are eaten with steaks or minced raw meat. Cooking is traditionally done with butter rather than oil; there is also a high consumption of dairy products. Immigration has ensured a diversity of ''ethnic'' restaurants and is gradually changing the eating habits of the residents in culturally mixed areas.

**Food Customs at Ceremonial Occasions.** Christmas is an occasion for large family meals with grandparents and cousins. There are many other occasions for long meals at public and private celebrations, such as weddings, funerals, and the days devoted to city and parish saints. Pastries are associated with religious and civil occasions. At Christmas, people eat sweet bread in the form of the child Jesus; at Easter, children are told that eggs are dropped in the gardens by flying churchbells; and sugar beans are distributed to those who visit a young mother.

**Basic Economy.** Belgium is heavily dependent on foreign trade. Since the closing of its coal mines in the 1960s, the country has had to import most of its fuel, although it is an important producer of nuclear energy. Although less then 3 percent of the population is involved in agriculture, farm production is very intensive. The southern part of the country has not recovered from the closing down of steel plants and coal mines; the economy of the north, traditionally based on trade and textile manufacturing, has fared better.

**Commercial Activities.** Belgium is considered the world's diamond capital. The annual turnover of the diamond industry was about $23 billion (U.S.) in 1996 and contributed nearly $3 billion (U.S.) to the Belgian economy. Belgium is also an important producer of several industrial minerals, including limestone, dolomite, whiting, sodium sulfate, silica sand, and marble. Livestock raising is the most important single sector of Belgian agriculture, accounting for over 60 percent of agricultural production. In 1998 there were about 3.2 million head of cattle, 7.4 million hogs, 147,000 sheep, and 22,000 horses. Belgian farmers breed some of the finest draft horses in the world, including the famous Percherons.

**Major Industries.** Industry, highly developed in Belgium, is devoted mainly to the processing of imported raw materials into semifinished and finished products, most of which are then exported. Steel production is the single most important sector of industry, with Belgium ranking high among world producers of iron and steel. In 1998, Belgium produced 342,000 tons of crude copper. The country also produces significant amounts of crude zinc and crude lead. The bulk of metal manufactures consists of heavy machinery, structural steelwork, and industrial equipment. The railroad equipment industry supplies one of the most extensive railroad systems in Europe. The textile industry, dating from the Middle Ages, produces cottons, woolens, linens, and synthetic fibers. The chemical industry manufactures a wide range of products, from heavy chemicals and explosives to pharmaceuticals and photographic supplies.

**Trade.** Belgium is heavily dependent on trade, mostly with neighboring European countries (76 percent of exports and 71 percent of imports are with EU partners). More than half the energy is nuclear produced, which makes the country less dependent on imports of fossil fuels. Most of the trade, for imports as for exports, is in machinery, chemicals and metal products. An exception is the important place of cut diamonds in exports. In the past decade, an increasing number of spin-offs of universities has reinforced Belgian exports in high-tech products.

**Division of Labor.** Less than 60 percent of the population was employed as of 1999, including 19.5 percent in part-time jobs. The repartition in sectors is as follows: 73 percent in services, 25 percent in industry, and 2 percent in agriculture.

*People stroll around the botanical gardens in Brussels.*

## SOCIAL STRATIFICATION

***Classes and Castes.*** There is a relatively even distribution of wealth, with 5 to 6 percent living close to the poverty line. The majority of the population is middle class. The vast majority has equal opportunities for education and a professional life. There is a very inclusive social security system.

Deep societal cleavages have led to the construction of "pillars," integrated social structures based on ideology. Although "pillarization" is becoming less important in social life, its influence is clearly noticeable. These pillars encompass every aspect of societal life, including youth, sports and leisure movements, education at all levels, trade unions, health funds, newspapers, and political parties. The three main pillars are the Christian-democrat pillar, the socialist pillar, and the liberal pillar. Until the 1990s, the positions of these pillars were mutually agreed on and anchored through a complex system of "political nominations" in which people with a philosophical affiliation to one of the pillars were appointed to key societal positions as magistrates, top public officials, and leaders of state-controlled companies. The public is turning against this aspect of the pillars, but their influence and power are considerable, especially when their interests are challenged.

The major cleavages are ethnocultural (Flemish speakers versus Francophones), philosophical (the church versus liberals) and economic. The importance of these cleavages has changed over time, often leading to the establishment of new coalitions.

***Symbols of Social Stratification.*** Wealth is most often expressed through houses and cars. In general, there are few external behavioral class markers. The upper classes act discreetly, and people make little distinction between classes or social strata. Exceptions sometimes appear in youth culture, where fashion can turn into a means of social distinction.

## POLITICAL LIFE

***Government.*** Belgium is a federal state, consisting of its three language communities that are responsible for the control of culture and education, and its three regions that are responsible for controlling the economic development, infrastructure, and environment. In Flanders, the institutions of the Dutch-speaking community and the Flemish region have merged, leaving the country with six governments and six parliaments. This complex structure has resulted from the increasing federalization of the country, which in turn has resulted from the de-

*The market square in Bruges. There are numerous ethnic restaurants in Belgium, due to immigration.*

mands for more cultural autonomy in each language community, as well as demands for control over local economic development.

The political system is based on discussion and compromise between different interest groups. The term ''Belgian compromise'' applies to solutions reached in this way: complex issues are settled by conceding something to every party. The resulting agreements often leave room for interpretation due to their complexity.

**Leadership and Political Officials.** The major political parties are the Liberals, Socialists, and Christian-Democrats, complemented by regionalist parties as the *VolksUnie* and the extreme right-wing *Vlaams Blok* in Flanders. Their Francophone counterpart is the Front Démocratique des Francophones (FDF). In some communes on the linguistic border and in Brussels, Francophone and Flemish parties form cross-political union lists such as Union des Francophones (UF) or Samen. The green parties entered the federal government coalition in 1999. All political parties (with the exception of the regionalist parties), have evolved from unitary parties into a Flemish party and a Walloon party since the 1970s. Politicians often rise through the pillars, mostly in Flanders; in Wallonia and Brussels, on the other hand, politicians usually have a stronger local

base, often as mayors. The few independent candidates with political potential are quickly recruited by the parties.

**Social Problems and Control.** Policing and the judiciary are organized at the national level. After a major police reform in 1999, there will be one police force with authority to operate in the entire nation. Delays in handling cases in Brussels are often related to a lack of bilingual magistrates. In recent years, civilian patrols without legal powers of intervention have come into existence, but their function is mainly to deter robbers.

Informal social control is much stronger in small villages and towns than it is in large cities. Organized crime is rare except in drug trafficking, prostitution, and illegal immigration. Organized crime is mostly controlled by foreign criminals such as the Russian mafia. There are relatively few murders and armed robberies. The most common crime is property theft.

**Military Activity.** Belgium is a member of NATO, and its military forces have been completely integrated into the alliance. The military has to live with tight budgets, and military expenditure is seen as a necessity, not a source of national pride. The military is professional and separate from the rest of society and is subject to strong parliamentary control.

## SOCIAL WELFARE AND CHANGE PROGRAMS

A series of Public Centers of Social Aid (CPAS) exist in the cities, supporting impoverished residents. A ministry of social promotion supports initiatives for the reduction of inequality.

## NONGOVERNMENTAL ORGANIZATIONS AND OTHER ASSOCIATIONS

Belgium hosts many international organizations and hundreds of lobbying-groups, but their presence has little direct impact on social life. The most influential organizations are the Catholic Church and its affiliates and social organizations related to the pillars, such as trade unions.

## GENDER ROLES AND STATUSES

**Division of Labor by Gender.** The occupational gender gap is decreasing, particularly among younger generations (67.5 percent of men working versus 50.2 percent of women working). In fact, the higher occupational rate of women is due to an increase in part-time jobs in services: less than 3 percent of men work part-time, but nearly 30 percent of women do.

**The Relative Status of Men and Women.** The unemployment rate in (1999) was slightly lower for men than for women. The wage differentials between men and woman are the lowest in the European Union, with women earning on average 91 percent of a man's salary.

## MARRIAGE, FAMILY AND KINSHIP

**Marriage.** There are no social or ethnic barriers to marriage, although proximity and social models influence the choice of a spouse. Young people marry and have children less often and later than former generations did. The divorce rate has increased to about one in three marriages.

**Domestic Unit.** The domestic unit usually is composed of the parents and up to three children, although immigrants from North Africa often have more children. Women still do more of the domestic work, but this is perceived as a matter of negotiation by the couple.

**Inheritance.** In the absence of a will, the children inherit equally from a deceased parent. However, if one spouse survives the other, he or she keeps the entire estate. The law limits the proportion of the estate that can be disposed of by will, depending on the number of children.

**Kin Groups.** The extension of the family group generally is limited to first cousins. However, there are a growing number of family associations in the upper and middle classes through which the descendants of an individual gather once or twice a year.

## SOCIALIZATION

**Child Rearing and Education.** The values parents attempt to transmit to their children are honesty, good manners, tolerance, and responsibility, but there are regional and class differences. Obedience and cleanliness are considered most important in Flanders and among workers, the unemployed, and shopkeepers; loyalty and courage are important in Wallonia; and independence and autonomy are more appreciated in Brussels and among university graduates, executives, civil servants and shopkeepers. The trend, however, shows a weakening of these oppositions, most notably between religious and hard work values in Flanders and socialist values in Wallonia.

Since 1956 all public and private schools have been supported by the state, and education is virtually free. In theory, access to the best schools depends on grades, language, location, and social position influence parental choice. Children must remain in full-time education until age sixteen and in part-time until age eighteen.

**Higher Education.** In arts, business, teacher training, and nursing, higher education is organized outside universities. Education is federalized and is conducted in the language of the individual region. Although language education in generally very good, there are no official bilingual institutions. The Catholic University of Louvain and the Free University of Brussels are divided into Flemish and Francophone parts. State universities are located in provincial towns. A high percentage of young people enter higher education (there were 307,000 students in higher education in 2000).

## ETIQUETTE

There are not many interactions in the streets, as residential, working and leisure areas tend to be distinct. Among young people, especially Franco-

*A stone bridge crossing a canal in Bruges. The north part of Belgium consists of isolated farms between villages, while the south tends to contain larger groups of farms.*

phones, girls rarely shake hands but kiss other girls and boys.

## RELIGION

***Religious Beliefs***. Catholicism is the main religious faith. The government financially supports the Catholic and Protestant churches as well as the Jewish and Muslim faiths. The Catholic Church controls an important network of schools with 70 percent of the pupils in secondary education and two main universities. Religious beliefs and practice declined during the twentieth century, but approximately 65 percent of Belgians believe in God. Many people who say they do not believe in God take part in religious rituals for major events such as baptisms, weddings, and funerals. Minority faiths include Muslims, Jews, and Protestants.

## MEDICINE AND HEALTH CARE

There is a modern health system with state, university, and private hospitals. Health insurance is mandatory and is paid for by employers. Self-employed people must have insurance for major risks and pay according to their income.

## SECULAR CELEBRATIONS

Many important secular celebrations are linked to the ethnic identity of the Flemish and the Francophones. Labor Day on 1 May and World War I Armistice Day are national holidays. The National Day on 21 July commemorates the taking of an oath of fidelity to the Constitution by the first king, Leopold I (1790–1865). Mardi Gras is celebrated in several cities.

## THE ARTS AND HUMANITIES

***Support for the Arts***. Aspiring artists and musicians receive training in evening schools that are free of charge and accessible in most of the country. At the postsecondary level, there are many state-supported conservatories and art schools. An extensive network of art galleries supports avant-garde and traditional artists. Museums in the main cities also support artists by buying some of their work and making it known to the public.

***Literature***. Sometimes it is denied that there is a Belgian literature, with only Flemish and Walloon or French and Dutch writers who happen to be Belgian citizens. However, authors such as Charles

*A typical farm in West Flanders. Livestock raising is the most important sector of Belgian agriculture.*

de Coster (1827–1879) and Emile Verhaeren (1855–1916), wrote in French on Flemish themes. Another important Francophone writer from Flanders was the symbolist Maurice Maeterlinck. The main nineteenth-century Flemish writers were Hendrik Conscience and Guido Gezelle. Flemish and Francophone writers contributed to important literary movements such as symbolism, surrealism, and magic realism. Important themes are the hardness of life, the questioning of the nature of reality, and the quest for original ways to get through life. The distrust of authority was present in one of the oldest Flemish tales, Reynard the Fox, in which the small fox outsmarts the larger animals.

***Graphic Arts.*** The golden age of graphic arts lasted from the fourteenth century to the seventeenth century and was embodied mostly in painting. The Flemish Primitives school of painting (fourteenth and fifteenth centuries) made the region the main artistic center of Europe outside of Italy. Artists such as Jan Van Eyck (1395–1441) and Rogier Van Der Weyden (1400–1464) were interested in spatial composition and psychology and rendered the colors and textures of living and material objects with realism. The main artistic figure of the next century was Pieter Breughel the Elder (1525–1569), with his lively paintings of peasant life.

Pieter Paul Rubens (1577–1640) was the most famous painter of his time, receiving commissions from European sovereigns. His main focus was on the human figure. Rubens influenced Anthony Van Dyk (1599–1641) and Jacob Jordaens (1593–1678). The graphic arts declined until the late nineteenth century, when James Ensor and René Magritte (in the twentieth century) revived the avant-garde. The most innovative works of living artists can be seen in contemporary art museums in Antwerp and Ghent.

**Performance Arts**. The Franco-Flemish style dominated European music in the fifteenth and sixteenth centuries, with composers such as Josquin des Prez and Orlando di Lasso. In the twentieth century, the most famous Belgian musician was the singer Jacques Brel. Several living classical composers are active. The harmonica player Toots Thielemans is the most famous jazz musician. The Blindman Kwartet combines jazz, pop, and classical music.

The presence in Brussels between 1959 and 1987 of the French choreographer Maurice Béjart stimulated a new generation of choreographers. The main theatrical centers are De Singel in Antwerp and the Kaai Teater in Brussels. Several theaters and orchestras are supported by the government.

## BIBLIOGRAPHY

Bawin-Legros Bernadette, ed. *Familles, Modes d'Emploi: Étude Sociologique des Ménages Belges*, 1999.

Cloet, M., and F. Daelemans, eds. *Godsdienst, Mentaliteit en Dagelijks Leven: Religieuze Geschiedenis in België sinds 1970/Religion, Mentalité et Vie Quotidienne: Histoire Religieuse en Belgique depuis 1970*, 1987.

Hoet, Jan, ed. *S.M.A.K. The Collections of the Museum of Contemporary Art/Ghent*, 1999.

Foblets, Marie-Claire. *Les Familles Maghrébines et la Justice en Belgique: Anthropologie Juridique et Immigration*, 1994.

Geirlandt K. J., ed. *L'Art en Belgique depuis 1945*, 1983.

Hasquin, Hervé, ed. *Dictionnaire d'histoire de Belgique: les hommes, les institutions, les faits, le Congo belge et le Ruanda-Urundi*, 2000.

Hermans, Theo, Louis Vos, and Lode Wils, eds. *The Flemish movement: A Documentary History*, 1992.

Heyrman, Peter. *Middenstandsbeweging en Beleid in Belgie, 1918–1940: Tussen Vrijheid en Regulering*, 1998.

Pearson, Raymond. *The Longman Companion to European Nationalism 1789–1920*, 1994.

Ruys, Manu. *The Flemings: A People on the Move–A Nation in Being*, 1973.

Schryver, Reginald de, ed. *Nieuwe Encyclopedie van de Vlaamse Beweging*. 1998.

Vande Putte G. *Belgica Creola: Le Contact des Langues en Périphérie Bruxelloise/Taalcontact in de Brusselse Periferie*, 1999.

Verstraete, Pieter Jan. *Bibliografie van de Vlaamse Beweging: Deel 5: 1986–1990*, 1998.

Voyé, Liliane, et al. *Belges, Heureux et satisfaits: Les Valeurs des Belges dans les Années 90*, 1992.

Witte, Els, Lode Vraeybeckx, Alain Meynen, *Politieke Geschiedenis van België*, 1990.

—JEAN DE LANNOY
AND RUBEN A. LOMBAERT

# BELIZE

## CULTURE NAME
Belizean

## ORIENTATION

**Identification.** Previously called British Honduras, the country now known as Belize derives its name from one of two historical sources: Maya root words or the surname of the Scottish buccaneer Peter Wallace, who maintained a camp near present-day Belize City in the seventeenth century. Belizeans affectionately refer to their country as "the Jewel."

The formation of a consciousness of a national culture coincided with the growth of the nationalist movement in the 1950s toward independence. It was a phenomenon that occurred simultaneously among neighboring British West Indian colonies.

Ethnic and geographic identification coincides with the areas where ethnic groups settled. In the north and west there are the *mestizos*, people formed by the union of Spaniards and Maya. In the central part, there are the Creoles, formed by the intermarriage of the British and their African slaves. In the south, there are the Garifuna, also called Black Caribs, along the coast and the Maya farther inland.

The building of the capital city, Belmopan, in the late 1960s was a crowning achievement of the nationalist movement, radically transforming the settlement pattern. The immediate reason was to rebuild after the massive destruction of the old capital, Belize City, by a hurricane in 1961; another reason was to attract the population into the hinterland to engage in agriculture, which the government was promoting to replace timber, the hallmark of the colonial economy. The government was attempting to build a national culture emerging from colonialism with a new settlement pattern and a new economy.

**Location and Geography.** Belize is at the southern end of the Yucatan peninsula, facing the Caribbean Sea. It covers 8,866 square miles (23,000 square kilometers) and has the second largest barrier reef in the world, which shelters scores of cays.

**Demography.** Immigration has been a major demographic factor. The latest massive inflow came from Latinos in the neighboring countries fleeing the civil unrest of the 1980s. Together with the long-resident Spanish-speaking group, they have become the largest ethnic group, according to the census of 1991. This group numbered 81,275, or 44 percent, of the national population of 189,392. The other main groups are the Creoles, 55,386 (30 percent); Maya, 20,447 (11 percent); and Garifuna, 12,343 (7 percent). While immigration has built the population, emigration has introduced a transnational fluidity between Belize and the United States. Since the 1960s thousands have left to settle in American cities, although many of those people retain family ties in Belize.

**Linguistic Affiliation.** The different groups speak their own languages, but the language spoken across ethnic lines is a form of pidgin English called Creole. There is much bilingualism and multilingualism. English is taught in all primary schools; however, its use is limited to official discourse and it appears more often in the written form than in the spoken.

**Symbolism.** The proponents of the nationalist movement introduced symbols as essential parts of the national culture they were crafting in the 1960s and 1970s. Prominent among them were the national bird, the toucan; tree, mahogany; and animal, tapir. In official discourse there was increasing use of the term "fatherland" to galvanize public sentiment away from a distant colonial power to a new nation state rooted in the cultural history of the Maya, the aboriginal settlers of the subregion.

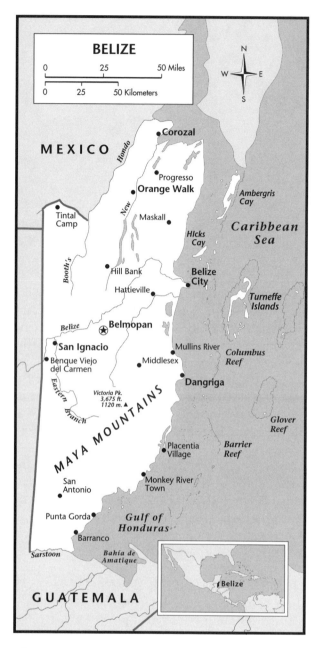

*Belize*

# HISTORY AND ETHNIC RELATIONS

**Emergence of the Nation.** The metamorphosis of Belize from a colony to a nation followed a set procedure postwar Britain had followed with dozens of other colonies: handing over the instruments of political power gradually to a democratically elected leadership. In Belize, the steps included introducing adult suffrage in 1954 and internal self-government in 1964, concluding an agreement with Guatemala to continue negotiations over its claims to Belizean territory, and gaining full independence on 21 September 1981.

**National Identity.** The development of a national identity became a task for the political party that won all the elections until 1984, becoming the voice of the nationalist movement and therefore earning the right to receive the instruments of statehood from Britain. Heading the party was an elite group whose members were Creole, urban-based, well educated, and mainly of lighter skin color.

**Ethnic Relations.** Transforming the nature of ethnic relations was a crucial task for the emerging political elite. The major change was from a British-imposed pecking order to a system in which all ethnic groups would have full access to the rights and privileges of citizenship. It was a deliberately inclusive approach that was popular and gave the impression of generating full public participation.

# URBANISM, ARCHITECTURE, AND THE USE OF SPACE

At a distribution rate of eight persons per square kilometer, Belize has one of the lowest population densities in the hemisphere. The impact of underpopulation and the dispersed location of communities becomes clear when traveling through the countryside for miles and finding clusters of small villages nucleated around small towns. Traditionally, communities were built along waterways—both seacoast and riverbanks— to facilitate the transportation of timber logs for export. This basic pattern still remains for almost all the towns.

Another trait reflective of the earlier easy availability of timber is the predominance of wood as the basic material for housing. Hurricane devastation, however, has led to the greater use of ferro-concrete for building after 1960.

The architecture has also changed with the use of the main building material. Up to the middle of this century the design of houses was influenced by styles from the turn of the twentieth century found throughout the British West Indies.

At the private level the current small sizes of houses for the large numbers of occupants leads to relatively small space available for individuals. On the other hand, there has been too little allocation of space for public parks, where children and adults can spend recreation time. The country's landscape, therefore, consists of a series of small but congested communities, an irony for a country with abundant land.

## FOOD AND ECONOMY

**Food in Daily Life.** Imported bleached wheat flour, corn, beans, rice, and poultry are the daily staples. There are hardly any food taboos, but there are beliefs across ethnic groups that certain foods, notably soups and drinks, help restore health.

**Food Customs at Ceremonial Occasions.** Apart from specific preferences for some food items at large religious ceremonies, especially among the Garifuna, the items eaten at ceremonies are basically those eaten daily. At such ceremonies, there are usually store-bought alcoholic beverages. Only in some rural communities are home-fermented fruit wines drunk.

**Basic Economy and Trade.** The national currency is known as the Belizean dollar. In the 1990s, there were periods when the country was self-sufficient in corn, rice, beans, poultry, pork, and beef, marking the first time that demand for those staples was satisfied consistently. However, the third largest import is food, which in 1996 amounted to 17 percent of total imports.

Food production for export receives favorable treatment by the government, including lobbying for international markets. The result is that food items—mainly sugar, citrus, and banana—accounted for 86 percent of exports in 1996 and contributed almost 80 percent of foreign exchange earnings.

**Land Tenure and Property.** The most pervasive legacy of colonialism in the modern economy is the concentration of land in large holdings owned by foreigners who use the land for speculation. This monopoly resulted in only 15 percent of the land available for agriculture being used for that purpose in the early 1980s. The government has never had a comprehensive land redistribution policy.

**Commercial Activities and Major Industries.** The gross domestic product (GDP) index shows the services sector (including banks, restaurants, hotels and personal services) as the largest, totaling 57 percent of a total GDP of $718 million in 1996. Within this sector, trades, restaurants, and hotels made up 18 percent. The main industry in the private sector remains agriculture, with fishing and logging lagging far behind.

**Division of Labor.** The most significant characteristic of the division of labor is the extensive movement of people, including foreign laborers entering agricultural industries andservice workers moving from their communities to areas where jobs are

*Two boys carry firewood in Maya Centre.*

available. Agriculture supplies about 30 percent of all jobs. It consists of manual labor dominated by men from Honduras and Guatemala. Belizeans predominate in professional jobs and white-collar services. They commute daily from various parts of the country or stay during the week in Belmopan, Belize City, and the cays, where tertiary-sector jobs are available.

## SOCIAL STRATIFICATION

**Classes and Castes.** While there is the traditional stratification into ethnic groups in the countryside, in urban communities there are conspicuous degrees of socioeconomic inequality in which skin color supersedes ethnicity. At the highest level, there are lighter-skinned Creoles, mestizos, and newly arrived North Americans, east Indians, and Middle Easterners. At the lower levels, there are darker-skinned Creoles and Garifuna. The highest levels retain control of the two political parties and the retail trade and other services in the tertiary sector. Those in the lower levels are largely unemployed.

The Maya and Garifuna demonstrate the surviving tribal traits of the aboriginal peoples. Both have the highest levels of poverty and participate least in the political and socioeconomic arenas. The

Maya are subdivided into the Mopan and Ketchi peoples.

## POLITICAL LIFE

***Government.*** The government is a parliamentary democracy, and there is separation of the executive, legislature, and judiciary. However, the political parties have virtually eliminated the power of the legislature in favor of a cabinet of ministers.

***Leadership and Political Officials.*** The Peoples United Party and the United Democratic Party provide the informal mechanisms that make the formal structures of the government function. Both draw support across all ethnic groups and social classes. All members of the government maintain openness to the public and encourage their constituents to communicate with them.

***Social Problems and Control.*** The police force is the first line of intervention against crime. However, the police are active only in urban communities and the few villages with police stations. The judiciary is a survival from the British system, and appeals can still proceed as far as the Privy Council in London. Locally, the formal functioning of the system is jeopardized by a lack of judges, magistrates, and prosecutors, resulting in a backlog of cases.

The violent crimes that occur most frequently are murder and manslaughter, rape, and indecent assault. The most prevalent property crimes are larceny, theft, burglary, and robbery.

***Military Activity.*** The national army provides protection against Guatemala, which in the past threatened to invade and implement its claim to Belizean territory. The army also is involved in drug interdiction efforts and assists in disaster preparedness and relief.

## SOCIAL WELFARE, CHANGE PROGRAMS, AND NONGOVERNMENTAL ORGANIZATIONS

The government provides minimal amounts of money as relief for the indigent and for the public in times of disaster. Social change programs are targeted at groups such as youth, refugees, and the poor, usually in cooperation with multilateral agencies. The programs have been primarily ameliorative rather than focusing on skills and entrepreneurial training.

Several nongovernmental organizations are the intermediaries for international funding for these

*The exterior of a healer's hut, Panti Maya Medicinal Trail. Most people go to Mexico or Guatemala for Western medical treatment.*

programs. Starting in the 1980s, the nongovernmental organizations have carried out many programs in raising social consciousness, research, environmental conservation, and economic development. With the steady dwindling of international support the nongovernmental organizations have declined in numbers. The few remaining are seriously attempting to finds alternative sources of support locally. They are increasingly factoring voluntarism within their support base. Such voluntarism had been the cornerstone of voluntary organizations that preceded the current crop of nongovernmental organizations in community self-help.

## GENDER ROLES AND STATUSES

***Division of Labor by Gender.*** Only a few women participate in the political, economic, social, and religious spheres; for example, among the twenty-nine elected members of the House of Representatives, there are only two women. A similar pattern exists in the religious ministries and the private sector.

***The Relative Status of Women and Men.*** Gender status tends to be more equitable at the levels of the household and the smaller community. Nominally there are more women-headed households among the Garifuna and Creole than among the Maya and mestizos. However, even among the Creole and Garifuna, deference is shown to male partners or relatives—whether they are co-resident or not—if they contribute financially and morally to the well-being of the household. In many rural communities, men and women function equally as shamans and healers.

## MARRIAGE, FAMILY, AND KINSHIP

**Marriage.** Despite a tradition of openly accepted liaisons, there has always been a high social value placed on church-blessed unions. Among the Creoles and Garifuna, there may be prolonged common-law unions that are eventually recognized. Among the Maya, men and women start their conjugal lives before age 18 years life. Mestizos start a few years later and tend to remain in long-lasting unions. There are stringent requirements for divorce, but partners of broken marriages often live with others in common-law unions.

**Domestic Unit and Kin Groups.** Childbearing is not confined within the domestic unit among many Belizeans. The first child or two may be born without any agreement between the parents to form a domestic unit. This leads to high rates of illegitimacy in some ethnic groups. For example, between 1970 and 1980, illegitimacy among the Creole and Garifuna was 70 to 80 percent, whereas among mestizos it was around 40 percent.

The separation of childbearing from domesticity leads to a need for extended families, which are primarily cognate kin groups. Apart from child rearing, the functions performed by kin groups include labor exchange and providing general support in times of need.

**Inheritance.** Most Belizeans die intestate but abide by the spirit of the laws governing inheritance. Priority is given to legal spouses and children whether from a legal marriage or not. Similar legislation was being planned in 1999 for surviving common-law spouses.

## SOCIALIZATION

**Child Rearing and Education.** Child rearing and early education are areas where urban people expect government support. Traditional practice persist in rural communities, where child rearing is provided by the extended family.

By law, a child has to attend primary school up to age fourteen. Through rote memory, a child learns the three R's and develops an appreciation of the national culture as well as learning basic Christian beliefs. Only 40 percent of primary school leavers go on to secondary schools because of poor performance in the national school-leaving examination and for lack space and limited funds for uniforms, textbooks, and fees.

**Higher Education.** Less than 1 percent of the population qualifies for higher education. A national university that was started in 1987 offers a limited range of programs; it has a student population of less than five hundred. The country also subscribes to the University of the West Indies, where annually about fifty Belizeans start their studies.

## RELIGION

**Religious Beliefs.** Christianity is the main religion. Most of the people are Roman Catholics, Anglican, Methodists, Baptists, or Mennonites. There are some Moslems and Hindus.

**Religious Practitioners.** The power of churches comes from their spiritual strength as well as from the state. State law allows for the incorporation of churches, relieving them from paying taxes. Ministers are state-sanctioned marriage officers, and the state integrates them as copartners in managing the vast majority of primary schools.

**Rituals and Holy Places.** Belize City and Belmopan are important sites for religious denominations. The Anglican Saint John's Cathedral was consecrated in Belize City in 1826. Roman Catholics have cathedrals in Belize City and Belmopan.

**Death and Afterlife.** In the areas of death and the afterlife, the non-Christian belief systems of the ethnic groups are most noticeable. Most groups celebrate elaborate ceremonies on behalf of the deceased. All the ethnic groups believe that their ancestors can intervene to influence events daily life.

## MEDICINE AND HEALTH CARE

Because of the inadequacy of the health care system, Belizeans use the medical services in Guatemala and Mexico. Many also resort to traditional systems, which employ amulets, plants, baths, incantations, and ancestral rituals. While Western-trained health workers once ostracized practitioners of the traditional system, the government has advocated some collaboration in the case of birth attendants.

*A house on stilts in Placencia. Hurricane damage has lead to more use of ferro-concrete in post-1960s dwellings.*

## SECULAR CELEBRATIONS

Three secular holidays predate the nationalist movement. Baron Bliss Day on 9 March celebrates a British benefactor who established a trust fund for the country's welfare. Commonwealth Day on the fourth Monday in May celebrates participation the British Commonwealth of Nations. Saint George's Caye Day on 10 September commemorates the victory by settlers in the last military effort of Spain to retake Belize in 1798. Holidays introduced as a result of the nationalist movement and later independence are 1 May, 21 September, 12 October, and 19 November. International Labour Day occurs on 1 May, 21 September marks the day Belize acquired independence in 1981, 12 October is Pan American Day, and 19 November commemorates the arrival and settlement of the Garifuna people.

## THE ARTS AND HUMANITIES

Artists support themselves primarily by selling their works at exhibitions and performing at concerts. The buyers include wealthy Belizeans who display art for their private pleasure. The National Arts Council promotes training and the display of various forms of art.

***Literature, Graphic Arts, and Performance Arts.*** A small body of written literature is published locally. There is a potentially rich source of oral literature, but hardly any is preserved in writing. The best developed graphic arts are painting and sculpture. Sculpture builds on a rich tradition of the use of wood. Mainly self-taught persons whose work demonstrates folkloric dimensions engage in painting and sculpture. A similar localized mode prevails in the performance arts, except drama and dance. Regional and international plays are performed in schools and occasionally for the public. There is much public support for those events.

*Punta* rock music is a component of the national culture that was created in the early 1980s by the Garifuna. It has become popular along the Caribbean coast of Central America.

## THE STATE OF THE PHYSICAL AND SOCIAL SCIENCES

Foreign scientists mainly from North America do almost all the scientific research in the country. Studies in the fields of Maya archaeology, natural history, and the physical environment are primary contributors to our understanding of the significance of Belize within the subregion. Plans for consolidation of the University College of Belize includes promoting research for its students and faculty.

## BIBLIOGRAPHY

Bolland, O. Nigel. *New Nation in Central America*, 1986.

————. *Colonialism and Resistance in Belize: Essays in Historical Sociology*, 1988.

Dobson, Narda. *A History of Belize*, 1973

Government of Belize. *Belize Estimates of Revenue and Expenditure for Fiscal Year 1999/2000 as Passed by the House of Representatives on Friday, 20 March 1999*, 1999.

————. *Abstract of Statistics, Belize 1998*, 1998.

Krohn, Hunter Lita, et al., eds. *Readings in Belizean History*, 2d ed., 1987.

Palacio, I. Myrtle. *Who and What in Belizean Elections 1954 to 1993*, 1993.

————. *Redefining Ethnicity: The experiences of the Garifuna and Creole*, 1995.

Palacio, Joseph O. *Development in Belize 1960–1980*, 1996.

Phillips, Michael D., ed. *Belize: Selected Proceedings from the Second Inter disciplinary Conference on Belize*, 1996.

Shoman, Assad. "The Birth of the Nationalist Movement in Belize 1950–1954." *Journal of Belizean Affairs* 2: 3–40, 1973.

————. *Party Politics in Belize 1950–1986*, 1987.

Stone, Michael Cutler. *Caribbean Nation, Central American State: Ethnicity, Race, and National formation in Belize, 1798–1990*, 1994.

UNICEF. *A Situation Analysis of Children in Belize 1997*, 1997.

Vernon, Dylan. *International Migration and Development in Belize: An Overview of Determinants and Effects of Recent Movement*, 1988.

Wilk, Richard, and Mac Chapin. *Ethnic Minorities in Belize: Mopan, Kekchi, and Garifuna*, 1990.

—JOSEPH O. PALACIO

# BENIN

## CULTURE NAME

Beninese

## ORIENTATION

**Identification.** Before 1975, the Republic of Benin was known as Dahomey, its French colonial name. Three years after the coup that brought Major Kérékou to power, the name was changed to the People's Republic of Benin, reflecting the Marxist-Leninist ideology of the new government. After the collapse of the Kérékou government in 1989, the name was shortened to the Republic of Benin. In the precolonial period, Dahomey was the name of the most powerful kingdom on the Slave Coast, which extended along the Bight of Benin to Lagos. Today Benin includes not only the ancient Fon kingdom of Dahomey but also areas inhabited by many other groups.

The nation's lack of cultural homogeneity is due to geographic factors and a history that has included waves of migration, competition between precolonial kingdoms, four centuries of commercial relations with Europe, and the impact of colonialism. In addition to language and ethnicity, there are divisions along lines of occupation and religion.

**Location and Geography.** The country has an area of 43,483 square miles (112,622 square kilometers). It shares borders with Niger, Burkina Faso, Nigeria, and Togo. There are five distinct geographic zones. In the south, coconut palms grow on a narrow coastal strip broken by lagoons and creeks. In the north, a plateau of fertile iron clay soil interspersed with marshy areas supports oil palms. The central area is a wooded savanna with some hilly areas. The Atacora mountain chain in the northwest is the area of greatest elevation, while the northeast is part of the Niger river basin. Most of the country has a tropical climate with a dry season from November to April and a rainy season from May to October. Rainfall and vegetation are heaviest in the south.

The country is divided into six departments containing eighty-four districts. The capital is Porto-Novo, but the seat of government is in nearby Cotonou, the largest city.

**Demography.** The current population is estimated to be about 6.5 million and is concentrated in the southern and central regions. The growth rate is high, and 48 percent of the people are less than fifteen years old.

**Linguistic Affiliation.** French is the national language, and English is taught in secondary schools. There are about fifty languages and dialects. Most people speak at least two languages. Fifty percent of the population speaks Fon; other important languages include Yoruba, Aja, Mina, Goun, Bariba, Dendi, Ditamarri, Nateni, and Fulfulde. Approximately 36 percent of the population is illiterate.

**Symbolism.** The flag first flown after independence was green, red, and yellow. Green denoted hope for renewal, red stood for the ancestors' courage, and yellow symbolized the country's treasures. In 1975, the flag was changed to green with a red star in the corner. In 1990, the original flag was reestablished to symbolize the rejection of Marxist ideology.

## HISTORY AND ETHNIC RELATIONS

**Emergence of the Nation.** Although several ethnic groups are assumed to be indigenous, migration that began four hundred years ago brought Aja-speaking peoples (the Gbe) into the southern part of the country, where they founded several kingdoms. The Yoruba presence in the southern and central regions also dates back several hundred years. The Bariba migrated west from what is now Nigeria and established a cluster of states. In the northwest,

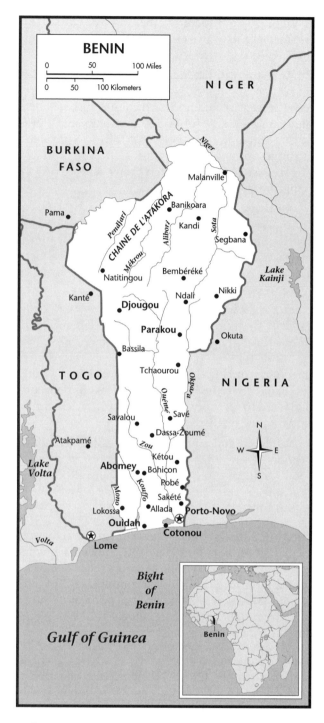

*Benin*

several indigenous groups remained independent of Bariba control.

The Portuguese were the first Europeans to make contact at Ouidah (Whydah) in 1580s; Dutch, French, and English traders followed. The coastal communities became part of an emerging trans-Atlantic trading system.

In the seventeenth century, slaves became the most important commodity, traded for manufactured items. At first the trade took place with coastal kingdoms, but the interior kingdom of Dahomey later conquered those kingdoms. Although a tributary of the Yoruba kingdom Oyo from 1740 to 1818, Dahomey dominated the regional slave trade. Traders dealt directly with the royalty of Dahomey, who continued to sell slaves to Brazilian merchants after the 1830s. Merchants and travelers wrote about the power of the Dahomean monarch, his army of "amazons" (female warriors), and ceremonies that included human sacrifice.

The French presence and influence increased after 1840 as a result of commercial and missionary activity. Tension with France increased as competition between European imperial powers escalated. France engaged in three military campaigns against Dahomey, and in 1894 King Behanzin surrendered and was exiled. By 1900, the Bariba had been defeated and the new boundaries had been determined. From 1904 to 1958, Dahomey was a colony in the federation of French West Africa.

Colonial rule forced the people to accept a new system of central administration, heavy taxation, forced labor, and harsh laws. France conscripted men to fight in both world wars. By the end of World War II, the economy was weak and growing discontent was difficult to manage.

After World War II, France followed a policy of increased representation and autonomy. During this period, a triumvirate of leaders emerged who would dominate national politics for decades. In 1958, Dahomey chose independence, which was declared in 1960. Hubert Maga was elected as the first president. His term was interrupted by a military coup in 1963, the first of six in the next nine years.

**National Identity.** Political turmoil before and after independence was not conducive to the formation of a national identity. The Kérékou regime and the seventeen-year experiment with socialism stabilized the country under a central bureaucracy. In the early years of his rule, Kérékou's called for the creation of a nation less aligned with French commercial and cultural interests. After the government adopted a Marxist-Leninist ideology in 1974, a rhetoric of national unity and "the revolution" permeated the media and government propaganda, but even today national identity is secondary to ethnic identity for much of the rural population.

**Ethnic Relations.** Beninese recognize about twenty sociocultural groups. In some cases, a cultural cluster is associated with one or more of the ancient kingdoms. The Fon (founders of the Dahomey kingdom) are the largest group. Their language is closely related to that of the Aja and Goun, and there are close ethnic ties with those groups as a result of shared precolonial history. Lines of cleavages create constantly changing northern, southern, and south-central coalitions of leaders who vie for control of limited resources and political power.

The Afro-Brazilian community in the south is descended from European traders, Africans who lived near European trading establishments, and traders and returned slaves from Brazil.

The educated peoples of the more urbanized southern region have dominated the nation's political and economic life. The teachers and civil servants who were given posts in the north were considered to be as foreign as the Europeans.

Benin is also home to Fulani herders known locally as the Peul. These herders move their livestock over long distances in search of grass. Even when they become sedentary, the Fulani maintain a unique cultural identity. Many of them serve in the military.

## URBANISM, ARCHITECTURE, AND THE USE OF SPACE

More than 40 percent of the population lives in urban environments, primarily in Cotonou. Cities have a mixture of modern and colonial architecture. Although some Cotonou residents live in multistory apartment buildings, their neighborhoods usually consist of walled compounds. In small towns and villages, new houses tend to be built from concrete block with metal roofs, but many are constructed from mud bricks and roofed with thatch. Large towns have both mosques and churches, and every town has at least one open-air market.

## FOOD AND ECONOMY

*Food in Daily Life.* Even in many urban areas, cooking is done outside or, when it rains, in a separate room or shelter. Women and girls cook family meals, although more young men are learning to cook. Because many homes do not have refrigeration, most people go to the market several times a week to purchase food.

The basic meal consists of a staple starch prepared as a sort of mush, eaten with a sauce that contains vegetables and meat or fish. Food is prepared at least twice a day: at midday and in the evening. The morning meal may consist of warmed-up leftovers from the previous evening's meal or food purchased from roadside vendors.

In the south, rice, corn, and manioc are the primary starches; millet, sorghum, and yams are preferred in central and northern communities. Sauces may contain okra, tomatoes, pumpkin seeds, peanuts, eggplant, peppers, and other vegetables. Legumes may be made into side dishes. In the marshy areas, carrots, green beans, and lettuce are being incorporated into the diet.

Beninese also eat many varieties of tropical fruits. Traditionally palm wine was produced in the south, while millet beer was brewed and consumed by the northern peoples. Today alcoholic beverages are likely to be imported.

Smoked, dried, or fresh fish is likely to accompany a meal in the south, while beef is more common in the north. Goats, sheep, and poultry are found throughout the country. Poor people often eat meals with no protein. "European" foods were introduced during the colonial period. Many young people perceive the traditional diet as monotonous and want to eat more expensive and often less nutritious imported foods.

Children and adults buy snacks from roadside vendors. Men without female family members to cook for them often eat in makeshift outdoor restaurants. In the cities, French cuisine is available in restaurants.

*Food Customs at Ceremonial Occasions.* Weddings, funerals, and holidays always involve eating. The Muslim feast day of Tobaski is celebrated by eating mutton, and families save to purchase a large sheep. Items such as pasta and canned peas are purchased by rural dwellers to eat on special occasions.

*Basic Economy.* The country is self-sufficient in food production, despite the increased production of cash crops. About half the population is engaged in agriculture, and traditional systems of internal trade still function to move food from one area to another. The lack of passable roads in rural areas makes it difficult to transport agricultural products to market. About nine hundred thousand people face intermittent food shortages.

Fishing is concentrated in the south, and pigs are raised by Christians. Most cattle are raised by Fulani herders.

During the socialist period, the government encouraged agro-business initiatives and increased production through rural development programs

*Traditional Benin applique cloth; these are associated with the ancient Beninese cultures of Dahomey.*

such as cooperatives, but farmers' incomes remained low. Forced to sell their products to government managed companies at artificially low prices, farmers were forced into additional subsistence agriculture to feed themselves.

In the last decade, increases in subsistence and cash crops and growth in manufacturing and industry have led to a higher economic growth rate. However, structural adjustment programs negotiated with the World Bank and the International Money Fund after the collapse of the socialist government have involved painful austerity measures, and in 1994 the currency (the Communate Financiere Africaine franc or CFAF) was devalued.

**Land Tenure and Property.** In the precolonial period, access to land was primarily through lineages and clans. However, private holdings existed before the colonial period as a result of gifts from kings to their supporters and purchases from lineage groups.

**Inheritance.** Patterns of inheritance vary according to the customs of individual groups; while national law permits women to inherit and own land, in patrilineal societies land is likely to be inherited by brothers and sons.

**Commercial Activities.** Agricultural products and consumer goods are sold wholesale and retail. Consumers can purchase goods at retail outlets for international import-export companies. Small stores called *boutiques* sell consumer goods and processed foodstuffs in most towns; many are run by Yoruba or Lebanese trading families. Modern stores are found only in the larger cities. Most people still depend on open-air markets to buy not only food but textiles, clothing, furniture, and manufactured goods. The informal economy is large.

Historically, women have played an important role in trade, and many women attempt to engage in commerce in addition to household or wage-earning labor.

**Major Industries.** After the fall of the socialist government, many inefficient industries were privatized. Most manufacturing is geared to processing agricultural products and import substitution of consumer goods. There has been increased foreign investment in cotton gins, but most industrial concerns operate at low capacity and serve the local market.

There are deposits of gold, oil, limestone, phosphates, iron ore, kaolin, and silica sand. Oil production has not been successful. The tourism industry will also require financial investment.

*Hooded and masked egunguns are present at a voodoo festival. Egunguns are the ghosts of ancestors, believed to visit earth at certain times of year by possessing living people.*

A hydroelectric power project on the Mono River is planned, and there is a project to build a natural gas pipeline.

**Trade.** Cotton, crude oil, palm products, and cocoa are the major exports. Major imports include textiles, machinery, food, and agricultural raw materials. After independence, France continued to be the main destination for exports. Other current trading partners include Brazil, Portugal, Morocco, and Libya.

**Division of Labor.** In rural areas, the division of labor is usually clearly prescribed, with specific tasks assigned to men and women. Children are expected to help with chores. In polygynous families, the division of labor among cowives is precise. The more senior a wife is, the more likely she is to have time to pursue commercial interests.

## SOCIAL STRATIFICATION

**Classes and Castes.** The system of social stratification has its roots in the precolonial kingdoms. Kingdoms in the south included royal and commoner families as well as slaves. At the top of the hierarchy was the ruling group of the Bariba, fol-

lowed by a class of Bariba cultivators. Next came the Fulani pastoralists, and on the bottom were the Gando, the slaves of the Wasangari. Colonization broke the power of the traditional rulers, but social status is still partially determined by a person's family roots. Wealth is another way to gain social status, and those who become wealthy through commerce are held in high regard.

One of the most significant social divisions is between the educated urban elite and the rural population. During the colonial period, educated Beninese in other states were expelled. Some found work in the bureaucracy at home, but many moved to European countries. The career goal of many students is to become a civil servant, although structural adjustment programs have reduced the civil service sector. The objectives of the new national employment program include developing the private sector and encouraging expatriates to contribute to the economic development process.

**Symbols of Social Stratification.** The dress, manners, activities, and worldview of the urban elite set them apart from other segments of society, and their lifestyle often is emulated by people in lower classes. Speaking French, wearing Western-style clothes, eating European foods, living in a house with a tin roof, and listening to modern music distinguish a person who is "civilized."

## POLITICAL LIFE

**Government.** Political instability has resulted from the inability of leaders to gain support outside their regional bases. Benin was the first country in the 1990s to make the transition from a dictatorship to a multiparty democracy. Under the new constitution, the president is directly elected to a five-year term and is limited to two terms. The president chooses the members of the cabinet. Members of parliament are elected to four-year terms. The National Assembly meets twice a year.

**Leadership and Political Officials.** Dozens of political parties have been formed since 1990, and the ability to negotiate alliances is essential to political success. Elections in the 1990s exhibited old patterns of patron-client relations, ethnic and regional fragmentation, brittle and shifting alliances, and isolated incidents of violence.

**Social Problems and Control.** The crime rate is low, and most disputes are resolved by local leaders. Few civilians have access to guns. Theft is a prob-

*A woman selling baguettes at a market in Cotonou. Many Beninese homes lack refrigeration, necessitating almost daily trips to the marketplace.*

lem, and many wealthier homeowners hire a night watchman.

***Military Activity.*** Military activity has been limited to domestic operations, and civilian rule has been toppled several times by factions of the military.

## SOCIAL WELFARE AND CHANGE PROGRAMS

Poverty has prevented the state from addressing the nation's health and educational needs, and it has relied on foreign aid and assistance from international organizations. Adjustment programs initiated after the collapse of the economy in 1989 limited the state's investment in health and social development. The National Family Planning Association was founded in 1972.

## GENDER ROLES AND STATUSES

***Division of Labor by Gender.*** In farming communities, men do the heavier tasks such as clearing land. Women help plant, harvest, and process many of the food products. Women carry wood and water and are responsible for household tasks involving food and children. Women are active in local and regional trade. The degree to which women work as

healers and ritual specialists varies between ethnic groups.

***The Relative Status of Women and Men.*** Although women in the Dahomey kingdom could increase their wealth and power as part of the royal palace organization and often served in primarily male occupations, the general pattern has always been for women to be socially and economically subordinate to men. The 1977 constitution conferred legal equality on women, but this was ignored in practice. Currently 65 percent of girls are not in school.

## MARRIAGE, FAMILY, AND KINSHIP

***Marriage.*** In the past, most marriages were arranged by families, but individual choice is becoming more common, especially among the educated elite. A couple may have both civil and traditional ceremonies. The wife joins her husband's family, or the new couple may relocate. Marriage is nearly universal because remarriage occurs quickly after divorce or the death of a spouse. Although cowives in polygamous marriages are supposed to get along, jealousy is not unusual.

*A fishing village on stilts. Ganvie, Lake Nokoue. Fish is more common as a daily meal in the southern part of Benin.*

Marriage may involve the transfer of money or goods to the bride's family. After a divorce, renegotiation of bridewealth may be necessary, especially if there are no children. Because women marry into a patrilineal descent system, the children belong to the father. Because wives do not become part of the husband's kin group, marriages tend to be brittle.

**Kin Groups.** Kinship ties involve loyalty as well as obligation. Outside the immediate family, the lineage and the clan are the most common descent groups. Kin are expected to attend important ceremonies and provide financial aid. Kin networks link members in urban and rural areas. Children may be sent to relatives to raise, but fostering sometimes results in country relatives being brought to large cities to work as domestic servants.

**Domestic Unit.** The average household contains six persons, but extended families and polygamous households may be much larger. Often close relatives live in the same vicinity in separate households but function as a cooperative economic unit.

## SOCIALIZATION

**Infant Care.** Infants are carried, often on the mother's back, and most are breast-fed. Children are cared for by siblings and other family members when they are not with the mother. Babies sleep anywhere, no matter how noisy it is.

**Child Rearing and Education.** Children are expected to be obedient and to show respect for their elders. Children learn gender-appropriate tasks early, especially girls. Most children have few toys and amuse themselves with simple games. It is estimated that 8 percent of rural children work as laborers on plantations and as domestic servants.

The educational system is modeled after that of France. School is free and compulsory for seven years beginning at age five. However, many families cannot afford uniforms and supplies or need their children's labor. It is recognized that education is the key to social advancement, and most parents sacrifice to send their children to school.

## ETIQUETTE

Good manners include taking time to greet people properly, using conventional oral formulas. Upon entering or leaving an appointment, it is appropriate to shake the hand of each person present. People who are well acquainted may greet each other by kissing on the cheek. Public displays of affection between members of the opposite sex are discouraged, but men frequently walk together holding

*This Benin village cooks food communally in a large pot. Most cooking is done outdoors, even in urban areas.*

hands. Offering food and drink to visitors is a key element of hospitality, and to refuse is considered rude. Many people eat in the traditional style, using the fingers of the right hand. It is considered bad taste to eat with the left hand or offer another person something with it.

## RELIGION

**Religious Beliefs.** About 15 percent of the population is Muslim, and 15 percent is Christian, mostly Roman Catholic. The rest of the population follows indigenous systems of belief. Vodun (voodoo) was taken with the coastal slaves to Brazil and the Caribbean. Some Vodun spirits were borrowed from the Yoruba religion, and Vodun involves divination and spirit possession. These supernatural powers help believers cope with illness and infertility and provide a philosophy for living.

**Death and the Afterlife.** In indigenous belief systems, ancestors are considered to remain part of the community after death. Shrines honor the ancestors, and offerings "feed" them. Among the Fon, circular metal sculptures on staffs called *asen* are made for each deceased person and kept in the family compound. In some communities, funerals involve a sequence of rituals before the person is con-

sidered to have made a complete transition to being an ancestor.

## MEDICINE AND HEALTH CARE

The birthrate and maternal mortality rate are high. Malaria and diarrheal dehydration are endemic. Only half the population is vaccinated. Over three-quarters of the population does not have access to primary health care. AIDS is straining the health care system. The rates of infection is three times higher in rural areas. People often employ more than one system of healing. Even those who have access to an infirmary or clinic may visit herbalists or other healers.

## SECULAR AND RELIGIOUS CELEBRATIONS

The major state holidays are New Year's Day (1 January), May Day (1 May), and National Day (1 August).

## THE ARTS AND HUMANITIES

**Support for the Arts.** Support for the arts and humanities is limited by poverty of the nation.

**Literature.** Benin has produced many scholars and writers from the educated urban class, such as the novelist and historian Paul Hazoumé and the philosopher Paulin Houndtonji.

**Graphic Arts.** The arts include fine craftsmanship in iron and brass and cloth appliqué banners associated with ancient Dahomey.

## THE STATE OF THE PHYSICAL AND SOCIAL SCIENCES

There is only one postsecondary institution, the University of Benin in Cotonou. The university serves as a base for international research teams, and its faculty members have produced important scholarly contributions. About twelve thousand students are enrolled.

## BIBLIOGRAPHY

Adam, Kolawolé Sikirou, and Michel Boko. *Le Bénin*, 1983.

Allen, Chris, "Benin," in *Benin, The Congo, Burkina Faso: Economics, Politics and Society*, 1989.

Bay, Edna G. *Wives of the Leopard: Gender, Politics, and Culture in the Kingdom of Dahomey*, 1998.

Blier, Suzanne. *African Vodun: Art, Psychology, and Power*, 1994.

Cornevin, Robert. *La Republique Populaire du Benin: Des Origines Dahoméennes a Nos Jours*, 1981.

Decalo, Samuel. *Coups and Army Rule in Africa: Studies in Military Style*, 1976.

———. *Historical Dictionary of Benin*, 3rd ed., 1995.

Eades, J. S., and Chris Allen. *Benin*, 1996.

Herskovits, Melville J. *Dahomey: An Ancient West African Kingdom*, 1938.

Kodjogbé, Nicaise, Gora Mboup, Justin Tossou, et al. *Enquête Démographique et de Santé, Republique de Bénin, 1996*, 1997.

Law, Robin. *The Kingdom of Allada*, 1997.

———. "The Politics of Commercial Transition: Factional Conflict in Dahomey in the Context of the Ending of the Atlantic Slave Trade." *Journal of African History* 38 (2): 213–233, 1997.

Lombard, Jacques. *Structures de Type "Feodal" en Afrique Noire: Études des Dynamismes Internes et des Relations Sociales chez les Bariba du Dahomey*, 1956.

Manning, Patrick. *Slavery, Colonialism and Economic Growth in Dahomey, 1640–1960*, 1982.

Mercier, Paul. *Tradition, Changement, Histoire: Les "Somba" du Dahomey Septentrional*, 1968.

Midiohouan, Thécla. "La Femme dans la Vie Politique, Économique et Sociale en RPB." *Presence Africaine* 141: 59–70, 1987.

Parrinder, Geoffrey. "Dahomey Half a Century Ago." *Journal of Religion in Africa* 19 (3): 264–273, 1989.

Ronen, Dov. *Dahomey: Between Tradition and Modernity*, 1975.

Ryan, Josephine Caldwell. "Changing Foodways in Parakou, Benin: A Study of the Dietary Behavior of Urban Bariba and Dendi Women." Ph.D. dissertation, Southern Methodist University, Dallas, Texas, 1996.

Sargent, Carolyn Fishel. *The Cultural Context of Therapeutic Choice: Obstetrical Care Decisions among the Bariba of Benin*, 1982.

———. *Maternity, Medicine and Power: Reproductive Decisions in Urban Benin*, 1989.

Whiteman, Kaye. "High Road to Nowhere: African Aftermath." *Encounter* 74 (4): 67–70, 1990.

—JOSEPHINE CALDWELL RYAN

# BERMUDA

## CULTURE NAME
Bermudian

## ORIENTATION

**Identification.** Bermuda is named after Juan de Bermudez, a Spanish explorer who first sighted the uninhabited islands probably in 1503.

**Location and Geography.** In a setting of turquoise waters, pink beaches and lush foliage on low hills, this small, subtropical coral island in the North Atlantic sits atop a long-extinct volcanic chain 570 miles (917 kilometers) southeast of Cape Hatteras, North Carolina, the nearest land. Only twenty-one square miles in area (fifty-five square kilometers), the island is comprised of many small islets around the Main Island and seven others that are bridged together. Bermuda is shaped like a fishhook, the eye being Saint George's Harbour at the northeast end, and the loop of the hook forming the Great Sound at the other, leading into Hamilton Harbour. Often mistakenly associated with the Caribbean, it is in fact nearer to Nova Scotia. Protected from extremes of weather by the Gulf Stream, temperatures range between 65 degrees Fahrenheit (18 degrees Celsius) in winter and 85 degrees Fahrenheit (29 degrees Celsius) in summer. There are nine parishes named after several of the primary English 'adventurers,' or investors in the 1607 Virginia colony who separately invested in the Somer Isles company.

**Demography.** The population of Bermuda is 62,997 (2000 estimate). Blacks have been in the majority since some point in the late eighteenth century, and now comprise between 60 and 70 percent of Bermudians. The majority of the remaining ethnic components are northern European, mainly British; they are followed by Portuguese, who are mainly of Azorean origin, and the descendants of a number of Native American tribes. While some 75 percent of Bermudians were born on the Island,

many or most of those born overseas have eventually become Bermudian by marriage. Fears of permanent overpopulation and of changes in the ethnic structure have made it nearly impossible to otherwise obtain Bermuda Status (as citizenship is called).

Nearly all the slaves were brought to Bermuda from the West Indies or as slaves on ships captured by Bermuda privateers. Few arrived directly from Africa. The northern European minority descend from the original English colonists and subsequent arrivals from all over Britain including indentured laborers. Some U.S. military personnel and some Scandinavians also settled here. A few Portuguese families arrived first in the 1840s from Madeira. Portuguese immigrants increasingly arrived in subsequent years to work in the growing agricultural industry.

**Linguistic Affiliation.** The language is a blend of British, North American, and various West Indian versions of the English language. Azorean Portuguese is still spoken and preserved in some Portuguese homes. In the Bermudian accent, sometimes *V*s and *W*s are transposed; a usage that derives from the Elizabethan English of the seventeenth century settlers.

**Symbolism.** The Bermudian flag is the British Red Ensign 'defaced' with the heraldic Bermuda Coat of Arms. The Union Flag occupies the upper, hoist quarter of an otherwise red flag and the Arms are within the red field. They consist of a white and green shield in which a heraldic red lion grasps a scroll displaying the sinking of Somers' ship *Sea Venture*.

## HISTORY AND ETHNIC RELATIONS

**Emergence of the Nation.** Bermuda was first settled in 1609, when the *Sea Venture*, a British flagship carrying settlers and provisions to Jamestown, Virginia, wrecked on the islands' shores. The senior

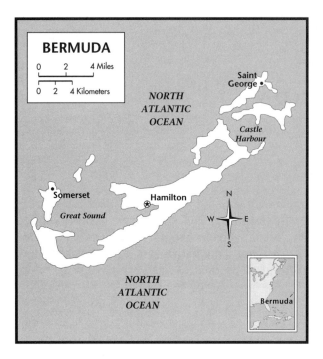

*Bermuda*

officer of the fleet, George Somers, and his ship-wrecked sailors built new vessels and continued on to Virginia, but, enchanted by the beauty and abundant natural resources, they made plans to settle the islands. Colonization began in July 1612, when sixty British settlers, led by Richard Moore, disembarked. Moore became the first governor. In 1616, the king issued a charter to form the Somers Isles Company, a commercial enterprise.

By 1620, the parliamentary Sessions House began to hold meetings of the colonial legislature. A system of land ownership developed as the territory was divided into parishes named after major stockholders in the Virginia Company. The Virginia Company ruled Bermuda much like a fiefdom and the colonists soon grew tired of the burdensome restrictions placed upon them. In 1684, Bermudian leaders sued to have the charter rescinded, and thereafter Bermuda was ruled as an English colony in a similar fashion to its American counterparts.

Slaves were first brought to the islands in the early seventeenth century. Most served as laborers and domestic workers rather than plantation workers. They were often treated brutally, and several slave revolts in the seventeenth and eighteenth centuries resulted in even harsher treatment.

The Bermudians launched into shipping, a highly successful industry until the advent of steam in the early nineteenth century. Taking advantage of the prolific Bermuda Cedar, they set to work to design and build the Bermuda sloops and schooners that became internationally famous. These ships were especially effective when sailing upwind or to windward. This was critical to their commercial value since they could deliver goods more quickly than their competitors. Crewed by Bermudians of all shades and degrees of servitude, they traded with ports all over the Atlantic coast of North America and the Caribbean. In wartime, armed with Letters of Marque or Warrants from the crown, they captured, depending on the war, French, Spanish, Dutch, and even American ships, bringing them to the Admiralty Prize Court in Bermuda for sale and prize money. Bermuda has been well known for privateering throughout its history.

Bermuda rose to prominence in the seventeenth century as a ship building and manning center from which ships sailed to carry on trade between the colonies and islands of North America and the Caribbean. It became a post for slave trading, as well as for West Indian rum, salt, and oranges. Whaling also added to the colony's income.

In 1815 the capital was moved from Saint George's to the increasingly busy port of Hamilton in the center of the island. As shipping declined, a new industry was needed to support the workforce, and Bermudians began to venture into organized farming.

The British Emancipation Act banned slavery in the Empire in 1834, although the practice was not actually ended in the English-speaking world until the U.S. Civil War a generation later. Much of Bermuda's trade was with the southern United States. While the islands remained officially neutral during the U.S. Civil War, their sympathies tended to lie with the Confederacy. The war in fact provided a boost to business, as the South paid high prices for weapons that came through Bermuda from Britain. Northern blockades were effective, and made the trip even more profitable for sailors who were willing to run a risk.

During the end of the nineteenth century, the export of vegetables, and onions in particular, provided Bermuda with a steady income. This industry fell as the United States began to produce more onions on its own soil. However, a new industry rose to take its place. Tourism brought money and development in the form of new hotels and growing towns.

World War I, in which exactly half of Bermuda's contingent died, brought this fledgling industry to a standstill. After the war, there was insufficient capital to renovate the few hotels, and inadequate shipping to bring the necessary visitors.

When the situation seemed most bleak, however, the Furness Steamship Company in England picked Bermuda as a destination for their new vacation ships. In the 1920s, the era of Prohibition in the United States, Bermuda became a popular escape where wealthy Americans could drink on steamships and in the hotels. In the 1930s, tourism carried Bermuda through the Great Depression with hardly a break in stride.

Soon after the beginning of World War II, when Britain "stood alone," Bermuda land was offered by a desperate Winston Churchill to entice President Franklin D. Roosevelt and the U.S. Congress to come to Britain's support. Roughly 10 percent of the country was leased for ninety years to the United States, displacing large numbers of Bermudian families. During World War II, Bermuda was used as a center of Allied operations. The British Royal Navy used it as a base for patrolling the Atlantic, and the United States built naval and military bases on the islands for protection against German submarines that posed a threat to American shipping. Bermuda was an important transit point for the Allies through the war. Winston Churchill, Dwight D. Eisenhower, and the British Prime Minister Harold Macmillan all held summits in Bermuda (as did John F. Kennedy, Richard Nixon, George Bush, and Margaret Thatcher in later years).

In the 1960s, racial tensions grew, as blacks began to protest unfair treatment. Grassroots movements formed to more thoroughly integrate blacks into Bermudian life. In 1968, a race riot erupted in Hamilton, caused by the perception that whites only were being given access to an overcrowded fair (they were in fact stall operators). Troops were called to Bermuda from Britain on two occasions but never were needed. In the spring of 1973, Bermuda's white governor, Sir Richard Sharples, and one of his aides were assassinated at the then unguarded Government House. Scotland Yard eventually prosecuted and obtained convictions for two of the men involved. The hanging of the two men resulted in further riots in the black communities. Injuries were minimal, but some business property was damaged. Some blacks began calling for independence from Britain as a way to end racial discrimination, and in 1977 continued political agitation led the government to discuss independence. In a vote in late 1995, Bermudians rejected a proposal of independence by a two-thirds majority, mainly in fear of opening the doors to the poverty independence brought to countries like the Bahamas and Jamaica, but also in fear of shaking the confidence of foreign firms who had invested in the country. Bermuda remains an Overseas Territory of the British crown, but the question of independence still arises.

**National Identity.** Bermudian identity is based largely in British cultural traditions. This is especially the case for wealthy white islanders and British expatriates. Blacks, poor whites, and those of Portuguese descent identify less with the British and their institutions. Cultural influences from the United States have also impacted life here.

Another ethnic group, the Mahicans, are descendants of American Indians who were brought to Saint David's Island from New York in the 1600s. They call themselves Mohawks, or "Mos" for short, and retain some of their unique cultural identity.

**Ethnic Relations.** The divide in Bermuda between blacks and whites began soon after the colony was established, as slaves were imported to serve the needs of the colonists. The so-called "Forty Thieves" families, descendents of the original white settlers, established a system of racial segregation in both government and social life that they perpetuated for over two centuries. Even today in the profusion of Bermuda's social clubs either blacks or whites tend to strongly predominate. Over the years, blacks have achieved important gains, but racial segregation still remains a source of tension.

## URBANISM, ARCHITECTURE, AND THE USE OF SPACE

Hamilton, the capital and largest city, is home to a number of interesting buildings, including the Anglican Cathedral of the Most Holy Trinity, built in 1894, and the Sessions House and Cabinet Building, which are the seat of government. However by far the most significant historical site is the original capital of Saint George's, a town largely unaltered since the seventeenth century. Among the many original buildings are the State House dating back to 1619 and Saint Peter's, the oldest Anglican Church in the Western Hemisphere.

Housing is now cement block, to preserve the native coral limestone, which is today used mostly for roofing slate in housing construction. Architectural styles were adapted to withstand the extreme winds and hurricanes Bermuda experiences, and as a result large numbers of the eighteenth century homes survive. Steep limestone roofs are whitewashed and designed to catch water to be stored in tanks beneath the houses. Slave quarters still survive as extensions to a number of the old houses.

Where space was at a premium in Saint George's, these were often ground floor with the family living above. Fireplaces, still widely popular, were an essential feature from the seventeenth through the nineteenth century, and were used as a source of heat, and for cooking and baking. The handsome and much-photographed chimneys doubled as buttresses for added roof support.

## FOOD AND ECONOMY

**Food in Daily Life.** Day-to-day food is identical with that of the United States, from where much of it is imported. Traditional Bermudian cuisine is a mixture of American, British, and West Indian influences. Once abundant seafood formed the basis of many local dishes. Chowder was made from a stockpot of leftover fish carcasses and flavored with hot pepper sauce and rum. Fritters were made from now-protected conch. Hoppin' John, a meal borrowed from the Carolinas, consists of rice cooked with beans or black-eyed peas. Johnnycakes (cornmeal pancakes, served with peas and rice) are also a traditional dish.

Rum is a popular drink. One local brand, Black Seal, when mixed with ginger beer, is appropriately called a Dark & Stormy.

**Food Customs at Ceremonial Occasions.** Sunday breakfast is generally a big meal of salt codfish from Nova Scotia, egg sauce, boiled potatoes, cooked bananas, and avocado when in season. Cassava Pie is served at Christmas. It is similar to cornbread when cooked, made from minced cassava or manioc root, eggs butter, and filled with pork and turkey or chicken. Good Friday is celebrated with a traditional breakfast of codfish cakes and hot-cross buns. Sweet potato pudding is often served on Guy Fawkes Day.

**Basic Economy.** Unemployment is virtually nonexistent in Bermuda. Roughly 15 percent of the population is made up of expatriates employed on temporary permits by employers that must first prove to the government there is no Bermudian available to fill the job. "Expats" range in qualification from dishwashers to highly qualified professionals. They and their dependants are significant contributors to the economy. Of the workforce, the vast majority are in professional or administrative work or services; only 2 percent are engaged in agriculture and fishing. Farmers produce bananas, vegetables, citrus fruits, flowers, and dairy products, but agriculture is limited by the fact that only 6 percent of the country's land is arable.

**Land Tenure and Property.** Bermuda's twenty-odd square miles are taxed on a progressive scale according to the assessed rental value. To protect Bermudian ownership, foreigners may only purchase at the top end of the scale, and only with permission. Corporations may only own the land allowed by their incorporating act. There is also public land, including several nature reserves, parks, and historic sites.

**Commercial Activities.** Most commercial activity revolves around the tourist industry. Hotels and restaurants, golf courses, and tour companies all cater to the constant influx of visitors (84 percent of whom come from the United States). Most of the goods sold in Bermuda are imported, and therefore costly.

**Major Industries.** Bermuda's dominant industry today is financial, and includes some of the world's largest re-insurance companies among other corporate enterprises of all kinds. The only restriction at this time has been a reluctance to accommodate foreign banks, for fear of losing local financial control. The earnings in this sector are now twice that of tourism, and as tourism has declined, the new housing and general services required by these corporate enterprises have absorbed much of the workforce once dependent on tourism.

**Trade.** Bermuda imports machinery and transportation equipment, construction materials, chemicals, food products, and live animals, primarily from the United States, but also from the United Kingdom and Mexico. The country's main export is pharmaceuticals, which are not processed in Bermuda, but merely stop there in transit. Bermuda also exports perfume, liqueurs, and Bermuda lilies (which are popular in the United States as Easter lilies) mostly to the United Kingdom and the United States.

**Division of Labor.** There is no shortage of jobs available, and people are free to choose their own professions. Blacks tend to occupy more of the lower paying positions than whites. Business ownership is substantially white, although board membership, and thus control of business, has become more diverse.

## SOCIAL STRATIFICATION

**Classes and Castes.** There is a uniformly high standard of living and little poverty in Bermuda. While racial discrimination continued to haunt the country long after the abolition of slavery, blacks

*Houses overlooking St. George's Harbor. St. George's is the most historical city in Bermuda, with an abundance of seventeenth century architecture.*

have made progress in entering the government and civic life.

***Symbols of Social Stratification.*** In general, attire is fairly formal. The famous Bermuda shorts, a legacy of the British Army's uniform, are worn by businessmen, along with jackets, ties, and knee socks. Otherwise, dress is similar to in the United States or Britain, and there are few distinguishing features among classes.

## POLITICAL LIFE

***Government.*** A 1977 constitutional conference effectively gave Bermuda full internal independence. Today, with a Westminster based parliamentary system of government, Bermuda has forty elected members in the Assembly. These choose the premier, and the premier selects a Cabinet of Ministers, each with a ministerial responsibility ranging from fiscal to education and health. The Senate is an appointed assembly, five seats by the premier, three by the opposition party, and three by the governor, of whom one is the president. The Senate cannot debate tax bills and may only delay others.

***Leadership and Political Officials.*** The Governor acts as Queen Elizabeth II's representative, as an advisor, and like the Queen has little actual power.

The present ruling party is the Progressive Labour Party (PLP), almost entirely African Bermudian and formed in 1963 with those interests at heart. The PLP won power in 1998 after some thirty-five years in opposition. Prior to this, the multi-racial United Bermuda Party (UBP) held a majority, with overwhelming support among the white population and a significant percentage of blacks as well.

***Social Problems and Control.*** Crime is dominated by drug-related offenses. Guns are prohibited, and violent crime is relatively rare. The legal system is based on that of Britain with Magistrates and a Supreme Court and Court of Appeal. The Privy Council of the British House of Lords is the final arbiter. The Supreme Court still retains the traditional British robes, wigs, and format. There is a maximum-security prison and a more relaxed prison farm.

***Military Activity.*** Britain assumes responsibility for the country's defense. The military consists of the Bermuda Regiment and the Bermuda Reserve Constabulary.

*Two men playing croquet. Bermuda is an Overseas Territory of the British Crown.*

## SOCIAL WELFARE AND CHANGE PROGRAMS

In 1965, funding for formalized pensions for all over the age of 65 was established and is paid for from payroll deductions. In 1997, legislation to substantially expand pensions was launched and now is in effect. Bermudians have basic hospitalization coverage, and employers customarily provide enhanced medical programs for all employees.

## NONGOVERNMENTAL ORGANIZATIONS AND OTHER ASSOCIATIONS

There are a large number of charities and service clubs active in Bermuda. The primary Bermudian provider of funds is the Centennial Trust of the Bank of Bermuda, which has donated nearly seven million dollars (U.S.) over ten years to numerous charities and organizations. The large international business sector provides significant funds. The two larger banks, the government, and many other interests provide comprehensive scholarships.

## GENDER ROLES AND STATUSES

***Division of Labor by Gender.*** While women are still responsible for most everyday domestic jobs, in Bermuda they are widely represented in all aspects of business and the professions. Most senior executives are still male, but significant top positions in business and the civil service are, and have been held by women. The present and previous premiers are women.

***The Relative Status of Women and Men.*** Women and men are equal in law; this is widely respected by employers and in most areas of society.

## MARRIAGE, FAMILY, AND KINSHIP

***Marriage.*** Religious ceremonies are followed by large receptions. The traditional cake is three-tiered, with one layer for the bride, one for the groom, and one that is served to the guests. The cake is topped with a cedar sapling, which the couple then plants at their new home.

***Domestic Unit.*** The domestic unit generally consists of the nuclear family. There is a considerable acceptance of single parenting. To be successful, and to provide role models for young males, this usually requires strong support from siblings, grandparents, and aunts and uncles in the wider family. There is often difficulty in realizing court child support rulings, and much remains unpaid.

**Inheritance.** While inheritance was once limited to the male line, today women as well as men are legally entitled to inherit property.

## SOCIALIZATION

**Infant Care.** Infant care is generally the domain of the mother, although those of the upper class often hire nannies.

**Child Rearing and Education.** Bermuda is well equipped with nursery and preschools set up to accept children of working mothers. Education is free and mandatory between the ages of five and sixteen. The school system is based on the British and American model. Several large private schools, once segregated, still lean to one race, religion, or the other. The literacy rate is near 100 percent.

**Higher Education.** Bermuda has one junior college, which enrolls about six hundred students. To obtain a four-year degree, it is necessary to leave the islands, and the government and private organizations provide scholarships to study in the United States, Canada, and the United Kingdom.

## ETIQUETTE

Politeness is highly valued, and there is a degree of formality in social interactions.

## RELIGION

**Religious Beliefs.** Thirty-nine percent of the population is non-Anglican Protestant; 27 percent is Anglican; 15 percent is Roman Catholic; and 19 percent practice other religions. Methodism first came to the islands in the mid-eighteenth century, and attracted a large percentage of the islands' black inhabitants. The African Methodist Episcopal (AME) church has historically been a significant unifying force in the black community. Catholicism first began to make inroads in the mid-nineteenth century, bolstered by the influx of Portuguese immigrants.

**Religious Practitioners.** The Archbishop of Canterbury in England is the central religious figure for members of the Anglican Church. The Bishop of Bermuda, who presides over the Anglican Cathedral in Hamilton, is next in the hierarchy. The Anglican church in Bermuda has many black pastors, including the bishop, and numerous black congregations.

**Rituals and Holy Places.** Bermuda has a number of historic churches. The oldest, Saint Peter's Church in Saint George's, was originally built in the early 1600s, and later rebuilt in 1713. The Anglican Cathedral in Hamilton is an elaborate Gothic structure with stained-glass windows and British oak sculpture. The Presbyterian Church in Warwick dates to 1719.

**Death and the Afterlife.** Both Catholics and Protestants believe in an afterlife. Funeral services in the church are generally followed by mourning in the home of relatives of the deceased.

## MEDICINE AND HEALTH CARE

The standard of health care is high. There are two hospitals on the islands, one medical and the other psychiatric, and there are adequate doctors to provide care for most of the population. There is an air-ambulance service to the United States and established medical relationships there, in Canada, and in the United Kingdom provide specialist care not locally available. Bermuda has a low infant-mortality rate, and life expectancy is seventy-five years for men and seventy-nine for women.

## SECULAR CELEBRATIONS

Holidays celebrated include New Year's Day, 1 January; Bermuda Day, 24 May (Queen Victoria's birthday); the monarch's official birthday, usually the third Monday in June; the two-day cricket, or Cup Match held on a Thursday and a Friday at the end of July or beginning of August; Labor Day, on first Monday in September; Armistice, or Remembrance Day, 11 November when wars are remembered; and Boxing Day, 26 December.

## THE ARTS AND HUMANITIES

**Literature.** Bermuda has produced a number of writers remarkable mostly for historical and cultural studies of the islands, including Walter B. Hayward, Dr. Henry Wilkinson, William S. Zuill, Terry Tucker, Nellie Musson, Cyril Packwood, and Frank Manning and Brian Burland. Bermuda has also provided refuge and inspiration for writers from other countries, including Mark Twain, Eugene O'Neill, Munro Leaf, Noel Coward, James Thurber, Vernon Ives, and Peter Benchley.

**Graphic Arts.** The Bermuda National Gallery in Hamilton, the Masterworks Foundation Gallery, and a number of smaller galleries throughout the Island display and sell work by many aspiring and successful resident artists. Hamilton's City Hall

*The Governor of Bermuda inspects troops of the Bermuda Regiment during the annual Peppercorn Ceremonies, St. George, Bermuda.*

Theatre and the Ruth Seaton James Hall at Prospect present numerous local and traveling productions.

Many local painters and sculptors have found a market in the tourist population. Much of their work takes its inspiration from the natural surroundings; watercolor is perhaps the most popular medium. Well-known painters include the late Alfred Birdsey, his daughter Joanne Birdsey Linberg, Carol Holding, and Joan Forbes. Desmond Fountain is the country's best-known sculptor.

**Performance Arts.** The Bermudian variety of Gombey, of West African origin but influenced and made unique by the early strong Native North American presence, has been passed down in family groups over centuries. Accompanied by rhythmic drums, wielding bows, arrows, and tomahawks, the dancers, including children, sport peacock feathered headdresses, masks, and capes. Many of the dances relate to biblical st. The four main Gombey troupes perform on Boxing Day and on unscheduled occasions throughout the year. West Indian calypso and reggae music are both popular.

## The State of the Physical and Social Sciences

The Bermuda Biological Station for Research (largely funded by the U.S. National Science Foundation) has laboratories and a library for the study of marine life and environmental issues such as acid rain. There are several including the Maritime Museum complex within the restored Royal Naval Dockyard at Ireland Island. The Bermuda Aquarium and Museum is privately and government supported; it is world famous.

## Bibliography

Adams, John. "The English Peopling of Bermuda," *The Bermudian Magazine*, special Heritage edition, May 1992.

———. "The Mixture of Races in Bermuda," *The Bermudian Magazine*, special Heritage edition, May 1992.

Boultbee, Paul G. and Raine, David F., compilers. *Bermuda*, 1998.

Craven, W. F. *Introduction to the History of Bermuda*, 1938; rev. ed., 1990.

Davies, Elizabeth W. *The Legal Status of British Dependent Territories: The West Indies and the North Atlantic Region*, 1995.

Ebbin, Meredith. "Women's Task Force Seeks Major Changes." *The Bermda Sun*, 24 December 1996.

"Gimme Shelter." *The Economist*, 1 January 2000.

Hendrick, Basil C. et al. *Anthropological Investigations in the Caribbean: selected papers*, 1984.

Lefroy, Major General J. H., CB, FRS, RA. *Discovery and Early Settlement of the Bermudas or Somers Islands, 1515 – 1687*, 1981.

Mudd, Patricia Marirea. "Bermudians of Portuguese Descent," *The Bermudian Magazine*, special Heritage edition, May 1992.

Packwood, Cyril Outerbridge. *Chained on the Rock: Slavery in Bermuda*, 1975.

———. "Origins of African Bermudians," *The Bermudian Magazine*, special Heritage edition, May 1992.

Theriault, Tania. "Women in Politics." *The Bermuda Sun*, 14 October 1998.

Tucker, Terry. *Bermuda: Today and Yesterday, 1503-1973*, 1975.

Ward, W. E. F. *The Royal Navy and the Slavers—The Suppression of the Atlantic Slave Trade*, 1969.

Wilkinson, Henry Campbell. *Bermuda from Sail to Steam, the History of the Island from 1784 to 1901*, 1973.

Ziral, James A. "People of the Great Spirit," *The Bermudian Magazine*, special Heritage edition, May 1992.

———. "Who Are We?" *The Bermudian Magazine*, special Heritage edition, May 1992.

—ELEANOR STANFORD
AND ANDREW SUSSMAN

# BHUTAN

**CULTURE NAME**

Bhutanese

**ALTERNATIVE NAMES**

Kingdom of Bhutan; Druk-Yul

**ORIENTATION**

*Identification*. Druk-yul means "Land of the Thunder Dragon." Most Bhutanese refer to their homeland as Druk-yul, the original and still official name. Bhutan, the name given to the country by the British, is the name used for most official and international business and reference. The name Bhutan may be derived from the ancient Indian term "Bhotania," which means "end of the land of the Bhots" (Tibet).

Because a number of stone tools and megaliths (large stones used in prehistoric monuments) have been found in Bhutan, it is believed that Bhutan was populated as early as 2000–1500 B.C.E.

The society of Bhutan today is made up of several ethnic groups. The Sharchops, who are believed to be ancestors of those earliest residents, live mostly in eastern Bhutan. Their early ancestor tribes may have originated from Burma (Myanmar) and northeast India. It is also believed that Indo-Mongoloids (usually referred to as Monpas, which means non-Tibetans) migrated into Bhutan two thousand years ago from Arunchal Pradesh, Nagaland, northern Burma, and Thailand. The Ngalops live in western Bhutan and migrated from the Tibetan plains; they are credited with being the first to bring Buddhism to the country. The other main ethnic group is the Lhotshampas, who were from Nepal originally. The Lhotshampas migrated to Bhutan toward the end of the nineteenth century.

*Location and Geography*. Bhutan is located in the northern area of South Asia and is also in the eastern Himalayan mountain area. It is 18,000 square miles (46,620 square kilometers) in size and is bordered in the north by the People's Republic of China and to the south, east, and west by India.

Geographically, Bhutan is divided into three zones: the southern zone, which has low foothills that are covered with dense tropical forests; the central zone, which primarily consists of fertile valleys at altitudes that range from 3,500 to 10,000 feet (1,060 to 3,050 meters); and the northern zone, which has valleys at heights that range from 11,000 to 28,000 feet (3,350 to 8,535 meters). It is this northern section that forms part of the Himalayas with its high peaks along the Tibetan borders.

The largest percentage of the population lives in the central zone. The federal capital of Thimphu is located along the river of the same name in this section of the country.

*Demography*. According to the most recent government census, Bhutan's population consists of approximately 600,000 people. However, Bhutanese dissident groups have argued that the population is, in fact, much bigger than government estimates. These groups contend that the Bhutanese government dramatically undercounted the number of ethnic Nepalese in the country as part of a campaign to limit the influence of this fast-growing minority population. Ethnic conflicts between the Buddhist majority and the largely Hindu Nepalese in the late 1980s and early 1990s forced tens of thousands Nepalese into refugee camps in Nepal and India. The Bhutanese government does not recognize the citizenship of the majority of these refugees, estimated at 112,000.

*Linguistic Affiliation*. Bhutan's national language is Dzongkha. Most of the schools conduct classes in English, although more textbooks are being written in Dzongkha. Different dialects are spoken by residents of the east and west, which sometimes makes it difficult for them to understand each other.

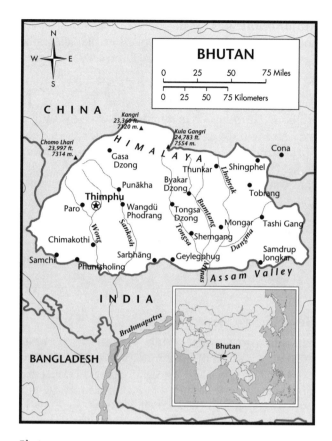

Bhutan

A large proportion of the population—especially urban residents—speak English. *Kuensel*, the national newspaper, is published in Dzongkha, English, and Nepali, both in print and on the Internet.

**Symbolism.** The national emblem is a circle with two double diamond thunderbolts placed above a lotus, topped by a jewel, and framed by two dragons. The thunderbolts represent harmony between secular and religious power. The lotus represents purity, the jewel represents sovereign power, and the two dragons represent Druk-Yul ("Land of the Thunder Dragon") the original name of Bhutan.

The national flag is divided diagonally by two blocks of different colors with a white dragon across the middle. The top part of the flag is golden yellow, which represents the secular power of the king, and the lower part is orange, which symbolizes the Buddhist religion. The dragon, who represents Bhutan, holds jewels in its claws, which stand for the wealth and perfection of the country.

The national flower is the blue poppy, which grows at the high altitudes. The national tree is the cypress. The Bhutanese people associate with it because it is straight and strong and can grow even in inhospitable soil. The national bird is the raven, which also adorns the royal hat. The national animal is an extremely rare mammal called the takin. It lives in flocks in areas 13,000 feet (4,000 meters) high and eats bamboo.

## HISTORY AND ETHNIC RELATIONS

**Emergence of the Nation.** Nearly all the historic records of early Bhutan were destroyed by fire, flood, earthquake, and war.

In the sixteenth century, the region came under Tibetan rule. Zhabdrung Ngawang Namgyal (1594–1651), who was referred to as "Zhabdrung Rinpoche" (which translates to "the precious jewel at whose feet one submits"), set up a dual system of administration headed by a spiritual leader and a civil government leader. This system endured until 1907 when a hereditary monarchy was established.

In the nineteenth century, the British sought to incorporate Tibet within their influence, which posed a threat to Bhutan, but this problem was successfully eliminated by Penlop Ugyen Wangchuck, who played the role of mediator between British India and Tibet. Wangchuck became the first hereditary monarch of Bhutan in 1907. In 1949 Bhutan officially became an independent nation.

**National Identity.** Bhutan's national identity is intimately bound up with its religious identity as a Buddhist nation. Buddhism influences both the daily lives of its people as well as the government, in which Buddhist religious leaders have considerable power.

**Ethnic Relations.** Bhutan has a wide diversity of ethnic groups, starting with a number of small tribal groups (related to similar tribes in India and Sikkim) whose ancestry goes back almost three thousand years. More recent centuries have seen large migrant groups from Tibet, Nepal and Mongolia. The rapid growth of the largely Hindu Nepalese population in Bhutan towards the end of the twentieth century resulted in significant ethnic conflicts with the Buddhist majority. The government responded by tightening immigration and citizenship laws to reduce the flow of Nepalese into Bhutan. When many Nepalese responded to this action with protests and demonstrations, ethnic violence and repression broke out against them in Bhutan's southern districts in the late 1980s and early 1990s. As a result, tens of thousands of Nepalese fled the country in 1991 and 1992. There are an estimated 112,000 Nepalese refugees currently residing in refugee camps in Nepal and India.

## URBANISM, ARCHITECTURE, AND THE USE OF SPACE

A large percentage of Bhutanese are rural residents who live in houses built to withstand the long, cold winters, with wood-burning stoves for both heat and cooking. Nearly all these rural houses are surrounded by some land that is used for growing vegetables. There are also a number of cities, including the capital of Thimphu, which is home to the royal family and government buildings. Other cities include Wangdue Phondrang and Tongsa. Bumthang is the spiritual region and has a number of monasteries and places of religious pilgrimage, as well as numerous religious legends associated with it.

The use of the space involves preserving both the environment and the quality of life of Bhutan residents and at the same time using space to preserve wildlife. As part of Bhutan's Buddhist heritage, this includes preserving the numerous *Dzongs* (monastery fortresses) that are located throughout the entire country.

## FOOD AND ECONOMY

*Food in Daily Life.* Because of the ethnic diversity of the people, there is a certain ethnic diversity in the food. Northern Indian cuisine is often mixed with the chilies of the Tibetan area in daily dishes. Mushrooms, apricots, asparagus, a variety of chilies and numerous spices are grown in abundance in nearly all the valleys. Spices, fruits, and vegetables are cooked with beef, chicken, pork, and dried yak, and resemble Chinese and Indian cuisine. The typical meal also features rice, dried beef or pork, and chilies sometimes cooked with soft, white cheese. The most popular beverage is tea, which is served in a variety of ways.

*Basic Economy.* The economy is based on agriculture and forestry and provides the livelihoods for 90 percent of the population. Agriculture is primarily subsistence farming and animal husbandry. The economy of Bhutan is aligned with that of India through strong trade and monetary links.

*Commercial Activities.* Cottage industries, which include weaving, account for the majority of production.

*Major Industries.* Manufactured goods include cement, wood products, processed fruits, alcoholic beverages, and calcium carbite. Electricity is another important industry.

*Trade.* The 1998 estimate of exports was $111 million. Electricity is a major export item and is exported to India. Other exports include spices, gypsum, cement, and precious stones. Chief imports are fuels, fabrics, and rice, and amounted to $136 million (estimate) in 1998. Major import partners are India, Japan, and the United Kingdom.

*Division of Labor.* The majority of Bhutanese are not skilled labor workers: 93 percent are in agriculture, 5 percent in services, and 2 percent in industry and commerce.

## SOCIAL STRATIFICATION

*Classes and Castes.* While Bhutan has no caste system, a pattern of discrimination against the minority Hindus of Nepalese origin exists. Thousands of Nepalese were deported from Bhutan in the late 1980s, and many others fled to refugee camps in Nepal. The government launched an effort to promote the cultural assimilation of the remaining Nepalese. Nepali was no longer taught in schools, and national dress was required for official occasions.

## POLITICAL LIFE

*Government.* Bhutan is a constitutional monarchy, ruled by a hereditary king, the "Druk Gyalpo," who governs with the aid of a Royal Cabinet and a National Assembly (the Tsongdu). In the past, the king appointed members to a Royal Advisory Council and to a Council of Ministers. Following the political reforms of 1998, however, these two councils were combined to form the cabinet. This body consists of six ministers elected by the National Assembly, six advisors also elected by the National Assembly, a member nominated by the king, and two representatives of the clergy.

The unicameral National Assembly (established in 1953), known as the Tsongdu, consists of one-hundred fifty members. Of these, thirty-five are appointed by the king to represent government and other secular interests; one-hundred five are elected to three-year terms by groups of village headmen, who are, in turn, elected by a one-family, one-vote system; and the remaining ten are chosen by the lamas acting in concert. The Tsongdu meets twice a year at Thimphu, the capital. Candidates file their own nominations. The assembly is charged with

*A Bhutanese woman weaving alongside a street. The majority of commercial production activity involves cottage industries.*

addressing the king on matters of national importance. It also enacts laws and approves senior government appointments. A simple majority is needed to pass a measure and is conducted by secret ballot. While the king may not veto legislation, he may return bills for further consideration; the king generally has enough influence to persuade the assembly to approve legislation he considers important or to withdraw proposals which he opposes.

Previously an autocracy, Bhutan moved closer to becoming a true constitutional monarchy when King Jigme Singye Wangchuk announced ambitious political changes in 1998. He relinquished his role as head of government and assigned full executive powers to a cabinet consisting of ministers and advisors to be elected by the National Assembly (in reality, the National Assembly chooses from a list of nominees proposed by the king, who also retains authority relating to security issues). The Council of Ministers, a subgroup of the cabinet, elects one of its members on a rotational basis to serve a one-year term as chairman. It is this official who is the head of government. As part of his reforms, King Jigme Singye Wangchuk also introduced legislation by which any monarch would have to abdicate in favor of his hereditary successor if the National Assembly supported a vote of no-confidence against him by a two-thirds majority.

The government discourages political parties and none operate legally.

***Social Problems and Control.*** The legal system is based on English common law and Indian law. Local headmen and magistrates (Thrimpon) hear cases in the first instance. Appeals may be made to an eight-member High Court, established in 1968. From the High Court, a final appeal may be made to the king. Criminal matters and most civil matters are resolved by application of the 17th century legal code as revised in 1965. Questions of family law are governed by traditional Buddhist or Hindu law. Minor offenses are adjudicated by village headmen. Criminal defendants have no right to court appointment of an attorney and no right to a jury trial. Under the 1979 Police Act, police need a warrant to arrest a person and must bring the detainees before a court within twenty-four hours of arrest.

In the past, Bhutan was virtually crime-free. However, with modernization and development, crimes such as burglary, theft and robbing of the ''chortens'' (religious stupas) are becoming common.

***Military Activity.*** The army consists of five thousand soldiers. The army headquarters are located in the capital city of Thimbhu. The regular activities of the soldiers include service with the palace guards, the royal police force, and the militia.

*A government official walking out of an administrative building in Tongsa. Bhutan is a constitutional monarchy.*

## NONGOVERNMENTAL ORGANIZATIONS AND OTHER ASSOCIATIONS

Nongovernmental associations include the National Women's Association of Bhutan and the Bhutan Youth Development Association.

## GENDER ROLES AND STATUS

**The Relative Status of Women and Men.** Bhutan's culture does not isolate or disenfranchise women. Dowry is not practiced, and land is divided equally between sons and daughters. Girls receive nearly equal educational opportunities, and, while accorded a lower status than boys, they are cherished because they are the ones who care for parents in old age.

**Division of Labor by Gender.** Men and women usually work side by side in the field. Women fill most of the nursing and teaching positions.

## MARRIAGE, FAMILY, AND KINSHIP

**Marriage.** Marriages may be arranged by the parents or by the individuals entering the marriage. To get married, a certificate is required from the Court of Law, but most marriages are performed by a religious leader. The Bhutanese are essentially monogamous. Polyandry (multiple husbands) has recently been abolished; the practice of polygamy is legal provided the first wife grants her consent.

A bride does not necessarily move into her husband's household, as is common throughout much of the Indian subcontinent. The new husband may reside with his wife's family if their need for labor warrants it. Alternatively, the new couple may set up their own household on their own plot of land. Divorce is permitted in Bhutanese society, although compensation is required from the party seeking the separation.

**Child Rearing and Education.** A modern educational system was introduced in Bhutan in the 1960s. Prior to that, education was provided only by monasteries. A growing number of children are attending school, but over 50 percent still do not attend. Education is not compulsory. The educational system consists of seven years of primary schooling followed by four years of secondary school. In 1994, primary schools enrolled 60,089 pupils. In the same year, secondary schools enrolled 7,299 students.

**Higher Education.** Bhutan has one college, which is affiliated with the University of Delhi. The Ministry of Education consists of the Department of Education, the Department of Adult and Higher Education, and the Department of Youth Culture and Sports. Scholarships are available for Hindu students to study at Venares Univesity in India.

## ETIQUETTE

As a traditional society, the Bhutanese follow a highly refined system of etiquette, which is called "driglam namzha." This traditional code of conduct supports respect for authority, devotion to the institution of marriage and family, and dedication to civic duty. It governs many different sorts of behavior, including how to send and receive gifts, how to speak to those in authority, how to serve and eat food at public occasions, and how to dress. A royal decree issued in 1989 promoted the driglam namzha as a means of preserving a distinct national identity and instituted a national dress code.

Men and women mix and converse freely, without the restrictions that separate the sexes among other groups in South Asia.

*A young monk playing a drum. The national religion is the Vajrayana form of Mahayana Buddhism.*

## RELIGION

**Religious Beliefs.** Buddhism, which was introduced in the seventh century, is the official religion of Bhutan. Bhutan is the only country in the world that has retained the Vajrayana form of Mahayana Buddhism as its national religion. Throughout all of Bhutan there are Buddhist *stupas*, believed to be a form of protection for tourists and residents.

Hinduism is practiced by the southern Bhutanese. In 1980 King Wangchuck declared Dus-

sera, one of the sacred festivals of Hinduism, a national holiday.

**Religious Practitioners.** There are ten thousand Buddhist monks and they are vitally involved in both the religious and social lives of the Buddhist population. Because of the religious significance of nearly every important event in the life of a Buddhist, the monks visit households and perform rites on such occasions as birth, marriage, sickness, and death.

**Rituals and Holy Places.** A number of annual festivals highlight different events in the life of Buddha. Many of the festivals feature symbolic dances, which are thought to bestow heavenly blessings on the participants or viewers.

During religious festivals, tourists are allowed to enter the *Dzong* (monastery/fortress) and view masked and sword dances; most of the dances date back to before the Middle Ages and are performed only once or twice a year. A fire dance performed at Bumthang is intended to help childless women who are at the festival conceive during the following year.

**Death and the Afterlife.** Both Buddhists and Hindus believe in reincarnation and the law of karma. The law of karma dictates that an individual's decisions and behaviors in one life can influence his or her transmigration into the next life; for example, if someone lived life in harmony with others, that person would transmigrate to a better existence after death. In contrast, someone who had lived selfishly would inherit a life worse than the previous one after death.

## MEDICINE AND HEALTH CARE

Bhutan suffers from a shortage of medical personnel with only 65 percent of the population having access to any form of medical care. The sick, indigent, and aged are cared for within the traditional family structure. Leading causes of death include respiratory tract infections, diarrhea and dysentery, various skin and parasitic infections, and malaria. Infant mortality rates are extremely high, running at one-hundred eighteen deaths per one thousand live births in 1995.

## SECULAR CELEBRATIONS

One of the largest annual festivals takes place on National Day, 17 December, which commemorates the establishment of the monarchy. At this event, the king participates by serving foods and joining the attendees in games and dances.

## BIBLIOGRAPHY

Aris, Michael, and Michael Hutt, eds. *Bhutan: Aspects of Culture and Development*, 1994.

Coelho, Vincent Herbert. *Sikkim and Bhutan*, 1971.

Crossette, Barbara. *So Close to Heaven: The Vanishing Buddhist Kingdoms of the Himalayas*, 1995.

Harris, George Lawrence. *Area Handbook for Nepal, Bhutan, and Sikkim*, 2nd ed., 1973.

Olschak, Blanche C. *Bhutan: Land of Hidden Treasures*, 1971.

———. *The Dragon Kingdom: Images of Bhutan*, 1988.

Rose, Leo. *The Politics of Bhutan*, 1977.

U.S. Dept of State, Editorial Division. *Background Notes: Bhutan*.

World Bank. *Bhutan: Development Planning in a Unique Environment*, 1989.

Zeppa, Jamie. *Beyond the Earth and the Sky: A Journey into Bhutan*, 1999.

—CONNIE HOWARD

# BOLIVIA

## CULTURE NAME

Bolivian

## ORIENTATION

**Identification.** Bolivia is named after Simón Bolívar, a leader in the nineteenth-century wars of independence against Spain. The national culture is an amalgam of Hispanic and pre-Hispanic elements with three cultural traditions: (1) Quechua/Aymara (roughly 34 percent and 23 percent of the population, respectively), centered in the high-altitude plateau and valley mountain regions (highlands) and corresponding to the two (Quechua- and Aymara-speaking) traditions that existed before the Spanish conquest of the sixteenth century; this ''Andean'' tradition extends from southern Colombia to northern Chile and Argentina and roughly corresponds to the boundaries of the Incan Empire, whose capital was Cuzco, Peru; (2) Spanish or Hispanic (roughly 87 percent of the population), derived from the cultural heritage of the conquering Spaniards; and (3) several dozen small Amazonian ethnic groups in the eastern lowlands.

**Location and Geography.** At 424,162 square miles (1,098,581 square kilometers), Bolivia is the fifth largest country in South America. Bordering Peru and Chile to the west, Argentina and Paraguay to the south, and Brazil to the north and east, it is divided into nine political–administrative units called departments. There are three major geographic–ecological landscapes: the high and cold plateau (*altiplano*) between the eastern and western Andean mountain chains (Cordillera Oriental and Cordillera Occidental) at 12,000 to 14,000 feet (4,000 to 4,500 meters) above sea level, the intermontane valleys (*valles*) in the easternmost part of the Cordillera Oriental at an average of 8,500 feet (2,600 meters) elevation, and the vast lowlands (Oriente) beyond the eastern flanks of the Cordillera Oriental. The sparsely populated Oriente—swamp,

grasslands, plains, and tropical and subtropical forest—constitutes over 70 percent of the country.

**Demography.** Historically, Bolivia has been predominantly rural, with most of its Quechua- and Aymara-speaking peasants living in highland communities. The 1992 census confirmed that 80 percent of the people live in the highlands and noted increasing rural to urban migration. In 1992, the population was 6,420,792, with 58 percent in urban areas (settlements of two thousand or more persons), an increase of 16 percent over the 1976 census. The fastest-growing urban centers include Cochabamba, Santa Cruz, and La Paz–El Alto, which account for over a third of the population. A low population density of fifteen inhabitants per square mile is paralleled by a young, fast-growing population (over 41 percent less than fifteen years old).

**Linguistic Affiliation.** Spanish, the national and official language, is spoken in urban centers, while the dominant languages in the rural highlands are Quechua (the Incan lingua franca) and Aymara and in the southeast Guaraní. Members of the Oriente ethnic polities (e.g., Guarayos, Mojeños, Tacanas, Movimas, Chimanes) speak Spanish and their indigenous languages, which are members of the Amazonian language family. Many trilingual (Spanish, Quechua, and Aymara) speakers live in Oruro and Potosí. Because of the greater prestige of Spanish, between 1976 and 1992, monolingual Spanish speakers increased almost 10 percent while those speaking only Quechua or Aymara dropped 50 percent. According to the 1992 census, at least 87 percent of all those over six years old spoke Spanish, an 11 percent increase over 1976 (although many are barely functional in Spanish). In 1992, 46 percent of residents were at least partly bilingual. Several varieties of Spanish, Quechua, and Aymara are spoken, and all have influenced one another in vocabulary, phonology, syntax, and grammar.

*Bolivia*

**Symbolism.** Two broad symbolic complexes help forge national pride and identity and an "imagined community." The first involves symbols and memories associated with disastrous wars and the subsequent loss of national territory. Schoolchildren are taught about the War of the Pacific (1879–1884), in which Chile overwhelmed Bolivia and Peru and seized Bolivia's coastal territories, and nationalism is intertwined with ongoing efforts to reclaim access to the Pacific. The War of the Chaco (1932–1935), in which Bolivia lost vast territories and oil deposits to Paraguay, was critical for national conscious-

ness-raising and the 1952 populist revolution. Other historical commemorations, such as Independence Day (6 August 1825) and the widely celebrated date of the signing of the agrarian reform law (2 August 1952), also serve as catalysts for collective memories. The second complex centers on commemorating the indigenous, non-Hispanic cultural heritage of most Bolivians, especially in the rural highlands, where many Quechua- and Aymara-speaking peasants see themselves as "descendants" of the "Incas," and in national folkloric music and festivals. These festivals are multilayered symbolic "sites" that index things "Bolivian,"—and the multiclass, multiethnic character of these celebrations fosters differential claims to and forging of culture, history, memory, and symbols.

## HISTORY AND ETHNIC RELATIONS

*Emergence of the Nation.* The highland regions were absorbed into the Incan Empire less than a hundred years before the Spanish conquest in 1532. For almost three hundred years Bolivia, or "Upper Peru" (Alto Perú), formed part of the Spanish Empire, and the Potosí silver mines were crucial for the colonial economy.

The wars of independence (independence was achieved in 1825) were led by Spanish-speaking Creoles who consolidated a highly exclusive social order. The disenfranchised majority in the colonial period fared little better after independence: power and privilege were monopolized by a tiny group of landowners and mine owners, and most Bolivians (primarily poor Quechua- and Aymara-speaking peasants and a smaller number of mine workers) were virtually excluded from national society. Only after the 1952 populist revolution did most Bolivians begin to enjoy the rights and privileges of citizenship.

*National Identity.* The sense of nationhood and national identity is shared by all Bolivians but, given the historical disenfranchisement of the peasant majority, probably is of recent origin. Most authors point to the wars of the Pacific and the Chaco and the 1952 populist revolution (along with subsequent state-building efforts) as the key events that created a sense of nationhood. A strong feeling of national identity coexists with other identities, some ethnic and some not, with varying levels of inclusiveness. Regional identities, such as Spanish speakers in the Oriente contrasting themselves with Quechua- or Aymara-speaking highland dwellers, have always been important. For members of lowland ethnic polities, self-identification as Mojeño or Tacana is important in everyday life. In southern highland ethnic politics, shared historical memories and cultural practices such as dress bolster ethnic identification as Macha, Sakaka, or Jukumani.

*Ethnic Relations.* The construction of a national identity that would override ethnic and other identities has been an important but only partly successful dimension of state-building efforts. With the exception of recent attempts by eastern ethnic polities to gain greater autonomy and enduring tensions between the large ethnic polities in the southern highlands (often exacerbated by land disputes), very little large-scale political and social action hinges on ethnic identification. Ethnicity does not underpin large-scale political action, and ethnic conflicts are rare.

## URBANISM, ARCHITECTURE, AND THE USE OF SPACE

Virtually all urban settlements—small towns and villages as well as large cities—are built around a central plaza where most church- and state-related buildings and offices are situated. This typically Mediterranean social, political and cultural "center" use of space is replicated in many urban and rural homes; most consist of compounds and internal patios surrounded by tall walls where cooking, eating, and socializing take place. Modern skyscrapers are found primarily in La Paz and Cochabamba. In the highlands, most dwellings are built of adobe.

## FOOD AND ECONOMY

*Food in Daily Life.* The typical diet is abundant in carbohydrates but deficient in other food categories. In the highlands, the primary staple is the potato (dozens of varieties of this Andean domesticate are grown), followed by other Andean and European-introduced tubers and grains (e.g., oca, quinua, barley, and, increasingly in the Oriente, rice), maize, and legumes, especially the broad bean. Freeze-dried potatoes (*chuño*) and air-dried jerky (*ch'arki*) from cattle or Andean camelids (llama, alpaca, and vicuña) are common, although beef forms an insignificant part of the daily diet. Maize beer (*chicha*) is a traditional and ritually important beverage in the highlands. In the Oriente, rice, cassava, peanuts, bananas, legumes, and maize constitute the cornerstone of the daily diet, supplemented by fish, poultry, and beef. Favorite national delicacies include guinea pig (also consumed during important ceremonial occasions) and deep-fried pork (*chicharrón*). Meals are served with hot pepper sauces. There are few food taboos, and almost all animal parts are eaten, although reptiles are not consumed. Most cultural restrictions center on food preparation, such as avoiding uncooked, unprocessed foods.

In cities and towns, the early-morning meal usually consists of coffee, tea, or a hot maize beverage (*api*), sometimes served with bread. In marketplaces, hot meals and stews are also consumed. In the countryside, breakfast sometimes consists of toasted ground cereals with cheese and tea, followed by a thick soup (*lawa*) at nine or ten. The major

*People involved in a festival procession. The prevailing religious practices center around the Cult of the Virgin Mary and devotion to the* Pachamama, *the earth mother.*

meal is lunch (*almuerzo*), which in upper-class urban households and restaurants typically is a four-course meal. A much lighter meal is eaten at around seven in the evening. Peasants and lower-income urban dwellers have a lunch of boiled potatoes, homemade cheese, a hard-boiled egg, and hot sauce (*lawa*) or a thick stew with rice or potatoes.

**Food Customs at Ceremonial Occasions.** The most elaborate and hearty meals, with abundant fresh vegetables and beef, chicken, or pork, are eaten at ceremonial occasions, such as the life cycle events of baptism, marriage, and death. Public displays of generosity and reciprocity, offering abundant food and drink not often available at other times of the year (e.g., bottled beer, cane alcohol [*trago*], and beef), are an important cultural imperative. On All Souls Day, meals are prepared for the recently deceased and those who are ill. Many important meals mimic those of upper-class restaurants in the major cities, including dishes such as *ají de pollo* (chicken smothered in hot chili sauce and served with rice and/or potatoes).

**Basic Economy.** Silver (and, later, tin) mining and agriculture in the highlands have historically been the twin pillars of the economy. The nation traditionally has produced and exported raw materials

and imported manufactured and processed goods. In 1994, agriculture accounted for 16 percent of the gross domestic product, mining and hydrocarbons almost 10 percent, and manufacturing and industry over 13 percent. Bolivia is self-sufficient in oil and natural gas and exports significant quantities of both. Tourism has emerged as an important economic force. The currency for Bolivia is Boliviano.

After the 1952 populist revolution, major mining concerns were converted into a state mining company (COMIBOL), while smaller companies were allowed to continue operating independently. With the exception of cocaine, a critical political and economic dilemma, no other economic sector rivals mining as a generator of foreign exchange. Since 1985, the neoliberal New Economic Policy (NEP), which was designed to break down barriers to capital flows and strengthen the state, has led to the almost total dismantling of COMIBOL and a surge in private mining. The NEP also has led to the privatization of other state concerns, such as telephones, airlines, and the national oil company.

Bolivia is self-sufficient in almost all food staples with the exception of wheat. Highland crops include tubers, maize, and legumes. Other crops (e.g., peanuts, citrus fruits, bananas, plantains, and rice) are grown in the Oriente, while large cattle ranches are prominent in the departments of Beni and Pando. In eastern Santa Cruz, large agricultural enterprises supply most of the country's rice, sugar, eating and cooking oils, and export crops such as soybeans. Enormous forests provide the raw materials for the lumber and wood products industry (deforestation is an increasing problem). The coca leaf, which is fundamental in Andean ritual, social organization, and health, has always been cultivated in the eastern regions, but the international drug trade has made Bolivia the third largest coca leaf producer and exporter in the world.

***Land Tenure and Property.*** Various legal and customary rights and obligations govern land tenure, such as rules and expectations that structure access to and transmission of use rights to land. Until recently, the legal cornerstone of land tenure was the 1953 agrarian reform law, which recognized various property regimes subject to different legal rights and obligations. In the highlands, where most peasants live, private property rights often are overshadowed by communal and customary forms of tenure, while among southern highland ethnic polities, land is communally held and private property rights do not apply. In frontier colonization areas, where most of the coca is grown and migrants have received land titles from the state, land fragmentation and commoditization are far more developed. Laws stressing partible inheritance (equal shares to all legitimate offspring, male or female) are constrained by informal, customary inheritance practices, and in the rural highlands there is a strong patrilineal bias, with most land inherited by males. There is also evidence of parallel inheritance (an ancient Andean norm), in which women inherit land from their mothers and men inherit from their fathers. Generally, only legally and socially recognized (legitimate) offspring have rights to the land and property of both parents, while illegitimate children are entitled only to a share of the mother's property. The agrarian reform law of 18 October 1996 was intended to stem the growing disparity in access to land, allow the state to reclaim (*revertir*) lands used mainly for speculative purposes, modernize the land reform agency, expropriate lands to protect biodiversity, and ensure the collection of land taxes. Bolivia has passed laws awarding greater autonomy to and delimiting and protecting the territories of the Oriente's ethnic polities.

***Commercial Activities.*** Many consumer goods such as television sets, radios, CD players, cars, motorcycles, and bicycles are sold, partly as a result of neoliberal economic reforms that lifted import bar-

riers. Most consumer goods are bought and sold in large, open periodic markets (*mercados*).

***Major Industries.*** Mining and oil and natural gas are the key industrial sectors. Spurred by an influx of international capital and the "coca economy," construction, including the production of lumber, cement, and other building materials, has taken off. The food and beverage industries (e.g., beer and soft drinks) are significant, as is the production of textiles and leather goods.

***Trade.*** Major exports include textiles, agricultural commodities, minerals, oil, and gas. Important agricultural commodities (excluding coca) that are exported include wood products, soybeans and soybean oils, and coffee. Significant amounts of oil and natural gas are exported to Chile, Argentina, and Brazil. In 1994, oil, natural gas, and mineral exports accounted for almost 50 percent of export earnings, while agricultural commodities (soybeans, lumber and wood products, sugar, cotton, and coffee) accounted for almost 30 percent. Almost half of all exports went to the United States and Europe. Bolivia imports mainly consumer goods, raw materials, and capital and manufactured goods, especially from the United States, Europe, and Brazil.

***Division of Labor.*** With the exception of political participation in the public sphere (which is profoundly gendered), there are few rigid rules in rural communities regarding the division of labor. Generally, all able-bodied adults and children—male or female—actively participate in tasks required for production. Most local-level government positions require some fluency in Spanish and the adoption of non-Andean cultural mores. Women and men of all ages, skills, and occupations are active in the economically and socially significant informal economy. Women and children are particularly prominent in marketplaces.

## SOCIAL STRATIFICATION

***Classes and Castes.*** An institutionalized system of unequal access to political, economic, and sociocultural resources is a direct outcome of the Spanish conquest of culturally and physically distinct Andean societies and is closely wedded to the nation's ethnic and cultural makeup. Class, culture (including ethnicity and language), and race (physical characteristics) overlap, solidify, and mark the social hierarchy. Class boundaries are permeable, but the shedding of the Andean cultural heritage is an important prerequisite for social mobility.

*A woman with a bundle of barley in the altiplano. The majority of Bolivians work in agriculture.*

At the bottom of the hierarchy are peasants, unskilled workers, and those in the "informal" economic sector who live in urban peripheries. Most are referred to as "Indian" and are likely to be monolingual in an Andean or indigenous language and/or barely functional in Spanish, have little formal education and a low income, be only nominally Catholic or Protestant, dress in "traditional" garb, and display Andean phenotypic characteristics (dark-skinned, relatively short, high cheekbones).

Members of a second broad, intermediate category are labeled mestizos, *cholos* (a disparaging term), or nonindigenous. (In the early colonial period "mestizo" originally referred to the offspring of native Andeans and Spaniards.) They are phenotypically almost identical to "Indians," are more assimilated to Hispanic cultural norms and more likely than peasants or unskilled laborers to have a command (though not fluent) of and preference for Spanish, and usually have more formal education.

At the apex of the social hierarchy is a small, "white" affluent elite class collectively referred to as "decent people" (*gente decente*) by peasants, who also address men of this category as "gentleman" (*caballero*) and women as "madam" (*señora*). (These labels also are used for members of the upper tier of the mestizo category.) Culture, class, and physical characteristics converge to mark and define inequal-

ity: Members of this elite class are more likely to be largely fair or white-skinned; be fluent and monolingual Spanish speaking; adopt "Western" clothing; live in major cities; occupy high positions in government, finance, or business; and not identify with the Andean heritage.

***Symbols of Social Stratification.*** Cultural differences and symbols such as language, dress, occupation, and residence are part of the class structure and function as pointers of the social hierarchy. A poor command of Spanish—speaking Spanish that is heavily influenced by Quechua or Aymara phonology or grammar—is an important marker of (lower) class position. Linguistic terms of reference and address also emphasize inferiority and/or social distance; a member of the elite may address a Quechua-speaking male adult peasant as "little child" (*hijito*), while the peasant will refer to him as "sir" or "gentleman." Clothing is also an important marker of cultural distinctiveness and class position. A woman who braids her hair and wears heavy, long pleated skirts (*polleras*) is classed as peasant, Indian, or *chola* and is presumed not to be at the top of the social hierarchy, as is a man who wears rubber sandals (*ojotas*) instead of shoes and wears a knitted wool cap with earflaps (*ch'ullu*). Other significant markers of class hierarchy and ethnic identity include coca chewing and participation in Andean religious rites.

## POLITICAL LIFE

**Government.** Bolivia is a constitutional republic with an elected president and national congress. Famous for its political instability, it has enjoyed unprecedented stability since 1985. There is a centralized political system (the president has always had the power to appoint the governors [prefectos] of the departments), yet recent (mid-1990s) laws were intended to decentralize state administration and increase political participation and decision making, especially at the municipal level. The executive and legislative branches of government are located in La Paz, the de facto administrative capital and seat of government, while the national judiciary is centered in Sucre, the legal capital.

**Leadership and Political Officials.** Formal political power is fragmented among numerous political parties spanning the ideological spectrum, and coalition governments have ruled since 1982. The most important political parties in the 1980s and 1990s were the Movimiento Nacionalista Revolucionario (MNR), Acción Democrática Nacionalista (AND), Movimiento Bolivia Libre (MBL), Conciencia de Patria (CONDEPA), Unidad Cívica Solidaridad (UCS), Frente Revolucionario de Izquierda (FRI), and Movimiento de Izquierda Revolucionaria (MIR). As a result of an alliance between AND, MIR, CONDEPA, and UCS, the former dictator General Hugo Bánzer was elected president in June 1997.

**Social Problems and Control.** Social control is exercised informally at the local level (neighborhood and village) and within networks of acquaintances and kin, and recourse to the police and the judiciary is rare. In peasant villages, disputes usually are settled internally by elected officials who follow customary practices. The drinking of alcoholic beverages and petty crime are growing in importance, as is the smoking of cocaine-laced cigarettes. Interpersonal violence is rare, although there is some domestic violence. Few people have a complete understanding of their constitutional rights and the complex judicial system. In addition to local and departmental courts, the government has set up special narcotics tribunals. The judicial branch is being restructured to streamline bureaucratic procedures.

**Military Activity.** The military has often intervened directly in politics, and many presidents have been military officers who achieved power through a coup d'état. The military has not fought an external war since the Chaco war. Major garrisons are based near cities and/or areas of major peasant concentrations. As a result of U.S. pressure, the military has become involved in anti-coca and anti-drug efforts.

## SOCIAL WELFARE AND CHANGE PROGRAMS

There is a poorly developed social safety net. Pension funds and retirement systems mainly benefit long-term wage earners, such as those employed by the state. Most Bolivians work in agriculture or the informal economy, sectors poorly covered by social welfare and security programs, and most rely on relatives for assistance during old age and in times of need. Since 1985, a variety of programs to ameliorate the impact of neoliberal policies and alleviate poverty and growing unemployment and underemployment have been financed by international development organizations.

## NONGOVERNMENTAL ORGANIZATIONS AND OTHER ASSOCIATIONS

Bolivia is a major recipient of international development aid. Development funds underwrite the many nongovernmental organizations (NGOs) that emphasize agricultural productivity and overall health. Many NGOs are involved in promoting sustainable agriculture in the Oriente, especially the search for tropical and subtropical crops that could compete with coca cultivation. Recent laws encouraging decentralization and popular participation have increased the roles and variety of NGOs.

## GENDER ROLES AND STATUSES

**Division of Labor by Gender.** Important positions of public authority are invariably held by men, while the domestic arena (symbolically associated with fire, kitchen, and hearth) is a female realm. Most ritual specialists, diviners, and healers are male. In agriculture, a flexible division of labor leads to men and women participating in all planting and harvest tasks. Women predominate, as they have since colonial times, in the marketing of crops and reproducing tradition and ethnic identity through weaving, transmitting the native language to their offspring, and their repertoire of songs. An especially gendered division of labor exists in the thriving domestic maid service, which depends on the recruitment of young, poor, usually Quechua- and/or Aymara-speaking, "Indian" girls to serve in upper-class, Spanish-speaking urban households.

*A man puts bread in the oven in a farm on the Rio Guapay near Santa Cruz. A typical Bolivian diet is high in carbohydrates.*

***The Relative Status of Women and Men.*** Gender complementarity—the idea of a necessary union of opposites and of the crucial role of women and men in human and social production—is a hallmark of Bolivian and Andean society and surfaces in many symbolic domains, such as the presence of male and female supernatural deities. The high status of women is bolstered in many rural communities by matrilineal ideology and inheritance, matrikin groups, and access to resources independent of the male spouse. Nevertheless, in many rural areas, the balance is tipping toward greater inequality as the economic position of women deteriorates. Recent research has focused on how notions of masculinity and the symbolism that center on the giving and taking of wives (the metaphors of bull and condor, respectively) are linked to violence against women, often in highly ritualized contexts.

## MARRIAGE, FAMILY, AND KINSHIP

***Marriage.*** Marriage, a fundamental rite of passage and a marker of adult status, often is linked to the formation of new households and is expected of all Bolivians. The typical Andean marriage pattern (customary in the highlands and Oriente but often frowned on by members of the elite) entails three highly ritualized steps: an initial period of coha-bitation (*juntados*) lasting up to three years in which the spouses set up a household and begin to bear children, a civil wedding, and a religious wedding followed by a two- to three-day marriage celebration. Although there are polygynous marriages in some Oriente ethnic groups, monogamy is the norm. The most important marriage prescription in the highlands is that of not marrying someone with an identical first (often paternal) surname and/or within the third cousin range. Village or hamlet exogamy is often the rule. Postmarital residence is usually neolocal (the couple sets up its own household independently of the parents), although this sometimes is preceded, especially in the case of cohabitation, by a patrilocal phase in which the couple temporarily resides with the groom's parents. Marriage expands alliances and networks of kin and generates obligations and reciprocities between the kin group, including godparents and other fictive kin, of both spouses. Divorce, while legal, is rare in rural communities. Remarriage among widows and widowers is common and expected.

***Domestic Unit.*** The basic urban and rural domestic unit is the household: single-family, nuclear (husband, wife, and children), or extended. Bolivians attach importance to bilateral kinship—the tracing of kin links through both the father and the mother—and households often include different

*Women sell fruit and vegetables at a street market in La Paz. Women play an important role in the marketing of crops, which are equally harvested by men and women.*

categories and generations of kin. Although males usually represent the household in public affairs, women control the kitchen, hearth, and household budget.

**Inheritance.** In many Quechua- and Aymara-speaking communities, the inheritance of non-communally held land and water rights is claimed to be bilateral and partible, although often a patrilineal bias in which males but not females inherit property is present. Both men and women

keep and control access to the property they inherit before marriage.

**Kin Groups.** Bolivians stress bilateral kinship, and virtually all recognize and stress kin groups beyond the nuclear family and household. Ritual kinship such as godparenthood is extremely important. In urban and rural areas, "family" (*familia*) often refers to a bilateral kin group (kindred) of the third cousin range. Patrilineally related kin groups (the members of which share an identical paternal surname), sometimes called *castas* ("castes"), are important in many rural villages, as they sometimes jointly manage and cultivate land. Members of southern highland ethnic polities such as the Macha, Jukumani, and Sakaka are organized in inclusive kin-based groups and categories called *ayllus*.

## SOCIALIZATION

**Infant Care.** Women have the primary responsibility for child care. Few deliver their babies in hospitals, relying instead on the help of midwives. Most rural and low-income women breastfeed, wrap, and swaddle their babies, sometimes for as long as two years. Young infants always accompany their mothers during productive activities such as cooking, gardening, and selling goods at marketplaces.

**Child Rearing and Education.** Infants and children usually are raised by their parents or other close kin. Adoption and fosterage are widely practiced. Children are taught early to contribute to the household economy and learn adult responsibilities. It is common for rural children to pasture flocks of sheep and help their parents and kin plant and harvest crops. In urban areas, children often help their mothers sell goods at marketplaces. Children are taught the importance of respect (*respeto*) for family, kin, and adults. Education is highly valued. Children are encouraged to attend school from about age six, although rural attendance and retention rates are considerably lower than urban ones. There is a definite gender bias, and young girls are less likely to complete their education than are boys. Cultural mores emphasize learning by watching, not necessarily by explicit teaching. Infants go through several rituals of socialization, such as the haircutting ceremony after about a year, followed by baptism and confirmation.

**Higher Education.** The illiteracy rate is 20 percent. According to the 1992 census, almost 37 percent of rural inhabitants are illiterate; gender inequalities are especially pronounced, as almost half of all women in rural areas cannot read or write. Poverty and, in the countryside, the wide cultural gap between students and teachers, contribute to high rates of illiteracy.

## ETIQUETTE

Social interaction is governed by norms emphasizing respect and formality and marking age, gender, status, and class differences. Shoppers are expected to be polite and convey deference to shopkeepers by using the adverb "please." The use of formal Spanish pronouns (*usted* but not *tu*) is especially important in addressing elders and older relatives, as are honorific titles for men and women (*don* for men and *doña* for women). Peasants address members of the urban, Spanish-speaking elite as "gentlemen." Cultural mores dictate that one stand very close to the person with whom one is interacting. Gazing and looking directly in the eye are acceptable. Physical greetings vary greatly. In rural areas, simple, short, firm handshakes are common; a hug (but short of a full bear hug), followed by a short pat on the back, is expected between kin and close friends. In rural settings, public touching, caressing, and kissing among couples are frowned on. Generosity and reciprocity are required in all social interactions, many of which involve the sharing of food and alcoholic beverages.

## RELIGION

**Religious Beliefs.** Bolivians are overwhelmingly Catholic (at least formally), and the Catholic Church has historically wielded enormous influence. However, religious beliefs and practices constitute a system of "popular religion" that encompasses formal elements of Catholicism and, increasingly, Protestantism (especially rituals) with only a partial understanding and acceptance of doctrine, coupled with pre-Hispanic Andean beliefs and rituals. In popular religion, complementary deities and supernatural beings coexist. Many people believe in a *k'harisiri*, a malevolent semihuman being who usually is identified as the soul of a priest, foreigner, or Spanish-speaking elite mestizo who, in a pact with the Devil (*supay*), attacks mainly indigenous travelers. Miners are especially devoted to the uncle (*tío*) deity, who ensures rewarding work and protects them against accidents and ill fortune. The widespread devotion to the cult of the Virgin Mary, which intersects with and is nurtured by the equally powerful devotion to the female *Pachamama* (earth mother), is a cornerstone of popular religion. Another distinguishing feature of Andean popular religion is the importance of rituals through which people maintain social relationships and reciprocal ties with supernatural deities. Such rituals sometimes entail the sacrifice of Andean camelids (such as llamas) but more often require constant libations (*ch'allas*) to them in the context of heavy drinking and ritualized coca chewing.

**Religious Practitioners.** The most important religious practitioners with whom the average person

*Buses and trucks line along the side of a cobbled street in the capital of La Paz. Since 1992 there has been increased migration from rural to urban areas.*

comes into contact are church officials (such as parish priests or bishops) and the leaders of Protestant sects. Popular religion includes religious practitioners (*yatiris*) who are diviners or claim knowledge of and ability to intercede with supernatural beings.

***Rituals and Holy Places.*** Social life is punctuated by many rituals that coincide with major agricultural seasons and/or are linked to the celebration of Christian deities, especially the Virgin Mary. The summer solstice is celebrated during the Night of Saint John (21 June) and has important pre-Hispanic antecedents. The carnival festival of Oruro (beginning on the Saturday before Ash Wednesday) is a crucial ritual event that blends Hispanic and pre-Hispanic cultural and religious elements; thousands of spectators and performers take part in musical and dance troupes that commemorate motifs, themes, images, and events, including veneration of the Virgin Mary. A similar festival is that of the Virgin of Urkupiña (14–16 August) in Quillacollo.

The cult of the Virgin of Copacabana, the religious patroness of the nation, whose image was sculpted in 1583, is an especially important ritual event. Many communities have their own ritual celebrations and holy places, almost all associated with the appearance of a Christian saint or the Virgin Mary or the presence of mountain deities.

**Death and the Afterlife.** Household shrines and the rituals that occur during All Souls and All Saints Day (1–2 November) point to the fact that the dead form part of the sociocultural universe of the living. During this solemn celebration, specially prepared ritual tables (*mesas*) with food and drink are offered to the souls of the recently deceased, who are expected to visit their kin (a return associated with the powers of reproduction, especially during the planting season). Funerary rituals typically include washing the body and clothes of the deceased; purchasing and preparing the casket; marshaling large quantities of coca, food, and drink for the all-night wake and subsequent burial; and sponsoring four masses within the next year.

## MEDICINE AND HEALTH CARE

Bolivia has one of the highest infant mortality rates in South America—between sixty-eight and seventy-five per one thousand live births. Major causes of infant and child mortality include respiratory infections, diarrhea, and malnutrition; almost 30 percent of infants under age three suffer from chronic malnutrition. Most people, particularly in the rural areas and low-income neighborhoods surrounding the large cities, lack access to basic biomedical care. Most sick people are cared for by family members and other kin. Many only partially understand and accept Western biomedical ideology and health care. Health beliefs and practices often include aspects of Western medicine and typically Andean elements. Traditional medical practices, often revolving around rituals and ritual practitioners (diagnostic specialists, curers, herbalists, and diviners)—among them the Callawaya of La Paz—are widespread. Divination, rituals, and ritual sacrifices are important in treating illness, as is the use of coca leaves, alcoholic beverages, and guinea pigs. Traditional medicine attaches importance to the social and supernatural etiology of illness and death, which often are attributed to strained social relations, witchcraft, or the influence of malevolent spirits. Dozens of illness categories, many psychosomatic, are recognized. Many curing rituals emphasize balanced, reciprocal relations with deities, who are "fed" and offered drink to dissipate illnesses.

## SECULAR CELEBRATIONS

Important secular celebrations include Independence Day (6 August) and the signing of the 1953 agrarian reform law (2 August), also known as the Day of the Indian (*Día del Indio*). Some of the best known and most meaningful secular celebrations are also national folkloric celebrations.

## THE ARTS AND HUMANITIES

The Bolivian Institute of Culture sponsors the arts and humanities and plays a role in preserving the nation's cultural heritage. Bolivia has a distinguished tradition in literature (especially the novel and short story), a popular oral tradition, and, to a lesser extent, graphic and performance arts. An important genre consists of world-class textile production in the regions of La Paz and Sucre. Supported by the Inter-American Foundation, Bolivian anthropologists are working with weavers and documenting their ancient techniques and traditions.

## THE STATE OF THE PHYSICAL AND SOCIAL SCIENCES

The system of higher education consists of nine state and more than a dozen private universities. Most offer degrees in law and the humanities and the social, health, and life sciences as well as engineering and the physical sciences. A National University Council of Science and Technology has been created. Teaching and research in the physical sciences are not well developed. In 1994, the social sciences received only about 10 percent of all research funds but accounted for 67 percent of university degrees. A doctoral degree is not offered in any field. Important privately funded social science research centers include CIPCA (Centro de Investigación y Promoción del Campesinado), based in La Paz; Cochabamba's CERES (Centro de Estudios de la Realidad Económica y Social); and ASUR (Asociación de Antropólogos del Sur) in Sucre.

## BIBLIOGRAPHY

Abercrombie, Thomas A. "To Be Indian, to Be Bolivian: 'Ethnic' and 'National' Discourses of Identity." In Greg Urban and Joel Sherzer, eds., *Nation–States and Indians in Latin America*, 1991.

———. *Pathways of Memory and Power: Ethnography and History among an Andean People*, 1998.

Albó, Xavier. "Bolivia: Toward a Plurinational State." In Marjorie M. Snipes and Lourdes Giordani, eds., *Indigenous Perceptions of the Nation State in Latin America*, 1995.

Albro, Robert. "Neoliberal Ritualists of Urkupiña: Bedeviling Patrimonial Identity in a Bolivian Patronal Fiesta." *Ethnology* 37 (2): 133–164, 1998.

Arnold, Denise Y. *Matrilineal Practice in a Patrilineal Setting: Rituals and Metaphors of Kinship in an Andean Ayllu*, 1998.

———, et al. "Simit'aña: Pensamientos compartidos acerca de algunas canciones a los productos de un ayllu Andino." In Denise Y. Arnold et al., eds., *Hacia un orden Andino de las cosas*, 1992.

CID. *Bolivia: Anuario estadístico del sector rural, 1994*, 1994.

Comité Ejecutivo de la Universidad Boliviana. *Inventario del potencial científico y tecnológico del sistema universitario Boliviano*, 1996.

Crandon-Malamud, Libbet. *From the Fat of our Souls: Social Change and Medical Pluralism in Bolivia*, 1991.

———. "Blessings of the Virgen in Capitalist Society: The Transformation of a Rural Bolivian Fiesta." *American Anthropologist* 95 (3): 574–596, 1993.

Durán, Jesús. *Las nuevas instituciones de la sociedad civil: Impacto y tendencias de la cooperación internacional y las ONG's en el área rural de Bolivia*, 1990.

Escobar, Ana María. "Andean Spanish and Bilingual Spanish: Linguistic Characteristics." In Peter Cole et al., eds., *Language in the Andes*, 1994.

Fernández Juárez, Gerardo. *El banquete Aymara: Mesas y yatiris*, 1995.

Fundación ASUR. *El renacimiento de un arte indígena: Los textiles jalq'a y tarabuco del centro sur de Bolivia*, 1996.

Gill, Leslie. *Precarious Dependencies: Gender, Class, and Domestic Service in Bolivia*, 1994.

Gisbert, Teresa, Silvia Arze, and Martha Cajías. *Arte textil y mundo andino*, 1992.

Godoy, Ricardo A. *Mining and Agriculture in Highland Bolivia: Ecology, History, and Commerce among the Jukumanis*, 1990.

Goldstein, Daniel M. "Performing National Culture in a Bolivian Migrant Community." *Ethnology*, 37 (2): 117–132, 1998.

Graham, C. "The Politics of Protecting the Poor during Adjustment: Bolivia's Emergency Social Fund." *World Development* 20 (9): 1233–1251, 1992.

Grütter, Jürg. *A Socio-Economic Evaluation of the Structural Adjustment Program of Bolivia*, 1993.

Hardman, M. J. "Aymara and Quechua: Languages in Contact." In Harriet E. Manelis Klein and Louisa R. Stark, eds., *South American Indian Languages: Restrospect and Prospect*, 1985.

Harris, Olivia. "Condor and Bull: The Ambiguities of Masculinity in Northern Potosí." In Penelope Harvey and Peter Gow, eds., *Sex and Violence: Issues in Representation and Experience*, 1994.

Instituto Nacional de Estadística. *Anuario estadístico 1994*, 1994.

———. *Características demográficas de la población en Bolivia*, 1997.

Johnsson, Mick. *Food and Culture among Bolivian Aymara: Symbolic Expressions of Social Relations*, 1986.

Klein, Herbert S. *Bolivia: The Evolution of a Multi-Ethnic Society*, 2nd ed., 1992.

———. *Haciendas and Ayllus: Rural Society in the Bolivian Andes in the Eighteenth and Nineteenth Centuries*, 1993.

———. "Recent Trends in Bolivian Studies". *Latin American Research Review* 31 (1): 162–170, 1996.

Lagos, Maria Laura. "'We Have to Learn to Ask': Hegemony, Diverse Experiences, and Antagonistic Meanings in Bolivia." *American Ethnologist* 20 (1): 52–71, 1993.

———. *Autonomy and Power: The Dynamics of Class and Culture in Rural Bolivia*, 1994.

Larson, Brooke. *Cochabamba, 1550–1900: Colonialism and Agrarian Transformation in Bolivia*, 1998.

León, Rosario. *El consumo alimentario en Bolivia*, 1992.

Léons, Madeline Barbara, and Harry Sanabria, eds. *Coca, Cocaine, and the Bolivian Reality*, 1997.

Mannheim, Bruce. *The Language of the Inka since the European Invasion*, 1991.

Marinissen, Judith. *Legislación Boliviana y pueblos indígenas: Inventario y análisis en la perspectiva de las demandas indígenas*, 1995.

Ministerio de Desarrollo Humano. *El pulso de la democracia: Participación ciudadana y descentralización en Bolivia*, 1997.

Morales, Edmundo. *The Guinea Pig: Healing, Food, and Ritual in the Andes*, 1995.

Nash, June. *We Eat the Mines and the Mines Eat Us*, 1979.

Orta, Andrew. "Converting Difference: Metaculture, Missionaries, and the Politics of Locality." *Ethnology* 37 (2): 165–186, 1998.

Paulson, Susan. *Gender and Ethnicity in Motion: Identity and Integration in Andean Households*, 1992.

Platt, Tristan. "Mirrors and Maize: The Concept of *yanantin* among the Macha of Bolivia." In John V. Murra, Nathan Wachtel, and Jacques Revel, eds., *Anthropological History of Andean Polities*, 1986.

Rasnake, Roger. *Domination and Cultural Resistance: Authority and Power among an Andean People*, 1988.

República de Bolivia. *Proyecto ley de los pueblos indígenas del Oriente, el Chaco y la Amazonía*, 1991.

Rivera Cusicanqui, Silvia, et al., eds. *Ser mujer indígena, chola o birlocha en la Bolivia postcolonial de los años 90*, 1996.

Salles-Reese, Verónica. *From Viraqocha to the Virgin of Copacabana: Representation of the Sacred at Lake Titicaca*, 1997.

Sanabria, Harry. *The Coca Boom and Rural Social Change in Bolivia*, 1993.

———. "Elusive Goals: 'Opción Cero' and the Limits to State Rule and Hegemony in Eastern Bolivia." In Marjorie M. Snipes and Lourdes Giordoni, eds., *Indigenous Perceptions of the Nation State in Latin America*, 1995.

———. "The Discourse and Practice of Repression and Resistance in the Chapare." In Madeline Barbara Leons and Harry Sanabria, eds. *Coca, Cocaine, and the Bolivian Reality*, 1997.

———. "Consolidating States, Restructuring Economies, and Confronting Workers and Peasants: The Antinomies of Bolivian Neo-Liberalism. *Comparitive Studies in Society and History* 41 (3): 535–562, 1999.

———. "Resistance and the Arts of Domination: Miners and the Bolivian State." *Latin American Perspectives* 27 (1): 56–81, 2000.

Spedding, Alison L. *Wachu wachu: Cultivo de coca e identidad en los Yunkas de La Paz*, 1994.

Stark, Louisa R. "The Quechua Language in Bolivia." In Harriet E. Manelis Klein and Louisa R. Stark, eds., *South American Indian Languages: Restrospect and Prospect*, 1985.

Strobele-Gregor, Juliana. "From Indio to Mestizo . . . to Indio: New Indianist Movements in Bolivia." *Latin American Perspectives* 21 (2): 106–123, 1994.

Tellería-Gieger, José L. *Documentos de análisis para la modernización de la universidad boliviana*, 1994.

Wachtel, Nathan. *Le Retour des Ancêtres: Les Indiens Urus de Bolivie, Xxe–XVIe siècle*, 1990.

———. *Gods and Vampires: Return to Chipaya*, 1994.

—HARRY SANABRIA

# BOSNIA AND HERZEGOVINA

## CULTURE NAME

Bosnian; Herzegovinan

## ORIENTATION

**Identification.** The name "Bosnia" is derived from the Bosna River, which cuts through the region. Herzegovina takes its name from the word *herceg*, which designated the duke who ruled the southern part of the region until the Ottoman invasion in the fifteenth century. The two regions are culturally indistinguishable and for much of their history have been united under one government. Although cultural variations in Bosnia and Herzegovina are minimal, cultural identity is currently extremely divisive. The three main groups are Muslims (Bosniacs), Serbs, and Croats. Before the recent civil war, many areas of the country had mixed populations; now the population has become much more homogeneous in most regions.

**Location and Geography.** Bosnia is in southeastern Europe on the Balkan Peninsula, bordering Slovenia to the northwest, Croatia to the north, and Serbia and Montenegro to the south and southwest; it has a tiny coastline along the Adriatic Sea. The land area is 19,741 square miles (51,129 square kilometers). Herzegovina is the southern portion of the country; it is shaped like a triangle whose tip (surrounded by Croatia and Yugoslavia) touches the Adriatic. Northern Bosnia is characterized by plains and plateaus. The central and southern regions are mountainous. The Dinaric Alps that cover this area also extend southward into Serbia and Montenegro. These regions, including the area around Sarajevo, the capital, are conducive to skiing and other winter sports and before the civil war were a popular tourist destination. Much of the land (39 percent) is forested; only 14 percent is arable. Most of the farmland is in the northern part of the country.

The climate varies from cold winters and mild, rainy summers in the mountains to milder winters and hot, dry summers in the rest of the country and a more Mediterranean climate near the coast. The entire region is vulnerable to severe earthquakes. Bosnia also suffers from air and water pollution because of poorly regulated industrial production in the years before the civil war.

**Demography.** The population was 4,364,574 in 1991. A U.S. estimate of the population in July 2000 was 3,835,777; however, that figure is not reliable as a result of dislocations and deaths from military activity and ethnic cleansing. In 1991, approximately 44 percent of the people were Bosniac, 31 percent were Serb, 17 percent were Croat, 5.5 percent were Yugoslav (of mixed ethnicity), and 2.5 percent were of other ethnicities. Since that time, the Bosniac population has declined and that of the Serbs has risen because of ethnic cleansing by the Serbian army. (The terms "Bosniac" and "Muslim" often are used interchangeably; "Bosniac" refers more explicitly to an ethnicity, to avoid confusion with the term "Muslim," which refers to any follower of the Islamic faith.)

Since 1995, the country has been internally divided into a Bosniac/Croat Federation, which controls 51 percent of the land and whose majority is Bosniac and Croat, and a Serb Republic, which has the other 49 percent and has a Serb majority. Herzegovina, which borders Croatia, has historically had a Croat majority.

**Linguistic Affiliation.** Croatian, Serbian, and Bosnian are virtually identical; the distinction among them is a matter of identity politics. Serbians write their language in the Cyrillic alphabet, whereas Croatian and Bosnian use the Latin script. Turkish and Albanian are spoken by a small minority.

**Symbolism.** The flag is blue, with a yellow isosceles triangle to the upper right and seven five-

*Bosnia and Herzegovnia*

pointed white stars and two half stars along the hypotenuse of the triangle.

## HISTORY AND ETHNIC RELATIONS

***Emergence of the Nation.*** The first known inhabitants of the region were the Illyrians. The Romans conquered the area in 167 B.C.E. In 395 C.E., the Roman Empire was split into Byzantium in the east and the Western Roman Empire in the west. The dividing line was the Drina River, which today forms the border between Bosnia and Serbia. Bosnia took on a special significance as the boundary region between the two empires.

The Slavs arrived in the Balkans around 600 C.E., migrating from the north. Bosnia changed hands numerous times. It first gained independence from Serbia in 960, although the relationship with its neighbor to the south continued to be negotiated.

Bosnia became part of the Hungarian Empire in the thirteenth century and gained independence again in the early 1300s. Internal fighting continued, however, until the Bosnian king Steven Tvrtko united the country. In 1376, he declared himself ruler not just of Bosnia but of Serbia as well.

The Ottoman Empire began to attack the region in 1383, eventually incorporating Bosnia as a Turkish province. During the almost four hundred years in which the Ottomans dominated the area, Bosnians adopted many elements of Turkish culture, including religion; the majority of the people converted from Roman Catholicism or Eastern Orthodox Christianity to Islam. Because of Bosnia's position on the border between the Islamic power to the east and the Christian nations to the west, the Turks held on to the area tenaciously, particularly as their empire began to weaken in the sixteenth and seventeenth centuries. In the mid-nineteenth century, Bosnians joined Slavs from Serbia and Croatia in an uprising against the Turks. Austria-Hungary, with the aid of the Russians, took advantage of the Turks' weakened position and invaded Bosnia-Herzegovina, annexing the region in 1908. The Bosnians were bitter at having repulsed the Turks only to be occupied by another outside force but were powerless to repel the new rulers.

In 1914, a Bosnian Serb nationalist assassinated Austrian Archduke Franz Ferdinand in Sarajevo, and Austria declared war on Serbia. World War I spread throughout Europe, ending four years later in the defeat of Austria-Hungary and its German allies. The Kingdom of the Serbs (Serbia, Montenegro, Croatia, and Slovenia) was formed in 1918, and Bosnia was annexed to the new nation. Dissension continued among the different regions of the kingdom, and in an effort to establish unity King Alexander I renamed the country Yugoslavia in 1929. The extreme measures he took, which included abolishing the constitution, were largely unpopular, and Alexander was assassinated in 1934 by Croatian nationalists.

In the 1930s, fascism began to claim many adherents in Croatia, fueled by strong nationalist sentiments and in response to the Nazi movement in Germany. In 1941, Yugoslavia was thrust into World War II when Germany and Italy invaded the country. Thousands of people were killed, and Belgrade was destroyed. Yugoslav troops resisted the invasion but fell after eleven days of fighting. The Germans occupied the country, installing a puppet government in Croatia. Croatian troops took part in the German program of ethnic cleansing, killing thousands of Jews, Gypsies, Serbs, and members of other ethnic groups. Two main resistance movements arose. The Chetniks were Serbian nationalists; the Partisans, under the leadership of the communist Josip Broz Tito, attempted to unite Yugoslavs of all ethnicities. The two groups fought each other, which weakened them in their struggle against the foreign powers. The Partisans managed to expel the Germans only after the Allies offered their support to the group in 1943.

When the war ended in 1945, Tito declared himself president of Yugoslavia. He won an election several months later, after outlawing opposing parties. Bosnia-Herzegovina was granted the status of a republic in 1948.

Tito nationalized businesses and industry in a manner similar to the Soviet system; however, Tito's Yugoslavia managed to maintain autonomy from the Soviet Union. He ruled with an iron fist, outlawing free speech and suppressing opposition to the regime. While ethnic and regional conflicts continued among the six republics (Serbia, Bosnia-Herzegovina, Croatia, Slovenia, Macedonia, and Montenegro), Tito suppressed them before they became a threat to the unity of the country.

Tito died in 1980 and his government was replaced by another communist regime. Power rotated within a state presidency whose members included one representative of each of the six republics and two provinces. This system contributed to growing political instability, as did food shortages, economic hardship, and the example of crumbling regimes in other Eastern European countries.

By the late 1980s, there was a growing desire in most of the republics for more autonomy and democratization. In 1989, however, the nationalist Slobodan Milosevic won the presidency in Serbia. Milosevic, with his vision of a ''Greater Serbia'' free of all other ethnicities, manipulated the media and played on Serbians' fears and nationalist sentiments.

Other Yugoslav republics held their first free elections in 1990. A nationalist party won in Croatia, and a Muslim party won in Bosnia-Herzegovina. The republics of Slovenia and Croatia declared independence in 1991. Because of its strong military and small population of Serbs, Milosevic allowed Slovenia to secede with little resistance. The Croatian declaration of independence, however, was met with a war that lasted into 1992.

In Bosnia, the Muslim party united with the Bosnian Croats and, after a public referendum, declared independence from Serbia in 1992. The Serbs in the republic's parliament withdrew in protest, setting up their own legislature. Bosnia's independence was recognized internationally, and the Muslim president promised that Bosnian Serbs would have equal rights. Those Serbs, however, supported by Milosevic, did not agree to negotiations. The Serbian army forced the Muslims out of northern and eastern Bosnia, the areas nearest to Serbia. They used brutal tactics, destroying villages and terrorizing civilians. Bosnians attempted to defend themselves but were overpowered by the Serbians' superior military technology and equipment.

One of the tactics Serb forces used throughout the war was the systematic rape of Bosnian women. Commanders often ordered their soldiers to rape entire villages. This atrocity has left permanent scars on much of the population.

In November 1992, the presidents of Serbia and Croatia decided to divide Bosnia between them. This resulted in increased fighting between Croats and Muslims as well as between Muslims and Serbs. In that month, six thousand United Nations (UN) troops were deployed in Bosnia as peacekeepers and to ensure the delivery of aid shipments. The UN troops were powerless to act, however, and the atrocities continued.

Many cities were in a state of siege, including Sarajevo, Srebrenica, and Gorazde. There were extreme shortages of food, water, fuel, and other necessities. Those who chose to flee often ended up in refugee camps with dreadful living conditions; the unlucky were sent to Serb-run concentration camps where beatings, torture, and mass murder were common.

In 1993, the UN declared six "safe havens" in Bosnia where fighting was supposed to cease and the population would be protected. This policy proved ineffective, as war continued unabated in all six areas. After a Serb attack on a Sarajevo market that resulted in the death of sixty-eight civilians, the UN decided to step in more forcefully.

In August 1995 a peace conference was held in the United States, resulting in the Dayton Peace Accords, an agreement that Bosnia-Herzegovina would revert to the boundaries in place before the fighting began and that the country would be divided into two parts: the Federation of Bosnia and Herzegovina (run jointly by Muslims and Croats) and the Serb Republic of Bosnia and Herzegovina. The agreement was signed in December, and NATO forces were sent to maintain the peace. The NATO troops are still a significant presence in Bosnia, with approximately thirty-four thousand in the area. The peace is tenuous, however, and recent fighting between Muslims and Serbs in nearby Kosovo has exacerbated ethnic tensions.

***National Identity.*** National identity for Bosnians is inextricably tied to ethnic and religious identity. The majority of Bosnians are Muslim, and their culture bears many traces of the Turkish civilization that predominated in the region for centuries. Bosnian Muslims tend to identify themselves in opposition to Serbia and its long-standing domination of the region. Bosnian Serbs, who are primarily Eastern Orthodox and share a culture with their Serb neighbors to the south, identify less as Bosnians and primarily as Serbs. Croats, who are mostly Roman Catholic, distinguish themselves from both Serbs and Bosnians. Before the civil war forced them into separate camps, all three groups also identified strongly as Bosnian.

***Ethnic Relations.*** The entire Balkan region has historically been called the powder keg of Europe because of volatile relations both among local groups and with outside forces. Bosnia, however, has a long history of relatively peaceful coexistence among its three main ethnic groups. Before the 1990s, intermarriage was common, as were mixed communities. When Milosevic rose to power in Yugoslavia in 1989, his extremist politics stirred latent distrust among the ethnic groups. When Bosnia declared independence in 1992, his government began a campaign of "ethnic cleansing" that has left millions dead, wounded, or homeless. While it is the Serbs, with the backing of Milosevic, who have been responsible for most of the atrocities, Croats also have persecuted Bosnian Muslims.

## URBANISM, ARCHITECTURE, AND THE USE OF SPACE

Approximately 42 percent of the population lives in towns or cities. Sarajevo, near the center of the country in a valley of the Dinaric Alps, is the capital and largest city. Once a cultural center and tourist destination (it was the site of the 1984 Winter Olympics), it has been devastated by the civil war. Before the war, it was a vibrant, cosmopolitan mixture of the old and the new, with skyscrapers and modern buildings standing alongside ancient Turkish mosques and marketplaces. Today many of these buildings are in rubble, and food and electricity are in short supply. Despite its desperate situation, Sarajevo has taken in many refugees from other parts of the country. Even amid the destruction, however, there is evidence of Sarajevo's glorious past. The Turkish Quarter boasts the Gazi

*Men work in a field in Maglaj, during the Yugoslavian Civil War. Most food must be imported because farming does not meet subsistence needs.*

Husrev-Bey mosque, which dates back to the sixteenth century. The religious architecture is varied and impressive; in addition to mosques, there are several Orthodox churches, a cathedral, and a Sephardic Jewish synagogue. The city also has a history museum and a national art gallery.

Mostar, the largest city in the Herzegovina region, also has been devastated by the civil war. Other major cities include Banja Luka, Zenica, and Tuzla. Before the war, housing in the cities consisted primarily of concrete apartment buildings. Many of those structures were destroyed during the war, and despite efforts at rebuilding, many remain unlivable. People have been forced into crowded living situations with little privacy.

In rural areas, which are much less densely populated, the effects of war have been less extreme. Most of those houses are small structures of stone or wood. Before the war, the majority of them were equipped with electricity and running water.

## FOOD AND ECONOMY

***Food in Daily Life.*** Bosnian food has been influenced by both Turkish and Eastern European cuisine. Grilled meat is popular, as are cabbage-based dishes. *Bosanski Ionac* is a cabbage and meat stew.

*Cevapcici* are lamb sausages that often are eaten with a flat bread called *somun.* Pastries, both sweet and savory, are common; *burek* and *pida* (layered cheese or meat pies), *zeljanica* (spinach pie), and *sirnica* (cheese pie) are served as main dishes. *Baklava*, a Turkish pastry made of phyllo dough layered with nuts and honey, is a popular dessert, as is an apple cake called *tufahije. Kefir*, a thin yogurt drink, is popular, as are Turkish coffee and a kind of tea called *salep.* Homemade brandy, called *rakija*, is a popular alcoholic drink. Alcohol use is down since the rise in Muslim influence, and in certain areas of the country drinking has been prohibited.

***Food Customs at Ceremonial Occasions.*** For Bosnian Muslims, the end of Ramadan (a month of fasting from sunrise to sunset) is celebrated with a large family meal and with Turkish-style sweets and pastries. Both Catholics and Eastern Orthodox believers celebrate Easter with special breads and elaborately decorated eggs. Christmas is an occasion for special family meals among the Christian population.

***Basic Economy.*** Bosnia is the second poorest republic of the former Yugoslavia. The agricultural sector, which accounts for 19 percent of the gross domestic product (GDP), does not produce enough

*Carpets and wool rugs produced by artisans in Sarajevo.*

to meet demand, and the country must import food. Industrial production fell 80 percent between 1990 and 1995 because of the civil war, and while it recovered somewhat between 1996 and 1998, the GDP is still significantly lower than it was in 1990. The unemployment rate is between 35 and 40 percent. Bosnia receives large amounts of money in the form of reconstruction assistance and humanitarian aid. In June 1998, a new currency, the convertible mark, replaced the dinar, which had been completely devalued as a result of inflation.

**Land Tenure and Property.** Tito nationalized many of Yugoslavia's farms into collectives. This proved unsuccessful, and he modified the system by giving farmers more control over production. Today, many farms are privately owned. While 90 percent of the country's firms are private, the large government conglomerates are still in place. This has hindered progress toward privatization, as has widespread corruption.

**Commercial Activities.** Crops produced for domestic sale include corn, barley, oats, wheat, potatoes, and fruits. The war has caused severe shortages of food, electricity, and other goods. There is an active black market on which some otherwise unavailable goods can be bought for exorbitant prices.

**Major Industries.** The main industries are mining (coal, iron ore, lead), vehicle assembly, textiles, domestic appliances, oil refining, and military supplies. Much of the production capacity has been damaged or shut down since the early 1990s. There is a negative growth rate of 5 to 10 percent in the country's industries.

**Trade.** The main imports are raw materials, petroleum-based fuels, and consumer goods. The primary exports are machinery, clothing and footwear, and chemicals. Other republics of the former Yugoslavia and Western European nations are the main trading partners. During the war, Serbia and Croatia placed strict restrictions on trade with Bosnia, further damaging the economy.

**Division of Labor.** Under communism, the composition of the workforce shifted from an agricultural base to an industrial one. The more desirable jobs in government often were obtained through connections. Today, as the economy is beginning to recover from the civil war, jobs are difficult to come by in many fields, and connections are still useful.

## SOCIAL STRATIFICATION

**Classes and Castes.** Before World War II, peasants formed the base of society, with a small upper class composed of government workers, professionals, merchants, and artisans and an even smaller middle class. Under communism, education, party membership, and rapid industrialization offered possibilities for upward mobility. The majority of the people had a comfortable lifestyle. The civil war drastically decreased the overall standard of living, and shortages and inflation have made necessary items unaffordable or unavailable. This situation has created more extreme differences between the rich and the poor, as those who have access to goods can hoard them and sell them for exorbitant rates. In general, the war stripped even the richest citizens of their wealth and left the majority of the population destitute.

**Symbols of Social Stratification.** Under Tito, Yugoslavia had a higher standard of living than did most countries in Eastern Europe; it was not uncommon for people in the cities to have cars, televisions, and other goods and appliances. The upper classes and higher-echelon government workers had more possessions and a higher standard of living. Today, luxuries of any sort are rare.

People generally dress in Western-style clothing. Muslim women can be distinguished by their attire; while they do not wear the full body covering common in other Islamic countries, they usually cover their heads with scarves. Traditional Serbian and Croatian costumes include caps, white blouses, and elaborately embroidered vests; they can be distinguished by the type of embroidery and other small variations. These outfits are worn only for special occasions such as weddings and festivals.

## POLITICAL LIFE

**Government.** The legislature is bicameral. In the National House of Representatives, or *Vijece Opcina*, two-thirds of the seats are designated for the Bosniac/Croat Federation and one-third for the Serbian Republic; in the House of Peoples, or *Vijece Gradanstvo*, each ethnic group is guaranteed five seats. The presidency rotates every eight months among members of the three groups. These three presidents are elected by popular vote for four-year terms.

**Leadership and Political Officials.** Since the war, politics has splintered along ethnic lines. More than twenty political parties are represented in the government, most of them identified as Bosnian Muslim, Serb, or Croat. Bosnians are currently extremely wary of trusting a leader from a different ethnic group to represent their interests.

**Social Problems and Control.** The high rate of unemployment has led to an increase in crimes such as petty theft and carjacking. Unexploded land mines throughout the country are still a major concern. The Federation and the Republic have separate legal systems with trial and appellate courts.

One of the primary concerns today is prosecuting war criminals. An international war tribunal at the Hague has tried some perpetrators, but many others remain at large, including Slobodan Milosevic.

**Military Activity.** The Federation Army consists of separate Croatian and Bosniac elements. The Bosniac Army (the official army of the Federation) consists of forty thousand troops; the Croatians have sixteen thousand. The Army of the Serb Republic is composed solely of Bosnian Serbs and numbers around thirty thousand. Both federation and republican forces have air and air defense components that are subordinate to ground forces.

*A child playing while wearing a United Nations helmet. Many schools were closed during the war, leaving children with no access to education.*

## SOCIAL WELFARE AND CHANGE PROGRAMS

Tito instituted a welfare system that provided for the poor, the elderly, and the mentally and physically disabled. His government also guaranteed women maternity leave and paid leave when their children were sick.

In independent Bosnia, the Muslim, Croat, and Serbian administrations provide aid for their respective populations. In the 1990s, the majority of the money for social services came from foreign aid organizations rather than from the government.

## NONGOVERNMENTAL ORGANIZATIONS AND OTHER ASSOCIATIONS

A number of international humanitarian groups have provided aid to help the country recover from the civil war. One of the largest of these groups is the International Committee of the Red Cross, which, in addition to providing aid and aid workers, investigated Serbian violations of the Geneva Conventions during the war. Other active groups include Christian Relief, World Vision, the Interna-

*A building with arched double doors in Mostar, the largest city in the Herzegovina region. Mostar was badly damaged by the civil war.*

tional Medical Corps, and numerous religious, governmental, and humanitarian associations.

## GENDER ROLES AND STATUSES

***Division of Labor by Gender.*** Women are responsible for all domestic tasks, including cooking, cleaning, and child rearing. Women who work outside the home generally have lower-paying and lower-status jobs than men do. Since the economic devastation of the civil war, men are more likely to occupy the few jobs that are available, and more women have returned to the traditional roles of housewife and mother. Women are more equally represented in agriculture than they are in other fields, and the majority of elementary schoolteachers are women.

***The Relative Status of Women and Men.*** Bosnia has a patriarchal tradition in which women are expected to be subservient to men. Both the Eastern European and Islamic traditions have contributed to this situation. Under Tito's administration, women were given complete civil and political rights. Educational and lifestyle opportunities have increased significantly since that time, although there are still disparities.

## MARRIAGE, FAMILY, AND KINSHIP

***Marriage.*** Marriages are not arranged, and love matches are the norm. In 1991, before the civil war, 40 percent of the marriages registered involved ethnically mixed couples. Since that time, mixed marriages have become extremely rare. Despite Muslim sanctioning of polygamy, the custom was practiced in only one region of the country and currently is not practiced at all. It used to be customary for a bride's parents to give the couple a specially woven dowry rug containing the couple's initials and the wedding date.

***Domestic Unit.*** The traditional domestic unit often includes parents, grandparents, and young children. This pattern has been disrupted in many cases, as the war forced thousands of people to flee their homes. Many were relocated to refugee camps or other countries, and thousands more were sent to concentration camps. Many mixed families have been torn apart by ethnic hatred, as children and spouses are forced to choose between ethnic affiliation and family ties.

***Inheritance.*** Traditionally, inheritance follows a system of primogeniture, passing from the father

*A scenic view of Mostar. The Bosna river, which flows through the country, is part of the country name.*

to the oldest son. Under communism it was legal for women to inherit property.

***Kin Groups.*** As in the neighboring Slavic countries, Bosnians traditionally lived in *zadruga*, agricultural communities that ranged from two or three related nuclear families to as many as a hundred. Those communities were patriarchal and hierarchical in organization, with a male *gospodar* as the head. Most important decisions were made communally by the male members. While zadruga no longer exist in their original form, a person's extended family is still considered extremely important, especially in rural areas.

## SOCIALIZATION

***Infant Care.*** Tito's government, which encouraged women to work outside the home, established state-run day-care centers for young children.

***Child Rearing and Education.*** The current generation of children has witnessed unspeakable atrocities. Children were a prime target of snipers, especially in Sarajevo. Survivors suffer flashbacks, nightmares, and severe depression; in one survey, 90 percent of children surveyed in Sarajevo declared that they did not want to live. The country will be

dealing with the effect of the war on these children for years.

Education is free and mandatory for children between the ages of seven and fourteen. There are Muslim schools where students study the Koran and Islamic law in addition to secular subjects and where boys and girls are taught in separate classrooms.

The educational system has been hard hit by the war. Schools were common targets of Serb mortar attacks, and many were forced to close. Some makeshift schools were organized in homes, but many children were left with no access to education. Since 1995, many schools have reopened.

***Higher Education.*** The country has universities at Sarajevo, Banja Luka, Tuzla, and Mostar. After the civil war, the university in Mostar split into a Croat university in the western part of the city and a Muslim university in the eastern part.

## ETIQUETTE

Bosnians are known as a friendly, hospitable people. In Muslim houses, it is traditional to remove one's shoes and put on a pair of slippers. Kissing is a common form of greeting for both men and women. Three kisses on alternating cheeks are cus-

*Stone houses with terracotta roofs cover a hill in the town of Lastovo on the island of Lastovo.*

tomary. Visiting is a common pastime. When entering a home as a guest, one often brings a small present. Hosts are expected to serve a meal or refreshment.

## RELIGION

**Religious Beliefs.** Forty percent of the population is Muslim, 31 percent is Eastern Orthodox, 15 percent is Roman Catholic, and 4 percent is Protestant; 10 percent of the people follow other religions. Most of the population is not particularly observant, but religion is an important aspect of national identity. (Islam is associated with the Bosniacs, Eastern Orthodox with the Serbs, and Catholicism with the Croatians.)

Icons, which are images representing Christ, angels, saints, and other holy figures, hold an important place in Orthodox practice and are considered a connection between the earthly and spiritual realms.

**Religious Practitioners.** The central religious figures in Islam are called *muezzins*, scholars of the Koran who call the faithful to prayer. The Koran is seen as the ultimate authority in the religion. In the Eastern Orthodox religion, priests are the primary

religious authorities; they are permitted to marry. The Eastern Orthodox religion does not recognize the authority of the Pope but follows a group of patriarchs who have equal status.

**Rituals and Holy Places.** Mosques are Muslim houses of worship. It is customary to remove one's shoes before entering. The prayer hall has no pews or seats; instead, worshipers kneel on prayer rugs. After Ramadan, people exchange small gifts, visit friends, and have a large family meal.

Eastern Orthodox religious ceremonies are held in elaborate, beautifully designed churches, many of which date back hundreds of years. Each family has a patron saint who is honored once a year in a large celebration called *Krsna Slava*. A candle is lit in the saint's honor, and special foods are consumed. Christmas (observed 6 and 7 January in the Orthodox Church) is a major holiday. Christmas Eve, called *Badnje Vece*, is celebrated with a large bonfire in the churchyard and the singing of hymns. In addition to church services, Easter is celebrated by dying eggs and performing traditional *kolo* dances.

**Death and the Afterlife.** Christians and Muslims mourn the death of a loved one by dressing in black and paying visits to the family of the deceased.

In the Eastern Orthodox tradition, funerals are large, elaborate occasions. In the cemetery, a spread of salads and roasted meats is presented in honor of the deceased; this is repeated a year after the death, at which point the gravestone is placed in the ground. Gravestones often bear photographs as well as inscriptions.

## MEDICINE AND HEALTH CARE

Tito's government significantly raised the standard of health, eliminating diseases such as typhus, tuberculosis, and whooping cough. More medical workers were trained, facilities were improved, and educational campaigns raised the general awareness of the population regarding health issues.

Many of the nation's health problems today stem from the destruction caused by the civil war. The medical system has been hard hit; facilities have been destroyed, and staffing and supplies are inadequate to deal with the enormous number of casualties. Despite the health workers and aid sent by charitable organizations, these problems continue to plague the health care system and have left it unable to meet even the basic medical needs of the population.

## SECULAR CELEBRATIONS

The main secular holidays are New Year's Day, 1 January; Republic Day, 9 January (25 November in the Federation); Independence Day, 1 March; Day of the Army, 15 April; Labor Day, 1 May; and Victory Day, 4 May. There is an annual Sarajevo Film Festival in late August and a Winter Festival in February and March that is observed with theatrical and musical performances.

## THE ARTS AND HUMANITIES

**Support for the Arts.** Under communism, artists who glorified the state received government funding; most other expression was censored. Since that time, artists have been given more creative freedom, although the religious establishment has used its political power to influence the art that is produced. There is virtually no money from public or private sources to support the arts.

**Literature.** The national literary tradition can be traced back to epic stories that were set to music and passed orally from one generation to the next. While not as prevalent today, this art form was still widely practiced as recently as the 1950s. Contemporary literature is concerned with history and identity politics. The most famous Bosnian writer is Ivo Andric, a Serbian Catholic who was raised in Bosnia and won the Nobel Prize in 1961 for the historical novel *Bridge over the Drina*. Mesa Selimovic, another novelist, was raised a Muslim but proclaimed himself a Serbian writer. Much of the literature produced in recent years has consisted of nonfiction accounts of the war. One such work is that of Zlata Filipovic, a twelve-year old girl whose diary describes everyday life in besieged Sarajevo.

**Graphic Arts.** Sarajevo and Mostar are well known for the wool rugs and carpets their artisans produce. Turkish influence is evident in the bright colors and geometric designs. Calligraphy and metalwork also reflect traditional Islamic styles. Silk embroidery is a traditional women's art. Contemporary graphic artists have used bullets, shrapnel, broken glass, ash, and other debris to make powerful statements.

The film director Emir Kusturica, a Bosnian with a Muslim background, achieved international acclaim for his 1984 film *When Father Went Away on Business*, which was nominated for an Academy Award in the United States. Since the civil war, Kusturica's work has been condemned by Muslim authorities, and he has moved to Serbia.

**Performance Arts.** Music in urban areas has strong echoes of the Turkish tradition. Singing is accompanied by the *saz*, a type of lute. In rural areas, the music draws more on Slavic influences. *Ravne pesme* is a "flat song" with little variation; *ganga* is a polyphonic song that sounds like shouting. The main instruments are the *shargija* (similar to the saz), the *diple* (a droneless bagpipe), and a wooden flute. Epic poems are performed to the accompaniment of a one-stringed fiddled called a *gusle*. *Sevdalinka* songs (from the Turkish word for love) are sentimental melodies usually sung by young women. They are performed throughout Bosnia and Herzegovina and have a strong cultural resonance in the entire country.

There are a variety of folk dances. Some are similar to the Serbian and Croatian forms. The *nijemo kolo* is a circle dance performed to foot stamping rather than music. There are also different line dances, some performed by men and others by women. Rock 'n' roll and popular dancing are popular and in some cases are replacing the more traditional forms.

## THE STATE OF THE PHYSICAL AND SOCIAL SCIENCES

The physical and social sciences are virtually nonexistent since the civil war, and there are no funds available for these pursuits. The National and University Library was destroyed by Serbian bombings in 1992 and has not been rebuilt.

## BIBLIOGRAPHY

Benedek, Wolfgang, ed. *Human Rights in Bosnia and Herzegovina after Dayton: From Theory to Practice* 1999.

Bildt, Carl. *Peace Journey: The Struggle for Peace in Bosnia,* 1998.

Campbell, David. *National Deconstruction: Violence, Identity, and Justice in Bosnia,* 1998.

Chandler, David. *Bosnia: Faking Democracy after Dayton,* 1999.

"The Dismantled State of Bosnia." *The Economist,* June 28, 1997.

Doubt, Keith. *Sociology after Bosnia and Kosovo: Recovering Justice,* 2000.

Filipovic, Zlata. *Zlata's Diary: A Child's Life in Sarajevo,* 1994.

Glenny, Mischa. *The Balkans: Nationalism, War, and the Great Powers, 1804–1999,* 2000.

Hemon, Aleksander. *Question in Bosnia,* 2000.

Malcolm, Noel. *Bosnia, A Short History* 1994.

Mazower, Mark. *The Balkans: A Short History,* 2000.

Milojkovíc-Djuríc, Jelena. *Panslavism and National Identity in Russia and the Balkans, 1830–1880: Images of the Self and Others,* 1994.

Mojzes, Paul, ed. *Religion and War in Bosnia,* 1998.

"A Precarious Peace." *The Economist,* January 24, 1998.

Thompson, Mark. *Forging War: The Media in Serbia, Croatia, and Bosnia-Hercegovina,* 1999.

### Web Sites

U.S. State Department, Central Intelligence Agency. "Bosnia." www.odci.gov/cia/publications/factbook/geos/bk.html

—ELEANOR STANFORD

# BOTSWANA

## CULTURE NAME

Batswana

## ORIENTATION

**Identification.** Formerly Bechuanaland Protectorate under the British, Botswana became independent in 1966. *Botswana* means "place of Tswana" in the dominant national language (*Setswana*), and the citizenry are called *Batswana*, or Tswana people. The term Batswana, however, bears a double meaning. In government rhetoric, it refers to all citizens of Botswana. But the word also refers to ethnically "Tswana" people, as distinct from the other ethnic groups present in the country. This double meaning allows for both the expression of strong civic national sentiments and debate about the dominance of Tswana people and ideology over the broader population. The double meaning has also permitted the fiction, widely accepted in outside reporting, that Botswana's success as a multiparty liberal democracy is based on an ethnically homogeneous population, when abundant state resources based upon diamond mining, responsibly and equitably distributed, are the more likely source of stability. This fiction may indeed have supported the building of an officially nonethnic, state-oriented society, but has come under sharp challenge in the 1990s, as minority groups request the privileges of official recognition.

**Location and Geography.** Botswana is a landlocked and arid country. Bordering on South Africa, Zimbabwe, Namibia, and Zambia, it is 224,607 square miles (581,730 square kilometers) in area, about the same size as France. Two-thirds of the country is comprised of the Kalahari Desert, which is covered with grasses and scrub but has scarce surface water. Mean annual rainfall ranges from under 10 inches (250 millimeters) per annum in the southwest to over 25 inches (635 millimeters) in the northeast. The entire country is prone to extended droughts, causing significant hardship to agriculturalists, pastoralists, and hunter-gatherers. The Okavango Delta, in the north, is a large inland delta, and people there fish and farm on its flooded banks; tourists are drawn to the large numbers of wildlife that congregate in the area. The eastern third of the country, with more rainfall and fertile soils, is home to most of the population. Prior to independence, the British administered the Protectorate from Mafiking in South Africa. The capital city today, Gaborone, was built on a village site in the southeastern corner of the country at independence, near the borders of several of the Tswana polities that dominated the country.

**Demography.** Botswana's population has grown from 600,000 people in 1971 to an estimated 1,600,000 in 2000. While very high growth rates in the 1970s and 1980s have declined, high birth rates and declining infant mortality have led to a population structure heavily skewed toward young people: 43 percent of the population was under fifteen in 1991. Although ethnically Tswana people are often said to be a majority, government censuses collect no information on ethnicity. Earlier studies indicated that in some regions, Tswana were a minority, and that all polities were composed of people of heterogeneous origins, including Kalanga, Yei, Mbukushu, Subiya, Herero, Talaote, Tswapong, Kgalagadi, Kaa, Birwa, and varied peoples known as Bushmen (or, in Botswana, Sarwa). There are also resident Europeans and Indians.

**Linguistic Affiliation.** Bantu, Khoisan, and Indo-European languages are spoken in Botswana. English is the official language and Setswana the national language. This means that the language of government and higher education is primarily English, but that Setswana is the dominant language spoken in the country. Ninety percent of the population is said to speak Setswana. The term Setswana refers both to Tswana language, and to Tswana practices/culture, and there has been increasing re-

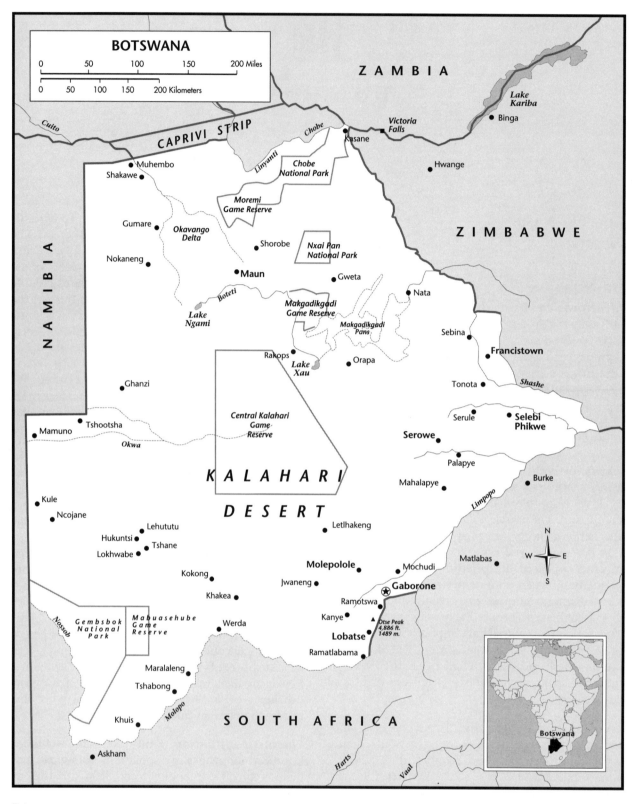

## BOTSWANA

0   50   100   150   200 Miles

0   50  100  150  200 Kilometers

ZAMBIA

*Lake Kariba*

Cuito

CAPRIVI STRIP

Chobe

Victoria Falls

Binga

Kasane

Linyanti

Muhembo

Hwange

Shakawe

Chobe National Park

Moremi Game Reserve

ZIMBABWE

Gumare

*Okavango Delta*

Shorobe

*Nxai Pan National Park*

NAMIBIA

Nokaneng

**Maun**

Gweta

Boteti

Nata

*Makgadikgadi Game Reserve*

*Lake Ngami*

*Makgadikgadi Pans*

Sebina

**Francistown**

Rakops

*Lake Xau*

Orapa

Tonota

Shashe

Ghanzi

*Central Kalahari Game Reserve*

Serule

**Selebi Phikwe**

Tshootsha

**Serowe**

Mamuno

Okwa

Palapye

**K A L A H A R I**

Mahalapye

Burke

Limpopo

Kule

**D E S E R T**

Ncojane

Letlhakeng

Lehututu

N

Hukuntsi

Tshane

W    E

Lokhwabe

**Molepolole**

Mochudi

Matlabas

S

Kokong

Jwaneng

Khakea

Ramotswa

⊛ **Gaborone**

Nossob

*Gembsbok National Park*

*Mabuasehube Game Reserve*

Werda

Kanye

▲ Otse Peak 4,886 ft. 1489 m.

**Lobatse**

Ramatlabama

Maralaleng

Tshabong

Molopo

Khuis

**S O U T H   A F R I C A**

Askham

Harts

Vaal

Botswana

*Botswana*

sistance to the dominance of Setswana as national language by speakers of other languages in the country; language-revival movements have also emerged. Most speakers of other languages are multilingual; some, however, have weaker competence in Setswana and have complained of disadvantages in primary schooling.

**Symbolism.** "Pula," the Setswana word for rain, is featured on the coat of arms, and is called out frequently at public gatherings as a salute and cry of approbation. It is also the term for the national currency. The national anthem is "Lefatshe la Rona," ("Our Country"), and its title captures the strong attachment most Batswana feel to the land and its resources, as well as some antiforeign sentiments. Cattle were tremendously important not just to a material economy but also to the symbolic economy of status, family, and social relations in the past, and cattle remain powerfully evocative to most Batswana today.

## HISTORY AND ETHNIC RELATIONS

**Emergence of the Nation.** People known colloquially to the west as Bushmen have lived in Botswana for thousands of years. Herders and agriculturalists from a Bantu tradition appeared more than two-thousand years ago. Tswana polities under Tswana chiefs moved into Botswana from the south and east in the seventeenth and eighteenth centuries, some responding to the rise of the Zulu state and European encroachments. Missionization of Tswana began in 1816, and throughout the nineteenth century Tswana polities were drawn into trade, Christianity, and the migrant labor economy centered in South Africa, while defending themselves against incursions from the north, east, and south. In 1885 the British declared the area the Bechuanaland Protectorate, and in a famous visit to Britain in 1895, three of the Tswana kings petitioned to remain under the British instead of being governed by the British South Africa Company. British administration in the twentieth century strengthened the role of the Tswana chiefs and the dominance of Tswana laws and customs over the country.

National political activity at first focused upon preventing the protectorate's annexation by South Africa. Later, as independence movements emerged across Africa, people from a variety of ethnic groups looked forward to independence and formed political parties. The move to independence was quite peaceful. Independence was granted to the newly named Republic of Botswana in 1966.

**National Identity.** As a new nation, Botswana emphasized nonethnic citizenship and liberal democracy. Diamonds were discovered soon after independence was granted, and the prudent and equitable use of their revenues has underwritten stability and the repeated reelection of the dominant political party.

**Ethnic Relations.** The domination of the country by the Tswana polities has persisted in a nonethnic government through the easy assumption of the predominance of Tswana people, language, and customs. Certain groups in the past were treated as serfs or subordinates by Tswana, such as the Sarwa, Kgalagadi, Yei, and Kalanga, and the latter two have been particularly active in the 1990s to secure official recognition for minority "tribes," and in ethnic revivalism. The nonethnic official rhetoric of civic participation, however, has also allowed many members of minority groups to move through the educational system into prominent management and bureaucratic positions.

## URBANISM, ARCHITECTURE, AND THE USE OF SPACE

Traditional architecture in Botswana is distinguished from modern architecture in three domains: the use of materials (mud/dung, wooden poles, thatch) that may be manufactured by members of a household; the round house form and/or thatched roofing; and/or the presence of a courtyard known as a lolwapa where much activity takes place. By contrast, modern architecture uses purchased materials (cement and bricks and roofing products) and involves the labor of specialized and commercial craftsmen, is square, and features rooms for specialized activities (bedrooms, kitchens). The traditional Tswana residential area is a compound, often housing several closely related family groups. Into the 1990s, much urban housing was financed and built by the government, and repeated a few basic patterns, including one that retained a courtyard structure, which later became unpopular.

Households in the Tswana polities often maintained three residential sites: one in a village, one at agricultural holdings around the village periphery, and one farther out at the cattlepost. Cattleposts, where livestock are kept, are today sometimes complex compounds with several houses and nearby agricultural fields, and sometimes just an animal pen or two and a ramshackle shelter for the herder(s). Many urban residents today continue to maintain a house in a village of origin, and many men and some women also develop cattleposts. Villages are distinguished from towns and cities by a significant engagement in agriculture by residents, and by the political structure of the settlement. At the heart of a village is the chief's central court and public forum, known as a kgotla. The village is divided into wards, each of which also has a kgotla where a headman hears lower-level disputes and matters of ward concern are aired.

Urban areas have grown rapidly in Botswana since independence. In 1991, 46 percent of the population was urban, a percentage that continues to grow. Cities are centered by a downtown area of shops, businesses, and government offices. Some larger villages have come to be known as "urban villages" or "agro-towns."

## FOOD AND ECONOMY

**Food in Daily Life.** Sorghum or corn meal porridge is the staple of most Botswana meals. People wake in the morning to a thinner version of the porridge, sometimes enriched with soured milk and/or sugar, and tea. A thicker version of the porridge, known as *bogobe*, anchors the substantial midday meal, accompanied by a stew of meat and/or cabbage, spinach (or wild greens), or beans. People also use rice, but it is considered more expensive and associated with Europeans. Meats include chicken, goat, sheep, cattle, fish, a caterpillar known as phane and various wild game. Village evening meals may include leftovers from midday, but for many people is often just tea and buttered bread.

There are many restaurants representing food from around the world in the urban areas. Fast food chains such as Kentucky Fried Chicken, Nando's chicken, and Pie City are quite popular. In smaller villages, there are likely to be no restaurants. Fatcakes, somewhat like round doughnut holes, are sold as snacks fairly ubiquitously. Locally brewed beer made from sorghum is popular in the rural areas and is available commercially as chibuku; people also drink the stronger honey/sugar-based khadi.

**Food Customs at Ceremonial Occasions.** At large public events, such as the opening of a new government building, and at weddings and funerals, men prepare the centerpiece: meat cooked in large iron pots until in shreds. Women prepare porridge and/or rice, pumpkin/squash, and often cole slaw or beet salad, and people are served heaping plates of food, arguing to get more meat for themselves. Beer is often served at weddings, and ginger beer at other events; tea and fatcakes are prepared for weddings and funerals that have all-night components.

**Basic Economy.** At independence in 1966, most people in Botswana relied on mixed agriculture (crops and livestock), hunting and gathering wild foods, and remittances from migrant labor in South Africa. But diamonds were found soon after independence, and since the 1970s mining has provided a strong backbone for economic development. Farming of sorghum, maize, millet, and beans, along with small stock and cattle, are still important for subsistence and also commercial returns. Because of drought and urban migration, Botswana no longer aspires to be self-sufficient in agriculture, but instead focuses on "food security" incorporating regular imports of grain and processed foods. Thirty-seven percent of formal employment is by the government (and almost 8 percent in state corporations), but employment in the private sector is now growing more rapidly; people work in service and retail, mines, construction, other industries, and in many small start-up businesses. Earnings are typically remitted rather broadly through extended kin networks.

**Land Tenure and Property.** About 5 percent of Botswana's land is freehold, and about 25 percent is state land in the form of national parks, game reserves, and wildlife management areas. The rest is communal land, also called "tribal land"; people are allocated rights to farm or build houses and pass the rights on to descendants, but they may not transfer the rights to someone else. Grazing land is generally not allocated, but people develop claims to grazing areas through registered wells and water rights. Some tribal grazing land was zoned for commercial development in the controversial Tribal Grazing Lands Policy of 1975, and is allocated in fifty-year leases. Land boards, composed of elected and appointed members, administer the allocation of tribal land. Although all citizens are guaranteed access to land, there have been many complaints about land board allocation; the association of "tribal" land with the dominant Tswana polities has produced demands by some minority groups for tribal lands of their own.

**Commercial Activities.** Agricultural products are marketed both through government marketing services and privately. Small-scale retailing of manufactured goods is widespread. Small home industries, such as sewing, cement block manufacture, other household goods, and construction are common activities, and the government is promoting larger industrial enterprises.

**Major Industries.** Botswana's diamond mines are jointly owned and operated with De Beers Consolidated Mines. Copper, nickel, and potash mines produce for an international market. Beef is exported as well, primarily to the European Union (EU) through the Lomé Conventions, designed by the EU to promote trade and development in third-world countries. Botswana has struggled to attract major industrial enterprise to the country. Textiles, clothing, and food processing constitute the major industries. Abundant wildlife, especially in the north, is the basis of a tourist sector that has focused primarily on high-end tours.

**Trade.** Botswana exports are dominated by diamonds, copper/nickel matte, beef and animal products; also exported are textiles and soda ash. In the 1990s, an automobile assembly plant added vehicles to the list of exports, but that plant was closed in 1999, and the government is seeking new operators for it. Around 80 percent of exports go to Europe. Diamonds account of about 80 percent of foreign exchange earnings. Botswana imports a wide variety of goods. Botswana is a member of the South African Customs Union.

**Division of Labor.** There was very little specialization in the "traditional" economy, with the exception of traditional doctors. Within the household, tasks were distributed based on age and gender. Tswana practices are often taken as representative of the country as a whole: hence the symbolically important area of cattle care is associated entirely with men. But women do care for and milk cattle in other cultures within the country (as, for example, the Herero). When ox-drawn plows, and later tractors, were introduced, men became more involved in crop agriculture. Apart from the heavy wooden supports, women did most of the construction and maintenance of traditional houses; today, men tend to specialize in modern construction techniques. Young boys and men, along with other dependent males, used to work at cattleposts, but now younger people attend school and Batswana complain frequently about finding reliable herders. In the "modern" economy, there is no formal division of labor by gender, age, or class.

## SOCIAL STRATIFICATION

**Classes and Castes.** In the past, class differentiation was not strongly marked in material life. Although cattle ownership was highly unequal, cattle themselves were distributed among many households for care and management purposes. In the Tswana polities, there was some differentiation between members of the chiefs' kin group ("royals"), commoners, and recent immigrants who had been incorporated into the polity. This differentiation was enacted at seasonal political rituals, such as the first-fruits ceremony. In the western and northern parts of the country, certain groups of people were essentially serfs, with few or no political rights, whose labor was compelled by citizens of the Tswana polities. These groups included Sarwa (Bushmen), Kgalagadi, and Yei in particular. These categories have, in contemporary Botswana, no legal standing, yet lingering prejudices and resentments of historical inequities continue to inform current social relations.

**Symbols of Social Stratification.** Late twentieth-century Botswana has developed one of the most skewed income distributions in the world. There is a developing bourgeoisie that has the ability to distinguish and reproduce itself through access to English-medium education, networks, and material lifestyle (including cars and electricity).

## POLITICAL LIFE

**Government.** Since independence in 1966, Botswana has been a multiparty democracy with elections held every five years to a unicameral legislature, the National Assembly, which has been dominated by the Botswana Democratic Party. There is also an advisory House of Chiefs, composed of the heads of the eight Tswana polities, and of chiefs elected from districts outside those polities. In 2000, the government undertook a review of the role of the House of Chiefs, and its constitution and role may be changed in coming years. Local government is organized around elected district and urban councils (with some appointed members), land boards, and village development committees. There is also a "tribal administration" organized under the Ministry of Local Government, Lands, and Housing. Chiefs and headmen are important figures both in villages and nationally, although they are forbidden to be active in party politics.

**Leadership and Political Officials.** Politics takes place in two forums, which are distinct in their underlying premises and the ways in which they are perceived by the citizenry, but which also overlap considerably. One forum is the liberal democratic party system and the bureaucratic apparatus of government. The other is focused on the chiefs (*dikgosi*; singular, *kgosi*), subchiefs, and headmen; and the distinctive center of Tswana village life, the

*The interior of a hut along the Okavango Delta. Fifty percent of Tswana households are headed by women.*

*kgotla*, an open-air chief's court and community forum.

Many Batswana look upon the consensual nature of kgotla debates, and the hearing of disparate opinions within them, as underpinning Botswana's successful constitutional democracy. It should be remembered, though, that the dikgosi were able to manipulate support through their great wealth and political power, that they declared many regulations without widespread support, and that only the voices of adult men were formerly admitted in kgotla. Indeed, in many dikgotla, ethnic minority groups were not allowed to speak, or their voices were significantly discounted. Furthermore, the emphasis on consensus at the end of debates meant that open disagreement was not tolerated—the illusion of homogeneity and consensus being created only through the silencing of difference and the exclusion of many possible voices.

Beneath the dikgosi were subordinate chiefs, in nesting levels like a pyramid, called *dikgosana* (literally "little chiefs"), going down to the headman of a ward, or neighborhood group within a village. The ward has often been represented as a microcosm of the tribe: composed of patrilineally linked families, headed by the senior male who negotiates disputes, and guarantees well-being through ritual/religious practices. Like the tribe overall, wards also include

nonfamily who choose to reside near an in-married relative, or who attach themselves to the family group as dependents. Succession to the position of kgosana or kgosi is ideally patrilineal to the first son; since monogamy became the dominant form of marriage, succession has largely followed these lines. Previously, however, polygamy and practices of substituting a sister for a childless wife, and of marrying women to men after the men's death, made the senior heir difficult to determine, and inheritance of the chiefship was often a complex political battle.

Today the chiefs represent both a politics based on familiarity (in the sense both of kinship, and of personal knowledge of lives lived in proximity) and a morality of consensus. By contrast, party politics represents continued disagreement and a morality of individualism. The chiefs, representing a morality of group unity, have become the focus of minority claims to recognition in the nation. The morality of the political parties and the bureaucracy is not viewed entirely negatively: this is the domain in which women, minorities, and junior males have been able to attain position, and its morality accords with ambitions of self-development promoted by government rhetoric.

The distinction between the two domains is becoming more blurred, as ethnic minorities see chiefs as representatives in government, as subchiefs are elected by villages, and as the entire "tribal" system is administered by the Ministry of Local Government, Lands, and Housing. The chiefs are effectively under the minister, and lower-level chiefs are clearly salaried state employees. With 85 percent of court cases in Botswana heard in the dikgotla, a considerable amount of bureaucratic oversight and procedure now surrounds the chiefs' courts.

***Social Problems and Control.*** Court cases are heard in magistrates' courts, based on Roman-Dutch law, and in chiefs' courts, based on customary law. Because the magistrates' courts are conducted in English and require a lawyer, most Batswana prefer to bring cases to the dikgotla, where lesser criminal cases are also heard. Here, much personal testimony is heard from all who wish to contribute, and chiefs' decisions are built upon the opinions of respected members of the community. Cases may be appealed in both systems, and there is an independent High Court. Theft, disputes over property, and personal relations are common court cases. There is an increasing fear of violent theft, and illegal immigrants and street youth are seen as particular problems. Batswana deal with social problems through gossip, witchcraft, and the courts. They tend to leave civic problems to the police; when they have taken matters into their own hands, the situation is considered a "riot" and police are called in.

***Military Activity.*** The Botswana Defense Force was established in 1977, in response to armed incursions from neighboring South Africa and Zimbabwe. The army has grown considerably, accounting for about 9 percent of government expenditures in 2000; the population is proud of its participation in United Nations peacekeeping efforts.

## SOCIAL WELFARE AND CHANGE PROGRAMS

Drought is a recurrent problem, and the government has provided drought-relief labor programs and has supported initiatives to combat declining interest in agriculture. Botswana's high population growth rate and an educational system oriented toward formal sector employment contribute to an official unemployment rate of around 20 percent in the 1990s. Many of these were youth, and youth disaffection was growing. Several nongovernmental and governmental programs targeted youth, focusing largely on sexuality, home-based

industries, and job skills. Urbanization has also created problems for elderly people in rural areas, and the government introduced old age pensions in 1997. With HIV/AIDS producing a large number of orphans, Orphans Rations were created in 2000 to assist families in caring for them.

## NONGOVERNMENTAL ORGANIZATIONS AND OTHER ASSOCIATIONS

International donors, drawn by the stable democratic environment and the relative absence of corruption, have aided infrastructural development and social welfare programs. As Botswana's own resources have grown, international aid has fallen off: the Peace Corps and the U.S. Agency for International Development, for example, withdrew from the country. Botswana-based nongovernmental organizations have supplemented the internationally based aid programs, targeting health, families, women, youth, the environment, human rights, unemployment, and the disabled. Among the most important associations that the broad population joins are churches. People may also join ethnic associations, burial societies, and other self-help groups; some of these serve as rotating-credit clubs where people pool small financial contributions to give members an occasional large sum or loan.

## GENDER ROLES AND STATUSES

***Division of Labor by Gender.*** Tasks were assigned by gender and age in the traditional households among the different ethnic groups in Botswana. Hunting was primarily a male activity everywhere, housebuilding and agriculture primarily female, while work with livestock varied among ethnic groups. Among Sarwa, women have been active participants in political affairs; among Tswana, women formerly were not allowed to participate in their own right, except as an occasional regent. To some extent, traditional divisions of labor persist in rural areas. In the "modern" economy, there is no formal division of labor by gender, but fewer women are in upper-level management and government positions, and certain positions are gender-based (herders are male; housemaids are female).

***The Relative Status of Women and Men.*** Today, after decades of labor migration, declining marriage rates, new laws guaranteeing women civil rights, and the modern economy, almost half of all households in Botswana are headed by women. Western education, the modern economy (particularly the service sector), and civil service positions have all

*A man repairs shoes in the street in Gaborone, Botswana.*

provided venues for women to improve their positions, but women's cash income in both rural and urban households lags far behind men's, and women's overall income is more dependent on non-cash items. Women have had trouble breaking into national politics except in supporting roles, but in the 1999 elections several women were elected to the National Assembly and others were appointed to seats, and one of the elected positions in the House of Chiefs was taken up by a young woman. Women now hold prominent ministerial positions. The legacy of women's unequal citizenship in Botswana was contested by a landmark case brought successfully against the government, challenging laws that allowed a man married to a foreign woman to transmit citizenship to his children, but not allowing a woman married to a foreigner to do the same.

## MARRIAGE, FAMILY, AND KINSHIP

**Marriage.** The various ethnic groups have different marriage traditions. In past practices, most groups permitted polygyny (the taking of more than one wife), a girl's first marriage would be arranged by her family, and marriages involved bride-wealth or bride-service. Tswana marriages in the past were best described as a process, attaining the full definition of marriage often only after many years; steps in the process included requesting marriage and preliminary exchanges, sexual relations but not cohabitation, children, a public celebration, the establishment of a household within the man's compound, and bride-wealth. Bride-wealth is still common, polygyny less so, and while most marriages are still negotiated by family members, the spouses choose each other. Most Batswana register a civil marriage, as well as conduct marriage ceremonies according to custom at home, and many have a church wedding too. People may marry according to customary property provisions or civil community property arrangements, but in both the woman is disadvantaged, and the husband is likely to control the property. Divorce may be sought by women and men, with common reasons including adultery, failure to provide support or household labor, and abuse. But many women today are choosing not to marry at all, opting for autonomy and to retain control over their own children.

**Domestic Unit.** Most people belong to extended families that share a compound; within the compound the domestic units based upon a woman and her children are discrete. The Tswana pattern of multiple residences meant that families were often not coresidential, as some members worked fields, others tended cattle, and others lived in the village. Modern village-based households are again dispersed, through school placements, labor migration, and urbanization. These patterns have placed strains on the cooperative extended family, but most people still expect demands on their resources and time, and cooperation, from a wide range of kin.

The senior male is traditionally the head of the household, and is responsible for mediating internal affairs and representing the group to larger society. Today, authority in a compound may be diffuse, as younger members with technocratic skills or special agricultural training make many decisions and represent the group to outside bureaucracies. Even more dramatically, almost half of all households in Botswana in 1991 were headed by women.

**Inheritance.** Inheritance practices vary between groups. Dominant Tswana tradition in the past allotted the management of property (cattle in particular), and offices to the senior son of the deceased. Today, widows and daughters also inherit property, but their claims may be judged less important in court disputes. Nondisputed smaller estates including houses, furniture, small business capital, and clothing, may be distributed among descendants and other relatives by the senior relatives of the deceased, according to perceived needs.

**Kin Groups.** Tswana patrilineal customs predominate through the court systems, though kin groups are organized according to patrilineal, matrilineal, double-descent, or bilateral principles depending on the ethnic group. Some groups have named clans, others have more fluid boundaries. Kin groups larger than the household or compound group may cooperate for a healing or strengthening ritual invoking ancestors, and should participate in funerals, which are significant events for defining relationships and obligations.

## SOCIALIZATION

**Infant Care.** Infants are carefully attended to and indulged. Mothers and older sisters carry infants almost everywhere in slings tied across the back. There is a prompt response to crying, with feeding, calming and jiggling, and attempts at distraction with keys or other small objects.

**Child Rearing and Education.** Toddlers continue to be indulged; adults encourage them to learn words, and jokingly threaten them with beatings or being taken away by passing police. As they get older, however, children are expected to contribute significantly to household work. They are often chastised for "just playing" and "not listening," and comments that they are lazy or bad outnumber praises of beauty or intelligence. By and large, children are spoken to, and should speak deferentially to their seniors.

Many women place children with their own mothers to raise, and the children do household chores for aging grandparents. Alternatively, working mothers will take in a (usually distant) young female relative, or a village girl, to help care for urban children. There is also an increasing use of preschools for the educational advantage they give.

As children become teenagers, they form groups and socialize more outside the household. Most Batswana consider teenagers children, being unable to make decisions or manage relationships; however, these ideas about age categories are changing. Initiation schools were formerly important, and are believed to have been where children learned about sex and relationships, but are held in only a few areas today. Formal education is considered the means to achievement in modern society, but many children receive little support at home to help them progress through school.

**Higher Education.** Higher education is considered very important by both the government and by Batswana at large. The country has invested considerable energy and money to improve primary and secondary schools, although there remains competition to secure places in senior secondary schools, and many students attend schools far from home. Students aspire to attend the University of Botswana.

## ETIQUETTE

Batswana emphasize extensive greetings and inquiries after each other. It is polite to address senior men as *Rra* and women as *Mma* (literally, father and mother). Grown women should keep their thighs covered, but more and more women are wearing tight pants, and short skirts are seen in urban areas. While younger people should be deferential to their elders, and women to men, these patterns are sustained more strongly in villages than in the urban areas.

## RELIGION

**Religious Beliefs.** Most Batswana are Christians of one form or another, although some still follow local practices. Small communities of Muslims, Hindus, and Baha'is are present. There are numerous small independent churches led by local pro-

*Villagers gather near thatch fences and huts in a Bayei village. Most urban residents still continue to maintain a house in their home village of origin.*

phets, larger churches with regional representation, and the major international Christian sects. Many of the local Christian churches incorporate recognition of older local religious practices and beliefs, including the influences of ancestors in people's lives, often focusing on healing and promoting well-being. Traditional beliefs among most ethnic groups focused on securing ancestral beneficence; Kalanga also followed the Mwali cult, and Sarwa rites focused upon troublesome but nonfamilial spirits. Many people who belong to a Christian church will also conduct private family ancestor rites to protect a new compound or house, or when repeated illness and misfortune afflicts members of the family.

***Religious Practitioners.*** Batswana hold positions of responsibility in the Christian worldwide sects. Women and men with charismatic powers to heal and contact God originate and lead their own sects. At events such as weddings or funerals, leaders of different churches preside cooperatively. Within households, senior males generally are the ones to make contact with ancestors and to act on their behalf. Traditional religious specialists may bring rain, diagnose misfortunes, or strengthen households against evil influences and witchcraft, using herbs, roots, and special medicines. Some are thought to practice witchcraft, called boloi, and use human body parts to assist their clients.

**Rituals and Holy Places.** Apart from churches, there are no national holy places, and national ceremonies for Independence Day and President's Day are predominantly civic, accompanied by Christian prayer. Some members of various ethnic groups maintain ritual and holy places; for example, Kalaŋga locate Mwali (God) in the Matopo Hills to the east, and Herero will maintain a "holy fire," or okuruo in their compounds.

**Death and the Afterlife.** Most Batswana believe in a Christian afterlife and anticipate resurrection. People also expect the deceased to maintain interest in their descendants, as ancestral spirits. People want to be buried in their home villages, even those who have not lived there for a long time. Today most people are buried in cemeteries, but some Batswana are still buried inside their compounds. Funerals are very important events, at which a wide range of relatives, neighbors, and other associates are expected to attend; the expenses are heavy for many families.

## MEDICINE AND HEALTH CARE

Some illnesses are considered "European" and some "African" and are brought to medical practitioners accordingly. Other illnesses are brought to Western medical doctors, traditional doctors, and church priests/healers for the same ailment, or to as many healers as people can afford. Physical ailments and general misfortune are both considered treatable, and the latter is brought to the attention of traditional doctors/diviners and church healers who are likely to diagnose social causes—jealousies, malevolence, and selfish ambitions. Women make extensive use of government clinics for prenatal and child medical care. Sexually transmitted diseases, tuberculosis, and malaria remain problems; the HIV infection rate is among the highest in the world.

## SECULAR CELEBRATIONS

Public holidays are scheduled for four-day weekends. Secular holidays include President's Day in mid-July, and Botswana Day on 30 September, which celebrates independence.

## THE ARTS AND HUMANITIES

**Support for the Arts.** The government provides limited support for performance and plastic arts. Schools have choral and dance groups, and young people may receive grants to develop song-drama groups. The National Museum and Art Gallery promotes local artists, and hosts annual exhibits of Western-style plastic arts and traditional crafts.

**Literature.** Praise poetry was highly elaborated in the Tswana chiefships and there are still a number of older men proficient at it, but modern literary forms are not extensively developed as yet. Botswana's best-known writer is Bessie Head, a South African emigree who lived in and wrote extensively about the country.

**Graphic Arts.** Crafts, particularly basketry, along with woven hangings and printed textiles, are developed for the urban and tourist markets. Traditions of house-painting in south-eastern Botswana have declined over recent decades.

**Performance Arts.** Choral groups proliferate, often associated with voluntary associations, and compete in neighborhoods, villages, and nationally; an annual Eisteddfod is held for school choir and traditional dance groups.

Song-drama groups are formed by the young; their performances focus on social problems facing youth, including pregnancy and HIV/AIDS. Some Tswana musical groups are becoming popular regionally.

## THE STATE OF THE PHYSICAL AND SOCIAL SCIENCES

The University of Botswana expanded considerably in the 1990s, and aspires to market higher education regionally. Scholarship tends to be parochial, although some faculty are active in international academic circles.

## BIBLIOGRAPHY

Andersson, Lars-Gunnar, and Tore Janson. *Languages in Botswana: Language Ecology in Southern Africa*, 1997.

Botswana, Government of, and Ministry of Finance and Development Planning. *National Development Plan 8, 1997/98–2002/03*, 1997.

———. "Authoritarian Liberalism: A Defining Characteristic of Botswana." *Journal of Contemporary African Studies* 14 (1): 29–51, 1996.

Griffiths, Anne M. O. *In the Shadow of Marriage: Gender and Justice in an African Community*, 1997.

Gulbrandsen, Ornulf. "To Marry—or Not to Marry: Marital Strategies and Sexual Relations in a Tswana Society." *Ethnos* 51: 7–28. 1986.

Hitchcock, R. Renee, and Mary R. Smith, eds. *Settlement in Botswana: The Historical Development of a Human Landscape*, 1982.

Holm, John, and Patrick Molutsi, eds. 1989. *Democracy in Botswana*, 4 (1). 1989.

Ingstad, Benedicte. "The Cultural Construction of AIDS and its Consequences for Prevention in Botswana." *Medical Anthropology Quarterly* 4: 28–40, 1988.

Larson, Thomas J. "The Hambukushu of Ngamiland." *Botswana Notes and Records* 2: 29–44, 1970.

———. *The Bayeyi of Ngamiland*, 1992.

Larsson, Anita. *Modernisation of Traditional Tswana Housing*, 1996.

Lee, Richard B. *The Dobe Ju/'hoansi*, 2 ed., 1993.

Molefi, Rodgers Keteng. *A Medical History of Botswana, 1885–1966*. 1996.

Morton, Fred, and Jeff Ramsay, eds. *The Birth of Botswana: A History of the Bechuanaland Protectorate from 1910 to 1966*, 1987.

Peters, Pauline E. "Maneuvers and Debates in the Interpretation of Land Rights in Botswana." *Africa* 62 (3): 413–434, 1992.

Procek, Eva, ed. *Changing Roles of Women in Botswana*, 1993.

Samatar, A. *An African Miracle: State and Class Leadership and Colonial Legacy in Botswana Development*, 1999.

Schapera, Isaac. *The Ethnic Composition of Tswana Tribes*, 1952.

———. *Praise-Poems of Tswana Chiefs*, 1965.

———. *A Handbook of Tswana Law and Custom*. London: Frank Cass and Company, 1955.

Schapera, Isaac, and John L. Comaroff. *The Tswana*, rev. ed., 1991.

Solway, Jacqueline. "Affines and Spouses, Friends and Lovers: The Passing of Polygyny in Botswana." *Journal of Anthropological Research* 46 (1): 41-66, 1990.

Stedman, Stephen John, ed. *Botswana: The Political Economy of Democratic Development*, 1993.

Tlou, Thomas, and Alec Campbell. *History of Botswana*, 1984.

Vivelo, Frank R. *The Herero of Western Botswana: Aspects of Change in a Group of Bantu-Speaking Cattle Herders*, 1977.

Werbner, Richard P., ed. *Land Reform in the Making: Tradition, Public Policy, and Ideology in Botswana*, 1982.

Wilmsen, Edwin N. *Land Filled with Flies: A Political Economy of the Kalahari*, 1989.

Zaffiro, James J. "Mass Media, Politics, and Society in Botswana: The 1990s and Beyond." *Africa Today* 40 (1): 7–26, 1993.

—Deborah Durham

# BRAZIL

## CULTURE NAME
Brazilian

## ALTERNATIVE NAMES
In Portuguese, Brasil; its citizens are *Brasileiros* or *Brasileiras* depending on gender.

## ORIENTATION

*Identification.* The Portuguese navigator Pedro Alvares Cabral arrived at present day Pôrto Seguro (Safe Harbor) in the state of Bahia on the Brazilian coast in April 1500 and named the new territory *Ilha de Vera Cruz*, Island of the True Cross, thinking he was on an island. A year later, Italian navigator Amerigo Vespucci sailed to Brazil on a voyage commissioned by the Portuguese crown and returned home with a cargo of hard, reddish wood. The wood was similar to an East Indian variety called *pau brasil*, which was then popular in Europe for making cabinets and violin bows. *Pau brasil* (brazilwood), the first product to be exploited by the Portuguese in this new territory, is the origin of the country's name, Brazil.

Because of its size and diversity, Brazil is one of the nations most deserving of the name "land of contrasts." The country is often divided into five regions: *Norte* (North), *Nordeste* (Northeast), *Centro-Oeste* (Central-West), *Sudeste* (Southeast), and *Sul* (South). These divisions are used for administrative purposes such as the national Brazilian census and they roughly correspond to geographic, demographic, economic, and cultural variation within this sprawling nation. The Northeast has the greatest proportion of people of African descent, the South and Southeast are home to the bulk of Brazilians of European and Japanese ancestry, while indigenous peoples live largely in the North and Central-West. Still, regional migration and extensive miscegenation (racial inter-breeding) has made Brazil one of the most racially diverse nations on earth.

Aside from the official fivefold regional division of Brazil, a simpler economic distinction is made between the poor, underdeveloped North and the wealthier, more industrialized South. This distinction is sometimes referred to as the "two Brazils" or "Belindia," with the wealthy South being compared to Belgium and the poor North to India. At times these contrasts are translated into negative stereotypes as when inhabitants of São Paulo, the huge metropolis in southeastern Brazil, blame their city's poverty and high crime rate on migrants from the North.

Those who consider themselves urban sophisticates—particularly inhabitants of Rio de Janeiro and São Paulo—have a long tradition of maligning people from smaller cities and towns in the Brazilian interior, calling them uneducated hicks and hillbillies. Urban, middle-class Brazilians are generally unfamiliar with the interior of their own country and misrepresent it as a region of unrelenting poverty and backwardness—a stark place of few creature comforts that is best avoided. One consequence of this attitude is that middle-class and wealthy Brazilians are more likely to have visited Miami, Orlando, or New York than to have traveled to tourist destinations in their own country.

Brazilians are aware of these regional and rural/urban distinctions and closely identify with their place of birth. One is a *nordestino* (northeasterner) or a *mineiro* (native of the state of Minas Gerais) or a *carioca* (native of the city of Rio de Janeiro). Nevertheless, Brazilians share a national culture—making Brazil a true case of unity in diversity. The legacy of the Portuguese in language, religion, and law serves to unify this vast land and its people. Until the mid-twentieth century almost all Brazilians were— at least nominally—Catholic and today, virtually all speak Portuguese and identify with the dominant Brazilian culture.

*Location and Geography.* Brazil, the world's fifth largest country in geographical expanse and the

*Brazil*

largest nation in Latin America, comprises slightly under half the land mass of the South American continent and shares a border with every South American country except Chile and Ecuador. It is the size of the continental United States excluding Alaska.

Brazil's physical environment and climate vary greatly from the tropical North to the temperate South. The landscape is dominated by a central highland region known as the *Planalto Central* (Brazilian Highlands, or Plateau of Brazil) and by the vast Amazon Basin which occupies over one-third of the country. The central plateau juts into the sea in a few areas along Brazil's 4,500-mile-long, (7,240-kilometer-long) coast, but it more often runs parallel to the ocean, creating a fertile, lowland area.

Brazil is a land rich in natural resources, principally iron ore, bauxite, manganese, nickel, uranium, gold, gemstones, oil, and timber.

The physical environment in each region determined the types of crops grown or the resources extracted and this, in turn, influenced the populations that settled there and the social and economic systems that developed. Brazil's economic history, in fact, has been marked by a succession of cycles, each one based on the exploitation of a single export commodity: timber (brazilwood) in the first years of colonization; sugarcane in the sixteenth and seventeenth centuries; precious metals (gold) and gems (diamonds) in the eighteenth century; and finally, coffee in the nineteenth and early twentieth centuries.

Brazil's northeast coast with its rich soils became the most prosperous region early on as vast sugar plantations were created to supply a growing demand for that product in Europe. Beginning in the seventeenth century, African slaves were imported to provide labor for these plantations. This is why even today the Northeast is the region with the strongest African influence.

The Southeast also received large numbers of African slaves during the gold boom of the eighteenth century and the coffee boom beginning in the nineteenth century. This region also attracted new immigrants from Europe, the Middle East, and Japan who established family farms and eventually urban businesses.

In contrast, the South—with a climate unsuited to either coffee or sugar—became the destination of many German and Italian immigrants who raised cattle and grew a variety of crops. The heritage of the Northeast coast, based on slave labor and a plantation economy, was distinct from that of the South and Southeast, where plantations existed along with small family farms. Such historical differences partly account for contemporary contrasts between these regions.

Another regional distinction, that between *litoral* (coast) and *interior* (inland), arises from the fact that settlement in Brazil has always been concentrated near the coast. To say that someone is from the "interior" usually implies that he or she is from a rural area, even though there are large cities located far from the coast. Although the gold boom of the eighteenth century and the rubber boom of the nineteenth century led to the growth of inland cities, the real movement to settle the heartland of the country began only in the late 1950s with the construction of the new national capital, Brasília, in the Central-West.

Brazil is probably best known as the land of the Amazon, the world's largest river in area drained and volume of water and second only to the Nile in length. The Amazon forest contains the world's largest single reserve of biological organisms, and while no one knows how many species actually exist there, scientists estimate the number could be as high as five million, amounting to 15 to 30 percent of all species on earth.

Although now a focus of Brazilian and international media attention because of the negative ecological consequences of development, the Amazon region had long been isolated from national culture. Still, early in colonial times Jesuit missionaries traversed the Amazon River and its major tributaries and established settlements at Manaus and Belem. Both became thriving urban centers during the rubber boom of the late 1800s and early 1900s. Beginning in the 1970s with the construction of the Trans-Amazon Highway and other feeder roads, the migrant flow into the Central-West—the site of Brasília—expanded into the Amazon region.

***Demography.*** The population of Brazil was about 170 million in 2000, the sixth largest in the world after China, India, the United States, Indonesia, and the Russian Federation. Despite its large population, Brazil's demographic density is relatively low. Although there has been significant population movement into the interior in recent decades, about 80 percent of all Brazilians still live within two hundred miles of the Atlantic coast.

Fertility rates have dropped dramatically in Brazil in the last three or four decades of the twentieth century, with the completed fertility rate at the turn of the twenty-first century down to an average of 2.1 children per woman. Nevertheless, the population will continue to grow in the first twenty or thirty years of the twenty-first century because of the nation's current youthful age structure.

The Brazilian population has three major components. Somewhere between 2.5 and 5 million Brazilian Indians inhabited Brazil when the Portuguese first arrived in the early sixteenth century. Divided into many different cultures with distinct institutions, Brazilian Indians spoke a large number of languages. Today they comprise only about .02 percent of the country's population. Their numbers fell rapidly as a result of displacement, warfare and, most importantly, the introduction of European diseases against which they had no immunity. By 1955, only 120,000 Brazilian Indians were left and they were thought to be on the road to extinction. This downward trend has been reversed, however.

Their numbers are now increasing owing to improved health care, lower incidence of disease, declining infant mortality, and a higher fertility rate. Contemporary estimates of the indigenous population range from 280,000 to 300,000; the population may reach 400,000 early in the new millennium.

Afro-Brazilians, the descendants of millions of slaves brought primarily from West Africa to Brazil over a three-hundred-year period, are the second major component of the national population. Afro-Brazilians and people of mixed racial ancestry account for at least 45 percent of the Brazilian population at the end of the twentieth century.

Brazil also has a large population of mixed European, mainly Portuguese, descent. In the late nineteenth and early twentieth centuries Brazil was the destination of many immigrants from Italy, Germany, and Spain. During the same era smaller numbers of immigrants arrived from Eastern Europe and the Middle East. Rounding out the demographic picture are, Japanese-Brazilians, descendants of Japanese who came to Brazil in the first decades of the 20th century, and Koreans who began arriving in the 1950s. Still, Brazil is among the most racially heterogeneous countries on earth and these distinct categories are somewhat misleading in that many, perhaps most, Brazilians are of mixed ancestry.

***Linguistic Affiliation.*** Nearly all Brazilians speak Portuguese, a Romance language, belonging to the Indo-European language family. The Portuguese language was introduced to Brazil by the Portuguese in the early sixteenth century. Prior to the arrival of the Portuguese, the native population spoke languages belonging to at least four major language families: Arawakan, Gê, Carib, and Tupi-Guarani. Tupi-Guarani—which was spoken by coastal Indians, the first to come into extensive contact with the Portuguese—served as the basis for *lingua geral*, a language developed by the Jesuits for their missionary work with the Indian population.

Aside from a small number of recently contacted indigenous peoples, all Brazilians speak Portuguese. Brazilian Portuguese differs somewhat in grammar, vocabulary, and pronunciation from the language of Portugal. Brazilian Portuguese contains a large number of indigenous terms, particularly Tupi-Guarani words for native plants, animals, and place-names that are not found in continental Portuguese. While regional accents exist in Brazil, they are not very pronounced and native Portuguese speakers from one region have no difficulty understanding those from other regions. The vast majority of Brazilians are monolingual in Portuguese, although many middle-class and elite Brazilians study English and to a lesser extent Spanish, French, and German. Brazilians are very proud of their linguistic heritage and resent that many foreigners, particularly North Americans, think Brazilians speak Spanish.

***Symbolism.*** Most Brazilians would agree that the symbols that best characterize their nation are the exuberant revelry of the pre-Lenten celebration of carnival and the wildly popular sport of soccer, called *futebol* in Brazil.

Carnival is a four-day extravaganza marked by parades of costumed dancers and musicians, formal balls, street dancing, and musical contests, a truly national party during which Brazilians briefly forget what they call the ''hard realities of life.'' Carnival is symbolic of the national ethos because it plays to many of the dualities in Brazilian life: wealth and poverty, African and European, female and male. The key to carnival's popularity is its break with and reversal of the everyday reality. Through the use of costume—notably called *fantasia* in Portuguese—anyone can become anybody at carnival time. Class hierarchies based on wealth and power are briefly set aside, poverty is forgotten, men may dress as women, leisure supplants work, and the disparate components of Brazilian society blend in a dizzying blaze of color and music.

Brazilians are also passionate about soccer and are rated among the best players of the sport in the world. Every four years when the world's best teams vie for the World Cup championship, Brazil virtually shuts down as the nation's collective attention turns to the action on the playing field. And when Brazil wins the World Cup—as it has on more occasions than any other country—the delirium of the populace is palpable. Brazilian flags are hoisted aloft, everyone wears green and yellow (the national colors), and thousands of Brazilians, seemingly intoxicated with pride, take to the streets in revelry.

## HISTORY AND ETHNIC RELATIONS

***Emergence of the Nation.*** In 1530 the Portuguese began to colonize the new land of Brazil, but during the sixteenth and early seventeenth centuries their hold on this vast territory remained tenuous as they struggled with an unfamiliar environment, indigenous peoples, and with French and later Dutch attempts to undermine Portuguese control.

*People harvesting sugar cane in Salvador. Northeast Brazil has the most African cultural influence, due to early plantation labor.*

A useful exercise is to compare the early colonization of the United States and Brazil since it sheds light on the ensuing differences between the two modern nations. Both countries imported large numbers of African slaves, but in Brazil the practice began earlier, lasted longer, and involved the importation of two to three times more slaves than in the United States. Estimates range from three to four million Africans forcibly taken to Brazil. Moreover, in contrast to the large number of families who came to settle in the North American colonies, the Portuguese colonists were more often single males. Thus, in the early 1700s, when the importation of slaves into North America was just beginning, the proportion of Africans to Europeans was much smaller in the United States than in Brazil, where the slave trade had been operating for more than a century. The smaller ratio of Portuguese colonists to slave and indigenous peoples in Brazil and the resultant tendency of single men to take African or indigenous women as concubines or wives led to the great racial mix that characterizes Brazilian society today. Extensive miscegenation occurred in Brazil among Africans, Portuguese, and indigenous peoples during colonial times, and later with the arrival of new immigrants from Europe, the Middle East, and Asia.

***National Identity.*** While many people today see Brazil's racial and cultural diversity as one of the nation's strengths, foreign visitors and Brazilians themselves have at times drawn a connection between extensive racial mixing and Brazil's "backwardness." The belief that Brazil was less able to develop due to its racial heterogeneity was at the root of governmental decisions regarding immigration. Nineteenth century government-sponsored colonization schemes, for example, hoped to attract white immigrants, especially northern Europeans. And, in the early twentieth century, when theories of eugenics were popular in many parts of the world, Brazilian elites were straightforward about their desire to "whiten" the country so that it would develop economically.

Others dissented from this view. In the 1930s well-known Brazilian anthropologist, Gilberto Freyre, argued that the richness of Brazilian society lay precisely in its mixed racial heritage. The Portuguese, he argued, had laid the foundation for a "new world in the tropics," a blending of African, Indian, and European elements that made Brazilian culture unique. While later criticized as a conservative romantic who downplayed the harsh realities of life for people of color in Brazil, Freyre nevertheless was instrumental in recasting discussions of the nation's multiracial heritage, making it a source of pride, rather than shame.

Historically the emergence of Brazilian national identity followed a pattern common to many other European colonial territories. During the colonial period (1500–1822), individuals born in Brazil were subject to rules and taxes that were decided in distant Portugal and most of the top posts in colonial administration were held by those born in the mother country. The relative lack of power over their own affairs encouraged the creation of a distinct identity among native-born Brazilians, albeit one made up of diverse elements.

In terms of wealth and power, colonial Brazil was dominated by a small white elite of Portuguese ancestry who owned sugar plantations worked by Indian and later, African slaves. Portuguese of more humble backgrounds and free people of color held the intermediate positions in colonial society; they were plantation foremen, artisans, small shopkeepers, low-level government bureaucrats, and members of militias.

Following Brazil's proclamation of independence from Portugal in 1822, Brazilian national identity was thrown into sharper relief, but its constituent parts remained largely unchanged. A small European elite still dominated Brazil's political and economic life, although gold had replaced sugar as the principle source of wealth (coffee would later replace gold). But the Brazilian masses still consisted of black slaves and free people of color who labored in gold mines, on coffee plantations, and as poverty-stricken sharecroppers and subsistence farmers.

Until the 1870s, in fact, Brazil was primarily a nation of people of color. In the first national census in 1872 over 60 percent of the population was classified as black or of mixed ancestry. Then a massive wave of immigration from Europe—eventually reaching some 2.5 million—helped shift the racial balance. At first a few thousand immigrants arriving from Germany and Spain added to the nation's existing ethnic melange, but once slavery was abolished in Brazil in 1888, immigration really took off. It reached a peak in the 1890s with over one million Italians settling in the South and Southeast and additional tens of thousands emigrating from Portugal. During those years immigrants from Eastern Europe, including many Jews, also came to Brazil. In the early 1900s, as the coffee economy continued to expand, new waves of immigrants arrived from the Middle East (mainly Lebanon) and Japan.

While some cities in southern Brazil swelled with burgeoning immigrant populations, other immigrants, especially Germans and Japanese, established themselves in isolated rural communities. In many small towns and rural areas in the South and Southeast during the 1920s and 1930s, children were educated in German or Japanese and Portuguese was rarely spoken. But when it was disclosed that the German government was aiding antigovernment groups in Brazil, the Brazilian authorities ordered the closing of schools in which the principal language of instruction was not Portuguese.

After World War II Brazil followed a pattern of assimilation common to many nations with a high percentage of immigrants. As the second and third generations settled in and moved up the economic ladder, they became "Brazilian" to varying degrees. They intermarried, no longer spoke the language of their ancestors, and came to think of themselves primarily as Brazilian.

Contemporary Brazilians not only share a common culture, they insist on distinguishing themselves linguistically and ethnically from other Latin Americans, a stance rooted in a sense of cultural pride, in the distinctiveness of their "race" as they call it. Brazilians have long been indifferent to their South American neighbors, dismissing their shared Iberian roots as of no particular consequence. As Brazilian anthropologist Darcy Ribeiro once remarked, "Brazil and Spanish America are divided into two worlds, back to back to each other."

***Ethnic Relations.*** Brazilians have a strong national ideology that their land is a "racial democracy," one without prejudice towards its darker skinned citizens. The ideology, although patently untrue, nevertheless shapes the contours of interracial behavior and discourse in Brazil, smoothing its edges. While racial prejudice and discrimination do, indeed, exist in Brazil, their expression is more subtle than in the United States and perhaps, therefore, more difficult to combat.

Unlike in the United States, in Brazil there is no "one drop" rule—the custom that defines anyone with any known or suspected African ancestry as "black." The Brazilian system of racial classification is both more complex and more in keeping with biological reality. First, Brazil has never had two discrete racial categories—black and white—and Brazilians recognize and have words for a wide variety of racial types. Moreover, how individuals are classified racially does not depend solely on their physical appearance, their skin color, hair type, and facial features or on those of their relatives. Social class, education, and manner of dress all come into play in assigning someone to a racial category. As Brazilians put it, "money whitens"—that is, the higher the social class, the lighter the racial category to which an individual belongs. A well dressed, well educated woman with dark skin and Negroid features might be referred to as a *moreno* (roughly, brunette), while an illiterate sharecropper with light skin might be assigned to a darker racial category than his physical appearance alone would warrant.

Ironically, some evidence suggests that since the 1960s Brazil has been moving toward a system of racial classification similar to that of the United States. That is, the multitude of racial terms commonly used by Brazilians may be giving way to a bifurcate system of *branco* and *negro*—white and black.

Whatever the trend in racial classification, Brazil is far from being a "racial paradise" as Freyre claimed. Some statistics bear this out. Dark-skinned people in Brazil are more likely to be poor than light skinned-people and whites have average monthly incomes almost two and a half times greater than nonwhites. Nonwhites have fewer years of schooling than whites, with illiteracy rates of 30 percent and 12 percent respectively.

In considering these figures, social scientists have long argued that discrimination in Brazil is more a matter of social class than of race. In other words, one's life chances as a poor person in Brazil are bleak, regardless of one's color. But recent research has questioned this assumption and has shown that even when holding markers of social class such as income and education as constants, nonwhites fare worse than whites in rates of infant mortality and average life expectancy.

The Brazil-as-a-racial-paradise ideology long served to dampen Afro-Brazilian social and political movements. Moreover, because of the absence of the one drop rule, racial consciousness has always been more muted in Brazil than in the United States, making it more difficult to organize on the basis of race. Nevertheless, the more inclusive term *Afro-brasileiro* (Afro-Brazilian) has gained popularity in recent years, more groups celebrating Brazil's African heritage and decrying racism have emerged, and an affirmative action program, called *discriminação positiva* (positive discrimination), has been instituted by the Brazilian government.

## URBANISM, ARCHITECTURE, AND THE USE OF SPACE

By far the most important demographic change in Brazil's recent history has been its shift from a predominantly rural to an urban society. As recently as 1940, more than two-thirds of Brazilians lived in rural areas, but by 2000 the proportion of rural dwellers had dropped to 22 percent. The "urban designation," however, includes many small cities as well as the large population centers of São Paulo and Rio de Janeiro.

With urbanization has come a number of intractable social problems. The large cities of southern Brazil have long attracted migrants from the impoverished north, but the economies of these cities have not expanded rapidly enough to absorb all these migrants. Unemployment, underemployment at subsistence wages, poverty, and crime have been the result. So, too, have been the growth of shantytowns, such as the famed hillside *favelas* of Rio de Janeiro. Favelas are extralegal settlements consisting of makeshift dwellings that lack urban services.

Until the late 1970s various municipal governments dealt with substandard housing through urban renewal, demolishing it to make way for "modern" buildings and thoroughfares and build-

ing public housing—often miles from the city center—for the displaced poor. Such benighted attempts to solve the problem were largely replaced in the 1980s with efforts to regularize the status of favelas by providing them with electricity, sewage, paved streets, schools, and clinics, a sign of the growing political clout of their inhabitants.

The desire of many of the urban poor to live in centrally located shantytowns stems from the fact that most Brazilian cities are ringed by miles of working class *suburbios* (suburbs) that necessitate long commutes to jobs in the city center. In other words, unlike in the United States, poor people in Brazil are more likely to live at the outskirts of urban areas—the suburbs—while the middle class and well-to-do tend to live in more conveniently located neighborhoods in the heart of the city.

Cities, especially big cities, have *movimento*—a quality of liveliness and bustle that most Brazilians value. And some Brazilian cities have a great deal of movimento indeed. São Paulo, a metropolitan area of sixteenth million people and one of the fastest growing cities in the world, is Brazil's New York, Chicago, and Detroit all rolled into one. Rural zones, in contrast, are generally viewed by urbanites as backlands, as dull places of unrelieved poverty.

Cities have played an important role in Brazilian history. After all, few other countries have had three national capitals. During the colonial period when sugar was king, the nation's locus was the northeast coast and Salvador was the colonial capital. Then with the eighteenth century gold boom centered in the state of Minas Gerais in the southeastern part of the country, the capital was moved to Rio de Janeiro where it remained until the founding of Brasília in 1960.

Urban architecture in Brazil owes much to the legacy of Portuguese colonialism. Cities such as Ouro Prêto and Rio de Janeiro grew in importance long before industrialization had brought the factory or the automobile to Brazil. These cities, which influenced patterns of urban construction throughout the country, were largely modeled on Portuguese cities. The neighborhoods built during colonial times have narrow streets with continuous building facades that converge on central plazas. These open areas are often the sites of churches or government buildings, constructions imbued with symbolic power by being set off from the solid mass of private dwellings that line the streets.

Brasília was designed to be the ideal modern city and its architecture and planning were meant to transform Brazilian society. But in Brasília today the distinctions between haves and have-nots are all

*The market at Belem Port.*

too apparent, concrete reflections of the nation's social and economic divisions. In planning Brasília no provision was made for housing the thousands of workers who built the city or the thousands more who would service it. The only provision for them was the inclusion of tiny maids' rooms in apartments built for the middle class. As a result, jerry-built satellite cities ringing the urban core grew up to house the workers the planners forgot.

The complaints of Brasília's residents illuminate the customary use of urban space in Brazil. Many express dislike for Brasília's traffic circles which replace the intersections and street corners found in most Brazilian cities. This highlights the importance of the street in Brazil as a site of social encounters and public activities.

## FOOD AND ECONOMY

***Food in Daily Life.*** Rice, beans, and manioc form the core of the Brazilian diet and are eaten at least occasionally by all social classes in all parts of the nation. Manioc is a root crop that is typically consumed as *farinha*, manioc flour sprinkled over rice and beans, or *farofa*, manioc flour sautéed in a bit of oil with onions, eggs, olives, or other ingredients. To this core, meat, poultry, or fish are added, but the frequency of their consumption is closely tied to

financial well-being. While the middle and upper classes may consume them on a daily basis, the poor can afford such protein sources far less often.

Traditionally the most important meal of the day is a multicourse affair eaten after midday. For middle-class and elite families it might consist of a pasta dish or a meat or fish course accompanied by rice, beans, and manioc and a sweet dessert or fruit followed by tiny cups of strong Brazilian coffee called *cafezinho*. For the poor it would be primarily rice and beans. The evening repast is simpler, often consisting of soup and perhaps leftovers from the midday meal.

As Brazil urbanizes and industrializes, the leisurely family-centered meal at midday is being replaced by *lanches* (from the English, ''lunch''), smaller meals usually consumed in restaurants, including ones featuring buffets that sell food by the kilo and such ubiquitous fast-food eateries as McDonalds. The poor, who cannot afford restaurants, are likely to eat the noon meal at home, to buy snacks sold on the street, or to carry food with them to work in stacked lunch buckets. In rural areas itinerant farm laborers who are paid by the day and who carry such buckets have been dubbed *bóias-frias*, ''cold lunches.''

*Portuguese colonialism shows its influence in large cities, with churches and market stalls converging on central plazas.*

Meals may be accompanied by soft drinks—including *guaraná*, made from a fruit that grows in the Amazon—beer, or bottled water.

***Food Customs at Ceremonial Occasions.*** While the principle foods consumed in Brazil are fairly uniform across the country, there are regional specialties, many of which are eaten on festive occasions. In the northeastern state of Bahia ingredients of African origin—palm oil (*dendê*), dried shrimp, peanuts, *malagueta* peppers—are the basis of regional cuisine in such dishes as *vatapá* (seafood stew) and *acarajé* (black-eyed pea fritters). A variety of fruit and fish native to the Amazon are featured in dishes of that region, while in southern Brazil, an area of extensive cattle ranches, meals of grilled meat (*churrasco*) are favored. Another southern specialty are *rodizios*, restaurants featuring barbecue in which waiters pass from table to table with large skewers of grilled meats and poultry.

Brazil's national dish, *feijoada* (literally "big bean" stew), is said to have originated during slave times. Traditionally feijoada contained inexpensive and less desirable cuts of meat such as tripe and pigs feet, Brazilian slaves having concocted the dish from the leftovers of the master's table. Today feijoada consists of a variety of meats slowly cooked with black beans and condiments. A *feijoada completa* or ''complete feijoada'' is accompanied by rice, fresh orange slices, a side dish of peppery onion sauce, chopped greens, such as collards, and *farinha*. *Caipirinhas*—a potent blend of Brazilian sugarcane alcohol (*cachaça*), crushed limes, and sugar—or *batidas* (*cachaça* and fruit juice) are usually served as aperitifs; beer is the drink of choice to accompany the meal. Feijoada is served in restaurants, typically on Wednesdays and Saturdays, and when made at home, it is a favorite dish for guests.

**Basic Economy.** Today Brazil has the eighth largest economy in the world. It is a major producer of such agricultural products as sugarcane, soybeans, oranges, coffee, cocoa, rice, wheat, and cotton. It is also a major supplier of beef with vast cattle ranches primarily in the southern and western regions of the country. Nevertheless, because of the tremendous growth of industry, agriculture accounts for only 13 percent of the nation' gross domestic product.

Agriculture employs—directly or indirectly—about one-quarter of the Brazilian labor force. Five million agricultural workers are wage laborers concentrated in the plantations of the North (sugarcane, cotton, coffee, cocoa) and the increasingly mechanized agricultural enterprises of the Southeast and South (soybeans, wheat, sugar, oranges). More than 70 percent of these workers lack contracts and social benefits and less than 40 percent are employed year round. There are also 4.8 million landless families who survive as tenant farmers, sharecroppers, and casual laborers.

In the last decades of the twentieth century, increasing mechanization and monopolization of the best farmlands by agribusinesses has accelerated the displacement of small family-owned farms. Nevertheless, there are still some five million family farms ranging in size from 12 to 250 acres (5 to 100 hectares) that occupy about 143 million acres (58 million hectares). In contrast, large commercial agricultural enterprises cover almost three times that area.

During the 1960s and 1970s Brazil experienced economic growth from agricultural modernization and, by the early 1980s, agricultural production had increased to the extent that Brazil had become the fourth largest food exporter in the world. But, at the same time, Brazil was not adequately feeding its own people. It is sixth worldwide in malnutrition,

ahead of only Bangladesh, India, Pakistan, Indonesia, and the Philippines.

**Land Tenure and Property.** Brazil's agrarian structure is dominated by large land holdings. Estates of more than 2,470 acres (1,000 hectares) make up less than 1 percent of the nation's holdings but occupy 44 percent of its agricultural lands, while farms of 25 acres (10 hectares) or less account for 53 percent of holdings and occupy under 3 percent of agricultural land. More than three million farmers work some 500 million acres (20 million hectares) of land, but the twenty largest landowners in the country themselves own a like amount.

Aside from inequalities of scale, there is also insecurity of land tenure in many parts of Brazil, particularly in the Amazon Basin. There, *capangas* (hired gunmen) are employed by wealthy landowners to ensure that squatters do not settle on their vast, ill-defined tracts of land. Insecurity of tenure, in fact, has led to a number of violent episodes in the region at the end of the twentieth century.

But there are some bright spots in terms of land security. Although encroachment on indigenous reserves—especially in the Amazon by gold miners, cattle ranchers, and others—is still a problem, today a majority of the 270 officially recognized indigenous groups in Brazil live on reserves protected for them by law. Land is now also being granted to the residents of several *quilombos*, communities in northern Brazil originally founded by runaway slaves.

**Major Industries.** Brazil has one of the most advanced industrial sectors in Latin America today and is a major producer and exporter of automobiles, textiles, shoes, durable consumer goods, steel, pharmaceuticals, and petrochemicals.

Industrial activity in Brazil is concentrated in the Southeast, with about half of the nation's industrial production in the state of São Paulo alone. Here, too, most of the country's unionized industrial jobs are found. For this reason, after the 1970s, migration from the Northeast to the Southeast and from rural to urban areas has been particularly intense. Later, however, as unemployment in the Southeast has climbed and tax incentives have led to increased industrial investments in the Northeast, the migrant flow has been reversed to some extent.

**Division of Labor.** One of the most significant distinctions in Brazilian society is between those who do manual labor and those who do not. Today, as in the past, it is only the working class and poor who work with their hands. This division has deep historical roots and is tied to the "gentleman's complex" that emerged during the colonial period when elite males, typically sugar planters, sported a long nail on the index finger as evidence that they never engaged in physical labor.

The Brazilian middle class is sometimes defined as those with *colarinho e gravata*—collar and tie—because a major marker of middle-class status is a white-collar job. In Brazil people who work with their hands are, by definition, not middle class. This is why middle-class Brazilian families are far more likely than their American counterparts to employ domestic servants; it would be unseemly for a middle-class housewife to get down on her knees to scrub the floor.

## SOCIAL STRATIFICATION

***Classes and Castes.*** "Brazil is no longer an underdeveloped country. It is an unjust country," Brazilian President Fernando Henrique Cardoso proclaimed in 1994. Today Brazil, although one of the ten largest economies in the world, has the most unequal distribution of income of any nation except South Africa. Moreover, inequality has been growing. In the mid-1990s, the poorest 20 percent of the population received only 3 percent of national income, while the richest 10 percent received 47 percent. Or, put in another way, the wealthiest 20 percent earn twenty-six times as much as the poorest 20 percent. It is estimated that some thirty-three million Brazilians live in poverty, including twenty million workers and ten million pensioners who receive the minimum wage of around $115 a month. In parts of Brazil, particularly the Northeast, infant mortality, a sensitive indicator of social inequality, has actually been rising.

This "social question," as Brazilians call the divide between rich and poor, has characterized the nation since colonial times. With industrialization and urbanization during the first decades of the twentieth century, however, the growth of the Brazilian middle class has made this simple division more complex. Today, depending on how it is defined, the middle class accounts for one-fifth to one-third of the population, but the resources and lifestyle of its members vary considerably. Some claim the Brazilian middle class admires elite values and aspires to elite status and it is indeed true that middle-class families in Brazil are far more likely to employ domestic servants and send their children to private school than their North American counter-

*Thousands of saqueiros (sack carriers) working on the Serra Pelada gold mine, which is now closed. Gold was one of the most important exports in the eighteenth century.*

parts. In the late 1980s, moreover, it was members of the Brazilian middle class who, hurt by then rampant inflation, began seeking their fortunes abroad as immigrants to North America, Europe, and Japan.

Still, a ray of hope emerged with the stabilization of the Brazilian currency and the rapid decline of inflation in the mid-1990s. Estimates suggest that some nineteen million Brazilians moved from the working poor to the lower middle class. For the first time these people had money to spend on consumer goods; those who remained poor also benefitted from stable prices and were better able to afford staples such as meat, chicken, eggs, and beans.

***Symbols of Social Stratification.*** Brazilians are preoccupied with class distinctions and are quick to size up the social distance that exists between themselves and others they meet. Yardsticks of such distance are general appearance and the "correctness" of a person's speech. The degree to which an individual's vocabulary and grammar is considered "educated" is used as a measure of schooling and, hence, social class. And this, in turn, establishes patterns of deference and authority between two individuals should they belong to different social strata. When such patterns are ignored, the "elite" persons may harshly demand of their "lessers," "Do you know *whom* you're talking to?"—a ritualized response when someone of higher status is not accorded due deference by someone lower on the social scale.

## POLITICAL LIFE

*Government*. The Federal Constitution of Brazil provides for three independent governing branches: executive, legislative, and judicial. Although the constitution has undergone several revisions in the last century, the most recent in 1988, it has always retained this division of governmental powers.

Voting in Brazil today is universal and compulsory for all literate citizens from eighteen to seventy years of age and optional for those who cannot read and write.

*Leadership and Political Officials*. Brazil's return to free elections in the mid-1980s after two decades of military dictatorship has not resulted in greater social and legal equity, and unequal treatment of rich and poor is ongoing. Government officials and well-to-do individuals who have committed crimes still are more likely to escape the long arm of the law than are those of lesser social status. In part, this is because Brazil is a country in which laws and regulations are passed, yet a significant proportion of them are ignored. Still, today there is growing intolerance of political corruption and a host of official inquiries are evidence that Brazilians are starting to reject impunity and demand accountability of their public officials.

One concept is key to understanding Brazilian political culture: *jeitos*, ways of cutting through obstacles—such as rules and red tape—to achieve a desired end. Jeitos are partly a response to Brazil's notorious bureaucratic thicket which makes getting a government document—be it a driver's license, passport, or marriage license—a cumbersome process. Those who can afford to hire *despachantes* (dispatchers), professional facilitators who know how to "do jeitos", to get things done. Others do jeitos on their own; perhaps a small "gratuity" to a low-paid government clerk will produce the desired document.

A personalistic system of patron-client relationships is another key to the nation's political culture. One becomes a government bureaucrat or politician and rises through the ranks by developing influential connections and getting help from personal networks. Ambitious individuals cultivate powerful patrons who promote and protect them, and their own career trajectories typically rise and fall with those of their patrons.

*Social Problems and Control*. Given the nation's stark economic inequalities, social control in Brazil has long been problematic, even more so at the end of the twentieth century than in the past. High rates of crime, particularly in large urban areas, are a frequent topic of conversation; kidnappings, assaults, and murder receive wide media coverage. The murder rate in greater São Paulo, for example, is some five times that of the New York metropolitan area. Killings by police are common particularly in poorer urban areas. Fearful for their security, corporate executives travel around in armored cars; elite neighborhoods are fortified as private, guarded condominiums surrounded by high walls. Also within this urban landscape of have and have-nots live tens of thousands of street children, eking out a bare existence, ever on their guard against being rousted, or worse, by the police.

*Military Activity*. The role of the military in Brazilian life declined significantly following the military dictatorship that lasted from 1964 to 1985. By 2000 the three forces of the military, the army, navy, and air force, had been subsumed under a new civilian defense ministry and were forced to give up their separate cabinet-level posts. Despite considerable grumbling about this reorganization, particularly among the nationalist wing of the Air Force, no evidence exists that the Brazilian armed forces have either the ability or the desire to regain their lost power through a military coup.

## SOCIAL WELFARE AND CHANGE PROGRAMS

Brazil has long had welfare and pension systems but they do little for poorer workers and largely benefit state functionaries. Brazil also has some of the most progressive social legislation of any developing country—such as paid maternity leave—but as with other legislation, it is more often honored in the breach.

One very successful social program that received national attention is *Viva a Criança* (Long Live Children), which was begun by the governor of the state of Ceará in the impoverished Northeast. A campaign of preventive health education, the program cut infant mortality in Ceará by one-third in only four years.

## NONGOVERNMENTAL ORGANIZATIONS AND OTHER ASSOCIATIONS

Arguably the most visible nongovernmental organization (NGO) in Brazil today is the *Movimento dos Trabalhadores Rurais Sem Terra* (MST), or Movement of Landless Rural Workers. Now with some 500,000 members, it began organizing the occupation of large unproductive estates in the mid-1980s after the federal government was slow to follow through on its promised program of land reform. A convoy of vehicles invade an estate at night so that by dawn too many people will have occupied the land for the police to be able to evict them. Such land occupations have escalated since the mid-1990s, enhanced by the Brazilian media's sympathetic portrayal of the MST as supporting a just cause.

Partly in response to the MST, by the end of 1998 the federal agrarian reform program had settled nearly 290,000 families on eighteen million acres (7.3 million hectares) of land, and Brazilian President Fernando Henrique Cardoso had promised an acceleration of the process.

Over the last decade or so many other Brazilian NGOs have been established dealing with the problems of street children, rural poverty, hunger, ecological issues, women's issues, and indigenous rights. Some have received international attention and foreign support.

## GENDER ROLES AND STATUSES

***Division of Labor by Gender.*** Gender roles in Brazil vary to some extent by social class, race, and place of residence. White, middle-class and elite women living in large urban centers generally have more occupational choices and greater behavioral flexibility than their poorer, darker, rural sisters. Nevertheless, even when women are employed, men are seen as the primary providers of the family, with women's monetary contributions viewed as supplementary. Moreover, whether employed outside the home or not, women remain responsible for the proper functioning of the domestic sphere, with or without the aid of domestic servants.

Today almost 40 percent of Brazilian women have jobs outside the home, although they hold only 2 percent of executive-level positions. And while the number of women in industry has more than tripled since 1970, they are primarily employed in low-skill, low-paying jobs in textiles and electronics. Poor women, especially those in the 20 percent of households with no permanently resident male, take whatever work they can get. Afro-Brazilian women are particularly disadvantaged in this regard; about 70 percent are employed in low-level agricultural, factory, and domestic service jobs.

***The Relative Status of Women and Men.*** The mostly male Portuguese colonizers of Brazil brought with them the concept of *machismo*, which identifies men with authority and strength and women with weakness and subservience. Still, machismo is tempered in Brazil. It lacks the sharp-edged stress on heterosexuality and obsessive dread of homosexuality that characterizes it in other Latin societies. Nevertheless, this world view, combined with the patriarchy of the Catholic Church, laid the foundation for male dominance. As in most of Latin America, Brazil has a double standard in sexual matters. Traditionally, at least, men were expected to demonstrate their virility through premarital and extramarital sexual escapades, while women were supposed to "save themselves" for their husbands and remain faithful after marriage. So-called "crimes of passion" are linked to this dual sexual standard. In the past—and occasionally even in modern times—men who killed their wives believing them to be unfaithful often went unpunished.

Women have been slow to receive legal equality in Brazil. They were not given the vote until 1932 and, until the 1960s, women were the equivalent of children under Brazilian law. They needed permission from their fathers or husbands to leave the country and could not open bank accounts on their own.

A women's rights movement emerged fairly late compared to that in the United States and has just started influencing legislation and the political process at the onset of the twenty-first century. While it has had some success, for example, in setting up special police stations for abused women, abortion is still illegal, although widespread. Moreover, the emphasis on youth and beauty as a measure of female worth remains unchanged and it is no coincidence that Brazilian plastic surgeons enjoy international renown.

## MARRIAGE, FAMILY, AND KINSHIP

***Marriage.*** Both civil and religious marriage exists in Brazil but the number of religious marriages is on the decline especially in urban areas. The poor continue to cohabit and are less likely to legalize their unions than those of higher social status. Owing to the strong opposition of the Catholic Church, divorce was made legal in Brazil only in 1977.

*Lace next to a lacemaker at work, Fortaleza, Brazil. Less than 50 percent of Brazilian women hold jobs outside the home.*

**Domestic Unit.** While the typical household in Brazil may consist of parents and children, this is not the isolated nuclear family unit familiar to Americans. Brazilian culture puts a high premium on extended family ties and Brazilians, regardless of social class, do not like to live any distance from their kin. Grown sons and daughters almost always remain at home until they marry and ideally live near their parents after marriage. Brazilians normally interact weekly, if not daily, with members of the extended kin group—cousins, aunts and uncles, married children and their spouses, and in-laws. Among the urban middle class it is not uncommon for members of an extended family to live in separate apartments in the same building.

**Inheritance.** Brazilians trace their ancestry and inherit through both maternal and paternal lines. They typically have two surnames, that of their mother's and father's families. When a woman marries she usually adds her husband's surname to her own and drops that of her mother's family, while her children are given the surnames of their mother's father and their own father, all indicating a patrilineal slant.

**Kin Groups.** When Brazilians speak of "family" they usually mean a large extended kin group rather than the immediate family of spouse and children. This large kin group, the *parentela*, consists of all maternal and paternal relatives, along with in-laws. The parentela is at the core of social life and in time of need ideally provides assistance to its members. Such support can also be obtained through ritual kinship (*compadrio*) in which parents select additional allies and protectors as godparents for their children. Some claim that the multiple functions of these extended kinship networks has inhibited the development of extrafamilial organizations in Brazil, such as parent–teacher associations and garden and civic clubs.

## SOCIALIZATION

**Child Rearing and Education.** Like so many aspects of Brazilian life, educational opportunities are tied to social class. Brazil has never invested heavily in public education and most middle-class and elite families send their children to private school. Education is also linked to race and geography. A white person in the Southeast has an average of 6.6 years of schooling, whereas a person of color living in the Northeast has spent an average of just 3.5 years in school.

Despite the low level of funding, the last four decades of the twentieth century witnessed a significant increase in the number of Brazilians attending school and a concomitant rise in the literacy rate—in 2000 about 82 percent of Brazilians are literate. In 1960 almost half the population had little or no schooling, a figure that fell to 22 percent by 1990. Notably, school is one setting in which females are often more successful than males. In some regions of Brazil, girls are more likely than boys to be in school and women tend to be more literate than men.

**Higher Education.** Two-thirds of all public monies spent on education in Brazil goes to universities, the other third to public primary and secondary schools. While public universities in Brazil—widely considered superior to their private counterparts—charge no tuition, they have very competitive entrance exams which generally favor students who have attended costly private schools with high academic standards.

The value placed on higher education by certain segments of Brazilian society may explain why it receives such a large share of revenue. Economic success in Brazil is said to come more from *who* one knows than *what* one knows, and where one is educated, influences who one knows. University education then, aside from training students in a particular profession, also confers (or confirms) social status which, in turn, provides the personal connections that can influence future success.

## ETIQUETTE

Brazilians have less sense of personal space than North Americans and are not bothered being packed together in crowded public places. They are physically expressive and convey emotional information through touch. While in some societies touching has sexual overtones, Brazilians equate it with friendship and a show of concern. Women tend to touch more than men and greet others with kisses on both cheeks, but men also welcome each other with hearty pats on the back and bear hugs. Such informality extends to conversation. Brazilians usually address teachers, doctors, priests, and other professionals using their title followed by their first name—Professor João, Doutora Maxine or Presidente Henrique.

Still, body language and terms of address vary with an individual's social standing. A domestic servant will greet her employer with a limp handshake, head slightly bowed and eyes lowered, and address her using the respectful "you" (*a senhora*), rather than the familiar "you" (*você*); the mistress of the house, by contrast always addresses her servants as *você*. University graduates or, at times,

even those who appear to be well educated, are addressed as *doutor* or *doutora* (doctor).

Brazilians also have relaxed attitudes towards nudity and toward the body in general. Witness the scanty costumes of carnival performers which consist of little more than a wisp of fabric and a few feathers, and the tiny string bikinis—called "dental floss" (*fio dental*) in Brazilian slang—that women of all shapes, sizes, and ages wear on Brazil's public beaches.

## RELIGION

**Religious Beliefs.** Brazil is the largest Catholic country in the world even though the percentage of Brazilians who belong to the Catholic Church has declined in recent years, down from 95 percent in the 1950s. Today about 73 percent of Brazilians identify themselves as Catholic but an unknown number are Catholics by tradition, not by faith.

Although church and state are separate in Brazil and, by law, there is freedom of religious belief and expression, a close relationship exists between the Catholic Church and the state. Major Catholic holidays are public holidays and a priest (or bishop) always presides at the inauguration of public buildings. Also, church-based welfare and educational institutions, such as religious seminaries, receive financial support from the federal government. At various times in Brazilian history the Catholic Church has either strongly endorsed the state or vigorously challenged the status quo, as in the case of liberation theology, a late-twentieth century movement that provided religious justification for questioning the yawning gap between haves and have-nots in Brazil.

Catholicism varies somewhat in rural and urban settings. What has been called "folk Catholicism," which includes beliefs and practices long abandoned in cities, is observed by people in the interior of the country. Such popular Catholicism survives in pilgrimage centers in the backlands which attract thousands of Brazilians, often from great distances. The faithful take vows to make a pilgrimage to honor the saint who fulfills their request—recovery from illness or getting a job are examples. Sometimes the grateful supplicant offers the saint a carved likeness of the body part that has been cured.

Brazilian Catholicism has always coexisted—generally in relative harmony—with other religions including those of the nation's indigenous people, African religions brought to Brazil by slaves, European spiritism, and various Protestant denomi-

*A house on the edge of the Amazon River. The Amazon forest is estimated to contain 15 to 30 percent of all species on earth.*

nations. Moreover, many Brazilian Catholics participate in the rituals of other religions but nevertheless consider themselves "good" Catholics.

*Candomblé*, the best known and most traditional of Brazil's African-derived religions, is centered in the city of Salvador and traces its origin to the Yoruba and Dahomey religions of West Africa. In Candomblé—a syncretic religion (one that combines elements of more than one religion) with both African and European elements—deities are called forth through the spirit possession of cult initiates. Despite police raids and other forms of social discrimination in years past, Candomblé has persisted and flourished as a vibrant symbol of Afro-Brazilian cultural identity.

*Umbanda* is another highly syncretic religion with spiritist elements that began in Rio de Janeiro in the late 1920s and spread to urban areas throughout the country. With some thirty million followers today, Umbanda has been called the one true national religion of Brazil because it embraces elements of all three of the nation's cultural traditions: African, European, and Indian.

Spiritism, based on the teachings of French philosopher Alain Kardec and introduced to Brazil in the nineteenth century, is yet another spiritual movement with a growing following. Spiritism is more an intellectual endeavor than an emotional

cry for salvation. Spiritists, most of whom are from the upper-middle-class and elite sectors of society, believe that humans are spirits trapped in bodies and that moral perfection is life's goal.

The live and let live stance of Brazilian Catholicism towards other forms of religious belief and expression is absent in Brazilian Protestantism, especially in its fundamentalist variant. The so-called "new Pentecostals" view Afro-Brazilian religions and Umbanda as the work of the Devil and dramatically exorcize new converts to rid them of such evil.

Pentecostal churches have enjoyed great success in recent years. In often highly emotional services, converts claim inspiration from the Holy Spirit, speak in tongues, and perform cures. Using radio and television, the sects target the poor and preach here-and-now self-improvement through individual initiative. One relatively new sect, the *Igreja Universal* (Universal Church), founded in Rio de Janeiro in the late 1970s, now has churches all over Brazil and throughout the world.

A development in the Brazilian religious panoply at the end of the twentieth century was the growth of the Charismatic movement within the Catholic Church. With its strong emphasis on the power of the Holy Spirit to heal physical, emotional, and material distress; its rituals involving speaking in tongues; and its lively, emotive reli-

*A view overlooking Rio de Janeiro. There is stark contrast between the wealthier, more industrialized south and the poorer, undeveloped north.*

gious services, Charismatic Catholicism has much in common with Pentecostalism.

## MEDICINE AND HEALTH CARE

Brazil has long had a public health system, but like other social programs that primarily serve the poor, it is vastly underfunded. In the early 1990s, per capita spending on health care was only about $50 annually, a paltry sum for a system on which over 60 percent of the Brazilian population depends. Many of the poor either self-medicate or get whatever remedies they can from local pharmacists who are the only health care providers in some rural areas. For those who can afford it at the other end of the social spectrum, Brazil has world class health care in modern medical centers, particularly in the prosperous Southeast and South.

## SECULAR CELEBRATIONS

Most secular celebrations in Brazil are tied to the liturgical calendar since many originally started as religious celebrations and then became secularized.

The Feast of the Three Kings, 6 January. Children go door to door singing songs and requesting gifts. This tradition has almost died out in urban areas, but survives in the interior.

Carnival, variable dates, from late January to March. Brazil's famous four-day "national party" preceding Ash Wednesday is marked by street parades, samba, music, parties, and elaborate costumes. Its forms vary from city to city and region to region. The most popular street carnivals are in Rio de Janeiro, São Paulo, Recife, Olinda, and Salvador.

Tiradentes Day, 2 April. Tiradentes (literally, tooth-puller) was leader of the Minas Conspiracy, the most important early movement for Brazilian independence. When the Portuguese Crown discovered Tiradentes was leading an independence movement, he was hanged and quartered in the public square in Vila Rica, a town in Minas Gerais.

Festas Juninas (June Festivals), June. Brazilians celebrate a series of popular festivals with origins in Roman Catholic tradition. The feasts of Saint Anthony (13 June), Saint John (24 June) and Saint Peter (29 June) are marked by huge bonfires, traditional foods and games, square dancing, and parties for children. Urban children dress up like hillbillies during these Festivals.

Brazilian Independence Day, 7 September. Brazil was a colony of Portugal until 1822 when Pedro I, the crown prince, declared its independence from the mother country.

Nossa Senhora Aparecida (Our Lady Aparecida), 12 October. The Feast of Nossa Senhora Aparecida, the patron saint of Brazil, is a legal holiday.

Proclamation of the Republic, 15 November. This holiday celebrates the demise of the Brazilian Empire and the proclamation of the republic in 1889.

New Year's Eve, 31 December. Thousands of followers of Afro-Brazilian religions celebrate New Year's Eve on Brazil's beaches to honor Yemanjá, goddess of he sea.

## THE ARTS AND HUMANITIES

**Literature.** The country has a rich literary tradition and several Brazilian writers have achieved international renown, including Jorge Amado, Brazil's best known contemporary author. His books have been translated into fifty languages and his writings vividly evoke the sensual and popular delights of Brazil, especially his native Bahia, the setting of most of his work.

Brazil also has a tradition of folk literature that is little known abroad. The *literature de cordel* (literally, literature on a string)—derived from the custom of displaying booklets of verse by hanging them from a thin string or cordel— is a form of rhymed verse still popular in the Northeast interior. In the region with the country's highest illiteracy rate, these verses disseminate news and carry on cultural traditions. The *cordel* singer, who travels from town to town performing his verses to the accompaniment of a guitar or accordion, writes the verses, composes the melody, prints the lyrics in a booklet—which he also sells—and may even illustrate the work with his own woodcuts or sketches.

**Performance Arts.** Music is not just entertainment in Brazil, it has been called the "soundtrack" of national life. Brazil gave the world samba and bossa nova, but other musical traditions—batuque, forró, maxixe—are less well known outside the country. Like so much of Brazilian culture, the country's music borrows from its three cultural elements, although in the musical realm it is the African tradition that has the largest influence. While Brazil's musical energies are mostly focused on popular, not classical, music, the country was also home to one of the world's most esteemed neoclassical composers, Heitor Villa-Lobos, who made

imaginative use of folk themes in his best known composition, *Bachianas Brasileiras*.

## THE STATE OF THE PHYSICAL AND SOCIAL SCIENCES

Research in both the physical and social sciences was hard hit by Brazil's economic crisis since almost all academic research is done at public universities which receive about 90 percent of their funds from state or federal governments. The private sector contributes very little to research.

The social sciences in Brazil have far more visibility than they do in the United States and a number of academics are known to the general public. Fernando Henrique Cardoso, a senator and two-term president of Brazil, was a renowned sociologist before he entered politics. This visibility may be linked to the fact that all of the social sciences focus on Brazil and on national issues. The vast majority of Brazilian anthropologists, for example, have conducted their field research within national territory.

Anthropologists in Brazil shifted their interests over the years from indigenous populations to the contact situation, including inter–ethnic friction. This was followed by research on peasants, urban populations, and popular culture. Sociology, which tends to be more quantitative than anthropology, often combines an interest in policy with research. Or as one Brazilian social scientist put it, "In Brazil theory is politics."

## BIBLIOGRAPHY

Alvarez, Sonia E. *Engendering Democracy in Brazil*, 1990.

Brown, Diana Deg. *Umbanda: Religion and Politics in Urban Brazil*, 1994.

Burdick, John S. *Looking for God in Brazil: The Progressive Catholic Church in Urban Brazil's Religious Arena*, 1993.

Costa, Emília Viotta da. *The Brazilian Empire: Myths and Histories*, 1985.

Cowell, Adrian. *The Decade of Destruction: The Crusade to Save the Amazon Rain Forest*, 1990.

DaMatta, Roberto. *Carnivals, Rogues, and Heroes: An Interpretation of the Brazilian Dilemma*, 1991.

———, and David Hess, eds. *The Brazilian Puzzle*, 1995.

Eakin, Marshall. *Brazil: The Once and Future Country*, 1998.

Harris, Marvin. *Patterns of Race in the Americas*, 1980.

Harrison, Phyllis. *Behaving Brazilian*, 1983.

Hecht, Tobias. *At Home in the Street: Street Children of Northeast Brazil*, 1998.

Hemming, John. *Red Gold: The Conquest of the Brazilian Indians, 1500–1760*, 1978.

Herrington, Elizabeth Ann. *Passport Brazil*, 1993.

Holston, James. *The Modernist City: An Anthropological Critique of Brasilia*, 1989.

Ireland, Rowan. *Kingdoms Come: Religion and Politics in Brazil*, 1991.

Kottak, Conrad Phillip. *Prime-Time Society*, 1990.

Lesser, Jeff. *Negotiating National Identity: Immigrants, Minorities, and the Struggle for Ethnicity in Brazil*, 1999.

Lever, Janet. *Soccer Madness*, 1983.

Levine, Robert M., and John J. Crocitti, eds. *The Brazil Reader*, 1999.

MacMillan, Gordon. *At the End of the Rainbow? Gold, Land, and People in the Brazilian Amazon*, 1995.

Margolis, Maxine L. *Little Brazil: Brazilian Immigrants in New York City*, 1994.

Mariz, Cecilia Loreto. *Coping with Poverty: Pentecostals and Christian Base Communities in Brazil*, 1994.

Mcgowan, Chris, and Ricardo Pessanha. *The Brazilian Sound: Samba, Bossa Nova, and the Popular Music of Brazil*, 1998.

Oliven, Ruben. *Tradition Matters: Modern Gaucho Identity in Brazil*, 1996.

Page, Joseph A. *The Brazilians*, 1996.

Parker, Richard G. *Bodies, Pleasures, and Passions: Sexual Culture in Contemporary Brazil*, 1991.

Patai, Daphne. *Brazilian Women Speak*, 1988.

Skidmore, Thomas E. *Black into White: Race and Nationality in Brazilian Thought*, 1993.

———. *Brazil: Five Centuries of Change*, 1999.

Slater, Candace. *Stories on a String: The Brazilian Literatura de Cordel*, 1990.

Summ, G. Harvey. *Brazilian Mosaic: Portraits of a Diverse People and Culture*, 1995.

Vianna, Hermano. *Samba Nation: Popular Music and National Identity in Brazil*, 1999.

Wagley, Charles. *An Introduction to Brazil*, 1971.

Weyland, Kurt. *Democracy without Equity: Failures of Reform in Brazil*, 1996.

—Maxine L. Margolis,
Maria Enedina Bezerra,
and Jason M. Fox

# BRITISH VIRGIN ISLANDS

## CULTURE NAME

British Virgin Islander

## ALTERNATIVE NAME

BVI, Virgin Islander

## ORIENTATION

**Identification.** The British Virgin Islands (BVI) is part of the Virgin Islands archipelago, which also includes the United States Virgin Islands (USVI) of Saint Thomas, Saint John, and Saint Croix. Christopher Columbus named the Virgin Islands after Saint Ursula and her eleven thousand martyred virgins. Tortola is the largest and most densely populated of the British Virgin Islands and is separated from Saint Thomas by a narrow and easily traversed sea channel. This physical proximity contributed to a long history of social and economic interaction and interdependence between the BVI and the USVI, and British Virgin Islanders reflect this history in their occasional use of the term "Virgin Islanders" to refer to themselves. Nevertheless, British Virgin Islanders express a strong sense of their distinctiveness, pointing to the more serene and rural nature of their island life, their economic well-being, and their independent and friendly character as key differences between the BVI and the USVI.

**Location and Geography.** Comprising thirty-six islands with a total landmass of 59 square miles (153 square kilometers), the BVI lie 50 miles (80 kilometers) east of Puerto Rico, in the northeastern Caribbean Sea. Tortola is the largest of the sixteen inhabited islands of the BVI, followed by Anegada, Virgin Gorda, and Jost Van Dyke. The capital of the BVI, Road Town, is on Tortola. With the exception of Anegada, which is a low-lying coral atoll, the islands of the BVI are hilly and dry, with rugged coastlines interrupted by coves, sandy beaches, and palm and mangrove swamps. The climate is sub-tropical and humid, with an annual rainfall of 27 inches (69 centimeters) and limited freshwater resources. Temperatures range from 72 to 88 degrees Fahrenheit (22 to 31 degrees Celsius) and are moderated by trade winds all year. BVI's tropical climate and sandy beaches attract 400,000 tourists annually.

**Demography.** The population of the BVI is approximately twenty thousand, with three-quarters on Tortola. Fifty percent of the population is made up of native British Virgin Islanders, with the remainder comprised largely of nationals from other Caribbean countries. Of the total BVI population, 90 percent is of African descent, with the remainder being of Amerindian, East Indian, and Middle Eastern descent, or white expatriates.

**Linguistic Affiliation.** English is the official language of the BVI, with both formal and creole variants spoken.

**Symbolism.** British Virgin Islanders are proud of the beauty of their islands and have a strong protective attitude toward their natural resources and their land. This is symbolized by the coat of arms that appears on the BVI flag and on many official publications that depict Saint Ursula framed by eleven oil lamps, which represent the eleven thousand virgins after whom the BVI were named. Beneath Saint Ursula is a scroll that reads, in Latin, *Vigilate* (Be careful). BVI flora and fauna are symbolized on national stamps, and the tourist board's depiction of the BVI as "Nature's Little Secrets" also is a source of national pride. However, the symbol that is most significant to BVI's national identity is land. British Virgin Islanders point proudly to the fact that the majority of BVI land remains in British Virgin Islanders' hands, and British Virgin Islanders attribute their independent character and strong economy to this fact.

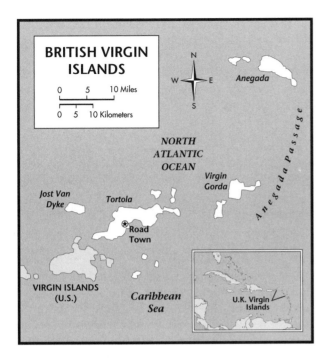

BRITISH VIRGIN
ISLANDS

0   5   10 Miles

0   5   10 Kilometers

*British Virgin Islands*

## HISTORIC AND ETHNIC RELATIONS

**Emergence of the Nation.** The Virgin Islands were settled by indigenous people in about 100 B.C.E., and were encountered by Columbus on 22 October 1493. Throughout the fifteenth and sixteenth centuries the BVI were under Spanish control, during which time the islands provided temporary anchorages for Spanish convoys hiding from English privateers. The Dutch on Tortola established the first permanent European settlement, in 1602, but by 1666 they had been replaced by English planters. Due to its arid climate and hilly terrain, the BVI were one of the more unprofitable of Great Britain's plantation islands during the colonial period. As a British colony, the BVI were administered as part of the Leeward Islands Federation from 1872 to 1956. From 1902, when the local BVI legislature was abolished, to 1950, when it was reconstituted, the BVI experienced little in the way of direct governance by Great Britain.

With the breakup of colonial rule in the eastern Caribbean in 1956, the BVI declined both amalgamation with the USVI and membership in the now defunct West Indies Federation of British Islands (1958–1962). Constitutional reform in 1967 established the BVI as a British dependent territory, with a locally elected legislature and chief minister, and also established the U.S. dollar as the official national tender. Increased BVI political autonomy was matched by increased economic autonomy, related to the development of a successful tourism economy beginning in 1962, and the development of an offshore financial services sector beginning in the early 1980s. The expansion of the BVI economy was accomplished through extensive reliance upon imported labor. Of the present-day BVI population of twenty thousand, half are non-British Virgin Islanders drawn to work in its burgeoning tourist and financial services economies. Throughout this period of rapid growth, the BVI maintained a high degree of political and social stability and its present-day per capita income of $26,903 (U.S.) is exceeded only by the per capita incomes of the Bahamas, Bermuda, and the Cayman Islands in the Caribbean. The economic development that fostered radical demographic and social change has gone hand in hand with a growth in BVI nationalist sentiment.

**National Identity.** As legislative changes abetted BVI political autonomy and consolidation and as economic prosperity fostered a sense of economic security, improved transportation and communication among far-flung BVI islands and communities made possible centralized banking and a national educational system. Concurrently, BVI economic dependence on the USVI diminished. Meanwhile, initiatives promoting a national culture also were launched, muting long-standing distinctions among different communities of British Virgin Islanders. The establishment in 1954 of a national beauty contest, in 1957 of Saint Ursula's Day as a national holiday, in 1979 of a national folk dance troupe, in 1982 of a Ministry of Culture, and the publication in 1984 of a comprehensive collection of BVI folk tales, songs, and recipes all provided bases for the people inhabiting the BVI to think of themselves as members of a nation.

**Ethnic Relations.** The present-day BVI is a more ethnically diverse country than it was in the mid-1970s. Legislation giving British Virgin Islanders preference in hiring and in the allocation of trade licenses, and restricting alien land ownership has resulted in some disaffection within the non-BVI population. While many British Virgin Islanders express the desire to retain BVI resources and land for British Virgin Islanders, they also recognize the need to acknowledge the contributions of non-British Virgin Islanders to the economy and society, and to provide for their inclusion in BVI public culture.

## URBANISM, ARCHITECTURE, AND THE USE OF SPACE

BVI architecture is strongly influenced by Caribbean vernacular style. One finds numerous examples of traditional wooden hip-roofed houses throughout the countryside, and even contemporary buildings, that are constructed of concrete and cinder block incorporate into their design wide verandas, high ceilings, hip roofs, and bright colors. Building codes establish strict guidelines for new home construction, and government legislation limits the size and height of hotels. While Road Town is the capital and urban center of the BVI, the traditional architecture along its main street, the lack of any traffic signals, the presence of open tracts of land, and open vistas to the sea provide a distinctly rural air. Most British Virgin Islanders live outside of "town" and tend to identify most closely with the community or region in which they live.

In communities throughout the BVI, a large, centrally located shade tree frequently serves as a spot for gathering, passing news, and discussing current events. All sporting events and the annual summer festival commemorating emancipation are held in Road Town and draw people from throughout the BVI. A cultural center in Road Town and the atrium of the main building of H. Lavity Stoutt Community College serve as sites for large indoor events.

## FOOD AND ECONOMY

**Food in Daily Life.** The BVI diet features johnnycake, peas and rice, fish and salt fish, mutton and goat, "ground provisions" such as tania, sweet potatoes and plantains, and an array of soups: fish soup, bullfoot soup, goat head soup, pea soup, and pumpkin soup. Most food is highly seasoned, and soups are commonly served with dumplings. A favorite local dish is fungi (cornmeal and okra) and fried fish; favored beverages are drinks made from local fruits, and include limeade, soursop, mauby, and passion fruit. Other Caribbean foods, such as jerk chicken, roti (a curry-filled pancake), and patties (meat and fish-filled dumplings) also are making their way into the BVI diet, as are imported processed foods and snacks.

**Food Customs at Ceremonial Occasions.** Secular and religious holidays are occasions for the preparation of special foods, with fish soup and dumplings, peas and rice, salt fish, stewed mutton, curried goat and grilled local fish preferred. Tradi-

tionally, Good Friday dinner is a meatless meal featuring salt fish, peas and rice, and *dukuna* (a spiced sweet potato and coconut pudding wrapped in plantain leaf and steamed). Traditional Christmas foods include guavaberry wine and guavaberry tart, both made from a small-berry-like fruit that grows on trees.

**Basic Economy.** Tourism and financial services are the mainstays of the BVI economy, generating 90 percent of the national income. The agricultural sector accounts for less than 10 percent of the national income, and is restricted to food crops and pasture.

**Land Tenure and Property.** Land is the basis of British Virgin Islanders' sense of autonomy and independence. The concept of "family land"—land held in common by members of a family—assumes a pivotal role in defining and structuring social relations and developing a concept of self. Although a Cadastral survey in the 1970s provided a map and registry of all BVI lands, disputes continue over the appropriate division of these lands among individuals making claims to their use. The conceptual and cultural importance of land is reflected in government legislation that places strict restrictions on alien land ownership and development.

**Commercial Activities.** Most commercial activities are related to tourism and financial services and include a flourishing charter yacht and water sports industry, restaurants and bars, guesthouses, villas and small luxury hotels, banks, trust companies, communications and telecommunications, and real estate sales and management.

**Major Industries.** The two major BVI industries are tourism and financial services. Light industries include a rum distillery, concrete block and construction aggregate manufacture, and yacht maintenance and repair.

**Trade.** The BVI trade with the United States, the USVI, Puerto Rico, and the United Kingdom. BVI exports include bananas, livestock, fresh fish, rum, and construction aggregates. Principal imports to the BVI are automobiles, building materials, foodstuffs, and machinery.

**Division of Labor.** In the contemporary economy most people work in commercial and service activities, and labor is divided along national lines. British Virgin Islanders hold the majority of jobs in the civil service, telecommunications, and banking. European and North American expatriates hold most of

*Colorful buildings along the waterfront in Tortola are indicative of Caribbean architecture.*

the senior positions in bank and hotel management and in the trust companies. Nationals from other Caribbean countries predominate in construction, the trades, and as service workers in tourism.

## SOCIAL STRATIFICATION

***Classes and Castes.*** BVI society is divided into "belongers" and "nonbelongers." As a term of identity "belonger" refers to people of BVI parentage or birth who hold BVI citizenship. Individuals of parentage from other Caribbean countries, and who constitute half of the total BVI population, are designated "nonbelongers," regardless of whether they were born in the BVI. Belongers have unrestricted rights to landownership and are given preference in hiring and in the allocation of trade licenses.

***Symbols of Social Stratification.*** There is an emerging structure of social and economic difference, based upon differential access to the country's economic resources. Most BVIslanders own their own home and most households have telephones, televisions, and stereos. Principle symbols of high social status are designer fashions, travel to Puerto Rico or the US to shop or for medical care, ownership of an expensive automobile, and a large house.

## POLITICAL LIFE

***Government.*** The BVI is a British dependent territory with a locally elected government that is responsible for the country's internal and financial affairs. A crown-appointed governor possesses reserved legislative powers in the areas of defense and internal security, external affairs, conditions of service of public officers, and the courts. The government is headed by a chief minister and a cabinet of three other ministers, all of whom are selected from among members of the Legislative Council. The Legislative Council consists of thirteen members elected by direct popular vote—one member from each of nine electoral districts, and four at-large members. Elections to the Legislative Council are held at least once every four years and are structured by a party system. The four major BVI political parties are the Virgin Islands Party (VIP), National Democratic Party (NDP), United Party (UP), and Concerned Citizens Movement (CCM).

***Leadership and Political Officials.*** Since 1986 the chief minister and his government have come from the Virgin Islands Party (VIP). The founder of the VIP, H. Lavity Stoutt, was the first popularly elected chief minister following constitutional reform in 1967. At the time of his death in office in 1995 Stoutt had served four terms and was the

*Shops and restaurants in Road Town, Tortola. Tourism is one of the leading mainstays of the economy.*

longest-serving politician in the Caribbean. The dominance of the VIP was challenged in the elections of 1998 by the newly formed National Democratic Party (NDP), which returned six representatives to the Legislative Council. Notwithstanding the popularity of the NDP, the post of chief minister is still held by a member of the VIP, Ralph T. O'Neal, who assumed the office upon Stoutt's death and who was returned to office in the 1998 elections. Although there is no formal movement toward full independence, its possibility is a central topic of public debate and party politics.

***Social Problems and Control.*** With economic and demographic growth, the BVI has experienced some increase in crime, and there is increased vigilance with respect to drug use and possession of fire arms. In general, however, the BVI is relatively crime-free and experiences little in the way of ethnic or racial strife.

***Military Activity.*** The BVI maintains no domestic military, depending entirely upon the UK for its external security.

## Social Welfare and Change Programs

Family and church play central roles in caring for the disabled, the sick, the indigent, and the elderly. The 1979 establishment of a Social Security Board and the 1981 completion of a new hospital in Road Town also provide formal structures for a national health and welfare policy. A Woman's Desk, established in the early 1990s as part of the Chief Minister's Office has developed highly successful educational and intervention programs in the areas of women's health and domestic violence, and community meetings held through the country in 1998–1999 motivated a series of reforms in citizenship law.

## Nongovernmental Organizations and Other Associations

Non-governmental organizations in the BVI provide assistance in areas as wide-ranging as environmental management and youth boating safety. The Rotary and Lions Clubs provide important assistance to youth groups and local schools, and the Hotel and Commerce Association is active in tourism development policies. Through its association with regional organizations such as OECS (Organization of Eastern Caribbean States) and international organizations such as UNESCO and the UN, the BVI has secured grants for development of roads and bridges, airport expansion and educational facilities.

## GENDER ROLES AND STATUSES

*Division of Labor by Gender.* Historically, women and men shared responsibility for the welfare of the household, with women gardening, cooking, sewing, and keeping household accounts and men opening new gardens, building houses, pasturing livestock, sailing, fishing, and traveling to other islands as agricultural laborers. Present-day BVI women hold the majority of positions in education and occupy a significant number of senior positions in the civil service. BVI men occupy almost all public offices as well as a significant number of upper-level management positions in the private sector. Nationals from other Caribbean countries are the majority of service workers, with men working in construction and boat maintenance and repair and as gardeners and cooks, and women working as clerks, secretaries, housekeepers, and waitresses.

*The Relative Status of Women and Men.* Men tend to participate in public life through membership in civic associations and daily information exchange, while women participate through the church and their positions in the civil service. Both men and women see their activities as contributing importantly to their community. While BVI men are more active in politics and law, women influence public life through their roles as educators and their leadership in community events such as Festival. Both men and women have suffrage at age of eighteen. The status of men and women alike is measured in terms of the strong independent and entrepreneurial spirit that is held to be characteristic of British Virgin Islanders of both genders.

## MARRIAGE, FAMILY, AND KINSHIP

*Marriage.* As is common throughout the Caribbean, individuals may enter into unions without marriage, although there is social preference for and a higher social status accrues to a legal marriage union.

*Domestic Unit.* While households made up of a married couple and their children are held to be the norm, the basic BVI family structure is extended, and households made up of a woman, her children, and their offspring, or of siblings and their offspring are common. Even a household headed by a married couple may include children from previous or "outside" relationships, godchildren, or children of other family members.

*Inheritance.* Inheritance of money and goods follows British Common Law, whereas inheritance of rights and tenancy to family land may or may not be transferred through legal mechanisms.

*Kin Groups.* The family, understood as a widespread association of kin linked by blood and common name, is the basis for social identity and standing and is a primary source of social and economic support. Members of an extended kindred tend to live in the same area or community, building their individual homes on jointly held family land. BVI family names are associated with specific BVI places or communities, and these in turn are associated with particular activities (such as sailing, business, agriculture, education) or proclivities. Upon meeting someone new, a British Virgin Islander might ask, "Who are you for?" The genealogy that is supplied in response will be used to locate that individual in the BVI social universe.

## SOCIALIZATION

*Child Rearing and Education.* The raising and care of children is considered to be a responsibility of the parents and their close relatives and friends. Infants are carried close to the body, protected from the sun by umbrellas and from breezes by hats, blankets and booties. Children are raised to dress neatly, to be clean, and to be respectful to all persons older than they are. Young girls are expected to stay close to home, while young boys are allowed to venture farther, with fewer constraints. The national literacy rate of 98 percent is a reflection of the value placed on education by British Virgin Islanders. Compulsory education was introduced for children ages five through twelve in 1890, and secondary education was introduced in 1943. Today there are eighteen public schools and eleven private primary schools on four islands, and two public high schools. Both girls and boys are expected to complete their education through high school.

*Higher Education.* A national college, H. Lavity Stoutt Community College, was opened in 1990.

## ETIQUETTE

British Virgin Islanders place great importance on mannerly behavior. The right of individuals to privacy also is held dear, so that one should not call out a person's name from afar, nor inquire about another person's whereabouts or business. Among the older generation, friends of either gender may be addressed formally as "Mr.," "Mrs.," or "Miss"

*A shipwright is building a boat on Carrot Bay on the island of Tortola. Fishing was historically one of a man's household responsibilities.*

and among the younger generation, friends of either gender may be greeted with a generic "How?" or "Everything safe?"

## RELIGION

**Religious Beliefs.** Christianity is the prevailing BVI religion, with 45 percent of the population Methodist, 21 percent Anglican, 18 percent Baptist or Pentecostal, and 6 percent Roman Catholic.

**Rituals and Holy Places.** BVI churches are the source of much social welfare and the center of regular social contact. The AM radio station opens its daily broadcast with a two hour devotional service, and public prayer opens the school day and most public events. During October and November, farm produce and home baked goods are brought into BVI churches, and children perform special hymns and recitations, in an annual Harvest Festival. In August, congregations join in commemorating emancipation with a special service at the site where the emancipation proclamation was read on 1 August 1834.

**Death and the Afterlife.** Deaths are principal occasions for family members to return home, and funerals and memorial services are announced and lists of relevant mourners are broadcast regularly over the radio.

## MEDICINE AND HEALTH CARE

A public hospital, opened in 1922, provides surgical and emergency care as well as some outpatient services and ambulatory care. However, there is no national health insurance, and most health care must be sought through private health providers. As is the case in many Caribbean countries, care is taken to avoid exposure to the chill night or early morning air, in the belief that it can cause bodily imbalance leading to sickness. For similar reasons, hot liquid taken in the morning is believed to be essential to restoring the balance that is the basis of good health. Seawater is believed to have healthful benefits, and many British Virgin Islanders start their morning with a "sea bathe." Colds, headaches, and chronic conditions may be treated with a variety of herbal remedies as prescribed by knowledgeable elders and "setters," individuals who also specialize in body manipulation and massage.

## SECULAR CELEBRATIONS

The major national holidays are New Year's Day (1 January), Commonwealth Day (13 March), Sover-

*A food stand at Carnival. Tortola.*

eign's Birthday, Territory Day, Festival (the first Monday, Tuesday, and Wednesday in August), Saint Ursula's Day (21 October), and Boxing Day (26 December). In November 2000 the Legislative Council replaced the holiday commemorating the birthday of the heir to the throne with a national holiday commemorating the birth of H. Lavity Stoutt (7 March). The most anticipated of national holidays are the three days of Festival in August that are set aside to commemorate the 1 August 1834 emancipation of African slaves. Festival is celebrated with beauty contests and calypso competitions, food fair, parades, and public musical performances and dances and also is an occasion for family reunions. Religious holidays include Christmas, Good Friday, and Easter Monday.

## THE ARTS AND HUMANITIES

**Support for the Arts.** The work of BVI artists is prominently displayed in public buildings, but there is no formal support of artists in the form of public grants or vigorous school training programs. H. Lavity Stoutt Community College has instituted a program of Virgin Islands studies to encourage and develop local art forms, as well as to revive traditional BVI crafts such as strawwork, boat-building, and iron work.

**Literature.** The British Virgin Islands has rich oral tradition, which includes the recitation of folktales in homes and at family gatherings, and more formal poetic recitations in schools and churches. A local group of writers convenes regularly to share their poems and stories, and several BVIslanders have had their poems, folktales and stories published locally and regionally. The memoir is another popular genre of BVI writing.

**Performance Arts.** A BVI folk dance troupe and local fungi bands (bands made up of guitar, ukulele, washtub bass, scratch gourd, and triangle that play calypso and folk tunes) perform regularly at local cultural events, and represent the BVI at regional cultural festivals and at BVI Tourist Board events abroad. Instruction in classical, jazz, and Caribbean music such as steel pan and fungi is offered as part of the school music curriculum, and local musical talent is showcased at school concerts, in public performance for tourists, and during the annual Festival commemorating emancipation. Local and international calypso performers also are central features of Festival shows, as are BVI fungi bands, steel pan orchestras and brass bands. A musical series sponsored by the community college brings classical and jazz performers to the BVI bimonthly from October to March.

## THE STATE OF THE PHYSICAL AND SOCIAL SCIENCES

The establishment in 1990 of a national tertiary educational institution has enhanced the development of BVI physical and social sciences. A nursing education program and a marine studies program contribute in the area of the physical sciences, and a Virgin Islands Studies program is developing a curriculum focused on the analysis of BVI cultural life and social and political institutions.

## BIBLIOGRAPHY

Bowen, W. Errol. "Development, Immigration, and Politics in a Preindustrial Society: A Study of Social Change in the British Virgin Islands in the 1960s." *Caribbean Studies* 16 (1): 67–85, 1976.

Cohen, Colleen Ballerino. "'This is de test': Festival and the Cultural Politics of Nation Building in the British Virgin Islands." *American Ethnologist* 25 (2): 189–214, 1998.

———. "Women as Tourism Producers and Product in the British Virgin Islands." In *Women as Producers and Consumers of Tourism in Developing Regions*, ed. Y. Apostolopoulos, S. Sonmez, and D. J. Timothy, 2000.

———. "Marketing Paradise, Making Nation." *Annals of Tourism Research* (22) 2: 404–421, 2001.

Cohen, Colleen Ballerino, and Mascia-Lees, Frances E. "The British Virgin Islands as Nation and Desti-Nation: Representing and Siting Identity in a Postcolonial Caribbean." *Social Analysis* 33 (September): 130–151, 1993.

Dookhan, Isaac. *A History of the British Virgin Islands 1672–1970*, 1975.

Encontre, Pierre. *Why Does the Tourist Dollar Matter? An Introduction to the Economics of Tourism in the British Virgin Islands*, 1989.

Harrigan, Norwell, and Varlack, Pearl. *The Virgin Islands Story*, 1988.

Maurer, Bill. *Recharting the Caribbean: Land, Law, and Citizenship in the British Virgin Islands*, 1988.

McGlynn, Frank. "Marginality and Flux: An Afro-Caribbean Community Through Two Centuries." Ph.D. dissertation, University of Pittsburgh, 1977.

O'Neal, Michael. "British Virgin Islands Transformations: Anthropological Perspectives." Ph.D. dissertation, Union Graduate School, Cincinnati, 1985.

O'Neal, Michael, and Maurer, Bill. "The Socioeconomic Context." In *Challenge and Change: The Awakening of a People, British Virgin Islands*, 1992.

Pickering, Vernon W. *A Concise History of the British Virgin Islands*, 1987.

—COLLEEN BALLERINO COHEN
AND MICHAEL E. O'NEAL

# BRUNEI DARUSSALAM

## CULTURE NAME

Bruneian

## ORIENTATION

**Identification.** Brunei Darussalam is a multiethnic society in which one ethnic group, the Barunay, has a monopoly of political power. Variations in tradition among other ethnic groups are not regional but cultural, social, and linguistic. Indigenous Muslims usually are referred to as Brunei Malays even if they are not native speakers of the Malay language.

Speculations about the etymology include derivations from the Malay (*baru nah* ("there!"), a Sanskrit form, and the Kelabit name for the Limbang River.

**Location and Geography.** The original home of Brunei culture is the area around the capital, Bandar Seri Begawan. Settlements of Barunay and Kadayan also are found along the coasts of northern Sarawak and southwestern Sabah in Malaysia; Tutong and Belait settlements are found exclusively in Brunei. Bisaya, Iban, and Penan people also live in Sarawak and Dusun and Murut people in both Sarawak and Sabah.

Brunei Darussalam is 2,226 square miles (5,763 square kilometers), with a coastline of about 100 miles (161 kilometers) on the South China Sea coast of northwestern Borneo and along the western shores of the southernmost portion of Brunei Bay. Brunei is completely surrounded by the Malaysian state of Sarawak. The climate is equatorial with high temperatures, high humidity, and heavy rainfall, although there is no distinct wet season. The country is divided into three contiguous administrative districts—Brunei-Muara, Tutong, and Belait—with a fourth, Temburong, separated by the Limbang Valley of Sarawak. The names of the districts derive from their main rivers.

Approximately 75 percent of the country is forested, although the exportation of whole logs has been banned. The country is covered with a wide range of mangrove, heath, peat swamp, mixed dipterocarp, and montane forests. There are numerous rivers, whose broad valleys contain most of the country's settlements. The southern portion of Temburong is mountainous and sparsely populated.

**Demography.** The 1998 population estimate was 323,600. Malays constitute about 67 percent of the total; Chinese, 15 percent; other indigenous peoples (Iban, Dayak, and Kelabit, all mainly from Sarawak), 6 percent, and others, 12 percent. In the late 1980s, 24,500 immigrants worked primarily in the petroleum industry. The population has increased more than twelve-fold since the first decade of the twentieth century. The distribution of population is Brunei-Muara, 66 percent; Belait, 20 percent; Tutong, 11 percent; and Temburong, 3 percent.

**Linguistic Affiliation.** Malay is the official language, but English is widely used in commerce. The Brunei dialect of Malay has many unique lexical items and a distinctive syntax. Malay is in the Western Malayo-Polynesian subgroup of the Austronesian language family, which also includes the other languages spoken in Brunei. Various Chinese languages, English, and Philippine and mainland south Asian languages are spoken by guest workers. Many individuals are multilingual.

**Symbolism.** The national flag is a yellow field of two trapeziums with a white diagonal parallelogram stripe above a black diagonal parallelogram stripe, representing the offices of the first vizier (a Muslim official), the Pengiran Bendahara, and the third vizier, the Pengiran Pamancha. These were the only vizier offices occupied in 1906, when the first British resident took up occupancy. The flag is emblazoned in the center by the state crest in

BRUNEI
DARUSSALAM

0   10   20   30 Miles

0   10   20   30 Kilometers

*South
China
Sea*

*Pulau
Labuan*

*Pulau
Kereman*

*Telok
Branei*

Muara   *Pulau
Muara Besar*

Jerudong

⊛ Bandar Seri
Begawan

Tutong

*Brunei*

Labu

Bangar

Kuala
Belait

Seria

Lumut   Kuala
Abang

Badas

Medit

*Tutong*

*Limbang*

*Pandaruan*

Batang
Duri

*Temburong*

Kerangan
Nyatan

Labi

Sukang

*Belait*

*Baram*

*Belait*

Mt. Pagon
6,070 ft.
1850 m.

M A L A Y S I A

N
W   E
S

Sarawak

• Brunei

*Brunei Darussalam*

red, which was added in 1959. The crest is composed of a flag and royal umbrella; four feathers symbolizing the protection of justice, tranquillity, prosperity, and peace; two hands representing the government's pledge to promote welfare, peace, and prosperity; and a crescent symbolizing Islam and inscribed in Arabic ''Always in service with God's guidance''; with a scroll inscribed in Arabic letters, *Brunei Darussalam* (''Brunei the Abode of Peace'').

## HISTORY AND ETHNIC RELATIONS

***Emergence of the Nation.*** The origins of the nation are only dimly known. Local traditions speak of a set of ancient local Bornean culture heroes, including Hawang Halak Batatar, who adopted Islam and became the first Muslim sultan of Brunei, Sultan Muhammad (reigned 1405–1415), and his brother, Patih Barbai, who became the second sultan, Sultan Ahmad (reigned 1415–1425). These heroes gave rise to the Barunay nobles. Many

Barunay aristocrats trace their origins to the Pagar Uyung area of the Minangakabau highlands of Sumatra. The third sultan, Sharif Ali (reigned 1425–1433), who married a daughter of Sultan Ahmad, came from Arabia and was a descendant of the Prophet Muhammad, as were all the following sultans.

Chinese documents record the ruler of Brunei sending a mission to the emperor of China in 977 C.E. The Brunei Empire, stretching to Manila and the southern Philippines and the coastal areas of western and northern Borneo, reached its height in the sixteenth century; the nadir occurred in the nineteenth century. Two ultimately unsuccessful Spanish invasions from Manila occurred in 1578 and 1580. A twelve-year civil war occurred in 1661–1673. Brunei became a British protected state in 1888 and became internally self-governing after the promulgation of the constitution in 1959. After achieving full independent sovereignty in 1984, Brunei joined the Association of Southeast Asian Nations (ASEAN), the Organization of Islamic Conference, and the United Nations. In 1992, Brunei joined the Nonaligned Movements.

***National Identity.*** In 1990, a new state ideology was launched to promote the unity of the diverse groups within a plural society. Malayu Islam Beraja (MIB, or Malay Muslim Monarchy) is based on the idea of Brunei as a traditional Malay state, a long-established Islamic state, and a monarchy.

***Ethnic Relations.*** All the ethnic groups in the nation have always been under the authority and rule of the sultan.

## URBANISM, ARCHITECTURE, AND THE USE OF SPACE

More than half the population lives in and around the capital. Other major towns include Tutong Town, seat of Tutong District; Kuala Belait, seat of Belait District; the small town of Bangar, seat of Temburong District; the deep-water port Muara, which opened in 1973 in Brunei-Muara District; and Seria, the center of the petroleum industry, in Belait District. There are also suburban developments around the capital and rural villages. The past two decades have seen a tremendous buildup around the capital. A network of roads and highways connects settlements in the three contiguous districts; Temburong is reached by boat from the capital area.

The architecture of the capital and its environs is dominated by the gold-domed Omar Ali Saifuddien Mosque (completed in 1958); the Nurul Iman Palace (1983), the largest residential palace in the world; the Royal Regalia Building (1992); the Royal Audience Hall (1968); and the Legislative Assembly (1968). The Tomb of the Fifth sultan is two miles downstream from the capital. The Royal Mausoleum has been used since 1786. The Hassanal Bolkiah National Stadium is the site of many large public celebrations. Numerous parks and recreation centers have been developed in the last decade.

## FOOD AND ECONOMY

**Food in Daily Life.** The diet consists of rice and curries of vegetables, fish, shellfish, and fruits. Curries of water buffalo, chicken, and beef are consumed on special occasions. Game birds and animals (especially mouse deer, barking deer, and sambar) are eaten in rural areas. Many kinds of Malay rice cakes and confections are also eaten. Pork products are forbidden to Muslims. There is a wide range of open-air markets and restaurants in the main towns. A popular local drink is iced unripe coconut milk. Coffee is widely consumed; alcoholic drinks are forbidden to Muslims.

**Food Customs at Ceremonial Occasions.** At large Malay wedding feasts and the forty-day funeral feast, rice and coconut cream-based meat curries (*santan*) are served, often to a hundred or more guests.

**Basic Economy.** Since World War II, the state's economy has been based on the exportation of petroleum and liquified natural gas (LNG), which account for about 36 percent of the gross domestic product (GDP). Brunei is the third largest oil producer in southeast Asia and the fourth largest producer of LNG in the world, exporting mainly to Japan, the United States, and ASEAN countries. Brunei produces only about 1 percent of its domestic needs for rice, 11 percent for fruit, 65 percent for vegetables, and some livestock (cattle and water buffalo). In early 1998, approximately 36,345 wage earners worked for the government and 106,000 were in the private sector. In rural areas an unknown number are still primarily subsistence producers. There are no sales, personal income, or capital gains taxes, only a 30 percent tax on corporate income. The workweek is Monday through Thursday and Saturday, with Friday and Sunday off. The national currency is known as the Bruneian dollar.

**Land Tenure and Property.** Before the land code of 1909, all land was either Crown Land, appanage land (held by high ranking nobles who were awarded "sacred" titles by the sultan), or private-heirloom land (held primarily by high-ranking nobles). Today any land not under private title is state land. Only citizens are allowed to own land. Rural villages have rights to state land for agricultural use.

**Commercial Activities.** Commerce is in its infancy. Local industry includes a water-bottling plant, a soft drink franchise, and garment companies. Foreign investment is encouraged but not highly developed. Priority is given to ensuring the stability of the natural environment, and all polluting industries are banned. Forest products and deep-sea fishing are not open to foreign investment. An international airport opened in 1974, and Royal Brunei Airlines began operation in 1975.

**Major Industries.** Commercial production of oil from land wells began in 1929. In 1963, production from offshore wells began. A major LNG production facility was completed in 1972.

**Trade.** The Bruneian economy is largely supported by exports of crude oil and natural gas, with revenues from the petroleum sector accounting for more than 50 percent of GDP. A 1990 study estimated that the commodities exported totaled approximately $2.2 billion, with the main exports including crude oil, liquid natural gas and petroleum. Brunei's main trading partners include Japan, the United Kingdom, and South Korea. The same 1990 study accounted for $1.7 billion in imported commodities. Brunei imports such goods as machinery and transport equipment, food, and manufactured goods. Singapore, the United Kingdom, and Switzerland are established as Brunei's main resources for these imported goods.

## SOCIAL STRATIFICATION

**Classes and Castes.** The dominant ethnic group, the Barunay, is composed of four ranked ascribed social classes: the nobles, the aristocrats, the ordinary people, and the slaves, although slavery is no longer practiced. Because class membership is strictly genealogical, a person assumes the class membership of his or her father and cannot rise or fall into any other class. There are no castes. The Kadayan have no social classes.

**Symbols of Social Stratification.** The only outward signs of social stratification are the prename titles of respect used in addressing or referring to nobles.

*Houses in the settlement are accessed by boats which travel on the waterways and canals within the community.*

## POLITICAL LIFE

***Government.*** Brunei Darussalam is an absolute constitutional monarchy. There are no political parties, elections, or legislature. Attempts to establish political parties in 1956 and 1985 did not succeed. In 1996, the first General Assembly of over a thousand elected village and *mukim* leaders met to give input to the Government. The first written constitution was promulgated in 1959, naming the sultan head of state, assisted by five councils (Religious Council, Privy Council, Council of Ministers, Legislative Council, and Council of Succession), with internal self-government and defense and foreign relations run by the United Kingdom. It was amended in 1971 to establish joint Bruneian-British responsibility for defense; in 1984, a cabinet-style government was introduced when Brunei resumed full sovereignty.

The sultan appoints judges to the Supreme Court, which consists of the high court and the court of appeals, and the Subordinate Court, which consists of the magistrate's courts. In 1991, an intermediate court was given civil and criminal jurisdiction. Syariah courts deal with Islamic law.

***Leadership and Political Officials.*** There are two forms of government administration—a modern administrative bureaucracy and a traditional system of ritual offices—which are awarded to nobles and aristocrats by the sultan. Individuals can rise through the ranks in both systems. The traditional system includes for the nobles five offices of vizier and about sixty additional various offices, and for the aristocrats about seventy-three offices of minister (*Pehin*). All occupants are males. Not all these traditional offices are always occupied at any given time; offices are not inherited on the death of their occupants but remain vacant until a sultan appoints a new occupant.

***Social Problems and Control.*** While the incidence of child abuse appears to be low, it is punished severely. Spouse abuse can be a cause for divorce. In general, Brunei is crime-free, especially in terms of violent crime.

***Military Activity.*** The Royal Brunei Armed Forces (RBAF) was founded in 1961. The RBAF was restructured in 1991 into land forces, an air force, a navy, support services, and a training corps. Service in the RBAF is voluntary. The main purpose of the military forces is defense.

## SOCIAL WELFARE AND CHANGE PROGRAMS

Since 1955, citizens, permanent residents, and persons who have worked in Brunei for thirty years have been entitled to a monthly pension. Elderly persons with dependents below working age receive additional allowances.

## NONGOVERNMENTAL ORGANIZATIONS AND OTHER ASSOCIATIONS

Muslims in Brunei may not belong to international service organizations.

## GENDER ROLES AND STATUSES

**Division of Labor by Gender.** Women have begun to assume positions of responsibility in government offices and departments. While women can be in the armed forces, they may not serve in combat.

**The Relative Status of Women and Men.** Compared to Islamic societies in the Middle East, women have very high status. Muslim women are encouraged to wear the *tudong*, a traditional head covering.

## MARRIAGE, FAMILY, AND KINSHIP

**Marriage.** Usually the parents of a young man arrange a marriage with the parents of a young woman. For a Muslim, the spouse must also be Muslim; thus, individuals, especially men, often convert to Islam in order to marry a Muslim. Interethnic group marriages are not uncommon. There is considerable minor variation in marriage ceremonies from group to group and within ethnic groups.

**Domestic Unit.** The domestic unit may be either a nuclear family or an extended family. This domestic arrangement is generated by a tradition in which a newly married couple joins the household of the bride's parents. After some time, young married couples may establish their own independent household.

**Inheritance.** Islamic inheritance law applies to Muslims. For non-Muslims, traditional practices apply.

**Kin Groups.** There are no descent-based kin groups. Malay kinship terminology is generational, with all "aunts" and "uncles" referred to as "mother" and "father," and Hawaiian, with all "cousins" referred to as "siblings." The kinship network of relatives may be very wide in the case of the Kadayan, who treat a relative by marriage the same as a blood relative, or narrower, in the case of the Barunay.

## SOCIALIZATION

**Infant Care.** Infants are watched over constantly by their parents, who often take them to the tasks in which they are engaged. Babies are fondly loved and appreciated by all.

**Child Rearing and Education.** Parents give young children responsibility for the care of their infant siblings at an early age, especially in rural areas.

**Higher Education.** The Universiti Brunei Darussalam opened in 1985 and offers a number of undergraduate degree programs, a few master's degrees, and a few certificate programs. Approximately two thousands government scholarship students study abroad, mainly in Commonwealth countries.

## ETIQUETTE

The following rules of etiquette are universal: pass items only with the right hand; refuse food by touching the container with the right hand, never verbally; use a thumb, never an index finger, to point; remove shoes whenever entering a home or public building, especially a mosque; shake hands gently and then gently touch the center of one's chest with the right hand afterward; never address a person by name alone; never consume items until specifically requested to do so; avoid public intersexual bodily contact; and never lose one's temper.

## RELIGION

**Religious Beliefs.** The national religion is the Shafeite sect of Islam. Religious holidays have variable dates that are set according to a lunar calendar. Early Ramadhan marks the beginning of the holy fasting month; the Anniversary of the Al-Quran commemorates the revelation of the Holy Book of Islam; Hari Raya Adilfitri or Hari Raya Puasa celebrates the end of the fasting month; Hari Raya Aidiladha or Hari Raya Haji celebrates the Haj or holy pilgrimage to Mecca; Hijrah celebrates the journey of the Prophet Muhammad Sallallahu Alihi Wassalam from Mecca to Medina; Mulaud, or the Birthday of the Prophet Muhammad, celebrates the birth of the founder of Islam; and Israk Mikraj commemorates the ascendancy of Muhammad into heaven.

**Religious Practitioners.** The sultan is the head of the Islamic faith. For all Muslims, matters of mar-

*A young boy watches the adults as they perform the noon prayer at a mosque in Bandar Seri, Begawan. The Shafeite sect of Islam is the national religion.*

riage, divorce, and the family as well as some sexual crimes are governed by Islamic law and fall under the jurisdiction of the religious court system.

***Rituals and Holy Places.*** Sixty mosques are maintained by the Ministry of Religious Affairs. Tombs of sultans are often treated as shrines.

## MEDICINE AND HEALTH CARE

Government health services are free for citizens, with minimal charges for permanent residents and immigrant government employees and their dependents. There are government hospitals in each of the four districts and two private hospitals, with the main referral hospital in the capital. Rural villages are served by scheduled Flying Medical Services by helicopter. Citizens are often sent abroad for treatment at government expense.

## SECULAR CELEBRATIONS

The national secular holidays are New Year's Day, 1 January; National Day, celebrating Brunei's resumption of full independent sovereignty in 1984, 23 February; Royal Brunei Armed Forces Day, marking the foundation day of the RBAF in 1961,

31 May; the Birthday of His Majesty the Sultan Haji Hassanal Bolkiah the Yang Dipertuan of Brunei Darussalam, 15 July; Christmas, 25 December; and Chinese New Year's Day, whose date is fixed by a lunar calendar.

## THE ARTS AND HUMANITIES

***Support for the Arts.*** History and local crafts are supported by a number of public institutions, including the Royal Regalia Building (1992), the Brunei History Center (1982) and the associated Churchill Memorial Museum, the Brunei Museum (1972), the Malay Technology Museum (1988), the Arts and Handicraft Center, and the Constitutional Museum.

***Literature.*** The Language and Literature Bureau promotes the development of literature and folklore and publishes textbooks in Malay and English for use in primary and secondary schools. A form of poetry known as *sajak* is popular with schoolchildren. A number of local authors have become well known. The most famous work of traditional literature is the epic poem *Sya'ir Awang Simawn*, which recounts the exploits of the culture hero

The Omar Ali Saifuddin Mosque on the Brunei River in Bandar Seri Begawan. Brunei is a constitutional monarchy; the Sultan is the head of state and all other political offices are held by men.

Simawn and constitutes a traditional history of the sultanate.

***Graphic Arts.*** Traditional arts and crafts form a large segment of Brunei's cultural heritage. Boat making, silver-smithing, bronze tooling, cloth weaving and basket making are examples of the types of artistry celebrated and emulated in modern-day culture.

## THE STATE OF THE PHYSICAL AND SOCIAL SCIENCES

The Hassanal Bolkiah Aquarium is in the capital. The Kuala Belalong Field Studies Center, set up in 1991 under the joint sponsorship of the University Brunei Darussalam's Department of Biology and the Brunei Shell Petroleum Company, is located in the Temburong District. A department of sociology and anthropology was opened at the University Brunei Darussalam in 1997.

## BIBLIOGRAPHY

Brown, Donald E. *Brunei: The Structure and History of a Bornean Malay Sultanate*, 1970.

———. *Principles of Social Structure: Southeast Asia*, 1976.

Brunei Shell Group of Companies, *Brunei Darussalam: A Guide*, 1992.

Cleary, Mark, and Hairuni H. M. Ali Maricar. "Aging, Islam and the Provision of Services for Elderly People in Brunei Darussalam. David R. Phillips, ed., in *Aging in East and South-East Asia*, 1992.

Government of Brunei. *Brunei Darussalam in Profile*, 1988.

Hussainmiya, B. A. *Sultan Omar Ali Saifuddin III and Britain: The Making of Brunei Darussalam*, 1995.

Leake, David, Jr. *Brunei, The Modern Southeast-Asian Sultanate*, 1989.

Maxwell, Allen R. "Kadayan Men and Women." In Vinson H. Sutlive, Jr., ed., *Female and Male in Borneo: Contributions and Challenges to Gender Studies*, 1991.

———. "Who is Awang Simawn?" In Victor T. King and A. V. M. Horton, eds., *From Buckfast to Borneo: Essays Presented to Father Robert Nicholl on the 85th Anniversary of His Birth, 27 March 1995*, 1995.

———. "The Place of the Kadayan in Traditional Brunei Society." *South East Asia Research* 4 (2): 157–196, 1996.

———. "The Origin of the Brunei Kadayan in Ethnohistoric Perspective." In Robert L. Winzeler, ed., *In-*

*digenous Peoples and the State: Politics, Land, and Ethnicity in the Malayan Peninsula and Borneo,* 1997.

Ranjit Singh, D. S. *Brunei 1839–1983: The Problems of Political Survival,* 1984.

Saunders, Graham *A History of Brunei,* 1994.

### Web Sites

Government of Brunei Darussalam Official Web Site, http://www.brunei.gov.bn

U.S. Department of State. "Brunei Country Report on Human Rights Practices for 1998," http://www.state.gov/www/global/human_rights/1998_hrp_report/brunei.html

—ALLEN R. MAXWELL

# BULGARIA

## CULTURE NAME
Bulgarian

## ALTERNATIVE NAMES
Bulgar, from the Bulgarian bŭlgar (Bulgarian person). In English, "Bulgar" is usually used only for the central Asian ancestors of the modern Bulgarians.

## ORIENTATION

**Identification.** The names "Bulgar", and "Bulgarian" most likely derive from a Turkic verb meaning "to mix." Ethnic Bulgarians trace their ancestry to the merging of Bulgars (or Proto-Bulgarians), a central Asian Turkic people, and Slavs, a central European people, beginning in the seventh century C.E. in what is now northeastern Bulgaria. Besides ethnic Bulgarians, there are several ethnic minorities, the most numerous being Turks and Gypsies, with smaller numbers of Armenians, Jews, and others.

The dominant national culture is that of the ethnic Bulgarians, and there is little sense of shared national culture among the three main ethnic groups. Turks usually do not self-identify as Bulgarians, whereas Gypsies often do. Both groups are generally considered outsiders by ethnic Bulgarians, in contrast to the more assimilated minorities such as Jews and Armenians. Nevertheless, since all citizens participate in the national economy and polity, a shared national bureaucratic-political culture does exist, both shaped by and shaping the cultural practices of the constituent ethnic groups.

**Location and Geography.** Bulgaria is located on the Balkan Peninsula in southeastern Europe. It is bordered on the east by the Black Sea, on the north by Romania and the Danube River, on the south by Greece and Turkey, and on the west by Macedonia and Serbia. The landscape consists of mountains, foothills, and plains. One-third of the territory is forested, and one-third is more than 2,000 feet (600 meters) above sea level. Major mountain ranges include Rila, Pirin, Balkan (Stara Planina), and Rhodope. For geographic reasons, Sofia was named the capital in 1879, after Bulgaria gained independence. Situated in an upland basin near the western border, Sofia was on the crossroads of major trade routes between the Aegean Sea and the Danube and between Turkey and central Europe. It also offered easy access to Macedonian lands, which were not part of the new Bulgarian state. Regional cultural variation sometimes reflects occupational specialization associated with local environmental conditions (e.g., fishing, animal husbandry), along with the influence of other cultural groups.

**Demography.** Bulgaria's population was 8,230,371 on December 31, 1998. The population increased gradually for most of the twentieth century, but has decreased by more than 700,000 people since 1988. This decline stems from out-migration and falling birthrates during the uncertain postsocialist period. About 68 percent of Bulgaria's population lives in urban areas, compared to 25 percent in 1946. In 1992, 86 percent of the population self-identified as ethnically Bulgarian, 9 percent as Turkish, and 4 percent as Roma (Gypsy). Smaller groups include Russians, Armenians, Vlachs, Karakachans, Greeks, Tatars, and Jews. The 1992 census did not include a category for Pomaks (Bulgarian Muslims), who are often identified as one of Bulgaria's four main ethnic groups and constitute an estimated 3 percent of the population. Through emigration, ethnic Turks have decreased as a share of the population since Bulgaria's 1878 independence. During the socialist period, ethnicity data were not made public, and there were efforts to assimilate Muslim minorities. This makes discussion of historical trends difficult, and some people may have self-identified on the census differently than they might in other contexts.

*Bulgaria*

**Linguistic Affiliation.** The national language is Bulgarian, a South Slavic language of the Indo-European language family, which uses the Cyrillic script. Bulgarian is very closely related to Macedonian, the two languages being largely mutually intelligible, and to Serbo-Croatian. Much vocabulary has been borrowed from Russian, Greek, and Turkish, and the latter two have had a strong influence on Bulgarian grammar. Bulgarian has two main dialectal variants, eastern and western, and also local dialects. National education and media are fostering homogenization of the language, particularly in urban settings.

The Turkish minorities speak Turkish, a Turko-Altaic language. Gypsies speak Romany, an Indic language of the Indo-European language family.

Many Gypsies also speak Turkish, and some speak Romanian. Bulgarian is necessary for interaction with the authorities and in commerce, and is the medium of instruction in schools, though minorities are entitled to be taught their mother tongue. The national media use Bulgarian, while some radio broadcasts and print media are available in Turkish.

**Symbolism.** The Bulgarian nation is symbolized in the coat of arms, which has at its center a crowned lion, a symbol of independence dating to the medieval Bulgarian state. During the state socialist period, the crown (a symbol of monarchy) was replaced by a star. After the fall of state socialism in 1989 the crown was replaced following a seven-year debate. The flag, a tricolor of horizontal stripes (from top: white, green, red), while a visible national emblem, is not so vested with specific meaning.

Among the most potent symbols of Bulgarian national identity are several key historical events: the founding of the Bulgarian states in 681 and 1878; the partition of Bulgaria in the Treaty of Berlin (1878); the union with Eastern Rumelia (an autonomous Ottoman province created by the partition) in 1885; the successful defense against Serbian encroachment in 1885; and territorial gains, losses, and humiliation in the Balkan wars (1912–1913) and World War I (1914–1918). Symbols of incompleteness and loss serve as powerful rallying points for national unity.

Images of the peasant, the merchant, the craftsman and entrepreneur, the teacher, and the nationalist revolutionary vie with each other in literature and folklore as icons of the true Bulgarian spirit, which incorporates qualities ranging from honesty and industry to resourcefulness and cunning.

## HISTORY AND ETHNIC RELATIONS

**Emergence of the Nation.** In the fifth century C.E., Slavs began to settle the Thracian-occupied eastern Danubian plains. In the seventh century, they joined with invading Bulgars to gain control of a sizable territory, which they defended against Byzantium in 681, gaining recognition as the first Bulgarian state. The Slav and Bulgar elements are then understood to have merged into one ethnic-cultural group, particularly after the official adoption of Byzantine-rite Christianity in 864 unified them around a common religion. With Christianity soon came vernacular literacy, and the development of a Slavic writing system by the Bulgaro-Macedonian Saints Cyril and Methodius. The local Slavic language became the language of liturgy and state administration, diminishing the ecclesiastical and cultural influence of Byzantium. In the tenth century Bulgaria was counted among the three most powerful empires in Europe.

The Ottomans invaded in the fourteenth century and ruled the Bulgarian lands for five centuries. The last century of Ottoman rule witnessed the reflowering of Bulgarian culture in the "National Revival." Bulgarian schools and cultural centers were established. In 1870 the Bulgarian church regained independence from Greek domination. The outside world took note in April 1876 when a Bulgarian uprising met bloody Ottoman reprisals. Russia defeated the Ottomans in 1878, leading to the reestablishment of a Bulgarian state. Hopes for a large Bulgaria were dashed in the Treaty of Berlin (1878), which left large numbers of ethnic Bulgarians in adjacent states. This partitioning of Bulgaria has been the cause of much conflict in the Balkans.

Following World War II (1939–1945), a socialist government was instituted under Soviet tutelage. The ouster of communist leader Todor Zhivkov on 10 November 1989 precipitated a reform process culminating in the dismantling of state socialism in 1990 and the establishment of a more democratic form of government.

**National Identity.** Bulgarian national identity is premised on the understanding that the Bulgarian nation (people) was formed with a distinctive ethnic identity during the Middle Ages (from a mix of Slavic, Bulgar, and other ethnicities). This identity, preserved throughout Ottoman rule, formed the basis for an independent nation-state. The history of the struggle for a Bulgarian state provides key symbols of national identity. Another premise is that ethnic and territorial boundaries should overlap. This has led at times to territorial conflicts with neighboring states. Moreover, this renders ambivalent the status of minorities, since they do not share the same ethnic and historical ties to the Bulgarian lands and state.

**Ethnic Relations.** Bulgaria officially espouses cordial relations with neighboring states. Relations with Macedonia, however, are complicated since many Bulgarians see Macedonia as historically a Bulgarian territory. The liberation of Macedonia was a central element in the nineteenth-century Bulgarian liberation movement and in early twentieth-century nationalism. Ottoman Macedonia was divided among Bulgaria, Greece, and Serbia in 1913. Bulgarian claims to the contrary, most Macedonians sought an independent Macedonian state, realized only after World War II within Yugoslav Macedonia. Bulgaria was quick to recognize Macedonia's independence from Yugoslavia in 1991, but does not acknowledge a distinct Macedonian culture. Since 1997 the Bulgarian government has acknowledged Macedonian as a separate language. Many Bulgarians, however, continue to consider Macedonians as Bulgarians, and the existence of a Macedonian minority within Bulgaria is generally denied.

There is both official and popular concern regarding the human rights (especially the right to ethnic self-determination) of Bulgarians living in neighboring states, particularly Serbia and Macedonia.

The relations among the various ethnic groups within Bulgaria are somewhat strained, partly as a legacy of brutal assimilation policies under state socialism, and partly out of fear on the part of ethnic Bulgarians that minority self-determination would threaten the integrity of the nation-state. Generally, in mixed settlements, relations with members of other ethnic groups are amicable, though much depends upon personal acquaintance.

## URBANISM, ARCHITECTURE, AND THE USE OF SPACE

Until World War II, Bulgaria's economy was largely agricultural. State socialism brought rapid industrialization and the collectivization of agriculture, leading to a significant population shift to the towns and cities. Soviet-style concrete apartment buildings and industrial developments ring towns and cities, with older-style homes and apartment buildings closer in. Educational and administrative facilities are dispersed in the major cities. Streets are wide, and often cobbled, and public parks, gardens, and playgrounds abound. Economic collapse in the 1990s has adversely affected the infrastructure and the maintenance of public spaces.

Commercial districts are by and large centrally located, and trips to central produce markets are essential for urban household survival. Residence and work are usually spatially separate, with most people relying on public transportation, which is extensive, but crowded.

Traditional houses in villages and towns are archetypally wooden, surrounded by high fences and with latticed windows. National Revival period houses are brightly painted with second floors projecting out over the street. Interiors often include carved wooden ceilings. Dwellings, whether apartments or traditional houses, are very much private spaces, with interiors hidden from public view and often decorated in highly individual manners.

Churches are prominent, many dating from the National Revival, and many Revival-era cultural centers (chitalishta) are preserved. Many mosques were destroyed following liberation and also during the state socialist period. Mosque restoration and rebuilding began after 1989 in Muslim areas.

## FOOD AND ECONOMY

**Food in Daily Life.** The everyday diet is based largely on local, in-season products. Bread, an important staple, is often purchased rather than home baked. Dairy products are widely consumed, partic-ularly yogurt and white-brined cheese. Home-cooked lunches and dinners often include soups, salads, stews, grilled meats, or stuffed vegetables, while meals away from home may consist of foods such as bread, cheese, sausage, and vegetables. Banitsa is a popular pastry filled with cheese and eggs, pumpkin, rice, spinach, or leeks. For snacks and breakfast, it is accompanied by a grain-based drink, boza, or yogurt-based airan. Popular alcoholic beverages include rakiya, a potent fruit-based brandy, and wine. Many people can fruits and vegetables and make sauerkraut for winter when fresh produce is unavailable or unaffordable. Regional culinary variation reflects local environmental conditions, for example, fish along the sea, vegetables in the plains, and dairy products in mountain areas. Some observant Muslims avoid eating pork. In response to postsocialist conditions, meat and dairy product consumption has declined relative to the less-expensive bread. Typical restaurant offerings are more limited than home cooking, with menus based around salads, soups, grilled meats, and perhaps a meatless offering. Coffee bars, pubs, and sweet shops are popular meeting places for a drink, coffee, or snack.

**Food Customs at Ceremonial Occasions.** Some Orthodox Christians observe a Lenten fast before Easter, and observant Muslims avoid eating and drinking during daylight hours during Ramadan. Within Islamic tradition, numerous dishes are served and sweets are exchanged on Ramazan (Ramadan) Bairam, and a ram or calf is ritually slaughtered for Kurban Bairam. Kurban means sacrifice and also refers to a boiled meat dish prepared for ceremonial occasions. Another popular celebration dish is spit-roasted sheep or goat. The Christmas Eve table includes numerous, predominantly meatless dishes, including stuffed cabbage leaves, beans, lentils, boiled wheat, dried fruit, and nuts. For Christmas or New Year's, fortunes in the form of coins, cornel cherry twigs, or slips of paper are inserted in banitsa or bread. Special holiday breads include Easter's braided kozunak, which is sometimes decorated with dyed eggs.

**Basic Economy.** Bulgaria's economy has experienced considerable disruption since communism's fall in 1989. Industrial and agricultural production have declined, unemployment has increased, and the purchasing power of pensions and wages has fallen. In 1986, agriculture made up 16 percent of the economy (measured as a share of gross value added); industry, 60 percent; and services, 24 percent. The figures for 1996 were 15 percent for agri-

*A mural on a wall in Varna. Before the fall of state socialism in 1989, art (especially folk art), was state-funded.*

culture, 30 percent for industry, and 55 percent for services. Private-sector activity, more prominent in agriculture and services than in industry, increased from 17 percent of the economy in 1991 to one-half in 1996. In principle, Bulgaria is self-sufficient in food production; however, periodic shortages of key crops, such as wheat, have been caused both by poor weather and by declines in agricultural production following liquidation of cooperative farms. With economic changes during the 1990s, household subsistence food production has increased substantially.

**Land Tenure and Property.** Significant changes in property ownership followed communism's collapse. Bulgaria's constitution declares as state property underground resources, coastal beaches, public roadways, waters, forests and parks of national significance, nature preserves, and archaeological sites. Ownership of agricultural land and forests is legally restricted to Bulgarian citizens, government entities, and organizations; foreigners, however, are permitted use rights. Private property rights to most agricultural land have been restored to their former (precollectivization) owners or their heirs, and the parliament passed legislation in 1997 to restore to their former owners forests that were privately owned before forest nationalization in 1947. Most precollectivization landholdings were

small, and this pattern continues. About 19 percent of forests were privately owned before nationalization, and churches, mosques, cooperatives, schools, and municipalities owned or managed some of the remainder. Some forests and pastures were communally managed before collectivization; it is unclear, however, the extent to which communal land management will reemerge.

**Major Industries.** Before World War II, Bulgaria's economy was based primarily on agriculture along with light manufacturing enterprises, such as food processing and textile production, which processed the resulting products. Rapid industrialization occurred during the socialist era, particularly in heavy industry such as machinery production, mining and metallurgy, and chemical and oil processing, and these sectors continued to dominate Bulgarian industry at the end of the twentieth century. Manufacture of food, beverages, and tobacco products also continues to be important.

**Trade.** Much of Bulgaria's socialist-era trade was with other socialist countries through their trading organization, the Council for Mutual Economic Assistance. In the last decade, trade with European Union countries has grown relative to that with former socialist bloc countries. Bulgaria's largest trading partners in 1997 were Germany, Greece, Italy, and the Russian Federation. Major export categories include chemical and petroleum products, machinery, electronics, mining and metallurgy, textiles and clothing, and processed food, beverages, and tobacco.

**Division of Labor.** Labor specialization increased during the socialist era, and many young people received vocational training preparing them for particular professions. Yet, many rural households have returned to private agricultural production in the postsocialist period, and people may be unable to find jobs for which they were trained.

## SOCIAL STRATIFICATION

**Classes and Castes.** During the socialist period, senior party officials, managers of state enterprises, and their kin formed an elite, the former bourgeois elite having had their property and means of wealth confiscated and nationalized. Since 1989, despite the restitution of much confiscated property, it is largely the socialist-era elite and those close to them who have managed to acquire the wealth that now defines status, mostly through illegal transfers of control of state-owned assets and the private exploitation of formerly state-controlled trade relationships. Much of the new private wealth is also derived from criminal activity, particularly organized crime.

**Symbols of Social Stratification.** During the state socialist period, elite status depended upon the maintenance of the right relationships and entailed privileges of access—to better housing, the best schooling, scarce (often imported) commodities, and foreign travel. Following the fall of state socialism, status began to be measured more in terms of monetary wealth, while the gap between the rich and the ordinary citizens grew sharply. Despite a general aversion to it, conspicuous consumption by the elite has become considerably more visible in the form of imposing dwellings and imported luxury goods and motor vehicles.

## POLITICAL LIFE

**Government.** Bulgaria's 1991 constitution, which established a parliamentary republic, provides for a multiparty parliamentary system and free elections with universal adult suffrage. Bulgaria's chief of state is an elected president, and the head of government is a prime minister selected by the largest parliamentary group. To enter the National Assembly, parties and electoral coalitions must receive at least 4 percent of the popular vote. The Council of Ministers, chaired by the prime minister, is the main body of the executive branch of government. Mayors and councilors of local municipalities are elected, while regional governors are appointed by the Council of Ministers. There is also an independent judiciary.

**Leadership and Political Officials.** Bulgaria experienced considerable political disruption during the 1990s. Postsocialist governments have changed frequently, and two parliaments failed to survive their four-year mandates. Growing disillusionment with government and its inability to effect postsocialist economic restructuring is seen in the decline in voter participation from 83 percent of eligible voters during the 1991 parliamentary election to 59 percent in 1997. More than thirty-five political parties and coalitions registered for parliamentary elections during the 1990s, yet only a handful gained enough votes to enter parliament. Politics are dominated by the Union of Democratic Forces, an anticommunist coalition that became a party in 1997, and the Bulgarian Socialist Party, successor to the Bulgarian Communist Party. The other party to play a major role in parliamentary politics is the Movement for Rights and Freedom, which is commonly identified with Bulgaria's Turkish minority. Despite the disillusionment, many Bulgarians continue to look to the government to solve problems and provide services—as it did during the socialist era.

**Social Problems and Control.** Formal systems for addressing crime include laws, police, and the courts. In the postsocialist period, crime is seen to be out of control, and the police are viewed as ineffective at best and involved in rapidly escalating crime rates at worst. The most common reported crimes are property and car theft, while allegations of corruption are widespread. Another common perception is that certain economic sectors are controlled by so-called mafia groups operating outside the law. Ordinary people often feel helpless to do anything about these situations. In some rural communities, less formal systems of social control continue to operate for addressing problems such as crop damage from livestock trespass, and local authorities may mediate disputes.

**Military Activity.** All Bulgarian men must perform military service, although Bulgaria has had little direct involvement in military conflicts since World War II. In the 1990s, the length of service was reduced, partly due to cost considerations, and movement began toward a voluntary military. Mil-

*Young women harvesting roses on a farm in Kazanluk. Women tend to do more hand labor, while men work with machinery and animals, in the agricultural sector.*

itary spending fell from 4.6 percent of gross domestic product in 1988 to 1.8 percent in 1996.

## SOCIAL WELFARE AND CHANGE PROGRAMS

Bulgaria's socialist-era social safety net included pensions, health care, maternity leave, and guaranteed employment. Some services had ideological goals, such as day care, which helped facilitate women's entrance into the workforce. The economic status of many households has fallen significantly in the postsocialist period because of unemployment and the declining purchasing power of wages and pensions. Meanwhile, the government's poor financial condition has made maintaining earlier services difficult. Nongovernmental organizations (NGOs), such as the Bulgarian Red Cross, are involved in activities such as supporting orphanages and feeding homeless children. Others promote civil rights or ethnic and religious tolerance. Yet, NGO activities are limited by their economic circumstances and reliance on foreign funding. Some foreign support for NGOs results from their perceived status as democratic institutions that are part of civil society, which was seen as lacking during the socialist era and thus needing support.

## NONGOVERNMENTAL ORGANIZATIONS AND OTHER ASSOCIATIONS

Few independent organizations existed in socialist Bulgaria. Previously established groups were incorporated into state structures or disappeared. Newly formed environmental organizations such as Ecoglasnost played a role in the 1989 political changes, and NGO numbers increased considerably following the collapse of the state socialist regime. These organizations address such concerns as environmental protection, economic development, human rights, social welfare, health care, the arts, and education. Most NGOs rely on financial support from non-Bulgarian sources interested in their activities or in the organizations themselves as democratic institutions. Many NGOs have been created by urban professionals, although some groups exist in rural areas. The mass mobilization around environmental issues seen in 1989 has decreased as many people struggle to survive the difficult economic situation. More generally, NGO impact on people's lives is limited by their small sizes, financial constraints, and the limited recognition of NGOs in some circles. Other organizations include trade unions and professional associations.

*A Bulgarian man draws water from a roadside well near Belogradchick.*

## GENDER ROLES AND STATUSES

***Division of Labor by Gender.*** Many women entered paid employment during the socialist era, when an ideology of gender equality was promoted, and they made up nearly half the workforce in the late twentieth century. Women are frequently employed as teachers, nurses, pharmacists, sales clerks, and laborers, and less often involved in management, administration, and technical sciences. Women are also largely responsible for household tasks—child care, cooking, cleaning, and shopping. Agricultural labor is divided according to gender, with men working with animals and machinery and women doing more hand labor in crop production, although flexibility exists in response to specific situations.

***The Relative Status of Women and Men.*** While Bulgaria is often described as a patriarchal society, women may have substantial authority in household budgeting or agricultural decision making. Both men and women have the right to vote and own property. Women lag behind men only slightly in educational achievement. Despite the socialist ideology of gender equality, women are often employed in lower paying jobs, remain responsible for most household chores, and represent more than half the registered unemployed. They also oc-

cupy leadership positions less frequently than men. Fewer than 14 percent of postsocialist parliamentary representatives have been women, and only one in five municipal councilors were women in 1996.

## MARRIAGE, FAMILY, AND KINSHIP

***Marriage.*** Bulgarians typically marry by individual choice, although families may exert pressure on the choice of spouse. Some groups, such as Pomaks and Gypsies, previously arranged marriages and may occasionally do so now. Only civil ceremonies are legally recognized, although couples may also have a religious ceremony. Marriages are monogamous, close relatives are not considered appropriate marriage partners, and spouses are usually from the same ethnic and religious group. Nearly all adults marry, typically in their early to mid-twenties. Divorce was rare in the past, but is less stigmatized today. Marriage rates declined in the 1990s in response to postsocialist uncertainty.

***Domestic Unit.*** Historical accounts of Balkan family structure often discuss the *zadruga*, an extended, joint-family household said to have disappeared by the early twentieth century. Contemporary households commonly consist of a married couple or couple with children, but they may include three generations—for example, a nuclear family with a grandparent or a married couple, their son and daughter-in-law, and grandchildren. Most couples have only one or two children, although birthrates are higher for Bulgaria's ethnic minorities. Households are the primary units of social and biological reproduction, and economic activity, especially in the case of agricultural production. Two wage earners are often required to support urban households. Since most women work, grandparents often care for grandchildren in three-generation households, and a grandmother may shop and cook. Other factors contributing to such households are housing shortages and the need to generate income through both wage labor and subsistence production. After marriage, patrilocal residence—with the new couple moving in with the husband's parents—is more likely than matrilocal residence, although couples may establish independent households if they have sufficient resources.

***Inheritance.*** In principle, both men and women own property such as land, buildings, and animals, and inheritance is partible (i.e., property is divided among all heirs rather than going to a single heir). In practice, some heirs may be disinherited or may receive more land than their siblings, and daughters may inherit less land than sons. The latter is sometimes explained in terms of the often large dowries of household goods and sometimes land or livestock that women take into marriage. Houses are often inherited by youngest sons, who bring their wives to live in the family home.

***Kin Groups.*** Bulgarians count as kin relatives by blood and marriage on both the male and female sides. Rather than formal structures, kindreds tend to be informal networks of relatives. One's inner circle of close kin, friends, and neighbors is referred to as *blizki*, or close people. The importance of more distant relatives depends on factors such as proximity and frequency of interaction. With the socialist era's rapid urbanization, relatives can be dispersed between rural and urban settings, although it is not uncommon to find clusters of kin in rural communities. In rural settings, kin and other blizki often cooperate in agricultural activities. Connections through rural and urban networks of kin and blizki are often mobilized to accomplish such objectives as obtaining scarce goods, accessing information, or gaining employment.

## SOCIALIZATION

***Infant Care.*** Early infant care is usually provided by the mother. Working mothers receive at least four months maternity leave on full pay, enabling them to care full time for young infants. The government in theory provides income supplements to families with children, but the economic collapse of the 1990s made the amounts mere tokens (when they were paid at all).

***Child Rearing and Education.*** Ethnic Bulgarians tend towards single-child families. They are thus able to devote considerable resources and attention to their children's well-being and education. Children aged three to six may attend state-run kindergartens, where available. Otherwise, their care often falls to grandparents, who are increasingly visible as caregivers in the economically insecure postsocialist era. Heavy-handed discipline is uncommon, but children are brought up to defer to parental authority.

Schooling is free and compulsory for children aged seven to sixteen (four years elementary; six to eight secondary). Ethnic Bulgarians value education, and children are encouraged to do well, with many parents paying for private tutoring to ensure that their children pass entrance examinations for the better secondary schools and universities or even resorting to bribery of officials. Since 1989, many private schools have been established, offering an educational alternative for the wealthy and often catering to those not accepted into elite state schools.

Turks and Gypsies have notably higher birthrates and tend to be lower on the socioeconomic scale, as well as culturally and linguistically disadvantaged. Levels of educational achievement are generally lower than among ethnic Bulgarians.

***Higher Education.*** Bulgaria has an extensive system of higher education, with state universities, technical institutes, and teacher's colleges in a number of cities. There is also a private American university in the city of Blagoevgrad. Competition for places in the state universities is rigorous. Most students receive subsidized housing and many receive scholarships to offset the costs of education. Fees are not high, but under the depressed economic conditions they are significant.

## ETIQUETTE

In Bulgaria, gestures for indicating "yes" and "no" are essentially opposite from those common in most of the rest of Europe. A sideways shaking of

*Muslims pray in a mosque on the first day of Bajram in the village of Breznica.*

the head indicates ''Yes,'' and a short upward and downward movement (nod) of the head indicates ''No.''

Bulgarians generally pride themselves on their hospitality and neighborliness. An uninvited visitor will first be greeted with a handshake or verbal greeting at the outermost doorway or gateway, and will be invited further into the private domestic space depending on the nature of the visit. At mealtimes, a guest will be offered food and drink, and at other times a drink (often homemade rakiya); it is impolite not to accept this hospitality. The obligation to accept a host's offer extends to situations outside of the home, such as when invited for a meal or a drink in a restaurant or other establishment. When visiting someone's home, it is customary to bring flowers or sweets.

On the street or in other public places, strangers will usually avoid making eye contact. In public transportation, it is expected that younger people will give up a seat to an older woman or to a parent with a young child. Failure to do so invites public censure from other passengers.

In ethnically-mixed areas, it is considered polite to greet a neighbor or acquaintance in that person's own language.

## RELIGION

***Religious Beliefs.*** Most ethnic Bulgarians belong to the Bulgarian Orthodox Church, though there are small numbers of Muslims (Pomaks), Protestants, and Roman Catholics. Most Turks and many Gypsies are Muslim, while some (especially Gypsies) are Christian. In Bulgaria, both Orthodox Christianity and Islam incorporate some pagan beliefs and rituals. Among the Pomaks and Gypsies, Christian and Islamic beliefs and practices often coexist. Other religions include Judaism, Armenian Orthodox Christianity, and a variety of Protestant churches and sects.

Orthodox Christianity is enshrined in the constitution as the traditional religion in Bulgaria, and the church has a legacy of ties to nationalist groups. State regulation of religious affairs has diminished since the fall of state socialism. Nevertheless, political interference remains a factor in religious affairs, and schisms in the Orthodox and Muslim communities in the 1990s (over challenges to the legitimacy of leaderships installed under state socialism) were dominated by partisan political interests. Proselytizing by foreign-based churches and sects is considered a threat to national identity.

Most Orthodox Bulgarians and Muslims are not observant, and many are atheists, partly a result of the state socialist government's attempts to discredit religion. Despite some resurgence of interest in religious observance since the fall of state socialism, religious practices have become largely markers of cultural identity.

**Religious Practitioners.** The Orthodox Church is headed by a patriarch, presiding over the Holy Synod (or Church Council), with a hierarchy of regional archbishops, bishops, and priests. There are also monasteries where monks and nuns practice a life of religious devotion and scholarship. The Muslim community is governed by the Supreme Muslim Council under the Chief Mufti (religious judge), with a hierarchy of regional muftis, imams (clergy), and religious teachers.

**Rituals and Holy Places.** For both Christians and Muslims, the most significant rituals are those associated with the passage of life: birth, marriage, and death, as well as christening (for Christians) and circumcision (for Muslims). Christian holidays include Christmas, Easter, Lent, and saints' days. Services are held on Sundays and often daily, and people often visit churches to pray to saints, burning candles in honor of loved ones. Muslim holidays include the month-long fast of Ramadan and the Festival of Sacrifice (Kurban Bairam). The observant attend mosques on Fridays and may observe daily prayers.

Churches and especially monasteries are considered sacred, not only to the Orthodox Church but also to the nation, as they played a significant role in the national emancipation.

**Death and the Afterlife.** Both Orthodox Christians and Muslims believe in an afterlife. For both, proper observance of death and burial-related rituals is considered crucial to the soul's proper passage into the afterlife.

## MEDICINE AND HEALTH CARE

Bulgaria has an extensive health-care system based around community polyclinics, with a network of general and specialized hospitals. This system is largely a legacy of the state socialist period, when universal healthcare was provided free of charge. Following health care reforms in 2000, consumers must now choose their own family doctor and pay for heath insurance. Health-care professionals may also operate private practices.

Bulgarians have long valued herbal remedies, and economic hardship in the 1990s led to increased reliance on herbs, with Western medicine becoming for many a last resort. Bulgarians on the whole are

A woman wears traditional dress in Talboukhin, Bulgaria.

very concerned with their health, and are knowledgeable about treating minor ailments with both Western and herbal medicines. Yet, consumption of tobacco and alcohol are extremely high, and the rate of strokes is among the highest in the developed world.

## SECULAR CELEBRATIONS

Efforts were made during the socialist era to replace religious holidays and life-cycle rituals with secular ones—for example, civil ceremonies replaced church weddings and Grandfather Frost delivered presents on 1 January instead of Grandfather Christmas on 25 December. With communism's fall, government-recognized holidays include Easter and Christmas, and some socialist holidays such as 9 September, marking the beginning of the socialist era, have disappeared.

New Year's is celebrated on 1 January with holiday foods and traditions designed to bring luck and health in the coming year. Baba Marta (Grandmother March), on 1 March, is a pre-Christian holiday welcoming spring, on which people exchange *martinitsas*, good luck charms made from red and white threads. Bulgaria's liberation from the Ottoman Empire is celebrated on 3 March, International Women's Day on 8 March, Labor Day on 1 May, and Bulgarian education and culture on 24 May, a day associated with Saints Cyril and Methodius, founders of the Cyrillic alphabet. Other celebrations—often associated with the agricultural calendar, the Orthodox Christian calendar, or both—include the day of the vintner on 14 February; Saint George's Day on 6 May, in honor of the patron saint of shepherds and the army; and festivals of masked *kukeri* (mummers) marking the beginning of spring and the agricultural season (dates vary). Important life-cycle celebrations mark births, high school graduations, send-offs to military service, weddings, and deaths. The latter are commemorated at specified intervals following death (e.g., nine days, forty days, six months, one year).

## The Arts and Humanities

**Support for the Arts.** During the state socialist period, the arts were state funded (and regulated). State-sponsored folk ensembles were charged not only with preserving heritage, but also with the task of transforming folk art forms to the level of high culture. State sponsorship allowed the arts to flourish, and ideological limits did not necessarily compromise artistry. Puppet theater, for instance, developed to a high standard of excellence. Since the fall of state socialism in 1989, state funding has evaporated, and entrepreneurship on the part of individuals and ensembles has become necessary for survival, where before salaries and programming emanated largely from the Ministry of Culture. This has been a tough transition for many practitioners of the arts. What state funding remains is granted subject to open competition.

**Literature.** Bulgarian literature begins with the advent of literacy in Old Church Slavonic (Old Bulgarian) in the late-ninth century C.E. The earliest writings were religious in nature. In the late-eighteenth century, secular writings began to be written using a more accessible modern vernacular Bulgarian. Several important writings on the history of the Bulgarian nation date from this period. In the early nineteenth century, the modern standard language developed through the promotion of literacy in the schools.

Literature and journalism flourished around the theme of national emancipation. Ethnologists began to collect and publish folklore, another vehicle for the development of national consciousness. Bulgarian Revival and early modern literature continues to form the core of literature studies within the Bulgarian education system. Several Bulgarian authors and poets have achieved international fame.

**Graphic Arts.** Bulgaria's graphic art traditions have their roots in Orthodox Christian icon and fresco painting, and some Bulgarian medieval works are world famous and significant in the history of world art, particularly the frescos in the Boyana church near Sofia. Folk arts and crafts thrive, and distinctive and beautiful traditions exist in wood carving, ceramics, and weaving and other textile arts.

**Performance Arts.** Bulgaria boasts a rich palette of music, dance, and theater, ranging from folk music and dance to classical and modern opera, jazz, and Western-style popular music. Of particular note here are the varieties of folk and folk-influenced musics, many of which have become well-known in the outside world since the mid-1980s, achieving status as virtual icons of Bulgarian national culture. Particularly prominent are women's vocal (choral) music and wedding band music. Traditionally, folk musicians are often gypsies, the music is sensuous, and performances involve a high degree of spontaneity, particularly at events such as weddings. In theater, opera, and ballet, the repertoire of Bulgarian artists includes a range of international and local productions. Bulgarian cinema had its heyday in the 1970s and 1980s under state sponsorship, but now produces only between five and ten films annually.

## The State of the Physical and Social Sciences

During the socialist era, the government supported the physical and social sciences; increased higher education opportunities resulted in the training of a cadre of scientists in such fields as linguistics, economics, history, philosophy, sociology, folklore, ethnography, physics, chemistry, biology, botany, geography, geology, forestry, agronomy, and medicine. Many scientists were employed in research institutes of the Bulgarian Academy of Sciences or at universities. Under postsocialist economic constraints, government support for these activities has fallen substantially. Some scientists have left the country as a result, while others have changed jobs or sought support for their activities through nongovernmental organizations.

## Bibliography

Anson, Jon, Elka Todorova, Gideon Kressel, and Nicolai Genov, eds. *Ethnicity and Politics in Bulgaria and Israel*, 1993.

Bates, Daniel G. "Uneasy Accommodation: Ethnicity and Politics in Rural Bulgaria". In David A. Kideckel, ed., *East European Communities: The Struggle for Balance in Turbulent Times*, 1995.

Bell, John D., ed. *Bulgaria in Transition: Politics, Economics, Society, and Culture after Communism*, 1998.

Buchanan, Donna A. "Wedding Music, Social Identity, and the Bulgarian Political Transition." In Mark Slobin, ed., *Retuning Culture: Musical Changes in Central and Eastern Europe*, 1996.

Crampton, Richard J. *A Concise History of Bulgaria*, 1997.

Creed, Gerald W. *Domesticating Revolution: From Socialist Reform to Ambivalent Transition in a Bulgarian Village*, 1998.

Dobreva, Stanka. "The Family Farm in Bulgaria: Traditions and Changes. *Sociologia Ruralis* 34 (4): 340–353, 1994.

Eminov, Ali. *Turkish and Other Muslim Minorities in Bulgaria*, 1997.

Flanz, Gisbert H. "Republic of Bulgaria. In Albert P. Blaustein and Gisbert H. Flanz, eds., *Constitutions of the Countries of the World*, 1992.

Genov, Nikolai. *Human Development Report: Bulgaria, 1997*, 1997.

Jones, Derek C., and Jeffrey Miller, eds. *The Bulgarian Economy: Lessons from Reform During Early Transition*, 1997.

Konstantinov, Julian, Gideon M. Kressel, and Trond Thuen. "Outclassed by Former Outcasts: Petty Trading in Varna. *American Ethnologist* 25 (4): 729–745, 1998.

Marushiakova, Elena, and Vesselin Popov. *Gypsies (Roma) in Bulgaria*, 1997.

Mosely, Philip E. "Distribution of the Zadruga within Southeastern Europe. In Robert F. Byrnes, ed., *Communal Families in the Balkans: Essays by Philip E. Mosely and Essays in His Honor*, 1976.

Panova, Rossica, Raina Gavrilova, and Cornelia Merdzanska. "Rethinking Gender: Bulgarian Women's Impossibilities." In Nanette Funk and Magda Mueller, eds., *Gender Politics and Post-Communism*, 1993.

Paskaleva, Krasimira, Philip Shapira, John Pickles, and Boian Koulov, eds. *Bulgaria in Transition: Environmental Consequences of Political and Economic Transformation*, 1998.

Pickles, John, and the Bourgas Group. "Environmental Politics, Democracy and Economic Restructuring in Bulgaria." In John O'Loughlin and Herman van der Wusten, eds., *The New Political Geography of Eastern Europe*, 1993.

Raikin, Spas T. "Nationalism and the Bulgarian Orthodox Church." In P. Ramet, ed., *Religion and Nationalism in Soviet and East European Politics*, 1989.

Roth, Klaus, and Juliana Roth. "The System of Socialist Holidays and Rituals in Bulgaria." *Ethnologia Europaea* 20: 107–120, 1990.

Sanders, Irwin T. *Balkan Village*, 1949.

Silverman, Carol. "The Politics of Folklore in Bulgaria." *Anthropological Quarterly* 56 (2): 55–61, 1983.

———. "Pomaks." In Richard V. Weekes, ed., *Muslim Peoples: A World Ethnographic Survey*, 2nd ed. 1984.

Smollett, Eleanor. "The Economy of Jars: Kindred Relationships in Bulgaria—An Exploration. *Ethnologia Europaea* 19: 125–140, 1989.

Todorova, Maria. "The Bulgarian Case: Women's Issues or Feminist Issues?" In Nanette Funk and Magda Mueller, eds., *Gender Politics and Post-Communism*, 1993.

### Web Sites

Consultative Group on Early Childhood Care and Development. *Who Is Caring for Children: An Exploratory Survey. A Study of the Situation in Bulgaria*, 1995. Available from http://www.ecdgroup.com/archive/bulfinal.html

—BARBARA A. CELLARIUS
AND TIM PILBROW

# BURKINA FASO

## CULTURE NAME
Burkinabè

## ALTERNATIVE NAMES
Formerly Upper Volta (Haute Volta)

## ORIENTATION

**Identification.** In 1984, Thomas Sankara's revolutionary government changed the name Upper Volta to Burkina Faso, thus discarding the name the French had given their former colony. Burkina Faso is an artificial word, using linguistic elements from the country's largest languages: Burkina means "free man" in Mooré; Faso means "land" in Dyula. Burkina Faso is thus identified as the "country of the free men." Its inhabitants are called Burkinabè; the "bè" is a suffix from another language of the country, Fulfulde.

Burkina Faso is a multiethnic nation with about sixty ethnic and linguistic groups. The country is roughly divided into two parts, each with different historical backgrounds and political cultures: the eastern and central regions were historically dominated by kingdoms, emirates, and chieftaincies such as the Mossi at the center, the Gurmanché in the extreme east and the Fulbe and Tuareg in the north. The western and southern regions contain a number of ethnic groups, which were politically less centralized. The largest of these groups are the Bisa and Gurunsi in the south, the Lobi and Dagara in the southwest, the Bobo in the west, and the Bwaba and Samo in the northwest.

**Location and Geography.** The country covers 105,869 square miles (274,200 square kilometers) in the center of West Africa, north of Ghana and Ivory Coast. It is a landlocked, flat country with an average altitude between 650 and 1,300 feet (200 and 400 meters) above sea level. There are some elevations in the west, the highest point being the Tenakourou (2,457 feet; 749 meters). The largest part of the former Upper Volta lies within the catchment area of the three northern tributaries of the Volta river, the Mouhoun, the Nazinon, and the Nakambe (formerly the Black, Red, and White Volta). The capital Ouagadougou lies almost in the geographical center of the country. It was the capital of a powerful Mossi kingdom and became the seat of French colonial administration in 1919.

The tropical climate has a wet season and a dry season. The northern Sahelian zone, which is adjacent to the Sahara desert, is much drier than the south, with only six to twenty-four inches (150 to 600 millimeters) of rain falling between June and September. In the southernmost Sudanic zone, rains usually start in May and end around October. Here the annual precipitation is from 35 to 51 inches (900 to 1300 millimeters). Rains show extreme variations from year to year, in both timing and quantity. They typically fall during short violent thunderstorms.

The country's vegetation varies with trees and thick bush in the south and near-desert conditions in the north. The landscape changes dramatically according to the seasons. In the driest months, extreme drought and the Harmattan, a dusty cold wind from the Sahara, desiccate all vegetation; widespread manmade bushfires add to the burnt aspect of the landscape. With the first rains, leaves sprout on trees and bushes and the savannah grass grows to several yards within a few months.

**Demography.** According to the 1996 census, there were 10,469,747 Burkinabè, with a population growth rate of about 2.5 percent. Central Intelligence Agency and World Bank estimates indicated a population of over 11 million by 1999. With an average life expectancy of forty-five years, 50 percent of the population is less than fifteen years old. The Mossi ethnic group makes up almost half of the population; Fulbe, Gurmanché, Bobo-Dyula, Bisa,

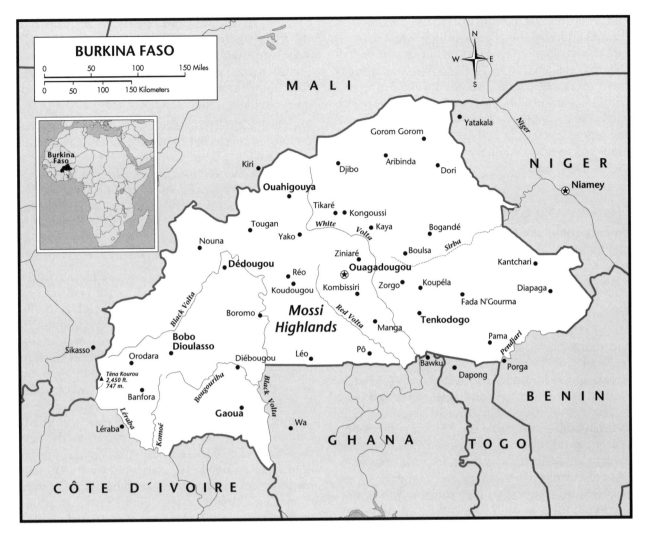

*Burkina Faso*

Dagara-Lobi, and Gurunsi are each between 5 and 8 percent of the total population.

**Linguistic Affiliation.** French, the language of the former colonizing power, is the official language. It is used in schools, the army, the media, and by people who attend school if they are not from the same ethnic group. Since many people do not go to school, they have little or no knowledge of the French language. Widespread vernacular languages include Mooré in the center of the country and Dyula in the west; a few other languages are also used in radio programs and on television news. Among more than sixty languages spoken in Burkina Faso, thirty-eight belong to the Gur or Voltaic language family, including Mooré, Bwamu, Dagara, and Lobiri. The Mande language family includes twelve languages, such as Bisa, Sane, Dyula, and Bobo. Other language families include only one or two languages; the most important of these is

Fulfulde spoken by the cattle rearing Fulbe people. Many Burkinabè grow up speaking several national languages as well as French.

**Symbolism.** The national flag is divided in two equal horizontal fields, with red on top and green below; a yellow five-pointed star sits in the center. The national motto has been changed to reflect the political changes since the country gained its independence from France in 1960. The first motto, ''Unity-Work-Justice,'' was changed 1984 during the socialist Sankara revolution to the Fidel Castro-inspired ''fatherland or death we shall overcome;'' the motto was changed again in 1991 during the ''rectification'' of Blaise Compaoré, to ''Unity-Progress-Justice.''

The years of Sankara's revolution in the 1980s had a profound impact on the national identity. The country's symbols, such as the country's name and national anthem, were given renewed importance and reflect a pride in being Burkinabè. The national hymn highlights the ongoing anti-colonial struggle and the ideology of national pride that are part of the national character of the "free and upright men." National identity was also forged during two frontier wars (1974–1975 and 1985–1986) with Mali. Another important rallying point for national feelings is soccer: the national team ("Etalons" or Stallions) uses the symbol of the military strength of the Mossi kingdoms.

## HISTORY AND ETHNIC RELATIONS

**Emergence of the Nation.** Burkina Faso's ancient and precolonial history is only known in fragments, due to the lack of early and consistent written sources and the limited archaeological information available. Recent excavations have shown that rich and stratified societies lived in permanent villages in the northeast around the year 1000 C.E. In the south, the origins of the impressive but still undated "Lobi" ruins remain a mystery. The Mossi appear to have founded their kingdoms—the most important being Wagadugu, Yatenga and Tenkodogo—around the fifteenth century C.E. Written sources mention the Mossi in connection with raids on the Sahelian towns of Timbuktu and Walata, and throughout the Middle Ages as anti-Islamic enemies of the Mali and Songhay kings. Another early important precolonial kingdom was Gurma in the east. In the nineteenth century, several smaller states with an Islamic ideology formed, such as the Fulbe states of Liptako, Jelgooji, Barani, and the Marka states of Wahabu and Boussé. States like Kong and Kenedugu expanded into southern Burkina Faso. Within or between the spheres of influence of these states, politically non-centralized societies could maintain their autonomy and sometimes even expand.

French colonial armies conquered and occupied the territory beginning in 1895, thus thwarting the northern advances of the concurring colonial powers Britain and Germany. After the First World War, which brought massive oppression, popular uprisings, and their bloody suppressions, the French carved out the Upper Volta colony as an administrative unit from French West Africa. In order to assure a supply of labor to the French coastal colonies, Upper Volta was dissolved in 1932 and its territory divided among the Ivory Coast, French Sudan (now Mali), and Niger.

The traditional Mossi aristocracy and the emerging intellectual elite protested against the dissolution of Upper Volta, and their continued agita-

tion was rewarded in 1947 by the reconstitution of the colony. After the reconstitution, some directly-voted deputies represented Upper Volta in the French parliament in Paris. These deputies, under their influential leader Ouezzin Coulibally, developed a true national conscience for the first time.

During the 1958 referendum, a majority of the population preferred to remain a largely autonomous colony within the French-African Community instead of becoming independent. Nevertheless, one year later Maurice Yaméogo of the Rassemblement Démocratique Africain (RDA) declared the Republic of Upper Volta and became its first president. On 5 August 1960, Upper Volta proclaimed its national independence from France.

Yaméogo adopted a pro-Western foreign policy while moving towards a single party political system and assuming almost dictatorial rights. In this, he followed the example of Félix Houphouët-Boigny, president of the Ivory Coast and leading RDA figure, who was very influential in Burkina Faso's politics following independence. In 1966, the army overthrew Yaméogo; the coup was encouraged by the trade unions, which were angered by Yaméogo's austerity measures. Sangoulé Lamizana, chief of army staff, served as the new president. The country alternated between periods of military and civil rule, and in 1977 and 1979 new constitutions were adopted, marking the short lived second and third republics. Colonel Saye Zerbo came to power in a 1980 coup, but was deposed in 1982 by a coalition of conservative and socialist officers; they installed Surgeon-Major Jean-Baptiste Ouedraogo as president. Thomas Sankara became his minister and later prime minister.

Sankara was young, ambitious, and charismatic, a popular hero of the 1975 frontier war with Mali. He was a strident anti-colonialist and Marxist. Tensions within the government grew until Sankara finally ousted the conservative faction and took over power on 4 August 1993, backed by a number of left-wing parties and trade unions. The following four years profoundly changed the country's political and social landscape as Sankara introduced many reforms. His foreign policy embraced socialist countries like Libya and Cuba, and he promoted an anti-imperialist ideology of autarchy and national pride; many foreign development organizations were forced to leave the county. Dropping the old colonial name, Upper Volta, and choosing the new name, Burkina Faso, was derived from the indigenous languages, but was perhaps the most symbolically important of his measures. The political leadership along with Comity for the Defense of the Revolution (CDR), a mass organization with a presence in almost every village, encouraged mass mobilization and self-help. In Ouagadougou and other towns, vast housing programs were instituted; in the countryside, numerous schools and community clinics were built. Sankara also curtailed the elite's privileges: civil servants were dismissed or were forced to give parts of their salary for development projects; all traditional authorities were abolished, especially the powerful Mossi aristocracy. Drastic measures virtually eradicated corruption.

The regime gradually moved towards a totalitarian system. Sankara, who became increasingly isolated, was killed on 15 October 1987 by the troops of his old friend and colleague, Blaise Compaoré. Sankara's violent death made him a martyr for his ideas; he remains an idol among the youth in Burkina Faso and other parts of Africa.

In the years following the bloody 1987 coup, Blaise Compaoré embarked on a policy called rectification, meant to change most of the revolutionary policies of his predecessor. In 1990 Compaoré's party, ODP-MT (Organization for Popular Democracy/Work Movement, later the Congress for Democracy and Progress or CDP), renounced Marxism-Leninism. In June 1991, a new constitution marked the return to multiparty democracy and the beginning of the fourth Republic. In the December 1991 elections however, Compaoré was voted president under unusual conditions: the opposition had boycotted the elections, Compaoré was the sole candidate, and only one quarter of the voters turned out. In the following years, the opposition was divided into old conservative parties and a multitude of revolutionary Sankarist groups disillusioned with Compaoré's rectification. The opposition, which denounced the government's lack of equity and transparency, again boycotted the 1997 presidential elections and presented no convincing candidate. Compaoré was reelected with 87.5 percent of the vote, and a voter turnout of 56 percent.

The fourth Republic is marked by a reorientation to the West. The International Monetary Fund (IMF) imposed a structural adjustment program that is meticulously followed; current political stability makes Burkina Faso, one of the world's poorest countries, a prime destination for Western donors. In the late 1990s, the amount of development funds flowing into the country exceeded the central government expenditures.

**Ethnic Relations.** The population of Burkina Faso has always been highly mobile. The landscape provides few natural barriers and the traditional economic activities of shifting cultivation, semi-nomadic pastoralism, and trade require some degree of migration. Today's ethnic groups are the result of this high level mobility. Cultural exchange—even assimilation—and linguistic flexibility were frequently more important than cultural difference. But clear ethnic identities did sometimes develop in precolonial times, and the colonial transformation of the political landscape sometimes favored the hardening of ethnic borders. Generally, though, community networks transcended ethnic boundaries; this is especially true for long distance traders like the Dyula or the Yarse, and for the semi-nomadic Fulbe. Limited economic resources in the overpopulated central plateau also resulted in the migration of the Mossi people to all parts of the country during the twentieth century.

The nation's boundaries were inherited from the colonial powers. These had demarcated them in a sometimes arbitrary way, separating people from the same ethnic group while enclosing people without any cultural or historical affinities. In spite of this, a national identity has formed and there are currently no serious separatist movements and no major ethnic conflicts. One reason may be the importance of a powerful cultural device, the joking relationship, which helps to ease potential tensions. When joking partners—they could be strangers or friends—meet, they insult each other in a sometimes rude but always humorous way; it is absolutely forbidden to take any offence. Joking relationships are highly developed among many ethnic groups, especially between the Mossi and Samo, the Bisa and Gurunsi, the Fulbe and Bwaba/Bobo, and the Guin/Karaboro and Lobi/Dagara.

## URBANISM, ARCHITECTURE, AND THE USE OF SPACE

A predominantly rural country, about 90 percent of the population lives in more than eight thousand villages. The highest population density (over fifty persons per square km) is in the center, in the so-called Mossi plateau. This contrasts with the large, virtually uninhabited spaces in the southwest, the extreme east, and the north—where the majority of the national parks are located and land use is highly restricted. The late twentieth century saw a rapid increase in urbanization, illustrated through the exponential growth of the capital Ouagadougou. Its population grew from approximately 100,000 in 1970 to 752,236 in 1996. One of every two people living in cities lives in Ouagadougou; the city's growth rate is estimated at 6.4 percent annually.

*A Bobo wears a fish mask and a cape made of vegetable fiber for an agricultural festival. The Bobo are the largest ethnic group in western Burkina Faso.*

The capital's growth is partly at the expense of the country's second town, Bobo-Dioulasso. With about the same number of inhabitants on the eve of independence, Bobo-Dioulasso is today less than half as populated as Ouagadougou (312,330 inhabitants in 1996). No other city approaches these two in population.

Traditional architecture varies by region and ethnic group. It ranges from the temporary straw hut of the Fulbe and the tent of the Tuareg to the round hut made of adobe bricks and covered by a straw roof (used by the Mossi, Bisa, and Gurmanché). In the south, the Bobo, Dagara, Gurunsi, and Lobi build huge, castle-like houses with solid wood and mud walls and flat roofs. Over a hundred persons can live in these structures, which are sometimes colorfully decorated. Villages in the south may consist of a dozen widely-dispersed huge houses. Markets in the center of villages and towns are not only spaces for commercial activities but communication centers were news is exchanged, marriages are arranged, and company is enjoyed.

Imported building material, such as the zinc sheets for roofing, is becoming increasingly important in the countryside. In cities, large boulevards, representative roundabouts, football stadiums, and multi-storied administrative buildings like the headquarters of the Economic Community of West African States in Ouagadougou symbolize modernity. An entire new quarter, called Ouaga 2000 and containing villas, embassies, and a congress center, has been built on the southern fringes of the capital. There is a drastic disparity between cities and the countryside in matters of revenue, health, education, and general infrastructure.

## FOOD AND ECONOMY

**Food in Daily Life.** The main staple food is tô, a kind of paste prepared with millet or corn flour. It is eaten lukewarm and accompanied by a sauce. The most popular sauces are made with baobab and/or sorrel leaves and contain condiments, which vary from region to region. Shea butter or groundnut paste is frequently added. In the southernmost regions yams are grown and eaten, while in the north, especially among the Fulbe, milk is an important part of diet. Local delicacies also include a kind of caterpillar which is highly cherished among the Bobo and which is very nourishing due to its high protein content. In rural areas, meat is rarely eaten. Livestock is primarily kept not for nutrition but to pay a bride price or to offer sacrifice. The exception is the weekly market where meat is prepared and sold. Frequently this is pork baked in an oven, considered a delicacy. In urban areas rice and pasta have replaced tô. In the morning wooden kiosks offer customers a breakfast of coffee, fried egg, and fresh French-style baguette. In Ouagadougou and Bobo-Dioulasso there is an array of international restaurants with French, Italian, Chinese, and Lebanese cuisine.

In the evenings, upperclass people sit outside in garden restaurants where beef barbecue, fried fish, and chicken are served with bottled beer. There are two national brands, Sobbra and Brakina. For the majority bottled beer is too expensive, and they drink the popular locally brewed millet beer called *dolo* instead. It is always prepared by a woman, the dolotière, who runs a bar called a cabaret. Dolo is served in a calabash after having been cooked for over three days in huge jars. The preparation of dolo is an important income for rural women and the millet beer varies in strength and taste according to region. Bangui is a palm wine made in the Banfora region. Other locally-prepared drinks are liquor, soured milk (*gappal*), and juice made from the fruit of the tamarind tree, ginger, or bissap leaves. In the north and west, tea plays an important role.

***Food Customs at Ceremonial Occasions.*** Meat is rare in daily dishes, but is eaten during ceremonial and ritual occasions including wedding ceremonies, celebrating the birth of a child, and funerals. All ethnic groups celebrate local festivals during which special food is prepared, and local beer is frequently consumed.

Muslims celebrate Tabaski, the Islamic 'Id al-Kabir (or 'Id al-Adha), which includes the sacrificing and eating of a ram by each family. During the month of Ramadan they are only allowed to eat and drink after sunset.

***Basic Economy.*** One of the poorest countries in the world, the average person has a yearly per capita purchasing power parity of only $860 (1997 World Bank estimate). The country is landlocked, and has few natural resources and a fragile tropical soil, which has to support a comparatively high population density. Overgrazing and deforestation are serious problems which have lead to soil degradation, erosion, and desertification.

About 85 percent of the population is engaged in agriculture, almost entirely at the subsistence level. Less than 10 percent of the agricultural production is cash crops. There is little irrigation and people practice mainly rainfall hoe culture, which is highly vulnerable to variations in precipitation. In all regions, the rainfall pattern tends to vary dramatically from year to year in timing, quantity, and regional distribution. There are good and bad years and this may change from one village to the next. Recurring droughts are the most dangerous natural hazards, sometimes leading to famine. The typical short, violent storms contribute to problems of soil erosion and crop damage.

The most important crop is millet (sorghum and penisetum). In certain regions corn, rice, groundnuts, vegetables, and yams are cultivated. The savannah environment is ideal for extensive livestock grazing, except for those southern areas infested by tsetse fly. The country supports an estimated four million cattle and almost fourteen million sheep and goats. Most agricultural communities do have some livestock, but the Fulbe and Tuareg of the northern regions are considered real pastoralists. Although most communities have permanently settled, they cherish the semi-nomadic lifestyle and many Fulbe still follow their herds of cattle. Meat is inexpensive and animals are exported to the coastal countries.

The main export remains labor. Since early colonial days, migrant laborers from Burkina Faso went to work in the gold mines and plantations of Ghana and the Ivory Coast. Today more than a million Burkinabè live permanently in the Ivory Coast and many more are seasonal migrants. A considerable number of Burkinabè live in France.

***Land Tenure and Property.*** According to law, the state owns all land. Large areas have been declared national parks or used for state-assisted development schemes. Wild hunting, fishing, and wood cutting are not allowed. Illegal access to these resources often brings villagers into conflict with the agents of the national water and forest administration.

In towns and cities, urban space is divided into plots for which individual property titles can be acquired. In recent years, the allotment of plots is speeding up in towns and on the outskirts of the bigger cities. In rural communities, access to land is dictated by length of settlement: the lineage or clan whose ancestor is said to have founded the settlement has special rights to land, and usually provides the earth-priest. This essentially religious office holder is also necessary to legalize land rights, regulate land-use claims, and determine where houses may be built. In former kingdoms or chiefdoms, land disputes were frequently settled before the traditional ruler or Muslim authorities. The co-existence of cattle herders and agriculturalist in many areas carries a high potential for conflict. The national body for land use planning attempts to mediate these conflicts at the local level.

Wealthy individuals, investors from the cities, and village associations sometimes work big fields in the bush to grow cash crops, mainly cotton. Other big agricultural enterprises are state owned, like the large irrigated sugar cane plantations near Banfora.

*Traditional household equipment stands on sale next to modern Western items in a market in Bobo-Diolasso. The trade deficit in Burkina Faso is $300 million.*

**Commercial Activities.** Most of the country's commercial activities fall within the informal economy. There are many small traders and craftsmen, with the most successful established in permanent shops in the urban central markets. A growing artisan community produces souvenirs such as woodcarvings, leather- and basketworks, and speciality fabrics for the expanding tourism market.

**Major Industries.** Generally, unprofitable government-controlled corporations still dominate industry. but in recent years more emphasis has been given to the private sector. In compliance with IMF guidelines, a number of state companies have been privatized since 1991. This rarely yielded the expected results, yet there are signs for economic progress. Following the African franc currency devaluation in January 1994, the government updated its development program in conjunction with international agencies, and exports and economic growth have increased. Agro-industry accounts for over 55 percent of the overall industrial production and is dominated by the powerful cotton processor Société de Fibres Textiles (SOFITEX). Bobo-Dioulasso was once the country's industrial center due to its fertile agricultural land and, since 1933, to the railway connection with the Ivory Coast. After indepen-

dence, industries and businesses are have progressively shifted towards the capital Ouagadougou.

Gold is the third most important export item after cotton and animal products and is a fast-growing industry. The nonindustrial mining sector employs thousands of mobile freelance miners who extract gold with primitive technology and are largely uncontrolled by the state. In the late 1990s, several dozen international mining companies began operations in the country, prospecting and exploiting the known gold deposits.

**Trade.** Almost all external trade is with countries to the south, especially with the harbors in the Ivory Coast and Togo. The few tarred roads are the connection to the coastal countries, along with a railway line to Abidjan. According to 1997 estimates, the country had a strong trade deficit: imports totaled $700 million, while exports were worth only $400 million. Main imports are machinery and food products, corn, barley, and rice, as well as fuel for transportation and to generate electricity. Cotton is of increasing importance, accounting for 73.4 percent of national exports. Meat, livestock, and hides are also important; gold and agricultural products such as green beans, mangos, sesame, groundnuts and shea butter make up the remaining exports.

***Division of Labor.*** The state is the country's largest employer. Civil service jobs are preferred to work in the private sector, as job security is much higher and while wages are low, they are paid regularly. Competence is important in civil service recruitment, but kinship and regional affinity play important roles. Since the implementation of a structural adjustment program, employment in the civil service has been drastically reduced, except in education, health, and tax administration. Frequently one person's income must feed many people. While the official pension age for employees is between the ages of fifty-three and fifty-five, people in subsistence agriculture work as long as their health permits. They also start at a young age, as work is considered part of children's education.

## SOCIAL STRATIFICATION

***Classes and Castes.*** Many of the country's traditional societies have their own hierarchies. The Mossi society differentiates between aristocrats (Nakomse), commoners (Talse), and slaves or captives (Yemse). The Nakomse are people of power whose ancestors were horse-riding warriors and founders of the Mossi kingdoms. They were not necessarily rich in a materialistic sense, but they controlled people. They had many followers and they took slaves, which were frequently integrated into their families. The offspring of these slaves can hardly be differentiated from other people, yet their slave origin may still be remembered. In other societies too, a family's slave origin is known; most obvious is the demarcation between nobles and slaves in the extreme north among the Tuareg.

Apart from class stratification, individuals are also categorized by occupation. In the west, which is influenced by Mande tradition, blacksmiths and praise singers (Griots) form caste-like groups (Nymakallaw) and are sometimes feared for their occult powers. There are also groups of traders, the Dyula in the west and the Yarse among the Mossi, who are generally respected.

Social and material inequality increased dramatically during the 1990s. Equality was one of the main principles during Sankara's time; flashy cars were confiscated and even high state officials had to work on farms and participate in the daybreak mass sports. Since the 1994 devaluation of the African franc, the situation has changed. Unemployment and poverty has increased in spite of a growing economy. A few individuals have acquired great wealth, seen by many as proof of growing corruption and a flawed privatization policy.

***Symbols of Social Stratification.*** Obvious social inequality is still shocking in an environment of widespread poverty, and wealth is not generally advertised. While more huge villas with satellite dishes are being built and expensive cars make their appearance on Ouagadougou's streets, there is a certain carefulness in the display of wealth. Thus the uniform dress code of the Sankara time, the Faso Danfani, is widespread even among the wealthy. An exception is the rich Lebanese community, which controls many profitable businesses.

## POLITICAL LIFE

***Government.*** The political system of the fourth Republic is based on a constitution which is inspired by the French presidential democracy. The parliament has two chambers. The Assemblée Nationale has 111 members elected by popular vote every five years. Each of the forty-five provinces has a fixed number of representatives. The Chambre des Représentants was instituted in 1999 and is purely consultative. The 120 appointed members are representatives of religious groups, traditional rulers, trade unions, women's organizations and other social groups. The cabinet with thirty-five ministers is headed by the prime minister who is named by the president. The president, the real power center in the political structure, is elected by popular vote for a seven-year term. There is no limit in the number of terms a president may serve. Constitutional changes may soon shorten the term of office to five years.

***Leadership and Political Officials.*** The political class is a limited group, where most personalities know each other well. This is both because Burkina Faso is a small country and also because much of the elite studied abroad in the same universities, in either Paris, where the country maintains a student hostel in the rue Fessart, in Dakar, or in Moscow. Political leaders who were student activists have replaced the first generation of politicians active before independence. Many of today's political class came up during the Sankara revolution and were part of the CDR, an institution created by Sankara to enforce revolutionary ideals. Political agendas are often secondary, and political parties are seen as pressure groups used to bring a certain set of people to power. Nevertheless, politicians are seen as regular people who may be approached like anybody else, not as a detached elite.

*People stand by huts in a Bobo village in Burkina Faso. The majority of citizens, about 90 percent, live in rural areas, among Burkina Faso's 8000 villages.*

The biggest political party is the Congrès pour la Démocratie et le Progrès (CDP). The main opposition parties are the Parti pour la Démocratie et le Progrès (PDP), mainly rooted in the west, and the Alliance pour la Démocratie et le Fédéralisme—Rassemblement Démocratique Africain (ADF-RDA), with a strong base in Yatenga province and in the town of Koudougou. Efforts have been made to unite the extra-parliamentarian opposition in the Group of Fourteenth, a coalition with changing constituent parties and political pressure groups founded on 14 February 1998.

***Social Problems and Control.*** Crime rates are rising, but traditionally have been very low. Thieves may be lynched in some rare cases, a practice disappearing due to campaigns of national human rights organizations. Criminals are usually delivered to the police or the gendarmerie, a military police with a reputation of an uncorrupted elite force. Armed robbery is still a very rare phenomenon.

Social unrest comes from students and politicized youth—political demonstrations sometimes turn into violent scenes. These demonstrations increased after the murder of the critical and very popular journalist Norbert Zongo in December 1998. This crime, attributed to the immediate entourage of president Compaoré, catalyzed widespread discontent with the political regime and created a volatile political situation with frequent strikes and social unrest.

***Military Activity.*** After the frontier wars with Mali in the mid-1970s and 1980s, the country had no military conflicts with its neighbors. However, some African countries criticize the nation for its contacts with rebel groups: According to a UN report, some political leaders are involved in illegal arms and diamond trafficking with rebel groups in Angola and Sierra Leone.

## SOCIAL WELFARE AND CHANGE PROGRAMS

State employees and employees in parastatals and larger private companies benefit from social security, but for the vast majority there is no social welfare.

## NONGOVERNMENTAL ORGANIZATIONS AND OTHER ASSOCIATIONS

The numerous development projects are an important economic and social factor. They can be multilateral like those financed by World Bank, United

Nations, or the European Union, or they can be initiated by national development agencies. The most important donor countries are France, Germany, Netherlands, Denmark, the United States, and Japan. Furthermore, hundreds of nongovernmental organizations (NGOs) such as charity organizations, churches, town partnerships, and initiatives by concerned groups and individuals are working on various development related issues in the fields of health, education, and poverty relief. Public education campaigns target issues like female excision and the sustained development of natural resources. In the villages, solidarity groups of men, women, and youth form to propose concrete development projects to donors.

## GENDER ROLES AND STATUSES

**Division of Labor by Gender.** In most rural areas both women and men work in agriculture. Men are expected to furnish the millet, while women are in charge of all other things. In an urban context, this is translated into the man's responsibility to give "Naā Songo," "the money for sauce." Male and female tasks in rural areas are clearly differentiated. Hunting and butchering is always a male activity while the collection of firewood and water is seen, among other duties, as female tasks. In the urban sector, women are employed in almost all positions, though to a lesser degree than men. Girls in the modern cities are encouraged to pursue higher education and many scholarships are reserved for them.

**The Relative Status of Women and Men.** A woman's role is considered to be that of a wife and mother; a woman in her thirties who is unmarried or childless carries a severe social stigma. A married woman who is childless— barrenness is usually attributed to the women—bears enormous pressure from her husband's family and is likely to be sent away without any material resources. The family head is always a man, who represents the family to the outside world. Nevertheless, women have a good deal of say in domestic and economic matters and they may be successful in commerce or other jobs. Besides her job, a career woman is expected to raise children and to fulfill domestic tasks. She is aided in this by relatives from the village who regularly perform household tasks for urban families.

## MARRIAGE, FAMILY, AND KINSHIP

**Marriage.** Today arranged marriages, which were the rule in former times, are rare, especially in ur-

ban contexts. In a customary marriage, the husband pays bride price to the bride's family. The amount varies according to ethnic group from symbolic to substantial contributions that take many years to acquire. The differences in bride price tend to hinder interethnic marriages, which are nevertheless practiced among a number of neighboring groups. Women join their husbands after marriage, and this forges an alliance between two families. Divorce is possible; any children stay with the husband's family, and the family receives the bride price should the woman remarry. If the husband dies, the widow is expected to marry a brother of her late husband. The World Bank estimates that about one-third of households are polygynous. Polygyny is practiced in traditional and Muslim contexts, but is opposed by the Christian churches.

Urban and educated people may choose to have a civil marriage. Progressive family law gives many rights to women; some men even refrain from marrying at the registrar for fear of having too many duties in case of divorce.

**Domestic Unit.** Extended family is very important and relatives from the husband's or wife's side may live together with the nuclear family. Three, four, or more generations living under one roof is common. Average household size is more than eight people in rural areas and more than six people in urban areas (World Bank). Especially in rural areas, a number of related households may live together in a compound. Old age and experience are highly regarded; generally the head and authority of the compound is a family elder.

**Inheritance.** A deceased man's widow and brothers decide the inheritance. If there are sons of a mature age, the property goes to them and they take care of their mother. According to modern family law, even illegitimate children have the right to inherit from their father. Customary law shows numerous variations according to ethnic group, but usually there are quite precise rules on inheritance. Belongings may be handed down both in the mother's as well in the father's line. Children are usually considered to belong to the father's family; illegitimate children, though, are considered to belong to their maternal uncles.

**Kin Groups.** The clan or lineage plays a major role in both traditional and urban settings. These are solidarity groups with a common name, customs, and taboos, and are founded on the idea of common descent. The most widespread type is the patri-clan, were belonging is defined through the male line. A

*A Burkinabè woman sweeping her compound kitchen. Men and women have equal responsibilties in the agricultural sector of rural areas.*

clan or lineage can be made up of several thousand persons which may be dispersed, with each settlement made up of members of different clans, or as a locally defined unit on its clan territory. Marriage partners come from outside the clan. While in precolonial times clans were important for assistance in economic matters and warfare, they now serve as mutual assistance networks for city dwellers and as pressure groups for political office.

## SOCIALIZATION

*Infant Care.* Infants and children up to two or three years have almost constant physical contactwith the mother, an aunt, or an elder sister. They are regularly tied with a wrapper to a woman or girl's back and carried around while the woman does domestic work or is farming. Elder siblings are strongly involved in rearing the younger ones; especially the first-borns have much responsibility.

*Child Rearing and Education.* Infant care and child rearing is the responsibility not only of the biological parents, but of the whole compound and, in rural areas, the entire village. The aim of all education is not to encourage an individual personality but to integrate children into the social environment.

Primary school education starts at age seven. About one third of all children go to primary school; in urban areas the rate is about three times as high as in the countryside. In many villages, children walk for hours to reach the school. Classes are quite large, with an average of about fifty pupils. School attendance varies according to region and gender: Most of the southern and western provinces have attendance rates of fifty percent and more, while in some northern and eastern provinces less than twenty percent attend school. Nationally, two girls for every three boys attend primary school, and only half as many girls as boys go to secondary school.

*Higher Education.* The University of Ouagadougou, founded only in 1974, dominates higher education with about eight thousand enrolled students. In 1997, the Polytechnic University of Bobo-Dioulasso opened its doors. The École Nationale d'Administration et de la Magistrature (ENAM) in Ouagadougou trains higher state officials, and the École Normale Supérieure (ENS) is in Koudougou. All together about ten thousand students are enrolled in post-secondary schools, less than one percent of the population. Only one-third are women. University graduates are a tiny and respected elite, carrying the hopes of their parents and sometimes of an entire ethnic group. Even for university graduates, however, it is increasingly difficult to find jobs.

## ETIQUETTE

Hospitality and politeness is important to the Burkinabè. Salutations are an elaborate procedure always involving shaking hands. Conversations are rarely direct, and general issues are discussed first to set everybody at ease. Women are expected to refrain from wearing very short skirts and low-cut dresses, and from smoking in public. Officials and uniformed people are always approached with respect. They and official buildings should not be photographed. When the national flag is lowered, everyone is expected to stand still. As a rule, elders, even if only a few years older, are treated with high respect.

## RELIGION

**Religious Beliefs.** A tolerant country in matters of religion, Burkina Faso has no major conflicts between the religions. Approximately 45 percent continue to hold traditional beliefs. About 43 percent practice Islam, which has been strong for centuries among the Marka, Dyula, and Fulbe, and since the colonial era among the Mossi. Christianity, spread by missionaries in colonial times, is mostly rooted in the south, the west, and among the urban elite; 6 percent are Roman Catholics and 6 percent Protestant.

**Religious Practitioners.** Muslims have the Iamam who leads the Friday prayer, and Christians have the standard clergy. In traditional religion, there are many religious offices and functions, but hardly any full-time religious specialists. Each ethnic group has its own specialists. The most important ones may be labelled earth priests, fortunetellers, rainmakers, or healers. Religious practitioners are chosen through family tradition or because they are called by a spirit. Traditional religion is tolerant, non-proselytizing, and flexible. Certain cults and religious specialists gain popularity beyond the local level because people feel that they can offer effective help for certain problems. Witchcraft and magic are powerful antisocial forces, but they are important in every-day life and ensure adherence to cultural norms.

**Rituals and Holy Places.** The sacrifice of chicken, guinea fowl, or even bigger livestock is the core ritual of traditional religious practice. The animals

*Man sitting at entrance to painted hut. There are stark differences in the infrastructure of the countryside versus the city.*

are offered to a wide range of spiritual forces symbolized by shrines or by conspicuous natural features such as hills, rocks, caves, trees, crossroads, termite hills, rivers, and ponds. Traditional compounds may contain dozens of shrines and power objects. A number of ethnic groups practice initiation rituals for youth. Others have powerful secret societies, which perform with masks on certain occasions.

The monotheistic religions have their own holy places. Among Catholics there is a strong cult of Saint Mary, and a number of sanctuaries have been erected for veneration. The Muslims honor some of the old mosques from the early times of Islamization, like the ones in Bobo-Dioulasso and Ouahabou.

**Death and the Afterlife.** Hardly any death is considered natural, especially in case of accident or the death of a younger person. Fortunetellers or necromancers may be consulted to find out whether the victim either transgressed certain socio-cultural norms or was a victim of witchcraft. Among Muslims, burial takes place within 24 hours, and is devoid of much ceremony. Traditional believers in most ethnic groups, however, celebrate long and elaborate funeral rituals to elevate the deceased to the sphere of the ancestors. The ancestors are integral part of the living community and are thought to affect lives; in many places, they are worshipped in special shrines. Christian churches adapt in different ways to these beliefs.

## MEDICINE AND HEALTH CARE

Knowledge of traditional healing methods is quickly declining. Some specialists still know much about herbs, roots, and barks and the traditional bonesetters are still consulted in rural areas. Psychological problems are treated through possession rituals. Western medicine, however, has made profound impact. Vaccination campaigns reach even remote settlements and at village markets medicinal pills and tablets can be purchased. They are comparatively cheap but of doubtful quality. Bigger villages have a dispensary run by a nurse. Although treatment is free, the prescribed drugs are quite expensive. Medical treatment by a doctor or in hospitals is much too expensive for the average person.

## SECULAR CELEBRATIONS

National holidays honor independence and the Sankara revolution: On 11 December 1959, the Republic was proclaimed and on 5 August 1960, Upper Volta became independent. The revolution is honored on 4 August, the date when Thomas Sankara came to power in 1983. His death in 1987 is remembered on 15 October.

In former kingdoms, royalty is celebrated in yearly festivals. Every Friday morning the Mogho Naaba, king of Ouagadougou, makes a public appearance with his court in front of the palace. A more modern introduction are carnival-like mask processions in Ouagadougou, such as Carnival Dodo or Carnival Salou. The National Week of Culture (SNC) is celebrated annually in Bobo-Dioulasso. All artistic expressions are united there: theater, music, dance, sculpture, literature, and cinema from all corners of the country, along with exhibitions, cooking contests, horse races, and traditional wrestling.

## THE ARTS AND HUMANITIES

**Support for the Arts.** The state promotes artistic expression through help in organization, logistics, and infrastructure more than by direct funding. A number of different festivals are organized, including the successful biennial Pan African Film Festival (FESPACO), held in Ouagadougou since 1965. The festival attracts more than 5,000 participants and has aided the development of francophone African cinema.

**Literature.** In a society where the majority is illiterate, oral tradition is central to pass history and culture from generation to generation. A number of ethnic groups have Griots, specialized narrators; in others youth is taught by elders during initiation rituals. There is also a written literature including works by well-known writers like Augustin Sondé Coulibally, Jean Baptiste Somé, and Monique Ilboudo which are read in schools and have been honored through national awards. A major obstacle for the development of a national literature is the scarcity of publishers.

**Graphic Arts.** Sculpture in wood, leather- and basketworks, hand-dyed fabrics, lost wax casting, and pottery are highly-developed traditional crafts. Many objects such as masks, figurines, and music instruments are produced for use in sacred contexts and are seen as power objects. A growing artisan group produces souvenirs and art pieces for the expanding tourism market. They may recall traditional forms or be of modern artistic expression. The showroom for this production is the biennial International Arts and Crafts Fair (SIAO) in Ouagadougou, attended by many artists of neighboring countries. Arts and craft production is also shown in Ouagadougou's National Center for Arts and Crafts (CNAA), where artists are trained and work together.

**Performance Arts.** A number of theater and music festivals are held; among the most important are the National Culture Week (SNC) in Bobo-Dioulasso and the Atypical Nights of Koudougou, a theater festival. Individuals also celebrate occasions like births or weddings with spontaneous music and dance. Dancing and music groups exist for all occasions, and Bobo-Dioulasso's Djembe drumming tradition is internationally famous.

## THE STATE OF THE PHYSICAL AND SOCIAL SCIENCES

Scientific research is aimed primarily at promoting economic and social development. The National Scientific Research Center (CNRST) has a number of institutes in many disciplines, sometimes working in cooperation with foreign research bodies. While the country adopts technological innovations from abroad, efforts are also made to understand indigenous knowledge systems and to enhance their status.

## BIBLIOGRAPHY

Atlas Jeune Afrique. *Burkina Faso*, 1998.

Balima, Salfo-Albert. *Légendes et histoires des peuples du Burkina Faso*, 1996.

Breuser, Mark. *On the Move: Mobility, Land Use and Livelihood Practices on the Central Plateau in Burkina Faso*, 1999.

Englebert, Pierre. *Burkina Faso: Unsteady Statehood in West Africa*, 1996.

Guissou, Basile. *Burkina Faso un espoir en Afrique*, 1995.

Ilboudo, Jean. *Burkina 2000: Une eglise en marche vers son centenaire*, 1996.

Kambou-Ferrand, Jeanne-Marie. *Peuples voltaïques et conquête coloniale 1885–1914, Burkina Faso*, 1993.

Klotchkoff, Jean-Claude. *Le Burkina Faso aujourd'hui*, 1998.

Kedrebéogo, Gérard. "Linguistic diversity and language policy: The challenges of multilingualism in Burkina Faso." *Hémisphères* 12: 5–27, 1997.

Lear, Aaron. *Burkina Faso*, 1986.

Madiéga, Géorges. "Les parties politiques et la question des fédérations en haute Volta (Burkina Faso)." In Ageron, Ch. and M. Michel, eds., *L'Afrique noire française, l'heure des indépendances*, 1992.

Massa, Gabriel and Georges Madiéga. *La Haute Volta Coloniale*, 1995.

Savonnet-Guyot, Claudette. *Etat et sociétés au Burkina*, 1986.

Skinner, Elliott P. *The Mossi of Burkina Faso: Chiefs, Politicians and Soldiers*, 1989.

Zagré, Pascal. *Les politiques économiques du Burkina Faso: Une tradition d'ajustement structurel*, 1994.

—RICHARD KUBA
AND PIERRE CLAVER HIEN

# BURMA

## CULTURE NAME

Burmese

## ORIENTATION

**Identification.** The name of the country of Burma (or Myanmar, as it is now officially known) is associated with the dominant ethnic group, the Burmese. Because of the current regime's lack of legitimacy and poor human rights record, it is common practice outside the country not to use the name Myanmar. The country fell under British colonial rule during the nineteenth century. When it became independent as the Union of Burma in 1948, the country almost immediately entered a state of civil war as ethnic minorities fought against the Burmese-dominated central government. Insurgencies by some ethnic groups continue. In 1962, the military leader Ne Win seized power. His regime sought to isolate the nation and institute nationalist policies under the label "the Burmese Road to Socialism." In 1972, the name of the country was changed to the Socialist Republic of the Union of Burma. After civil unrest in 1988, the military government changed the name to the Union of Myanmar.

Efforts to create a broadly shared sense of national identity have been only partly successful because of the regime's lack of legitimacy and tendency to rely on coercion and threats to secure the allegiance of non-Burmese groups. The low level of education and poor communications infrastructure also limit the spread of a national culture.

**Location and Geography.** The state has an area of 261,789 square miles (678,034 square kilometers). It is bordered by Bangladesh to the west, India and China to the north, and Laos and Thailand to the east. The southern portion faces the Bay of Bengal and the Andaman Sea. The middle portion centers on the Irrawaddy River, with a large delta area at its mouth and the area above the delta featuring floodplains. Most of the population and agricultural lands are found along the Irrawaddy, which is navigable for about one-thousand miles. The western, northern, and eastern regions have mountains and high valleys and plateaus. The western region has the Arakan, Chin, and Naga hills. The most important geographic feature to the east is the Shan Plateau. The Burmese live primarily in the central lowlands, while the other ethnic groups live mainly in the highlands. Under British rule, the political capital was moved from Mandalay in the center to Rangoon on the eastern edge of the Irrawaddy delta in 1885. That city was built in 1755 and named Dagon. Rangoon remained the capital after independence (its name was changed later to Yangon) and continues to be politically and economically the most important city. Both Rangoon and Mandalay lie within the area occupied primarily by Burmese peoples, although both cities have a significant Indian population as a legacy of British rule.

**Demography.** The official population figure in 1995 was 44.74 million, but it may range from 41.7 million to 47 million. Linguists have identified 110 distinct ethnolinguistic groups, and the government recognizes 135 ethnic groups (referred to as races). The Burmese account for about 68 percent of the population. Other major ethnic groups include the Shan (about four million), Karen (about three million), Arakanese or Rakhine (about two million), Chinese (over one million), Chin (over one million), Wa (about one million), Mon (about one million), Indians and Bengalis (about one million), Jingpho (about less than one million), and Palaung (less than one million). With the exception of the Chinese, Indian, and Belgalis, each minority group occupies a relatively distinct area.

**Linguistic Affiliation.** Burmese is a Tibeto-Burman language whose alphabet is derived from south Indian scripts. The largest ethnic group that speaks Burmese is the Myanma; there is a smaller Burmese-speaking ethnic group known as

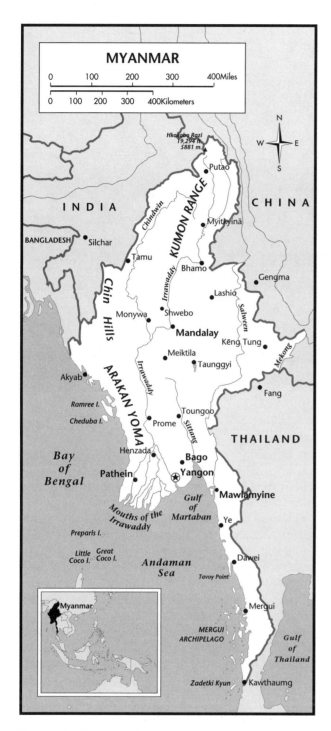

## MYANMAR

*Burma, also known as Myanmar*

ucated urban residents speak English as a second language, but English is not widely spoken among the population as a whole. The teaching of English in schools was banned from 1966 to 1980. Shan is as an important second language for many ethnic groups in Shan State, while Jingpho is spoken as a second language by many smaller ethnic groups in Kachin State.

**Symbolism.** Since 1962, the government has used an array of slogans urging discipline and support for the regime and the military. The promotion of nationalist sentiments through the media, public events, and the display of related images is especially marked on holidays. Among architectural sites with national symbolism, two of the most important are the archaeological site of the old capital of Pagan and Shwedagon Pagoda in Rangoon.

## HISTORY AND ETHNIC RELATIONS

**Emergence of the Nation.** The earliest civilizations associated with what is now Burma were the Mon (also called Taliang) in the south and the Pyu in central Burma which flourished during the first half of the first millennium. The Mon were strongly influenced by Indian culture through trade and the Buddhist religion. The Pyu went into decline in the 800s. Around that time, the ancestors of the Burmese, known as Mranma, settled to the south of Mandalay. With the former Pyu city of Pagan (known as Arimadanapura) as his capital, the Burmese ruler Anaw-rahta (ruled 1044–1077) founded the first Burmese kingdom. His conquest of Thaton resulted in the spread of Theravada Buddhism and the adoption of many aspects of Indian-inspired Mon art and architecture. The lowland area along the Irrawaddy River under the control of Pagan often is referred to as ''Burma Proper,'' since it is the heartland of the region that has been most securely under Burmese rule. In the late 1200s, Pagan declined and the Burmese lost control over much of the territory. Over the next few centuries, the Burmese slowly regained control over portions of lowland Burma from their new capital of Pegu. However, the Mon remained independent until 1539 and the Arakanese until 1784, while most of the upland territory occupied by the Shan was outside their control or only loosely under Burmese domination. The capital was moved to Ava during the reign of King Tha-lun (1629–1648).

During the reign of Ling Alaung-hpaya (1752–1760), a new dynasty was founded known as the Kon-baung, and the Burmese began a new period of military expansion. The Mon were conquered

Baramagyi (or Barua). A few regional dialects of Burmese are associated with subgroups. Closely related Southern Burmish languages include Arakanese, Intha, and Taungyo (or Tavoyan). Burmese is the national language. It is spoken as a second language by most educated members of other ethnic groups, but some of those groups have little contact with the national language. Many ed-

347

*Floating gardens on Lake Inle. Most Burmese live along the Irrawaddy River, which has one thousand miles of navigable length.*

again, Burmese migration into Mon territory was instituted, and many Mon were resettled in the western Irrawaddy delta. Burmese migrants were sent to the east to serve as a barrier against the Shan. Efforts at expansion beyond the lowland area met with little success.

In the early nineteenth century, incursions into border areas to the west brought Burmese rulers into conflict with the British in India, leading to the first Anglo–Burmese War in 1824. At the end of the war in 1826, the Burmese were forced to give up claims to territories in eastern India and a portion of southern Burma that included territories associated largely with non-Burmese ethnic groups. Continued poor relations resulted in the loss of the province of Pegu. This territory became known as Lower Burma. Although foreign relations improved under the reign of King Min-don (1853–1878), unstable conditions following his death and Prince Thibaw's overtures to the French led the British to invade Upper Burma again in 1885. In the face of local resistance that lasted until 1890, the British established colonial rule over not only the lowland territory but the Shan states as well. Over the next few decades, the British tried to bring the other highland areas under their control, but some territories remained free throughout the colonial period.

In the 1920s and 1930s, the British implemented reforms aimed at granting eventual self-rule. The proindependence forces were not unified, and there was infighting between factions. In addition to sporadic anti-British violence, nationalist sentiments took on a Burmese ethnic tone that resulted in violent outbursts against local Indians and Chinese. Burma was occupied by the Japanese during World War II. The British returned toward the end of the war, but the colony quickly moved toward independence. An independent Union of Burma was declared in 1948 under Prime Minister U Nu. It was a fragile new nation beset by political infighting and civil war involving ethnic minorities and communists backed by China.

***National Identity.*** Before colonial rule, Burma consisted essentially of the central lowland areas and a few conquered peoples, with highland peoples only nominally under Burmese control. The British brought most of the highlands peoples loosely under their control but allowed highland minorities to retain a good deal of their own identity. This situation changed after independence as the Burmese-dominated central government attempted to assert control over the highland peoples. Despite continued resistance to the central government, those in the lowland areas and the larger settlements in the highlands have come to share more of a common national culture. The spread of Burmese language usage is an important factor in this regard.

***Ethnic Relations***. The majority of the people speak Tibeto-Burman languages. Tibeto-Burman speakers in Burma can be divided into six distinct groups. The Burmish constitute the largest of these groups by population. Nungish speakers live in upland areas in Kachin State. The main Baric-speaking group is the Jingpho in Kachin State. The Kuki-Naga-speaking peoples include a large number of ethnic groups in the mountains along the border with India and Bangladesh. The Luish group includes the Kado, who live near the border with the Indian state of Manipur. The Karen groups live in the hills along the border with Thailand and the southern lowlands. The Lolo-speaking groups tend to be the most recent immigrants to Burma; they live in the highlands of Shan and Kachin states.

There are also large numbers of speakers of Austro-Tai languages. The largest Daic-speaking group is the Shan, who constitute the majority in Shan State. Smaller, related groups include the Tai Khun, Lue, Tai Nua, and Khamti. Other Austro-Tai speakers include the Austronesian-speaking Moken and small groups of Hmong and Mien in Shan State.

Under the British, ethnic minorities generally were able to retain some autonomy. Negotiations for independence after World War II brought suspicions among the political leaders of several ethnic minorities that their status would be undermined. Immediately after independence in 1948, serious divisions emerged between Burmese and non–Burmese political leaders, who favored a less unified state. Between 1948 and 1962, armed conflicts broke out between some of these minority groups and the central government. Although some groups signed peace accords with the central government in the late 1980s and early 1990s, others are still engaged in armed conflict. The Wa have signed a peace agreement but have retained a great deal of autonomy and control of much of the drug trade in northern Burma.

Military operations in ethnic minority areas and government policies of forced resettlement and forced labor have dislocated many ethnic groups, and have caused large numbers of refugees to flee to neighboring countries. At present there are around three hundred thousand refugees in Thailand, Bangladesh, and India, mostly from ethnic minorities.

Before independence, Indians were a dominant presence in urban-centered commercial activities. With the outbreak of World War II, a large number of Indians left for India before the Japanese occupation. Through the 1950s, Indians continued to leave in the face of ethnic antagonism and antibusiness policies. The Indians remaining in Burma have been treated with suspicion but have avoided overt opposition to the regime.

## URBANISM, ARCHITECTURE, AND THE USE OF SPACE

About 80 percent of the population lives in rural areas. Rangoon has a population of 4 million, and Mandalay has almost 1 million residents. The ethnic composition of Rangoon and Mandalay is overwhelmingly Burmese, although these cities are also where most of the Indian population lives.

Architecture reflects the country's Buddhist and colonial heritage. Buddhist temples are the most important architectural features throughout the country. The Buddhist temple serves as a religious school, a community center, a guest house, a place where the government and other agencies post information, a site for sports activities, a center for welfare services for those who are poor and ill, a morgue, and a center for music and dance. It also carries out economic services such as providing loans and renting lands and homes. Temples are also important in urban areas. While most temples in central Burma are Burmese in style, the temples of Shan State tend to have a distinctive look that is referred to as the Shan style. Temples tend to be surrounded by small shops that sell sacred and secular items.

The traditional house is made largely of bamboo. Flattened pieces of bamboo made into large plaited sections are used to make the walls. The floors are made of bamboo planks or wood. The frame of the house is made of wood, with hard and durable wood being used for the house posts. Roof coverings are made of a variety of materials, including thatch made from broad-leafed grass or palm fronds. Roofs may be covered with tiles, wooden shingles, or zinc sheets. The front of the house usually has a veranda that is raised a few feet off the ground. This is the public area where guests are entertained. The center of the house is the living area for the family. Behind it is a covered cooking area where rice is stored. Especially in urban areas, these houses are being replaced by more generic ones made from cement.

Some ethnic minorities have distinctive styles of houses. Many Palaung traditionally lived in multiple-family houses. Today, these structures are very rare, and most Palaung live in single-family houses.

*Small boat traffic on Lake Inle. Men are primarily responsible for the transportation of commercial goods.*

## FOOD AND ECONOMY

***Food in Daily Life.*** Rice is the staple food except among those in highland areas where rice is difficult to grow. In those areas, rice, millet, sorghum, and corn are the staples. Rice is accompanied by a raw salad of leaves, fruit, or vegetables; a soup; and curries of fish, meat, prawns, or eggs. In addition to turmeric and chili, curries are seasoned with fermented fish or shrimp paste. A variety of cultivated vegetables and wild greens are eaten as well as bamboo shoots. Meals often are accompanied by lentils, pickled relishes, and *balachaung* (made from fried dry prawns). There are a variety of rice-noodle dishes. After a meal, it is common to eat fresh fruit.

Burmese traditionally eat a morning meal and an evening meal that is taken before dark. The meals are served in a large platter or on a low table, with members of the household sitting on mats. Food is eaten with the fingers, although sometimes utensils are used. It is common to drink water and eat fruit after the main meal. Throughout the day people eat betel and smoke tobacco. Burmese not only drink tea made from dried tea leaves but also eat pickled tea as a snack. Other snacks include chappatis, fried insects, and Chinese pastries.

Tea shops are found in every city, town, and large village. These establishments are important locales for social gathering. Street stalls sell a variety of foods in the cities and towns. Relatively few restaurants serve Burmese food. The majority serve Indian or Chinese food, and English food is served in many hotels and guest houses.

***Food Customs at Ceremonial Occasions.*** Feasting and sharing food are an important feature of traditional agricultural and religious rites. Often special foods are prepared for those occasions. *Htamane,* which is served during the rice harvest festival February, is made of glutinous rice mixed with sesame seeds, peanuts, shredded ginger, and coconut. Alcoholic beverages are drunk during some secular festivities but are not drunk during most religious festivals. In urbanized areas, commercial beer and other forms of alcohol are consumed, while in more remote rural areas, locally made alcohol is more common. Alcoholic drinks are made from fermented palm juice and a distilled rice-based solution. Fermented grain-based alcoholic drinks are more commonly consumed among highland groups.

***Basic Economy.*** The economy is dominated by agriculture, which accounts for over 59 percent of the gross domestic product and employs about two-thirds of the labor force. Rice is the main product. Production declined after independence but increased during the late 1970s and early 1980s because of the introduction of high-yielding varieties, fertilizer, and irrigation. Since that time, production has barely kept pace with population growth, and Burma, once the world's leading exporter of rice, is barely able to meet subsistence needs of its own population. It continues to export some rice to earn foreign exchange. The production of narcotics from poppies and other sources is widespread in the northern highlands, and Burma is the world's leading supplier of opiates.

**Land Tenure and Property.** In areas under Burmese rule, land traditionally was held on the basis of service to the court and could be leased or sold and passed on to one's heirs; it also could be taken away by the court. In more remote areas, land ownership tended to be related to continual cultivation and occupancy. Under the British, private ownership became widespread in the central areas and a system of land taxation was introduced in which failure to pay property taxes could result in the loss of land. Before World War II, in the southern delta area absentee ownership of productive land was widespread. In the central area, agricultural land tended to be in the hands of small-scale owner-producers. Shortly after independence, the government passed a land nationalization act that was intended to turn land owned by wealthy landlords over to those who worked the land. However, that act was not implemented. A second act passed in 1954 met with only partial success.

The revolutionary government that seized power in 1962 nationalized the larger commercial and manufacturing establishments, including those of Indian traders. This created a large black market economy as people attempted to circumvent government control of commerce. The revolutionary government attempted to remove the landlord class and turned all land over to peasant producers while retaining ultimate ownership for itself. In practice, agricultural tenancy was not eliminated, and producers had the added burden of state intervention. After 1988, the government allowed a greater role for the private sector and foreign investment. While these reforms have allowed greater private ownership, considerable insecurity remains among those who own property.

**Commercial Activities.** Since 1992, the military regimes have emphasized self-sufficiency and tried to limit imports. The largest companies and financial institutions are state-owned, with the private sector limited mainly to small-scale trading. In recent years, however, more imported goods, especially from China, have appeared in local markets

*A Burmese woman at a lacquer factory.*

and there has been growth in the private sector. The main cities and many smaller towns have one or more central markets that sell a wide variety of domestic and imported goods, including clothing and cloth, tobacco, food, baskets, jewelry, toiletries, and electronic goods. There are also specialized markets, such as the iron bazaar in Rangoon's Chinatown.

**Major Industries.** Industrial production focuses on goods for local consumption, although a handful of factories produce for exportation. Local industries include textiles and footwear, wood processing, mining, the production of construction materials, pharmaceuticals, and fertilizer manufacturing. Although the country has substantial gem, oil, and natural gas reserves, extraction and processing capabilities are limited. There is a small tourist industry. There has been a dramatic growth in the number of hotels built since the introduction of economic reforms. Travel restrictions and poor infrastructure have concentrated the tourist industry in a few areas.

**Trade.** Legal exports include timber, rice, beans and pulses, fish, garments, precious stones, and rice. Legal imports include construction materials, plant equipment, and consumer goods. The difference in the value of imports and exports is covered in large part by revenue from narcotics and other illegal exports. Under British colonial rule, Burma was the world's leading exporter of rice, and rice remains the major legal export. Logging was also important in the colonial economy, but excessive harvesting and poor forestry management have resulted in a sharp drop in the availability of teak. China, Thailand, and India are their main markets for timber, but most wood is exported illegally. Burma is famous for rubies and jade, but since 1962, a lack of capital and expertise has hindered that industry. As with timber, most ruby and jade exports go through illegal channels.

Burma is the world's largest supplier of illegal opiates (opium and heroin), and the export of amphetamines has increased. Money from the illegal narcotics trade plays a crucial role in the national economy and in keeping the regime solvent. Much of the production of illegal narcotics, however, is in the hands of ethnic rebels in Shan State. Recent peace accords between the government and some rebel groups have given the regime access to income from narcotics.

Thailand and India are Burma's primary sources of legal and illegal imported goods. Small amounts are also imported from other neighboring countries such as India, Malaysia, and Singapore.

***Division of Labor.*** There is little specialization in the agricultural sector. Small-scale commercial trading is done by both men and women, with men being primarily responsible for the transportation of goods. Ethnic Indians and Chinese are an important segment in commercial trading, but many Burmese and others are involved in commercial activities. Few tasks or professions are the monopoly of a single ethnic group. There are various forms of traditional craft specialization. This includes making lacquer ware, stone working, fine wood carving, and working with metal. Modern technical professions such as medicine and engineering are related to one's level of education and specialized training. Those in the higher levels of commerce and administration generally come from the families of prominent members of the regime, and connections with the regime are important factors in amassing wealth and power.

## SOCIAL STRATIFICATION

***Classes and Castes.*** Not only is poverty widespread, there is marked inequality. Essentially, the society is divided into a tiny elite, a fairly small middle class, and a large number of very poor people. While there are traditional elites within most of the ethnic groups and new elites in some groups whose wealth comes from smuggling, the national elite is overwhelmingly Burmese. In recent years income from the narcotics trade has been an important source of wealth for members of the elite. Although some segments of the middle class have prospered from the economic reforms of the late 1980s, most have not done well and remain poor.

## POLITICAL LIFE

***Government.*** The military has ruled the country since 1962. In the face of growing opposition to the government and its socialist policies, Ne Win and President San Yu resigned in July 1988, and widespread civil unrest followed. General Saw Muang formed a new military regime known as the State Law and Order Restoration Council (SLORC) and abolished much of the socialist system. Elections were held for the 485-member People's Assembly in 1990. The opposition National League for Democracy (NLD) won 396 seats, while the military-backed party won only 10. The People's Assembly was never convened, and many of its leaders were arrested or forced into exile. The military began drafting a new constitution in 1992, but this task has not been completed. The regime changed its name to the State Peace and Development Council (SPDC) in 1997. The council includes a chairman and twenty other members. The government formed by the council consists of a prime minister, two deputy prime ministers, and thirty-seven ministers.

***Leadership and Political Officials.*** Political leadership revolves around political intrigues and struggles for power within the military. From 1962 until 1988, General Ne Win was the dominant political figure, with other officers and their associates jockeying for positions underneath him. General Than Swe's hold on power since 1988 has been far less absolute. The officers holding positions in SLORC/SPDC tend to be roughly the same age and have roughly similar backgrounds and values.

The National League for Democracy is led by Aung San Suu Kyi, the daughter of the assassinated independence leader Aung San. She is currently under house arrest in Rangoon. The majority of the small inner circle around Aung San Suu Kyi are former military officers and associates or followers of Aung San. Both the regime and its leading opponents therefore form a small political elite.

There is an ethnic dimension to political office holding and leadership. The 1948 and 1962 govern-

*A young child at an initiation ceremony in Mandalay. Ninety percent of Burmese follow the Theravada form of Buddhism, also know as Hinayana Buddhism.*

ments were predominantly Burmese in composition and pursued pro-Burmese policies. Those policies sparked ethnic insurgencies led by ethnic elites, and the situation deteriorated when the regime passed a law in 1983 that created three tiers of citizenship rights based largely on ethnicity. At the bottom was a category of "other races" that included naturalized immigrants, mainly from India and China, whose ancestors arrived during the colonial period. Those assigned to this tier cannot run for political office or hold senior government posts. The 1988 regime signed peace accords with most of the insurgent groups, but national leadership has remained in the hands of the Burmese.

***Social Problems and Control.*** The authoritarian military regime has been harsh in its treatment of ethnic minorities and rules by decree, without a constitution or legislature. The regime systematically violates human rights and suppresses all forms of opposition. The judiciary is not independent of the military regime, which appoints justices to the supreme court. These justices then appoint lower court judges with the approval of the regime. Prison conditions are harsh and life-threatening. The regime reinforces its rule with a pervasive security apparatus led by a military intelligence organization known as the Directorate of Defense Services Intelligence (DDSI). The regime engages in surveillance of government employees and private citizens, harassment of political activists, intimidation, arrest, detention, and physical abuse. The movements and communications of citizens are monitored, homes are searched without warrants, and people are forcibly relocated without compensation. There is no provision for judicial determination of the legality of detention. Before being charged, detainees rarely have access to legal counsel or their families. Political detainees have no opportunity to obtain bail, and some are held incommunicado for long periods. After being charged, detainees rarely have counsel. In ethnic minority areas, human rights abuses are widespread, including extrajudicial killings and rape. The regime justifies its actions as being necessary to maintain order and national unity.

Although the regime officially recognizes the NLD, political rights are limited. There is virtually no right of assembly or association. Intimidation of NLD supporters forced the party to close its offices throughout the country. Opponents of the regime have disappeared and been arrested. Detainees often face torture, beatings, and other forms of abuse. There is little academic or religious freedom. Under the 1974 constitution, the regime required religious organizations to register with it. Religious meetings are monitored, and religious publications are subject to censorship and control. Buddhist monastic orders are under the authority of the state-sponsored State Clergy Coordination Committee. The regime has attempted to promote Buddhism and suppress other religions in ethnic minority areas. Workers' rights are restricted, unions are banned, and forced labor for public works and to produce food and other goods and perform other services for the military is common. Military personnel routinely confiscate livestock, fuel, food supplies, alcoholic drinks, and money from civilians.

**Military Activity.** Since 1962, the military (the *Tatmadaw*) has been the dominant political and economic force, with a large proportion of the population serving in the armed forces since the 1960s. In 1985, there were an estimated 186,000 men and women in the military; another 73,000 were in the People's Police Force and 35,000 served in the People's Militia. Reflecting the country's poverty and international isolation, the military is poorly armed and trained. Direct spending on the military declined from about 33 percent in the early 1970s to about 21 percent in 1987, representing less than 4 percent of the gross domestic product. This decline in personnel and expenditure was reversed in 1988. By 1997, the military had grown to over 350,000 and military spending had increased greatly. At present, military spending by the government is greater than nonmilitary spending. Military officers and their families play an important role in economic affairs outside the formal activities of the military. This is true both in the formal economy through government economic entities and in the black market, especially narcotics smuggling. The military's formal role includes intimidation of the population and waging war against ethnic insurgents.

## GENDER ROLES AND STATUSES

**Division of Labor by Gender.** Both men and women do agricultural work, but individual tasks are often gender-specific. Men prepare the land for planting and sow seeds, and women transplant rice seedlings. Harvesting is done by both men and women. Men thresh the rice. Most domestic work is done by women. During ceremonies, however, men are involved in food preparation. A variety of traditional handicrafts are made within the household or by specialists. Items of metal, wood, or stone generally are made by men, and weaving usually is done by women. Pottery, basketry, plaiting, making lacquerware, and making umbrellas can be done by men or women. Small-scale market selling and itinerant trading are conducted by both sexes. Transportation of goods or people by animal, carts, boat, or motor vehicle is done mainly by men. Religious specialists and traditional curers generally are male, but sometimes they are female. Spirit mediums can be male or female. Traditional theatrical and musical performances involve both genders. Women work mainly in teaching and nursing.

**The Relative Status of Women and Men.** Traditional society was known for the relatively high status of women. If a couple divorces, for example, common goods are divided equally and the wife retains her dowry as well as the proceeds from her commercial activities. However, military rule has undermined the status of women, especially at the higher levels of government and commerce. Women, however, play a significant role in the political opposition to the regime. The higher levels

*Mingalla Market, Mandalay. Men and women engage equally in small marketplace selling and trading.*

of business are in the hands of men, but many medium-size and small businesses are run by women.

## MARRIAGE, FAMILY, AND KINSHIP

**Marriage.** Individuals usually find their own marriage partners. Arrangements for the marriage may be made by the parents of sometimes an intermediary is employed. If the parents oppose the union, often the children elope and later the parents condone the marriage. When a man asks a woman's parents for their consent, it is common practice for him to bring a gift for the woman. Wedding ceremonies are relatively simple except among wealthy families. After speeches by the parents, members of the families and guests share pickled tea. Polygyny is rare. Far more common is the practice of wealthy and powerful men having an informal second wife. Divorce is relatively common and usually involves the couple ceasing to live together and dividing their property.

**Domestic Unit.** A newly married couple may live with the parents of one partner (often the parents of the wife) but soon establish their own household. The nuclear family is the primary domestic unit, but it may include extended family members such as unmarried siblings, widowed parents, or more

distant unmarried or widowed relatives. The husband is nominally the head of the household, but the wife has considerable authority. Women are responsible for most domestic chores.

**Inheritance.** Property generally is divided equally among the children after the parents die.

**Kin Groups.** Descent is reckoned bilaterally. Traditionally, there were no family names.

## SOCIALIZATION

**Infant Care.** Young children receive a great deal of attention. Newborns are placed in very carefully made cradles. A mother keeps her baby with her when she leaves the house. Burmese women carry babies on the hip, while most hill-dwelling peoples hold them in a sling on the back. Young children are pampered, given considerable freedom of movement, and allowed to handle virtually anything that catches their attention. Weaning usually takes place when a child is two to three years old. Relative or friends may nurse an infant. Adults take a great deal of interest in children, including those who are not their own.

**Child Rearing and Education.** Young children undergo several rites of passage. When a child is a

*A child carrying baskets on a shoulder pole. Traditionally, all boys of eight to ten years of age attended school in a Buddhist monastery.*

**Higher Education.** There are forty-five universities and colleges and 154 technical and vocational schools. There has been a steady erosion of higher education since 1962. After the civil unrest in 1988, during which many students were involved in antigovernment activities, there were widespread closures of universities and colleges. Since that time there has been a repeated cycle of opening and closing the universities and colleges that has made serious study virtually impossible. The universities and colleges were closed in 1996, and only a few were reopened in 2000.

## ETIQUETTE

It is considered improper to lose one's temper or show much emotion in public, but the Burmese are a very friendly and outgoing people. The Burmese and other Buddhists follow the Buddhist custom of not touching a person on the head, since spiritually this is considered the highest part of the body. Patting a child on the head not only is improper but is thought to be dangerous to the child's well-being. A person should not point the feet at anyone. Footwear is removed upon entering temple complexes for religious reasons, and it is polite to remove footwear when entering a house.

## RELIGION

*Religious Beliefs.* Almost 90 percent of the people are Buddhists, and the proportion is higher among the Burmese majority. Burmese follow the Theravada form of Buddhism, which is also known as Hinayana Buddhism and the doctrine of the elders or the small vehicle. In Theravada Buddhism, it is up to each individual to seek salvation and achieve nirvana. Buddhism is believed to have been introduced to Burma by missionaries sent by the Indian emperor Ashoka in the third century B.C.E.

few years old, a ceremony is held to give the child a name. Children in rural areas grow up surrounded by the implements that they will use when they grow up and watch adults performing domestic, agricultural, and artisanal tasks. In the past, all boys eight to ten years of age would begin attending school in a nearby Buddhist monastery, where they would learn about Buddhism and be taught to read and write. Those schools gradually gave way to public schools, but many young men continue to receive some education in monasteries. Under that system, few women were educated; their education took place mainly at home as they learned how to perform domestic tasks.

Modern education began under King Mindon (1853–1878), who built a school for an Anglican missionary. Under the British, secular education spread and the country achieved a relatively high level of education. Since 1962, the educational infrastructure has deteriorated. Today two-thirds to three-quarters of children drop out of elementary school before the fifth grade. The curriculum is scrutinized by the military regime, and it often is forbidden to teach in languages other than Burmese.

Buddhism is followed by many of the non-Burmese ethnic groups. While all these groups follow Theravada Buddhism, there are some differences between the in beliefs and practices and those of the Burmese. Buddhist beliefs and practices include animistic elements that reflect belief systems predating the introduction of Buddhism. Among the Burmese, this includes the worship of *nats*, which maybe associated with houses, in individuals, and natural features. An estimated 3 percent of the population, mainly in more isolated areas, who adhere solely to animistic religious beliefs.

Another 4 percent of the population is Christian (3 percent Baptist and 1 percent Catholic), 4 percent is

Muslim, 4 percent is Hindu, and 1 percent is animist. Christian missionaries began working in the country in the nineteenth century. They had relatively little success among Buddhists but made numerous converts among some of the minority groups.

***Religious Practitioners.*** Between ages of ten and sixteen, most young Burmese men and some young women become Buddhist novices and go to live in a monastery. While most young men remain at the monastery for only a short time before returning to the secular life, some become fully ordained monks. A person who wants to become a monk is expected to be free of debt and certain diseases, have the permission of his parents or spouse, agree to follow the disciplinary rules of the monkhood, and not become involved in secular life. While monks are expected to lead a life of aestheticism, they perform important functions in the community, especially as counselors. A variety of religious practitioners are associated with the animistic beliefs of most Buddhists, including spirit dancers who become possessed by spirits and may engage in healing and fortune-telling. There are also astrologers, other types of healers, tattoists with occult knowledge, and magicians.

***Rituals and Holy Places.*** Thingyan, the water festival, marks the advent of the new year in mid-April. Buddha images are washed, and monks are offered alms. It is also marked by dousing people with water and festive behavior such as dancing, singing, and theatrical performances. Kason in May celebrates Buddha's birth, enlightenment, and entrance into nirvana. The day includes the ceremonial watering of banyan trees to commemorate the banyan tree under which Buddha sat when he attained enlightenment. A ceremony is held in July to mark the start of the three-month lenten period and commemorate Buddha's first sermon. It is at this time that young males become novices. Lent is a period of spiritual retreat for monks, who remain in their monasteries. During this time people may not marry. Lent ends in October. Over a three-day period, candles, oil lamps, paper lanterns, and electric bulbs are lit to show how angels lit Buddha's return from heaven. Many marriages are held at this time. A celebration is held in November to produce new garments for monks and Buddha images. People come to complete the production of the cloth within a single day.

***Death and the Afterlife.*** Buddhists believe that those who die are reborn in a form that is in keeping with the merit they accumulated while alive. The cycle of death and rebirth is believed to continue as long as ignorance and craving remain. The cycle can be broken only through personal wisdom and the elimination of desire. Funerals involve either burial or cremation. The ceremony includes a procession of monks and mourners who accompany the coffin to the cemetery or crematorium, with the monks chanting and performing rites. Funerals for monks tend to be elaborate, while those who have died a violent death generally are quickly buried with very little ceremony, since their spirits are believed to linger as malevolent ghosts.

## MEDICINE AND HEALTH CARE

The use of traditional forms of medicine remains important, especially among the ethnic minorities. Few young people, however, receive training in these forms of medicine by an aging group of traditional healers and many traditional practices and the knowledge of traditional remedies are being lost. Serious health problems are reaching crisis proportions, and nontraditional health care by the public and private sectors has deteriorated.

Malaria, AIDS, and malnutrition and related diseases are a serious problem. Intravenous drug use formerly was a problem mainly in the northeast among ethnic minorities, but since 1988, drug used has spread to the lowlands and the urban areas inhabited by the Burmese majority. There are only 703 hospitals and 12,464 doctors. These facilities are in very poor condition, and funding for medical care and training is inadequate.

## SECULAR CELEBRATIONS

The major state holidays are Independence Day (4 January), Union Day (12 February), Peasants' Day (2 March), Resistance or Armed Forces Day (27 March), May Day or Workers' Day (1 May), Martyr's Day (19 July), and National Day (late November or early December). These are occasions for the regime to promote nationalist sentiments, and some are accompanied by festive events. Far more important for most Burmese are the older celebrations associated with agriculture and the Buddhist religion.

## THE ARTS AND HUMANITIES

***Support for the Arts.*** Until the 1880s, the nobility was an important source of support for artists. After the fall of the monarchy, support came from newly rich merchants and British colonial officers. From the 1920s to the 1940s, there was relatively little support from the government or the public. State schools for the fine arts were opened in

*A woman carrying grasses in Maymio, Burma. Women had high status in traditional society, which has been lessened today by the militaristic government.*

Rangoon and Mandalay in 1953, and there was a revival of interest in traditional art forms. The military regime of 1962 encouraged art forms supportive of its nationalist and socialist agenda. Since 1988, there has been little government support.

**Literature.** The focus of writing within Burmese society was, and to a large extent still is, focused on writing for theater performances (*pwe*) and producing texts relating to Buddhism. In addition, since the nineteenth century there is a fair amount of popular fiction. There is also some British fiction from the colonial period that is set in Burma. Among the early British works of fiction concerned with the Burmese are two novels by H. Fielding: *The Soul of a People* (1898) and *Thibaw's Queen* (1899). By far the best known British novel set in Burma is George Orwell's *Burmese Days* (1934), a critical examination of British colonial rule.

**Graphic Arts.** The graphic arts include temple sculpture in wood, stucco, stone, and wood; temple mural painting, usually in tempera; other forms of wood carving; ivory carving; work in bronze, iron, and other metals; jewelry; ceramics; glassware; lacquerware; textiles and costume; items made of palm and bamboo; and painting on paper or canvas.

Lacquerware entails the covering of an object made of bamboo or wood with a liquid made from tree sap. These objects include containers as well as tables, screens, and carved animal figures. The process preserves, strengthens, and waterproofs objects and has been developed into a decorative art form. Its origins are ancient. Pagan is the largest and most important center for lacquerware. The Government Lacquerware School was established by local artists in Pagan in 1924. The Shan also have a distinctive lacquerware tradition.

Weaving is a highly developed traditional art form. Among the Burmese, it reached its highest form in the production of *lun-taya acheik* cloth. The technique was brought from Manipur in the eighteenth century, but the complex motifs are distinctly Burmese. This style of cloth is still woven near Mandalay for sale to elite Burmese. There are distinctive textile traditions among the ethnic minorities.

Traditional painting on paper made from tree bark or bamboo pulp is known as *parabaik* painting. The earliest known example dates back to the eighteenth century. Pigments were made of tempera, with gold and silver inks used for the costumes of nobles and deities. The paintings also formed folded pages in books. Initially these paintings depicted religious scenes, court scenes, or astrological charts, medicines, tattoo designs, and sexual techniques, and the painters were itinerant artists employed by the court. In the nineteenth century, the court in Mandalay employed full-time artists, and a system of apprenticeship was put in place. Among the new styles of painting that emerged after the fall of the monarchy were paintings of happy families sold to the newly rich. Traditional painting declined in the 1920s as local patrons and artists became more interested in European styles. A revival of interest in Burmese themes took place after the 1962 military takeover. The new regime held an annual painting exhibition to promote select painters. The exhibitions ended in 1988, but the military regime allowed the fine arts school to remain open. Most painters today are dependent on sales through a handful of private galleries that cater largely to resident expatriates. The themes of newer paintings continue to be Burmese, especially religious paintings and landscapes.

***Performance Arts.*** Popular performances often combine music, dance, and drama in a pwe ("show"). These shows take place at fairs, religious festivals, weddings, funerals, and sporting events. They generally are held at night and can go on all night long. A pwe typically includes performances based on legends and Buddhist epics; comedy skits; singing, dancing, and music; and sometimes a puppet show. Traditional music and dance have been influenced by Thailand. Traditional instruments played in an ensemble include a circle of drums, a thirteen-stringed boat-shaped harp, a circle of gongs, a xylophonelike instrument, an oboelike instrument, a bamboo flute, a bass drum, small cymbals, and bamboo clappers. Today these traditional instruments are combined with Western ones, including a guitar. The Kon-baung court employed performers specializing in recitation, singing, dancing, and acting. Highly stylized dramatic performances were accompanied by music. There is also a tradition of popular public performances such as the *nebhatkhin* (a pageant depicting the birth of Buddha) and the more secular *myai-waing* (an earth-circling performance) conducted by traveling actors and musicians. After 1885, entertainers performed for a new public, and more lively forms of entertainment were developed, including all-female dance troupes. Western-style stage plays were introduced at that same time. There was interest in newer forms of performance in the late nineteenth and early twentieth centuries. Such performances ended with the outbreak of World War II. After of independence, there was a revival of interest in traditional dance, drama, and music. The 1950s saw a revival of traditional art forms and the emergence of a new form of modern melodrama called *pya-zat*. These were modern plays that rarely dealt with traditional subjects. While secular performance arts now dominate popular entertainment, the military regime has continued to support more traditional performances and the fine arts schools still teach traditional forms of dance and drama, although the audiences consist largely of tourists, resident expatriates, and members of the ruling elite.

## THE STATE OF THE PHYSICAL AND SOCIAL SCIENCES

Training in the physical and social sciences at national institutions such as Yangon University and Yangon Technical University is very limited. Since 1962, the social sciences have been almost nonexistent. Some social science research continues to take place, but most of it focuses on the relatively distant past. Institutions involved in such work include the

Myanmar Historical Commission, Cultural Institute, Department of Archaeology, and Religious Affairs Department.

## BIBLIOGRAPHY

Aung San Suu Kyi. *Freedom from Fear: And Other Writings*, 1991.

———. *Aung San Suu Kyi: Conversations with Alan Clements*, 1997.

———. *Letters from Burma*, 1997.

Aung-Thwin and Michael A. Pagan. *The Origins of Modern Burma*, 1995.

———. *Myth and History in the Historiography of Early Burma: Paradigms, Primary Sources, and Prejudices*, 1998.

Carey, Peter, ed. *Burma: The Challenge of Change in a Divided Society*, 1997.

Fraser-Lu, Sylvia. *Burmese Lacquerware*, 1985.

———. *Burmese Crafts Past and Present*, 1994.

Fredholm, Michael. *Burma: Ethnicity and Insurgency*, 1993.

Gravers, Mikael. *Nationalism as Political Paranoia in Burma: An Essay on the Historical Practice of Power*, 1999.

Howard, Michael C. *Textiles of the Hill Tribes of Burma*, 1999.

Isaaca, Ralph, and T. Richard Blurton. *Visions from the Golden Land: Burma and the Art of Lacquer*, 2000.

Lintner, Bertil. *Outrage: Burma's Struggle for Democracy*, 2nd ed., 1990.

———. *Burma in Revolt: Opium and Insurgency since 1948*, 1999.

Luce, Gordon H. *Phases of Pre-Pagan Burma Languages and History*, 1995.

Maring, Joel M. and Ester G. Maring. *Historical and Cultural Dictionary of Burma*, 1973.

Maung, Mya. *The Burmese Road to Poverty*, 1991.

Renard, Ronald D. *The Burmese Connection: Illegal Drugs and the Making of the Golden Triangle*, 1996.

Silverstein, Josef, ed. *Independent Burma at Forty Years: Six Assessments*, 1989.

Singer, Noel F. *Burmese Puppets*, 1992.

———. *Burmese Dance and Theatre*, 1995.

Smith, Martin. *Burma: Insurgency and the Politics of Ethnicity*, 1991.

Spiro, Melford. *Burmese Supernaturalism*, 2nd ed., 1974.

———. *Kinship and Marriage in Burma*, 1977.

———. *Buddhism and Society: A Great Tradition and Its Burmese Vicissitudes*, 1982.

———. *Anthropological Other or Burmese Brother? Studies in Cultural Analysis*, 1992.

Strachan, Paul, ed. *Essays on the History and Buddhism of Burma*, 1988.

———. *Imperial Pagan: Art and Architecture of Burma*, 1990.

Taylor, Robert H. *The State in Burma*, 1987.

—MICHAEL C. HOWARD

# BURUNDI

## CULTURE NAME

Burundian

## ORIENTATION

**Identification.** Burundi has to two distinct ethnic groups: the Hutu and the Tutsi. While these cultures have coexisted in the area for centuries and now share a common language and many common cultural elements, they remain separate in terms of group identification.

**Location and Geography.** Burundi is a small landlocked country in east central Africa, bordering Rwanda, Tanzania, and the Democratic Republic of the Congo. Its total area is 10,750 square miles (27,830 square kilometers). The country is situated on a high plateau, with the altitude ranging from 2,532 feet (772 meters) at Lake Tanganyika in the east, to 8,760 feet (2,670 meters) at the highest point, Mount Heha. The country lies along the East African rift and experiences occasional tremors and earthquakes. Forty-four percent of the land is arable, but only 9 percent is planted with permanent crops. One-third of the country is used as pastureland. The most fertile areas are in the highlands, where temperatures are moderate and rainfall averages sixty inches (152 centimeters) a year. The mountain slopes are dense with trees. The plateau is also wooded, particularly at the higher altitudes. The wildlife includes elephants, hippopotamus, crocodiles, buffalo, warthogs, baboons, and antelopes. These animals are being threatened as development encroaches on their natural habitat, and the country has not established national park areas or sanctuaries where species are protected. Laws against poaching are not strictly enforced. The country also is experiencing deforestation and soil erosion because of overgrazing and the spread of farming.

**Demography.** The population was estimated at 6,054,714 in 2000, with one of the highest population densities in Africa. Through much of the country's history, the majority (around 85 percent) of the people have been Hutu. The Tutsi, the largest minority, traditionally have accounted for about 14 percent of the population. One percent of the people are Twa. The ethnic balance has begun to shift as Hutu from Burundi have fled to neighboring Rwanda to escape ethnic persecution and Tutsi have escaped violence in Rwanda and settled in Burundi. The Tutsi now make up closer to 20 percent of the population. There is a small population of three thousand Europeans and two thousand South Asians; most of these immigrants live in the capital, Bujumbura, and are involved in church-related activities.

**Linguistic Affiliation.** Both the Hutu and the Tutsi speak Kirundi, a Bantu language. The Twa also speak Kirundi, although theirs is a slightly different dialect. Along with French, Kirundi is the official language. Swahili, a mixture of Arabic and Bantu languages that is the language of trade and business in much of East Africa, also is spoken, mostly in the region of Lake Tanganyika and in the capital city. English is taught in some schools.

**Symbolism.** The Tutsi are historically a herding society, and the cow therefore holds a great deal of symbolic power in the national culture. This is reflected in the language: a typical Kirundi greeting, *Amashyo*, translates as "May you have herds of cattle." The language is full of references in which cattle stand for health, happiness, and prosperity.

## HISTORY AND ETHNIC RELATIONS

**Emergence of the Nation.** The original inhabitants of present-day Burundi are thought to be the Twa people, descendants of the pygmies. The Hutu arrived from the west in a gradual migration between the seventh and the eleventh centuries. They outnumbered the Twa and put their own regional kings, called *bahinza*, in place. Most of the Twa

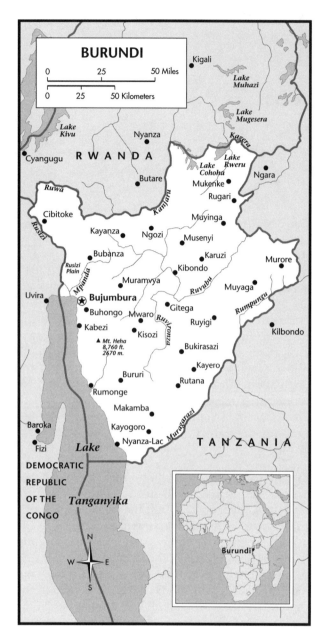

*Burundi*

centralized, following a system similar to that of feudal lords, and internal conflicts led to a situation in which the king controlled only half the land that was nominally part of his domain by 1900.

In 1885, Germany declared present-day Burundi and Rwanda part of its sphere of influence, forming a territory it called German East Africa; however, Germans did not begin to settle in the area until 1906. They made a deal with the Tutsi king, guaranteeing him protection from his enemies in exchange for following German commands, thus making the king a puppet. The European conflict of the World War I spread to the African continent, and in 1916 Belgium sent 1,400 troops to Burundi. They wrested control of the land from the Germans with little opposition. In 1923, Burundi and Rwanda were officially declared a Belgian mandate by the League of Nations. The territory was known as Ruanda-Urundi.

After the World War II, the mandate was superseded by a United Nations trusteeship. Throughout colonial times, internal strife continued to build. When independence was declared in 1962, the area reverted to Tutsi rule. In the first elections, which were overseen by the Belgians, the Tutsi-led Union for National Progress and Unity (UPONA) won a majority in the National Assembly. The first prime minister, Louis Rwagasore, from the UPONA party, was assassinated a few weeks after the election and was succeeded by his brother-in-law, Andre Muhirwa. Because Burundi and Rwanda were populated by the same ethnic groups and spoke the same language, the United Nations thought that they should remain one nation, but the two wanted independence separately, and the United Nations acquiesced. Rwanda, unlike Burundi, was controlled by the Hutu, and before European rule, the two had never constituted a single political entity.

Anti-Tutsi sentiment began to intensify among the Hutu in Burundi. In a 1964 election, a Hutu won the popular vote but the Tutsi refused to accept a Hutu prime minister. In 1965, a Hutu rebellion was put down violently. A coup in 1966 replaced the monarchy with a military government and put Michel Micombero in power. Micombero's party, UPONA, was declared the only legal political party, and Micombero consolidated his power by declaring himself both president and prime minister. The coup resulted in further Hutu deaths. A civil war that began in 1971 caused some Tutsi deaths in addition to the Hutu toll of 100,000 to 150,000 dead and 100,000 displaced or homeless.

Another coup in 1976 left the country with a one-party government and elected the coup's

retreated farther into the forested highlands. The Tutsi began to appear in the fifteenth and sixteenth centuries, migrating from the Nile region in present-day Sudan and Ethiopia south and west in search of new cattle pastures. The Tutsi are tall, martial people, and while they never accounted for more than their current 15 percent of the population, they established economic and political control of the region, effectively subduing the Twa and the Hutu majority. From the seventeenth through the nineteen centuries, the kingdom continued to expand, eventually encompassing parts of present-day Rwanda and Tanzania. However, rule was de-

leader, Jean-Baptiste Bagaza, as president. Bagaza declared the goal of eliminating corruption in the government; however, in the subsequent election in 1982, he was the only candidate. Bagaza's regime harbored suspicion toward Catholics, who were considered dangerously sympathetic to the Hutu. In 1986, the government seized control of the seminaries, banned Catholic prayer meetings, and arrested and jailed several priests. These policies were largely unpopular, however, and Bagaza began to soften his stance.

The year 1987 saw the coup engineered by Major Pierre Buyoya. Buyoya suspended the constitution that had been in place since 1981 and installed a transitional government. In the following year, twenty thousand Hutu were killed in the ongoing ethnic conflict. As president, Buyoya attempted to make peace between the two groups, including representatives of both parties in the cabinet.

In 1992, a new constitution established a multiparty system, and in the following year, Melchior Ndadaye, the nation's first Hutu ruler, was elected president. Five months after assuming office, Ndadaye and several other Hutu leaders were assassinated in a failed coup attempt. A further outbreak of violence ensued, resulting in the deaths of 150,000 people (both Hutu and Tutsi) in two months and the emigration of an estimated eighty thousand.

The National Assembly named another Hutu, Cyprien Ntaryamira, to replace Ndadaye in 1994. Later that year, he and Juvenal Habyarimana, the president of Rwanda, died in a plane crash under suspicious circumstances. The next president, Sylvestre Ntibantunganya, held office for two years, until a 1996 coup by the Tutsi installed Pierre Buyoya as president again. The president of Tanzania, who had led peace talks between the Hutu and the Tutsi, called for sanctions against the Buyoya regime, and the rest of the world responded by halting trade and international flights. Despite the crippling effect on the economy, no change was effected; the bloodshed that had begun in 1993 continued with little sign of abatement, and the peace process was put on hold. In 1999, the sanctions were lifted, and at the end of that year Nelson Mandela was appointed as moderator of the peace talks. However, no clear end to the fighting is in sight.

**National Identity.** The country's history of ethnic strife goes back centuries. Cultural identity stems from tribal affiliation rather than from any unify-

ing national characteristic. The domination of the Hutu majority by the Tutsi minority has not resulted in a fusion but in extreme divisiveness in terms of national identity. Neither tribe is contained within the borders of current-day Burundi; the Hutu-Tutsi conflict also has affected neighboring Democratic Republic of Congo and Rwanda, the latter of which was part of the same territory under colonial rule. Belgium's influence as a colonial power did little to unite the two tribes.

**Ethnic Relations.** Relations between the Hutu and the Tutsi are extremely antagonistic. While the two tribes share a good deal culturally, their mutual disdain is evident. The Hutu have a number of sayings reflecting the rapacious nature of the Tutsi, and the Tutsi, traditionally cattle herders, look down upon the farming tradition of the Hutu. Animosity and resentment have led to continued violence and political unrest. The violence and hatred extend beyond the borders of the country; Rwanda is engaged in similar ethnic warfare. Whereas in Burundi much of the violence is perpetrated on the Hutu by the Tutsi, in Rwanda the situation is reversed. However, the two nations are closely linked, and events in one often influence and precipitate events in the other. The small population of Twa in Burundi remain isolated from both groups, preferring to live in the forest as hunter-gatherers, although as their land has been lost, some have adopted different trades and have settled closer to the Hutu and the Tutsi.

## URBANISM, ARCHITECTURE, AND THE USE OF SPACE

The capital city, Bujumbura, is the populous and most industrialized city. It is located on the north shore of Lake Tanganyika, and its port is the country's largest. Cement, textiles, and soap are manufactured there, and it is home to one of the country's two coffee-processing facilities. Bujumbura, once known as Usumbura, was also the colonial capital, and many of its buildings reveal a European influence. The majority of foreigners in the country are concentrated in the capital, which gives the city a cosmopolitan feel. Large sections of the city, however, are almost entirely untouched by colonial influence. The second-largest city, Gitega, is east of Bujumbura on the Ruvuvu River. It was the old capital of the kingdom under Tutsi rule and has grown rapidly in the last several decades from a population of only five thousand in 1970. Gitega is in the fertile highlands and is surrounded by coffee, banana, and tea plantations. It has a coffee-processing plant and a brewery that manufactures beer from bananas.

These are the only two urban centers. Ninety-two percent of the population lives in a rural setting, mostly in family groupings too small to be called villages that are scattered throughout the highlands. A number of market towns draw inhabitants of surrounding rural zones to buy, sell, and trade agricultural products and handicrafts.

Burundians traditionally built their houses of grass and mud in a shape reminiscent of a beehive and wove leaves together for the roof. The traditional Tutsi hut, called a *rugo,* was surrounded by cattle corrals. Today the most common materials are mud and sticks, although wood and cement blocks also are used. The roofs are usually tin, since leaves are in short supply as a result of deforestation. Each house is surrounded by a courtyard, and several houses are grouped together inside a wall of mud and sticks.

## FOOD AND ECONOMY

*Food in Daily Life.* The most common foods are beans, corn, peas, millet, sorghum, cassava, sweet potatoes, and bananas. The diet consists mainly of carbohydrates; vitamins and minerals are provided by fruits, vegetables, and combinations of grains, but little fat and protein are available. Meat accounts for 2 percent or less of the average food intake. As a result, kwashiorkor, a disease caused by protein deficiency, is common. Fish is consumed in the areas around Lake Tanganyika. Meal production is labor-intensive. The cassava root is washed, pounded, and strained, and sorghum is ground into flour for pancakes or porridge. The porridge is rolled into a ball with one hand and dipped in gravy or sauce.

*Food Customs at Ceremonial Occasions.* Beer is an important part of social interactions and is consumed at all important occasions, such as the marriage negotiations between two families. It is drunk through straws. A number of food customs revolve around the treatment of cows, which are considered sacred. For example, milk cannot be heated or boiled or drunk on the same day that peas or peanuts are consumed. When a cow dies, the family eats its meat and then plants its horns in the soil near the house to bring good luck.

*Basic Economy.* Burundi has one of the lowest gross national products in the world. It is moving toward a free-enterprise economy, with a system that is partly state-run and partly private. There is a severe trade imbalance as the country imports twice as much as it exports. The entire economy has been severely altered by the ethnic warfare that has plagued the country since 1993, resulting in 250,000 deaths and the displacement of 800,000 people and leaving the country with limited supplies of food, medicine, and electricity. In 1990, before the violence began, 36 percent of the population lived below the poverty line; in rural areas, this number approached 85 percent. Ninety percent of the population supports itself through subsistence farming, growing cassava, corn, sweet potatoes, bananas, and sorghum. Four percent of the population is employed by the government, 1.5 percent by industry and commerce, and 1.5 percent in the service sector.

*Land Tenure and Property.* In the system imposed by the Tutsi in the fifteenth century, Hutu worked as serfs for Tutsi landholders. This system, which is called cattle clientage, meant that the Hutu cared for the land and the cattle but did not own it. In fact, they were in effect possessions of the Tutsi. This contract was called *ubugabire.* After independence, the Tutsi did not want to relinquish their land and managed to keep the ubugabire system in place until 1977. The legacy of this system remains, as much of the land is still owned by the Tutsi minority.

*Commercial Activities.* Farmers cultivate a large number of crops for domestic consumption, including bananas, dry beans, corn, sugarcane, and sorghum. They also raise goats, cattle, and sheep. These products are transported to local markets and to the capital. Bartering is still common, particularly the use of cattle as currency.

*Major Industries.* There is little industry and development is slow because of a lack of trained workers and little investment or aid from foreign countries. It is difficult to develop industry in a country in which most people cannot afford to purchase the goods industry would produce. Currently, the country is involved mainly in processing food (primarily coffee), brewing beer, and bottling soft drinks. There is some production of light consumer goods, including blankets, shoes, and soap. The country also engages in the assembly of imported components and public works construction.

*Trade.* Coffee, which was introduced to the area in 1930, is the main cash crop, accounting for 80 percent of foreign revenue. This leaves the economy vulnerable to variations in weather and to fluctuations in the international coffee market. To combat

*A car drives on a quiet street in the downtown capital of Bujumbura. Only about 8 percent of the population live in the two largst cities: Bujumbura and Gitega.*

this problem, Burundi has been attempting to diversify its economy by increasing the production of other products, such as tea and cotton. Other exports include sugar and cattle hides. It exports mainly to the United Kingdom, Germany, Benelux nations, and Switzerland. Burundi receives goods from the Benelux nations, France, Zambia, Germany, Kenya, and Japan. The main imports are capital goods, petroleum products, and food. While the country produces some electricity from dams on the Mugere River, it receives the majority of its power from a hydroelectric station at Bukavu in the Congo and by importing oil from the Persian Gulf. Burundi had a large trade deficit in the 1980 and 1990s, but this was mostly alleviated by foreign aid from Belgium, France, and Germany.

**Division of Labor.** The Hutu have a long tradition of working the land. The Tutsi were originally cattle herders, although much of the labor of caring for their cattle was done by the Hutu. This class division is still evident, as most of the few prestigious jobs are held by the Tutsi, who dominate both the government and the military. A few Hutu have attained positions in business and government, but the majority are farmers.

## SOCIAL STRATIFICATION

**Classes and Castes.** Since the Tutsi came to power in the fourteenth or fifteenth century, they have occupied a higher social position than the Hutu. Agricultural Hutu were forced to become caretakers for the large Tutsi cattle herds. The ruling class was composed entirely of Tutsi. It was possible, although rare, for Hutu (or even occasionally Twa) to join the Tutsi class through acts of unusual bravery or honor, and Tutsi could fall into the Hutu class by committing a dishonorable act. The Tutsi still are represented disproportionately in the government and among the wealthy. This discrepancy has been exaggerated by Tutsi violence specifically targeting Hutu with professional jobs and training. Thus, the Hutu as a whole have been left even more disproportionately illiterate and poor.

**Symbols of Social Stratification.** The possession of a large number of cattle is traditionally the sign of a wealthy person. Even today, especially among rural people, cattle are a visible token of prosperity, and people are reluctant to slaughter them even when the sale of the meat could bring money to the family. Other traditional status symbols include the spear, which is carried on ceremonial occasions, and

*Students at a school watch a performance representing the Hutus and Tutsis groups. The Hutus and Tutsis have a longstanding history of ethnic differences, which has split not only Burundi, but extends into Rwanda and the Democratic Republic of Congo.*

drums. The ultimate symbol of power traditionally was the drum of the *mwami*, or king. Being selected to play this drum was considered one of the highest achievements a young man could attain. Traditional attire consists of brightly colored wraps for women and white clothing for men. Today, especially in the cities and among the wealthier classes, Western-style clothes are common.

## POLITICAL LIFE

***Government.*** The constitution ratified in 1992 established a plural political system that was suspended after a military coup in 1996. In 1998, it was replaced by a transitional constitution that enlarged the National Assembly and created two vice presidents. The president, who is elected for a maximum of two five-year terms, is both chief of state and head of the government. The legislative branch is the unicameral National Assembly, which has 121 members elected by popular vote to serve five-year terms. Technically there is universal suffrage, but the current president came to power through a coup, at which point he suspended all elections for the National Assembly. The country is divided into

fifteen provinces that are administered by governors appointed by the president. These regions are further subdivided into *arrondissements*, then into communes or townships.

***Leadership and Political Officials.*** Political leaders are not trusted among the population. Instability and frequent changes in regime, as well as the disregard for the democratic process shown by many rulers, have led to a feeling of disenfranchisement and bitterness, especially among the Hutu. A number of elected Hutu leaders have been assassinated since independence. While it has been exacerbated in recent years, this sentiment of distrust dates back centuries to the long standing domination by the Tutsi in a nonrepresentative governmental system.

***Social Problems and Control.*** The legal system is based on traditional tribal customs and the German and French models introduced by the Belgians. The highest level of legal recourse is the Supreme Court, under which there are several lower levels of courts. Crime rates are high in and around the capital. The most pressing social problem is the ongoing ethnic violence, which often is dealt with brutally by the police and military forces.

**Military Activity.** At independence, the country had a separate army and police force. The two were consolidated in 1967. Since that time a navy and an air force have been added. The armed forces include an army, an air force, a navy, and a paramilitary organization for police action and riot control. The army is dominated by the Tutsi, who have used it since independence to ensure their control of the government. Males are eligible for military service at sixteen.

## SOCIAL WELFARE AND CHANGE PROGRAMS

The social welfare system provides health care only for people who are employed and earn a salary and therefore is largely ineffective in dealing with the country's health problems. Money is scarce, and the government has no effective mechanism in place for dealing with the many widespread problems that affect the country, ranging from unemployment, to illiteracy and lack of education, to AIDS.

## NONGOVERNMENTAL ORGANIZATIONS AND OTHER ASSOCIATIONS

The United Nations has been a presence since the country gained independence in 1962, especially through the World Health Organization, which has provided money and training to combat smallpox, tuberculosis, malaria, malnutrition, and AIDS. Catholic and Protestant churches have a long history of sending missionaries and aid workers to the region.

## GENDER ROLES AND STATUSES

**Division of Labor by Gender.** Women's primary duties are childbearing and child care. They are also responsible for household chores, including cleaning and food preparation. In rural regions, women also work in agriculture and do most of the work of planting, as their fertility is believed to be transferred to the seeds. Women are almost entirely unrepresented in business and at all levels of government.

**The Relative Status of Women and Men.** Women are respected, particularly for their power as life bearers. The role of the mother is highly honored, but in practice, women have little decision-making authority in the family or in society as a whole. Fatherhood is considered an important responsibil-

ity, and it is the man who is in charge of the family. Women's status is little higher than that of children, and like them, women are expected to defer to the wishes of any adult male.

## MARRIAGE, FAMILY AND KINSHIP

**Marriage.** Polygamy was practiced traditionally. Despite being forbidden by both civil law and the Christian churches, it still exists. Traditionally, it was the duty of the father to find a first wife for his son. It is still common practice for the parents of a young man to meet with his potential bride and her parents and discuss issues such as the bridewealth. This is the equivalent of a dowry, but it is given by the groom's family to the bride's. Traditionally, it consisted of cattle, goats, and hoes, but today it can include cash, clothing, and furniture. The bridewealth is delivered on the wedding day, when the bride leaves her parents (who do not attend the wedding ceremony) to participate in the festivities at the husband's home.

**Domestic Unit.** Each family generally has its own house, and these houses are grouped together in compounds that include the homes of extended family members. Upon marriage, a woman becomes part of her husband's family. In Tutsi tradition, wives and husbands live separately, but in Hutu practice, they share a house.

**Inheritance.** Inheritance passes from the male head of the family to his oldest son after the father's death. This is symbolized by the bequest of the ceremonial spear.

**Kin Groups.** Family ties are very powerful, and extended families live in close proximity as a clan. Particularly in the countryside, the extended family is the primary social unit, as kin groups live together in relative isolation from other groups. The Tutsi divide themselves into four *ganwa* (royal) clans—the Batare, Bezi, Bataga, and Bambutsu—descendants of the four dynasties that once ruled the country.

## SOCIALIZATION

**Infant Care.** Birth usually occurs at home, assisted by midwives and other women. Six days after a baby is born, a ceremony called *ujusohor* is observed in which he or she is presented to the family. The mother receives a crown of flowers and gifts of beer and money. Children are named in the *kuvamukiriri* ceremony. The paternal grandfather bestows on the child a proper name, a clan name, and one or two

*Tutsi schoolboys in a class in Bujumbura. Lack of supplies, teachers, and overall political instability have led to low school attendance figures, which average only 50 percent.*

nicknames. If the family is Christian, baptism occurs at the same time. This is not done until the child reaches the age of about one year, as infant mortality is high.

Children are breast-fed for as long as possible. At age two or three, they begin to be fed the typical national diet. Mothers generally tie their babies to their backs (or when they are older, perch them on their hips) and carry them everywhere.

**Child Rearing and Education.** Children are highly valued. They are viewed partly as insurance for the future, as one proverb suggests: "The greatest sorrow is to have no children to mourn for you." Traditionally, male Tutsi children are given extensive training in public speaking, storytelling, traditional dances, and military skills. In the agricultural Hutu culture, the work ethic is inculcated early; both boys and girls begin to be assigned chores at around the age of five. They also are schooled in proper behavior and in communal and family values. Those values include treating elders with supreme respect and responding promptly and willingly to their commands.

The overall literacy rate is 35 percent: 49 percent for men and 22 percent for women. Education

is free and technically mandatory for children between the ages of seven and twelve, but only an estimated 50 percent of eligible children attend primary school; for secondary school, the figure is only 8 percent. The functioning of the schools has been hindered by political instability, a severe shortage of teachers, and a lack of supplies. Many families prefer to keep their children at home to work in the fields and care for younger siblings. School is taught in Kirundi in the lower grades and in French at the secondary level.

**Higher Education.** There is one university, located in Bujumbura, which was opened in 1960. There are two technical colleges in the capital that train people in crafts, mechanics, carpentry, and other skilled labor. Several institutions provide training in teaching and other professions.

## ETIQUETTE

Exchanges often include literal or figurative references to cattle. A typical greeting involves both parties wishing each other large herds. Handshakes are important, and the type varies by location. One version involves touching one's left hand to the other person's elbow. People stand close together in

*Gitaga drummers perform a folk dance. Dance is an essential part of Burundian culture that has received international recognition.*

conversation and often continue holding hands for several minutes after shaking. Social gatherings, whether large or small, formal or informal, often include food and drink, especially beer. It is considered rude to turn down food or drink when it is offered.

## RELIGION

***Religious Beliefs.*** Sixty-seven percent of the population is Christian (62 percent Roman Catholic and 5 percent Protestant); 23 percent of the people follow exclusively traditional beliefs, and the remaining 10 percent are Muslim. The first Roman Catholic mission was set up in 1898, and the Protestants arrived in 1926. In addition to converting a large percentage of the population, they established schools and hospitals. Although the majority of the people today profess to be Christian, many retain some animist beliefs and practices.

Traditional beliefs place a strong emphasis on fate as opposed to free will. Everything is in the hands of Imana, the source of all life and goodness. The traditional religion is a form of animism in which physical objects are believed to have spirits. There is great respect for dead ancestors. In the Hutu tradition, these spirits often visit with evil intent, whereas in Tutsi belief, the ancestors' influence is more benign. Cattle are invested with a special spiritual force. They are cared for according to specific customs dictated by the religion and are objects of prayer and worship.

***Religious Practitioners.*** Diviners, or fortune-tellers, are believed to have a special connection with the spirit world and can be called upon as go-betweens. The Hutu sometimes use their services to appease the spirits of their ancestors. When Burundi was a Tutsi kingdom, the *mwami*, or king, played an important role in some religious ceremonies.

***Rituals and Holy Places.*** *Kubandwa* is one of the most important religious festivals. It celebrates the grain harvest and pays homage to Kiranga, a spirit who is the leader of all the dead ancestors. At this ceremony, young men decorate their bodies and engage in traditional chants and dances; one of them dresses as Kiranga. At the end of the festival, people bathe in a stream in a cleansing ritual. Another central ritual is a fertility ceremony called *umuganuro*, in which a sacred drum is played and a virgin plants the first sorghum seeds to assure a good harvest.

*Cultivated terrace farming in the Nyanza region. Coffee crops account for 80 percent of foreign revenue.*

**Death and the Afterlife.** Departed ancestors are considered an essential part of the culture. There are various practices and ceremonies to exalt and appease their spirits, which are seen as powerful influences in the world of the living.

## MEDICINE AND HEALTH CARE

Burundi has extremely poor health conditions and few doctors to alleviate those problems. Malaria, influenza, diarrhea, and measles are common. Diseases are spread through poor sanitation and contaminated drinking water. While access to potable water has increased in the last decades, it is still low, particularly in rural areas. Epidemics of infectious diseases such as cholera are relatively rare, but when they occur, the death toll is high. The country has a high birthrate and a high infant mortality rate. As in much of Africa, AIDS is the major health problem today. As a result, life expectancy is one of the lowest in the world: forty-seven years for females and forty-five years for males. The AIDS epidemic has resulted in lower population growth and a low proportion of males to females.

## SECULAR CELEBRATIONS

Independence Day is celebrated on 1 July.

## THE ARTS AND HUMANITIES

**Support for the Arts.** The Center of Burundi Culture, founded in 1977, provides support for traditional art forms. Located in Bujumbura, it sponsors a "living museum" that honors the artistic aspects of people's daily lives as well as an open-air theater, a botanical garden, a music pavilion, and a crafts village. Gitega is home to a national museum that contains folk art, historical artifacts, and a library. That city also has an art school. Cultural programs have suffered as a result of poverty and political upheaval.

**Literature.** Because of widespread poverty and illiteracy written literature is virtually nonexistent. However, there is a strong oral tradition consisting of stories, legends, fables, poems, riddles, and songs. In this way, history and culture are passed from one generation to the next. Storytellers are highly respected, and it is part of their duty to train young people in the art. There are a number of epic poems about cattle. Storytelling is used as a way to report news, but subtlety and creative figures of speech are more valued than is strict accuracy.

**Graphic Arts.** While people value the artistic expression of craftsmen, all the items they produce are functional as well as decorative. Baskets traditionally are woven by Tutsi women with the help of their servants. They are made from papyrus root, bast fiber, and banana leaves and are decorated with mud dyes in elaborate patterns. The baskets serve a variety of purposes, from water canisters, to carrying containers for the head, to storage vessels for food and seasonings. Other handicrafts include leather goods and ironwork, both of which are often decorated with geometric patterns similar to those used in baskets. Blacksmiths fashion spears for warfare and hunting, which are handed down from father to son. The Twa are famous for pottery, a tradition that dates back thousands of years.

**Performance Arts.** Burundi has a unique and long-standing musical heritage. At family gatherings *imvyino* songs with a short refrain and a strong beat that often include improvised verses, are sung. The *indirimbo* song is a more subdued form that is performed by a single singer or a small group. Men sing *kwishongora*, a rhythmic song with shouts and trills, whereas the *bilito*, a sentimental musical expression, is generally a female form. "Whispered singing" is also typical of Burundian music. It is performed at a low pitch so that the accompaniment of the instruments can be heard more clearly. Songs are played on the *inanga*, an instrument while six to eight strings stretched over a hollow wooden bowl; the *idono*, a fiddle with one string; the *ikihusehama*, a clarinetlike woodwind; and the *ikimbe*, a linguaphone. Drums are important not only as musical instruments but as symbols of power and status. Several men play one drum at the same time and alternate playing solos.

Dance is an integral part of the culture. One form of Tutsi dance, performed by a group of highly trained men, has gained international attention. The troop Les Tambouinaires du Burundi has performed in New York and Berlin. The dancers dress in leopard fur and headdresses and enact an elaborate choreography of leaps. This form has its roots in the dances of the royal court in the time of the Tutsi kingdom.

## THE STATE OF THE PHYSICAL AND SOCIAL SCIENCES

Because of the extreme poverty and lack of education, facilities for the study of the social and physical sciences are virtually nonexistent. There is a run-down geology museum and a reptile park in the capital.

## BIBLIOGRAPHY

Bonvin, Jean. *Social Attitudes and Agricultural Productivity in Central Africa*, 1986.

Daniels, Morna, compiler. *Burundi*, 1992.

Economist Intelligence Unit. *Country Report: Rwanda, Burundi*, 1999.

Eggers, Ellen K. *Historical Dictionary of Burundi*, 1997.

Jennings, Christian. *Across the Red River: Rwanda, Burundi, and the Heart of Darkness*, 2000.

Lemarchand, René. *Rwanda and Burundi*, 1970.

Longman, Timothy. *Proxy Targets: Civilians in the War in Burundi*, 1998.

Melady, Thomas Patrick. *Burundi: The Tragic Years*, 1974.

Ndarubagiye, Léonce. *Burundi: The Origins of the Hutu-Tutsi Conflict*, 1996.

Webster, John B. *The Political Development of Rwanda and Burundi*, 1966.

Weinstein, Warren. *Political Conflict and Ethnic Strategies: A Case Study of Burundi*, 1976.

Wolbers, Marian F. *Burundi*, 1989.

### *Web Sites*

United Nations Children's Fund (UNICEF). *State of Burundi's Children*, 1995, http://www.HORN/ burundi/UNICEF/burundi

U.S. State Dept. Central Intelligence Agency. *Burundi*, http://www.odci.gov/cia/publications/factbook/ geos/by

—ELEANOR STANFORD

# CAMBODIA

**CULTURE NAME**

Cambodian

**ALTERNATIVE NAMES**

Kampuchean, Khmer

## ORIENTATION

**Identification.** The name "Cambodia" derives from the French *Cambodge*, which comes from the Khmer word *Kâmpuchea*, meaning "born of Kambu." During the socialist regimes of Democratic Kampuchea (DK) (1975–1979) and the People's Republic of Kampuchea (PRK) (1979–1989), the country was known internationally as Kampuchea, but more recent governments have returned to using Cambodia, and the official name in English is now the Kingdom of Cambodia.

Khmer as a noun or adjective can refer to the Cambodian language, people, or culture and thus suggests an ethnic and linguistic identity more than a political entity. From 1970 to 1975, the country was known as the Khmer Republic (KR).

**Location and Geography.** Cambodia lies between Thailand and Vietnam in mainland southeast Asia, with a smaller stretch of the northern border adjoining Laos. The most central region culturally and economically is the lowland flood plain of the Mekong River and Tonle Sap Lake. The Sap River meets the Mekong at Phnom Penh, where the river soon divides again into the Bassac and the Mekong, which flow through southern Vietnam to the South China Sea. Although Cambodia also has a coastline on the Gulf of Thailand, the coast is separated from the central flood plain by mountains; only since the 1950s have railroads and roads provided ready access to the coastal port towns.

The economy is dominated by wet rice agriculture. The iconic image of the countryside is one of rice paddies among which are scattered sugar palms. Until recently, much of the area outside the flood plains was forested.

The ancient capital of the Khmer Empire was at Angkor, close to present-day Siem Reap. In the fifteenth century, the capital was moved to the area of the intersection of the Sap and Mekong rivers, near present-day Phnom Penh, perhaps to enhance trade. The most densely populated areas now are along the rivers in the provinces near Phnom Penh.

**Demography.** According to a 1998 census, the population is 11.42 million. There are no reliable statistics for ethnic populations, although the Khmer population is certainly the largest. A 1993 demographic study estimated that Khmer represented 88.7 percent of the population; Vietnamese, 5.2 percent; Cham, 2.5 percent; Chinese, 1 percent; and others (Thai, Lao, and smaller minority groups in the north and northeast), 2.6 percent.

**Linguistic Affiliation.** The dominant Khmer language belongs to the Austroasiatic language family and is related to Vietnamese, Mon, and a number of other Asian languages. Khmer writing, derived from Indian systems, may have begun as early as the third century C.E.; the first dated inscriptions in Khmer are from the seventh century C.E. While Khmer is closer to Vietnamese than to Thai, a shared literate tradition related to a common religion and centuries of cultural contact has resulted in much vocabulary being shared with Thai. As in Thailand, Laos, and Burma, the language of Theravada Buddhist scriptures, Pali, often is studied by young men during temporary periods as monks and is an important influence on literary Khmer.

A scarcity of written materials resulting from the colonial dominance of French and later periods of political turmoil had left the educated population highly dependent on second languages, and in urban areas there is a great desire to learn English and French. Despite the efforts of France to promote the continued use of French as a second language, it is

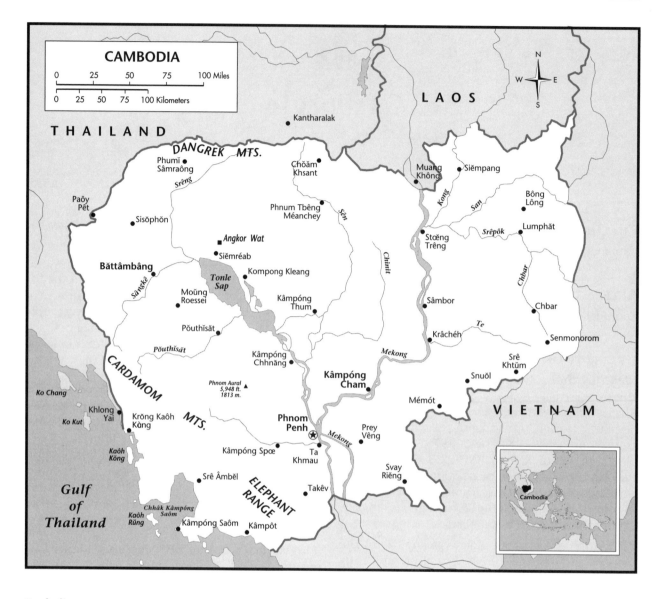

*Cambodia*

probably giving way to English. Vietnamese, Chinese, and Cham, who are often bilingual, freely use their own languages, and Vietnamese and Chinese newspapers are published in Phnom Penh.

***Symbolism.*** The most important cultural symbol is the ancient Khmer temple Angkor Wat, along with the ancient Khmer Empire and its monumental antiquities. Pictures and bas-relief carvings of the four-faced tower of the Bayon at Angkor Thom and of *âpsâras* (celestial dancing girls) are ubiquitous in homes and public buildings. Since independence, every flag except the one used by the United Nations when it administered the country in 1993 has featured the image of Angkor Wat. Classical dance, also an important national symbol, consciously

tries in costume and gesture to recreate Angkorean bas-reliefs.

The institution of kingship, which was reestablished in 1993, is an important national symbol, especially in rural areas, where devotion to the king never died out during the socialist period. It is not clear to what extent the symbolism of kingship can be separated from its current embodiment in Norodom Sihanouk.

In the 1980s, the government promoted the memory of the atrocities of 1975–1979 DK period, also known as the Pol Pot regime, including holidays to commemorate bitterness (20 May) and national liberation (7 January). However, the DK atrocities symbolize Cambodian identity much less for its people than they do for foreigners. Nevertheless, many Cambodians express a sense that their culture has been lost or is in danger, and this cultural vulnerability stands as a kind of national symbol.

National identity sometimes is mobilized around the idea of hostility to Vietnam. This derives in part from the ways in which national identity was defined by resistance groups during the PRK period, when there was a strong Vietnamese military and cultural presence.

## HISTORY AND ETHNIC RELATIONS

**Emergence of the Nation.** The roots of the nation lie in the systematization of wet rice agriculture and the gradual development of a more extensive political organization that climaxed in the Khmer Empire in the period 802–1431. The Khmer Empire was not a nation in the modern sense and varied in size from king to king. However, at different times the empire ruled large parts of what is now Thailand, Laos, and Vietnam. The population of the empire included Siamese and probably other Austroasiatic peoples who gradually assimilated to the Khmer. Khmer culture and language were clearly dominant during that period, and the Khmer population extended well beyond the current boundaries.

The rise of Siam (now Thailand) as an empire and nation and the gradual expansion of Vietnam drastically decreased Khmer territory and led to a period when Cambodia was dominated by those kingdoms. It is generally accepted that if Cambodia had not been colonized by France, it would have been swallowed by its neighbors.

**National Identity.** True national identity was created during the French colonial presence. The French fixed boundaries, systematized government and ecclesiastical bureaucracies, promoted the empire as a national symbol, encouraged an increasingly elaborate ceremonial role for the king, and introduced secular education.

**Ethnic Relations.** There are significant populations of ethnic Khmer in Thailand and Vietnam. The Khmer in Thailand are well integrated into the Thai state, with few significant links to Cambodia. The Khmer in southern Vietnam, called Khmer Kraom, have historically had much stronger ties to Cambodia proper, and several important Cambodian political leaders have been Khmer Kraom. There continues to be migration of Khmer Kraom to Cambodia, including young men who come as Buddhist monks; many Khmer Kraom have a strong sense of identity with the nation. Their role in Cambodia is complex in that while they are glorified as a symbol of lost territory, they are sometimes distrusted as being Vietnamese.

Large numbers of the Cambodian refugees who fled to camps in Thailand during the DK period and the early PRK period resettled in the United States, France, Australia, and New Zealand. The largest ethnic minority population is Vietnamese, whose numbers range between 500,000 and a million. However, those numbers are hotly contested for political reasons. Tension between ethnic Khmer and Vietnamese is strong. Scholars disagree about whether this hostility has a long history or is a recent political construction. State-sponsored killing and forced expulsion of Vietnamese occurred during the KR and the DK periods. Since the 1991 Paris Agreements, there have been two well-publicized massacres of Vietnamese villagers and numerous smaller incidents of violence against Vietnamese, mostly attributable to Khmer Rouge guerrillas. Other new political parties employ strong anti-Vietnamese rhetoric. Vietnamese influence in Cambodia dates at least to the seventeenth century. A significant Vietnamese population in Phnom Penh predated French colonialism; however, the pattern of migration increased when the French brought Vietnamese to Cambodia as administrators, plantation workers, and urban laborers. As rice farmers, Vietnamese have often been in direct economic competition with Khmer. There are also large fishing communities of Vietnamese, and in urban areas, Vietnamese engage in a number of small trades, including construction work, another area where they compete with ethnic Khmer.

The Cham, a predominantly Muslim people, began migrating to Cambodia in the fifteenth century from the South China Sea coast as that area came under Vietnamese political domination. Their population is between 240,000 and 300,000. Many Cham live in riverfront communities and engage in fishing, small business, and raising and slaughtering of livestock (an occupation avoided by Khmer Buddhists for religious reasons). Cham suffering during the DK period was especially severe, when resistance to Khmer Rouge communal discipline led to brutal pogroms. In recent years the Cham have cultivated links to Muslims in Malaysia, Indonesia, and Arabic countries.

A recent estimate of the Chinese population is 100,000, although because of the numbers of Chinese who have historically lived in Cambodia, the numbers of persons with some Chinese blood, and Chinese cultural influence, the impact is much greater. There has traditionally been much more

*A family attempts to net fish in their backyard after a flood. Next to rice, fish is the most important staple in Cambodia.*

intermarriage between Khmer and Chinese than between Khmer and Vietnamese, and ethnic relations are considered much better, although there has been periodic discrimination. There has been a Chinese presence since the time of Angkor, but immigration increased dramatically during the colonial period. Chinese are particularly associated with urban areas; before 1970, there were more Chinese and Vietnamese than Khmer in Phnom Penh.

## URBANISM, ARCHITECTURE, AND THE USE OF SPACE

Phnom Penh, the capital and the only major city, is relatively small, but rapidly increasing in population. At the time of the 1998 census, it was 997,986. A lack of political and economic integration with rural Cambodia and peasant resentment of the urban population probably influenced the decision of the DK government in 1975 to evacuate the entire urban population to the countryside. Since 1979, Phnom Penh has experienced only a gradual rebuilding. Architecturally, the city is a mixture of pre-1975 French colonial, Chinese, and modernist styles alongside the simple socialist styles of the 1980s, garish new buildings, and shanty towns.

The Royal Palace compound and the nearby National Museum lie on Phnom Penh's park-lined central riverfront and form a prominent cultural focal point of the country and city. Norodom Boulevard, lined with embassies, government buildings, and villas, runs between Independence Monument and the Wat Phnom temple. Several key markets, Buddhist temples, and luxury hotels serve as major landmarks. City streets are full of people, evoking a sense of social flux with no clear boundaries. Communication is easy and natural.

Provincial capitals have compounds of government buildings, large central markets in pre-1975 modern buildings, and several Buddhist temples. At the district and subdistrict levels, there are more modest temples, makeshift markets, and simple school buildings. Distinctions between public and private buildings tend to be free-flowing.

## FOOD AND ECONOMY

*Food in Daily Life.* The staples are rice and fish. Traditionally, a home meal is served on a mat on the floor or with the diners seated together on a raised bamboo platform. Meals are eaten in shifts according to status, with adult males and guests eating first and food preparers last. Breakfast typically consists of rice porridge or rice noodles. Lunch and dinner may be a combination of a spiced broth with fish or meat and vegetables, fish, fresh vegetables eaten with a fish-based paste, and stir-fried vegetables with chopped meat. A strong-smelling fermented fish paste called *prâhok* is the quintessential flavoring of Khmer food. Fruit is savored, and its display is considered a mark of abundance. It often is given as a gift. *Teuk tnaot*, a liquid tapped from sugar palms and drunk in various degrees of fermentation, generally is not taken with meals.

The tradition of Khmer cuisine in restaurants is undeveloped, and restaurants typically serve what is regarded as Chinese food. There are no food taboos, although devout Buddhists refrain from alcohol. Monks also cannot eat after noon and are enjoined to eat whatever they are given without making special requests.

***Food Customs at Ceremonial Occasions.*** During festivals, elaborate and painstakingly seasoned dishes are prepared, such as curries, spiced fish sauces, complex stir fries, and a variety of sweets. At a temple festival, each family brings dishes that are ritually presented to the monks. After the monks have eaten, the remaining food is eaten by the lay community.

***Basic Economy.*** The basis of the economy continues to be rice agriculture, and much of the population farms at a subsistence level, linked by a relatively undeveloped market system for rice, fruits, and vegetables, and using the riel for currency. Rice farmers are vulnerable to market fluctuations and to drought and insect infestation. State-owned rubber plantations dating back to the colonial period have remained a peripheral part of the economy.

***Land Tenure and Property.*** Radical attempts to communalize property during the DK period and more modest attempts to encourage collective agriculture under PRK met with strong cultural resistance. Cambodians have a strong sense of personal property shared within the domestic unit. Constitutionally, the PRK recognized only three kinds of economic organization: state, cooperative, and family. Only after 1989, with the conscious shift to a market economy, did corporate enterprises and foreign investment become legal.

***Commercial Activities.*** Cambodian artisans are known for silk and cotton weaving, silver work, silver and gold jewelry, and basketry. Handmade pottery is sold from oxcarts that travel from city to city. Straw mats made by hand at local workshops are available in markets; they also are made for personal use. In rural areas, plows, machetes,

*A young Cambodian monk burning incense. Monkhood offers a means to education for boys in Cambodia.*

looms, fish traps, and winnowing trays are often made for personal use, although imported factory-made products now are used more often.

Tourism is an important part of the economy, but it was hindered by fear of political unrest during most of the 1990s. It increased dramatically in 1999 and 2000.

***Major Industries.*** Industry is undeveloped. State-owned sawmills, soap and cigarette factories, and small workshops for the construction of aluminum products, together with larger state-owned textile and rubber tire factories, have been privatized, and new breweries and cement factories have opened. After 1994, foreign-owned garment factories began to appear, employing mostly female laborers at extremely low wages. The economic role of those factories has expanded rapidly.

***Trade.*** The government lacks effective controls over cross-border trade. In the 1980s, resistance groups near the Thai border financed their activities by trading in gems and timber. Illegal timber exports to Thailand and Vietnam are uncontrolled, and the country is rapidly becoming deforested. Illegal sales of rice to Thailand and Vietnam are also considerable and in 1998 resulted in domestic shortfalls. Besides rice and wood products, Cambodia exports fish products, cement, brewery products, and handicrafts to nearby Asian countries. The garment industry is linked to markets in the United States and the European Union.

## SOCIAL STRATIFICATION

**Classes and Castes.** Ideas about status and the display of wealth have changed dramatically since 1991. Under socialism, the state promoted an ideology of egalitarianism, and personal wealth was not easily detected. Since 1991, extremely wealthy individuals have emerged among high-ranking government officials and well-placed businesspersons in a country where the population remains very poor. Cambodians have traditionally cultivated the practice of exaggerated respect for a small class of civil servants and other "big men," perhaps defined in terms more by influence than by wealth. There is great sensitivity to degrees of relative wealth, especially in decisions about marriage partners. A relative status hierarchy figures conspicuously in personal relations.

**Symbols of Social Stratification.** There is a general assumption that degrees of wealth can and should be publicly known. In the absence of banks, wealth was traditionally worn on the person as jewelry, which still is an important marker of status. Folk categorization distinguishes between the poor family's house of bamboo and thatch, the more economically secure family's traditional wood house on stilts, and the richer family's house of stone or cement. In Phnom Penh, the wealthiest families live in villas as opposed to apartments or wood houses. More contemporary markers involve cars and consumer goods.

## POLITICAL LIFE

**Government.** The 1993 constitution established a constitutional monarchy devoted to the principles of liberal democracy. The national government consists of a 120-member National Assembly, a Council of Ministers, and a Constitutional Council. In 1999, the Assembly voted to create a Senate. At the beginning of the twenty-first century, the government was still in transition from the one-party system of the 1980s to a liberal democracy. Although 1993 United Nations-sponsored elections instituted a multiparty system at the national level, and multiparty elections determined the membership of the National Assembly and the choice of prime ministers in 1993 and 1998, there have not been local multiparty elections. While provincial

governorships and ministerial positions were decided by negotiations between the major parties after the national elections, officials at the district level and below were usually persons who had been in office since the socialist 1980s. Local elections were tentatively scheduled for early 2002.

**Leadership and Political Officials.** The Cambodian People's Party (CPP) is an outgrowth of the People's Revolutionary Party of Kampuchea (PRPK), which through the 1980s served as the single party, providing discipline and leadership for the socialist state. It is not clear to what extent the transition to a multiparty democracy has taken place.

**Social Problems and Control.** There is much distrust of the police and judicial systems, which are believed to be corrupt. Traffic disputes and claims to property often are negotiated outside the legal system. Common criminals are dealt with brutally, and there is a widespread assumption that persons with wealth and political power are effectively outside the law. There have been many cases of violence against opposition politicians and journalists.

**Military Activity.** The military continues to dominate the national budget despite the collapse of the Khmer Rouge insurgency. In 1997, defense and security represented 53.9 percent of government expenditures. Fighting on the streets of Phnom Penh at the time of a 1996 coup is remembered with resentment. Individual soldiers often break the law with impunity. The military is not a particularly cohesive social force and has not threatened to seize power.

## SOCIAL WELFARE AND CHANGE PROGRAMS

While a basic government framework to address the needs of widows, orphans, veterans, and those handicapped by war has been in place since the PRK period, those programs have been plagued by a lack of funds. International organizations (IOs) and nongovernmental organizations (NGOs) played an important role in the emergency reconstruction of the country in 1979–1982, providing food and helping to rebuild the agricultural infrastructure. The issue of aid was complicated in the 1980s by an international embargo. Some aid organizations chose to provide relief to Cambodians on the Thai border; other organizations were restricted from working in the provinces. A small number of international NGOs continued to offer assistance in health care, rehabilitation for mine victims, food relief, and agricultural training and assistance. After the beginnings of a negotiated political settle-

*A Cambodian boy pulls a forty-four gallon drum full of water on his cart, a trip he makes eight to ten times a day.*

ment at the end of the 1980s, rapidly increasing numbers of NGOs and IOs have played a role in the country.

## NONGOVERNMENTAL ORGANIZATIONS AND OTHER ASSOCIATIONS

Local NGOs usually are funded by IOs, donor countries, or international NGOs. In 1999, there were over two hundred local NGOs, all but two formed since 1992. Given a traditional absence of associations outside the state and religious institutions, NGOs represent a significant development. Some have focused on rural development, welfare, education, and women's issues. Perhaps the NGOs with the greatest immediate impact have been local human rights organizations, which have established extensive grassroots networks to document human rights abuses.

## GENDER ROLES AND STATUSES

***Division of Labor by Gender.*** In most spheres, there is some flexibility in gender roles. Most tasks performed by men occasionally are performed by women, and vice versa. Traditionally among villagers, men fished, plowed, threshed rice, made and repaired tools, and cared for cattle. Women trans-

planted seedlings; did washing, mending, and housecleaning; performed most of the child care; and did the everyday shopping. Women are traditionally responsible for a family's money and engage in small-scale marketing.

In the DK period, communal work further broke down gender barriers, and in the post-DK period, when conscription created a shortage of men in civilian life, women were forced to do more hard physical labor. This gender imbalance meant that a small number of women played important roles in civil service and politics. The numbers of women in civil service and politics decreased somewhat in the 1990s, but new foreign-owned textile factories employ almost exclusively women laborers. Only men can enter the monkhood. While women assume ascetic lifestyles and take up residence in temples, they are considered part of the lay population.

***The Relative Status of Women and Men.*** Bilateral kinship and a strong tendency toward matrilocality leave women in a position of relative strength. The fact that women control family finances may not be regarded as a sign of superiority but represents real power in practical terms. However, women have much less access than men to the highest positions of political and economic power.

Traditional codes of behavior for women are more elaborate and strict than those for men. Their role is often marked symbolically as inferior. While traditional art and contemporary media images of women show them as active agents, they often are depicted as physically vulnerable to men. Domestic violence against women at the village level is widespread, and those women have little legal recourse.

## Marriage, Family, and Kinship

**Marriage.** Marriage traditionally is arranged by the parents of the bride and groom or by someone acting as their representative. Ideally, the groom originates the courtship process by asking his parents to approach the parents of a woman to whom he is attracted. Neither the groom nor the bride is forced to take a marriage partner, although parents may have considerable influence in choosing a partner. Considerations of the benefits to the two families often figure more prominently in the choice of a marriage partner than does romantic love. It is not unusual for decisions about marriage to be made before a couple has had much contact. Specialists in reading horoscopes typically are consulted about the appropriateness of a wedding, although their advice is not always followed. The groom pays bride-wealth to the family of the bride; this money sometimes is used to buy jewelry or clothing for the bride or defray the cost of the wedding.

Although polygyny was legal before 1989, true polygyny, sanctioned by ceremony and both wives living in the same house, was rarely practiced outside of royalty in modern times. However, a mistress is referred to as a second wife, and even though bigamy was prohibited by the 1993 constitution, the practice of keeping a second or third wife does not carry a social stigma. There is strong social pressure to marry and for those who marry to have children. Divorce is a socially recognized option, although there is social pressure against it and some reluctance to grant it.

**Domestic Unit.** The domestic unit is classically a nuclear family consisting of parents and children; however, there is much flexibility in allowing other arrangements. Residence after marriage is ideally neolocal but often, for practical reasons, with the parents of one of the spouses. The preference is for matrilocality, although this is not a rigid rule. Aged parents often live with their adult children. Major family decisions are shared by the husband and wife.

**Inheritance.** An inheritance is ideally divided equally among children without regard to gender or age order, although the child who supported the parents in their old age may be favored and a child no longer living in the village may receive less property.

**Kin Groups.** Kin groups larger than the family have no socially prescribed role, although they can be a source of emotional bonds and personal alliance.

## Socialization

**Infant Care.** Infant care is characterized by almost constant attention to the child, who is rarely left alone. The child is carefully observed to determine the character it is believed to already possess; it is considered from birth an active agent and its wishes, such as who should hold it, are observed and respected.

**Child Rearing and Education.** Children are socialized early to respect the authority of parents and older siblings. There is a strong cultural value of ''study,'' but little sense of study as oriented toward a specific goal or profession. Schools in Cambodia emphasize the copying of texts and memorization. Since the DK period, education has been plagued by the poor condition of buildings, lack of books and trained teachers, and the inability of the government to pay teachers. Boys sometimes enter the monkhood as an alternative to state education.

**Higher Education.** Tertiary education has only gradually been re-instituted since 1979 and is still on unsteady foundations. Over the course of the 1980s, different universities were reopened: The Faculty of Medicine, Pharmacy, and Dentistry in 1979, teacher training schools in 1980, a technical school in 1981, an Institute of Economics in 1984, and the Agricultural Institute in 1985. The University of Phnom Penh was not reopened until 1988. Tertiary education has been very dependent on foreign aid, foreign faculty, and overseas training of students.

## Etiquette

Khmer has a complex system of pronouns and terms of address that distinguishes between people of formal rank, people with whom the speaker is in everyday interaction (further distinguished by relative age), and those with whom one assumes a marked informality, including people of clear inferior status and those with whom the speaker shares a long-standing familiar equality. Those addressing monks or royalty are expected to use even more complex linguistic systems, which, in addition to special pronouns and terms of address, include spe-

*A women registers to vote in Phnom Penh. Despite this right, women wield little political power.*

cial vocabulary for sleeping, eating, walking, and, in the case of royalty, for body parts. Relative rank is also distinguished by the order by which traditional greetings, palms together raised in supplication, are made, the degree of the hands' elevation, and the consideration of whether this greeting or a Western handshake is used. A major part of etiquette involves knowing these systems and how to negotiate their ambiguities; the systems were partially abandoned during the socialist periods, but since 1991 have been revived with new emphasis.

There is a much stronger taboo against public touching between men and women than in Western countries, but same-sex touching is more accepted than, for example, in the United States. Conventional wisdom holds that the head is the highest part of the body and the feet the lowest, and it is rude to touch another adult's head, just as it is rude to point one's foot at another person. However, a certain kind of intimacy among equals is characterized by the breaking of the norm, with friendly cuffs to the other person's head.

## RELIGION

***Religious Beliefs.*** Theravada Buddhism spread in the later years of the Khmer Empire and is tradition-

ally considered the religion of ethnic Khmer. Animist practices and what are called Brahmanistic practices are also part of the culture and are deeply intermingled with the everyday practice of Buddhism. They are not considered separate religions but part of the spectrum of choices for dealing with moral, physical, and spiritual needs. Buddhism is a national tradition, with a bureaucracy and a written tradition. Brahmanist and spirit practices are more localized and are passed on from person to person rather than as a formal institution.

All religious traditions were weakened by the banning of religious observances by the DK and by the religious policies of PRK, which restricted religion and emphasized a Buddhism consistent with socialist modernity. Since restrictions were lifted in 1989, religion has enjoyed a revival. Christian converts returned from refugee camps and foreign countries, and Christianity has established a strong foothold among ethnic Khmers. A number of other religious movements draw on the appeal of powerful traditional cultural icons and funding by overseas Khmer.

***Religious Practitioners.*** Theravada Buddhist monks can be seen in saffron robes walking in procession in the early mornings, when they go from door to door asking for food. A lay specialist, the

*These two Buddha factory workers are representative of the female-dominated industrial work force in Cambodia.*

achar, also plays an important role as the person who leads public chanting and an expert in the formulas for different rituals.

Outside the formal sphere of Buddhism there are other practitioners. The *krou* (or *krou khmaer*) specializes in traditional medicine and magic, including the making of amulets, and negotiating with certain kinds of spirits; the *thmuap* is a kind of *krou* specializing in black magic. The *roup* or *roup arâkk* is a spirit medium through whom special knowledge can be obtained.

***Rituals and Holy Places.*** The Buddhist temple complex, or *vott*, is central to community life, as is the calendar of Buddhist holidays, which is linked to the seasons and the agricultural cycle. Monks must reside in a single temple for the length of the rainy season, and ceremonies mark the beginning and end of the retreat. The period around the end of the rainy season, after rice has been transplanted but before the harvest takes place, includes two major holidays: Pchum Ben (a two-week period of rituals in honor of the spirits of the dead) and Kâthin (a day for processions and the ceremonial presentation of monks' robes). The day of the Buddha's birth and enlightenment (May) and the day of the Buddha's last sermon (February) are also important holidays.

The beginning of the Buddhist lunar calendar occurs in April and has both religious and secular aspects.

***Death and the Afterlife.*** Cambodian Buddhists believe in reincarnation, although this may include temporary periods in realms resembling heaven or hell. The dead usually are cremated after an elaborate procession. Ceremonies in memory of the dead are held on the seventh and hundredth days after death.

## MEDICINE AND HEALTH CARE

Western and Chinese medicine and health care coexist with traditional Cambodian practices that partly derive from Ayurvedic tradition, under the guidance of *krou khmaer*. Western medicine enjoys great prestige, but there is a lack of professionals. Widespread use of imported western drugs, including intravenous serums and other injections, involves the role of semi-skilled professionals. Even when the medicine is "western," its practice is deeply shaped by Khmer folk categorizations of the nature of illness and the properties of medicine.

## SECULAR CELEBRATIONS

In Phnom Penh the most popular secular holiday is the Water Festival, 21–23 November, with its colorful longboat races and the nighttime display of illuminated boats. Spirit practices also associated with the boat races mean that the holiday is not completely secular.

Independence Day (9 November) and the King's Birthday (31 October) have in recent years involved large government-sponsored celebrations. However these holidays, and other smaller ones, like Constitution Day, the Day of the Royal Plowing Ceremony, and the Victory Day over Genocidal Crime, do not have the widespread cultural resonance of more religious celebrations such as New Year's, Pchum Ben, and Kathin.

## THE ARTS AND HUMANITIES

***Support for the Arts.*** Since 1979, there has been a governmental effort to restore aspects of traditional culture destroyed during the DK period. Most state and international funding has gone toward the restoration of Angkorean antiquities, but there also has been support for classical dance and for recording traditional music and setting up workshops for making traditional instruments. In recent years, there has been NGO support for preserving and developing marketing strategies for traditional weavers. Some musicians, singers, and theater groups earn money by performing at village festivals and weddings. The most successful perform on radio and television and market their work on cassette tapes. Overseas Cambodian musical groups and video producers also sell their work in Cambodia.

**Literature.** There is a long tradition of the use of writing, with important religious texts, royal chronicles, and epic poetry, but modern literature is undeveloped. Oral traditions are strong: domestic storytelling and a genre of narrative singing to a banjolike instrument play important cultural roles.

Virtually no literature was produced during the DK period, and many writers were killed or fled. Literature in the 1980s had a socialist orientation. Since 1991, there has been greater freedom to publish pre-1975 literature but little money to publish new books. Small newspapers have flourished, and some satirical writing has appeared. Pre-1975 authors living overseas and younger writers have published Khmer books in their countries of resettlement.

**Graphic Arts.** While much work in graphic arts is produced, it often is seen as mere artisanship and has received little attention. Some art is produced for tourists and the decoration of homes and offices. Since the early 1990s, the most important project for painters has been the restoration of murals in Buddhist temples. Graphic art is rarely seen as the individual expression of the artist.

**Performance Arts.** Classical dance and music, originally associated with the court, enjoy great prestige, although live performances by the national companies are not frequent. Less professional musicians, singers, and theater artists keep alive local traditions. Virtually every village has musicians who play at weddings. A pop tradition has revived since the end of socialism.

While filmmaking was revived in the 1980s, the output remains small and the budgets are low.

Television is dominated by films and soap operas from Thailand and Hong Kong, dubbed into Khmer.

## BIBLIOGRAPHY

Center for Advanced Study. *Interdisciplinary Research on Ethnic Groups in Cambodia: Executive Summaries,* 1996.

Chandler, David. *A History of Cambodia, 22d ed.,* 1996.

Charny, Joel R. *NGOs and the Rehabilitation of Cambodia,* 1992.

Curtis, Grant. *Cambodia: A Country Profile,* 1989.

Desbarats, Jacqueline. *Prolific Survivors: Population Change in Cambodia, 1975–1993,* 1995.

Ebihara, May. *Svay, a Khmer Village in Cambodia,* 1971.

———, Carol Mortland, and Judy Ledgerwood, eds. *Cambodian Culture Since 1975: Homeland and Exile,* 1994.

Edwards, Penny. *Cambodge: The Cultivation of a Nation, 1860–1945,* 1999.

Heder, Steve, and Judy Ledgerwood, eds. *Propaganda, Politics, and Violence in Cambodia: Democratic Transition under United Nations Peace-Keeping,* 1996.

Kiernan, Ben. *The Pol Pot Regime: Race, Power, and Genocide in Cambodia under the Khmer Rouge, 1975–79,* 1996.

Ledgerwood, Judy. *Analysis of the Situation of Women in Cambodia: Research on Women in Khmer Society,* 1992.

Mabbett, Ian, and David Chandler. *The Khmers,* 1995.

Marston, John. *Cambodia 1991–94: Hierarchy, Neutrality, and the Etiquettes of Discourse,* 1997.

Martel, Gabrielle. *Lovea: Village des Environs d'Angkor,* 1975.

Smith-Hefner, Nancy J. *Khmer-American,* 1999.

Steinberg, David J., et al. *Cambodia: Its People, Its Society, Its Culture,* 1959.

Zimmerman, Cathy. *Plates in a Basket Will Rattle: Domestic Violence in Cambodia,* 1994.

—JOHN MARSTON

# CAMEROON

## CULTURE NAME

Cameroonian

## ORIENTATION

**Identification.** The name of the country derives from the term used for the Wouri River by Portuguese explorers. Reaching the Cameroon coast near the modern port city of Douala around 1472, those explorers named the river *Rio dos Camaroes* ("River of Prawns") after the variety of crayfish they found there. This name later was applied to the coastal area between Mount Cameroon and Rio Muni.

Cameroon has distinct regional cultural, religious, and political traditions as well as ethnic variety. The division of the country into British- and French-ruled League of Nations mandates after World War I created Anglophone and Francophone regions. The English-speaking region consists of the Southwest and Northwest provinces, where Pidgin English (Wes Cos) is the lingua franca and English is taught in school. The educational system and legal practices derive from those of England. The French-speaking region consists of the remaining eight provinces, where French is the lingua franca, the French school system is used, and the legal system is based on the statutory law of continental Europe. This region is dominant in numbers and power. Tension between the two regions increased after the introduction of a multiparty political system in the 1990s.

The English-speaking region is divided into two cultural regions. The Grassfields peoples of the Northwest Province consist of nearly one hundred chiefdoms each ruled by a divine king *(fon)*. Most of these chiefdoms have patrilineal or dual descent kinship systems, although some groups, such as the Kom, are matrilineal. Polygyny and fertility are important cultural values, although this varies by wealth and education. The social organization and culture of the Grassfielders are closely related to those of the French-speaking Bamiléké peoples of

the Western province. Like the Bamiléké, Grassfielders often are in opposition to the central government.

The peoples of the Southwest province had less hierarchical systems of governance and social organization. The British appointed warrant chiefs to aid their colonial rule, and in many instances the population rallied behind those chiefs in the postcolonial period. The peoples of the Southwest province include the Bakweri, who live along the slopes of Mount Cameroon. The Bakweri practice rites of healing and initiation in associations of spirit mediums that distinguish between male and female roles and between village and bush.

In the French-speaking area, the largely Muslim north is culturally distinct from the largely Christian and animist south. The northern area includes three provinces: Adamoua, North, and Extreme North. Since the jihad led by an Islamic cleric in 1804, the northern region has been culturally dominated by the Fulani. Urban Fulani are renowned as clerics in the Sunni branch of Islam. Most Fulani are cattle herders. An important subgroup are the Bororo'en, noted for the size of their cattle herds. With their Hausa colleagues, they engage in long-distance trade involving cattle. Other northern ethnic groups include the Mandara, Kokoto, and Arab Choa. Major crops include cotton and millet.

Most of the southern peoples are Christian or engage in traditional, animist religious practices. The Center, South, and East provinces are characterized by dense tropical rain forest. The Center and South are culturally dominated by the Beti peoples, which include the Ewondo, Eton, and Bulu, and are linguistically and culturally related to the Fang of Gabon. They are patrilineal, grow root crops and peanuts for their own consumption, and grow cocoa as a cash crop. The Ewondo were early converts to Catholicism. The current president is Bulu, and many prominent authors are Beti. Peoples in the East include the Maka and Gbaya, both with relatively egalitarian forms of social organization in

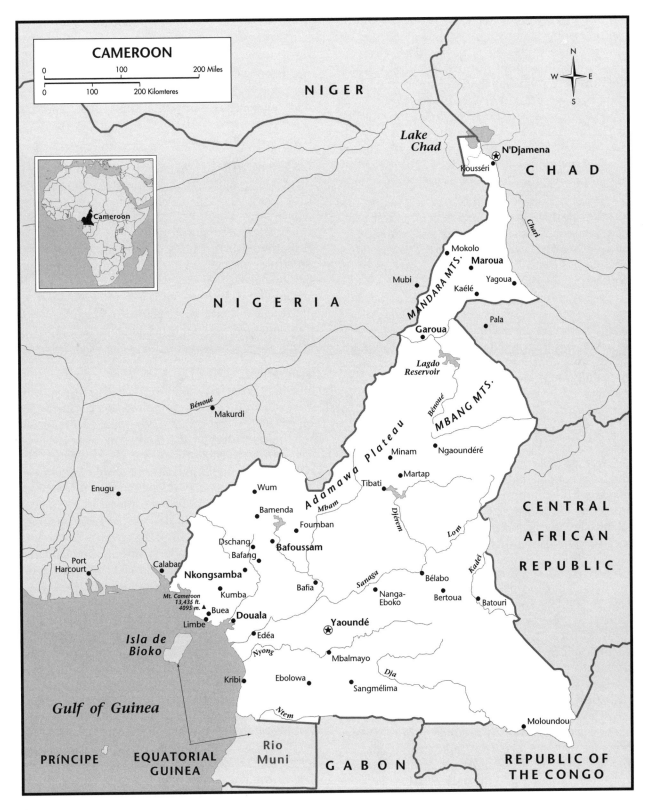

Cameroon

which reciprocity is a key value. Forestry and tobacco farming are important sources of income. The East province is also home to the Baka, a tropical forest forager (pygmy) group of about thirty thousand to forty thousand living in small camps that exchange forest products with nearby farmers. The Littoral province is in the coastal rain forest region in the southwest. It includes the largest city, the port of Douala, and the industrial, hydroelectric, and bauxite mining area near Edea. The major ethnic groups are the Duala and Bassa.

The southern part of the French-speaking area includes the high plateau region of the West province, which includes the Bamiléké and Bamoun peoples. Both are culturally similar to the Grassfielders. The Bamiléké constitute roughly 25 percent of the population. In rich volcanic soils they grow food crops and coffee. The population is dense, and the Bamiléké served as a labor reserve population in the twentieth century, resulting in large, entrepreneurial urban émigré population. The large urban population is prominent in commerce and higher education. Since the conversion of Sultan Njoya to Islam early in the twentieth century, the Bamoun have been a largely Muslim people. Sultan Njoya, a man of unusual intellect, developed an original alphabet and wrote a history of his people and dynasty.

A sense of a common national culture has been created through shared history, schooling, national holidays and symbols, and enthusiasm for soccer. However, ethnic distinctiveness remains, and ethnic identity became an increasingly important source of social capital during the 1990s.

**Location and Geography.** Cameroon is situated by the Gulf of Guinea on the west coast of Africa. Its area is 179,527 square miles (465,000 square kilometers). Nigeria lies to the west, Chad and the Central African Republic to the east, and the People's Republic of Congo, Equatorial Guinea, and Gabon to the south. The climate is hot and humid in the forested south and west, cooler in the highland Grassfields region of the West and Northwest provinces, and hotter and drier in the savanna and sahel of the north. The capital, Yaoundé, is in the Center province. It has experienced rapid growth and increasing strife between immigrant groups (particularly the Bamiléké) and the native Beti.

**Demography.** The population in 1987 was 10,498,655; it was estimated to be nearly 14 million in 1997. In 1987, 46 percent of the population was under fifteen years old. The population is growing at an average annual rate of almost 3 percent, with declining mortality and high fertility.

Thirty-eight percent of the population lives in urban centers.

There are no reliable population figures for the major cultural groups. The Bamiléké account for approximately 25 percent of the total population, and northerners, including the Fulani, approximately 20 percent. These two groups also have the highest fertility rates.

**Linguistic Affiliation.** French and English are the official languages. The approximately two hundred fifty local languages include Ewondo and Bulu, Duala, the Bamiléké languages, and Fulfulde. Among the less educated, the Wes Cos dialect of Pidgin English functions as a lingua franca in the English-speaking area and in many neighborhoods in Douala. Both French and English are taught in school, but only those with a secondary education are fluent in both. Most people speak at least one local language and one official language, and many people are multilingual.

**Symbolism.** The flag has three equal vertical stripes of green, red, and yellow, with a five-pointed gold star in the center of the red stripe. The stripes represent the three major geographic areas: green for the rain forest, red for the laterite soils of the savanna, and yellow for the sands of the sahel. The national anthem begins with the words *O Cameroun, berceau de nos ancetres* ("Oh, Cameroon, cradle of our ancestors"), reflecting the importance of ancestors and kinship and the desire to forge an imagined community with a common ancestry. The feeling of national unity is strongest among schoolchildren and has been stressed since the end of the cold war.

## HISTORY AND ETHNIC RELATIONS

**Emergence of the Nation.** Before colonization, Cameroon was a territory of diverse climatic zones populated by a variety of peoples and polities. The Muslim states in the north traded with trans-Saharan merchants and Arabic peoples. The coastal peoples in the south traded with Portuguese and Dutch seafarers beginning in the late fifteenth century. In 1884, Cameroon became a German protectorate (Kamerun). The Germans were defeated by British and French forces in 1916, and the territory was divided between those nations in 1916. In 1922, the French and British zones became League of Nations mandates, with the French controlling over 80 percent of the national territory. Those zones were transformed into United Nations Trusteeships in 1946. The frontier between the French and British zones cut through the territories of several ethnic groups, particularly the Bamiléké and Grassfields peoples of the western highlands. This later served as an impetus for the reunification of those zones at the time of independence. French Cameroon (Cameroun) became independent in 1960, and after a plebiscite in 1961, British Cameroon gained independence. The southern part of the British territory joined the Federal Republic of Cameroon, while the northern part, ethnically united with the Hausa-city states, joined Nigeria. In 1965, Cameroon came under single-party rule. It was renamed the United Republic of Cameroon in1972 and the Republic of Cameroon in 1984.

**National Identity.** A national culture was first formed by external powers through colonization. Even regional cultural differences emerged originally during the periods of mandate and trusteeship. A sentiment of common national identity is particularly strong in major institutions of socialization such as schools and during international soccer matches, visits by foreign dignitaries, and times of international dispute. Ahmadou Ahidjo, a Muslim from the northern city of Guider, who was president from independence until 1982, attempted to foster national integration by posting civil servants to areas outside their ethnic homelands. His successor, Paul Biya, is a Catholic of the Bulu (Beti) people of the South province. In 1983 and 1984, alleged coup attempts by those loyal to Ahidjo led to martial law and ethnic tensions between groups in the northern and southern regions. Since the legalization of multiparty politics in 1992, political parties have been increasingly associated with specific ethnic groups or regions.

**Ethnic Relations.** In addition to regional and ethnic distinctions, coalitions and tensions exist on a local level. People from the northern areas are collectively referred to as "northerners" by their southern compatriots and share some cultural attributes related to their Islamic religion. Anglophone and Francophone peoples of the Grassfields (Grassfielders, Bamiléké, and Bamoun) share common attributes and have practiced their own interchiefdom diplomacy for several centuries. In February 1992, violence between the Arab Choa and Kokoto ethnic groups during voter registration led to the death of more than one hundred people. Violence reemerged two years later, leading over one thousand people to seek refuge in Chad. In the Grassfields of the Northwest and Western provinces, interdependence and conflict between farmers and grazers coincide with ethnicity. The ethnicization of party politics and the increasing importance of ethnicity in relation to

economic claims have led to conflicts between "autochthonous" (indigenous) and migrant populations.

## URBANISM, ARCHITECTURE, AND THE USE OF SPACE

The major cities include Douala (the shipping and industrial center), Yaoundé (the capital), Nkongsamba (the end point of the railroad through the southern plantations of the colonial period), Maroua and Garoua, Bafoussam and Bamenda (the provincial capitals of the West and Northwest provinces), Kumba, and Limbe. Yaoundé has several monuments to national unity.

Most villages and small towns in rural areas have a marketplace in a central location that may house a weekly, biweekly, or daily market, depending on their size. Most markets have separate areas for women's products (produce and palm oil), and men's products (livestock and bush meat). Official buildings are often located near these markets or along the central axis leading through smaller towns.

Architecture varies by region. In the rain forest and the Grassfields, *poto-poto* (earthen plaster on a wooden frame) and mud brick rectangular buildings roofed in palm thatch or corrugated iron are common. Traditional Grassfields architecture was constructed of "bamboo" (the spines of raffia palm fronds); square or rectangular buildings with sliding doors were topped by conical thatched roofs. The doorposts of royalty had elaborate carvings. Traditional architecture in the north includes round mud buildings crowned in thatch. Walled compounds usually include a separate granary. Throughout the nation, structures built of concrete bricks, corrugated iron roofs, and iron grillwork have replaced other forms of housing.

Much of daily life occurs in public areas such as the courtyards of polygynous compounds. Privacy is often suspect, especially among peoples with a strong belief in malevolent and occult powers.

## FOOD AND ECONOMY

**Food in Daily Life.** The sharing of cooked food is one of the major ways to cement social relationships and express the high value placed on human company. Sharing food and drink demonstrates hospitality and trust. Social support networks among kin and friends, particularly between country folk and their urban relatives, are held together symbolically with gifts of cooked and uncooked

*An initiation ritual of a Bwiti cult in Cameroon. The ritual involves the use of the psychotropic drug iboga, and represents a journey to the land of the dead.*

food. Sacks of beans, maize, or peanuts "from home" can be seen on the roofs of bush taxis traveling between the countryside and urban centers.

Meals consist of a cooked cereal or root staple accompanied by a sauce or stew. In the southern areas, the major staples are root crops such as cassava and cocoyams, and plantains; in the moist savanna and Grassfields, maize and plantains; and in the arid north, sorghum and millet. Rice and pasta have become popular. Staples may be boiled, pounded, or fried; most commonly they are made into a thick porridge shaped into oblong balls. Sauces usually have a base of palm oil and ground peanuts. Vegetables such as greens, okra, and squashes are common. Hot peppers, onions, ginger, and tomatoes are popular condiments. Dried or fresh fish or meat may be included in the sauce. Uncooked fruits such as bananas, mangoes, papayas, oranges, and avocados are popular snacks and desserts; they are not considered part of meals.

In many regions, men and guests eat before women and children. Hand washing is part of the etiquette of meals. Whether from a separate dish or a common pot, a small ball of porridge is formed by three fingers of the right hand and then dipped in sauce. Westernization has led families to eat to-gether around a common table, using separate place settings and cutlery.

Food taboos vary by ethnic group. The Bassa of the Littoral province serve a gourmet dish of viper steaks in black sauce, but only the oldest males among the Ewondo (Beti) of the Center province may eat viper. Totems of specific clans, healers, or royal dynasties are taboo to certain members of some ethnic groups.

***Food Customs at Ceremonial Occasions.*** At the visit of an honored guest, a wedding, or a funeral, a chicken, goat, sheep, or steer is served to guests. Special drinks, such as palm wine and millet beer as well as bottled carbonated drinks, beer, and wine are served at these occasions. Among the Bamiléké, as part of coronation festivities, the newly installed paramount chief ceremoniously serves each subject a handful of beans mixed with palm oil to symbolize the chief's ability to ensure food and fertility in his realm.

***Basic Economy.*** The country is basically self-sufficient in food, although the distribution of food is variable. Seasonal famines occur in the arid north. Per capita gross national product (GNP) was $610 in 1996. From 1990 to 1996, the GNP declined and it has shown slight increases since that time. Cameroon has a trade surplus but is burdened by debt. Agriculture, including the production of food and cash crops such as coffee, cocoa, and cotton, employs almost two-thirds of the labor force. Many people produce mainly for themselves, selling the "surplus" at local markets.

**Land Tenure and Property.** Among the Fulani, land is inherited patrilineally. In the Grassfields, land is held by fons, with use rights devolving to specific patrilineages and matrilineages. Throughout the country, the privatization of land tenure is increasing. Access to private land titles depends on money, understanding of the bureaucracy, and connections. Women, the main producers of food crops, are often at a disadvantage when land is privatized.

**Commercial Activities.** In the towns, there are grocery and dry goods stores. Restaurants and bars, taxis, and domestic labor involve an increasing proportion of the labor force.

**Major Industries.** Major industries include mining and aluminum processing, forestry, and the manufacture of beverages. Petroleum is a significant source of national income.

**Trade.** Wood, coffee, cocoa, cotton, and palm oil are the principal exports. The trading partners are France, Nigeria, the United States, and Germany. Principle imports include consumption goods; semifinished goods; minerals; industrial and transportation equipment; and food, beverages, and tobacco.

**Division of Labor.** The division of labor is determined largely by formal education (for civil servants) and gender. There is some specialization by ethnic group such as herding by Fulani, the butchering and meat trade by Hausa, and transportation by Bamiléké.

## SOCIAL STRATIFICATION

**Classes and Castes.** There is a high degree of social inequality. Among the Fulani, Grassfielders, Bamiléké, and Bamoun the traditional social organization included hierarchical relations between members of groups with different status (royalty, nobility, commoners, and slaves). Other ethnic groups have a more egalitarian social organization in which age and gender are the major factors in social stratification. New forms of social inequality based on access to political power and level of formal education coexist with indigenous forms of stratification. Although a cosmopolitan lifestyle has developed among the wealthy and the intelligentsia, markers of cultural distinctiveness and obligation to kin and ethnic compatriots remain. Regional differences in wealth also exist: the far northern and eastern areas have less access to wealth and infrastructure.

**Symbols of Social Stratification.** Housing styles differ by class, in both urban and rural areas. The wealthiest people have concrete houses painted in bright colors and surrounded by high walls. Those houses have flower gardens and interior furnishings such as upholstered furniture and armoires. The poorest people live in mud houses with thatched or corrugated iron roofs, sparsely furnished with beds and stools made of local materials. Styles of dress also vary by class; the wealthiest can afford Italian leather shoes to accompany the latest European and African wardrobes, while poorer people wear cloth wrappers and secondhand European-style clothing. The wealthiest tend to speak French or English even at home, while the poorest speak local languages and Pidgin English.

## POLITICAL LIFE

**Government.** Since the 1992 amendment of the constitution, Cameroon has been a multiparty state. Executive power is held by the president, who serves for seven years and, since 1992, for a maximum of two terms.

**Leadership and Political Officials.** The twenty-seven-year period of single party rule left a legacy of an authoritarian political culture. At the national level, government leadership resides in the president and his cabinet. On the local level, the *prefet* (district officer) and *sous-prefet* are the most powerful administrative officials. Positions in government are determined through a combination of know-how, party loyalty, and ethnic and regional background. In many areas, local and national forms of leadership coexist. For example, the chiefdoms of the Northwest and West provinces form states within a state, with fons sharing power with government officials. Some chiefs served as rallying points for opposition groups during the political crises of the 1990s.

**Social Problems and Control.** There are several police forces, including internal security police, gendarmes, and military police. The legal system combines the case law system of the British with the statutory law system of the French. Theft is a com-

*Many Cameroonians have a highly stratified social structure. The intricately beaded calabashes (gourds) and carvings indicate this tribal king's royal status.*

mon crime, and the U.S. State Department issues regular warnings about bandits in the tourist regions of the northern provinces. Local chiefs serve as justices of the peace and receive a small salary. Officially, criminal law is no longer in their jurisdiction, although they often settle disputes regarding theft, trespass, and personal injury or assault via witchcraft.

Customary law combined forms of dispute resolution ranging from rituals of reconciliation to banning and capital punishment. A combination of discussion and the use of oracles still is used in most cultures. Since the colonial era, the jurisdiction of local chiefs and councils has eroded. Informal social control mechanisms include gossip, ostracism, and fear of occult, ancestral, or divine retribution for wrongdoings.

**Military Activity.** Cameroon has a bilateral defense agreement with France. In the 1980s and

*A woman carrying water back to her home to help care for and feed her family.*

1990s, the military was involved in border disputes with Nigeria regarding the Bakassi peninsula.

## SOCIAL WELFARE AND CHANGE PROGRAMS

The government sponsors many social welfare programs, largely through the community development and extension services of the Ministry of Agriculture. Nongovernmental organizations (NGOs) have become increasingly involved in social welfare and the development of civil society. Their importance has increased as government functions have been cut back during a period of economic and political crisis.

## NONGOVERNMENTAL ORGANIZATIONS AND OTHER ASSOCIATIONS

Most NGOs fall into one of two types: those with a focus on social problems such as AIDS awareness, condom distribution, and street children; and ethnic development associations that link urban migrants with their home villages, build hospitals, schools, and bridges ''back home,'' and organize urban ethnic festivals. Ethnic associations often are organized as rotating credit associations, building on a long tradition of mutual aid in both rural and urban areas. They reflect the increasing importance of ethnicity in national and local politics.

## GENDER ROLES AND STATUSES

***Division of Labor by Gender.*** In most areas, women are responsible for feeding their families. They grow staple food crops, while men clear the land and provide meat, oil, and salt. Men grow the cash crops. Among the pastoral populations, men herd the livestock and women process dairy products.

***The Relative Status of Women and Men.*** In general, men have higher social status than women. They have more rights with regard to marriage, divorce, and land tenure within most local systems of social organization and more access to government bureaucracy and the courts. However, women may have informal power within households, enforced through their control of subsistence activities and their role as conduits to female ancestors. Many women are prominent in higher education and government ministries.

## MARRIAGE, FAMILY, AND KINSHIP

***Marriage.*** Among many ethnic groups, first marriages historically were arranged with varying degrees of veto power by the potential bride and groom, but individual choice stressing companionship is becoming more common. Most southern groups prefer exogamous marriage, while the Fulani tend to be endogamous. Polygyny is a goal within many groups but is not always financially attainable. Some women prefer small-scale polygyny for the company and mutual aid a co-wife might provide.

***Domestic Unit.*** Domestic organization varies widely throughout Cameroon. Rural polygynous compounds are composed of a male head of a household surrounded by his wives and their children. Wives and children usually sleep in separate dwellings within the compound. In both urban and rural areas, child-rearing by a close relative (a kind of foster arrangement) is common.

***Inheritance.*** The organization of kinship varies widely, as do local rules of inheritance. The inheritance of land is often separated from that of movable property. The inheritance of wives may serve as a form of old-age insurance for women without grown children, since marriage provides access to land. Among many groups, traditional titles and honors may be inherited.

**Kin Groups.** Most northern groups, such as the Fulani, are patrilineal. The kinship organization of most Grassfielders, Bamiléké, and Bamoun is variously described as patrilineal or dual descent. The Kom of the Grassfields are a notable matrilineal exception. Most forest peoples are patrilineal.

## SOCIALIZATION

**Infant Care.** Child bearing is highly valued, and infants are given a great deal of daily and ritual attention. Generally, infants are kept close to the mother and breast fed on demand. Once they can hold the head upright, they are carried by siblings. Infants generally sleep with their mothers. The arrival of a baby is the occasion for visits during which the newborn is cuddled, bounced, bathed, and spoken to.

**Child Rearing and Education.** Beliefs and practices concerning child rearing vary by ethnic group. Commonalities include the importance of learning by example and through play and imitation of the tasks of adults. Children are taught to observe astutely but remain reserved and prudent in what they report. Remembering one's ancestors, elders, and origins is an increasing concern of parents whose children spend long hours in public schools and often leave their homelands to find work in urban centers and on industrial plantations.

Since independence, the country has achieved a high level of school attendance. Primary enrollment in 1994 included 88 percent of children. Secondary education is much less common (27 percent), with boys attending secondary school more frequently than girls. Instruction is in French and English, although the second national language usually is introduced only in secondary school. Primary education lasts for six years in Francophone areas and seven years in Anglophone areas. Secondary education lasts for an additional seven years. School attendance is highest in the cities, especially Yaoundé and Douala, and lowest in rural areas. Despite the relatively high level of school attendance, 21 percent of men and 35 percent of women had no formal education in 1998.

**Higher Education.** While less than 3 percent of men and 1 percent of women attend institutions of higher learning, advanced study is widely regarded as a route to upward mobility. Originally, the University of Yaoundé was the only comprehensive university, while regional universities specialized in particular subject areas. Yaoundé also housed the University Centre for Health Sciences, a medical school servicing several African countries. In the 1990s, the University of Yaoundé was broken up into several campuses, each devoted to a different field of study. The regional universities became more comprehensive, leading to some decentralization in higher education. Many people pursue a doctoral degree overseas.

## ETIQUETTE

Greetings, use of proper names, and use of praise names are important parts of daily etiquette in many regions of Cameroon. At meetings, each person should be greeted by name or with a handshake. Serving and graciously receiving food is an important symbol of hospitality and trust throughout the country. Respect is accorded to elders throughout Cameroon. Protocol regarding speaking and seating during an audience with a chief is highly developed in regions with hierarchically organized cultures (Fulani, Bamiléké, Banoun, and Grassfields).

## RELIGION

**Religious Beliefs.** Cameroonians have a variety of religious beliefs, and many individuals combine beliefs and practices of world religions with those of their own culture groups. Approximately 53 percent of the population are members of Christian denominations, about 25 percent practice mainly "traditional" religions, and approximately 22 percent are Muslim. Most Christians live in the southern areas, and most Muslims in the north. Christian missions constituted an informal second layer of colonialism.

Traditional religions are systems of practices and beliefs that adapt to changing social conditions. Most involve the veneration of ancestors and the belief that people, animals, and natural objects are invested with spiritual power.

**Religious Practitioners.** In addition to Christian and Muslim clerics, religious practitioners include the ritual specialists of cultural groups. These specialists may be political leaders, spirit mediums, or healers. Their spiritual power may be inherited, learned, or acquired through their own affliction and healing. Generally, they combine their religious activities with other forms of livelihood.

**Rituals and Holy Places.** For Muslims, a pilgrimage to Mecca is a source of honor. Among animists, holy places often include sacred trees or groves, unusual rock formations, and the burial places of ancestors. These places are often sites of propi-

*A Bamiléké tribesman wearing a mask during a traditional ritual in Cameroon.*

tiatory offerings to ancestors or spirits. Offerings include special foods, palm oil, libations of palm wine, and chickens. Among the monarchies of the Grassfields, sacred places include sites of former palaces where rituals that promote fertility and good fortune for the chiefdom are performed.

***Death and the Afterlife.*** Several cultures, including the Bamiléké in the west and the Maka in the east, practice divination and/or perform public autopsies to determine the cause of death. These peoples are particularly concerned with death caused by witchcraft. In many cultures, a death is announced through public wailing by women. Grassfields peoples bury their dead quickly but observe a week of public mourning called cry-die. Close relatives shave their heads. Approximately a year later, lavish death celebrations honor the deceased, who has become an ancestor. Death provides the occasion for the most important ceremonies of the forest forager groups (Baka, Kola, and Medzan). The forest spirit is believed to participate in death ceremonies by dancing under a raffia mask. The honoring and veneration of ancestors are common to nearly all

*Cameroonian dancers from the Mabeas tribe. Dance is an essential part of many celebrations such as weddings and coronations.*

groups. Ancestors may be remembered in oral literature (the Fulani), buried in elaborate tombs in the family courtyard (Catholic Ewondo), or reburied and provided offerings of prayer, food, and shelter (the Bamiléké). The Fulani, like other Muslims, believe in an afterlife of material rewards for those who obey Allah's laws.

## MEDICINE AND HEALTH CARE

Health care consists of biomedical treatment, traditional practices (often closely bound to traditional

religion), and Islamic medicine in various combinations that depend on belief, cost, proximity, and the advice of kin and neighbors.

Biomedical health care facilities are provided through the national government and Christian missions as well as by private physicians. There are health centers, maternal child health centers (offering prenatal, childbirth, well-baby, and under-five care), and private, general, and central hospitals. In rural health centers, nurses often play a direct role in diagnosis and treatment, and perform surgical operations. Pharmacists are an important source of biomedical advice. Vendors of prescription medicines also give advice to patients and their families, although their understanding of disease may differ from that of physicians and pharmacists.

Traditional practitioners include herbalists, bone setters, diviners, and ritual specialists who may supplicate spirits or ancestors. These practitioners adapt to changing conditions by incorporating new ideas and medicines into their practices. There has been a tendency toward the predominance of herbalists and individual treatment and away from the use of ritual specialists and community-wide treatments. Many practitioners specialize in the treatment of particular afflictions. Patients readily consult practitioners from different cultural groups.

The Islamic medical system is derived from Arabic and Greco-Roman sources. These medical practitioners not only are important sources of treatment for northern Muslims but also are popular among other peoples. Many non-Muslims seek protection from evil by displaying symbols of Islamic blessings in their houses.

## SECULAR CELEBRATIONS

Secular celebrations such as New Year (1 January), Youth Day (11 February), Labor Day (1 May), and National Day (20 May) include public parades involving public officials, party loyalists dressed in commemorative cloth with party insignia, and schoolchildren as well as dance troupes.

## THE ARTS AND HUMANITIES

**Support for the Arts.** Artists are mostly self-supporting, although 7 percent of the national budget was devoted to recreational and cultural activities in 1996 and 1997.

**Literature.** The Fulani are known for their oral literature, including poetry, history, stories, legends, proverbs, magic formulas, and riddles. Since the colonial period, written literature has had a strong history in the southern areas. Ewondo and Douala authors have contributed classics to modern African literature.

**Graphic Arts.** Many groups produce pottery, textiles, and sculptures that are used as everyday household objects. Grassfielders (including the Bamiléké and Bamoun) are noted for blue and white royal display cloth, elaborately beaded calabashes, and sculptures that include royal reliquaries. The Bamoun are known for lost-wax bronze sculptures.

The graphic arts of pastoral groups such as Fulani and Hausa are largely related to cattle herding.

**Performance Arts.** Music and dance styles are essential to the celebration of funerals, weddings, and succession to high office.

## THE STATE OF THE PHYSICAL AND SOCIAL SCIENCES

In addition to the university system, there are a number of institutions of applied and basic research in the physical and social sciences. Many are run and funded in coordination with the research institutions of donor countries, the United Nations, or NGOs. Social sciences are popular among university students. Because of insufficient library resources, students have formed their own organizations to create subject-specific libraries that are completely student-run.

## BIBLIOGRAPHY

Alexandre, P., and J. Binet. *Le Groupe Dit Pahouin*, 1958.

Ardener, E. *Coastal Bantu of the Cameroons*, 1956.

Bailey, Robert C., Serge Bahuchet, and Barry S. Hewlett. ''Development in the Central African Rainforest: Concern for Forest Peoples.'' In K. Cleaver, et al., eds. *Conservation of West and Central African Rainforests*, 1992.

Bayart, J.-F. *The State in Africa: The Politics of the Belly*, 1993.

Dugast, I. *Inventaire ethnique du Sud-Cameroun*, 1949.

Feldman-Savelsberg, P. *Plundered Kitchens, Empty Wombs: Threatened Reproduction and Identity in the Cameroon Grassfields*, 1999.

Fotso, M. et al. *Enquête Démographique et de Santé, 1998*.

Geschiere, P. *The Modernity of Witchcraft: Politics and the Occult in Postcolonial Africa*, 1998.

Goheen, M. *Men Own the Fields, Women Own the Crops: Gender and Power in the Cameroon Grassfields*, 1996.

Konings, P. and F. B. Nyamnjoh. ''The Anglophone Problem in Cameroon.'' *Journal of Modern African Studies* 35 (2): 207–229, 1996.

LeVine, V., and R. P. Nye. *Historical Dictionary of Cameroon*, 1974.

Njoya, I. M. *Historire et Coutumes des Bamum*, 1951.

Nkwi, P. N. and A. Socpa. ''Ethnicity and Party Politics in Cameroon: The Politics of Divide and Rule.'' In P. N. Nkwi and F. B. Nyamnjoh, eds. *Regional Balance and National Integration in Cameroon*, 1997.

Riesman, Paul. *Freedom in Fulani Social Life: An Introspective Ethnography*, 1977.

Salamone, Frank A. "Colonialism and the emergence of Fulani ethnicity." *Journal of Asian and African Studies* 20: 170–201, 1985.

Schultz, Emily A. *Image and Reality in African Interethnic Relations: The Fulbe and Their Neighbors*, 1981.

—PAMELA FELDMAN-SAVELSBERG

# CANADA

## CULTURE NAME
Canadian

## ORIENTATION

**Identification.** The name Canada is derived from the Iroquoian word *kanata*, which means village.

**Location and Geography.** Canada is located in the northern portion of the continent of North America, extending, in general, from the 49th parallel northward to the islands of the Arctic Ocean. Its eastern and western boundaries are the Atlantic and Pacific Oceans respectively. Its land area totals 3,851,809 square miles (9,976,185 square kilometers). The easternmost portion of the country is a riverine and maritime environment, consisting of the provinces of Newfoundland, Labrador, Nova Scotia, Prince Edward Island, and New Brunswick. The central portion of the country, in its southern areas, is primarily boreal forest (the provinces of Ontario and Quebec). This forest region extends across the entire country from the eastern slopes of the Rocky Mountains through to the Atlantic coast, and is dominated by coniferous trees. A section of the country westward from the Great Lakes basin along the southern extent of this forest region is a prairie made up mostly of flat grasslands (in the provinces of Manitoba, Saskatchewan and Alberta). The westernmost portion of the country is dominated by the Rocky Mountains, with a narrow riverine environment, made up of northern rain forests, west of the mountains (in the province of British Columbia). Between the southern Carolinian forest of the central regions of the country lies a region in Ontario and Quebec characterized by numerous lakes and expanses of exposed rock known as the Canadian Shield, an area left exposed after the most recent glacial retreat. Across the northernmost portion of the country from east to west lies a region dominated by tundra and finally at its most northern reach, an arctic eco-zone (in north-

ern Ontario and Quebec and in the territories of Nunavut, Northwest Territories, and the Yukon).

These variations have had important social and cultural effects. The largest segment of the population resides in the central Carolinian region, which has the richest and most varied agricultural land and, because the Great Lakes waterway system dominates the central portion of the country, is also where most of the major manufacturing is located. The savanna or prairie region is more sparsely populated, with several large urban centers in a network across the region, which is dominated by grain farming, cattle and other livestock production, and more recently, oil and natural gas extraction. The two coastal regions, which have some agricultural production, are best characterized by the dominance of port cities through which import and export goods move. In the northern section of the center of the country, also sparsely populated, resource extraction of minerals and lumber, has predominated. The effect of this concentration of the population, employment, and productive power in the central region of the country has been the concentration of political power in this region, as well as the development over time of intense regional rivalries and disparities in quality of life. Equally important, as employment in the center came to dominate gross national production, immigration has tended to flow into the center. This has created a diverse cultural mix in the central region of the country, while the prairie and the eastern maritime region have stabilized ethnically and culturally. The consequence of these diverse geographies has been the development of a rhetoric of regional cultures: Prairie, Maritime, Central, and because of its special isolation, West Coast.

A final differentiation is between urban and rural. Local cultural identity is often marked by expressions of contrasting values in which rural residents characterize themselves as harder working, more honest, and more deeply committed to community cooperation, in contrast to urban dwellers

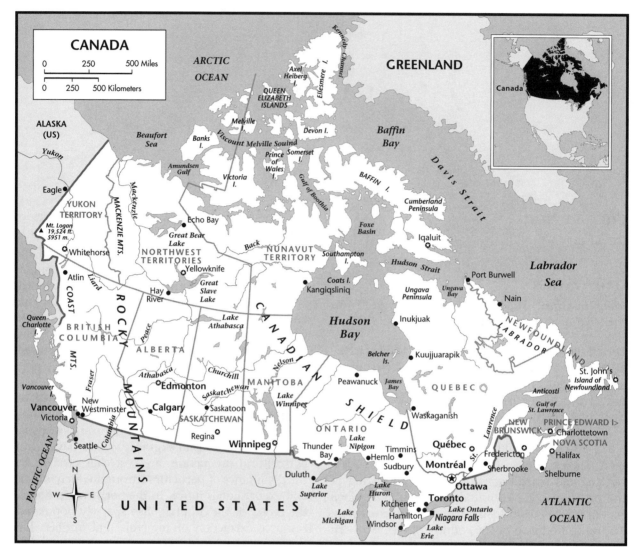

*Canada*

who are characterized by rural residents as greedy, dishonest, arrogant, and self-interested. Urban dwellers express their own identities as more modern and forward looking, more sophisticated, and more liberal in their overall social values, and perceive rural residents as conservative, overdependent on outmoded traditions, unsophisticated, and simple minded. This distinction is most explicit in Quebec, but also plays a key role in political, social, and cultural contentions in Ontario.

***Demography.*** The official population at the last census calculation, in 1996, was 29,672,000, an increase over the previous census in 1991 of about 6 percent in five years. The previous five-year increase was almost 7 percent. There has been a slowing population increase in Canada over the last several decades, fueled in part by a decline in the crude birthrate. This slowing of growth has been offset somewhat by an increase in immigration over the last two decades of the twentieth century, coupled with a slowing of emigration. Statistics Canada, the government Census management organization, is projecting a population increase of as much as 8 percent between 2001 and 2005, mostly through increased immigration.

***Linguistic Affiliation.*** Canada is bilingual, with English and French as the official languages. English takes precedence in statutory proceedings outside of Quebec, with English versions of all statutes serving as the final arbiter in disputes over interpretation. As of 1996, the proportion of Canadians reporting English as their mother tongue was just under 60 percent while those reporting French as their mother tongue was slightly less than 24 percent.

The percentage of native English speakers had risen over the previous decade, while that of French speakers had declined. At the same time, about 17 percent of all Canadians could speak both official languages, though this is a regionalized phenomenon. In those provinces with the largest number of native French speakers (Quebec and New Brunswick), 38 percent and 33 percent respectively were bilingual, numbers that had been increasing steadily over the previous twenty years. In contrast, Ontario, which accounts for more than 30 percent of the total population of Canada, had an English-French bilingualism rate of about 12 percent. This is in part a result of the immigration patterns over time, which sees the majority of all immigrants gravitating to Ontario, and in part because all official and commercial services in Ontario are conducted in English, even though French is available by law, if not by practice. English-French bilingualism is less important in the everyday lives of those living outside of Quebec and New Brunswick.

First Nations language groups make up a significant, if small, portion of the nonofficial bilingual speakers in Canada, a fact with political and cultural importance as First Nations groups assert greater and more compelling claims on political and cultural sovereignty. The three largest First Nations languages in 1996 were Cree, Inuktitut, and Ojibway, though incomplete census data on First Nations peoples continues to plague assessments of the extent and importance of these mother tongues.

Changing immigration patterns following World War II affected linguistic affiliation. In the period, from 1961 to 1970, for example, only 54 percent of immigrants had a nonofficial language as mother tongue, with more than two-thirds of this group born in Europe. Almost a quarter of them reported Italian, German, or Greek as mother tongue. In contrast, 80 percent of the 1,039,000 immigrants who came to Canada between 1991 and 1996 reported a nonofficial language as mother tongue, with over half from Asia and the Middle East. Chinese was the mother tongue of just under 25 percent, while Arabic, Punjabi, Tagalog, Tamil, and Persian together accounted for about 20 percent. In 1971, the three largest nonofficial mother tongue groups were German, Italian, and Ukrainian, reflecting patterns of non-English and non-French immigration that have remained relatively constant through most of the twentieth century. In the period ending in 1996, this had changed, with the rank order shifting to Chinese, Italian, and German. This is reflected in regional concentrations, with Italians concentrated heavily in Ontario, Germans in both Ontario and the Prairie regions, and Chinese and other Asians most heavily represented in southern Ontario and in British Columbia. A gradual decline in out-migration from Europe, coupled with political changes in China and throughout Asia, leading to increased out-migration from these areas, is changing the ethnic and linguistic makeup of Canada. It should be stressed, however, that these changes are concentrated in two or three key urban centers, while linguistic affiliation elsewhere in the country remains stable. This is likely to change in the early twenty-first century as an aging cohort of European immigrants declines and out-migration from Europe continues to decrease. These shifts will come to have increasingly important cultural effects as immigrants from Asia and, most recently, from certain areas throughout the continent of Africa, come to influence the political and social life of the core urban centers in which they settle.

**Symbolism.** This is an area of considerable dispute in Canada, in large part because of the country's longstanding history of biculturalism (English and French) and perhaps most importantly because of its proximity to the United States, whose symbolic and rhetorical influence is both unavoidable and openly resisted. Ethnic and cultural diversity in Canada, in which different cultural groups were expected to maintain their distinctiveness rather than subsume it to some larger national culture, which is the historical effect of the English-French biculturalism built into the Canadian confederation, means that national symbols in Canada tend to be either somewhat superficial or regionalized. There are, however, certain symbols that are deployed at both official and unofficial events and functions which are generally shared across the entire country, and can be seen as general cultural symbols, even if their uses may not always be serious.

Canada is often symbolically connected with three key images—hockey, the beaver, and the dress uniform of the Royal Canadian Mounted Police. Hockey, often described as Canada's national sport, is a vigorous, often violently competitive team sport and, as such, it carries the same kind of symbolic weight as baseball does for many Americans. What gives it its profound symbolic importance is the way in which hockey events, such as the winning goal scored by the Canadian national team during a competition with the Russian national team in the 1970s, are used as special cultural and historical markers in political discourse. Hockey is used, in its symbolic form, to signify national unity and a national sense of purpose and community. That most

Canadians do not follow hockey in any serious way does not diminish its role as a key cultural symbol.

The beaver, which appears often on Canadian souvenirs, might seem to be an odd animal to have as a national symbol. It is a ratlike character, with a broad flat tail and, in caricature, a comical face highlighted by front chewing teeth of considerable prominence. What gives the beaver its special merit as a cultural symbol, however, are its industriousness, toiling to create elaborate nesting sites out of mud and twigs, and its triumph over the seasons. The beaver is humble, nonpredatory, and diligent, values that form a fundamental core of Canadian self-identification.

The Royal Canadian Mounted Police (RCMP), often represented in their dress uniform which includes a tight-fitting red coat, riding pants, high black boots, and broad-brimmed felt hat, also represent this Canadian concern with diligence and humility. Canada was opened to European occupation not by a pioneering spirit fighting against all odds to push open a wild and dangerous frontier, as in the United States, but by a systematic effort to bring the vastness of the Canadian landscape under police control. The RCMP, along with agents of colonial economic interests such as the Hudson's Bay Company, expanded the scope of colonial control and occupation of Canada in a systematic and orderly way, not so much by conquest as by coordination. That is, Canada was opened to European occupation and control almost as a bureaucratic exercise in extending the rule of law. Where the American frontier was a lawless and wild place, later brought under control by centralizing government bodies, the Canadian frontier never quite existed. Instead, Canada was colonized by law rather than by force.

The core values that inform these symbols are cooperation, industriousness, and patience—that is, a kind of national politeness. The Canadian symbolic order is dominated by a concern for order and stability, which marks Canadian identity as something communal rather than individualistic.

## HISTORY AND ETHNIC RELATIONS

**Emergence of the Nation.** Canada throughout its history might best be described as a nation of nations. Two European colonial powers dominate the history of Canada and its emergence as a nation: France and Great Britain. In time Britain emerged as the dominant political and cultural force in Canada, but that emergence exemplifies the sense of compromise and cooperation on which Canadian social

identity is founded. While Britain, and later English Canada, came to be and remain the most powerful part of the Canadian cultural landscape, this dominance and power exists in a system of joint cultural identity, with French Canada, in Quebec and in other parts of eastern Canada, remaining a singular and distinctive cultural entity in its own right.

The Canadian novelist Hugh McLennan, writing in the 1940's, spoke of the two solitudes which in many ways govern the cultural and political life of Canada. Two communities, distinguished by language, culture, religion, and politics live in isolation from each other with divergent aspirations and very divergent views of the history of Canada as a nation. The peace between the French and English sides of the Canadian coin is a peace born in war, with Britain defeating French colonial forces in the late eighteenth century. It is a peace born of common purpose when the now English colony of Canada withstood invasion from the newly formed United States, with the sometimes uneven assistance of the remaining French community in Lower Canada, later to be called Quebec. It is also a peace driven by controversy and scandal. During the opening of the westward railroad in the late nineteenth century, a process of pacification of the Canadian frontier most noteworthy for its having been planned and carried out by a series of government committees, French Canadians felt, not without cause, that they were being excluded from this nation building. And it is a peace marked, even today, by a deep sense of ethnic antagonism, most particularly in Quebec, where French Canadian nationalism is a vibrant, if not the dominant political force.

This complex antagonism, which has been a thread throughout Canada's emergence as a nation, has also led to a particular kind of nation. Most important, the development of the Canadian nation, however uneven the power of the English and the French, has been characterized by discussion, planning, and compromise. The gradual opening of all of Canada to European control, and its coming together in 1867 as a national entity, was not the result of war or revolution but instead, of negotiation and reconciliation. It was an orderly transition managed almost like a business venture, through which Canada obtained a degree of sovereignty and Great Britain continued to hold Canada's allegiance as a member of the British Empire. When, in the early 1980s Canada would take the final step towards political independence by adopting its own constitution, it would do so through negotiation as well, and again, the antagonism between English and French Canada, which resulted in the Government of Quebec refusing to sign the constitutional enabling agreement would provide both the drama of the moment, and its fundamental character, one of compromise and collaboration.

It is these qualities of combining co-operation with ethnic independence which continue to shape Canada's development as a nation. Developments in human rights law, for example, with a new emphasis on the importance of group rights and in particular group rights under conditions of inequality among groups, were pioneered in Canada. The model of universal health care for all citizens in Canada which, while currently stressed by economic changes in the final decades of the twentieth century, illustrates how a system of co-operative engagement between multiple and independent political partners can produce institutions which benefit everyone. While Canada remains an often contentious and divided place in many ways, with regional and ethnic communities making greater demands for independence, they do so because the history of Canada's emergence as a nation has been a history of interdependence in which these polarities and debates are not so much a sign of dissolution but evidence of a continued vitality. An early colonial governor of Canada is reputed to have said that it is "nearly impossible to govern a nation where one half the people are more British than the Queen, and the other more Catholic than the Pope." While he may have been right about the difficulty, nearly a century and a half of Canadian nationhood has demonstrated that it is indeed possible to build a nation where diversity serves as the keystone of unity.

**National Identity.** Leading up to and following the emergence of Canada as an independent political state in 1867, English Canada and English identity dominated the political and cultural landscape. The remaining French presence, in Quebec and throughout the eastern part of the country, while a strong cultural entity in itself, exercised only limited influence and effect at the national level. English symbols, the English language, and the values of loyalty to the English crown prevailed throughout the nation as the core underpinnings of national identity.

**Ethnic Relations.** The dominance of English Canada in terms of national identity, especially in a federal system in which binationalism and biculturalism were enshrined in the founding legislation of the country, exercised a powerful effect on ethnic relations, but that effect was not ethnic homogenization. Instead, the dominance of English Canada

served as a major locus of ongoing tension between the two national identities of Canada, a tension which, in the period from the 1960s onward, has come to be expressed in growing French-Canadian nationalism and so far unsuccessful attempts on the part of French Canada to secede from the Canadian confederation. This tension—which is built into the principles of the confederation itself, which recognizes the duality of Canadian national identity—while regularly threatening the unity of the federation, has also had a mollifying effect on ethnic divisions more generally.

Canada has seen successive waves of immigration, from the Netherlands, Germany and Italy, England and Ireland, China and Japan, and more recently from south and east Asia and from many countries throughout Africa. While some of these migration waves have resulted in considerable political and social conflict, as in the large-scale migration of Chinese laborers brought into Canada to work on the national railroad, the overall pattern of in-migration and settlement has been characterized by relatively smooth transitions. This is in large part an effect of the legislated binationalism and biculturalism on which Canada is founded. Such a model of confederation, which institutionalizes cultural diversity, has meant the new cohorts of migrants have not experienced the kind of assimilationist and acculturationalist pressures which have characterized ethnic relations in the United States. Where, in the United States, there was considerable pressure on migrant cohorts to become "American," in Canada these cohorts have more often than not retained their identity of birth. This has created a kind of mosaic-like quality in Canadian ethnic relations in which being Canadian does not necessarily take precedence over being Japanese or Italian or Somalian or Pakistani. Instead, the two identities can and often do carry the same social and political weight, creating in Canada a diversity of identity unlike that found in other large nation-states. This cooperative national identity, with its multiple cultural orientations, has not been without its tensions and conflicts. English Canadian cultural domination has created flash points of assimilationist sentiment, and the fact that Japanese-Canadians, for example, were seen as being both Japanese and Canadian, helped justify the imprisonment of people of Japanese ancestry throughout Canada during World War II. Overall, however, ethnic relations in Canada have tended to not be exclusionary and assimilationist.

The main exception to this has been the relationship between the dominant French-English state and aboriginal peoples. Colonial relations with indigenous ethnic groups worldwide have often been marked by violent conquest. While violence did play a role in these relationships in Canada, more often than not aboriginal peoples simply had their ethnic and cultural identities erased. The use of forced schooling, including the removal of children from their families, for example, sought to annul aboriginal cultural identities through a process of denial. Historically the policy in Canada has been to not recognize aboriginal cultural and ethnic identity as an identity at all. In more recent years, First Nations people throughout Canada have adopted a renewed expression of ethnic and cultural identity, as part of the process of asserting claims to sovereignty and their right of historical redress. These claims have been only moderately successful, in part because First Nations people are asserting an identity and a claim to ethnic coherence that had been denied them for more than one hundred years, and in part because the dominating ethic of multicultural cooperation in Canadian ethnic relations, which gives their claim to ethnic identity legitimacy in the Canadian system, also diminishes and undermines their claim to a special ethnic status. While First Nations peoples are indeed emerging as real ethnic, cultural, and political entities, they do so in a system that relegates them to the position of one among many. The future direction of First Nations ethnicity, and their position within this Canadian mosaic, is likely to be complex, contentious, and a long time in its resolution.

## URBANISM, ARCHITECTURE, AND THE USE OF SPACE

Space has symbolic importance for Canadian culture, in part because of the vastness of Canadian geography coupled with its sparse population, and in part because a sense of distance in Canada has tended to create regional tensions based on the isolation of the larger pockets of the population. Most Canadians live in towns and cities, a trend away from rural residence not unlike that found throughout the rest of the industrialized world. Canadian cities are found at important hubs of interchange between agriculture and manufacturing, such that most Canadian cities emerged as points of connection between farm production and industrial development. Because of this, Canadian cities have tended to develop haphazardly as the larger scale processes of industrialization and changes in farming have developed. Such historical processes are not amenable to planning.

Canadian cities look like cities almost anywhere in the industrialized world, save the fact they tend to be cleaner due to an effect of the way that orderliness has been a dominant feature of the history of Canadian material culture. Canadian cities, even during phases of urban decay, have tended to be more carefully planned and better run, at least in terms of amenities and services, than those in many other industrialized nations.

Unlike European cities, however, space in Canadian cities tends to be privatized. While most cities have some space, such as a formal plaza at a city hall, at which public events are held, in general there are no large communal spaces in which social interactions occur. Instead, Canadians in cities of whatever size socialize in private spaces: their homes or commercial sites, such as restaurants. Like cities throughout North America, space in Canadian cities is dominated by movement, and Canadian cities are designed as networks through which goods, vehicles, and people move on their way to or from some place. As such, streets are designed to control the flow of vehicular traffic, to in some way isolate foot traffic, and in all instances to direct traffic toward destinations rather than allow traffic to accumulate. This has led, over the last several decades, to the gradual disappearance of urban commercial streetscapes, replaced by indoor shopping malls as a key destination of traffic flow. Rural towns, however, counter this trend somewhat. Many smaller towns have endeavored to revitalize their commercial streetscapes in recent decades and the decline of this streetscape is often seen as a sign of the decline and decay of the town as a whole.

Residence in Canadian cities is generally private rather than communal, dominated by private homes or residences. Vertical residence structures, such as apartment buildings, dominate much of the urban renewal of core areas in cities, while expansion of cities has been dominated by the development of large tracts of private single-family dwellings.

Official architecture in Canada has, historically, been neoclassical though not to the same extent as one finds in the United States. While official buildings in the early part of the twentieth century were often modeled on massive classical buildings, in the latter part of the century these buildings took on shapes not unlike other functional commercial buildings. Key symbolically important buildings, such as courthouses and city halls, are often grand in scale; what marks them today is their diversity rather than the application of a single stylistic model.

*A house and pond in rural Nova Scotia. Most Canadians live in private homes.*

## FOOD AND ECONOMY

***Food in Daily Life.*** The agricultural and ethnic richness of Canada has led to two distinctive characteristics of everyday food consumption. The first is its scale. Canadians are "big eaters," with meat portions in particular dominating the Canadian meal. There are generally three regular meals in a given day. Breakfast, often large and important in rural areas, but less so in urban areas, is most often not eaten in a group. Lunch, at midday, is most often a snack in urban areas, but remains a substantial meal in rural centers. Dinner, the final formal meal of the day, is also the meal most likely to be eaten by a residential group as a whole, and it is the largest and the most socially important meal of the day. It is the meal most often used as a social event or to which invitations to nonfamily members are extended, in contrast with lunch which is often, for adults, shared with coworkers. Meat plays a key role in all three of the formal meals, but with increasing importance at breakfast and dinner. Dinner should have some special, and most often, large, meat portion as its key component. Each of these three meals can be, and often are, very substantial. There are general rules concerning appropriate foods for each meal, rules that can be quite complex. For example, pork can figure in each meal, but only particular kinds of pork would be consid-

ered appropriate. Pork at breakfast may appear as bacon, or sausage, in small portions. Both of these products are made with the least valuable portion of the pig. At lunch, pork may appear in a sandwich in the form of processed meats, also made from the least valuable portion of the pig. For dinner, pork appears in large and more highly valued forms, such as roasts or hams, which require often elaborate preparation and which are presented to diners in a way that highlights their value and size.

The other main feature of Canadian food is diversity. The complex ethnic landscape of Canada and the tendency of ethnic groups to retain a dual cultural orientation have meant that Canadian cuisine is quite diverse in its content, with many ethnic dishes seen as somehow quintessentially Canadian as well. Whether pizza or chow mein, cabbage rolls or plum pudding, Canadian cuisine is best characterized as eclectic rather than consistent in content. There are a small number of food items that are considered distinctively Canadian, such as maple syrup, but overall the Canadian diet is drawn from a panoply of ethnic sources.

***Food Customs at Ceremonial Occasions.*** Ceremonial food does not generally differ greatly in content from everyday foods. What distinguishes food in ceremonial settings, such as state dinners, is not the type of food but the amount of food served and the complexity of its presentation and consumption. Ceremonial dinners are often made up of a long list of dishes served in a rigid sequence, eaten with utensils specified for each portion, and presented in often elaborate arrangement either generally, on the table as a whole, or in the particular portions placed on each diner's plate.

The same general consideration applies to meals for more private special occasions, such as those marking important religious holidays such as Christmas. The number of discrete dishes is usually quite large, the preparation of each is often specialized and involved, and portions consumed are more often than not greater than what one would consume under other circumstances. These more private special occasion meals often involve entire extended families sharing in both preparing and eating the meal.

There is another special meal worth mentioning, the potluck. "Potluck" is derived from the word *potlatch*, a special occasion of many West Coast First Nations peoples. The potluck involves each guest preparing and bringing a dish to the event, to be shared by all the diners. The key component of this particular kind of meal is food sharing among friends as opposed to food making for family. In general, potluck meals are meals shared by friends or coworkers. They express the symbolic importance of the meal as a part of the moral geography of social relations among nonkin, but distinguish this meal as an act of food sharing rather than an act of food preparation. That is, the potluck meal expresses a sense of community and kindness, while the family meal expresses a sense of service, duty, and family solidarity.

**Basic Economy.** Canada is a resource rich, but land and people poor, country. While physically vast, there are geographic limitations on where people can live such that most of the population is located around the Great Lakes, and in the Saint Lawrence River Valley. This has meant, however, that the natural resources throughout the country can be exploited more fully.

Key to Canada's basic economy is its role as a resource base, not only for its own manufacturing, but for export as well. Minerals and ore, forestry products, and in particular in the twentieth century, oil and gas, have been the foundation of the Canadian economy since European conquest of the area.

Farming is also key to the Canadian economy, although most of Canada's agricultural production

*A father and son celebrate their lumber heritage during the winter Lumberjack Parade in Chicoutimi, Quebec.*

is exported, primarily though not exclusively, to the United States. This is a function of the scale of agricultural production in Canada in relation to the smallness of the Canadian population. Very few Canadians produce at the subsistence level; so few in fact, that it is fair to say all agricultural production in Canada is production for sale. Equally important, even that agricultural production consumed in Canada itself is not sold directly by producers to consumers but rather through a network of secondary distributers. Because of the shortness of Canadian growing seasons, a significant portion of all food consumed in Canada is imported from elsewhere in the world.

Manufacturing in Canada is dominated by automobile production, and by the manufacture of other large equipment and farm equipment. Canada also produces a wide range of consumer products, including furniture, electronics and building material. Since the 1980s production of high technology equipment, and especially communication equipment, has become a key sector of the economy as well.

The single largest area of economic growth in Canada since the 1970s has been in the "service" sector, the part of the economy which provides services rather than goods for sale. The financial, research, and tourist sectors have shown substantial increases during this period. Taken together, the resource sector and the service sector dominate the economy of Canada, such that Canada remains primarily a provider of resources, either in material or in labor through service, and equally important, an importer of manufactured goods. While balance of trade in the import and export of manufactured goods tends to favor Canada, factoring in service export means Canada is always somewhat at a trading deficit with its partners globally.

***Land Tenure and Property.*** Property in Canada is primarily by rental and freehold. Immediate, and some closely related secondary kin have some claims on the disposition of property, usually through inheritance. Some land, and other kinds of property, may be held in cooperative ownership, such as, for example, land held by religious communities or farmers co-op groups. To a limited extent, the property of married couples, and some property of common-law couples, is also held in common, each partner having some degree of claim on the total joint property. This joint ownership is also being extended to same-sex conjugal partners, whose property rights are now similar to those of common-law opposite sex couples. The state has right of expropriation of privately held land, and the right of criminal seizure of other properties. Private ownership of both land and moveable property is also subject to statues governing financial solvency, such that bankrupts, for example, can have their land and other property sold to balance their debt.

***Major Industries.*** Canadian manufacturing is dominated, in terms of economic effect, by automobile manufacturing, and to a lesser extent by resource processing such as steel and other metals production. The automotive sector is the single largest sector, but resource extraction and processing, including mineral, chemical, and forestry products taken together, is the most important productive and commercial activity in Canada. In general, Canada exports more than it imports, in large part because of the combination of its raw material resource-based economy and the automotive sector.

The provision of services is the second most important commercial activity in Canada in terms of number of people employed, accounting for slightly less than half the labor force, but manufacturing, resource extraction, and agriculture dominate employment and commercial activity.

***Trade.*** Canada exports around the world, but its most important export and import trading partner is the United States. In recent decades Canada has had a slight balance of trade advantage with all its trading partners, including the United States, by exporting more goods than it imports from others. The automotive sector dominates Canadian manufacturing and trade, due to a preferential trade agreement with the United States through which American automobile manufacturers agreed to produce one vehicle in Canada for every vehicle it exports to Canada from its American based plants. In return, Canada waived all tariffs on vehicles exported by American manufacturers to Canada. Under pressure from non-American car makers worldwide, this agreement, which expired in February 2001, is likely not to be renewed, a change which could affect the overall importance of automobile manufacturing for Canadian trade relations.

The manufacturing and export of large equipment, and in particular farm equipment, is the second largest component of Canadian manufacturing and trade. The export of farm equipment in particular is a major component of Canada's international aid programs. Some economic analysts project that large equipment manufacturing, including the recent advance of airplane building in Canada, may supplant automobile manufacturing as the dominant sector of Canadian trade.

At the same time, Canada remains a major resource exporter. In particular, Canada exports raw materials such as petro-chemicals and oil, minerals and ores, and forestry products. This is a key trading role which Canada has played in the global economy throughout its history. This sector of the economy is subject to the most stringent rules governing foreign ownership, but the importance of resource extraction and trade for Canada is such that these rules are being loosened under pressure from bodies such as the World Trade Organization, of which Canada is a member.

Farm product export ranks fourth in overall trade importance for Canada, with special emphasis on wheat, canola and corn, soybeans and non-citrus fruit. Livestock trade, including beef, pig, and chicken products, while substantial, makes up only a very small part of Canada's agricultural exports, with most of Canada's livestock production being consumed domestically. Increased restrictions on the import, in particular of beef products due to health concerns over Bovine Spongiform Encephalopathy (mad cow disease), has led to a gradual increase in overall livestock production in Canada, but no significant increase in export of these goods. This is likely to change as more and more countries world wide turn to Canada and the United States for "safe" beef and other livestock products.

Finally, Canada, along with the United States and Mexico, belongs to a North American Free Trade Zone, the result of a treaty between these three countries. The North American Free Trade Agreement (NAFTA) establishes preferential trading rules between the three signatories, though its administration has not been without dispute. The effect over time may be an increasing reliance on exports to and imports from NAFTA partners, with trade production in each of the three countries under pressure to address the import and export needs of the other partners, possibly limiting trade expansion in other global areas. Canada appears to be resisting this limitation on trade development by pursuing special trade arrangements with such countries as China and Indonesia. At the same time, Canada is an active participant in negotiations to extend the NAFTA agreement to include all countries in the Western Hemisphere in a mutual trade agreement.

**Division of Labor.** Labor in Canada is unevenly divided between skilled professional, skilled manufacturing, and general unskilled such as service workers. With increased manufacturing efficiency, the skilled manufacturing labor force has declined in size, though not in economic impact, while the general unskilled labor force has increased; at the same time skilled professionals—whether doctors, computer programmers, and other new economy professionals—has also increased. Access to different jobs is determined in part by education and training and in part by social networks. There has been a strong tendency for children to follow their parents into similar positions in the labor force, but shifts away from stable employment in manufacturing, along with the growth of the unskilled labor market in the services sector, has seen this change in recent decades. While access to and advancement in both the skilled professional and skilled manufacturing sectors is described as meritocractic, there remain strong class, ethnic, and regional factors that affect access to and promotion within labor markets.

## SOCIAL STRATIFICATION

**Classes and Castes.** Class is a contentious issue in Canada, in no small part because the rhetoric of Canadian identity, with its emphasis on equality, unity in diversity, and mutual respect and cooperation, does not match the actual distribution of economic wealth and political power. Indeed, this culture of diversity has had the effect, on the one hand, of disguising class divisions, and on the other, of allowing them to flourish. Combined with ethnic diversity and strong regional disparities, class in Canada is a complex web of factors, which make easy descriptions of working and upper class, for example, difficult.

The number of people in Canada defined as being low income by the government increased from about 17 percent in 1991 to about 19 percent in 2000. Average incomes in the central provinces are closest to the national average, but in eastern provinces average incomes can be as much as 25 percent lower than the national average. This has led to the emergence of low-skill, low-pay service sector jobs being located in the eastern provinces, creating a strong regional class division.

Class divisions can been seen in educational participation rates, with lower-class individuals less likely to participate beyond, or in some regions, to complete secondary school. Urban centers, both large and small, are divided into neighborhoods by class; in large urban centers undergoing the most recent phase of urban redevelopment, the large cohort of urban poor are increasingly being confined to smaller and smaller areas of older rental housing stock. This reaggregation of upper-class residential enclaves in revitalized urban cores is also producing greater demand for low-skill service sector employment, which reproduces the class divisions by dividing urban centers into networks of microregions defined by the class position of the residents.

**Symbols of Social Stratification.** Class symbolism in Canada is mostly modest, again in large part as a result of the rhetoric of identity that prizes diversity and even humility. Signs of class excess, such as massive residences, or conspicuous overconsumption, are not common in Canada, except in rare cases. Some symbolic sites of class expression, such as purchasing subscription tickets to and attending local symphony concerts, constitute a dual discourse of class. In one sense, members of a particular class express cultural solidarity, and in another sense, it is an avenue for class mobility, with members of lower classes using these events as a way of marking their movement between classes. Unlike in England, for example, where accent and dress can clearly mark class position, the symbolic expression of stratification in Canada is less obvious and so more difficult to decipher. Dark business suits, jewelry, hairstyles, and types of leisure activities and leisure sites, such as exclusive clubs, can express status, but in the absence of enforced rules concerning admission and even who may or may not em-

*Agriculture is a key element of Canada's economy, especially the cultivation of grains such as corn and wheat for export.*

ploy particular symbols, stratification is not often explicitly expressed.

## POLITICAL LIFE

**Government.** Canada is a confederation of ten provinces and three territories, with a central federal government managing national services and international relations. Each province and, to a lesser extent, each territory has constitutional sovereignty over at least some aspects of its affairs. Each level of government is a constitutionally governed democracy, modeled on the British parliamentary system with representatives chosen in statutorily scheduled elections. Suffrage is universal for all citizens over the age of eighteen, except, in some instances, those in prison or citizens living overseas. Political control at each level of government is determined by the political party that wins the largest number of representative seats, not by proportion of popular vote. The election of each representative, however, is direct and proportional, the winner being the candidate who receives the single largest percentage of the votes cast.

**Leadership and Political Officials.** Leadership is dominated, in particular at the provincial and national levels, by professionals, often though not exclusively, lawyers, and most often though not ex-

clusively, men. These political leaders are selected for election by political parties, and there is an informal network of control that governs these nominations which requires service to the political party as part of the process of gaining access to that party's nomination for election by the citizens. There are no limits on the number of terms a political leader may serve. In general, these elected political officials serve two functions: representing the interests of their constituents at whatever level of government they serve, and advancing the political interests and the platform of the party that nominated them. Where these two functions come into conflict, the interests of their political party most often takes precedence, resulting occasionally in elected government officials being punished by their political parties.

Leadership and governing is carried out as well, however, by appointed officials who form a large bureaucracy that implements the decisions of elected officials. This bureaucracy is mostly drawn from middle-and upper-class, well-educated sectors of the population, and apart from a small percentage of appointments at the pleasure of the governing party, their positions in this system are lifelong if they choose. Access to this bureaucracy is in part through training and merit and in part through a network of connections outward from the bureaucracy to the business and higher educational communities.

Statutory prohibitions exist against bribery and other kinds of influence peddling in dealings with politicians and government officials, although violations do occur and often result in considerable scandal and criminal sanction.

***Social Problems and Control.*** Social control is effected by a system of courts of law, and by local, provincial, and a national police force. The most common crimes are crimes against property, although violent crimes are also common. In recent years, the incidence of violent crime has declined somewhat, although at the same time the incidence of crime against certain vulnerable sectors of the population, such as the elderly and women, has increased. There is a strong class component to the prosecution of some crimes. Prosecution for drug offenses, which in Canada are for the most part minor offenses related to possession or small-scale trafficking of controlled substances, is most often focused on lower-class individuals. While the prison population in Canada is relatively small compared to many other industrialized nations, the percentage of the prison population who are of First Nations descent remains very high, in spite of the small number of First Nations people in the population as a whole. This suggests that other kinds of disparity are also operating in the apprehension and prosecution of crime.

All accused persons are constitutionally guaranteed an open trial and rules of evidence, fairness of prosecution, and judicial review, with several levels of appellate courts in place to oversee this process. Judges are appointed for life, though they are subject to removal by judicial review boards. Such action is rare. Police forces, which are empowered by both federal and provincial statute, are relatively independent from political interference or control, and in many instances are self-governing within the limits of their statutory authority.

***Military Activity.*** The Canadian military was engaged almost exclusively in peacekeeping or disaster relief, both nationally and internationally, during the last four decades of the twentieth century. While Canada maintains a small standing army, at least small for the size of the country physically, because it has no border disputes with its neighbors, the army's primary role has been to assist other countries in either disputes or in the event of emergencies. Canada provided conflict forces to joint warfare efforts during this period, but these engagements have been small and most often highly specialized. Canada has about twenty-five hundred military personnel deployed worldwide in support and emergency situations in the Balkans, the Middle East, and Africa. As of 2001, the Canadian military was undergoing restructuring and reorganization. It was engaged in a major recruiting effort, as its numbers had declined steadily for nearly twenty years. What role the miliary will play in Canada in the coming decades remains unclear.

## SOCIAL WELFARE AND CHANGE PROGRAMS

Canada is an example of a capitalist welfare state, in that tax-base-funded programs exist to provide some measure of protection to the impoverished and those at risk of impoverishment. These programs, usually administered at the town or city level, but funded from taxes collected at the provincial and federal level, take two main forms. The first is an insurance program designed to provide income support in the event of unemployment. Individual workers pay premiums based on their wages, and the fund is supplemented by general tax revenue as needed. There are strict guidelines for qualification and the income support paid out of the fund represents a percentage of the unemployed person's previous income. There are also time limits on this support. This is a national program, and while guidelines regarding qualification vary from region to region, it is generally available to all employed persons. The second program, a general welfare program, provides subsistence support for persons and families unable to work or unemployed for longer periods than those covered by the insurance program. Levels of support in this program are often very low, providing incomes to both individuals and families well below the low-income cutoff points used by governments to measure poverty. Recently these programs have been altered to require recipients to perform some labor for the community in order to qualify. This change, along with reductions in levels of actual income support, have been controversial in Canada, with the debate focusing on the role of the state in providing support to the economically disadvantaged, a basic principle of the welfare state.

## NONGOVERNMENTAL ORGANIZATIONS AND OTHER ASSOCIATIONS

Nongovernmental organizations (NGOs) take many shapes and have many different purposes in Canada. At least three distinctive types are quite common in all regions. The first are organizations whose aim is to raise and distribute funds to assist

*The neoclassical buildings of the Canadian Parliament and the modern architecture of Hull, the city across the river, are representative of the diversity found in Canada.*

people in some distress or at some disadvantage. The largest of these, the United Way, raises funds from individuals and corporations and uses this money to fund community-based assistance and improvement programs focused on such diverse social issues as health, poverty, social development, adjustment of new immigrants, disaster assistance, and education. A second type of NGO, associations of mutual interest, takes several forms. The most common are community aid organizations whose membership share certain social or political values, such as the Kinsmen or the Shriners. These organizations raise funds both from members and from the general public in support of particular kinds of projects such as hospitals, and recreation facilities. A second common type of NGO in this category focuses on specific aspects of community improvement and development such as economic health and revitalization, as in the case of the Chamber of Commerce whose members are drawn from the local business community.

The third type of NGO in Canada is activist-oriented organizations. These come in several forms. There are politically focused organizations advancing particular ideological or political interests. For example, there is a national organization made up of small business owners, while another works as a

taxation watchdog. Others are organized around pressing social issues, and in particular disease related issues. Many activist NGOs have as their purpose fund-raising and lobbying on behalf of research into or care for such diseases as breast cancer, arthritis, and HIV/AIDS. Other activist-oriented NGOs work on behalf of broader social issues such as poverty, homelessness, and the environment.

In all cases, NGOs rely on fund-raising from the general public, although funding assistance from different levels of government is also available. Most NGOs are staffed either completely or almost completely by volunteers. Of all the industrialized countries, Canada has the distinction of having the highest level of volunteering and the highest level of charitable support of NGO activity. It should be noted, however, that this success has also allowed tax-funded social support and improvement programs to be reduced or eliminated, placing greater and greater emphasis on voluntarism for the sustaining of the social safety net, as the welfare state comes under increasing economic pressure.

## GENDER ROLES AND STATUSES

***Division of Labor by Gender.*** There are no specific gender-based prohibitions on participation in labor, but cultural and political values enforce a system of differential access and participation in the labor force. Health-care provision exemplifies this implicit division. Medical doctors, the highest paid and highest status health-care providers, are overwhelmingly male. In contrast, so-called ancillary health-care providers such as nurses are overwhelmingly women. Several factors contribute to this division. A distinction between healing and caring, where healing is seen as the province of science and caring the province of nurturing, has the effect of steering men into the "scientific" area of health and women, culturally more closely associated with nurturing, into the "caring" area. While this tendency continues to change, the implicit rules of division of labor persist as expressions of cultural values.

Statutory prohibitions exist against gender-based discrimination in labor, but their interpretation and enforcement has been complex and highly controversial because they come in conflict with often deeply held values of gender difference and gender roles. For example, the work-related recommendations of a federal commission on the status of women, which was convened in the 1960s, have not yet been implemented.

**The Relative Status of Women and Men.** In terms of explicit rules, women and men have equal standing and equal status in Canadian society. Both men and women may participate in political life, serve in government, own and dispose of property, and so on. That few women do successfully participate in official political life remains a contentious issue for many Canadians, because male-dominated networks of access to political authority and political participation continue, implicitly, to exclude women. Perhaps more important than political participation, however, are certain economic realities which indicate that the status of women relative to men remains uneven. Women are more likely to live below the poverty line, are more likely to head single-parent households, are more likely to work in the service sector, the lowest paying and most volatile sector of the labor market, and are more likely to be the subject of violence by their conjugal partner. It is important to note that the status of gender relations in any society has at least two components—the official version, that is the explicitly stated values and ideals of the society as a political entity, and the practical version, the actual nature and quality of life, risk, and participation of women relative to men.

## MARRIAGE, FAMILY, AND KINSHIP

**Marriage.** Except for some ethnic sectors, marriages are freely chosen by the two partners. Marriage is restricted to the union of a man and a woman by statute, although this is currently under review by the country's courts. Official marriages, officiated by either religious authorities or by municipal clerks or judges, must be dissolved by the legal procedure of divorce.

A second form of marriage, the de facto or common-law union, gives the couple almost all the same privileges and obligations as official marriage. Common-law union is a matter of informal declaration by the partners. Common-law conjugal recognition has recently been extended to include same-sex partners. The dissolution of common-law unions or same-sex partnerships requires no special legal proceedings, although resolution of shared property rights and support responsibilities arising from the union often require legal intervention and enforcement.

In both cases, the marriage union involves mutuality of financial support, some degree of joint ownership of property, and joint responsibility for the care and support of children. Under Canadian law, all marriages must be monogamous. The de facto or common-law union is considered to be annulled should either partner take on a new conjugal partnership.

Marriages are most often celebrated privately between the two families involved. There is, however, an interesting rural/urban distinction. Engagement or marriage celebrations in smaller communities are often community events at which anyone may attend, usually for a small fee.

**Domestic Unit.** The most common domestic unit is the nuclear family, made up of both parents and their children. Almost all newlywed couples start their own family unit independent of their parents. A demographic shift, which has seen a slow and steady increase in the number of elderly in Canada, has led to an increase in the number of domestic units in which one or more elderly relative can also be present. Increases in rate of divorce since the 1970s has also meant an increase in the number of single-parent households, most often headed by women.

Authority in domestic units is generally shared by adult members, though men most often exercise more power in financial and disciplinary matters than their female partners.

*Skaters on the frozen Rideau Canal celebrate the Winterlude, a festival held annually in Canada.*

**Inheritance.** Inheritance radiates outward from the nuclear family to more distance relatives, with members of the immediate nuclear family taking precedence. All manner of property, as well as most if not all of a deceased person's debt, can be inherited. There are no gender differences in what can be bequeathed and what can be inherited, although in rural communities and areas there is a tendency for male children to inherit land, while female children inherit more liquid forms of property. In most instances, spouses take precedence over children in matters of inheritance. All inheritances can be contested through legal proceedings.

**Kin Groups.** Allowing for some ethnic variation, in general, kinship is a dispersed system of relatedness in Canada, and while there are general expectations of mutual support along kin lines, levels of which diminish with kin distance, there are no formal rules of kinship observance, other than those statutory prohibitions against marrying close kin, or criminal code provisions regarding incest. Kinship does not determine residence, though kin networks are often used to gain access to employment.

## SOCIALIZATION

**Infant Care.** Infant care is most often the responsibility of the female partner in a family and is most often a private matter. As more mothers of small children enter the labor market, some professional infant care is available, though this is unevenly distributed nationally and is most often found in urban settings. Siblings may play a role in infant care, but there is no general expectation of this.

Young children are expected to be quiet in public, and mothers will take steps necessary to keep their infant children calm in public settings. Breast-feeding, though not prohibited, is rare in public, although feeding in other forms is common.

**Child Rearing and Education.** Child rearing is under the control of the natal family during the first several years of a child's life. While some monitoring of the treatment of very young children is done by the state, through child welfare organizations, for the most part children are cared for by their parents until the age of four or five, and parents have almost total control over how their children are cared for. Most child care responsibilities are carried out by the mother, in families with two resident parents of the opposite sex. In same sex parent families, child rearing responsibility is most likely to be shared by the two parents, and an increasing, though still very small number of opposite sex parent families are adopting this practice. However, the overwhelming majority of single parent headed households are headed by women, which reflects the key role women are expected to play in child rearing. While experts in childhood development have been active in promoting such things as early childhood education, the fact the majority of single parent female headed households with children have incomes at or below the poverty level suggests that the rearing and care of very young children is not considered socially important work by many Canadians.

Children are expected to be quiet, well-behaved, and relatively docile and are taught to show respect and deference to authority and to be obedient and submissive. Girls and boys are socialized into conventional gender roles early, through differences in dress and through limitations or direct instruction in appropriate play activities. Young children are, for the most part, excluded from important ceremonial activities such as church attendance. Their presence at public functions is considered to be at least potentially disruptive, and they are usually excluded. There has also been an increase in the number of child-free apartments, condominiums, and even housing developments in some suburban areas.

Children are required by law to attend school, or to be instructed at home under government guidelines, from the age of six to sixteen. In the 1980s and 1990s, the age at which children first attend school dropped, in some areas, to as young as four. This reflects the increase in two income households in Canada, which also lead to growth in professional daycare services for very young children. State funding of this early child care, however, was cut substantially in the final years of the 1990s making pre-school child care outside the home almost entirely the financial responsibility of parents.

In general, early childhood is a period of relative helplessness for the child, and during this period children are expected to be irresponsible and troublesome. Most of the effort of child rearing during this period is directed at controlling children's behavior and teaching the appropriate social roles. Corporal punishment, though allowed in Canada, is subject to criminal prosecution if it is excessive. Children under the age of twelve cannot be charged with criminal offenses, although their parents may be held financially responsible for their misdeeds. There has been some political lobbying to either lower that age to as low as six or, alternatively, to increase it to sixteen or eighteen. Once children enter school, child rearing becomes politically and socially complex, as state interests often come into conflict with the values and interests of parents, or with the concerns of communities as a whole. With increasing ethnic diversity, the potential for conflicts expands. Such issues as arranged marriage, male and female circumcision and other genital modification, and religious schooling are just three areas of child rearing and parental control producing substantial concern and debate in Canada.

**Higher Education.** Canada has the highest per capita level of postsecondary education participation of any industrialized country. All of its universities are publicly funded institutions, although students do pay tuition fees. National and provincial support programs are in place to assist students in postsecondary education.

## ETIQUETTE

The ethnic diversity of Canada means that rules of social propriety are quite complex. There are certain general expectations. Greeting, except in formal settings, does not require touching in the form of embraces or handshakes. Behavior in public should be subdued. Rowdiness and loud speech, for example, are considered inappropriate except under special circumstances or in places such as bars or other venues. As a community, Canadians are in general soft spoken, patient, and almost apologetic in their public behavior. They are also in general tolerant of the complex network of cultural differences in public behavior, more so in cities perhaps, where such diversity is more common place.

## RELIGION

**Religious Beliefs.** Religious affiliation is more prevalent than religious observance, though this varies by ethnic and religious group. Most Canadians claim some religious affiliation, most often Christian, although between the 1981 and 1991 census periods, the number of people claiming no religious affiliation has almost doubled from about 1.7 million to a little under 3.4 million. Nevertheless, there are significant practitioners of all the major world religions in Canada. Officially, Canada is a Christian nation, with respect for the Christian God enshrined in statute. Swearing on the Bible, for example, is part of most legal proceedings, though nonsecular alternatives are also practiced. Prayers open many official functions.

Personal religious observance has declined in the last several decades, a phenomenon similar to that found in most industrialized countries. This appears to be mostly a Christian phenomenon. Often new Canadians will make special efforts to maintain their religious observances as part of the process of retaining their original ethnic or cultural identity. Some religious groups have grown in membership, such as those associated with evangelical Christianity, but overall the trend in Canada has been toward increasing secularism in public and in private lives. An exception is the increase in the observance of traditional religious practices among First Nations peoples in recent decades, which should be seen both as a spiritual revitalization and as part of the historic process of reasserting their ethnic and political identities in Canada.

**Religious Practitioners.** Most religious officials are associated with the mainstream world religions, although there are some ethnic differences. For example, specialist religious practitioners such as healers are common in Portuguese communities such as the one in Toronto. With changes in migration patterns, important religious practitioners associated with non-world religions, such as local religious traditions found among different people from Africa, are becoming common. Excepting

*A group of children play hockey on the snow in Cape Dorset, Northwest Territories. Hockey, considered to be Canada's national sport, is popular across the nation.*

those religious practitioners who function for political bodies, such as the chaplain of the federal parliament, religious practitioners in general have authority in, and serve the needs of, only their own locally defined communities.

One exception is the increasing importance of First Nations spiritual leaders, who also serve as political leaders in their communities. These practitioners are often directly involved in negotiations with the wider Canadian community, and their spiritual and political roles are indivisible.

***Rituals and Holy Places.*** There is too much religious diversity throughout Canada to make any general observations on rituals and sacred sites. Churches of many types are important locales in almost all communities, not only to practitioners of the particular religion, but also as community centers and bases of operation in community emergencies. In both large and small communities, churches are often the site of community activism and the provision of community services, such as shelter for homeless people. While religion might be said to play less and less of a role in the cultural life of Canada, religious institutions and practitioners play significant roles in nonspiritual aspects of community life.

***Death and the Afterlife.*** The majority of Canadians believe in the Christian model of the afterlife, of heaven and of hell. Burial practices vary by religious group, but for the most part funeral and burial observances are the responsibility of the deceased's family. Funerals are both private functions, attended by family and friends, and public, as in the funeral procession from a church to a burial site. The funerals of important political or cultural figures may be televised.

## MEDICINE AND HEALTH CARE

Basic health care is provided in all places by a tax-funded system of hospitals and practitioners. Some specialist services require either complete or partial payment by the patient. The dominant medical model is Western biomedicine, though, as is the case in all ethnically diverse societies, other traditions do flourish serving local community needs, and increasingly, also serving the needs or health interests of the larger community. These ''alternative'' health providers may be spiritual practitioners or practitioners from other healing traditions such as acupuncture or Asian Ayurvedic systems. There is also a system of non-biomedical Western practitioners, such as chiropractors and homeopaths, who have their own training institutions and professional organizations. Except in restricted cases, these practitioners do not participate in the publicly funded health service system.

Canada has a system of public health surveillance which monitors infectious diseases, the safety of food and drinking water, and other health risks and problems.

## SECULAR CELEBRATIONS

Canadian holidays may be either political or religious. The major celebrations, which are often marked by a statutory holiday away from work, include two religious holidays: Christmas, 25 December; and Easter, which varies from year to year. There are five main political or secular celebrations: Canada Day, 1 July; New Year's Day, 1 January; Victoria Day, which honors Queen Victoria of England and varies from year to year; Labor Day, September; and Thanksgiving, in October.

## THE ARTS AND HUMANITIES

**Support for the Arts.** Most artists in Canada are self supporting and there are very few artists whose entire income is drawn from their artistic efforts. Several tax-funded programs, at all levels of government, do exist to provide financial assistance to artists of all types. The Governor General's Awards are presented each year to artists, writers, musicians, and other performers. There is a federal National Art Gallery, and most provinces also have one major tax-funded art gallery, usually in the provincial capital.

**Literature.** Canada does not have a single national literary tradition, participating instead in the wider English world of literature. While there are many internationally known writers from Canada, in general there is no single canon of Canadian literature. One exception is the province of Quebec, which has a longstanding "national" literature known for its social criticism and experimentation.

In recent decades, the number of published Canadian authors has increased dramatically, and Canadians as a community buy and read more books than in most other industrialized countries. Nevertheless, there is no special preference given to Canadian literature.

**Graphic Arts.** Canada has a large cohort of artists working in all media. Most small cities, and all larger ones, have many art galleries, including the tax-funded galleries. Several artist cooperatives ex-

ist in cities across the country, providing artistic and financial support for members. There is no single model for artistic presentation operating across the country.

**Performance Arts.** Theater ranges from professional theaters, mostly in large cities, which offer mainstream entertainment such as musical theater, to small community theater companies which can be found throughout the country. Several specialist companies or events, such as the Stratford Shakespeare Festival and the Shaw Festival, both in Ontario, take place each year and are international draws.

The city of Toronto has the distinction of hosting more theater openings per year than any other city in the English-speaking world. Its theaters include large commercial venues offering mostly musical theater, several large venues for other kinds of musical performance, and a diverse range of theaters and theater companies offering both new works original to the company and works from almost every linguistic and cultural tradition.

For the most part, attendance follows class lines but with important exceptions. Smaller theaters and theater companies, and in particular those offering new, experimental or political theater, encourage and attract audiences from all classes. Indeed, that is part of their role and their goal. Many of these theater companies see themselves as activists promoting social change. This makes these theaters both performance spaces and informal NGOs, a dual role that, while not unique to Canada, is an important aspect of its political culture.

## THE STATE OF THE PHYSICAL AND SOCIAL SCIENCES

Canada has a network of publicly funded educational and research institutions; in particular, the system of universities and colleges. These institutions train successive generations of researchers and practitioners. The physical sciences dominate these institutions, attracting most of the government sponsored funding of university research. Research in the physical sciences, and increasingly in the social sciences as well, is most often done in collaboration with industry and business interests, who also provide substantial funding for university based research. The majority of students attending these institutions receive training in the physical sciences.

The social sciences and humanities, however, do not receive the same collaborative support. Cana-

*A church and townhouses line a street, with Quebec City, Quebec, behind them.*

dian postsecondary education is based on a "liberal arts" model which recognizes the importance of breadth of scholarship in all fields of human endeavor as a key to a successful education and to success as a citizen. Both economic constraints in recent decades, as well as ideological shifts in how education is defined and valued, has led, however, to the erosion of financial support for both the social sciences and the humanities. While Canada maintains a major funding body for research in the social science and humanities, its resources have declined in recent years, which has been the object of considerable political dispute.

Although the official commitment to the humanities and social sciences, among politicians, educators, and most of the public, remains substantial, the trend has been toward an increasingly technocratic model of higher education. While education has often celebrated, championed, and enhanced the ethnic and cultural diversity of Canada, economic and political changes are shifting emphasis away from diversity in the direction of a kind of practical homogenization in which practical application and financial benefit takes precedence over the breadth and depth of knowledge and understanding. This puts the social sciences and humanities in a precarious position, as the political culture of Canada changes.

## BIBLIOGRAPHY

Angus, Ian. *A Border Within: National Identity, Cultural Plurality, and Wilderness*, 1997.

Atwood, Margaret. *Surfacing: A Thematic Guide to Canadian Literature*, 1972.

Avery, Donald. *Dangerous Foreigners: European Immigrant Workers and Labour Radicalism in Canada, 1896–1932*, 1979.

Axtell, James. *The Invasion Within: The Contest of Cultures in Colonial North America*, 1985.

Basran, G. S., and David A. Hay. *The Political Economy of Agriculture in Western Canada*, 1988.

Berry, J. W., and J. A. Laponce, eds. *Ethnicity and Culture in Canada: The Research Landscape*, 1994.

Brown, Graham L., and Douglas Fairbairn. *Pioneer Settlement in Canada, 1763–1895*, 1981.

Cairns, Allan C. *Citizens Plus: Aboriginal Peoples and the Canadian State*, 2000.

Clark, S. D. *The Social Development of Canada: An Introductory Study with Select Documents*, 1942.

———. *Church and Sect in Canada*, 1945.

———. *The Developing Canadian Community*, 1968.

Corsianos, Marilyn, and Kelly Amanda Train. *Interrogating Social Justice: Politics, Culture and Identity*, 1999.

Driedger, L., ed. *Ethnic Canada: Identities and Inequalities,* 1987.

Easingwood, Peter, et al, eds. *Difference and community: Canadian and European Cultural Perspectives,* 1996.

Fleras, Augie, and Jean Leonard Elliott. *Unequal Relations: An Introduction to Race, Ethnic, and Aboriginal Dynamics in Canada,* 1999.

Fowke, Edith. *Canadian Folklore,* 1988.

Fry, A. J., and C. Forceville, eds. *Canadian Mosaic: Essays on Multiculturalism,* 1988.

Gleave, Alfred. *United We Stand: Prairie Farmers, 1901–1975,* 1991.

Helms-Hayes, Rick, and James Curtis. *The Vertical Mosaic Revisited,* 1998.

Horn, Michael. *Academic Freedom in Canada: A History,* 1999.

Hunter, Alfred A. *Class Tells: On Social Inequality in Canada,* 1981; 2nd ed., 1986.

Innis, H. A. *The Fur Trade in Canada,* 1927.

Keohane, Kieran. *Symptoms of Canada: An Essay on the Canadian Identity,* 1997.

Kershen, Jeffrey, ed. *Age of Contention: Readings in Canadian History, 1900–1945,* 1997.

Kymlicka, Will. *Finding Our Way: Rethinking Ethnocultural Relations in Canada,* 1998.

Levitt, Cyril. *Children of Privilege: Student Revolt in the Sixties: A Study of Student Movements in Canada, the United States, and West Germany,* 1984.

MacLennan, Hugh. *Two Solitudes,* 1945.

Mannion, John J. *Irish Imprints on the Landscape of Eastern Canada in the Nineteenth Century,* 1971.

McRae, T., et al. *Environmental Sustainability of Canadian Agriculture: Report of the Agri-environmental Indicator Project,* 2000.

Morgan, Henry J., and Lawrence J. Burpee. *Canadian Life in Town and Country,* 1905.

Morton, Desmond. *Canada and War: A Military and Political History,* 1981.

Naiman, Joanne. *How Societies Work: Class, Power and Change in a Canadian Context,* 2nd. ed., 2000.

Novak, Mark. *Aging and Society: A Canadian Perspective,* 1997.

Palmer, Bryan D. *The Character of Class Struggle: Essays in Canadian Working-Class History, 1850–1985,* 1986.

Porter, John. *The Vertical Mosaic: An Analysis of Social Class and Power in Canada,* 1965.

Ralston, Helen. *The Lived Experience of South Asian Immigrant Women in Atlantic Canada: The Interconnections of Race, Class, and Gender,* 1996.

Russell, Loris. *Everyday Life in Colonial Canada,* 1973.

Trudeau, Pierre E. *Fatal Tilt: Speaking Out about Sovereignty,* 1991.

Vallières, Pierre. *White Niggers of America: The Precocious Autobiography of a Quebec "Terrorist,"* 1971.

Wade, Mason. *Regionalism in the Canadian Community, 1867–1967,* 1969.

Wood, Louis A. *A History of Farmers' Movements in Canada,* 1924, 1975.

Woodcock, George. *The Century that Made Us: Canada, 1814–1914,* 1989.

—Douglass Drozdow-St.Christian

# CAPE VERDE

## CULTURE NAME

Cape Verdean

## ORIENTATION

**Identification.** The islands are named for the Cap Vert peninsula in West Africa, the nearest land formation. Cape Verdeans identify strongly with the culture of their individual islands.

**Location and Geography.** Cape Verde comprises ten islands, nine of which are inhabited, and is located 375 miles (600 kilometers) off the coast of Senegal. The combined area of all the islands is 1,557 square miles (4,033 square kilometers), roughly the size of Rhode Island. The islands vary in geographical characteristics. Sal, Boavista, Maio, and São Vicente are flat and desert-like, with stretches of sand dunes. Santiago, Santo Antão, Fogo, and São Nicolau are more mountainous and arable, although all the islands have a long history of drought. They are all of volcanic origin; Fogo, the only volcano still active, last erupted in 1995. The capital, Praia, is on the island of Santiago which is the largest in terms of area and population and the first one to be settled.

**Demography.** The population of Cape Verde is 430,000. Of these, 85,000 live in the capital. Because of the country's long history of emigration, there are an additional estimated one million Cape Verdeans living abroad, mainly in the United States, western Europe, and Africa. The United States Cape Verdean population, concentrated in the New England states, is estimated to be as large as the population in Cape Verde itself.

**Linguistic Affiliation.** The official language is Portuguese. It is used in school, for official functions, and for all written communication. The vernacular is a Creole, which is essentially fifteenth-century Portuguese with a simplified vocabulary and influences from Mandingo and several Senegambian languages. Each island has its own distinctive Creole in which its inhabitants take pride.

## HISTORY AND ETHNIC RELATIONS

**Emergence of the Nation.** The Cape Verde Islands were uninhabited until the Portuguese first landed in 1460. They settled in an area of Santiago which they called Ribeira Grande and which they used as a slave-trade post between Africa and the New World. Some Africans stayed on the island and worked as slaves on the *latifundas*, or plantations, there. Ribeira Grande experienced several pirate attacks, and was abandoned after a French assault in 1712. After 1876, with the decline of slave trade, the islands lost much of their economic value to the Portuguese. The effects of drought and famine were compounded by poor administration and government corruption. Cape Verde regained some wealth in the late nineteenth century due to its convenient location on major trade routes between Europe, South America, and Africa and to the opening of a coal and submarine cable station in the port city of Mindelo. This prosperity again declined after World War I, however, and the country experienced several devastating famines. It was not until after the second world war that relative prosperity began to return.

In 1951, the Portuguese changed Cape Verde's status from colony to overseas province and in 1961, granted full Portuguese citizenship to all Cape Verdeans. A war of independence was fought from 1974 to 1975 in Guinea-Bissau, another Portuguese colony on the mainland also seeking autonomy. The islands became an independent republic in 1975.

**National Identity.** Cape Verdean culture is a unique mixture of European and African elements. National identity is rather fragmented, mainly as a result of the geographical division of the islands. The northern, or *barlavento* islands, tend to identify more with the Portuguese colonizers, whereas the

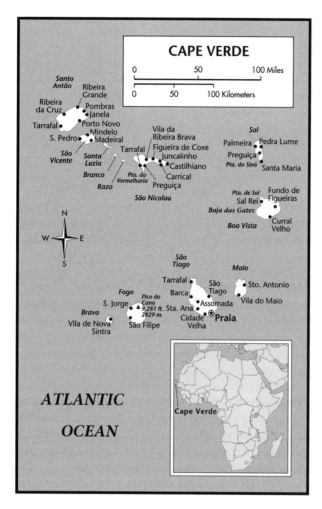

*Cape Verde*

southern, or *sotavento* islands (Santiago in particular) have a closer cultural affinity with Africa. Cape Verdeans have a strong sense of pride in the specific culture of their own island.

**Ethnic Relations.** Cape Verde is a *mestizo* society. Seventy-eight percent of the population is Creole, that is, of mixed African and European blood. Of the remainder, 28 percent is black African, and 1 percent is white.

## URBANISM, ARCHITECTURE, AND THE USE OF SPACE

Praia, the capital of Cape Verde, is a rapidly growing urban center. Its growth has been unimpeded by zoning laws or organization which has allowed it to spread out into nearby land in a haphazard way. Mindelo, the second largest city with a population of 47,000, is located on the northern island of São Vicente and provides a marked contrast as a clean, orderly city with a European feel. Many of the

islands combine old colonial architecture with the new cinderblock structures that are sprouting up to house the burgeoning population. The traditional houses that dot the countryside are stone structures with thatched or tiled roofs.

## FOOD AND ECONOMY

**Food in Daily Life.** Corn is the staple food of Cape Verde. The national dish, *cachupa*, is a stew of hominy, beans, and whatever meat or vegetables may be available. Other common foods include rice, beans, fish, potatoes, and manioc. A traditional breakfast is *cuscus*, a steamed cornbread, eaten with honey and milk or coffee. Cape Verdeans generally eat a large lunch in the mid-afternoon and a small, late dinner. Grog, or sugar cane liquor, is manufactured on the islands and is a popular drink, particularly among the men.

**Food Customs at Ceremonial Occasions.** Many Catholic saints' days are observed throughout the year. Food and its preparation play a large part in these celebrations. Women usually spend the few days prior to the feast pounding corn for the cachupa, cleaning and cutting vegetables, and preparing meat. *Xerem*, a form of cachupa in which the corn is more finely ground, is often served.

**Basic Economy.** The economy is primarily based on agriculture although only 10 percent of the land is arable. Roughly one-third of the population are farmers. The islands produce bananas, corn, beans, sugarcane, coffee, and some fruits and vegetables, but supply less than one-fifth of the country's needs. Much of the rest comes in the form of aid from the United States, Portugal, Holland, and other countries in western Europe. Remittances from Cape Verdeans living abroad also make a considerable contribution to the economy and GNP.

**Land Tenure and Property.** Cape Verdeans have a communal attitude towards property and freely borrow and lend possessions. Farm land is generally privately owned but many farming communities form organizations to oversee its use and distribute pooled funds in the development of such things as corrals or plant nurseries.

**Commercial Activities.** The majority of goods produced in Cape Verde are agricultural. Most towns have a small market where fruits, vegetables, meat, and fish are sold.

**Major Industries.** Agriculture accounts for one-third of the GNP, services and transportation for

**418**

one-half. This is due, in part to the growth of tourism which has been enhanced by the construction of luxury hotels and resorts on several islands. Construction comprises nearly one-fourth of the GNP as the country continues to urbanize and the population expands.

**Trade.** Cape Verde's main trade partners are countries of the European Union (Portugal, France, Holland, Germany, Spain, and Italy). Small amounts of fish, salt, lobster, bananas, shoes, and pharmaceutical products are exported. Large quantities of food, construction and building materials, machinery, and textiles are imported.

**Division of Labor.** Labor is not strictly divided along gender lines. Women and men do heavy physical labor; however, domestic work is an exclusively female domain. Children often follow the same trade as their parents. They begin at a very young age, especially if they come from farming or fishing families. Older people continue to work as long as they are able, sometimes modifying strenuous tasks. It is not unusual to see men and women in their seventies harvesting beans or hauling rocks at a construction site.

## SOCIAL STRATIFICATION

**Classes and Castes.** There is little class distinction in Cape Verde because the vast majority of the population is poor. There is a small but growing middle class in the towns and cities and virtually no upper class. Those of higher socio-economic backgrounds tend to identify culturally with Europe and to think of themselves as more ''European,'' often because they have spent time abroad.

**Symbols of Social Stratification.** Cape Verdeans take pride in their dress and personal appearance. The most highly valued attire is American brand names popular among African Americans. These clothes are often an indicator of class; however, the poorest Cape Verdeans sometimes have relatives in the United States who send gifts of clothing.

## POLITICAL LIFE

**Government.** Since Cape Verde won independence from Portugal in 1975, it has had a democratic multi-party system of government with proportional representation through electoral districts. The unicameral national assembly is made up of seventy-two elected deputies including six chosen by the Cape Verdean population abroad.

**Leadership and Political Officials.** The president is elected for a five-year term and appoints a prime minister. There are two main political parties: African Party for the Independence of Cape Verde (PAICY) and Movement for Democracy (MPD). In the general population identification with one party or the other is strong and highly personal. Local elections are occasions for rallies with music and dancing, parades, and public shouting matches.

**Social Problems and Control.** What little crime there is in Cape Verde consists mainly of petty theft and robbery. This is more common in the cities, particularly in Praia. The code of conduct is implicitly enforced by social pressure. Personal reputation is of paramount importance; for this reason, the court system is overrun with slander cases.

**Military Activity.** Cape Verde has a small military of eleven hundred active duty personnel. Of these, 91 percent are in the army and 9 percent are in the air force. Cape Verde spends roughly 1 percent of its GNP on its military.

## SOCIAL WELFARE AND CHANGE PROGRAMS

Social security programs have been introduced, but are limited in scope. The government provides some assistance for the poor and the elderly, as well as free health care, but the majority of social welfare is provided by individual families and communities.

## NONGOVERNMENTAL ORGANIZATIONS AND OTHER ASSOCIATIONS

Several foreign nongovernmental organizations (NGOs) are a presence; among these, the German organization Dywidag has helped develop the ports. The U.S. Peace Corps sends volunteers to work in the education system and local government. Portuguese aid groups are also present in Cape Verde.

## GENDER ROLES AND STATUSES

**Division of Labor by Gender.** Women take care of all domestic tasks including cooking, cleaning, and child rearing. At the same time, they also make substantial contributions in other sectors of the work force, including farming, construction, and commerce. Women are often the sole economic supporters of their families. However, they are proportionally under-represented in the white-collar professions and in the political system.

*People, dressed in Western clothing, stand in front of a mural depicting the importance of safe sex, another Western import.*

**The Relative Status of Women and Men.** While the genders are legally recognized as equal, there are broad de facto disparities in rights and power. Women (mothers in particular) are respected for the immense workload they shoulder, yet they often are expected to defer to men.

## MARRIAGE, FAMILY, AND KINSHIP

**Marriage.** Legal and church weddings are uncommon in Cape Verde. More often than not, a woman will simply *sai di casa* (leave her family's house) to move in with her boyfriend. This is often occasioned by the woman becoming pregnant. After four years of cohabitation, a relationship acquires the status of common-law marriage. While polygamy is not legal, it is customary for men (married or not) to be sleeping with several women at once.

**Domestic Unit.** Traditionally, several generations of a family live together in the same house. Childrearing is communal, and living situations are fluid; children often stay with aunts, uncles, or other relatives, especially during the school year. Due to emigration and de facto polygamy, there are a great many households headed by single mothers.

## SOCIALIZATION

**Infant Care.** Seven days after a baby is born, the parents throw a big party called a *sete*. Like any other party, it is an occasion for dancing and drinking. At midnight the guests file in to the baby's room and sing to it as a protection against evil spirits. Infants are coddled and held. Mothers often tie small babies to their backs and carry them along to work.

**Child Rearing and Education.** Children are treated with affection, but are reprimanded strictly for misbehavior. Corporal punishment is not uncommon. Children are expected to work at the family's trade, and even if the parents are professionals, children do a good deal of housework. Obedience and deference to elders is inculcated early. It is not uncommon for an adult to grab any child on the street and ask him or her to run an errand.

Education is mandatory and free between the ages of seven and fourteen. About 90 percent of children attend school. Each island has a high school that goes through at least eleventh grade. High school students pay an education tax on a sliding scale based on their parents' income.

**Higher Education.** Cape Verde is still in the process of establishing an institution of higher learn-

*Old colonial style architecture is reminiscent of the past European influence in Cape Verde.*

ing. There are teacher certification schools in Praia and one in Mindelo. To obtain any other degree past high school, it is necessary to go abroad. A higher degree is of little use in the Cape Verdean job market, and the vast majority of those who leave to study do not return.

## ETIQUETTE

Cape Verdeans are an extremely generous and hospitable people. Even the poorest take pride in presenting guests with a meal. It is considered rude to eat in front of others without sharing, and for this reason one does not eat in a public setting such as on the street or on a bus.

Cape Verdeans stand close together when talking and are physically demonstrative, often touching and holding hands (men as well as women). Greetings are somewhat lengthy, and include shaking hands (or kissing for women), and inquiring about each other's health and family. This is usually done each time two people meet, even if it is more than once in the same day.

## RELIGION

***Religious Beliefs.*** Ninety-eight percent of Cape Verdeans are Roman Catholic. The Nazarene church is also represented as are Seventh Day Adventists, Mormons, and Evangelical Christians. There is a history of several Jewish settlements that dates back to the inquisition, but they are now extinct.

***Rituals and Holy Places.*** Each town has a church, but most Cape Verdeans are non-practicing Catholics. However, saints' days are often the basis of community-wide parties involving dancing, drinking, and food. One family, neighborhood, or town usually takes charge of the celebration for a given saint.

***Death and the Afterlife.*** Despite its relatively secular atmosphere, rituals surrounding death are strictly observed. Funerals are large events attended by much of the community. The procession is accompanied by mourners who perform a highly stylized, musical wailing. Family members of the deceased dress in black for a full year after the death and are forbidden to dance or play music.

## MEDICINE AND HEALTH CARE

Cape Verde provides its citizens with free health care through small hospitals on each island. Facilities and resources are poor but are more advanced than many in West Africa. The best hospitals are in Praia and Mindelo, and people are often sent there for

*Fogo Islanders in a truck loaded with firewood.*

treatment. The main health concerns are infectious and parasitic diseases such as tuberculosis, pneumonia, bronchitis, and gastrointestinal ailments. These are caused mainly by malnutrition and poor sanitation. The average life expectancy is 62 years, and the infant mortality rate is the lowest in West Africa.

## SECULAR CELEBRATIONS

New Year's Day is celebrated on 1 January. Amilcar Cabral Day (24 January), recognizes the birthday of the liberator of Cape Verde, one of the leaders in the war of independence. Independence Day is celebrated on 5 July.

## THE ARTS AND HUMANITIES

**Support for the Arts.** There is a Cape Verdean Cultural Center in Praia, which stages performances and exhibitions and sells books, music, and artifacts.

**Literature.** There is a small but growing body of Cape Verdean literature. Most of it is written in Portuguese, but a movement to develop a standardized written form of Creole has caused several books to be published in this language as well. Written literature is strongly influenced by the tradition of

oral story telling which finds its roots in both Africa and Europe. A predominant theme in both literature and music is *saudade*, a sense of longing or homesickness, usually the result of emigration and the ensuing separation of families.

**Graphic Arts.** Graphic art production is limited. Crocheting is popular among women. Textiles were traditionally produced on large looms in a time-consuming process but this is rare today. The island of Boavista is known for its clay pottery; Fogo is known for small carvings made from hardened lava. There is also some basket weaving, embroidery, woodworking, and other craft production, but the preponderance of artifacts sold at the markets is imported from Africa.

**Performance Arts.** Music and dance are a focal point of Cape Verdean culture. Traditional forms of music include *funana*, which is played on an accordion and an iron bar that serves as a rhythm instrument. *Batuque* is performed by a circle of women who beat out rhythms on plastic sacks held between their legs. Both types of music are very African-influenced and are particular to the island of Santiago. Another traditional form of music is the *morna* which is a slower, more Portuguese-influenced ballad. Each type of music has a specific dance that goes with it. Popular music has a largely synthesized feel.

## THE STATE OF THE PHYSICAL AND SOCIAL SCIENCES

There are no research facilities or laboratories for physical sciences in Cape Verde.

## BIBLIOGRAPHY

Bratton, Michael. "Deciphering Africa's Divergent Transitions." *Political Science Quarterly*, Spring 1997.

Carreira, Antonio. *People of the Cape Verde Islands: Exploitation and Emigration.* Trans. and ed. by Christopher Fyfe, 1982.

Davidson, Basil. *Fortunate Isles: A Study in African Transformation*, 1989.

Davidson, Basil. *No Fist Is Big Enough to Hide the Sky: the Liberation of Guinea and Cape Verde*, 1981.

Hills, C. A. R. "Portugal and Her Empire, 1497-1997." *Contemporary Review*, July 1997.

Irwin, Aisling and Colum Wilson. *Cape Verde Islands: The Bradt Travel Guide*, 1998.

Khouri-Dagher, Nadia. "Teachers Under Pressure." *UNESCO Sources*, April 1998.

Lobban, Richard A. *Cape Verde: Crioulo Colony to Independent Nation*, 1998.

Meintel, Deirdre. *Race, Culture and Portuguese Colonialism in Cabo Verde*, 1984.

Mozer, Gerald M. "Neglected or Forgotten Authors of Lusophone Africa." *World Literature Today*, Winter 1999.

Shaw, Caroline S., ed. *Cape Verde*, 1991.

Teixeira, Erin. "Exploring a Racial Riddle in Cape Verde." *Los Angeles Times*, 18 December 2000.

### *Web Sites*

Cape Verde Reference Page. http://www.users.erols.com/kauberdi/

Embassy of the Republic of Cape Verde to the United States and Canada Homepage. http://www.capeverdeusembassy.org

—ELEANOR STANFORD

# CAYMAN ISLANDS

## CULTURE NAME

Caymanian

## ALTERNATIVE NAMES

Crown Colony of the Cayman Islands; Caymans

## ORIENTATION

**Identification.** Christopher Columbus discovered the Cayman Islands on 10 May 1503 when his ships were blown off course by strong winds. He saw two small islands so full of turtles that he named them *Las Tortugas*, Spanish for "the turtles." It was the presence of the marine crocodile, however, that gave the islands their name, after the Carib word *caymanas*. The capital, George Town, was named after King George III of England.

**Location and Geography.** The three islands Grand Cayman, Little Cayman, and Cayman Brac lie in the Caribbean Sea about 200 miles (320 kilometers) northwest of Jamaica. Total land area is 100 square miles (264 square kilometers). The islands are outcrops of the Cayman Ridge, which extends from Cuba to Belize, and are formed primarily of limestone. Two of the deepest parts of the Caribbean, the Cayman Trough to the east and the Bartlett Trough to the south, together with the shallower Cayman Bank west of Grand Cayman lie in close proximity. Grand Cayman, the largest island, is approximately 22 miles (35 kilometers) long and 8 miles (13 kilometers) wide; its most striking feature is the North Sound, a shallow reef-protected lagoon. Cayman Brac, about 90 miles (145 kilometers) northeast of Grand Cayman, is about 12 miles (19 kilometers) long and a mile (1.6 kilometers) wide; its name derives from its most striking feature, the *brac* (Gaelic for "bluff") that runs the length of the island and drops 140 feet (43 meters) into the sea at its highest point. The flattest and least developed of the three islands, Little Cayman, lies about 5 miles (8 kilometers) west of Cayman Brac. There are no natural freshwater resources.

**Demography.** The population of 40,000 (2000 estimate) is diverse, with people of European stock comprising about 25 percent of the total, those of African descent another 25 percent, and the remaining 50 percent being of mixed ancestry. The capital, George Town (estimated population 35,000), is on Grand Cayman. According to 1999 estimates, the population growth rate is 4.2 percent. Women slightly outnumber men.

**Linguistic Affiliation.** English is the official language. A Creole language, Bay Islands English, is thought to have developed in the Caymans during the eighteenth century, and spread to islands farther west. Creole forms are more common on Cayman Brac and Little Cayman.

**Symbolism.** Turtles, pirates, and the British have all played a large part in the culture. The Department of Tourism combined the three when it chose a peg-leg "Sir Turtle" as a mascot and symbol for the country. The flag is blue, with the flag of the United Kingdom in the upper hoist-side quadrant and the Caymanian coat of arms on a white disk on the outer half of the flag. The coat of arms features a pineapple (a symbol of hospitality) and a turtle above a shield with three stars, representing the islands, and a scroll with the motto "He hath founded it upon the seas." Caymanians voted on new national symbols in 1996; the national flower is the wild banana orchid, the national tree is the silver thatch palm, and the national bird is the Cayman parrot.

## HISTORY AND ETHNIC RELATIONS

**Emergence of the Nation.** The islands became British following the Treaty of Madrid in 1670. During 1661–1671 settlers came from Jamaica; records show that Cayman Brac and Little Cayman

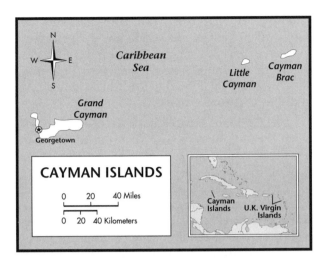

*Cayman Islands*

were settled before Grand Cayman, but these settlements were abandoned after attacks by pirates, who continued to use the islands as a hideout well into the eighteenth century. The first census, taken in 1803, showed 933 residents, half of whom were slaves. When slavery was abolished in 1835, most freed slaves remained on the islands. The first constitution was adopted in 1959. Jamaica administered the islands until 1962, when the Caymans opted to remain under British rule as a British Crown Colony after Jamaica became independent.

***National Identity.*** The remoteness of the islands, and the social integration following the emancipation of slaves in 1835, resulted in a socially homogeneous society. Out of necessity, Caymanians relied on the sea. Shipbuilding and "sailorizing," the old term for seafaring, were important. They used local ingredients—coral fans for sieving flour, fish skins for scrubbing, the washwood plant for soap. The silver thatch palm was used for hats, baskets, roofs, and rope that was prized because it did not rot in saltwater and could be traded for other necessities. In the nineteenth century many of the locals left Cayman for jobs on neighboring islands and in Nicaragua, Honduras, and the southern United States; after World War II, a number of Caymanians left to work on ships, particularly oil tankers. These emigrants sent money and gifts home to relatives, continued to think of Cayman as home, and often returned after long periods abroad. There is a well-documented tradition of circular migration; the national anthem contains several references to "coming back to the island homeland" after traveling to distant cities. As late as the 1950s, the government's annual report stated that the main export was "seamen," and their remittances

the mainstay of the economy. Persons of Caymanian descent, but born outside the islands, make up a significant part of the workforce today, and there is a strong feeling that the current immigration law should be changed to make it easier for these residents to obtain full Caymanian citizenship. Caymanians have resisted independence, and any hint that Britain may wish to divest itself of the islands is met with strong opposition.

***Ethnic Relations.*** Relations between the various ethnic groups are good. There are no restrictions on applications for work permits, although current policy aims at insuring a balance among the various nationalities. The Immigration Board may restrict applications if any particular geographic category is thought to be excessive. The areas of friction do not involve ethnicity so much as who is entitled to citizenship. As of 2000, the islands had approximately ten thousand foreign workers, comprising almost a quarter of the population.

## URBANISM, ARCHITECTURE, AND THE USE OF SPACE

Older houses were made from wattle and daub. Some cottages are raised off the ground, with large porches and gabled roofs. The local silver thatch palm, traditionally used for roofing, was supplanted by corrugated tin. Rainwater was collected from the roof and stored in a cistern beneath the house. Houses are usually painted in pastel colors of pink, turquoise, and green. "Sand gardens" are popular, decorated with native flowering plants and shells; at Christmas, it is traditional to bring white sand from the beach and spread it around the house to resemble snow.

The rapid growth in construction on Grand Cayman, which began during the 1980s to meet demand for new homes, hotels, and condominiums, has caused concern that the human dimension to urban design is being lost and that much of the island's architecture will eventually fall victim to new development. Efforts are being made to preserve some of the traditional landmarks, such as the Old Courts Building, one of the few surviving nineteenth century structures, and the Harry Piercy House, built in 1916 and recently renovated to become the National Museum offices. The Heritage Garden in the Queen Elizabeth II Botanic Park on Grand Cayman has a restored Caymanian farmhouse, complete with original furnishings, cook room, cistern, outbuildings, and fences and walls built of old coral.

## FOOD AND ECONOMY

### Food in Daily Life.

Seafood is predominant. The traditional national dish is turtle; conch is also popular, either served raw with lime juice and onions, or cooked as a stew, chowder, or fritters. A number of recipes show influences from other Caribbean countries such as Jamaica and Trinidad. "Jerking," a slow-smoking process using a blend of spices, and "heavy cake," a dense sweet dessert made with "breadkind" (starchy vegetables such as cassava, papaya, and yams) are two examples. "Fish rundown" is fish stewed with "breadkind." "Swankie" is lemonade. Other common local ingredients include key limes, honey, rum, and coconut. A microbrewery produces beer for local consumption. Other than fish, turtle meat, and a few local fruits and vegetables, almost all food must be imported.

### Food Customs at Ceremonial Occasions.

At Christmas, beef (a luxury item) is featured, along with heavy cake and non-native fruits such as apples, pears, and grapes. Drinks based on corn, sorrel, and pineapple are also traditional during the holiday season.

### Basic Economy.

The country has the highest per capita income in the Caribbean—$23,800, according to a 1996 estimate. The economy is based largely on tourism and the islands' status as an offshore financial center. There is no business or personal income tax; legend has it that King George III of England granted this freedom from taxation, along with a permanent exemption from military service, as a reward for the islanders' heroism in saving British seamen wrecked off the coast in 1788. Major sources of government revenue include import duties, a tax of 7.5–10 percent on land or property transfers, a 10 percent tax on tourist accommodations, airport and cruise ship passenger departure fees, company registration fees, work permits, and business licenses. Inflation, which had been less than 3 percent for much of the 1990s, increased to over 4 percent in the first half of 2000. A stock exchange opened in January 1997. There is also a large shipping registry, with 1,080 ships registered as of 1997.

### Land Tenure and Property.

There are no restrictions on who may own property, although foreigners may own no more than two residences. As the government insures property titles, and all titles are registered, no title search or title insurance is needed. As of late 1999, the National Trust for the Cayman Islands owns 1,980 acres of nature reserves in perpetuity.

### Commercial Activities.

Tourism accounts for about 70 percent of the (GDP) and 75 percent of foreign currency earnings, with the bulk of the visitors from the United States. Tourist arrivals average about 1.2 million annually. The tourist industry is aimed at the luxury market.

The Caymans became an offshore banking center in the 1980s. More than six hundred banks are registered, with assets in excess of $500 billion, making the islands the fifth largest financial center in the world and a leader in the global eurocurrency market. Currently, at least forty of the world's top banks are represented. There are no exchange control or reporting requirements; deposits earn tax-free interest; funds can be moved in and out freely; and there is an excellent telecommunications system. The banking sector employs about a tenth of the labor force and contributes 16 percent of the GDP. Accusations of illegal activities, specifically "money laundering," have been leveled at some Cayman banks. In 1990 the Cayman Islands signed the Mutual Legal Assistance Treaty with the United States, and in 1996 enacted Britain's "proceeds of criminal conduct" law. Banks may now disclose information in cases of criminal activity (excluding tax-related matters), but there is still criticism of Caymanian banking in the international financial press.

### Major Industries.

Construction, the third major commercial activity, expanded in the 1980s to meet tourist accommodation demand, and labor had to be imported. Indications are that the rate of new construction slowed somewhat in 2000.

### Trade.

Major trading partners are the United States, Great Britain, Trinidad and Tobago, the Netherlands Antilles, and Japan. Exports include turtle products and manufactured consumer goods.

### Division of Labor.

The Immigration Law of 1992 gives preference in employment to those holding Caymanian status. Caymanians hold the majority of the clerical, secretarial, and lower management jobs. Foreign workers fall into two categories: temporary construction laborers hired during high-growth periods and professional and senior management staff in areas where there are no qualified locals available.

## SOCIAL STRATIFICATION

### Classes and Castes.

The largely affluent, well-educated resident population mixes well, without racial problems or noticeable class distinctions.

*A cottage on Grand Cayman. Large porches and gabled roofs are not uncommon.*

Crime, which had been almost nonexistent on the islands, has increased on Grand Cayman, but remains at a low level.

***Symbols of Social Stratification.*** Education is the primary factor in attaining high social status. It is seen as not only leading to better economic prospects, but also as enabling one to associate with people who are more cultured and conscious of upper-class values.

## POLITICAL LIFE

***Government.*** Formerly a dependency of Jamaica, the islands chose to remain a direct dependency of the British Crown when Jamaica achieved independence in 1962. The governor is appointed by the British Crown. An eight-member Executive Council advises the governor. Five of the council members (called ministers) are elected from the fifteen Legislative Assembly representatives. Three members are appointed by the governor: the chief secretary, who acts in the governor's absence; the financial secretary; and the attorney general. The Legislative Assembly is composed of two members from each of Cayman's six electoral districts, plus the three appointed members of the Executive Council.

There are no recognized political parties. Groups or "teams" of candidates run for office, and there is little or no difference in political ideology among them. In the November 2000 election, the National team, which had governed since 1992, was defeated in a surprise return to campaigning by independent candidates. There is universal suffrage, and the voting age is eighteen.

***Leadership and Political Officials.*** Peter Smith was appointed governor in May 1999. There is a Cayman Islands representative to the United Kingdom. The late Jim Bodden, a legislative leader from the mid-1970s to the mid-1980s and founder of the International College of the Cayman Islands, was named the first "National Hero"; his statue stands opposite the assembly building in George Town.

***Social Problems and Control.*** The most pressing social problems result from the rapid growth due to immigration. Caymanians now make up less than 50 percent of the workforce and are a bare majority of the population, as indicated by the 1999 census results. The country is a melting pot of nations and cultures (more than one hundred countries are represented); there is ongoing debate over who should be granted "Caymanian status" and allowed to live and work permanently in the Cayman Islands. Currently, foreigners must apply for a work permit that is valid for one year, which may be renewed.

Dependence upon tourism and finance puts Caymanians at the mercy of forces beyond their control. The islands' high standard of living, which is reflected in higher costs, may be contributing to a decline in tourism, as vacationers seek cheaper destinations. Cayman financial institutions have come under repeated scrutiny, criticism, and threats of tighter outside controls. The islands' economic welfare depends on these two sectors, so any decline in revenues would bring significant hardship.

**Military Activity.** The Royal Cayman Islands Police Force, first established in 1907, now has 266 officers.

## SOCIAL WELFARE AND CHANGE PROGRAMS

The Progress with Dignity team, which took control of the Legislative Assembly in 1984, emphasized greater government control of spending and development, and a social welfare approach to economic growth.

## NONGOVERNMENTAL ORGANIZATIONS AND OTHER ASSOCIATIONS

Concern about preserving Caymanian culture resulted in the establishment of the National Cultural Foundation, the National Museum, the National Trust, and the National Archive in the 1980s. An important part of the National Archive is the Memory Bank, an oral history program intended to preserve social history and culture via taped interviews with longtime residents.

There is an active Chamber of Commerce with members on Grand Cayman and Cayman Brac, and a number of business organizations, primarily in the tourism and financial services areas.

## GENDER ROLES AND STATUSES

**Division of Labor by Gender.** Traditional society was matriarchal; Caymanian women took over in family, business, and government when the men went to sea. Starting in the 1930s, there was a growing feeling that women's roles and expectations had to change if the society was to progress. Women began to play more active roles in social and economic life. With the birth of trade unionism, women became important in the economic sphere, although the male-dominated society did not accept women as political equals.

**The Relative Status of Women and Men.** After World War II, universal adult suffrage resulted in women being grudgingly accepted as partners in the political process. Today, in the major businesses and social services, women play important roles; in the political arena, however, women are still under represented, making up just 26 percent of the candidates in the November 2000 election.

## MARRIAGE, FAMILY, AND KINSHIP

**Marriage.** Only monogamy is permitted. Homosexual acts are illegal, which has caused friction between the local Cayman authorities (especially the religious leaders) and Great Britain, which is pressing for liberalization throughout its territories. The pattern of circular migration meant that many men lived apart from their families for long periods, continuing to support them financially from abroad.

**Domestic Unit.** Households range from single persons (now most commonly expatriate workers) to single-parent families, traditional nuclear families, and extended family units with women usually predominating, both in numbers and in amount of control exercised within the family.

**Inheritance.** Property is inherited by descendants of the original owner; land is generally divided among the children.

**Kin Groups.** Family networks extend not only throughout the country but also overseas. Maintaining ties with relatives at home gives emigrants the possibility of a base should they decide to return. For those remaining on the islands, the relationships traditionally provided financial support, knowledge of distant events and cultures, and a place of temporary shelter should they also decide to emigrate.

## SOCIALIZATION

**Infant Care.** Child care is seen as the responsibility of the mother. During much of the islands' history, when men were obliged to be absent for long periods at sea, women stayed behind and received assistance from relatives.

**Child Rearing and Education.** Parents are expected to control their children's behavior. A high value is placed on education, which is free and compulsory to age sixteen; the literacy rate is 98 percent. At least one parent has been expected to be available to help students with homework, but recently there

*Stingray City is just one of the attractions making the Cayman Islands a popular tourist destination.*

has been a marked increase in both parents working, or single parents working multiple jobs, and in complaints that parents are "losing control" of their children. Schools follow the British educational system; the government operates ten primary, one special education, and three high schools.

**Higher Education.** Institutions of higher education are the Community College of the Cayman Islands, the International College of the Cayman Islands, and the Cayman Islands Law School.

## ETIQUETTE

There is a strong emphasis on politeness and modesty, partly due to the history of Cayman as a matriarchal society and partly due to the strong British influence. Handshaking is the usual greeting. A person may be introduced by his or her first name (such as "Mr. Tom" or "Miss Lucy"), because of the large number of people with similar surnames (such as Ebanks or Bodden). Unlike many tourist destinations, there is no "beach-hawking" culture; topless bathing is illegal, and wearing swimsuits off the beach is frowned on, although casual dress is acceptable. Homosexuality is illegal, and recent British government efforts to encourage liberalization in this area have been strongly opposed.

## RELIGION

**Religious Beliefs.** The most important denomination is the United Church (Presbyterian and Congregational). Roman Catholic, Anglican, Baptist, and other Protestant denominations are also present. Sunday is a day of churchgoing, and visitors are welcome in most churches.

**Religious Practitioners.** Although women comprise the majority of the congregations, there has been resistance to allowing women to serve in positions of authority in the churches, and the majority of church leaders are male.

**Rituals and Holy Places.** No information is currently available on rituals and holy places in the Cayman Islands.

**Death and the Afterlife.** Family graveyards, where several generations were buried, have been supplanted by public cemeteries.

## MEDICINE AND HEALTH CARE

Health-care coverage is mandatory. Health facilities include a state-of-the-art hospital, opened on Grand Cayman in May 2000; a government health-care complex; and a medical clinic. Life expectancy for males is seventy-six years, for females, eighty-one

*A group of smiling Cayman Island children playing on the beach. There is no natural freshwater on the islands.*

years; the infant mortality rate, based on a 2000 estimate, is ten deaths per one thousand live births.

## SECULAR CELEBRATIONS

Public holidays include: New Year's Day, 1 January; the Easter season holidays of Ash Wednesday, Good Friday, and Easter Monday; Discovery Day, the third Monday in May; the Queen's official birthday, a Monday in mid-June; Constitution Day, the first Monday in July; the Monday after Remembrance Sunday in November; Christmas Day, 25 December; and Boxing Day, 26 December.

The national festival, Pirates' Week, is the last week of October, and is celebrated with parades, regattas, fishing tournaments, and special events. The costume carnival of Batabano takes place on Grand Cayman during the last week of April or beginning of May; Cayman Brac has a similar celebration, called Brachanal, held a week after Batabano. Cayfest is the national arts festival, usually held during April, and features exhibitions, displays, dance, and drama.

## THE ARTS AND HUMANITIES

**Support for the Arts.** Support for the arts comes from the government, private enterprise, community-based organizations, and individuals. The primary organization is the Cayman National Cultural Foundation (CNCF). Its projects have included hosting the Carib Art Exhibition and supporting Cayman's participation in CARIFESTA, the Caribbean Festival of Creative Arts.

**Literature.** Perhaps the best-known novel about Cayman life, Richard Matthiessen's *Far Tortuga* (1975) focuses on the life of a turtle boat captain and the relationship between man and nature in a changing society.

**Graphic Arts.** The most famous artist is Gladwyn Bush, known as "Miss Lassie," a fourth-generation Caymanian who began painting at the age of sixty-nine and has had exhibits in many countries. Her works, which she calls "markings," are painted not only on canvas but also on the walls, windows, and furnishings of her home, which is a local landmark on Grand Cayman. Other contemporary artists include Bendel Hydes and Kamal Singh Matthews. Local artists also work with such materials as coral, wood, limestone, and caymanite (multicolored limestone).

**Performance Arts.** The F.J. Harquail Theatre on Grand Cayman is the main venue for local and visiting companies. The CNCF provides training in the art of creating and staging plays through annual writing workshops, and stages performances of plays by local writers. Workshops are given in dance, drama, choral singing, and storytelling. "Gimistory," the Cayman Islands International Storytelling Festival, was established in November 1999 and is expected to become an annual cultural event.

## BIBLIOGRAPHY

Amit-Talai, Vered. "In Precarious Motion: From Territorial to Transnational Cultures." *Canadian Review of Sociology and Anthropology* 34 (3): 319–332, 1997.

Babiuk, Dale. "Canucks in the Caymans." *CA Magazine* 132 (2): 20–25, 1999.

George, Shurland, and Andrew F. Clark. "Tourism Educational and Training Policies in Developing Countries: A Case Study of the Cayman Islands (Caribbean)." *Journal of Third World Studies* 15 (1): 205–220, 1998.

Graham, William Ross. "Bay Islands English: Linguistic Contact and Convergence in the Western Caribbean." Ph.D. dissertation, University of Florida, 1997.

Maingot, Anthony P. *The United States and the Caribbean*, 1994.

McLaughlin, Heather R. *Cayman Yesterdays: An Album of Childhood Memories*, 1991.

———. "The Cayman Islands Memory Bank: Collecting and Preserving Oral History in Small Island Societies." Paper presented at the 65th IFLA Council and General Conference, Bangkok, Thailand, August 1999.

Meditz, Sandra W., and Dennis M. Hanratty. *Islands of the Commonwealth Caribbean: A Regional Study*, 1989.

Williams, Neville. *A History of the Cayman Islands*, 1970.

### *Web Sites*

Island Connoisseur. *Destinations: Cayman Islands*. Electronic document. Available from http://www.caribbeansupersite.com/cayman

U.S. State Department. *Background Notes: Cayman Islands*, May 1996. Electronic document. Available from http://dosfanlib.uic.edu/ERC/bgnotes/wha/caymans9605.html

—SUSAN W. PETERS

# CENTRAL AFRICAN REPUBLIC

## CULTURE NAME

Central African

## ORIENTATION

**Identification.** The official name of the country is the *République Centrafricaine* (CAR). Previously it had been Oubangui-Chari, one of the four territories of French Equatorial Africa, bound by the Ubangi River to the south and the Shari to the north. Before independence, there was no sense of a common culture among the indigenous peoples, who thought of themselves as members of lineages and clans, and as villagers. After colonization, when members of different ethnolinguistic groups came into contact, there developed a sense of being riverine (Sango, Gbanzili, and Ngbaka on the Ubangi River), forest (Mbati and Isungu) or grassland peoples (Gbaya and Banda). There is also the hunting, gathering and patron-dependent culture of the *Babinga* (pygmies) in the forests of the southwest.

**Location and Geography.** The country lies at the center of Africa in a region where wooded grasslands adjoin dense rain forests and has an area of about 239,400 square miles (620,000 square kilometers). The capital, Bangui, originated at the site of a French military post established on the banks of the Ubangi River in June 1889.

**Demography.** The population in 1988 was 2,688,426, of whom 43 percent was less than fifteen years old. Bangui's population has increased because of forced labor in the hinterlands in the colonial period and, since independence, urban attractions and economic opportunities.

There are fifteen secondary urban centers of populations with from twenty to thirty thousand inhabitants that consist of villages inhabited by persons with different employment and ethnic identities. The vast majority of residents speak languages belonging to the Ubangian family, the most important of which are Banda and Gbaya, some of whose dialects are mutually unintelligible; Nilo-Saharan languages are spoken near the Chad border, and Bantu languages near the Congo (Brazzaville). Although Muslims have been in the territory since it was first colonized, their numbers have increased in the last two decades. In 1992, there were estimated to be forty thousand Mbororo, or nomadic Fulfulde pastoralists. Although it is forbidden to use ethnic names in governmental documents, the average person is very much aware of the *mara* ("ethnic group") of others, and ethnicity figures highly in daily life and politics. Tribes in the technical sense never existed in this region, although in the east there were two indigenous non-Muslim sultanates.

**Linguistic Affiliation.** After colonization, the conquered people began to communicate in Sango, the pidgin that emerged quickly out of contacts between the diverse foreign Africans who were brought by the French—and the Belgians who preceded them in 1887— to be used as militia, workers and personal servants, and the inhabitants of the upper Ubangi River. By 1910, Sango had become a stable lingua franca spread by soldiers and others serving the whites. Never used by the French in a serious manner, the language was adopted in the early 1920s by Protestant missionaries and later by Roman Catholics as a religious language. Written material in Sango was first published by Protestants. Since independence, competence in spoken Sango has become almost universal except among the Mbororo. In Bangui, Sango is the most frequently used language even in households where an ethnic language is traditional. In 1996, Sango was declared co-official with French. It remains primarily a spoken language in government and education, while French is used in written communications.

**Symbolism.** The state's "linguistic unity" was declared in the constitution of 1986, and Sango's his-

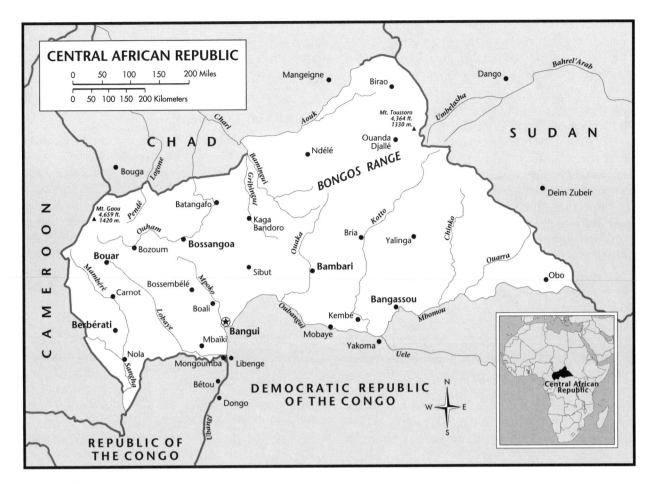

*Central African Republic*

tory of denigration by the French, ubiquity, and distinctness from co-territorial languages has made it the primary national symbol.

## HISTORY AND ETHNIC RELATIONS

**Emergence of the Nation.** The plebiscite offered to its colonies by France initiated the steps taken toward independence. The CAR first became a member of the newly established French Community, eventually becoming a fully independent state in 1960.

**Ethnic Relations.** Barthélemy Boganda, the first president, had an ambitious view of French-speaking central Africa, but the government was controlled by riverine ethnic groups until the election of Ange-Félix Patassé, a person of mixed ethnicity from the populous northwest in 1993. The animosity between the riverine and grassland groups manifested in civil and military strife in 1996 in Bangui, can be traced to the earliest years of the territory. In most cases, however, members of indigenous and foreign ethnic groups get along satisfactorily.

## URBANISM, ARCHITECTURE, AND THE USE OF SPACE

Villages, mostly inhabited by the male descendants of a lineage or clan, are located along and face the roads. This practice was introduced in the 1920s, to create "plantation villages" for cotton cultivation. In the 1970s, villages often were consolidated, ostensibly to modernize agriculture.

The typical dwelling, which must be replaced frequently because of termites, is made with sun-dried brick and thatched with wild grass; in the deep forest area palm fronds are tiled on. Mud-and-wattle structures were discouraged under French rule but still exist. Floors are made of pounded earth, on which people sleep on mats with adults sometimes using home-made beds. A whole family lives in a single dwelling, the interior of which is divided, especially when the owners have been influenced by Western culture. Nearby may be a goat pen, but there rarely is a latrine, which are more common in urban centers. Dwellings are used primarily for storage and sleeping. However, in the six-month dry and hot season in the savannah, people frequently sleep outdoors. Family life occurs in open spaces or on a narrow ground-level verandah, and food is prepared at a family hearth situated in the front of the dwelling.

The village interior extends up to the road and is kept cleared and swept by women, while the *ngonda* "bush" (uncultivated land) begins a few yards behind the houses. Village space is therefore completely open, so that one's activities are visible to all and passers by can be seen, greeted, and engaged in conversation. There are no enclosures except among the Muslims and the few people who have adopted their cultural traits. For indigenous Central Africans, concealment and secrecy violate cultural norms.

Urban centers are the sites of prefectural (provincial) and subprefectural administration. They are conglomerates of villages, but wealthier people such as civil servants and merchants live in dwellings constructed of cement blocks, laid with a cement floor, and roofed with metal sheets. Larger buildings of that construction type from the colonial period are used by government departments and religious organizations. These secondary centers are connected by a dirt-road system created between 1925 and 1938 with indigenous labor that has facilitated migration and travel, contributing to quasi-urbanization and the nationalization of the culture. Because links between the members of a lineage are maintained, much travel—often as paid passengers on the tops of transport trucks—is associated with illness and death among kin. An extensive network of privately owned bus systems serving the interior has degenerated into "bush-taxi" services. The increase in the population of secondary centers and the agricultural practices of Central Africans have led to disastrous ecological changes, because trees are used for both house construction and firewood, and deforestation around all the urban centers has caused a need for the importation of wood from afar.

Bangui is more a huge agglomeration of habitats clustered chaotically around a colonial core than a city. The cost of Bangui's increasing size is the loss of agricultural land on its perimeter. Permanent buildings of cement block and metal roofing are backed by houses adapted to the country with sun-dried brick walls and roofs thatched in grass or palm fronds. These clusters of buildings belong to close kin and resemble precolonial familial villages. Their style is determined in part by ethnicity but largely by wealth; the number of partitioned rooms, by acculturation and number of inhabitants. Few of these houses have electricity, running water, or access to roads. Most people walk to their destinations, but even the poor have been able to afford private buses or taxi-buses while wealthier people have motorbikes or automobiles.

## FOOD AND ECONOMY

**Food in Daily Life.** The staple is a doughlike mixture of processed and dried detoxified cassava (*gozo*) or sorghum. This is accompanied by a sauce made of vegetables, poultry, meat, or fish. Traditionally, beer was made from sorghum, although locally manufactured beer is now more common along with soft drinks. A hard liquor is made from cassava or sorghum. Chickens and goats in the villages are used as currency in marriages and as gifts and occasionally are sold for cash; wild game, killed in the dry-season grass-burning hunts, supplements the rural diet.

At roadside stands, bakery bread and homemade fried bread (*makara*), sandwiches, barbecued meat, and other snacks are sold by women. Restaurants are frequented mostly by expatriates. Coffee and tea, prepared with sugar and canned evaporated milk, are popular in urban centers.

The inhabitants of the forest area subsist on cassava, bananas, plantains, palm-nut-oil, forest caterpillars, and the leaf of a wild plant (*koko*). Individuals, in turn, bring these foods to Bangui to sell at the market. Protein is at a low level in the diet throughout the country.

**Basic Economy.** Central Africans are mostly self-sufficient, growing their own staples (manioc, sorghum, peanuts, sesame, corn, and squash), supplemented by wild tubers, leaves, and mushrooms. Peanut oil is produced commercially. Most products in the stores are imported from other African countries, Europe, and Asia. The most sought-after employment is in government service. In 1989, there were 25,000 persons in government service and only about 4,300 in the private sector, most of them in Bangui.

**Commercial Activities.** Cotton production was obligatory under French rule as early as 1925 and had an irreversible influence on population movements and the politicization of residents. In 1961, 50 percent of one's hours at work were devoted to cotton agriculture, and in 1971, 90 percent of the income from exports was attributed to cotton. Coffee plantations and lumbering are also important.

**Major Industries.** There is one factory that produces cloth. Industry is at a low level, and com-

*A boatman brings home a bat for soup to the banks of the Ubangi River in his dugout canoe. His wife wears a traditional print wrap dress.*

merce is carried on by entrepreneurs. Diamonds and gold are surface-mined mostly by individuals in the Haute-Sangha and Haute-Kotto prefectures; their purchase and sale are dominated by recent Muslim immigrants from nearby countries. The importance of this immigration is reflected in the establishment of diplomatic relations and air service to Cairo and Djedda that provides transportation to those making a pilgrimage to Mecca. Uranium has been found around Bakouma.

***Trade.*** Cotton, coffee, and tobacco make up a major proportion of exports, grown by about 80 percent of the population.

## SOCIAL STRATIFICATION

***Classes and Castes.*** Social class is differentiated by place of residence and work: rural versus urban. In recent years, the imitation of French culture has led people to refer to the "provinces" and to their inhabitants as *paysans*—"peasants." Power differentiates the bureaucrats from the governed. People with power, economic security, and education are considered intellectuals. These constitute the upper class. The middle class consists of people in com-

merce and business, most of whom are Muslims. Employees in the public sector support at least a tenth of the population. In 1982, only 52,000 people had regular employment. The vast majority of people are either farmers, self-employed, or are unemployed, including in urban centers the partially educated.

***Symbols of Social Stratification.*** Traditionally, people avoided the display of power and wealth because they were shared in the lineage. In spite of the acquisition of wealth and Western goods, egalitarianism continues to be the ideal.

## POLITICAL LIFE

***Government.*** The government, patterned after that of France, has a parliament consisting of the National Assembly and an Economic and Regional Council that is led by the president. The president is elected by universal direct suffrage and serves a six-year term. There are ministers with domestic and international portfolios, but the president has personal control of the radio and television systems. The nation is divided into prefectures and subprefectures. At the village level, the government is represented by an appointed "chief" approved by the government whose main role is to represent the villagers and enforce laws such as the annual head tax imposed on males. In urban centers, there are wards and neighborhoods also headed by chiefs.

***Leadership and Political Officials.*** Leadership at the highest level has usually come from the military, and sometimes from the civil service. Those holding high office play their roles with formality and a sense of invulnerability. Distance from the mainstream is maintained by the use of the French language.

***Social Problems and Control.*** Very little has been done to control forced payments from drivers of cars and trucks at road blockades by young men and the violent highway banditry in the hinterland. Under most regimes, the security forces have not been paid regularly, leading to civil strife. Structures for social control resemble those of France; the *gendarmerie* (police), like the military, is largely ineffectual in controlling theft, a crime which often takes the form of armed robbery. There are two parrallel systems in the judiciary system, one similar to that in France, and one based on customary law.

***Military Activity.*** An army serves to protect the presidency and maintain civil order.

*A group of children surround a boatman near Bangassou. Children are taught at a young age to respect adults.*

## GENDER ROLES AND STATUSES

***Division of Labor by Gender.*** Women traditionally are responsible for the production and preparation of food. Women also work in private holdings growing cotton and other products to participate in the money economy. They are the principal vendors of food products in markets. Men contribute heavy work in rural areas and constitute most of the employed workforce.

***The Relative Status of Women and Men.*** In politics, the civil service, the military, and the police force, women are well represented despite being less educated. Women are less likely to attend, much less finish, primary school.

## MARRIAGE, FAMILY, AND KINSHIP

***Marriage.*** Traditionally, and to some extent in modern-day rural areas, marriages were arranged by the members of a family's lineage. Few could afford polygamous marriages, although polygamy varies both between rural areas and urban centers, and between ethnic groups. The young man is obliged to work for the girl's family for as long as up to four years, after which his family pays a brideprice. With the increased emphasis on acquiring monetary wealth, the brideprice and the accompa-

nying gifts have become onerous or unachievable for many in urban centers. Due to the increased expenses associated with weddings, the number of church weddings among Christians has dropped. Stable common-law marriages are parallelled by *liaisons* ("relationships") in Africa, in which a woman remains with a man as long as he cares for her. A man can "divorce" his wife by putting her belongings in front of the house and locking the door. Divorce traditionally depends on the return of the brideprice, with added contributions that depend on the number of children. The woman's family can continue exacting payments as long as she bears children, who become members of the man's lineage.

***Domestic Unit.*** The basic unit consists of the biological father and mother, their children, and other close kin for varying periods of time. The parents' siblings also take part in the rearing of the children and their resident cousins. Children in rural areas are sent away to serve adult kin, sometimes to receive a formal education in a larger village or town.

## SOCIALIZATION

***Infant Care.*** Infants traditionally were not weaned until about age two, and everyone in the family was involved in their care. Children are lectured by their

*Men marched in traditional dress to celebrate the coronation of Emperor Bokassa I.*

parents on social behavior, and corporal punishment is never severe. A child's exaggerated screams bring adults to mediate on behalf of the child. Siblings avoid fighting.

***Child Rearing and Education.*** A child's most important responsibilities are to respect, obey, and serve adults and to avoid causing trouble (such as theft) with non-kin. Respect for age is encoded in the language. Education follows the French system, and is available to all, although the system is handicapped by insufficient funding. The educational system is frequently disrupted by walkouts by unpaid teachers. Attendance in primary school is around 50 percent but drops progressively in the upper grades. Dependence on foreigners for teachers has been almost eliminated, but the quality of teaching has fallen.

***Higher Education.*** With a baccalaureate degree a person may enroll at the University of Bangui to prepare for a career in public service or to emigrate to France. The majority of the students attending higher education are male.

## ETIQUETTE

People adjust their speech according to the age and role of their interlocutors. Although the second per-

son plural pronoun is used to express deference in speaking to an individual, among young urban dwellers there is an ideology of equality and solidarity that leads to the use of the singular pronoun.

## RELIGION

***Religious Beliefs.*** The practice of traditional religion has declined since the 1950s in favor of various forms of Christianity. The first missionaries established Saint Paul des Rapides at Bangui in 1894, and Protestant missionaries, mostly American, arrived in the early 1920s. Protestant Central African churches, once aligned with the denominations of the early missions, have splintered into several factions as a result of competition for leadership in the clergy. Charismatic forms of Christianity are practiced in independent churches. There are also syncretistic movements with traits from Catholicism, Protestantism, and Islam. Islam is growing through immigration and conversion; boys sometimes convert to gain employment.

***Rituals and Holy Places.*** Traditional religious practices continue in the annual grass-burning hunts of the dry season and in rare initiation rites. More common are ceremonies associated with clitorectomy, although modern-day circumcision has been almost entirely secularized with boys being sent to a local clinic. Expressions of traditional religion in Bangui are rare, but marches and parades, especially among Christian youth and women, are common, with uniforms and banners displaying one's allegiances. Members of syncretistic churches wear special clothing.

**Death and the Afterlife.** Most people believe that death is the consequence of ill will (sorcery). At traditional wakes, kin frequently charge each other with having killed the deceased; all-night dancing and mourning last for several days. There may have been traditional burial grounds, but cemeteries were introduced by Christians and Muslims. In Bangui and other urban centers, burial in cemeteries is obligatory.

## MEDICINE AND HEALTH CARE

The only major hospital is in Bangui, but there are mission-operated, private, and governmental clinics. By the 1950s, specialists in traditional medicine began to decline in importance. Belief in sorcery is widespread even among Christians, and protective charms on a person's body may be more common among some Muslims than among other Central Africans. The most common causes of death are AIDS, malaria, and schistosomiasis. Epidemics of meningitis occur frequently.

## SECULAR CELEBRATIONS

Mother's Day has become a holiday of considerable importance in urban centers, used by women to exact gifts and privileges. The political celebrations are Independence Day and Memorial Day in honor of Barthélemy Boganda, the first president.

## THE ARTS AND HUMANITIES

**Literature.** The CAR is an oral society and the percentage of literate people in both French and Sango is very low. There have been only intermittent and ephemeral periodicals, mostly in French. A poorly stocked nonreligious bookstore for readers of French exists in Bangui.

**Performance Arts.** Popular dance music, a local version of the style characteristic in Kinshasa, Democatic Republic of Congo, and Brazzaville, Republic of Congo, has been recorded and sold commercially and played on the radio.

## BIBLIOGRAPHY

Cordell, Dennis. *Dar al-Kuti: A History of the Slave Trade and State Formation on the Islamic Frontier in Northern Equatorial Africa (Central African Republic and Chad) in the Nineteenth and Early Twentieth Centuries,* 1977.

——. *Dar al-Kuti and the Last Years of the Trans-Saharan Slave Trade,* 1985.

Decalo, Samuel. *Psychoses of Power: African Personal Dictatorships,* 1989.

Hewlett, Barry S. *Intimate Fathers: The Nature and Context of Aka Pygmy Paternal Infant Care,* 1991.

Kalck, Pierre. *Central African Republic: A Failure in Decolonisation,* 1971.

——. *Historical Dictionary of the Central African Republic,* 1980, 1992.

——, compiler. *Central African Republic,* 1993.

Le Vine, Victor T. *Political Leadership in Africa: Post-Independence Generational Conflict in Upper Volta, Senegal, Niger, Dahomey, and the Central African Republic,* 1967.

Mangold, Max. *A Central African Pronouncing Gazetteer,* 1985.

O'Toole, Thomas. *The Central African Republic: The Continent's Hidden Heart,* 1986.

Samarin, W. J. "The Attitudinal and Autobiographic in Gbeya Dog-Names." *Journal of African Languages* 4: 57–72, 1965.

——. "The Art of Gbeya Insults." *International Journal of American Linguistics* 35: 323–329, 1969.

——. "French and Sango in the Central African Republic." *Anthropological Linguistics* 28: 379–397, 1986.

——. "Damned In-Laws and Other Problems." In Mohammad Ali Jazayery and Werner Winter, eds. *Languages and Cultures: Studies in Honor of Edgar C. Polomé,* 1988.

——. "The Creation and Critique of a Central African Myth." In *Revue française d'histoire d'outre-mer* (318): 55–81, 1998.

——. "The Status of Sango in Fact and Fiction: On the One-Hundredth Anniversary of its Conception." In J. H. McWhorter, ed., *Language Change and Language Contact in Pidgins and Creoles,* 2000.

——. "Explaining Shift to Sango in Bangui." In R.Nicolai, Ph. Dalbera, and De Feral, eds. *Leçons d'Afrique: Filiations, Ruptures et Reconstitutions des Langues: Un Hommage à Gabriel Manessy,* 2001.

Titley, Brian. *Dark Age: The Political Odyssey of Emperor Bokassa,* 1997.

Villien, François. *Entre Oubangui et Chari vers 1890,* 1981.

—WILLIAM J. SAMARIN

# CHAD

## CULTURE NAME

Chadian

## ORIENTATION

**Identification.** Chad is a vast, ethnically diverse African country. It gained independence from France in 1960 after a sixty-year colonial period rule that did not create a meaningful national unity. Within the country's borders one may distinguish several national cultures that are based on the ethnoregional and religious affiliations of the population groups. Many of the cultures can be traced back to a complex precolonial history of competing indigenous states and sultanates.

The name Chad is derived the from designation of the great Lake Chad (originally called Kuri) by the sixteenth century author and imam Ibn Fortu. Chad is somewhat similar to Sudan in that it has a northern part inhabited by an Islamic (and partly Arabic-speaking) population of pastoralist semidesert peoples, and a southern part of Christians and traditional religious people, engaged in mixed agriculture, crafts, and trade. These two parts each comprise about half of the population. Postcolonial Chad has, like Sudan, been marked by deep regional-ethnic divisions and a violent history of struggle for power among the various elites that have alternative visions of the state and their place within it. Armed rebellions and years of protracted and destructive civil war, in which the role of Libya was at times notable, have characterized Chad's recent history. Starting in 1993, the armed conflicts subsided and some sort of democratization process was instigated.

**Location and Geography.** Chad is a resource-poor, landlocked country, bordered by the Sudan, the Central African Republic, Cameroon, Nigeria, Niger, and Libya. It has an area of 495,752 square miles (1,284,000 square kilometers), most of it desert, semidesert, or savannah. In the extreme south there are lush forests and agricultural areas. The country is divided into three climatic-ecological zones from north to south: the Saharan zone (dry and hot, with livestock raising, minor cultivation, and some trade), the Sahelian zone (more rainfall, livestock raising, and cereal cultivation), and the southern semitropical zone (with good rainfall of up to 48 inches (1,200 millimeters) per year, large-scale cultivation, cash-crop production, trade, and crafts). The country is drought-prone and suffers from periodic famine. Chad is basically a large plain, with some mountain ranges, including the Guéra massif in the center and the Ouaddaï or Ennedi massif in the east; in the north in the middle of the desert lies the spectacular Tibesti range, where cultivation is possible due to higher rainfall. In the southwest, on the border with Cameroon, Niger, and Nigeria, is Lake Chad, a shrinking water mass lying at an altitude of about 790 feet (240 meters). The two main rivers—the Logoni and the Chari—are in southwest Chad and run into Lake Chad. They are navigable for most of the year and are also used extensively for fishing.

**Demography.** Chad's population is some 7 million (1999), giving a population density of 14.2 people per square mile (5.5 per square kilometer). The fertile southern third of the country has a density of 77.7 per square mile (30 per square kilometer). There are an estimated 180 ethnic groups in Chad (although their boundaries are often hard to establish). The largest are the Sara (approx. 32 percent of the total population), the Arabs (22 percent), the Maba, the Tubu, and the Mbum. Many of the ethnic groups are also found in neighboring countries such as Cameroon, Niger, the Sudan, and Nigeria, having been separated by the colonial and postcolonial boundaries. Most Chadians live in rural areas. Urban centers include the capital N'Djamena (approx. 800,000 people, most of them now Arabs or Arabic-speaking), Sarh (120,000), Moundou (110,000), Bongor, Abéché, and Doba. Life expectancy is approximately forty-eight years, while the

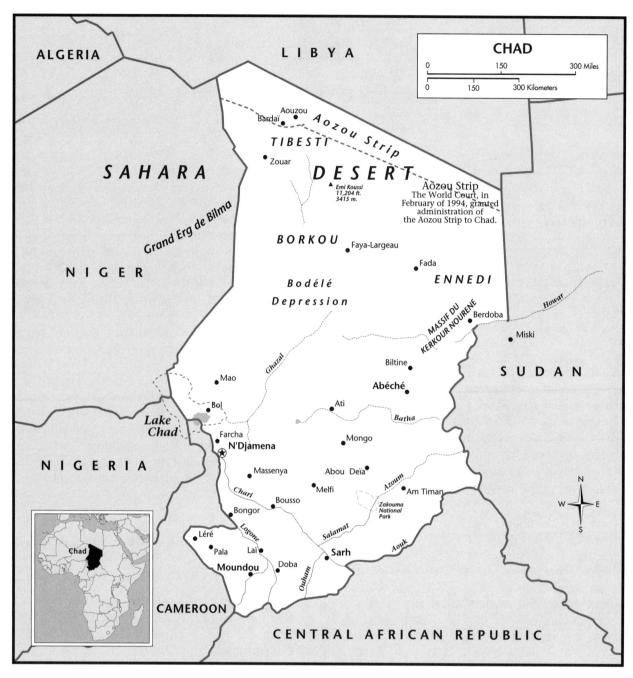

*Chad*

annual population growth rate is 2.5 percent. About 90 percent of the population lives in the southern 15 percent of Chadian territory.

**Linguistic Affiliation.** There are more than 100 languages spoken in Chad, virtually all belonging to two great languages families: Nilo-Saharan and Afro-Asiatic. The precise extent and variety of the linguistic situation are not known, because of a notable lack of research. Language does not overlap with ''ethnic group'' identity, as some languages

are spoken by groups identifying themselves with different ethnic/regional labels. Arabic, Sara, and French are widely spoken, the latter used in education and the administration, especially in the south. The use of Arabic, traditionally an important commercial language, is expanding across the country.

**Symbolism.** The main symbol of Chad is the national flag, consisting of three vertical fields of blue, yellow, and orange-red, without any figurative decoration. Additional national symbols are not known, although various parties and rebel fronts have used their own flags.

## HISTORY AND ETHNIC RELATIONS

***Emergence of the Nation.*** Chad did not exist as a political unit before the French conquest of 1900, but was an area of important indigenous state formation and had seen Arab immigration (of groups collectively called Djoheina and Hassaouna) and Islamization since the fourteenth century. There was a conglomerate of kingdoms (such as Bagirmi and the pre-Islamic state of Kanem-Bornu), chiefdoms and sultanates (such as Ouaddaï and Tama) of varying size and ethnic composition; amongst these states, war and raiding were frequent. The descendants of these states in the north and east are today's seminomadic pastoralist peoples and cultivators in the northern and central parts of the country.

Southern Chad is inhabited by a variety of ethnic groups that, although culturally related, traditionally had no strong centralized polities. The largest group among them are the Sara, although they themselves form a combination of twelve "tribal" groups that never showed any strong unity. Other groups are the Mundang, the Massa, and the Mbum. The southerners were the victim of a tradition of slave raiding by such northern groups as the Barma, Fulani, Bagirmi, Tubu, and Maba; this has left deep scars in the fabric of Chadian society. It was because of the promise to end slave raiding (and the killing of the notorious warlord and slave raider Rabih az-Zubayr, who was of Sudanese origin) that the Sara peoples welcomed the French colonists in 1900.

Under French colonial rule, the southern part of the country received most of the attention in the domains of economic and educational investment, and many people there converted to Christianity. The Islamized north, seen as a vast expense of inhospitable desert with little productive resources except livestock, dates, and some cereals, was mistrusted and relatively neglected, and people there kept more to their "traditional" ways in a cultural and educational sense. In the first decade of Chadian independence the northerners also remained relatively excluded from national politics; Northerners have had the upper hand in Chadian politics since 1979. It must be kept in mind that, before colonization, the "north-south" divide, so often referred to now, was nonexistent in Chad.

In 1960, when independence was granted by France, Chad had no "national identity" recogniz-

able to the population at large. Ethnoregional traditions formed the framework for group identification, with the "nation" only as an abstract concept. Southerners (who were the first to clamor for independence) formed the state elite, but did not succeed in building a representative or democratic political system. Rebellion in northern regions emerged, notably that of the FROLINAT (National Liberation Front) movement in 1966. The civil wars of the 1970s and 1980s, though resulting from exclusionist state policies, authoritarianism, and divergent views on the role of the state, fueled group tensions. But despite these divisive conflicts and the opposition between the north and the south, there seems to be no great desire on either side to split up the country and go it alone, except perhaps in a federal arrangement.

There is the constant danger that the perceived ethnoreligious and territorial divide between the Arabized "Islamic north" and the "Christian south" will solidify into a polarization between the two (although the post-1960 civil wars were not fought on the basis of religion). This would fuel rivalry even more and inhibit the emergence of a democratic system based on equity and resource sharing. There is a basic, perhaps unsolvable, contradiction between the identity and aspirations of the south and those of the north, although both regions have their internal divisions as well.

In the late 1960s, when the southerner N'Garta (François) Tombalbaye was president, there was an effort by his government to create cultural "unity" between the various groups of the south vis-á-vis the north. This was done by making it obligatory for all people holding public office (at some point even Muslims) to undergo an initiation ritual based on the Sara ethnic tradition. This "cultural revolution," however, became a violent and intimidating exercise that completely failed and even antagonized many southerners. In the years of the regime of Hissen Habré (1982–1990), there was suppression and terror in the south, perpetrated by northern-dominated government forces. This created the fear that southern rights and identity would be trampled. There is often talk of a "superiority complex" of northern people vis-á-vis the south.

One of the domains where the north-south tension is now becoming apparent is education, where the government (emanating from the northern and eastern Islamic groups) is urged to further Islamic orientation. While Chad is still a "secular state," the rivalry between the faiths and the strengthening of Islam in public life may become another threat to long-term stability.

**National Identity.** Chad's national identity is precarious, and first and foremost derived from the inherited postcolonial administrative state structure. Constitutionally, Chad is unitary and secular, but in recent years a struggle has occurred to redefine the identity of the nation. In the wake of the civil war that ended in 1990, contrasting views on what kind of nation Chad can, or should be, are emerging. Core issues are the roles of ethnic traditions, religious identity, and balanced ethnoregional representation in the state apparatus. The issue of how this would have to be reflected in the nation's legal system has not even been posed. Language policy also reveals the problems: French and Arabic were chosen as the official languages of the state—both long established in Chad but neither of them indigenous.

**Ethnic Relations.** A relatively understudied subject, traditional Chadian society—in all its ethnic and religious variety and complexity—is not well-known to the outside world. Little recent field research has been done in either the countryside or the urban areas on the various societies and diverse ethnocultural traditions. One could say that group relations have suffered from the burden of longtime slave raiding (formally ended only in 1926) and communal political violence. Peoples with no particular affinity toward each other are bound together in a state that was largely externally created and not the outcome of local political processes. There is therefore a continuous challenge to create patterns of cooperation and a durable society in the midst of regional and ethnic (and increasingly religious) antagonism. Violent insurgency and rebellion were until recently the prime means used to establish political power of one group over the others. The question is whether a resilient state can come out of this process. In this respect, the long-term problems of Chad may be as serious as those of Sudan, because some groups do not feel deeply committed to the nation as a whole nor to other Chadians as partners in the venture of developing an inclusive polity. The Sara, initially dominant, are now a disenchanted group because they see their rights and identity being threatened.

It is likely that ethnic relations in Chad will benefit from a decentralization of the political structure that retains unity in diversity. When the rights and regional interests of the various ethnic groups are respected, few groups will desire to dissolve the state except some diehards of the north.

## URBANISM, ARCHITECTURE, AND THE USE OF SPACE

The rate of urbanization in Chad is low, with most of the people still living as cultivators and pastoralists in dispersed hamlets, cattle camps, villages, and oases. Old capitals of the sultanates and kingdoms (for example, Njimi, capital of the Kanem kingdom, Wara of the Ouaddaï sultanate, and Niere of the Tama sultanate) have dwindled in size and few historical structures remain except for some palaces and mosques. There is a significant variety of building styles, use of space, mobility patterns, and material culture across the ethnic groups and climatic conditions. In the countryside, the traditional house- and hut-building styles are maintained, although the construction of corrugated iron and concrete buildings has rapidly expanded. In the sparsely populated north, with its vast expenses of desert plains, distances are great between pasture areas and human settlements. Several nomadic groups live in tents and shelter structures. The sedentary cultivators in the south live in villages and have a much higher population density. Abéché is perhaps the most characteristic town of Chad, with its clay buildings, monuments, and small winding streets.

The capital N'Djamena is a new town, founded by the French in 1900 as Fort-Lamy. It suffered huge damage in the 1980–1982 war instigated by Hissen Habré. Because of continuous immigration and the influx of refugees from the civil war period, the city has grown rapidly without a proper expansion of services and infrastructure.

## FOOD AND ECONOMY

**Food in Daily Life.** Patterns of food production and consumption are rather diverse across the various ethnic groups. There is no shared "national food culture," although the one dish fairly common throughout the country is a kind of set grain porridge, made of sorghum or millet flour, served with sauces that contain meat, dried fish, tomatoes, onions, and good spices. Some north-south divide is apparent in food traditions. In the south (in contrast to the north) there is no fish in the diet, and there is less consumption of milk products from livestock herds. The diet of southern peoples also shows more variety in the forest products, tubers, spices, and fruits that are consumed. Staple foods, apart from sorghum and millet, are maize, manioc, potatoes, rice, sesame, and some bean species.

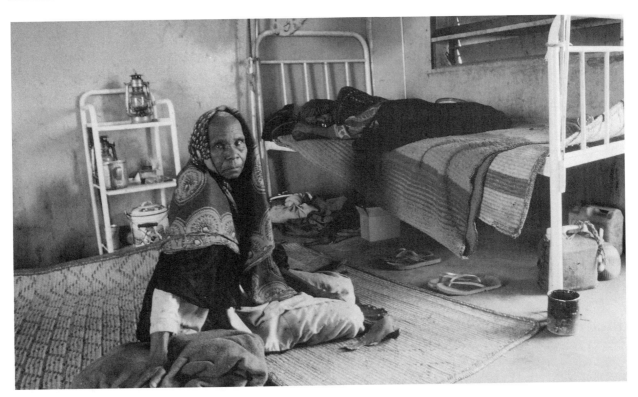

*A woman dressed in traditional clothing, sits on the floor of her more modern, concrete house in Chad.*

**Basic Economy.** Chad is one of the poorest countries on the African continent. The great distances and poor infrastructure have hampered the development of a national market and a nationwide, shared food economy. Local communities outside the cities are largely self-sufficient in food production. Commercial food production is concentrated in the South. Chad has a thoroughly agrarian economy, with about 40 percent of the workforce engaged in livestock herding, 40 percent in agricultural production (including cotton farming), and the rest in manufacturing, services, and the military. Most of the economy is geared to subsistence cultivation (including sorghum, millet, groundnuts, vegetables, and fruits) and livestock raising. About 40 percent of the gross domestic product is generated from agriculture, and approximately 18 percent from the livestock economy (which includes cattle, goats, sheep, and camels).

Because of political problems, violent conflict, an almost nonexistent infrastructure, and the lack of a national government, there was hardly any attention given to development-oriented, long-term economic strategy during the last three decades of the twentieth century. The potential of the country, however, is great: there are good chances for the development of cattle herding (on the large central grass plains), mineral deposits, commercial farm-

ing, and oil production. Chad is still strongly dependent on foreign aid, especially from France, which supplies on average about 30 percent of the national budget.

**Land Tenure and Property.** Most of the land is held in communal tenure, especially in the pastoral north, although the state has the final claim on all land in Chad. A claim on land was traditionally established by the person who started developing and cultivating it. Customary law according to local tradition is important everywhere in settling land claims and disputes and allocating access to resources, such as fishing places, pasture, date groves, and water holes. In the cotton-producing south, a class of entrepreneurs has concentrated much land in its own hands. Property law in Chad is underdeveloped, and the judicial system does not apply everywhere because of a lack of courts and manpower. In the areas of the old kingdoms and sultanates, much landed property is still owned by old aristocratic families. In the cities there is a private property market. Big traders and well-placed government people have acquired substantial pieces of property over the years.

**Commercial Activities.** Chad has a narrow commercial base. Since independence, both Chad's internal and external markets remain undeveloped; the nation never succeeded in developing a successful commercial export economy. Persistent structural deficits of up to 30 percent of the national budget have been common. Following the period of turmoil and civil conflict, an increase in commerce with Sudan, Cameroon, and other neighboring countries has become essential for Chad to further develop its economy. Cameroon will most likely be the link to the sea for future Chadian exports (notably oil). There are plans for a pineline and a railroad from Chad to the Cameroon coast.

With its varied landscapes, ruins of ancient capitals, and spectacular scenery in the central and northern parts of the country (such as the Tibesti Mountains), Chad has significant tourism potential. The number of annual visitors, however, is minuscule (seven to eight thousand), resulting in little impact on the national economy.

**Major Industries.** Industries in Chad are very limited in number and size, and are all located in or close to N'Djamena. The largest one is cotton production. There is also a large oil refinery. Minor industries include the production of beer, cigarettes, textiles, and natron (a mineral), as well as the processing of sugarcane and meat. New industries could develop around the exploitation of resources such as gold, uranium, kaolin, bauxite, or tungsten, although exploration has not been sufficiently carried out because of the past civil wars.

In the 1970s, oil was struck in Kanem, near Lake Chad. Production started in 1977, allowing Chad to develop a rate of fuel self-sufficiency of 75 percent. In the 1980s and 1990s new finds were made in the south, such as near Doba. Oil exploitation in the south started only in 1998 but is eventually expected to have a major impact on Chad's economy, assuming that the country as a whole benefits from the proceeds. There is tension emerging about the appropriation of oil proceeds between the northern-dominated elites and the southern peoples on whose land the oil was found.

**Trade.** Historically, Chad was at the crossroads of major long-distance trade routes such as the Trans-Sahara caravan route to the Libyan and Egyptian coast, to the west, and to the east (into Sudan). Goods traded included slaves, gold, cattle, ivory, arms, and textiles. The kingdoms of the Middle Ages partly emerged on the basis of their establishing control over the southern end of this trade line. Under French rule, much trade was redirected through the south, into Cameroon.

In the twentieth century, Chad's trade position steadily declined, the only major trade items being cotton and livestock. Food imports are very limited, except in times of drought. Raw cotton generates over 65 percent of export revenues, while livestock exports account for another 20 percent of revenue. Minor additional exports are dates, rice, meat, gum arabic, and natron.

## SOCIAL STRATIFICATION

**Classes and Castes.** In modern Chad, social stratification is seen in the emergent class of big traders, landowners and government people (who invest in property, industry, and livestock keeping); the large majority of common peasants and pastoralists, fighting for survival with little means; and a small but vocal urban working class of some sixty thousand. There is no clear-cut division of elites according to regional provenance; for example, the elite does not consist only of northerners. Since the 1970s, membership in a successful armed movement could serve as a way to social advancement, since the resources of the state were then within reach.

Many societies in Chad traditionally have different low-prestige occupational castes, such as hunters, potters, tanners, and blacksmiths (*haddad*). There are also groups of slave descendants that live in pockets of the north, such as the Kadjidi near Lake Chad, and the Kamadja, who form relatively self-contained communities and do not intermarry with their Tubu masters/employers. A similar group in the south are the Yalna in the Salamat region. Modern education, social change, and the mobilizing effect of the armed movements have partially invalidated traditional prejudices and divisions relating to caste membership.

**Symbols of Social Stratification.** Stratification is evident in wealth differences, dress style, leisure activities, and location and style of residences.

## POLITICAL LIFE

**Government.** Since independence Chad has had a variety of governments, none of them successful in establishing an inclusive system of governance for the various population groups. In 1960 Chad started out as a multiparty parliamentary republic. Two years later, the then-president N'Garta (François) Tombalbaye, a southerner, dismantled this system to install a one-party state (in line with the political trend in postcolonial Africa at the time). His authoritarian and repressive policies, combined with a compulsory cultural revolution, provoked dissatisfaction in the south and revolts in the north,

*Children and adolescents rarely pursue a complete education in Chad. These young men and boys are helping their households by drawing water from a well.*

including one by the National Liberation Front (FROLINAT), founded in 1966. In a 1975 coup, Tombalbaye was killed and General Félix Malloum took over. He did not stem the tide of revolt, and was forced out of office in 1979 by FROLINAT, led by Goukouni Oueddei and Hissen Habré. In 1982, after three years of social unrest and armed struggle led by local warlords, President Oueddei was replaced as head of the government by his former comrade Habré, who was supported by France because of his campaign to kick the Libyans (who were supporting Oueddei) out of Chad. A period of repression and abuse followed, however, with many casualties in the south. Northern groups also came to resent Habré's heavy-handed, authoritarian approach; they supported the guerrilla war started by his former ally (and rival) Idriss Déby in April 1989 that culminated in the defeat of Habré's government forces twenty-one months later.

Under the Déby regime, which took over in 1990, an effort was made to set up a new type of republican government, with all the trappings of a democratic system. A two-chamber parliament consisting of the National Assembly and the Senate was set up. A High Court and a Constitutional Court were also installed. More political parties were allowed (although recruitment on a religious or ethnic basis was prohibited), freedom of the press and of organization was accorded, and multiparty elections were promised. At the same time, there was never any doubt that Déby would maintain a tight hold on the reigns of power. Suppression of occasional insurgencies and massacres by government forces of members of suspected opposition groups have marred the transition to a secure democratic political system. Nevertheless, the groundwork for democratic institutions was laid, and there is still a possibility that a better system of inclusive governance may entrench itself.

### Leadership and Political Officials.

A new National Assembly was elected in 1997, in relatively free multiparty elections. Among 49 parties, Déby's MPS party (Patriotric Salvation Movement) won, gaining 63 of the 123 seats. The major opposition party is the Union for Renewal and Democracy (URD), led by the senior southern politician W.A. Kamougué. Another opposition party is the National Union for Development and Democracy (UNDR). Some armed movements (like FNTR and MDD) are still active, showing that the use of force to press political claims remains an option in Chadian life.

The maintenance of political power is a balancing act, based on neo-patrimonial principles of co-operation and the monitoring of personal loyalties and in which the meting out of positions and privileges, in an often informal manner, is crucial.

### Social Problems and Control.

Chad's many social problems include widespread poverty and displacement of people, ethnic and social group tensions, poor education and health care, and the orphans and broken families that have resulted from the devastating civil conflicts. There is still a sense of insecurity in many areas, reinforced by the spread of small weapons. Common criminal behavior includes banditry and road robbery, and in the cities, theft and burglary; many young men from the rural areas who were active in the armed rebel groups have had trouble in adapting to civilian life and have therefore turned to such crimes. There is also a substantial informal (non-taxpaying) economy on which the government has no hold (but from which it also profits). Corruption is still widespread. One underestimated problem aggravated by the civil wars and the resulting social and economic

crises is environmental damage, most notably the rapid decline of the country's trees, forests, and wildlife.

### Military Activity.

In Chad's political system, the military and the use of armed force in general have played a crucial role in establishing power. Violence was the chief political means with which claims to hegemony in Chadian politics were established. (The only president ever voted into office since 1960 was the first one, Tombalbaye.) The current president, Déby, though elected in 1995, came to power in 1990 by the force of arms, and support of the reformed national army (ANT) is important in ultimately securing his power base. There are currently various small-scale rebel groups, but they do not pose a serious threat to the national government and its army. One of the challenges for the Déby government is to broaden the recruitment base of the army and make it more representative of the country's various population groups. Chad has never had a real national army that was independent of political struggles and insurgent movements.

The national army under President Déby (ANT) numbers about thirty thousand men. There is also a 5,500-strong Republican Guard who are the elite troops of the Déby regime and are under his personal command. France maintains a small military presence as well.

Tibesti in the north (the former stronghold of Oueddei) is still an insecure area, not fully under government control. It is also made unsafe because of a large number of land mines left by the Libyans when they occupied the Aozou Strip from 1973 to 1994.

## SOCIAL WELFARE AND CHANGE PROGRAMS

These are conspicuous in their absence. A government without funds and social programs has forced citizens to rely on their own resources, though some are occasionally assisted by foreign (many French) nongovernmental organizations, such as Doctors without Borders and various missionary organizations. Islamic and Christian as well as some ethnic associations of self-help also exist.

## NONGOVERNMENTAL ORGANIZATIONS AND OTHER ASSOCIATIONS

One important group is the Chadian Labour Union (Union Syndicale du Tchad), which is independent and has organized various crucial strikes of political significance. In addition, two Chadian human

*Blacksmiths' workshop in the town of Fort Lamy (now N'djamena). Blacksmithing is considered a "low-prestige" trade in Chad.*

rights organizations play a substantial public role by monitoring the abuse of both government forces and rebel movements, and by maintaining diplomatic contact with Western donor countries.

## GENDER ROLES AND STATUSES

***Division of Labor by Gender.*** Men predominate in government, the military, and public life. Political life (including insurgency) is almost exclusively the domain of men. The pastoral economy and commercial farming are dominated by men as well.

Women do the main work in the rural subsistence economy across the country, handling family responsibilities and household tasks, including child care. They also care for small livestock, tend family gardens, and are involved in the small-scale trade of agricultural surpluses. There is also an emerging small group of female traders in the urban centers. Women are not, however, significantly organized in public associations.

***The Relative Status of Women and Men.*** Men's status is seen to be higher than that of women, but this is related to conceptions about religious roles and public functions, not necessarily to ideas of inherent inferiority. There are some differences across the country's regional or ethnic groups as to the status and roles of men and women in social and religious duties, but in practice, women are economically active and freely move about in most spheres of life, although the northern Islamic groups are more conservative than the southerners and city people. There is, however, no Islamist discourse that limits the social role of women or forces them to go veiled. The new 1996 constitution accords many more rights to women, though practice lags behind.

## MARRIAGE, FAMILY, AND KINSHIP

**Marriage.** Polygyny (the taking of more than one wife) is known among both the southern peoples such as the Sara and the northern Islamic groups. Bride-wealth payment is also common among most Chadian groups.

**Domestic Unit.** Nuclear families independently living their own lives are rare except in the towns. The effective social unit for most Chadians is an extended family or joint family of married brothers.

**Inheritance.** Patrilineal systems of inheritance predominate in the country, modified by modern, French-inspired law as well as by *Shari'a* (Islamic law) in the regions where Islam is important.

**Kin Groups.** The framework of clans is of great importance to most Chadians, be they northerners or southerners, though clans are of declining relevance in the towns. Kinship determines people's social and cultural allegiances. Political affiliation tends to follow ethnoregional lines. This was reinforced in the course of the past civil wars. Lineage and clan membership is important among the pastoralists, such as the Tubu; and in southern village societies, such as the Nar and the Tupuri. Such membership, however, does not subvert the importance of individual agency, much cherished among Chadians.

## SOCIALIZATION

**Child Rearing and Education.** The rearing of young children is done by the mother and by relatives; at a later stage there is more involvement by the father. Of greatest importance for all Chadians is the socializing role of the family and the ethnocultural group later in life through, for example, initiation, the taking on of religious and ritual

*People buying flour at a market in the town of N'Djamena.*

duties, mutual help, and social support. Children necessarily remain dependent on their families until their early twenties.

About 60 percent of Chadian children attend primary school, but the literacy rate in Chad is estimated at only 20 percent, a comparatively low rate within Africa. Further formal education is pursued by a minority, and most children are educated by their families, taking on domestic and economic tasks in their early teens.

After decades of neglect because of civil conflict, isolation, and neglect, education, particularly Islamic education, is expanding among the peoples of the north, although its quality leaves much to be desired. Koranic schools in the north and east have existed for a long time but they have a very limited curriculum.

**Higher Education.** Higher education is seriously underdeveloped in Chad, except for the small and underfunded University of Chad, founded in 1971, and some technical-administrative colleges, such as the Ecole Nationale de Télécommunication in Sarh and the Ecole Nationale d'Administration in N'Djamena. The university was often closed due to civil war and the resulting damage to its facilities. Chad's economic and demographic base is too narrow to sustain a good higher education system.

Many young people go to France or other French-speaking West African countries for further education.

## ETIQUETTE

Chadians, being of quite different religious and cultural backgrounds, do not observe a common standard of etiquette except that respect for community elders, moderation, and reserve in public life is universally appreciated. Some groups are very sensitive to verbal abuse and insult, which can lead to serious personal conflict. Traditional community standards and values are in decline, since in the past decades social life has been subverted by civil war and communal conflicts, which in turn allowed violent behavior to be an acceptable mode of expression for many young people.

## RELIGION

*Religious Beliefs.* Two religions predominate in Chad: Christianity and Islam. About half of the population, and particularly in the northern and eastern parts of the nation, follow Islam, while some 30 percent are Christians, who are concentrated in the south and among formally educated people. A further 20 percent, mainly in the south, adhere to traditional religions, most of them not well known. Across the spectrum, traditional local beliefs and cults are important, often in conjunction with one's allegiance to the Islamic or Christian faith. Ancestor veneration, belief in certain spirits, use of oracles and divination, and ideas of fertility and cosmic harmony are central. The discourse of ''witchcraft'' is not prevalent in Chad as compared to, for instance, central and southern Africa.

Despite the southern peoples' association of Islam with slave raiding and violence, communal-religious relations between Christians and Muslims has historically been characterized by mutual tolerance and cooperation. Indeed, in Chad's civil wars, religious antagonisms never played an important role. Islam in Chad also has a very diverse character. There is no strong basis for Islamist ''fundamentalist'' movements in Chad, although some groups of this nature exist. Missionary groups of both Islam and Christianity are active in Chad. Conversion is an ongoing process, but the use of pressure or force is rejected. The public role of traditional religions is very limited, that of Christianity and especially of Islam is much more visible.

*Religious Practitioners.* The Imam of N'Djamena is the spiritual leader of Chad's Muslims. The Catholic archbishop, also residing in the capital, heads the country's 550,000 Catholic believers. Islamic Sufi orders such as the Tijjaniya and the Sanusiyya are popular in northern and central Chad. Traditional religions in the south have their own ritual leaders and practitioners.

*Rituals and Holy Places.* Apart from the rites and ceremonies central in Islam and Christianity, there are important initiation and healing rituals among many ethnic groups that define their cultural tradition and personal identity. These have strong localized character. Islam and Christianity in Chad have no specific holy places (such as graves of saints or pilgrimage centers) that attract a nationwide or cross-border audience, but the number of mosques and churches is on the rise.

*Death and the Afterlife.* Adherents of both Christianity and Islam believe in an afterlife in Heaven or Hell, with the deceased to be resurrected when God so decides. Traditional religions also cherish the idea of a life after death, as evident from the beliefs in the continued presence of ancestors, and the presence of the dead in dreams and in spirit form. The diversity and complexity of the southern traditional religions in this respect is far from explored.

## MEDICINE AND HEALTH CARE

Due to an underdeveloped and neglected state health-care system and the absence of alternatives in the private sphere, Chadians are mostly dependent on basic primary health care and polyclinical aid and, especially, on traditional medicine. In the larger towns, such as N'Djamena, Sarh, Moundou, and Abéché, there are hospitals, but with very poor facilities. There is one doctor per 38,000, a very low ratio. Prevalent tropical diseases are malaria, schistosomiasis, and river blindness, especially in the south. The north often has suffered from drought and famine.

## SECULAR CELEBRATIONS

The annual national holiday is Independence Day on 11 August. Major Christian and Muslim holidays are recognized by the state as public holidays.

## THE ARTS AND HUMANITIES

*Support for the Arts.* There is no government support for the arts, except if one considers the maintenance of the small Musée National as such. Some individual artists have galleries in N'Djamena.

*A traditional mud hut stands in the village of Massaguet, but modern, iron-and-concrete buildings are being built more frequently throughout Chad.*

**Literature.** The various ethnic cultures have their own traditions of oral literature, including narratives, epics, and ritual drama. Literary creativity of Chadians is notable in the diaspora community in France, but less so in Chad itself, where market demand and the conditions for a literary culture are very limited. Languages of literary expression (in poetry, novels, memoirs, and theatre) are French and, to a lesser extent, Arabic.

**Graphic Arts.** Various ethnic groups in the country have their distinct artistic traditions related to the decoration of houses, clothing, leatherwork, and artifacts. Modern graphic artists are few and are located in the capital of N'Djamena.

**Performance Arts.** Performance arts in theaters are virtually nonexistent; traditional religious and other rituals, however, are alive and well in both the south and the north, as part of the everyday cultural life of the Chadians. Not much is known about the remaining traditional material cultures of the various ethnic groups.

## THE STATE OF THE PHYSICAL AND SOCIAL SCIENCES

The sciences have only a token presence in Chad. Lack of funding and institutions and the stagnating effect of the civil wars have long inhibited any development of the scientific research and teaching. The University of Chad has only about seventeen hundred students and has to make do with a library of fourteen thousand books for all fields. The Chadian National Institute for the Humane Sciences has only six researchers and a library of one thousand books. Finally, there is a Veterinary Research Center and a Cotton Research Center.

## BIBLIOGRAPHY

Azevedo, Mario J. *Roots of Violence: A History of War in Chad*, 1998.

Azevedo, Mario J., and Emmanuel U. Nnadozie. *Chad: A Nation in Search of its Future*, 1998.

Buijtenhuijs, Robert. *Le Frolinat et les guerres civiles au Tchad; 1977–1984: La Révolution introuvable*, 1987.

————. *Transition et élections au Tchad, 1993–1997: Restauration autoritaire et recomposition politique*, 1998.

Centre Culturel Al-Mouna. *Tchad: "Conflit nord-sud": Mythe ou réalité?*, 1996.

Chapelle, Jean. *Le peuple Tchadien: Ses racines, sa vie quotidienne et ses combats*, 1980.

Decalo, Samuel. *Historical Dictionary of Chad*, 3rd ed., 1997.

Feckoua, Laoukissam L. *Tchad: La solution fédérale*, 1996.

Fuchs, Peter. "Nomadic Society, Civil War, and the State in Chad." *Nomadic Peoples* 38: 151–162, 1996.

Hallaire, Jacques. *Naissance d'une église Africaine: Lettres et chroniques du Pays Sar, Tchad (1952–1989)*, 1998.

Nolutshungu, Sam C. *Limits of Anarchy: Intervention and State Formation in Chad*, 1996.

Owens, Jonathan, ed. *Arabs and Arabic in the Lake Chad Region*, 1994.

Tubiana, Marie-José. *Women of the Sahil; Chad-Sudan: Reflections*, 1994.

—JON G. ABBINK

# CHILE

## CULTURE NAME
Chilean

## ALTERNATIVE NAMES
The self-name is cultura chilena

## ORIENTATION

**Identification.** There exist different explanations about the origins of the name "Chile." The most accepted one is that it is derived from the native Aymará word *chilli* meaning "the land where the earth ends." Chile is considered to be one of the most homogeneous nations of Latin America in both ethnic and cultural terms. In contrast to many other Latin American nations, Chile has not experienced the emergence of strong regionalism or conflicting regional cultural identities. Since the late nineteenth century, both the northern and southern regions have been mainly populated by people coming from the central region, helping to strengthen the country's cultural homogeneity.

Notwithstanding the existence of a strong dominant national culture, some cultural regional traditions can be identified. In the northern provinces near Bolivia, Aymará Indians have been able to preserve many aspects of their Andean culture. In the southern region the Mapuche Indians are a large cultural group who strongly contributed to the formation of Chilean culture. On Chiloé Island also in the south, a distinct *chilote* culture emerged over the centuries from a relatively harmonious blending of Indian and Spanish backgrounds; this culture is characterized by rich traditions of music, dance, and mythological tales. Some two thousand miles off the coast of Chile lies the remote Eastern Island, which is inhabited by twenty-eight hundred native islanders who still keep alive many of their Polynesian cultural traditions.

Since the late nineteenth century, Chilean culture has also been nurtured by the arrival of a large group of immigrants, mainly Germans, British, French, Italians, Croatians, Palestinians, and Jews. Today they fill leading positions in academic and cultural circles as well as within the country's political leadership. Nevertheless, many Chileans are often not even aware of their ethnic and cultural backgrounds and they firmly embrace the dominant culture of mainstream society.

**Location and Geography.** Chilean culture is located within the confines of the Republic of Chile, although today some 800,000 Chileans are living abroad. Most of them left the country since the mid-1970s as a result of the political and economic hardships of the military regime that ruled from 1973 to 1990.

Chile is a large and narrow strip situated in southwest South America, bounded on the north by Peru, on the east by Bolivia and Argentina, and on the west and south by the Pacific Ocean. Formidable natural barriers mark present-day Chile's boundaries, isolating the country from the rest of South America. To the north the arid Atacama Desert separates it from Peru. The high Andes peaks constitute its natural frontier with Bolivia and Argentina. To the south, the cold waters of the Drake Sea announce the nearness of Antarctica. To the west, Chile looks at endless masses of the South Pacific water.

Between the huge Andes Mountains (to the east) and the lower Coastal mountains (to the west) is the great Central Valley, which extends from Salamanca, north of Santiago, for over 620 miles (1,000 kilometers) south to Puerto Montt. The country has a total area of 292,260 square miles (756,950 square kilometers).

Chile's geographical shape is quite peculiar. Chile has a longitude of 2,650 miles (4,265 kilometers) making of it one of the longest countries in the world. This is in dramatic contrast with the country's average width, which does not exceed 221 miles (356 kilometers). In some places Chile is so

452

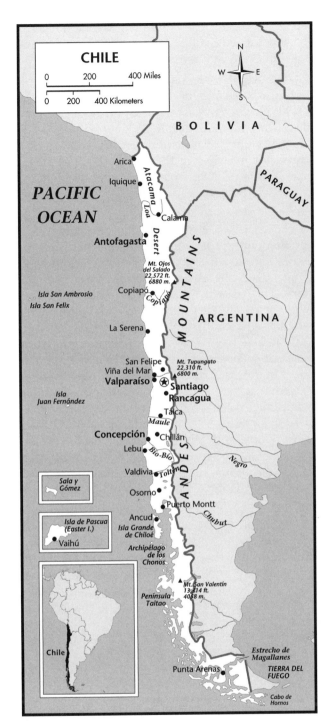

*Chile*

gion by contrast is chilly and rainy, having icy fjords and glaciers at the southernmost tip.

The capital city, Santiago, is located in the central region and constitutes the political, cultural, and economic center of the country, and the homeland of the historically dominant Central Valley culture. Chile is administratively divided in twelve regions (subdivided in thirty-one provinces) and a metropolitan region that includes the capital city.

**Demography.** Chile has a population of 15,017,800 inhabitants (from a June 1999 estimate) with an annual growth rate of 1.8 percent. The national population density is 46.5 persons per square mile. Almost six million people live in the metropolitan region of Santiago, while the northern and southern regions are sparsely populated. Most Chileans (84 percent) reside in urban areas, while the rest live in an increasingly urbanized rural environment. As of 1997, life expectancy at birth was seventy-two years for males and seventy-eight years for females, while the infant mortality rate was ten per thousand live births.

The majority of Chileans (65 percent) are of mixed European-indigenous descent ("mestizos," though this term is not in use in Chile). Some 25 percent of Chileans are of European ancestry (mainly from Spanish, German, Italian, British, Croatian, and French origins, or combinations thereof). Chile also has a large Palestinian community (some 300,000 persons, the largest outside Palestine). The indigenous population represents some 7 percent of the population. There are about 500,000 Mapuche Indians in Chile, constituting the country's largest Native American population. Since the late 1980s, the country's economic prosperity and sociopolitical stability have attracted an increasing number of immigrants from Korea and from other Latin American countries (largely from Peru, Argentina, and Cuba).

**Linguistic Affiliation.** The official language of Chile is Spanish (*castellano* as Chileans call it), which is spoken by practically all the country's inhabitants. In the northern region some twenty thousand indigenous people also speak Aymará, while most of Chile's Mapuche population speak or at least understand their ancestral language, Mapudungu. In Eastern Island the two thousand native inhabitants speak their own language of Polynesian origin. Chileans of foreign ancestry do sometime also speak their mother tongue but do so almost exclusively in the intimacy of their home.

One of the most spectacular expressions of the existing cultural homogeneity is the relative ab-

narrow that the Andes peaks of its eastern border can be seen from the Pacific coastline.

Its length explains the great variety of climates and regions one can find from north to south. While the northern region is extremely dry (including the great Atacama Desert and numerous places where no rain has ever been recorded), the central region is a fertile area with a mild climate. The southern resence of recognizable regional accents, despite the country's extreme geographic length. For instance, the differences in accent between middle-class Chileans from Antofagasta, Santiago, Valdivia, and Punta Arenas are almost inaudible. The national coverage of many Santiago-based radio and television stations also helps to homogenize Chilean Spanish. In contrast, there are in Chile very sharp accent distinctions among the different social classes.

Chilean Spanish is quite characteristic and is immediately identified in other Latin American countries for its distinctive "melody." Chileans generally speak very fast and terminal consonants are often not even spoken. They also often add the suffix –"ito" or –"ita" (meaning "little") to the end of words. In addition, Chilean speech contains many words adopted from the Mapuche language as well as much *chilenismos* (Chilean slang).

**Symbolism.** The national flag and the national anthem are the two most important symbols of national identity. The flag consists of two horizontal bands of white (above) and red (below), representing, respectively, the Andean snow and the Indians' blood fallen in their heroic struggle against the Spanish invaders. The flag also has a blue square at the hoist-side end of the white band with a white five-pointed star in the center. The blue represents Chile's clear blue sky while the white star was the Araucanian Indians coat of arms used in their battlefield banners.

The national day, 18 September, commemorates the country's declaration of independence from Spain, in 1810. This is a day of celebration and national unity in which Chileans enjoy traditional food and folklore-type music and honor the martyrs of independence. During that day Chileans visit *fondas* (traditional palm-roofed shelters) where they eat *empanadas* (meat pastries), drink Chilean red wine, and dance the *cueca*, the country's national dance. In the days surrounding this festivity children, adolescents, and their fathers fly kites in public parks. During "the 18" as Chileans call it, numerous expressions of Chilean culture are proudly praised by the entire nation. A special symbol of the culture is the figure of the *huaso* (the Chilean cowboy), who is dressed Seville style with a flat-topped hat, colorful short-cropped *poncho* or *manta*, and shiny high-heeled boots with large spurs, and is present everywhere during the national celebrations. Another important symbol is the figure of the *roto chileno*, a poorly educated and clothed lower class Chilean who has a great sense of humor and is also smart and courageous. The *roto*

represents the humble Chileans who fought against the Spanish rule and later against the Peruvian-Bolivian Confederation.

The country's geographical isolation and remoteness (the idea of living at "the end of the world") represents a major symbol of national identification. Many Chileans almost glorify the country's physical isolation, as they consider it a key factor in allowing the creation of a homogeneous society. This isolated geography is symbolized in the national imagery by the impressive Andes.

Another key element in the generation of a national cultural identity is the idea that Chileans descend from a perfect blend of two exceptional people: the Basks (Basques) and the Araucanian Indians. The Basks represent perseverance and a high working ethos. They populated the Chilean territory in significant numbers and worked the land with their own hands under difficult conditions and in a permanent state of war with the native population. On the other hand, Chileans are also proud of descending from the brave and indomitable Araucanian Indians. Representing the sole exception in Latin America, the Araucanians successfully resisted Spanish attempts to conquer their territory for more than three centuries. It is not uncommon to find Chileans who bear the names of great Araucanian leaders such as Lautaro, Lincoyán, Tucapel, or Caupolicán.

Climate also plays an important role in the construction of the national cultural identity. Many Chileans believe that the existence of cold winters in their country shaped a laborious and foreseeing people. In the same vein, Chileans generally dislike and distrust everything that can be cataloged as "hot," "tropical," or "exotic"; they assume these elements encourage laxity and indolence and hence consider them synonyms for underdevelopment.

## HISTORY AND ETHNIC RELATIONS

**Emergence of the Nation.** The emergence of the Chilean nation is intimately related to the cultural and social features of the country's rural society. This evolved in the Central Valley since the late colonial period. A land aristocracy of Bask-Castilian lineage succeeded in creating a well-established social order within the confines of their huge estates (haciendas). Living often for generations in the same haciendas, Chilean peasantry (largely of mestizo backgrounds) evolved into a submissive and loyal class towards their "patrons." So during the war of independence in the early nineteenth century, the

Chilean rural population fought dutifully side by side with the local national elite against the Spanish army. During the rest of the nineteenth century, war functioned as a successful mechanism in strengthening the sense of nation and the cultural unity among Chileans. In the years 1836–1839, Chile fought a successful war against Peru and Bolivia. But what certainly represents the most important landmark in the nation-building process is the War of the Pacific (1879–1883) in which the Chilean army defeated the allied forces of Peru and Bolivia. This victory led to the annexation by Chile of huge territories in the north that had belonged to the two defeated nations. Following this victory the Chilean army was sent to the southern region to crush the resistence of the Araucanian Indians and integrate their homeland in the Chilean national territory.

In the nineteenth century, while most Latin American countries were submerged in endless civil wars and constant social upheaval, Chile was a relatively prosperous nation with stable constitutional governments. The Chilean nation became highly respected in the rest of the continent and Chileans soon fully realized their country was in many aspects an honorable exception in this restless part of the world. This idea of representing an exception has heavily nurtured the sense of nation among Chileans and has helped them to differentiate themselves from the neighboring countries.

**National Identity.** During the nineteenth century, several leading intellectuals of the so-called "1848 generation," such as Francisco Bilbao and José Victorino Lastarria, played an important role in studying and criticizing several aspects of the emerging national culture and identity. For instance, they strongly criticized the country's Spanish cultural legacy. They saw in it the source of many national characteristics they rejected, such as the strong political and religious conservatism existing among the country's elites. They instead sought inspiration in the cultural experience of industrious nations such as Great Britain, France, Germany, and the United States.

In the meantime, however, the Chilean state substantially expanded public education and academic formation, which served to disseminate national values and to fortify the sense of national identity among the population. While Chilean elites were conservative in political and religious matters, they adopted technical and scientific knowledge coming from Europe. They actively attracted many men of science from European nations to improve the Chilean educational system and the country's

cultural development in general. Chilean national identity has thus been constructed in the shadows of European progress. Chileans have always been more preoccupied in trying to follow the pace of cultural and scientific transformations in Europe and the United States (often unsuccessfully) than in comparing themselves with neighboring countries and realities. During the last two decades, as a result of the outstanding performance of the Chilean economy, the country is close to shedding its status as a Third World nation.

The strong insertion of the country into the world economy in the last two decades has enormously enlarged the awareness among Chileans of a collective entity ("us") that competes in a larger global environment with other nations. On the other hand, the national identity experiences a clear schism when Chileans are confronted with the recent authoritarian past and the figure of General Augusto Pinochet. With respect to this issue, Chile continues to be divided into two fronts, with supporters and opponents of the former dictator constantly accusing each other of being "anti-patriotic" and of not defending the real interests of the nation.

**Ethnic Relations.** The facts that most Chileans are of mixed ancestry and that the country has a high degree of cultural homogeneity have prevented the germination of open hostilities between the nation's different ethnical groups. Chilean mestizos are often not even aware of being of mixed descent as most of them consider themselves to possess Spanish backgrounds.

Chileans are not habituated to consciously think in terms of race or color in the way people frequently do in other Latin American countries with large Amerindian and Afro-American populations. Ethnic differences in Chile are not expressed in terms of skin color because Afro-Americans are almost nonexistent and Mapuche Indians have a relatively light skin. Rather, ethnic differences in Chile take the form of facial appearances, hair and eye color, body length, and family names.

Chileans are quite nationalistic and patriotic. This implies, for instance, that the stressing of one's French or German background can be totally counterproductive as this makes the person in a sense "less Chilean." So most nationals prefer not to talk about their cultural roots and very often do not even know their ancestral tree. Chileans are accustomed to national leaders and members of the intellectual elites without Spanish names. For instance three recent presidents possessed French (Pinochet),

*A view of the presidential palace. Santiago, Chile.*

Welsh (Aylwin), and Swiss (Frei) ethnic backgrounds.

The immigration of western European people in the late nineteenth century was relatively limited (compared to Argentina or southern Brazil) and did not disturb the traditional domination of Bask-Castilian families in the country. These immigrants were soon absorbed by mainstream Chilean culture and they mostly became members of the growing middle classes. Chileans are also accustomed to several nationalities possessing their own schools, sporting clubs, and even first division football teams and fire brigades. Most Chileans experience this expression of cultural diversity as an integral part of the Chilean cultural landscape.

Mapuche Indians are socially and economically segregated in Chile. So while they are praised in Chile's national mythology they are, in practice, largely discriminated against by the rest of the population. Chileans of Mapuche backgrounds usually work in poorly paid jobs with little or no prestige—as nannies or cleaners or in construction. Since the restoration of democratic rule in the country in 1990 tensions between Mapuche organizations in southern Chile and the state have increased. Mapuches have strongly protested against discrimination and demanded the return of their ancestral land. In addition, some of them have participated in violent actions directed against the exploitation of native forests by large timber enterprises and the construction of water dams in their historical homeland. This increasing conflict, however, has not altered the traditional pacific nature of ethnic relations between Mapuches and the rest of the population because the Mapuche reaction is not directed against Chileans but against the national authorities.

The recent arrival of Korean immigrants and darker skinned people from Cuba and other Latin American countries has led to some xenophobic reactions among Chileans. This recent immigration, however, does not constitute a major issue in Chilean society as the number of immigrants is small.

## URBANISM, ARCHITECTURE, AND THE USE OF SPACE

Most Chilean towns and cities were originally designed following the classical Spanish pattern. They normally possess a central square (*plaza de armas*) from which lanes and streets extend in a straight line to four cardinal points. In the past, the central square was surrounded by a town hall (*cabildo*), a Catholic church or cathedral, and houses of notable families. Today there are only a few examples left of colonial architecture (which was mainly adobe-built). This has largely been the result of earthquakes that frequently hit the country. In addition, since the mid-nineteenth century, many colonial buildings in downtown Santiago have been replaced by newer edifications in neoclassical style. This occurred after many Santiago families who became extremely rich from mining activities in northern Chile constructed large palaces in the Italian and French neoclassical style. Today affluent Santiago citizens live in exclusive neighborhoods close to the foothills of the Andes Mountains in large houses of mainly French and American style. In the large middle-class neighborhoods (dating from the 1930s on) one finds an ample variety of architectural styles with strong Spanish, French, and British features. Since the 1960s American-style bungalow houses have become dominant among middle-class citizens. Starting in the mid-1980s a new financial center emerged in an exclusive area of Santiago with huge modern tower buildings, reflecting the economic bonanza of the last two decades.

Until very recently, poor Chileans lived in large shanty towns (called *callampas*, ["mushrooms"]) at the periphery of large cities and towns. Their homes were self-constructed, one or two room cardboard and tin huts. These shanty towns have been gradually eradicated by the authorities and replaced by low-income housing.

In the countryside, the peasantry traditionally lived in small adobe houses constructed within the haciendas, at a prudent distance from the landowner's house, the so-called *casa patronal*. Today a considerable number of casas patronales are still conserved in the Central Valley. They constitute historical tourist attractions that keep the flavor of Chile's traditional rural society. Most peasants now live in small semi-urbanized settlements (the so-called *villorrios rurales*), which have emerged at the margins of highways and main rural roads.

## FOOD AND ECONOMY

**Food in Daily Life.** Food has a very special place within Chilean culture. Chileans normally eat four times a day. The first meal of the day is breakfast, which mostly consists of rather light fare including toasted bread with butter and instant coffee with milk. Lunch (served between 1:00 and 2:00 P.M.) is the big meal of the day. Traditionally two main dishes are served. The first course may be a salad of some kind. A common salad is the *ensalada chilena*, including sliced onions, chopped and peeled tomatoes, an oil and vinegar dressing, and fresh cilantro (coriander). The second dish generally includes beef

or chicken, accompanied by vegetables. Around 5:00 P.M. Chileans take *once*, an afternoon tea with bread and jam, that often also includes cheeses and *palta* (avocados). Once, which means "eleven," is evidently named after the British tea time—11:00 A.M. Around 9:00 P.M. most families serve dinner, which is usually a single but substantial dish, most often accompanied with wine grown in the many Central Valley vineyards.

Chilean cuisine has both Indian and European influences. The national dish, *porotos granados*, for instance, has ingredients characteristic of Indian cooking (corn, squash, and beans), with distinctly Spanish contributions (onion and garlic). As may be expected in a country with an extremely long coast, seafood has a prominent role in local culinary preferences. Traditional Chilean seafood includes *locos* (abalone), *machas* (razor clams), *erizos* (large sea urchins), and *cochayuyo* (seaweed). Another national delicacy is *caldillo de congrio*, a soup of conger eel, tomatoes, potatoes, onions, herbs, and spices.

**Food Customs at Ceremonial Occasions.** During the celebrations of Independence Day (18 September) Chileans eat a large variety of traditional food. As a snack or the first course of a large meal, Chileans normally eat empanadas. This pastry of Spanish origin is stuffed with meat, cheese, or seafood, as well as onion, raisins, and olives. Another popular starter is *humitas*, which contains a paste of white corn, fried onions, and basil, wrapped in corn husks and cooked in boiling water. A classic second dish is *pastel de choclo* (choclo is the Mapuche word for corn). It is a white corn and beef casserole topped with sugar and mostly cooked in traditional black ceramic dishes, handmade in the small town of Pomaire. Also on Independence Day, large *parrilladas* (barbecues) are organized across the country. Large quantities of wine, *chicha* (fermented apple brew), and *pisco* (grape brandy) accompany the celebrations.

**Basic Economy.** In the mid-1970s, Chile pioneered the adoption of market-oriented structural reforms. For almost two decades Chile was the best performing economy in the region and its economic and financial policy reforms served as an example for other Latin American nations. From 1983 to the late 1990s, Chile experienced constant economic growth at an annual average rate of 6.4 percent.

Manufacturing accounts for about 17 percent of the gross domestic product (GDP), while agriculture, forestry, and fishing contribute 8 percent and mining another 8 percent. Chile's GDP reached the

*Downtown Santiago features a mix of modern and colonial buildings.*

figure of $80 billion (U.S.) in 1997, representing a per capita GDP of $5,700 (U.S.).

**Land Tenure and Property.** Prior to 1960, land concentration in Chile was among the highest in the Western Hemisphere. In the period 1964–1973, a profound land reform was implemented that eliminated latifundium in the countryside. During the military government (1973–1990) land tenure became entirely privatized, while agrarian producers were forced to modernize their enterprises in order to survive foreign competition. The 1997 agricultural census showed that 84.8 percent of the country's farmland was privately owned, 5 percent was tenant-farmed, and 1.6 percent was exploited through sharecropping. Since the democratic restoration in 1990, the Chilean government has returned to the Mapuche Indians part of their ancestral land.

**Major Industries.** Chile's major industries are copper and other minerals, foodstuffs, fish processing, iron and steel, wood products, transport equipment, cement, and textiles.

**Trade.** Foreign trade constitutes one of the main motors of the Chilean economy, accounting for about 20 percent of GDP. In 1999, exports amounted to $15.6 billion (U.S.). Chilean foreign commerce is quite diversified as some thirty-eight hundred products are shipped to 170 markets. Chile's major export products are copper (45 percent of the total), other minerals (10 percent), industrial goods (33 percent), and agricultural and sea products (12 percent). Chile's export markets are fairly balanced between Europe (29 percent), Asia (26 percent), Latin America (23 percent), and North America (19 percent).

**Division of Labor.** Most Chileans do not join the labor market before their sixteenth birthday. Primary education is compulsory, and the educational level has expanded enormously in recent years with the literacy rate reaching 95.2 percent. Because of the very competitive nature of the local labor market, most employers will hire only persons with full secondary school educations, even for unskilled jobs. Upper- and middle-class males commonly do not participate in the labor market before their mid-twenties, as they normally work for the first time following the completion of their academic or professional education. In 1997 Chile had a labor force of 5.7 million, with 38.3 percent occupied in services (including 12 percent in public services), 33.8 percent in industry and commerce, 19.2 percent in agriculture and forestry, 19.2 percent in fishing, 2.3 percent in mining, and 6.4 percent in construction. In the late 1990s the unemployment rate fluctuated between 6 and 8 percent of the labor force.

## SOCIAL STRATIFICATION

**Classes and Castes.** Chile is, on the one hand, the most modern country in Latin America and has relatively low levels of poverty. On the other hand, however, Chile shows the second worst distribution of wealth in the entire region (after Brazil). So while the richest 10 percent of the population obtains 46.1 percent of the national income, the poorest 10 percent gets only 1.4 percent.

While color does not constitute the main source of social discrimination in Chile, class does. In contrast to many other Latin American countries, most Chileans constantly think and act in terms of traditional class divisions (largely expressed as lower, middle, and upper). The Chilean educational system is primarily meritocractic-oriented. For instance, entrance to university is based on the points obtained at a single national academic test. Nevertheless, getting an academic degree or even a good job does not automatically guarantee social acceptance among the middle and upper classes. The same is true for people from lower-class origins who have made money and live in middle- or upper-class neighborhoods. They are often disdainfully called *rotos con plata* ("vulgar people with money"). Generally, it can be stated that most Chileans of European roots belong to the upper and middle classes, while most Chileans of mestizo and indigenous backgrounds belong to the lower classes.

***Symbols of Social Stratification.*** Class differences are first of all expressed in the strong spatial segregation existing in large Chilean cities. Upper, middle, and lower classes live largely isolated from each other in quite distinctive neighborhoods and city sectors. Also, primary and secondary schools express social stratification. Chileans automatically categorize a person socially based only on the *comuna* (municipal division within the city) where the person lives and the name of the school he or she has attended.

Speech is another important marker of social stratification. Upper-class Chileans exaggerate their particular way of speaking to indicate their social predominance. On the other end of the social ladder, lower-class Chileans speak in a very idiosyncratic way. Chileans are so speech-conscious that even the slightest difference in pronunciation of some consonants immediately "betrays" social background.

## POLITICAL LIFE

***Government.*** For most of its independent life Chile has had constitutional and democratic governments. In the period 1973–1990 the country experienced a military regime led by General Augusto Pinochet. Since 1990 democratic rule has been restored.

Chile is a unitary republic with a democratic presidential system. The president of the republic is both head of government and chief of state and is elected by direct balloting for a period of six years (and is not eligible for a direct second term). The legislative branch consists of a bicameral National Congress. The Senate has forty-seven seats of which thirty-nine are elected by popular vote for a period of eight years. The remaining eight senators are nominated (the so-called *senadores designados*), while former presidents are automatically senators for life. The Chamber of Deputies has 120 members who are elected by popular vote to serve four-year terms.

***Leadership and Political Officials.*** Since the restoration of democracy in 1990 Chile has been ruled by a center-left political coalition called Concertación. Its main members are the Christian Dem-

ocrat Party, the Socialist Party, and the Party for Democracy. Two main parties, the National Renewal Party, and the Independent Democratic Union, compose the right-wing opposition, which have formed an electoral alliance during past presidential and congressional elections. The Communist Party, the main opposition party from the left, has not won a parliamentary seat since democratic restoration.

Traditionally, Chile's political party system has been one of the strongest in Latin America. Politicians with long careers within a political party filled most top-level government and parliamentary positions. In the last two decades, however, Chilean politics have become increasingly "technocratic." The possession of technical expertise, particularly in finance and economics (rather than the possession of political skills), has become the most important requirement for top-level posts.

***Social Problems and Control.*** Chile ranks rather low on the world crime scale. The country has an annual murder rate of 1.7 per 100,000 inhabitants. Violent robberies or robberies with assault, however, have been increasing during the last decade. Criminality has recurrently been mentioned by a large majority of Chileans as one of the country's most serious problems. The Chilean police force, *Carabineros*, enjoys high prestige among the population, as it is known to be relatively efficient and incorruptible. Chile has a relatively high imprisonment rate—165 out of 100,000 citizens—almost twice the rate of leading European countries. This could be related to the country's judiciary system which, according to many, needs desperately to be modernized. As a result, there are long delays prior to trials, and preventive detention thus pushes the rate up. Moreover, European countries have alternative sentencing methods, whereas Chile does not.

***Military Activity.*** The Chilean army played a central role in the process of nation building in the nineteenth century. Until 1973 the Chilean armed forces were characterized by their high professional standards and their noninterference in political matters. After the 1973 military takeover, military officers filled key positions in state enterprises and in central and regional governmental institutions. Following the democratic restoration in 1990, the presence of the military in national events continues to be considerable. The armed forces as an institution has firmly defended Pinochet and until very recently they openly resisted accepting any responsibility in the human rights abuses committed during his regime. In 1998 Chilean military expendi-

*Minerals have long been an important part of Chile's economy, as this antiquated silver smelting facility at Huanchaca, Antofagasta demonstrates.*

tures amounted to $2.12 billion (U.S.), constituting 3.5 percent of the gross domestic product.

## SOCIAL WELFARE AND CHANGE PROGRAMS

Since the restoration of democratic rule in 1990 the fight against poverty has become one of the primary goals of successive governments. In that year the Fund for Solidarity and Social Investment was set up to finance the application of huge social programs. In recent years social expenditures increased to 70 percent of total fiscal expenditures. The combination of high levels of economic growth and successful social policies have led to a remarkable reduction in the levels of poverty in the country. While in 1987 45.1 percent of the population was classified as poor, in 1996 this figure was reduced to 23.2 percent. In absolute figures, around 2 million people escaped poverty between those years.

## NONGOVERNMENTAL ORGANIZATIONS AND OTHER ASSOCIATIONS

Chile has one of the largest numbers of nongovernmental organizations (NGOs) in Latin America. Most NGOs were created during the military government (1973–1990) with the support of the Chil-

ean Catholic Church and foreign humanitarian institutions. Their main objective was to defend the rights of persecuted groups and to provide jobs to professionals who were dismissed from state institutions and academic centers for political reasons. Many NGOs created research centers to analyze several facets of Chilean society (such as women, employment, the agrarian situation, and human rights). Since 1990, many NGO professionals have became officials of the Chilean state. This has allowed close cooperation between state officials and NGO members.

## GENDER ROLES AND STATUSES

***Division of Labor by Gender.*** Women make up 51 percent of the country's population. Although female participation in the labor market has grown significantly in recent decades (by 83 percent between 1970 and 1990), women today form only 37 percent of Chile's total labor force. Despite the increasing attention of democratic governments attempting to improve the labor and social conditions of women, women still have to work under less favorable conditions than men. Unemployment among women is persistently higher than that of men, and female workers earn about 65 percent of the income earned by males for equivalent jobs.

In terms of education, women do not lag behind men as females under thirty-five either have equal or more education than men. Middle- and upper-class women are generally well educated and are not only employed in traditional fields (such as nursing, teaching, and social services) but also as doctors, engineers, lawyers, and economists.

**The Relative Status of Women and Men.** Women and men are equal under Chilean law and the state is obliged to provide both sexes equal employment opportunities. Women possess a great deal of influence and are very active in almost all fields of Chilean society. In the private sphere Chilean men almost always socialize with their friends in the company of their girlfriends or wives, and the latter do participate in conversations and discussions on equal footing. Also due to the strong class nature of Chilean society, women of middle- and upper-class backgrounds have immensely more social status, power, and access to good jobs than males from the lower classes. Nevertheless, as a whole women in Chile possess a lower status than men. This is particularly visible in the political field where power relations find its main expression. Women obtained full electoral rights only in 1949 and they have seldom filled more than 7 percent of the parliamentary seats.

## MARRIAGE, FAMILY AND KINSHIP

**Marriage.** Marriage is one of the most significant rites of passage among Chileans. Although inscription of the marriage at the civil register is sufficient for it to be officially recognized under Chilean law, most Chileans find that a wedding is not really complete without a church ceremony. Everyone is free to marry whomever he or she wants, but because Chile is a class-conscious society, people in general marry persons from similar social and educational backgrounds.

Weddings are normally not ostentatious and wedding parties are mostly organized at home or in a small hall near the church. Commonly, Chileans marry young (in their early or mid-twenties) and tend to have children relatively soon after marriage. Only 12 percent of Chilean women are still single at the age of forty-five. People have quite conventional views about premarital sex, and living together before marriage is still relatively rare (only 3 percent of women between the ages of twenty-five and forty-four). Because of the considerable religious and political influence of the Roman Catholic Church, Chile is the only country in Latin America without a divorce law. Instead, couples who want to end their marriage request an annulment of the civil marriage, under the pretext that a procedural error was made during the civil marriage ceremony. As this implies a costly legal procedure, many Chileans just informally terminate a marriage, but this bars them from marrying again under Chilean law.

**Domestic Unit.** The nuclear family is by far the dominant household unit in Chile. Ninety percent of the population lives with their family while only 8.1 percent live alone. Family size has strongly decreased in recent decades. The average family consists of four persons, and the average number of children is 2.5 per woman. Chile is among the countries with the lowest fertility rate in Latin America, and with the most rapid rate of decrease. In most households (79 percent) authority is held by men. Female-led households can mainly be found among low-income sectors. Particularly among the middle and upper classes, housewives possess a large degree of discretional power in decisions concerning the ruling of their homes (including acquisition of furniture and financial matters) and the children's education.

**Inheritance.** According to Chilean law and customs, when the father passes away half of the estate passes to his wife. The other half is divided by the number of children plus two parts for the mother. So in a family with two children, the mother inherits three-quarters of the estate. Age or gender differences among the children do not alter their rights to equal parts of the inheritance. Until very recently, however, Chilean legislation made a differentiation between "legitimate" (born within the marriage) and "illegitimate" children. Depending on the specific situation, the latter had fewer or no rights for obtaining a part of the estate. In early 2000 this discriminatory legislation was abolished.

**Kin Groups.** Although the nuclear family constitutes the basis of Chilean households, grandparents continue to exert considerable authority in family affairs. Moreover, and either by necessity or by choice, grandparents (especially widowed grandparents) frequently live with the family of one of their daughters or sons. Married children normally visit their parents over the weekend and it is not uncommon for them to talk with their parents by phone almost daily. Aunts, uncles, and cousins are also considered to be close relatives and they frequently meet at family and social gatherings. Particularly in the lower classes, the extended family represents an indispensable source of support for coping with difficulties in hard times.

*Chile's mountainous regions force architects to be creative, as these apartments built into a hillside in Renaca show.*

## SOCIALIZATION

*Infant Care.* Chilean children are primarily cared for by their mothers. In most middle- and upper-class families, however, mothers often can count on the vital full-time support of *empleadas domésticas* (nannies), who for the most part also live with the family at home. Both in the lower classes and within indigenous groups, however, older brothers and sisters do fill an important role in caring for toddlers, as their parents often work outside the home. In an increasing number of public services, ministries, and large factories, day care facilities for children are at the disposition of working mothers.

*Child Rearing and Education.* Young children are generally raised in a relatively relaxed manner. They are not sent to bed very early and fully participate in social and family gatherings, sometimes until very late at night. Chilean parents are generally inclined to pampering their children, by buying what they demand or by surprising them with presents at any time of the year. Children are not explicitly encouraged to learn to become independent but rather are coaxed to remain close and loyal to the family whatever their age. So youngsters in Chile tend to become independent at a relatively late age, as they often leave home only when they marry. Parental authority remains even after children have an independent life, as parents believe they have still the right to get involved in important decisions and personal problems.

*Higher Education.* Chileans from all social backgrounds are very conscious about the importance of providing a good education for their children. As a rule, parents are geared up to make immense financial sacrifices to send their children to good schools and to finance their further education. The number of higher education centers in Chile has dramatically increased during the last decade. In 1980 Chile had eight universities, while by 1990 this number increased to sixty, most of them being private institutions. In addition, the country has eighty professional institutes and 168 technical training centers. Among young people aged eighteen to twenty-four, 19 percent attend an institution of higher education.

## ETIQUETTE

Chilean etiquette does not differ very much from that of Western societies. Although Chileans are in general less formal than other Latin Americans, they definitely follow certain rules in social gatherings. During formal occasions people shake hands in a restrained way, while good friends may shake hands and embrace. Chilean women normally salute acquaintances (both male and female) with one kiss on the right cheek.

Chileans commonly use the formal "you" (*usted*) to address persons, independently of the interlocutor's social status. Also parents-in-law are respectfully addressed with *usted* and with *don* or *doña* before their Christian name. The informal "you" (*tú*) is largely used between people who know each other very well and among youngsters, but it is avoided when one speaks to an elder.

Chileans are generally quite punctual for their business appointments. When invited into a home for dinner, however, it is expected that the guest will not show up before some twenty minutes after the agreed time.

Chileans are quite restrained in public spaces and restaurants and it is particularly bad form to talk too loudly. Waiters are called "señor" and are addressed in formal "you" form. It is also considered imprudent to talk about the authoritarian past, Pinochet, the armed forces, and the like in social gatherings, as Chileans are quite divided on these sensitive subjects.

## RELIGION

**Religious Beliefs.** A large majority of Chileans (73 percent) are affiliated with the Roman Catholic Church. Some 15 percent of the population identifies itself with several Protestant groups. This includes Anglicans and Lutherans, but the vast majority of Chilean Protestants (90 percent) belong to the Pentecostal Church. Another 4 percent of the population belongs to other religious groups (Jews, Muslims, and Greek Orthodox), while 8 percent claim not to profess any religion. Chileans profoundly respect the religious beliefs of others, and religion seldom constitutes a source for conflict or disagreement.

**Religious Practitioners.** The national authorities of the Roman Catholic Church have historically exerted a high degree of influence in Chile. For instance, during the Pinochet regime the chief of the Chilean Catholic Church, Cardinal Raúl Silva Henríquez, took a firm stand against the government's human rights abuses. The Church also offered legal support and institutional protection to many persecuted people. Traditionally, the Chilean clergy (made up of about two thousand priests, half of them foreign, and fifty-five hundred nuns) have firmly embraced the cause of social justice. Following democratic restoration, Chilean bishops have actively participated in national debates about divorce, abortion, and the role of the family in modern society.

**Rituals and Holy Places.** Many popular religious celebrations and processions are held in Chile. One of the most colorful is the Festival of La Tirana. This festival is celebrated for three days in July in the village of La Tirana, some 40 miles (64 kilometers) inland from the northern port of Iquique, near the Atacama Desert. This celebration is strongly influenced by the carnival of Oruro, Bolivia. During the celebrations, some 150,000 people dance through the streets in colorful costumes and devil masks. The Festival of La Tirana is an expression of the religious blend between Catholicism and ancient indigenous practices.

On 8 December, Chileans celebrate the Immaculate Conception (of the Virgin Mary). During that day many people from Santiago make a pilgrimage to the Santuario de la Virgen de lo Vásquez (a shrine some 50 miles [80 kilometers] from Santiago) to show their religious devotion. Some people walk many miles on their knees to show their respect to the virgin and as recompense for the favors she has granted them.

**Death and the Afterlife.** Chileans pay great tribute to loved ones who have passed away. Following death a wake and a funeral are held at a church where close friends and the extended family assist to the religious service. Most Chilean prefers graves, but in recent years an increasing number of people choose to be cremated. It is common practice that each year on the anniversary of the death, a Catholic mass is offered in the deceased's memory. On November 1, All Saints' Day, a large number of Chileans visit the cemetery to bring flowers to the grave of family members and friends. Most Chileans believe that there is an afterlife.

## MEDICINE AND HEALTH CARE

Chile has one of the best health care systems in Latin America. Around 90 percent of the population is insured through public (61 percent) and private (28 percent) schemes to obtain access to all types of health services. National health expenditure is 8 percent of the country's GDP. The public health system has 9.14 physicians and 3.83 nurses for every ten thousand beneficiaries. There are, however, big differences in the quality of medical help among the different income groups. While upper- and middle-class Chileans normally make use of the services of private clinics with excellent physicians and the latest medical technology, the lower class are forced to make use of relatively poorly-equipped public care centers and hospitals. Behind the modern health care system, there is a habit in Chile of self-medication and the use of traditional herbs. In southern Chile, elderly Mapuche Indians still consult their female shamans (*machis*) when they have health problems.

## SECULAR CELEBRATIONS

Labor Day (1 May) is a national holiday. Union leaders and government officials participate in worker gatherings that celebrate the importance of labor to the nation.

Día de las Glorias Navales (21 May) commemorates the 1879 naval battle of Iquique during the War of the Pacific, where Chile's national hero, Captain Arturo Prats, lost his life in naval combat against Peruvian vessels. In coastal cities, people commemorate Prats and his crew by boarding small boats covered with Chilean flags and throwing flowers into the sea.

The celebration of Chilean independence in 1810 takes place on 18 September. Chileans go into the streets to celebrate with folk dances and national dishes. This is the country's most important secular celebration.

*Horses pull fishing boats with the morning catch onto a beach in Papudo.*

Día de la Raza (12 October) commemorates the discovery of America by Christopher Columbus and cheers the Spanish background of Chilean culture. In recent years, indigenous groups have made it clear that this celebration does not represent everyone in the country.

On New Year's Eve (31 December), and New Year's Day (1 January), Chileans gather with their families and friends, normally around an *asado* (barbecue). These holidays also mark the initiation of the summer vacation period for many people. The New Year is traditionally received with a spectacular fireworks display at the port of Valparaíso that is transmitted by television to the entire nation.

## THE ARTS AND HUMANITIES

**Support for the Arts.** Until very recently, Chilean artists rarely obtained any financial support for their work from the state or other institutions. In 1992 the Chilean Ministry of Education created Fondart, a national fund for the development of art and culture. In the period 1992–2000 Fondart has financed 3,626 artistic projects with a total of $26 million (U.S.) and has become the main source of financing for cultural activities in Chile.

**Literature.** Poetry has been the leading form within Chilean literature. The epic poem *La Araucana*, written in the sixteenth century by the Spanish poet Alonso de Ercilla, is considered Chile's first major literary work. In this classical work, Ercilla wonders at the natural beauty of Chile and expresses his admiration for the brave Araucanian Indians. In the twentieth century two great Chilean poets were awarded the Nobel prize in literature. In 1945 Lucila Godoy Alcayaga (who wrote under the pseudonym Gabriela Mistral) became the first Latin American to receive this award. Pablo Neruda received the Nobel prize in 1971. Both poets expressed in their work their love for both the nature and the people of Chile and the rest of Latin America.

In the 1980s and 1990s a series of Chilean novelists obtained international recognition, including Isabel Allende, Ariel Dorfman, José Donoso, Francisco Coloane, Luis Sepúlveda, and Antonio Skarmeta.

**Graphic Arts.** Chilean graphic arts have been dominated by paintings. A good collection of the work of major Chilean painters since the nineteenth century are displayed in the Museum of Fine Arts and the Museum of Contemporary Art in Santiago. Nineteenth century painters such as Pedro Lira and Juan Francisco González show rustic Chilean landscapes and portraits of common people. During the twentieth century Chile produced several painters who have achieved fame outside the country, particularly in Europe and the United States. For instance, the works of Nemesio Antunez, Claudio Bravo, and Roberto Matta are present in major world art collections.

***Performance Arts.*** Traditional folk music offers the best of Chile's performance arts. One of the country's greatest folk musicians has been Violeta Parra. During the 1950s and 1960s she travelled through the Chilean countryside to collect folk music and began to perform it in Santiago artistic circles. Her music motivated many young artists who in the mid-1960s formed a new musical stream called the *Nueva Canción Chilena* ("Chilean New Song"). This was the beginning of a fruitful and creative period for Chilean folk music. Artists such as Víctor Jara and Patricio Manns and well-known musical groups such as Inti-Illimani and Quilapayún belong to this musical current. The classical pianist Claudio Arrau was Chile's most prominent performance artist of the twentieth century.

## THE STATE OF THE PHYSICAL AND SOCIAL SCIENCES

Most scientific research in the physical sciences is conducted at two of the oldest and largest universities, Universidad de Chile and Pontificia Universidad Católica. In 1967 the National Commission for Scientific and Technological Research was created. Its main role is to advise the Chilean authorities in all matters referring science and technology. This commission also provides scholarships for M.A. and Ph.D. degrees. In the period 1988–1997 a total of 479 individuals obtained a four-year scholarships for their Ph.D, and 236 for a M.A. In 1992 a National Fund for Scientific and Technological Development was established to finance first-rate research projects. Through 1997 it had financed some 6,000 scientific projects for more than $2.5 billion (U.S.).

Chilean social sciences are very prestigious in Latin America. They are practiced not only in universities but also in a large number of well-known private institutions that are mainly concentrated in Santiago.

## BIBLIOGRAPHY

Arroyo, Gonzalo et al. "Chilenidad: En búsqueda de una nueva alma." *Mensaje* 462: 27–39.

Bauer, Arnold. *Chilean Rural Society*, 1975.

Bengoa, José. *Historia del pueblo Mapuche*, 2 ed., 1991.

Bethell, Leslie, ed. *Chile since Independence*, 1993.

Brennan, John, and Alvaro Taboada. *How to Survive in the Chilean Jungle? An English Lexicon of Chilean Slang and Spanish Sayings*, 1996.

Caistor, Nick. *Chile in Focus: A Guide to the People, Politics, and Culture,* 1998.

Castillo-Feliu, Guillermo. *Culture and Customs of Chile*, 2000.

Collier, Simon, and William F. Sater. *A History of Chile, 1808–1994*, 1996.

Encina, Francisco A. *Nuestra inferioridad económica*, 1912.

Flacso. *Mujeres latinoamericanas en cifras: Chile*, 1992.

Instituto Nacional de Estadísticas. *Compendio estadístico 1999*, 1999.

Kohen Winter, Jane. *Cultures of the World: Chile*, 1991.

Loveman, Brian. *Chile: The Legacy of Spanish Capitalism*, 2nd ed., 1980.

MacBride, George M. *Chile: Land and Society*, 1936.

Ministerio de Agricultura. *Chilean Agriculture Overview, 1999*, 1999.

Montecino, Sonia. *Madres y huachos: Alegorías del mestizaje chileno*, 1997.

Palacios, Nicolás, *Raza Chilena*, 1904.

Perrottet, Tony, ed. *Chile: Insight Guides*, 1998.

Pickering, Marianne. *Chile: Where the Land Ends*, 1997.

Roraff, Susan, and Laura Camacho. *Chile, Cultural Shock: A Guide to Customs and Etiquette*, 1998.

Subercaseaux, Benjamín. *Chile o una loca geografía*, 1940. Published in English by Macmillan as *Chile: A Geographical Extravaganza*, 1943.

———. *Chile: un país moderno?*, 1996.

———. *Historia de las ideas y de la cultura en Chile*, 2 vols., 1997.

Sznajder, Mario. "Who is a Chilean? The Mapuche, the Huaso and the Roto as the Basic Symbols of Chilean Collective Identity," In Luis Roninger and Mario Sznajder, eds., *Constructing Collective Identities and Shaping Public Spheres*, 1998.

Turismo y Comunicaciones. *Chile: A Remote Corner on Earth*, 1992.

Umana-Murray, Mirtha. *Three Generations of Chilean Cuisine*, 1997.

Wheeler, Sara. *Travels in a Thin Country: A Journey through Chile*, 1994.

—PATRICIO SILVA

# CHINA

**CULTURE NAME**

Chinese

**ALTERNATIVE NAMES**

The Chinese call their country Zhonghua Renmmin Gogheguo, or Zhong Guo for short.

**ORIENTATION**

*Identification.* The Chinese refer to their country as the Middle Kingdom, an indication of how central they have felt themselves to be throughout history. There are cultural and linguistic variations in different regions, but for such a large country the culture is relatively uniform. However, fifty-five minority groups inhabit the more remote regions of the country and have their own unique cultures, languages, and customs.

*Location and Geography.* China has a land area of 3,691,502 square miles (9,596,960 square kilometers), making it the world's third largest nation. It borders thirteen countries, including Russia and Mongolia to the north, India to the southwest, and Myanmar, Laos, and Vietnam to the south. To the east, it borders the Yellow Sea, the South China Sea, and the East China Sea. The climate is extremely diverse, ranging from tropical in the south to subarctic in the north. In the west, the land consists mostly of mountains, high plateaus, and desert. The eastern regions are characterized by plains, deltas, and hills. The highest point is Mount Everest, on the border between Tibet and Nepal, the tallest mountain in the world.

The Yangtze, the longest river in the country, forms the official dividing line between north and south China. The Yangtze sometimes floods badly, as does the Yellow River to the north, which, because of the damage it has caused, is called "China's sorrow."

The country is divided into two regions: Inner China and Outer China. Historically, the two have been very separate. The Great Wall, which was built in the fifteenth century to protect the country against military invasions, marks the division. While the areas of the two regions are roughly equal, 95 percent of the population lives in Inner China.

The country is home to several endangered species, including the giant panda, the golden monkey, several species of tiger, the Yangtze alligator, and the red-crowned crane. While outside organizations such as the World Wildlife Fund have made efforts to save these animals, their preservation is not a top priority for the government.

*Demography.* China is the most populous nation on earth; in 2000, the estimated population was 1,261,832,482 (over one-fifth of the world's population). Of these people, 92 percent are Han Chinese; the remaining 8 percent are people of Zhuang, Uyhgur, Hui, Yi, Tibetan, Miao, Manchu, Mongol, Buyi, Korean, and other nationalities. Sichuan, in the central region, is the most densely populated province. Many of the minority groups live in Outer China, although the distribution has changed slightly over the years. The government has supported Han migration to minority territories in an effort to spread the population more evenly across the country and to control the minority groups in those areas, which sometimes are perceived as a threat to national stability. The rise in population among the minorities significantly outpaces that of the Han, as the minority groups are exempt from the government's one-child policy.

*Linguistic Affiliation.* Mandarin Chinese is the official language. It is also called Putonghua and is based on the Beijing dialect. Modern spoken Chinese, which replaced the classical language in the 1920s, is called *bai hua*. The writing system has not changed for thousands of years and is the same for all the dialects. It is complex and difficult to learn

*China*

and consists of almost sixty thousand characters, although only about five thousand are used in everyday life. Unlike other modern languages, which use phonetic alphabets, Chinese is written in pictographs and ideographs, symbols that represent concepts rather than sounds. The communist government, in an attempt to increase literacy, developed a simplified writing system. There is also a system, called *pinyin*, of writing Chinese words in Roman characters.

Chinese is a tonal language: words are differentiated not just by sounds but by whether the intonation is rising or falling. There are a number of dialects, including Yue (spoken in Canton), Wu (Shangai), Minbei (Fuzhou), Minnan (Hokkien–Tai-wanese), Xiang, Gan, and Hakka. Many of the dialects are so different that they are mutually unintelligible. Some minority groups have their own languages.

**Symbolism.** The flag has a red background with a yellow star in the upper left-hand corner and four smaller yellow stars in a crescent formation to its right. The color red symbolizes the revolution. The large star stands for the Communist Party, and the four small stars symbolize the Chinese people; the position of the stars stands for a populace united in support of the state.

The main symbol of the nation is the dragon, a fantastical creature made up of seven animals. It is accorded the power to change size at will and to bring the rain that farmers need. New Year's festivities often include a line of people in a dragon costume. Another patriotic symbol is the Great Wall. Spanning a length of 1,500 miles, it is the only human-made structure visible from the moon. Work began on the wall in the third century B.C.E. and continued during the Ming Dynasty in the fifteenth century. The emperor conscripted criminals and ordinary farmers for the construction; many died while working, and their bodies were buried in the wall. It has become a powerful symbol of both the oppression the Chinese have endured and the heights their civilization has achieved.

## HISTORY AND ETHNIC RELATIONS

**Emergence of the Nation.** Records of civilization in China date back to around 1766 B.C.E. and the Shang Dynasty. The Zhou defeated the Shang in 1059 B.C.E. and went on to rule for nearly one thousand years, longer than any other dynasty.

China was a feudal state until the lord of Qin managed to unite the various lords and became the first emperor in 221 B.C.E. He ruled with an iron fist, demanding that the teachings of Confucius be burned, and conscripting thousands of people to construct canals, roads, and defensive walls, including the beginning of what would become the Great Wall. The Qin Dynasty was short-lived; it lasted only three years, until the death of the emperor. The Han Dynasty, which held sway from 206 B.C.E. until 220 C.E., saw the introduction of many of elements that would later characterize Chinese society, including the Imperial Examination System, which allowed people to join the civil service on the basis of merit rather than birth. This system remained in effect until the beginning of the twentieth century.

The Han Dynasty was followed by the Period of Disunity, which lasted more than three hundred years. During that time, the country was split into areas ruled by the Mongols and other tribes from the north. It was during this period that Buddhism was introduced in the country. The Sui Dynasty rose to power in 581, connecting the north and the south through the construction of the Grand Canal.

The Tang Dynasty ruled from 618 until 907 and saw a blossoming of poetry and art. It was also a period of expansion, as the nation increased its territory in the west and north. The Five Dynasties period followed, during which the empire once again split. The Song Dynasty (960–1279) was another artistically prolific era. The Song fell to Mongol invasions under the leadership of Kublai Khan, who established the Yuan Dynasty. It was during this time that the capital was established in Beijing.

The Ming took over in 1368 and ruled for nearly three hundred years. During that period, trade continued to expand.

The Qing Dynasty ruled from 1644 until 1911 and saw the expansion of China into Tibet and Mongolia. Especially in later years, the Qing practiced strict isolationism, which ultimately led to their downfall, as their military technology did not keep pace with that of the Western powers. Foreign traders came to the country by sea, bringing opium with them. The Qing banned opium in 1800, but the foreigners did not heed that decree. In 1839, the Chinese confiscated twenty thousand chests of the drug from the British. The British retaliated, and the four Opium Wars began. The result was a defeat for China and the establishment of Western settlements at numerous seaports. The foreigners took advantage of the Qing's weakened hold on power and divided the nation into "spheres of influence."

Another result of the Opium Wars was the loss of Hong Kong to the British. The 1840 Treaty of Nanjing gave the British rights to that city "in perpetuity." An 1898 agreement also "leased" Kowloon and the nearby New Territories to the British for one hundred years. A group of rebels called the "Righteous and Harmonious Fists," or the Boxers, formed to overthrow both the foreigners and the Qing. The Qing, recognizing their compromised position, united with the Boxers to attack the Western presence in the country. The Boxer Rebellion saw the end of the Qing Dynasty, and in 1912, Sun Yatsen became president of the newly declared Chinese Republic. In reality, power rested in the hands of regional rulers who often resorted to violence. On 4 May 1919, a student protest erupted in Beijing in opposition to continued Western influence. The student agitation gained strength, and the years between 1915 and the 1920s came to be known as the May Fourth Movement, a period that saw a large-scale rejection of Confucianism and a rise in social action, both of which were precursors to the communist revolution.

The politically weakened and disunified state of the country paved the way for two opposing political parties, each of which had a different vision of a modern, united nation. At Beijing University, several young men, including Mao Zedong, founded the Chinese Communist Party. Their opposition, the Kuomintang, or Nationalist Party, was led by Chiang Kaishek. The two tried to join forces, with

Chiang as the head of the National Revolutionary Army, but dissension led to a civil war.

The Sino-Japanese war began in 1931 when Japan, taking advantage of China's weakened and divided state, invaded the country. An attack on the city of Nanjing (the capital at that time) in 1937 resulted in 300,000 deaths and large-scale destruction of the city. Japan did not withdraw its forces until after World War II.

The Kuomintang, with its military superiority, forced the communists into a retreat to the north that lasted a year and became known as the Long March. Along the way, the communists redistributed land from the rich owners to the peasants, many of whom joined their fight. The Nationalists controlled the cities, but the communists continued to grow in strength and numbers in the countryside; by the late 1940s, the Nationalists were surrounded. Many Kuomintang members abandoned Chiang's army and joined the communists. In April 1949, Nanjing fell to the communists; other cities followed, and Chiang, along with two million of his followers, fled to Taiwan. Mao Zedong, the chairman of the Chinese Communist Party, declared the establishment of the People's Republic of China on 1 October 1949.

Mao began a series of Five Year Plans to improve the economy, beginning with heavy industry. In 1957, as part of those reforms, he initiated a campaign he named the Great Leap Forward, whose goals were to modernize the agricultural system by building dams and irrigation networks and redistributing land into communes. At the same time, industries were established in rural areas. Many of those efforts failed because of poor planning and a severe drought in the northern and central regions of the country. A two-year famine killed thirty million people.

The government launched the so-called One Hundred Flowers campaign in the spring of 1956 with the slogan "Let a hundred flowers bloom, let a hundred schools of thought contend." The intent was to encourage creative freedom; the next year, it was extended to include freedom of intellectual expression. Many people interpreted this to mean an increased tolerance of political expression, but the government did not agree, and the result was a large-scale purge of intellectuals and critics of the Communist Party. This was part of what became known as the Cultural Revolution. In an attempt to rehabilitate his popularity, Mao initiated an attack on his enemies in the Communist Party. Those attacks extended beyond the government to include intellectuals, teachers, and scientists, many of whom were sent to work camps in the countryside for "reeducation." Religion was outlawed, and many temples were destroyed. Tens of thousands of young people were enlisted in Mao's Red Guards, who carried out his orders and lived by the words of the *Little Red Book* of Mao's quotations.

In the early 1970s, toward the end of Mao's regime, Zhou Enlai, an influential politician, worked to restore relations between China and the outside world, from which it had been largely cut off during the Cultural Revolution. In 1972, U.S. President Richard Nixon made a historic trip to China to meet with Mao, beginning a period of improvement in diplomatic relations with the United States.

When Mao died in 1976, the country was in a state of virtual chaos. His successor was Hua Guofeng, a protégé whom the chairman had promoted through the ranks of the party. However, Mao's widow, Jiang Qing, along with three other bureaucrats (Zhang Chunqiao, Wang Hongwen, and Yao Wenyuan), assumed more power in the transitional government. Known as the Gang of Four, they were widely disliked. When the gang publicly announced its opposition to Hua in 1976, Hua had them arrested, a move that was widely approved. The four politicians were imprisoned but did not come to trial until 1980.

In 1977, Deng Xiaoping, a Communist Party member who had been instrumental in the Civil War and the founding of the People's Republic, rose to power and began a program of modernization and moderation of hard-line economic policies. He was faced with the great challenge of updating a decrepit and wasteful government system and responding to demands for increased freedom while maintaining order. Dissatisfaction was widespread, particularly among students, who began calling for an end to government corruption and the establishment of a more democratic government. In 1989, Beijing University students organized demonstrations in Tiananmen Square that lasted for weeks. The People's Liberation Army finally opened fire on the protesters. The June Fourth Massacre (Tiananmen Square Massacre) garnered international attention and sparked worldwide indignation. The United States responded by imposing trade sanctions.

Deng died in 1997, marking the end of government by the original founders of the communist state. Jiang Zemin, the mayor of Shanghai, became president. His government has faced a growing but unstable economy and a system beset by official corruption as well as several regions threatening the

一对夫妇只生一个孩子

保 护

*A man stands in front of a family planning billboard in Beijing. Due to China's huge population, most families are allowed to have only one child.*

unity of the country as a whole. There is a boundary dispute with India, as well as boundary, maritime, and ownership disputes with Russia, Vietnam, North Korea, and several other nations.

In 1997, following a 1984 agreement, the British returned Hong Kong and the New Territories to Chinese control. The handover occurred at midnight on 1 July. Although it had been agreed that Hong Kong would retain the financial and judicial systems installed by the British at least until 2047, an estimated half-million people left the city between 1984 and 1997 in anticipation of the takeover, immigrating to the United States, Canada, and Singapore.

Macao, a Portuguese colony, was given back to China in December 1999 under conditions similar to those in the Hong Kong deal, in which the territory would be permitted to retain much of its economic and governmental sovereignty. Taiwan remains another territory in question. The island broke away from the mainland government in 1949 after the relocation there of Chiang Kaishek and his nationalist allies, who have governed since that time. The Nationalists still maintain their mandate to govern the nation as a whole, and many are opposed to reunification, while the communists claim that Taiwan is a province of China.

Tibet is a contested region that has gained international attention in its quest for independence. China first gained control of the area during the Yuan Dynasty (1271–1368) and again early in the eighteenth century. While it was part of China through the Qing Dynasty, the government did not attempt to exercise direct control of Tibet again until the communists came to power and invaded the territory in 1950. The Dalai Lama, Tibet's religious and political leader, was forced into exile in 1959. The region became autonomous in 1965 but remains financially dependent on China. The question of its independence is a complex one, and resolution does not appear imminent.

***National Identity.*** The vast majority of Chinese people are of Han descent. They identify with the dominant national culture and have a sense of history and tradition that dates back over one thousand years and includes many artistic, cultural, and scientific accomplishments. When the communists took over in 1949, they worked to create a sense of national identity based on the ideals of equality and hard work.

Some minority groups, such as the Manchu, have assimilated almost entirely. While they maintain their own languages and religions, they identify with the nation as well as with their own groups. Other minority ethnic groups tend to identify more with their individual cultures than with the Han. For example, the Mongolians and Kazakhs of the north and northwest, the Tibetans and the Zhuangs in the southwest, and the inhabitants of Hainan Island to the southeast are all linguistically, culturally, and historically distinct from one another and from the dominant tradition. For some minority groups, the Tibetans and Uigurs of Xinjiang in particular, the issue of independence has been an acrimonious one and has led those groups to identify themselves deliberately in opposition to the central culture and its government.

***Ethnic Relations.*** China is for the most part an extremely homogeneous society composed of a people who share one language, culture, and history. The government recognizes fifty-five minority groups that have their own distinct cultures and traditions. Most of those groups live in Outer China, because the Han have, over the centuries, forced them into those harsh, generally less desirable lands. The Han often consider the minority groups inferior, if not subhuman; until recently, the characters for their names included the symbol for "dog." The minority groups harbor a good deal of resentment toward the Han. Tibet and Xinjiang in particular have repeatedly attempted to separate from the republic. The Tibetans and the Uighurs of Xinjiang have expressed animosity toward the Han Chinese who live in bordering regions, and as a result, China has sent troops to those areas to maintain the peace.

## URBANISM, ARCHITECTURE, AND THE USE OF SPACE

While the majority of the population is still rural, the cities are growing, as many people migrate in search of work. Forty cities have populations over one million.

The largest city is Shanghai, which is near the center of the country's east coast. Because of its strategic location as a port on the Huangpu River, near the Yangtze, areas of the city were taken over by the British, French, and Americans after the Opium Wars. Although those concessions were returned to China in 1949, Shanghai retains a European feel in some districts. It is a city of skyscrapers and big business, a cultural locus, and a center of both extreme wealth and extreme poverty.

Beijing, the capital, is the second largest urban center. Its history goes back three thousand years, and it has been the capital since the late thirteenth century. Beijing is divided into the Inner City (to the north) and the Outer City (to the south). The Inner City contains the Imperial City, which contains the Forbidden City. This spectacular architectural aggregation of temples, palaces, and man-made lakes, whose construction began in 1406, is where the emperor and his court resided. Although it once was off limits to civilians, today sightseers and tourists can admire its gardens, terraces, and pavilions. Tienanmen Square, the site of several demonstrations and events, as well as the location of Mao's tomb, is at one end of the Forbidden City. Despite the city's size, it is still possible to navigate Beijing without a car, and most people do; bicycles are one of the most common modes of transportation—this cuts down greatly on air pollution.

Other important cities include Tianjin, a northern port and industrial center; Shenyang in the northeast, another industrial city; and Guangzhou, the main southern port city.

Architecture varies with the diverse climate. In the north, people sleep on a platform called a *kang*. Mongolians live in huts called yurts. In the south, straw houses built on stilts are common. In much of the country, traditional houses are rectangular and have courtyards enclosed by high walls. The roofs are sloped, curving upward at the edges.

## FOOD AND ECONOMY

***Food in Daily Life.*** Rice is the dietary staple in most of the country. In the north and the west, where the climate is too dry to grow rice, wheat is the staple grain. Here, breakfast usually consists of noodles or wheat bread. In the south, many people start the day with rice porridge, or *congee*, served with shrimp, vegetables, and pickles. Lunch is similar to breakfast. The evening meal is the day's largest. Every meal includes soup, which is served as the last course.

People cook in a wok, a metal pan with a curved bottom; this style of cooking requires little oil and a short cooking time. Steaming in bamboo baskets lined with cabbage leaves is another cooking method. Meat is expensive and is served sparingly.

The cuisine can be broken down into four main geographic varieties. In Beijing and Shandong, specialties include Beijing duck served with pancakes and plum sauce, sweet and sour carp, and bird's nest soup. Shanghaiese cuisine uses liberal amounts of oil and is known for seafood and cold meat dishes. Food is particularly spicy in the Sichuan and Hunan provinces. Shrimp with salt and garlic, frogs' legs, and smoked duck are popular dishes.

471

*Neighborhood houses in Dali reflect traditional Chinese urban architecture.*

The southern cuisine of Canton and Chaozhou is the lightest of the four. Seafood, vegetables, roast pork and chicken, and steamed fish are served with fried rice. *Dim sum*, a breakfast or lunch meal consisting of a combination of different appetizer style delicacies, is popular there.

Cooking reflects the country's history of famines caused by factors such as natural disasters and war. The Chinese eat parts and species of animals that many other cultures do not, including fish heads and eyeballs, birds' feet and saliva, and dog and cat meat.

Tea is the most common beverage. The Han drink it unsweetened and black, Mongolians have it with milk, and Tibetans serve it with yak butter. The Chinese are fond of sugary soft drinks, both American brands and locally produced ones. Beer is a common beverage, and there are many local breweries.

**Food Customs at Ceremonial Occasions.** Special occasions and large family gatherings often entail big, elaborate meals. In the north, dumplings called *jiaozi* are served at the Spring Festival and other special occasions. For the Moon Festival in midautumn, "moon cakes" are served, baked pastries filled with ground sesame and lotus seeds or dates. Banquets originating in the imperial tradition

are ceremonial meals common to important state gatherings and business occasions. They usually are held at restaurants and consist of ten or more courses. Rice is not served, as it is considered too cheap and commonplace for such an event.

**Basic Economy.** In 1978, the country began the slow process of shifting from a Soviet-style economy to a more free market system, and in twenty years managed to quadruple the gross domestic product (GDP) and become the second largest economy in the world. However, the decentralization of the economy has often conflicted with the tight reign exercised by the highly centralized political system. The economy is burdened with widespread corruption, bureaucracy, and large state-run businesses that have been unable to keep pace with economic expansion. Inflation rates, which rose steeply in the 1980s, fell between 1995 and 1999 as a result of stricter monetary policies and government control of food prices. While the economy appears to be improving, the standard of living in rural areas remains poor, and the government faces problems collecting taxes in provinces that are becoming increasingly autonomous, such as Shanghai and Guangzhou.

The labor force consists of 700 million people, of whom 50 percent work in agriculture, 24 percent in industry, and 26 percent in services. The unemployment rate is roughly 10 percent in the cities and higher in the countryside. A large number of migrants move between the villages and the cities, barely supporting themselves with part-time jobs and day labor. The national currency is named the yuan.

One of the largest economic challenges has been feeding the enormous population. The government has taken a two-pronged approach, instituting a series of modernization projects to improve irrigation and transportation and trying to curb population growth by allowing each family to have only one child. The one-child law, which does not apply to minority groups, has faced widespread popular resistance.

***Land Tenure and Property.*** One of Mao's priorities was a program of land reform. He turned over the previous sharecropper-like system and in its place established collective, government-run farms. Deng did away with many of the large-scale communes. While safeguarding the system of government-owned land, he allowed individual farmers to rent land and gave them more freedom in decision making. This shift saw a large increase in agricultural productivity; output doubled in the 1980s.

While farmers and other individuals have much more control over their land than in the past, the majority of it is still owned by the government.

***Commercial Activities.*** Much commercial activity revolves around agriculture. Products vary from region to region. The main goods produced for domestic sale are rice, wheat, soybeans, fruits, and vegetables. From 1958 to 1978, all farms were run as communes and were required to sell all of their output to the government at predetermined prices. Today, farmers still must sell a portion of the yield to the government, but the rest goes on the open market where supply and demand determine the price. In government stores, there is no negotiating of prices, but the increasing numbers of privately owned shops often welcome bargaining.

There is a large black market in foreign goods such as cigarettes, alcohol, and electronic products. Connections (called *guanxi*) are of supreme importance in acquiring such goods. It is not uncommon for products made in state-owned factories for sale by the government to find their way into private stores.

Hong Kong, with a fully capitalist economy, developed under British rule into an international financial center. The main commercial activities there are banking and high-technology product and services.

***Major Industries.*** The larger industries include iron and steel, coal, machine building, armaments, textiles and apparel, petroleum, footwear, toys, food processing, automobiles, and consumer electronics. Metallurgy and machine building have received top priority in recent years and account for about one-third of industrial output. In these, as in other industries, the country has consistently valued quantity in production over quality, and this is reflected in many of the products. Tourism, which increased during the 1980s, fell sharply after Tiananmen Square; however, it has picked up again as the economy has continued to open to Western investors.

***Trade.*** China imports machinery and equipment, plastics, chemicals, iron and steel, and mineral fuels, mainly from Japan, the United States, Taiwan, and South Korea. Exports include machinery and equipment, textiles and clothing, footwear, toys and sporting goods, mineral fuels, and chemicals. These products go primarily to the United States, Hong Kong, Japan, and Germany. Trade has shifted dramatically over the years. In the 1950s, the main trading partners were other communist countries; however, the decline of the Soviet Union as a world power changed that. Most trade today is conducted with the noncommunist world.

***Division of Labor.*** Initially, under communism, urban workers were assigned jobs by the government. Wages were predetermined and did not reward productivity. That system was modified in 1978 and again in 1986 to allow for wage increases and firings in relation to productivity. Under Deng Xiaoping, people were encouraged to develop their entrepreneurial skills as shopkeepers and taxi drivers and in other small business ventures. Older people often become caretakers for their young grandchildren. Many continue to engage in community work and projects.

## SOCIAL STRATIFICATION

***Classes and Castes.*** Confucian philosophy endorses a hierarchical class system. At the top of the system are scholars, followed by farmers, artisans, and finally merchants and soldiers. A good deal of social mobility was possible in that system; it was common practice for a family to save its money to invest in the education and advancement of the oldest son. When the communists took control, they overturned this traditional hierarchy, professing the

*A view of the Great Wall of China, which is more than 1,500 miles long and is the only man-made structure visible from the moon.*

ideals of a classless society. In fact, the new system still has an elite and a lower class. Society is divided into two main segments: the *ganbu*, or political leaders, and the peasant masses. According to the philosophy of the Communist Party, both classes share the same interests and goals and therefore should function in unison for the common good. In reality, there is a large and growing gap between the rich and the poor. Weathy people live in the cities, while the poor tend to be concentrated in the countryside. However, farmers have begun to migrate to the cities in search of work in increasing numbers, giving rise to housing and employment problems and creating a burgeoning class of urban poor people.

***Symbols of Social Stratification.*** Cars, a rare commodity, are a symbol of high social and economic standing. Comfortable living accommodations with luxuries such as hot running water are another. Many government employees who could not otherwise afford these things get them as perks of the job. As recently as the 1980s, most people dressed in simple dark-colored clothing. Recently, more styles have become available, and brand-name or imitation brand-name American clothes are a marker of prosperity. This style of dress is more common in the cities but is visible in the countryside among the better-off farmers.

Many minority groups maintain their traditional attire. Tibetans dress in layers of clothes to protect themselves from the harsh weather. The women wrap their heads in cloth. Uighur women wear long skirts and bright-colored scarves; the men wear embroidered caps.

## POLITICAL LIFE

***Government.*** China is a communist state. The president is the chief of state and is elected by the National People's Congress (NPC) for a five-year term. However, the president defers to the decisions and leadership of the NPC. The NPC is responsible for writing laws and policy, delegating authority, and supervising other parts of the government. The highest level in the executive branch of the government is the State Council, which is composed of a premier, a vice premier, councillors, and various ministers. The State Council handles issues of internal politics, defense, economy, culture, and education. Its members are appointed and can be removed by the president's decree.

The country is divided into twenty-three provinces, five autonomous regions, and four municipalities. (Taiwan is considered the twenty-third province.) At the local level, elected deputies serve in a local people's congress, a smaller-scale version of the national body, which is responsible for governing within the region and reports to the State Council.

**Leadership and Political Officials.** The Chinese Communist Party (CCP) is in effect the only political party. Eight registered small parties are controlled by the CCP. There are no substantial opposition groups, but there are two—the Falun Gong sect and the China Democracy Party—that the government sees as potential threats. The Falun Gong in particular has received international attention because of the government's attempts to suppress it. The organization claims that it is a meditation group based on Buddhist and Taoist philosophies; the government considers it a cult that threatens public order and the state. The government has sent hundreds of Falun Gong members to labor camps and has imprisoned many of its leaders. The group is legal in Hong Kong.

**Social Problems and Control.** The legal system is a complex mixture of tradition and statute. A rudimentary civil code has been in effect since 1987, and new legal codes since 1980. The country continues to make efforts to improve its laws in the civil, administrative, criminal, and commercial areas. The highest court is the Supreme People's Court, which supervises lower courts, hears appeals, and explains national laws.

The crime rate is rising. Pickpocketing and petty theft are the most common offenses, but there are increasing numbers of incidents of violent crime. Prostitution and drug use are also growing problems.

Public humiliation is a common punishment for crimes such as petty theft. Prisons often put inmates to work in farming or manufacturing. The death penalty is assigned not only for violent crimes but also for acts such as bribery and corruption. The government has been known to deal harshly with political dissidents. Many participants in the 1989 Tiananmen Square protests were imprisoned, and the government continues to punish severely any displays of opposition. The country has been cited numerous times for human rights violations.

**Military Activity.** The People's Liberation Army (PLA) includes the Ground Forces, the Navy (both marines and naval aviation), the Air Force, and the Second Artillery Corps (strategic missile force). The People's Armed Police, consisting of internal security troops, is supposedly subordinate to the Ministry of Public Security but is included in the "armed

forces" and in times of war acts as an adjunct to the PLA. The government quotes a figure of over $12 billion (1.2 percent of the GDP) for military expenses, but many Western analysts place the amount several times higher. Service in the PLA is voluntary and highly selective. Both women and men can serve, and the army conscientiously upholds communist ideals of equality; there are no ranks in the army.

As of 1998, there were 2.8 million people in the armed forces: 1,830,000 in the army, 420,000 in the air force, and 230,000 in the navy. That year, however, the government introduced a plan to cut the armed forces by half a million.

## SOCIAL WELFARE AND CHANGE PROGRAMS

State-run corporations or groups of factories often provide housing, child care, education, medical care, and other services for their employees. These organizations are called *danwei*, or work units. They also provide compensation for injury and disability, old age, and survivors' pensions. Many of the government's social welfare initiatives are concentrated in the cities where housing, education, and food are subsidized; in the countryside, the burden of social welfare often falls to companies, organizations, and individual families. The government supplies emergency relief in the case of natural disasters, including floods and crop failures. The government offers financial incentives to families that comply with its one-child policy, giving them preference in housing, health care, and other social services.

## NONGOVERNMENTAL ORGANIZATIONS AND OTHER ASSOCIATIONS

China is a member of a number of international associations, including the United Nations, UNESCO, and the World Health Organization. It has applied for membership in the World Trade Organization. There are a number of foreign health, development, and human rights organizations active in China, including the Red Cross, the World Health Organization, the U.S. Peace Corps, Amnesty International, and others.

## GENDER ROLES AND STATUSES

**Division of Labor by Gender.** Before the twentieth century, women were confined to the domestic realm, while men dominated all other aspects of society. The only exception was agriculture, where women's work had a somewhat wider definition. Western influence began to infiltrate the country in

*A merchant rents books from a sidewalk rack on a street in Tunxi.*

the nineteenth century, when missionaries started schools for girls. Opportunities increased further as the country began to modernize, and under communism, women were encouraged to work outside the home. Today women work in medicine, education, business, sports, the arts and sciences, and other fields. While men still dominate the upper levels of business and government and tend to have better paying jobs, women have made considerable progress.

***The Relative Status of Women and Men.*** Confucian values place women as strictly subordinate to men, and this was reflected in traditional society. Women had no rights and were treated as possessions, first of their father's and later of their husband's. The practice of foot binding was symbolic of the strictures women faced in all aspects of life. From the age of seven, girls had their feet wrapped tightly, stunting their growth and virtually crippling them in the name of beauty. This practice was not outlawed until 1901. The procedure was inflicted mainly on upper-class and middle-class women, as peasant women needed full use of their feet to work in the fields.

The rejection of many traditional values early in the twentieth century resulted in increasing equality and freedom for women. The Western

presence in the nineteenth century also had an influence. Raising the status of women was a priority in the founding of the modern state. Women played an important role in the Long March and the communist struggle against the Kuomintang, and under Mao they were given legal equality to men in the home and the workplace as well as in laws governing marriage, divorce, and inheritance. Despite these legal measures, women still face significant obstacles, including spousal abuse and the practice of selling women and young girls as brides.

## MARRIAGE, FAMILY, AND KINSHIP

***Marriage.*** According to custom, marriages are arranged by the couple's parents. While this system is less rigid than it once was, it is still common for young people to use matchmakers. People take a pragmatic approach to marriage, and even those who chose their own spouses often take practical considerations as much as romantic ones into account.

Weddings are usually large, expensive affairs paid for by the groom's family. For those who can afford it, Western-style weddings are popular, with the bride in a white gown and the groom in a suit and tie.

The legal age for marriage is twenty for women and twenty-two for men. A marriage law enacted by the communists in 1949 gave women the right to choose their husbands and file for divorce. While it is difficult to obtain a divorce, rates are rising.

**Domestic Unit.** It is common for several generations to live together under one roof. After marriage, a woman traditionally leaves her parents' home and becomes part of her husband's family. The husband's mother runs the household and sometimes treats a new daughter-in-law harshly. Although today practical reasons compel most children to leave the parents' home, the oldest son often stays, as it is his duty to care for his aging parents. Even today, many young adults continue to live with their parents after marriage, partly because of a housing shortage in the cities.

**Inheritance.** The estate generally passes to the oldest son, although, especially in the case of wealthy and powerful men, most of their personal possession traditionally were buried with them. The remaining property went to the oldest son. Since the communists came to power in 1949, women have been able to inherit property.

**Kin Groups.** Extended family is extremely important, and the wealthy and well educated often hire genealogists to research their family trees. Family members, even distant relations, are valued above outsiders. The passing on of the family name is of great importance. If the oldest son in a family has no son of his own, he often is expected to adopt the son of his next youngest brother. If no sons are born in the clan, a sister's son may be adopted to carry on the name.

## SOCIALIZATION

**Infant Care.** Traditionally, male babies were valued much more highly than female offspring. Girls were looked at as a liability and in times of economic hardship often were sold into lives of servitude or prostitution. While this has changed somewhat, those attitudes have again become prevalent with the government's one-child policy. When families are allowed to have only one child, they want to ensure that it is a boy; for this reason, rates of female infanticide and abandonment have risen. While babies are highly valued, it is considered bad luck to praise them aloud. It is common to offer backward compliments, remarking on a child's ugliness.

A baby usually is not washed for the first three days after birth. On the third day, he or she is bathed, and friends and relatives come to view the

new addition to the family. When a male child turns one month old, the parents throw a First Moon party. The boy's head is shaved, and the hair is wrapped in a red cloth, which, after a hundred days, is thrown in the river. This is thought to protect the child.

Women usually are granted maternity leave between two months and one year, but rural women tend to go back to work earlier.

**Child Rearing and Education.** From a very young age, children are assigned responsibilities in both the family and the community. In the countryside, this means farm chores; in the city, it consists of housework or even sweeping the street. Schoolchildren are responsible for keeping the classroom clean and orderly.

Under communism, when women were encouraged to take jobs outside the home, child care facilities became prevalent. Grandparents also play a significant role in raising children, especially when the mother works outside the home.

Education is mandatory for nine years. Ninety-six percent of children attend kindergarten and elementary school, and about two-thirds continue on to secondary school, which lasts for three years. In high school, students pursue either technical training or a general education. Those who receive a general education can take the extremely difficult qualifying exams to enter a university. The educational system stresses obedience and rote learning over creativity. Both traditional Confucians and the Communist Party view education as a method for inculcating values in the young. Under Mao, the educational system suffered from propaganda and the devaluation of intellectual pursuits. Because of the size of the population, classrooms and teachers are in short supply.

The country has made great progress in increasing the literacy of the general population. When the communists came to power, only 15 percent of the population could read and write. Today, thanks to mandatory schooling for children and adult education programs, the rate is over 75 percent.

**Higher Education.** Higher education is not accessible to many. Admission to the universities is extremely competitive; only 2 percent of the population attends college. In addition to the rigorous entrance examination, students are required to demonstrate their loyalty to the Communist Party. During the summers, university students perform manual labor. The curriculum emphasizes science

*A mother and her children in a farming commune in Canton. Only ethnic minority families are allowed to have more than one child.*

and technology. It is considered a great honor to undertake advanced study, and a university degree virtually guarantees a comfortable position after graduation. The most prestigious universities are in Beijing and Qinghua, but there are more than a hundred others scattered throughout the country. There are technical and vocational schools that train students in agriculture, medicine, mining, and education.

### ETIQUETTE

Deference and obedience to elders is considered extremely important. There is a hierarchy that places older people above younger and men above women; this is reflected in social interaction.

Chinese people are nonconfrontational. Saving face is of primary importance; appearing to be in the right or attempting to please someone is more important than honesty. It is considered rude to refuse a request even if one is unable to fulfill it. The fear of losing face is a concern that governs social interactions both large and insignificant; failure to perform a duty brings shame not just on the individual, but on the family and community as well. Individuality is often subsumed in the group identity. There is little privacy in the home or family,

and housing shortages and cramped living quarters often exaggerate this situation.

People touch often, and same-sex hand holding is common. However, physical contact between men and women in public is limited. Smiling is not necessarily a sign of happiness; it can be a display of worry or embarrassment.

Visiting is an important part of social life. Guests often drop in unannounced and are invited to join the family for a meal. It is customary to bring a small gift when visiting.

### RELIGION

***Relgious Beliefs.*** As a communist state, the country is officially atheist. Fifty-nine percent of the population has no religious affiliation. Twenty percent of the people practice traditional religions (Taoism and Confucianism), 12 percent consider themselves atheists, 6 percent are Buddhist, 2 percent are Muslim, and 1 percent are Christian. The teachings of Confucius are laid out in *The Analects*. It is a philosophy that stresses responsibility to community and obedience and deference to elders.

Taoism, founded by Lao Tse Tsu, is more mystical and less pragmatic than Confucianism. The *tao*, which translates as "the way," focuses on ideals of balance and order and often uses nature as a metaphor. It also includes elements of animism. Taoism, unlike Confucianism, rejects rank and class. Taoists shun aggression, competition, and ambition.

Buddhism, which came to the country from India, is similar to Taoism in its rejection of striving and material goods. The goal of Buddhism is nirvana, a transcendence of the confines of mind and body. Confucianism, Taoism, and Buddhism are not mutually exclusive, and many people practice elements of all three in addition to worshiping various gods and goddesses, each of which is responsible for a different profession or other aspect of life. Luck is of supreme importance in popular belief, and there are many ways of bringing good fortune and avoiding badluck. A type of geomancy called *fengshui* involves manipulating one's surroundings in a propitious way. These techniques are used to determine everything from the placement of furniture in a room to the construction of skyscrapers.

Many of the minority groups have their own religions. Some, such as the Dais in Yunnan and the Zhuangs in the southwest, practice animism. The Uighurs, Kazakhs, and Huis are Muslim. Tibetans follow their own unique form of Buddhism, called Tantric or Lamaistic Buddhism, which incorporates many traditions of the indigenous religion called *bon*, including prayer flags and prayer wheels and a mystical element.

Despite the numerous Catholic and Protestant missionaries who arrived in the country beginning in the nineteenth century, Christianity has managed to gain few converts. Christians are mostly concentrated in big cities such as Beijing and Shanghai.

***Religious Practitioners.*** Confucianism and Taoism do not have central religious figures. In Buddhism, there are monks who devote their lives to prayer and meditation. Worship is usually not communal; the only group services are performed at funerals.

The central figure in Tibetan Buddhism is the Dalai Lama, a name that translates as "Ocean of Wisdom." When one Dalai Lama dies, it is believed that he is then reincarnated, and it is the duty of the monks to search out his spirit in a newborn child. Today the position has political as well as religious significance. The current Dalai Lama lives in exile in India and pursues the cause of Tibetan independence.

***Rituals and Holy Places.*** Taoist temples are dominated by the roof, usually yellow or green, which is adorned with images of gods and dragons. The interior usually consists of a courtyard, a main hall with an altar where offerings are placed, and sometimes small shrines to various deities. Buddhist temples incorporate pagodas, a design which came from India around the first century C.E. (the time when the religion made its way to China). These temples also display statues of the Buddha, sometimes enormous sculptures in gold, jade, or stone.

Worship generally takes the form of individual prayer or meditation. One form of spiritual practice that is very popular is physical exercise. There are three main traditions. *Wushu*, a self-defense technique known in the West as *gong fu* (or kung fu), combines aspects of boxing and weapon fighting. Shadow boxing, called *taijiquan* (or tai chi chuan), is a series of slow, graceful gestures combined with deep breathing. The exercises imitate the movements of animals, including the tiger, panther, snake, and crane. *Qidong* is a breathing technique that is intended to strengthen the body by controlling the *qi*, or life energy. These exercises are practiced by people of all ages and walks of life; large groups often gather in parks or other public spaces to perform the exercises together.

Buddhist and Taoist temples hold special prayer gatherings to mark the full moon and the new moon.

The largest festival of the year is the celebration of the new year or Spring Festival, whose date varies, falling between mid-January and mid-February. People clean their houses thoroughly to symbolize a new start, and children are given money in red envelopes for good luck. Activities include fireworks and parades with dancers dressed as lions and dragons. It is a time to honor one's ancestors.

The birthday of Guanyin, the goddess of mercy, falls between late March and late April and is observed by visiting Taoist temples. The birthday of Mazu, the goddess of the sea (also known as Tianhou), is celebrated similarly. It falls in May or June. The Water-Splashing Festival is observed in Yunnan Province in mid-April. It involves symbolic bathing and water splashing that are supposed to wash away bad luck. The Zhuangs mark the end of the plowing season in the spring with a cattle-soul festival, which includes a sacrificial ceremony and offerings of food to the cattle. Moon Festival, or Mid-Autumn Festival, in September or October is celebrated with fireworks, paper lanterns, and moon gazing. The birthday of Confucius (28 September) is a time to make pilgrimages to his birthplace in Shandong Province.

*A group of people practice tai chi along the main thoroughfare in Shanghai. The popular form of exercise emphasizes slow, graceful movements.*

***Death and the Afterlife.*** Funerals are traditionally large and elaborate. The higher the social standing of the deceased, the more possessions and people were buried with him or her to ensure entry into the next world. Traditionally, this included horses, carriages, wives, and slaves. Chinese mourners dress in white and wrap their heads in white cloths.

Ancestor worship is an important part of the religion, and it is common Buddhist practice to have a small altar in the house dedicated to deceased family members. Tomb-Sweeping Day, or *Qingming*, on 5 April, is dedicated to visiting the burial place of one's ancestors and paying one's respects. Food is often placed on graves as an offering. Ghost Month (late August to late September) is a time when the spirits of the dead are thought to return to earth. It is not a propitious time for new beginnings, and anyone who dies during this period is not buried until the next month.

## MEDICINE AND HEALTH CARE

Traditional medicine is still widely practiced. It is an ancient, intricate system that places an emphasis on the whole body rather than specific ailments. All natural elements, including human beings, are thought to be made up of *yin* (the female force) and *yang* (the male force). These opposing forces are part of the body's *qi*. Health problems are considered a manifestation of an imbalance of *yin* and *yang*, that disrupts a person's qi. Remedies to right the imbalance include snake gallbladder, powdered deer antlers, and rhinoceros horn, as well as hundreds of different combinations of herbs. Another method of treatment is acupuncture, which involves the insertion of thin needles into the body to regulate and redirect the flow of qi. Massage techniques are also used, and doctors avoid cutting into the body.

Western medical facilities are much more accessible in the cities than in the countryside. Even those who have access to Western medicine often use a combination of the two systems, but the government, which runs all the major health facilities, places a priority on Western medical practices.

Health conditions have improved significantly since 1949. Life expectancy has risen, and many diseases, including plague, smallpox, cholera, and typhus, have been eliminated. Smoking is a growing health concern, particularly since American cigarette companies have begun large-scale marketing campaigns. HIV and AIDS are increasingly a problem, particularly in Yunnan province, which borders Vietnam, Laos, and Myanmar. It is exacerbated by prostitution, a rise in intravenous drug use, and lack of education.

## SECULAR CELEBRATIONS

New Year's Day on 1 January is observed in addition to the traditional Chinese New Year. Other holidays include International Working Women's Day on 8 March, International Labor Day on 1 May, Youth Day on 4 May, Dragon Boat Festival in May or June, Children's Day on 1 June, Founding of the Communist Party of China Day on 1 July, Founding of the People's Liberation Army Day on 1 August (celebrated with music and dance performances by military units), Teacher's Day on 10 September, and National Day on 1 and 2 October.

## THE ARTS AND HUMANITIES

**Support for the Arts.** The government censors the output of all artists; it is forbidden to produce work that criticizes the Communist Party or its ideals. There is a long tradition of imperial patronage of the arts that continues today in the form of state-funded literary guilds that pay writers for their work. While providing support to writers, this system also suppresses their creative freedom. As the economy has become more open, however, the government has decreased its support, and artists are becoming more dependent on selling their work.

**Literature.** Chinese poetry is not just a linguistic feat but a visual one. Classical poems express balance through both rhyme and tone as well as through the physical layout of the characters on the page. The oldest known anthology of poetry, *The Book of Songs*, was put together in 600 B.C.E. One of the first individual poets, whose work is still read today, is Qu Yuan, best known for his piece called *Li Sao*, or *The Lament*.

A more popular and less elitist literary tradition developed during the Ming Dynasty with the dissemination of prose epics. The most famous of these are work *The Water Margin* and *The Dream of the Red Chamber*.

Western influence in the nineteenth century led to a literature based more on the vernacular. The first writer to emerge in this new movement was Lu Xun, whose best known work is *The Rickshaw Boy*, which details the life of rickshaw drivers in Beijing. During the communist revolution, literature was seen as a tool for promoting state-sponsored ideology. While the years after the Cultural Revolution saw some opening in terms of what was permissible, freedom of expression is still curtailed. Contemporary writers include Zhang Xianliang, whose work is known for its controversially sexual subject matter, and Lao Gui, whose *Blood Red Dusk* examines the events of the Cultural Revolution.

**Graphic Arts.** Painters are best known for their depictions of nature. Landscapes strive to achieve a balance between yin, the passive female force, represented by water, and yang, the male element, represented by rocks and mountains. These paintings often have writing on them, sometimes by the artist and sometimes by a scholar from a later era. The inscription can be a poem, a dedication, or a commentary on the work. Communist politicians also took to this practice, and many paintings bear the writing of Chairman Mao.

Writing is considered the highest art form, and calligraphy is said to be the deepest expression of a person's character.

China has been known for sculpture and pottery since before the earliest dynasties. The art of pottery reached its pinnacle during the Song Dynasty, when porcelain was developed.

Bronze vessels have been used for thousands of years as religious artifacts. They were engraved with inscriptions, and often buried with the dead. Jade was believed to have magical powers that could ward off evil spirits. Sculptures made of that material were placed in tombs, and sometimes corpses were buried in suits made of jade.

Embroidery is practiced by women who decorate clothes, shoes, and bed linens with colorful, elaborate designs of animals and flowers.

**Performance Arts.** Unlike the Western scale, which has eight tones, the Chinese has five. There is no harmony in traditional music; all the singers or instruments follow the melodic line. Traditional instruments include a two-stringed fiddle (*erhu*), a three-stringed flute (*sanxuan*), a vertical flute (*dongxiao*), a horizontal flute (*dizi*), and ceremonial gongs (*daluo*).

Opera is a popular traditional art form. There are at least three hundred different forms of opera from different geographic areas. The performances are elaborate and highly stylized, involving acrobatic movements and intricate makeup and costumes. Actors play one of four types of roles: the leading male (usually a scholar or official), the leading female (usually played by a man), the painted-face roles (warriors, heroes, demons, adventurers, and other characters), and the clown. The subject matter is usually historical, and the language is archaic. Opera is not an entertainment only for the

*Bicycles are one of the most common modes of transportation in China's crowded cities.*

elite; it is often performed in the marketplace for a few pennies a ticket.

There is a lively rock music scene. The most famous performers are Cui Jian and Lui Huan.

Chinese film gained international acclaim in the 1980s and 1990s. The films of the director Zhang Yimou deal with social issues, including women's lives in the precommunist period and the ramifications of the Cultural Revolution. His films, which include *Raise the Red Lantern* and *To Live*, have often been subject to disapproval or censorship from the government. The director Xie Fei is beginning to win recognition accolades for his social commentary films, which include *Our Fields* and *The Year of Bad Luck*.

## THE STATE OF THE PHYSICAL AND SOCIAL SCIENCES

The Chinese have long been known for their scientific accomplishments; many discoveries and inventions credited to Western scientists were first made in China. Among those inventions are the seismoscope (an instrument used to detect earthquakes), first created in 132 C.E., the mechanical clock (1088), and the compass (eleventh century). A Chinese alchemist discovered gunpowder by accident in the eleventh century. Before its use in fire-

arms was developed, its use was in fireworks. Paper was invented in China in the first century B.C.E., woodblock printing in the eighth century C.E., and movable type in the eleventh century.

Despite its contributions to technological development, Chinese science is no longer in the forefront. The country began to fall behind during the nineteenth century, and as the infrastructure and economy weakened, it could no longer keep up with the Western powers. Today, schools stress science and technology in an effort to catch up with other countries. The government prefers to concentrate its efforts on practical projects rather than in basic research, a policy that does not always please scientists and has made progress uneven. In the 1980s and 1990s, China developed its technology in satellites and nuclear weaponry as well as creating a supercomputer and a hybrid form of high-yield rice.

The social sciences, like the arts, have faced censorship from the communist government, and the educational system gives science and technology priority over the social sciences.

Both Beijing and Shanghai have numerous museums dedicated to national history and archaeology. There are also a number of archaeological museums in the provinces. The main libraries are in

Beijing and Shanghai, and Beijing is home to the Historical Archives.

## BIBLIOGRAPHY

Bracker, Paul. "Will China Be Number One?" *Time*, 22 May 2000.

Cook, Sarah, et al., eds. *Chinese Economy under Transition*, 2000.

Davis, Deborah S. *Consumer Revolution in Urban China*, 2000.

"Demystifying China." *The Economist*, 4 April 2000.

Diamant, Neil J. *Revolutionizing the Family: Politics, Love, and Divorce in Urban and Rural China*, 2000.

Diemberger, Maria Antonia Sironi. *Tibet: The Roof of the World between Past and Present*, 2000.

Donald, Stephanie Hemelryk. *Public Secrets, Private Spaces: Cinema and Civility in China*, 2000.

Dorgan, Michael. "Fueled by Prostitution Boom, AIDS Virus Spreads in China." *Philadelphia Inquirer*, 22 December 2000.

Duke, Michael S. "World Literature in Review: China." *World Literature Today*, Autumn 1999.

Edmonds, Richard Louis, ed. *People's Republic of China after Fifty Years*, 2000.

Elliot, Dorinda. "More Rights—At a Cost." *Newsweek*, 29 June 1998.

Esherick, Joseph, ed. *Remaking the Chinese City: Modernity and National Identity, 1900–1950*, 2000.

Florcruz, Jaime A., et al. "Inside China's Search for Its Soul." *Time*, 4 October 1999.

Hsu, Immanuel Chung-yueh. *The Rise of Modern China*, 2000.

Hu, Shao-hua. *Explaining Chinese Democratization*, 2000.

Knapp, Ronald G. *Walled Cities*, 2000.

Leicester, John. "China Details Crackdown on Group." *Philadelphia Inquirer*, 16 January 2001.

Liang, Zhang, compiler, and Nathan, Andrew J., ed. *The Tiananmen Papers*, 2001.

Lloyd, John. "Will This Be the Chinese Century?" *New Statesman*, 10 January 2000.

Mitter, Rana. *Manchurian Myth: Nationalism, Resistance, and Collaboration in Modern China*, 2000.

Perry, Elizabeth J., and Mark Selden. *Chinese Society: Change, Conflict, and Resistance*, 2000.

Roberts, J. A. G. *A Concise History of China*, 1999.

Shaughnessy, Edward J., ed. *China: Empire and Civilization*, 2000.

Tien, Hung-mao, and Yun-han Chu. *China under Jiang Zemin*, 2000.

"Wealth and Power: Those Elusive Goals." *The Economist*, 8 April 2000.

Zang, Xiaowei. *Children of the Cultural Revolution: Family Life and Political Behavior in Mao's China*, 2000.

### Web Sites

U.S. Department of State, Central Intelligence Agency. *World Fact Book: China*, www.odci.gov/publications/factbook/geos/ch

—ELEANOR STANFORD

# COLOMBIA

## CULTURE NAME

Colombian

## ORIENTATION

**Identification.** Since declaring independence on 20 July 1810 and achieving it in 1819, Colombia has changed its name seven times. Regional cultural traditions are diverse, with a broad range of distinct groups that have unique customs, accents, social patterns, and cultural adaptations. These groups are classified into three cultures: those in the interior, the countryside, and the coastal regions. Only during elections, sporting events, and beauty pageants do the regional cultures unite for a common goal.

**Location and Geography.** Covering about 440,000 square miles (1.14 million square kilometers), Colombia has coast on the Atlantic and Pacific oceans. Lowland coastal areas give way to rain forest, the Andes, and the Inland *Ilanos* (plains).

Colombia is connected to Central America by the Isthmus of Panama. It contains several small islands in the Atlantic, including San Andrea and Providencia, and in the Pacific, the Malpelo and Gorgona islands have been set aside as natural wildlife reserves. Colombia borders Ecuador and Peru to the south, Brazil and Venezuela to the east, and Panama to the northwest.

The Atlantic or Caribbean coastal lowlands receive less rainfall than the area along the Pacific. Many industries are located within this area, along with 20 percent of the population. The fertile land supports banana and sugarcane plantations along with cattle ranches. Lush rain forest and swamps characterize the Pacific lowlands. Because of the abundant rainfall and poor soil quality, few people inhabit this region.

The three Andean *Cordilleras* (mountain ranges) running the entire length of the country from the north to the south, occupy only 30 percent of the landmass. Most of the population lives in the inland Andean region, which begins along the Caribbean coast near Venezuela. Climatic effects are accentuated on the high elevations of these mountain ranges. The hot zone is marked by heavy annual rainfall along the Pacific coast. The temperate zone, in which 40 percent of the population lives, has moderate rainfall and moderate temperatures.

The treeless regions adjacent to the cold zone usually are referred to as *paramos* (high plains), above which begin the *nevados* (snowcapped peaks). The cold zone receives heavy rainfall during the wet seasons from April to June and September to December. The northern end of this range is characterized by volcanic eruptions and earthquakes. Despite the tectonic activity, almost 80 percent of the population lives in the Andean region. The highlands to the east of the Magdalena Valley include Cundinamarca, where Bogota, the capital, is located. Set in the central range to the west of the Magdalena are two of the most important cities: Medellín (the second largest city) and Manizales. Farther to the south in the Cauca Valley is Cali, the third largest city, which has some of the richest farmland. This area contains some of the richest mineral deposits in the world, including gold and emeralds. Coffee plantations are plentiful in the mild climate, which also supports banana, cassava, and coca.

To the east of the Andes is the broad expanse of the *Ilanos*, which contains more than 60 percent of the land area. The high plateau is striped with tributaries of the Amazon River and rain forest to the south. While few crops are grown in this hot, flat region, the grassland provides ample space to graze cattle.

Colombia has great biodiversity with 1,550 species of birds and over 13,000 species of plants.

**Demography.** With a population of 42.3 million (30 June 2000), Colombia is a nation of mixed race. It is estimated that about 75 percent of the population is of mixed heritage, with 55 percent of this

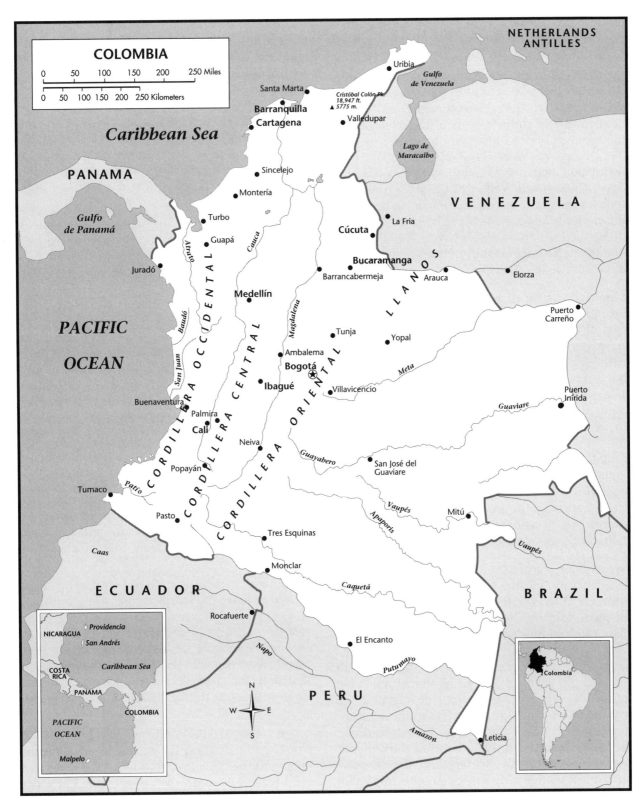

Colombia

group being *mestizos*, 16 percent *mulattoes*, and 4 percent *zambos*. The other 20 percent of the population is of European, African, or Indian ancestry.

Caucasians, mainly descendants of Spaniards, constitute about 20 percent of the population. Antioquia and the coffee region are considered "white" departments or states because of the reluctance of European settlers to mix with blacks or Indians. Black people represent about 4 percent of the total population and live primarily on the Caribbean coast, the historical center of the slave trade. The Indian population, which is estimated to have been between 1.5 and 2 million people in the pre-conquest period, numbers between 300,000 and 400,000. There are over fifty Indian groups, many of which live in relative isolation.

***Linguistic Affiliation.*** The official language is Spanish, which was imposed during the colonial period. All Colombians speak it except some of the indigenous populations in the Amazonian basin. In major cities, English is used, particularly by the upper class, but it is not commonly understood or spoken. Outside urban areas, Spanish is virtually the only medium of communication. Colombia takes great care to preserve the linguistic "purity" of Castilian Spanish. The Colombian Academy of Language was founded in 1871 by a commission from the Spanish Royal Academy of Language; it was the first such body established in Latin America. Colombian Spanish is marked by the presence of numerous cultural expressions. In addition to Spanish, over 200 indigenous languages and dialects are spoken.

***Symbolism.*** Patriotic symbols represent the war of independence and the founding fathers. Francisco Miranda, a Venezuelan, designed the national flag in 1806. Adapting the red and yellow of the Spanish flag, Miranda divided the two colors by a stripe of blue to symbolize the ocean separating the independent country from the motherland. The upper half of the flag is yellow, symbolizing the natural riches of the country, while the lower half is divided into two equal parts of blue and red, with the red symbolizing the blood shed in the war for independence. In 1834, the national shield, Arms of the Republic, was added to the flag to represent the defensive armament used in early battles. Another important national symbol is the condor, which signifies liberty and sovereignty.

## HISTORY AND ETHNIC RELATIONS

***Emergence of the Nation.*** The discovery of the country's coastal lands in 1499, followed by Span-

ish occupation for the next 300 years, indicates the integral role Spain played in the region's cultural, religious, and political development. In the early part of the 1500s, Spain attempted to control the Caribbean and Pacific coastlines, establishing Santa Marta in 1525 and Cartagena de Indias in 1533. In that year, the conquest of the Incas in Peru gave the Spaniards strategic positions in the north and south for the subjugation and colonization of Colombia. By the middle of the sixteenth century, the Spaniards had established a major foothold in the Americas.

During this period, the Andes were occupied by a number of indigenous groups that ranged from stratified agricultural chiefdoms to tropical farm villages and nomadic hunter-gatherer groups. The social structures of these groups were destroyed during the conquest, as Indians were forced into slavery to exploit the natural riches of the country. As the number of casualties in the Indian population increased due to starvation and disease brought by the conquistadors and to the intense labor of slavery, Spain imported slaves from Africa for gold and silver mining on the Pacific coast. The tri-ethnic composition of the population during this period led to the ethnic terminology still used today. Spaniards were referred to as *Peninsulars*, while their South-American-born descendants were called *criollos* (Creoles). Miscegenation produced people of mixed race known to the Spaniards as the *castas* (castes). These were *mestizos* from the intermarriage of whites and natives, *mulattoes* from that of blacks and whites, and *zambos* from that of blacks and Indians.

Unfair practices and decrees by the Spaniards created a desire for independence. Most traumatic was the practice of *encomiendas*, an institutionalized system in which Indians were "entrusted" to the care of Spaniards called *Encomienderos*. These "caretakers" provided the Indians with religious instruction and a livelihood in exchange for their labor. In practice, this system amounted to enslavement.

In 1781, 20,000 Indians and mestizos attempted to march on the capital in what became known as the *Comuneros* revolt, but the revolt was crushed and its leaders were executed. There was little or no support from the Creole population, but some Creoles were appalled by the brutality of the Spaniards and began to spread the rebellious sentiment. The call for vengeance spread to other provinces, as government officials excluded Creoles from high governmental positions. After several minor uprisings, Colombia achieved independence after the decisive battle of Boyacá on 9 August 1819 under Simon Bolivar, a Creole who joined the patriotic movement in 1810.

***National Identity.*** There is not a unique national culture separate from the cultural influence of colonial Spain. Instead of resisting Spanish cultural influences, most indigenous groups embraced them. Rather than having a common culture, Colombia is a country with many distinct regional cultures.

***Ethnic Relations.*** Past relations with other regional cultures were based on the hierarchical society imposed by Spain, in which the upper echelon of "white" Spaniards enjoyed wealth, power, and prestige while blacks and Indians were at the bottom of the socioeconomic hierarchy. After independence, Creoles quickly replaced Spaniards in the upper echelons of the new society. Qualified mestizos and mulattoes also ascended to high positions, but their inclusion was based on their level of education, wealth, and "whiteness." Colombians continue to identify themselves according to their regional heritage, physical appearance, and socioeconomic status.

*Apartment towers in Bogota. High-density public housing projects are common in the cities.*

## URBANISM, ARCHITECTURE, AND THE USE OF SPACE

The nation's architecture reflects seventeenth century Spanish colonial origins. Regional differences derive from those in Spain. Thus, hints of Moorish and Castilian architecture are evident in many cities. Many areas have had difficulty maintaining older structures, and the climate has destroyed many Baroque buildings. Some of the architectural gems are the many churches that dot the landscape. The detailed interiors of the country's churches are reflective of the Medieval and Renaissance churches in Spain. Newer buildings in larger cities utilize modern styles with adaptations of the Baroque style supplemented with wood and wrought-iron elements.

In the nineteenth century, a new form of architecture began to develop from the efforts of artisans who incorporated elements of Greek, Roman, and Renaissance art. This style, known as *republicano*, represented the independence of Colombian art. This movement incorporated cement and steel building materials. Many government buildings follow the *republicano* architectural style.

In the 1930s, Colombia began to embrace modern architecture. The new Liberal Party government tore down many older buildings to reject the conservative past. In their place, it constructed modern buildings with an international flavor.

*Republicano* homes are typically built on a single level with an A-frame roof. Houses in the more crowded cities often have two or more stories and reflect a European influence. Most people lived in single-family dwellings until the migration to urban centers in the late 1940s and early 1950s. The need for adequate housing persuaded the government to invest in high-density public housing projects during the early 1950s. In the poorer areas, large families live in small houses constructed from cinder blocks and covered with an adobe made of clay, cow manure, and hay.

Park space is limited to larger towns and cities that were founded by the Spanish. Parks have areas where social activity is encouraged; long benches are placed close together so that people can have space around them without restricting communication. Few formal parks exist outside the cities, although people congregate around churches or other local monuments.

## FOOD AND ECONOMY

***Food in Daily Life.*** Most middle-class families eat elaborate meals that reflect Spanish and indigenous traditions. A typical meal is identified by size rather than content, such as a light breakfast, a substantive midday lunch, and a lighter meal in the early evening. Dinner consists of fresh fruit, homemade soup, and a main dish with meat or fish accompanied by rice and/or potatoes. Lower-income people eat a more carbohydrate-rich diet. Meals usually end with a very sweet dessert, frequently made from *panela*, a type of brown sugar.

There are regional differences in foods. In the interior rural regions, a hearty breakfast consists of a strip of pork, rice and beans, sweet plantains, and a large steak with fried eggs. Dinner is similar, except for the eggs. In the coastal region, the emphasis is on seafood. In Cartagena, the typical lunch consists of rice with coconut, fried plantains, and shrimp. Colombians enjoy a variety of national and international cuisines.

Specialty dishes are eaten during holidays. A dish associated with the capital is *ajiaco*, a stew with three types of potato, chicken, and corn, that is served with capers, cream, and avocado. Another dish served during religious holidays is *pasteles*, while along the coast, people eat *sancocho*, a fish or chicken stew. Colombians consume large quantities of beer and coffee and relatively little milk or wine. *Aguardiente* combines local rum and a corn of sugar brandy.

**Basic Economy.** The economy is dependent on manufacturing and agricultural exports, but this domestic production relies on expensive imports such as tractors, power generators, and industrial machinery. Commercial agriculture stresses bananas, cut flowers, sugar, and coffee. In the world's second leading exporter of coffee, the economy is sensitive to fluctuations in the market price. Manufacturing exports include textiles, garments, chemicals, and metal products. Despite rich mineral deposits, Colombia derives less than 4 percent of the gross domestic product (GDP) from mining.

Economic progress has resulted from the government's efforts to make the economy more specialized and productive by encouraging trade, deregulation, and financial investment. While the executive and legislative branches can intervene in economic matters, the hands-off policy of the government has resulted in a 3 percent annual growth of the economy since the ending of government subsidies.

**Land Tenure and Property.** Most of the productive agricultural land forests are privately owned. The structure of owner-operator relationships varies: coffee is grown on small plots by share-croppers, whereas plantation agriculture and forestry involve multinational joint ownership using local labor. Land containing valuable minerals and hydrocarbons generally reverts to the government, which arranges contracts between domestic and foreign corporations. Public land includes 43 national parks. The government has designated special lands for the indigenous groups. Land distribution has been a difficult issue, and deforestation is being examined in the context of management practices and trade policies.

**Commercial Activities.** Fifty-one percent of the GDP comes from the commercial sector, which includes utilities, transportation, communications, wholesale commerce, real estate, retail banking, and stock exchanges. While these business sectors operate domestically, many have an international presence, including investment banking, insurance, commercial real estate, hotels, and advertising.

**Major Industries.** The primary industries are in the manufacturing sector, which employs over 35 percent of the workforce. The largest industries in this sector are textile, garment, furniture, and corrugated box manufacturing. Heavy industries also make a significant contribution to the GDP, including oil production, coal mining, chemical and resin-producing plants, and forestry. Although tourism is a major industry, the growth of this sector has been hindered by instability in the Andean and forested regions.

**Trade.** Exports include coffee, cut flowers, emeralds, and leather goods—most of which go to the United States and Europe. Other significant exports are oil, coal, and bananas. A free-market economy has allowed the country to benefit from foreign trade and foreign investment. After the North American Free Trade Agreement, Colombia established a similar trade pact between itself and several Latin American nations. Colombia is seeking similar trade pacts with it neighbors to the north, including the United States.

**Division of Labor.** The labor force consists of manual and semi-skilled, highly skilled, managerial, and professional segments. In the agricultural and manufacturing sectors, manual or semi-skilled labor is physically demanding and wages are low. Workers who are classified as highly skilled include artisans and carpenters and supervisors in industrial plants and farms. Managers and professionals include highly educated individuals who occupy the top decision-making or policy-making roles in industries, universities, and the government.

*Bananas are a staple crop in Colombia's thriving agricultural sector.*

## SOCIAL STRATIFICATION

*Classes and Castes.* The massive urban migration that began in the 1950s saw a middle class emerge, resulting in a three-class system: upper, middle, and lower. The upper class, which includes 20 percent of the population, accounts for about 75 to 80 percent of the gross national product. This group tends to be made up of individuals of unmixed European ancestry. Within this class, there is an elite referred to as the "oligarchy" that enjoys wealth and financial security, political power, and education. This group may be considered a caste, since membership is largely due to birthright, not to individual ability. A wide gap separates the elite from the masses. Unlike the elite, this group has few opportunities for social mobility. Social inequality is evident in the lower class, whose members are often malnourished, poorly housed, disease-ridden, and illiterate.

White people continue to dominate the upper class, while mestizos and mulattoes constitute the middle and lower classes. Blacks and Indians make up a significant portion of the lower class. Historically, blacks felt socially superior to Indians despite the fact that Indians occupied an officially higher position in society.

*Symbols of Social Stratification.* White or light skin is associated with being Spanish. Today, people may not be aware of this association, but they still equate being white with being wealthy.

The style of clothing preferred by urban professionals and the middle and upper classes is similar to that in the United States. White, mestizo, and mulatto men and women prefer conservative dark suits. Individuals from rural areas often wear the same clothes in the fields and at home. Men usually wear loose-fitting pants, while women wear loose-fitting skirts. Cloaks are worn by both sexes in the cold, rural highlands.

All three classes in the interior, especially in Bogotá, speak a deliberate and grammatically correct Spanish, whereas coastal speech patterns have a rapid tempo. People from the interior are more proper and ceremonial in social interactions, while coastal inhabitants are usually more trusting and carefree.

## POLITICAL LIFE

*Government.* The government has an executive branch led by an elected president, a bicameral (House of Representatives and Senate) legislative branch, and a judicial branch. The president is elected to a four-year term by popular vote and may not be reelected. The president runs for office with his vice president, and names the cabinet, which consists of ministers with administrative powers. The president's duties include enforcing laws, conducting foreign affairs, supervising public finances, maintaining public order, and serving as commander-in-chief of the armed forces.

In the Congress, senators are elected by national vote, while representatives are elected by the people in their districts. Members of both houses may be re-elected to an unlimited number of terms. Congress meets only twice a year but may be called for additional sessions by the president. The House of Representatives appoints an attorney general. The responsibilities of the Senate include approving military promotions, declaring war, permitting foreign troops to enter the national territory, litigating impeachment proceedings against the president, and electing supreme court justices.

Under the constitution of 1991, the Constitutional Court and Council of State were added to the Supreme Court, which is the court of final appeals for ordinary legal matters, annulments, and contractual disputes. It also tries public officials for misconduct in office. The Council of State hears cases involving administrative issues and proposes laws regarding administrative practices, while the Constitutional Court is charged with reviewing laws, treaties, and other public policies to ensure that they do not violate the constitution.

### Leadership and Political Officials.
One of the most important informal decision-making groups among the upper class is referred to as *roscas*, a term that symbolizes the interconnecting networks in the political system. These groups have a membership structure that parallels the society of colonial Spain. These informal groups are found in the political, social, economic, and financial sectors. *Roscas* have been successful in monitoring and controlling some social, political, and economic changes. At this level, most political decisions are made and many careers are determined. *Roscas* link influential individuals and institutions so that universities, banks, industries, and agricultural interests may be coordinated and controlled by a few people. Inclusion in these such groups is limited to members of the upper-middle and upper classes. Another informal custom is the *palanca* ("leverage"), in which an influential friend or relative tries to help an individual gain a position. Allegiance to political parties and family ties are the source of most *palancas*.

After independence, the founding fathers formed the Centralist and Federalist parties, which later became the Conservative and Liberal parties. The Liberal Party advocates the separation of church and state, free enterprise, free commerce, no taxes on exportation, no intervention in matters of state by foreign nations, a free press, political liberty, decentralization of government, universal suffrage, and equal justice for all. The Conservative Party defends moral values, supports good customs, maintains close ties between church and state, protects traditional values, maintains a central government and central bank, favors tariffs, maintains the *status quo* and federal support of education, and calls for equal justice for all.

### Social Problems and Control.
The modern National Police, a branch of the armed forces, was created in 1891 to enforce federal laws. With the escalation of violence during the 1980s, the size of the national force increased. However, the National Police lack a presence in many municipalities. In a country racked by violence, some judges wear masks to hide their faces in order to avoid reprisal. These "judges without faces" demonstrate the inability of the judicial system to protect its members and the general public.

Over 50 years ago, many politicians tried to reform a corrupt political system that acted in favor of the privileged few. However, after the assassination of Jorge Eliécer Gaitán in 1948, old-line politicians fell into disfavor. Elected to many political positions, including his appointment as mayor of Bogotá, Gaitán had captivated the country with his dynamic oratory and articulation of social problems. The elite feared that Gaitán's popularity would ensure his election to the presidency. Gaitán's death resulted in an escalation of violence, especially in the countryside. The period between 1946 and 1956 is known as *La Violencia*; over 350,000 people died in an armed uprising against social and political injustice. After Gaitán's assassination, the guerrilla movements began to organize into large centralized groups.

Today the two major guerilla organizations—the Revolutionary Armed Forces of Colombia (FARC) and the Army of National Liberation (ELN)—have attempted to disrupt the government and the national economy to bring about reform and social justice. They have generally targeted government buildings, military positions, and police stations, but also have attacked energy distribution and communication networks, and engaged in extortion, kidnapping, and assassination.

Drug trafficking is a major economic and social problem that has enriched the drug cartels and fi-

Two boys in a canoe on the bank of the Amazon River, near San Martin. The Amazonian basin is home to several indigenous populations.

nanced the guerrillas. To counter the effects of the drug trade, informal social control systems have risen to combat crime, including paramilitary organizations. Many people take the law upon themselves, and many crimes are committed in the context of personal or group retaliation.

***Military Activity.*** Numbering 150,000, the military is divided into an army, a navy, and an air force. Mandated with protecting the country's borders and territorial waters, the military has been involved in internal conflicts such as fighting against guerrillas.

## SOCIAL WELFARE AND CHANGE PROGRAMS

The social security system developed in 1843 applied only to military personnel. Other social security programs have been slow to develop. While many programs available to the average laborer are relatively new, they provide health, pension, social security, and death benefits. Individual benefits in the public sector exceed those in the private sector. The social welfare system has been expensive and inequitably applied, with only 16 percent of the population currently covered by social insurance. The poorest segment of the population is not cov-

ered by any program. These groups rely on nongovernmental organizations to supplement the limited support provided by the government.

## NONGOVERNMENTAL ORGANIZATIONS AND OTHER ASSOCIATIONS

Nongovernmental organizations (NGOs) have been involved in agricultural, educational, and health programs. With the backing of the government and community leaders, organizations such as the Magdalena Medio Project have influenced public affairs. Among the priorities of NGOs are land reform projects to redistribute farmland in favor of family farming and the poor, human capital development in education to give communities control over local education, and public sector efficiency. Groups such as the Pasto Education Project and the Rural Education Project have advocated better-equipped public schools and teacher training.

In 1982, with help from the World Bank, the Women's World Bank was established to provide very small, low-interest loans to women micro-entrepreneurs in rural and remote regions. The Carvajal Foundation paved the way for other institutions promoting micro-enterprise, such as the

*A street scene in the Colombian town of Cartagena. Houses in Colombia's cities often have two or more stories and reflect a European style.*

Women's World Bank and the Solidarios Financial Cooperative. Other NGOs focus on diverse aspects of the nation's economy, education, and people. The Colombian Indigenist Institute, is an advocate for many native groups. The first national labor organization, the Confederation of Colombian Workers (CTC), promotes labor reform. Having lost much of its influence, the CTC was supplanted by the Union of Colombian Workers backed by the Catholic Church and then by the Unified Central of Workers.

## GENDER ROLES AND STATUSES

***The Relative Status of Women and Men.*** Gender roles have changed with the migration from rural to urban areas, but family and household organization is still marked by sexual segregation and a difference between male and female goals and aspirations. As a result of colonial influence, Colombian society adopted a culture in which men occupy a dominant role within the household as breadwinner

**492**

and disciplinarian and assume responsibility for maintaining family pride and position within the community. The role of machismo is an important characteristic of public life. Machismo is not synonymous with strict male dominance—it applies to the public personification of the male family head. Machismo requires separate male and female roles in economic life and consumption, the reliance of women on men, and distinct sets of life goals for men and women. With more women holding higher-paying jobs and occupying prominent positions in society, the role of machismo is now less dominant in urban centers but is still evident in rural regions.

Machismo defines a woman's role as a mother in addition to her conjugal role. The traditional male-female relationship assumes that the woman puts her husband's wishes before her own. She is responsible for the care of the children and household, but the husband makes decisions about the household's basic necessities.

While male familial roles are relatively consistent across economic groups, female roles vary as a result of the modern economy. In upper class and some middle class families, women avoid working outside the home in order to preserve family status, honor, and virtue. Women from lower class and lower-middle class families often hold jobs outside the home or work in the fields to contribute to the family's subsistence, giving them a greater degree of equality. Many couples farm fields owned through the wife's family, and in this case it is difficult for a husband living with his wife's family to exercise control over the wife.

Women have assumed visible and important roles in society. Upper class and middle class women dedicate themselves not only to the family but also to social issues and the church. Women from these groups hold a number of prominent public positions and are considered among the most politically active in Latin America.

## MARRIAGE, FAMILY, AND KINSHIP

**Marriage.** Arranged marriages are no longer common, especially among the upper-middle and upper classes, but the members of these groups are encouraged to marry within their own class. While men and women can date whomever they wish, they must be accompanied by a chaperone. Before marrying, couples usually court for at least a year.

Members of the lower and middle classes strive to marry someone outside of their class; mestizos, mulattoes, and blacks prefer to marry into white families. However, when intermarriage takes place, it is generally white males who marry Indians or blacks.

Most people, especially in urban centers, are married in the Catholic Church. Upper class people use this religious rite to create powerful family unions. Church weddings are expensive and allow families to demonstrate their financial and social status. Because of the expense, members of the lower middle class may opt for a civil marriage. Others choose a consensual marriage. Divorce for civil marriages was not permitted until 1970.

**Domestic Unit.** The nuclear family consisting of a father, a mother, and their children is the basic household unit. Upper class families usually have many children. The father is the head of the household, while the mother is responsible for child rearing, homemaking, and the basic education of the children. Lower class and some middle class wives work in the city or next to kin in the fields.

**Inheritance.** Parents bequeath property to their children in equal shares. In rural families, sons and daughters may inherit property with the condition that they will continue to work the land. In urban centers, parents may leave a family business to their children to share and run.

**Kin Groups.** Large upper class families have an extended kin group in which the oldest member receives the most wealth and prestige. Family and kin group members interact regularly and generally live close to each other in urban areas or on the same land or estate in rural locations. Family members participate in social activities to expand the family's wealth. In times of severe financial difficulties, families lacking a socioeconomic network, may be displaced into a lower class.

## SOCIALIZATION

**Infant Care.** Mothers from the upper class prefer to give birth in clinical settings, while those in the lower class usually have babies at home, sometimes with the help of a midwife. Upper class families use cribs and playpens. The sleeping quarters of the child are usually separate from those of the parents. In poorer families, a child usually sleeps in the same bed as the mother or next to the mother on the floor.

Parents encourage a child to behave properly. From birth to adolescence, parents nurture children very carefully, inculcating moral values and raising them to respect themselves and their elders. Chil-

*Churches, like the one shown here in Anitoquia, are some of the last examples of Medieval or Renaissance architecture in Colombia.*

dren are taught right from wrong, encouraged to be obedient, and informed about the need for higher education. Obedience to adults, conformity to social expectations, and religious devotion are important qualities in a "good" child.

The only ceremonial initiations rural and urban children receive are the religious rites of the Catholic Church. Within the first year, a baby is baptized. Families often use the rite of baptism to achieve upward social mobility. Choosing distinguished godparents brings prestige to the parents and offers the child social and economic networks.

At age four or five, children enroll in elementary school where they learn to read, write, and do simple math as well as study geography and history. Completion of secondary school leads to a diploma that qualifies a student for college.

***Higher Education.*** The Catholic Church established the first universities before 1700; the first public universities were founded much later. Today there are over 40 universities. National universities receive funding from the government, which in the 1958 constitution was mandated to spend at least 10 percent of the national budget on education.

Higher education is considered necessary to achieve professional goals and to contribute to the progress and prosperity of the country. However, the university system reinforces social stratification. Higher education is coveted by all, but only the middle and upper classes can afford to attend a university.

## ETIQUETTE

Social interaction in the upper class is generally formal and respectful. The members of lower socioeconomic groups from the interior pride themselves on their good manners. Unlike their coastal counterparts, lower class individuals in the interior express mutual respect for each other and their elders; women are treated respectfully and given special attention.

Personal space is highly regarded, so conversations take place at arm's length. The violation of this space even in crowded stores and museums is considered disrespectful and hostile. Exceptions occur in crowded bus stations and on buses. Formal greetings among strangers are mandated, whereas salutations among acquaintances are informal.

## RELIGION

***Religious Beliefs.*** Ninety-five percent of the people consider themselves members of the Roman Catholic Church and attach great importance to Catholic sacraments. More than 85 percent of Catholics in urban parishes attend mass regularly.

People in rural areas are said to be more devout than those in the cities, but their Catholicism is different from that of the urban upper and middle classes. In the countryside, Catholic practices and beliefs have been combined with indigenous, African, and sixteenth-century Spanish customs. People pray to a patron saint, who is considered to be more accessible than God. Rural villages have a patron saint who is honored each year with a fiesta. Traces of rural folk religion also are found in urban lower class communities, particularly those with many rural migrants.

Although the 1991 constitution established religious freedom and does not mention the Church by name, the Catholic Church continues to have significant influence. A Protestant movement has attracted more than 260,000 people. Protestants are a minority on the mainland but a majority on San Andres and Providencia islands. There are also small contingents of Muslims and Jews.

*A farmer, his wife, and their donkey cross a wooden footbridge to the market at Puente de Calamate, Colombia.*

The Spanish began a process of conversion among the Indians in the sixteenth century, and the institutionalization of the Catholic Church was a high priority for the colonial government. That church destroyed most of the indigenous rituals and religious customs. The Inquisition had the authority to summon and interrogate, often using torture, any subject accused of heresy and had the power to confiscate the property of convicted persons.

**Religious Practitioners.** Local priests are often the primary authority figures in small communities. Most priests and bishops were born in the country. Like most elites, priests have gravitated toward urban areas, leaving a void of religious leadership in some areas. Colombia supports more than 30 monasteries and 80 convents.

**Rituals and Holy Places.** Priests in churches perform most Catholic sacraments. The rite of baptism is the sacramental entry into Christian life, and communion is a memorial of Christ's death and resurrection.

**Death and the Afterlife.** Christian dogma holds that the spirit lives on after the body has died. A divine judgment of the person's life determines the well-being of the spirit after death. An elaborate ceremony involving the preparation of the deceased for burial by relatives is accompanied by prayer and followed by a period of mourning.

## MEDICINE AND HEALTH CARE

Health care has improved dramatically over the last 30 years, but this has occurred mostly in upper class and middle class urban areas. The urban poor and people in remote regions have limited access to food, housing, and medical treatment. There has been a reduction in the infant mortality rate and an increase in life expectancy over the last decade.

In rural areas, women must contend with cultural and legal restrictions on health care. Twenty percent to thirty percent of maternal deaths in those areas are due to induced abortions, which usually are performed outside of medical facilities.

*Sangre muertes* ''blood deaths,'' are violent criminal attacks and murders related to activity by drug cartels that primarily affect men under age forty-five. The increase in guerilla activities also has resulted in many deaths, especially in remote areas.

Malaria affects approximately 15 percent of the population, although the prevalence of AIDS is low. The health care system has taken an aggressive role in controlling the spread of AIDS by giving patients free access to therapy. Colombians have been exposed to a number of endemic tropical diseases,

*Villagers of all ages dig through a hill to build a road in rural Colombia.*

including dengue and yellow fever, and a variety of tropical parasitic infections.

Traditional remedies are commonly used, particularly in rural and remote areas. Many forms of traditional medicine rely on indigenous plants. Traditional healers called *Taitas* from the *yagé* culture have tried to maintain their indigenous medical practices. In recognition of the importance of the plants used in traditional medicine, those healers have attempted to preserve the forest in the Amazonian region.

## SECULAR CELEBRATIONS

Numerous national holidays celebrate the country and its culture, and many religious holidays are celebrated as national holidays. Important church holidays include the Epiphany (6 January); Holy Week, which includes Easter (March or April); All Saints Day (1 November); the Immaculate Conception (8 December); and Christmas (25 December). Colombia also celebrates the feast days of various saints on both a national and a local level.

Feminine beauty is considered very important, and the country celebrates it each November with the crowning of Miss Colombia. Apart from soccer, the Reinado de Belleza is the most popular sports event.

Other important national holidays are Independence Day (20 July), which celebrates the declaration of independence in 1810, and 7 August, which commemorates the Battle of Bocayá, where Bolívar defeated the Spanish. Other holidays center on regional and local cultures, such as the Carnaval of Barranquilla, the Cartagena International Caribbean Music Festival, the Medellín flower fair, and the Festival of the Devil in *Rio Sucio*.

## THE ARTS AND HUMANITIES

***Support for the Arts.*** Art is considered one of the defining features of Colombian culture. The arts are supported through private individuals and foundations such as the Telefonica Foundation, the Chamber of Commerce of Medellín, the Tobacco Company of Colombia, Federation of Coffee Producers, and the Bank of the Republic of Colombia, which supports the world renowned Museum of Gold. The government, through the Ministries of the Interior and Education, also provides substantial support for numerous museums, theaters, and libraries throughout the country. Among the government supported institutes are the National Museum of Colombia, and the Colombian Institute of Culture, both of which support artists while striving to preserve Colombia's rich history. In addition to these traditional institutes, local governments and private transportation companies support local artists by hiring them to colorfully decorate city and town buses.

**Literature.** Colombia did not begin to develop a literary tradition until the arrival of the Spanish, and its literature still shows a strong European influence. After independence, writers began to develop their own styles, and wrote about national themes instead of European ones. Early writers such as Jorge Isaacs and José Eustacio Rivera addressed the values of rural peasants and their struggle for existence. These and other stories about the regional populations influenced the development of distinct regional literary styles. One of the writers whose style grew out of the artistic influences of the Caribbean coast is Gabriel García Márquez, winner of the Nobel Prize in 1982. As a member of José Félix Fuenmayor's Group of Barranquilla, García Márquez became known for his juxtaposition of myths, dreams, and reality ("magic realism"). García Márquez and other writers are influencing a group of writers who embrace modern and postmodern themes.

**Graphic Arts.** Over 2,000 years ago, native peoples in the Andes produced intricate artwork. After colonization, native artistic influences were abandoned in favor of European styles. However, Colombia is attempting to carve a niche in the international art world with the production of works by painters such as Fernando Botero and Alejandro Obregón and the sculptor Edgar Negret.

One of the leaders of national art was Pedro Nel Gómez, whose murals featured social criticism. Other artists followed the nationalistic and indigenous themes of the movement, although their technique was more traditional. Colombia takes pride in its artists, many of whom still use nationalistic and indigenous themes while incorporating international elements.

**Performance Arts.** The diversity of Colombia's music is intimately linked to its many distinct regional differences. *Vallenato*, a type of Colombian music and dance, originated on the Atlantic coast and is enjoyed throughout the country. *Currulao*, a type of music from the Pacific coast, uses the sea, rain, and rivers as its central themes and employs mostly ordinary wooden instruments. In the interior of the country, the two traditional types of music played throughout the Andean region are the *Bambuco* and the *Guabina*. Both types of music have considerable mestizo influence, often using as their undercurrents themes that emphasize the earth, mountains, and lakes. *Joropo* is considered to be "fierce" or Plains' music because it is played in the *Llanos Orientales*, or Eastern Plains, and reflects the cattle ranch workers' arduous way of life. *Cumbia* music and dance are considered Colombian national treasures whose rhythmic cadence and melodies echo the mulatto and indigenous flavor; it has become the flagship of Colombia's musical genres. Special mention should be paid to the "musical city" of Ibagué, which has contributed to the enrichment and dissemination of Colombian music.

## THE STATE OF THE PHYSICAL AND SOCIAL SCIENCES

The country has produced important work in biology, medicine, geology, mathematics, physics, genetics, psychology, and anthropology. As the home of several pre-Colombian archaeological sites, Colombia has become the source of much of what is known about Latin America before European settlement.

Colombia also has been at the forefront of studies of volcanology and seismology. Medical research in the country is considered among the best in Latin America. Individuals who have made important contributions to the field include José Ignacio Barraquer, Rodolfo R. Llinás, and Manuel Patarroyo. Research in the physical and social sciences is funded largely by the government, although numerous private organizations also provide assistance.

## BIBLIOGRAPHY

Bagely, Bruce M. "The Society and Its Environment." In *Colombia: A Country Study*, 1990.

Berquist, Charles W. *Coffee and Conflict in Colombia, 1886–1910*, 1986.

Blossom, Thomas. *Narino: Hero of Colombian Independence*, 1967.

Brusco, Elizabeth E. *The Reformation of Machismo: Evangelical Conversion and Gender in Colombia*, 1995.

Bushnell, David. *The Libertor, Simón Bolívar*, 1970.

———, and Neill Macaulay. *The Emergence of Latin American in the Nineteenth Century*, 1988.

———, and Wilheim G. M. Hegel. *The Making of Modern Colombia: A Nation in Spite of Itself*, 1993.

Davis, Robert H. *Historical Dictionary of Colombia*, 2nd ed., 1993.

Griffin, Charles C. "Enlightment and Independence." In John Lynch, ed., *Latin American Revolutions, 1808–1826,* 1994.

LeGrand, Catherine. *Frontier Expansion and Peasant Protest in Colombia, 1830–1936,* 1986.

Martz, John D. *The Politics of Clientelism: Democracy and the State of Colombia,* 1997.

Pearce, Jenny. "The People's War." *NACLA Report on the Americas,* 23 (6): 13–21, 1990.

Reichel-Dolmatoff, G. *Colombia: Ancient People and Places,* 1965.

Sánchez, Gónzalo. "The Violence: An Interpretive Synthesis." In Charles Bergquist, Ricardo Penaranda, and Gónzalo Sánchez, eds., *Violence in Colombia,* 1992.

Schultes, Richard Evans. *Where the Gods Reign: Plants and Peoples of the Colombian Amazon,* 1988.

Sharpless, Richard E. *Gaitán of Colombia: A Political Biography,* 1988.

Smith, T. Lynn. "The Racial Composition of Colombia." *Journal of Interamerican Studies,* 8: 213–235, 1965

———. *Colombia: Social Structure and the Process of Development,* 1967.

Wade, Peter. *Blackness and Race Mixture: The Dynamics of Racial Identity in Colombia,* 1993.

Williams, Raymond L., and Kevin G. Guerrieri. *Culture and Customs of Colombia,* 1991.

—SAMUEL MÁRQUEZ
AND DOUGLAS C. BROADFIELD

# COMOROS

## CULTURE NAME
Comorian

## ORIENTATION

**Identification.** Comorian residents call their Country *Masiwa*, "the islands," or refer to the individual name of each island. Zisiwa za Komor is a translation of the French words for the country. "Comoro" comes from the Arabic *qumr*, "the moon" or *qamar* "whiteness".

Although Comorians practice Sunni Islam of the Chafeite rite, their social organization is matrilineal and residency is matrilocal. Social life is characterized by a widespread system of exchange, which, in turn, creates customary ceremonies and rituals (*aida*, *shungu*), particularly the Great Weddings (*ndoola nkuu*, *arusi*). Everyone participates as a member of a given lineage or age group, or as a member of a gender-specific association.

**Location and Geography.** The Federal Islamic Republic of the Comoros is a group of three volcanic islands totaling 719 square miles (1,862 square kilometers), lying between Africa and Madagascar. The capital, Moroni, is on Ngazidja, which has an active volcano, no rivers, rocky coasts, and beaches. The climate is tropical and humid. Wildlife is rich in rare species, including coelacanths, sea turtles, and lemurs.

**Demography.** The population of the three islands is estimated at 539,000 in 1999, a number that has doubled in twenty-five years. Forty-five percent of the population is under age fifteen, and only 6 percent is over age sixty. Close to 20 percent of the population, essentially from Ngazidja, has migrated, mostly to France. Many farmers from the overpopulated island of Ndzuani have migrated to Mwali.

**Linguistic Affiliation.** Comorian is a Bantu language that looks like, but is not related to, Swahili; each island has its own way of speaking it. The language contains many words of Arabic and French origin. All Comorians receive a Koranic education and learn to write their language in Arabic characters. Formal education is given in French.

**Symbolism.** The national emblem is a green flag (the color of Islam) with a crescent moon and four white stars, that symbolize the four islands (including Mayotte). In 1996, the names of Allah and the Prophet Mohammed were added to the flag. The national anthem is *Udzima wa Masiwa* ("Island Unity"), and the motto is "Unity, Justice, and Progress."

## HISTORY AND ETHNIC RELATIONS

**Emergence of the Nation.** The islands were colonized by Africans in the eighth century. The presence of Islam is recorded as early as the eleventh century. With the arrival of Muslim Arabs, chiefdoms evolved into sultanates in the fifteenth century. The era of "battling sultans" saw the flourishing of commerce and the slave trade as well as numerous Madagascan raids. At the end of the nineteenth century, colonial occupation imposed unity and peace in the archipelago. That unity ended in 1975 with the removal of Mahore (Mayotte), which remained French; it was threatened again in 1997 by the secession of Ndzuani.

**National Identity.** Comorians, whose ancient African origins can be seen in their matrilineal social organization, have been influenced culturally by Arabian Islam and the West. Islam is considered synonymous with civilization, but Comorians also have appropriated many aspects of French culture. The official languages—French, Arabic, and Comorian—reflect that cultural diversity.

**Ethnic Relations.** Family ties have made the islands a single cultural and social group. The secession of Ndzuani, which the majority of the

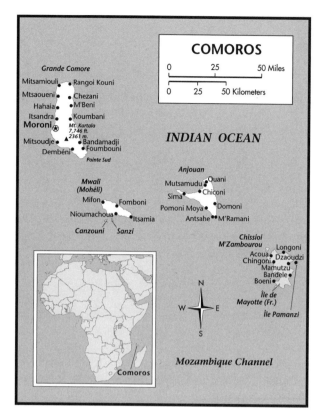

Comoros

**Food in Daily Life.** Rice is the staple of the daily diet, along with manioc and other root vegetables, plantains, fresh and dried fish, and milk from grated coconuts. Food taboos provide a way to establish connections and acknowledge identity.

**Food Customs at Ceremonial Occasions.** Ceremonial dishes include beef and castrated goat served with white rice and curdled milk as well as enormous cakes. Another traditional dish is gruel or porridge made with the dried fruit of sago palms. French cuisine and imported beverages are becoming prevalent.

**Basic Economy.** Seventy percent of the active population engages in subsistence and commercial farming. Overexploited forests on Ndzuani produce kitchen wood. Cattle and goats are slaughtered during festivals. Six thousand state employees and two South African tourist hotels account for the service sector. In a small and very poor country, the informal sector is very active. The basic unit of currency is the Comorian franc.

**Land Tenure and Property.** Three legal land systems coexist: customary oral law, the Islamic title to property, and modern identification. Land used to be split among families in the absence of the concept of individual property: land was community property, and its use was sufficient to allow people to live on it. On Ngazidja, these undivided properties are handed down to the girls but may be used by their brothers or husbands to provide for the household.

**Commercial Activities.** A long tradition of small commerce has led to the multiplication of stores selling basic products, fabrics, and imported clothes. There are many informal trade links with France, Reunion Island and Mauritius, and Saudi Arabia, where gold and appliances are purchased for the great weddings.

**Major Industries.** Industry accounts for only 4 percent of the gross national product and is essentially represented by companies that prepare spices and fragrant plants for exportation.

**Trade.** Vanilla, cloves, copra, and ylang ylang, which gave the Comoros the name "Perfume Islands," account for most exports to France, Germany, and the United States. Comorians import construction materials, food, and petroleum. France provides the largest amount of aid, followed by the European Union and the World Bank. Large finan-

population disavows, resulted from poor political, social, and economic management rather than ethnic conflicts.

## URBANISM, ARCHITECTURE, AND THE USE OF SPACE

Comorians live in villages and cities, some of which are fortified. Mosques, palaces, public squares, stone and coral archways called the doors of peace, and tombs decorated with domes and pillars are examples of stone-built monuments. Sculpted wood and coral decorate niches, ceilings, and doors, featuring geometric or floral patterns and Koranic calligraphy.

Houses are made of dark basalt plastered with coral lime, cob (mud mixed with straw from rice plants), and braided coconut fronds. Cement is slowly replacing stone, while sheet metal replaces braided coconut fronds. A typical house has two rooms, one private and one for to receiving visitors, and sometimes a living room. The courtyard is used for domestic activities. Boys sleep in bachelor quarters. Women dominate in houses, indoor courtyards, and alleys. Men's territory includes mosques and public squares.

cial transfers come from Comorians from Ngazidja who live in France.

***Division of Labor.*** Children help their parents collect water and wood; girls often work inside the house, while boys work outside. Men and women share agricultural work; men cut down trees and are in charge of money-making crops, while women tend to the food-producing fields. Men fish in canoes or in small imported motorboats, and women sell the fish. Women fish at low tide, using a piece of fabric as a net or a plant that releases a substance that paralyzes small fish. Traditionally, wealthy women do not work in the fields but do kitchen work or embroidery.

Comorians engage in formal and informal commerce. Construction materials and automobile parts are sold by Indian merchants. Comorians prefer civil service jobs that provide clean, satisfying, and regular work to farm labor, which they view as dirty, tiring, and unreliable.

## SOCIAL STRATIFICATION

***Classes and Castes.*** Society is made up of three classes. Princely descendants of the ancient sultans trace their lineage back to Arab immigrants who married into local leaders' matrilineal families. The title of *sharif*, a descendant of Muhammad, is handed down through the male line. Farming families are organized in a local hierarchy that reflects their role in the foundation or development of the village. In the cities, fishermen form a separate and socially inferior class, although they can be wealthier than other city residents. Descendants of the African slaves, who arrived in the fourteenth to the nineteenth centuries, live in distinct neighborhoods or villages. The lifestyle of the urban Arab aristocracy in Ndzuani differs greatly from that of the farming population.

***Symbols of Social Stratification.*** The great wedding ceremony identifies accomplished men, who wear a ceremonial coat and a special scarf on Fridays and in some villages enter the mosque through a special door. At Ngazidja, only women who participate in great weddings can wear the *bwibwi*, a black garment. Village women often wear great wedding jewels to work. In the cities, the size of the house a family builds for its daughter reflects its wealth.

## POLITICAL LIFE

***Government.*** The president is assisted by the Federal Assembly made up of forty-two representa-

tives and a supreme court. Religious opinion on legal matters is given by a mufti or a council of ulemas.

Although the constitution specifies that an elected official should rule each island with the assistance of a cabinet, a governor is appointed and works alone. In 1998, a temporary government was supposed to organize elections, which never took place. In April 1999, Colonel Azali Assoumani took power, and appointed a civil government (State Committee) and a State Council largely staffed by the military, with the goal of bringing about an agreement between the islands to establish a new form of federalism.

***Leadership and Political Officials.*** Relations between the government and local leaders (accomplished men) depend on family and local ties. Political parties are more like personal networks than political movements, and electoral campaigns are directed toward and dominated by the accomplished men, who tell their constituents in the village how to vote.

***Social Problems and Control.*** The fundamental social unit is the village or city neighborhood. On Ngazidja, the classification of the male population into age and traditional groups gives each person a role in the village hierarchy. Customary oral law (*ada na mila*) includes sanctions against disrespect toward elders, disobedience, theft, and adultery. Until a fine is paid in money or cattle, a convicted person is banished, and he and his family are cut off from the village's social life. Men convicted of incest are dragged across the village in a shaming procession. If a crime has been committed, the criminal's village may be banished by the regional leaders. Customary law and Muslim law are carried out by the cadis (Islamic judges) in matters of personal rights and inheritance. Modern courts try penal cases.

***Military Activity.*** The army consists of about a thousand men. It has intervened only once: at Anjouan at the beginning of the secession crisis. From 1978 to 1989, the Presidential Guard was overseen by French-speaking mercenaries.

## SOCIAL WELFARE AND CHANGE PROGRAMS

Development programs are financed by international public assistance, the Association of Comorians of France, and the Organization for International Solidarity. Their efforts are mostly in the area of health services.

*Wedding guests on Grand Comore Island. Men and women marry an average of two to four times each, sometimes more often.*

## NONGOVERNMENTAL ORGANIZATIONS AND OTHER ASSOCIATIONS

Male social organization rests on age group and status. Musical associations and sports clubs exist in every village. Female social organization, which is less formal, occurs through help groups and customary associations for development. Most women's organizations are devoted to community development and the training of women and youths.

## GENDER ROLES AND STATUSES

***Division of Labor by Gender.*** Men work to provide for the household and meet the needs of the family. Fear of ridicule keeps men away from housework; an adolescent boy who sleeps in his mother's house is labeled a "girl." Women band together and use their power to influence village affairs through their associations. Modern political life includes women, and one cabinet post is usually staffed by a woman. In the Islamic religious context, women are limited to functioning as Koranic instructors.

***The Relative Status of Women and Men.*** Despite the practice of polygamy and men's near-monopoly of religious offices, women have a com-

fortable social status as they are owners of the conjugal house. On Ngazidja, the eldest daughter and her brother are the head of the household and of their mother's lineage. Women have a degree of material autonomy, the role of the mother is praised, and women receive prestige in the organization of the traditional festivals.

## MARRIAGE, FAMILY, AND KINSHIP

***Marriage.*** On average, men and women marry two to four times but sometimes much more often. Very few men are polygamous and even then have no more than two wives at a time. The great wedding must be held in the village and within the family so that the wealth being exchanged remains within the community. It must be the woman's first wedding even if it is celebrated years after a religious marriage took place. Only the husband may repudiate his spouse, although the wife may provoke him to make that decision.

***Domestic Unit.*** Residency is matrilocal. The domestic unit is dominated by the mother's relatives, including children from earlier marriages and other people for whom the mother is responsible. Some family members eat in the household but sleep elsewhere. Transfers of children within the family

*Scenic view of Nioumachoua Town. Moheli, Comoros.*

occur frequently. If he is from the same village, the father often visits his mother's and sisters' houses.

**Inheritance.** When she marries, every woman is given a house and arable land. On Ngazidja, land owned jointly matrilineally and passed down through women, may be sold only to escape dishonor. Personal property is handed down by declaration or testament; Islamic law is rarely invoked.

**Kin Groups.** On Ngazidja, one belongs to one's mother's lineage, called the "belly" or "house," which has its own name. On the other islands, matrilineal transmission is less formalized but one still lives with one's maternal family. Patrilineal transmission, which is of Arab origin, exists on Ndzuani, and three *sharif* lineages live in the islands.

## SOCIALIZATION

**Infant Care.** The birth of a child is considered a divine blessing. A child is always held by adults or by its brothers and sisters. Children are rarely scolded, though rowdiness is sometimes criticized. Chronic malnutrition affects a third of children below age three; this situation is worse in Ndzuani.

**Child Rearing and Education.** Familiarly nicknamed "Mom" and "Dad," children are trained for their future roles at an early age, especially girls, who do heavy domestic work. A boy's circumcision at around age four is celebrated by prayer and a special meal. All children attend a religious school, where they memorize the Koran. The instructor, often a local parent, is a respected educator. French secular education favors urban residents and men. Public education is disorganized, and private schools open their doors when teachers at public schools go on strike. Boys enter into the age-class system between ages fifteen and twenty. Pubescent girls are watched closely because pregnancy eliminates the possibility of a great wedding.

**Higher Education.** There is one school of higher education in the capital. Students must go abroad for training, often at their own expense, because scholarships are scarce. Arab countries pay for Arabic–language education and theology, but access to desirable jobs in the administration requires a French diploma.

## ETIQUETTE

One must respect and greet one's elders regardless of their social status. A woman may not go out without a head veil. The wife eats in the kitchen with the children; the husband eats at the dinner table or in the living room, where he may invite a parent or friend. Master in his wife's house, a man must behave with dignity and authority.

## RELIGION

**Religious Beliefs.** Sunni Islam of the Chafeite rite is the dominant religious and cultural standard. Many Comorians also believe in the power of *djinn*, and other spirits of the earth. These beliefs derive from Arab, African, and Madagascan traditions. People also believe in a concept of cosmic balance that grew out of Arab astrology.

**Religious Practitioners.** There are many ways of practicing Islam, and religious roles may overlap. Some roles and practices are clearly defined and institutionalized: conducting prayer on Fridays, preachers and muezzin who organize community prayer at the mosque, and Koranic masters. Sheiks and Sufi brotherhoods have a strictly Islamic mystical experience; *walimu* masters, who are numerous in the countryside, may be Koranic instructors, healers, astrologists, and masters of the Mus-

*A man taps water from a baobab tree, which acts as a natural water reservoir, Grand Cormore Island.*

lim *djinn*. Communication with the invisible is a common experience.

**Rituals and Holy Places.** In addition to Sunni Islam's religious holidays, Comorians celebrate the Birth of the Prophet and the birthdays of local saints. Most prayer services are held at neighborhood and Friday mosques, while the special devotions of the *shadhuliyya*, *kadiriyya*, and *rifayya* brotherhoods are held in the orders' mosques' courtyards (*zawiya*), where local saints are buried in tombs where people come to pray. Cults of spirits in the bush constitute a less visible religious practice.

**Death and the Afterlife.** People bury the dead according to Islamic rites that exclude women and organize special prayers for the third, ninth, and fortieth days of mourning. Seeing one's dead parent in a dream informs a person about that relative's happiness, facilitating prayer.

## MEDICINE AND HEALTH CARE

The failure of the public health care system has led to the opening of many small private clinics in the cities. Comorians do not separate sickness from other misfortunes that may be revealed by tradi-

tional practitioners who offer herbal remedies, protective amulets with Koranic texts, astrological calculations, or propitiation of possessor spirits. People use these remedies according to the nature of their need (health, love, work, social relations) and wealth.

## SECULAR CELEBRATIONS

The national holiday, commemorating independence, is celebrated on 6 July.

## THE ARTS AND HUMANITIES

**Support for the Arts.** Customary celebrations (*ada*) are occasions for male and female dancing, violin concerts, and the recitation of important literary texts. Religious and secular musical events are transmitted by the national radio and independent radio and television stations.

**Literature.** Oral literature includes stories about the creation of villages, war epics, philosophical poetry, tales, riddles, and proverbs. Novels and poetry in French are available.

**Graphic Arts.** Artisans produce everyday objects, including sculpted wood coconut graters and abacus-style number games, makeup tables in carved coral, basketry, pottery, embroidery (ceremonial coats, Islamic bonnets, openwork curtains), and jewelry.

**Performance Arts.** Traditional musical genres coexist with music performed by modern village orchestras. Comedic and tragic theatrical works deal with historical themes and often are critical of society.

## THE STATE OF THE PHYSICAL AND SOCIAL SCIENCES

The National Center for Research and Scientific Documentation at Moroni coordinates studies in the human and natural sciences. The center is also home to an archive, a museum, and a library.

## BIBLIOGRAPHY

Ahmed-Chamanga, Mohammed. *Lexique Comorien (Shindzuani)-Francais*, 1992.

Blanchy, Sophie. ''Famille et Parente dans L'Archipel des Comores.'' *Journal des Africanistes* 62 (1): 7–53, 1992.

———. "Le Partage des Boeufs dans les Rituels Sociaux du Grand Mariage a Ngazidja (Comores)." *Journal des Africanistes*, 66 (1–2): 169–203, 1996.

———, and Moinesha Mroudjae Said Islam. *The Status and Situation of Women in the Comoros*, 1989.

———, Moinecha Cheikh, Moussa A. Saïd, Masseande Allaoui, and Moussa Issihak. "Therapies Traditionnelles aux Comores." *Cahiers des Sciences Humaines de l'ORSTOM* 29 (4): 763–791, 1993.

———, Moinecha Cheikh, Moussa A. Saïd, Masseande Allaoui, and Moussa Issihak. "Rituels de Protection dans l'Archipel des Comores." *Islam et Societes au Sud du Sahara* 10: 121–145, 1996.

Chanfi, Ahmed A. *Islam et Politique aux Comores*, 1999

Chanudet, Claude, and Jean-Aime Rakotoarisoa. *Moheli, une Ile des Comores a la Recherche de Son Identite*, 2000.

Chouzour, Sultan. *Le Pouvoir de l'Honneur: Tradition et Contestation en Grande Comore*, 1994.

Damir Ben Ali, George Boulinier, and Paul Ottino. *Traditions d'une Lignee Royale des Comores*, 1985.

Gevrey, A. *Essai sur les Comores*, 1870.

Lafon, Michel. "Le Shingazidja, une Langue Bantu sous Influence Arabe." Ph.D. dissertation, INALCO, Paris, 1987.

Martin, Jean. *Comores, Quatre Iles entre Pirates et Planteurs*, 1983.

Otteinheimer, Martin. *Marriage in Domoni*, 1985.

——— and Harriet Otteinheimer. *Historical Dictionary of the Comoro Islands*, 1994.

Saïd, Moussa A. *Princes, Guerriers et Poetes dans la Litterature Comorienne*, 2000.

Sidi, Aïnouddine. *Anjouan: L'Histoire d'une Crise Fonciere*, 1998.

Vérin, Pierre. *Les Comores*, 1994.

Wright, Henry, "Early Seafarers of the Comoro Islands: The Dembeni Phase of the IX–X Centuries A.D." *Azania* 19: 13–60, 1984.

—SOPHIE BLANCHY

**SEE ALSO:** MAYOTTE

# DEMOCRATIC REPUBLIC OF THE CONGO

## CULTURE NAME

Congolese

## ALTERNATIVE NAMES

Congo (Kinshasa)—which distinguishes this country from the other Congo, which is often called Congo (Brazzaville). Formerly: Zaire, Zairians, Belgian Congo, Congo (Léopoldville).

## ORIENTATION

**Identification.** Named after the enormous Congo River and the large ethnic group living at its mouth, the Kongo, the Democratic Republic of the Congo first had its borders drawn at the Berlin Conference of 1884–1885. During this conference, Africa was arbitrarily divided in ways that benefitted the European colonial powers, with no regard for existing tribal systems and linguistic groups. In some instances, these new borders separated families, while other people without previous contact suddenly became part of one nation. Many of Congo's leaders have favored certain ethnic groups and areas over others, exacerbating differences between ethnic groups. The future of the Congo depends upon average citizens transcending the political rhetoric of hatred and uniting within an African-style democracy.

**Location and Geography.** Located in Central Africa, the Congo shares an extremely long border with the Republic of Congo, Central African Republic, Sudan, Uganda, Rwanda, Burundi, Tanzania, Zambia, and Angola. Largely landlocked, the DRC depends on the mighty Congo River for transportation and livelihood. Second in power only to the Amazon River, the Congo River is said to have enough hydroelectric power to light up every home in all of southern Africa. The regular flow of the river is due to its various tributaries, which feed from both sides of the equator.

As Africa's third largest country, the Democratic Republic of the Congo boasts 905,356 square miles (2,344,872 square kilometers), including deep forests, the famous Ruwenzori mountain range, the Central Basin, the Highland Plateau, beautiful rivers, cities, villages, and mining towns.

Kinshasa is the capital and largest city in the Democratic Republic of the Congo. Formerly known as Léopoldville, after King Leopold II of Belgium, Kinshasa is a vibrant and modern town of over 5 million people located on the Congo River. Other cities include the southern diamond-mining center, Lubumbashi (850,000 inhabitants), river-oriented Kolwezi (417,810), Kisangani (600,000), Mbuji-Mayi (810,000) and Matadi (172,730), the country's primary seaport. Various communities throughout the nation's interior make their livelihoods by fishing, hunting, and working the soil.

**Demography.** With an estimated population of nearly 52 million in 2000, the Democratic Republic of the Congo is home to over two hundred different ethnic and linguistic groups. In the far north of the country, near the Sudanese border, live people with ethnic and linguistic backgrounds similar to that of Saharans. Their culture is strongly influenced by Arabic- and Berber-speaking people of the Middle East. People of Bantu origin populate most of the rest of the country, including Lunda, Luba, Kuba, Kongo, and Mongo, groups. In addition, some 240,000 people are temporary residents, as neighboring wars have led to huge migrations into the region. The vast population of the DRC is divided into ten administrative regions.

The copper industry in eastern Zaire created several urban areas that sprang up around the mines. Currently, 60 percent of the population lives in rural areas, although many people migrated to the cities during the 1980s and 1990s in the hopes of finding food and work. Rapid urbanization has increased the squalor of shantytowns located outside

*Democratic Republic of the Congo*

city centers, where many families have to share space, water, and food.

***Linguistic Affiliation.*** Most Congolese speak several languages; it is not uncommon for someone to fluently speak four or more languages. French, introduced by Belgian colonists, is still used by the government and in radio broadcasts as Congo's official language. Other major languages include Swahili, Lingala, Kikongo, and Tshiluba. Used by the colonial military in the 1800s as the language of trade and travel, Lingala remains the lingua franca of the region. It is the most popular language for communicating across ethnic lines, and the majority of popular music heard on the radio is sung in Lingala.

The flight of many Congolese to cities and mining towns outside linguistic boundaries has caused new varieties of language to arise. Such dialects are often a synthesis of several languages that formed as people from different backgrounds learned to speak with one another. Migration and modernization has also led to changes within specific language groups. For example, the Swahili taught during the colonial era in missionary schools has evolved into a new dialect called Kingwana. Language choice carries inherent political overtones. For example, the use of French in conversation implies an official tone.

**Symbolism.** National holidays include Independence Day, Constitution Day, and Armed Forces Day, indicating that the ruling party wishes to solidify feelings of nationalism and remind the nation of its freedom from a colonial past.

The country's flag has a light blue background with six stars on the left-hand side and one large yellow star in the center. Because the current president wanted to honor the Congo's first freely elected president, Patrice Lumumba, he chose the same flag that Lumumba used in 1960. Originally, the six stars represented the six administrative districts; though there are currently ten such provinces, the president selected this older version out of respect for the nation's hero.

## HISTORY AND ETHNIC RELATIONS

**Emergence of the Nation.** Throughout Congo's prehistory, most ethnic groups were isolated from one another by the thick forests that engulf the country. For several hundred years before the arrival of Europeans in the late fifteenth century, many kingdoms were highly organized and efficient administrators of health, education, and trade. Regions located along the Congo River were most easily accessible to outside traders. Therefore, they were the first to open themselves up to Christianization and the Portuguese slave trade in the 1480s. Throughout the sixteenth century, the worldwide demand for slaves increased, triggering violence between ethnic groups as European slave traders kidnapped people and encouraged African men to capture members of other ethnic groups for money. Even missionaries, who thought of themselves as bringing the "pure light" of Europe to shine on the Congolese "darkness," sometimes participated in the lucrative business of slavery.

In the 1885 scramble for Africa, King Leopold II of Belgium declared himself the dictator and sole proprietor of the new Congo Free State. Leopold garnered public support at home by publicly announcing his intent to Christianize and modernize the Congolese population, all the while planning the forced labor of men, women, and children for the lucrative ivory and rubber business. When people did not meet the king's quotas, his army killed them or cut off their hands. The overall population of the country greatly diminished during the early twentieth century due to such cruelty and to the susceptibility of many Congolese to new European diseases.

Mounting international criticism forced Leopold to sell his colony to Belgium in 1908. The Belgians, unfortunately, failed to contain his bloodthirsty troops, who were responsible for managing the rubber trade that caused over five million people to perish. From 1890 to 1910, between 5 and 8 million people perished as a direct result of the rubber trade.

By 1903, the economy for rubber in the Congo had collapsed, so the new Belgian colony focused on exploiting the Katanga province for copper, diamonds, and oil. So-called "vacant land" could be used by businesses from many countries willing to exploit one of the world's richest areas. Both forced labor and high taxes continued the horrors of Leopold. Families were split as many men went far away from their villages to the mines to work, nearly destroying the fabric of traditional society.

During the 1930s and 1940s, the Belgian colonial government tried to enforce mass cultivation standards, but without proper transportation mechanisms in place, large amounts of food lay wasted and unsold. The demand for copper grew during the World War II era, creating peripheral markets for household goods such as soap and sugar. Though economic growth increased and education improved during this time, the Belgians remained staunchly authoritarian. Local chiefs were used as pawns of the government; often they were removed from power if rumored to be anticolonialist.

**National Identity.** Increased poverty and aggravation over colonial rule united this extremely large country, despite its lack of roads, telephones, and newspapers. Under the administration of the Belgians, for example, Congolese were not permitted to travel without a permit and were not allowed to drink hard liquor. Such inequality fed the flames of desire for independence, as did the news of neighboring countries achieving freedom from colonial rule. Liberation movements from around the country began to cooperate and consolidate their power against the Belgians. Religious movements formed, strongly espousing antiwhite, anticolonialist rule. Massive strikes and retaliatory massacres helped motivate opposition groups in the extremely large and ethnically diverse country.

When the Belgians abruptly left the Congo and independence was declared on 30 June 1960, there

*Canoeing on the Zambezi River. Rivers are a common mode of transportation in the Democratic Republic of the Congo.*

was only one trained Congolese lawyer, no Congolese physicians or officers, and only five men otherwise trained as administrators in the whole country. This small group suddenly had to run the third largest nation in Africa. Between 1960 and 1964, Congo was convulsed by a series of coups, mercenary-led rebellions, the arrival of United Nations (UN) peacekeeping forces, and secessionist movements. The most telltale event was the outcome of Congo's first free and fair election in May of 1960: because of his charismatic qualities, Patrice Lumumba and his party, the MNC (Mouvement National Congolais) won the most parliamentary seats. While other parties traditionally were based along ethnic lines, Lumumba enjoyed popular support across racial divisions. His goal for the new country was gradual Africanization and development. After the Americans refused to assist the new president, Lumumba sought a small token of support from the Soviet Union. This caused the United States, caught up in the Cold War, to fear the Congo's newest leader. In addition, some U.S. business leaders wondered if Lumumba would be receptive to U.S. business interests. These factors led to an alledged U.S.-backed plot against President Lumumba, ending in his death on January 17, 1961. The United States had engineered his demise and execution after less than a year in office.

The United States was preparing Joseph Mobutu, an army strongman, for leadership. Mobutu remained in power for twenty-three years, until 1997. Mobutu proceeded to declare all political parties illegal, except for his party, the Mouvement Populaire de la Revolution, or MPR. He also abolished the parliament.

President Mobutu asked that everyone drop his or her missionary-given, Christian names in an effort to re-Africanize the nation. He changed his own name to Mobutu Sese Seko Kuku Ngbendu Wa Za Banga, "The warrior who dares and cannot know defeat because of his will and is all powerful, leaving fire in his wake as he goes from conquest to conquest." In addition, he changed the country's name to Zaire, and several city names as well. Many people were executed within Mobutu's circles and in the business community for allegedly planning coups, and most business operations were overrun by government officials and eventually collapsed. Mobutu did what Leopold had done: he enslaved his people, got extremely wealthy at their expense, and watched as everyone outside of his small circle endured an ever-increasing cycle of poverty and repression. After over fifty university students, rumored to be part of a demonstration against the government, were murdered in their beds by Mobutu's guard, the international community began to take notice of the brutality of the regime, and some countries withdrew their financial support from Zaire.

Mobutu's personal fortune at his death was estimated to be $5 billion. His name became synonymous with corruption around the world. In the 1970s and 1980s, the Congo economy suffered because of Mobutu's excessive expenses, the fall of copper on the world market, extremely high inflation and a simultaneous devaluation of the currency, the government defaulting on International Monetary Fund and World Bank payments, and the near ubiquitous nationalization of businesses.

**Ethnic Relations.** Laurent Kabila's ascension to power culminated on 16 May 1997, when he was named the head of the Democratic Republic of the Congo. Kabila, originally from the Katanga province, was the leader of rebel troops who, fed up with Mobutu's rule, marched across the country capturing each town along the way. When Kabila took the capital, Mobutu fled into exile in Europe where he died a few months later, in September 1997. The initial celebrations gave way to an internal conflict that as of 2000 involved five other African nations.

Nearly one year after Mobutu's death, Kabila announced war against the Tutsi. Ironically, they were the ethnic group that most supported his campaign to overthrow the Mobutu regime. Because of the lack of civil rights and equality in the Congo, ethnic Tutsis have never had citizenship, even those born in the country. Their goal was to overthrow Kabila in favor of a more democratic regime.

Forty years after independence, the political struggle for power still continues as this war has claimed over one million lives. Inspired by decades of colonialism, Leopold's Rule, and the multinational push to control the Congo's natural resources, this war is about more than ethnic rivalries; intertwined is a complex history, broken allegiances and promises, Mobutu's policy of divide and conquer and billions of dollars of natural resources hanging in the balance.

The conflict is not confined to Rwanda and the Congo, however; Zimbabwe, Namibia, Angola, and Uganda have each taken their sides, creating what some have called "Africa's World War I."

The future of the region remains uncertain, especially in the light of President Laurent Kabila's assassination by one of his bodyguards on January 16, 2001. The late president's son Joseph Kabila was sworn in as the country's new president on January 26. The new Kabila has promised that free and fair elections would take place in the near future.

## URBANISM, ARCHITECTURE, AND THE USE OF SPACE

In rural areas, several round or rectangular mud huts enclosed in an area comprise a family's homestead. The frame is built by tying vines around sticks and palm frond stems. A mixture of sand, water, and often cement is then used to fill in the structure and a grass roof completes the home. Families often move their homestead to be near their new fields, or if termites have destroyed their roof. At times, new homes are built on top of the old field, so that after several years, the newly fertilized land can be used again. Each hut serves a different purpose: some are for cooking, others are for storage, and there are guest huts and separate rooms for the male and female children, who usually sleep on handwoven raffia mats placed upon the ground. Traditional homesteads are as diverse as their owners. They may be large or small, extremely clean or left in neglect.

In the areas surrounding cities, large shantytowns have emerged. Usually the small homes are made of corrugated iron in these areas. Given the extreme heat during most of the year, these homes are often swelteringly hot. In general, the quality of life in the urban shanties is lower than that of the rural areas. In some urban areas, however, better homes or apartments are available for the rich who drive Western automobiles and wear suits. Large government buildings made of modern materials symbolize the wealth of the politically powerful.

## FOOD AND ECONOMY

**Food in Daily Life.** Unfortunately, for many in the Congo, food is not necessarily a part of daily life. And, when food is available, it usually does not contain the vitamins and minerals required to help ward off disease and maintain proper health. The primary staple, pasty white *fufu* (manioc tubers, pounded into the texture of oatmeal), is eaten out of a communal bowl. This chunky carbohydrate is accompanied by varying side dishes, depending on wealth, season, and availability. Examples include sweet potatoes, perch, bananas, and plantains. For many rural people, meat is a delicacy reserved for special days or when the family can afford the luxury. Only the right hand is used in eating because it is an insult to conduct any transaction with the left hand, which is used only for bathroom purposes. In the traditional way of eating, the women first serve the men, who usually sit on the chairs in the home. After the men are finished eating, the women and children usually sit on the floor and share the remaining items, resulting in poorer nutrition. In

*A congregation prays at an Assembly of God in Bukavu. Due to the efforts of missionaries, the majority of Congolese practice Christianity.*

some areas, however, the women first set aside good morsels of meat for the children and themselves, resulting in better child nutrition rates in these regions.

Fish is a primary food source for many, depending on their proximity to rivers and streams. Some families build their own ponds by diverting small rivers to an area, using bamboo for pipes. Manure, bits of food, and other materials are used as compost in the bottom of the pond to promote the growth of plankton. Fish are then harvested after six months of feeding. Often the women fry or salt the fish that the family did not consume for sale in markets throughout the year.

Many edible treats abound from the palm tree, including wine, oil, fruits, and nuts. Youth learn early to climb high into the trees for nuts, process them by boiling and pounding the nut to make oil, and to tap the base of the tree for wine. This wine starts out not very potent, but as it sits, the alcohol content greatly increases. The palm fruits can also be used for cosmetic purposes.

Riverboats are seen throughout the country, as the river acts as a vital artery for trade and transportation along the populated river banks. On the riverboats, large communal kitchens serve tea and bread for breakfast and rice and beans for lunch and dinner. Urban life has changed many traditional customs, and a thriving restaurant culture exists in Kinshasa. Usually catering to business people and the rich, these expensive places offer French, Chinese, Greek, and Tunisian food as well as traditional chicken cooked in oil with rice.

***Food Customs at Ceremonial Occasions.*** A tradition ingrained into the villager's lifestyle is to be extremely generous and giving to all people. Starting with a family's closest kin, members share with one another and especially with the most needy in the community, even when their own health suffers from lack of food. Lavish gifts are bestowed upon visitors, guests, and distant cousins alike. A family's only chicken or goat is often slaughtered for holiday celebrations, funerals, and weddings, and to celebrate births. Traditional beer and palm wine is brewed for these special occasions, which usually involve singing and dancing. Above the drums, singing, and stomping of feet, women ululate shrilly to express their excitement. This encourages the dancers, who then begin to move with a renewed vigor.

***Basic Economy.*** The per capita gross national product (GNP) of the country stands as the world's third lowest, according to a 1998 report. In 2000, as

*A number of female students at a college in Kinshasa, learning dance. There are four universities located in the Congo.*

the government continues printing money to fund the war, the inflation rate of the Congolese franc continued to rise (standing at 84 percent in May 2000), and hopes for a healthy national economy dwindled. Congolese industry was operating at only about 10 percent of its capacity.

***Land Tenure and Property.*** In the past, the chief or village headman had authority over village land and ownership, but the European notion of individual land ownership led to a law in 1966 stating that the government owned all land, creating two simultaneous legal systems. Both laws exist side by side, and the unclear status of land ownership is usually "solved" by postponing land dispute investigations with bribes. Some people want to officially own the land they and their ancestors have been tending for centuries so that they can use the property as collateral for a loan. This legal issue caused by the parallel legal systems, however, prevents many from obtaining such a loan, making it difficult for would-be entrepreneurs to finance a new business. In addition, women cannot own land without their husband's consent.

***Commercial Activities.*** People are forced to find food for themselves and their families by any means necessary. Since the Congo fails to perform the functions of a state, has a very ineffective administrative system, fails to uphold civil rights, and often neglects to pay even its few salaried workers, Congolese citizens must find a way to carry on with their lives to survive. The origin of this problem lies in the Belgian colonial days and the subsequent Mobutu era, in which the real function of the regime was to consolidate wealth in the hands of the few at the expense of the rest.

It is estimated that the total economy of the DRC is three times larger than the official gross domestic product. The unofficial economy is not a backseat player; it is the real economy on the ground. This is because the vast majority of economic activity takes place behind the official system. Rather than go through the excessive bureaucratic formalities (a single export alone requires thirty-nine separate administrative procedures), people take the matter of survival into their own hands. Exports such as copper, diamonds, gold, and coffee are bound for Europe, South Africa, and Angola. People bicycle in common goods from neighboring countries to sell in the DRC for less. The consistently overvalued price of items in the official economy prevents everyone but the excessively rich from buying even the most basic necessities, and forces more people to operate within the black market. In fact, the primary reason to obtain a "regular job" (such as, teacher or police officer) is to use the new job as a springboard to new connections that enhance the operations of the work that takes place outside the traditional sector. Women have especially taken advantage of the booming informal sector, thereby avoiding official requirements for licensing, since they would normally need their husband's permission to open any sort of bank account or to obtain a trading permit. Tenacious entrepreneurs even continue their business under the extremely difficult conditions inside refugee camps. Hair salons, discos, bars, wrestling arenas, and shops selling basic goods have sprung up inside these camps.

***Major Industries.*** Subsistence agriculture accounts for a vast majority of the industry in the Congo. People farm corn, manioc, potatoes, beans, and rice for their personal use. Textiles, food products, cement, and plastic shoes are manufactured.

Powerful players from around the world compete for access to the DRC's rich natural resources, which include diamonds, cobalt, copper, gold, and oil. In order to pass customs, traders may eat gold pellets or hide illegal goods in the spaces of a car engine in order to successfully make it through a border, where they then sell these items on the black market.

***Trade.*** One of the most severe hindrances to trade and marketing in the Congo is the lack of adequate internal transportation. Most roads through the country's vast interior are not paved, and its 1,550 miles (2,500 kilometers) of paved roads remain in serious disrepair. Rain damages the terrain, creating huge potholes which make transport across the country virtually impossible. Estimates in the early 1990s suggested that it could take up to six months to travel from the east to the west of the country over the deeply rutted dirt tracks, even with a car in excellent condition. In addition, airline services are unreliable. Therefore, the most effective method of transport in the country is by river barge. These boats float down the Congo River, carrying large numbers of people and their goods on deck.

***Division of Labor.*** Rural children learn from a young age to tend fields, carry water, cook, and clean the homestead. Everyone, regardless of talent, ability, or age, is involved in work for the family's survival.

## SOCIAL STRATIFICATION

***Classes and Castes.*** Congo's richest people primarily live in Kinshasa. Referred to as Kinois, these government officials and Western businessmen are few in number. Non-Congolese expatriates—businesspeople of higher wealth and class from West Africa, Greece, Asia, the United States, and Japan—enjoy a higher standard of living than the majority of the population. Missionaries and foreign aid workers are socially fragmented into their respective groups and each attend separate schools, churches, and social clubs. Some Western workers, however, do live in rural areas, without the comforts of an elite lifestyle. The urban sub-bourgeoisie—those seen by the majority of the very poor as rich, but not enjoying much actual income since they are rarely paid—include teachers, clerks, and low-level bureaucrats. This disgruntled group is dependent on the state for their salaries. Teachers often bribe their students with threats of failure in order to survive. The rest of the city-dwelling population includes soft drink vendors, shoe repairmen, taxi drivers, salespeople, artisans, smugglers, and prostitutes, all of whom survive in the urban sprawl by operating in the unofficial economy.

*The Institut de Medicine Tropicale Princesse Astrid. In the Congo, modern medical practices work together with traditional forms of African medicine.*

Congolese are known for their extreme tenacity and ability to weather difficult situations. Rural peasants are hardest hit by the economic collapse, since state officials collect 50 percent of the peasants' income through taxation. In rural areas, respect and authority comes from being old and/or male. Many communities have chiefs, and most of them still wield a considerable amount of power in their villages.

***Symbols of Social Stratification.*** With the introduction of Western imports and a monetary sys-

tem, life in the Congo became increasingly stratified and based upon material acquisition. In the traditional sense, being rich meant owning lots of cattle or having many children. The idea of acquiring goods, trinkets, and other material things, however, is seen as the way to move forward in this modern age.

Some of the youth, fascinated with European styles and envisioning Europe as a place with an almost magical quality, are greatly influenced by the few people who have traveled abroad. A few men, concerned with their outward appearance, spend all their money on expensive, fashionable brand-name clothes, often while living in unhealthy conditions. This phenomenon is widely observed in male youth in Kinshasa, who believe, if they dress well, that more doors will open to them socially, politically, and economically. The desire for foreign clothes still fascinates the rich few, who are seen in the cities in designer clothes, driving Mercedes and talking on cellular phones.

Rural women often wear scarves on their heads, carry their babies on their backs, and wear light, brightly colored clothes. The tattered clothes of the majority of shoeless, rural and urban poor are outward signs of the poverty they endure.

## POLITICAL LIFE

*Government.* Leopold's rule, Belgian colonialism, and Mobutu laid the framework for the current form of government. Mobutu established what some have called a ''kleptocratic'' dictatorship, in which the constitution and separate executive, legislative, and judicial branches existed on paper only, and the primary role of the government was extracting money from the land and people. On paper, Kabila answered to a bicameral parliament including a Senate, Chamber of Representatives, and an independent judiciary. In reality, he allowed himself to operate the entire country with the help of only twelve men, who comprised his interim assembly, citing civil war as a deterrent to democratic rule. Kabila's rhetoric included the goal of transferring power to the people through the use of People's Power Committees, which were slated to begin operations in each province sometime in the future. Kabila dissolved his own party, the Alliance of Democratic Forces for the Liberation of Congo-Zaire (AFDL) in January 1999, and subsequently engaged in fighting several armed factions opposed to his rule. Allegiances to a political party or faction are usually based along ethnic and clan lines.

*Leadership and Political Officials.* Everyone in the path of the president is ordered to stand perfectly still when he marches through Kinshasa's city streets. When an average citizen happens to meet a government official, the citizen will usually try to avoid conflict by conceding to the official's demands, and by keeping overall contact to a minimum. Those who spoke negatively of the Kabila regime faced probable prison, torture, and execution.

*Social Problems and Control.* With political parties officially banned and demonstrations outlawed,

it is not difficult to imagine the social problems in the country. Rather than a government, a military, and a police force protecting its citizens, the ordinary people going about their daily life are harassed, stolen from, and lied to by the very people who are supposed to protect them. Journalists such as Kalala Kalaos, who was awarded the International Freedom of the Press Award in 1995, have endured countless prison sentences and torture for openly criticizing the government. Years of colonialism, brutality, and the general misunderstanding of the role of government will take more than a few years to overcome. It would be difficult for any new government, given this history, to come in and change things overnight since much of the illegal activity is promoted by the rich and powerful.

Problems of all sorts are solved in local courts, in which issues are discussed and resolved through legal or religious ceremonial actions such as purification and consecration. Traditional systems remain the primary method for solving disputes.

*Military Activity.* The role of the unpaid Congo Military is to set up numerous roadblocks in order to earn their money from the bribes of road-weary travelers. Soldiers rape women, inflict arbitrary fines on citizens, and pillage and harass the villagers. Most of the rest of the military is involved in fighting to protect Kabila's regime against several factions that wish to overthrow the government.

*Social Welfare and Change Programs.* Since less than 1 percent of the GNP is devoted to the health care of the citizens, little is being done by the government to assist its population. The few people in large cities who are salaried and are actually receiving pay also enjoy social security and pension benefits, but this does little for the vast majority of the population, which receives no support from the government.

## NONGOVERNMENTAL ORGANIZATIONS AND OTHER ASSOCIATIONS

International relief organizations fly food in to refugees and people displaced because of the war. At times the food does not reach the innocent masses; rather, it often falls into the hands of the military, who can then strengthen themselves for more fighting.

As an institution, the Roman Catholic Church has been a major player in the Congo throughout modern history, often condemning state-sponsored human rights violations. In 1993 Catholic leaders

*A village market, where people buy food, baskets, pottery, and other necessities.*

sent a memo to Mobutu denouncing state-sponsored terrorism and asking him to stop torturing and executing political prisoners. The church has served an important role throughout Congo's history as an intermediary to the state.

## GENDER ROLES AND STATUSES

*Division of Labor by Gender.* Most political, economic, and religious institutions have male leadership. Historically, Congolese men have been treated with respect and have been given positions of authority more often than Congolese women. The way a woman is treated in the Congo depends on her immediate environment and racial background. It has been argued that lower-class urban women enjoy fewer freedoms than their rural counterparts. Because women in cities are often more dependent on their husbands and other males for their livelihoods, the rural lifestyle may sound appealing to some; rural women find some independence through gardening, preparing meals, and generating small crafts for sale. These women spend so much time with their daily work, however, that they have little opportunity to organize for social change. Women living in Kinshasa are more able to form groups that collectively challenge the notion of male superiority.

*The Relative Status of Women and Men.* Though many ethnic groups in the Congo practice matrilineal succession, in which inheritance is passed through the mother's side of the family, women are regarded as lower than males on the scale of social hierarchy. There is a high degree of societal pressure placed upon young women to marry, and an urban single woman is regarded as a prostitute, regardless of her professional status. In many cases, women must detail everything they purchase for their husband, while the male usually does not have to account for his own expenses. The goal is to keep women dependent on and subservient to men.

Women often band together in groups to resist unfair treatment or taxation. Some led popular efforts against Mobutu, such as organizing prayer groups in Kinshasa to mobilize efforts for his removal; many women continue to play a prominent role in challenging traditional roles of authority.

## MARRIAGE, FAMILY, AND KINSHIP

*Marriage.* In the past, single women in the Congo belonged to their fathers, and, upon marriage, their ownership would be transferred to the husband. The man's father would give gifts such as knives, food, or slaves to the new wife's father, in exchange for his loss of precious labor and kinship.

*Young Rwandan refugees sit on a blanket outside an orphanage in Goma, Democratic Republic of the Congo.*

In rural areas it is common for men to have many wives. Village chiefs or headmen usually have more than one wife. The goal is to have many children who survive until adulthood, providing the household with enough hands to complete the many chores necessary for survival. At times, however, the women married to one man compete amongst each other for kitchens, food, affection, and children.

***Domestic Unit.*** Women are responsible for the majority of the day-to-day survival tasks, such as cutting wood for cooking fires; hauling on their heads large buckets of water for cooking; cleaning clothes; reaping; sowing, and harvesting the fields; collecting palm fruits; cooking, pounding, and sifting the local cassava root; child rearing; and making baskets and pottery for sale at local markets. Traditionally, men went off on hunts for several days, using traps, spears, and bows and arrows to kill animals large and small. Now there are fewer animals to hunt, but the work of women does not diminish by proportion. In fact, the responsibility of the household falls more squarely on their shoulders, as the society becomes ever more dependent on farming. Many women have recently flocked to urban areas in the hopes of selling their handiwork, becoming hairstylists, or participating in the underground economy. Often the woman is the family's

principal breadwinner. Many women have hopes that their children will advance out of poverty, and they are therefore burdened with the additional responsibility of paying school fees. Male children typically advance further in school than their female counterparts, since men are the head of the household and make financial decisions on behalf of the entire family and will benefit more from the education.

***Kin Groups.*** In the traditional African model of kinship rules, there is a clear delineation of power, starting with the male head of the family. Chiefs come to rule based on their popularity within the village, their personal charisma, and their overall prestige. Whatever elders command is adhered to unconditionally, out of respect. Respect for elders, chiefs, and ancestors is an extremely important facet of daily life in the Congo.

Methods of solving problems must be based on traditional practices. For example, in the case of the Ebola virus, discovered in Kikwit in 1995, an immediate plan of action was necessary in order to ensure that this airborne and extremely deadly disease did not cause a local, and perhaps worldwide, pandemic. It was local elders who were responsible for stemming the deadly virus. Since these elders are the most respected men in their community, they were

*An overcrowded refugee camp in Kibumba. Ongoing military conflicts have led to the creation of the overpopulated refugee camps.*

summoned by health-care workers to explain the severity of the disease. Workers persuaded each elder to share with each head of the family the vital information required to stop the disease from spreading; the family heads in turn informed their kin. The elders persuaded the entire community not to touch or kiss their dead, as was common burial practice. Because the traditional way of disseminating information was followed, the disease was eliminated.

## SOCIALIZATION

*Infant Care.* It is common to see women carrying their babies on their backs as they work in the field, care for other children, carry water, cook, gather firewood, and clean their clothes and homes. Young girls learn from a very young age to take care of their younger siblings. Babies are seen on the backs of girls as young as five years of age.

*Child Rearing and Education.* Some authors argue that there really is no period of life called "childhood" in the Congo, at least in the Western sense of the concept. From the time babies are able to walk, they are thrust into the realm of adult responsibilities. Youth learn from their parents and elders how to manage the homestead. Young girls, especially, are expected to do lots of work for the

family and are usually the ones found endlessly pounding cassava roots with a large mortar and pestle. Good children treat their elders with utmost respect and perform chores without complaint.

Traditionally, male children go to an initiation camp away from their villages for one year. Culminating in a festival and circumcision, this rite of passage into adulthood provides an opportunity for boys to learn to hunt, make handicrafts, and perfect their singing and dancing. The festival usually culminates in a dance ceremony where one dancer gets to wear an elaborate secret mask the village-mask-maker has worked all year to create. After this induction into adulthood, the boys travel back to their communities as men.

The Catholic Church has several mission schools for children that enjoy great popularity, since many national schools have understaffed classrooms. In state schools, the teachers' salaries are often unpaid, forcing many to bribe students for a high test score. Some male teachers solicit sexual acts from female students, offering a good grade or money in exchange. Such obstacles usually do not deter most females from pursuing education and a better life.

Some Africanists have questioned the role that school-based education has played in the rural communities, suggesting that youth may learn more about survival, farming, and raising a homestead from their parents. They argue that students waste precious hours each day learning useless facts in schools, rather than spending time inheriting wisdom from their elders.

**Higher Education.** The Congo has four universities. Two are located in Kinshasa with one each in Lubumbashi and Kisangani. There are also a number of other technical and teacher-training schools scattered around the country.

Some college applicants feel frustrated with the national policy of regional affirmative action in which a disproportionate number of students from remote areas are accepted into a university, leaving students with better scores and a higher level of education fewer available spots. Discouraged and angry, some students claim that the overall level of education in the universities declines because of this policy. This policy, however, is intended to give students from all parts of the country the chance to attend an institution of higher learning.

## ETIQUETTE

Casual clothes are permitted, but unwritten rule is that the nicer one looks, the more respect one will receive. Most local Congolese dress in clean, crisp clothes and colorful outfits. Women wear long skirts, never pants.

Taking pictures is highly sensitive and should be avoided, especially around military areas, checkpoints, and border controls. Greetings are very important in Congolese life; saying hello and inquiring about the other person's situation must be attended to before other matters are discussed. Special respect is given when greeting elders or village headmen, especially if the person who approaches is younger than the other.

## RELIGION

**Religious Beliefs.** The missionaries in the colonial past greatly influenced the Congo's society, and most Congolese profess Christianity as their primary religion. The Roman Catholic Church is extremely prominent, both as a religion and organized group. Over half of the population is Roman Catholic, owing to the large number of missions, schools, hospitals, and foundations run by the church. The Catholics have the most extensive social network of schools, hospitals, and churches in the country.

Traditional beliefs pervade nearly every aspect of life, even for churchgoing Christians. Several syncretic sects have combined traditional ancestral worship and ancient beliefs with Christianity to create new faiths, such as Kimbanguism. Started in 1902 by Simon Kimbangu, who claimed to receive visions of Moses healing, this faith combines anti-European sentiment with traditional African religion. Other Christian based-faiths include the Jamaa, the Kitawala, and the Protestant Church of Christ. There are also a small number of Muslims, who were converted by the influence of Zanzibari slave traders in the 1870s.

People in the Congo who still primarily adhere to traditional African religions believe in the presence of a supreme being who is best accessed through ancestors rather than by direct prayer. Traditional beliefs hold that divine spirits inhabit inanimate objects, and that god can be found as a rock, a tree, or any other object. Having respect and reverence for one's ancestors is part of daily life in the Congo, and people hold a continual dialogue with their ancestors. Angry ancestral spirits looming around villages are offered sacrifices and gifts to placate them. People prayerfully ask the ancestors to bring them good harvests, and ceremonies are held specifically for that purpose.

Illnesses, poor harvests, impotence, and death may arise because of a number of causes. Problems may be attributed to the will of god, angry ancestors, enemies, or witches, depending on the circumstance. Many Congolese fear witches, which are believed to bring all sorts of destruction to communities. People may pay village diviners, known to have special powers including healing and intuition, to find out the cause of the problem. Once the cause has been determined, the solution is remedied according to the healer's knowledge.

**Religious Practitioners.** Spiritual healers, often called *ngangas*, use sacred medicines made of a variety of herbs to cure patients. Someone seeking advice or a cure may go to a healer to remedy a headache, skin disease, or AIDS; to ask for good crops or to become pregnant; or to be told the future. During certain rituals inside the healer's home, specific rules must be followed, depending on the consultation. This usually involves killing chickens, eating special herbs, uttering specific phrases, and consulting the *nkisi*. The nkisi may be a box, bag, or gourd with medicines inside. It is thought to be a force raised from the dead that has chosen to submit itself to human control during rituals. *Ngangas* wear around their waist the nkisi and small bags with herbs. Often the patient is told to come back for his or her solution in the morning, so the nganga can wait for ideas to arise through dreams

*A guard stands at the gate to the palace of the governor of Kivu.*

and communications with ancestors. These healers, who are paid for their services, pass on to one of their children their knowledge of herbs and of divination through the throwing of bones, and their other talents. Many politicians regularly consult diviners and traditional healers.

***Rituals and Holy Places.*** Most Congolese mix their indigenous practices with the Christian faith, depending on circumstances and desired outcomes. When someone falls ill, the whole community works together to help the patient. First, it must be determined whether the illness comes "from God," or if it is of natural or human causes. If it is determined that a witch or enemy caused the sickness, then traditional healing methods and beliefs are used, such as offering sacrifices to God and the ancestors. If, however, the disease seems to be from God, members of the community will most likely go to church to pray for the person.

***Death and the Afterlife.*** Many Congolese believe that the spirits of people who have died remain with the family in very obvious ways. Ancestors are very much alive and remain active in the life of the family for generations. People communicate with their ancestors, who act as intermediaries between humans and God. People often ask their ancestors for rain, health, good crops, or the solution to a

difficult problem. White cloth is tied around trees to welcome these ancestral spirits. When someone dies, small gifts are placed around the corpse so the person will have these items when he or she enters the spirit world. The body is then buried in a shroud. Women wear white paint on their faces to symbolize both their mourning and strength in overcoming difficulties.

## MEDICINE AND HEALTH CARE

Since many people drink, bathe, wash their clothes, and defecate in the same river, most water that is accessible to the population carries a host of diseases. Only 14 percent of the population has access to safe drinking water. Standards of living are even lower in refugee camps, where disease spreads much faster because of squalid living conditions and high the population density. Other problems in the Congo relate to the wartime conditions, which have led to the closure of some hospitals and to the government not paying some nurses and doctors.

Some common ailments affecting the Congolese include malaria, parasites, tuberculosis, schistosomiasis, diarrhea, AIDS, and malnutrition. The increasing problem of AIDS has led to education programs targeting youth. In addition, there has been a strong shift in Congolese health care toward redis-

*Copper ready for exportation at a mine in the Shaba region.*

covery of ancient methods, especially after many Western doctors and clinics shut their doors. A health survey, conducted in the Mobutu era, was coordinated to find common ground between Western and traditional medicine, so that all health-care practitioners could use their specific knowledge for the greater good of the whole community.

## SECULAR CELEBRATIONS

National holidays include New Year's Day, 1 January; Commemoration of the Martyrs of Indepen-

dence, 4 January; Labor Day, 1 May; Anniversary of the New Constitution, 24 June; Independence Day, 30 June; Parents' Day, 1 August; Youth Day, 14 October; Armed Forces Day, 17 November; Christmas, 25 December. Celebrations often include parades, singing, dancing, and feasting on large animals.

## THE ARTS AND HUMANITIES

*Support for the Arts.* Government support for the arts has been limited to those who bolster the political agendas of the ruling party. Therefore, many artists also farm, fish, or engage in underground commercial activity to supplement their income. Informal groups of artists have been established to serve as moral support for the numerous artisans who display their works on city streets.

*Literature.* Congolese writers have focused on issues of identity in relation to their colonial past, the differences and similarities between ethnic groups, and conflicts between old and new ways. Some popular poets, playwrights, and novelists include Elebe ma Ekonzo, Valerin Mutombo-Diba, Paul Lomami-Tshibamba, Lisembe Elebe, and Mwilambwe Kibawa.

*Graphic Arts.* Introduced by the Portuguese missionaries of the late fifteenth century, the Ingot Cross continues to be a symbol of both religion and wealth in the Congo. Similar in shape to the square Christian cross, local metalworkers cast these objects from a copper mold. People still use Ingot Crosses as currency and in bride-wealth transactions, especially in the Katanga region.

A large copper industry in the southern Katanga province has sparked a new artistic form in which portraits are sketched into a copper sheet, which is then covered with clay for unique color and texture. Many famous African heads-of-state have had their likenesses imprinted on copper. This art form is gradually gaining recognition in Europe and around the world.

In large towns and cities, tourists can buy handcrafted art, including wood carvings, paintings, baskets, jewelry, and masks. In addition, clothing and mats are popular wares, which are often made from the ubiquitous raffia palm tree.

Postindependence paintings depict exploitation, poverty, and inequality. Such paintings give voice to a Congolese interpretation of history separate from the colonial mind-set pervasive in schools.

*Performance Arts.* Kwasa-kwasa can be heard in circles throughout Africa. This extremely popular dance music originated in Kinshasa, considered by many to be the African music capital. Congolese music and dance of all types can be heard on radios and seen on televisions throughout the world. Congo jazz and soukous, played on a guitar, are popular varieties for such dances. Traditional instruments, such as the thumb piano and various drums, are often used to accompany singers and dancers, who may be singing about anything from love and gender roles to issues of power abuse and government. When artists are afraid to discuss such controversial topics openly, they hint about them through the poetry of song.

The Mbuti people are renowned for a vocal style in which many voices simultaneously sing different, independent melodies. Most types of artistic talent are learned from family members or village elders.

## THE STATE OF THE PHYSICAL AND SOCIAL SCIENCES

Museums in Kinshasa and Lubumbashi and an Academy of Fine Arts in Kinshasa contribute to the understanding of Congo history. Universities, government offices, and many nongovernmental organizations maintain libraries. Ethnographers, scientists, and those studying the humanities find these institutions valuable places to conduct their research.

## BIBLIOGRAPHY

Aronson, David. "The Dead Help No One Living." *World Policy Journal* 14 (4): 81–96, 1998/1998.

Ball, George W. *The Elements in Our Congo Policy*, 1961.

Brittain, Victoria. "The Congo Quagmire." *World Press Review*, November 1998, 14–15.

Callaghy, Thomas M. *The State-Society Struggle: Zaire in Comparative Perspective*, 1984.

Caputo, Robert. "Lifeline for a Nation: Zaire River." *National Geographic*, November 1991, 2–35.

"Congo's Hidden War." *Economist*, 17 June 2000, 45–46.

"Democratic Republic of the Congo: Country Profile." *Economist Intelligence Unit*, 1999.

Elliot, Jeffrey M., and Mervin Dymally. *Voices of Zaire: Rhetoric or Reality?*, 1990.

Emizet, Kisangani. "The Massacre of Refugees in Congo." *Journal of Modern African Studies* 38 (2): 162–174, 2000.

Fabian, Johannes. *Moments of Freedom*, 1998.

"Far from Congo's Battlefield." *Economist*, 29 July 2000, 46.

Gondola, Ch. Didier. "Dream and Drama." *African Studies Review*, 42 (1): 23–48, 1999.

Griggs, Matt. "Life on the Inside," *Geographical*, July 2000, 40–43.

Himmelheber, Hans. *Zaire 1938/39: Photographic Documents of the Yaka, Pende, Tshokwe, and Kuba*, 1993.

Hochschild, Adam. *King Leopold's Ghost: A Story of Greed, Terror, and Heroism in Colonial Africa*, 1998.

Kabwasa, Antoine Nsang-O'Khan. ''African Cosmogony, Life's Philosophy and Development.'' Lecture, University of Nairobi, 17 February 1998.

Kingsolver, Barbara. *The Poisonwood Bible*, 1998.

''The Lusaka Accords May Create More Instability.'' *Defense and Foreign Affairs Strategic Policy*, 27 (7): 3, 1999.

MacGaffey, Wyatt. *Art and Healing of the Bakongo*, 1991.

Meditz, Sandra W., and Tim Merrill, eds. *Zaire: A Country Study*, 1994.

Nelson, Samuel H. *Colonialism in the Congo Basin, 1880–1940*, 1994.

Packham, Eric S. *Success or Failure?: The UN Intervention in the Congo after Independence*, 1998.

Pepin, Jacques. ''Zaire (Congo): Resurgence of Trypanosomiasis.'' *Lancet*, June 1997, S10–S11.

Tanner, Henry. ''A Congo: Reporters Nightmare.'' *Nieman Reports*, 53/54 (4/1): 187–189, 1999/2000.

Tidwell, Mike. *The Ponds of Kalambayi: An African Sojourn*, 1990.

U.S. Congress. House. Committee on Foreign Affairs. Subcommittee on Africa. *Political and Economic Situation in Zaire*, Fall, 1981.

U.S. Embassy, Kinshasa. *Marketing in Zaire: Overseas Business Reports*, July 1991.

—JENNIFER J. ZIEMKE

# REPUBLIC OF CONGO

## CULTURE NAME

Congolese

## ORIENTATION

**Identification.** The Kongo Kingdom was one of the great early empires in central Africa. That kingdom is the source of the official name of the Republic of Congo.

**Location and Geography.** The land area is 132,046 square miles (approximately 342,000 square kilometers). The equator passes through the country, which has one hundred miles (161 kilometers) of coastline on the Atlantic Ocean. The nation borders the Angola enclave of Cabinda, Cameroon, the Central African Republic, the Democratic Republic of the Congo, and Gabon.

The four major topographic regions are a coastal plain that reaches forty miles into the interior, a fertile valley in the south-central area, a central plateau between the Congo and Ogooue rivers, and the north Congo Basin. Most of the country is covered by dense tropical forest. The climate is humid and hot, with heavy rainfall.

The Congo River forms the eastern and southern borders and is one of the most important natural resources. The local peoples have long used the river for food, transportation, and electricity. The river flows between Kinshasa, the capital of the Democratic Republic of Congo, and Brazzaville, the capital and largest city of the Republic of the Congo.

**Demography.** The population was estimated at 2.8 million in 2000. About 60 percent of the people live in urban areas, particularly Brazzaville and Pointe Noire. Another 12 percent live along the main railway between those cities. The remainder of the population resides in isolated rural areas.

**Linguistic Affiliation.** French is the official language and is used in governmental activities.

Lingala and Monokutuba are commonly spoken trade languages. Over sixty local languages and dialects are spoken, the most widely used of which are Kikongo, Sangha, and Bateke. A talking drum language developed in the villages as a form of long-distance communication. Specific beats are broadcast for marriages, deaths, births, and other information.

**Symbolism.** For the residents, the mythology of the region is tied closely to the mystical powers of animals. Families take a specific animal spirit to represent them and often raise totem poles to signify this event.

## HISTORY AND ETHNIC RELATIONS

**Emergence of the Nation.** The first inhabitants are believed to have been forest dwellers such as the Teke. Other ethnic groups joined them to form the three kingdoms that ruled the area before the arrival of Europeans: the Kongo, Loango, and Teke. The mouth of the Congo River was the base for the Kongo Kingdom which encountered the Portuguese in 1484. Trading contracts gave the Congolese textiles, jewelry, and manufactured goods in return for ivory, copper, and slaves. Western education and Christianity were introduced into the region at that time.

The Portuguese did not venture into the interior but bought goods and slaves through African brokers on the coast. When the slave trade diminished because of depopulation, the Portuguese bought slaves from other tribes. Fighting between the tribes weakened them as a group, including the Kongo. This increased the power of the Europeans and strengthened the slave trade. This situation continued until the European powers outlawed slavery in the late 1800s.

The Teke Kingdom of the interior signed a treaty with the French in 1883 that gave the French land in return for protection. Pierre Savorgnan de Brazza

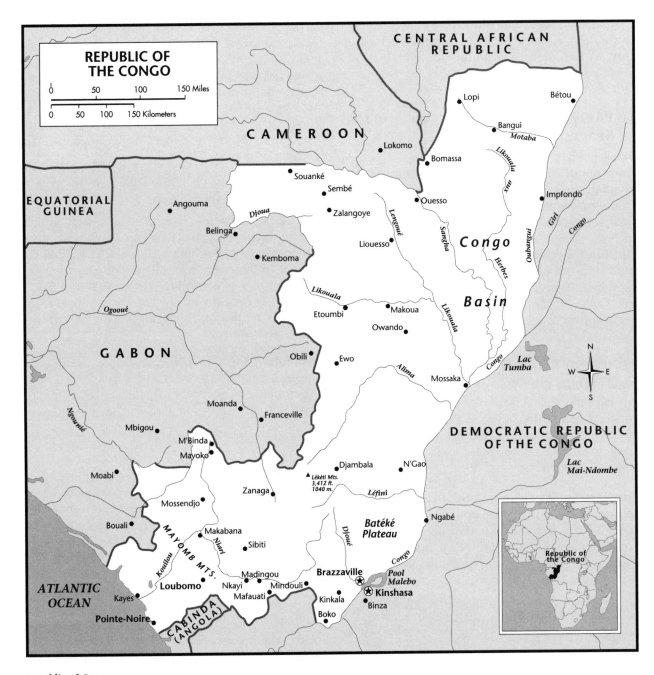

*Republic of Congo*

oversaw French interests. A small settlement along the Congo River was renamed Brazzaville and became the capital of the area now called the Middle Congo.

Gabon, the Central African Republic, and Chad were combined with Middle Congo to become French Equatorial Africa in 1910. French citizenship was granted to local residents in 1946. In 1956, the Republic of Congo and the other three countries became autonomous members of the French Community.

***National Identity.*** Internal self-government was achieved in 1958 as a stage in a series of reforms that started in the mid-1940s. In 1960, the Republic of Congo became an independent nation. The new nation maintained its ties with the French community both economically and politically.

***Ethnic Relations.*** There are fifteen main ethnic groups and seventy-five subgroups. The largest ethnic groups are the Bakongo (48 percent of the population), the Sangha (20 percent), the Teke (17 percent), and the M'Bochi (12 percent). The Teke group suffers from widespread discrimination from all the other ethnic groups in Central Africa because they are unorganized forest dwellers with little political power.

## URBANISM, ARCHITECTURE, AND THE USE OF SPACE

The Republic of Congo is one of the most urbanized countries in Africa, with almost two-thirds of the population living in the urban conglomeration from Brazzaville to Pointe Moiré. Urban houses are made of concrete, often with a small garden attached. Villages are arranged with one large dirt street in the middle and many smaller streets running perpendicular to it. Many houses are built of mud brick with thatched or metal roofs. Cooking takes place in the front of the house, along with social interaction.

## FOOD AND ECONOMY

**Food in Daily Life.** The rain forest soil is not nutrient-rich; less than 3 percent of the land is cultivated for food production. Meat is expensive because it has to be hunted or imported. For this reason, little meat is eaten. Bananas, pineapples, taro, peanuts, manioc, cassava, rice, and bread are the staples.

**Food Customs at Ceremonial Occasions.** Food taboos depend on the tribe and village. If a family has a totem, it cannot eat that animal, which is considered a spiritual protector. At major festivals, meat, usually chicken, is eaten. Plum wine and beer are consumed at these times.

**Basic Economy.** Agriculture, industry, and services dominate the economy. The most important products are lumber, plywood, sugar, cocoa, coffee, diamonds, and especially oil.

**Land Tenure and Property.** Under communist rule, the government was the owner of all commercial property. After the civil war, privatization was decreed. Almost 90 percent of homes are now owned by individuals or families.

**Commercial Activities.** Minor agricultural products and light manufactured goods are sold in informal street markets.

**Major Industries.** The major industry is petroleum extraction. Cement kilning, forestry, brewing, sugar milling, palm oil, soap, and cigarette making also are important industries.

**Trade.** The largest export partner is the United States, followed by Belgium and Luxembourg, Taiwan, and China. Oil accounted for 50 percent of the gross national product in 1997. Imported items include manufactured goods, capital equipment, petroleum products, construction materials, and food. These items are imported from France, Italy, the United States and the United Kingdom. The country is deeply in debt.

## SOCIAL STRATIFICATION

**Classes and Castes.** Under communism, urban and educated people had jobs and could make more money than rural people, who had a lifestyle closer to that of the ethnic tribes. Discrimination against the pygmies, known as Teke, Aka, or forest dwellers, is widespread. They are turned away from hospitals, receive lower pay, and are not represented in the government.

**Symbols of Social Stratification.** Because of communism and local social customs, few people have accumulated personal wealth. General indicators of prosperity are education, large houses, and money.

## POLITICAL LIFE

**Government.** A transitional government has ruled since 1997, when President Denis Sassou-Nguesso forcefully took over the government with the aid of Angolan troops. He defeated Pascal Lissouba, who had won the 1992 elections, the first democratic election in twenty-eight years. Under Lissouba, the government had experienced accusations of mismanagement and conflict with other political parties that led to a civil war.

When Sassou-Nguesso regained power, he replaced the constitution of 1992 with the Fundamental Act. This act gave the president the power to appoint all the members of the government and military officers, serve as commander in chief, and direct the policy of the government. Thus, the act created a highly centralized government with the president as the head of state and head of government. The legislative and judicial branches currently exist in a weakened form.

From 1965 to 1990, a Marxist form of government was in place.

**Leadership and Political Officials.** Fubert Youlou became the first president in 1960. Within three years, he was forced to resign because of military and economic pressures. Socialist forces gained strength, and the government nationalized

countries. Both national and rebel forces committed summary executions and rapes. Civilians were convicted of being rebels and executed without a trial. Many soldiers on both sides were undisciplined, and mob violence was common. Electricity and the infrastructure were disrupted during the civil war, causing water and food shortages, disease, and displacement that involved almost a third of the population.

**Military Activity.** The military includes trained and untrained soldiers. The available force consists of 641,543 males, about half of whom are fit for service.

## SOCIAL WELFARE AND CHANGE PROGRAMS

Internal strife placed international organizations in the lead role in revealing government and human rights abuses. The country began receiving economic and social aid before it became officially independent. International economic aid ended with the onset of the civil war, but local and international humanitarian groups continued to operate.

## NONGOVERNMENTAL ORGANIZATIONS AND OTHER ASSOCIATIONS

The government has allowed nongovernmental organizations (NGOs) to operate in some areas. This has given the NGOs considerable power. Among the forty major organizations active in the country are the United Nations, Medecins sans Frontieres, the UN Food and Agriculture Organization, the International Monetary Fund, UNESCO, and the World Health Organization. The country is a member of the Organization of African Unity, the Economic Commission for Africa, and the Central African Customs and Economic Union and an associate member of the European Commission.

## GENDER ROLES AND STATUSES

**Division of Labor by Gender.** According to the Fundamental Act, discrimination based on race or sex is illegal, and equal pay for equal work is mandated. In the workplace, women are underrepresented. This forces them into the informal sector, where no rules are enforced. Employment benefits are therefore negligible. It is estimated that 51 percent of women are economically active, compared to 84 percent of men. Women accounted for 39 percent of economically active persons in 1990.

Women typically are responsible for labor in and around the house; this includes planting, har-

*A man waits to see the pope, who was on a state visit to the Republic of Congo in 1980.*

economic interests under the second president, Alphonse Massamba-Debat, who was forced out by a military coup in 1968. Major Marien Ngouabi then took over the leadership, establishing a one-party state and a people's republic. In 1977, he was assassinated.

After a short period of military rule, Colonel Joachim Yhomby-Opango was appointed president. He found former president Massamba-Debat and others guilty of planning Ngouabi's assassination. Less then two years after Yhomby-Opango became president, his own party forced him from office.

The presidency was then conferred on Colonel Denis Sassou-Naguesso. Former president Yhomby-Opango was tried for treason and stripped of possessions and power. Sassou-Naguesso served until 1992, when Lissouba was elected. After the civil war, in which Lissouba lost to Sassou-Naguesso, high-level officials, including Lissouba and former Prime Minister Kolelas, left the country, fearing a war-crimes trial.

**Social Problems and Control.** Civil war and political instability have caused large-scale violence. The rebels were mostly from the south, and nationalist forces came from the north and from neighboring

A group of women and soldiers during a 1980 visit by Pope John Paul II to Brazzaville, Congo. Roughly 50 percent of Congo natives practice Christianity.

vesting, food preparation, water fetching, minor housework, and child rearing. Men in rural areas hunt; those in urban areas are the family money earners.

**The Relative Status of Women and Men.** Women are underrepresented in politics and the higher levels of the government. In rural areas, women are often discouraged from attaining paid employment and education at the high school level. They are instead encouraged to focus on family and child-rearing activities. This gives them limited power in social dealings with men, who typically are better educated and have more money. Nongovernmental organizations such as the Ministry of Public Service and the Promotion of Women have started government initiatives to improve the status of women.

## MARRIAGE, FAMILY, AND KINSHIP

**Marriage.** Traditionally, family members arranged marriages. Today, this is less common, especially in the cities. A practice that dates back to ancient times is the dot, or brideprice. Once price has been set between the two families, the groom must pay it to the wife's family. The dot is often very high.

After the marriage, a ritual is performed to demonstrate the virginity of the bride. The morning after the wedding night, women from both sides of the family go to the couple's bed. Questions are asked about the wedding night, and the presence of blood provides evidence of virginity. If virginity is not proved, the marriage can be annulled and the groom can ask for the return of the brideprice.

After a divorce the man can ask for his brideprice back. Because most women can not repay it, divorce is mostly a male option. Polygyny is allowed, but polyandry is illegal. Adultery is illegal only for women.

**Domestic Unit.** The concept of the nuclear family does not apply in much of the country. The family includes many relatives, such as grandparents, uncles, aunts, cousins, nephews, and nieces. The average woman bears five children, although in rural areas the number is often twice that high.

**Inheritance.** The Legal Code states that 30 percent of a husband's estate must go to his widow. Very often this code is not adhered to, and a surviving wife may not get any of her husband's assets.

**Kin Groups.** Many of the ethnic groups, including the Bakongo, are matrilineal. The oldest uncle on

*A group of women holding papal flags and wooden crosses on the streets of Congo.*

the mother's side is considered the most important male and sometimes has more influence over a child's life than does the father. This uncle can be responsible for the child's education, employment, and marriage selection. Cousins on the mother's side are considered siblings. The family is responsible for sick, handicapped, and elderly members. Any care that is needed is distributed throughout the entire family system.

## SOCIALIZATION

*Infant Care.* The infant mortality rate is high, and for this reason women tend to bear many children. Care of infants is largely a female responsibility, though forest dwellers tend to share parental duties.

*Child Rearing and Education.* For decades, Brazzaville was the capital of education in Central Africa. A mostly urban population and the need for civil servants in a Marxist society fueled the system. The education was of such high quality that neighboring countries sent students to study in the secondary schools and the university. The civil war caused a decline in funding for schools and a subsequent decline in enrollment. Adult literacy is are around 70 percent, one of the highest levels in sub-Saharan Africa. There are many rural schools.

*Higher Education.* Marien Ngouabi University is the main center for higher education and once had an enrollment of ten thousand students. Parts of the school were destroyed during the civil war and families that can afford it send their children abroad.

## ETIQUETTE

The Congolese take great pride in their appearance and manner of dress. Regardless of financial status, it is common to wear clean and pressed handmade garments. There is a certain formality in social interactions in both urban and rural areas. An inquiry must be made about one's health and family to indicate the required level of respect. Older people are shown respect through physical gestures, and agreement with them is considered more important than frankness.

## RELIGION

*Religious Beliefs.* There is no official state religion; the Fundamental Act mandates freedom of religion. About 50 percent of the people are Christian. Forty-eight percent of the people adhere to native religions and the remaining 2 percent are Muslim. Varying combinations of Christianity and animism have developed. In some rural areas, Christian missionaries have had little success in converting the forest dwellers.

Before the coming of Christianity, all the native religions were animist. The monotheistic religion of Nzambi is widely practiced among the Bakongo. In this tradition, Nzambi created the world after a great sickness, vomiting first the sun, then the stars, animals, and people. After the creation, he went to live with the ancestral spirits. It is believed that family members join the ancestral world after death to protect the living. In cases of wrongful or violent death, they roam until retribution has occurred. Medicine and religion are often indistinguishable in the native religions.

## MEDICINE AND HEALTH CARE

In 1996, life expectancy was forty-nine years for men and fifty-three years for women. AIDS affected 100,000 residents in 1997. The civil war and the financial crisis have hindered anti-AIDS programs and worsened public health. Sixty percent of the people have access to safe water and immunization, but only 9 percent have access to sanitary services.

## SECULAR CELEBRATION

The major holidays are Christmas, New Year's, Easter, All Saints Day, National Reconciliation Day (10 June), Tree Day (6 March), and Independence Day (15 August).

## ARTS AND HUMANITIES

**Literature.** Storytelling is part of the cultural tradition. Since the introduction of written language, novels, plays, and poems have become more popular.

**Performance Arts.** The Congolese are known for their singing. Songs fill the air during the performance of chores and recently have been recorded. Rumba and other forms of music are played with native and Western instruments.

## THE STATE OF THE PHYSICAL AND SOCIAL SCIENCES

The civil war has had a deleterious effect on the sciences and education.

## BIBLIOGRAPHY

Gall, Tim, ed. *Worldmark Encyclopedia of Cultures and Daily Life*, 2000.

Fegley, Randall. *The Congo.*

Rajewski, Brain, ed. *Countries of the World*, 1998.

Schmittroth, Linda, ed. *Statistical Record of Women Worldwide*, 1995.

Stewart, Gary. *Rumba on the River.*

Thompson, Virginia and Richard Adloff. *Historical Dictionary of the People's Republic of Congo*, 1984.

U.S. Department of State. *Country Reports on Human Rights Practices.*

U.S. Department of State, Central Intelligence Agency. *CIA World Factbook*, 2000.

—DAVID MATUSKEY

# COOK ISLANDS

## CULTURE NAME

Cook Islander

## ORIENTATION

**Identification.** The country is named after Captain James Cook, who landed there in 1773.

**Location and Geography.** The Cook Islands are part of Oceania, a group of islands in the South Pacific roughly halfway between Hawaii and New Zealand, lying between American Samoa and Tahiti. Their total area is 93 square miles (240 square kilometers). The islands are dispersed over nearly two million square kilometers of ocean. The southern islands, which make up 90 percent of the land area, are hilly terrain of recent volcanic origin; Rarotonga is the most mountainous. The northern islands are coral atolls that have formed over ancient sunken volcanoes and are characterized by outer reefs surrounding a lagoon. There are several species of birds but few native plants and animals; the only indigenous mammal is the Pacific fruit bat.

**Demography.** The population is 20,407 (July 2000 estimate). Among the residents, 81 percent are full-blooded Polynesian, 8 percent are mixed Polynesian and European, 8 percent are mixed Polynesian and non-European, and 2 percent are European. Among the Polynesian people, there are slight variations from island to island; northerners, for example, are more closely related to Samoans than they are to other Cook Islanders. More than 90 percent of the population is concentrated in the southern islands, and over 50 percent on Rarotonga. The population is declining, as many residents have emigrated to Australia and New Zealand; there are more Cook Islanders in New Zealand than in the islands.

**Linguistic Affiliation.** English is the official language and is taught in school. The common vernacular is Cook Islands Maori, also called Rarotongan, which is similar to the Maori spoken in New Zealand and Tahiti. Dialects vary, and in the north, some islands have their own languages.

**Symbolism.** The flag has a blue background with a Union Jack in the upper lefthand corner. In the center of the flag is a circle of fifteen white five-pointed stars, one for each of the fifteen islands.

## HISTORY AND ETHNIC RELATIONS

**Emergence of the Nation.** Archeologists trace the settlement of the islands to the fourth century C.E.; the oral history of Raratonga (the most influential island and the first one to be settled) dates back about 1,400 years.

The first European sighting occurred in 1595, when the Spaniard Alvaro de Mendana glimpsed Pukapuka, one of the northern islands. In 1606, Pedro Fernandez de Quirós landed on Rakahanga in the north. Captain Cook was the first European to explore the land extensively. He arrived in 1773 and returned in 1777. Cook's name was bestowed on the southern islands in an 1835 atlas. At that time, the northern group was known as the Penrhyn Islands or the Manihiki Islands.

Christian missionaries had an important large impact on the islands. They decimated the population by introducing diseases such as whooping cough, measles, and smallpox. However, culturally they did not attempt to eradicate all indigenous traditions. The first missionary on the islands was the Reverend John Williams of the London Missionary Society, who landed on Aitutaki in 1821. Another influential figure was Papeiha, a convert from the Society Islands who moved to Rarotonga in 1823.

In 1888, the British declared the islands a protectorate to counter the French, who were increasing their colonial holdings in the South Pacific. In 1900, New Zealand annexed Rarotonga and the other main islands in the southern group; this was

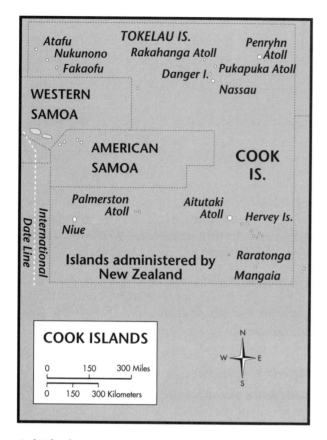

*Cook Islands*

extended the next year to include the northern islands. The goal was eventual self-sufficiency for the islands, but despite their agricultural potential, this has not happened. In 1965, the islands gained the right to self-government in internal affairs, but defense and foreign policy remain under the control of New Zealand.

Albert Henry of the Cook Islands Party (CIP), a major figure in the independence movement, was elected prime minister in 1968. He was knighted in 1974, but the honor was revoked in 1980 because of claims of corruption. When Henry died in 1981, Dr. Thomas Davis of the Democratic Party became prime minister. Several years of relative political instability followed; power changed hands a few times between 1983 and 1989, when Geoffrey Henry, Henry's nephew, became prime minister. His government did not have widespread popular support, but Geoffrey Henry was knighted in 1992, and the CIP won by a large majority in the 1994 elections.

In the mid 1990s, a controversy known as the "winebox affair" surfaced: the islands were accused by New Zealand of illegal practices in offshore banking and international tax evasion. The affair developed into an international scandal, but the nation's misdeeds were never proved in court. However, economic problems continued to beset the country, including a trade imbalance. In April 1996, Prime Minister Henry announced a 50 percent cut in government departments and privatized a number of government-owned businesses. Many of the recently fired government employees left for New Zealand and Australia. The tourism industry suffered for several years as well.

**National Identity.** Cook Islanders identify first with their individual islands and secondarily with the country as a whole. There is a strong sense of connection with New Zealand; Cook Islanders have citizenship, and many emigrate or have relatives there.

**Ethnic Relations.** There is some resentment toward Europeans because of the islands' colonial heritage, but it is acknowledged that Europeans generate a large proportion of the nation's income in the form of tourism.

## URBANISM, ARCHITECTURE, AND THE USE OF SPACE

The capital, Avarua, is the largest city but is more like a small town. Located on the northern coast of Rarotonga, it has an old harbor and one main road that follows the waterfront. Much of the architecture is colonial, including the Cook Islands Christian Church, which was built in 1855.

Traditional houses, called *kikau*, have panadus-thatched roofs. Few of these structures remain, mostly on the northern islands. In the south, this architecture remains only on the island of Aitutaki in a village called New Jerusalem. On Rarotonga, this style of building is prohibited because it is considered inferior to European architecture and bears a certain stigma.

## FOOD AND ECONOMY

**Food in Daily Life.** *Rori* (sea cucumbers) are eaten raw or cooked with butter, garlic, and spices. Fish is eaten both raw and cooked. Raw fish, called *ika*, is marinated in lemon juice or a mixture of vinegar, oil, and salt and served with chopped onion and coconut cream. Young taro leaves are mashed and mixed with coconut cream, salt, and chopped onion in a dish called *rukau*.

Coconut water is a popular beverage, as are fruit juices and coffee. Beer, called bush beer, is brewed from oranges, bananas, pawpaws, or hops.

Traditional cooking is elaborate and time-consuming. Food is prepared in an *umu*, an oven dug in the earth and filled with firewood and basalt rocks. A grill of banana wood is placed over the hot stones. Food is wrapped in banana leaves and then in sacks and thrown into the pit, which is covered with soil and allowed to sit for about three hours.

**Food Customs at Ceremonial Occasions.** Special occasions are marked by a feast called an *umukai* (literally "food from the oven"). Meat is the main dish, supplemented with ika and potato salad. Kava, made from the root of the pepper plant, is a traditional ceremonial drink. It is nonalcoholic but can be consciousness-altering. Christian missionaries virtually eliminated the drink from the islands; today, the word "kava" is used for any alcoholic beverage.

**Basic Economy.** Economic development has been hampered by geographic isolation, a lack of natural resources, and natural disasters. The country has a severe trade imbalance that is partly compensated for by foreign aid from New Zealand and by remittances sent by islanders living abroad. The New Zealand dollar is the currency used. Most economic growth is in tourism, offshore banking, and the mining and fishing industries.

**Land Tenure and Property.** There are laws prohibiting the buying or selling of land. Ownership is hereditary; land can be leased, but outsiders are not allowed to own land. Land is divided among the descendants after the death of the owner. As a result of this system, a family may possess several plots scattered over an island.

**Commercial Activities.** Commercial activity centers on the tourist industry. The islands (Rarotonga in particular) are dotted with hotels, resorts, and restaurants that cater to tourists.

**Major Industries.** The major industries are fruit processing and tourism. Rarotonga receives nearly fifty thousand tourists a year.

**Trade.** The islands import large quantities of products, including food, textiles, fuels, timber, and capital goods. Forty-nine percent of imports come from New Zealand, and the remainder primarily from Italy and Australia. Exports include agricultural products (copra, papayas, fresh and canned citrus fruit, coffee, and fish), pearls and pearl shells, and clothing. Eighty percent of exports go to New Zealand; the rest are sent to Japan and Hong Kong.

**Division of Labor.** People are relatively free to work in the profession of their choice. Twenty-nine percent of the labor force works in agriculture, 15 percent in industry, and 56 percent in services.

## SOCIAL STRATIFICATION

**Classes and Castes.** Class traditionally was determined by a hereditary system of titles. Today, status is determined more by education and profession, and there is a good deal of social mobility.

**Symbols of Social Stratification.** The majority of residents today wear Western-style clothing. Dress is often casual, with the exception of churchgoing on Sundays. The traditional outfit of short, fringed grass skirts, headbands, and collars is worn mainly for dances and other celebrations. Both men and women wear flowers in their hair. Traditionally, fat is a symbol of wealth and beauty, and at puberty boys and girls undergo ritual seclusion and feedings to gain weight. However, this is changing as Western standards of beauty have begun to exert more influence.

## POLITICAL LIFE

**Government.** The chiefs of state are the British monarch and the New Zealand high commissioner. The head of the government is the prime minister, who appoints a cabinet. The unicameral parliament has twenty-five members elected by popular vote for five-year terms. Twenty-four members represent different districts, and one represents islanders living in New Zealand. The prime minister is not chosen by election; this position goes to the leader of the party that wins the most seats in the parliament. The indigenous ruling body is the House of Arikis (chiefs). The chiefs advise the government on matters relating to tradition but do not have legislative power.

**Leadership and Political Officials.** The Cook Islands Party was the party largely responsible for independence. The two other parties are the Democratic Alliance Party and the New Alliance Party.

**Social Problems and Control.** Violent crime is rare, but petty theft is becoming more common, particularly on Rarotonga. The legal system is based on New Zealand law and English common law.

**Military Activity.** The Cook Islands do not have a military. They depend on New Zealand, which defends the islands at their request, in consultation with the islands' government.

*Thatched cottages and plants line a street in New Jerusalem, Aitutaki. These are some of the last remaining examples of traditional houses, called Kikau.*

## NONGOVERNMENTAL ORGANIZATIONS AND OTHER ASSOCIATIONS

The country participates in several international organizations, including UNESCO and the World Health Organization.

## GENDER ROLES AND STATUSES

***Division of Labor by Gender.*** Women are responsible for domestic work; men do all the fishing and heavy labor such as construction. Women often work outside the home. Until recently, men dominated most positions in management and government, but this situation is changing.

***The Relative Status of Women and Men.*** Women are treated with respect, primarily in relation to their roles as wives and mothers. Women are in charge of family finances and oversee the land, determining which crops to plant. At the level of the church and village, women are the primary administrators. Domestic violence against women is punished strictly.

## MARRIAGE, FAMILY, AND KINSHIP

***Marriage.*** Polygamy has been eliminated because of the influence of the Christian churches. There is a good deal of freedom in choosing one's spouse, and it is not uncommon for couples to have a trial marriage before wedding. Divorce and separation are fairly common, as are common-law marriages.

***Domestic Unit.*** The extended family is highly valued, and it is common for various relatives and generations to live under the same roof. A newly married couple usually lives with one set of in-laws until they have the means to establish a residence of their own.

***Inheritance.*** Inheritance is not gender-specific. When a mother dies, land passes jointly to all her children.

***Kin Groups.*** Society is divided into family clans, each of which is linked to the ancient system of chiefs. Rarotonga has six clans (*ariki*), which were established centuries ago, when the Maoris first settled on the island and divided the land.

## SOCIALIZATION

***Infant Care.*** Infants are given a lot of attention and are treated with indulgence.

534

*A village store in Arutanga. Stores often cater to tourists, who make up a large portion of the Cook Island economy.*

**Child Rearing and Education.** The teaching of Christian values and respect for elders is an important aspect of child rearing. Education is free and compulsory from age five through age fifteen. There are twenty-eight primary schools and seven secondary schools.

**Higher Education.** There are several institutions of post secondary education. There are training programs for nurses and teachers as well as an apprenticeship program for various trades and a Cook Island Christian Church theological college that trains ministers. There is a branch of the Fiji-based University of the South Pacific in Avarua. Many people send their children to New Zealand, Australia, or other South Pacific countries to receive higher education. The government provides scholarships to students for studying abroad.

## ETIQUETTE

Cook Islanders are known for their hospitable and generous, if somewhat reserved, nature. When invited to someone's home, it is customary to bring a small gift for the host. Upon returning from a voyage, travelers are greeted with a garland of flowers placed around their necks; they are seen off the same way before departures.

## RELIGION

**Religious Beliefs.** Virtually all the people are Christian; 70 percent belong to the Protestant Cook Islands Christian Church (CICC) and 30 percent are Roman Catholic, Seventh Day Adventist, Mormon, or members of other denominations. Little is known about the indigenous religion, which had a complex system of seventy-one gods, each of which was responsible for a specific aspect of life; this religion also believed in twelve levels of heaven, some of which were located above the earth, and some below.

**Religious Practitioners.** Ministers are the central figures in the CICC. They are held in high esteem and have a great responsibility to their congregations. People express approval or dissatisfaction with a minister through the size of their donations to the local church.

**Rituals and Holy Places.** There are churches throughout the islands, and many residents attend regularly, dressing up in white straw hats. Sermons are in Maori. (The Bible was translated into Maori in the 1880s.) Singing is an integral part of services, and hymns often incorporate traditional Polynesian harmonies.

*A woman sits on the floor making a colorful quilt in the city of Aitutaki.*

The site of worship in traditional religious practice is called a *marae*. Despite the fact that the indigenous religion has been supplanted by Christianity, *marae* still hold significance for many people, particularly on Rarotonga.

**Death and the Afterlife.** Burial vaults are located in the front yards of houses. Usually, the woman who built the house is buried there. Women's coffins are sealed in these concrete structures because it is considered disrespectful to cover their bodies in dirt after death. Graves are only cared for by friends or family of the deceased. When no survivors remain, the tops of the burial vaults are removed and the land is plowed over.

## MEDICINE AND HEALTH CARE

Health care is provided by the government, but the system is relatively primitive. Each island has a hospital, but some of the more remote hospitals are very poorly equipped. People generally are sent to the hospital in Rarotonga or New Zealand for serious illnesses. Some people rely on traditional medicines and faith healers in addition to the Western medicine that is available.

## SECULAR CELEBRATIONS

New Year's Day is celebrated 1 January. Anzac Day on 25 April commemorates Cook Islanders killed in World War II. The queen's birthday is celebrated on the first Monday in June. Constitution Day is celebrated on 4 August; the ten-day festivities include sports and dancing. Flag Raising Day occurs on 27 October. Tiare (Floral) Festival Week is held in the last week in November; it includes parades and other festivities.

## THE ARTS AND HUMANITIES

**Support for the Arts.** Avarua is home to the National Library, which has a collection of rare books and literature about the Pacific. The National Museum displays traditional arts and handicrafts. The capital has the Sir Geoffrey Henry National Cultural Centre, which was built in 1992.

**Literature.** The literary tradition is primarily one of legends and stories passed orally from one generation to the next. Many of these stories have been written down and published. One of the best known writers in the twentieth century was Manihikan Kauraka Kauraka, who published both renderings of traditional tales and original poetry, stories, and nonfiction writings.

**Graphic Arts.** The islands are known for a textile art called *tivaevae*, practiced by women, which combines appliqué and embroidery. Tivaevae decorates bedspreads and cushion covers. Flower art is popular in the form of *ei* (necklaces) and *ei katu* (tiaras). Jewelry made from black pearls is another specialty. Other traditional arts and crafts include woven pandanus mats, baskets, purses, and fans.

**Performance Arts.** The islands are known for music (primarily fast, complex drumming) and dance, in particular the fast, hip-swinging *tamure*, which is performed in traditional costumes consisting of grass skirts and headbands. Many of these performances are held for tourists on so-called Island Nights at hotels. They also are staged during the annual Dance Week every April and during Constitution Week in the summer.

## THE STATE OF THE PHYSICAL AND SOCIAL SCIENCES

There are few facilities for the study of the physical and social sciences.

## BIBLIOGRAPHY

Baltaxe, James Bernard. *Transformation of the Rangatira: A case of the European Reinterpretation of Rarotongan Social Organization*, 1975.

Beaglehole, Ernest. *Social Change in the South Pacific: Rarotonga and Aitutaki*, 1957.

Buck, Peter Henry. *Arts and Crafts of the Cook Islands*, 1944.

———. *Material Culture of the Cook Islands (Aitutaki)*, 1976.

Campbell, Andrew Teariki, ed. *Impressions of Tongareva (Penrhyn Island) 1816–1901*, 1984.

———. *Social Relations in Ancient Tongareva*, 1985.

Crocombe, R. G. *Land Tenure in the Cook Islands*, 1964.

Feizkhah, Elizabeth. "Large Load, Heavy Soil, High Spin." *Time South Pacific*, February 28, 2000.

Gilson, Richard. *Cook Islands 1820–1950*, 1980.

Harmon, Jeff B. "Ignoring the Missionary Position." *New Statesman*, August 21, 1998.

Kauraka, Kauraka. *Legends from the Atolls*, 1984.

### Web Sites

U.S. State Department, Central Intelligence Agency. *The Cook Islands*, www.odci.gov/cia/publications/factbook/geos/cw

—ELEANOR STANFORD

# COSTA RICA

**CULTURE NAME**

Costa Rican

**ALTERNATIVE NAMES**

Ticos

## ORIENTATION

**Identification.** In 1502, Columbus stopped near present-day Limón, Costa Rica. Natives with "golden mirrors around their necks" told of "many places ... [with] gold and mines." Subsequent chroniclers called the region "Costa Rica"—Rich Coast—although it turned out to be among the poorest of Spain's colonies.

Costa Ricans are called *ticos*, which derives from their appending the Spanish *-ico* diminutive to the standard *-ito*.

**Location and Geography.** Costa Rica is located in Central America with Nicaragua to its north and Panama to its south. Its territory is 19,652 square miles (51,022 square kilometers). Volcanic mountains—several of which produce sporadic eruptions— run northwest to southeast, dividing Costa Rica into Pacific and Atlantic zones. There are frequent earthquakes.

The capital, San José, is on the *meseta central*, a plateau twenty-five miles by twelve miles (40 kilometers by 20 kilometers). The *meseta* is in the Central Valley—an area five times as large as the plateau— which includes three other cities in addition to San José.

Temperature varies with altitude, averaging over 86 degrees Fahrenheit (30 degrees Celsius) in the coastal lowlands, but only 64 degrees Fahrenheit (18 degrees Celsius) at the higher elevations. The Atlantic zone receives trade winds and has high rainfall year-round. The Pacific zone has fertile volcanic and alluvial soils and distinct wet and dry seasons. The northern Pacific suffers frequent droughts, associated with the Niño phenomenon.

There are many rivers, but few are navigable. Pacific ports include Puntarenas, Quepos, and Golfito. Two modern ports, Caldera and Punta Morales, were built near Puntarenas in the 1980s. The major Atlantic port, Limón, is unprotected from tropical storms. Moín, north of Limón, has container and petroleum facilities.

Costa Rica's broken topography creates myriad microenvironments. One-quarter of the territory endures practically in its wild state with rainforests, dry tropical forest, and savannas. Costa Rica has a level of biodiversity—4 to 7 percent of the world total—unmatched by any other nation its size.

**Demography.** In 2000, Costa Rica's population was four million, with 60 percent living in the Central Valley in and around Cartago, San José, Heredia, and Alajuela. Thirty-two percent of the population was 14 years old or under, while 5 percent was 65 or older. Annual population growth was 2.03 percent.

The country had 21.9 births and 4.0 deaths per 1,000 population in 2000, and a net migration rate of 2.4. Average fertility was 2.7, down from 5.4 in 1973 and 7.3 in 1960. The drop in birth rates was attributed to rising female literacy, to a decline in the proportion of the population working in agriculture, and to increased access to family planning. Despite the influential Catholic Church's opposition to contraception, in 1990, 86 percent of sexually active women of childbearing age used birth control.

**Linguistic Affiliation.** Spanish is the official language, but the variant spoken has features particular to Costa Rica. On the Atlantic coast, however, descendants of Caribbean immigrants speak English, as do many others throughout the country who learned it to better their employment prospects.

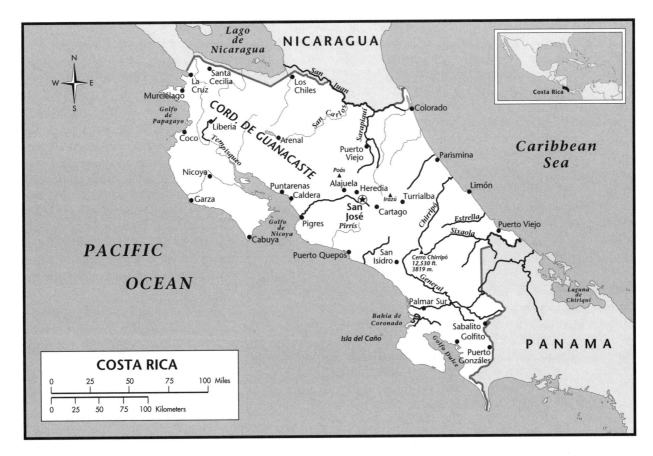

Costa Rica

**Symbolism.** The national flag, a partial imitation of the French tricolor, consists of blue horizontal stripes on the top and bottom of the flag and two white inner stripes divided by a wide red stripe, which contains the national coat of arms to the left of center. Aside from the flag and religious icons, important symbols include flags of the major political parties (green and white for the National Liberation Party; red and blue for the Social Christians) and of the most popular soccer teams.

## HISTORY AND ETHNIC RELATIONS

**Emergence of the Nation.** Costa Rica gained independence from Spain as part of the Mexican Empire (1821–1823) and the Central American Federation (1823–1838). In 1824 it annexed much of the province of Guanacaste from Nicaragua. In the 1850s, Costa Rican troops joined Nicaraguans and Hondurans to defeat William Walker's pro-slavery filibusters. This campaign sparked proto-nationalist sentiment, and it was only then that the term *nación* began to be used to refer to Costa Rica rather than to all of Central America.

**National Identity.** Elites had to improvise a national identity following independence. The main hero of the campaign against the United States filibusters, martyred drummer boy Juan Santamaría, was "discovered" as a national icon decades after the conflict ended. Border disputes with Nicaragua and Colombia (to which Panama belonged until 1903) fanned feelings of distinctiveness in the late nineteenth century, as did the creation of a national school system.

Costa Ricans pride themselves on having a society "different" from the rest of Central America. They point to their country's high levels of education and health, its renowned national parks, and its history of democracy and political stability. Despite this "exceptionalism," the country shares many social, economic, and environmental problems with its neighbors.

**Ethnic Relations.** As much as 95 percent of Costa Ricans consider themselves "white." "Whiteness" figures importantly in national identity. The indigenous population that survived the conquest was small and, for the most part, rapidly became Hispanic. In the eighteenth and nineteenth centuries, successful males of African, Indian, or mixed ancestry married poorer ''Spanish'' women, using ''whitening'' to assure their children's upward mobility. In the nineteenth century, immigration from Europe and the United States ''whitened'' the population, particularly the elite. During the twentieth century, the definition of ''whiteness'' became more inclusive, as elites sought to convince mestizos that they were part of a ''homogeneous'' nation distinct from the ''Indians'' elsewhere in Central America.

In Guanacaste and northern Puntarenas, much of the population is descended from Indians and colonial-era slaves. They are Hispanic in culture and language, though their pronunciation resembles Nicaraguan more than central Costa Rican Spanish.

Concentrated in Limón Province, Afro-Costa Ricans—the descendants of Jamaican and other British West Indians who immigrated in the nineteenth century for work on the Atlantic Railroad, plantations, and docks—are more widely perceived as ''black.'' (These Afro-Costa Ricans are part of an English-speaking Protestant group extending along the entire Caribbean coast of Central America.) Blacks—denied Costa Rican nationality until 1948—were blocked by law and discrimination from working elsewhere, so Limón remained culturally distinct until the mid-twentieth century.

On the Atlantic side of the Talamanca mountains, the Bribri and Cabécar—the largest indigenous groups—speak related languages and share a culture that varies only slightly from one locality to another, depending on the degree of contact with Hispanic society. They maintain clan marriage rules, collective agricultural production, and a religion centered around the deity Sibö the Creator. The six reserves on the Pacific side of the Talamanca cordillera and in the nearby lowlands also are home to the Bribris and Cabécares and to smaller numbers of Borucas (or Bruncas) and Teribes (or Térrabas), the latter two groups having assimilated into the peasant population.

Guaymí Indians live in southern Puntarenas. Many move between these communities and Panama, and until 1991 those born in Costa Rica lacked identity documents and access to state services. The Guaymíes maintain their language and distinct way of life, despite growing reliance on wage labor.

At the end of the twentieth century, five hundred Indians—descendants of a group that numbered well over one thousand in the late nineteenth century—lived in the north along the Río Frío in Alajuela Province. The Guatusos (or Malecus) violently repulsed outsiders' incursions until the 1870s when rubber tappers began to kill Indian men and kidnap women and children, who were sold as slaves in Nicaragua. The population plummeted to below two hundred, never recovering even half its pre-contact size.

Matambú, in Guanacaste, is the only indigenous reserve in the northern Pacific area once populated by peoples whose culture resembled that of central Mexico. The Chorotegas practiced maize agriculture and were among the first targets of the Spanish conquest in the area that became Costa Rica. Culturally, members of the Matambú community are indistinguishable from the surrounding peasantry, participating in saints' brotherhoods (something emblematic of ''Indian'' identity) and producing ceramics with indigenous motifs for tourists.

Many of the first Spanish colonists in Costa Rica may have been Jewish converts to Christianity who were expelled from Spain in 1492 and fled to colonial backwaters to avoid the Inquisition. The first sizable group of self-identified Jews immigrated from Poland, beginning in 1929. From the 1930s to the early 1950s, journalistic and official anti-Semitic campaigns fueled harassment of Jews; however, by the 1950s and 1960s, the immigrants won greater acceptance. Most of the 2,000 Costa Rican Jews today are not highly observant, but they remain largely endogamous.

In 1873 the Atlantic Railroad imported 653 Chinese indentured laborers, hoping to duplicate the success of rail projects that used Chinese labor in Peru, Cuba, and the United States. Many Chinese fled the snake-infested lowlands, while others died from malaria, landslides, and overseers' brutality. In 1897 the government banned Chinese immigration and anti-Chinese feeling did not subside until World War II.

Other Central Americans had long come to Costa Rica to work in agriculture, especially in the banana zones. In the 1980s, Nicaraguans and Salvadorans fled violence and economic crises to work as farmhands, laborers, servants, and street vendors.

Many foreigners have taken advantage of the *Pensionado* Law, which grants residency to investors and exempts them from import duties. Most are retired United States citizens, but Chinese, Iranians, Arabs, Europeans, and Latin Americans also settled in Costa Rica under this law.

By the late twentieth century, allusions in textbooks and political discourse to ''whiteness,'' or to Spain as the ''mother country'' of all Costa Ricans, were diminishing, replaced with a recognition of the multiplicity of peoples that make up the nation.

## URBANISM, ARCHITECTURE, AND THE USE OF SPACE

Almost all towns have a central plaza with a Catholic church, government buildings, bandstand, and benches. Rural villages have grassy squares that double as soccer fields. Beyond the downtown grids are "urbanizations" that resemble U.S. subdivisions and then rural homesteads. There is little notable architecture aside from San José's ornate neo-classical National Theater. Few colonial constructions survive, and many contemporary buildings would elsewhere be considered kitsch. The cities suffer from severe air, water, and noise pollution.

## FOOD AND ECONOMY

**Food in Daily Life.** Maize is consumed as tortillas, which accompany rice and beans—typically eaten three times a day with eggs, cheese, meat, or chicken and with *chayote* stew or salad at lunch or supper. The midday meal was once the largest, but the long lunch break has succumbed to a fondness for fast food.

Beverages include coffee, sugary fruit drinks, and soda. Alcohol consumption is high.

**Food Customs at Ceremonial Occasions.** Salty appetizers are served at parties and at bars and restaurants. Maize *tamales* are prepared by hand for Christmas. Other special occasions (birthdays, graduations, marriages) may merit a roasted pig, an elaborate cake, or other sweets.

**Basic Economy.** Until the 1960s, Costa Rica depended on coffee and bananas for most of its export earnings. Coffee income was well distributed, which fueled a dynamic commercial sector. After the 1948 Civil War, nationalized banks channeled subsidized loans to neglected regions and new activities. In the 1960s, beef and sugar assumed greater importance, and the country began to industrialize, protected by Central American Common Market tariffs. Following a debt crisis in the early 1980s, the state reduced its role in the economy and promoted export-oriented agriculture and industries. Since the late 1990s, tourism has been the second largest source of dollars, after bananas.

**Land Tenure and Property.** Costa Rica has an image as an "agrarian democracy," but land distribution is highly unequal. Coffee farms are mostly

The National Theater of Costa Rica in San José, which is a national landmark due to its neo-classical style.

small, but sugar, banana, rice, and cattle farms may reach 24,700 or more acres (ten thousand hectares). Land reform programs in the 1960s and 1970s broke up some estates and distributed plots to peasants. Conflicts between large farmers and squatters are frequent and sometime result in violence.

**Commercial Activities.** City and town residents now rely on supermarkets rather than neighborhood stores and farmers' markets. Growing consumerism has spurred construction of malls where the affluent acquire the latest fashions and gadgets and the poor come to gawk and marvel at the high prices.

**Major Industries.** Since the mid-1980s, Costa Rica has become a center for factories that assemble garments, electronic components, and other goods for export. Other key manufactures include baseballs, agricultural chemicals, and processed foods. The economy is increasingly integrated into global circuits of trade, production, and finance.

**Trade.** Coffee and bananas are the country's chief agricultural exports, along with beef, sugar, flowers, nuts, and root vegetables.

***Division of Labor.*** The economy diversified after 1950, and new groups emerged. In 1997, agriculture accounted for 19 percent of employment and 15 percent of gross domestic product (GDP), under half of 1950 levels.

## SOCIAL STRATIFICATION

***Classes and Castes.*** Many upper-class families are descended from a few Spanish conquistadores. Levels of interaction between social classes were nonetheless high well into the twentieth century. Members of prominent families intermarried with other groups, especially wealthy European, Latin American, and North American immigrants. In Guanacaste and northern Puntarenas more rigid patterns of class relations are the norm.

The coffee elite, which dominated politics and society from the mid-nineteenth to the mid-twentieth century, derived most of its wealth from coffee processing and the export trade, not from ownership of plantations. Coffee also gave rise to a rural middle class. The Costa Rican middle class constitutes a larger proportion of the population—perhaps one-quarter—than in other Central American countries.

Costa Rica is no longer a country of peasants. The opening of the University of Costa Rica in 1940 and the expansion of the public sector after 1948 provided new opportunities for upwardly mobile young people. Yet poverty remained significant, affecting one-fifth of the population at the close of the twentieth century. Nonetheless, in 1999, the United Nations ranked Costa Rica fourth among developing nations worldwide that have made progress in eliminating severe poverty.

***Symbols of Social Stratification.*** The culture of consumption—in which clothes, cars, houses, and trips abroad are markers of status—is most conspicuous among members of the upper middle class, roughly 10 percent of the population.

## POLITICAL LIFE

***Government.*** The government has four branches: the executive, the unicameral Legislative Assembly, the judiciary, and the Supreme Electoral Tribunal. In addition, many autonomous public sector institutions were created in the 1960s and 1970s. Most were privatized, downsized, or abolished in the 1980s and 1990s.

***Leadership and Political Officials.*** Presidential and legislative elections are held every four years.

Presidents generally appoint cabinet ministers and many other central government officials and employees. Legislative deputies consolidate support through dispensing special budget appropriations (*partidas específicas*) in their districts.

Costa Ricans are passionate about party loyalties, which often run in families and generally date to the 1940s when a social democratic insurgency overthrew a Catholic-Communist reformist coalition government and ushered in the modern welfare state. The National Liberation Party (PLN) was social democratic, but embraced free-market policies in the 1980s. The Social Christian Unity Party (PUSC) has roots in social Christian reformism, but became more conservative than the PLN. Leftist parties declined. Regionalist parties occasionally elected legislative deputies or local officials.

***Social Problems and Control.*** With the economic crisis of the early 1980s, violent street crime skyrocketed and remains high today. Firearms from wars elsewhere in Central America were easily acquired. Costa Rica became a transshipment point for Colombian cocaine bound for the United States. The emergence of private financial institutions in the 1980s facilitated money laundering.

***Military Activity.*** The military was abolished following the 1948 Civil War. Security forces include the Civil Guard, Rural Guard, Judicial Police, and several smaller intelligence units. Private guards protect businesses and middle- and upper-class communities.

In the 1970s and 1980s, northern Costa Rica served as a base for armed Nicaraguan Sandinistas and then for anti-Sandinistas.

## SOCIAL WELFARE AND CHANGE PROGRAMS

Costa Rica has made remarkable strides in improving living standards. Most Costa Ricans enjoy access to free health care, basic education, and social services. Free-market policies have forced reductions in spending, but health and education indicators remain impressive.

## NONGOVERNMENTAL ORGANIZATIONS AND OTHER ASSOCIATIONS

Costa Rica hosts dozens of nongovernmental organizations, many of which operate throughout Central America. The business elite is organized in sectoral *cámaras* (chambers), which exercise enormous political influence. Public-sector and banana-worker unions were important until the 1980s.

*Farmers attending a cattle sale in Capelin, Liberia. Agriculture, especially bananas and coffee, is one of the biggest parts of the Costa Rican economy.*

Since then, employee-sponsored *solidarista* associations—which provide loans and other benefits—have replaced many unions.

## GENDER ROLES AND STATUSES

***Division of Labor by Gender.*** Women are still responsible for food preparation, childcare, and cleaning. Men rely on mothers and wives or hired help. The middle and upper classes employ servants for housework and childcare. Heavy agricultural labor is performed by men and adolescent boys. Women harvest coffee, cotton, and vegetables.

***The Relative Status of Women and Men.*** Gender relations are similar to those elsewhere in Latin America, although women have achieved greater equality than in some other countries. "Macho" practices—flirtatious remarks on the street, physical violence in the home—are widespread.

Gender relations are in flux, with marked differences between generations and social groups. Women increasingly combine traditional responsibilities with work and education. Men dominate business and politics, but many women have held cabinet posts or are prominent in arts and professions. A 1994 Law for Promoting the Women's Social Equality prohibited discrimination and established a women's rights office.

## MARRIAGE, FAMILY, AND KINSHIP

***Marriage.*** Costa Ricans' median age at first union is twenty-one for women and twenty-four for men. Premarital sex, expected of men, has become more common for women. Divorce and separation are frequent. Many upper-class men maintain mistresses and second families. The National Child Welfare Board garnishes wages of men who fail to pay child support and blocks them from traveling abroad.

***Domestic Unit.*** Most families are in practice extended, with elderly or other kin in the household and other relatives nearby. Female-headed, multigenerational households are common among the poor.

***Inheritance.*** Costa Ricans use their fathers' and mothers' last names to reckon descent. Inheritance is partible, but practiced with flexibility. Since 1994, the property of unmarried couples must be registered in the woman's name.

## SOCIALIZATION

*Infant Care.* Infants are dressed warmly, because "air" is considered harmful. Girls have their ears pierced shortly after birth. Almost half of mothers no longer breast feed. Most parents request that a friend or affluent neighbor be a godparent to their newborn.

*Child Rearing and Education.* Children are treated with indulgence until age four or five, when they tend to be disciplined more consistently. Disciplinary practices vary greatly, from corporal punishment to withholding treats. Poor children often help with chores at an early age. Primary school attendance is universal; secondary school enrollment rates are very high. The educational system emphasizes rote learning and memorization, rather than analytical thinking. The adult literacy rate is 95.1 percent (1997).

*Higher Education.* One-quarter of the university-age population enrolls in higher education. Four public universities enroll four-fifths of the students; the rest attend three dozen private institutions. The undergraduate curriculum consists of a year of education in liberal arts and sciences followed by three or four years of specialized courses, leading to a university bachelor's degree. Students may opt for a year of additional work, involving a written thesis, that leads to a *licenciatura*, the main credential required for most advanced positions. Medicine and law are undergraduate careers.

## ETIQUETTE

Costa Ricans consider themselves "cultured" and polite. Children, parents, and age-mates are often addressed in the formal second-person. Men greet each other with a handshake, while women greet female and male friends and relatives with a kiss. Dating and courtship, once highly ritualized, are approaching U.S. patterns. Much socializing goes on in restaurants and bars. Malicious gossip is common and a source of both delight and apprehension.

## RELIGION

*Religious Beliefs.* The Catholic heritage remains important in everyday language and culture. *Cristiano* is used as a synonym for "human being." Even those who are not religious like to have a religious medallion or picture of a saint in their cars or homes.

Costa Ricans demonstrate their Catholic faith mainly at baptisms, weddings, and funerals or dur-

*A brightly painted ox cart wheel, for which the town of Sarchi, Costa Rica, is famous.*

ing holy week and on saints' days. Although the official religion and a required subject in schools, Catholicism nevertheless coexists with other supernatural beliefs such as spirits and spells, even among the highly educated.

The principal challenge facing Catholicism is the rise of evangelical Protestantism, which now claims the loyalty of more than one-tenth of the population. Adherents report finding the participatory evangelical services more satisfying than staid Catholic liturgy. Converts generally abstain from alcohol and abide by stern codes of conduct.

*Religious Practitioners.* In the 1940s, the Church was involved in social reform. Following the 1948 Civil War and the defeat of the Catholic-Communist alliance, the Church abandoned activism. The broad reach of the welfare state meant that the Church did not have to be as concerned with social questions as its counterparts elsewhere. Some priests participated in action campaigns among peasants and shantytown dwellers, but most Church institutions remained conservative, with the Catholic hierarchy keeping a low profile.

*Rituals and Holy Places.* On the eve of the 2 August celebration for the national patron saint—Our Lady of the Angels—pilgrims throughout the country fulfilling "promises" to her hike to Cartago's Basílica of Our Lady of Los Angeles. Most churches sponsor local saints' celebrations, which are smaller and more secular in comparison with the national holiday for Our Lady of Los Angeles.

**Death and the Afterlife.** Catholics are typically buried following a church funeral. Wakes are held in the home of the deceased or in a funeral parlor. When a middle- or upper-class person dies, family members and associates place condolence advertisements in newspapers. Masses are held and rosaries recited at regular intervals after the event.

## MEDICINE AND HEALTH CARE

Costa Rica leads Central America in health, largely because of the extension to the entire population of free care through the Health Ministry and Social Security System. (The affluent, however, prefer to use private clinics.) Costa Rica's disease profile increasingly parallels that of industrialized societies. By the early 1990s, Costa Rica had as many doctors per one thousand population as the United States.

## SECULAR CELEBRATIONS

Secular celebrations occur at regular intervals—election days, soccer championships—and when a Costa Rican team or individual attains international prominence. Festivities are marked by caravans of automobiles flying flags and blaring horns.

Middle- and upper-class girls often have fifteenth-year celebrations marking their formal entrances into society. Rodeos, with equestrian and bull-riding competitions, are held in many towns, sometimes in connection with religious celebrations.

## THE ARTS AND HUMANITIES

**Support for the Arts.** Beginning in the 1950s, the state provided extensive support for the arts and arts education, funding a National Symphony and Youth Orchestra, a major publishing house, dance and theater troupes, and several major museums, as well as offering awards and prizes in numerous fields. With the economic cut backs that began in the 1980s, the Ministry of Culture's budget plummeted, although many arts institutions and artists have managed to survive through private donations, concerts or gallery sales, and tourist patronage.

**Literature.** In the early twentieth century, Joaquin Garcia Monge edited the literary journal *Repertorio Americano*, which was widely read throughout Latin America. Costa Rica's most distinguished early twentieth-century writers, such as novelists Carlos Luis Fallas, Joaquin Gutiérrez, Fabián Dobles, and Luisa González, as well as more contemporary ones, such as novelists Carmen Naranjo and Alfonso Chase and poet Jorge Debravo, have focused on social protest as a major theme. Political essays and biographies are also quite common, traditionally, as is sentimental, regionalist fiction that evokes a largely problem-free, idyllic past.

**Graphic Arts.** Costa Rica has little of the artisan or craft production so noticeable in Mexico or Guatemala. The "traditional" painted oxcart that is featured in tourist shops actually dates only to the early twentieth century.

Graphic artists Francisco Amighetti, Manuel de la Cruz González, and Margarita Berthau are among those who have attained an international following. Sculptor Francisco Zúñiga also has an international reputation, although he lived most of his life in Mexico and emphasizes Mexican topics in his work.

**Performance Arts.** The world of Costa Rica drama expanded significantly in the 1970s with the arrival of exiled Argentine and Chilean actors, playwrights, and directors, who founded new theater companies that had a more contemporary and broader repertoire. Several small theater companies have significant public followings, as do the productions staged at the major universities. In addition to the small, but vibrant, classical music scene, there are several folk groups devoted to Latin American "new song" and to recording and performing the country's vanishing heritage of Caribbean calypso, Spanish-style peasant ballads, and labor songs. American-, Brazilian-, and Cuban-influenced jazz combos enjoy a small but dedicated following. Modern dance has become popular since the 1970s, reflecting in part a breakdown of traditional inhibitions about exhibitions of physicality and the body.

## THE STATE OF THE PHYSICAL AND SOCIAL SCIENCES

The University of Costa Rica is the main research institution. Other public universities are the Technological Institute, the National University—whose religion department became an important center for Latin American liberation theology advocates—and the State University at a Distance,

545

which provides correspondence courses. Specialized institutions include the Central American Business Administration Institute, the Peace University, and the Center for Tropical Agronomic Research and Teaching. Since the mid 1980s, private universities have proliferated, specializing in law, business administration, tourism, and technical programs.

## BIBLIOGRAPHY

Biesanz, Mavis Hiltunen, Richard Biesanz, and Karen Zubris Biesanz, *The Ticos: Culture and Social Change in Costa Rica*, 1998.

Bozzoli de Wille, María E. *El indígena costarricense y su ambiente natural*, 1986.

Chomsky, Aviva. *West Indian Workers and the United Fruit Company in Costa Rica 1870–1940*, 1996.

Edelman, Marc. *The Logic of the Latifundio: The Large Estates of Northwestern Costa Rica Since the Late Nineteenth Century*, 1992.

———. *Peasants Against Globalization: Rural Social Movements in Costa Rica*, 1999.

———, and Joanne Kenen (eds.). *The Costa Rica Reader*, 1989.

Evans, Sterling. *The Green Republic: A Conservation History of Costa Rica*, 1999.

Gudmundson, Lowell. *Costa Rica Before Coffee: Society and Economy on the Eve of the Export Boom*, 1986.

Honey, Martha. *Hostile Acts: U.S. Policy in Costa Rica in the 1980s*, 1994.

Janzen, Daniel H. (ed.) *Costa Rican Natural History*, 1983.

Lara, Silvia, Tom Barry, and Peter Simonson. *Inside Costa Rica: The Essential Guide to its Politics, Economy, Society, and Environment*, 1995.

Leitinger, Ilse Abshagen (ed.). *The Costa Rican Women's Movement: A Reader*, 1997.

Molina, Iván, and Steven Palmer. *The History of Costa Rica: Brief, Up-to-Date and Illustrated*, 1998.

Morales, Abelardo, and Carlos Castro. *Inmigración laboral nicaragüense en Costa Rica*, 1999.

Palmer, Steven. "Getting to Know the Unknown Soldier: Official Nationalism in Liberal Costa Rica, 1880–1935." *Journal of Latin American Studies* 25 (1): 45–72, 1993.

Sandoval García, Carlos. *Sueños y sudores en la vida cotidiana: Trabajadores y trabajadoras de la maquila y la construcción en Costa Rica*, 1996.

Stone, Samuel Z. "Aspects of Power Distribution in Costa Rica." In Dwight Heath, ed., *Contemporary Cultures and Societies of Latin America*, 1974.

Williams, Robert G. *States and Social Evolution: Coffee and the Rise of National Governments in Central America*, 1994.

Wilson, Bruce M. *Costa Rica: Politics, Economics, and Democracy*, 1998.

Winson, Anthony. *Coffee and Democracy in Modern Costa Rica*, 1989.

—MARC EDELMAN

# CÔTE D'IVOIRE

## CULTURE NAME

Ivoirian

## ALTERNATIVE NAMES

Republic of Côte d'Ivoire; République de Côte d'Ivoire

## ORIENTATION

**Identification.** Often called the "jewel of West Africa," Côte d'Ivoire has been a model of economic prosperity and political stability for its neighboring African countries since its independence in 1960. In the fifteenth century, French and Portuguese merchants in search of ivory named the region the Ivory Coast for its abundance of the natural resource. The country changed its name to Côte d'Ivoire in 1985; its official name is the *République de Côte d'Ivoire*—a reflection of French control of the country from 1843 until independence. Today, the nation's rich economy lies in juxtaposition to its turbulent political climate. Whether Côte d'Ivoire will continue its rich history of socio-economic development amidst this unstable political climate remains uncertain as of late 2000.

**Location and Geography.** Côte d'Ivoire occupies approximately 124,500 square miles (322,460 square kilometers), an area slightly larger than New Mexico. Located on the south coast of West Africa, it borders the North Atlantic Ocean, with Liberia and Guinea on the west; Mali and Burkina Faso on the north; and Ghana on the east. The country is made up of three distinct geographic regions: the southeast is marked by coastal lagoons; the southern region, especially the southwest, is densely forested; and the northern region is called the savannah zone. The population of Côte d'Ivoire is ethnically diverse and delineated by the places the more than sixty indigenous ethnic groups live, although this number is often reduced to four major cultural regions—the southeast, sometimes referred to as the Atlantic East (Akan), the southwest, sometimes referred to as the Atlantic West (Kru), the northeast/north-central (Voltaic), and the northwest (Mande). The official capital is Yamoussoukro; Abidjan is the administrative capital. The country's three largest population centers are Abidjan (2.6 million), Daloa (1 million), and Man (957,706), and almost one-half of the country's population is concentrated in the urban cities of Abidjan and Bouaké.

**Demography.** The current population estimate is approximately 16 million. The largest group is the ethnic Baoule, who comprise over 23 percent of the population. Other significant ethnic groups include the Bete (18 percent), Senufo (15 percent), and Malinke (11 percent). The remaining population is comprised of the Agni, Africans from other countries (mostly Burkinabe and Malians), and non-Africans (primarily French and Lebanese). Of the more than 5 million non-Ivoirian Africans living in Côte d'Ivoire, one-third to one-half are from Burkina Faso; the rest are from Ghana, Guinea, Mali, Nigeria, Benin, Senegal, Liberia, and Mauritania. The country's population growth rate, estimated to increase at 3.8 percent per year, has led to rapid growth and a population of which almost half is under fifteen years of age.

**Linguistic Affiliation.** French is the official language used throughout the country, however there are over sixty native languages. Four of the major branches of the Niger-Congo language are spoken among Ivoirians, including the Kwa, Atlantic, Mande, and Voltaic. Language areas correspond closely to the four cultural regions of the nation. Agni and Baoule, both Kwa languages, are the most widely spoken languages in the south. In the north, variants of Mande and Senofu are the most widely spoken, but are also heard in almost all southern trading areas. No single African language is spoken by a majority of the population,

*Côte d'Ivoire*

and most Ivoirians speak two or more languages fluently. French is used in schools and business and is spoken more frequently by men than by women. Arabic is taught in Quranic schools, which are most common in the north, and is spoken by immigrants from Lebanon and Syria. Many Ivoirians understand English, which is taught in high school and the National University of Côte d'Ivoire, but English is not a language of choice, even among the educated. Almost half the adult population is literate.

***Symbolism.*** The most prominent symbol of Côte d'Ivoire is its national emblem, which depicts a shield displaying the profile of an elephant's head, surrounded by two palm trees, with the rising sun above the head and a banner bearing the words *République de Côte d'Ivoire* beneath it. The country's flag is a vertical tricolor of orange, white, and green; orange represents the savannahs of the north, green represents the forests of the south, and white represents unity. The national anthem is *L'Abidjanaise*, which means "Greetings, O Land of Hope."

## HISTORY AND ETHNIC RELATIONS

***Emergence of the Nation.*** Very little is known about the early history of Côte d'Ivoire. As early as 1 C.E., the area now called Côte d'Ivoire had become a melding place of various African people. Between the fourteenth and eighteenth centuries, as kingdoms rose and fell, many ethnic groups moved in and settled permanently in the region. France made its initial contact with Côte d'Ivoire in 1637, and in the eighteenth century the country was invaded by two related groups: the Anyi and the Baoule. In 1843 and 1844, the French government signed treaties with the kings of the Grand Bassam and Assinie regions, placing their territories under a French protectorate. The French gradually extended the area under French control until they dominated in 1915.

Today, the sixty distinct ethnic groups that make up the Côte d'Ivoire are loosely grouped into four main cultural regions which are differentiated in terms of environment, economic activity, language, and overall cultural characteristics. Most representatives of southeast cultures are Akan peoples, descendants of eighteenth-century migrants from the kingdom of Asante. The largest Akan populations in Côte d'Ivoire are the farming communities of the Baoule and the Agni. Smaller groups live in the southeastern lagoon region, where contact and intermarriage between the Akan and other groups have resulted in a multicultural lifestyle. Dependent on fishing and farming for their livelihood, they are not organized into centralized polities above the village level. The southwest Kru peoples are probably the oldest of Côte d'Ivoire's present-day ethnic groups, the largest tribe of which is the Bete. Traditional Kru societies were organized into villages that relied on hunting and gathering for sustenance, and they rarely formed centralized chiefdoms. In the north, descendants of early Mande conquerors occupy territory in the northwest, stretching into northern Guinea and Mali. The Mande peoples are comprised primarily of the Malinke, Bambara, and Juula. To the east of the Mande are Voltaic peoples. The most numerous of these, the Senufo, migrated to their present location from the northwest in the sixteenth and nineteenth centuries.

Amidst the settling of these unique cultures, the peoples of Côte d'Ivoire have been influenced by the French. The Ivory Coast became an autonomous republic in the French Union after World War II, and achieved independence on 7 August 1960. As Côte d'Ivoire has emerged as a nation—amidst colonization, exploitation, native revolts against the French,

the prominence of French culture, and finally independence—its people have lived in ethnic diversity, strong economic prosperity, and a cultural mosaic. Only in the latter part of the twentieth century did several decades of political tensions culminate with the country's first coup d'etat.

***National Identity.*** Since their independence the people of Côte d'Ivoire began to develop a national consciousness. Most of the country's people consider themselves Ivoirians first, and then as members of a particular ethnic group. Yet the concept of a national identity is complex. National boundaries reflect the impact of colonial rule as much as twenty-first century politics, bringing nationalism into conflict with centuries of evolving ethnicity. Each of Côte d'Ivoire's large cultural groups has more members outside the nation than within, resulting in strong cultural and social ties with people in neighboring countries.

***Ethnic Relations.*** For the most part, the multiethnic groups live together in harmony, with certain group tensions. Conflict between the majority Muslims and native peoples exists, and societal discrimination on the basis of ethnicity is sometimes practiced by members of all ethnic groups. According to the U.S. State Department Country Report on Human Rights, differences between members of the Baoule group and other ethnic groups, especially the Bete, are a major source of political tension and have erupted repeatedly into violence, most recently in 1997. During the latter part of 1999, tensions arose between several Ivoirian and non-Ivoirian ethnic groups.

## URBANISM, ARCHITECTURE, AND THE USE OF SPACE

Côte d'Ivoire is a juxtaposition of the urban and rural. Its cities, particularly the fashionable Abidjan, are replete with modern office buildings, condominiums, European-style boutiques, and trendy French restaurants. They stand in sharp contrast to the country's many villages—accessed mainly by dirt roads—whose architecture is comprised of huts and simple abodes reminiscent of an ancient time. While the cities are described as crowded urban enclaves with traffic jams, high crime rates, an abundance of street children, and a dichotomy of rich and poor, the villages are filled with farmers tending their fields, native dress, homemade pottery, and traditional tribal rituals. Most traditional village homes are made of mud and straw bricks, with roofs of thatched straw or corrugated metal. The Baoule live in rectangular structures, while the Senufo compounds are set up in a circle around a courtyard. High fences surround many Malinke village of mud-brick homes with cone-shaped straw thatched roofs. The artistic Dan paint murals with white and red clay onto their mud-brick homes.

## FOOD AND ECONOMY

***Food in Daily Life.*** In Côte d'Ivoire, grains such as millet, maize (corn), and rice and tubers such as yams and cassava make up most meals. These staples are complemented by legumes such as peas, beans, or peanuts, and smaller quantities of vegetables, oils, spices, and protein—usually meat or fish. Women prepare the grains by grinding them in large wooden bowls with long wooden pestles. For the most part, the family meals are cooked outdoors in ceramic or metal pots on stone hearths. Ivoirian food is very spicy and eaten with the hands. Well-known dishes consist of rice with a pepper-flavored peanut sauce, which is found in the northern savannah; and fish and fried plantains, served in the coastal regions. The national dish is *foutou* (also spelled *futu*) a thick, heavy paste made of mashed plantains or yams eaten with a spicy sauce or stew made of fish or meat. Because of its ability to keep well, dried, grated cassava, known as *gari*, is a popular food. Côte d'Ivoire's most popular culinary treat, *maquis*, normally features braised chicken and fish in onions and tomatoes. Favorite drinks among the villagers include palm wine and home-brewed beer.

***Food Customs at Ceremonial Occasions.*** Food plays an important role in the ceremonial and religious ceremonies of most native people groups. Feasting and drinking are used in coming-of-age ceremonies, religious ceremonies, and funeral/memorial services. Among the Akan peoples, the most important of these is the yam festival, a time of thanksgiving for good harvests and an opportunity to remember the discovery of the yam. One of Côte d'Ivoire's most famous festivals involving food is the Festival of Masks, which takes place in villages in the Man region every February. Every March, the Carnival in Bouaké is filled with festivities and food. Côte d'Ivoire's major Muslim holiday, Ramadan, is a month-long celebration during which everyone fasts between sunup and sunset in accordance with the fourth pillar of Islam, and then ends the fast with a huge feast. *Eid al-Fitr* is another Muslim holiday focused on feasts, prayer, fellowship, and gift giving. In native traditions, fetish priests often use food to create magic potions or amulets; the future may be divined by tossing rice grain into a box; certain foods may be forbidden to improve illness or misfortune. Ancestral spirits are offered food and drink before being consulted.

***Basic Economy.*** Despite economic hardship in the 1980s and early 1990s, Côte d'Ivoire is still the most prosperous of the tropic African nations, primarily because of its diversified export goods, close ties to France, and foreign investment. Côte d'Ivoire is among the world's largest producers and exporters of coffee, cocoa beans, and palm oil. Consequently, the economy is highly sensitive to fluctuations in international prices for these products and to weather conditions. Despite attempts by the government to diversify the economy, it is still largely dependent on agriculture. The Ivoirian economy began a comeback in 1994, due to the devaluation of the CFA franc (the Ivoirian currency unit) and improved prices for cocoa and coffee, growth in non-traditional exports such as pineapple and rubber, limited trade and banking liberalization, offshore oil and gas discoveries, and generous external financing and debt rescheduling by France and other countries. According to 1999 statistics, the Gross National Product is $25.7 billion; $1,600 per capita.

***Land Tenure and Property.*** Historically, the government has viewed the use of land as equating ownership. After independence, Ivoirian law on landownership required surveys and registration of land, which then became the irrevocable property of the owner and his or her successors. However, the National Assembly enacted the Land Use Law in 1988, which established that land title does not transfer from the traditional owner to the current user simply by virtue of use. However, in rural areas, tribal rules of land tenure still exist, which generally uphold that members of the tribe that dominates a certain territory have a native right to take that land under cultivation for food production and in many cases cash crops. Throughout the country, land tenure systems are changing from those in which rights are secured by traditional village authorities (communal systems) to those in which land can be bought and sold without approval from customary authorities.

***Commercial Activities.*** Cities and villages feature open markets, where foodstuffs are sold liberally, along with common household items. Merchants deal in locally grown products and few imported items. Additionally, cultural items are often found for sale, including clay pots, masks, drums, baskets, jewelry, and sculpture. In the major cities, including Abidjan and Bouaké, there are speciality shops for

*Skyscrapers and office buildings dot the skyline of Abidjan, the main city and former capital.*

dry goods, foodstuffs, hardware, electrical appliances, and consumer electronics. Generally, items are sold on a cash basis, but bartering is common in the smaller villages. Shopkeepers also extend credit to farmers until the end of the harvest season, and vendors allow installment purchases for automobiles and major appliances.

***Major Industries.*** Côte d'Ivoire's major industries include agriculture (coffee, cocoa beans, bananas, palm kernels, corn, rice, manioc [tapioca], sweet potatoes, sugar, cotton, rubber), timber, wood products, oil refining, automobile assembly, textiles, fertilizer, construction materials, and electricity. In 1998, the country's industrial production growth rate was 15 percent. Small manufacturing factories produce food, wood products, cloth, chemicals, cement, lumber, furniture, and corrugated-steel roofing; heavy industries produce air conditioners, freezers, refrigerators, paint, varnish, railroad cars, and heavy metal.

***Trade.*** Historically, Côte d'Ivoire has had strong economic ties with France. During the 1990s, Côte d'Ivoire's principal markets for exports were France and the Netherlands, which purchased approximately one-third of its total exports, a trend that continues today. The United States is the third largest export market, with Italy following. Current statistics indicate that Côte d'Ivoire exports $3.9 billion worth of goods annually, primarily cocoa, coffee, tropical woods, petroleum, cotton, bananas, pineapples, palm oil, cotton, and fish. France, which provides one-third of Côte d'Ivoire's imports, is the country's largest supplier. The United States, Italy, and Germany each supply about 5 percent of the country's imports, which include food, consumer goods, capital goods, fuel, and transport equipment. Due to the 1999 coup, Côte d'Ivoire received only limited assistance from international financial institutions during that year, and the European Union stopped its assistance programs altogether.

***Division of Labor.*** In Côte d'Ivoire, men, women, and children of all ages work. Almost 70 percent of the labor force is engaged in agriculture, livestock raising, forestry, or fishing. Both men and women work in the fields and harvest the crops, while men perform heavier agricultural work, as well as mining, construction, and industrial work. Men dominate civil and military positions, such as police officers, soldiers, customs officials, top-level bureaucrats, and foreign-salaried government officials. Children often work on family farms, and in the cities some children work as vendors, shoe shiners, errand runners, and car washers. Labor legislation is based on the French overseas labor code of 1952, which allows for collective bargaining, trade unions, and a government-set minimum wage, however the majority of the labor force works in agriculture or in the informal sector where the minimum wage does not apply. Forced labor is prohibited by law.

## SOCIAL STRATIFICATION

**Classes and Castes.** While the growing economy of Côte d'Ivoire has greatly improved the quality of life for some citizens, gross financial inequality exists. High population growth coupled with the economic stagnation of the 1980s and early 1990s resulted in a steady fall in living standards overall. Access to land, housing, secondary education, and jobs are the key determinants of social mobility in Ivoirian society, which allows for a wealthy, urban minority to receive most of society's benefits. The vast majority of the population is poor; 1998 statistics indicate that at least 60 percent of the country's active population is unemployed and most of those who have jobs earn wages that are not enough to cover their basic monthly expenses. When Gross Domestic Product declined by an average 2.7 percent between 1985 and 1990, the proportion of the population in poverty increased from 14 percent to 20 percent. The Ivoirian middle class is still a small minority—primarily traders, administrators, teachers, nurses, artisans, and successful farmers—whose opportunity for social mobility is fairly limited.

**Symbols of Social Stratification.** Urban housing is a measure of status, since most urban land concessions are granted to people in government and administration and to their relatives and clients. Secondary education is also an important urban resource and vehicle of social mobility. Although primary schools are found throughout the country, secondary schooling is an urban activity, channelling graduates into urban occupations in medical and legal fields. By the 1990s, employment had become the most significant indicator of social status. Like many other nations, consumer goods are another prominent symbol of social stratification, especially for the city population. Among the administrative and civil-servant class, imported cars and clothes, home furnishings, and broad cultural and recreational activities mark a high standard of living.

## POLITICAL LIFE

**Government.** Côte d'Ivoire is a constitutional multiparty republic dominated by a strong presidency. Côte d'Ivoire's Constitution provides for its presidency within the framework of a separation of

*Rice planting in the Kohrogo region. Rice is a staple food in the diet of most Ivoirians.*

powers between its three branches: executive, legislative, and judicial. The president is the chief of state; the prime minister is the chief of government. The unicameral National Assembly is composed of 175 members elected by direct universal suffrage for a five-year term. It moves forward legislation typically introduced by the president although it also can also introduce legislation. In June 1998, the National Assembly enacted amendments to the Constitution that diminished the authority of the prime minister relative to the president, authorized the president to annul elections or to postpone announcing election results, extended the presidential term from five to seven years, mandated the creation of a second legislative chamber (senate), provided for the president of the senate to succeed the president in the event of his death or incapacitation, and wrote into the Constitution the presidential eligibility restrictions of the 1994 electoral code. A draft of a new constitution was overwhelmingly approved by voters in July 2000.

State entities exist on several levels, including 16 regions, 58 departments, 230 subprefectures, and 196 communities. At all levels, all subnational government officials are appointed by the central government, with the exception of communities, which are headed by mayors elected for five-year terms, and traditional chieftaincies, which are headed by elected chiefs. The judicial system is headed by a Supreme Court and includes the Court of Appeals and lower courts. The High Court of Justice has authority to try government officials, including the president.

***Leadership and Political Officials.*** Côte d'Ivoire's contemporary political history is characterized by one-party rule and the leadership of President Felix Huphouet-Boigny, leader of the Parti Democratique de la Côte d'Ivoire (PDCI) until his death in 1993. He was one of the founders of the Rassemblement Democratique Africain (RDA), the leading pre-independence inter-territorial political party in French West African territories. Members of a single political party, the PDCI, occupied both the presidency and a majority of seats in the national legislature since independence in 1960, although other parties have been legal since 1990. Massive protests forced the president to legalize opposition parties. Both Houphouet-Boigny and his successor, President Henri Konan Bedie, helped build a nation of political stability and economic prosperity by repressing democratic opposition.

The country's first military coup overthrew President Bedie's administration in December 1999, and Retired General Robert Guei assumed control of the country. After suspending the Constitution, dissolving the National Assembly, and forming the National Committee for Public Salvation (CNSP), which consists of himself and eight military officers, Guie lost the presidential elections of October 2000. The National Electoral Commission announced that Laurent Gbagbo, the leader of the Ivorian Popular Front, won the controversial presidential elections with 59 percent of the vote, ushering in a new era of multi-party legitimacy and the power of free popular elections.

***Social Problems and Control.*** Security forces include the army, navy, and air force, all under the Ministry of Defense; the Republican Guard, a well-funded presidential security force; the national police; and the gendarmerie, a branch of the armed forces roughly equivalent in size to the army, which is responsible for general law enforcement, maintenance of public order, and the country's security, including the suppression of crime and street violence. According to the U.S. State Department, before the 1999 coup, the armed forces were in charge of maintaining civil order. In rural areas, traditional institutions often administer justice at the village level, handling domestic disputes and minor land issues in accordance with customary law. However,

the formal court system increasingly is superseding these traditional avenues. In 1996 the government appointed a Grand Mediator to settle disputes that cannot be resolved by traditional means, representing Côte d'Ivoire's trend to bridge traditional and modern methods of dispute resolution.

***Military Activity.*** The Côte d'Ivoire's government invests in its armed forces (FANCI), which include an army, navy, air force, and gendarmerie. In times of national crisis the gendarmerie can be used to reinforce the army. Formed in 1996, the National Security Council upholds both internal and external security policy. The civilian Directorate of General Intelligence is responsible for countering internal threats. A security staff (*L'Etat Major de la Securité*) collects and distributes information about crime and coordinates the activities of the security forces in times of crisis. The Special Anticrime Police Brigade (SAVAC) is also active. Military expenditures totalled $94 million in 1996, or 1 percent of the GDP. Following the coup d'etat, the structure of the military did not change.

## SOCIAL WELFARE AND CHANGE PROGRAMS

A high population growth rate, a high urban crime rate, a high incidence of AIDS, and a high poverty rate characterize Ivoirian society. Recognizing these issues, in the 1990s the government announced its commitment to implement social welfare and change programs, specifically in the areas of literacy, education, health, women and family development, economic development, and poverty alleviation—with a specific goal of reducing poverty from 36.8 percent of the population in 1995 to 30 percent in 2000. Numerous offices under the Ministries of Public Health and of Employment, Public Service, and Social Security are dedicated to these goals, but their efforts are constrained by a lack of funding and the unique multiplicity of Ivoirian tribes. As a result, many of these policies are coordinated by religious, private, and international organizations—from the far-reaching United Nations to small, specialized groups that work in only one community. The programs they finance and implement include safeguarding human rights, poverty alleviation, infectious disease control, contraception, literacy, and rescuing street children.

## NONGOVERNMENTAL ORGANIZATIONS AND OTHER ASSOCIATIONS

Many humanitarian nongovernmental organizations (NGOs) operate within Côte d'Ivoire, including

*Christian churches, mosques, and other holy places are important meeting places.*

the International Committee of the Red Cross (ICRC), UNICEF and other United Nations programs, Prisoners without Borders, and Doctors without Borders. The Ivorian Human Rights League (LIDHO), a domestic human rights NGO, actively investigates alleged human rights violations. Other NGOs such as Amnesty International and the Ivoirian MIFED also monitor government human rights abuses and publish critical reports. Despite this and other criticism, the government has encouraged the formation of NGOs and generally cooperates with them.

## GENDER ROLES AND STATUSES

***Division of Labor by Gender.*** In rural areas, women and men divide the labor, with men clearing the land and harvesting cash crops like cocoa and coffee, while women grow vegetables and other staples and perform most household tasks. Women also collect water and fuel, care for their families, spin and weave, and produce handicrafts and pottery to sell. In general, men hold most prominent civic and government positions, as well as the role of tribal chief in the villages. Religious roles, from shamans to Catholic priests to Muslim imams, are dominated by men.

***The Relative Status of Women and Men.*** Government policy encourages full participation by women in business, but generally there is a bias among employers to hiring women, whom they consider less dependable because of their potential pregnancy. Women are underrepresented in most professions and in the managerial sector as a whole. Some women also encounter difficulty in obtaining loans, as they cannot meet the lending criteria mandated by banks, including title to a house and production of profitable cash crops, specifically coffee and cocoa. However, women are paid on an equal scale with men in the formal business sector. Men continue to dominate managerial positions and enjoy the most career mobility, usually due to a higher level of education and connections with other businessmen.

## MARRIAGE, FAMILY, AND KINSHIP

***Marriage.*** Ivoirian marriages center on the combining of two families. The creation of a new household is significant to wedding rituals. The government abolished polygamy in 1964, and set the legal marriage age at eighteen for boys and sixteen for girls, although polygamy is a widely accepted lifestyle among many native ethnic groups. Additionally, the government does not recognize forced marriage or dowries ("bride prices") paid to the mother's family to legitimize the marriage. Although marriage customs are changing and becoming more Westernized, a large majority engage in traditional native wedding rituals. Divorce, although not common, is socially acceptable among most ethnic groups.

***Domestic Unit.*** Whether the family lives in an urban or rural setting, the extended family is the basic social unit. Despite lineage, men are generally seen as the power head of the household, while women tend to domestic needs and childrearing. In the Baoule village, the women live with their husbands' families; among the Senufo, husbands and wives live separately with men living in rectangular houses and their wives occupying round ones. When girls get married and leave home, it is the responsibility of the sons to care for the elders of the household.

***Inheritance.*** Men dominate inheritance practices in traditional societies. Both Baoule and Senufo people belong to their mother's family group; power and land are passed down through a mother's family line to her sister's sons. In the Bete and Nyula groups, inheritance is passed down to the through the father's line to the sons. In most traditional societies in Côte d'Ivoire, women do not have the right to inherit land, but only to use that of their husbands or families. Legislation was enacted in 1983 to allow women greater control of their property after marriage.

***Kin Groups.*** The family is linked to a larger group, the clan, primarily through lineages. One of the most important kin groups is the patrilineage, a group formed by tracing descent through male forebears to a male ancestor. In eastern Côte d'Ivoire, however, many societies are organized into matrilineage, which trace descent through female forebears to one female ancestor. Both men and women are included in both type of lineage, sometimes five or six generations removed from the founding ancestor, but the linking relatives are of one gender. Lineages generally share corporate responsibility for socializing the young and maintaining conformity to social norms. Lineage elders often meet to settle disputes, to prescribe or enforce rules of etiquette and marriage, to discuss lineage concerns, and preserve the group overall. They also pressure nonconformists to adhere to group mores. Lineages are generally grouped in villages and united as a chiefdoms.

## SOCIALIZATION

***Infant Care.*** While infant care may vary across cultures, the mother is the primary caregiver, usually with support from older siblings and extended family. The childrearing practices related to the care of the infant include breastfeeding on demand and up to several years, carrying the child on the mother's back, and sleeping with the child, all of which create a close and intimate relationship between the mother and child and security for the child. In most Ivoirian cultures, there is little understanding of the value of interacting with infants, and adults don't really play with children in the traditional Western sense until the child reaches preschool age.

***Child Rearing and Education.*** In Côte d'Ivoire, children are highly valued and play a very special role in perpetuating the family and culture and providing care for other family members. Girls are taught by their mothers, and boys learn from their fathers and other male figures. Overall, children are the responsibility of the community, and when primary caregivers are not available the community creates a system for caring for children. Parental and community goals for children are centered around social and human values, including respect, self-reliance, helpfulness, cooperation, and obedience, and often folktales or stories are used to reinforce these values. The more modern the culture, the more likely there is to be a shift to more materialistic values. Many rural ethnic cultures engage in rituals and initiation ceremonies: for example, the *Senufo* is a ritual in which every seven years a new group of boys pass through three stages of initiation that are completed when they are in their thirties. Education is free, and primary education is compulsory; however, in the early 1990s only about 1.5 million students annually attended primary schools.

***Higher Education.*** Higher education is very prestigious and available only to a select minority of the population. In the early 1990s, only about 423,000 attended secondary and vocational schools. Secondary education is viewed as an important urban resource and vehicle of opportunity. Although primary schools are found throughout the country, secondary schooling channels graduates into urban occupations. A large proportion of students who enter primary school are eliminated at crucial points in the education ladder, especially as they encounter stringent admissions requirements for secondary schools and universities, but many also drop out throughout the system. In general, students' educa-

*At the funeral of Nanan Toto Kra, a Baoule Akan, Mossi men dance with calabash rattles. Funerals, held 40 days after death, are important and elaborate ceremonies for Ivoirians.*

tional attainments reflect their parents' level of education.

## ETIQUETTE

Often relaxed in character and very polite, Ivoirians always great each other and inquire about a person's health, family, or work. It is considered rude to conduct business without first greeting. Men shake hands with one another; women instead kiss each other three times on the cheeks, alternating sides. At social functions, it is polite to shake hands with everyone upon entering and leaving. Eye contact is usually avoided, particularly between father and child, and it is considered rude to stare. Gift giving is customary, especially to those who are respected in the community.

## RELIGION

***Religious Beliefs.*** The constitution guarantees freedom of religion to all citizens. About 60 percent of the population adhere to indigenous beliefs, 25 percent are Muslim, and about 12 percent are Christian (mostly Roman Catholic). Only about 3 percent follow other religions, including some 100,000 Ivoirians who follow Harrisism, a unique Ivoirian

Christian religion that upholds a simple lifestyle. Christianity dominates in the south and the center of the country; Islam is predominant in the north and northeast (although many Muslims have moved south in search of work); and indigenous belief systems are present throughout the land. Both Islam and Christianity have been adapted to indigenous religions in a variety of ways, and many Ivoirians who have converted to Christianity still observe rituals that worship the spirits of their ancestors. Most Ivoirian Muslims are Sunni, following the Maliki version of Islamic law. Sufism is also widespread, infused with indigenous beliefs and practices. Beyond these localized versions of world religions, however, are complex systems of belief and practice that incorporate multiple elements of several religions, including animism, fetishism, and witchcraft. According to most local belief systems, spiritual beings—a creator, ancestral spirits, and spirits associated with places and objects—can influence a person's life and play a large role in religious worship and practice.

***Religious Practitioners.*** Each of the main religious traditions has its own practitioners, such as the Christian priests, nuns, and ministers, the Islamic clerics, and the priests and diviners of traditional religions. In Islam, a significant religious authority is the marabout—a miracle worker, physician, and mystic who exercises both magical and moral authority. He is also respected as a dispenser of amulets, which protect the wearer against evil. In the south, Akan religious practitioners include lineage heads, village chiefs, and priests who officiate at ritual observances for cults honoring specific deities. These priests (*akomfo*) also act as diviners, many of whom are believed to be clairvoyant and able to locate the source of spiritual difficulty for their followers, who consult them for a fee. Priests sometimes act as doctors, since many diseases are believed to have a spiritual basis.

***Rituals and Holy Places.*** Collective ceremonies and rituals are important to many indigenous religions, and include ceremonial dancing, ancestor worship sacrifices, mask carving and ceremonies, fetish priest ceremonies, and divination ceremonies. To the Akan, the most important of these is the yam festival, which serves as a memorial service for the dead and asks for their protection in the future, is a time of thanksgiving for good harvests, and is a ritual of purification that helps purge the group of evil influences. Ivoirians conduct rites in a variety of sacred spaces, including a variety of shrines dedicated to spirits, Christian and Roman Catholic churches, and mosques. Missions with churches, schools, and seminaries appear throughout the country. Yamoussoukro is home to the Grand Mosque and the largest church in Africa, the Basilica of Our Lady of Peace.

***Death and the Afterlife.*** The vast majority of Ivoirians believe that a person's soul lives after death. Because often death is considered the transformation of an ordinary human into an honored ancestor, funerals are elaborately celebrated. Relatives spend a great deal of money to provide the proper funeral services and memorials for their loved ones, which usually take place forty days after the death, and involve dancing, drumming, singing, and feasting that goes on for days, even weeks.

## MEDICINE AND HEALTH CARE

Ivoirians experience a number of health issues, including a large incidence of HIV-AIDS, female genital mutilation (FGM), unsanitary living conditions, unsafe drinking water, and a host of infectious diseases, including malaria, gastrointestinal ailments, respiratory infections, measles, and tetanus. The first case of AIDS was diagnosed in 1985; as of January 1999 the number of AIDS patients reached nearly 40,000. According to the World Health Organization, as many as 60 percent of women have undergone FGM. Studies show that in 1993 only 60 percent of the population had access to health care services, and a little over 80 percent had access to safe water. The average life expectancy is forty-three years for males, and forty-six years for females. Infant and child mortality rates remain high in rural areas, where access to clean water and waste disposal systems is limited, and malnutrition is widespread. An estimated 95 infants per 1,000 births die in their first year of life. Close spacing of births contributes to high rates of malnutrition in the first two years of life.

During the 1990s, the government increased its information, education, and communication regarding health and family planning. Public health expenditures increased steadily during the decade, but the health care system was unable to meet the health care needs of the majority of the population. Medical care for wealthy urban households is superior to that available to rural families. Chronic shortages of equipment, medicine, and health care personnel also contribute to overall poor service, even where people have access to health care facilities. In many rural areas, health care remains a family matter, under the guidance of lineage elders and traditional healers. The World Health Organization and the United Nations Children Fund provide child vaccinations for polio myelitis, diphtheria, tetanus, pertussis, tuberculosis, yellow fever, and measles, and vaccinate pregnant women against tetanus.

## SECULAR CELEBRATIONS

The Ivorian government recognizes the following holidays: New Year's Day (1 January), Labor Day (1 May), Assumption (15 August), All Saints' Day (1 November), Independence Day (celebrated on 7 December), and Christmas (25 December). Movable religious holidays that vary based on the Islamic lunar calendar include *Id al-Fitr* and *Id al-Adha*, as well as the Christian holidays based on the Gregorian calendar, such as Good Friday, Easter Monday, Ascension Day, and Pentecost Monday.

## THE ARTS AND HUMANITIES

***Support for the Arts.*** The arts are largely self-supporting, although the government encourages and provides support to dance troupes, artists, writers, and the museum. Village cultural groups receive some government assistance.

*Mud and straw homes with thatched roofs are still common in villages.*

**Literature.** Côte d'Ivoire has enjoyed a long history of storytelling, primarily because of its high illiteracy rate. By passing on traditional poetry, folktales, and myths, the storytellers, called *griots* by the Malike, impart societal values, history, and religion. French is the dominant language for written literature, as little exists in native languages. Bernard Dadie is perhaps Côte d'Ivoire's best-known writer to emerge in the twentieth century. He wrote the country's first play, *Assémiwen Déhylé*, and one of its first novels, *Climbié*, as well as several other successful works. Other authors have contributed to the vast array of literature from Côte d'Ivoire, including Aké Loba, Pierre Dupré, Ahmadou Kourouma, Jean-Marie Adiaffi, Isaïe Biton Koulibaly, Zegoua Gbessi Nokan, Tidiane Dem, Amadou Kone, Grobli Zirignon, and Paul Yao Akoto. Women entered the literary scene during the mid-1970s with Simone Kaya's autobiographical work. Among the best-known women writers are Fatou Bolli, Anne-Marie Adiaffi, Véronique Tadjo, Flore Hazoumé, and Gina Dick.

**Graphic Arts.** Indigenous graphic art traditions are found in abundance in Côte d'Ivoire, including wood sculpting, weaving, pottery making, mask making, jewelry making, carving, sculpting, and painting. All traditional Ivoirian art is made first for practical purposes—usually in relation to religious,

health, or village matters. Ivoirian artists combine traditional materials—such as wood, ivory, clay, and stone—and folktales and religious or mythical elements to make their art, which often transcends several cultures. Many Senufo and Baoule woodcarvers make art specifically for tourists searching the open markets for souvenirs.

**Performance Arts.** In Côte d'Ivoire performance art embodies music, dance, and festivals. Music exists almost everywhere—in everyday activities and religious ceremonies—and most singing is done in groups, usually accompanied by traditional instruments. Along with the native melodies of the indigenous groups, Ivoirians participate in more contemporary music from Europe and America. Dichotomies—from the Abidjan Orchestral Ensemble that performs classical music to street rock and roll—can be found in the cities. Traditional dance is alive in ceremonies and festivals, and is usually linked to history or ethnic beliefs. The Senufo N'Goron dance, for example, is a colorful initiation dance where young girls wearing a fan of feathers and imitate birds. Malinke women perform the Koutouba and Kouroubissi dances before Ramadan. The various traditions have unified the masquerade, music, and dance as an expression of the continuation of creation and life, and during these events the mask takes on deep cultural-spiritual significance.

## THE STATE OF THE PHYSICAL AND SOCIAL SCIENCES

The Ivoirian government is committed to the development of the physical and social sciences. Since 1982, IDESSA (*Institut des Savanes*) and IDEFOR (*Institut des Forêts*) have replaced the numerous commodity-specific agricultural research institutions once active in the country. IDESSA has departments for food crops, industrial crops, and livestock husbandry. IDEFOR's departments research coffee and cocoa, fruit crops, rubber, oil palm and coconut, and forestry in general. Some agricultural and scientific research is also conducted at the National University and at ENSA, the school of agronomy. Both educational institutions have helped to abate the formerly critical shortage of human resources for agricultural research, and both are supported by public funds. The National University of Côte d'Ivoire in Abidjan has faculties of sciences, medicine, and pharmacy, as well as an institute of renewable energy. The French Institute of Scientific Research for Cooperative Development is also located in Abidjan.

## BIBLIOGRAPHY

Center for Environment and Development in Africa (CEDA). *Côte d'Ivoire: Environmental Profile of the Coasts*, 1997.

Central Intelligence Agency. *CIA World Factbook 2000*, 2000.

Cohen, Michael A. *Urban Policy and Political Conflict in Africa: A Study of the Ivory Coast*, 1974.

Eloundou-Enyegue, Parfait M. *Poverty and Rapid Population Growth in Africa: The Links between High Fertility and Poverty at the Household Level*, Rand Working Papers in Economics, 1998.

Foster, Philip, and Zolberg, Aristide R., eds. *Ghana and the Ivory Coast: Perspectives on Modernization*, 1971.

Grootawrt, Christian. *Analyzing Poverty and Policy Reform: The Experience of Côte d'Ivoire*, 1996.

Grinker, Roy Richard, and Christopher B. Steiner, eds. *Perspectives in Africa: A Reader in Culture, History and Presentation*, 1997.

Ikenga-Metuh, E. *Comparative Studies of African Traditional Religions*, 1987.

International Monetary Fund. *Enhanced Structural Adjustment Facility Policy Framework Paper, 1998–2000*, 2000.

Kashambuzi, Eric. *Critical Issues in African Development*, 1997.

Khapoya, Vincent B. *The African Experience: An Introduction*, 2d ed., 1998.

Library of Congress, Federal Research Division. *Côte d'Ivoire: A Country Study*, 3d ed., 1991.

Mbiti, J. S. *African Religions and Philosophy*, 1990.

Meekers, Dominique. "The Process of Marriage in African Societies." *Population and Development Review* 1 (18): 61-78, March 1992.

Moss, Joyce, and Wilson, George. *Peoples of the World: Africans South of the Sahara*, 1991.

Mundt, Robert J. *Historical Dictionary of the Ivory Coast*, 2d ed., 1995.

Osae, T. S., S. N. Nwabara, and A. T. O. Odunsi. *A Short History of West Africa—A.D. 1000 to the Present*, 1973.

Rapley, John. *Ivoirian Capitalism: African Entrepreneurs in Côte d'Ivoire*, 1993.

United Nations, Sustainable Development. *National Implementation of the Rio Commitments: Côte d'Ivoire Country Information*, 2000.

U.S. State Department Bureau of African Affairs. *Country Background Notes: Côte d'Ivoire*, July 1988.

U.S. State Department Bureau of Economic and Business Affairs. *Country Commercial Guide: Côte d'Ivoire*, 2000.

The World Bank, *Africa Region, A Continent in Transition: Sub-Saharan Africa in the Mid-1990s*, 1995.

———. *Poverty in Côte d'Ivoire: A Framework for Action*, 1997.

—GINA MISIROGLU

# CROATIA

## CULTURE NAME
Croatian

## ORIENTATION

*Identification.* Historical references to Croats in the Holy Roman Empire date back to the ninth century. Stories connect the name "Croat" (*Hrvat*) with a powerful military chieftain in the early Middle Ages and an Alan word for "friend." Regional cultures are considered variations on the larger category of "Croatian," including the cultures of Dalmatia, Istria, Slavonia, and Zagorija. These regions are characterized by differences in geography, traditional economy, food, folkloric tradition, and dialect. Croats share an overall sense of national culture; people often feel strongly about regional identities and local cultural variations, particularly food and language.

A small percentage of non-Croat groups identify with a different culture. Serbs usually identify with Serbian culture. Slovenes, Muslims, Jews, Albanians, and Roma (Gypsies) generally identify with their own national groups and cultures.

In two cases non-Croats constitute a significant minority in a local population and have maintained group identities as non-Croats. In Istria, an Italian minority prefer the Italian language, and identify strongly with Italian culture. In Slavonia, along the Hungarian border, ethnic Hungarians (Magyars) prefer the Hungarian language and identify with Hungarian culture. This is not generally true of non-Croat and non-Slav populations in other regions, such as Italians in Dalmatia and Hungarians in Zagreb.

Before the recent war (1991–1995), there was a large Serb population in the region known as the Military Frontier (*Vojna Krajina*) who did not identify with Croatian culture. As tensions built between Croats and Serbs in the late 1980s, Krajina

Serbs began to express animosity toward the Croatian culture and language. In 1991, Croatia lost political control of this region (and 30 percent of its land); in 1995, it regained legal and political control. In 1997, when the region was restored to Croatian administration, most Krajina Serbs left for Serbia, where many now live as refugees.

The Roman Catholics of Herzegovina identify with the Croatian national culture. Herzegovinans generally believe that they should be part of Croatia, not linked to Bosnia. Croats in the diaspora are represented in the national parliament.

*Location and Geography.* Croatia was one of the six republics of the former Yugoslavia. It shares borders with Italy, Slovenia, and Hungary to the north and with the Federal Republic of Yugoslavia (Serbia) and Bosnia-Herzegovina to the east and south. Croats think of themselves as more closely linked with Austria than with the other territories and cultures of the former Yugoslavia. They do not refer to themselves as a Balkan country but as a European one.

Croatia occupies approximately 21,825 square miles (56,540 square kilometers). The region along the Adriatic coast has a Mediterranean climate with mild winters and hot, dry summers. The inland region has a continental climate with very cold winters, hot, humid summers, and spring and autumn seasons that are often rainy. Seventy percent of the land is farmland. The largest portion of the country consists of the Pannonian plain, a flat, fertile agricultural region that extends into Hungary and Serbia. The Drava and Sava rivers drain into the plain, making it an excellent region for agriculture. Cultural variations, particularly regional cuisine, are related to geographic variations within the country; traditional economies are also linked to geography. The capital, Zagreb, is centrally located but was not chosen for that reason. It is the largest city, and historically the political, commercial, and intellectual center.

### CROATIA

| | | | |
|---|---|---|---|
| 0 | 25 | 50 | 75 Miles |
| 0 | 25 | 50 | 75 Kilometers |

*Croatia*

**Demography.** The population was approximately 5 million in 2000. Croats make up 78 percent of the population and are the dominant ethnic group. Serbs account for 12 percent, and the remaining 10 percent includes Bosnians, Hungarians, and Slovenes as well as a very small number of Jews and Kosova Albanians. The religious makeup of the nation reflects this ethnic breakdown. Roman Catholics constitute 77 percent of the population; Serbian Orthodox, 11 percent; and Muslims, 1 percent. The Serb population has decreased since Croatian independence from Yugoslavia and the war that began in 1991. In 1981, Serbs accounted for approximately 17 percent of the population.

**Linguistic Affiliation.** The Croatian language has three major dialects, identified by three different words for "what"—sto, kaj, and ca. From 1945 to 1991, the official language was Serbo-Croatian. Even under socialism, Croats often referred to their language as Croato-Serbian (instead of Serbo-Croatian) or as Croatian. Croatian and Serbian variants of the language were always recognized as different dialects, and had different alphabets. Since independence, Croatian and Serbian have been declared separate languages. The government has been working to establish an official Croatian language, resurrecting vocabulary that fell out of general usage under socialism.

Croatian and related Southern Slav languages are modern versions of the languages of the Slavic peoples who moved into the lands of the former Yugoslavia around 500 C.E. Today, language is an important part of personal and group identity, but historically the Croatian language was not always spoken by a majority of Croats. Under the Hapsburgs, urban Croats spoke German, and Latin was the official language of government. A national reawakening in the nineteenth century focused on the establishment of a national language.

The dialects reflect not only regional variation but contact with and domination by different peoples. Thus, Istrians speak a Croatian influenced by Italian, while the people of Zagreb speak a Croatian strongly influenced by German. Regional dialects, such as Dalmatian, are sometimes regarded as provincial or indicative of less education and exposure to high culture. There is a counter tendency, however, to regard the regional dialects as more authentic forms of Croatian than those spoken by urban, cosmopolitan populations.

**Symbolism.** The newly independent state has had to recreate a national culture by drawing from history and folk culture. In this sense, Croatia is an imagined community. The modern national identity draws on its medieval roots, association with Viennese "high culture," culturally diverse rural traditions, and Roman Catholicism.

Croats use the metaphor of a single related people with shared blood to describe themselves as a nationality. Religion is probably the most powerful symbol of national identity today. Most Croats consider themselves Roman Catholic whether they practice their religion or not. Language and history are also important symbols of identity. Croat language and its regional dialects are much spoken of by Croats themselves. Feelings about ancient ties to a territory and a direct link to the independent Kingdom of Croatia are part of the modern Croatian national identity.

The most important national symbol is the flag, which has three bands of color: red on top, white in the middle, and blue on the bottom. This flag was first used in 1848 under Austro-Hungarian rule. Under socialism, a red star was added in the center. The present-day flag has a coat of arms in the center that includes a symbol of each of the five parts of the country on top of a red and white chessboard shield. The chessboard dates to the Middle Ages but was also used by Croatian fascists (Ustasha) during World War II. Serbs saw the resurrection of this symbol as provocation.

In the nineteenth century, Croats rediscovered their folk traditions. Folk songs, folk dances, and village customs were taken as symbols of national pride. This interest in village culture went along with a quest for a stronger national identity under Hapsburg rule. Rural people were romanticized and taken to represent the soul of the country and the character of particular regions. The word *narod* means both "folk" and "nation." The symbols of regional culture are costumes, dances and songs, and village customs. These folk traditions were appropriated and modified by the middle classes in the nineteenth century and celebrated as well under socialism. Folklore performances that drew from regional cultures throughout the former Yugoslavia highlighted Yugoslav "brotherhood and unity."

Important culture heroes are symbols of the long history of Croat people. Two prominent figures are King Tomislav, the first king, and Ban Josip Jelacic, a noble military leader under Austro-Hungarian rule. Foods, both national and regional, and language are important symbols of national and regional identity.

## HISTORY AND ETHNIC RELATIONS

**Emergence of the Nation.** Croats as a people and a country trace their history to the medieval Kingdom of Croats. Through much of their history, Croats were ruled by another political body, but there were movements to establish national recognition or independence.

Slavic peoples migrated into the Balkans and along the Dalmatian coast in the sixth century. They displaced or absorbed the Illyrians, who may be the ancestors of modern Albanians. These Slavs encountered other nomadic peoples, primarily from the Middle East, including the Avars, Alans, and Antes. The mixture of these peoples produced the southern Slavs. The various southern Slavs remained disparate tribal groups with no clear identity as Croats or Serbs until the ninth century.

The Kingdom of Croatia had been established by the tenth century. In 1102, the Croats came under Hungarian rule. Croatia agreed to follow the king of Hungary but retained its own governmental body, the Sabor, and its own governor, or Ban. Through the years of Hungarian rule, the relationship shifted back and forth from more or less equal partners in

*Agriculture is still the most important industry in Croatia.*

the administration of Croatia to clear domination by Hungary.

Since the twelfth century, Croatia has been largely under the domination of others. The Ottoman Empire took a portion of the country for approximately 100 years, after the mid-sixteenth century. Croatia then asked the Austrian Hapsburgs for help against the Turks. This may have been the start of a Croatian preference for the Austrians and dislike for the Hungarians. The Hapsburgs established the Military Frontier creating a buffer zone between Croatia and Austria to the north, and the Ottoman empire to the south. It also created a large pocket of non-Croat people within Croat lands. Orthodox Slavs who fled Bosnia were moved into the Military Frontier to serve as resident soldiers and were given free title to land.

Croatia remained under Hapsburg rule until the late eighteenth and early nineteenth centuries, when Napoleon conquered Croatia in 1809. The so-called Illyrian Empire lasted until the fall of Napoleon, and Croatia returned to Austro-Hungarian rule. In 1840 a Croatian National Party was formed. Croats began to search for a national identity, including a Croatian language, literature, and history. Rural populations were believed to be the curators of "authentic Croatian culture." Croats also began to

look to Serbs and other southern Slavs as people with whom they shared a linguistic and cultural affinity. After World War I, Croatia joined other southern Slavs in the first Yugoslavia. The Kingdom of Serbs, Croats and Slovenes (the Kingdom of Yugoslavia) was born out of the Treaty of Versailles. At first, Croats welcomed the union but soon resented the Serbian monarch and the fact that the seat of government was in Belgrade, the Serbian capital. In 1928, the Ustasha Party was formed with the goal of winning independence. Italy and Germany supported this movement and its terrorist activities. In 1941, when the Axis powers occupied Yugoslavia, the Ustasha Party became the ruling faction in the Independent State of Croatia (NDH). It is not clear, however, that a majority of Croats supported or identified with the Ustasha Party. Modern Croats generally disclaim association with the NDH.

Fascist Croatia was responsible for the extermination of Serbs, Jews, and Gypsies. In the recent war (1991–1995), Serbs used the term "Ustasha" as a very negative term to refer to any Croat. This term, and the Croat term "Chetnik" for Serbs, also harking back to the time of World War II, served to distance the Serbs and Croats from each other, and remind both sides of a time when atrocities were committed.

During World War II, there was also a war in the Yugoslav territories for internal control of the region By then the first Yuboslavia had come apart. Josip Broz (Tito) was the leader of the Partisans; he was born and raised in Croatia. Many Croats joined the Partisans. Eventually Partisans prevailed. Modern Croats claim they were the dominant national group in the Partisan army, though Serbs and Bosnians make the same claim.

Under socialism, a Yugoslav identity was promoted and nationalism was suppressed. Singing Croatian songs said to be nationalistic could lead to a jail term. Maspok, or the "Croatian Spring," the only large-scale nationalist movement under Tito's regime, was put down in 1971. It was led by important Croatian communists and was based on economic disagreement with the Serb elite in Belgrade.

Economic and political problems escalated after Tito died. Some of the socialist leaders recast themselves as nationalist leaders. Croats began to express resentment against the Yugoslav government and the favoritism they believed Serbs received in government jobs. Many believed themselves to be economically superior and able to stand alone. Economically, the entire country was in a crisis, but Slovenia and Croatia had some advantages, including proximity to western Europe and a tourist industry on the Dalmatian coast. The first free elections were held in Slovenia and Croatia in 1990. The Croatian Democratic Union (HDZ) was formed, and Franjo Tudjman, a former communist and nationalist, rose to power.

In the late 1980s tension began to build between Croats and Serbs in the former Yugoslavia. Violent incidents began to erupt in Croatia in February 1991. Croatia declared independence from socialist Yugoslavia in 1991. War broke out in 1991 with Yugoslav National Army (JNA). At the end of 1991 there was full-scale war in Croatia. The war was between the Serbs, in what had been the Republic of Serbia in the former Yugoslavia, and Croats in the newly independent Croatia. The reasons for the war are very complex. Very simply, while Croatia wanted to separate from Yugoslavia, Serbs were largely unwilling to allow this to happen, probably largely for economic reasons.

The first president of the new democratic Croatia, Franjo Tudjman, died in 1999. The HDZ no longer controls the parliament, and young people feel that the country is becoming a democratic and modern European nation.

## URBANISM, ARCHITECTURE, AND THE USE OF SPACE

Architecture reflects the influence of the bordering nations. Austrian and Hungarian influences are visible in public space and buildings in the north and central regions. Large squares named for culture heroes, well-groomed parks, and pedestrian-only zones, are features of these orderly towns and cities. Above-ground trams provide excellent transportation. Muted colors prevail, especially tones of yellow and gold.

Zagreb, the largest and most important city, includes an upper city (Gornji Grad) and a lower city (Kaptol). The heart of the city is the Square of Ban Jelacic. In 1848, the Austrian government presented Jelacic with a bronze statue of himself that was placed in this central square. Croatian names for streets and squares were often replaced with socialist names after 1945, only to be returned to their original names in 1991.

The University of Zagreb was established in 1669. Its faculties are spread around the central portion of the city. Important public buildings include the Sabor as well as ministries, embassies, and government offices. One of the most important public buildings is the Gothic cathedral of Saint Stefan. Inside the cathedral, there is a carved stone inscription in Glagolithic, the alphabet first used in Croatia. The Dolac is the large central farmer's market. Perhaps the most important public place in daily life is the café, and in Zagreb there are many. People rarely meet in their homes, which are small and crowded. When visitors do enter a private home, they are usually invited only into a parlor or living room area, or the kitchen. Whether in a café or a home, people generally socialize around a table. In public spaces, people maintain privacy by avoiding conversation or using formal terms of address.

In the suburbs beyond the older, central section of Zagreb, there are apartment buildings and a smaller open market. There is almost always a Catholic church. The most remote suburbs of New Zagreb have high-rise Soviet-style apartment blocks.

The rural areas of Zagorija and Slavonia still have some traditional houses that are mostly built of brick or stone. In cities, houses are built right up to the street. An inner courtyard sometimes provides space for a small garden. Modern houses in cities and villages usually have two or three stories with masonry and stucco. Many people build their own houses, beginning with a simple bedroom—

*Photos decorate a family grave within a cemetery on the island of Susak. It is common in Croatia to decorate graves with candles, flowers, and photos.*

living room structure and adding on as time and money allow.

Along the coast, the architecture is Mediterranean. Houses usually are made of stucco and painted white, and have red tile roofs. Cities and towns still have the characteristic open markets, squares, and Catholic churches, but are less likely to be laid out in a neat grid.

## FOOD AND ECONOMY

***Food in Daily Life.*** The main meal of the day is a late lunch. In the north and inland, the majority of the foods has an Austrian or Hungarian flavor. A typical lunch includes chicken or beef soup, cooked meat (often pork), potatoes, and bread. Greens with vinegar and oil are served in the spring and summer, and pickled vegetables in the winter. Along the coast, a meal usually includes fish and pasta, risotto, or polenta. Lamb is common in the Dalmatian highland region. Breakfast is simple, usually consisting of strong coffee and bread with jam. The traditional dinner typically consists of leftovers from lunch, cold meats, and cheese with bread. People usually eat in their own homes, although they also eat snacks on the streets. Restaurants are usually very formal and expensive. A variety of fast foods are available, including foods typical of ethnic minorities. While people rarely eat in restaurants, almost everyone has coffee in cafés on a regular basis.

***Food Customs at Ceremonial Occasions.*** For holidays or special occasions, there are larger quantities of food, particularly meat. Roast pork with the skin (*pecenka*) is popular in Zagreb and Slavonia. Special cakes are also prepared. Fried cheese, octopus salad, spicy grilled meats, and dishes made with phyllo reflect different cultural influences. Large quantities of alcohol are part of any celebration. In Slavonia, this is usually a plum brandy; in Zagreb and on the coast, grape or herb brandies are popular. Whenever people get together, they usually drink together. Strong Turkish-style coffee and espresso are important symbols of hospitality. Men usually are offered an alcoholic drink.

***Basic Economy.*** People no longer produce food primarily for their own consumption; although, during the war from 1991 to 1995 people depended on kitchen gardens and subsistence fishing, particularly on the coast. Agriculture, however, remains an important industry. Steel manufacture, chemical production, and oil refineries are also important, as are textiles, shipbuilding, and food processing.

*Children play in the ruins of a building. The war for Croatian independence that lasted from 1991 to 1995 took a heavy toll on the country.*

Tourism, which was the major industry on the coast until 1991, is again important. Croatia depends on imported goods and the revenue from exports.

***Land Tenure and Property.*** Since the end of socialism, the country has been in the process of transferring property to private ownership. There have been difficulties in the cases of apartments and houses that were confiscated under socialism, and have been occupied for many years by families other than the original owners. The inhabitants of government-owned apartments have been given opportunities to buy their homes. The transformation of industries from government to private ownership is largely complete.

***Division of Labor.*** Division of labor in the workplace is based largely on skill and educational level. Individuals whose families are professional are likely to enter the professions, while working-class families largely produce working-class children.

Under socialism, family connections could help one achieve a position. This was consistent with the national culture and was not necessarily a product of socialism. Communist Party membership increased one's potential for good employment. It is not uncommon for people to retire to help care for a grandchild, while younger men and women continue to work after becoming parents.

## SOCIAL STRATIFICATION

**Classes and Castes.** An unofficial class system is based on one's family name and professional status rather than wealth. Communist Party membership challenged this class system, although it was not uncommon for prominent families to join the party. In more recent years, Croats increasingly became discontented with the socialist government, particularly people who were well educated, professional, and from prominent families.

**Symbols of Social Stratification.** Economic indicators of high social status include style of dress, material wealth such as a house or apartment in a city, an automobile, a vacation house, and international travel. Less obvious indicators are educational level and occupation. Most high-status individuals speak English well and are likely to speak one other European language. Dialect is also an indicator of social status. People from a city have higher status than people from villages, though many urban dwellers have village family connections. High-status individuals are usually Croats. They may be of mixed ethnicity but are members of a predominantly Croatian family. Jewish families are likely to be of relatively high status. Ethnic Albanians are usually at the bottom of the social system, and Gypsies are completely outside it.

## POLITICAL LIFE

**Government.** Croatia is a democratic republic with a parliamentary government based on a constitution established in 1990. The parliament (Sabor) has a House of Representatives and a House of Counties. The latter is advisory only and has equal representation from every region. Seats are set aside in the House of Representatives for ethnic minorities and Croats in the diaspora. Representatives are elected for four-year terms.

**Leadership and Political Officials.** The president of the republic is elected for a five-year term and may only serve two consecutive terms. There is also a prime minister.

There are thirteen parties with representatives in the government. The dominant party since 1991 has been the HDZ. Some of the smaller parties formed a coalition and won the elections after Tudjman's death.

**Social Problems and Control.** Since the war of 1991–1995, there is increased crime, particularly of a petty nature. There are more beggars visible on the streets. Most of the individuals are people who are displaced or refugees, or otherwise left out of the current system as a result of war and political change. Some elderly people, for example, had pensions that were paid in another of the republics of the former Yugoslavia. Others who had money in banks outside Croatia may have lost their savings. For the most part, however, people are coping with the help of family. Croatia and non-governmental organizations provide some safety net for refugees.

**Military Activity.** In the former Yugoslavia, all men were required to serve one year of military duty, either right after high school, or if they went on to university, during or at the end of their university education. Usually people served their military duty in a republic other than the one in which they were born and lived. Beginning in 1983, women could voluntarily join the military. The new Croatian Army grew out of a para-military established originally as Croatia began to feel threatened and vulnerable before the outbreak of war in 1991. As tensions built in the former Yugoslavia, Croats began to refuse to serve in the Yugoslav Army. During the war, all young men were expected to register for military service. Generally men from the same village or locality served together during the war, even though this meant that a village could lose a number of its young men in one battle. Because the different sides spoke the same language (more or less), and dressed more or less the same, regional dialects, and actually knowing one's comrades in arms became important. In the new state of Croatia, young men are now required once again to register for a year of military duty.

## SOCIAL WELFARE AND CHANGE PROGRAMS

Social problems since independence, include the needs of refugees and other victims of war. There is a School of Social Welfare in the University of Zagreb. There is a very small social welfare system. In the former Yugoslavia, there was little unemployment or welfare, though a social security system existed. However, if one did not have a job, one

*A woman sells produce at an open air market within the Diocletian Palace walls in Split.*

depended on his or her family for support. When there were crises, other family members stepped in.

Active programs of change pertain primarily to the shift to democracy and free-market capitalism, including related issues such as intellectual property rights.

## NONGOVERNMENTAL ORGANIZATIONS AND OTHER ASSOCIATIONS

Many nongovernmental organizations (NGOs) came to the country during and just after the Serb-Croat war (1991–1995). They included international relief organizations such as the International Red Cross, church-based organizations such as Catholic Relief Services and Caritas (Care), and other private voluntary groups, including Doctors without Borders. Some of these groups attempted to address problems in Croatia, while others used Croatia as a base of operations to carry out work in Bosnia. United Nations peacekeeping forces were a visible presence just after the war.

## GENDER ROLES AND STATUSES

**Division of Labor by Gender.** Traditionally, a loose division of labor allocates housework and child care to women and outside work to men. But women have long been part of the labor force. Before socialism, rural women worked alongside men in fields and on the farm. They also prepared meals and processed food for storage, kept the house, did laundry, and minded the children. Under socialism, women were encouraged to join the workforce. Today, most women expect to have a job or career.

When women work for wages, men share some of the duties at home. Grandfathers traditionally spend time with grandchildren, and fathers take a fairly active role in raising children. Men are less likely to clean, do laundry, cook, and to think of domestic work or child care as their responsibility.

***The Relative Status of Women and Men.*** Croatia is portrayed as a patriarchal society, but women have fairly equal status with men. Men enjoy more privileges and have a higher status and many families prefer sons to daughters. Women are represented in most professions, politics, and the arts and are not likely to take a secondary role in public life. Women are as likely as men to pursue higher education. Status differences are as marked between older and younger people, and between professional or working- class individuals, as they are between the genders. Gender differences are more pronounced among farmers and the working classes than among professionals.

*A Croatian woman makes sausages. Pork is a common food, especially in northern Croatia.*

## MARRIAGE, FAMILY, AND KINSHIP

*Marriage.* Couples arrange their own marriages. Young people usually meet in school, through friends, or at work. They often begin to spend time together in the company of a larger group of friends. A young man and woman usually have a serious relationship before they meet each other's families. Individuals theoretically have a great deal of choice about marriage partners, but Croats tend to marry people of the same nationality and religion and with the same educational level and social status. Most men and women marry in their early 20s. Monogamous marriage is the rule. Divorce is increasingly common, although it is still considered undesirable. Pregnancy before marriage is not uncommon, but is not usually the sole reason for getting married.

*Domestic Unit.* In the past, three-generation households were the norm. A married couple usually lived with the husband's parents. Today young people are ambivalent about living with their parents or grandparents after marriage. There is still a cultural preference for extended families, but young people tend to want privacy.

Young married couples usually live with one set of parents or a grandparent because of a shortage of housing. There is also a preference for keeping small children in the care of resident grandparents and for caring for the elderly at home. Young children are often placed in day care or kindergarten. Increasingly, elderly people spend some time in a nursing home, which usually creates a huge financial burden for their families.

*Inheritance.* The most important property passed from one generation to another is a house or apartment. Usually one child in a family inherits a residence, which he or she occupies. Family wealth, however, ideally is distributed equally among all the sons and daughters. In the past only sons inherited, and in some regions, only eldest sons. Daughters usually were given a dowry; in rare cases, this might include some land.

*Kin Groups.* Croats practice bilateral kinship. In principle they favor the father's side of the family. Couples traditionally resided with the husband's parents after marriage, and were expected to have more to do with the husband and father's relatives. Traditional kinship terms reflect this, with different terms for the husband's parents and the wife's parents, and for the two mothers-in-law. In practice, however, many families have resided with or near the wife's parents. Whether a couple live with or are closer to one set of parents or another depends to some extent on personal preference, and also on economic matters (who has room in their house for the couple, who is likely to leave a house or apartment to the couple).

## SOCIALIZATION

*Infant Care.* Infants are cared for at home, primarily by the mother. They usually are swaddled tightly in blankets when they are very small. As toddlers, they are dressed in multiple layers of clothing to protect them against the cold. Infants stay close to their caretakers, usually sleeping with their parents or in the same room. They often are breast fed, although bottle feeding is not uncommon. Women do not breast feed in any public settings. Infants and toddlers are supervised very closely and are not encouraged to explore or move about on their own. Mothers or other adult caretakers feed children, dress them, and perform routine physical care well into the young childhood years.

*Child Rearing and Education.* Family members are the preferred caretakers for children. Young children are placed in day care when they are not taken care of by their parents or grandparents. Kin-

*A man sits among the ruins of Vukovar, destroyed by fighting in 1991. The four-year struggle between Croats and Serbs destroyed many cities.*

dergartens are provided free by the government and accept children from the ages of one to six years. Children begin their formal public education at age seven. There are now private kindergartens, mostly run by the Catholic Church. Croats do not use nannies or unrelated babysitters. Children are verbally corrected for misbehavior. Spanking is not common now, especially among urban professional people. Good children obey their parents and other adults, show respect for elders and property, play quietly, eat what adults prepare for them, and go to sleep at a regular bedtime. Children are less likely to act out physically than verbally. They do not bring other children home to play because homes are small and for the family and adult guests. Parents take responsibility for the behavior of children. Most adults see the personality or behavioral traits of an older relative in a child.

***Higher Education.*** People value higher education, although families that have been working class through the generations tend to expect their children to stay in that class. The University of Zagreb is the largest of the five universities. There are fifty one schools and colleges (faculties) associated with the universities. Zagreb has a central National and University Library, which all citizens may use. In-

dividuals who do not attend university usually attend a secondary school to prepare for work. Secondary curricula include gymnasium (college preparatory general education), technical education (mechanical training), and specialized education (bookkeeping or office skills).

## ETIQUETTE

People stand close to one another and talk loudly. Strangers stare openly at one another. Formality is maintained in language and behavior when people do not know each other well. Strangers nod their heads in passing. In stores, offices, and places of business, people use formal language for greetings and good-byes. Failure to greet someone in a context that requires a greeting and an overly familiar greeting are serious breaches of etiquette. People who are on friendly terms greet each other more informally and usually kiss on both cheeks. Men and women kiss, women and women kiss, and men kiss other men who are family members or very close associates. Young people are expected to offer the first greeting to older people, and women to men. The formal "you" is used unless people are age mates, good friends, or coworkers or have reached a stage where the dominant person invites the person of lesser status to address him or her informally.

## RELIGION

**Religious Beliefs.** For many people, Catholicism is a symbol of nationality even though they may not attend mass or participate in other religious activities or ceremonies. Most young people are baptized, and most marriages are conducted in a church. Other religions include Eastern or Serbian Orthodox, Islam, Judaism, and Protestantism. Since the war, there has been a more visible presence of Protestant missionaries, including members of the Church of the Latter Day Saints and Jehovah's Witness. There is some interest in Eastern religions, such as Buddhism, among young adults.

**Religious Practitioners.** Catholic priests and nuns are the most visible religious practitioners in Croatia. There are ministers of a few Protestant sects (particularly the Jehovah's Witnesses and Seventh Day Adventists), and religious leaders for some of the minority ethnic and religious communities. Likewise, there is evidence of some interest in non-Western religions, particularly in Zagreb. (Zagreb has a restaurant run by Hari Krishnas, for example). Since Croatian independence, however, Catholicism is more visible and more significant in Croatian daily life.

**Rituals and Holy Places.** Most families now observe Catholic rites of passage, including Baptism, First Communion, Confirmation and Marriage ceremonies in the Church. Funerals complete with a Funeral Mass are also important. Christmas and Easter are once again important national holidays, and are widely celebrated. Churches and cemeteries are important places in most peoples' lives. Many people have made pilgrimages to nearby Medjugorje in Herzegovina. This is a site where five young people claim to have seen repeated apparitions of the Virgin Mary, and where many people claim to have been cured of debilitating illnesses.

**Death and the Afterlife.** Most Croats hold to a Roman Catholic vision of death and resurrection of the soul. Interestingly, all Saints' Day (Day of the Dead) is the only Catholic holiday that was celebrated by most of the ethnic groups in the former Yugoslavia. It is still a very important observance in Croatia. Families wash and prepare graves, and decorate them with candles, flowers and photographs. People often make several trips to graveyards during the days just before and after All Saints' Day.

## MEDICINE AND HEALTH CARE

Under socialism, all citizens had access to medical care, and this is still the case. Physicians begin training at the start of their university education. The usual period of training for a physician is six years.

## SECULAR CELEBRATIONS

Secular holidays include New Year's Day, International Labor Day (1 May), Croatian Statehood Day (30 May), Antifascist Uprising Day (22 June), and the Day of National Gratitude (5 August). International Women's Day (8 March) is still popularly observed.

## THE ARTS AND HUMANITIES

**Support for the Arts.** The arts are generally well supported in Croatia, including literature, fine arts, graphic arts and performance arts. Folk art, music and dance are also important, and part of the Croatian national identity. In the former Yugoslavia, all these activities were supported directly by the state. This is no longer entirely true, although the state is still involved in support of the arts, and the general Croat population pays attention to and appreciates many forms of art.

## THE STATE OF THE PHYSICAL AND SOCIAL SCIENCES

The Croatian Academy of Arts and Sciences oversees all research and activities in science, the humanities, the social sciences and the fine arts. It is considered the successor organization of the Yugoslav Academy of Arts and Sciences. Twenty research institutes are associated with this academy. There is a new National and University Library in Zagreb.

## BIBLIOGRAPHY

Banac, Ivo. *The National Question in Yugoslavia: Origins, History, Politics*, 1984.

Denich, Bette S. ''Unmaking Multi-Ethnicity in Yugoslavia: Metamorphosis Observed.'' In David Kideckel and Joel Halpern, eds., *The Anthropology of East Europe Review* Special issue: *War among the Yugoslavs*. 11 (1 and 2), 1994.

Despalatovic, Elinor. *Peasant Culture and National Culture: Balkanistica*, vol. 2, 1976.

Dubinskas, Frank A. *Performing Slavonian Folklore: The Politics of Reminiscence and Recreating the Past*, 1983.

Erlich, Vera St. *Family in Transition: A Study of 300 Yugoslav Villages*, 1966.

Eterovich, Francis H., and Christopher Spalatin. *Croatia: Land, People and Culture*, vols.1 and 2, 1964, 1970.

Gilliland, Mary K. "Nationalism and Ethnogenesis in the Former Yugoslavia" In Lola Romanucci-Ross and George DeVos, eds., *Ethnic Identity*, 3rd ed., 1995.

———, Sanja Spoljar-Vrzina and Vlasta Rudan. "Reclaiming Lives: Variable Effects of War on Gender and Ethnic Identities in Narratives of Bosnian and Croatian Refugees." *Anthropology of East Europe Review*, 13 (1): 30–39, 1995.

Glenny, Misha. *The Balkans: Nationalism, War and the Great Powers, 1804–1999*, 2000.

———. *The Fall of Yugoslavia*, 3rd ed., 1996.

Guldescu, Stanko. *History of Medieval Croatia*, 1964.

Huseby-Darvas, Eva V. "But Where Can We Go? Refugee Women in Hungary from the Former Yugoslavia." In Jeffrey L. MacDonald and Amy Zaharlick, eds., *Selected Papers on Refugee Issues*, vol. 3, 1994.

Jelavich, Charles. *South Slav Nationalisms: Textbooks and Yugoslav Union before 1914*, 1990.

Kim, Julie, and Erich Saphir. *Yugoslavia: Chronology of Events June 15, 1991–August 15, 1992*, 1992.

Kirin, Renata Jambresic, and Maja Povrzanovic, eds., *War, Exile, Everyday Life: Cultural Perspectives*, 1996.

Macan, Kresimir, and Vesna Sijak. *Croatia for Everyone*, 1996.

Magas, Branka. *The Destruction of Yugoslavia*, 4th ed., 1993.

Malcolm, Noel. *Bosnia: A Short History*, 1994.

Povrzanovic, Maja. "War Experience and Ethnic Identities: Croatian Children in the Nineties." *Collegium Antropologicum*. 19 (1), 1995.

Rihtman-Augustin, Dunja. "Ethnology between Ethnic and National Identification." *Studia Ethnologica Croatica*, 6: 1994.

Silber, Laura, and Allan Little. *Yugoslavia: Death of a Nation*. 3rd ed., 1995.

Simic, Andrei. "Machismo and Cryptomatriarchy: Power, Affect and Authority in the Contemporary Yugoslav Family." *Ethos*, 11 (1 and 2), 1983.

Singleton, Fred. *Twentieth Century Yugoslavia*, 1976.

West, Richard. *Tito and the Rise and Fall of Yugoslavia*, 1994.

—MARY KATHERINE GILLILAND

# CUBA

## CULTURAL NAME
Cuban

## ALTERNATIVE NAME
Republic of Cuba

## ORIENTATION

**Identification.** Christopher Columbus landed on the island in 1492 and named it Juana after Prince Juan, the heir apparent to the throne of Castille. The name "Cuba," an abbreviation of the indigenous word *Cubanacán*, held sway.

**Location and Geography.** The island lies about ninety miles south of the Florida Keys. Its western tip begins about 125 miles (210 kilometers) from Cancún and extends 750 miles (1,207 kilometers) east-southeast. The area of the country is 48,800 square miles (110,860 square kilometers). About a third of the island is mountainous, consisting of the Guaniguanco chain in the western province of Pinar del Rio, the Escambrey in the south-central province of Las Villas, and the largest system, the Sierra Maestra, in the western province of Oriente. Between these mountain systems is a large plain in the western province of Matanzas and another in the eastern province of Camaguëy. Since the European conquest, the western third of the island has exercised military, political, economic, and cultural dominance.

The capital is Havana on the northern coast of the western third of the island. The second largest city is Santiago de Cuba in the province of Oriente, where the Roman Catholic archbishopric was established in the colonial era. Although Santiago sometimes is called the "second capital," the economic importance of the port of Havana has given it a hugely disproportionate role in the definition of the national culture.

**Demography.** Recent population estimates range from 11.06 million to 11.17 million. At least 50 percent of the population is classified as mulatto (mixed African and European descent), although the cultural privilege assigned to whiteness probably causes many mulattos to minimize their African heritage. Thirty-seven percent of the population claims to be exclusively white, and 11 percent is classified as "negro." The remaining 1 percent is Chinese, the result of the importation of 132,000 Chinese indentured laborers between 1853 and 1872 to replace the loss of labor caused by the impending end of African slavery. In 1862 the African population was larger than that of whites. Although the larger slave-holding plantations were in the west, escaped and emancipated slaves often fled east, where they could more easily hide or establish themselves on small unclaimed plots of land in Oriente. Thus, it is there that Afrocuban art, religion, and music were most strongly expressed and the cultural movement "afrocubanismo" began.

**Linguistic Affiliation.** Nearly all Cubans speak Spanish exclusively. The dialect is similar to that in the other Hispanic Caribbean islands, although the rhythmic speaking and the use of highly expressive hand gestures are distinctly Cuban. Languages spoken by the indigenous population are extinct. French was spoken for a short time by slave-holding European refugees from the 1791 Haitian revolution but this has since died out.

**Symbolism.** The three major symbols of national identity have arisen from the three struggles for independence. The national anthem was composed at the start of the first war for independence, the Ten Years War (1868-1878). It is a call to arms that evokes the image of the peasants of the town of Bayamo in the eastern heartland. The second national symbol is the flag. It has a white star imposed on a red triangle, modeled on the triangular symbol of the Masonic lodges in which the struggle against Spain was organized. The triangle is imposed on

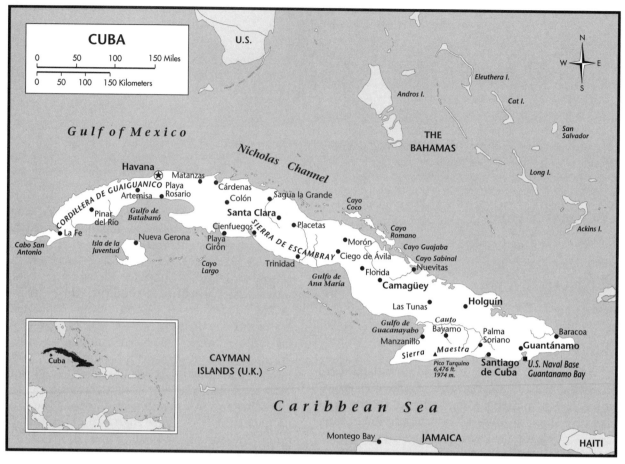

*Cuba*

three blue stripes alternating with two white stripes. The third symbol of national pride and independence is the flag of the 26th July Movement, which contains the black initials M26J (Movimiento 26 de Julio) on a field of red. The M26J flag commemorates Castro's attack on the army barracks at Moncada and served as a symbol of resistance to the dictatorship of Fulgencio Batista and the imperialism of the United States, which openly supported him. Afrocuban music and dance were also appropriated as symbols of the nation beginning in 1898, when the United States invaded the island, and especially after the triumph of the Revolution in 1959.

## HISTORY AND ETHNIC RELATIONS

**Emergence of the Nation.** The Cuban nation has arisen from a history of colonial and imperial domination. Formal colonial status under Spain was ended only by the invasion by the United States in 1898, when military and corporate interests made the island a de facto colony of the United States.

After the triumph of the Revolution on 1 January 1959, Cuba became truly independent for the first time since the colonial invasion of 1511.

The Pre-Columbian population was about 112,000, consisting mostly of Arawak (Taino and Sub-Taino) in the central and eastern region and a few Ciboneys (also called Guanahacabibes) who had fled the advance of the Arawak and moved west to Pinar del Rio. Indigenous lands were quickly distributed to European conquistadors and gold prospectors, and indigenous persons were enslaved and given to Europeans for use in mining and agricultural projects (a system called the *encomienda*). Indigenous people who resisted were murdered. Malnutrition, overwork, suicide, and brutality made the indigenous population virtually extinct within fifty years of the conquest.

The indigenous past was largely abandoned and forgotten, save only a few cultural survivals in language and architecture. The only people left on the island were *peninsulares* (those born in Spain), creoles (colonists of European decent who were born on the island), and African slaves. The struggle between these three groups determined the character of the colony and the meaning of Cuban-ness (*cubanidad*). Peninsulares came to earn their fortunes and return to Spain. Their privileged status as colonizers depended on the maintenance of colonial structures; thus, their loyalty was to Spain even if they were lifelong residents of the colony. Peninsulares had an almost exclusive claim to administrative (governmental) offices and ecclesiastical appointments and a near monopoly on much trade with Spain and other nations.

The peninsulares' privileges and wealth evoked the resentment of the creoles, who outnumbered them. There were creole elites, especially merchants in Havana, whose privilege was dependent on the colonial status of the island, but most eastern creoles increasingly saw their interests as opposed to those of Spain. Their emerging nationalist sentiment was countered by increasing anxiety among the African majority. After the British occupation of Havana in 1752, slaves who had been stolen from Africa comprised the majority of the population. After the Haitian revolution of 1791, creoles and peninsulares thought that only the presence of the Spanish army could maintain order and their privilege. This fear added to the reluctance of the slaveholding creole elite to support the movement for independence. But the eastern planters had less to fear from a slave revolt, since their farms were much smaller and had far fewer slaves.

Hence, the contestation over the meaning of Cubanness was between eastern planters, African slaves, freed blacks, impoverished white farmers, and urban workers one the one side, and peninsulares and western creole elites on the other side. Planters in Oriente organized for revolution in Masonic lodges, since the Catholic churches were staffed by Spanish clergy. In 1868, the eastern planters, loosely organized into a Liberation Army, declared war on Spain by issuing the "Shout from Yara," which called for complete freedom from colonialism, declaring gradual and indemnified emancipation of slavery, and imploring western planters to join the struggle for independence. This "Ten Years War" failed, but not before causing economic ruin, especially in Oriente and Camagüey. The Pact of Zanjón in 1878 ended the war and promised reform, but many of the surviving belligerents were dissatisfied with the maintenance of colonial authority, and the reforms were not forthcoming. The Afrocuban General Antonio Maceo continued skirmishing but finally conceded defeat in 1880.

Over the next seventeen years, the efforts of the poet and statesman José Martí, "Father of the Cuban Nation," gave the independence cause a cohesive political ideology which the first insurrection had lacked. Working from the United States, he formed the Revolutionary Junta to raise money and awareness. United States capitalists largely favored independence, since the removal of Spain would leave the island defenseless against an economic invasion; using "freedom" and "democracy" as the ideological excuse, they asked the United States government to intervene on behalf of the independence movement.

That movement had become stronger economically and militarily, and even some western planters began to favor independence. When war broke out in Oriente in 1895, the belligerents had a better organized civil organization and a more aggressive military strategy. Indeed, the war was almost won by 1898, and Spain was ready to negotiate independence. However, when an explosion sank the *USS Maine* in Havana harbor, U.S. businessmen and war-hungry Secretary of the Navy Theodore Roosevelt seized on the excuse to invade Cuba. The United States blamed Spain for the explosion and declared war on it. Spain was quickly defeated, and in the Treaty of Paris in 1898, the United States claimed ownership of the remaining Spanish colonies (Cuba, Puerto Rico, and the Philippines).

Imminent victory for Cuban independence fighters had been stolen by another colonial power, the United States. Cubans protested. In 1901, the United States agreed to withdraw from Cuba militarily, but only under extreme conditions, including a ninety-nine year lease to a naval base at Guantánamo in Oriente, veto power over trade and military treaties, and the right to intervene in the island's internal affairs. The legislation containing these conditions, the Platt Amendment, was drafted in Washington and inserted verbatim into the first Cuban constitution of 1902.

In 1906, Cubans again protested United States intervention, prompting another military occupation that lasted until 1909. The United States ambassador became the de facto head of state by virtue of his ability to command another invasion. The Cuba Colonizing Company, a U.S. corporation, sold land to any United States citizen who wished to profit from cheap lands, gradually transforming ownership of the island to non-Cubans. Some Cubans benefitted from this arrangement, but most resented it to no small extent. When the United States allowed President Gerado Machado y Morales to make himself a dictator (1924–1933) and ignore civil law in favor of violence and corruption, Cubans promulgated a new constitution that abnegated the hated Platt Amendment, although it left the Guantánamo naval base intact. But hopes for independence were again dashed when Fulgencio Batista, who had in 1934 staged a coup to install himself as a military dictator, seized power again in 1952 and removed the elected president. United States support of the Batista dictatorship enraged the majority of Cubans.

One year later in 1953 a small group of independence fighters attacked the Moncada army barracks in Oriente. They were quickly defeated, and most were summarily executed. The leader of the attack, a lawyer named Fidel Castro Ruz, was saved by the intervention of the Roman Catholic archbishop of Santiago de Cuba. At his trial, Castro delivered a five-hour speech entitled "History Will Absolve Me," the publication of which disseminated his message of true independence. The date of the attack became the name of a national revolutionary movement, the Movimiento 26 de Julio.

When Castro was released from jail, he, along with his brother Raul Castro, Che Guevara, and a small group of revolutionaries fled to Mexico to plan another military attack. Castro himself traveled to New York and Miami to raise funds. On 2 December 1956, the small group landed about one hundred miles west of Santiago in a small ship named "Granma." Nearly all were captured, but the three leaders and a few others fled into the Sierra Maestra mountains, where they were joined by thousands of Cubans. The guerillas were supported with food, water, and shelter by the peasants of Oriente, nearly all of whom wanted an end to not only the Batista dictatorship but also to its chief sponsor, the United States military.

The guerillas were vastly outgunned by Batista's U. S. army-trained and equipped military forces, but they had the support of the population, knowledge of the terrain, the cooperation of some army deserters, and the work of nonmilitary revolutionaries in other parts of the island. The "Revolutionary Directorate" of University of Havana students, the Communist Party, and the 26 July Movement had been sabotaging Batista since the Moncada attack. With such a cooperative effort, it took only three years to topple the dictator.

When they entered Havana in tanks at the end of December 1958, the guerrillas were greeted by millions of ebullient Cubans. Batista had fled to Miami with $300 million (U.S.) of embezzled funds, soon to be joined by other wealthy Cubans who had profited from his dictatorship. For the first time since the European conquest, Cuba was free. When on 8 January 1959 Castro spoke to the masses in

Havana, a white dove is said to have alighted on his shoulder, proving to many Cubans that the Revolution had indeed been an act of God.

***National Identity.*** There are several ways in which the development of a national culture can be traced. Afrocuban cultural forms, particularly music and dance, were crucial to the definition of the new nation during the neocolonial republic. Afrocubanismo, the syncretic result of the African majority's culture and that of the dominant European minority, was the "conceptual framework of modern Cuban culture." African rhythms were inserted into popular music, and the Eurocuban dances "danza" and "contra-danza" and the Afrocuban dances "son" and rhumba became popular. When Cuba was threatened with a diminution of its national identity because of the U.S. economic colonialism beginning in 1898, nationalist sentiment found in the Afrocuban music and dance of Oriente province a unique Cubanness free of foreign cultural and ideological influence. For a time, Afrocubanismo was the centerpiece of nationalist representation.

But a different political/ideological agenda stresses the appropriation of United States cultural, ideological, and political ideas in the development of the Cuban character. Though products and ideas did flow from north to south and back again, this argument contains an extreme privileging of the upper classes and white Cubans over the majority, reducing all of culture to the materialism of the rich, who bought American fashion, Cadillacs, and appliances, and sent their children to expensive North American private schools. But there was a world of cultural production which had nothing at all to do with North America and was quite independent of its influences, such as Afrocubanism in Oriente. Probably since 1898 and certainly since 1959, Cubanness has been informed by a proud nationalism, and Cuban nationalism is configured as precisely the opposite of everything "American." Resentment over the two military invasions of 1898 and 1906, the suffocating economic imperialism from 1902-1959, and the internationally-censured economic embargo has caused most Cubans to reject everything North American. Indeed, the more the United States government tries to strangle the Cuban people with its clearly unsuccessful embargo, and the more right-wing the Cuban American Foundation becomes, the stronger Cubans' commitment to the Revolution grows. Even those who might otherwise resist the Castro government are moved to defend the ideal of *Cuba Libre*. And since the most vehement opponent of the Revolution is the United States, a country which attempted to colonize Cuba just 50 years ago, the Revolution can convincingly claim to be the sole option for freedom.

**Ethnic Relations.** Martí declared in the 1890s that there were no blacks or whites in Cuba, only Cubans, but this was more an ideological call to unity against the colonial powers than a description of reality. Neither the gradual abolition of slavery from 1880 to 1886 nor the transfer of power from Spain to the United States alleviated the racial tension that was a heritage of slavery. After the abolition of slavery in 1886, Afro-Cubans organized in the Central Directorate of Societies of the Race of Color. Nine years later, as much as 85 percent of the rebel army was composed of black soldiers, who expected that when the war was won they would have an improved position in society. When that did not happen, Afro-Cubans founded the Independent Party of Color in 1908, but this was banned in 1910. In 1912, a protest of that ban led to a massacre of Afro-Cubans in Oriente. In the following years, the marginalization of darker mulattos and Afro-Cubans continued despite the popularity of Afrocuban music and dance.

The Revolution of 1952–1959 declared the establishment of an egalitarian society, and since racism was a product of capitalism it was assumed that it would disappear under socialism. But even today, Afro-Cubans are effectively absent in the highest levels of the government. Castro admitted in 1986 that more Afro-Cubans and women should be represented in the Central Committee, but racism is deeply embedded in the white Cuban ideology. Cubans are acutely aware of fine gradations in phenotypes and have words to describe every shade of brown and black.

## URBANISM, ARCHITECTURE, AND THE USE OF SPACE

In the colonial period, the port of Havana was strategically valuable as a military post, administrative center, and shipping port. For this reason, Havana has been privileged in terms of public expenditures, economic investment, health and educational institutions, and physical infrastructure. When the Revolution came to power, it faced the task of equalizing differential development within Havana and between it and the rest of the island. When the wealthiest Cubans fled to Miami, their mansions were distributed to poor working people. Unequal urban–rural development was dramatically transformed by the state's installation of plumbing and electricity in remote rural areas; the building of

hospitals, schools, and day care centers in small towns; and a raising of the rural standard of living so that it was closer to that in Havana. Since 1990, the economic crisis has again so impoverished the countryside that rural people have poured into Havana to seek jobs in the tourism sector. To stem this tide, the regime has made it illegal for persons from other provinces to reside in the city.

Cubans are accustomed to being in close quarters both at home and in public; the culture does not value privacy and private space as highly as does United States culture. Socializing often takes place on the street or in line for food and goods. Cubans are not defensive even of bodily space: physical affection is commonly displayed, and physical contact among strangers is not problematic. Being in constant relation with others, socializing in groups, and sharing both social space and body space are the norm. In this way, the socialist preference of collectivity and community over individuality and privacy coincides with the Latin American tendency toward group cohesion and commitment.

But this closeness in Cuba is also a necessity, since new housing construction has been a failure of the Revolution. Construction materials have been in constant shortage because of the U.S. embargo and the need to concentrate construction efforts on Import Substitution Industrialization. To solve this problem, in the early 1970s, the Revolution tried a novel new approach to self-help: the microbrigades. Coworkers would build new housing together; in exchange, they would be supplied with material, granted paid leave from their jobs, and given ownership of the new housing. The microbrigades created not only new housing but also day care centers, schools, and other public buildings. Private construction using black market materials has also compensated somewhat for the housing shortage, but most people live in cramped quarters. This creates tremendous stress, especially for couples who are hard pressed to find privacy.

## FOOD AND ECONOMY

**Food in Daily Life.** Normal daily diet in Cuba is rather simple. Rice and beans are a staple, supplemented by fried plantains, tubers, and vegetables. Cucumbers are a cheap and abundant vegetable complement. While beef once was eaten by all segments of the population, pork and chicken have overtaken it as a more economical alternative. Pork is made into a low-quality ham called *jamon vikin*, which cost about $2 (U.S.) per pound in Havana in

*Workers in a cigar factory, Havana. In the socialist system, all workers collectively "own" the factories they work in.*

the summer of 2000. Beef is virtually unavailable to city dwellers.

Historically, more than half the daily caloric intake has been imported. Despite efforts to reverse this situation, agriculture has been dedicated mostly to sugar. Both the United States, and later the Soviet Union, discouraged Cuba from diversifying agricultural production by penalizing it with negative terms of trade if it did not accept foreign imported grain. For this reason, the country has been unable to supply its citizens with adequate food since the collapse of the socialist trading network. Daily food rations have long been governed by the *libretta*, a booklet that rations monthly allowances of staples such as rice, oil, sugar, beans, and soap. Since the economic crisis of the 1990s (labeled "Special Period During Peacetime") caused the adoption of extreme austerity measures and a hugely diminished state sector, food allowances have been decreased to below-subsistence levels. Despite innovative attempts to feed themselves, many Cubans are going hungry. To improve food distribution and alleviate hunger, the free farmer's markets (MLCs), closed in 1986 because they had enabled some Cubans to become wealthy at the expense of others, have been reopened.

**Food Customs at Ceremonial Occasions.** Cubans are very fond of sweets, and a cake is a special treat normally reserved for birthdays. Ice cream is also a special treat and a national obsession; the national ice cream manufacturer "Copelia" is quite renowned for its very fine ice cream, and Cubans believe it is the best in the world. A "salad" of ice cream costs a Cuban 5 pesos, or twenty-three cents (U.S.).

**Basic Economy.** The economy is socialist, meaning that the population as a whole owns most of the means of production and collectively benefits from national economic activity. Private property is minimal, and private wealth is seen as a breach of the social contract by which all Cubans benefit equally from the resources of their island. Soon after the Revolution, most of the means of production were collectivized; agricultural plantations, industrial factories, and nickel mines were converted to "social property" of all Cubans collectively. The voluntary departure in the period 1960–1962 of many people who had become wealthy under the neocolonial dictators (1898-1959) facilitated this process as privileged Cubans fled to Miami and New Jersey. The state has used social property to pay for health care, social security, and education. Unfortunately, the state has reproduced the same two errors as have other socialist economies: first, a focus on production levels at the expense of efficiency; and second, an insistence on centralized planning in lieu of market forces. The first Revolutionary constitution established the "System of Direction and Planning of the Economy" (SDPE), a mechanism of centralized planning and establishment of production quotas. The mechanism of planning was the Central Planning Board (JUCEPLAN). The SDPE was a slightly more flexible system than was the Soviet model, but ultimately it too stifled innovation. But since the Special Period, the state has shown some willingness to compromise, allowing a great deal of private economic initiative and requiring state ventures to be fully self-sufficient.

There is a tension in Cuba between ideological purity and economic exigency; this is especially visible in the tourism sector, which has been growing rapidly since 1990. In 1987, the state created the corporation Cubanacán to negotiate joint ventures between the state and foreign enterprises for the construction of new facilities for tourism. Foreign capital has boosted tourism and saved the economy but has created ideological problems for the socialist Revolution: foreign capitalists and tourists are exploiting resources that belong to Cubans and have brought a culture and ideology that may not be compatible with socialist egalitarianism. To protect against ideological corruption, the state has separated tourism from the general economy by making some resorts inclusive, and by banning Cubans from some tourist areas. Tourist dollars thus do not benefit the general economy, and this situation has caused resentment among citizens banned from parts of their own country.

**Land Tenure and Property.** Before the 1959 revolution, Cuba was a highly stratified society in which 8 percent of the population held 79 percent of the arable land. Rural farm workers experienced extreme poverty and malnutrition, and almost no workers owned land. The Agrarian Reform Law of 1959 divided the largest estates and distributed land to two hundred thousand landless farm workers. In 1975, the National Association of Small Farmers led the effort to form agricultural cooperatives. By 1986, 72 percent of private farmers had chosen to participate in agricultural cooperatives. In exchange, the state provided them with seeds, fertilizer, mechanization, social security, modern housing, and lower income taxes. No small farmer was forced off his land against his will.

**Commercial Activity.** Under the extreme duress of the Special Period, the state has decentralized economic activity, allowing an explosion of private enterprise. In 1992, a constitutional amendment recognized the right to private ownership of the means of production. In 1993, President Castro announced one hundred new categories of authorized private economic activity. Commercial activity is now a mixture of social ownership of the major means of production, private ownership of some agricultural lands whose products are sold both to the state and in the free farmers' markets, small-scale artisans who sell to other Cubans and tourists, and the import of oil and other non-indigenous resources.

**Major Industries.** Tobacco and coffee have competed with sugar since the early nineteenth century, but land has always been most profitably used for sugar cultivation and external factors have discouraged crop diversification. Diversification of the economy has been hampered because first one superpower then another has traditionally used Cuba as nothing more than a sugar and citrus plantation. The revolutionary government has tried to engage in Import Substitution Industrialization to lessen its dependency on imported manufactured goods, but this effort has been hurt by a lack of fuel since Soviet and Russian oil subsidies ended in 1990. Much industrial equipment was of Soviet manufacture, and hence replacement parts are no longer available. Lack of fuel and replacement parts has led to the reintroduction of animal traction for agriculture in a retrenchment to a preindustrial past. Nickel is an abundant mineral resource, and its exportation was a major element of trade with the socialist states until 1989. The Revolution has had some success in developing biotechnology as an export sector, but there is has been hampered by a lack of bioindustrial inputs. Tourism has become the most promising new activity for the earning of hard currency. The most urgent need aside from food is petroleum, and the government is exploring offshore drilling.

**Trade.** The economic catastrophe that began in 1989 resulted from the collapse of the Council of Mutual Economic Assistance (COMECON), the trade network of socialist states. COMECON had facilitated the trading of sugar, citrus, and nickel at above-market prices in exchange for Soviet oil at below-market prices. Cuba was allowed to resell the Soviet oil and keep the profit. This advantageous arrangement allowed the country to construct an egalitarian society, but when the subsidy ended the economy was shown to be unstable. Cuba was suddenly forced to trade in a global capitalist market

*View overlooking Havana. Cuban cities are extremely overcrowded.*

ing trading partner, followed by Canada and Japan in volume of trading. Cuba has been aggressively pursuing an improvement in trade relations with Mexico, Brazil, and other Latin American states, and at least since 1991 has been seeking membership into CARICOM (Caribbean Common Market), which might partially replace the now-defunct COMECON.

***Division of Labor.*** The Revolution was committed to offering higher education to all citizens who wanted partly it in order to replace the professionals who left in the early 1960s and partly to redress economic inequality. But the availability of a higher education has caused increasing numbers of young people to be dissatisfied with agricultural and industrial occupations, causing a chronic shortage of workers. Despite the efforts of the regime to reverse this situation, professional careers, including higher governmental positions, are disproportionately held by whiter Cubans, while Afro-Cubans are over-represented in agriculture and assembly line industry.

The austerity measures of the Special Period have caused massive worker displacement as lack of fuel, industrial inputs, and spare parts for machinery has forced the state to downsize or close many offices and factories. In 1991, the Cuban Communist Party (PCC) confirmed that the opportunity to work is a fundamental human right of every citizen, and so people whose workplaces are closed or downsized are given a generous package of material support and the opportunity to be transferred to the agricultural sector.

## SOCIAL STRATIFICATION

***Classes and Castes.*** After 1959, class distinction became far less dramatic, so that occupation and class no longer determined access to health care, food, clothing, schooling, and shelter. Before the socialist revolution, only 45 percent of the population had completed primary education, 9 percent secondary, and 4 percent higher education. But by 1988, those numbers were 100 percent, 85 percent, and 21 percent respectively. The percentage of income earned by those in the lowest salary bracket rose dramatically, indicating a rapid and dramatic redistribution of wealth.

The reemergence of a privileged class in the Special Period is the direct result of capitalist "reform," as those who run the new private enterprises have access to imported luxury items while some of their fellow citizens starve. Those who live in a tourist area and have an extra room in their house or apartment are allowed to rent that room

based on cash transactions and not on ideological compatibility.

The need to develop new trading partners is an urgent matter, and here again pragmatic exigency runs afoul of ideological coherence. Cuba can no longer afford to limit its trading partners to those who share its visions of justice and equality. It has been forced to cooperate economically with capitalist states whose political-economic ideologies are anathema to the socialist ideal. Spain is Cuba's lead-to tourists at market rates. Despite the heavy payments the state requires in return for authorization to do this, some citizens have amassed enormous material privileges in the midst of economic catastrophe for the majority. Throughout the Revolution, Cubans have accepted material hardship because, in a socialist country, everybody suffers equally when there are hard times. But now the poverty of the island is becoming increasingly distributed in a grossly inequitable manner. Capitalism assumes that wealth and poverty are not distributed equally, and the increasing presence of small pockets of wealth in a sea of poverty is rather distressing to most Cubans who were reared with socialist ideals of justice and equity in economic relations.

***Symbols of Social Stratification.*** Along with capitalism and social stratification, commodification has begun to lay claim to the hearts and souls of Cubans who for 40 years have been shielded from the values of conspicuous consumption. For the young, who do not remember what capitalism was like before the Revolution, it is United States fashion which symbolize status. Anything with a label is in vogue, and a pair of Nike shoes or Levi's jeans are highly coveted. Material excess is increasingly embraced as indicative of social value.

## POLITICAL LIFE

***Government.*** The political system is termed "Democratic Centralism." Every citizen has the right to participate in discussions of political, social, and economic issues, but that participation is somewhat constrained by the hierarchical structure of society and government. Authority ultimately rests with the central executive branch; both the issues discussed and the decisions made are determined by the President of the Republic. The 1976 constitution established a system of representative legislative bodies called the Organs of People's Power (OPP). Municipal, provincial, and national levels of the Peoples' Power debate issues and send the results to the next level of the hierarchy. The National Assembly of the OPP elects from its ranks a Council of State that can act on its behalf when it is not in session. From the Council of State is chosen the Council of Ministers, who have direct administrative responsibility for the executive departments. This is but one example of the conflation of the executive and legislative functions of the revolutionary government so that a system of checks and balances does not exist.

***Leadership and Political Officials.*** Although according to the Constitution the OPP is technically independent of the Cuban Communist Party (PCC), in effect the party selects candidates for every level of the OPP, especially the National Assembly and the Councils of State and Ministers. In theory, the PCC only provides ideological guidance, but in practice, it exercises direct political power. While appointment or election to governmental posts does not require party membership, those who are not party members are far less likely to be approved as candidates for local OPP and therefore cannot easily begin a political career. The party is directed by its Central Committee, which is chosen every five years at a Party Congress. The First Secretary of the party chooses a smaller body of 25 persons called the Political Bureau that makes daily decisions. Since Fidel Castro is currently President of the Republic, First Secretary of the PCC, President of the Councils of State and the Council of Ministers, and Commander in Chief of the Revolutionary Armed Forces (FAR), no decision can be made that does not meet with his approval. This limits citizens' abilities to genuinely participate in decision-making.

The ideals of the revolution are supported by a majority of the population, and even Cubans who do not support Castro recognize that the socialist government has vastly improved the standard of living of most Cubans. They do not want neocolonial status under the United States, nor do they long for the gulf between wealth and poverty that capitalism produces. Most Cubans probably will support the socialist project even after Castro is gone. To ensure continuity in leadership, Fidel has appointed his brother Raul to succeed him when he dies.

***Social Problems and Control.*** The state has taken advantage of the propensity of Cubans to gossip and spy on their neighbors. Under the threats of invasion and internal turmoil, the government relied on an effective but potentially repressive mechanism for social control, the Committees for the Defense of the Revolution (CDR). These are groups of citizens who observe and document illegal, subversive, or terrorist activity and organize education, health, and community improvement projects. The CDRs were founded in September 1960 to discover and combat sabotage and internal terrorism. In April 1961, they were mobilized to fight against the invasion at the Playa Girón (Bay of Pigs). Once the invasion was defeated and the major counter revolutionary saboteurs and terrorists were expelled or fled, continuing external aggression from the

United States provided an excuse to maintain the CDRs.

In their zeal to defend socialism, the CDRs have sometimes become oppressive organs of state police power. In the 1960s, social deviants denounced by the CDRs were sent to work camps under army supervision, called the Military Units to Aid Production (UMAPS), that were designed to reeducate counter revolutionaries, gays, and other deviants in revolutionary ideology and behavior. Those camps lasted only for two years before being disbanded, but fear of the CDRs and the National Police still operates as a powerful force for social control.

*Military Activity.* Critics of the Revolution point to the CDRs and to teenagers' compulsory one-year military service to claim that Cuba is a highly militarized society. In fact this claim is not true, since the unarmed CDRs are more gossip mills than militia-like brigades, and since a year of agricultural service is an acceptable substitute for the military service. It is true that the Cuban military has historically been very active internationally and is well known for its role in supporting liberation movements worldwide. The Cuban army has traveled all over the world fighting with subaltern peoples in the third world as they struggle for independence from neo-colonial powers or liberation from oppressive dictators. The most renowned effort in this regard has been in Angola, where Cuban soldiers fought against (apartheid) South Africa when it invaded its northern neighbor. Indeed, Nelson Mandela has credited Cuban efforts with a major role in bringing an end to Apartheid. In the fiscal crisis of the 1990s, Cuba has been forced to retrench almost completely from its military and extensive humanitarian commitments around the world.

## SOCIAL WELFARE AND CHANGE PROGRAMS

Social change programs usually are instituted by a ministry or institute of the state. Changes initiated by citizens are channeled through five mass organizations: Federation of Cuban Women (FMC), Confederation of Cuban Workers (CTC), Union of Cuban Youth (UJC), the Committees for the Defense of the Revolution (CDC), and the National Association of Small Farmers (ANAP), through which the state both receives feedback from the people and implements its decisions. Aside from mass organizations and scholarly research institutes associated with a university, there is not much room for private initiative. The state claims that private-sphere movements for change are unneces-

sary, since the Revolution itself is deeply committed to the well-being of all citizens in the realms of employment, health care, education, housing, and food.

## NONGOVERNMENTAL ORGANIZATIONS AND OTHER ASSOCIATIONS

The state assumes full responsibility for all development projects and the well-being of its citizens and is reluctant the to admit need for external assistance. It is true that "freedom brigades" of supporters of socialism from North America and elsewhere have come to work during the sugar harvest, but these have been symbols of ideological support, not material charity. Another North American organization, Pastors for Peace, annually sends a shipment of medicine, food, and medical computers. Several agencies of the United Nations work in Cuba, including the United Nations Development Program, the United Nations Population Fund, the World Health Organization, and the World Bank. And the World Heritage Committee of UNESCO, (United Nations Educational, Scientific, and Cultural Organization) is involved in the architectural restoration of the colonial city of Trinidad and of Old Havana.

## GENDER ROLES AND STATUSES

*Division of Labor by Gender.* As part of its commitment to constructing an egalitarian society, the Revolution has successfully incorporated women into agricultural, industrial, and professional occupations. By 1990, half the doctors and most of the dentists in the country were women.

In 1961, the Revolution began to construct day care centers to free women from constant child care long enough to develop a career or contribute to industrial, agricultural, or intellectual activity. Women's economically productive activity is thought to serve the country as a whole, and in fact women who choose not to work outside the home are sometimes subjects of censure for failing to contribute economically to the Revolution.

But men continue to expect women to perform housework and maintain child-rearing responsibilities even if they have full-time careers outside the home and participate in FMC and PCC activities. The People's Power attempted to address this recalcitrance by enacting a generous maternity law in 1974 and the "Family Code" in 1975. This code defined domestic chores as the responsibility of both partners and required husbands to do half the

*Men harvesting tobacco in Pinar del Rio. Tobacco is an important crop in Cuba, and high–quality Cuban cigars are famous around the world.*

housework if their wives worked outside the home. This is ideologically consistent with socialism, but enforcement of the codes has been difficult, as men are reluctant to relinquish their privilege.

**The Relative Status of Women and Men.** As in the United States, despite women's formal legal equality, they are grossly under-represented in the highest levels of the party, the government, and the military. The resilience of Cuban gender norms is not only a matter of entrenched misogyny; it is encoded into the Revolution itself. Victorious guerillas entered Havana in tanks sporting machetes, machine guns, and long beards from their years in the jungle, having defended their women and motherland. A 1965 newspaper editorial declared that the Revolution is ''a matter for men.'' Nonetheless, iniquitous gender relations have indeed been disrupted by the socialist revolution, and Cuban women are far better off than women in most of Latin America and the rest of the world in terms of education and career options, reproductive rights and health, formal legal protections against discrimination and domestic violence, social supports during child-rearing, and aggressive enforcement of paternity laws.

## MARRIAGE, FAMILY, AND KINSHIP

**Marriage.** In the nineteenth century, anxiety about the Afrocuban majority gave rise to efforts to ''whiten'' the population. This agenda, combined with a chronic shortage of women, led to the development of both a legal code and an informal code which calculated not only ethnicity but also wealth, family reputation, and virginity status to determine which mixed-ethnicity marriages were permissible. The turning of illicit unions into acceptable marriages was part of a social agenda that sought to alleviate anxiety over race relations, illegitimacy, and the shortage of white women, especially in rural areas.

In the countryside, marriage, as with all civil institutions before the Revolution, was far less formal than it was in Havana province. Most rural areas in the east did not have the regular services of a priest, and colonial governmental institutions did not function well. The result was a tradition of marriages that followed regional customs but did not have the benefit of legal or ecclesiastical sanctioning.

In its early years, the Revolution made provisions to formalize ''common-law'' couplings. While some social-reproduction functions of the family

*A group of women walk past apartments in Havana. Housing is at a premium in Havana, and it is not uncommon for families to share an apartment.*

were taken over by the revolutionary state, marriage itself has been encouraged. But the institution of marriage has suffered because of the new legal equality of women. Men have become resentful that their privilege has been disrupted, and women struggle to participate in the PCC and FMC, raise children, maintain their homes, and work full-time outside the home. Under these conditions, marriages are often strained, and the divorce rate is much higher than it was under the neocolonial dictators.

**Domestic Unit.** In addition to liberating women economically, the Revolution has attempted to liberate women's bodies and sexuality. Safe, legal, and free abortion is available on demand for any woman who has reached the age of majority (sixteen years). Contraceptives are widely available, even to young girls, along with effective sex education which is more progressive and honest than that in most other nations. However, the liberation of female sexuality, allowing young girls as well as boys to experiment sexually without social censure, has resulted in a high rate of pregnancy among girls under age sixteen. Adolescent boys have thus enjoyed increased sexual access but are not psychologically or economically prepared to participate in the care and upkeep of their children, resulting in a high number of very young single mothers. The state

has exhorted men to take greater responsibility, and child support payments are extracted from some irresponsible men's salaries, but these efforts have met with only partial success. Hence a typical domestic unit includes a grandmother who is involved in the rearing of the youngest generation, often without the presence of the children's father. Ironically, the participation of grandmothers in child rearing allows men to ignore their parental responsibility and household chores. Domestic units are thus likely to be multigenerational and defined around women, while men come and go in search of work or extramarital recreations.

**Inheritance.** Inheritance is not a major issue in a poor socialist country where significant private property is an exception. Some houses and apartments are privately owned and can be inherited, but the state limits the freedom of an heir to dispose of an inherited housing unit if other Cubans live in it. Most agricultural land has been collectivized or is part of a cooperative and thus is not inheritable. Smaller private property such as heirlooms, clothing, and cars are inherited according to kinship lines without state intervention.

**Kin Groups.** The family has lost some of its importance as the Revolution has taken over some of its economic and social functions. Families are much smaller now and less likely to include wide horizontal connections (though vertical, intergenerational connections continue, and libretta combining is sometimes necessary). It may be, though, that as the state loses its ability to meet the basic material needs of its citizens in the current economic crisis, the family will again increase in prominence.

## SOCIALIZATION

*Infant Care.* Beginning in infancy, the government attempts to instill in citizens the values of socialism. For children, this means teaching the values of collective cohesion and self-forgetting in the interest of the group. Tendencies toward individualism and selfishness, including the use of favorite pacifiers and blankets, are discouraged. It is in the child care centers that this early socialization occurs.

*Child Rearing and Education.* Socialization for integration into the socialist project continues throughout childhood. The general lesson is that individual achievement should be harnessed for the good of the whole; children are encouraged to think about their classmates and have concern for other people's well-being. By the teenage years, high school education includes a year of socialization into the productive life of the nation, as children spend a year away from home in a combination boarding school with agricultural work. This gives the youth a chance to develop social skills with others from different areas, teaches the values of cooperative participation in a common project, gives parents a break from caring for teenagers, teaches agricultural skills to those who wish to make farming their career, and adds to the agricultural workforce.

*Higher Education.* All children receive a primary education. Youths who are preparing for college and pass the entrance examinations attend an academically-oriented school called *pre-universitario*. Those who are best suited for agricultural or industrial careers attend technical schools. Higher education is fully funded by the socialist government, and the state pays university and technical students a monthly stipend for food and lodging. Higher education is so accessible that more people attend universities than there are white-collar jobs available.

## ETIQUETTE

Being generous and hospitable is a highly valued quality. Unlike in Central America, houses are not protected by metal fences, doors are left open, and visitors are always welcomed. It is rude not to greet every man with a handshake and every woman with a kiss on the cheek. Touching as a demonstration of affection is not taboo and does not carry a sexual connotation. Cubans do like to complain and argue heatedly; it is said that an argument is not finished until everyone collapses from exhaustion. But this kind of argument is performative and relieves social tension. More intense interpersonal conflict requires a more subtle approach; Cubans loath open conflict, and so the social norm is to minimize interpersonal conflicts by expressing them through innuendo rather than direct accusation.

## RELIGION

*Religious Beliefs.* Religious faith and practice have not been as influential in the culture of Cuba as in other Latin American nations, for two reasons: first, in the colonial period the Catholic clergy were almost entirely peninsular (born in Spain). They represented the external power of Spain, and hence Catholicism itself was suspect, especially with the population which supported independence. Secondly, there simply were not very many priests in the rural areas, especially in Oriente. Those Cubans who chose to maintain a faith practice were left to produce a religiosity of their own design. The popular religiosity which did develop among white and creole Cubans was a local version of Catholicism enriched with African influences.

Santería is a product of this religious syncretism. Because of the demographic history of the island, Santería—a religious system of the Yorubá people of Nigeria who were brought as slaves—is more prevalent in the eastern region. It is based on the maintenance of relationships, both among people and between people and deities called *orishas*. Since orishas were comparable to and interchangeable with Catholic saints, slaves could put on a face of Catholic piety while worshiping their own gods.

Since the relaxation of state censure in the 1990s there has been an increase of Protestant missionary activity on the island. Catholic church membership is on the rise, and Pope John Paul II was welcomed to the island in January 1998 to the cheering of crowds of both the faithful and the curious. Evangelical Protestantism is growing at an even faster rate, fed perhaps by the desperate mate-

*People during a street festival.*

rial conditions prevalent on the island and the population's need for hope in a sea of poverty and despair.

**Religious Practitioners.** Many religious persons, including priests, participated in the Revolution and supported its ideals, but when it was discovered in 1961 that churches were being used as bases of counterrevolutionary plotting, all foreign priests were invited to leave the island. This hostility was cemented by the declaration of atheism in the first socialist constitution in 1976. Practicing religious leaders and the faithful were thereafter excluded from some professions and promotion to high governmental offices. However, Castro was impressed by the Liberation Theology of Latin America, which sided with the poor in their struggles against oppressive governments and neoliberal capitalism. The leading role of Christian religious leaders in the socialist Nicaraguan revolution was particularly noted by Castro, whose attitude toward religion softened considerably as a result. In the 1980s, more freedom was given to print religious materials and preach, and in 1991, faith was removed as an impediment to party membership.

**Rituals and Holy Places.** Because of the unpopularity and suppression of religion in the early revolutionary period, public Christian rituals are rare.

There are no holy sites to which pilgrimages are made, although the cathedrals in Santiago and Havana are symbolic and continue to offer Mass. More common is a home altar that may include both Catholic and African elements. Afrocuban religion is more likely to be celebrated publicly in Oriente. The churches continue to celebrate events on the Christian calendar, but these rituals do not generally spill out into the streets.

**Death and the Afterlife.** There is no common pattern of belief regarding the afterlife. Santería maintains a belief in the survival of ancestor spirits, and the Christian faithful have a theology of heaven. Funerals are celebrated and may invoke religious imagery, but more common is a secular ceremony in which the deceased is remembered for her contribution to the socialist project.

## MEDICINE AND HEALTH CARE

The Revolution's greatest success has been an astonishing improvement of the health of the population since 1959: Cubans have benefitted dramatically in the last forty years, with lower infant and maternal mortality rates, a higher average caloric consumption, and a vastly reduced number of persons served by each doctor. Cuba has joined the United States and Canada as the only three nations in the Western

Hemisphere to have been granted "best health status" by the United Nations. Since health care is not a matter of profit, and there are no insurance companies in search of wealth, Cuba can provide high-quality health care at a reasonable cost.

Part of this success is due to an innovative system of distribution of health services and a focus on preventive medicine. "Polyclinics" in the municipalities have specialists who treat any number of illnesses. These specialists have been supplemented since 1985 with family physicians, who are even more widely distributed throughout the neighborhoods and focus on prevention and health maintenance.

There are rural areas in which alternative medical practitioners use traditional methods of healing, and there is an element of Santería that seeks spiritual aid to cure physical illness. However, the revolutionary government has great faith in biomedical science as the vehicle for modernization and has invested heavily in biotechnological research. Cuba has engaged in a massive program of humanitarian overseas aid, placing thousands of doctors, nurses, and public health technicians all over the second and third worlds.

Several factors threaten the stability and efficacy of Cuba's health care system. The worsening of the United States embargo as a result of congressional legislation means that not only can medical equipment and medicines not reach Cuban ports, but neither can the latest research reports and scholarly journals. Also, the hierarchical nature of government and society discourages popular participation. The result is a top-down approach to treatment with little patient-doctor consultation. Finally, in the severe spending restrictions of the Special Period, the state can not provide the same level of services it did when the economy was stable. Some health care professionals have been forced to abandon medical practice in favor of work in the more lucrative tourism industry.

## SECULAR CELEBRATIONS

Two significant events in the history of Cuba are celebrated annually with great fanfare. The first is the symbolic date of the triumph of the Cuban Revolution on 1 January 1959, when Batista fled to Miami and the Sierra Maestra guerillas arrived in Havana. This celebration coincides neatly with New Year's. The second event is the attack on the Moncada barracks by Fidel and his fellow revolutionaries on 26 July 1953, symbolically beginning the final and triumphant Cuban Revolutionary

movement. This celebration coincides with the annual "carnival" in both Santiago and Havana. Carnival, consisting of song and dace, outlandish costume, and much drinking and eating, has a history which far precedes the Revolution.

## THE ARTS AND HUMANITIES

**Support for the Arts.** The Revolution's stated goal is to nurture the development of each citizen's abilities, even if those talents are not economically productive. The state supports promising artists and art schools, creating the Cuban Film Institute, the National Cultural Council, and the National School for the Arts. There has recently been some external funding as the international art world has taken great interest in Cuban artistic production.

**Literature.** Writers enjoy the privileged position of visionary thinkers, partly a result of the fact that the hero of Cuban nationalism was a poet, José Martí. In the early years of the Revolution, there was considerable censorship, but the state relaxed censorship in 1987 and now allows critical ideas to be debated openly as long as they do not incite treason.

**Graphic Arts.** Though artistic production is supported by the state, in the past it was also ideologically constrained by state censors. But now that Cuban art has become popular in the United States and Europe, it has become a potential source of external revenue from tourists and art dealers. The state has become more permissive toward protest art since it became financially lucrative.

Film has been a popular and successful form of art since 1959. Havana hosts the internationally renowned New Latin American Film Festival every year. Cubans love going to the cinema; it is a favored and inexpensive form of recreation, and since film production has been socialized, going to the movies only costs about fourteen cents.

**Performance Arts.** Expressive language, music, and dance are a cultural heritage that Cubans express frequently. Any Cuban can dance and enjoys performing at Carnival, for tourists, or at parties. Afrocuban music is performed on street corners and in living rooms all over the island. Cuba is also known worldwide for the National Ballet of Cuba, whose founder and artistic director, Alicia Alonso, continues to guide the company and attend performances. In keeping with the ideals of the socialist state, the ballet is supported by public funds, so that it is accessible to all citizens, costing only about twenty-five cents per performance.

## THE STATE OF THE PHYSICAL AND SOCIAL SCIENCES

Scientists in all fields are supported by the state, which sees scientific advancement as the key to the success of the socialist project. Medical research has been especially successful. But in the current economic crisis, the state has been unable to maintain its scientists and laboratories as it did in the past. The United States embargo makes it difficult to obtain even basic laboratory supplies.

As to the social sciences, the government has supported thousands of historians, anthropologists, philosophers, and economists. There is some limitation on social scientific research, since the state does not permit the publication of findings that suggest an abandonment of the socialist project or of the PCC. Within that constraint, any investigation or finding can be published and debated, even if it calls for reform.

## BIBLIOGRAPHY

Balari, Eugenio. "Agricultural Policy with Social Justice and Development." In Sandor Halebsky and John Kirk, eds., *Transformation and Struggle: Cuba Faces the 1990s*, 1990.

Dilla, Haroldo. *Comrades and Investors: The Uncertain Transition in Cuba*, translated by Michael Gonzales, 1998.

Halebsky, Sandor, and John Kirk, eds. *Transformation and Struggle: Cuba Faces the 1990s*, 1990.

Hatchwell, Emily, and Simon Calder. *Cuba in Focus: A Guide to the People, Politics, Culture*, 2000.

Helg, Aline. *Our Rightful Share: The Afro-Cuban Struggle for Equality, 1886–1912*, 1995.

Monreal, P. "Sea Changes: The New Cuban Economy." *Report on the Americas* XXXII 5: 21–29, 1999.

Moore, Robin. *Nationalizing Blackness: Afrocubanismo and Artistic Revolution in Havana, 1920–1940*, 1997.

Pérez-López, Jorge, ed. *Cuba at a Crossroads: Politics and Economics after the Fourth Party Congress*, 1994.

Pérez, Louis. *Cuba: Between Reform and Revolution*, 1996.

———. *On Becoming Cuban: Identity, Nationality, and Culture*, 1999.

Peters, P. and J. Scarpaci, *Cuba's New Entrepreneurs: Five Years of Small-Scale Capitalism*, 1998.

Smith, Lois, and Alfred Padula. *Sex and Revolution: Women in Socialist Cuba*, 1996.

Thomas, Hugh. *Cuba, or the Pursuit of Freedom*, 1998.

—G. DERRICK HODGE

# Cyprus

**CULTURE NAME**
Cypriot

**ALTERNATIVE NAMES**
Greek Cypriot, Turkish Cypriot

**ORIENTATION**

*Identification.* Cyprus is an island in the eastern Mediterranean that was divided into a Greek southern side and a Turkish northern side after a coup instigated by the dictatorship ruling Greece in 1974 and a subsequent Turkish military offensive. Interethnic violence had earlier caused the partial separation of the two communities. With a Greek majority of around 77 percent of the population at the time of independence in 1960, many people regard Cyprus as part of the wider Greek culture. Although the island became part of the Byzantine Empire in the fourth century, it was part of the Ottoman Empire from 1571 to 1878 and had an 18.3 percent Turkish minority in 1960. Greek Cypriots are Christian Orthodox, while Turkish Cypriots are Sunni Muslim.

*Location and Geography.* The island is close to Turkey, Syria, and Egypt. Both Greek and Turkish Cypriots prefer to think of themselves as living close to Europe rather than Africa and the Middle East. The island appears barren and yellow in the long summertime and greener in the winter, with carob and olive trees along with pine forests on the mountains. The centrally located capital, Nicosia (called *Lefkosia* by Greek Cypriots and *Lefkosha* by Turkish Cypriots), is divided and functions as the capital of each side.

*Demography.* In 1960, the island emerged as an independent state after almost a century of British colonial rule. At that time, the demographics were as follows: Greek Cypriots, 77 percent (441,656); Turkish Cypriots, 18.3 percent (104,942); Arme-

nians–Gregorians, 0.6 percent (3,378); and Roman Catholics and Maronites, 0.5 percent (2,752); with a total population of 573,566. Since the 1974 division, the population statistics have been disputed. Many Turkish Cypriots left because of declining economic conditions on their side of the island, while many Turkish settlers moved in because they viewed northern Cyprus as being better off than Turkey. Greek Cypriot official sources provided the following breakdown for the island as a whole in 1977: 735,900 total, of whom 623,200 are Greek (84.7 percent), 90,600 are Turkish (12.3 percent), and 22,100 (3 percent) are foreigners. Those sources claim that there are now 85,000 Turkish settlers on the Turkish Cypriot side and that around 45,000 Turkish Cypriots have emigrated.

*Linguistic Affiliation.* Greek Cypriots are taught at schools and employ in writing and orally, on formal and public occasions, standard modern Greek (SMG), while Turkish Cypriots employ standard modern Turkish (SMT). For informal oral exchanges, each community employs what could be called the Cypriot dialect. Cyprus has a high degree of literacy, and much of the population can communicate in English, especially the younger generation.

Until the 1970s, Turkish Cypriots could communicate adequately in Greek and a significant number of elderly Greek Cypriots could understand some Turkish. However, political conflict gradually led to increasing linguistic barriers. As animosity increased, the act of speaking the enemy's language was considered unpatriotic. Now, after twenty-six years of complete separation, very few Greek Cypriots can understand Turkish and no young Turkish Cypriots speak or understand Greek.

For informal oral exchanges, each community employs a different idiom, known within each side as "the Cyprus dialect." Those dialects are sometimes regarded as intimate, local, and authentic idioms vis–a–vis the two standard varieties, while in

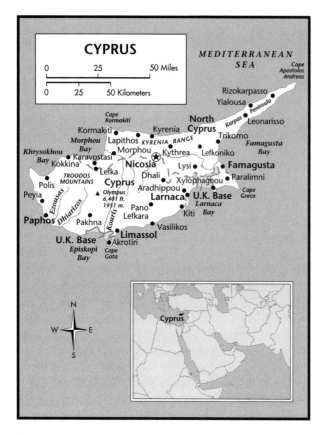

## CYPRUS

0     25     50 Miles

0   25   50 Kilometers

*MEDITERRANEAN SEA*

Cape Apostolos Andreas

Rizokarpasso
Yialousa
*Karpas Peninsula*
Cape Kormakiti
Kormakiti
Kyrenia
North Cyprus
Leonarisso
Morphou Bay
Lapithos *KYRENIA RANGE*
Trikomo
Khrysokhou Bay
Morphou
Kythrea
Famagusta Bay
Kokkina
Karavostasi
Nicosia
Lefkoniko
Lefka
Lysi
Famagusta
Polis
*TROODOS MOUNTAINS*
Cyprus
Dhali
Xylophaghou
Paralimni
Peyia
Olympus 6,401 ft. 1951 m.
Aradhippou
Larnaca
U.K. Base
Cape Greco
*Exousas*
Pano
Lefkara
Kiti
Larnaca Bay
Paphos
*Dhiarizos*
Pakhna
*Kouris*
Vasilikos
U.K. Base
Akrotiri
Limassol
Episkopi Bay
Cape Gata

N
W   E
S

Cyprus

*Cyprus*

other contexts they may be seen as low, vulgar, or peasant idioms.

**Symbolism**. When Cyprus emerged as a state in 1960, it acquired a flag but not a national anthem. The flag shows a map of the island in orange–yellow against a white background, symbolizing the color of copper, for which the island was renowned in ancient times. Under this lies a wreath of olive leaves. The symbolism of the flag thus draws on nature rather than culture or religion. The official symbol of the 1960 state, the Republic of Cyprus, is a dove flying with an olive branch in its beak in a shield inscribed with the date 1960, all within a wreath of olive leaves, symbolizing the desire for peace. Until 1963, when interethnic conflict broke out, a neutral piece of music was played on official state occasions; after 1963, the two communities fully adopted the national anthems of Greece and Turkey.

The flag of the Republic of Cyprus was rarely used before 1974. Greek Cypriots, who after 1960 were striving for union with Greece (*enosis*), used the Greek flag, while Turkish Cypriots hoping for the division of the island (*taksim*) used the flag of Turkey. The flag of the republic was used more commonly after the 1974 separation of the island, but only by Greek Cypriots. It was employed as a state symbol of the Republic of Cyprus, which in practice meant the Greek side. Turkish Cypriots declared their own state in 1983 under the name of the Turkish Republic of Northern Cyprus (TRNC), which has been recognized only by Turkey. In striving to prevent international political recognition of the Turkish Cypriot polity, Greek Cypriots started to employ the official flag of the republic. In practice, however, Greek Cypriots often fly both the Greek flag and that of the republic, while Turkish Cypriots fly both their own flag and that of Turkey.

The largest left-wing parties on both sides, which are antinationalist and progressive, often jointly support the "Cypriot identity thesis," in which people are considered first and foremost Cypriots. The largest right–wing Greek and Turkish parties, which are nationalist and conservative, emphasize ethnic and cultural affiliations with the two other states.

The national days of Greece and Turkey are commemorated, along with dates from the history of Cyprus. Such commemorations often stir feelings of animosity. The most important commemorations for Greek Cypriots are the start of the anticolonial struggle (1 April 1955), the independence of the Republic of Cyprus in 1960 (1 October), and the two days of mourning for the events of July 1974: the Greek attempted coup of 15 July 1974, and the subsequent Turkish military offensive on 20 July 1974, known among Greek Cypriots as the "Anniversaries of the Treacherous Coup and the Barbaric Turkish Invasion." Turkish Cypriots commemorate the establishment of the Turkish Cypriot nationalist resistance organization in 1958 (1 August 1958). During December, a week is devoted to the period spanning 1963 to 1967, mourning those who died in the interethnic fighting that erupted around Christmas 1963. This is called the "Week of Remembrance of the Martyrs and the Struggle." The Turkish armed offensive of 20 July 1974 is celebrated as the anniversary of the "Happy Peace Operation." Turkish Cypriots also commemorate 15 November 1983 as "Independence Day," when they declared themselves as a state.

## HISTORY AND ETHNIC RELATIONS

**Emergence of the Nation**. The processes of nation building, which transformed Christian and Muslim peasants in Cyprus from colonial subjects to Greeks and Turks, followed those of nation building in Greece and Turkey. Only in the twentieth century was there a widespread emergence of Greek and Turkish national consciousness in Cyprus. During the colonial period, both communities employed teachers from the two states, or their own teachers were educated in Greece or Turkey. Both actively encouraged those states to support them, as Greek Cypriots were striving for enosis and Turkish Cypriots initially wanted the island to remain under British rule or be returned to Turkey. As both groups identified with their mainland "brothers," their respective cultures were transformed in ways that drew them apart from each other. This process began with the identification of each group with the history of the "motherland" rather than the history of Cyprus per se.

During the nineteenth and twentieth centuries, the peasants of Cyprus shared a number of cultural traits, but as ethnic boundaries became stronger, those syncretic cultural traits gradually disappeared. Muslims might visit Christian churches to pray and offer votive offerings to Christian saints. There were people who came to be known as Cotton–Linens (*Linopambakoi*), who practiced both religions at the same time. Even more widespread commonalities existed with regard to folk religion and medicine. People would visit a local healer or spiritual leader of either creed to solve all daily problems, be cured of illnesses, and avoid becoming bewitched. Those common elements gradually were abolished as Orthodox Christianity and Sunni Islam became established. Similar processes took place with regards to language as the mostly oral mixed varieties were replaced by the written official national languages of Greece and Turkey.

Greek Cypriot folklorists attempted to legitimize the struggle for enosis by emphasizing links to contemporary or ancient Greeks, while Turkish Cypriot folklore studies emphasized the commonalties of Turkish Cypriots with the people of Turkey. These attempts at proving a group's purity and authenticity often were accompanied by attempts to prove the impurity and mixed culture (and blood) of the other community in order to deny those people an identity and even existence as political actors who could voice demands. Those conflicts were exacerbated by British colonialism, which tried to disprove the presence of Greeks and Turks in Cyprus in order to counter their anticolonial political strivings, advocating instead the existence of a Cypriot nation with a slave mentality that required benevolent British guidance.

**National Identity.** In 1960, the new state was composed of people who considered themselves Greeks and Turks rather than Cypriots; these people did not support the state. Interethnic conflict erupted in 1963 and continued until 1967, when Turkish Cypriots found themselves on the losing side. When an extreme right–wing military junta emerged in Greece in 1967, its policies in Cyprus led to resentment and made Greek Cypriots wary of joining Greece. As interethnic strife begun to abate, Greek Cypriots tried to reverse the separatist situation. Turkish Cypriots had moved into enclaves under their own administration, and Greek Cypriots tried to reintegrate them in social and political life. In the late 1960s, the two sides negotiated their differences in a relatively peaceful environment. Turkish Cypriots emerged from their enclaves and began, at least in economic terms, to reintegrate with Greek Cypriots. During this period, some Greek Cypriots started to regard themselves as Cypriots, in control of an independent state whose sovereignty they tried to safeguard both from Greek interference and from the threat posed by Turkish enclaves. A group of right–wing Greek Cypriots, with the encouragement of the junta and against the wishes of the vast majority of Greek Cypriots, launched a coup in 1974. The aim was to depose Archbishop Makarios, the president of the republic, and join Greece. Turkey reacted with a military offensive that caused enormous suffering among Greek Cypriots, 170,000 of whom were displaced from the 37 percent of the island that came under the control of Turkey. Population exchanges led to the creation of two ethnically homogeneous sides, although negotiations for a solution still take place.

**Ethnic Relations.** Greek Cypriots who want a unified state claim that people peacefully coexisted in mixed communities in the past. Turkish Cypriots argue that the two groups always lived in partial separation and conflict.

After 1974, reunification emerged as the major Greek Cypriot political objective. This change in political aspirations led to major revisions. First, the "peaceful coexistence thesis" was established as a historical argument that proposed that if the past was characterized by coexistence, so would a united future. A policy of rapprochement toward Turkish Cypriots necessitated measures of goodwill toward Turkish Cypriots. Turkish Cypriots no longer were regarded as enemies but as compatriots, and all animosity was directed toward Turkey. Gradually, the term "brother," once used only for Greeks (living in Greece) has begun to refer to Turkish Cypriots. Greek Cypriots officially started to talk of "one people" who should live in one state, while Turkish Cypriots officially spoke of "two peoples" or "two nations" which should live separately.

*Boats moored in the harbor at Kyrenia. In seaside towns and villages, tourism and fishing are important parts of the economy.*

However, Greek Cypriot society became more culturally integrated with Greece through education and the reception of Greek television channels. The Turkish Cypriot authorities actively encouraged even stronger measures of integration with Turkey, both economically and culturally.

The strongest proponents of a distinct Cypriot identity come from the largest left–wing party, AKEL. Supporters of that party were in the past victimized for being communist and treated as unpatriotic traitors by right–wingers speaking in the name of Greek nationalism. They had many contacts with Turkish Cypriots through left–wing organizations, such as joint trade unions.

On the Turkish Cypriot side, Turkey generally is considered as having liberated Turkish Cypriots, but after 1974 various groups came to identify themselves ethnically and culturally as Cypriots rather than Turks. Politically, these groups are more in favor of a unified state than are the right–wing Turkish Cypriot parties. As a result of the enormous influx of Turkish people into the island, they feel threatened by cultural assimilation by Turkey. Turkish workers also provide an unwelcome source of cheap labor that competes with Turkish Cypriot workers and their trade unions. For this reason, they began to stress that jobs and resources should belong to the "Cypriots" rather

than the outsiders (Turks). As a result of these developments, a new school of folklore studies emerged after 1974 on the Turkish Cypriot side that stresses cultural commonalties with Greek Cypriots. Turks are sometimes called *karasakal* ("black–bearded") by Turkish Cypriots, a term with connotations of backwardness and religious fanaticism.

People on both sides are mostly secular, especially on the Turkish Cypriot side, since Turkish national identity emerged as a secular antireligious ideology. Greek nationalism eventually acquired strong religious overtones in the form of the Hellenic–Christians ideals, but the influence of religion is also on the decline on the Greek Cypriot side.

## URBANISM, ARCHITECTURE, AND THE USE OF SPACE

The most striking examples of monumental architecture during the British colonial period were schools built by Greek Cypriots emphasizing a Greek classical facade. After 1960 school buildings utilized a "modern" and functional style. The most imposing examples of contemporary monumental architecture are the glass and marble-covered bank buildings on the more affluent Greek Cypriot side. In terms of officially built monuments, which abound on both sides, the largest ones are those

*Meals commonly feature bread, yogurt, and a variety of vegetables, salads, and dips.*

depicting living and deceased political leaders. On the Greek Cypriot side, an enormous statue of past-president Archbishop Makarios stands opposite another monument symbolizing the EOKA fight against anticolonialism (1955–1960), with freedom as a woman opening the prison door to emerging fighters and civilians. On the Turkish Cypriot side, the largest such monument lying outside Famagusta is dedicated to Ataturk (the founder of the state of Turkey), whose head appears on the top. Another, multisided, monument is outside Nicosia with the inscription "We Will Not Forget;" it features Denktash, the current Turkish Cypriot leader, and Kuchuk, a once prominent politician. Perhaps the most striking feature in the landscape of the whole island is the "stamping" of the mountain range in the Turkish Cypriot side with two enormous flags, those of Turkey and the TRNC, visible from miles away with an inscription by Ataturk: "How Happy to Say I am a Turk." This could be seen as an attempt by the internationally unrecognized Turkish Cypriot state to engrave its presence on the land and remind all—Greek Cypriots, Turkish Cypriots, and foreign visitors alike—that it exists and is in control of the north side of the island.

From the middle of the twentieth century, the dominant trend was for people to move towards the urban centers and abandon the villages, a trend ex-acerbated by ethnic conflict. These demographic shifts took place as people searched for employment in government jobs, in the expanding industry, and later in the tourism sector. The social and political upheavals caused significant numbers of Greek Cypriots and Turkish Cypriots to become, at one time or other, dislocated. This meant that town planning could never be seriously enforced, giving a rather cluttered character to urban space. The 'traditional' one room-type village house gradually disappeared as the emergence of a more individualized society necessitated separate rooms, at least for each adult. Related to this were changes in settlement patterns. While in the past relatives often formed neighborhoods, as land plots were divided and subdivided among children, the emergence of the nuclear family gradually changed this pattern. Overall, despite rapid industrialization and other changes of a capitalist nature, once couples are married, they build on the assumption of marital, occupational and geographical stability. This entails the construction of often large and expensive houses, which may place the couple in debt for ten to twenty years.

## FOOD AND ECONOMY

***Food in Daily Life.*** Fresh salad and plain yogurt accompany most meals, which usually consist of vegetables cooked in various ways and includes what is known by both communities as *yahni* (with olive oil, tomatoes and onions). When people eat out they often order *meze*, a large collection of small dishes starting with various dips and salads and ending with grilled meat or fish.

**Basic Economy.** Both sides in Cyprus are fairly self-sufficient in terms of food production and both export a variety of fruit and vegetables. The agrarian sector of the economy is gradually diminishing as the service sector assumes prominence.

**Major Industries.** On the Greek Cypriot side, beyond a significant sector of light industry, the tourism and services sectors have been growing very rapidly. Cyprus has become a fairly typical Mediterranean tourist resort, attracting millions of tourists annually, mainly from northern Europe. Its position at the crossroads of Europe, Asia, and Africa has led to a significant expansion of the service sector (which has lately been reaching markets such as the ex-Soviet Union and Eastern Europe). Various incentives have made it very popular as a site for offshore trading, shipping, and other offshore activities. The even more turbulent political climate in some of the nearby Middle Eastern countries (such as Lebanon) has led to various companies choosing Cyprus as a base for their activities in the area.

On the Turkish Cypriot side, agrarian production is much more significant, as it has been less able to develop tourism and industry. This is partly a result of a lack of funds for necessary investments and infrastructure improvements, but it is also an outcome of an international trade embargo that the Republic of Cyprus has been successful in levying against the Turkish Cypriot regime. This means, for example, that international air companies do not fly directly to northern Cyprus and that tourists wishing to travel there must work their way through Istanbul, raising expenses and travel time. For these reasons, there has been a steady migration of Turkish Cypriots abroad, to places such as Turkey and the United Kingdom, in search of employment. The unemployment problem in the north contrasts with the full-employment status of the south, one it has been enjoying continuously for more than 20 years, which leads to a net import of workers from abroad.

## SOCIAL STRATIFICATION

**Classes and Castes.** On the Greek Cypriot side, one of the strongest social movements has been that represented by the communist party, AKEL. It has consistently commanded about a third of the total votes cast in elections during the post-independence period. Related and linked to this is the strong and effective presence of trade unions, which have successfully defended and promoted workers' rights. Highly organized and well represented, the working class movement has managed to claim significant benefits for its members and has kept up with the rise in living standards. This has, to a significant extent, reduced the possibility of wide-ranging class distinctions, giving rise to a large middle class with few instances of poverty and almost no evidence of destitution, such as homelessness. The full-employment status in Greek Cyprus has contributed to this state of affairs.

On the Turkish Cypriot side, the political left has also been a significant political force, commanding 25 to 30 percent of the vote. However, high unemployment and grave economic problems, along with an influx of destitute migrant workers from Turkey who are prepared to work for very low wages, have prevented Turkish workers from organizing and effectively protecting workers' rights. The prevalence of patronage and clientilism has meant that those close to right-wing parties, which have the most political power, are also favored economically, giving rise to more rigid wealth distinctions.

## POLITICAL LIFE

**Government.** The Republic of Cyprus is a democracy with a presidential system of government. On some issues, notably defense and international politics it may act in cooperation or in consultation with Greece. The Turkish Cypriot regime is a parliamentary democracy with a marked political, military, and economic dependence on Turkey.

**Leadership and Political Officials.** In general the practice of patronage politics is widespread on both sides of Cyprus, more so on the Turkish side due to the much smaller size of the population, the poorer economic conditions, and the fact that political leader Rauf Denktash has remained in power for almost three decades. With the exception perhaps of the largest left-wing parties on both sides, other parties tend to be more person- than principle- or policy-focused.

Both sides have a similar political party structure in terms of left and right. The right-wing parties on each side (Democratic Rally on the Greek Cypriot side, National Unity Party and Democratic Party on the Turkish Cypriot side) tend to be na-

*A Turkish boundary line in Nicosia, Cyprus, limits Greeks from entering the area.*

tionalistic, with strong links to ex-freedomfighters' associations, encompassing a spectrum of supporters from the far right to more liberal elements, and persistently advocating links with the two "motherlands." The two left-wing parties (AKEL on the Greek Cypriot side and CTP on the Turkish Cypriot side) are composed mainly of communist supporters and have a strong antinationalist stance that advocates more links between the people of the two sides instead of with Greece and Turkey.

## GENDER ROLES AND STATUSES

**Division of Labor by Gender.** On both sides, there is a strong, though contested and decreasing, element of patriarchy. Economic, social, and political power are concentrated in the hands of men, and only men can become religious functionaries, whether Christian or Muslim. Women are almost absent from political offices, although they are entering the workplace in increasing numbers. However, in general they are employed in jobs of lesser status and lower remuneration than men. The entry of women into the job force, while offering a financial base for more independence and security, often means that women undertake both the role of working outside the house while still retaining

their responsibilities in the home, resulting in a double burden. A solution is often found, especially on the richer Greek Cypriot side, by importing female workers (notably from Sri Lanka, Thailand, and the Philippines) to take over the domestic responsibilities.

## MARRIAGE, FAMILY, AND KINSHIP

**Marriage.** Whereas half a decade ago a significant proportion of marriages were arranged (often by the father), this has largely disappeared, although parents may still exert strong control and influence over marital choices. Most people consider getting married to be the normal course of action, so the vast majority do in fact marry; those who don't are often viewed as being either eccentric or unlucky, or both. Whereas previously the provision of a dowry, mostly for women, was considered mandatory, parents still feel they should provide as much economic support as possible for their children when they marry. Ideally, the parents hope to provide the newlywed couple with a fully furnished house and other basic needs, such as one or two cars.

**Domestic Unit.** The typical family arrangement on both sides is the nuclear family, often with fairly strong ties towards a more extended family, especially the parents. Most couples hope to have two children, preferably one of each sex. The more traditional division between the public domain (work, etc.), which is overseen by the male, and the private domain (the home), which is overseen by the female, is still strong, despite women's entry into the labor market. Since people usually move into city apartments or build their own home, relatives do not live in as close proximity as in the past, when they lived in clusters of houses in the same town or village.

## SOCIALIZATION

**Infant Care.** Children are considered to be important, whether they are toddlers or as teenagers. As babies they are usually the woman's responsibility, and the social environment on both sides is very accepting of children in public spaces, such as restaurants. Parents put significant energy into providing a rich and stimulating environment for their children.

**Child Rearing and Education.** Parents take their children's education very seriously, carefully considering which school the children should attend and becoming actively involved in the whole

*A man and woman repair fishing nets in a boat in Paphos, Cyprus.*

schooling process. Providing a good education is considered as one of the most important parental responsibilities and is very highly valued in general. A child is viewed as being economically dependent on parents, with parents responsible for shouldering a child's expenses at least until the child graduates from university, if not up until marriage itself.

***Higher Education.*** Most parents strive to provide a university education for their children, and the percentage of people with university degrees is very high by any standard. To achieve this goal, parents start to save early in order to cover the large expenses (since until a few years ago there were no universities in Cyprus), or they ask for a bank loan or sell property, as they feel it is their responsibility to pay their children's expenses until they graduate from university.

## ETIQUETTE

Cyprus as a whole could be characterized as a rather informal place. People easily and casually enter into physical contact and in general, personal space is not rigidly marked. There are more formal and polite forms of address that are employed in particular circumstances (such as toward elders, or in a professional situation, for example), but the absence of entrenched historical hierarchies and strong class distinctions allows daily exchanges to proceed in a mostly casual fashion. Because both societies are small, individuals usually know many of the people with whom they come into contact, thus decreasing the need for formalities. Visitors from larger Western countries often remark that Cyprus seems to be a place where "everyone knows each other," or even "where everyone is related to each other."

## RELIGION

***Religious Beliefs.*** The vast majority of Greek Cypriots are Greek Orthodox, while most Turkish Cypriots are Sunni Muslim.

## SECULAR CELEBRATIONS

Secular celebrations are mostly national commemorations of historical events, including those of Cyprus itself and those from Greece (for the Greek Cypriots) or Turkey (for the Turkish Cypriots).

The main secular celebrations of Greek Cypriots include the following: 25 March: Greek National Day (commemorating the 1821 start of the struggle for independence from the Ottomans in Greece); 1 April: Anniversary of EOKA (commemorating the 1955 start of the Greek Cypriot anti-colonial struggle by the National Organization of Cypriot Fighters [EOKA]); 1 October: Independence Day (commemorating the 1960 creation of the Republic of Cyprus); 28 October: *OHI* (NO) Day (commemorating the 1940 refusal of Greece to surrender to Germany leading to the involvement of Greece in the World War II).

The main secular celebrations of Turkish Cypriots are: 19 May: Youth and Sports Day; 20 July: Peace and Freedom Day (commemorating the Turkish military intervention in Cyprus starting on 20 July 1974); 1 August: Communal Resistance Day (commemorating the 1958 founding of the Turkish Resistance Organization [TMT], also commemorating the Ottoman conquest of Cyprus and Day of Armed Forces); 30 August: Victory Day (anniversary of the victory of Turkish army in 1922 against the Greeks leading to the emergence of an independent Turkish state); 29 October: Turkish National Day (commemorating the creation of the state of Turkey in 1923); 15 November: Independence Day (unilateral declaration of the Turkish Republic of Northern Cyprus as an independent state in 1983).

## STATE OF PHYSICAL AND SOCIAL SCIENCES

The 1980s were a period of rapid growth in the local provision of college and university education on both sides. Many state and private universities or colleges were created during that time period in order to cater to the already present and rapidly rising demand for university-level education. The new universities have also been successful in attracting students from other countries, notably the ex-Soviet Union, Eastern Europe, Turkey, Africa, Asia, and the Middle East. These institutions have provided a significant increase in the amount of research conducted in the social and physical sciences, which was previously almost nonexistent. Due to the colonial presence and subsequent political problems, research in Cyprus used to be mainly focused on disciplines such as history, folklore, and politics, which both sides could use to support and legitimize their political goals.

## BIBLIOGRAPHY

Ali, Aydin Mehmet, ed. *Turkish Cypriot Identity in Literature*, 1990.

Argyrou, Vassos. *Tradition and Modernity in the Mediterranean: The Wedding as Symbolic Struggle*, 1996.

Attalides, Michails, ed. *Cyprus Reviewed*, 1977.

———. *Cyprus: Nationalism and International Politics*, 1979.

Azgin, Bekir, and Yiannis Papadakis. "Folklore." In K. Grothusen, W. Steffani, and P. Zervakis, eds., *Cyprus: Handbook on South Eastern Europe*, 1998.

Beckingham, Charles. "Islam and Turkish Nationalism in Cyprus." *Die Welt des Islam* 5: 65–83, 1957.

Calotychos, Vangelis, ed. *Cyprus and its People: Nation, Identity and Experience in an Unimaginable Community 1955–1997*, 1998.

Ertekun, Necatigil. *The Cyprus Dispute and the Birth of the Turkish Republic of Northern Cyprus*, 1981.

Gazioglu, Ahmet. *The Turks in Cyprus*, 1990.

Given, Michael. "Inventing the Eteocypriots: Imperialist Archaeology and the Manipulation of Ethnic Identity." *Journal of Mediterranean Archaeology* 11 (1): 3–29, 1998.

———. "Star of the Parthenon, Cypriot Melange: Education and Representation in Colonial Cyprus." *Journal of Mediterranean Studies*, 7 (1): 59–82, 1997.

Grothusen, Klaus–Detlev, Winfried Steffani, and Peter Zervakis, eds. *Handbook on South Eastern Europe*, 1998.

Harbottle, Michael. *The Impartial Soldier*, 1970.

HAS–DER. *Halkbilim Sempozyumlari (Folklore Symposiums)*, 1986.

Hill, George. *A History of Cyprus*, 1948–1952.

Islamoglu, Mehmet. *Kibris Turk Kultur ve Sanati [Cypriot Turkish Culture and Art]*, 1994.

Ismail, Sabahetin. *20 July Peace Operation: Reasons, Developments, Consequences*, 1989.

King, Russel, and Sarah Ladbury. "The Cultural Reconstruction of Political Reality: Greek and Turkish Cyprus since 1974." *Anthropological Quarterly* 55: 1–16, 1982.

Kitromilides, Paschalis. "Greek Irredentism in Asia Minor and Cyprus." *Middle Eastern Studies* 26 (1): 3–15.

Kizilyurek, Niyazi. *Oliki Kypros [Whole Cyprus]*, 1990.

Kyrris, Kostas. *Peaceful Coexistence in Cyprus under the British Rule (1878–1959)*, 1977.

Loizos, Peter. *The Greek Gift*, 1975.

———. *The Heart Grown Bitter: A Chronicle of Cypriot War Refugees*, 1979.

———. "Intercommunal Killing in Cyprus." *Man* 23: 639–653.

Markides, Kyriakos. *The Rise and Fall of the Cyprus Republic*, 1977.

*North Cyprus Almanac*, 1987.

Papadakis, Yiannis. "Greek Cypriot Narratives of History and Collective Identity: Nationalism as a Contested Process." *American Ethnologist* 25 (2): 149–165, 1998.

Patrick, Richard. *Political Geography and the Cyprus Conflict*, 1976 Press and Information Office of the Republic of Cyprus. *The Almanac of Cyprus*, 1997.

Peristianis, John. "Anthropological, Sociological and Geographical Fieldwork in Cyprus." In M. Diemen and E. Fried, eds., *Regional Variation in Modern Greece and Cyprus*, 1976.

Purcell, H. *Cyprus*, 1969.

Salih, Hikmet. *Cyprus: The Impact of Diverse Nationalism on a State*, 1978.

Sant Cassia, Paul. "The Archbishop in the Beleaguered City: An Analysis of the Conflicting Roles and Political Oratory of Makarios." *Byzantine and Modern Greek Studies* 8: 191–212, 1983.

———. "Patterns of Covert Politics in Post–Independence Cyprus." *Archives of European Sociology* 24: 115–135, 1983.

———. "Religion, Politics and Ethnicity in Cyprus during the Turkokratia." *Archives of European Sociology* 27: 3–28, 1986.

Stavrinides, Zenon. *The Cyprus Conflict: National Identity and Statehood*, 1975.

Tachau, Frank. "The Face of Turkish Nationalism as Reflected in the Cyprus Dispute." *Middle East Journal* 13: 262–272, 1959.

Volkan, Vamik. *Cyprus: War and Adaptation*, 1978

Worsley, Peter, and Paschalis Kitromilides, eds. *Small States in the Modern World: The Conditions of Survival*, 1979.

—YIANNIS PAPADAKIS

# CZECH REPUBLIC

## CULTURE NAME

Czech

The term "Czech" refers to the cultural characteristics of the Czech-speaking inhabitants of the Czech Republic (*Česká republika*), which includes Bohemia (*Čechy*), the larger western part, and Moravia (*Morava*), the eastern part. Northern Moravia includes Silesia (*Slezsko*), a historical region that lies mostly in southwestern Poland. The Silesians (*Slezané*) of the Czech Republic tend to maintain their ethnic character, but many agree that they constitute a subculture within the Czech culture.

## ALTERNATIVE NAMES

Czechs call their culture *česká kultura*. The historical and geographic term "Bohemian" is misleading, as it not only excludes Czech-speaking Moravians but includes members of several ethnic minorities that live in Bohemia but do not speak Czech.

## ORIENTATION

*Identification.* The origin of the words *Čechy* (Bohemia) and *Čech* ([a] Czech) is not clear. *Čechy* originally may have referred to a dry place, or it may have been a place-name that eventually gave rise to the name of its inhabitants. Alternatively, the ethnic designation *Čech* (pl. *Češi* or *Čechové*) is explained as an abbreviated pet name for a groom (a person responsible for the care of horses, *čeledín*), or it might have been someone's name. The words *Čech*, *Čechy*, and *česká* ("Czech" or "Bohemian") first occur in the oldest rhymed Czech chronicle (*Dalimilova kronika*), which dates back to the beginning of the fourteenth century.

*Location and Geography.* The area of the Czech Republic is 30,450 square miles (78,866 square kilometers), with Bohemia being twice as large as Moravia. The republic is bounded by Poland on the north, Germany on the northwest and southwest,

Austria on the south, and the Slovak Republic on the east.

Bohemia is ringed by low mountain ranges. Sněžka in the north is the highest point at 5,256 feet (1,602 meters). The chief rivers are the Labe (Elbe) and its main tributaries, the Vltava (Moldau) and the Ohře (Eger); the Elbe flows into the North Sea. Moravia's dominant geographic feature is the basin of the Morava River, which empties into the Danube west of Bratislava, the capital of the Slovak Republic.

*Demography.* The population of the Czech Republic in 1999 was about 10.3 million according to the Statistical Yearbook of the Czech Republic, (in recent years there have been small population losses). The ethnic composition is 94 percent Czech (Moravians and Bohemian Czechs), 3 percent Slovak, 0.6 percent Polish, 0.5 percent German, 0.3 percent Romany (Gypsy) officially but perhaps as much as 2.5 percent, and about 0.4 percent Ukrainian. Other ethnic minorities are numerically insignificant. For example, the Jewish population is probably no more than 12,000 because over 80,000 Jews died in Nazi concentration camps during World War II.

The border regions, which began to be inhabited by many German-speaking people in the second half of the twelfth century, were resettled after World War II by Czechs after nearly three million Bohemian and Moravian Germans were expelled or chose to leave.

*Linguistic Affiliation.* The Czech language (čeština or česky jazyk) belongs to the West Slavic sub-branch of the Slavic languages and is an Indo-European language. It is mutually intelligible with Slovak. Spoken Czech has several regional dialects. The differences among those dialects mainly involve the pronunciation of vowels and the names of local or regional dishes, plants, and costumes. Czech was one of the Slavic languages at least as early as the ninth century, the time of the Great Moravian

*Czech Republic*

Empire. The oldest Czech literary monuments go back to the second half of the thirteenth century.

**Symbolism.** The official state symbols are the national anthem, flag, and coat of arms. The presidential flag (standard) bears the slogan *Pravda vítězí* ("Truth Prevails"), attributed to the first president of Czechoslovakia, Tomáš Garrigue Masaryk (1850–1937, president 1918–1935).

The national anthem, *Kde domov můj?* ("Where Is My Home?"), was originally a song in a popular satirical play of 1834. The first stanza extols the beauty of the countryside, and the second the nobility of the Czech people. In 1918, when the Austro-Hungarian Empire disintegrated and the Czechs and Slovaks were given a country of their own, this gentle song became one of the two national anthems of Czechoslovakia, along with the Slovak national anthem. The Czech flag consists of a lower red field and an upper white field with a blue wedge reaching from the flagpole side of the flag to its center. There are two coats of arms. The central feature on the small coat of arms is a split-tailed lion wearing a crown. The large coat of arms makes pictorial references to Bohemia, Moravia, and Silesia. Several historical personalities have special meaning for Czechs. The earliest is Václav I (Wenceslas I, familiar from the popular Christmas carol), who was killed by the order of his younger brother and successor, Boleslav I, in 929 or 935. Wenceslas has been revered as a saint since the second half of the tenth century and as a patron and protector of the country and a symbol of statehood since the eleventh century. The ancient chorale "Saint Wenceslas, Ruler of the Czech Land" (*Svatý Václave, vévodo české země*) has been a national hymn since the end of the thirteenth century. To honor Saint Wenceslas, in 1848 the large central boulevard

**5 9 9**

in Prague was renamed Wenceslas Square (*Václavské náměstí*), and in 1913 an equestrian statue memorializing him was erected there.

A monument in Prague's Old Town Square (*Staroměstské náměstí*) commemorates Jan Hus (John Huss), a religious reformer who was burned as a heretic in Constance (Konstanz) in southern Germany in 1415. The Hussite movement, originally religious and nationalist, culminated in 1419 when the Hussite forces defeated several armies sent to Bohemia by the pope to put an end to reformational ideology. A compromise between the Hussites and the Catholic Church was not reached until 1436. Another Czech whose memory is still cherished is Jan Amos Komenský (1592–1670), known outside the country as Comenius. A religious reformer, Comenius also was a scientist and a founder of modern pedagogy and is referred to as the "teacher of nations." As the bishop of a Czech Protestant denomination, he was forced to go into hiding after 1620, when education fell under the control of the Catholic Church. When Comenius went into permanent exile in 1628, a number of European countries invited him for extended visits. He died in the Netherlands, where he is buried. During the religious conflicts of the Thirty Years War (1618–1648), Comenius proposed the establishment of an ecumenical council of churches and an international academy of scientists. Among his writings were a seven-volume manuscript with recommendations for the improvement of human affairs and a textbook with illustrations (*Orbis pictus* [1658]) that is said to be the first such textbook. Comenius was a revered figure throughout the Western world. He was even offered the presidency of the very young Harvard College but refused, preferring to remain in Europe, because he hoped he could eventually return to his native Moravia.

One of the symbols of the Czech national revival that took place from near the end of the eighteenth century to the 1880s is the National Theater (*Národní divadlo*) in Prague. The theater was opened in 1881 but was destroyed by fire later that year. Restored and reopened in 1883, it continues to be one of Prague's landmarks. An inscription on the ornate auditorium, *Národ sobě*, translates freely as "By the people to the people." A symbol of the Nazi occupation is Lidice, a community in central Bohemia. As punishment for the assassination of the Nazi deputy administrator of Bohemia and Moravia, Reinhard Heydrich, on 10 June 1942, the village was razed, with all of Lidice's 192 men shot and 196 women and most of the 105 children sent to concentration camps. After the war, a new village was built nearby and the tragedy was commemorated by a monument and a memorial rose garden. Several communities in the United States, Brazil, Mexico, Australia, and elsewhere were named Lidice in memory of the innocent people who lost their lives.

A world-famous fictional character is the "good soldier Švejk" in the novel of that name published between 1921 and 1923 by Jaroslav Hašek (1883–1923). *The Good Soldier Švejk* portrays a complex character who, although discharged from military service for idiocy, is resourceful, expresses great compassion, and never stops making fun of the bureaucracy of the Austro-Hungarian Empire. Garrulous and ready to follow orders to the letter, Švejk is the epitome of someone whose obtuseness helps him survive. The novel has been translated into many languages, filmed several times, adapted for theatrical presentations, and made into an opera.

## HISTORY AND ETHNIC RELATIONS

*Emergence of the Nation.* The first ethnically identifiable inhabitants of the area, a Celtic people, lived there from the fourth century B.C.E. until about the second century C.E. They were followed by a Germanic people who left during the so-called migration of nations in the fifth century. Slavic-speaking groups made the area their homeland no later than the sixth century. Among them were the Czechs in central Bohemia and the Moravians along the Morava and Dyje rivers to the east. In the first half of the eleventh century, Oldřich of the princely and later royal Czech dynasty of the Přemysls (Premyslid dynasty) brought Moravia under his control, and Bohemia and Moravia then became the foundation of the Czech state.

The crowning of the first Bohemian king took place in 1085, and the first university in central Europe was founded in Prague in 1348. The development of Czech national culture came to a temporary halt in 1620, when the Czech estates (social classes possessing political rights) were defeated in the Battle of White Mountain (*Bílá hora*). The Bohemian kingdom lost its independence, and its provinces were declared the hereditary property of the Hapsburgs. Forcible re-Catholization of a people who from the beginning of the fifteenth century had been influenced by the reformist teachings of Jan Hus resulted in a wholesale emigration that, together with epidemics of plague and other diseases, reduced the population of Bohemia by about one-half and that of Moravia by one-fourth. A period referred to as "the darkness" (*temno*) lasted until the end of the eighteenth century, when the Czech national revival—the formation of the modern Czech nation—began.

**National Identity.** West Slavic tribes inhabiting the Bohemian territory gradually were united by the politically dominant Czechs and came under their leadership by the ninth century. Moravian tribes were united even earlier than those of Bohemia. The ethnic badge of all these groups consisted of the various dialects of the Czech language.

**Ethnic Relations.** Until the end of the twelfth century, the population was almost exclusively Czech-speaking. Over the next two centuries, its makeup underwent a change. Large numbers of German colonists settled in Bohemian cities and rural areas, some of which subsequently became completely Germanized. Population statistics for Bohemia in 1851 gave the ratio of Czechs to Germans as 60 to 38.5. The historical territory of the Bohemian state did not become more Germanized over the centuries because of the anti-German feelings of the Czechs.

After World War II, the ethnic makeup of Czechoslovakia changed profoundly. Most Jews did not survive the war, and after the war, settlers of Czech origin arrived from Romania, Yugoslavia, and Volhynia in the Soviet Union. By 1950, about 95 percent of all Czechoslovak citizens of German nationality had left.

With the exception of the World War II period, Czechs and Slovaks shared a common state between 1918 and 1992. Until 1969, the relationship between the two groups was asymmetrical: Slovakia was considered an agrarian appendage to the highly industrial Czech nation, and the Czechs viewed Slovak culture as lacking in maturity and refinement. Even though the Czech and Slovak languages are closely related and mutually intelligible, many Czechs viewed Slovak as a caricature of Czech. The peaceful separation of Czechs and Slovaks into two independent countries on 1 January 1993 was largely a consequence of the paternalistic attitude of the Czechs toward the Slovaks and the desire of the Slovaks to assert their ethnic identity through political independence.

There has always been a special relationship between Czechs and the United States. The Austrian Empire, of which Bohemia and Moravia were a part from 1620 to 1918, was one of the most densely populated areas of Europe when the empire began to experience a rapid increase in population growth around the middle of the nineteenth century. Population pressures soon forced many Czechs to look for employment and a new life abroad. Lower Austria and the United States were the countries to which most of these people migrated. The places in the United States to which Czech immigrants were drawn included not only large cities but also rural areas, especially in the prairie states of the Mississippi Valley as well as Nebraska, Kansas, and Texas. In the early 1990s, about 1.3 million people in the United States claimed a Czech background.

## URBANISM, ARCHITECTURE, AND THE USE OF SPACE

The Czech Republic is a fairly densely populated country, with about 340 persons per square mile. The highest population density is in metropolitan Prague (*Praha*), which has 1.3 million inhabitants. The next three largest cities are the capital of Moravia, Brno, with approximately 400,000 people; Ostrava in northern Moravia, with about 350,000; and Plzeň (Pilsen), with approximately 180,000. Seven cities have populations just below or above 100,000. Overall, about 65 percent of the Czech people live in cities or towns of 5,000 or more.

The tendency of Czechs to move from rural areas to cities predates the founding of the nation in 1918. As a consequence, Prague has continued to grow steadily even though the national population is virtually stationary. The result is a tight housing market despite the constant construction of monotonous blocks of prefabricated multistory apartment houses on the outskirts of the city.

These new districts stand in sharp contrast to the historic parts of Prague with their great variety of architectural styles. Some of the city's monumental but stylistically restrained buildings date from the last third of the nineteenth century (National Theater, National Museum, and the Rudolfinum concert hall) and the first third of the twentieth (Municipal House, with a concert hall and restaurants, and the ministries in central Prague along the Vltava).

The Czech Republic is essentially a country of small cities and towns. However, there have always been hundreds of small villages in the countryside, frequently only a few miles apart. In the past several decades, there has been a tendency to consolidate them administratively.

The rooms of Czech apartments and family houses are small, and bedrooms, which usually have no closets, are made smaller by the use of wardrobes. Family houses are constructed of cinder block or brick rather than wood.

*Astronomical clock on Old Town Hall.*

## FOOD AND ECONOMY

***Food in Daily Life.*** The traditional Czech diet may be considered heavy, with an emphasis on meat, potatoes, and dumplings and the use of substantial amounts of animal fats, butter, and cream. Meats—primarily pork, beef, poultry, and organ meats such as liver, kidneys, brains, and sweetbreads—are frequently prepared with gravy and eaten with potatoes or dumplings (*knedlík*, pl. *knedlíky*). Soups are an important part of the noon meal. Potato and tripe soup are favorites, as well as beef or chicken broth with tiny liver or marrow dumplings. The most commonly used vegetables are carrots, peas, and cabbage. Salads were eaten only seasonally until recent years.

Czechs have always enjoyed sweets. The most common are fruit dumplings (made with plums or, in winter, preserved apricots) served with grated farmer cheese and bread crumbs browned in butter, with sugar sprinkled on top. Dumplings often are served as a meal. Popular sweet baked goods include *buchty* (sing. *buchta*), small, roughly rectangular yeast buns with a filling of jam or preserves; *koláče* (sing. *koláč*), small cakes made of white flour with an indentation on the surface for a filling of poppy seeds, plum jam, or sweetened farmer cheese; a semisweet cake (*bábovka*) made of yeast dough and baked in a fluted tube pan; thin pancakes spread with jam, rolled, and topped with powdered sugar (*palačinky*); small raised pancakes (*lívance*); and apple strudel (*jablkovy závin* or *štrúdl*).

The national beverage is beer (*pivo*); some good domestic wines are produced in Moravia. The domestic plum brandy is called *slivovice* (slivovitz).

Especially during the past ten to twenty years, marked changes have occurred in the Czech diet. More fresh vegetables are eaten year-round by those who can afford imported food; vegetable shortenings, oils, and margarine are replacing animal fats; and a variety of mixes are used to prepare soups and dumplings. What people eat today is greatly influenced by what they can afford: good cuts of beef and pork are expensive, but poultry is much more affordable.

***Food Customs at Ceremonial Occasions.*** A typical Sunday dinner menu continues to be *svíčková* (known in English by the German name *sauerbraten*): fillet of beef marinated in vinegar and spices before roasting, served with a rich sour-cream sauce and almost always accompanied by dumplings. Also popular for special meals is roast duck, pork, or goose with dumplings and sauerkraut. On Christmas Eve, nearly the entire country eats the traditional breaded and fried carp, and on

Christmas Day, roast turkey is found on many tables.

***Basic Economy.*** In the first half of the 1990s, the Czech economy was transformed from a centrally planned economy to an essentially privatized, market-oriented economy. Small businesses nationalized during the 1950s by the communist regime were returned to the rightful owners or their heirs; small businesses created during the socialist period were auctioned off to employees or outsiders. Large enterprises were privatized through the sale of vouchers to citizens over 18 years of age, who then became shareholders. Some of the heavy industries and banks still owned by the state may be privatized in the future. For basic needs, particularly temperate-zone food products, Czech society is self-sufficient, but it imports oil and gas. The republic has supplies of coal and lignite (brown coal) and uranium ore. Well over half the country's electrical energy is generated by coal-fired thermal power stations, some is supplied by nuclear plants, and a relatively small amount is produced by waterpower.

***Land Tenure and Property.*** Prior to World War I, noble families had extensive holdings of farmland and forests (for example, the Schwarzenberg family owned 248,000 hectares of land). After Czechoslovakia was established at the end of World War I (1918), the new government considered land reform a priority. The first land reform restricted considerably the economic power of both the nobility and the large landowners by reducing their holdings of agricultural and forest land. The land subject to expropriation was allotted to smallholders, farming cottagers, small craftspeople, landless persons, etc. After 1948, when the communists took over, collectivization and nationalization of land became almost total; by 1977 only 2.4 percent of all persons permanently active in agriculture owned land, and all of these were small farmers in mountainous regions. Aside from agricultural cooperatives, private holdings of land are now very modest: the rural summer cottages owned by many urban residents generally occupy lots of only a fraction of an acre.

Restitution of property began after the velvet revolution of 1989. With respect to the former nobility, restitution has had mixed results. Many children of the original owners were living in foreign countries and had no experience with or desire to become entrepreneurs in large-scale agriculture or forest management. In many cases their castles or mansions were found to be in such a state of neglect that restoration and maintenance have been beyond their means. Nevertheless the heirs and the few original owners still living are pleased to have the option of owning their former homes once again.

***Major Industries.*** The Czech Republic has long been highly developed industrially. The leading industries include the manufacture of machinery, automobiles, chemicals, refined petroleum products, fertilizers, cement, iron and steel, glass, textiles, footwear, and beer. Many industrial enterprises have been undergoing restructuring to catch up with those in the West. After an initial decline in aggregate output in 1990, modest growth resumed in 1994.

Under communism, agriculture was almost completely collectivized. Postcommunist privatization did not result in a return to small-scale private farming because agricultural workers prefer to be shareholders in privatized cooperatives. The collectivization of the 1950s resulted in rapid mechanization of agricultural work, which is now the most advanced in central and eastern Europe. Today the agricultural labor force is only about a quarter of a million, or 5 percent of the total labor force. The most commonly cultivated crops are grains, fodder, sugar beets, rape, potatoes, and hops. Hops, which are used in the production of beer and for pharmaceutical products, are exported. Livestock production involves primarily cattle, pigs, and poultry. Lumber is another export, especially from southern Bohemia.

Under communism, industry was the priority sector and service-oriented industries were neglected; heavy industry's share of output was larger than that in developed capitalist economies. The neglect of services gave rise to a so-called second economy in which services were obtained by barter or by paying someone on a private basis. In the 1990s, service industries began to grow rapidly.

A consequence of the communist regime's stress on industrial production without proper safeguards against polluting the environment was ecological devastation of certain regions, especially in northern Bohemia (in and around the city of Most) and northern Moravia (the city of Ostrava). Even Prague is polluted, mainly from the many cars in the city center.

***Trade.*** The Czech economy is highly dependent on foreign trade. The republic imports mainly from the same countries it exports to: Germany, Slovakia, the United States, Austria, Italy, and Russia. Exports consist primarily of manufactured goods, machinery and transport equipment (including automobiles), and chemicals; imports include goods of those types as well as fuels and lubricants. The Czech economy runs a large trade deficit with Russia, importing energy and raw materials but exporting relatively little. Because the Czech crown is now freely convertible, there is practically no limit to what can be purchased by those who have the funds. Since 1994, inflation has been 10 percent or less per year (in 1999 it was only 2.1 percent, and the estimate for 2000 is 4 percent).

## SOCIAL STRATIFICATION

***Classes and Castes.*** After World War I, when Czechoslovakia became an independent country, the middle class was the largest socioeconomic class. Poverty and unemployment were most noticeable in the large cities and least prevalent in farming villages. The wealthy included those owning businesses and the relatively few members of noble families, who had lost their titles with the establishment of the republic in 1918 but not much of their property, which included castles and large tracts.

Under the communist regime after World War II, the economic status of manual workers rose and that of highly specialized people declined steeply (physicians were paid no more than street pavers, who were paid reasonably well). A new elite consisted of the most active members of the Communist Party. They enjoyed numerous privileges, such as large apartments, access to special hospitals, special stores with merchandise not available to others, and for those in high government positions, state automobiles with chauffeurs. Ethnicity was of no consequence; what mattered was political activity and dependability.

This political elitism ended after 1989. Successful businesspeople now have visible wealth: luxury cars, expensive villas, and maids and chauffeurs. By contrast, older people complain that their pensions do not keep pace with the cost of living; pensioners therefore often vote for leftist parties that advocate controlled prices.

## POLITICAL LIFE

***Government.*** The Czech Republic is a parliamentary democracy. The president is elected for a five-year term and may not be elected for more than two consecutive terms. The president appoints and dismisses the prime minister, appoints certain high officials, and can veto any bills (other than constitutional ones) passed by parliament. Václav Havel

*Two boys in Prague, Czech Republic.*

(1936–), a playwright, essayist, and political dissident during the communist regime, became president of the postcommunist republic (1989–1992) and in 1993 was the first president of the Czech Republic.

The parliament consists of the Chamber of Deputies (two hundred deputies elected for four-year terms) and the Senate (eighty-one senators elected for six-year terms). The government consists of the prime minister, his or her deputies, and the ministers who make up the cabinet; the cabinet is the supreme body of executive power. The highest judicial body is the supreme court.

***Leadership and Political Officials.*** Since the end of the communist regime, political life has again been characterized by a considerable number of political parties. In the 1992 elections, forty-two parties and movements participated, with eight receiving 5 percent or more of the popular vote. Because of the large number of parties, no party receives a majority, and the government is formed by a coalition of the parties with the most votes. Parties range from conservative, to Christian democratic, to social democratic, to communist. The strongest in the 1998 election were the Czech Social Democratic Party (32.3 percent), the Civic Democratic Party

(27.7 percent), and the Communist Party of Bohemia and Moravia (11 percent).

***Social Problems and Control.*** The most common crime is pickpocketing, usually in crowded streetcars and subways. Prague is among the European capitals with the highest rates for this type of crime. Czechs attribute these thefts and more serious criminal acts to non-Czech minorities and citizens of poorer eastern European countries who have entered the republic legally or illegally. The privatization of formerly state-owned businesses and enterprises has resulted in many cases of embezzlement and, to a lesser extent, bribery. Violent crimes are more common than they were under communism. Many citizens feel that the police are not as numerous or efficient as they should be and that the courts are too lenient.

***Military Activity.*** Military service of one year is compulsory for all males without physical limitations, but a civilian work assignment of eighteen months may be substituted. Active duty personnel in 1996 totaled forty-four thousand, of whom 36.4 percent were in the air force. Military expenditures in 1995 accounted for 2.3 percent of gross national product compared to the world average of 2.8 percent.

## SOCIAL WELFARE AND CHANGE PROGRAMS

Social programs cover old age, invalidism, death, sickness and maternity, work injury, unemployment, and allowances per child. Under the communist regime, every person had the right to employment; however, some jobs would have been unnecessary in a market-oriented economy. There was a saying, ''The state pretends to pay us, and we pretend to work.'' Even though many of these superfluous jobs have been eliminated, unemployment was only 6 percent in 1998.

## NONGOVERNMENTAL ORGANIZATIONS AND OTHER ASSOCIATIONS

There are few formal social clubs or organizations. Most socializing takes place in pubs or outdoors during summer holidays. The few organizations that exist are of a serious nature, such as scholarly associations and political clubs. Sports organizations and groups interested in such activities as fishing and stamp collecting are quite active. In general, however, Czechs prefer to use their free time according to their own tastes, especially in the large cities.

## GENDER ROLES AND STATUSES

***Division of Labor by Gender.*** Before World War II, most middle-class women did not work, remaining at home to run the household and take care of the children. Women constituted no more than a third of the labor force. This began to change during World War II, when the occupying German authorities required many women to replace men forced into work for the war effort. Under the postwar communist regime, many women worked to improve the economic situation of their families; the state facilitated women's employment by making day nurseries available. In 1976, about 87 percent of women of working age were employed. The latest available figures (1995) show a high proportion of women in the total labor force: 46.2 percent compared to 53.8 percent for men.

***The Relative Status of Women and Men.*** Women have made significant strides since World War II in terms of employment opportunities and participation in public life. However, a disproportionate number of women are in the lower half of the pay scale. Women remain concentrated in the traditional sectors of female employment: retail sales, health care, elementary schools, and social work. While the concept of equality between men and women is recognized, the husbands of women who are fully employed seldom perform half the household duties. Because a number of the mechanical conveniences taken for granted in the West are not widely affordable, most women work harder at home than American women do. However, women have a large say in how money is spent and how the family uses its free time and are becoming increasingly active in political life, business (banks and insurance companies), and civil service (post offices).

## MARRIAGE, FAMILY, AND KINSHIP

***Marriage.*** For much of the twentieth century, the selection of a spouse has rested with the young couple. Before World War II, socioeconomic standing and education were of considerable importance in the selection of a husband or wife. Middle-class men usually did not marry until they were launched in their careers, typically in their late twenties or early thirties; women usually married in their early or middle twenties. More recently, men have begun to marry earlier. There are no legal restrictions on who can marry except for marriages between close relatives. The number of legal marriages in 1996 was 5.2 per 1,000. This number is low because the percentage of young adults in the age range 15–29 is among the lowest in the world

*Buildings line the Vlatava River in Prague, Czech Republic.*

(because this is also true for the 0–14 age group, the low number of marriages is expected to continue). Relative to the low marriage rate, the divorce rate of 3.2 per 1,000 population is quite high.

Czech newlyweds prefer to live separately from their families, but because of housing shortages in the larger cities, that goal is not easy to attain. Both spouses usually work unless a very young child keeps a mother temporarily at home.

**Domestic Unit.** The typical household unit is the nuclear family, consisting of husband, wife, and children or stepchildren. Because of the housing shortage, a widowed mother of one of the spouses may be included in the household; she is a valuable addition to the nuclear family if the young couple has children because she can provide child care while the mother works. In the Moravian countryside, where people own family houses, parents commonly live with their adult children. Typically, when Moravians build a family house, they include space in it for their parents.

**Inheritance.** The importance of inheritance diminished under the communist regime because all businesses and properties except for family houses were nationalized. Privatization began after the velvet revolution in 1989, and most property owned pri-

vately before 1948 has been returned to the owners or their descendants.

**Kin Groups.** For urban Czechs, the effective kin group is limited to the closest relatives. For most people, collateral relatives more distant than uncles, aunts, and first cousins are seen only on special occasions such as weddings and funerals. However, most villagers, especially in Moravia, continue to maintain relations with more distant relatives. Descent is bilateral, that is, through both the mother's and the father's lines, but the husband's surname becomes the family name.

## SOCIALIZATION

**Infant Care.** The birthrate in the Czech Republic was 8.8 per 1,000 in 1996, compared with the world average of 25. About 84 percent of children are born to parents who are married. Because of the small size of a typical Czech family, the birth of a child is a special event. Baby showers are not common, but close friends frequently give a gift when a child has been born. Before World War II, most women were expected to stay at home and take care of the children and the household. Since the 1950s, many women of childbearing age have held jobs to help maintain a decent economic standard. Women were given generous maternity leaves—usually six months at 90 percent of full pay and at 60 percent of full pay until the child was 3 years old. Since the 1990s, the rules governing maternity leave have been much less generous. However, if a new mother has help from her mother or mother-in-law, she is likely to return to work as soon as possible.

During the first two years, children are given much attention. Most babies are bottle-fed, but some mothers still breast-feed their babies until the first teeth appear. When babies no longer awaken for feedings during the night, they are moved to a separate room if space is available. It is customary to take children outdoors every day in prams or strollers. In cities, two or three mothers from the neighborhood are likely to be found sitting and talking in a nearby park while their babies are getting fresh air and sunshine.

**Child Rearing and Education.** Although fathers are usually the heads of families, mothers exercise authority over young children. Czech children are expected to be obedient after being admonished. They are reprimanded whenever they are considered to be out of line and usually are made to feel guilty for unacceptable behavior. Praise for good behavior is not dispensed often. Children are taught to be orderly, hardworking, practical, and egalitarian and are expected not to resort to physical violence.

If a family can live on the father's income, the mother stays at home during a child's early years. At about age 3, many children are sent to day nurseries, and a year or two later to kindergarten. Since 1990, some of these preschool services have been discontinued or have become more costly.

**Higher Education.** Education is highly valued, and academic titles receive great respect. School teachers used to enjoy fairly high status and wield a great deal of authority on school premises; in recent years, their pay has become relatively low and their prestige has suffered. Most parents pressure their children to do well in school. For a child to have to repeat a grade is embarrassing for the family.

Children begin school at age 6 and must remain in school until age 15. All students attend elementary school for the first five years. Those who plan to go to a university move on to an eight-year *gymnázium*, a secondary school that prepares them for higher education. To be accepted at a gymnasium, students must pass written examinations in mathematics and Czech. At the end of the eighth year, they take a final school-leaving examination (*maturita*). An alternative is to take nine years of basic education with the option of continuing with either the last four years of gymnasium or a four-year specialized training program in schools that prepare students to become nurses, electricians, and so on, or to enter business or management. Public kindergartens and primary and secondary schools are free. Recently, a few private and parochial schools became available at the primary and secondary levels. Their quality is good, but not many parents can afford the tuition. University students are not charged tuition but must pay for their textbooks as well as board and lodging.

## ETIQUETTE

Social interaction is not much different from that in other central European countries; compared to that in the United States, it is rather formal. This formality is in part caused by the Czech language, which has two forms of the second-person personal pronoun. The "familiar" form is used to address a member of the family, a good friend of long standing, or a child or by a child addressing another child. The "polite" form is used in more formal situations. It is not uncommon for colleagues of similar age in neighboring offices to use the formal form when talking with each other.

The tendency toward formal behavior is strengthened by the tradition of using titles. The use of someone's first name is limited to older family members addressing younger ones and to very good friends. It usually takes daily contact over a number of years before people are on a first-name basis. Much less informal contact reinforces the social distance between people. Because Czech apartments are small, invitations to visit and casual dropping by occur only among good friends.

Czechs stand at arm's length from each other unless they are conveying information that should not be overheard. Like other Europeans, Czechs do not show as much consideration as one finds in Britain or in smaller cities in the United States when several people are boarding a streetcar, bus, or train or waiting to be served in a store. Their tendency to get ahead of others may reflect the experience of the socialist years, when people had to stand in lines for scarce goods.

Because there are no significant differences in social equality by virtue of position or ethnic background (with the exception of the Romany [Gypsies], who are disapproved of for allegedly committing petty thefts), the rules of etiquette are alike for all members of the society. Because Czechs emphasize cleanliness, most remove their shoes when entering private homes. They eat in the Continental style, with the fork in the left hand and the knife in the right, and there is no special attempt to converse at meals. When attending cultural events, Czechs dress for the occasion, and young women try to follow the latest styles. Younger people tend to be more informal and self-confident than their elders.

## RELIGION

**Religious Beliefs.** Christianity was brought to the area of the Czech Republic during the ninth century by missionaries from Germany to the west (the Latin rite) and the Byzantine Empire to the southeast (the Eastern rite). The missionaries of the Eastern rite were the brothers Constantine (later renamed Cyril) and Methodius, natives of Thessalonica in Macedonia. They arrived in 863, invited by Rostislav (or Rastislav), ruler of the Great Moravian Empire, and devised the first Slavic writing system, in which they published parts of the Bible in a Slavic language that was intelligible to the local population. The arrival of the Magyars in the middle Danube area near the end of the ninth century and their subsequent raids to the north led to the disintegration of the Great Moravian Empire and weakened the influence of the Eastern rite. By

*People walking through the public square in Prague, Czech Republic.*

the time a bishopric was established in 973 in Prague, Roman Catholic missionaries had prevailed and Latin had become the liturgical language.

A breach with Rome took place during the first half of the fifteenth century as a consequence of the reform movement begun by Jan Hus. After Hus was burned at the stake in Constance in 1415, his legacy became a lasting aspect of the national heritage. It was reinforced in the middle of the sixteenth century by the attempts of Ferdinand I, the Holy Roman emperor and Bohemian king, to bring the population back under the influence of the Roman Catholic Church. After the army of the Bohemian estates was defeated by Ferdinand II in the Battle of White Mountain in 1620, Catholicism and Hapsburg rule tended to be equated as symbols of foreign oppression.

Precise numbers of the members of various denominations are not available; approximate percentages are Roman Catholics, 40 percent; Protestants, 4 to 5 percent; Orthodox, 1 percent; and uncommitted, atheists, and agnostics, 54 percent. Many Czech Catholics tend to be lukewarm in their faith. Moravian Catholics are more committed. Religious sentiments have always been more strongly felt and expressed in rural areas. Since the end of World War I, strong secularist tendencies have been

evident. The forty-one years of communist rule (1948 to 1989) further undermined religious practices and expression: Those who regularly attended religious services were discriminated against in terms of professional advancement. After 1989, a resurgence of religious beliefs and observances became noticeable, especially among young people.

Before World War II, about 120,000 Jews lived in the Czech lands. Except for those who married non-Jews and the relatively few who were able to emigrate, most Jews—about 80,000—died in Nazi concentration camps. After the war, only a very few of those who escaped the Holocaust returned.

***Religious Practitioners.*** The Roman Catholic Church has archdioceses in Prague, founded in 1344, and Olomouc (Moravia), founded in 1777. The archbishop of the Prague archdiocese is the only Czech cardinal. In addition, there are six dioceses headed by bishops: four in Bohemia and two in Moravia.

The Protestant churches (in Czech usually referred to by a term translated as "Evangelical") are small, less hierarchical, and diversified. Among those registered in 1995 were the Baptists, Czech Brethren, the Czechoslovak Hussite Church, Jehovah's Witnesses, Methodists, Pentecostalists, Seventh-Day Adventists, and the Silesian Evangelical Church of the Augsburg Confession. Other denominations include the Czech Orthodox Church, the Old Catholic Church, the Unitarians, and the Federation of Jewish Communities in the Czech Republic.

***Rituals and Holy Places.*** Catholic churches or chapels are found in even the smallest communities. Other denominations and religious organizations have church buildings only in areas where a congregation is large enough to support them. Smaller groups gather for worship in private homes or hold meetings in rented quarters.

There were several places of pilgrimage—all Catholic—where the devout used to travel every year to attend a mass commemorating the local saint. Most of those sites were of only regional significance, but a few were known throughout the country. For example, pilgrimages began in 1647 to the church at *Svatá hora*, a hill above Příbram in central Bohemia. Beginning in 1990, pilgrimages were resumed in eastern Moravia (Hostýn and Velehrad). Many of these yearly ceremonies have turned into events resembling country fairs and are attended by thousands of people. An example is Matthew's Fair (*matějská pout'*), which takes place on the outskirts of Prague every spring.

***Death and the Afterlife.*** Serious church members, whether Catholic or Protestant, believe in an afterlife. Even lukewarm Catholics frequently arrange for a dying family member to receive the last rites before death. In the past, the dead usually were buried in a casket and their graves were provided with elaborate headstones. Over the last fifty years, cremation has become the accepted practice, but in rural Moravia, burying in the ground still predominates.

## MEDICINE AND HEALTH CARE

The extensive use of medicinal plants was replaced during the first half of the twentieth century by the use of synthetic drugs. Many of these drugs are produced by a well-developed domestic pharmaceutical industry. Czech medicine has always followed the course of Western medicine and kept up with modern advances.

Health spas using thermal mineral waters and/ or mud or peat baths are numerous and popular. Some are world-famous, such as Marienbad (*Mariánské Lázně*) and Karlsbad (*Karlovy Vary*). Karlsbad was well known by the end of the eighteenth century; members of the European aristocracy often visited it to regain or improve their health.

Health insurance was widely available before World War II. Under communism, free health care was provided to all citizens, but its quality varied. Most Czechs would agree that the system was abused. Medical waiting rooms were crowded not only with people who had good reason to be there but also with those who wanted to leave their places of employment to take care of private matters such as standing in line for items in short supply. Free health care continues to be available, but the system is monitored more closely. To avoid long waits, patients who have the financial means often see private physicians.

In general, health services in the Czech Republic are much better than the world average: the number of persons per physician is one of the lowest in the world, and the number of hospital beds per capita is among the highest. Equally impressive is the infant mortality rate of 6 per 1,000 live births. Life expectancy at birth is 70.5 years for males, and 77.5 years for women (1997). The major causes of death are diseases of the circulatory system and cancer.

## SECULAR CELEBRATIONS

Holidays include New Year's Day; Easter Monday; Labor Day (1 May); 8 May, which commemorates the day in 1945 that saw the end of the occupation by Nazi Germany and the German signing of an unconditional surrender to the Allies; 5 July, which celebrates the arrival in 863 of the Slavic missionaries Constantine and Methodius; 6 July, in memory of the burning at the stake of Jan Hus in 1415; 28 September, Czech Statehood Day; 28 October, which marks the founding of Czechoslovakia in 1918; 17 November, Day of the Struggle for Freedom and Democracy; and Christmas Eve, Christmas Day, and the following day (December 24–26).

Although state television and radio present special commemorative programs on many of these holidays, most Czechs spend their days off with the family, visiting relatives, and attending sports events, theaters, and concerts. Those who live in Prague spend their holidays in country cottages working in the garden and enjoying the outdoors.

## THE ARTS AND HUMANITIES

***Support for the Arts.*** Under the communist regime, prominent writers, painters, and sculptors as well as museums, theaters, art galleries, and major orchestras were supported by the state. This generous support of theaters and orchestras meant that tickets to artistic events, from play readings to costly productions such as operas in Prague's National Theater, were affordable by all. Those in the arts who received state money had to conform to political and ideological dictates, or at least make certain that they did not offend the Soviet Union, those in power in their own country, and the Communist Party. Working under such strictures became unbearable for some of the most creative writers, such as Josef Škvorecký (1924–) and Milan Kundera (1929–), both of whom left the country to write and publish abroad.

Since the velvet revolution of 1989, artists have enjoyed freedom of expression and most support themselves. However, prestigious artistic institutions and ensembles such as the National Theater, the National Gallery, and the Czech Philharmonic continue to receive state support.

***Literature.*** The first literary language in the area of the present-day Czech Republic was Old Church Slavic, which was used by the missionaries Constantine and Methodius. Although Latin predominated from the eleventh through the fourteenth centuries, Czech began to be used during the thirteenth century, and during the fourteenth was employed in a great variety of genres: legends, tracts, dramatic compositions, satires, and fables. The activities of the United Brethren, especially a translation of the Bible toward the end of the sixteenth

*People relax by the river in the picturesque town of Rozmberk.*

century, contributed greatly to the stabilization of the Czech literary language.

Modern Czech literature began to develop during the nineteenth century. The founder of modern Czech poetry was Karel Hynek Mácha (1810–1836), whose long poem *Máj* (May) was published in 1836. Celebrating the beauty of the spring countryside and romantic love, Mácha's work made masterful use of the sound qualities of the Czech language in dealing with death and faith, the execution of a young man who killed his father for having seduced the girl the son loved, and the girl's suicide; those themes were quite daring for their time. In prose, the most enduring early work was *Babička* (Grandmother) by Božena Němcová (1820–1862). The author depicted rural life during the first half of the nineteenth century, including the folk customs that took place in the different seasons. By 1998, more than 350 editions of this work had appeared.

Another popular writer, Alois Jirásek (1851–1930), produced both novels and plays based on themes of Czech history ranging from the Hussite movement to the national revival. The poet Otokar Březina (1868–1929) had a great influence on lyrical poetry in the twentieth century; his five collections of poems reflected a profound knowledge of world literature, philosophy, and theology. Karel Čapek (1890–1938) is known the world over in translation. His literary production includes plays, children's books, informal essays about his travels in Europe, utopian novels, and novels in which he explores the nature and foundations of knowledge. The English word ''robot'' comes from Čapek's play *RUR* (*Rossum's Universal Robots* [1920]).

In general, Czech lyric poetry has surpassed in quality both prose and dramatic writing. The Czechs are enthusiastic readers and often read in trains and buses and on the Prague subway. Translations of foreign books are readily available.

***Graphic Arts.*** Stone architecture in the Czech lands dates from the second half of the ninth century (rotundas). By the thirteenth century, the Romanesque style had been replaced by the Gothic, which reached its peak during the reigns of Charles IV (1346–1378) and his son Václav IV (1378–1419). Prague has thousands of architectural and artistic monuments of every style, attesting to its long history (the fortified settlement around which Prague developed was founded toward the end of the ninth century). The palaces and mansions of Prague are small, but what they lack in size is compensated for by their intimacy and their setting in old Prague's narrow, curving streets. Foreign visitors consider Prague one of the most beautiful cities in the world.

Painting and sculpture have a long history, ranging from the works of Theodorik, court painter of Charles IV, to the newest postmodernist styles. Among the most revered painters are Josef Mánes (1820–1871), a landscape and portrait painter and the author of ethnographic sketches and illustrations; Mikoláš Aleš (1852–1913), who depicted Czech historical events and scenes from folklife; and Alfons Mucha (1860–1939), an internationally known representative of Art Nouveau. Mucha was one of the founders of modern poster art, and reproductions of his posters remain popular. Among modern painters is František Kupka (1871–1957), who lived in France after 1906. He was a pioneer of abstract art and is best known for nonfigurative representations.

Among Czech sculptors are Josef Václav Myslbek (1848–1922), a representative of monumental realism exemplified by the statue of Saint Wenceslas in Prague's main square, and Jan Štursa (1880–1925), whose female figures are admired for their sensuously shaped forms.

***Performance Arts.*** In the Czech Republic, music is the most popular art, and Czech music is well known in the rest of the world. The old saying "Co Čech, to muzikant" ("Every Czech is a musician") is a succinct characterization of the Czech disposition. Renaissance vocal polyphonic music was composed and performed during the sixteenth century, Italian operas were presented not only in Prague but in smaller towns in the eighteenth century, and at the time when the Baroque was giving way to classicism, numerous musicians from the Czech lands were active in many European countries. Among Czech composers, four are heard in the concert halls and opera houses around the world. Bedřich Smetana (1824–1884) composed the six symphonic poems *My Country* (*Má vlast*) and the folk opera *The Bartered Bride* (*Prodaná nevěsta*). Antonín Dvořák (1841–1904), who composed works in many genres, is known especially for his sixteen *Slavonic Dances* (*Slovanské tance*) and Symphony No. 9, *From the New World*; he was also the founder and the director for three years of the National Conservatory of Music in New York (1892–1895). Leoš Janáček (1854–1928) was a Moravian composer known for strongly rhythmic and dramatic operas, such as *Jenufa* (*Její pastorkyňa*), and Bohuslav Martinů (1890–1959) composed operas, symphonies, and chamber music.

Every May since 1946, music lovers from many countries come to Prague to attend the concerts, recitals, and other musical events offered every day. Not only the best Czech musicians but foreign ensembles and soloists take part in this music festival known as Prague Spring (*Pražské jaro*).

Drama and ballet are well represented not only in Prague but also in several Bohemian and Moravian cities. There is a long tradition of puppetry, ranging from well-known nomadic puppeteers in the eighteenth century to a professional network of puppet theaters today. Prague is also known for its *Laterna magika* (*Magic Lantern*), founded in 1958, a mixed-media spectacle that combines live performance with film, slides, and music. *Laterna magika* was shown at world's fairs in Brussels in 1958 and Montreal in 1967. Czech filmmakers have had great successes, and several of their works have received Oscars, including *Kolya* in 1997. Probably the best-known Czech director is Miloš Forman (1932–), who left the country in 1968 because of its lack of artistic freedom. Among his films made in the United States are *Taking Off* (1971), *One Flew Over the Cuckoo's Nest* (1975), and *Amadeus* (1984).

## THE STATE OF THE PHYSICAL AND SOCIAL SCIENCES

The physical sciences in the Czech Republic are of respectable quality, and research in some fields is well known abroad, for example, in polymer chemistry. Among Czechs who distinguished themselves internationally were Jaroslav Heyrovský (1890–1967) and Václav Hlavatý (1894–1969). Heyrovský was a physical chemist who won the Nobel Prize in 1959 for his discovery of polarography and its use in analytic chemistry. One of the craters on the moon bears his name. Hlavatý's specialties were differential and algebraic geometry and the general theory of relativity, on which he closely collaborated with Albert Einstein. After World War II, Hlavatý became politically active. After the communist takeover in 1948, he settled in the United States.

During the communist regime, work in the social sciences was severely limited, especially in sociology and political science. Since the application of Marxist-Leninist theory and practice was supposed to lead inevitably to the best possible society, what was there to study at home? Also, research that showed injustice or other defects in Czechoslovak society would disagree with the official view.

Several disciplines in the social sciences did manage to carry on but remained relatively unproductive—for example, ethnography. Ethnographic research was done almost exclusively in Czechoslovakia and was concerned mainly with history and variations of regional subcultures. However, there were several outstanding scholars in Egyptology, Indology, and Celtic languages and cultures.

The highest scientific institution in Czechoslovakia was the Czechoslovak Academy of Sciences with headquarters in Prague. It consisted of over fifty institutes, most of them devoted to research in the empirical sciences. The scientific activities of the academy were guided by the state plan of basic research, itself part of a government-approved plan for the development of science and technology. The activities of the various institutes were therefore tightly controlled. For example, sociology and philosophy were combined in the same academic institute, and the few sociological research projects that were undertaken had to conform to Marxist ideology.

The succeeding institution, the Academy of Sciences of the Czech Republic, was established in 1992. Although the personnel of the institutes was reduced, as was their funding, politics was taken out of the sciences. Research projects in the various institutes are limited by the scarcity of researchers and funds. However, scientists outside the institutes of the academy, for example university faculty, can apply for research funds to the Grant Agency of the Czech Republic.

## BIBLIOGRAPHY

Agnew, Hugh L. *Origins of the Czech National Renascence*, 1993.

Bradley, John F. *Lidice: Sacrificial Village*, 1972.

Demetz, Peter. *Prague in Black and Gold: Scenes in the Life of a European City*, 1997.

Dubček, Alexander. *Hope Dies Last: The Autobiography of Alexander Dubček*, edited and translated by Jiří Hochman, 1993.

Hašek, Jaroslav. *The Good Soldier Švejk and His Fortunes in the World War*, translated by Cecil Parrott, 1973.

Hermann, A. H. *A History of the Czechs*, 1975.

Heymann, Frederick G. *John Žižka and the Hussite Revolution*, 1955.

———. *George of Bohemia: King of Heretics*, 1965.

Holy, Ladislav. *The Little Czech and the Great Czech Nation: National Identity and the Post-Communist Transformation of Society*, 1996.

Horecky, Paul L., ed. *East Central Europe: A Guide to Basic Publications*, Part 2: "Czechoslovakia," 1969.

Iggers, Wilma A. *Women of Prague: Ethnic Diversity and Social Change from the Eighteenth Century to the Present*, 1995.

———, ed. *The Jews of Bohemia and Moravia: A Historical Reader*, 1992.

Kerner, Robert J., ed. *Czechoslovakia: Twenty Years of Independence*, 1945.

Korbel, Josef. *The Communist Subversion of Czechoslovakia, 1938–1948: The Failure of Coexistence*, 1959.

———. *Twentieth-Century Czechoslovakia: The Meaning of Its History*, 1977.

Kovtun, George J., comp. *Czech and Slovak History: An American Bibliography*, 1966.

Kriseová, Eda. *Václav Havel: The Authorized Biography*, translated by Caleb Crain, 1933.

Leff, Carol Skalnik. *The Czech and Slovak Republics: Nation versus State*, 1997.

Linehan, Edward J. "Czechoslovakia: The Dream and the Reality." *National Geographic* 133 (2): 151–193, 1968.

Morison, J. *Czech and Slovak Experience*, 1992.

Nyrop, Richard F., ed. *Czechoslovakia: A Country Study*, 1982.

Odložilík, Otakar. "Slavonic Cities III: Prague." *Slavonic and East European Review* 24 (1):81–91, 1946.

Pounds, Norman J. G. *Eastern Europe*, chap. 9, 1969.

Rechcígl, Miloslav, Jr., ed. *The Czechoslovak Contribution to World Culture*, 1964.

———. *Czechoslovakia Past and Present*, 1968.

Sadler, John E., ed. *Comenius*, 1969.

Salivarova, Zdena. *Summer in Prague*. Transl. by Marie Winn, 1973.

Salzmann, Zdenek. "Interethnic Relations in a Multinational State: The Czech-Slovak Case." In *Three Contributions to the Study of Socialist Czechoslovakia*, University of Massachusetts Department of Anthropology Research Reports, no. 22, 1983.

———. "Czechs." In David Levinson and Melvin Ember, eds., *American Immigrant Cultures: Builders of a Nation*, 1997.

———, and Vladimír Scheufler. *Komárov: A Czech Farming Village*, 2nd enlarged ed., 1986.

Sayer, Derek. *The Coasts of Bohemia: A Czech History*, 1998.

Selver, Paul. *Masaryk: A Biography*, 1975.

Skilling, H. Gordon, ed. *Czechoslovakia 1918–88: Seventy Years from Independence*, 1991.

Spinka, Matthew. *John Hus: A Biography*, 1968.

Suda, Zdeněk L. *Zealots and Rebels: A History of the Communist Party of Czechoslovakia*, 1980.

Thomson, S. Harrison. *Czechoslovakia in European History*, 2nd ed., 1953.

Wallace, William V. *Czechoslovakia*, 1976.

Wechsberg, Joseph. *Prague: the Mystical City*, 1971.

Wheaton, Bernard, and Zdenek Kavan. *The Velvet Revolution: Czechoslovakia, 1988–1991*, 1992.

Wolchik, Sharon L. "The Status of Women in a Socialist Order: Czechoslovakia, 1948–1978." *Slavic Review* 38 (4): 583–602, 1979.

———. *Czechoslovakia in Transition: Politics, Economics and Society*, 1991.

———. "Czechoslovakia." In *The Columbia History of Eastern Europe in the Twentieth Century*, edited by Joseph Held, 1992.

———. "Women and Work in Communist and Post–Communist Czechoslovakia." In Hilda Kahne and Janet Z. Giele, *Women's Work and Women's Lives: The Continuing Struggle Worldwide*, 1992.

—ZDENEK SALZMANN